Business Mathematics

Business Mathematics

THIRTEENTH EDITION

Gary Clendenen

Siena College

Stanley A. Salzman

American River College

PEARSON

Boston Columbus Indianapolis New York San Francisco Upper Saddle River
Amsterdam Cape Town Dubai London Madrid Milan Munich Paris Montréal Toronto
Delhi Mexico City São Paulo Sydney Hong Kong Seoul Singapore Taipei Tokyo

Editorial Director: Chris Hoag
Editor in Chief: Michael Hirsch
Content Editor: Christine Whitlock
Editorial Assistant: Matthew Summers
Senior Managing Editor: Karen Wernholm
Project Manager: Beth Houston
Digital Assets Manager: Marianne Groth
Supplements Production Coordinator: Katherine Roz
Media Producer: Audra Walsh
QA Manager, Assessment Content: Marty Wright
Executive Content Manager: Rebecca Williams
Senior Content Developer: John Flanagan
Executive Marketing Manager: Michelle Renda
Associate Marketing Manager: Alicia Frankel
Marketing Assistant: Emma Sarconi
Image Manager: Rachel Youdelman
Procurement Specialist: Carol Melville
Associate Director of Design, USHE North and West: Andrea Nix
Program Design Lead: Barbara Atkinson
Text Design: PreMediaGlobal
Composition: PreMediaGlobal
Illustrations: PreMediaGlobal
Cover Art: currency: Russell Shively/Shutterstock; handshake: EDHAR/Shutterstock; stock-market numbers:
Photofriday/Shutterstock; blue barcode: Mark Oleksiy/Shutterstock; for-sale/foreclosure sign: Andy Dean Photography/
Shutterstock; Wall St bull: Ushuaia2001/Fotolia; red bike helmet: Kati Molin/Shutterstock; neon coffee sign:
Donald R. Swartz/Shutterstock; wind turbines: TebNad/Shutterstock; couple with yard-sale sign: David Sacks/Lifesize/
Getty Images; squares & cubes: Petr Vaclavek/Fotolia

Credits appear on page P-1.

Library of Congress Cataloging-in-Publication Data
Clendenen, Gary.
  Business mathematics / Gary Clendenen, Siena College, Stanley A. Salzman,
  American River College.—13th edition.
    pages cm
  Includes index.
  ISBN 978-0-321-95505-0 (alk. paper)
  1. Business mathematics.   2. Business mathematics—Programmed instruction.   I. Salzman, Stanley A.
II. Title.
  HF5691.M465 2015
  650.01'513—dc23

                                                                    2013023130

10   17

www.pearsonhighered.com

ISBN 10: 0-321-95505-6
ISBN 13: 978-0-321-95505-0

Contents

Preface   viii
The Business Mathematics, 13th Edition, Learning System   ix
Learning Tips for Students   xiv
Business Mathematics Pretest   xv
Index of Applications   xvi

Chapter 1
Whole Numbers and Decimals   1

1.1   Whole Numbers   2
1.2   Application Problems   15
1.3   Decimal Numbers   21
1.4   Addition and Subtraction of Decimals   25
1.5   Multiplication and Division of Decimals   29
   Chapter 1 Quick Review   37
   Chapter Terms   37
   Case Study: Cost of Getting Married   39
   Case in Point Summary Exercise: Subway   40
   Chapter 1 Test   41

Chapter 2
Fractions   43

2.1   Fractions   44
2.2   Addition and Subtraction of Fractions   50
2.3   Addition and Subtraction of Mixed Numbers   58
2.4   Multiplication and Division of Fractions   63
2.5   Converting Decimals to Fractions and Fractions to Decimals   71
   Chapter 2 Quick Review   75
   Chapter Terms   75
   Case Study: Operating Expenses at Woodline Moldings and Trim   77
   Case in Point Summary Exercise: Home Depot   78
   Chapter 2 Test   79

Chapter 3
Percents   81

3.1   Writing Decimals and Fractions as Percents   82
3.2   Finding Part   89
3.3   Finding Base   96
   Supplementary Application Exercises on Base and Part   100
3.4   Finding Rate   102
   Supplementary Application Exercises on Base, Rate, and Part   106
3.5   Increase and Decrease Problems   110

Chapter 3 Quick Review   117
Chapter Terms   117
Case Study: Self Employed Retirement Plan   119
Case in Point Summary Exercise: Century 21   120
Chapter 3 Test   121

Chapter 4
Equations and Formulas   123

4.1   Solving Equations   124
4.2   Applications of Equations   132
4.3   Business Formulas   141
4.4   Ratio and Proportion   150
   Chapter 4 Quick Review   159
   Chapter Terms   159
   Case Study: Forecasting Sales at Alcorn's Boutique   161
   Case in Point Summary Exercise: General Motors   162
   Chapter 4 Test   164
   Chapters 1–4 Cumulative Review   168

Chapter 5
Bank Services   173

5.1   Electronic Banking, Checking Accounts, and Check Registers   174
5.2   Checking Services and Credit-Card Transactions   184
5.3   Bank Statement Reconciliation   189
   Chapter 5 Quick Review   198
   Chapter Terms   198
   Case Study: Banking Activities of a Retailer   200
   Case in Point Summary Exercise: Jackson & Perkins   201
   Chapter 5 Test   203

Chapter 6
Payroll   205

6.1   Gross Earnings: Wages and Salaries   206
6.2   Gross Earnings: Piecework and Commissions   216
6.3   Social Security, Medicare, and Other Taxes   224
6.4   Income Tax Withholding   230
   Chapter 6 Quick Review   242
   Chapter Terms   242
   Case Study: Payroll: Finding Your Take-Home Pay   245
   Case in Point Summary Exercise: Payroll at Starbucks   246
   Chapter 6 Test   247

Chapter 7
Mathematics of Buying   249

7.1   Invoices and Trade Discounts   250
7.2   Series Discounts and Single Discount Equivalents   260
7.3   Cash Discounts: Ordinary Dating Methods   264
7.4   Cash Discounts: Other Dating Methods   270
   Chapter 7 Quick Review   277
   Chapter Terms   277
   Case Study: George Foreman   279
   Case in Point Summary Exercise: Discounts at Bed Bath & Beyond   280
   Chapter 7 Test   281

Chapter 8
Mathematics of Selling   283

8.1   Markup on Cost   284
8.2   Markup on Selling Price   291
   Supplementary Application Exercises on Markup   299
8.3   Markdown   301
8.4   Turnover and Valuation of Inventory   307
   Chapter 8 Quick Review   316
   Chapter Terms   316
   Case Study: Markdown: Reducing Prices to Move Merchandise   320
   Case in Point Summary Exercise: Recreational Equipment Inc. (REI)   321
   Chapter 8 Test   322
   Chapters 5–8 Cumulative Review   324

Chapter 9
Simple Interest   327

9.1   Basics of Simple Interest   328
9.2   Finding Principal, Rate, and Time   339
9.3   Simple Discount Notes   347
9.4   Discounting a Note Before Maturity   356
   Supplementary Application Exercises on Simple Interest and Simple Discount   364
   Chapter 9 Quick Review   368
   Chapter Terms   368
   Case Study: Banking in a Global World: How Do Large Banks Make Money?   372
   Case in Point Summary Exercise: Apple, Inc.   373
   Chapter 9 Test   374

Chapter 10
Compound Interest and Inflation   377

10.1   Compound Interest   378
10.2   Interest-Bearing Bank Accounts and Inflation   389
10.3   Present Value and Future Value   399
   Chapter 10 Quick Review   405
   Chapter Terms   405
   Case Study: Valuing a Chain of McDonald's Restaurants   407
   Case in Point Summary Exercise: Bank of America   408
   Chapter 10 Test   409
   Chapters 9–10 Cumulative Review   411

Chapter 11
Annuities, Stocks, and Bonds   413

11.1   Annuities and Retirement Accounts   414
11.2   Present Value of an Ordinary Annuity   422
11.3   Sinking Funds (Finding Annuity Payments)   430
   Supplementary Application Exercises on Annuities and Sinking Funds   438
11.4   Stocks and Mutual Funds   440
11.5   Bonds   449
   Chapter 11 Quick Review   456
   Chapter Terms   456
   Case Study: Financial Planning   459
   Case in Point Summary Exercise: American River College   460
   Chapter 11 Test   461

Chapter 12
Business and Consumer Loans   463

12.1   Open-End Credit and Charge Cards   464
12.2   Installment Loans   475
12.3   Early Payoffs of Loans   483
12.4   Personal Property Loans   490
12.5   Real Estate Loans   498
   Chapter 12 Quick Review   506
   Chapter Terms   506
   Case Study: Consolidating Loans   510
   Case in Point Summary Exercise: Underwater on a Home   512
   Chapter 12 Test   514
   Chapters 11–12 Cumulative Review   516

Chapter 13
Taxes and Insurance   519

13.1   Property Tax   520
13.2   Personal Income Tax   527
13.3   Fire Insurance   541
13.4   Motor-Vehicle Insurance   551
13.5   Life Insurance   559
   Chapter 13 Quick Review   565
   Chapter Terms   565
   Case Study: Financial Planning For Property Taxes and Insurance   568
   Case in Point Summary Exercise: Mattel Inc.—Taxes and Insurance   569
   Chapter 13 Test 571

Chapter 14
Depreciation   573

14.1 Straight-Line Method   574

14.2 Declining-Balance Method   582

14.3 Sum-of-the-Year's-Digits Method   589

Supplementary Application Exercises on Depreciation   596

14.4 Units-of-Production Method   600

14.5 Modified Accelerated Cost Recovery System   605

Chapter 14 Quick Review   613

Chapter Terms   613

Case Study: Comparing Depreciation Methods   615

Case in Point Summary Exercise: Ford Motor Company   616

Chapter 14 Test   617

Chapter 15
Financial Statements and Ratios   619

15.1 The Income Statement   620

15.2 Analyzing the Income Statement   625

15.3 The Balance Sheet   632

15.4 Analyzing the Balance Sheet   636

Chapter 15 Quick Review   644

Chapter Terms   644

Case Study: Bicycle Shop   647

Case in Point Summary Exercise: Apple, Inc.   649

Chapter 15 Test   651

Chapter 16
Business Statistics   653

16.1 Frequency Distributions and Graphs   654

16.2 Mean, Median, and Mode   665

Chapter 16 Quick Review   673

Chapter Terms   673

Case Study: Watching a Small Business Grow   675

Case in Point Summary Exercise: Bobby Flay   676

Chapter 16 Test   677

Appendix A
The Metric System A-1

Appendix B
Basic Calculators B-1

Appendix C
Financial Calculators C-1

Appendix D
Exponents and Order of Operations D-1

Appendix E
Graphing Equations E-1

Answers to Selected Exercises AN-1

Glossary G-1

Index I-1

Photo Credits P-1

Preface

FROM THE AUTHORS

The thirteenth edition of *Business Mathematics* has been revised to improve readability and currency and to motivate students by using interesting examples from business and personal finance. Additional focus has been placed on real-world business applications. A different, well-known company is highlighted at the beginning of each chapter and used throughout that chapter in discussions, examples, exercises, and a case. Each chapter ends with two business application cases that help students integrate the concepts using a business setting. Numerous new graphs, news clippings, and photographs have been added to increase the relevance of the material to the world that students know, and discussion of the recent financial crisis has been added to help students better understand what has happened. The globalization of our society is also emphasized through examples and exercises that highlight foreign countries and international topics.

This text teaches math calculations in the context of business applications. An important goal of the text is to develop students' understanding of both to the point where they can figure out which calculations apply when presented with an unfamiliar situation. In this sense, we seek to develop a level of business "intuition" by having them work through the integrative cases, a wide-range of application exercises, writing and investigative questions, and discussions about current and relevant data. Additionally, we also seek to help students develop intuition related to business by discussing topics such as global supply chains, inventory, the financial crisis, debt, etc. These topics are widely discussed in advanced courses in four year programs at colleges and universities throughout the world.

The new edition reflects the extensive business and teaching experience of the authors, college faculty who have previously worked in and owned businesses. It also incorporates ideas for improvement from reviewers nationwide as well as students who have taken the course. We focus on providing solid, practical, and up-to-date coverage of business mathematics topics beginning with a brief review of basic mathematics, and go on to introduce key business topics, such as bank services, payroll, business discounts and markups, simple and compound interest, stocks and bonds, consumer loans, taxes and insurance, depreciation, financial statements, and business statistics. Two appendices have been added to this edition for those who have requested more algebra and/or who have an interest in graphs.

The traditional concept of learning has evolved based on knowledge that students learn in a variety of ways and that many classes are at least partly taught online or in labs. To support student learning in this multidimensional world, we have developed an outstanding supplemental learning package of print and digital products including the industry-leading MyMathLab. Numerous studies have shown that MyMathLab can greatly increase student learning and retention by presenting material in a variety of formats to suit all types of student learning styles.

Our state-of-the-art supplements package includes revised video lectures, case study videos, an enhanced PowerPoint package, student's solutions manual, an extensive instructor's manual, printed quick reference tables, and a wealth of online resources for instructors and students including MathXL online and MyMathLab. We hope this text and package satisfies all of your classroom needs. Please feel free to contact us with any questions or concerns. Use "Business Math" in the regarding line.

Gary Clendenen
gclendenen@yahoo.com
Stanley Salzman
stan.salzman@comcast.net

The Business Mathematics, 13th Edition, Learning System

This textbook has evolved over the years as thousands of students and hundreds of instructors have used the book and told us what works and what doesn't. *Business Mathematics*, 13th edition, Learning System is the result of this process of refinement that informs both the printed textbook and our new MathXL and MyMathLab applications for online. The goal of this textbook is for students to develop the computational skills they will need to be successful in the world of business along with a better understanding of business concepts and situations that require a mathematical solution. Each chapter is set up to teach a math concept and its applications in the following pattern:

1. A **'Case in Point' company profile** introduces the student to a company and a situation that requires math calculations.

2. A **clear explanation** of the math concept is presented, followed by **examples with detailed solutions**.

3. Students immediately apply the math concept to a similar problem in a **Quick-Check problem** to test their understanding.

4. **Solution steps,** detailing how to solve problems, are summarized in a shaded box.

5. **Quick Tips** provide students with helpful tips and cautions.

6. **Business applications** are found in examples, exercises, cases and discussion, and features such as Numbers in the News and newspaper clippings providing business and economic information.

7. **An Exercise Set** follows each section of the book providing a wealth of practice opportunities to develop computational skills. The exercises are paired, graded from simple to more complex, and conclude with numerous titled application word problems. Each type of exercise is preceded with a **Quick Start** worked example to help get students started.

8. **Additional Problem Sets** and **Supplementary Exercises** are embedded in select chapters for topics that students find difficult and typically require additional work.

9. A **Quick Review** section at the end of the chapter presents students with an overview of the math concepts covered in the chapter.

10. Two case studies require students to use math concepts to solve business problems in real companies. The first **Case Study** is a shorter case application, while the second **Case in Point Summary Exercise** revisits the chapter opening company with a more in-depth application. Both cases end with Discussion or Investigate questions that encourage further thinking.

11. Finally, a chapter concluding **Test** allows students to gauge their mastery of all chapter concepts and applications.

12. **Cumulative Review Problem Sets** appear every 2–4 chapters. These problems cover all math concepts covered in the preceding chapters and help students retain math concepts throughout the course.

BUILDING CALCULATOR SKILLS

This text provides the following resources to help students build calculator skills:

Calculator Solutions Calculator solutions, identified with the calculator symbol 🖩, appear after selected examples. These solutions show students the keystrokes needed to solve the problem in the Example.

Basic Calculator Instruction in Appendix B presents detailed coverage of basic calculators for professors who allow students to use calculators.

Financial Calculator Instruction in Appendix C reviews the basic functions of financial calculators using present value and future value. The financial calculator solutions are shown in shaded boxes along with the 🖩 for some examples in the text.

NEW CONTENT HIGHLIGHTS

Many changes have been made in the 13th edition. Here is a list of the changes by chapter:

- Chapters 1 through 3 have been reworked and several examples have been updated. The figures in Chapter 3 (Percents) related to increase and decrease problems have been modified to improve student learning.

- Chapter 4 (Equations and Formulas) has been updated and significant additional material related to algebra has been added with the addition of Appendix D (Exponents and Order of Operations) and Appendix E (Graphing Equations). Appendix E can be used, in combination with the many figures and charts throughout the book, to improve students' abilities to interpret data.

- Chapter 5 (Bank Services) has been extensively reworked to bring it up-to-date in the continually changing world of banking in a global, wired world. Discussion has been added explaining how electronic banking is a backbone for business. Discussion about how important it is to control costs in business as well as how internet transactions have reduced costs for businesses has been included.

- Chapter 6 (Payroll) has been updated and includes the most recent information related to Social Security, Medicare, and income tax withholding. Figures in the chapter show percent of workers living on the edge due to insufficient savings, the value of higher education, average salaries for various sales careers, and a chart listing the median wage of a wide range of workers by job/career. The history of Social Security and Medicare are outlined. The Case in Point Summary exercise asks students to take on the role of a manager preparing a payroll at a Starbucks.

- Chapter 7: Mathematics of Buying introduces e-commerce and the resulting changes in business operations. A new topic is introduced: the retail supply chain. Students are encouraged to think as managers about invoices and discounts based on the amount purchased or the timing of payments. The importance of controlling costs is emphasized in the chapter and in the case on managing inventory at Bed, Bath and Beyond.

- Chapter 8: Mathematics of Selling is introduced using Recreational Equipment, Inc. (REI) which is one of the premier sporting goods and mountaineering stores in the country. To enhance student understanding of supply chain issues in retail, the discussion on tracking inventory has been expanded and data showing the growth of online retail sales is included. Figures have also been changed to enhance student understanding.

- Chapter 9: Simple Interest has been updated to reflect current interest rates. Rather than just giving formulas and calculations, this chapter was written to help students gain insights about the importance of interest rates in business and life. For example, a graph showing housing starts and interest rates is included along with a discussion of why high interest rates usually result in lower housing starts. Also, an explanation is given about how the government uses interest rates to help control the growth rate of the economy which in turn affects the number of jobs. The company highlighted is Apple, Inc.

- Chapter 10: Compound Interest and Inflation shows the benefits of compounding interest over periods of time. Inflation is defined and examples are included to show the effect of inflation on earning power. Deflation is also defined since it is a topic currently in the news. One of the cases at the end of the chapter describes the serious financial effects of the recent collapse in real estate prices on a home builder.

- Chapter 11: Annuities, Stocks, and Bonds uses both examples and exercises to emphasize the value of long-term saving for students and businesses. It includes descriptions of the basic types of retirement accounts and explains how divorced couples can use annuities for alimony and child support payments. The chapter highlights a recent graduate that works for a community college as he makes choices about the retirement plan offered by his employer. It also discusses stocks and bonds as investments.

- Chapter 12: Business and Consumer Loans now has a greater emphasis on student debt. The sections on Credit Cards, Installment Loans, and Real Estate Loans will be of special interest to students. A discussion of FICO score has been added and tips are given to help students improve their own score which will improve their ability to obtain credit. One of the cases at the end of the chapter shows how a family reduces monthly payments by refinancing. The second case highlights a family that is "under water" on their home, meaning that the debt on the home is greater than its market value.

- In Chapter 13: Taxes and Insurance, additional discussion has been added showing students where tax dollars go and all personal income tax applications have been updated using the most current tax laws. A new figure shows where the government gets its money from and where it goes. All personal income tax applications have been updated using the most current tax laws. The company highlighted in the chapter Mattel Inc., has significant international sales. Discussion has been added showing the effects of the recent financial crisis on the budget in a local school district.

- Chapter 14: Depreciation contains the most recent federal laws and guidelines.

- Chapter 15: Financial Statements and Ratios features Apple, Inc. Recent financial statements from the company are shown so that students can learn based on a company they know and from which they buy products.

- Many of the problems in Chapter 16: Business Statistics have been changed. It includes numerous graphs with data related to business or the economy, including average credit card debt, states with serious budget problems, top tax rates, and average costs of medical treatment. Concepts are introduced throughout the chapter using a deli and highlighted in a case related to cooking show host Bobby Flay in a case at the end of the chapter.

Student and Instructor Supplements

RESOURCES FOR STUDENTS

Classroom Lectures and Case Studies contain a comprehensive lecture for each section of the text, along with case study videos that profile real companies from the in-text Case Studies. These videos are available in MyMathLab.

Student's Solutions Manual This supplement contains the complete, worked-out solutions to all of the odd-numbered exercises in the text. This manual can be ordered alone or packaged with the textbook for an additional cost. ISBN: 0-321-95870-5

RESOURCES FOR INSTRUCTORS

Online Instructor's Solutions Manual (Download only) This supplement contains the complete, worked-out solutions to all of the exercises in the text. Available for download in MyMathLab and the Instructor's Resource Center. ISBN: 0-321-95872-1

Online Instructor's Resource Manual (Download only) contains teaching suggestions; two pretests—one in basic mathematics and one in business mathematics; six different test forms for each chapter (four short answer and two multiple choice); two final examinations; numerous application exercises (test items) for each chapter; answers to all test materials; suggested answers to the writing questions in the text; and a selection of tables from the text. Available for download in MyMathLab and the Instructor's Resource Center. ISBN: 0-321-95871-3

MEDIA RESOURCES

MYMATHLAB® ONLINE COURSE (ACCESS CODE REQUIRED)

MyMathLab from Pearson is the world's leading online resource in mathematics, integrating interactive homework, assessment, and media in a flexible, easy to use format. MyMathLab delivers **proven results** in helping individual students succeed. It provides **engaging experiences** that personalize, stimulate, and measure learning for each student. And, it comes from an **experienced partner** with educational expertise and an eye on the future.

To learn more about how MyMathLab combines proven learning applications with powerful assessment, visit **www.mymathlab .com** or contact your Pearson representative.

MYMATHLAB® READY TO GO COURSE (ACCESS CODE REQUIRED)

These new Ready to Go courses provide students with all the same great MyMathLab features, but make it easier for instructors to get started. Each course includes preassigned homework and quizzes to make creating a course even simpler. Ask your Pearson representative about the details for this particular course or to see a copy of this course.

MATHXL® ONLINE COURSE (ACCESS CODE REQUIRED)

MathXL® is the homework and assessment engine that runs MyMathLab.
(MyMathLab is MathXL plus a learning management system.)

With MathXL, instructors can:

- Create, edit, and assign online homework and tests using algorithmically generated exercises correlated at the objective level to the textbook.
- Create and assign their own online exercises and import TestGen tests for added flexibility.
- Maintain records of all student work tracked in MathXL's online gradebook.

With MathXL, students can:

- Take chapter tests in MathXL and receive personalized study plans and/or personalized homework assignments based on their test results.
- Use the study plan and/or the homework to link directly to tutorial exercises for the objectives they need to study.
- Access supplemental animations and video clips directly from selected exercises.

MathXL is available to qualified adopters. For more information, visit our website at www.mathxl.com, or contact your Pearson representative.

TESTGEN®

TestGen® (www.pearsoned.com/testgen) enables instructors to build, edit, print, and administer tests using a computerized bank of questions developed to cover all the objectives of the text. TestGen is algorithmically based, allowing instructors to create multiple but equivalent versions of the same question or test with the click of a button. Instructors can also modify test bank questions or add new questions. The software and testbank are available for download from Pearson Education's online catalog.

POWERPOINT® LECTURE SLIDES

The PowerPoint Lecture Slides contain coverage of all chapter concepts illustrated with new problems not found in the book and many of the even numbered exercises from the exercise set.

▼ Acknowledgments

We would like to thank the many users of the thirteenth edition for their insightful observations and suggestions for improving this book. We also wish to express our appreciation and thanks to the following reviewers of this and previous editions for their contributions:

Joe Adamo, *Cazenovia College*

Julia Angel, *North Arkansas College*

John Angeline, *Bucks County Community College*

Yvonne Block, *College of Lake County*

Kathy Blondell, *St. Johns River Community College*

Jesse Cecil, *College of the Siskiyous*

Carolyn Chapel, *Western Wisconsin Technical Institute*

Janet Ciccarelli, *Herkimer County Community College*

Vittoria Cosentino, *Metropolitan Community College*

Diallo Cummings, *Aiken Technical College*

Ron Deaton, *Grays Harbor College*

Elaine DiPerna, *Community College of Allegheny County—Allegheny*

Jacqueline Dlatt, *College of DuPage*

Dana Dye, *Gulf Coast State College*

James Grippe, *Central Maine Community College*

Perry Haan, *Tiffin University*

Mysti Hobson, *Zane State College*

Chris Howell, *New Mexico Junior College*

Jeanette Landin, *Empire College*

Young Jin Lee, *University of Wisconsin Green Bay*

Ping Lin, *California State University, Long Beach*

Chuck Lyons, *Hibbing Community College*

Krista Mahan, *Walla Walla Community College*

Jennie Mitchell, *Saint Mary-of-the-Woods College*

Gary Rattray, *Central Maine Community College*

Frederick Reed, *Eastern New Mexico University–Ruidoso*

Bob Reese, *Illinois Valley Community College*

Randall Rinke, *Mercyhurst University*

Pam Rogers, *Spartanburg Community College*

Ellen Sawyer, *College of DuPage*

Farooq Sheikh, *SUNY Geneseo*

Robin Sirkis, *Delaware Technical and Community College—Owens*

Catherine Skura, *Sandhills Community College*

Our appreciation goes to Deana Richmond, Ellen Sawyer, and Perian Herring, who checked all of the exercises and examples in the book for accuracy. We would also like to express our gratitude to our colleagues at American River College and Siena College who have helped us immeasurably with their support and encouragement: Vivek Pandey, Jim Booker, Robert Gonzalez, Meg Pollard, James Bralley, and Rob Diamond.

The following individuals at Pearson Education had a large impact on this thirteenth edition of *Business Mathematics,* and we are grateful for their many efforts: Michael Hirsch, Editor in Chief; Christine Whitlock, Content Editor; Beth Houston, Project Manager; and Matthew Summers, Editorial Assistant. Thanks are due as well to PreMediaGlobal, and Greg Johnson and Tracy Duff in particular, for adeptly handling the production of this thirteenth edition.

As an author team, we are committed to providing the best possible text to help instructors teach and students succeed. As we continue to work toward this goal, we would welcome any comments or suggestions you might have via e-mail to gclendenen@yahoo.com. Please use "Business Math" in the regarding line.

Gary Clendenen

Stanley A. Salzman

About the Authors

Gary Clendenen received bachelor's and master's degrees in mathematics before going into business for himself in the oil industry. He returned to academia and earned his Ph.D. in Business Management in 1993 and has been a faculty member since then. His business experience includes working as an actuary for an insurance company and owning commercial real estate. He has published papers in numerous refereed journals and does volunteer work with several organizations. His hobbies include long bicycle rides, traveling, and reading on diverse topics such as the history of the Apache Indians of the Southwest, economics, and issues related to potential shortages of energy, water, and minerals. He has two sons and several grandchildren.

Stanley A. Salzman has taught Business Math, Marketing, and Real Estate courses at American River College in Sacramento for 35 years. He says, "Some of my greatest moments in teaching have been seeing the look on the face of a student who understands a business math concept or idea for the first time." Stan and his wife have four children and eight grandchildren. Stan likes outdoor activities, exercising, and collecting antique toy trains.

Charles D. Miller (deceased) was instrumental in writing the early editions of this book as well as several other books. We continue to find inspiration and guidance in his passion for excellence.

Learning Tips for Students

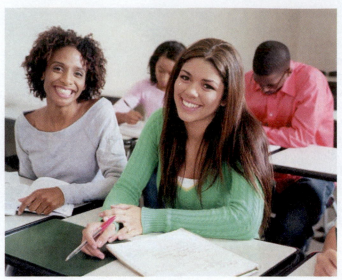

SUCCESS IN BUSINESS MATHEMATICS

This text applies mathematics to solve problems in business. Your success in future business courses and pursuits will be enhanced by the knowledge and skills you will gain in this course. It is very important to realize that your future employer is far more interested in your ability to solve problems than whether you remember a particular formula or how to work one type of problem. So, the goal of this book is both to educate you about business mathematics and importantly to also help you become a better problem solver.

Studying business mathematics is different from studying subjects like English or history. The key to success is *regular practice*. This should not be surprising. After all, can you learn to ski or play a guitar without regular practice? The same is true for learning mathematics. Working problems nearly every day *is the key to becoming successful*. Here are some suggestions to help you succeed in business mathematics.

1. **Attend class regularly. Try to pay careful attention and take notes.** In particular, write down the problems the instructor works on the board.

2. **Ask questions in class.** It is not a sign of weakness, but of strength. There are always other students with the same question who are too shy to ask.

3. **Read the book carefully, maybe twice, and spend time using the online materials.** Studying each topic will help you solve the homework problems. Most exercises are keyed to specific examples or objectives that will explain the procedure for working them.

4. **Before doing your homework, look at the problems the teacher worked in class.** This will reinforce what you have learned. Many students say, "I understand it perfectly when you do it, but I get stuck when I try to work the problem myself."

5. **Read the section and review your notes before starting your homework.** Check your work against the answers in the back of the book. If you get a problem wrong and are unable to understand why, mark that problem and ask your instructor about it. Then practice working additional problems of the same type to reinforce what you have learned.

6. **Work as neatly as you can using a pencil, and organize your work carefully.** Write your symbols clearly, and make sure the problems are clearly separated from each other. Working neatly will help you to think clearly and also make it easier to review the homework before a test.

7. **After you complete a homework assignment, look over the text again.** Try to identify the main ideas that are in the lesson. Often they are clearly highlighted or boxed in the text.

8. **Use the chapter test at the end of each chapter as a practice test.** Work through the problems under test conditions, without referring to the text or the answers until you are finished. You may want to time yourself to see how long it takes you. When you finish, check your answers against those in the back of the book, and study the problems you missed.

9. **Keep all quizzes and tests that are returned to you, and use them when you study for future tests and the final exam.** These quizzes and tests indicate what concepts your instructor considers to be most important. Be sure to correct any problems on these tests that you missed so you will have the corrected work to study.

10. **Don't worry if you do not understand a new topic right away.** As you read more about it and work through the problems, you will gain understanding. Each time you review a topic, you will understand it a little better. Few people understand each topic completely right from the start.

Business Mathematics Pretest

This pretest will help you determine your areas of strength and weakness in the business mathematics presented in this book.

1. Round 5.46 to the nearest tenth.

2. Round $.064 to the nearest cent.

3. Round $399.49 to the nearest dollar.

4. Multiply: $\begin{array}{r} 7801 \\ \times\ 1758 \end{array}$

5. Divide: $35\overline{)11{,}032}$

6. Change $8\frac{7}{8}$ to an improper fraction.

7. Change $\frac{40}{26}$ to a mixed number.

8. Write $\frac{15}{21}$ in lowest terms.

9. Add: $\begin{array}{r} \frac{3}{4} \\ \frac{1}{2} \\ +\ \frac{7}{8} \end{array}$

10. Add: $\begin{array}{r} 2\frac{2}{3} \\ 7\frac{1}{4} \\ +\ 10\frac{1}{2} \end{array}$

11. Subtract: $\frac{3}{8} - \frac{7}{24}$

12. Subtract: $\begin{array}{r} 83\frac{3}{4} \\ -21\frac{2}{5} \end{array}$

13. Multiply: $\frac{3}{8} \times \frac{3}{5}$

14. Divide: $15\frac{1}{4} \div 5\frac{1}{8}$

15. Express .625 as a common fraction.

16. Express $\frac{3}{5}$ as a decimal.

17. Subtract: $\begin{array}{r} 598.316 \\ -\ 79.839 \end{array}$

18. Multiply: $\begin{array}{r} 30.67 \\ \times\ 5.39 \end{array}$

19. Divide: $1.2\overline{)309.6}$

20. Express $\frac{7}{8}$ as a percent.

21. Intelnet spent 5.2% of its sales on advertising. If sales amounted to $864,250, what amount was spent on advertising?

22. What annual rate of return is needed to receive $930 in one year on an investment of $18,600?

23. Home Entertainment Systems offers a 60-inch LCD HDTV at a list price of $2459 less trade discounts of 20/10. What is the net cost?

24. A department head at Old Navy is paid $16.80 per hour with time and a half for all hours over 40 in a week. Find the employee's gross pay if she worked 43 hours in one week.

25. How long will it take an investment of $12,500 to earn $125 in interest at 4% per year? (*Hint:* Use Bankers Interest, i.e., assume 360 day year.)

26. An invoice from Collier Windows amounting to $20,250 is dated October 6 and offers terms of 3/10, n/30. If the invoice is paid on October 14, what amount is due?

27. Find the percent of markup based on selling price if some home exercise equipment costing $1584 is sold for $1980.

28. Find the single discount equivalent to a series discount of 30/20.

29. Using the straight-line method of depreciation, find the annual depreciation on a Bobcat loader that has a cost of $18,750, an estimated life of six years, and a scrap value of $750.

30. Whiting's Oak Furniture sells a dining room set for $1462.98 after deducting 26% from the original price. Find the original price.

1. _____
2. _____
3. _____
4. _____
5. _____
6. _____
7. _____
8. _____
9. _____
10. _____
11. _____
12. _____
13. _____
14. _____
15. _____
16. _____
17. _____
18. _____
19. _____
20. _____
21. _____
22. _____
23. _____
24. _____
25. _____
26. _____
27. _____
28. _____
29. _____
30. _____

Index of Applications

A

Agriculture
  Alligator hunting, 434
  Christmas tree farm, 353
  Commercial fertilizer, 69
  Commercial fishing boats, 587, 612
  Egg production, 14
  Farmland prices, 115
  Forestry operations, 495
  Gardening, 55
  Land area, 19
  Land sale, 435
  Landscaping, 487
  Long-stemmed roses, 300
  Pecan trees, 482
  Race horses, 354
  Trucks & sprayers, 353
Automotive/Transportation
  Antilock brakes, 114
  Automotive, 276
  Auto parts startup, 148
  Auto production, 157
  Auto repair, 55, 140
  Auto sales, 115
  Big rims and tires, 34
  Camaros and Mustangs, 100
  Company vehicles, 610
  Diesel tractor, 598
  Driving distractions, 93
  Driving tests, 99
  Fire truck, 436
  Fuel consumption, 70
  Garbage truck, 489
  Harley Davidson, 140
  Heavy-duty truck, 604
  Hybrid Toyota, 34
  International airline, 642
  Map reading, 156
  Motorcycles, 526
  Motorcycle safety, 106
  Mustang, 147
  Petroleum transport, 56
  Police cruisers, 268
  Shuttle van, 597
  Ski boat, 481
  SUV sales, 19
  Tractor parts, 290
  Tractor purchase, 362, 481, 495
  Trailer load, 61
  Transmission, 56
  Transmission repair, 642
  Truck accessories, 306
  Vehicle depreciation, 580
  Weighing freight, 19
  Wheels with bling, 275
  Yard Maintenance, 20

B

Banking
  Accumulating $1,000,000, 434
  Amortizing a loan, 496
  Amount due, 276
  Amount owed the IRS, 240
  Bad credit history, 354
  Bank balances, 182
  Bank loan, 344
  Benefit increase, 108
  Budgeting, 108

Capital improvement, 337
Checking account records, 28
Check processing, 19
Commission with returns, 223
Completing check stubs, 181
Compounding, 396
Corporate finance, 337, 387
Corporate savings, 397
Credit card balance, 472
Credit-card deposits, 187, 188
Credit union, 386
Current checking balance, 193
Emergency cash, 397
Financing college expenses, 403
Financing construction, 362
Finding interest, 148
Finding time, 148
Home loan, 505
Inflation and retirement, 397
Inheritance, 149, 397
Interest earnings, 345
Interest rate, 345
International finance, 354, 386, 387
Loan amount, 149
Loan collateral, 396
Loan qualification, 99
Loans between banks, 337
Loan to an uncle, 148
Maturity value, 148
Maximizing interest, 387
Minority loans, 116
Partial invoice payment, 276
Partial payment, 487
Payment due, 276
Penalty on late payment, 345
Poor credit, 353
Promissory note, 345
Putting up collateral, 397
Reconciling checking accounts, 194, 195
Retirement account, 100, 345
Retirement funds, 454
Retirement income, 397
Retirement planning, 421
Salary plus commission, 223
Saving for a home, 421
Saving for retirement, 344
Savings, 148, 386
Savings account, 396
Short-term savings, 344
Student loan, 148
Time of deposit, 345, 346, 396
Time or rate?, 387
United Kingdom, 386
Variable-commission payment, 223
Writing a will, 448
Business
  Abbreviations on invoices, 256–257
  Advertising expenses, 104, 105
  Automotive supplies, 299
  Barge depreciation, 581
  Battery store, 362
  Best Buy, 215
  Book publishing, 663
  Bridal shop, 147
  Business expansion, 403
  Business fixtures, 580
  Business ownership, 95
  Business safe, 597
  Cadillac dealer, 641

Calculation gross earnings, 33–34
Call center, 20
Catering company, 268
Chiquita Brands International, 116
Clothing store, 146
Coffee shop, 629
Commercial carpeting, 69
Comparing discounts, 263
Corporate profits, 92
Cost after markdown, 106
As of dating, 269
Dealer's cost, 114
Dental-supply company, 624
Discount dates, 276
Entrepreneur, E-12
Evaluating inventory, 315
Expanding manufacturing operations, 403
Finding discount dates, 269
Flower shop, 629
Food inflation, 114
Gift shop, 623
Grocery chain, 634
Grocery store, 429
Guitar shop, 629
Hotel room costs, 19
Ice cream shop, 623
Independent bookstore ownership, 612
International business, 337
International shipments, 139
Inventory, 336, 488
Inventory purchase, 346
Juice company, 641
Luxury hotels, 20
Managerial earnings, 34
New product failure, 94
New showroom, 435
Offshore drilling, 611
Oil profits, 156
Opening a restaurant, 495
Paint store, 338, 593
Paper products manufacturing, 115
Partial invoice payment, 275
Partnership profits, 156
Print shop, 396
Product purchases, 10
Quality, E-11
Retail giants, 14
Russian electrical supplies, 268
Sewing center, 362
Ship building, 139
Shopping center, 612
Simple discount rate, 354
Soft-drink bottling, 599
Spray-paint inventory, 314
Stock turnover at cost, 314
Stock turnover at retail, 314
Stock value, 116
Using invoices, 255–256
Value of a business, 403, 404
Walmart supercenter, 525
Woman's clothing shop, 156
Women in business, 12
Business equipment
  Business signage, 597
  Canning machine, 481
  Car-wash machinery, 598
  Ceiling fans, 299
  Commercial carpet, 595
  Commercial fishing boats, 587, 612

Commercial freezer, 594
Communication equipment, 300
Company vehicles, 610
Deep fryer, 604
Dental office furniture, 612
Depreciating computer equipment, 581
Depreciating machinery, 581
Depreciating office furniture, 593
Double-pane windows, 299
Drilling rig, 581
Electronic equipment, 496
English soccer equipment, 275
Forklift depreciation, 594
George Foreman grill, 269
Hospital equipment, 595
Industrial forklift, 598
Jewelry display cases, 597
Kitchen equipment, 20, 274
Laboratory equipment, 580
Machinery depreciation, 579
Oak desk, 305
Printer, 495
Refrigerated display case, 599
Scuba equipment, 497
Storage tank, 610
Surplus-equipment auction, 115
Woodworking machinery, 596
X-ray equipment, 435

C
Construction
Airplane hangar, 548
Apartment owner, 525
Asphalt crumb, 489
Cabinet installation, 55, 56
Commercial building, 139, 436, 548
Concrete footings, 70
Construction power tools, 588
Conveyor system, 587
Delivering concrete, 62
Elderly housing, 505
Excavating machinery, 588
Financing construction, 362
Finish carpentry, 68
Forklift depreciation, 594
Home construction, 346
Landscape equipment, 595, 596
New kitchen, 436
New roof, 353, 436
Office complex, 525, 612
Offshore drilling, 611
Parking lot fencing, 61
Perimeter of fencing, 57
Remodeling, 488
Road paving, 337
Rock crusher, 361
Security fencing, 61
Stainless steel grill, 263
Theater renovation, 20
Triplex, 549
Warehouse construction, 596
Weather stripping, 70
Window installation, 61
Yacht construction, 640

D
Domestic
Electricity rates, 68
Home beverage fountains, 258
Home-value appreciation, 114
Household lubricant, 100
Lights out, 106
Personal budgeting, 99
Producing crafts, 68
Tailored clothing, 62

E
Education
College bookstore, 186–187
College enrollment, 98, 116
College expenses, 115, 428
College textbooks, 19, 147
Exchange program, 139
High school dropouts, 107
Paying for college, 428
Private school equipment, 588
Saving for college, 436
Student union, 434
Textbooks, 290
University fees, 116
Vocabulary, 105
Employment/Employee benefits
Aiding disabled employees, 101
Computer consultant, 487
Earnings calculation, 68
Employee net pay, 239
Employee population base, 98
Female lawyers, 93
Guaranteed hourly work, 222
Heating-company representative, 241
Hiring, 99
Insurance office manager, 214
Job cuts, 104
Key employee insurance, 564
Layoff alternative, 107
Managerial earnings, 34
Marketing representative, 240
Nurses, 94
Nursing, 105
Office assistant, 214
Part-time work, 61
Payroll, 228, 229, 344
Piecework with overtime, 223
Retail employment, 214
Retirement, 421
River raft manager, 241
Self-employment, 229, 403
Starbucks district manager, 240
Store manager, 215
Video player, 257
Women in the military, 104
Women in the Navy, 93
Working in China, 158
Entertainment/Sports
Athletic shoes, 315
Athletic socks, 314–315
Bowling equipment, 300
Casino, 353
Competitive cyclist training, 19
Dance shoes, 258
Drums, 299
DVD rentals, 115
Eating out, 114
Elliptical trainer, 305
Exercycle, 289
Fishing boat, 19
Fly-fishing, 299
Gambling payback, 99
Gaming, 147
Golf cart, 299
Golf clubs, 290
Home-workout equipment, 298
Kayak, 305
Lost overboard, 106
Motorcyclists, 105
Mountain bike, 300
Movie projectors, 489
Movies, 147
Musical instruments, 146
New auditorium, 435
NINTENDO, 263
NY Yankees, 93

Parachute jumps, 12
Piano repair, 315
Recreation equipment, 597
Rock concert, 157
Scuba diving, 434
Scuba equipment, 497
Scuba shoppe, 629
Ski jackets, 289
Snowboard, 299
Sports complex, 436
Sportswear, 300
Sport T-shirts, 314
Sprint training, 56
Summer vacation, 92, E-13
Super Bowl advertising, 94
Swimming, 155
Swimming pool pump, 298
Table-tennis tables, 290
Tanning salon, 105
Theater seating, 597
Vacation mistakes, 106
Water skis, 139
Weight-training books, 290
Yachts, 641
Youth soccer, 20
Environment
Earthquake damage, 354
Effects of global warming, 106
Flooding, E-10
Global warming, 156
Hurricane Katrina, 12
Sea levels, 156
Water scarcity, 108
Winter-wheat planting, 115

F
Family
Alimony, 28
Child-care payments, 421
Child support, 100
Divorce settlement, 403
Family budget, 94
Family restaurant, 114
Family size, 99
Head of household, 540
Married, 540
Saving to buy a home, 108
Food service industry
Bakery, 403
Beef/turkey cost, 28
Biscuits, 155
Cake recipe, 56
Campus vending machines, 13
Canadian food products, 275
Chicken noodle soup, 108
Coffee shop, 629
Fast-food restaurants, 595
Frozen yogurt, 275
Goat cheese, 482
Health food, 337
Hershey Kisses, 13
Hershey mini chips, 13
Kitchen island, 258
McDonald's, E-10
Pizza, 147, 354
Restaurant tables, 599
Sales of health food, 156
Selling bananas, 298
Subway sandwiches, 18
Tiger food, 155
Wine, 299

G
General interest
Airport improvements, 435
Antiques, 149, 306

Apparel, 623
Bar soap, 93
Bed in a bag, 299
Beer consumption, 105
Blouses, 298
Bracelet, 263
Crystal from Ireland, 275
Custom-made jewelry, 290
Engagement ring, 488
Fires, 116
Furniture, 662
Iceberg volume, 157
Island area, 157
Japanese Yen, 157
Liquid fertilizer, 258
Making jewelry, 70, 362
Man's best friend, 99
Native-American jewelry, 57
Population forecasts, 107
Rare stamps, 435
Responder backpack, 289
Restaurant tips, 28
Sewer drain service, 595
Shampoo ingredients, 100
Social Security, 429
Songbird migration, 157

Government
American Chiropractic Association, 106
Biker helmet laws, 107
Criminal justice, 338
Disaster relief, 428
Gross national product, 12
Injury lawsuit, 428
Law enforcement, 344
Salvation Army, 12
Salvation army loss, 549
Total World War II veterans, 19
U.S. Paper money, 35
U.S. Patent recipients, 109
Voter registration, 99
War deaths, 663
World War II Veterans, 19

H

Healthcare
Bad medicine, 74
Blood-alcohol levels, 109
Blood cells, 155
Blood-cholesterol levels, 100
Calories from fat, 100
Cone zone deaths, 116
Criminology lab, 214
Dental office furniture, 612
Dispensing eye drops, 70
Flu pandemic of 1918, 100
Gambling with health, 74
Health food, 337
Health in a machine, 108
Hospital equipment, 595
Medicine dose, 35
Motor Vehicle Accidents, 12
Overweight, 93
Oxygen supply, 641
Physically impaired, 20
Sick pet, 101
Side-impact collisions, 108
Smoking and cancer, 74
Smoking and lung disease, 93
Smoking or nonsmoking, 99
Social Security and Medicare, 228, 229
Weight-training equipment, 586

I

Insurance
Adult auto insurance, 557
Bodily injury insurance, 557

Coinsured fire loss, 549
Fire insurance premium, 548
Fire loss, 548
Gift-shop fire loss, 549
Industrial building insurance, 548
Insurance company payment, 558
Key employee insurance, 564
Life insurance, 564
Major fire loss, 549
Medical expenses and property damage, 558
Multiple carriers, 549
Partial coverage, 549, 550
20-Pay life policy, 564
Premium factors, 564
Property insurance, 100
Universal life insurance, 564
Whole life insurance, 564
Youthful-operator auto insurance, 557
Youthful operator—no driver's training, 557

R

Real estate
Home ownership, 98
Home prices, 107
Real estate commissions, 94
Real estate development, 155
Real estate fees, 34
Residential rental property, 611

S

Sales/Marketing
Auto purchase, 481
Auto sales, 115
Auto sales in China, 94
Boat purchase, 353
Computer sales, E-13
Condominium purchase, 505
Consumer internet sales, 95
Crayon sales, 12
Deli sales, 114
Department sales, 10
Determining purchasing power, 397
Educational sales, 240
Firewood sale, 70
Hardware purchase, 258
Home purchase, 505
Hot tub purchase, 472
Inside sales, 214
iPad sales, 13
iPhone discount, 106
Jell-O sales, 12
Jetson aircraft sales, 635
Monthly sales, E-11
National home sales, 115
Nissan sales, 140
Nursing-care purchases, 257
Pottery-shop sales, 298
Purchase of T-bills, 354, 363
Real estate fees, 34
Recreation equipment rental, 13
Refrigerator purchase, 481
River-raft sales, 298
Sales of health food, 156
Selling a restaurant, 428
Selling bananas, 298
Soda sales, 139
Subway sales, 27
Telemarketing teamwork, 13
Ticket sales, 155
Total cost, 94
Total sales, 108
Tractor purchase, 362, 481, 495
Travel-agency sales, 240
Tripod purchase, 258
Van purchase, 428
Vegetable sales, 140
Wholesale auto parts, 258

Science/Technology
Apple, Inc., E-11
Canning machine, 481
Carpet-cleaning equipment, 587
Ceiling fans, 299
Cell phones, 353, E-12
Chip fabrication, 481
Communication equipment, 588
Computer chips, 147
Computer replacement, 428
Computer system, 481
Construction power tools, 588
Conveyor system, 587
Copy machines, 596
Device assembly, 55
Digital camera, 94
Digital thermometers, 299
Electric guitar, 480
Electronic analyzer, 587
Facebook users, 115
Fiber optics, 259
Flash drive, 300
Global Positioning Systems (GPS), 263, 275, 305
Graphic arts, 258
iPad, 263
Laptops, 345, 612
Lawn-mower, 345, E-13
Measuring brass trim, 61
Metal lathe, 480
Notebook, 19
Outdoor lighting, 290
Personal organizers, 596
Playset, 480
Printing, 489
Refrigerators, 146
Smart phones, 496, E-14
Sound system, 139
Studio sound system, 586
Surveillance cameras, 488
Video equipment, 598
Web design, 337, 353, 489
Wind energy, 105
Wind turbine, 594

Stocks/Investments
Bond fund, 454, 455
Bond purchase, 454
CDS or global stocks, 448
Fixed rate or stocks, 448
Investing in bonds, 344
Investment, 386, 387
Investment decision, 386
Mutual fund investing, 421
Stock price, E-12
Stock purchase, 448
T-bill and stock investing, 421
Trade-discount comparison, 258

T

Taxes
Commercial property tax, 525
Comparing property tax rates, 526
Federal withholding tax, 238
Gasoline taxes, 93
Income tax payment, 353
Married—income tax, 539, 540
Penalty on unpaid income tax, 338
Penalty on unpaid property tax, 337
Real estate taxes, 525
Sales tax, 93, 114
Sales-tax computation, 94
Single—income tax, 539
State withholding tax, 238
Taxes on home, 526
Top tax rates, 664

Business Mathematics

1 Whole Numbers and Decimals

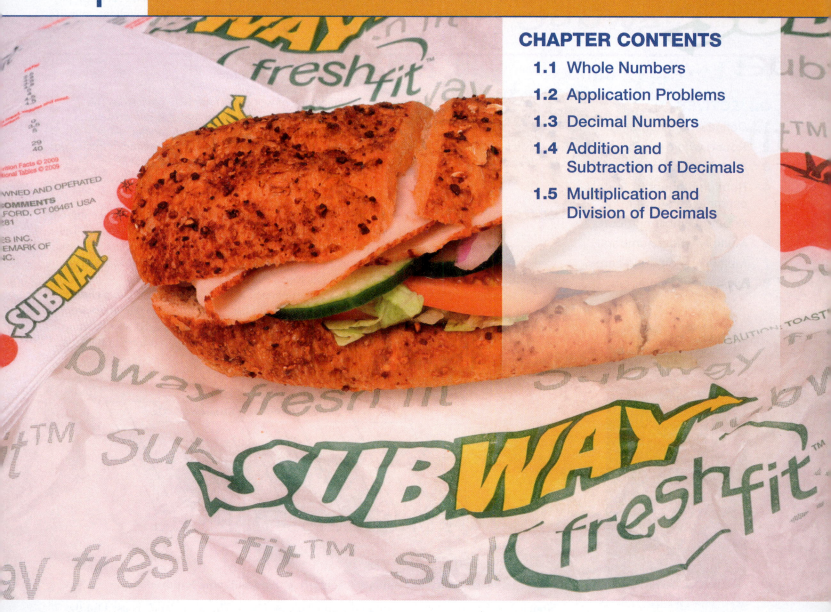

CHAPTER CONTENTS

1.1 Whole Numbers

1.2 Application Problems

1.3 Decimal Numbers

1.4 Addition and Subtraction of Decimals

1.5 Multiplication and Division of Decimals

▼ CASE IN POINT

JESSICA FERNANDEZ worked part time for SUBWAY when taking classes at a local community college, but she is now a manager that oversees 18 employees. She looks for employees that have a good work ethic, are honest and friendly, and who can work with numbers. She uses numbers daily to schedule employees, compute sales, figure sales taxes, complete the payroll, and order inventory.

This text will improve your ability to work with numbers which is important! It also teaches you important concepts that relate to your personal life (debt, savings, investment, home mortgages, insurance, and taxes) and the workplace (markup, markdown, bank services, payroll, and simple interest). You will use the concepts covered in this book throughout your life.

▼ 1.1 Whole Numbers

OBJECTIVES

1 Define whole numbers.

2 Round whole numbers.

3 Add whole numbers.

4 Round numbers to estimate an answer.

5 Subtract whole numbers.

6 Multiply whole numbers.

7 Multiply by omitting zeros.

8 Divide whole numbers.

CASE IN POINT   To improve the efficiency of workers at the SUBWAY store she manages, Jessica Fernandez cross-trains each employee so that she can do several tasks, including food preparation, cleanup, and operating the cash register. After watching an employee give a customer too much change for a second time, a frustrated Jessica Fernandez decided that any new hire must pass a basic math test.

OBJECTIVE 1   Define whole numbers.   The **decimal system** uses the ten one-place **digits:** 0, 1, 2, 3, 4, 5, 6, 7, 8, and 9. Combinations of these digits represent any number needed. The starting point of this system is the **decimal point (.)**. This section considers only the numbers made up of digits to the left of the decimal point—the **whole numbers**. The following diagram names the first fifteen places held by the digits to the left of the decimal point.

A researcher estimated that 581,075,900 smart phones will be sold in 2015. Use a **comma** to work with numbers this large. Starting at the decimal place and moving to the left, place a comma between each group of three digits. Although commas are always used when writing numbers, they are not shown on some calculators. Commas are not required for numbers with four digits such as 8475.

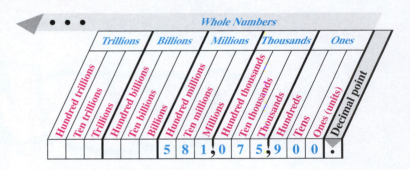

The number 581,075,900 is read as

five hundred eighty-one million, seventy-five thousand, nine hundred.

Notice that the word "*and*" is not used with whole numbers. The word "*and*" is used for the decimal place, as discussed in Section 1.3.

Expressing Whole Numbers in Words

 EXAMPLE 1   Write the following numbers in words.

(a) 7835   (b) 111,356,075   (c) 17,000,017,000

SOLUTION

(a) seven thousand, eight hundred thirty-five

(b) one hundred eleven million, three hundred fifty-six thousand, seventy-five

(c) seventeen billion, seventeen thousand

Quick TIP

Do not use the word "*and*" when reading or writing a whole number.

QUICK CHECK 1

At one point in 2013, the national debt of the United States was $16,810,680,391,540. Write the number in words.

OBJECTIVE 2   Round whole numbers.   Business applications often require **rounding** numbers. For example, money amounts are often rounded to the nearest thousand or million dollars. Use these steps to **round whole numbers**.

Rounding Whole Numbers

Step 1	Locate the **place** to which the number is to be rounded. Draw a line under that place.
Step 2	If the first digit to the *right* of the underlined place is **5 or more, increase** the digit in the place to which you are rounding by 1. If the digit is **4 or less, do not change**.
Step 3	**Change** all digits to the right of the underlined digit to zeros.

Rounding Whole Numbers **EXAMPLE 2** Round each number as indicated.

(a) 579 to nearest ten

(b) 34,127 to nearest thousand

(c) 475,871 to the nearest ten thousand

(d) 79,625 to nearest thousand

SOLUTION

(a) **Step 1** Locate the tens place and underline.

579

Round to this place.

Step 2 The first digit to the right of the underlined digit is 9, which is greater than 5. Therefore, increase the digit in the tens place from 7 to 8.

Step 3 Change all digits to the right of the tens place to zero. In other words, change the 9 in the ones place to a zero.

579 rounded to the nearest ten is 580.

(b) **Step 1** Locate the thousands place and underline. 34,127

Step 2 Since the digit to the right of the thousands place is 1 (less than 5), do not change the 4 in the thousands place.

Step 3 Change all digits to the right of the thousands place to zeros.

34,127 rounded to the nearest thousand is 34,000

(c) **Step 1** Locate the ten thousands place and underline. 475,871

Step 2 Since the digit to the right of the ten thousands place is 5, which falls in the category of 5 or more, increase the 7 to an 8.

Step 3 Change all digits to the right of the tens thousands place to zeros: **480,000**

(d) **Step 1** Locate the thousands place and underline. 79,625

Step 2 The number to the right of the underlined number 9 above is 5, which falls in the 5 or more category. Thus, increase the 9 by 1 to 10. Place a 0 in the thousands place and carry 1 to the ten thousands place changing the 7 to an 8.

Step 3 Change all digits to the right of the thousands place to zeros: **80,000**

Quick TIP

When rounding a number, look at the first digit to the right of the digit being rounded. Do not look beyond this digit.

QUICK CHECK 2

Round each number.

(a) 653,781 to the nearest ten thousand (b) 6,578,321 to the nearest million

(c) 499,100 to the nearest thousand (d) 499,100 to the nearest hundred thousand

We will now review four basic **operations** with whole numbers: **addition, subtraction, multiplication,** and **division**.

OBJECTIVE 3 Add whole numbers. In **addition**, the numbers being added are **addends**, and the answer is the **sum**, or **total**, or **amount**.

$$8 \quad \text{addend}$$
$$\underline{+\ 9} \quad \text{addend}$$
$$17 \quad \text{sum (answer)}$$

Add numbers by arranging them in a column with units above units, tens above tens, hundreds above hundreds, thousands above thousands, and so on. Use the decimal point as a reference for arranging the numbers. If a number does not include a decimal point, the decimal point is assumed to be at the far right. For example, 85 = 85. and 527 = 527.

Adding with Checking   To find the one-day total amount of purchases at the SUBWAY store, manager Jessica Fernandez needed to add the following amounts.

$$
\begin{array}{r}
\color{red}{\$4028} \\
\$738 \\
63 \\
125 \\
2617 \\
+ \quad 485 \\
\hline
\$4028
\end{array}
$$

First, add down the columns   ↓   Then, check by adding up.   ↑

> **Quick TIP**
>
> Always be sure to check your work.

Adding from the top down results in an answer of $4028. Check for accuracy by adding again—this time from the bottom up. If the answers are the same, the sum is probably correct. If the answers are different, there is an error in either adding down or adding up, and the problem should be reworked. Both answers agree in this example, so the sum is correct.

> **QUICK CHECK 3**
>
> Find the total of the following expenses: $2805 + $871 + $28 + $169 + $1196

OBJECTIVE 4   Round numbers to estimate an answer.   Answers can be quickly estimated using **front-end rounding**. This requires the first number to be rounded and all the following digits to be changed to zero. Only one nonzero digit remains.

Using Front-end Rounding to Estimate an Answer   The graphic shows the top oil producing areas in the U.S. Notice that a lot of oil is produced offshore in the Gulf of Mexico. Apply front-end rounding to estimate total oil production from these areas.

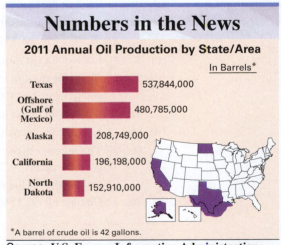

Numbers in the News

2011 Annual Oil Production by State/Area

In Barrels*

Texas	537,844,000
Offshore (Gulf of Mexico)	480,785,000
Alaska	208,749,000
California	196,198,000
North Dakota	152,910,000

*A barrel of crude oil is 42 gallons.

Source: U.S. Energy Information Administration

> **Quick TIP**
>
> In front-end rounding, only one nonzero digit (first digit) remains. All digits to the right are zeros.

SOLUTION

	Actual		Front-end Rounded
Texas	537,844,000	→	500,000,000
Offshore (Gulf)	480,785,000	→	500,000,000
Alaska	208,749,000	→	200,000,000
California	196,198,000	→	200,000,000
North Dakota	152,910,000	→	200,000,000
	Estimated Total		1,600,000,000 barrels of oil

Oil consumption in the U.S. is about 7,000,000,000 barrels. The U.S. must buy the difference between what is consumed and what is produced in the U.S. It buys oil from Canada, Saudi Arabia and other oil exporting nations.

QUICK CHECK 4

Use front-end rounding to estimate the total of the following numbers.

621,150; 38,400; 9682; 27,451; 435,620

OBJECTIVE 5 **Subtract whole numbers.** A subtraction problem is set up much like a addition problem. The top number is the **minuend**, the number being subtracted is the **subtra hend**, and the answer is the **difference**.

$$
\begin{array}{rl}
23 & \text{minuend} \\
-\;7 & \text{subtrahend} \\
\hline
16 & \text{difference}
\end{array}
$$

Subtract one number from another by placing the subtrahend directly under the minuend with columns aligned. Begin the subtraction from the right-most column. When a digit in the subtrahend is *larger* than the corresponding digit in the minuend, **borrow** as shown in the next example.

Subtracting with Borrowing

 EXAMPLE 5

Subtract 2894 SUBWAY drink cups from 3783 SUBWAY drink cups in inventory. First, write the problem as follows.

$$
\begin{array}{r}
3783 \\
-2894
\end{array}
$$

In the ones (units) column, subtract 4 from 3 by borrowing a 1 from the tens column in the minuend to get 1 ten + 3, or 13, in the units column with 7 now in the tens column. Then subtract 4 from 13 for a result of 9. Complete the subtraction as follows.

$$
\begin{array}{c c c c c}
2 & 16 & 17 & 13 & \\
3 & 7 & 8 & 3 & \\
-\;2 & 8 & 9 & 4 & \\
\hline
8 & 8 & 9 & & \text{drink cups}
\end{array}
$$

In this example, the tens are borrowed from the hundreds column, and the hundreds are borrowed from the thousands column.

Check the answer to a subtraction problem by adding the answer (difference) to the subtrahend. The result should equal the minuend.

Subtracting with Checking

EXAMPLE 6

Subtract 1635 from 5383 and check the answer.

Quick TIP

Do not change the order of the numbers when subtracting. For example, $(9 - 5)$ is not the same thing as $(5 - 9)$.

Problem		Check	
Problem (subtract down) ↓	5383 minuend	5383 ↑	This result should equal the minuend.
	− 1635 subtrahend	+ 1635	
	3748 **difference**	3748	Check (add up)

OBJECTIVE 6 **Multiply whole numbers.** Multiplication is actually a quick method of addition. For example, 3×4 can be found by adding 3 a total of 4 times, since 3×4 means $3 + 3 + 3 + 3 = 12$. However, it is not practical to use the addition method for large numbers. For example, 103×92 would be found by adding 103 a total of 92 times. Instead, find

6. TIP

okay to change the order
en multiplying two numbers.
or example, $8 \cdot 5 = 5 \cdot 8$.

this result with multiplication. The multiplication of 103 by 92 can be written in any of the following ways:

$$103 \times 92 = 103 \cdot 92 = 103 \cdot 92 = (103)(92)$$

The number being multiplied is the **multiplicand**, the number doing the multiplying is the **multiplier**, and the answer is the **product**.

$$\begin{array}{rl} 3 & \text{multiplicand} \\ \times\ 4 & \text{multiplier} \\ \hline 12 & \text{product} \end{array}$$

When the multiplier contains more than one digit, **partial products** must be used, as in the next example, which shows the product of 25 and 34.

Multiplying Whole Numbers

 EXAMPLE 7

Multiply 25×34 by first multiplying 25 by the 4 in the ones place as shown in Step 1. Then multiply 25 by 3 in the tens place as shown in Step 2, before adding to find the answer in Step 3.

Problem	Step 1	Step 2	Step 3	
25	25	25	25	multiplicand
× 34	× 34	× 34	× 34	multiplier
	100	100	100	partial product (25 × 4)
		75	+ 75	partial product (25 × 3)
			850	product

Step 1   Multiply 25 by 4 and write 100 aligning ones places.

Step 2   Multiply 25 by 3 and write 75 one position to the left since 3 is in the tenths place. The 5 in 75 will be in the ten's place.

Step 3   Add the two partial products to get the answer.

QUICK CHECK 7

Multiply 18 telemarketers by 36 phone calls per telemarketer per hour to estimate the number of calls made in one hour.

OBJECTIVE 7 **Multiply by omitting zeros.** If the multiplier or multiplicand end in zero, first omit any zeros at the right of the numbers and then replace omitted zeros at the right of the final answer. For example, find the product of 240 and 13 as follows.

$$\begin{array}{rl} 24\cancel{0} & \text{Omit the zero in the calculation.} \\ \times\ 13 & \\ \hline 72 & \\ 24\ \downarrow & \\ \hline 3120 & \text{Replace the omitted zero at the right of} \\ & \text{312 for a final answer (product) of 3120.} \end{array}$$

Multiplying, Omitting Zeros

EXAMPLE 8

In the following multiplication problems, omit zeros in the calculation and then replace omitted zeros to obtain the product.

(a)

$$\begin{array}{rr} 150 & 15 \\ \times\ 70 & \times\ 7 \\ \hline & 105 \\ & 10,500 \end{array}$$ ← omit zeros   attach 2 zeros   answer

(b)

$$\begin{array}{rr} 300 & 3 \\ \times\ 90 & \times\ 9 \\ \hline & 27 \\ & 27,000 \end{array}$$ ← omit zeros   attach 3 zeros   answer

QUICK CHECK 8

Multiply 400 by 50. Omit zeros in the calculation and replace them in the product.

A shortcut for multiplying by 10, 100, 1000, and so on is to just attach the number of zeros to the number being multiplied. For example,

$$33 \times 10 \quad = \quad 33 \text{ and } \mathbf{1} \text{ zero } = 330$$
$$56 \times 100 \quad = \quad 56 \text{ and } \mathbf{2} \text{ zeros } = 5600$$
$$732 \times 1000 = 732 \text{ and } \mathbf{3} \text{ zeros } = 732{,}000$$

OBJECTIVE 8 Divide whole numbers. The **dividend** is the number being divided, the **divisor** is the number doing the dividing, and the **quotient** is the answer. **Division** is indicated in any of the following ways.

$$\underset{\text{dividend}}{15} \; \div \; \underset{\text{divisor}}{5} \; = \; \underset{\text{quotient}}{3} \qquad\qquad \underset{\text{divisor}}{5} \overline{)\underset{\text{dividend}}{15}} \; \; \overset{3}{} \; \text{quotient}$$

$$\underset{\text{divisor}}{\overset{\text{dividend}}{\dfrac{15}{5}}} = 3 \; \text{quotient}$$

Dividing Whole Numbers   **EXAMPLE 9**

To divide 1095 baseball cards evenly among 73 collectors, divide 1095 by 73 as follows.

$$73\overline{)1095}$$

Since 73 is larger than 1 or 10, but smaller than 109, begin by dividing 73 into 109. There is one 73 in 109, so place 1 *over the digit 9* in the dividend as shown. Then multiply 1 and 73.

$$\begin{array}{r} 1 \\ 73\overline{)1095} \\ \underline{73} \quad 1 \times 73 = 73 \\ 36 \end{array}$$

Subtract 73 from 109 to get 36. The next step is to bring down the 5 from the dividend, placing it next to the remainder 36. This gives the number 365. The divisor, 73, is then divided into 365 with a result of 5, which is placed to the right of the 1 in the quotient. Since 73 divides into 365 exactly 5 times, the final answer (quotient) is exactly 15.

$$\begin{array}{r} 15 \\ 73\overline{)1095} \\ \underline{73} \\ 365 \\ \underline{365} \\ 0 \end{array}$$

Check the answer by multiplying.

$$\begin{array}{r} 73 \\ \times \; 15 \\ \hline 365 \\ 73 \\ \hline 1095 \end{array}$$ **Since this is the original number of cards, the answer checks.**

QUICK CHECK 9

Divide $7506 evenly among 18 winners. How much will each receive?

Often, the divisor does not divide evenly into the dividend, leaving a remainder. The next example shows that remainders can be also be written using fractions or decimals. Fractions and decimals are covered in the next chapter. For now, write a remainder of 6 as R6.

Dividing with a Remainder
in the Answer

EXAMPLE 10

Divide 126 by 24. Express the remainder in each of the three forms.

Remainder	Fraction	Decimal

$$
\begin{array}{r}
5\ \text{R6} \\
24\overline{)126} \\
120 \\
\hline
6
\end{array}
\qquad
\begin{array}{r}
5\frac{6}{24} \\
24\overline{)126} \\
120 \\
\hline
6
\end{array}
\qquad
\begin{array}{r}
5.25 \\
24\overline{)126.00} \\
120 \\
\hline
60 \\
48 \\
\hline
1\ 20 \\
1\ 20 \\
\hline
0
\end{array}
$$

QUICK CHECK 10

Divide 19 by 5.

If a divisor contains zeros at the far right, first drop the zeros in the divisor and then move the decimal point in the dividend the same number of places to the left as there were zeros dropped from the divisor.

$$900\overline{)108{,}000} \qquad \text{becomes} \qquad 9\overline{)1080}$$

Drop 2 zeros. ————   Move decimal point
                                        2 places left.

Dropping Zeros
to Divide

EXAMPLE 11

To divide 108,000 by 900, first drop two zeros from each number. Then divide.

$$
\begin{array}{r}
120 \\
9\overline{)1080} \\
9 \\
\hline
18 \\
18 \\
\hline
0 \\
0 \\
\hline
\end{array}
$$

Check Answer

$$
\begin{array}{r}
120 \\
\times\ 9 \\
\hline
1080
\end{array}
$$ so the division is correct

You must change 9 back to 900 and multiply by 120 to get the original dividend of 108,000.

Quick TIP

After dropping zeros and dividing, do not add trailing zeros back to the answer.

Therefore, $108{,}000 \div 900 = 120$.

QUICK CHECK 11

First drop zeros, and then divide $19{,}200 \div 300$.

Checking Division
Problems with
Remainders

EXAMPLE 12

In a division problem, check the answer by multiplying the quotient (answer) and the divisor. Then add any remainder. If the result is not the same as the dividend, an error exists and the problem should be reworked. Check the following division problems.

(a)
$$
\begin{array}{r}
37\ \text{R3} \\
716\overline{)26{,}495} \\
21\ 48 \\
\hline
5\ 015 \\
5\ 012 \\
\hline
3 \quad \text{remainder}
\end{array}
$$

(b)
$$
\begin{array}{r}
85\ \text{R6} \\
418\overline{)35{,}536} \\
33\ 44 \\
\hline
2\ 096 \\
2\ 090 \\
\hline
6 \quad \text{remainder}
\end{array}
$$

Quick TIP

Be sure to add the remainder to the product when checking a division problems with a remainder.

SOLUTION

(a)

```
      716
  ×    37
     5012
    2148
   26,492
  +     3     add remainder
   26,495     correct
```

(b)

```
      418
  ×    85
     2090
    3344
   35,530
  +     6     add remainder
   35,536     correct
```

QUICK CHECK 12

Divide 9897 by 215. Check the answer by multiplying the quotient (answer) by the divisor.

▼ 1.1 Exercises

MyMathLab®

The shaded sections below contain solutions to help you get a **QUICK START** *on the various types of exercises.*

Write the following numbers in words. (See Example 1.)

1. 7040 seven thousand, forty
2. 5310 five thousand, three hundred ten
3. 37,901 _____
4. 725,069 _____
5. 4,650,015 _____
6. 3,765,041,000 _____

Round each of the following numbers first to the nearest ten, then to the nearest hundred, and finally to the nearest thousand. Go back to the **original number** *each time before rounding to the next position. (See Example 2.)*

	Nearest Ten	*Nearest Hundred*	*Nearest Thousand*
7. 2065	2070	2100	2000
8. 8385	8390	8400	8000
9. 46,231	_____	_____	_____
10. 55,175	_____	_____	_____
11. 106,054	_____	_____	_____
12. 359,874	_____	_____	_____

13. Explain the three steps needed to round a number when the digit to the right of the place to which you are rounding is 5 or more. (See Objective 2.)

14. Explain the three steps needed to round a number when the digit to the right of the place to which you are rounding is 4 or less. (See Objective 2.)

Add each of the following. Check your answers. (See Example 3.)

15.	16.	17.	18.
75	57	875	135
63	26	364	594
45	43	171	415
+ 27	+ 18	+ 776	+ 276
210			

19.	20.	21.	22.
750	371	311,479	803,526
91	45	77,631	759,991
8	839	+ 594,383	+ 36,024
540	3		
+ 7	+ 47		

Subtract each of the following. Check your answers. (See Examples 5 and 6.)

23.	24.	25.	26.
896	757	3715	6215
− 228	− 286	− 838	− 767

27.	28.	29.	30.
65,198	445,193	7,025,389	9,807,943
− 43,652	− 62,785	− 936,490	− 959,489

Solve the following problems. To serve as a check, the vertical and horizontal totals must be the same in the lower right-hand corner.

31. PRODUCT PURCHASES   The following table shows monthly purchases at a Best Buy by product line for each of the first six months of the year. Complete the totals by adding horizontally and vertically.

Product	Jan.	Feb.	Mar.	Apr.	May	June	Totals
Software	$49,802	$36,911	$47,851	$54,732	$29,852	$74,119	**$293,267**
Computers	$86,154	$72,908	$31,552	$74,944	$85,532	$36,705	
Printers	$59,854	$85,119	$87,914	$45,812	$56,314	$91,856	
Mobile Phones	$73,951	$72,564	$39,615	$71,099	$72,918	$42,953	
Totals							

32. DEPARTMENT SALES   The following table shows Jameson's Fashion expenses by department for the last six months of the year. Complete the totals by adding horizontally and vertically.

Department	July	Aug.	Sept.	Oct.	Nov.	Dec.	Totals
Office	$29,806	$31,712	$40,909	$32,514	$18,902	$23,514	
Production	$92,143	$86,599	$97,194	$72,815	$89,500	$63,754	
Sales	$31,802	$39,515	$58,192	$32,544	$41,920	$48,732	
Warehouse	$15,746	$12,986	$32,325	$41,983	$39,814	$20,605	
Totals							

Multiply each of the following. (See Example 7.)

33.
```
    218
  × 43
   654
   872
  9374
```

34.
```
   672
 ×  56
```

35.
```
   1896
 ×   62
```

36.
```
   7318
 ×   38
```

37.
```
     6452
 ×    263
```

38.
```
     7143
 ×    295
```

39.
```
     1109
 ×   7311
```

40.
```
     9503
 ×   3411
```

Estimate answers using front-end rounding. Then find the exact answers. (See Example 4.)

41. **Estimate**   **Exact**
```
  8000  ←rounds   8215
    60  ←  to       56
   700  ←          729
+ 4000  ←       + 3605
 12,760          12,605
```

42. **Estimate**   **Exact**
```
        ←         2685
        ←           73
        ←          592
  +     ←       + 7183
```

43. **Estimate**   **Exact**
```
        ←          783
  -     ←        - 238
```

44. **Estimate**   **Exact**
```
        ←          942
  -     ←        - 286
```

45. **Estimate**   **Exact**
```
        ←          638
  ×     ←        × 47
```

46. **Estimate**   **Exact**
```
        ←          864
  ×     ←        × 74
```

Multiply, omitting zeros in the calculation and then replacing them at the right of the product to obtain the final answer. (See Example 8.)

47.
```
    370
  × 180
     37
   × 18
    666    2 zeros
  66,600
```

48.
```
    520
  × 400
```

49.
```
   3760
 × 6000
```

50.
```
   7200
 × 1300
```

Divide each of the following. (See Examples 9 and 10.)

51.
```
     1241 R1
  4)4965
    4
    09
     8
    16
    16
    05
     4
     1
```

52. 7)13,214

53. 43)19,715

54. 93)81,452

55. Explain why checking the answer is a very important step in solving math problems.

56. In your personal and business life, when is it most important to check your math calculations? Why?

Divide each of the following, dropping zeros from the divisor. (See Examples 10 and 11.)

57. 180)‾429,350 **58.** 320)‾360,990 **59.** 1300)‾75,800 **60.** 1600)‾253,100

```
         2 385 R5
    18)42,935
       36
        6 9
        5 4
        153
        144
          95
          90
           5
```

Rewrite the following numbers in words. (See Example 1.)

61. MOTAR VEHICLE ACCIDENTS According to the NHTSA, the number of people injured in accidents in 2011 was 2,240,000.

62. WOMEN IN BUSINESS A.G. Edwards reports that there are 8,534,350 businesses owned by women in the United States.

63. PARACHUTE JUMPS There are 3,200,000 parachute jumps in the United States each year according to the History Channel.

64. GROSS NATIONAL PRODUCT The market value of goods and services created in the U.S. increased last quarter to $15,461,800,000,000.

Rewrite the numbers from the following sentences using digits. (See Example 1.)

65. JELL-O SALES The average number of boxes of Jell-O gelatin sold each day is eight hundred fifty-four thousand, seven hundred ninety-five. (*Source:* Kraft Foods.)

65. 854,795 boxes

66. CRAYON SALES The Binney & Smith Company makes about two billion Crayola Crayons each year.

66. _____

67. SALVATION ARMY During the past year, the Salvation Army served fifty-five million, five hundred seventy-two thousand, six hundred thirty-three meals to hungry men, women, and children.

67. _____

68. HURRICANE KATRINA At a New Orleans pumping station, one of the pumps designed by Alexander Baldwin Wood pumped six hundred forty-eight million gallons of flood water (7500 gallons per second) in one day.

68. _____

Solve the following application problems.

69. HERSHEY MINI CHIPS A student estimated that there are approximately 5000 Mini Chips semisweet chocolate chips in 1 pound. How many chips are in 40 pounds?

69. **200,000 chips**

5 × 4 = 20   4 zeros
↙
200,000

70. HERSHEY KISSES Each day 33,000,000 Hershey Kisses can be produced. Find the number of Hershey Kisses that can be produced in 30 days.

70. _____

71. CAMPUS VENDING MACHINES On a normal weekday, the vending machines at American River College dispense 900 sodas, 400 candy bars, 500 snack items, and 200 cups of coffee. If it takes Jim Wilson four hours to restock the vending machines, how many items does he restock each hour?

71. _____

72. IPAD SALES The numbers of iPads sold weekly in one city were 1801, 927, 2088, 580, and 1049. Find the average number sold per week.

72. _____

WHITE WATER RAFTING *American River Raft Rentals lists the following daily raft rental fees. Notice that there is an additional $3 launch fee payable to the park system for each raft rented. Use this information to solve Exercises 73 and 74.*

American River Raft Rentals		
Size	**Rental Fee**	**Launch Fee**
4 persons	$70	$3
6 persons	$95	$3
10 persons	$165	$3
12 persons	$180	$3

73. On a recent Sunday, the following rafts were rented: 6 4-person rafts, 15 6-person rafts, 10 10-person rafts, and 5 12-person rafts. Find the total receipts, including the $3-per-raft launch fee.

73. _____

74. During the July 4th weekend, the following rafts were rented: 38 4-person rafts, 73 6-person rafts, 58 10-person rafts, and 46 12-person rafts. Find the total receipts including the $3-per-raft launch fee.

74. _____

EGG PRODUCTION   *The following pictograph shows the states with the largest number of egg-laying chickens. Use this information to answer Exercises 75–78.*

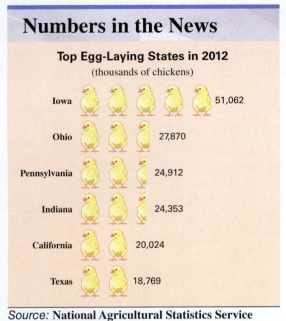

Numbers in the News

Top Egg-Laying States in 2012
(thousands of chickens)

Iowa   51,062

Ohio   27,870

Pennsylvania 24,912

Indiana   24,353

California   20,024

Texas   18,769

Source: **National Agricultural Statistics Service**

75. Find the number of egg-laying chickens in the top four states.
$51{,}062 + 27{,}870 + 24{,}912 + 24{,}353 = 128{,}197$ thousand or $128{,}197{,}000$

75. 128,197 thousand or 128,197,000

76. Use front-end rounding to estimate the total number of egg-laying chickens from all states shown.

76. _____

77. How many more egg-laying chickens are there in Iowa than in Texas?

77. _____

78. How many more egg-laying chickens are there in Iowa and Ohio combined compared to California and Texas combined?

78. _____

RETAIL GIANTS   *The following pictograph shows the number of retail stores worldwide for the seven companies with the greatest number of outlets. Use the pictograph to answer Exercises 79–84.*

Numbers in the News

The Retail Giants

Dollar General

Wal-Mart

7-Eleven

CVS

Family Dollar

Walgreens   = 1000 stores

Rite-Aid

Source: **Company Web sites.**

79. Find the number of Family Dollar retail stores.
$6.5 \times 1000 = 6500$ stores

79. 6500 stores

80. Estimate the number of stores for 7-Eleven.

80. _____

81. Which company has the largest number of retail stores? How many does it have?

81. _____

82. Which of the seven retailers has the fewest number of retail stores? How many does it have?

82. _____

83. How many more retail stores does Dollar General have than Walgreens?

83. _____

84. How many more stores does CVS have compared to its competitor Walgreens?

84. _____

QUICK CHECK ANSWERS

1. Sixteen trillion, eight hundred ten billion, six hundred eighty million, three hundred ninety-one thousand, five hundred forty

2. (a) 650,000, (b) 7,000,000, (c) 499,000
   (d) 500,000

3. $5069

4. 1,080,000

5. 1679 customers

6. 1791

7. 648 phone calls

8. 20 attach 3 zeros = 20,000

9. $417

10. 3 R4

11. 64

12. 46 R7

▼ 1.2 Application Problems

OBJECTIVES

1 Find indicator words in application problems.

2 Learn the four steps for solving application problems.

3 Learn to estimate answers.

4 Solve application problems.

▼ CASE IN POINT   When Jessica Fernandez became a manager at a SUBWAY store, she had to brush up on her math skills. She remembered that certain words indicate addition, subtraction, multiplication, and division.

Many business-application problems require mathematics. You must read very carefully to decide how to solve the problem.

OBJECTIVE 1 **Find indicator words in application problems.** Look for **indicator words** in the application problem—words that indicate the necessary operations: addition, subtraction, multiplication, or division. Some of these words appear below.

Addition	Subtraction	Multiplication	Division	Equals
plus	less	product	divided by	is
more	subtract	double	divided into	the same as
more than	subtracted from	triple	quotient	equals
added to	difference	times	goes into	equal to
increased by	less than	of	divide	yields
sum	fewer	twice	divided equally	results in
total	decreased by	twice as much	per	are
sum of	loss of			
increase of	minus			
gain of	take away			
	reduced by			

The word *and* is not listed above since it can have many different meanings, including all the following:

1. sum of 3 **and** 4,
2. product of 6 **and** 8,
3. seventeen **and** one-half, or
4. six **and** seven tenths.

OBJECTIVE 2 **Learn the four steps for solving application problems.** When working difficult problems, try to take your time and relax as if you were at the gym or a pool. Believe it or not, you are training your brain when working problems. It is okay if you do NOT know how to solve a problem when first reading it.

Quick TIP

Do NOT make the mistake that some students do, which is to try and solve a problem before knowing what is being asked.

Solving Application Problems

Step 1   Read the problem carefully, two or three times if needed. Be sure that you understand what is being asked.

Step 2   Identify given facts and *look for indicator words*. Then work out a plan to solve the problem.

Step 3   Estimate a *reasonable answer* using rounding.

Step 4   Solve the problem. Does the answer make sense? If not, work it again.

OBJECTIVE 3 **Learn to estimate answers.** Each of the steps in solving an application problem is important, but special emphasis should be placed on step 3, estimating a reasonable answer. Many times an answer just *does not fit* the problem.

What is a *reasonable answer*? Read the problem and estimate the approximate size of the answer. Should the answer be part of a dollar, a few dollars, hundreds, thousands, or even millions of dollars? For example, if a problem asks for the retail price of a shirt, would an answer of $20 be reasonable? $1000? $.65? $65?

Always make an estimate of a reasonable answer. Always look at the answer and decide if it is reasonable. These steps will give greater success in problem solving.

Using Word Indicators to Help Solve a Problem

EXAMPLE 1

Total sales at a neighborhood yard sale were $3584. The money was divided equally among the boys soccer club, the girls soccer club, the boys softball team, and the girls softball team. How much did each group receive?

SOLUTION

Sales of $3584 are to be *divided equally* among the four groups. Estimate the answer by first rounding $3584 to the nearest hundred ($3600); then divide by 4.

$$\$3600 \div 4 = \$900 \quad \textbf{estimate of amount to each group}$$

Divide to find the exact answer.

$$
\begin{array}{r}
\$896 \\
4\overline{)3584} \\
\underline{32} \\
38 \\
\underline{36} \\
24 \\
\underline{24} \\
0
\end{array}
$$

Check Work

$$
\begin{array}{r}
\$896 \\
\times \quad 4 \\
\hline
\$3584
\end{array}
$$
The answer is correct.

Each group should get $896.

QUICK CHECK 1

A library budget surplus of $13,280 is divided evenly among four branch libraries. How much did each receive?

OBJECTIVE 4 **Solve application problems.** To improve your accuracy, use the four steps and estimate answers when solving application problems.

Solving an Application Problem

EXAMPLE 2

The daily sales figures at a SUBWAY RESTAURANT were $2358 on Monday, $3056 on Tuesday, $2515 on Wednesday, $1875 on Thursday, $3978 on Friday, $3219 on Saturday, and $3008 on Sunday. Find the total sales for the week.

SOLUTION

 CASE IN POINT The sales for each day are given, and the total sales are needed. The word indicators *total sales* tell you to add the daily sales to arrive at the weekly total. Since the sales are about $3000 each day for a week of 7 days, a reasonable estimate would be around $21,000 ($7 \times \$3000 = \$21,000$). Find the actual answer by adding the sales for each of the 7 days.

$$
\begin{array}{r}
\textbf{\$20,009} \\
\$2358 \\
\$3056 \\
\$2515 \\
\$1875 \\
\$3978 \\
\$3219 \\
+ \; \$3008 \\
\hline
\$20,009
\end{array}
$$

Add.

Check

$20,009 **sales for the week**

The answer of $20,009 is reasonable.

QUICK CHECK 2

The numbers of visitors to a war veterans' memorial during one week are 5318, 2865, 4786, 1898, 3899, 2343, and 7221. First estimate the total attendance for the week. Then calculate exactly.

Solving an Application Problem

Many experts believe that water shortages will soon be a major problem. The chart below shows an estimate of fresh water resources per person, by country.

(a) Find the difference in the water resources per person between China and India.

(b) Use division to compare water per person in the United States to that in India.

Water Shortages in India

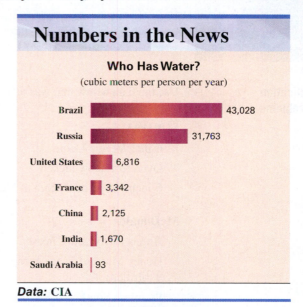

Numbers in the News

Who Has Water?
(cubic meters per person per year)

Country	
Brazil	43,028
Russia	31,763
United States	6,816
France	3,342
China	2,125
India	1,670
Saudi Arabia	93

Data: CIA

(a) The indicator word *difference* suggests a subtraction problem.

$$\begin{array}{r} 2125 \\ -\ 1670 \\ \hline 455 \end{array}$$ cubic meters per person per year

(b) $6816 \div 1670 = 4.08$ (rounded), or about 4 times as much water per person in the United States as in India.

Note that the figure suggests nothing about the geographic distribution of water within a country or whether the water is clean enough for human consumption. Clearly, some countries have far fewer water resources than others. In addition, water pollution is a terrible problem in many poor countries.

QUICK CHECK 3

Find the difference in the water resources per person between Brazil and Saudi Arabia.

Solving a Two-Step Problem

In May, the landlord of an apartment building received $940 from each of eight tenants. After paying $2730 in expenses, how much money did the landlord have left?

SOLUTION

Multiply the amount of rent by the number of tenants to arrive at the monthly income. Since the rent is about $900 and there are eight tenants, a *reasonable estimate* would be around $7200 ($900 × 8 = $7200).

$$\begin{array}{r} \$940 \\ \times\quad 8 \\ \hline \$7520 \end{array}$$ monthly income (this is reasonable)

Now subtract the expenses from the monthly income.

$$\begin{array}{r} \$7520 \\ -\ 2730 \\ \hline \$4790 \end{array}$$ amount remaining

QUICK CHECK 4

A homeowner's association collected $385 from each of 62 homeowners. If the association paid $18,280 in expenses, how much remained?

SUBWAY promotes healthy, low-fat food choices and fresh vegetables. Perhaps you have seen the SUBWAY advertising featuring Jared Fogle. As a college student, he weighed 425 pounds. By eating just two (a 6-inch and a foot-long) SUBWAY sandwiches each day, he lost 225 pounds in one year. However, other fast-food chains such as McDonalds also now offer items with fewer calories and less fat as shown in the next example.

Solving Application Problems

EXAMPLE 5   Use the data below that was taken from company websites to answer each question.

SUBWAY	Calories	Total Fat (gms)
6-inch Veggie Delite	230	2.5
Oven Roasted Chicken	320	5.0
6-inch Pepperoni Meatball Melt	600	29.0

McDonalds		
Angus Bacon and Cheese	790	39
Honey Mustard Snack Wrap (grilled)	250	8
Premium Southwest Salad (grilled chicken)	290	8

(a) How many fewer calories and grams of fat are in a 6-inch Veggies Delite Sandwich (SUBWAY) compared to an Angus Bacon and Cheese sandwich (McDonalds)?

(b) How many fewer calories and grams of fat are in a Premium Southwest Salad with grilled chicken (McDonalds) compared to a 6-inch Pepperoni Meatball Melt (SUBWAY)?

SOLUTION

(a) The indicator word fewer suggests subtraction should be used.

$$\begin{array}{r} 790 \\ -\ 230 \\ \hline \textbf{560 fewer calories} \end{array} \qquad \begin{array}{r} 39 \\ -\ 2.5 \\ \hline \textbf{36.5 fewer grams of fat} \end{array}$$

(b)
$$\begin{array}{r} 600 \\ -\ 290 \\ \hline \textbf{310 fewer calories} \end{array} \qquad \begin{array}{r} 29 \\ -\ 8 \\ \hline \textbf{21 fewer grams of fat} \end{array}$$

QUICK CHECK 5

From the information given above, find the total calories and grams of fat if an individual eats both a Honey Mustard Snack Wrap (grilled) and a Premium Southwest Salad (grilled chicken) from McDonalds.

▼ 1.2 Exercises

MyMathLab®

The shaded sections below contain solutions to help you get a **QUICK START** *on the various types of exercises.*

Solve the following application problems.

 1. SUBWAY SANDWICHES   Last week, SUBWAY sold 602 Veggie Delite sandwiches, 935 ham sandwiches, 1328 turkey breast sandwiches, 757 roast beef sandwiches, and 1586 SUBWAY Club sandwiches. Find the total number of sandwiches sold.

$602 + 935 + 1328 + 757 + 1586 = $ **5208 sandwiches**

1. 5208 sandwiches

2. **COMPETITIVE CYCLIST TRAINING** During a week of training, Rob Andrews rode his bike 80 miles on Monday, 75 miles on Tuesday, 135 miles on Wednesday, 40 miles on Thursday, and 52 miles on Friday. What is the total number of miles he rode in the five-day period?

Total miles traveled = 80 + 75 + 135 + 40 + 52 = 382 miles

2. __382 miles__

3. **MILES DRIVEN** The Federal Highway Administration estimates that total miles driven fell from 3020 billion miles last year to 2920 billion miles this year due to the recession. Find the reduction in miles driven.

3. _____

4. **SUV SALES** In a recent three-month period, there were 81,465 Ford Explorers and 70,449 Jeep Grand Cherokees sold. How many more Ford Explorers were sold than Jeep Grand Cherokees? (*Source*: J. D. Power and Associates.)

4. _____

5. **WORLD WAR II VETERANS** According to the Department of Veterans Affairs, U.S. World War II veterans are dying at the rate of 607 per day. How many World War II veterans are projected to die in the next 365 days? (*Source*: Department of Veteran's Affairs.)

5. _____

6. **TOTAL WORLD WAR II VETERANS** According to the Department of Veterans Affairs, there are roughly 1,100,000 U.S. World War II veterans alive today. If only 1 in 16 is still alive, find the total number who were World War II veterans. (*Source*: Department of Veteran's Affairs.)

6. _____

7. **FISHING BOAT** A fishing boat weighs 8375 pounds. If its 762-pound engine is removed and replaced with a 976-pound engine, find the weight of the boat after the engine change.

7. _____

8. **COLLEGE TEXTBOOKS** Tatum Palmer needs to buy three textbooks this semester and shops first at her college bookstore. The cost of new books are: $195, $180, and $205. The cost of used books are: $85, $62, and $92. Find the savings if she buys all three books used.

8. _____

9. **NOTEBOOK** The price of a mini notebook was lowered from $499 to $435. Find the decrease in price.

9. _____

10. **WEIGHING FREIGHT** A truck weighs 9250 pounds when empty. After being loaded with firewood, the truck weighs 21,375 pounds. What is the weight of the firewood?

10. _____

11. **LAND AREA** There are 43,560 square feet in 1 acre. How many square feet are there in 140 acres?

11. _____

12. **CHECK PROCESSING** Bank of America processes 40 million checks each day. Find the number of checks processed by the bank in a year. (Use a 365-day year.)

12. _____

13. **HOTEL ROOM COSTS** In a recent study of hotel–casinos, the cost per night at Harrah's Reno was $75, while the cost at Harrah's Lake Tahoe was $225 per night. Find the amount saved on a seven-night stay at Harrah's Reno instead of staying at Harrah's Lake Tahoe.

13. _____

⚠ indicates an exercise that is related to the Case in Point feature.

14. LUXURY HOTELS   A luxury hotel room at the Ritz-Carlton in San Francisco costs $645 per night, while a nearby room at a Motel 6 costs $74 per night. What amount will be saved in a four-night stay at Motel 6 instead of staying at the Ritz-Carlton?

14. _____

15. PHYSICALLY IMPAIRED   The Enabling Supply House purchased 6 wheelchairs at $1256 each and 15 speech compression disc players at $895 each. Find the total cost.

15. _____

16. KITCHEN EQUIPMENT   Find the total cost if SUBWAY buys 32 baking ovens at $1538 each and 28 warming ovens at $887 each.

16. _____

17. YOUTH SOCCER   A youth soccer association raised $7588 through fund-raising projects. There were expenses of $838 that had to be paid first, and the remaining money was divided evenly among the 18 teams. How much did each team receive?

17. _____

18. YARD MAINTENANCE   Doug Smith hires a crew of three men to mow yards. His total costs of wages, taxes, expenses, and the costs of equipment and truck is about $98 per hour. He charges an average of $60 per yard and his crew can mow and edge two yards per hour. Find his profit for a week in which his crews worked 35 hours.

18. _____

19. THEATER RENOVATION   A theater owner is remodeling to provide enough seating for 1250 people. The main floor has 30 rows of 25 seats in each row. If the balcony has 25 rows, how many seats must be in each row of the balcony to satisfy the owner's seating requirements?

19. _____

20. CALL CENTER   Beverly Stratton was hired to manage a call center for a market research firm that makes calls asking about consumer preferences. She anticipates about 82 outgoing calls per hour, 40 hours per week, 5 days a week, 50 weeks a year. Estimate the total number of calls per year. Also estimate the minimum number of call center operators needed if each can make about 17,000 calls a year. Round up to the next larger whole number.

20.

_____

QUICK CHECK ANSWERS

1. $3320

2. 28,000; 28,330 visitors

3. 42,935 cubic meters per person per year

4. $5590

5. 540 calories; 16 grams of Fat

1.3 Decimal Numbers

OBJECTIVES

1   Read and write decimal numbers.

2   Round decimal numbers.

OBJECTIVE 1 Read and write decimal numbers. A **decimal number** is any number written with a decimal point, such as 6.8, 5.375, or $7.50. Decimals, like fractions, can be used to represent parts of a whole. **Section 1.1** discussed how to read the digits to the *left* of the decimal point (whole numbers). Now we will see how to read the digits to the right of the decimal point, which always end in "th" or "ths."

Read the decimal number .039475 as "39475 millionths," where millionths comes from the fact that the last digit of this number falls in the millionths place. Write this number using words as follows.

thirty-nine thousand, four hundred seventy-five millionths

When reading a number with digits both to the left and the right of the decimal place, use the word *and* to show the location of the decimal point. Here are some examples.

9.7	nine **and** seven tenths
11.59	eleven **and** fifty-nine hundredths
1045.658	one thousand, forty-five **and** six hundred fifty-eight thousandths
5,600,000.0072	five million, six hundred thousand **and** seventy-two ten thousandths

Reading Decimal Numbers   **EXAMPLE 1**

Write the following decimals in words.

(a) 19.08   (b) .097   (c) 7648.9713   (d) 3,068,001.7

SOLUTION

(a) nineteen **and** eight hundredths

(b) ninety-seven thousandths

(c) seven thousand, six hundred forty-eight **and** nine thousand, seven hundred thirteen ten-thousandths

(d) three million, sixty-eight thousand, one **and** seven tenths

QUICK CHECK 1

Write (a) 0.068 and (b) 4,370.15 in words.

OBJECTIVE 2 Round decimal numbers. It is important to be able to round decimals. For example, Walgreens sells two candy bars for $.79, but you want to buy only one candy bar. The price of one bar is $.79 ÷ 2, which is $.395, but you cannot pay part of a cent. So the store rounds the price up to $.40 for one bar. The steps to round decimal numbers are the same as those used to round whole numbers, which have already been discussed.

Rounding Decimals

Step 1   Find the **place** to which the number is to be rounded. Draw a vertical line after that place to show that you are cutting off the rest of the digits.

Step 2   Look at only the first digit to the right of your cut-off line. If the first digit is **5 or more, increase** the digit in the place to which you are rounding by 1. Otherwise, do not change the digit in the place to which you are rounding.

Step 3   **Drop** all digits to the right of the place to which you have rounded.

To round 97.3892 to the nearest tenth, first draw a vertical line to the right of the 3 in the tenths place. The digit to the right of the vertical line is 5 or more, so round the 3 in the tenths position up to 4 and drop all digits to the right.

$$97.3 \mid 892$$

digit to the right of tenths place

tenths place

97.3892 rounded to the nearest tenth is 97.4.

Rounding Decimal Numbers   **EXAMPLE 2**   Round each as indicated.

(a) 87.562 to the nearest tenth

(b) 3678.5928 to the nearest hundredth

SOLUTION

(a) Step 1   Locate the tenths place and put a vertical line immediately to the right.

$$87.5 \mid 62$$

tenths place

Step 2   The number to the right of the line is 6, which is in the category of 5 or more. Therefore, round the 5 in the tenths place up to 6.

Step 3   Drop all digits to the right of the tenths place.

87.562 rounded to the nearest tenth is 87.6.

(b) Step 1   Locate the hundredths place and put a vertical line to the right.

$$3678.59 \mid 28$$

Step 2   The number to the right of the line is 2, or less than 5. Therefore, leave the 9 as it is in the hundredths place.

Step 3   Drop all digits to the right of the hundredths place.

3678.5928 rounded to the nearest hundredth is **3678.59.**

Rounding 3678.5928 to the nearest tenth would result in 3678.6, and rounding it to the nearest whole number would result in 3679.

QUICK CHECK 2

Round 72.8479 to the nearest thousandth.

Rounding the Same Decimal Number to Different Places   **EXAMPLE 3**   Round 24.998 to the nearest (a) hundredth, (b) tenth, and (c) whole number.

SOLUTION

Use the method just described.

(a) 24.998 rounded to the nearest hundredth is 25.00.

(b) 24.998 rounded to the nearest tenth is 25.0.

(c) 24.998 rounded to the nearest whole number is 25.

Interestingly, in this particular situation all three round to the same number. However, that will usually not be the case.

Quick TIP

Always refer back to the original number before rounding.

QUICK CHECK 3

Round 518.4464 to the nearest (a) thousandth, (b) hundredth, and (c) tenth.

▼ 1.3 Exercises

MyMathLab®

*The shaded sections below contain solutions to help you get a **QUICK START** on the various types of exercises.*

Write the following decimals in words. (See Example 1.)

1. .38 thirty-eight hundredths

2. .91 ninety-one hundredths

3. 5.61 _____

4. 6.53 _____

5. 7.408 _____

6. 1.254 _____

7. 37.593 _____

8. 20.903 _____

9. 4.0062 _____

10. 9.0201 _____

11. "My answer is right, but the decimal point is in the wrong place." Can this statement ever be correct? Explain. (See Objective 1.)

12. In your own words, explain the difference between thousands and thousandths.

Write the following decimals, using numbers.

13. four hundred thirty-eight and four tenths **438.4**

14. six hundred five and seven tenths **605.7**

15. ninety-seven and sixty-two hundredths _____

16. seventy-one and thirty-three hundredths _____

17. one and five hundred seventy-three ten-thousandths _____

18. nine and three hundred eight ten-thousandths _____

19. three and five thousand eight hundred twenty-seven ten-thousandths _____

20. two thousand seventy-four ten-thousandths _____

GROCERY SHOPPING   *Alan Zagorin is grocery shopping. The store will round the amount he pays for each item to the nearest cent. Write the rounded amounts. (See Examples 2–4.)*

21. Claim Jumper apple pies are two for $11.99. So one pie is $5.995. Zagorin pays _____.

22. Four 12-packs of soda cost $11.90. So one 12-pack costs $2.975. Zagorin pays _____.

23. Muffin mix is three packages for $1.75. So one package is $.58333. Zagorin pays _____.

24. Candy bars are six for $3.94. So one bar is $.65666. Zagorin pays _____.

25. Barbeque sauce is three bottles for $11.98. So one bottle is $3.993. Zagorin pays _____.

26. Tony's Pizzas are five for $37.46. So one pizza is $7.492. Zagorin pays _____.

 indicates an exercise that is related to the Case in Point feature.

Round each of the decimals to the nearest tenth, the nearest hundredth, and the nearest thousandth. Remember to use the original number each time before rounding. (See Examples 2–4.)

	Nearest Tenth	Nearest Hundredth	Nearest Thousandth
27. 3.5218	3.5	3.52	3.522
28. 4.836	4.8	4.84	4.836
29. 2.54836			
30. 7.44652			
31. 27.32451			
32. 89.53796			
33. 36.47249			
34. 58.95651			
35. .0562			
36. .0789			

Round each of the dollar amounts to the nearest cent.

37. $5.056 **$5.06**	**38.** $16.519 **$16.52**	**39.** $32.493 _____
40. $375.003 _____	**41.** $382.005 _____	**42.** $12,802.965 _____
43. $42.137 _____	**44.** $.846 _____	**45.** $.0015 _____
46. $.008 _____	**47.** $1.5002 _____	**48.** $7.6009 _____
49. $1.995 _____	**50.** $28.994 _____	**51.** $752.798 _____

Round each of the dollar amounts to the nearest dollar (nearest whole number).

52. $8.58 **$9**	**53.** $26.49 **$26**	**54.** $.57 _____
55. $.49 _____	**56.** $299.76 _____	**57.** $12,836.38 _____
58. $268.72 _____	**59.** $395.18 _____	**60.** $666.66 _____
61. $4699.62 _____	**62.** $11,285.13 _____	**63.** $378.59 _____
64. $233.86 _____	**65.** $722.38 _____	**66.** $8263.47 _____

67. Explain what happens when you round $.499 to the nearest dollar. (*See Objective 2.*)

68. Review Exercise 67. How else could you round $.499 to obtain a result that is more helpful? What kind of guideline does this suggest about rounding to the nearest dollar?

▼ 1.4 Addition and Subtraction of Decimals

OBJECTIVES

1 Add decimals.

2 Estimate answers.

3 Subtract decimals.

▼ **CASE IN POINT** As manager of a SUBWAY, Jessica Fernandez is responsible for making bank deposits to the company checking account. These banking activities require the ability to accurately add and subtract decimal numbers.

OBJECTIVE 1 Add decimals. To add, write the numbers so that the decimal points are aligned, which causes the place values to be aligned. As with adding whole numbers, add decimal numbers in columns, beginning on the right and moving to the left.

You may wish to add **trailing zeros** to the right of the decimal point so that each number being added has the same number of digits to the right of the decimal point. This does not change the number and can make it easier to keep track of things.

$$45.93 = 45.93\textbf{0} = 45.93\textbf{00}$$

— two trailing zeros added

— one trailing zero added

Adding Decimal Numbers

EXAMPLE 1 Add $45.93 + 14.017 + 96.5432$.

SOLUTION

First, align place values by lining up the decimal points.

— decimals aligned

```
45.93
14.017
96.5432
```

Although not required, you can add trailing zeros if you wish so that each number has the same number of digits to the right of the decimal point. Then, add from right to left.

    11   1

— trailing zeros added

```
 45.9300
 14.0170
 96.5432
156.4902
```

QUICK CHECK 1

Add 3.8, 14.604, 5.76, and 27.152.

OBJECTIVE 2 Estimate answers. Check that the numbers in Example 1 were correctly added by estimating the answer. Apply front-end rounding to the numbers as follows.

Problem		Estimate
45.93	⟶	50
14.017	⟶	10
+ 96.5432	⟶	+ 100
156.4902		160

The answer is relatively close to the actual value found of 156.4902 giving confidence that the original decimal numbers were added correctly.

Another option is to round each of the numbers to the nearest whole number and then compare as follows.

Problem		Estimate
45.93	$\longrightarrow$	46
14.017	$\longrightarrow$	14
+ 96.5432	$\longrightarrow$	+ 97
156.4902		157

The sum of 156.4902 is very close to the estimate of 157, so it appears the addition was done correctly.

Adding Dollars and Cents

 EXAMPLE 2

During a recent week, a manager made the following bank deposits to a business account: $1783.38, $4341.15, $2175.94, $896.23, and $2562.53. Use front-end rounding to estimate the total deposits and then find the total deposits.

SOLUTION

Estimate		Problem
$ 2000	$\longleftarrow$	$ 1783.38
4000	$\longleftarrow$	4341.15
2000	$\longleftarrow$	2175.94
900	$\longleftarrow$	896.23
+ 3000	$\longleftarrow$	+ 2562.53
$11,900		$11,759.23

The total deposits for the week were $11,759.23, which is close to our estimate.

QUICK CHECK 2

The following bills were paid last week; $1268.72, $228.35, $2336.19, $176.68, and $1560.75. Use front-end rounding to estimate the total amount of the bills paid, and then find the total bills paid.

OBJECTIVE 3 Subtract decimals. Subtraction is done in much the same way as addition. Line up the decimal points and place as many zeros after each decimal as needed. For example, subtract 17.432 from 21.76 as follows.

$$\begin{array}{r} 21.76\mathbf{0} \\ -\ 17.432 \\ \hline 4.328 \end{array}$$ Place one trailing zero after the top decimal.

Estimating and Then Subtracting Decimals

 EXAMPLE 3

First estimate using front-end rounding and then subtract.

(a) $\begin{array}{r} 11.7 \\ -\ 4.923 \end{array}$ (b) $\begin{array}{r} 39.428 \\ -\ 27.98 \end{array}$

SOLUTION

Attach zeros as needed and then subtract.

(a)
Estimate		Problem
10	$\longleftarrow$	11.700
− 5	$\longleftarrow$	− 4.923
5		6.777

(b)
Estimate		Problem
40	$\longleftarrow$	39.428
− 30	$\longleftarrow$	− 27.980
10		11.448

QUICK CHECK 3

First estimate using front-end rounding, and then subtract 5.32 from 26.952.

▼ 1.4 Exercises

MyMathLab®

*The shaded sections below contain solutions to help you get a **QUICK START** on the various types of exercises.*

First use front-end rounding to estimate and then find the exact answer. (see Examples 1 and 2.)

1. Estimate | Problem
```
  40  ←    43.36
  20  ←    15.8
+  9  ←  +  9.3
 ───      ─────
  69       68.46
```

2. Estimate | Problem
```
  600  ←     623.15
  700  ←     734.29
+ 700  ←  +  686.26
 ────       ───────
 2000        2043.70
```

3. Estimate | Problem
```
        6.23
        3.6
        5.1
        7.2
     +  1.69
       ──────
```

4. Estimate | Problem
```
       12.79
        2.15
       16.28
        4.39
     +  7.61
       ──────
```

5. Estimate | Problem
```
     2156.38
        5.26
        2.791
   +    6.983
     ─────────
```

6. Estimate | Problem
```
     1889.76
       21.42
       19.35
   +    8.1
     ─────────
```

7. Estimate | Problem
```
     6133.78
      506.124
       18.63
   +    7.527
     ─────────
```

8. Estimate | Problem
```
      743.1
     3817.65
        2.908
     4123.76
   +   21.98
     ─────────
```

9. Estimate | Problem
```
     1798.419
       68.32
      512.807
      643.9
   +  428.
     ─────────
```

Place each of the following numbers in a column and then add. (See Example 1.)

10. 45.631 + 15.8 + 7.234 + 19.63 = **88.295**

11. 12.15 + 6.83 + 61.75 + 19.218 + 73.325 = **173.273**

12. 197.4 + 83.72 + 17.43 + 25.63 + 1.4 =

13. 27.653 + 18.7142 + 9.7496 + 3.21 =

14. 73.618 + 19.18 + 371.82 + 355.125 =

15. It is a good idea to estimate an answer before actually solving a problem. Why is this true? (See Objective 2.)

16. Explain why placing zeros after any digits to the right of the decimal point does not change the value of a number. (See Objective 1.)

Solve the following application problems.

 17. SUBWAY SALES Sales for each day of the week at the SUBWAY managed by Jessica Fernandez were $1815.79, $2367.34, $1976.22, $2155.81, $1698.14, $2885.26, and $2239.63. Find the total weekly sales.

17. _____

 indicates an exercise that is related to the Case in Point feature.

18. RESTAURANT TIPS   Becky Waterton wants to know what her total
tips were for the three days she worked as a waitress at a Spanish tapas
restaurant. Her tips for Thursday, Friday, and Saturday were $85.25,
$114.60, and $129.40. Find the total.

18. _____

19. BEEF/TURKEY COST   At one store, the cost of T-bone steak is $6.71 per pound, while the cost of
turkey is $1.39 per pound. How much more per pound is the price of T-bone steak than turkey?

19. _____

20. ALIMONY   The average alimony paid to divorced spouses in one city is $1238.73 per month.
However, the court ordered James Tuxon to pay his ex-spouse $1530 per month. Find the
amount he is paying above the average.

20. _____

First use front-end rounding to estimate the answer and then subtract. (See Example 3.)

21. Estimate	Problem	22. Estimate	Problem	23. Estimate	Problem
20	19.74	40	35.86		51.215
− 7	− 6.58	− 8	− 7.91		−19.708
13	13.16	32	27.95		

24. Estimate	Problem	25. Estimate	Problem	26. Estimate	Problem
	27.613		325.053		3974.61
	− 18.942		− 85.019		− 892.59

27. Estimate	Problem	28. Estimate	Problem	29. Estimate	Problem
	7.8		27.8		5
	− 2.952		− 13.582		− 1.9802

© CHECKING-ACCOUNT RECORDS   *Jessica Fernandez, manager of SUBWAY, had a bank
balance of $5382.12 on March 1. During March, she deposited $60,375.82 received from sales,
$3280.18 received as credits from suppliers, and $75.53 as a county tax refund. She paid out
$27,282.75 to suppliers, $4280.83 for rent and utilities, and $12,252.23 for salaries and
miscellaneous. Find each of the following.*

30. How much did Fernandez deposit in March?

   $60,375.82 (sales) + $3280.18 (credits) + $75.53 (refund) = $63,731.53

30. _____

31. How much did she pay out?

31. _____

32. What was her final balance at the end of March?

32. _____

QUICK CHECK ANSWERS

1. 51.316   **3.** 25; 21.632
2. $5400; $5570.69

1.5 Multiplication and Division of Decimals

OBJECTIVES

1 Multiply decimals.

2 Divide a decimal by a whole number.

3 Divide a decimal by a decimal.

▼ CASE IN POINT Managing a business requires the ability to multiply and divide decimal numbers. The manager at SUBWAY applies these skills in many ways to find payroll, purchasing, and sales.

OBJECTIVE 1 Multiply decimals. Decimals are multiplied as if they were whole numbers. It is not necessary to line up the decimal points. The decimal point in the answer is then found using the following steps.

Positioning the Decimal Point

Step 1   Count the total number of digits to the *right* of the decimal point in each of the numbers being multiplied.

Step 2   In the answer, count from *right to left* the number of places found in step 1 and write the decimal point. It may be necessary to attach zeros to the left of the answer in order to correctly place the decimal point.

Multiplying Decimals   EXAMPLE 1

Multiply each of the following.

(a) 8.34 × 4.2   (b) .032 × .07

SOLUTION

(a) First multiply the given numbers as if they were whole numbers.

$$
\begin{array}{r}
8.34 \quad \longleftarrow \text{ 2 decimal places} \\
\times \quad 4.2 \quad \longleftarrow \text{ 1 decimal place} \\
\hline
1668 \\
3336 \quad\quad \\
\hline
35.028 \quad \longleftarrow \text{ 3 decimal places in answer}
\end{array}
$$

There are two decimal places in 8.34 and one in 4.2. This means that there are $2 + 1 = 3$ decimal places in the final answer. Find the final answer by starting at the right and counting three places to the left:

35.028   3 places to the left

(b) Here, it is necessary to attach zeros at the left in the answer:

$$
\begin{array}{r}
.032 \quad \longleftarrow \text{ 3 decimal places} \\
\times \quad .07 \quad \longleftarrow \text{ 2 decimal places} \\
\hline
.00224 \quad \longleftarrow \text{ 5 decimal places in answer}
\end{array}
$$

Attach 2 zeros.

QUICK CHECK 1

Multiply each of the following

(a) 6.7 × 4.32   (b) .086 × .05

The next example uses the formula for the gross pay or pay before deductions.

Gross pay = Number of hours worked × Pay per hour

Multiplying Two Decimal Numbers

EXAMPLE 2

Find the gross pay of a SUBWAY employee working 31.5 hours at a rate of $8.65 per hour.

SOLUTION

▼ CASE IN POINT   Find gross pay by multiplying the number of hours worked by the pay per hour.

$$
\begin{array}{r}
31.5 \quad \longleftarrow \text{1 place} \\
\times\ 8.65 \quad \longleftarrow \text{2 places} \\
\hline
1575 \\
1890 \\
2520 \\
\hline
272.475 \quad \longleftarrow \text{3 places in answer}
\end{array}
$$

This worker's gross pay, rounded to the nearest cent, is $272.48.

QUICK CHECK 2

A college student earns $9.28 per hour. How much is earned for 26.5 hours of work?

Applying Decimal Multiplication

EXAMPLE 3

Assume the cost of each 30-second television ad at the 2013 Super Bowl game was $2.7 million. If there were 60 advertising spots of 30 seconds during the game, find the total amount charged for advertising.

SOLUTION

Find the total amount charged for advertising during the 2013 Super Bowl by multiplying the number of 30-second advertising spots during the game by the charge for each advertisement.

$$
\begin{array}{r}
2.7 \quad \longleftarrow \text{1 place} \\
\times\ 60 \quad \longleftarrow \text{0 places} \\
\hline
00 \\
162 \\
\hline
162.0 \quad \longleftarrow \text{1 place}
\end{array}
$$

The total amount charged for advertising was $162 million ($162,000,000).

QUICK CHECK 3

Find the total amount charged for Super Bowl ads in 2013 if two advertisers canceled, resulting in fifty-eight 30-second ads.

OBJECTIVE 2 Divide a decimal by a whole number. Divide the decimal number 21.93 by the whole number 3 by first writing the division problem as usual. Place the decimal point in the quotient directly above the decimal point in the dividend and perform the division.

Place a decimal point directly above dividend's decimal point.

$$
\begin{array}{r}
7.31 \\
3\overline{)21.93}
\end{array}
$$

Check by multiplying the divisor and the quotient. The answer should equal the dividend.

$$
\begin{array}{r}
7.31 \\
\times\ \quad 3 \\
\hline
21.93 \quad \longleftarrow \text{matches dividend}
\end{array}
$$

Sometimes it is necessary to place zeros after the decimal point in the dividend. Do this if a remainder of 0 is not obtained. Attaching zeros *does not change* the value of the dividend. For example, divide 1.5 by 8 by dividing and placing zeros as needed.

Problem	Check
.1875	.1875
8)1.5000	× 8
8	1.5000
70	
64	
60	
56	matches
40	
40	
0	

By the check,
$1.5 \div 8 = .1875$

Sometimes, a remainder of 0 is never obtained when dividing. For example, dividing 4.7 by 3 results in repeating 6s that continue without end, as you can see from the following division. Continue the division to one decimal place more than needed so that you can **round the decimal** to the desired place. In this case, the division is carried out to the nearest ten thousandth so that the final answer can be rounded to the nearest thousandth.

> **Quick TIP**
>
> Carry the division one place further than the position to which you wish to round.

```
   1.5666
3)4.7000
   3
   17
   15
    20
    18
     20
     18
      2
```

The number 1.5666 rounded to the nearest thousandth is 1.567.

Dividing a Decimal by a Whole Number

EXAMPLE 4

Divide the following; then check using multiplication.

(a) 27.52 ÷ 32   (b) 153.4 ÷ 8

SOLUTION

Problem	Check
.86	.86
(a) 32)27.52	× 32
25 6	172
1 92	258
1 92	27.52
0	

Problem	Check
19.175	19.175
(b) 8)153.400	× 8
8	153.400
73	
72	
14	
8	
60	
56	
40	
40	
0	

QUICK CHECK 4

Divide the following; then check using multiplication.

(a) 15)823.26   (b) 78.562 ÷ 4

OBJECTIVE 3 Divide a decimal by a decimal. To divide by a decimal, first convert the divisor to a whole number. For example, to divide 27.69 by .3, convert .3 to a whole number by moving the decimal one place to the right. Then move the decimal point in the dividend, 27.69, one place to the right so that the value of the problem does not change. You may need to attach one or more trailing zeros to do this.

$$.3\overline{)27.6\,9}$$

First, convert the decimal to a whole number.

Then move the decimal point in the dividend the same number of places to the right as done in the divisor.

Then divide as follows:

$$
\begin{array}{r}
92.3 \\
3\overline{)276.9} \\
\underline{27} \\
06 \\
\underline{6} \\
0\,9 \\
\underline{9} \\
0
\end{array}
$$

Dividing a Decimal by a Decimal

EXAMPLE 5

Divide and check the answers.

(a) 17.6 ÷ .25   **(b)** 5 ÷ .42

SOLUTION

(a)
$$
\begin{array}{r}
70.4 \\
.25\overline{)17.60.0} \\
\underline{17\ 5} \\
10 \\
\underline{0} \\
100 \\
\underline{100} \\
0
\end{array}
$$

Check
$$
\begin{array}{r}
70.4 \\
\times\ .25 \\
\hline
3520 \\
1408 \\
\hline
17.600
\end{array}
$$

(b)
$$
\begin{array}{r}
11.9047 \\
.42\overline{)5.00.0000} \\
\underline{42} \\
80 \\
\underline{42} \\
38\ 0 \\
\underline{37\ 8} \\
200 \\
\underline{168} \\
320 \\
\underline{294} \\
26
\end{array}
$$

Rounding the answer to the nearest thousandth gives 11.905.

Check
$$
\begin{array}{r}
11.905 \\
\times\ .42 \\
\hline
23810 \\
47620 \\
\hline
5.00010
\end{array}
$$

(The check is off a little due to rounding.)

Quick TIP

For an answer that has been rounded, the check answer will not be exactly equal to the original dividend.

QUICK CHECK 5

Divide; then check using multiplication.

(a) 22.5 ÷ .8   **(b)** 8.6 ÷ .32

▼ 1.5 Exercises

*The shaded sections below contain solutions to help you get a **QUICK START** on the various types of exercises.*

First estimate using front-end rounding and then multiply. (See Example 1.)

1. Estimate	Problem	2. Estimate	Problem
100 ←	96.8	20 ←	16.6
× 4 ←	× 4.2	× 4 ←	× 4.2
400	406.56	80	69.72

C indicates an exercise that is related to the Case in Point feature.

3. Estimate   Problem
34.1
× 6.8

4. Estimate   Problem
70.35
× 8.06

5. Estimate   Problem
43.8
× 2.04

6. Estimate   Problem
69.3
× 2.81

Multiply the following decimals.

7. .532
× 3.6
.532 ← **3 decimals**
× 3.6 ← **1 decimal**
1.9152 ← **4 decimals**

8. .259
× 6.2
.259 ← **3 decimals**
× 6.2 ← **1 decimal**
1.6058 ← **4 decimals**

9. 21.7
× .431

10. 76.9
× .903

11. .0408
× .06

12. 2481.9
× .003

CALCULATING GROSS EARNINGS   *Find the gross pay for each employee at the given rate. Round to the nearest cent. (See Examples 2 and 3.)*

13. 18.5 hours at $8.25 per hour
18.5 × $8.25 = $152.63

13. $152.63

14. 36.6 hours at $9.85 per hour

14. _____

15. 27.9 hours at $11.42 per hour, and 6.8 hours at $14.63 per hour

15. _____

16. 11.4 hours at $8.59 per hour, and 23.9 hours at $10.06 per hour

16. _____

Divide the following, and round your answer to the nearest thousandth. (See Examples 4 and 5.)

17. 6)48.45

18. 5)62.38

19. 411.63 ÷ 15

20. $2.43\overline{)9.6153}$ **21.** $.65\overline{)37.6852}$ **22.** $15.62 \div .28$

23. In your own words, write the rule for placing the decimal point in the answer of a decimal multiplication problem. (See Objective 1.)

24. Describe what must be done with the decimal point in a decimal division problem. Include the divisor, dividend, and quotient in your description. (See Objectives 2 and 3.)

Solve the following application problems:

25. REAL ESTATE FEES   Robert Gonzalez recently sold his home for $246,500. He paid a commission of .06 times the price of the house. What was the amount of the commission?

$246,500 × .06 = $14,790

25. $14,790

26. FABRIC   To make curtains for her new apartment, Janitha Williams needs 2.75 yards of material for each window. Find the total amount of material needed if she decides to do four windows.

26. _____

27. HYBRID TOYOTA   To reduce his driving costs as a salesperson, Bill Chen bought a Toyota Prius. One week, he drove 519 miles in and around the city and used 10.2 gallons of gasoline. Find the miles per gallon to the nearest tenth.

27. _____

28. MANAGERIAL EARNINGS   A SUBWAY assistant manager earns $2528 each month for working a 48-hour week. Find **(a)** the number of hours worked each month and **(b)** the assistant manager's hourly earnings (1 month = 4.3 weeks). Round to the nearest cent.

(a) _____

(b) _____

29. BIG RIMS AND TIRES   Henry Barnes has a loan balance of $2872.26 on the new 23-inch rims and tires he bought for his SUV. If his payments are $106.38 per month, how many months will it take to pay off the balance?

29. _____

30. MEDICINE DOSE Each dose of a medication contains 1.62 milligrams of a certain ingredient. Find the number of doses that can be made from 57.13 milligrams of the ingredient. Round to the nearest whole number.

30. _____

31. U.S. PAPER MONEY The thickness of a $100 bill is .0043 inch.

(a) If you had a pile of one hundred $100 bills, how high would it be?

(b) How high would a pile of 1000 bills be?

(a) _____

(b) _____

32. (a) Use the information from Exercise 31 to find the number of $100 bills in a pile that is 43 inches high.

(b) How much money would you have if the pile was all $20 bills, which have the same thickness as a $100 bill?

(a) _____

(b) _____

Use the information from the Look Smart online catalog to answer Exercises 33–36.

43-2A   43-2B

43-3A   43-3B

KNIT SHIRT ORDERING INFORMATION	
43–2A Short sleeve, solid colors	$14.75 each
43–2B Short sleeve, stripes	$16.75 each
43–3A Long sleeve, solid colors	$18.95 each
43–3B Long sleeve, stripes	$21.95 each
XXL size, add $2 per shirt.	
Monogram, $4.95 each. Gift box, $5 each.	

TOTAL PRICE OF ALL ITEMS (EXCLUDING MONOGRAMS AND GIFT BOXES)	SHIPPING, PACKING, AND HANDLING
$0–25.00	$3.50
$25.01–75.00	$5.95
$75.01–125.00	$7.95
$125.01+	$9.95
Shipping to each additional address add $4.25.	

33. Find the total cost of ordering four long-sleeve, solid-color shirts and two short-sleeve, striped shirts, all size XXL and all shipped to your home.

33. _____

34. What is the total cost of eight long-sleeve XXL shirts, five in solid colors and three striped? Include the cost of shipping the solid shirts to your home and the striped shirts to your brother's home.

34. _____

35. (a) What is the total cost, including shipping, of sending three short-sleeve, solid-color shirts, with monograms, in a gift box to your uncle for his birthday?

(b) How much did the monogram, gift box, and shipping add to the cost of your gift?

(a) _____

(b) _____

36. **(a)** Suppose you order one of each type of shirt for yourself, adding a monogram on each of the solid-color shirts. At the same time, you order three long-sleeve, striped, size-XXL shirts to be shipped to your father at a different address in a gift box. Find the total cost of your order.

(a) _____

(b) _____

(b) What is the difference in total cost (excluding shipping) between the shirts for yourself and the gift for your father?

QUICK CHECK ANSWERS

1. **(a)** 28.944   **(b)** .0043
2. $245.92
3. $156.6 million or $156,600,000

4. **(a)** 54.884   **(b)** 19.6405
5. **(a)** 28.125   **(b)** 26.875

▼ Chapter 1   Quick Review

Chapter Terms   *Review the following terms to test your understanding of the chapter. For each term you do not know, refer to the page number found next to that term.*

addends [p. 3]

addition [p. 3]

amount [p. 3]

borrow [p. 5]

comma [p. 2]

decimal number [p. 21]

decimal part [p. 2]

decimal point [p. 2]

decimal system [p. 2]

difference [p. 5]

digits [p. 2]

dividend [p. 7]

dividing decimals [p. 30]

division [p. 3]

divisor [p. 7]

front-end rounding [p. 4]

indicator words [p. 15]

minuend [p. 5]

multiplicand [p. 6]

multiplication [p. 3]

multiplier [p. 6]

multiplying decimals [p. 29]

operations [p. 3]

partial products [p. 6]

product [p. 6]

quotient [p. 7]

rounding [p. 2]

round decimals [p. 31]

round whole numbers [p. 2]

subtraction [p. 3]

subtrahend [p. 5]

sum [p. 3]

total [p. 3]

trailing zeros [p. 25]

whole numbers [p. 2]

CONCEPTS

EXAMPLES

1.1 Reading and writing whole numbers

The word *and* is not used. Commas help divide thousands, millions, and billions. A comma is not needed with a four-digit number.

Write 795 and 9,650,036 using words.

seven hundred ninety-five

nine million, six hundred fifty thousand, thirty-six

1.1 Rounding whole numbers

Rules for rounding:

1. Identify the position to be rounded. Draw a line under that place.
2. If the digit to the right of the underlined place is 5 or more, increase by 1. If the digit is 4 or less, do not change.
3. Change all digits to the right of the underlined digit to zero.

Round:

7 2 6 to the nearest ten

     5 or more, so add 1 to tens position

tens position

So, 726 rounds to 730.

1,498,586 to the nearest million

     4 or less, so do not change

millions position

So, 1,498,586 rounds to 1,000,000.

1.1 Front-end rounding

Front-end rounding leaves only the first digit as a nonzero digit. All other digits are changed to zero.

Round each of the following, using front-end rounding.

76 rounds to 80

348 rounds to 300

6512 rounds to 7000

23,751 rounds to 20,000

652,179 rounds to 700,000

1.1 Addition of whole numbers

Add from top to bottom, starting with the ones place and working to the left. To check, add from bottom to top.

$$
\begin{array}{r}
\mathbf{1140} \\
687 \\
26 \\
9 \\
+\ 418 \\
\hline
\mathbf{1140}
\end{array}
$$

Problem (add down)   **Check** (add up)

1.1 Subtraction of whole numbers

Subtract the subtrahend from the minuend to get the difference, borrowing when necessary. To check, add the difference to the subtrahend to get the minuend.

Problem   **Check**

$$
\begin{array}{r}
621 \\
4738 \\
-\ 649 \\
\hline
4089
\end{array}
\qquad
\begin{array}{r}
4089 \\
+\ 649 \\
\hline
\mathbf{4738}
\end{array}
$$

CONCEPTS	EXAMPLES

1.1 Multiplication of whole numbers

The multiplicand is multiplied by the multiplier, giving the product. When the multiplier has more than one digit, partial products must be used and then added.

```
     78    multiplicand
  ×  24    multiplier
    312    partial product
    156    partial product (one position left)
   1872    product
```

1.1 Division of whole numbers

÷ and $\overline{)}$ mean divide.

A —, as in $\frac{25}{5}$, means divide 25 by 5.

Also, the /, as in 25/5, means to divide 25 by 5. Remainders are usually expressed as decimals.

```
                    44    quotient
        divisor  2)88    dividend
                   88
                    0
```

If answer is rounded, the check will not be perfect.

1.2 Application problems

Follow these steps.

1. Read the problem carefully.
2. Work out a plan using *indicator words* before starting.
3. Estimate a reasonable answer.
4. Solve the problem. If the answer is reasonable, check. If it is not, start over.

Shauna Gallegos earns $118 on Sunday, $87 on Monday, and $63 on Tuesday. Find her total earnings for the three days. Total means to add. An estimate using front-end rounding is $100 + $90 + $60 is $250.

```
  $268      Check
  $118
  $ 87
 +$ 63
  $268      total earnings are reasonable
```

1.3 Reading and rounding decimals

1.3 is read as "one and three tenths."
Round .073265 to the nearest ten-thousandth.

```
.0732|65
```

↑ ten-thousandth position

Since the digit to the right is 6, increase the ten-thousandths digit by 1 and drop all digits to the right. So, .073265 rounds to .0733.

1.4 Addition and subtraction of decimals

Decimal points must be in a column. Attach zeros to keep digits in their correct columns.

Add: 5.68 + 785.3 + .007 + 10.1062
Line up the decimal points and add from right to left.

```
    5.6800  ←
  785.3000  ← Attach zeros.
     .0070  ←
+  10.1062
  801.0932
```

1.5 Multiplication of decimals

Multiply as if decimals are whole numbers. Place the decimal point as follows.

1. Count digits to the right of decimal points.
2. Count from right to left the same number of places as in step 1. Zeros must be attached on the left if necessary.

Multiply: .169 × .21

```
    .169     3 decimal places
  × .21      2 decimal places
    169
    338
  .03549     5 decimal places in
             answer
```

Attach one zero.

1.5 Division of decimals

1. Move the decimal point in the divisor all the way to the right.
2. Move the decimal point the same number of places to the right in the dividend.
3. Place a decimal point in the answer position directly above the dividend decimal point.
4. Divide as with whole numbers.

Divide 52.8 by .75

```
              70.4              Check
  .75.)52.80.0                  70.4
        52 5                  ×  .75
          30                   3520
           0                   4928
          30 0                52.800
          30 0
             0
```

Case Study

COST OF GETTING MARRIED

Interested in getting married? You might be surprised at the cost. A local newspaper said that the average costs of a wedding with 200 guests increased from $24,168 in 2005 to $28,540 in 2013. The bar graph gives the breakdown of average costs. Use the information to answer the questions that follow.

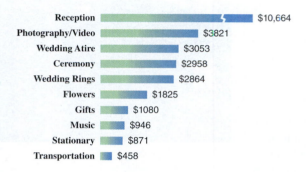

Reception	$10,664
Photography/Video	$3821
Wedding Attire	$3053
Ceremony	$2958
Wedding Rings	$2864
Flowers	$1825
Gifts	$1080
Music	$946
Stationary	$871
Transportation	$458

1. Find the combined cost of the reception, photography, wedding attire, and the ceremony.

    1. _____

2. Find the difference in the average costs of a wedding in 2005 versus 2013.

    2. _____

3. If you budget $7500 for the wedding reception and the cost per person is $42, find the number of guests you can invite and the amount remaining.

    3. _____

4. If costs force you to limit the number of guests to 115 and the cost of the reception to $5325, find the amount spent per person rounded to the nearest cent.

    4. _____

5. A couple plans to spend $22,000 for their wedding. Their parents have agreed to pay $8000 of the costs. If the couple has excess income of $650 per month, how many months will it require for them to pay their share of the costs?

    5. _____

INVESTIGATE

List five expenses associated with a wedding that are not mentioned. List five things that could be changed to bring the cost of the wedding down.

▼ Case in Point Summary Exercise

SUBWAY

www.subway.com

Facts:

- 1965: First store opened in Connecticut
- 1974: First store franchised to an individual
- 1995: Supports cancer research
- 2013: Over 37,000 restaurants in 100 countries

With the help of a family friend, seventeen-year-old Freed DeLuca opened the first SUBWAY store in 1965. DeLuca believed in using only the freshest ingredients and drove many miles each week in his Volkswagen bug to buy fresh produce. Later management decided to "give back" to the community and now supports research related to both heart disease and cancer. The firm differs from other fast-food firms by offering heart-healthy meals.

Profit margins are surprisingly small in most businesses, so managers must work very hard to control costs. A primary responsibility of a store manager at SUBWAY is to control costs. Of course, the store manager is also responsible for many issues related to employees, the quality of food and service, and also sales.

1. Jessica Fernandez is the manager of a SUBWAY store. Find the total of an invoice with the following costs: produce, $486.12; meat and cheese, $1236.14; bread dough, $364.76; shipping charges, $103.75.

    1. _____

2. One employee worked the following hours during the week: Thursday, 3.5 hours; Friday, 4.5 hours; Saturday, 6 hours; and Sunday, 5.5 hours. He is paid $8.65 per hour. Find the total number of hours worked and the pay for the week rounded to the nearest cent.

    2. _____

3. Fernandez notes that meat and cheese costs went up from $1864.92 last week to $2065.48 this week and attributes it to additional customers. Find the difference between the two. If the average cost of meat and cheese per sub sandwich is $.94, estimate the number of additional customers this week compared to last week, rounded to the nearest whole number.

    3. _____

4. This month, Fernandez plans to spend four times as much on advertising as the $168.32 spent last week. Find the amount spent on advertising. If the increased advertising brings in 1.3 times last week's revenue of $10,984.76, estimate the revenue.

    4. _____

Discussion Question: *If sales increase by $1500 in a week, do you think profit for the week will also increase by about $1500? Why or why not?*

Source: SUBWAY, www.subway.com

▼ Chapter 1 Test

To help you review, the bracketed numbers indicate the section in which the topic is discussed.

Round as indicated. **[1.1]**

1. 844 to the nearest ten

2. 21,958 to the nearest hundred

3. 671,529 to the nearest thousand

Round each of the following, using front-end rounding. **[1.1]**

4. 50,987

5. 851,004

6. One week, Katie Nopper earned the following commissions: Monday, $124; Tuesday, $88; Wednesday, $62; Thursday, $137; Friday, $195. Find her total amount of commissions for the week. **[1.2]**

7. A rental business buys three airless sprayers at $1540 each, five rototillers at $695 each, and eight 4-foot ladders at $38 each. Find the total cost of the equipment purchased. **[1.2]**

Round as indicated. **[1.3]**

8. $21.0568 to the nearest cent

9. $364.345 to the nearest cent

10. $7246.49 to the nearest dollar

Solve each problem. **[1.4 and 1.5]**

11. $9.6 + 8.42 + 3.715 + 159.8 =$ _____

12.
$$\begin{array}{r} 2.715 \\ 32.78 \\ 426.3 \\ +\ 37 \\ \hline \end{array}$$

13.
$$\begin{array}{r} 341.4 \\ -\ 207.8 \\ \hline \end{array}$$

14. $3.8 - .0053$

15.
$$\begin{array}{r} 21.98 \\ \times\ .72 \\ \hline \end{array}$$

16.
$$\begin{array}{r} 218.6 \\ \times\ .037 \\ \hline \end{array}$$

17. $21.8\overline{)252.008}$

18. $24,500 \div 70 =$ _____

19. $57.358 \div 2.41 =$ _____

1. _____

2. _____

3. _____

4. _____

5. _____

6. _____

7. _____

8. _____

9. _____

10. _____

🔺 indicates an exercise that is related to the Case in Point feature.

20. A manager at SUBWAY wants to find the total cost of 24.8 pounds of sliced turkey at $1.89 a pound and 38.2 pounds of provolone cheese at $2.05 a pound. Find the final cost.   **[1.4 and 1.5]**

20. _____

21. Roofing material costs $84.52 per square (10 ft × 10 ft). The roofer charges $55.75 per square for labor, plus $9.65 per square for supplies. Find the total cost for 26.3 squares of installed roof. Round to the nearest cent.   **[1.4 and 1.5]**

21. _____

22. A federal law requires that all residential toilets sold in the United States use no more than 1.6 gallons of water per flush. Prior to this legislation, conventional toilets used 3.4 gallons of water per flush. Find the amount of water saved in one year by a family flushing the toilet 22 times each day (1 year = 365 days).   **[1.4 and 1.5]**

22. _____

23. Steve Hamilton bought 135.5 meters of steel rod at $.86 per meter and 12 meters of brass rod at $2.18 per meter. How much change did he get from eight $20 bills?   **[1.4 and 1.5]**

23. _____

24. Capital Hills Supermarket sells bananas for $1.74 per kilogram. Find the price per pound by dividing $1.74 by 2.2 pounds. Round to the nearest cent. **[1.5]**

24. _____

25. A concentrated fertilizer must be applied at the rate of .058 ounce per seedling. Find the number of seedlings that can be fertilized with 14.674 ounces of fertilizer.   **[1.5]**

25. _____

26. A veterinarian decides that a cat with a kidney infection should get .65 milliliters of antibiotic twice a day for 7 days. Find the total amount of antibiotic needed rounded to the nearest milliliter.

26. _____

27. A family has budgeted $1000 so that all four of them can convert to the newest iPhone at the same time. The cost of each iPhone is $199 and the sales tax is calculated by multiplying .08125 times the combined cost of the four phones. Find the amount left over from the budgeted amount.

27. _____

2 Fractions

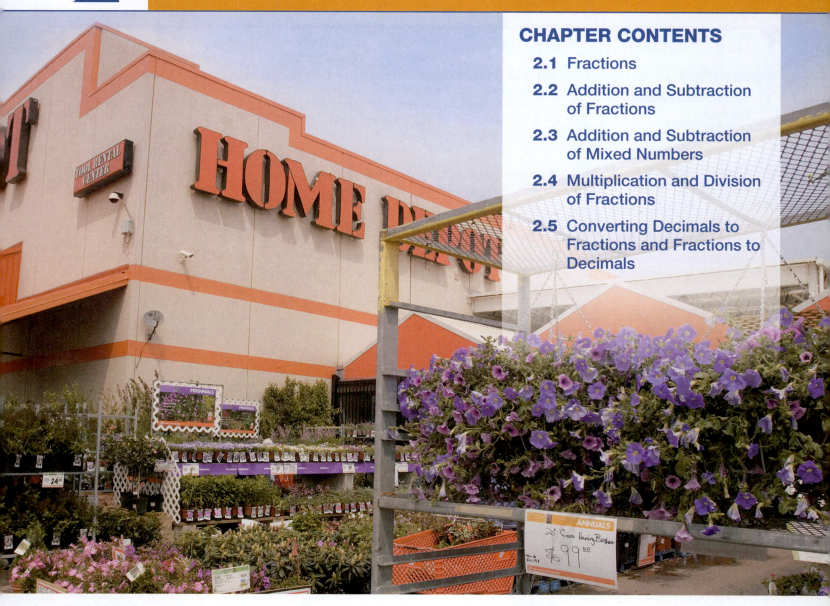

CHAPTER CONTENTS

2.1 Fractions

2.2 Addition and Subtraction of Fractions

2.3 Addition and Subtraction of Mixed Numbers

2.4 Multiplication and Division of Fractions

2.5 Converting Decimals to Fractions and Fractions to Decimals

▼ CASE IN POINT

KARA OAKS has been employed at The Home Depot for several years. During this time, she has worked in the hardware and plumbing departments and she now manages the cabinetry department and helps people design replacement cabinets. Knowing and using fractions is a key part of Oaks's job. As shown in the Summary Case at the end of the chapter, she must be very accurate when determining the specifications for cabinets.

Chapter 1 discussed whole numbers and decimals. This chapter looks at *fractions*, numbers that can be used to represent parts of a whole. Fractions and decimals are two ways of representing the same quantity. Fractions are used in business and our personal lives.

▼ 2.1   Fractions

OBJECTIVES

1   Recognize types of fractions.

2   Convert mixed numbers to improper fractions.

3   Convert improper fractions to mixed numbers.

4   Write a fraction in lowest terms.

5   Use the rules for divisibility.

Home Depot

▼ CASE IN POINT   The employees in the cabinetry department at Home Depot must be able to use decimals, fractions, and mixed numbers in order to work with customers. The measurements of cabinets, trim pieces, and room sizes never seem to be an even number of inches—they often involve fractions.

A **fraction** represents part of a whole. Fractions are written in the form of one number over another, with a line between the two numbers, as in the following.

$$\frac{5}{8} \quad \frac{1}{4} \quad \frac{9}{7} \quad \frac{13}{10} \quad \leftarrow\text{— numerator} \\ \quad\quad\quad\quad\quad\quad \leftarrow\text{— denominator}$$

The number above the line is the **numerator**, and the number below the line is the **denominator**. In the fraction $\frac{2}{3}$, the numerator is 2 and the denominator is 3. The denominator is the number of equal parts into which something is divided. The numerator tells how many of these parts are needed. For example, $\frac{2}{3}$ is "2 parts out of 3 equal parts," as shown in the figure.

$\frac{2}{3}$ means 2 parts
out of 3 equal parts

OBJECTIVE 1   Recognize types of fractions.   Proper fractions, also called **common fractions**, have numerators that are smaller than their denominators. Proper fractions have a value of less than 1. **Improper fractions** have numerators that are equal to or greater than the denominators. Improper fractions have a value of 1 or more. Here are some examples.

$$\text{Proper fractions:} \quad \frac{1}{2}, \frac{3}{4}, \frac{7}{13}, \frac{91}{100}$$

$$\text{Improper fractions:} \quad \frac{3}{3}, \frac{9}{7}, \frac{125}{4}, \frac{13}{12}$$

To write a whole number as a fraction, place the whole number as the numerator on top of a denominator of 1, as shown here.

$$8 = \frac{8}{1} \quad\quad 25 = \frac{25}{1} \quad\quad 4 = \frac{4}{1} \quad\quad 135 = \frac{135}{1}$$

A **mixed number** is the sum of a whole number and a fraction. So, $5\frac{3}{8}$ is a mixed number that means $5 + \frac{3}{8}$. It is even read as *five and three-eighths* or as the sum of a whole number and a fraction. Here are some other mixed numbers.

$$17\frac{3}{5} \quad\quad \text{seventeen and three-fifths}$$

$$92,407\frac{3}{4} \quad\quad \text{ninety-two thousand, four hundred seven and three-fourths}$$

It is important to realize that the number 0 is never used in the denominator of any fraction, since division by 0 is not defined.

OBJECTIVE 2 Convert mixed numbers to improper fractions. Follow the steps shown to convert a mixed number to an improper fraction.

> **Converting a Mixed Number to an Improper Fraction**
>
> Step 1   Multiply the whole number by the denominator of the fraction.
>
> Step 2   Add the product to the numerator of the fraction to find the new numerator.
>
> Step 3   Keep the same denominator.

Here is an example.

$$4\frac{5}{8} = \frac{(4 \times 8) + 5}{8} = \frac{37}{8}$$

Step 1 Multiply the whole number by the denominator.

Step 2 Add the product to the numerator.

Step 3 Keep the same denominator.

Converting Mixed Numbers to Improper Fractions

EXAMPLE 1

Kara Oaks read the instructions that came with a new microwave oven. The opening in the kitchen cabinet needed to be $25\frac{3}{4}$ inches wide by $16\frac{1}{2}$ inches tall in order to install the micro-wave oven. Convert both of these mixed numbers to improper fractions.

(a) $25\frac{3}{4}$ **(b)** $16\frac{1}{2}$

SOLUTION

(a) Multiply the whole number 25 by the denominator 4 to find 100. Add the product to the numerator of the fraction 3 to find 103. Keep the same denominator of 4.

$$25\frac{3}{4} = \frac{(25 \times 4) + 3}{4} = \frac{103}{4}$$

(b) $16\frac{1}{2} = \frac{(16 \times 2) + 1}{2} = \frac{33}{2}$

> **QUICK CHECK 1**
>
> Convert to improper fractions.
>
> **(a)** $15\frac{1}{3}$ **(b)** $21\frac{3}{8}$

OBJECTIVE 3 Convert improper fractions to mixed numbers. Use the steps shown here to convert an improper fraction to a mixed number.

> **Converting an improper fraction to a mixed number**
>
> Step 1   Divide the numerator of the fraction by the denominator.
>
> Step 2   The quotient is the whole-number part of the mixed number.
>
> Step 3   The remainder is the numerator of the fraction.
>
> Step 4   Keep the same denominator in the fraction part of the mixed number.

For example, to convert $\frac{17}{5}$ to a mixed number, first divide 17 by 5. The **quotient** is the whole-number part and the remainder is the numerator of the fraction. Keep the same denominator.

$$\begin{array}{r} 3 \text{ R2} \\ 5)\overline{17} \\ \underline{15} \\ 2 \end{array} \qquad \text{So, } \frac{17}{5} = 3\frac{2}{5}.$$

Check the calculation by converting the mixed number $3\frac{2}{5}$ back to an improper fraction.

$$3\frac{2}{5} = \frac{(3 \times 5) + 2}{5} = \frac{17}{5}$$

The answer checks, so the fraction $\frac{17}{5}$ equals the mixed number $3\frac{2}{5}$. These are two different ways to write the same number.

Converting Improper Fractions to Mixed Numbers

EXAMPLE 2

Convert the following improper fractions to mixed numbers.

(a) $\dfrac{27}{4}$ (b) $\dfrac{29}{8}$ (c) $\dfrac{42}{7}$

SOLUTION

(a) Convert $\frac{27}{4}$ to a mixed number by dividing 27 by 4.

$$\begin{array}{r} 6 \\ 4\overline{)27} \\ \underline{24} \\ 3 \end{array} \qquad \frac{27}{4} = 6\frac{3}{4}$$

Therefore, $\dfrac{27}{4} = 6\dfrac{3}{4}.$

(b) Divide 29 by 8 to convert $\frac{29}{8}$ to a mixed number.

$$\begin{array}{r} 3 \\ 8\overline{)29} \\ \underline{24} \\ 5 \end{array} \qquad \frac{29}{8} = 3\frac{5}{8}$$

(c) Divide 42 by 7.

$$\begin{array}{r} 6 \\ 7\overline{)42} \\ \underline{42} \\ 0 \end{array} \qquad \frac{42}{7} = 6$$

QUICK CHECK 2

Convert to mixed numbers.

(a) $\dfrac{73}{4}$ (b) $\dfrac{32}{5}$

OBJECTIVE 4 Write a fraction in lowest terms. If both the numerator and denominator of a fraction cannot be divided without a remainder by any number other than 1, then the fraction is in **lowest terms**. For example, 2 and 3 cannot be divided without a remainder by any number other than 1, so the fraction $\frac{2}{3}$ is in lowest terms. In the same way, $\frac{1}{9}$, $\frac{4}{11}$, $\frac{12}{17}$, and $\frac{13}{15}$ are in lowest terms.

When both numerator and denominator *can* be divided without a remainder by a number other than 1, the fraction is *not* in lowest terms. For example, both 15 and 25 can be divided by 5 with no remainder, so the fraction $\frac{15}{25}$ is not in lowest terms. Write $\frac{15}{25}$ in lowest terms by dividing both numerator and denominator by 5, as follows.

$$\frac{15}{25} = \frac{15 \div 5}{25 \div 5} = \frac{3}{5} \qquad \text{lowest terms}$$

Divide by 5.

Writing Fractions in Lowest Terms   **EXAMPLE 3**   Write the following fractions in lowest terms.

(a) $\dfrac{15}{40}$ (b) $\dfrac{33}{39}$

SOLUTION

Look for a number that can be divided without a remainder into both the numerator and denominator.

(a) Both 15 and 40 can be divided by **5**.

$$\frac{15}{40} = \frac{15 \div \mathbf{5}}{40 \div \mathbf{5}} = \frac{3}{8} \quad \text{lowest terms}$$

(b) Divide both numbers by 3.

$$\frac{33}{39} = \frac{33 \div \mathbf{3}}{39 \div \mathbf{3}} = \frac{11}{13} \quad \text{lowest terms}$$

QUICK CHECK 3

Write in lowest terms.

(a) $\dfrac{36}{45}$ (b) $\dfrac{48}{66}$

OBJECTIVE 5 Use the rules for divisibility. It is sometimes difficult to tell which numbers will divide evenly into another number. The following rules may help.

> **Quick TIP**
>
> There is not easy rule to see if a number is evenly divisible by 7.

Rules for Divisibility

A whole number can be evenly divided by

2 if the last digit is an even number, such as 0, 2, 4, 6, or 8

3 if the sum of the digits is divisible by 3 with no remainder

4 if the last two digits are divisible by 4 with no remainder

5 if the last digit is 0 or 5

6 if the number is even and the sum of the digits is divisible by 3 with no remainder

8 if the last three digits are divisible by 8 with no remainder

9 if the sum of all the digits is divisible by 9 with no remainder

10 if the last digit is 0

Using the Divisibility Rules   **EXAMPLE 4**   Determine whether the following statements are true.

(a) 3,746,892 is evenly divisible by 4.

(b) 15,974,802 is evenly divisible by 9.

SOLUTION

(a) The number 3,746,892 is evenly divisible by 4, since the last two digits form a number divisible by 4 without remainder.

$$3, 746, 8\underline{92}$$

92 is divisible by 4.

> **Quick TIP**
>
> Testing for divisibility by adding the digits works only for 3 and 9.

(b) See if 15,974,802 is evenly divisible by 9 by adding the digits of the number.

$$1 + 5 + 9 + 7 + 4 + 8 + 0 + 2 = \mathbf{36}$$

36 is divisible by 9.

Since 36 is divisible by 9, the given number is divisible by 9.

The rules for divisibility help determine *only whether a number is evenly divisible by another number*. They cannot be used to find the result. The division must actually be done to find the quotient.

QUICK CHECK 4

Determine (a) whether 628,375,210 is evenly divisible by 5, and (b) whether 825,693,471 is evenly divisible by 3.

2.1 Exercises

MyMathLab®

*The shaded sections below contain solutions to help you get a **QUICK START** on the various types of exercises.*

Convert the following mixed numbers to improper fractions. (See Example 1.)

1. $3\dfrac{5}{8} = \dfrac{29}{8}$

   $\dfrac{(8 \times 3) + 5}{8} = \dfrac{29}{8}$

2. $2\dfrac{4}{5} = \dfrac{14}{5}$

   $\dfrac{(5 \times 2) + 4}{5} = \dfrac{14}{5}$

3. $4\dfrac{1}{4} = $ ____

4. $3\dfrac{2}{3} = $ ____

5. $12\dfrac{2}{3} = $ ____

6. $2\dfrac{8}{11} = $ ____

7. $22\dfrac{7}{8} = $ ____

8. $17\dfrac{5}{8} = $ ____

9. $7\dfrac{6}{7} = $ ____

10. $21\dfrac{14}{15} = $ ____

11. $15\dfrac{19}{23} = $ ____

12. $7\dfrac{9}{16} = $ ____

Convert the following improper fractions to mixed or whole numbers and write in lowest terms. (See Examples 2 and 3.)

13. $\dfrac{13}{4} = 3\dfrac{1}{4}$

    $\begin{array}{r} 3 \\ 4\overline{)13} \\ 12 \\ \hline 1 \end{array}$ $3\dfrac{1}{4}$

14. $\dfrac{9}{5} = 1\dfrac{4}{5}$

    $\begin{array}{r} 1 \\ 5\overline{)9} \\ 5 \\ \hline 4 \end{array}$ $1\dfrac{4}{5}$

15. $\dfrac{8}{3} = $ ____

16. $\dfrac{23}{10} = $ ____

17. $\dfrac{38}{10} = $ ____

18. $\dfrac{56}{8} = $ ___

19. $\dfrac{40}{11} = $ ____

20. $\dfrac{78}{12} = $ ____

21. $\dfrac{125}{63} = $ ____

22. $\dfrac{195}{45} = $ ____

23. $\dfrac{183}{25} = $ ____

24. $\dfrac{720}{149} = $ ____

25. Your classmate asks you how to change a mixed number to an improper fraction. Write a couple of sentences explaining how this is done. (See Objective 2.)

26. Explain in a sentence or two how to change an improper fraction to a mixed number. (See Objective 3.)

Write the following in lowest terms. (See Example 3.)

27. $\dfrac{8}{16} = \dfrac{1}{2}$

$\dfrac{8 \div 8}{16 \div 8} = \dfrac{1}{2}$

28. $\dfrac{15}{20} = \dfrac{3}{4}$

$\dfrac{15 \div 5}{20 \div 5} = \dfrac{3}{4}$

29. $\dfrac{25}{40} = \underline{}$

30. $\dfrac{36}{42} = \underline{}$

31. $\dfrac{27}{45} = \underline{}$

32. $\dfrac{112}{128} = \underline{}$

33. $\dfrac{165}{180} = \underline{}$

34. $\dfrac{12}{600} = \underline{}$

GOLD Pure gold is 24 karat gold. Due both to the high cost of pure gold and the fact that pure gold is soft and can be bent, gold jewelry is often mixed with an alloy and sold as 18-karat, 14-karat, or 10-karat. Write each fraction in lowest terms.

35. 24 karat = (24 parts gold, no alloy) $\dfrac{24}{24} = 1$

35. 1 _____

36. 18 karat = (18 parts gold, 6 parts alloy)

36. _____

37. 14 karat = (14 parts gold, 10 parts alloy)

37. _____

38. 10 karat = (10 parts gold, 14 parts alloy)

38. _____

39. What does it mean when a fraction is expressed in lowest terms? (See Objective 4.)

40. Eight rules of divisibility were given. Write the three rules that are most useful to you. (See Objective 5.)

Put a check mark in the blank if the number at the left is evenly divisible by the number at the top. Put an X in the blank if the number is not divisible. (See Example 4.)

	2	3	4	5	6	8	9	10
41. 32	√	X	√	X	X	√	X	X
42. 45	X	√	X	√	X	X	√	X
43. 60	_	_	_	_	_	_	_	_
44. 72	_	_	_	_	_	_	_	_
45. 90	_	_	_	_	_	_	_	_
46. 105	_	_	_	_	_	_	_	_
47. 4172	_	_	_	_	_	_	_	_
48. 5688	_	_	_	_	_	_	_	_

─────────── **QUICK CHECK ANSWERS** ───────────

1. (a) $\frac{46}{3}$ (b) $\frac{171}{8}$

2. (a) $18\frac{1}{4}$ (b) $6\frac{2}{5}$

3. (a) $\frac{4}{5}$ (b) $\frac{8}{11}$

4. (a) 628,375,210 is evenly divisible by 5
   (b) 825,693,471 is evenly divisible by 3

2.2 Addition and Subtraction of Fractions

OBJECTIVES

1 Add and subtract like fractions.

2 Find the least common denominator.

3 Add and subtract unlike fractions.

4 Rewrite fractions with a common denominator.

OBJECTIVE 1 Add and subtract like fractions. Fractions with the same denominator are called **like fractions**. Such fractions have a **common denominator**. For example, $\frac{3}{4}$ and $\frac{5}{4}$ are *like* fractions with a common denominator of 4, while $\frac{4}{7}$ and $\frac{4}{9}$ are *not like* fractions.

Adding (or Subtracting) Like Fractions (Which Have Common Denominators)
Step 1   Add (or subtract) the numerators
Step 2   Place the sum (or difference) over the common denominator.

Adding and Subtracting Like Fractions

Add or subtract.

(a) $\dfrac{3}{4} + \dfrac{1}{4} + \dfrac{5}{4}$ (b) $\dfrac{11}{15} - \dfrac{4}{15}$

SOLUTION

The fractions in both parts of this example are like fractions. Add or subtract the numerators and place the result over the common denominator.

(a) $\dfrac{3}{4} + \dfrac{1}{4} + \dfrac{5}{4} = \dfrac{\mathbf{3+1+5}}{\mathbf{4}}$ ⟵ Add the numerators.
                                                          ⟵ Write the common denominator.

  $= \dfrac{9}{4} = 2\dfrac{1}{4}$ ⟵ Write the answer as a mixed number.

(b) $\dfrac{11}{15} - \dfrac{4}{15} = \dfrac{\mathbf{11-4}}{\mathbf{15}} = \dfrac{7}{15}$

Quick TIP

When adding or subtracting like fractions, keep the same denominator.

QUICK CHECK 1

Add or subtract.

(a) $\dfrac{5}{8} + \dfrac{7}{8} + \dfrac{1}{8}$ (b) $\dfrac{17}{21} - \dfrac{4}{21}$

Fractions are commonly used in construction trades as shown in the drawing below. The fractions in the shelf-end base cross section on the left are *like fractions,* whereas the fractions in the shelf-end peninsula base on the right are *unlike fractions,* which do not have common denominators.

Shelf-End Base:
Cross Section

Shelf-End Peninsula Base:
Cross Section

OBJECTIVE 2 Find the least common denominator. Fractions with different denominators, such as $\frac{3}{4}$ and $\frac{2}{3}$, are **unlike fractions**. Add or subtract unlike fractions by first writing the fractions with a common denominator. The **least common denominator (LCD)** for two or more fractions is the smallest whole number that can be divided, without a remainder, by all the denominators of the fractions. For example, the LCD of the fractions $\frac{3}{4}$, $\frac{5}{6}$, and $\frac{1}{2}$ is 12, since 12 is the smallest number that can be divided evenly by 4, 6, and 2.

There are two methods of finding the least common denominator:

Inspection. With small denominators, it may be possible to find the least common denominator by inspection. For example, the LCD for $\frac{1}{3}$ and $\frac{1}{5}$ is 15, the smallest number that can be divided evenly by both 3 and 5.

Method of prime numbers. If the LCD cannot be found by inspection, use the method of prime numbers, as shown in the next two examples. First, we define a prime number.

> A **prime number** is a whole number that can be divided without a remainder by exactly two distinct numbers: itself and 1. Prime numbers are 2, 3, 5, 7, 11, 13, 17, and so on. The number 1 is *not* prime because it can be divided evenly by only *one* number: the number 1.

Finding the Least Common Denominator

EXAMPLE 2

Use the method of prime numbers to find the least common denominator for $\frac{5}{12}$, $\frac{7}{18}$, and $\frac{11}{20}$.

SOLUTION

First write the three denominators: 12   18   20

Begin by trying to divide the three denominators by the smallest prime number, 2. Write each quotient directly above the given denominator as follows.

$$\begin{array}{r} 6 \quad 9 \quad 10 \\ 2)\overline{12 \quad 18 \quad 20} \end{array}$$

This way of writing the division is just a handy way of writing the separate problems $2)\overline{12}$, $2)\overline{18}$, and $2)\overline{20}$. Two of the new quotients, 6 and 10, can still be divided by 2, so perform the division again. Since 9 cannot be divided evenly by 2, just bring up the 9.

$$\begin{array}{r} 3 \quad 9 \quad 5 \qquad \text{Just bring 9 up.} \\ 2)\overline{6 \quad 9 \quad 10} \\ 2)\overline{12 \quad 18 \quad 20} \end{array}$$

Quick TIP

It does not matter which prime number you start with; the final list of prime numbers will be the same.

None of the new quotients in the top row can be divided by 2, so try the next prime number, 3. The numbers 3 and 9 can be divided by 3, and one of the new quotients can still be divided by 3, so the division is performed again.

$$\begin{array}{r} 1 \quad 1 \quad 5 \\ 3)\overline{1 \quad 3 \quad 5} \\ 3)\overline{3 \quad 9 \quad 5} \\ 2)\overline{6 \quad 9 \quad 10} \\ 2)\overline{12 \quad 18 \quad 20} \end{array}$$

Since none of the new quotients in the top row can be divided by 3, try the next prime number, 5. The number 5 can be used only once, as shown.

$$\begin{array}{r} 1 \quad 1 \quad 1 \\ 5)\overline{1 \quad 1 \quad 5} \\ 3)\overline{1 \quad 3 \quad 5} \\ 3)\overline{3 \quad 9 \quad 5} \\ 2)\overline{6 \quad 9 \quad 10} \\ 2)\overline{12 \quad 18 \quad 20} \end{array}$$

Now that the top row contains only 1s, find the least common denominator by multiplying the prime numbers in the left column: $2 \times 2 \times 3 \times 3 \times 5 = 180$.

QUICK CHECK 2

Use prime numbers to find the least common denominator for $\frac{3}{5}$, $\frac{5}{6}$, and $\frac{3}{20}$.

Finding the Least Common Denominator

EXAMPLE 3

Find the least common denominator for $\frac{3}{8}$, $\frac{5}{12}$, and $\frac{9}{10}$.

SOLUTION

Write the denominators in a row and use the method of prime numbers.

$$\begin{array}{r} 1 \quad 1 \quad 1 \\ 5)\overline{1 \quad 1 \quad 5} \\ 3)\overline{1 \quad 3 \quad 5} \\ 2)\overline{2 \quad 3 \quad 5} \\ 2)\overline{4 \quad 6 \quad 5} \\ \text{Start here} \longrightarrow 2)\overline{8 \quad 12 \quad 10} \end{array}$$

The least common denominator is $2 \times 2 \times 2 \times 3 \times 5 = 120$.

OBJECTIVE 3 Add and subtract unlike fractions. Unlike fractions may be added or subtracted using the following steps.

> **Adding or Subtracting Unlike Fractions**
>
> Step 1   Find the least common denominator (LCD).
>
> Step 2   Rewrite the unlike fractions as like fractions having the least common denominator.
>
> Step 3   Add or subtract numerators, placing answers over the LCD and reducing to lowest terms.

To add or subtract unlike fractions, rewrite the fractions with a common denominator. Since Example 2 shows that 180 is the least common denominator for $\frac{5}{12}$, $\frac{7}{18}$, and $\frac{11}{20}$, these three fractions can be added if each fraction is first written with a denominator of 180.

Step 1 $\dfrac{5}{12} = \dfrac{}{180}$ $\dfrac{7}{18} = \dfrac{}{180}$ $\dfrac{11}{20} = \dfrac{}{180}$

OBJECTIVE 4 Rewrite fractions with a common denominator. To rewrite the preceding fractions with a common denominator, first divide each denominator from the original fractions into the common denominator.

Step 2 $12\overline{)180}^{\,15}$ $18\overline{)180}^{\,10}$ $20\overline{)180}^{\,9}$

Next multiply each quotient by the original numerator.

$15 \times 5 = 75$ $10 \times 7 = 70$ $9 \times 11 = 99$

Now, rewrite the fractions.

$\dfrac{5}{12} = \dfrac{75}{180}$ $\dfrac{7}{18} = \dfrac{70}{180}$ $\dfrac{11}{20} = \dfrac{99}{180}$

Finally, add.

Step 3
$$\dfrac{5}{12} + \dfrac{7}{18} + \dfrac{11}{20} = \dfrac{75}{180} + \dfrac{70}{180} + \dfrac{99}{180} = \dfrac{75 + 70 + 99}{180}$$
$$= \dfrac{244}{180} = 1\dfrac{64}{180} = 1\dfrac{16}{45} \quad \text{Write the answer as a mixed number with the fraction in lowest terms.}$$

Adding and Subtracting Unlike Fractions

EXAMPLE 4   Add or subtract.

(a) $\dfrac{3}{4} + \dfrac{1}{2} + \dfrac{5}{8}$ (b) $\dfrac{9}{10} - \dfrac{3}{8}$

SOLUTION

(a) Inspection shows that the least common denominator is 8. Rewrite the fractions so each has a denominator of 8, then add.

$$\dfrac{3}{4} + \dfrac{1}{2} + \dfrac{5}{8} = \dfrac{6}{8} + \dfrac{4}{8} + \dfrac{5}{8} = \dfrac{6 + 4 + 5}{8} = \dfrac{15}{8} = 1\dfrac{7}{8}$$

(b) The least common denominator is 40. Rewrite the fractions so each has a denominator of 40, then subtract.

$$\dfrac{9}{10} - \dfrac{3}{8} = \dfrac{36}{40} - \dfrac{15}{40} = \dfrac{36 - 15}{40} = \dfrac{21}{40}$$

QUICK CHECK 4

Add or subtract.

(a) $\dfrac{2}{3} + \dfrac{5}{8} + \dfrac{3}{4}$ (b) $\dfrac{4}{5} - \dfrac{1}{3}$

Fractions can also be added or subtracted vertically, as shown in the next example.

Adding and Subtracting Unlike Fractions

EXAMPLE 5

Add or subtract.

(a) $\dfrac{2}{9} + \dfrac{3}{4}$ (b) $\dfrac{11}{16} + \dfrac{7}{12}$ (c) $\dfrac{7}{8} - \dfrac{5}{12}$

SOLUTION

First rewrite the fractions with a least common denominator.

(a)
$$\begin{array}{r} \dfrac{2}{9} = \dfrac{8}{36} \\[6pt] + \dfrac{3}{4} = \dfrac{27}{36} \\ \hline \dfrac{35}{36} \end{array}$$

(b)
$$\begin{array}{r} \dfrac{11}{16} = \dfrac{33}{48} \\[6pt] + \dfrac{7}{12} = \dfrac{28}{48} \\ \hline \dfrac{61}{48} = 1\dfrac{13}{48} \end{array}$$

(c)
$$\begin{array}{r} \dfrac{7}{8} = \dfrac{21}{24} \\[6pt] - \dfrac{5}{12} = \dfrac{10}{24} \\ \hline = \dfrac{11}{24} \end{array}$$

🖩 All calculator solutions are shown using a basic calculator. The calculator solution to part (b) uses the fraction key on the calculator.

11 $\boxed{a^{b/c}}$ 16 $\boxed{+}$ 7 $\boxed{a^{b/c}}$ 12 $\boxed{=}$ $1\frac{13}{48}$

Note: Refer to Appendix B for calculator basics.

QUICK CHECK 5

Add or subtract.

(a) $\dfrac{11}{12} + \dfrac{2}{3}$ (b) $\dfrac{9}{10} - \dfrac{7}{15}$

2.2 Exercises

MyMathLab®

*The shaded sections below contain solutions to help you get a **QUICK START** on the various types of exercises.*

Write each fraction with the indicated denominator. (See Objective 3.)

1. $\dfrac{4}{5} = \dfrac{16}{20}$
   $20 \div 5 = 4$
   $4 \times 4 = 16$

2. $\dfrac{3}{4} = \dfrac{12}{16}$
   $16 \div 4 = 4$
   $4 \times 3 = 12$

3. $\dfrac{9}{10} = \dfrac{}{40}$

4. $\dfrac{7}{8} = \dfrac{}{56}$

5. $\dfrac{6}{5} = \dfrac{}{40}$

6. $\dfrac{7}{8} = \dfrac{}{64}$

7. $\dfrac{6}{7} = \dfrac{}{49}$

8. $\dfrac{11}{15} = \dfrac{}{120}$

Find the least common denominator for each group of denominators using the method of prime numbers. (See Example 2.)

9. 3, 8, **24**

```
    1 1
3)3 1
2)3 2
2)3 4
2)3 8
```

2 × 2 × 2 × 3 = 24

10. 18, 24, **72**

```
     1    1
3) 3    1
3) 9    3
2) 9    6
2) 9   12
2)18   24
```

2 × 2 × 2 × 3 × 3 = 72

11. 12, 18, 20, _____

12. 18, 20, 24, _____

13. 15, 24, 32, _____

14. 6, 8, 10, 12, _____

15. 10, 35, 50, 60, _____

16. 5, 18, 25, 30, 36, _____

17. Prime numbers are used to find the least common denominator. Write the definition of a prime number in your own words. (See Objective 2.)

18. Explain how to write a fraction with an indicated denominator. Give the example of changing $\frac{3}{4}$ to a fraction having 24 as a denominator. (See Objective 4.)

Add or subtract. Write answers in lowest terms. (See Examples 4 and 5.)

19. $\frac{2}{5} + \frac{1}{5} = \frac{3}{5}$

$\frac{2+1}{5} = \frac{3}{5}$

20. $\frac{2}{9} + \frac{4}{9} = \frac{2}{3}$

$\frac{2+4}{9} = \frac{6}{9} = \frac{2}{3}$

21. $\frac{3}{10} + \frac{5}{10} =$ ____

22. $\frac{5}{8} + \frac{7}{8} =$ _____

23. $\frac{11}{12} - \frac{5}{12} =$ ____

🔺 indicates an exercise that is related to the Case in Point feature.

24. $\dfrac{5}{7} - \dfrac{1}{7} =$ ___

25. $\dfrac{5}{12} - \dfrac{1}{16} =$ ___

26. $\dfrac{2}{3} - \dfrac{3}{8} =$ ___

27. $\dfrac{3}{4} + \dfrac{5}{9} + \dfrac{1}{3} =$ ___

28. $\dfrac{1}{4} + \dfrac{1}{8} + \dfrac{1}{12} =$ ___

29. $\dfrac{3}{7} + \dfrac{2}{5} + \dfrac{1}{10} =$ ___

30. $\dfrac{5}{6} + \dfrac{3}{4} + \dfrac{5}{8} =$ ___

31. $\dfrac{7}{10} + \dfrac{8}{15} + \dfrac{5}{6} =$ ___

32. $\dfrac{3}{10} + \dfrac{2}{5} + \dfrac{3}{20} =$ ___

33.
$$\begin{array}{r} \dfrac{3}{4} \\ \dfrac{2}{3} \\ +\dfrac{8}{9} \\ \hline \end{array}$$

34.
$$\begin{array}{r} \dfrac{7}{12} \\ \dfrac{5}{8} \\ +\dfrac{7}{6} \\ \hline \end{array}$$

35.
$$\begin{array}{r} \dfrac{8}{15} \\ \dfrac{3}{10} \\ +\dfrac{3}{5} \\ \hline \end{array}$$

36.
$$\begin{array}{r} \dfrac{1}{6} \\ \dfrac{5}{9} \\ +\dfrac{13}{18} \\ \hline \end{array}$$

37.
$$\begin{array}{r} \dfrac{7}{10} \\ -\dfrac{1}{4} \\ \hline \end{array}$$

38.
$$\begin{array}{r} \dfrac{4}{5} \\ -\dfrac{2}{3} \\ \hline \end{array}$$

39.
$$\begin{array}{r} \dfrac{5}{8} \\ -\dfrac{1}{3} \\ \hline \end{array}$$

40.
$$\begin{array}{r} \dfrac{19}{24} \\ -\dfrac{5}{16} \\ \hline \end{array}$$

41. Where are fractions used in everyday life? Think in terms of business applications, hobbies, and home life. Give three examples.

42. With the exception of the number 2, all prime numbers are odd numbers. However, not all odd numbers are prime numbers. Explain why these statements are true. (See Objective 2.)

Solve the following application problems.

43. GARDENING   Zalia Todd is planting her flower bed and has ordered $\frac{1}{4}$ cubic yard of sand, $\frac{3}{8}$ cubic yard of mulch, and $\frac{1}{3}$ cubic yard of peat moss. Find the total cubic yards that she has ordered.

43. _____

44. AUTO REPAIR   Chuck Manly has used his savings to repair his car. He spent $\frac{1}{4}$ of his savings for new tires, $\frac{1}{6}$ of his savings for brakes, $\frac{1}{10}$ of his savings for a tune-up, and $\frac{1}{12}$ of his savings for new belts and hoses. What fraction of his total savings has he spent?

44. _____

45. DEVICE ASSEMBLY   When installing a cable to a computer, Ann Kuick must be certain that the proper type and size of mounting hardware is used. Find the total length of the bolt shown.

45. _____

46. CABINET INSTALLATION   When installing cabinets for The Home Depot, Kara Oaks must be certain that the proper type and size of mounting screw are used. Find the total length of the screw.

46. _____

47. PETROLEUM TRANSPORT   Ken Faulk drives a tanker truck for Chemlake Transport. He leaves the refinery with his tanker filled to $\frac{7}{8}$ of capacity. If he delivers $\frac{1}{4}$ of the tank's contents at the first stop and $\frac{1}{3}$ of the tank's contents at the second stop, find the fraction of the tanker's contents remaining.

47. _____

48. TRANSMISSION   A transmission contains $\frac{7}{8}$ gallon of hydraulic fluid. A cracked seal resulted in a loss of $\frac{1}{6}$ gallon of fluid in the morning and another $\frac{1}{3}$ gallon in the afternoon. Find the amount of fluid remaining.

48. _____

49. CAKE RECIPE   Melissa Staple plans to triple the recipe for her favorite carrot cake in order to have enough for her grandmother's 88th birthday party. The recipe calls for ¼ cup of butter. Use addition to find the number of cups of butter needed.

49. _____

50. NATURAL-FOODS STORE   Joan McKee wants to open a natural-foods store and has saved $\frac{2}{5}$ of the amount needed for start-up costs. If she saves another $\frac{1}{8}$ of the amount needed and then $\frac{1}{6}$ more, find the total portion of the start-up costs she has saved.

50. _____

51. CABINET INSTALLATION   The mounting bracket shown was purchased at The Home Depot. Find the diameter of the hole which is the distance across it.

$\leftarrow \frac{3}{8}$ inch $\rightarrow$ $\leftarrow \frac{3}{8}$ inch $\rightarrow$

$\leftarrow \frac{15}{16}$ inch $\rightarrow$

51. _____

52. SPRINT TRAINING   Rona Martin competes in 100-meter sprints in high school. Today, she only has time to run $\frac{3}{4}$ miles. After stretching to warm up, her trainer has Martin sprint $\frac{1}{8}$ mile, $\frac{1}{4}$ mile, and $\frac{1}{4}$ mile. Find the additional distance she must run.

52. _____

STUDENT TIME MANAGEMENT   *Refer to the circle graph to answer Exercises 53–56.*

One Day of a Student

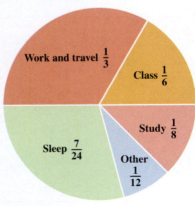

Work and travel $\frac{1}{3}$

Class $\frac{1}{6}$

Study $\frac{1}{8}$

Sleep $\frac{7}{24}$

Other $\frac{1}{12}$

53. What fraction of the day was spent in class and study?

53. _____

54. What fraction of the day was spent in work and travel, and other?

54. _____

55. In which activity was the greatest amount of time spent? What fraction of the day was spent on this activity and class time?

55. _____

56. In which activity was the least amount of time spent? What fraction of the day was spent on this activity and study?

56. _____

Use the newspaper advertisement for this four-piece chisel set to answer Exercises 57 and 58. (*Source*: Harbor Frieght Tools.)

57. Find the difference in the cutting-edge width of the narrowest chisel and the second to widest chisel. The symbol " is for inches.

57. _____

58. Find the difference in the cutting-edge width of the two chisels with the narrowest blades. The symbol " is for inches.

58. _____

4-Piece Chisel Set   Lot NO. 42429

• sizes: $\frac{1}{4}$", $\frac{1}{2}$", $\frac{3}{4}$", and 1"

• Heat-treated, high-carbon steel

• $7\frac{1}{4}$" overall length

• Straight bevel

SALE!
$4.97   REGULAR PRICE $7.99

59. PERIMETER OF FENCING   A hazardous-waste site will require $\frac{7}{8}$ mile of security fencing. The site has four sides, three of which measure $\frac{1}{4}$ mile, $\frac{1}{6}$ mile, and $\frac{3}{8}$ mile. Find the length of the fourth side.

59. _____

60. NATIVE-AMERICAN JEWELRY   Chakotay is fitting a turquoise stone into a bear-claw pendant. Find the diameter of the hole in the pendant. (The diameter is the distance across the center of the hole.)

60. _____

$\frac{3}{16}$ in. $\frac{3}{16}$ in.

$\frac{7}{8}$ in.

▼ **2.3** Addition and Subtraction of Mixed Numbers

OBJECTIVES

1 Add mixed numbers.
2 Add with carrying.
3 Subtract mixed numbers.
4 Subtract with borrowing.

▼ **CASE IN POINT**   Total customer satisfaction is very important to managers at The Home Depot. Some important aspects of quality include:

1. quality products,
2. excellent prices and a wide selection,
3. making sure customers feel comfortable in the store, and
4. accuracy in design and installation.

OBJECTIVE 1 Add mixed numbers. To add mixed numbers, first add the fractions. Then add the whole numbers and combine the two answers. For example, add $16\frac{1}{8}$ and $5\frac{5}{8}$ as shown.

$$\text{First add the fractions:} \quad \frac{1}{8} + \frac{5}{8} = \frac{1+5}{8} = \frac{6}{8} = \frac{3}{4} \quad \textcolor{blue}{\text{reduced}}$$

$$\text{Then add the whole numbers: } 16 + 5 = 21$$

Finally, write the sum of the fraction and whole-number parts as a mixed number.

$$21 + \frac{3}{4} = 21\frac{3}{4}$$

So, $16\frac{1}{8} + 5\frac{5}{8} = 21\frac{3}{4}$.

To add mixed numbers, change the mixed numbers, if necessary, so that the fraction parts have a common denominator.

Adding Mixed Numbers   ▼ **EXAMPLE 1**   Add $9\frac{2}{3}$ and $6\frac{1}{4}$.

SOLUTION

Inspection shows that 12 is the least common denominator. Write $9\frac{2}{3}$ as $9\frac{8}{12}$, and write $6\frac{1}{4}$ as $6\frac{3}{12}$. Then add. The work can be organized as follows.

$$9\frac{2}{3} = 9\frac{8}{12}$$
$$\underline{+\, 6\frac{1}{4} = 6\frac{3}{12}}$$
$$15\frac{11}{12}$$

QUICK CHECK 1

Add $5\frac{1}{4}$ and $8\frac{3}{8}$.

OBJECTIVE 2 Add with carrying. If the sum of the fraction parts of mixed numbers is greater than 1, carry the excess from the fraction part to the whole-number part.

Adding with Carrying   ▼ **EXAMPLE 2**   A rubber gasket must extend around all four edges (perimeter) of the dishwasher door panel shown on the following page before it is installed. Find the length of gasket material needed by adding $34\frac{1}{2}$ inches, $23\frac{3}{4}$ inches, $34\frac{1}{2}$ inches, and $23\frac{3}{4}$ inches.

To add mixed numbers:
1. add fractions,
2. add whole numbers, and
3. combine the two to write as a mixed number.

SOLUTION

▼ **CASE IN POINT**   Write using the least common denominator and then add.

$$34\frac{1}{2} = 34\frac{2}{4}$$

$$23\frac{3}{4} = 23\frac{3}{4}$$

$$34\frac{1}{2} = 34\frac{2}{4}$$

$$+23\frac{3}{4} = 23\frac{3}{4}$$

Dishwasher door panel $23\frac{3}{4}''h$

$34\frac{1}{2}''w$

$$114\frac{10}{4} = 114 + \frac{10}{4} = 114 + 2\frac{2}{4} = 116\frac{2}{4} = 116\frac{1}{2} \text{ inches}$$ length of gasket needed

---

QUICK CHECK 2

The four sides of a vegetable garden are $15\frac{1}{2}$ feet, $18\frac{3}{4}$ feet, $24\frac{1}{4}$ feet, and $30\frac{1}{2}$ feet. How many feet of fencing are needed to go around the garden?

OBJECTIVE 3   Subtract mixed numbers. To subtract two mixed numbers, change the mixed numbers, if necessary, so that the fraction parts have a common denominator. Then subtract the fraction parts and the whole-number parts separately. For example, subtract $3\frac{1}{12}$ from $8\frac{5}{8}$ by first finding that the least common denominator is 24. Then rewrite the problem as shown.

$$8\frac{5}{8} = \quad 8\frac{15}{24}$$ First subtract the fraction parts.
Then subtract the whole-number parts.

$$-3\frac{1}{12} = -3\frac{2}{24}$$

$$5\frac{13}{24}$$ ←——— Subtract numerators.

←——— Subtract whole numbers.

OBJECTIVE 4   Subtract with borrowing. The following example shows how to subtract when borrowing is needed.

Subtracting with Borrowing

EXAMPLE 3

(a) Subtract $6\frac{3}{4}$ from $10\frac{1}{8}$.   **(b)** Subtract $15\frac{7}{12}$ from 41.

SOLUTION

Start by rewriting each problem with a common denominator.

(a)
$$10\frac{1}{8} = 10\frac{1}{8}$$

$$-6\frac{3}{4} = -6\frac{6}{8}$$

Subtracting $\frac{6}{8}$ from $\frac{1}{8}$ requires borrowing from the whole number 10.

$$10\frac{1}{8} = 9 + 1 + \frac{1}{8}$$

$$= 9 + \frac{8}{8} + \frac{1}{8} = 9\frac{9}{8} \quad 1 = \frac{8}{8}$$

Rewrite the problem as shown. Check by adding $3\frac{3}{8}$ and $6\frac{3}{4}$. The answer should be $10\frac{1}{8}$.

$$10\frac{1}{8} = 9\frac{9}{8}$$

$$-6\frac{6}{8} = -6\frac{6}{8}$$

$$3\frac{3}{8}$$

(b)
$$41$$

$$-15\frac{7}{12}$$

To subtract the fraction $\frac{7}{12}$ requires borrowing 1 whole unit from 41.

$$41 = 40 + 1 = 40 + \frac{12}{12} = 40\frac{12}{12} \quad 1 = \frac{12}{12}$$

Rewrite the problem as shown. Check by adding $25\frac{5}{12}$ and $15\frac{7}{12}$. The answer should be 41.

$$41 = 40\frac{12}{12}$$

$$-15\frac{7}{12} = -15\frac{7}{12}$$

$$25\frac{5}{12}$$

Quick TIP

You do not have to write fractions using the least common denominator when adding or subtracting on a calculator.

The calculator solution to part (a) uses the fraction key.

$$10 \boxed{a^{b/c}} 1 \boxed{a^{b/c}} 8 \boxed{-} 6 \boxed{a^{b/c}} 3 \boxed{a^{b/c}} 4 \boxed{=} 3\tfrac{3}{8}$$

QUICK CHECK 3

Subtract **(a)** $5\tfrac{2}{3}$ from $12\tfrac{3}{8}$ and **(b)** $17\tfrac{5}{9}$ from 73.

▼ 2.3 Exercises   MyMathLab®

*The shaded sections below contain solutions to help you get a **QUICK START** on the various types of exercises.*

Add. Write each answer in lowest terms. (See Examples 1 and 2.)

1.
$$82\tfrac{3}{5} \qquad 82\tfrac{3}{5}$$
$$+\,15\tfrac{1}{5} \quad +\,15\tfrac{1}{5}$$
$$\overline{\quad 97\tfrac{4}{5} \qquad 97\tfrac{4}{5}}$$

2.
$$25\tfrac{2}{7} \qquad 25\tfrac{2}{7}$$
$$+\,14\tfrac{3}{7} \quad +\,14\tfrac{3}{7}$$
$$\overline{\quad 39\tfrac{5}{7} \qquad 39\tfrac{5}{7}}$$

3.
$$41\tfrac{1}{2}$$
$$+\,39\tfrac{1}{4}$$
$$\overline{\qquad}$$

4.
$$28\tfrac{1}{4}$$
$$+\,23\tfrac{3}{5}$$
$$\overline{\qquad}$$

5.
$$46\tfrac{3}{4}$$
$$12\tfrac{5}{8}$$
$$+\,37\tfrac{4}{5}$$
$$\overline{\qquad}$$

6.
$$26\tfrac{5}{8}$$
$$17\tfrac{3}{14}$$
$$+\,32\tfrac{2}{7}$$
$$\overline{\qquad}$$

7.
$$32\tfrac{3}{4}$$
$$6\tfrac{1}{3}$$
$$+\,14\tfrac{5}{8}$$
$$\overline{\qquad}$$

8.
$$16\tfrac{7}{10}$$
$$26\tfrac{1}{5}$$
$$+\,8\tfrac{3}{8}$$
$$\overline{\qquad}$$

Subtract. Write each answer in lowest terms. (See Example 3.)

9.
$$16\tfrac{3}{4} \qquad 16\tfrac{6}{8}$$
$$-\,12\tfrac{3}{8} \quad -\,12\tfrac{3}{8}$$
$$\overline{\quad 4\tfrac{3}{8} \qquad 4\tfrac{3}{8}}$$

10.
$$25\tfrac{13}{24} \qquad 25\tfrac{13}{24}$$
$$-\,18\tfrac{5}{12} \quad -\,18\tfrac{10}{24}$$
$$\overline{\quad 7\tfrac{1}{8} \qquad 7\tfrac{3}{24}=7\tfrac{1}{8}}$$

11.
$$9\tfrac{7}{8}$$
$$-\,6\tfrac{5}{12}$$
$$\overline{\qquad}$$

12.
$$374$$
$$-\,211\tfrac{5}{6}$$
$$\overline{\qquad}$$

13.
$$19$$
$$-\,12\tfrac{3}{4}$$
$$\overline{\qquad}$$

14.
$$71\tfrac{3}{8}$$
$$-\,62\tfrac{1}{3}$$
$$\overline{\qquad}$$

15.
$$6\tfrac{1}{3}$$
$$-\,2\tfrac{5}{12}$$
$$\overline{\qquad}$$

16.
$$72\tfrac{3}{10}$$
$$-\,25\tfrac{8}{15}$$
$$\overline{\qquad}$$

17. In your own words, explain the steps you would take to add two large mixed numbers. (See Objective 1.)

🔺 indicates an exercise that is related to the Case in Point feature.

18. When subtracting mixed numbers, explain when you need to borrow. Explain how to borrow using an example. (See Objective 4.)

Solve the following application problems.

19. PART-TIME WORK Loren Kabakov, a college student, works part time at the Cyber Coffeehouse. She worked $3\frac{3}{8}$ hours on Monday, $5\frac{1}{2}$ hours on Tuesday, $4\frac{3}{4}$ hours on Wednesday, $3\frac{1}{4}$ hours on Thursday, and 6 hours on Friday. How many hours did she work altogether?

19. $22\frac{7}{8}$ hours

$$3\frac{3}{8} + 5\frac{1}{2} + 4\frac{3}{4} + 3\frac{1}{4} + 6 = 3\frac{3}{8} + 5\frac{4}{8} + 4\frac{6}{8} + 3\frac{2}{8} + 6 = 21\frac{15}{8} = 22\frac{7}{8} \text{ hours}$$

20. TRAILER LOAD A trailer is to be loaded with plasma televisions weighing $2\frac{5}{8}$ tons, DVD players weighing $6\frac{1}{2}$ tons, personal computers weighing $1\frac{5}{6}$ tons, and computer monitors weighing $3\frac{1}{4}$ tons. If the truck weighs $7\frac{3}{8}$ tons empty, find the total weight after it has been loaded.

20. $21\frac{7}{12}$ tons

$$2\frac{5}{8} + 6\frac{1}{2} + 1\frac{5}{6} + 3\frac{1}{4} + 7\frac{3}{8} = 21\frac{7}{12} \text{ tons}$$

21. WINDOW INSTALLATION A contractor who installs windows for The Home Depot must attach a lead strip around all four sides of a custom-made stained glass window. If the window measures $34\frac{1}{2}$ by $23\frac{3}{4}$ inches, find the length of lead stripping needed.

$23\frac{3}{4}''$

$34\frac{1}{2}''$

21. $116\frac{1}{2}$ inches

$$34\frac{1}{2} + 23\frac{3}{4} + 34\frac{1}{2} + 23\frac{3}{4} =$$

$$34\frac{2}{4} + 23\frac{3}{4} + 34\frac{2}{4} + 23\frac{3}{4} = 114\frac{10}{4} = 116\frac{1}{2} \text{ inches}$$

22. MEASURING BRASS TRIM To complete a custom order, Kara Oaks of The Home Depot must find the number of inches of brass trim needed to go around the four sides of the lamp base plate shown. Find the length of brass trim needed.

22. _____

$5\frac{1}{8}''$

$9\frac{7}{8}''$

23. SECURITY FENCING The exercise yard at the correction center has four sides and is enclosed with $527\frac{1}{24}$ feet of security fencing around it. If three sides of the yard measure $107\frac{2}{3}$ feet, $150\frac{3}{4}$ feet, and $138\frac{5}{8}$ feet, find the length of the fourth side.

23. _____

24. PARKING LOT FENCING Three sides of a parking lot are $108\frac{1}{4}$ feet, $162\frac{3}{8}$ feet, and $143\frac{1}{2}$ feet. If the distance around the lot is $518\frac{3}{4}$ feet, find the length of the fourth side.

24. _____

$108\frac{1}{4}$ ft

$162\frac{3}{8}$ ft

? ft

$143\frac{1}{2}$ ft

25. **DELIVERING CONCRETE**   Chuck Stone has $8\frac{7}{8}$ cubic yards of concrete in a truck. If he unloads $2\frac{1}{2}$ cubic yards at the first stop, 3 cubic yards at the second stop, and $1\frac{3}{4}$ cubic yards at the third stop, how much concrete remains in the truck?

25. _____

26. **TAILORED CLOTHING**   Marv Levenson bought 15 yards of Italian silk fabric. He made two tops with $3\frac{3}{4}$ yards of the material, a suit for his wife with $4\frac{1}{8}$ yards, and a jacket with $3\frac{7}{8}$ yards. Find the number of yards of material remaining.

26. _____

QUICK CHECK ANSWERS

1. $13\frac{5}{8} = 14\frac{1}{8}$

2. $87\frac{8}{4} = 89$ feet

3. (a) $6\frac{17}{24}$ (b) $55\frac{4}{9}$

2.4 Multiplication and Division of Fractions

OBJECTIVES

1. Multiply proper fractions.
2. Use cancellation.
3. Multiply mixed numbers.
4. Divide fractions.
5. Divide mixed numbers.
6. Multiply or divide by whole numbers.

▼ **CASE IN POINT** Most of the cabinets sold by The Home Depot are standard size units and modules that can be combined to satisfy varied applications and room sizes. However, all too often, Kara Oaks finds that various components and trim pieces must be custom sized which requires her to work with fractions and mixed numbers.

OBJECTIVE 1 Multiply proper fractions. To multiply two fractions, first multiply the numerators to form a new numerator and then multiply the denominators to form a new denominator. Write the answer in lowest terms if necessary. For example, multiply $\frac{2}{3}$ and $\frac{5}{8}$ by first multiplying the numerators and then the denominators.

$$\frac{2}{3} \times \frac{5}{8} = \frac{2 \times 5}{3 \times 8} = \frac{10}{24} = \frac{5}{12} \quad \text{in lowest terms}$$

Multiply numerators.
Multiply denominators.

OBJECTIVE 2 Use cancellation. To **cancel**, find a number that divides evenly into both a numerator and denominator of fractions being multiplied. That number can be canceled, or divided out of the numerator and denominator before multiplying the fractions. For example, divide 2 into both 2 and 8 in the problem below. Once simplified, the fractions can be multiplied.

$$\frac{\overset{1}{2}}{3} \times \frac{5}{\underset{4}{8}} = \frac{1 \times 5}{3 \times 4} = \frac{5}{12}$$

EXAMPLE 1

Multiplying Common Fractions

Multiply.

(a) $\dfrac{8}{15} \times \dfrac{5}{12}$ (b) $\dfrac{35}{12} \times \dfrac{32}{25}$

SOLUTION

Use cancellation in both of these problems.

(a) $\dfrac{\overset{2}{8}}{\underset{3}{15}} \times \dfrac{\overset{1}{5}}{\underset{3}{12}} = \dfrac{2 \times 1}{3 \times 3} = \dfrac{2}{9}$

Divide 4 into both 8 and 12.
Divide 5 into both 5 and 15.

(b) $\dfrac{\overset{7}{35}}{\underset{3}{12}} \times \dfrac{\overset{8}{32}}{\underset{5}{25}} = \dfrac{7 \times 8}{3 \times 5} = \dfrac{56}{15} = 3\dfrac{11}{15}$

Divide 4 into both 12 and 32.
Divide 5 into both 35 and 25.

Quick TIP

When canceling, be certain that the numerator and the denominator are both divided by the same number.

QUICK CHECK 1

Multiply using cancellation.

(a) $\dfrac{7}{8} \times \dfrac{4}{21}$ (b) $\dfrac{36}{15} \times \dfrac{45}{24}$

OBJECTIVE 3 Multiply mixed numbers. To multiply mixed numbers, change the mixed numbers to improper fractions, cancel, and then multiply. For example, multiply $6\frac{1}{4}$ and $2\frac{2}{3}$ as follows.

$$6\frac{1}{4} \times 2\frac{2}{3} = \frac{25}{4} \times \frac{8}{3} = \frac{25}{\underset{1}{4}} \times \frac{\overset{2}{8}}{3} = \frac{25 \times 2}{1 \times 3} = \frac{50}{3} = 16\frac{2}{3}$$

Cancel.
Change to improper fractions.

Multiplying Mixed Numbers

EXAMPLE 2

Multiply.

(a) $3\frac{3}{4} \times 8\frac{2}{3}$ (b) $1\frac{3}{5} \times 3\frac{1}{3} \times 1\frac{3}{4}$

SOLUTION

Quick TIP

Be sure to change each mixed number to a fraction before multiplying.

(a) $3\frac{3}{4} = \frac{15}{4}$ and $8\frac{2}{3} = \frac{26}{3}$

$$\frac{\overset{5}{\cancel{15}}}{\underset{2}{\cancel{4}}} \times \frac{\overset{13}{\cancel{26}}}{\underset{1}{\cancel{3}}} = \frac{\mathbf{5 \times 13}}{\mathbf{2 \times 1}} = \frac{65}{2} = 32\frac{1}{2}$$

(b) $1\frac{3}{5} = \frac{8}{5}, 3\frac{1}{3} = \frac{10}{3}$, and $1\frac{3}{4} = \frac{7}{4}$

$$\frac{\overset{2}{\cancel{8}}}{\underset{1}{5}} \times \frac{\overset{2}{\cancel{10}}}{3} \times \frac{7}{\underset{1}{\cancel{4}}} = \frac{\mathbf{2 \times 2 \times 7}}{\mathbf{1 \times 3 \times 1}} = \frac{28}{3} = 9\frac{1}{3}$$

The calculator solution to part (b) uses the fraction key.

$1 \boxed{a^{b/c}} 3 \boxed{a^{b/c}} 5 \boxed{\times} 3 \boxed{a^{b/c}} 1 \boxed{a^{b/c}} 3 \boxed{\times} 1 \boxed{a^{b/c}} 3 \boxed{a^{b/c}} 4 \boxed{=} 9\frac{1}{3}$

QUICK CHECK 2

Multiply.

(a) $3\frac{3}{5} \times 1\frac{2}{3}$ (b) $2\frac{2}{3} \times 1\frac{5}{9} \times 3\frac{3}{4}$

You can double the following recipe by multiplying the amount of each item by 2.

Chocolate/Oat-Chip Cookies

1 cup (2 sticks) margarine or butter,
  softened
$1\frac{1}{4}$ cups firmly packed brown sugar
$\frac{1}{2}$ cup granulated sugar
2 eggs
2 tablespoons milk
2 teaspoons vanilla
$1\frac{3}{4}$ cups all-purpose flour
1 teaspoon baking soda

$\frac{1}{2}$ teaspoon salt (optional)
$2\frac{1}{2}$ cups uncooked oats
One 12-ounce package (2 cups)
  semi-sweet chocolate morsels
1 cup coarsely chopped nuts (optional)

Heat oven to 375°F. **Beat** margarine and sugars until creamy.
Add eggs, milk, and vanilla; beat well.
Add combined flour, baking soda, and salt; mix well. **Stir** in oats, chocolate morsels, and
  nuts; mix well.
Drop using rounded measuring tablespoonfuls onto ungreased cookie sheet.
Bake 9 to 10 minutes for a chewy cookie or 12 to 13 minutes for a crisp cookie.
Cool 1 minute on cookie sheet; remove to wire rack. Cool completely.

MAKES ABOUT 5 DOZEN

Multiplying a Mixed Number by a Whole Number

EXAMPLE 3

(a) Find the amount of uncooked oats needed if the preceding recipe for chocolate/oat-chip cookies is doubled (multiplied by 2).

(b) How many cups of all-purpose flour are needed when the recipe is tripled (multiplied by 3)?

SOLUTION

(a) $2\frac{1}{2} \times 2 = \frac{5}{2} \times \frac{\overset{1}{\cancel{2}}}{\underset{1}{1}} = \frac{\mathbf{5 \times 1}}{\mathbf{1 \times 1}} = \frac{5}{1} = 5$ cups

(b) $1\frac{3}{4} \times 3 = \frac{7}{4} \times \frac{3}{1} = \frac{\mathbf{7 \times 3}}{\mathbf{4}} = \frac{21}{4} = 5\frac{1}{4}$ cups

OBJECTIVE 4 Divide fractions. To divide fractions, first invert the divisor by exchanging the numerator and denominator. For example, when dividing $\frac{3}{8}$ by $\frac{7}{9}$, first invert $\frac{7}{9}$ to $\frac{9}{7}$. Then multiply the two remaining fractions.

$$\frac{3}{8} \div \frac{7}{9}$$

$$\frac{3}{8} \cdot \frac{9}{7}$$ Invert second fraction and change to a multiplication problem.

$$\frac{3 \cdot 9}{8 \cdot 7}$$ Multiply numerators and denominators.

$$\frac{27}{56}$$

so, $\dfrac{3}{8} \div \dfrac{7}{9} = \dfrac{27}{56}$.

Dividing Common Fractions   **EXAMPLE 4**   Divide.

(a) $\dfrac{7}{8} \div \dfrac{1}{4}$ (b) $\dfrac{25}{36} \div \dfrac{15}{18}$

Quick TIP

Only invert the second fraction, the divisor, when dividing fractions.

SOLUTION

First, invert the second fraction, and then multiply.

(a) $\dfrac{7}{8} \div \dfrac{1}{4} = \dfrac{7}{\overset{}{\underset{2}{8}}} \times \dfrac{\overset{1}{4}}{1} = \dfrac{7 \times 1}{2 \times 1} = \dfrac{7}{2} = 3\dfrac{1}{2}$

(b) $\dfrac{25}{36} \div \dfrac{15}{18} = \dfrac{\overset{5}{25}}{\underset{2}{36}} \times \dfrac{\overset{1}{18}}{\underset{3}{15}} = \dfrac{5 \times 1}{2 \times 3} = \dfrac{5}{6}$

OBJECTIVE 5 Divide mixed numbers. To divide mixed numbers, first change all mixed numbers to improper fractions. Then divide as above by inverting the divisor and, finally, multiplying the fractions.

For example, work $3\dfrac{5}{9} \div 2\dfrac{2}{5}$ as follows.

$$3\dfrac{5}{9} \div 2\dfrac{2}{5}$$

$$\dfrac{32}{9} \div \dfrac{12}{5}$$ Convert to improper fractions.

$$\dfrac{32}{9} \cdot \dfrac{5}{12}$$ Invert second fraction and change to a multiplication problem.

$$\dfrac{32 \cdot 5}{9 \cdot 12}$$ Multiply fractions.

$$\dfrac{160}{108}$$

$$1\dfrac{13}{27}$$ Change to a mixed number

So, $3\dfrac{5}{9} \div 2\dfrac{2}{5} = 1\dfrac{13}{27}$.

OBJECTIVE 6 Multiply or divide by whole numbers. To multiply or divide a fraction by a whole number, write the whole number as a fraction over 1.

Multiply: $3\dfrac{3}{4} \times 16 = 3\dfrac{3}{4} \times \dfrac{16}{1} = \dfrac{15}{4} \times \dfrac{16}{1} = \dfrac{15}{4} \times \dfrac{\overset{4}{16}}{\underset{1}{1}} = 15 \times 4 = 60$

Write as a whole number over 1.

Divide: $2\dfrac{2}{5} \div 3 = \dfrac{12}{5} \div \dfrac{3}{1} = \dfrac{\overset{4}{12}}{5} \times \dfrac{1}{\underset{1}{3}} = \dfrac{4 \times 1}{5 \times 1} = \dfrac{4}{5}$

Write 3 as $\dfrac{3}{1}$.

Base-End Panel

$23\frac{3}{4}''$ wide

$34\frac{1}{2}''$ high

$\frac{3}{4}''$ deep

Mills Pride manufactures cabinets for kitchens and baths. The specifications for base-end panels are shown in the diagram. The lumber used is $\frac{3}{4}$ inch deep and is cut down from 24 inches to a $23\frac{3}{4}$-inch width. The panel is then cut to a height of $34\frac{1}{2}$ inches. The materials used in the manufacture of cabinets, solid oak in this case, are very expensive. Every precaution is taken to minimize waste.

Multiplying a Whole Number by a Mixed Number

EXAMPLE 5

A cabinetmaker will need 80 base-end panels, shown above and to the left, to complete a job. If each panel is $34\frac{1}{2}$ inches in length, how many inches of oak material are needed, assuming no waste?

SOLUTION

Multiply the number of panels needed by the length of each panel: $34\frac{1}{2}$ (which is $\frac{69}{2}$).

$$80 \times \frac{69}{2} = \frac{\overset{40}{80}}{1} \times \frac{69}{\underset{1}{2}} = \frac{40 \times 69}{1 \times 1} = \frac{2760}{1} = 2760 \text{ inches}$$

The length of material needed by the cabinetmaker is 2760 inches.

QUICK CHECK 5

A plumber needs 68 pieces of 1-inch-diameter copper tubing. If each piece of tubing must be $28\frac{1}{2}$ inches long, how many total inches of tubing are needed?

Dividing a Whole Number by a Mixed Number

EXAMPLE 6

To complete a custom-designed cabinet, oak trim pieces must be cut exactly $2\frac{1}{4}$ inches long so that they can be used as dividers in a spice rack. Find the number of pieces that can be cut from a piece of oak that is 54 inches in length.

SOLUTION

To divide the length of the piece of oak by $2\frac{1}{4}$, first change the mixed number $2\frac{1}{4}$ to the fraction $\frac{9}{4}$. Then invert the divisor and multiply. The divisor is the number that follows the ÷ sign.

$$54 \div 2\frac{1}{4} = 54 \div \frac{9}{4} = \frac{\overset{6}{54}}{1} \times \frac{4}{\underset{1}{9}} = \frac{6 \times 4}{1 \times 1} = \frac{24}{1} = 24$$

The number of trim pieces that can be cut from the oak stock is 24.

QUICK CHECK 6

A welder needs angle iron pieces that are $3\frac{1}{3}$ inches long. Find the number of pieces that can be cut from a piece of angle iron that is 70 inches in length, assuming no waste.

2.4 Exercises

MyMathLab®

The shaded sections below contain solutions to help you get a **QUICK START** on the various types of exercises.

Multiply. Write each answer in lowest terms. (See Examples 1–3.)

1. $\dfrac{3}{4} \times \dfrac{2}{5} = \dfrac{3}{10}$

$\dfrac{3}{\overset{}{\underset{2}{4}}} \times \dfrac{\overset{1}{2}}{5} = \dfrac{3}{10}$

2. $\dfrac{2}{3} \times \dfrac{5}{8} = \dfrac{5}{12}$

$\dfrac{\overset{1}{2}}{3} \times \dfrac{5}{\underset{4}{8}} = \dfrac{5}{12}$

3. $\dfrac{9}{10} \times \dfrac{11}{16} = $ _____

4. $\dfrac{2}{3} \times \dfrac{3}{8} = $ _____

5. $\dfrac{9}{22} \times \dfrac{11}{16} = $ _____

6. $\dfrac{5}{12} \times \dfrac{7}{10} = $ _____

7. $1\dfrac{1}{4} \times 3\dfrac{1}{2} = $ _____

8. $1\dfrac{2}{3} \times 2\dfrac{7}{10} = $ _____

9. $3\dfrac{1}{9} \times 3 = $ _____

10. $\dfrac{3}{4} \times \dfrac{8}{9} \times 2\dfrac{1}{2} = $ _____

11. $\dfrac{1}{4} \times 6\dfrac{2}{3} \times \dfrac{1}{5} = $ _____

12. $\dfrac{2}{3} \times \dfrac{9}{8} \times 3\dfrac{1}{4} = $ _____

13. $\dfrac{5}{9} \times 2\dfrac{1}{4} \times 3\dfrac{2}{3} = $ _____

14. $3 \times 1\dfrac{1}{2} \times 2\dfrac{2}{3} = $ _____

15. $5\dfrac{3}{5} \times 1\dfrac{5}{9} \times \dfrac{10}{49} = $ _____

Divide. Write each answer in lowest terms. (See Example 4.)

16. $\dfrac{1}{4} \div \dfrac{3}{4} = \dfrac{1}{3}$

$\dfrac{1}{\overset{}{\underset{1}{4}}} \times \dfrac{\overset{1}{4}}{3} = \dfrac{1}{3}$

17. $\dfrac{3}{8} \div \dfrac{5}{8} = \dfrac{3}{5}$

$\dfrac{3}{\overset{}{\underset{1}{8}}} \times \dfrac{\overset{1}{8}}{5} = \dfrac{3}{5}$

18. $\dfrac{13}{20} \div \dfrac{26}{30} = $ __

19. $\dfrac{9}{10} \div \dfrac{3}{5} = $ _____

20. $\dfrac{7}{8} \div \dfrac{3}{4} = $ _____

21. $2\dfrac{1}{2} \div 3\dfrac{3}{4} = $ _____

22. $1\dfrac{1}{4} \div 4\dfrac{1}{6} = $ _____

23. $5 \div 1\dfrac{7}{8} = $ _____

24. $3 \div 1\dfrac{1}{4} = $ _____

indicates an exercise that is related to the Case in Point feature.

25. $\dfrac{3}{8} \div 2\dfrac{1}{2} =$ _____

26. $1\dfrac{7}{8} \div 6\dfrac{1}{4} =$ _____

27. $2\dfrac{5}{8} \div \dfrac{5}{16} =$ _____

28. $5\dfrac{2}{3} \div 6 =$ _____

29. In your own words, explain how to multiply fractions. Make up an example problem of your own showing how this works.

30. Describe how cancellation works in fractions and give an example. (See Objective 2.).

Find the time-and-a-half pay rate by multiplying the hourly wage given by $1\dfrac{1}{2}$ (See Example 5.)

31. $8 $12 _____

$\$8 \times 1\dfrac{1}{2} = \$12$

32. $17 _____

33. $12.50 _____

(*Hint:* $12.50 = $12\tfrac{1}{2}$)

34. $9.50 _____

35. Your classmate is confused about how to divide by a fraction. Write a short explanation telling how this should be done.

36. When multiplying two proper fractions, the product is smaller than either of the fractions. For example, $\dfrac{1}{2} \cdot \dfrac{1}{3} = \dfrac{1}{6}$. Is the same thing true when multiplying a proper fraction by a mixed number? Explain and show some examples.

Solve the following application problems.

37. ELECTRICITY RATES   The utility company says that the cost of operating a hair dryer is $\dfrac{3}{10}$ ¢ per minute. Find the cost of operating the hair dryer for 30 minutes.

37. _____

38. ELECTRICITY RATES   The cost of electricity for brewing coffee is $\dfrac{2}{5}$ ¢ per minute. What is the cost of brewing coffee for 90 minutes?

38. _____

39. CHRISTMAS WREATHS   Matthew Genaway wants to make 16 wreaths to sell at the craft fair. Each wreath needs $2\dfrac{1}{4}$ yards of ribbon. How many yards does he need?

39. _____

40. EARNINGS CALCULATION   Jack Horner worked $38\dfrac{1}{4}$ hours at $10 per hour. How much money did he make?

40. _____

41. FINISH CARPENTRY   Kara Oaks at The Home Depot estimates that a certain design for a kitchen and bathroom needs $109\dfrac{1}{2}$ feet of cabinet trim. How many homes can be fitted with cabinet trim if there are 1314 feet of cabinet trim available?

41. _____

42. COMMERCIAL FERTILIZER For 1 acre of a crop, $7\frac{1}{2}$ gallons of fertilizer must be applied. How many acres can be fertilized with 1200 gallons of fertilizer?

42. _____

43. A manufacturer of floor jacks is ordering steel tubing to make the handles for this jack. How much steel tubing is needed to make 135 of these jacks? (The symbol for inch is ".)

43. _____

CENTRAL HYDRAULICS
2-Ton Compact Floorjack

4000 LB CAPACITY

- $19\frac{1}{2}$" handle
- Lifts 5" to $15\frac{1}{4}$"
- Fully rolled edge for added tray strength
- 21" L × $9\frac{1}{2}$" W × 6" H
- Compact & lightweight for portability—perfect for the trunk

44. A wheelbarrow manufacturer uses handles made of hardwood. Find the amount of wood that is needed to make 182 handles. The longest dimension shown is the handle length.

44. _____

6.0 CUBIC FT
WHEELBARROW

- Steel construction with hardwood handles
- 14" tubeless pneumatic tire
- Fully rolled edge for added strength
- Overall dimensions: $61\frac{1}{2}$" L × 27" W × 24.9" H

45. STRAWBERRY CHEESECAKE The manager of a commercial kitchen has 40 cups of graham cracker crumbs on hand. Find the number of strawberry cheesecakes that can be made if each requires $1\frac{1}{4}$ cup of graham cracker crumbs.

45. _____

46. COMMERCIAL CARPETING The manager of the flooring department at The Home Depot determines that each apartment unit requires $62\frac{1}{2}$ square yards of carpet. Find the number of apartment units that can be carpeted with 6750 square yards of carpet.

46. _____

47. **FUEL CONSUMPTION**   A fishing boat uses $12\frac{3}{4}$ gallons of fuel on a full-day fishing trip and $7\frac{1}{8}$ gallons of fuel on a half-day trip. Find the total number of gallons of fuel used in 28 full-day trips and 16 half-day trips.

47. _____

48. **MAKING JEWELRY**   One necklace can be completed in $6\frac{1}{2}$ minutes, while a bracelet takes $3\frac{1}{8}$ minutes. Find the total time that it takes to complete 36 necklaces and 22 bracelets.

48. _____

49. **DISPENSING EYEDROPS**   How many $\frac{1}{8}$-ounce eyedrop dispensers can be filled with 11 ounces of eyedrops?

49. _____

50. **CONCRETE FOOTINGS**   Each building footing requires $\frac{5}{16}$ cubic yard of concrete. How many building footings can be constructed from 10 cubic yards of concrete?

50. _____

51. **ALASKA WILDERNESS**   "Grizzly" Hanson needs 40 crates of trapping and other supplies to make it through the winter at his remote cabin. If he can carry only $8\frac{1}{2}$ crates with each load behind his snowmobile, find the number of round trips required. You may need to round up.

51. _____

52. **WEATHER STRIPPING**   Bill Rhodes, an employee at The Home Depot, sells a 200-yard roll of weather stripping material. Find the number of pieces of weather stripping $\frac{5}{8}$ yard in length that may be cut from the roll.

52. _____

QUICK CHECK ANSWERS

1. (a) $\frac{1}{6}$ **(b)** $\frac{9}{2} = 4\frac{1}{2}$

2. (a) 6 **(b)** $15\frac{5}{9}$

3. (a) $3\frac{3}{4}$ cups **(b)** $7\frac{1}{2}$ teaspoons

4. (a) $\frac{4}{3} = 1\frac{1}{3}$ **(b)** $\frac{16}{21}$

5. 1938 inches

6. 21 pieces

2.5 Converting Decimals to Fractions and Fractions to Decimals

OBJECTIVES

1 Convert decimals to fractions.

2 Convert fractions to decimals.

3 Know common decimal equivalents.

Decimals and fractions are used to represent part of a whole. In this section, you will learn how to convert a decimal to a fraction and vice versa.

OBJECTIVE 1 Convert decimals to fractions. Recall from the previous chapter that place values to the right of the decimal point are named as shown.

A decimal number can be written as a fraction just by reading it. For example, we learned in the previous chapter that the number .025 is read as twenty-five thousandths. Write it is a fraction by placing 25 in the numerator and 1000 in the denominator.

$$\frac{25}{1000} \text{ which reduces to } \frac{1}{40}$$

Decimal	Read as	Fraction Equivalent
0.6	six tenths	$\frac{6}{10} = \frac{3}{5}$
0.38	thirty-eight hundredths	$\frac{38}{100} = \frac{19}{50}$
0.875	eight hundred seventy-five thousandths	$\frac{875}{1000} = \frac{7}{8}$

Another method of converting a decimal to a fraction is by first removing the decimal point. The remaining number is the numerator of the fraction. The denominator of the fraction is 1 followed by as many zeros as there were digits to the right of the decimal point in the original number.

Converting Decimals to Fractions

EXAMPLE 1

Convert the following decimals to fractions.

(a) .3   **(b)** .98   **(c)** .654

SOLUTION

(a) After removing the decimal point in .3, you can see that the numerator of the fraction is 3. Since there is only one digit to the right of the decimal point, the denominator is 1 followed by one zero, or 10.

$$.3 = \frac{3}{10}$$

↑————————1 followed by 1 zero

(b) The numerator of the fraction is 98. Since there are two digits to the right of the decimal point, the denominator is 1 followed by two zeros, or 100.

$$.98 = \frac{98}{100} = \frac{49}{50} \text{ (lowest terms)}$$

↑————————1 followed by 2 zeros

(c) Since there are three digits to the right of the decimal point, the denominator is 1 followed by three zeros, or 1000.

$$.654 = \frac{654}{1000} = \frac{327}{500} \text{ (lowest terms)}$$

↑————————1 followed by 3 zeros

QUICK CHECK 1
Convert the following decimals to fractions.

(a) .75   (b) .64   (c) .875

OBJECTIVE 2 Convert fractions to decimals. Convert a fraction to a decimal by dividing the numerator of the fraction by the denominator. Place a decimal point after the numerator and attach one zero at a time to the right of the decimal point as the division is performed. Keep going until the division produces a remainder of zero or until the desired degree of accuracy is reached.

Converting Fractions to Decimals

EXAMPLE 2

Convert the following fractions to decimals.

(a) $\frac{1}{8}$ (b) $\frac{2}{3}$

Decimal Equivalents

$\frac{1}{16} = .0625$

$\frac{1}{10} = .1$

$\frac{1}{9} = .1111$ (rounded)

$\frac{1}{8} = .125$

$\frac{1}{7} = .1429$ (rounded)

$\frac{1}{6} = .1667$ (rounded)

$\frac{3}{16} = .1875$

$\frac{1}{5} = .2$

$\frac{1}{4} = .25$

$\frac{3}{10} = .3$

$\frac{1}{3} = .3333$ (rounded)

$\frac{3}{8} = .375$

$\frac{2}{5} = .4$

$\frac{1}{2} = .5$

$\frac{3}{5} = .6$

$\frac{5}{8} = .625$

$\frac{2}{3} = .6667$ (rounded)

$\frac{7}{10} = .7$

$\frac{3}{4} = .75$

$\frac{4}{5} = .8$

$\frac{5}{6} = .8333$ (rounded)

$\frac{7}{8} = .875$

$\frac{9}{10} = .9$

SOLUTION

(a) Convert $\frac{1}{8}$ to a decimal by dividing 1 by 8. Add trailing zeros after the 1 as needed.

```
      .125
  8)1.000      Add zeros as needed.
    8
    ──
    20
    16
    ──
    40
    40
    ──
     0      remainder of 0      Therefore, 1/8 = .125.
```

(b) Divide 2 by 3.

```
       .6666
  3)2.0000      Keep attaching zeros.
    1 8
    ──
     20
     18
     ──
     20
     18
     ──
     20
     18
     ──
      2
```

The division continues without ending and has a repeating decimal, which is often written as $.\overline{6}$, $.6\overline{6}$, or $.66\overline{6}$. It would be written as .67 when rounded to the nearest hundredth and as .667 when rounded to the nearest thousandth.

The calculator solution to this example is

2 ÷ 3 = 0.666666667

QUICK CHECK 2

Convert the following fractions to decimals.

(a) $\frac{4}{5}$ (b) $\frac{5}{8}$

OBJECTIVE 3 Know common decimal equivalents. Some of the more common **decimal equivalents** of fractions are listed in the margin. These decimals appear from least to greatest value and are rounded to the nearest ten-thousandth.

Quick TIP

Do not use both a decimal and a fraction in the same number.

▼ 2.5 Exercises

MyMathLab®

The shaded sections below contain solutions to help you get a **QUICK START** *on the various types of exercises.*

Convert the following decimals to fractions, and write each in lowest terms. (See Example 1.)

1. $.75 = \dfrac{3}{4}$

$\dfrac{75}{100} = \dfrac{3}{4}$

2. $.55 = \dfrac{11}{20}$

$\dfrac{55}{100} = \dfrac{11}{20}$

3. $.24 = $ _____

4. $.64 = $ _____

5. $.73 = $ _____

6. $.33 = $ _____

7. $.85 = $ _____

8. $.68 = $ _____

9. $.34 = $ _____

10. $.288 = $ _____

11. $.444 = $ _____

12. $.125 = $ _____

13. $.625 = $ _____

14. $.875 = $ _____

15. $.805 = $ _____

16. $.791 = $ _____

17. $.096 = $ _____

18. $.012 = $ _____

19. $.0375 = $ _____

20. $.0875 = $ _____

21. $.1875 = $ _____

22. $.9845 = $ _____

23. $.0016 = $ _____

24. $.0085 = $ _____

25. A classmate of yours is confused about how to convert a decimal to a fraction. Write an explanation of this for your classmate, including changing the fraction to lowest terms. (See Objective 1.)

26. Explain how to convert a fraction to a decimal. Be sure to mention rounding in your explanation. (See Objective 2.)

Convert the following fractions to decimals. If a division does not come out evenly, round the answer to the nearest thousandth. (See Example 2.)

27. $\dfrac{1}{4} = .25$

$$\begin{array}{r} .25 \\ 4\overline{)1.00} \\ \underline{8} \\ 20 \\ \underline{20} \\ 0 \end{array}$$

28. $\dfrac{7}{8} = $ _____

29. $\dfrac{3}{8} = $ _____

30. $\dfrac{5}{8} =$ ____

31. $\dfrac{2}{3} =$ _____

32. $\dfrac{5}{6} =$ _____

33. $\dfrac{7}{9} =$ _____

34. $\dfrac{1}{9} =$ _____

35. $\dfrac{7}{11} =$ _____

36. $\dfrac{8}{25} =$ ____

37. $\dfrac{22}{25} =$ ____

38. $\dfrac{14}{25} =$ ____

39. $\dfrac{181}{205} =$ _____

40. $\dfrac{1}{99} =$ _____

41. GAMBLING WITH HEALTH   A hospital study of 1521 heart-attack patients found that 1 out of 8 quit taking the life-saving drugs prescribed to them. **(a)** What fraction stopped taking their medicine? **(b)** Convert this fraction to a decimal. **(c)** How many patients in the study quit taking their medicine? Round to the nearest whole number.

(a) _____

(b) _____

(c) _____

42. SMOKING AND CANCER   A study found that one out of every five smokers developed lung cancer. (a) Write the fraction as a decimal. (b) Out of a group of 8000 smokers, find the number expected to develop lung cancer.

(a) _____

(b) _____

QUICK CHECK ANSWERS

1. (a) $\dfrac{3}{4}$ **(b)** $\dfrac{16}{25}$ **(c)** $\dfrac{7}{8}$ **2. (a)** .8 **(b)** .625

▼ Chapter 2   Quick Review

Chapter Terms *Review the following terms to test your understanding of the chapter. For each term you do not know, refer to the page number found next to that term.*

cancel **[p. 63]**

common denominator **[p. 50]**

common fraction **[p. 44]**

decimal equivalent **[p. 72]**

denominator **[p. 44]**

fraction **[p. 44]**

improper fraction **[p. 44]**

inspection **[p. 50]**

least common denominator (LCD) **[p. 50]**

like fractions **[p. 50]**

lowest terms **[p. 46]**

method of prime numbers **[p. 50]**

mixed number **[p. 44]**

numerator **[p. 44]**

prime number **[p. 51]**

proper fraction **[p. 44]**

quotient **[p. 35]**

unlike fractions **[p. 50]**

CONCEPTS

2.1 Types of fractions

Proper: Numerator smaller than denominator
Improper: Numerator equal to or greater than denominator
Mixed: Whole number plus proper fraction

$$4 + \frac{2}{3} = 4\frac{2}{3}$$

2.1 Converting fractions

Mixed to improper: Multiply whole number by denominator and add numerator.
Improper to mixed: Divide numerator by denominator and place remainder over denominator.

2.1 Writing fractions in lowest terms

Divide the numerator and denominator by the same number.

2.2 Adding like fractions

Keep the same denominator, add numerators, and reduce to lowest terms.

2.2 Finding a least common denominator (LCD)

Inspection method: Look to see if the LCD can be found.
Method of prime numbers: Use prime numbers to find the LCD.

2.2 Adding unlike fractions

1. Find the LCD.
2. Rewrite fractions using the LCD.
3. Add numerators, placing answers over the LCD, and reduce to lowest terms.

EXAMPLES

proper fractions $\quad \dfrac{2}{3}, \dfrac{3}{4}, \dfrac{15}{16}, \dfrac{1}{8}$

improper fractions $\quad \dfrac{17}{8}, \dfrac{19}{12}, \dfrac{11}{2}, \dfrac{5}{3}, \dfrac{7}{7}$

mixed numbers $\quad 2\dfrac{2}{3}, 3\dfrac{5}{8}, 9\dfrac{5}{6}$

$$7\frac{2}{3} = \frac{(7 \times 3) + 2}{3} = \frac{23}{3}$$

$$\frac{17}{5} = 3\frac{2}{5} \qquad 5\overline{)17} \\ \quad\;\; \underline{15} \\ \qquad\;\; 2$$

$$\frac{30}{42} = \frac{30 \div 6}{42 \div 6} = \frac{5}{7}$$

$$\frac{3}{4} + \frac{1}{4} + \frac{5}{4} = \frac{3 + 1 + 5}{4} = \frac{9}{4} = 2\frac{1}{4}$$

$$\frac{1}{3} + \frac{1}{4} + \frac{1}{10}$$

$$5\overline{)1 \quad 1 \quad 5} \\ 3\overline{)3 \quad 1 \quad 5} \\ 2\overline{)3 \quad 2 \quad 5} \\ 2\overline{)3 \quad 4 \quad 10}$$

Multiply the prime numbers.

$$2 \times 2 \times 3 \times 5 = 60 \text{ LCD}$$

$$\frac{1}{3} + \frac{1}{4} + \frac{1}{10} \quad \text{LCD} = 60$$

$$\frac{1}{3} = \frac{20}{60}, \frac{1}{4} = \frac{15}{60}, \frac{1}{10} = \frac{6}{60}$$

$$\frac{20 + 15 + 6}{60} = \frac{41}{60}$$

CONCEPTS   **EXAMPLES**

2.2 Subtracting fractions

1. Find the LCD.
2. Rewrite fractions using the LCD.
3. Keep the LCD as denominator and subtract numerators.
4. Reduce to lowest terms.

$$\frac{5}{8} - \frac{1}{3} = \frac{15}{24} - \frac{8}{24} = \frac{15 - 8}{24} = \frac{7}{24}$$

2.3 Adding mixed numbers

1. Find the LCD, then add fractions and reduce.
2. Add whole numbers.
3. Combine the sums of whole numbers and fractions.

$$9\frac{2}{3} = 9\frac{8}{12}$$
$$+ 6\frac{3}{4} = -6\frac{9}{12} \qquad \text{LCD} = 12$$
$$\overline{\qquad\qquad} $$
$$15\frac{17}{12} = 16\frac{5}{12}$$

2.3 Subtracting mixed numbers

1. Find the LCD and subtract fractions, borrowing if necessary.
2. Subtract whole numbers.
3. Combine the differences of whole numbers and fractions.

$$8\frac{5}{8} = 8\frac{15}{24}$$
$$- 3\frac{1}{12} = -3\frac{2}{24} \qquad \text{LCD} = 24$$
$$\overline{\qquad\qquad}$$
$$5\frac{13}{24}$$

2.4 Multiplying proper fractions

1. Multiply numerators and multiply denominators.
2. Reduce the answer to lowest terms if cancelling was not done.

$$\frac{6}{11} \times \frac{7}{8} = \frac{\overset{3}{\cancel{6}}}{11} \times \frac{7}{\underset{4}{\cancel{8}}} = \frac{21}{44}$$

2.4 Multiplying mixed numbers

1. Change mixed numbers to improper fractions.
2. Cancel if possible.
3. Multiply fractions.

$$1\frac{3}{5} \times 3\frac{1}{3} = \frac{8}{\underset{1}{\cancel{5}}} \times \frac{\overset{2}{\cancel{10}}}{3} = \frac{8}{1} \times \frac{2}{3}$$
$$= \frac{16}{3} = 5\frac{1}{3}$$

Always reduce to lowest terms.

2.4 Dividing proper fractions

Invert the divisor, multiply as proper fractions, and reduce the answer to lowest terms.

$$\frac{25}{36} \div \frac{15}{18} = \frac{\overset{5}{\cancel{25}}}{\underset{2}{\cancel{36}}} \times \frac{\overset{1}{\cancel{18}}}{\underset{3}{\cancel{15}}} = \frac{5}{2} \times \frac{1}{3} = \frac{5}{6}$$

2.4 Dividing mixed numbers

Change mixed numbers to improper fractions. Invert the divisor, cancel if possible, and then multiply fractions.

$$3\frac{5}{9} \div 2\frac{2}{5} = \frac{32}{9} \div \frac{12}{5} = \frac{\overset{8}{\cancel{32}}}{9} \times \frac{5}{\underset{3}{\cancel{12}}}$$
$$= \frac{40}{27} = 1\frac{13}{27}$$

2.5 Converting decimals to fractions

Think of the decimal as being written in words and write in fraction form. Reduce to lowest terms.

Convert .47 to a fraction.
Think of .47 as **"forty-seven hundredths."**
Then write as $\frac{47}{100}$.

2.5 Converting fractions to decimals

Divide the numerator by the denominator. Round if necessary.

Convert $\frac{1}{8}$ to a decimal.

$$\begin{array}{r} .125 \\ 8\overline{)1.000} \\ \underline{8} \\ 20 \\ \underline{16} \\ 40 \\ \underline{40} \\ 0 \end{array} \qquad \frac{1}{8} = .125$$

▼ Case Study

OPERATING EXPENSES AT WOODLINE MOLDINGS AND TRIM

It is often said that a picture is worth a thousand words. Visual presentation of data is often used in business in the form of graphs. A commonly used graph that shows the relationships of various data is the circle graph, also called a pie chart. The circle, which contains 360 degrees, is divided into slices, or fractional parts. The size of each slice helps to show the relationship of the various slices to each other and to the whole.

The annual operating expenses for Woodline Moldings and Trim are shown below. Use this information to answer the questions that follow.

WOODLINE MOLDINGS AND TRIM OPERATING EXPENSES			
Expense Item	Monthly Amount	Annual Amount	Fraction of Total Expenses
Salaries	$10,000	_____	_____
Rent	$6,000	_____	_____
Utilities	$2,000	_____	_____
Insurance	$1,500	_____	_____
Advertising	$1,500	_____	_____
Miscellaneous	$3,000	_____	_____
Total Expenses		_____	

1. Find the total annual operating expenses for Woodline Moldings and Trim.
2. What fraction should be used to represent each expense item as part of the total expenses?

1. _____

2. _____

3. Draw a circle (pie) graph using the fractions you found in part (b) to represent each expense item. Approximate the fractional part of the circle needed for each expense item. Label each segment of the circle graph with the fraction and the expense item.

4. Since there are 360 degrees in a circle, find the number of degrees that would be used to represent each expense item in the circle graph.

4. _____

INVESTIGATE
Business and economic data are often shown using pie charts. Find two pie charts with business or economic data and explain the contents. Look in newspapers such as *USA Today* or on the Internet.

▼ Case in Point Summary Exercise

HOME DEPOT

www.homedepot.com

Facts:

- 1978: Founded in Atlanta, Georgia
- 2005: More than $80 billion in annual sales
- 2010: More than 2200 retail stores

The Home Depot is the world's largest home-improvement retailer, employing more than 300,000 employees called associates. Its goal is to provide a very high level of service, broad selection of products, and very competitive prices in a one-stop shopping environment. Management also believes in taking care of its employees by offering many benefits. It even has a program that matches employee charitable donations. Management also tries to encourage employees to donate their time to needy organizations.

1. Kara Oaks manages the cabinetry department. She has been asked to take measurements for a set of custom cabinets made of cherry wood. The side panel is $32\frac{1}{4}$ inches tall. If she needs 6 side panels, find the number of inches of cherry wood needed, assuming no waste when cut.

    1. _____

2. The width of each side panel is $14\frac{1}{2}$ inches. Find the area of each panel by multiplying the height of the panel given in (a) by the width. The resulting area is in square inches.

    2. _____

3. Find the total area of cherry wood needed for all six side panels in square inches.

    3. _____

4. Ignoring waste, how many side panels can be made if the cabinetmaker has only 2250 square inches of cherry wood panels of the appropriate width?

    4. _____

Discussion Question: *Do you think that exact measurements are an important component of quality from the standpoint of a customer at The Home Depot? What are other important components of quality?*

Source: HOME DEPOT, www.homedepot.com.

Chapter 2   Test

To help you review, the numbers in brackets show the section in which the topic was discussed.

Write the following fractions in lowest terms.   **[2.1]**

1. $\dfrac{25}{30} = $ _____

2. $\dfrac{875}{1000} = $ _____

3. $\dfrac{84}{132} = $ _____

Convert the following improper fractions to mixed numbers, and write using lowest terms.   **[2.1]**

4. $\dfrac{65}{8} = $ _____

5. $\dfrac{56}{12} = $ _____

6. $\dfrac{120}{45} = $ _____

Convert the following mixed numbers to improper fractions.   **[2.1]**

7. $7\dfrac{3}{4} = $ _____

8. $18\dfrac{4}{5} = $ _____

9. $18\dfrac{3}{8} = $ _____

Find the LCD of each of the following groups of denominators.   **[2.2]**

10. 2, 6, 5, _____

11. 6, 8, 15, _____

12. 6, 9, 12, 24, _____

Solve the following problems.   **[2.2–2.4]**

13.
$$\begin{array}{r} \dfrac{1}{5} \\ \dfrac{3}{10} \\ + \dfrac{3}{8} \\ \hline \end{array}$$

14.
$$\begin{array}{r} 32\dfrac{5}{16} \\ - 17\dfrac{1}{4} \\ \hline \end{array}$$

15.
$$\begin{array}{r} 126\dfrac{3}{16} \\ - 89\dfrac{7}{8} \\ \hline \end{array}$$

16. $67\dfrac{1}{2} \times \dfrac{8}{15} = $

17. $33\dfrac{1}{3} \div \dfrac{200}{9} = $

Solve the following application problems.

18. Becky Finnerty, a pastry chef, used $23\frac{1}{2}$ pounds of powdered sugar for one recipe, $34\frac{3}{4}$ pounds powdered sugar for another recipe, and $17\frac{5}{8}$ pounds of powdered sugar for a third recipe. If Finnerty started with two 50-pound sacks of powdered sugar, find the amount of powdered sugar remaining. **[2.3]**

18. _____

19. Rhonda Goedeker received her Social Security check of \$1275. After paying $\frac{1}{3}$ of this amount for rent, she paid $\frac{3}{5}$ of the remaining amount for food, utilities, and transportation. How much money does she have left?

19. _____

20. A painting contractor arrived at a 6-unit apartment complex with $147\frac{1}{2}$ gallons of paint. If his crew sprayed $68\frac{1}{2}$ gallons on the interior walls, rolled $37\frac{3}{8}$ gallons on the masonry exterior, and brushed $5\frac{3}{4}$ gallons on the window trim, find the number of gallons of paint remaining. **[2.3]**

20. _____

21. A pizza restaurant has 1000 ounces of mozzarella cheese in inventory. Find the number of regular pizzas that can be made if each uses $8\frac{1}{2}$ ounces of mozzarella cheese. Find the number of ounces of cheese remaining.

21. _____

Convert the following decimals to fractions. **[2.5]**

22. .625 =

23. .82 =

*Use the advertisement for this four-piece chisel set to answer Exercises 24 and 25. The symbol " is for inches. (**Source:** Harbor Freight Tools.)* **[2.5]**

24. Convert the cutting-edge width of the smallest chisel from a fraction to a decimal.

24. _____

25. Convert the cutting-edge width of the largest chisel from a fraction to a decimal.

25. _____

3 Percents

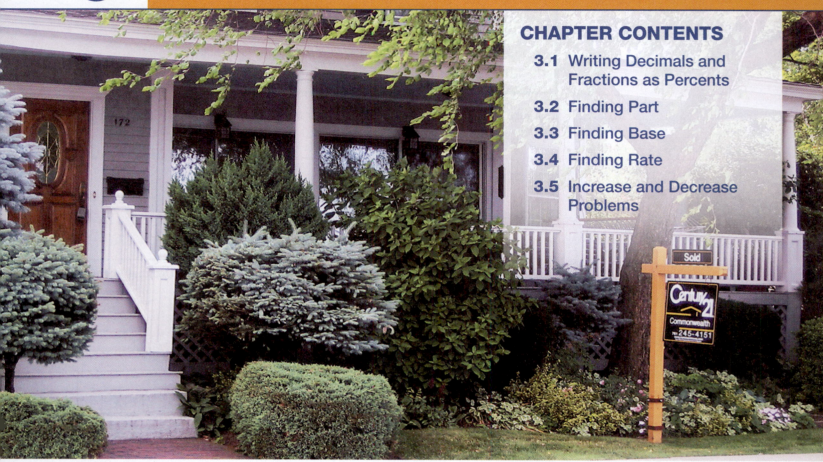

CHAPTER CONTENTS

3.1 Writing Decimals and Fractions as Percents

3.2 Finding Part

3.3 Finding Base

3.4 Finding Rate

3.5 Increase and Decrease Problems

▼ CASE IN POINT

TOM DUGALLY is a real estate agent with Century 21. He loves the business since it allows him to be his own boss. However, it is a tough business with many ups and downs. For example, his income collapsed as the recent financial crisis began in late 2008 as shown in the graph. Luckily, Dugally's wife had a good job with benefits including medical insurance, so he was able to stay in business. He is hopeful the real estate market continues to improve.

Dugally uses percents on a daily basis to calculate monthly payments, determine the commission on a sale, determine whether someone will qualify for financing, and estimate real estate taxes. He

Real Estate Commissions Earned by Tom Dugally

simply *could not do his job* without knowing how to work with percents.

As you can see from these examples, percents are very common in business.

> Markdown on an iPhone is 10% of the original price.
>
> Interest rate on a certificate of deposit is 2% of amount on deposit.
>
> Sales taxes in one city are 8.5% of the total amount of the sale.
>
> Real estate commission is 6% of the selling price of a house.
>
> Unemployment is 7.3% of the workforce.

Learn the topics in this chapter well—percents will be used throughout this course and you will see them throughout your life!

▼ 3.1 Writing Decimals and Fractions as Percents

OBJECTIVES

1 Write a decimal as a percent.

2 Write a fraction as a percent.

3 Write a percent as a decimal.

4 Write a percent as a fraction.

5 Write a fractional percent as a decimal.

Similar to fractions and decimals, **percents** represent parts of a whole. However, percents (**hundredths**) mean parts out of 100. They are written using a percent sign (%). For example 1% means 1 of 100 equal parts. The number 12% is read "twelve percent."

	Fraction Form	Decimal Form
12% = 12 out of 100 equal parts	$= \dfrac{12}{100}$	$= .12$
25% = 25 out of 100 equal parts	$= \dfrac{25}{100}$	$= .25$
100% = 100 out of 100 equal parts	$= \dfrac{100}{100}$	$= 1.00$
150% = 150 out of 100 equal parts	$= \dfrac{150}{100}$	$= 1.50$

Since 100% is 1, it is the whole or entire amount. Any percent greater than 100% is more than the whole. You can make 100% on a test, but not 150%, unless there is extra credit of some type. However, a swimmer may eat $1\frac{1}{2}$ granola bars, thereby eating 150% of a granola bar.

OBJECTIVE 1 Write a decimal as a percent. From the table above, we see that $.12 = \frac{12}{100} = 12\%$. Effectively, the decimal point in .12 was moved two places to the right and then a percent sign (%) was attached to the end when converting to a percent.

> **Converting a decimal number to a percent**
>
> **Step 1**   Move the decimal point two digits to the right attaching trailing zeros as needed. You are effectively multiplying by 100.
>
> **Step 2**   Attach a percent sign.
>
> For example, to convert .75 to a percent:
>
> $$.75 \Rightarrow .75, \Rightarrow 75\%$$
>
> Attach percent sign.
> Move decimal point 2 places to the right.

Changing Decimals to Percents   **EXAMPLE 1**   Change the following decimals to percents.

(a) .35   (b) .42   (c) 2.75

SOLUTION

Move the decimal point two places to the right and attach a percent sign.

(a) 35%   (b) 42%   (c) 275%

> **QUICK CHECK 1**
>
> Change the decimals to percents.
>
> (a) .72   (b) .25   (c) 1.1

If there is no digit in the hundredths position, place zeros to the right of the number to hold the hundredths position.

$$.5 = .50.\% = 50\% \qquad 1.2 = 1.20.\% = 120\%$$

attach zero   attach zero

Writing Decimals as Percents

EXAMPLE 2 Write the following decimals as percents.

(a) .8   (b) 2.6   (c) .1   (d) 4

SOLUTION

It is necessary to attach zeros here.

(a) 80%   (b) 260%   (c) 10%   (d) 400%

attach zero   attach zero   attach zero   attach 2 zeros

> **QUICK CHECK 2**
>
> Write the decimals as percents.
>
> (a) .6   (b) 3.5   (c) 8

If the decimal extends past the hundredths position, the resulting percent includes decimal parts of whole percents.

Writing Decimals as Percents

EXAMPLE 3 Write these decimals as percents.

(a) .625   (b) .0057   (c) 1.25

SOLUTION

(a) 62.5%   (b) .57%   (c) 125%

> **QUICK CHECK 3**
>
> Write the decimals as percents.
>
> (a) .875   (b) .0038   (c) 3.5

It is important to notice that in part (b) of the last example, the percent .57% is less than 1%, so .57% is less than 1 part out of 100 equal parts. In fact, .57% = .0057 is *a very small number.*

OBJECTIVE 2 Write a fraction as a percent. Write the fraction as a decimal by dividing the numerator by the denominator. Then, write the decimal number as a percent by moving the decimal point two places to the right and attaching a percent sign.

fraction   decimal   percent

$$\frac{2}{5} \quad = \quad .4 \quad = \quad 40\%$$

Writing Fractions as Percents

EXAMPLE 4 A marketing manager is given the following data in fraction form and must change the data to percents.

(a) $\frac{1}{4}$ (b) $\frac{3}{8}$ (c) $\frac{6}{5}$

SOLUTION

First write each fraction as a decimal, and then write the decimal as a percent.

(a) $\frac{1}{4} = .25 = 25\%$ (b) $\frac{3}{8} = .375 = 37.5\%$ (c) $\frac{6}{5} = 1.2 = 120\%$

QUICK CHECK 4

Change the fractions to percents.

(a) $\dfrac{3}{4}$ (b) $\dfrac{2}{5}$ (c) $1\dfrac{5}{8}$

A second way to write a fraction as a percent is by multiplying the fraction by 100%. For example, write the fraction $\frac{4}{5}$ as a percent by multiplying $\frac{4}{5}$ by 100%.

$$\frac{4}{5} = \frac{4}{5} \times 100\% = \frac{400\%}{5} = 80\%$$

OBJECTIVE 3   Write a percent as a decimal. Since percent means parts out of 100, change a percent to a decimal by dividing by 100.

Converting Percents to Decimals

Step 1   Drop the percent sign.

Step 2   Move the decimal point two places to the left. You are effectively dividing by 100.

For example, we show that 25% = .25.

```
            ┌→ Drop the percent sign.
25% ⟹ ‸25. ⟹ .25
         └──── Move the decimal point two places to the left.
```

Writing Percents as Decimals

EXAMPLE 5

To calculate some insurance claims, an insurance agent must change the following percents to decimals.

(a) 35%   (b) 50%   (c) 325%   (d) $37\frac{1}{2}\%$ $\left(\textit{Hint: } 37\frac{1}{2}\% = 37.5\%.\right)$

Quick TIP

Change any fraction part of a percent to a decimal before converting from a percent to a decimal.

SOLUTION

Move the decimal point two places to the left and drop the percent sign.

(a) .35   (b) .5   (c) 3.25   (d) .375

QUICK CHECK 5

Change the percents to decimals.

(a) 75%   (b) 40%   (c) 280%

OBJECTIVE 4   Write a percent as a fraction. To write a percent as a fraction, first change the percent to a decimal, then write the decimal as a fraction in lowest terms.

Writing Percents as Fractions

EXAMPLE 6

Even though smoking is believed to account for 1 of every 5 deaths in the United States, more than 45 million Americans smoke. The bar chart shows the percent of people in each age group that smoke. Convert each percent to a fraction and reduce to lowest terms.

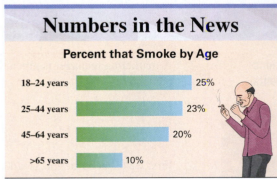

Numbers in the News

Percent that Smoke by Age

18–24 years	25%
25–44 years	23%
45–64 years	20%
>65 years	10%

DATA: *America Lung Association*

SOLUTION

Write each percent as a decimal and then as a fraction in lowest terms.

(a) $25\% = .25 = \dfrac{25}{100} = \dfrac{1}{4}$

(b) $23\% = .23 = \dfrac{23}{100}$

(c) $20\% = .20 = \dfrac{20}{100} = \dfrac{1}{5}$

(d) $10\% = .10 = \dfrac{10}{100} = \dfrac{1}{10}$

QUICK CHECK 6

Change the percents to fractions. Reduce to lowest terms.

(a) 35%   **(b)** 22%   **(c)** 88%

We did not always believe that smoking was harmful. During World War II, cigarettes were given to soldiers, who often traded them as currency. By the 1960s, a lot of scientific evidence indicated that smoking had serious negative consequences related to heart and lung disease, in particular. Today, smoking is considered to be *the* leading cause of preventable death in the world killing more people than HIV/AIDS, tuberculosis, and malaria combined.

OBJECTIVE 5 Write a fractional percent as a decimal. A fractional percent such as $\frac{1}{2}\%$ is smaller than 1%. In fact, $\frac{1}{2}\%$ is equal to $\frac{1}{2}$ of 1%. Write a fractional percent as a decimal by first changing the fraction to a decimal, followed by the percent sign. Then, write that number as a decimal by moving the decimal point two places to the left and dropping the percent sign.

$$\frac{1}{2}\% = .5\% = .00.5 = .005$$

written as a decimal with percent sign remaining   move the decimal point two places to the left

---

Writing Fractional Percents as Decimals

EXAMPLE 7

The following percents appear in a newspaper article. Write each fractional percent as a decimal and drop the percent sign.

(a) $\dfrac{1}{5}\%$ **(b)** $\dfrac{3}{4}\%$ **(c)** $\dfrac{5}{8}\%$

SOLUTION

Begin by writing the fraction as a decimal percent.

(a) $\dfrac{1}{5}\% = .2\% = .002$

(b) $\dfrac{3}{4}\% = .75\% = .0075$

(c) $\dfrac{5}{8}\% = .625\% = .00625$

QUICK CHECK 7

Write the fractional percents as decimals.

(a) $\dfrac{1}{2}\%$ **(b)** $\dfrac{1}{4}\%$ **(c)** $\dfrac{7}{8}\%$

The following chart shows the decimal and percent equivalents for several fractions.

Fraction, Decimal, and Percent Equivalents

$\frac{1}{100} = .01 = 1\%$	$\frac{9}{16} = .5625 = 56.25\%$ or $56\frac{1}{4}\%$
$\frac{1}{50} = .02 = 2\%$	$\frac{3}{5} = .6 = 60\%$
$\frac{1}{25} = .04 = 4\%$	$\frac{5}{8} = .625 = 62\frac{1}{2}\%$
$\frac{1}{20} = .05 = 5\%$	$\frac{2}{3} = .66\overline{6} = 66\frac{2}{3}\%$
$\frac{1}{16} = .0625 = 6.25\%$ or $6\frac{1}{4}\%$	$\frac{11}{16} = .6875 = 68.75\%$ or $68\frac{3}{4}\%$
$\frac{1}{12} = .083\overline{3} = 8\frac{1}{3}\%$	$\frac{7}{10} = .7 = 70\%$
$\frac{1}{10} = .1 = 10\%$	$\frac{3}{4} = .75 = 75\%$
$\frac{1}{9} = .111\overline{1} = 11\frac{1}{9}\%$	$\frac{4}{5} = .8 = 80\%$
$\frac{1}{8} = .125 = 12.5\%$ or $12\frac{1}{2}\%$	$\frac{13}{16} = .8125 = 81.25\%$ or $81\frac{1}{4}\%$
$\frac{1}{7} = .142\overline{8} = 14\frac{2}{7}\%$	$\frac{5}{6} = .833\overline{3} = 83\frac{1}{3}\%$
$\frac{1}{6} = .166\overline{6} = 16\frac{2}{3}\%$	$\frac{7}{8} = .875 = 87\frac{1}{2}\%$
$\frac{3}{16} = .1875 = 18\frac{3}{4}\%$	$\frac{9}{10} = .9 = 90\%$
$\frac{1}{5} = .2 = 20\%$	$\frac{15}{16} = .9375 = 93.75\%$ or $93\frac{3}{4}\%$
$\frac{1}{4} = .25 = 25\%$	$1 = 1.00 = 100\%$
$\frac{3}{10} = .3 = 30\%$	$1\frac{1}{10} = 1.1 = 110\%$
$\frac{5}{16} = .3125 = 31.25\%$	$1\frac{1}{4} = 1.25 = 125\%$
$\frac{1}{3} = .333\overline{3} = 33\frac{1}{3}\%$	$1\frac{1}{3} = 1.1333\overline{3} = 133\frac{1}{3}\%$
$\frac{3}{8} = .375 = 37\frac{1}{2}\%$	$1\frac{1}{2} = 1.5 = 150\%$
$\frac{2}{5} = .4 = 40\%$	$1\frac{2}{3} = 1.666\overline{6} = 166\frac{2}{3}\%$
$\frac{7}{16} = .4375 = 43.75\%$ or $43\frac{3}{4}\%$	$1\frac{3}{4} = 1.75 = 175\%$
$\frac{1}{2} = .5 = 50\%$	$2 = 2.00 = 200\%$

▼ 3.1 Exercises   MyMathLab®

*The shaded sections below contain solutions to help you get a **QUICK START** on the various types of exercises.*

Write the following decimals as percents. (See Examples 1–3.)

1. .25 = **25%**   **2.** .4 = **40%**   **3.** .72 = _____   **4.** 1.3 = _____

5. 2.034 = _____   **6.** .625 = _____   **7.** 3.625 = _____   **8.** 4.6 = _____

9. .875 = _____   **10.** .005 = _____   **11.** .0005 = _____   **12.** .0012 = _____

13. 3.45 = _____   **14.** .2108 = _____   **15.** .0308 = _____

Write the following as decimals. (See Examples 4–6.)

16. $\frac{1}{5}$ = **.2**   **17.** $\frac{5}{8}$ = **.625**   **18.** 64% = _____   **19.** 65% = _____

20. $\frac{1}{100}$ = _____   **21.** $\frac{1}{8}$ = _____   **22.** $8\frac{1}{2}\%$ = _____   **23.** $12\frac{1}{2}\%$ = _____

24. $\frac{1}{200}$ = _____   **25.** $\frac{1}{400}$ = _____   **26.** $50\frac{3}{4}\%$ = _____   **27.** $84\frac{3}{4}\%$ = _____

28. $3\frac{3}{8}$ = _____   **29.** $1\frac{3}{4}$ = _____   **30.** 350% = _____

Determine the fraction, decimal, or percent equivalents for each of the following, as necessary.
Write fractions in lowest terms and convert to a mixed number if appropriate.

	Fraction	Decimal	Percent
31.	$\frac{1}{2}$	.5	50%
32.	$\frac{3}{50}$	.06	6%
33.	_____	.875	_____
34.	$\frac{4}{5}$	_____	_____
35.	_____	_____	.8%
36.	_____	.00625	_____
37.	$10\frac{1}{2}$	_____	_____
38.	_____	_____	675%
39.	_____	.65	_____
40.	$4\frac{3}{8}$	_____	_____
41.	_____	.005	_____
42.	_____	_____	$\frac{1}{8}\%$
43.	$\frac{1}{3}$	_____	_____
44.	_____	_____	12.5%
45.	_____	2.5	_____
46.	$\frac{7}{20}$	_____	_____
47.	_____	_____	$4\frac{1}{4}\%$
48.	_____	1.25	_____
49.	$2\frac{1}{2}$	_____	_____
50.	_____	5.125	_____
51.	_____	_____	1037.5%
52.	_____	_____	$\frac{3}{4}\%$

Fraction	*Decimal*	*Percent*
53. _____	.0025	_____
54. $\frac{5}{8}$	_____	_____
55. _____	_____	$37\frac{1}{2}\%$
56. _____	_____	$6\frac{3}{4}\%$

57. Fractions, decimals, and percents are all used to describe a part of something. The use of percents is much more common than fractions and decimals. Why do you suppose this is true?

58. List five uses of percent that are or will be part of your life. Consider the activities of working, shopping, saving, and planning for the future.

59. Select a decimal percent and write it as a fraction. Select a fraction and write it as a percent. Write an explanation of each step of your work. (See Objectives 2 and 3.)

60. The fractional percent $\frac{1}{2}\%$ is equal to .005. Explain each step as you change $\frac{1}{2}\%$ to its decimal equivalent. (See Objective 4.)

QUICK CHECK ANSWERS

1. (a) 72%   **(b)** 25%   **(c)** 110%

2. (a) 60%   **(b)** 350%   **(c)** 350%

3. (a) 87.5%   **(b)** .38%   **(c)** 162.5%

4. (a) 75%   **(b)** 40%   **(c)** 62.5%

5. (a) .75   **(b)** .4   **(c)** 2.8

6. (a) $\frac{7}{20}$ **(b)** $\frac{11}{50}$ **(c)** $\frac{22}{25}$

7. (a) $\frac{1}{2}\% = .5\% = .005$

(b) $\frac{1}{4}\% = .25\% = .0025$

(c) $\frac{7}{8}\% = .875\% = .00875$

3.2 Finding Part

OBJECTIVES

1 Know the three components of a percent problem.
2 Learn the basic percent formula.
3 Solve for part.
4 Recognize the terms associated with base, rate, and part.
5 Calculate sales tax.
6 Learn the standard format of percent problems.

CASE IN POINT As a real estate agent, Tom Dugally is paid on commission. When he produces income as a result of a sale, a sale of his listing by someone else, or a rental agreement that is completed, he is paid a portion of this income. Currently, Dugally is looking for a home in the $210,000 price range for Scott and Andrea Abriani, a couple he met at an open house. He believes this is the most they can reasonably afford.

OBJECTIVE 1 Know the three components of a percent problem. Problems in percent contain three main components. Usually, two of these components are given, and the third component must be found.

Three components of a percent problem

1. **Base:** The whole or total, starting point, or that to which something is being compared.
2. **Rate:** A number followed by % or **percent**.
3. **Part:** The result of multiplying the base and the rate. The part is a *part* of the base. For example, sales tax is a part of total sales.

OBJECTIVE 2 Learn the basic percent formula. The base, rate, and part are related by the basic **percent formula**.

$$P = R \times B$$
$$\textbf{Part = Rate} \times \textbf{Base}$$

OBJECTIVE 3 Solve for part. Tom Dugally finds a house that the Abrianis purchase for $210,000. A 6% real estate commission must be paid. The $210,000 price of the house is the whole (or base), and the 6% percent commission is the rate. The unknown is the actual commission, which is the part. Find the commission as follows.

$$P = R \times B$$
$$P = 6\% \times \$210,000$$
$$= .06 \times \$210,000 \quad \text{Change percent to decimal.}$$
$$= \$12,600$$

The real estate commission of $12,600 will be split between the listing agent, the selling agent, and their two brokers. So, only part of it goes to Dugally.

Solving for Part Solve for part, using $P = R \times B$.

(a) 4% of 50   (b) 1.2% of 180   (c) 140% of 225   (d) $\frac{1}{4}$% of 560
(*Hint:* $\frac{1}{4}$% = .25%.)

SOLUTION

	50	180	225	560
(a) × .04	(b) × .012	(c) × 1.4	(d) × .0025
2.00	2.160	315.0	1.4000

QUICK CHECK 1

Solve for part.

(a) 6% of 200   (b) 1.8% of 150   (c) 210% of 310   (d) $\frac{1}{2}$% of 1300

EXAMPLE 2 The bar graph shows the unemployment rate by category in the midst of a serious recession. Use the data provided to estimate the number of unemployed teenagers out of a total of roughly 32,000 working-age teenagers in one city.

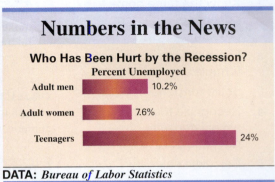

Numbers in the News

Who Has Been Hurt by the Recession?

Percent Unemployed

Adult men	10.2%
Adult women	7.6%
Teenagers	24%

DATA: *Bureau of Labor Statistics*

SOLUTION

The base is 32,000. The rate for unemployed teenagers is 24%. The number of unemployed teenagers is part of the whole, so part (P) is the unknown.

$$P = R \times B$$
$$P = 24\% \times 32,000$$
$$= .24 \times 32,000$$
$$= 7680$$

About 7680 of the 32,000 working-age teenagers in the city are unemployed.

▦ The calculator solution to this example is

$$24 \boxed{\%} \boxed{\times} 32,000 \boxed{=} 7680$$

Note: Refer to Appendix B for calculator basics.

QUICK CHECK 2

How many of the 83,200 working-age adult men in a city would you expect to be unemployed?

OBJECTIVE 4 Recognize the terms associated with base, rate, and part. Percent problems have certain similarities. For example, some phrases are associated with the base in the problem. Other phrases lead to the part, while % or *percent* following a number identifies the rate. The following chart helps distinguish between the base and the part.

Words and Phrases Associated with Base and Part

Usually indicates the base (*B*)	Usually indicates the part (*P*)
Sales ⟶	Sales tax
Investment ⟶	Return on investment
Savings ⟶	Interest
Retail price ⟶	Discount
Last year's figure ⟶	Increase or decrease
Old salary ⟶	Raise
Earnings ⟶	Expenditures

OBJECTIVE 5 Calculate sales tax. Calculating **sales tax** is a good example of finding part. States, counties, and cities often collect taxes on retail sales to the consumer. The sales tax is a percent of the sale. This percent varies from as low as 3% in some states to 8% or more in other states. The formula used for finding sales tax follows.

$$P = R \times B$$
$$\text{Sales tax} = \text{Sales tax rate} \times \text{Sales}$$

Calculating Sales Tax Becky Smith finally saved enough to buy the guitar she had dreamed about. Her goal was to start a band with her two sisters as backup and a friend as a drummer. The list price on the guitar was $1199.99 and the sales tax was 8.5%. Find the sales tax and total cost.

SOLUTION

The whole (*B*) is $1199.99, and the rate (*R*) is 8.5%.

$$P \;=\; R \;\times\; B$$
$$P = 8.5\% \times \$1199.99$$
$$= .085 \times \$1199.99$$
$$= \$101.99915, \textbf{ or } \$102.00 \textbf{ rounded to the nearest cent}$$

Now, add the sales tax cost to the cost of the guitar to find the total.

$$\text{Total} = \$1199.99 + \$102 = \textbf{\$1301.99}$$

QUICK CHECK 3

One day, the Lock Shoppe had sales of $1485 and charged a sales tax of 6%. Find the sales tax and the total sales including the tax.

Identify the rate, base, and part with the following hints.

> **Base** tends to be preceded by the word *of* or *on*; tends to be the *whole*.
> **Rate** is followed by a percent sign or the word *percent.*
> **Part** is in the same units as the base and is usually a portion of the base.

OBJECTIVE 6 Learn the standard format of percent problems. Percent problems can be written in the form "% of whole is/are part," as shown by these common examples.

Rate	Whole		Part
7.5% of the	total	is	the sales tax
8.5% of the	workers	are	unemployed
74% of the	students	are	full-time students
18% of the	children	are	obese

The following data shows the percent of 1582 people surveyed that purchased each type of ice cream. To find the number out of 1582 surveyed that bought Breyers, multiply the rate (*R*) of 14.7% by the whole (*B*) of 1582.

14.7% × 1582 = 232.554, or 233 people (rounded)

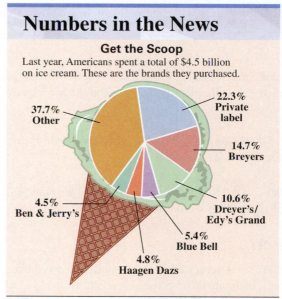

Numbers in the News

Get the Scoop

Last year, Americans spent a total of $4.5 billion on ice cream. These are the brands they purchased.

- 37.7% Other
- 22.3% Private label
- 14.7% Breyers
- 10.6% Dreyer's/Edy's Grand
- 5.4% Blue Bell
- 4.8% Haagen Dazs
- 4.5% Ben & Jerry's

DATA: Information Resources Inc., NPD Group.

Since $B \times R = R \times B$, it makes no difference which term is used first in multiplication. To prove the point, the same data is used, but with whole written first.

$$1582 \times 14.7\% = 232.554, \text{ or } 233 \text{ people (rounded)}$$

Identifying the Pieces in Percent Problems

 EXAMPLE 4

Identify the whole and rate in the following; then find the part.

(a) A refrigerator with an original price of $949 was marked down 10%.

(b) Expenses for the weekend were 92% of total sales of $1850.

(c) Corporate income taxes were 30% of total profit of $18,240,000.

SOLUTION

	Rate	×	Base	=	Part
(a)	10%	×	$949	=	$94.90 discount
(b)	92%	×	$1850	=	$1702 expenses
(c)	30%	×	$18,240,000	=	$5,472,000 corporate income taxes

QUICK CHECK 4

A video game is priced at $280 less a 15% discount. First, identify the whole and rate. Then calculate the part (the discount).

▼ 3.2 Exercises

MyMathLab®

The shaded sections below contain solutions to help you get a **QUICK START** *on the various types of exercises.*

Solve for part in each of the following. Round to the nearest hundredth. (See Example 1.)

1. 10% of 620 homes = **62 homes**

2. 25% of 3500 Web sites = **875 Web sites**

3. 75.5% of $800 = _____

4. 20.5% of $1500 = _____

5. 4% of 120 feet = _____

6. 125% of 2000 products = _____

7. 175% of 5820 miles = _____

8. 15% of 75 crates = _____

9. 17.5% of 1040 cell phones = _____

10. 52.5% of 1560 trucks = _____

11. 118% of 125.8 yards = _____

12. 110% of 150 apartments = _____

13. $90\frac{1}{2}$% of $5930 = _____

14. $7\frac{1}{2}$% of $150 = _____

15. Identify the three components in a percent problem. In your own words, describe how to identify each of these components. (See Objective 1.)

16. There are words and phrases that are usually associated with base and part. Give three examples of words that usually identify the base and the accompanying word for the part. (See Objective 4.)

Solve for part in each of the following application problems. Round to the nearest cent unless otherwise indicated. (See Examples 2 and 3.)

17. **SUMMER VACATION**   Of 350 people surveyed recently in New York, 68% said they prefer to vacation in Florida. Find the number preferring Florida.

    $P = R \times B$
    $P = .68 \times 350 = 238$

17. **238 people** _____

18. **CORPORATE PROFITS**   A survey of 30 large retailers showed that expenses averaged 92.4% of total sales. Estimate the expenses for a firm with $138 million in quarterly sales to the nearest tenth of a million dollars.

18. _____

19. SALES TAX A real estate broker wants to purchase a new Personal Digital Assistant priced at $399. If the sales tax rate is 7.75%, find the total price including the sales tax.

19. _____

20. Thomas Dugally of Century 21 Real Estate is working with a mortgage company that charges borrowers $350 plus 2% of the loan amount. What is the total charge to get a home loan of $190,000?

20. _____

21. WOMEN IN THE NAVY The navy guided-missile destroyer USS *Sullivans* has a 335-person crew of which 13% are female. Find the number of female crew members. Round to the nearest whole number.

21. _____

22. NY YANKEES The average price of a ticket for the better box seats at Yankee Stadium was $90 in 2005. Estimate the average cost today if it has increased by 250%.

22. _____

23. BAR SOAP A bar of Ivory Soap is $99\frac{44}{100}$% pure. If the bar of soap weighs 9 ounces, how many ounces are pure? Round to the nearest hundredth.

23. _____

24. GASOLINE TAXES An economics class estimated that about 22% of the price of gasoline is used to pay the various taxes along the supply chain including income taxes, property taxes, and excise taxes. If the price of gasoline is $3.60 per gallon, find the amount going to pay taxes rounded to the nearest cent.

24. _____

25. DRIVING DISTRACTIONS It is estimated that 29.5% of automobile crashes are caused by driver distractions, such as texting. If there are 16,450 automobile crashes in a study, what number would be caused by driver distractions? Round to the nearest whole number.

25. _____

26. SMOKING AND LUNG DISEASE According to one study by Danish scientists, at least 25% of all long-term smokers get a chronic lung disease known as COPD. Out of every 1000 smokers, find the minimum number expected to get COPD.

26. _____

27. FEMALE LAWYERS There are 1,094,751 active lawyers living in the United States. If 71.4% of these lawyers are male, find **(a)** the percent of the lawyers who are female and **(b)** the number of lawyers who are female. Round to the nearest whole number.

(a) _____

(b) _____

28. OVERWEIGHT According to the World Health Organization, about 65% of the roughly 8 billion people in the world are overweight. Find (a) the percent of people who are not overweight and (b) the number who are not overweight.

28. _____

29. DIGITAL CAMERA   A Sony 12 megapixel digital camera priced at $319 is marked down 25%. Find the price of the camera after the markdown.

29. _____

30. NURSES   In a survey of 146 hospital managers, 30% said they have difficulty recruiting enough nurses willing to work the hours needed to do the job. Find the number of managers making this claim rounded to the nearest whole number.

30. _____

31. NEW PRODUCT FAILURE   Marketing Intelligence Service says that there were 15,401 new products introduced last year. If 86% of the products introduced last year failed to reach their business objectives, find the number of products that did reach their objectives. Round to the nearest whole number.

31. _____

32. FAMILY BUDGET   A family of four with a monthly income of $5150 spends 90% of its earnings and saves the balance for the down payment on a house. Find **(a)** the monthly savings and **(b)** the annual savings of this family.

(a) _____

(b) _____

33. AUTO SALES IN CHINA   General Motors' sales in China were up 21.3% compared to the 218,097 vehicles sold last year. Find this years' sales rounded to the nearest whole number.

33. _____

34. SUPER BOWL ADVERTISING   The average cost of 30 seconds of advertising during the Super Bowl 6 years ago was $2.3 million. If the increase in cost over the last 6 years has been 17%, find the average cost of 30 seconds of advertising during the Super Bowl this year. Round to the nearest tenth of a million. (**Source:** NFL Research.)

34. _____

35. SALES-TAX COMPUTATION   As the owner of a copy and print shop, you must collect $6\frac{1}{2}\%$ of the amount of each sale for sales tax. If sales for the month are $48,680, find the combined amount of sales and tax.

35. _____

36. TOTAL COST   A NuVac is priced at $524 with an allowed trade-in of $125 for an old unit. If sales tax of $7\frac{3}{4}\%$ is charged on the price of the new NuVac unit, find the total cost to the customer after receiving the trade-in. (*Hint:* Trade-in is subtracted last.)

36. _____

37. REAL ESTATE COMMISSIONS   Thomas Dugally of Century 21 Real Estate sold a home for $174,900. The commission was 6% of the sale price. Since Dugally both listed and sold the home, he receives 60% of the commission, and his broker receives the remainder. Find the amount received by Dugally.

37. _____

38. **BUSINESS OWNERSHIP**   Jimmy Ruiz has an 82% ownership in a company called Jimmy's Cell Phones. If the company has a value of $98,400 and Ruiz receives an income of 45% of the value of his ownership, find the amount of his income.

38. _____

CONSUMER INTERNET SALES   *Country Store has a unique selection of merchandise that it sells by catalog and over the Internet. Use the shipping and insurance delivery chart below and a sales tax rate of 5% to solve Exercises 39–42. There is no sales tax on shipping and insurance. (**Source:** Country Store Catalog.)*

Shipping and Insurance Delivery Chart

Up to $15.00	add $3.95
$15.01 to $25.00	add $5.95
$25.01 to $35.00	add $6.95
$35.01 to $50.00	add $7.95
$50.01 to $70.00	add $8.95
$70.01 to $99.99	add $9.95
$100.00 or more	add $10.95

39. Find the total cost of 6 Small Fry Handi-Pan electric skillets at a cost of $29.99 each.

39. _____

40. A customer ordered 5 sets of flour-sack towels at a cost of $12.99 each. What is the total cost?

40. _____

41. Find the total cost of 3 pop-up hampers at a cost of $9.99 each and 4 nonstick minidonut pans at $10.99 each.

41. _____

42. What is the total cost of 5 coach lamp bird feeders at a cost of $19.99 each and 6 garden weather centers at $14.99 each?

42. _____

QUICK CHECK ANSWERS

1. (a) 12 (b) 2.7 (c) 651 (d) 6.5
2. 8486 men
3. $89.10 sales tax; $1574.10 total
4. $B = \$280; R = .15;$
   $P = $ discount amount
   $= \$42$ discount

3.3 Finding Base

OBJECTIVES

1   Use the basic percent formula to solve for base.

2   Find sales when tax amount and tax rate are known.

3   Find the investment when interest payment and rate of interest are known.

▼ **CASE IN POINT**   Thomas Dugally of Century 21 Real Estate helps buyers select properties that they can afford. Real estate lenders have strict guidelines that determine the maximum loan that they will give a buyer. Usually, the lender will limit the borrowers' monthly house payment to no more than about 28% of their monthly income.

OBJECTIVE 1 Use the basic percent formula to solve for base. In some problems, the rate and part are given, but the base, or whole, must be found. The formula $P = R \times B$ can be used to get the **formula for base**. The following circle diagram may help. To find the formula for base, cover B with your finger. This leaves P divided by R, so $B = \dfrac{P}{R}$.

$$\text{Base} = \frac{\text{Part}}{\text{Rate}} \quad \text{or} \quad B = \frac{P}{R}$$

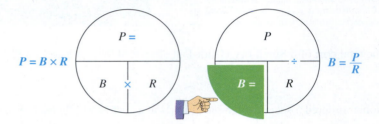

Scott and Andrea Abriana can afford a monthly house payment of only 28% of their income, or $1386. To find their monthly income, insert the rate of 28% and the part, or monthly payment of $1386, into the formula. Be sure to first convert 28% to its decimal equivalent, .28.

$$B = \frac{P}{R}$$

$$B = \frac{1386}{.28} = 4950$$

Their monthly income is $4950.

Solving for Base   ▼ **EXAMPLE 1**

Solve for base, using the formula $B = \frac{P}{R}$.

(a) 8 is 4% of _____.   (b) 135 is 15% of _____.   (c) 1.25 is 25% of _____.

SOLUTION

(a) $\dfrac{8}{.04} = 200$ (b) $\dfrac{135}{.15} = 900$ (c) $\dfrac{1.25}{.25} = 5$

QUICK CHECK 1

Solve for base, using $B = \frac{P}{R}$.

(a) 15 is 10% of _____.   (b) 62 is 1% of _____.   (c) 1.6 is 40% of _____.

OBJECTIVE 2 Find sales when tax amount and tax rate are known. In business problems involving sales tax, the amount of sales is always the base.

Finding Sales When Sales Tax Is Given

EXAMPLE 2

One week, a Famous Footware store collected sales taxes of $780. If the sales tax rate is 5%, find total sales for the week.

SOLUTION

Here, the rate of tax collection is 5%, and taxes collected are a part of total sales. The rate in this problem is 5%, the part is $780, and the base, or total sales, must be found. Arrange the problem in standard form.

$$R \quad \times \quad B \quad = \quad P$$

%	of	**something**	is	**something**
5%	of	**total sales**	is	**$780 (tax)**

Using the formula $B = \frac{P}{R}$, we get

$$B = \frac{780}{.05} = \$15{,}600 \text{ total sales}$$

 The calculator solution to this example is

$$780 \boxed{\div} .05 \boxed{=} 15600$$

QUICK CHECK 2

The number of people who passed the real estate license exam was 832. If this was a 65% pass rate, how many took the exam?

It is very important to check the reasonableness of an answer. Intuitively, total sales should be much higher than the sales tax. This is true in the last example because the sales tax is $780 and total sales are $15,600. If $780 had mistakenly been used as the base, the resulting answer would be $780 × 5% = $39, which would not be a reasonable figure for total sales.

OBJECTIVE 3 Find the investment when interest payment and rate of interest are known.

Finding the Amount of an Investment

EXAMPLE 3

Roberta Gonzales received $162.50 in interest from an account that paid 1.25% interest for the year. Find the amount of money invested in the account.

SOLUTION

The part (P) is the $162.50 in interest and the rate (R) is 1.25%. The whole, or base (B), is unknown.

$$B = \frac{P}{R}$$

$$B = \frac{\$162.50}{1.25\%}$$

$$= \frac{\$162.50}{.0125}$$

$$= \$13{,}000$$

The original investment was $13,000.

QUICK CHECK 3

One quarter, the administrator of a school district's retirement funds received $37,500 interest from an investment in bonds that paid 1.5% for the quarter. Find the amount invested.

▼ 3.3 Exercises

MyMathLab®

*The shaded sections below contain solutions to help you get a **QUICK START** on the various types of exercises.*

Solve for base in each of the following. Round to the nearest hundredth. (See Example 1.)

1. 530 firms is 25% of ___2120___ firms.

2. 240 letters is 80% of ___300___ letters.

3. 130 salads is 40% of _____ salads.

4. 32 shipments is 8% of _____ shipments.

5. 110 lab tests is 5.5% of _____ lab tests.

6. $850 is $4\frac{1}{4}$% of _____.

7. 36 students is .75% of _____ students.

8. 23 workers is .5% of _____ workers.

9. 66 files is .15% of _____ files.

10. 54,600 boxes is 60% of _____ boxes.

11. 50 doors is .25% of _____ doors.

12. 39 bottles is .78% of _____ bottles.

13. $33,870 is $37\frac{1}{2}$% of _____.

14. $8500 is $27\frac{1}{2}$% of _____.

15. $12\frac{1}{2}$% of _____ people is 135 people.

16. $18\frac{1}{2}$% of _____ circuits is 370 circuits.

17. 375 crates is .12% of _____ crates.

18. 3.5 quarts is .07% of _____ quarts.

19. .5% of _____ homes is 327 homes.

20. 6.5 barrels is .05% of _____ barrels.

21. 12 audits is .03% of _____ audits.

22. 8 banks is .04% of _____ banks.

23. The basic percent formula is $P = R \times B$. Show how to find the formula to solve for *B* (base). (See Objective 1.)

24. A problem includes amount of sales, sales tax, and a sales-tax rate. Explain how you could identify the base, rate, and part in this problem. (See Objective 2.)

Solve the following application problems. (See Examples 2 and 3.)

25. **HOME OWNERSHIP**   Due to the financial crisis, the number of U.S. households owning homes last year fell to 72.1 million or 65.4% of all households. Find the total number of households to the nearest tenth of a million.

   $$B = \frac{P}{R} = \frac{72.1}{.654} = 110.2 \text{ million (rounded)}$$

25. 110.2 million households

26. **EMPLOYEE POPULATION BASE**   In a large metropolitan area, 81% of the employed population is enrolled in a health maintenance organization (HMO). If 700,650 employees are enrolled, find the total number of people in the employed population.

26. _____

27. **COLLEGE ENROLLMENT**   This semester there are 1785 married students on campus. If this figure represents 23% of the total enrollment, what is the total enrollment? Round to the nearest whole number.

27. _____

🔺 indicates an exercise that is related to the Case in Point feature.

28. VOTER REGISTRATION   Registered Republican voters make up 13.8% of the population of one county. If there are 345,000 registered Republican voters in the county, find the total population in the county.

28. _____

29. LOAN QUALIFICATION   Thomas Dugally found a home for Scott and Andrea Abriani that will require a monthly loan payment of $1350. If the lender insists that the buyer's monthly payment not exceed 30% of the buyer's monthly income, find the minimum monthly income required by the lender.

29. _____

30. DRIVING TESTS   In analyzing the success of driver's license applicants, the state finds that 58.3% of those examined received a passing mark. If the records show that 8370 new driver's licenses were issued, what was the number of applicants? Round to the nearest whole number.

30. _____

31. PERSONAL BUDGETING   Jim Lawler spends 28% of his income on housing, 15% on food, 11% on clothing, 15% on transportation, 11% on education, 7% on recreation, 7% on miscellaneous, and saves the balance. If his savings amount to $200 per month, what are his monthly earnings?

31. _____

32. FAMILY SIZE   One survey among college students found that 28.4% grew up in a home with two or more siblings and 44.7% grew up in a home with one sibling. If 194 students grew up in a home with no siblings, find the size of the survey group.

32. _____

33. MAN'S BEST FRIEND   In a recent survey of dog owners, it was found that 901, or 34%, of the owners take their dogs on vacation with them. Find the number of dog owners in the survey who do not take their dogs on vacation.

33. _____

34. HIRING   Apple, Inc. recently announced that it will be hiring 1800 employees. If this is about 4.3% of the current workforce, estimate the number of people who work for Apple.

34. _____

35. GAMBLING PAYBACK   An Atlantic City casino advertises that it gives a 97.4% payback on slot machines, and the balance is retained by the casino. If the amount retained by the casino one day is $4823, find the total amount played on the slot machines.

35. _____

36. SMOKING OR NONSMOKING   A casino hotel in Barbados states that 45% of its rooms are for nonsmokers. If the resort allows smoking in 484 rooms, find the total number of rooms.

36. _____

▼ Supplementary Application Exercises on Base and Part

Solve the following application problems. Read each problem carefully to determine whether base or part is being asked for.

1. **SHAMPOO INGREDIENTS**   Most shampoos contain 75% to 90% water. If there are 12.5 ounces of water in a bottle of shampoo that contains 78% water, what is the size of the bottle of shampoo? Round to the nearest whole number.

   1. _____

2. **HOUSEHOLD LUBRICANT**   The lubricant WD-40 is used in 82.3 million U.S. homes, which is 79% of all homes in the United States. Find the total number of homes in the United States. Round to the nearest tenth of a million.

   2. _____

3. **PROPERTY INSURANCE**   Thomas Dugally of Century 21 Real Estate sold a commercial building valued at $423,750. If the building is insured for 68% of its value, find the amount of insurance coverage.

   3. _____

4. **FLU PANDEMIC OF 1918**   The Spanish Flu epidemic of 1918 killed more than 50 million people worldwide. Among others, Eskimos had little resistance to this flu strain. Ninety percent of the 80 villagers of Brevig Mission, Alaska, died of the flu within five days, killing entire families. Find the number of villagers that died in five days.

   4. _____

5. **CAMAROS AND MUSTANGS**   The Chevrolet Camaro was introduced in 1967. Camaro sales that year were 220,917, which was 46.2% of the number of Ford Mustangs sold in the same year. Find the number of Mustangs sold in 1967. Round to the nearest whole number.

   5. _____

6. **CHILD SUPPORT**   Sean Eden has 12.4% of his earnings withheld for child support. If this amounts to $396.80 per month, find his annual earnings.

   6. _____

7. **CALORIES FROM FAT**   Häagen-Dazs vanilla ice cream has 270 calories per serving. If 60% of these calories come from fat, find the number of calories coming from fat.

   7. _____

8. **BLOOD-CHOLESTEROL LEVELS**   At a recent health fair, 32% of the people tested were found to have high blood-cholesterol levels. If 350 people were tested, find the number having a high blood-cholesterol level.

   8. _____

9. **RETIREMENT ACCOUNT**   Erin Joyce has 9.5% of her earnings deposited into a retirement account. If this amounts to $308.75 per month, find her annual earnings.

   9. _____

10. SICK PET   Mary Johnson was very upset when her golden Labrador Retriever lost 6 pounds due to a kidney Infection. If that was 6.9% of the Lab's original weight, find the original weight to the nearest pound.

10. _____

AIDING DISABLED EMPLOYEES   The bar graph below shows how companies have accommodated their employees with disabilities. The data were collected from personnel directors, human resource directors, and executives responsible for hiring at 501 companies. Use this information to solve Exercises 11–14. Round to the nearest whole number.

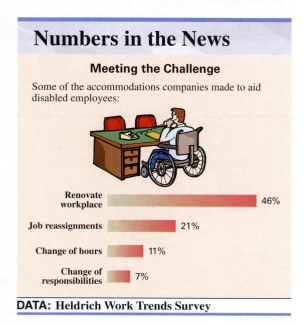

Numbers in the News

Meeting the Challenge

Some of the accommodations companies made to aid disabled employees:

Renovate workplace   46%
Job reassignments   21%
Change of hours   11%
Change of responsibilities   7%

DATA: Heldrich Work Trends Survey

11. How many companies have renovated the workplace to aid employees with disabilities?

11. _____

12. How many companies changed worker responsibilities to aid employees with disabilities?

12. _____

13. Find the number of companies that changed worker hours to aid employees with disabilities.

13. _____

14. Find the number of companies that made job reassignments to aid employees with disabilities.

14. _____

─── **QUICK CHECK ANSWERS** ───

1. (a) 150   **(b)** 6200   **(c)** 4   **3.** $2,500,000

2. 1280 took exam.

▼ 3.4 Finding Rate

OBJECTIVES

1 Use the basic percent formula to solve for rate.

2 Solve for the rate in application problems.

▼CASE IN POINT As managing broker at a Century 21 Real Estate office, Tom Dugally must prepare monthly, quarterly, and annual reports. He often calculates each expense item as a percent of income. He watches these numbers carefully to better control costs.

OBJECTIVE 1 Use the basic percent formula to solve for rate. In this type of percent problem, the part and base are given, and the rate must be found. The **formula for rate** is found from the formula $P = B \times R$. To find the rate using the diagram, cover R to get $\frac{P}{B}$, or part ÷ base.

$$\text{Rate} = \frac{\text{Part}}{\text{Base}} \quad \text{or} \quad R = \frac{P}{B}$$

Actually, the formula $P = B \times R$ can be used to find either P, B, or R as long as the values of two of the three components are known.

To find P: Use $P = B \times R$.

To find R: $P = B \times R$

$\dfrac{P}{B} = \dfrac{B \times R}{B}$ **Divide both sides by B.**

$\dfrac{P}{B} = R$,   or $R = \dfrac{P}{B}$

To find B: $P = B \times R$

$\dfrac{P}{R} = \dfrac{B \times R}{R}$ **Divide both sides by R.**

$\dfrac{P}{R} = B$,   or $B = \dfrac{P}{R}$

Solving for Rate   **EXAMPLE 1**   Solve for rate.

(a) 26 is _____ % of 104.   (b) _____ % of 300 is 60.   (c) 54 is _____ % of 12.

SOLUTION

(a) $\dfrac{26}{104} = .25 = 25\%$ (b) $\dfrac{60}{300} = .2 = 20\%$ (c) $\dfrac{54}{12} = 4.5 = 450\%$

Quick TIP

When finding rate, be sure to change your decimal answer to a percent.

QUICK CHECK 1

Solve for rate.

(a) 63 is _____ % of 84.   (b) _____ % of 128 is 544.

OBJECTIVE 2 Solve for the rate in application problems. Total revenue at Dugally's busy Century 21 Real Estate office one month was $113,000. The $9884 cost of maintaining the computer system that month was unusually high. Find the percent of revenue that went to maintain the computer system. Note first that the base is $113,000 and the part is $9884. The unknown is rate.

$$R = \frac{P}{B}$$

$$R = \frac{\$9884}{\$113,000}$$

$$= .0875 \quad (\mathbf{rounded})$$

$$= 8.75\%$$

Investors constantly try to invest funds where they can get the best rate of return on investment. The rate of return is found using the basic percent formula.

Finding the Rate of Return **EXAMPLE 2** An investment officer at Graham Bank placed $3,000,000 in a government security. It remained there for one year and earned $48,000 in interest. Find the rate of return.

SOLUTION

The whole is $3,000,000 and the part is $48,000. Find the rate as follows.

$$R = \frac{P}{B}$$

$$R = \frac{\$48,000}{\$3,000,000}$$

$$= .016, \quad \text{or} \quad 1.6\%$$

The investment earned 1.6% for the year.

QUICK CHECK 2

An investment of $40,500 resulted in a profit of $1012.50. What was the rate of return?

Solving for the Percent Remaining **EXAMPLE 3** One of the toughest races in the world is the 26.2-mile-long marathon. After running 22 miles, Sheila James is exhausted. Find the percent of the race that she must still run.

SOLUTION

$$\text{Distance yet to be run} = 26.2 - 22 = 4.2 \text{ miles}$$

$$R = \frac{P}{B}$$

$$R = \frac{4.2}{26.2}$$

$$= .160 \quad (\mathbf{rounded})$$

$$= 16\%$$

James still has to run 16% of the total distance.

QUICK CHECK 3

As long as it is maintained, an inexpensive hot-water heater should last 12 years before it needs to be replaced. If a water heater is 10 years old, find the percent of the water heater's life that remains, to the nearest percent.

▼ 3.4 Exercises   MyMathLab®

*The shaded sections below contain solutions to help you get a **QUICK START** on the various types of exercises.*

Solve for rate in each of the following. Round to the nearest tenth of a percent. (See Example 1.)

1. __10__ % of 2760 listings is 276 listings.

2. __40__ % of 850 showings is 340 showings.

3. 35 rail cars is _____ % of 70 rail cars.

4. 144 desks is _____ % of 300 desks.

5. _____ % of 78.57 ounces is 22.2 ounces.

6. _____ % of 728 miles is 509.6 miles.

7. 114 tuxedos is _____ % of 150 tuxedos.

8. $310.75 is _____ % of $124.30.

9. _____ % of $53.75 is $2.20.

10. _____ % of 850 liters is 3.4 liters.

11. 46 shirts is _____ % of 780 shirts.

12. 5.2 smart phones is _____ % of 28.4 smart phones.

13. _____ % of 600 acres is 7.5 acres.

14. _____ % of $8 is $.06.

15. 170 cartons is _____ % of 68 cartons.

16. _____ % of 425 orders is 612 orders.

17. _____ % of $330 is $91.74.

18. _____ % of 752 employees is 470 employees.

19. The basic percent formula is $P = B \times R$. Show how to find the formula to solve for R (rate). (See Objective 1.)

20. A problem includes last year's sales and this year's sales and asks for the percent of increase. Explain how you would identify the base, rate, and part in this problem. (See Objective 4.)

Solve for rate in the following application problems. Round to the nearest tenth of a percent. (See Examples 2–5.)

 21. **ADVERTISING EXPENSES**   Thomas Dugally of Century 21 Real Estate reports that office income last month was $315,600, while advertising expenses were $19,567.20. What percent of last month's income was spent on advertising?

$$R = \frac{P}{B} = \frac{19{,}567.20}{315{,}600} = .062 = 6.2\%$$

21. __6.2%_____

22. **JOB CUTS**   One Carrier Corporation factory builds air conditioning systems for commercial buildings. Sales are traditionally low as summer draws to an end and the manager decides he must layoff 80 of the 760 employees working on the assembly lines. Find the percent of workers that will be laid off.

22. _____

23. **WOMEN IN THE MILITARY**   A recent study by Rand's National Defense Research Institute examined 48,000 military jobs, such as Army attack-helicopter pilot and Navy gunner's mate. It was found that only 960 of these jobs are filled by women. What percent of these jobs are filled by women?

23. _____

 indicates an exercise that is related to the Case in Point feature.

24. **VOCABULARY**   There are 55,000-plus words in *Webster's Dictionary*, but most educated people can identify only 20,000 of these words. What percent of the words in the dictionary can these people identify?

24. _____

25. **ADVERTISING EXPENSES**   Advertising expenditures for Bailey's Roofers are as follows.

Newspaper	$2250	Television	$1425
Radio	$954	Yellow Pages	$1605
Outdoor	$1950	Miscellaneous	$2775

What percent of the total advertising expenditures is spent on radio advertising?

25. _____

26. **TANNING SALON**   Thai Beach says that of its 1100 customers, only about 250 tan regularly. Find the percent that tan regularly.

26. _____

27. **BEER CONSUMPTION**   Cricket's is a popular club for students from the nearby college. The club had 840 customers during Labor Day weekend. If 487 of those customers were under 26 years of age, find the percent under 26.

27. _____

28. **MOTORCYCLISTS**   Of the 2380 motorcycle riders that participated in a recent bike rally through the California mountains, 2041 were men. Find the percent who were men.

28. _____

29. **NURSING**   In a recent survey of 230 nurses, 159 were unhappy with their jobs due to the difficult working hours and work-related stresses. Find the percent unhappy with their jobs.

29. _____

30. **WIND ENERGY**   In the early 1980s, wind-generated electricity cost about 30 cents per kilowatt hour. Today, the best wind systems can produce electricity for 3 cents per kilowatt hour. Find today's cost as a percent of the cost in the 1980s.

30. _____

QUICK CHECK ANSWERS

1. (a) 75%   **(b)** 425%   **3.** 17%

2. 2.5%

▼ ## Supplementary Application Exercises on Base, Rate, and Part

In the equation $P = B \times R$, $P = part$, $B = base$, or whole, and $R = rate$, or percent. Use the following forms of the equation to solve the application problems.

$$P = B \times R \qquad B = \frac{P}{R} \qquad R = \frac{P}{B}$$

You will first need to read the problem carefully to determine whether base, part, or rate is unknown. Round rates to the nearest tenth of a percent.

1. **VACATION MISTAKES**   Out of 571 employees interviewed, 17% said they thought about work while on vacation. How many people thought about work?

   1. _____

2. **AMERICAN CHIROPRACTIC ASSOCIATION**   There are 60,000 licensed chiropractors in the United States. If 25% of these chiropractors belong to the American Chiropractic Association (ACA), find the number of chiropractors in the ACA.

   2. _____

3. **MOTORCYCLE SAFETY**   Only 20 of the 50 states require all motorcycle riders to wear helmets. What percent of the states require motorcycle riders to wear helmets?

   3. _____

4. **EFFECTS OF GLOBAL WARMING**   Periodically, 50% or more of all species of animals have gone extinct in a relatively short period of time. Many scientists believe we are entering such a period now as the Earth warms. In fact, one scientist predicts that as many as 5 million out of the estimated 8.7 million species on earth will disappear by 2100. Find the percent that may go extinct.

   4. _____

5. **LOST OVERBOARD**   In a recent insurance company study of boaters who had lost items overboard, 88 boaters or 8% said that they lost their cell phones. Find the total number of boaters in the survey.

   5. _____

6. **LIGHTS OUT**   There are still 88,000 households in the United States that do not have electricity. If this is .08% of the homes, find the total number of households.

   6. _____

7. **COST AFTER MARKDOWN**   A commercial copier and fax machine priced at $398 is marked down 7% to promote the new model. Find the reduced price.

   7. _____

8. **IPHONE DISCOUNT**   An older model iPhone was marked down by 15% from its original price of $199. Find the reduced price of the old model.

   8. _____

A monthly sales report for the top four salespeople at Active Sports is shown below. Use this information to answer Exercises 9–12.

Employee Commission	Sales	Commission Rate	Commission
Strong, A.	$18,960	3%	**$568.80**
Ferns, K.	$21,460	3%	**$643.80**
Keyes, B.	$17,680	4%	$707.20
Vargas, K.	$23,104	5%	$1152.20

9. Find the commission for Strong.

9. _____

10. Find the commission for Ferns.

10. _____

11. What is the rate of commission for Keyes?

11. _____

12. What is the rate of commission for Vargas?

12. _____

13. **BIKER HELMET LAWS**   There were 2.48 million motorcycle riders in the country who supported biker helmet laws. If this was 62% of the total motorcycle riders in the country, what is the total number of motorcycle riders?

13. _____

14. **HOME PRICES**   In one city, century 21 estimates that the average selling price of a home increased 2.4%, or by $5088, compared to last year. Find the average selling price of a house last year.

14. _____

15. **HIGH SCHOOL DROPOUTS**   In one inner city school district in a large city, 257 out of 414 entering students dropped out before graduating. Find the percent of dropouts.

15. _____

16. **LAYOFF ALTERNATIVE**   Instead of laying off workers, a company cut all employee hours from 40 hours a week to 30 hours a week. By what percent were employee hours cut?

16. _____

POPULATION FORECASTS   *The figure shows current population with a forecast of population for 2050 for the six most populated countries of the world. Use the data to answer Exercises 17–20.*

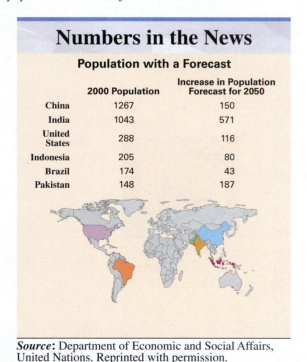

Numbers in the News

Population with a Forecast

	2000 Population	Increase in Population Forecast for 2050
China	1267	150
India	1043	571
United States	288	116
Indonesia	205	80
Brazil	174	43
Pakistan	148	187

Source: Department of Economic and Social Affairs, United Nations. Reprinted with permission.

17. For each country, find the percent increase in population forecast for 2050 rounded to the nearest percent.

18. List the countries from those growing most rapidly (in percent growth) to those growing slowest.

19. Find the 2050 forecast population for China and India, and write using digits.

20. China was the most populous country in the world in 2000. What country is forecast to be the most populous by 2050? What is the difference between the forecast population of this country and China in 2050?

20. _____

21. HEALTH IN A MACHINE   Vending machines on campus must include healthy food choices such as fruits, fruit juices, and healthy snacks. Of the total items sold in the machines this past month, 1440 or 25% have been in the healthy foods group. Find the total number of items sold in the vending machines.

21. _____

22. TOTAL SALES   If the sales tax rate is $7\frac{1}{2}$% and the sales tax collected is $942.30, find the total sales.

22. _____

23. SAVING TO BUY A HOME   Shamus and Kathleen McCoy want to save to buy a home. They set up the following budget based on percent of take-home income: 25% for rent and utilities, 22% for food and pharmacy, 12% for health care, and 32% for other, with the remainder to savings. Their take-home pay after taxes is $5450 per month. Find the annual savings.

23. _____

24. CHICKEN NOODLE SOUP   In one year, there were 350 million cans of chicken noodle soup sold (all brands). If 60% of this soup is sold in the cold-and-flu season (October through March), find the number of cans sold in the cold-and-flu season.

24. _____

25. BUDGETING   The owner of Omni Web Designs decides to save in order to purchase the small building he currently rents. Currently, after tax income averages $6800 per month. The owner budgets the following: 35% for rent, 17% for utilities and insurance, and 40% for salaries and supplies, with the remainder to savings. Find the annual savings.

25. _____

26. BENEFIT INCREASE   One 80-year-old couple gets $1582 in monthly Social Security benefits. They receive a letter saying that their benefits will go up by 2.4% per month. Find the amount of the increase and the new total monthly benefit, both to the nearest dollar.

26. _____

27. SIDE-IMPACT COLLISIONS   Automobile accidents involving side-impact collision resulted in 9000 deaths last year. If automobiles were manufactured to meet a side-impact standard, it is estimated that 63.8% of these deaths would have been prevented. How many deaths would have been prevented?

27. _____

28. WATER SCARCITY   A bottling company in India is installing new equipment that will reduce its current water consumption of 6.2 million gallons per year by 4.2%. Find the amount of water used after the installation of the new equipment and round to the nearest tenth of a million gallons.

28. _____

29. **U.S. PATENT RECIPIENTS**   Among the 50 companies receiving the greatest number of U.S. patents last year, 18 were Japanese companies. **(a)** What percent of the top 50 companies were Japanese companies? **(b)** What percent of the top 50 companies were not Japanese companies?

(a) _____

(b) _____

30. **BLOOD-ALCOHOL LEVELS**   In the United States, 15 of the 50 states limit blood-alcohol levels for drivers to .08%. The remaining states limit these levels to .10%. **(a)** What percent of the states have a blood-alcohol limit of .08%? **(b)** What percent have a limit of .10%?

(a) _____

(b) _____

▼ **3.5** Increase and Decrease Problems

OBJECTIVES

1 Learn to identify an increase or decrease problem.

2 Apply the basic diagram for increase word problems.

3 Use the basic percent formula to solve for base in increase problems.

4 Apply the basic diagram for decrease word problems.

5 Use the basic percent formula to solve for base in decrease problems.

▼ CASE IN POINT   Tom Dugally of Century 21 Real Estate knows that real estate values are always changing, usually going up, occasionally going down, but never staying the same. Dugally needs to keep track of the market and must be able to calculate increases and decreases in value on a regular basis.

OBJECTIVE 1 **Learn to identify an increase or decrease problem.** Businesses commonly look at how amounts change, either up or down. For example, a manager might need to know the percent by which sales have **increased** or costs have **decreased**. A consumer might want to know the percent by which the price of an item has changed. Identify these **increase** and **decrease** problems as follows.

Identifying Increase and Decrease Problems

Increase problem. The base (100%) *plus* some portion of the base gives a new value, which is the part. Phrases such as *after an increase of, more than,* or *greater than* often indicate an increase problem. The basic formula for an increase problem is

$$\text{Original} + \text{Increase} = \text{New value}$$
$$\quad\text{(base)}\qquad\qquad\qquad\text{(part)}$$

Decrease problem. The part equals the base (100%) *minus* some portion of the base, giving a new value. Phrases such as *after a decrease of, less than,* or *after a reduction of* often indicate a decrease problem. The basic formula for a decrease problem is

$$\text{Original} - \text{Decrease} = \text{New value}$$
$$\quad\text{(base)}\qquad\qquad\qquad\text{(part)}$$

OBJECTIVE 2 **Apply the basic diagram for increase word problems.**

Using a Diagram to Understand an Increase Problem ▼ EXAMPLE 1   The value of a home sold by Tom Dugally this year is $203,500, which is 10% more than last year's value. Find the value of the home last year.

SOLUTION

▼ CASE IN POINT   The phrase "10% more than last year's value," tells us that last year's value is the base and that it is the unknown. The figure below shows last year's value as 100% and this year's value which is:

(the base + 10% more than last year's value) = 110% of the base

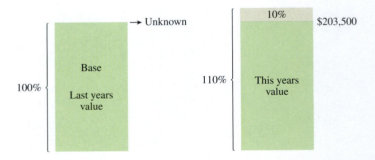

The diagram shows that the 10% increase is based on last year's value which is not known. It is not based on this year's value of $203,500. This year's value is last year's value plus 10% of last year's value.

OBJECTIVE 3 Use the basic percent formula to solve for base in increase problems.

Original	+	Increase	=	New value
100%	+	10%	=	110%

Substituting in the percent formula with part = $203,500 and rate = 110% results in the following.

$$\$203{,}500 = 110\% \times B$$

Solving for B results in the following equation, which is solved for B.

$$B = \frac{\$203{,}500}{110\%}$$

$$B = \frac{\$203{,}500}{1.1}$$

$$B = \$185{,}000$$

So the value of the house last year was $185,000. Now check the answer.

$185,000	← last year's value
+ 18,500	← 10% of $185,000
$203,500	← this year's value

$203,500 is 110% of $185,000.

QUICK CHECK 1

The total sales at Office Products this year are $713,340, which is 35% more than last year's sales. What is the amount of last year's sales?

Finding Base after Two Increases

Due to increased demand for a patented process that will help analyze the DNA of mice, Biotics Genome has increased production of testing kits by 20% per year for each of the two past years. This year's production is 93,600 kits. Find the number of kits produced two years ago.

SOLUTION

The two 20% increases cannot be added together since the two increases act on different bases. Solve this problem in two steps, one for each of the 20% increases. First, use a diagram to find last year's production of DNA kits.

Last year's production plus 20% of last year's production equals this year's production. So, part $(P) = 93{,}600$ and rate $(R) = 120\%$.

$$B = \frac{P}{R} = \frac{93{,}600}{120\%} = \frac{93{,}600}{1.2} = 78{,}000 \qquad \text{last year's production}$$

The number of DNA testing kits produced last year was 78,000. Use this number and knowledge that the sales volume increased 20% from 2 years ago to last year to find production 2 years ago.

It is important to realize that the two 20% increases cannot be added together to equal one increase of 40%. Each 20% increase is calculated on a different base.

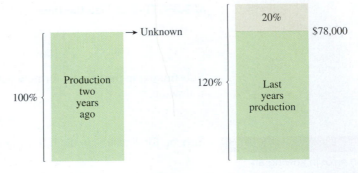

Production two years ago added to 20% of that production equals last year's production. So, part (P) = 78,000 and rate (R) = 120% once again.

$$B = \frac{P}{R} = \frac{78{,}000}{120\%} = \frac{78{,}000}{1.2} = 65{,}000 \qquad \text{production two years ago}$$

The calculator solution to this example is done by dividing in a series.

$$93600 \;\boxed{\div}\; 1.2 \;\boxed{\div}\; 1.2 \;\boxed{=}\; 65000$$

Check the answer.

65,000	production 2 years ago
+ 13,000	20% increase
78,000	production last year
+ 15,600	20% increase
93,600	production this year

QUICK CHECK 2

Due to a large gift from a donor, Blalock College has increased the number of scholarships by 10% per year for each of the past two years. If 1815 scholarships will be offered this year, find the number offered two years ago.

OBJECTIVE 4 Apply the basic diagram for decrease word problems.

Using a Diagram to Understand a Decrease Problem

EXAMPLE 3

After Nike deducted 10% from the price of a pair of competition running shoes, Katie Small paid $135. What was the original price of the shoes?

SOLUTION

The phrase "deducted 10% from the price" indicates it is a decrease problem. The original price is the unknown.

The common error made in decrease problems is thinking that the reduced price is the base. The original price is actually the base.

OBJECTIVE 5 Use the basic percent formula to solve for base in decrease problems.
Ten percent was deducted from the original price. The resulting price paid of $135 is 90% of the original price. So, part (P) = $135 and rate (R) = 90%.

$$B = \frac{P}{R} = \frac{135}{90\%} = \frac{135}{.9} = \$150 \qquad \text{Original price.}$$

Check the answer.

$150   original price
−   15   10% discount
$135   price paid

QUICK CHECK 3

A 40-inch HD LCD television is discounted 25% from the original price. If the discounted price is $1799.99, what was the original price of the television?

▼ 3.5 Exercises   MyMathLab®

The shaded sections below contain solutions to help you get a **QUICK START** *on the various types of exercises.*

Solve for base in each of the following. Round to the nearest cent.
(Hint: Original + Increase = New Value.) (See Examples 1 and 2.)

Part (after increase)	Rate of Increase	Base
1. $450	20%	$375
2. $800	25%	_____
3. $30.70	10%	_____
4. $10.09	5%	_____

Solve for base in each of the following. Round to the nearest cent.
(Hint: Original − Decrease = New Value.) (See Example 3.)

Part (after decrease)	Rate of Decrease	Base
5. $20	20%	$25
6. $1530	15%	_____
7. $598.15	30%	_____
8. $98.38	15%	_____

9. Certain words or word phrases help to identify an increase problem. Discuss how you identify an increase problem. (See Objective 1.)

10. Certain words or word phrases help to identify a decrease problem. Discuss how you identify a decrease problem. (See Objective 1.)

△ indicates an exercise that is related to the Case in Point feature.

Solve the following application problems. Read each problem carefully to decide which are increase or decrease problems, and work accordingly. (See Examples 1–3.)

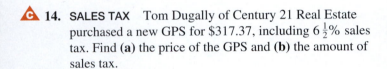

C **11. HOME-VALUE APPRECIATION** Thomas Dugally of Century 21 Real Estate just listed a home for $205,275. If this is 5% more than what the home sold for last year, find last year's selling price.

$$B = \frac{P}{R} = \frac{205{,}275}{1.05} = \$195{,}500$$

11. $195,500

12. DEALER'S COST Cruz Electronics sold an Xbox 360 Gaming and Entertainment System for $345, a loss of 8% of the dealer's original cost. Find the original cost.

$$B = \frac{P}{R} = \frac{345}{.92} = \$375$$

12. $375

13. FAMILY RESTAURANT Santiago Rowland owns a small restaurant and charges 8% sales tax on all orders. At the end of the day he has a total of $1026 including the sales and sales tax in his cash register. **(a)** What were his sales not including sales tax? **(b)** Find the amount that is sales tax.

(a) _____

(b) _____

C **14. SALES TAX** Tom Dugally of Century 21 Real Estate purchased a new GPS for $317.37, including $6\frac{1}{2}$% sales tax. Find **(a)** the price of the GPS and **(b)** the amount of sales tax.

(a) _____

(b) _____

15. EATING OUT There are 177,000 fast-food restaurants in the United States. If fast food represents 21% of the total restaurants, find the total number of restaurants. Round to the nearest whole number.

15. _____

16. ANTILOCK BRAKES In a recent test of an automobile antilock braking system (ABS) on wet pavement, the stopping distance was 114 feet. If this was 28.75% less than the distance needed to stop the same automobile without the ABS, find the distance needed to stop without the ABS.

16. _____

17. FOOD INFLATION Food inflation refers to the annual rate of increase in food prices. Food inflation in one South American country was 10% for each of the past two years. Estimate the cost, two years ago, of a basket of food that costs $80 today. Round each calculation to the nearest cent before proceeding.

17. _____

18. DELI SALES Sara Rasic, owner of Sara's Deli, says that her sales have increased exactly 20% per year for the last two years. Her sales this year are $170,035.20. Find her sales two years ago.

18. _____

19. **DVD RENTALS** Netflix, a DVD-rental company, has 26,000,000 subscribers, an increase of 220% from five years ago. Find the number of subscribers five years ago. Round to the nearest whole number.

19. _____

20. **FARMLAND PRICES** The value of Iowa farmland increased 4.3% this year to a statewide average value of $7003 per acre. How much per acre did Iowa farmland increase this year? Round to the nearest dollar.

20. _____

21. **AUTO SALES** Automobile sales in Asia were 23.4 million this year, a 9.4% increase over last year. Find the number of auto sales in Asia last year, rounded to the nearest tenth of a million.

21. _____

22. **FACEBOOK USERS** The number of Facebook users increased 10% in the past six months to 1 billion. Estimate the number of users six months ago to the nearest million.

22. _____

23. **SURPLUS-EQUIPMENT AUCTION** In a three-day public auction of Jackson County's surplus equipment, the first day brought $5750 in sales and the second day brought $4186 in sales, with 28% of the original equipment left to be sold on the third day. Find the value of the remaining surplus equipment.

23. _____

24. **COLLEGE EXPENSES** After spending $3450 for tuition and $4350 for dormitory fees, Edgar Espina finds that 35% of his original savings remains. Find the amount of his savings that remains.

24. _____

25. **PAPER PRODUCTS MANUFACTURING** The world's largest paper-manufacturing company reported a 16% drop in third-quarter earnings. If earnings had dropped to $122 million, find the earnings before the drop. Round to the nearest hundredth of a million.

25. _____

26. **NATIONAL HOME SALES** During the recession, sales of existing homes decreased 2.3% to an annual number of 4.87 million units. Find the annual number of homes sold before the decrease. Round to the nearest hundredth of a million.

26. _____

27. **WINTER-WHEAT PLANTING** Even though wheat prices rose during the planting season, farmers planted only 50.2 million acres of winter wheat varieties. If this is 2% fewer acres than last year, find the number of acres planted last year. Round to the nearest tenth of a million.

27. _____

28. CHIQUITA BRANDS INTERNATIONAL Shares of Chiquita Brands stock fell 14%, to close at $4.94 per share. What was the value of the stock before the fall? Round to the nearest cent.

28. _____

29. COLLEGE ENROLLMENT The enrollment at one college has grown 6% per year for the past two years. If the current enrollment is 33,708 students, find the number of students enrolled two years ago.

29. _____

30. UNIVERSITY FEES Students at one state university are outraged. The annual university fees were 30% more last year than they were the year before. If the fees are $3380 per year this year, which is 30% more than they were last year, find the annual student fees two years ago.

30. _____

31. CONE ZONE DEATHS This year there were 1181 deaths related to road construction zones in the United States. If this is an increase of 70% in the last five years, what was the number of deaths five years ago? Round to the nearest whole number.

31. _____

32. MINORITY LOANS A large mortgage lender made 52% more loans to minorities this year than last year. If the number of loans to minorities this year is 2660, find the number of loans made to minorities last year.

32. _____

33. FIRES One city reported that the number of fires caused by arson had dropped 17% in one year to 182. Find the number of fires caused by arson in the previous year.

33. _____

34. STOCK VALUE The stock value of drugstore operator CVS dropped 7.4% to close at $46.25 per share. Find the value of each share of stock before the drop. Round to the nearest cent.

34. _____

QUICK CHECK ANSWERS

1. $528,400

3. $2399.99 (rounded)

2. 1500 scholarships

▼ Chapter 3   Quick Review

Chapter Terms   *Review the following terms to test your understanding of the chapter. For each term you do not know, refer to the page number found next to that term.*

base [**p. 91**]   formula for rate [**p. 102**]   part [**p. 91**]   percents [**p. 000**]
decrease problem [**p. 110**] hundredths [**p. 82**]   percent [**p. 82**]   rate [**p. 91**]
formula for base [**p. 96**]   increase problem [**p. 110**]   percent formula [**p. 89**]   sales tax [**p. 90**]

CONCEPTS	EXAMPLES
3.1 Writing a decimal as a percent Move the decimal point two places to the right and attach a percent sign (%).	$.75(.75.) = 75\%$
3.1 Writing a fraction as a percent First change the fraction to a decimal. Then move the decimal point two places to the right and attach a percent sign (%).	$\frac{2}{5} = .4$ $.4(.40.) = 40\%$
3.1 Writing a mixed number as a percent First change the mixed number to a decimal. Then move the decimal point two places to the right and attach a percent sign.	$\frac{13}{8} = 1.375 \quad (1.37.5\%) = 137.5\%$
3.1 Writing a percent as a decimal Move the decimal point two places to the left and drop the percent sign (%).	$50\% (.50.\%) = .5$
3.1 Writing a percent as a fraction First change the percent to a decimal. Then write the decimal as a fraction in lowest terms.	$15\% (.15.\%) = .15 = \frac{15}{100} = \frac{3}{20}$
3.1 Writing a fractional percent as a decimal First change the fraction to a decimal, keeping the percent sign. Then move the decimal point two places to the left and drop the percent sign (%).	$\frac{1}{2}\% = .5\%$ $.5\% = .005$
3.2 Solving for part, using the percent formula $$\textbf{Part} = \textbf{Base} \times \textbf{Rate}$$ $$P = B \times R$$ $$P = BR$$	A company offered a 15% discount on all sales. Find the discount on sales of $1850. $P = B \times R$ $P = \$1850 \times 15\%$ $P = \$1850 \times .15 = \$277.50$ discount
3.2 Using the standard format to solve percent problems Express the problem in the format $$R \quad \times \quad B \quad = \quad P$$ $$\underline{\quad\quad}\% \text{ of } \underline{\quad\quad} \text{ is } \underline{\quad\quad}$$ Notice that *of* means $\times$ and *is* means $=$.	A shop gives a 10% discount on all repairs. Find the discount on a $175 repair. Rate = 10%, Base = $175, and discount is unknown. $$P \quad = \quad R \quad \times \quad B$$ Discount = 10% $\times \$175 = \$17.50$

CONCEPTS	EXAMPLES

3.3 Using the percent formula to solve for base

Use $P = B \times R$.

If the sales tax rate is 4%, find amount of sales when the sales tax is $18.

$$R \times B = P, \quad \text{or} \quad B = \frac{P}{R}$$

$$B = \frac{18}{.04} = \$450 \text{ sales}$$

3.4 Using the percent formula to solve for rate

Use $P = R \times B$.

The return is $307.80 on an investment of $3420. Find the rate of return.

$$R \times B = P, \quad \text{or} \quad R = \frac{P}{B}$$

$$R = \frac{307.8}{3420} = .09 = 9\%$$

3.5 Drawing a diagram and using the percent formula to solve increase problems

Solve for the base when given the rate (110%) and the part (after increase).

This year's sales are $121,000, which is 10% more than last year's sales. Find last year's sales.

Original + Increase = New value
100% + 10% = 110%

Use $B = \frac{P}{R}$.

$$B = \frac{\$121,000}{110\%} = \frac{\$121,000}{1.1}$$

$$= 110,000 \text{ last year's sales}$$

Check:
$110,000	last year's sales
+ 11,000	10% of $110,000
$121,000	this year's sales

3.5 Drawing a diagram and using the percent formula to solve decrease problems

Solve for the base when given the rate (90%) and the part (after decrease).

After a deduction of 10% from the price, a customer paid $270. Find the original price.

Original − Decrease = New value
100% − 10% = 90%

Use $B = \frac{P}{R}$.

$$B = \frac{270}{.9} = \$300 \text{ original price}$$

Check:
$300	original price
− 30	10% discount
$270	price paid

Case Study

SELF EMPLOYED RETIREMENT PLAN

Betty and Juan Martinez are self-employed and have a retirement plan. They have decided to invest in stocks in the plan and are looking at the companies listed below trying to figure out which to buy. Find the stock price last year, the percent of change from last year, or the stock price this year as indicated. Round dollar amounts to the nearest cent and percents to the nearest tenth.

Numbers in the News

Many Stock Prices Increase after Sharp Recession Wanes				
Company	Stock Symbol	Stock Price Last Year	Stock Price This Year	% Change from Last Year
APPLE	AAPL	$352.15	$587.41	_____
Exxon-Mobile	XOM	$78.32	_____	7.9%
McDonald's	MCD	_____	$89.60	9.0%
Coke	KO	$65.82	_____	15.1%

INVESTIGATE

List five large publicly held companies that you know or whose products and services you enjoy. Then use the Web to find the most recent closing stock price. Ignoring commissions, estimate the cost if you purchased ten shares of each of the five companies at the close price for the day.

Case in Point Summary Exercise

CENTURY 21

www.century21.com

Facts:

- 1971: Founded in California
- 1977: Went Public
- 2006: Bought by Apollo Investments
- 2013: Offices and Listings in over 70 countries

Century 21 Real Estate Corporation franchises real estate offices. It has more than 8500 independently owned and operated offices, with locations in all 50 states and more than 70 countries. The firm's Web site, Century21.com, is the fifth most visited real estate Web site on the Internet.

Tom Dugally worked as an agent for Century 21 for several years before he received his broker's license. A few years later, he contacted Century 21 and they helped him set up his own real estate office under a Century 21 franchise. He uses percents on a daily basis to find real estate commissions, monitor costs, follow interest rates, estimate property taxes, and keep up with home prices.

1. Dugally owned a small apartment complex that was worth $865,000 last year. He sold it for $892,680 this year. Find the percent increase in value.

   1. _____

2. Mr. Makin wants Dugally's agency to sell a similar property. Last year, this property had a value of $1,145,000. Use the percent increase from (1) to estimate the current value of this property.

   2. _____

3. A home owner has a large home overlooking a river that is currently valued at $435,000. If his home price has increased by the amount indicated in (1), find the amount by which it increased in value compared to one year ago. Round all dollar values to the nearest dollar.

   3. _____

4. The total real estate commissions paid to Dugally's real estate agency for the quarter were $237,075. If 65% of those funds are paid directly to the self-employed real estate agents that work in the office under Dugally, find the amount the real estate office keeps. He uses these funds to pay for office, computer, advertising expenses, unilities, etc.

   4. _____

Discussion Question: *It is very difficult for a new real estate agent to earn enough to live on while learning the business. What can Dugally do to train and help a new agent?*

Source: CENTURY 21, www.century21.com.

▼ Chapter 3 Test

To help you review, the numbers in brackets show the section in which the topic was discussed.

Determine the fraction, decimal, or percent equivalent for each of the following as necessary. Write fractions in lowest terms. **[3.1]**

FRACTION	DECIMAL	PERCENT
1. $\frac{3}{8}$	.375	_____
2. _____	.35	35%
3. $\frac{3}{125}$	_____	2.4%
4. ____	.14	14%
5. $5\frac{7}{8}$	5.875	_____
6. $1\frac{3}{4}$	_____	175%

Solve the following problems. **[3.1–3.4]**

7. 36 home sales is 12% of what number of home sales?

7. _____

8. What is $\frac{1}{4}$% of $1260?

8. _____

9. Find the fractional equivalent of 24%.

9. _____

10. 48 purchase orders is $2\frac{1}{2}$% of how many purchase orders?

10. _____

11. Change 87.5% to its fractional equivalent.

11. _____

12. Change $1\frac{3}{8}$ to a percent.

12. _____

13. The Los Angeles Lakers made 46.7% of their 92 field goal attempts in a recent game. Find the number of field goals made.

13. _____

14. An underwriter at an insurance company rejected 32 applications for car insurance in one month due to the poor driving record of the applicants. If this was 2.3% of the total number of applications, find the total number of applications. **[3.3]**

14. _____

15. The Honda Civic GX runs on natural gas so that it uses no gasoline. It gets 38 miles per gallon on the highway and has one of the cleanest engines available. Although it is listed at one dealer at $28,350, it is offered at a discount of 6.3% based partly on a rebate from the state. Find the sale price. **[3.5]**

15. _____

16. There are 40.6 million Americans who are 65 or older which makes up 13.1% of the population. Estimate the population of the U.S. to the nearest tenth of a million. **[3.3]**

16. _____

17. A retail store with a monthly advertising budget of $3400 decides to set up a media budget. It plans to spend 22% for television advertising, 38% for newspaper advertising, 14% for outdoor signs, 15% for radio advertising, and the remainder for bumper stickers.
(a) What percent of the total budget do they plan to spend on bumper stickers?
(b) How much do they plan to spend on bumper stickers for the entire year?   **[3.2]**

(a) _____
(b) _____

18. Americans lose about 300 million golf balls each year, and about 225 million of these are recovered and resold in what has become a $200-million annual business. What percent of the lost golf balls are recovered and resold?   **[3.4]**

18. _____

19. A Digital Media Player is marked "Reduced 20%, Now Only $149." Find the original price of the media player.   **[3.5]**

19. _____

20. Last year's backpack sales were 10% more than they were the year before. This year's sales are 1452 units, which is 10% more than last year. Find the number of backpacks sold two years ago.   **[3.5]**

20. _____

21. The local real estate board reports that the number of condominium listings last month was 379. If 357 condominiums were listed in the same month last year, find the percent of increase. Round to the nearest tenth of a percent.   **[3.4]**

21. _____

22. Proctor & Gamble, the maker of Tide detergent, Pampers diapers, and Clairol hair-care products, had quarterly earnings that rose 20% to $1.76 billion. Find the earnings in the previous quarter. Round to the nearest hundredth of a billion.   **[3.4]**

22. _____

4 Equations and Formulas

CHAPTER CONTENTS

4.1 Solving Equations

4.2 Applications of Equations

4.3 Business Formulas

4.4 Ratio and Proportion

▼ CASE IN POINT

BEN JAMES works in the research department of General Motors (GM) as a statistician. His duties include making forecasts of demand for individual vehicle models produced by the company. He uses a variety of tools, including equations, to make the forecasts.

It is very important that management have an accurate forecast of demand. A forecast of demand that is too low results in lost sales, since customers often will not wait to buy. A forecast that is too high results in too much inventory, which is expensive to carry in stock. Sometimes, excess inventory must be marked down in order to sell it. Either way, the firm loses money, potentially a *lot* of money. So, James has a very important job at GM.

Equations and formulas are often used in business. For example, they are used to find markup, interest, depreciation, the future value of annuities, and many other things. In this chapter, we show how to solve and work with basic equations and formulas.

▼ 4.1 Solving Equations

OBJECTIVES

1   Learn the basic terminology of equations.
2   Use basic rules to solve equations.
3   Solve equations requiring more than one operation.
4   Combine like terms in equations.
5   Use the distributive property to simplify equations.

OBJECTIVE 1 Learn the basic terminology of equations. Some of the basic terms related to equations are given in the table.

Definitions	Examples
A **variable** is a letter used to represent an unknown value. Any letter can be used for a variable.	x, t, s, z, R, y, or A
A **term** is a number, a variable, or the product or quotient of a number and a variable.	$53, y, 6x, 9.5z, \dfrac{4}{5}y, \dfrac{s}{3}$
An **expression** can be a single term, but it is often the sum or difference of two or more terms. An expression does not contain an *equal* sign.	$7b, 6x + 9, z - \dfrac{1}{2}y, 19.4t - 5$
An **equation** is two expressions that are equal to one another.	$x + 5 = 9$
Each equation has a **left side** and a **right side**.	$x + 5 = \mathbf{9}$
A **solution** to an equation is the number that can be substituted in place of a variable that makes the equation true.	$x = 4$ is a solution to the equation $x + 5 = 9$.

To see that $x = 4$ is a solution to the equation $x + 5 = 9$, **substitute** 4 in place of x and determine if the resulting equation is true.

$$x + 5 = 9$$
$$4 + 5 = 9 \qquad \text{Substitute 4 in place of } x \text{ in the equation.}$$
$$9 = 9 \qquad \text{Replace } 4 + 5 \text{ with 9 on the left side.}$$

Since the final equation is true, we know that $x = 4$ is a solution to the equation.

OBJECTIVE 2 Use basic rules to solve equations. To solve a basic equation for the unknown, change it so that:

  1. all terms with a variable are on one side of the equation and
  2. all terms with only numbers are on the other side of the equation.

It makes no difference whether the variables are on the left side or the right side of the equation.

To move a term to the other side of the equation, do the opposite operation, or "undo," as shown in Example 1, using the following two rules. It is important that what you do to one side of the equation is done to the other side.

Rules for Solving Equations

Addition Rule The same number (or term) may be added or subtracted on both sides of an equation.

Multiplication Rule Both sides of an equation may be multiplied or divided by the same nonzero number (or term).

Solving a Linear Equation Using Addition

EXAMPLE 1

Solve $x - 9 = 15$ for the unknown.

SOLUTION

The goal is to end up with an equation equivalent to the original equation in which the variable x is isolated on one side and the numbers are on the opposite side. The number 9 is being subtracted from the x on the left side. Undo this operation and move 9 to the other side of the equation by adding 9 to both sides.

$$x - 9 = 15$$
$$x - 9 + \mathbf{9} = 15 + \mathbf{9} \qquad \text{Add 9 to both sides.}$$
$$x + 0 = 24$$
$$x = 24$$

To confirm that the value of the unknown is 24, substitute 24 for x in the original equation.

$$x - 9 = 15 \qquad \text{Original equation}$$
$$24 - 9 = 15 \qquad \text{Let } x = 24.$$
$$15 = 15 \qquad \text{True}$$

Therefore, x is equal to 24. This is the solution to the equation.

QUICK CHECK 1

Solve $y - 22 = 45$.

Solving a Linear Equation Using Subtraction

EXAMPLE 2

Solve $k + 7 = 18$.

SOLUTION

To isolate k on the left side, do the opposite of adding 7, which is *subtracting* 7 from both sides.

$$k + 7 = 18$$
$$k + 7 - \mathbf{7} = 18 - \mathbf{7} \qquad \text{Subtract 7 from both sides.}$$
$$k = 11$$

QUICK CHECK 2

Solve $m + 19 = 32$.

Solving a Linear Equation Using Division

EXAMPLE 3

Solve $5p = 60$.

SOLUTION

The term $5p$ indicates the multiplication of 5 and p. Since division is the inverse of multiplication, solve the equation by *dividing* both sides by 5.

$$5p = 60$$
$$\frac{5p}{\mathbf{5}} = \frac{60}{\mathbf{5}} \qquad \text{Divide both sides by 5.}$$
$$p = 12$$

Check by substituting 12 for p in the original equation.

QUICK CHECK 3

Solve $17g = 153$.

Solving a Linear Equation Using Multiplication

 EXAMPLE 4

Solve $\dfrac{y}{3} = 9$.

SOLUTION

The bar in $\frac{y}{3}$ means to divide. Since multiplication is the opposite of division, multiply both sides by 3.

$$\frac{y}{3} = 9$$

$$\frac{y}{3} \cdot 3 = 9 \cdot 3 \qquad \text{Multiply both sides of the equation by 3.}$$

$$y = 27$$

QUICK CHECK 4

Solve $\frac{t}{4} = 28$.

Example 5 shows how to solve an equation using a reciprocal. To get the **reciprocal** of a nonzero fraction, exchange the numerator and the denominator. For example, the reciprocal of $\frac{7}{9}$ is $\frac{9}{7}$. The product of two reciprocals is 1.

$$\frac{\overset{1}{\cancel{7}}}{\underset{1}{\cancel{9}}} \cdot \frac{\overset{1}{\cancel{9}}}{\underset{1}{\cancel{7}}} = 1$$

So, $\dfrac{9}{7}$ is the reciprocal of $\dfrac{7}{9}$.

Solving a Linear Equation Using Reciprocals

 EXAMPLE 5

Solve $\dfrac{3}{4}z = 9$.

SOLUTION

Solve this equation by multiplying both sides by $\frac{4}{3}$, the reciprocal of $\frac{3}{4}$. This process will give $1z$, or just z, on the left.

$$\frac{3}{4}z = 9$$

$$\frac{3}{4}z \cdot \frac{4}{3} = 9 \cdot \frac{4}{3} \qquad \text{Multiply both sides by } \tfrac{4}{3}.$$

$$z = 12$$

QUICK CHECK 5

Solve $\frac{1}{2}z = 99$.

OBJECTIVE 3 Solve equations requiring more than one operation. To solve equations that require more than one step, first isolate the terms involving the unknown (or variable) on one side of the equation and the constants (or numbers) on the other side by using addition and subtraction.

Solving a Linear Equation Using Several Steps

 EXAMPLE 6

Solve $2m + 5 = 17$.

SOLUTION

$$2m + 5 = 17$$

$$2m + 5 - 5 = 17 - 5 \qquad \text{Subtract 5 from both sides.}$$

$$2m = 12$$

Now divide both sides by 2.

The unknown can be on either side of the equal sign, so $6 = m$ is the same as $m = 6$.

$$\frac{2m}{2} = \frac{12}{2} \qquad \text{Divide both sides by 2.}$$

$$m = 6$$

As before, check by substituting 6 for m in the original equation.

QUICK CHECK 6

Solve $3y + 9 = 45$.

Solving a Linear Equation Using Several Steps

EXAMPLE 7

Solve $3y - 12 = 52$.

SOLUTION

$$3y - 12 = 52$$
$$3y - 12 + 12 = 52 + 12 \qquad \text{Add 12 to both sides.}$$
$$3y = 64$$
$$\frac{3y}{3} = \frac{64}{3} \qquad \text{Divide both sides by 3.}$$
$$y = 21\frac{1}{3}$$

QUICK CHECK 7

Solve $9q - 14 = 58$.

OBJECTIVE 4 Combine like terms in equations. Some equations have more than one term with the same variable. Terms with the same variables are called **like terms**. They can be *combined* by adding or subtracting the coefficients just as 5 apples + 2 apples can be combined to be 7 apples.

$$5y + 2y = (5 + 2)y = 7y$$
$$11k - 8k = (11 - 8)k = 3k$$
$$12p - 5p + 2p = (12 - 5 + 2)p = 9p$$
$$2z + z = 2z + 1z = (2 + 1)z = 3z$$

Terms with different variables in them *cannot* be combined into a single term just as 5 apples + 2 bananas cannot be combined to be either 7 apples or 7 bananas. These are called **unlike terms**. For example, $12y + 5x$ cannot be combined to make one term, since y and x are different variables.

Solving a Linear Equation Using Several Steps

EXAMPLE 8

Solve $8y - 6y + 4y = 24$.

SOLUTION

Start by combining terms on the left: $8y - 6y + 4y = 2y + 4y = 6y$.

$$8y - 6y + 4y = 24$$
$$(8 - 6 + 4)y = 24 \qquad \text{Combine like terms.}$$
$$6y = 24$$
$$\frac{6y}{6} = \frac{24}{6} \qquad \text{Divide both sides by 6.}$$
$$y = 4$$

QUICK CHECK 8

Solve $17z - 12z = 42$.

Solving a Linear Equation

EXAMPLE 9

Solve $7z - 3z + .5z = 15$.

SOLUTION

$$7z - 3z + .5z = 15$$
$$(7 - 3 + .5)z = 15 \qquad \text{Combine like terms.}$$
$$4.5z = 15$$
$$\frac{4.5z}{4.5} = \frac{15}{4.5} \qquad \text{Divide both sides by 4.5.}$$
$$z = 3\frac{1}{3}$$

QUICK CHECK 9

Solve $3t - .5t = 17$.

OBJECTIVE 5 Use the distributive property to simplify equations. An equation may include a number being multiplied by the sum of two or more terms in parentheses. Use the **distributive property** to multiply the number by each term in the parentheses.

$$a(b + c) = ab + ac$$

The following diagram may help in remembering the distributive property.

Multiply a by b and by c.

$$a(b + c) = ab + ac$$

More examples:

Multiply 2 by m and 7.

$$2(m + 7) = 2m + 2 \cdot 7 = 2m + 14$$
$$8(k - 5) = 8k - 8 \cdot 5 = 8k - 40$$

Solving a Linear Equation Using the Distributive Property

EXAMPLE 10

Solve $8(t - 5) = 16$.

SOLUTION

First use the distributive property on the left to remove the parentheses.

$$8(t - 5) = 16$$
$$8t - 40 = 16$$
$$8t - 40 + \mathbf{40} = 16 + \mathbf{40} \qquad \text{Add 40 to both sides.}$$
$$8t = 56$$
$$\frac{8t}{8} = \frac{56}{8} \qquad \text{Divide both sides by 8.}$$
$$t = 7$$

QUICK CHECK 10

Solve $9(s - 16) = 135$.

Now that you have seen how to solve a few equations, look at the steps to keep in mind when solving equations.

> **Solving an Equation**
>
> **Step 1** Remove all parentheses on both sides of the equation using the distributive property.
>
> **Step 2** Combine all like terms on both sides of the equation.
>
> **Step 3** Place all terms containing a variable on the same side of the equation and all terms not containing a variable on the other side of the equation.
>
> **Step 4** Multiply or divide the variable term by numbers as needed to produce a term with a coefficient of 1 in front of the variable.

Solving a Linear Equation Using the Distributive Property

EXAMPLE 11 Solve $5r - 2 = 2(r + 5)$.

SOLUTION

$$5r - 2 = 2(r + 5)$$
$$5r - 2 = 2r + 10 \quad \text{Use the distributive property on the right side.}$$
$$5r - 2 + 2 = 2r + 10 + 2 \quad \text{Add 2 to both sides to get all terms with only numbers on the right side.}$$
$$5r = 2r + 12$$
$$5r - 2r = 2r + 12 - 2r \quad \text{Subtract } 2r \text{ from both sides to get all terms with only variables on the left side.}$$
$$5r - 2r = 12$$
$$3r = 12 \quad \text{Combine like terms on the left side.}$$
$$\frac{3r}{3} = \frac{12}{3} \quad \text{Divide both sides by 3.}$$
$$r = 4$$

Quick TIP

Be sure to check the answer in the *original* equation.

Check by substituting 4 for r in the original equation.

> **QUICK CHECK 11**
>
> Solve $5(s - 4) = 3(s + 9)$.

Solving a Linear Equation Using the Distributive Property

EXAMPLE 12 Solve $3(t - .8) = 14 + t$.

SOLUTION

$$3(t - .8) = 14 + t$$
$$3t - 2.4 = 14 + t \quad \text{Use the distributive property.}$$
$$3t - 2.4 - t = 14 + t - t \quad \text{Subtract } t \text{ from both sides.}$$
$$2t - 2.4 = 14 \quad \text{Combine like terms on the left side.}$$
$$2t - 2.4 + 2.4 = 14 + 2.4 \quad \text{Add 2.4 to both sides.}$$
$$2t = 16.4$$
$$\frac{2t}{2} = \frac{16.4}{2} \quad \text{Divide both sides by 2.}$$
$$t = 8.2$$

> **QUICK CHECK 12**
>
> Solve $12u - 8 = 8(u + 4)$.

▼ 4.1 Exercises   MyMathLab®

The shaded sections below contain solutions to help you get a **QUICK START** *on the various types of exercises.*

Solve each equation for the unknown.

1. $s + 12 = 15$ **3**____
$$s + 12 = 15$$
$$s + 12 - 12 = 15 - 12$$
$$s = 3$$

2. $k + 15 = 22$ **7**____
$$k + 15 = 22$$
$$k + 15 - 15 = 22 - 15$$
$$k = 7$$

3. $b - 7 = 24$ ____

4. $P - 13 = 52$ ____

5. $12 = b + 9$ ____

6. $7 = m - 3$ ____

7. $8k = 56$ ____

8. $3q = 120$ ____

9. $60 = 30m$ ____

10. $94 = 2z$ ____

11. $\dfrac{m}{5} = 6$ ____

12. $\dfrac{r}{7} = 1$ ____

13. $\frac{2}{3}a = 5$ ____

14. $\frac{3}{4}m = 18$ ____

15. $\dfrac{9}{5}r = 18$ ____

16. $2x = \dfrac{5}{3}$ ____

17. $3m + 5 = 17$ ____

18. $2y - 5 = 39$ ____

19. $4r + 3 = 9$ ____

20. $2p + \dfrac{1}{2} = \dfrac{3}{2}$ ____

21. $11r - 5r + 6r = 84$ ____

◭ indicates an exercise that is related to the Case in Point feature.

22. $5m + 6m - 2m = 72$ _____   **23.** $3(2x + 3) = 3x + 12$ _____   **24.** $4z + 2 = 2(z + 3)$ _____

25. Define variable, term, expression, and equation.

26. Explain the difference between an expression and an equation. Then explain what is meant by the *solution to an equation*.

▼ 4.2 Applications of Equations

OBJECTIVES

1. Translate phrases into mathematical expressions.
2. Write equations from given information.
3. Solve application problems.

CASE IN POINT   At General Motors, Ben James studies historical sales, looking for trends and patterns. He also analyzes the current economic conditions that affect those who buy vehicles. He uses the knowledge gained to develop equations that help him make forecasts of demand. Without a good forecast, managers would not know how many cars to build and suppliers would not know how many parts to produce.

OBJECTIVE 1 Translate phrases into mathematical expressions. Most problems in business are expressed in words. Before these problems can be solved, they must be converted into mathematical language.

Word problems often have certain phrases that occur again and again. The key to solving word problems is to correctly translate these expressions into mathematical expressions. The next few examples illustrate this process.

Translating Verbal Expressions Involving Addition

 EXAMPLE 1 Write the following verbal expressions as mathematical expressions. Use x to represent the unknown quantity. Note that other letters can also be used to represent this unknown quantity.

SOLUTION

Verbal Expression	Mathematical Expression	Comments
(a) 5 plus a number	$5 + x$	x represents the number, and *plus* indicates **addition**.
(b) Add 20 to a number	$x + 20$	x represents the number, and *add* indicates **addition**.
(c) The sum of a number and 12	$x + 12$	x represents the number, and *sum* indicates **addition**.
(d) 6 more than a number	$x + 6$	x represents the number, and *more than* indicates **addition**.

QUICK CHECK 1

Write a number plus 7 as a mathematical expression using y for the unknown.

Translating Verbal Expressions Involving Subtraction

 EXAMPLE 2 Write each of the following verbal expressions as a mathematical expression. Use p as the variable.

SOLUTION

Verbal Expression	Mathematical Expression	Comments
(a) 3 less than a number	$p - 3$	p represents the number, and *less than* indicates **subtraction**.
(b) A number decreased by 14	$p - 14$	p represents the number, and *decreased by* indicates **subtraction**.
(c) 10 fewer than p	$p - 10$	p represents the number, and *fewer than* indicates **subtraction**.

QUICK CHECK 2

Use s for the unknown, and write a mathematical expression for 19 minus an unknown.

Translating Verbal Expressions Involving Multiplication and Division

EXAMPLE 3

Write the following verbal expressions as mathematical expressions. Use y as the variable.

SOLUTION

Verbal Expression	Mathematical Expression	Comments
(a) The product of a number and 3	$3y$	y represents the number, and *product* indicates **multiplication**.
(b) Four times a number	$4y$	y represents the number, and *times* indicates **multiplication**.
(c) Two-thirds of a number	$\frac{2}{3}y$	y represents the number, and *of* indicates **multiplication**.
(d) The quotient of a number and 2	$\frac{y}{2}$	y represents the number, and *quotient* indicates **division**.
(e) The sum of 3 and a number is multiplied by 5	$5(3 + y)$	This requires **parentheses**.
(f) 7 is multiplied by the difference of an unknown number and 14	$7(y - 14)$	This requires **parentheses**.

QUICK CHECK 3

Use t for the variable, and write an expression for the product of 7 and the sum of 9 plus an unknown.

When multiplying or adding, it does not make any difference which variable is written first. For example.

$$15 \times y = y \times 15 \qquad x + 3 = 3 + x$$

However, the order *does* make a difference when dividing or subtracting, as you can see.

$$\frac{10}{x} \neq \frac{x}{10} \quad (\text{unless } x = 10) \qquad z - 150 \neq 150 - z \quad (\text{unless } z = 150)$$

OBJECTIVE 2 Write equations from given information. Read the problem carefully as you develop the equation(s) needed to solve it.

Writing an Equation from Words

EXAMPLE 4

Translate "the product of 5 and a number decreased by 8 is 100" into an equation. Then, solve the equation.

SOLUTION

Use the letter y as the variable and translate as follows.

The product of 5		and a number	decreased by	8	is	100.
↓	↓	↓	↓	↓		↓
5	·	(y	−	8)	=	100

Simplify and complete the solution of the equation.

$$5 \cdot (y - 8) = 100$$
$$5y - 40 = 100 \qquad \text{Apply the distributive property.}$$
$$5y = 140 \qquad \text{Add 40 to both sides.}$$
$$y = 28 \qquad \text{Divide by 5.}$$

QUICK CHECK 4

Write "ninety-four is the product of 12 and the sum of a number and 2.5" as an equation, using p for the variable.

Writing an Equation from Words

 EXAMPLE 5

Write "the sum of an unknown and 6, when divided by 15, is equal to 7" as an equation, using r as the variable.

SOLUTION

The sum of an unknown and 6	when divided by 15	is equal to	7.
↓	↓	↓	↓
$(r + 6)$	$\div 15$	$=$	7

Simplify and solve the equation.

$$(r + 6) \div 15 = 7$$
$$(r + 6) \div 15 \cdot \mathbf{15} = 7 \cdot \mathbf{15} \qquad \text{Multiply both sides by 15.}$$
$$r + 6 = 105$$
$$r + 6 - \mathbf{6} = 105 - \mathbf{6} \qquad \text{Subtract 6 from both sides.}$$
$$r = 99$$

QUICK CHECK 5

Write "the quantity 17 minus an unknown, divided by 12, is equal to 14" as an equation, using r as the variable.

OBJECTIVE 3 Solve application problems. Now that statements have been translated into mathematical expressions, you can use this knowledge to solve problems.

Solving Application Problems

Step 1   Read the problem carefully. A sketch may help.

Step 2   Identify the unknown and choose a variable to represent it. If possible, write any other unknowns in terms of the same variable.

Step 3   Translate the problem into an equation.

Step 4   Solve the equation.

Step 5   Answer the question(s) asked in the problem.

Step 6   Check your solution using the original words of the problem.

Step 7   Be sure your answer is reasonable.

Step 3 is often the most difficult. To write an equation from the information given in the problem, convert the facts stated in words into mathematical expressions. These expressions are used to build a *mathematical model* of the situation.

Solving a Business Problem

 EXAMPLE 6

Ben James is studying monthly demand for Chevrolet Impalas in two different regions of the country. He has 14,200 new Impalas to ship to the two regions, and he decides to ship 3350 more to the Southeast region than to the mid–Atlantic Coast region. Find the number to be shipped to the mid–Atlantic Coast region.

▼ **CASE IN POINT** If m = number of Impalas to be shipped to the mid–Atlantic Coast region, then $(m + 3350)$ = number to be shipped to the Southeast region. The sum of the two shipments is 14,200.

SOLUTION

Number to mid–Atlantic Coast region	+	Number to Southeast region	=	Total
m	+	$(m + 3350)$	=	$14{,}200$

$$m + m + 3350 = 14{,}200 \qquad \text{Remove parentheses}$$
$$2m + 3350 = 14{,}200 \qquad \text{Combine like terms.}$$
$$2m + 3350 - \mathbf{3350} = 14{,}200 - \mathbf{3350} \qquad \text{Subtract 3350 from both sides.}$$
$$2m = 10{,}850 \qquad \text{Simplify.}$$
$$\frac{2m}{2} = \frac{10{,}850}{2} \qquad \text{Divide both sides by 2.}$$
$$m = 5425$$

So, the numbers to be shipped are:

$$m = \quad 5425 \text{ to the mid–Atlantic Coast region}$$
$$(m + 3350) = \quad \underline{8775} \text{ to the Southeast region}$$
$$= 14{,}200 \text{ to be shipped}$$

Since this agrees with the total to be shipped, the answer checks.

> **QUICK CHECK 6**
>
> A professor was taking 28 students to Guadalajara, Mexico, on a two-week, travel-study program. If there were 14 more women than men, find the number of men and the number of women.

Applying Equation Solving

 EXAMPLE 7

A mattress for a single bed is on sale for $200, which is $\frac{4}{5}$ of its original price. Find the original price.

SOLUTION

Let p represent the original price, $200 is the sale price, and the sale price is $\frac{4}{5}$ of the original price. Use this information to write the equation.

Sale price	is	$\frac{4}{5}$	of	original price.
↓	↓	↓	↓	↓
$200	=	$\frac{4}{5}$	×	p

Solve the equation.

$$200 = \frac{4}{5} \cdot p$$

$$\frac{5}{4} \cdot 200 = \frac{5}{4} \cdot \frac{4}{5} \cdot p \qquad \text{Multiply by reciprocal.}$$

$$\frac{1000}{4} = \mathbf{1} \cdot p$$

$$250 = p$$

The original price is $250.

> **QUICK CHECK 7**
>
> Fearful of bankruptcy, the top manager of a company laid off enough people so that the workforce was only $\frac{2}{3}$ of the original workforce. Find the original number of employees if there were 34 employees after the layoff.

Solving Investment Problems

 EXAMPLE 8

Laurie Zimmerman has $15,000 to invest. She places a portion of the funds in a passbook account and $3000 more than twice this amount in a retirement account. How much is put into the passbook account? How much is placed in the retirement account?

SOLUTION

Let z represent the amount invested in the passbook account. To find the amount invested in the retirement account, translate as follows.

3000	more than	2 times the amount
↓	↓	↓
3000	+	$2z$

Since the sum of the two investments must be $15,000, an equation can be formed as follows.

Amount invested in passbook		Amount invested in retirement account		Total amount invested
z	+	$(3000 + 2z)$	=	$15,000

Now solve the equation.

$$z + (3000 + 2z) = 15{,}000$$
$$3z + 3000 = 15{,}000$$
$$3z = 12{,}000 \qquad \text{Subtract 3000.}$$
$$z = 4000 \qquad \text{Divide by 3.}$$

The amount invested in the passbook account is z, or \$4000. The amount invested in the retirement account is $3000 + 2z$ or $3000 + 2(4000) = \$11{,}000$.

QUICK CHECK 8

A mutual fund company has \$24 million to invest. They place part of the funds in the bonds of a utility company and \$4 million more than three times that amount in New York City bonds. Find the amount placed in utility bonds and the amount in New York City bonds.

Solving a Business Problem

 EXAMPLE 9   The Eastside Nursery ordered 27 tree seedlings. Some of the seedlings were elms, costing \$17 each. The remainder of the seedlings were maples at \$11 each. The total cost of the seedlings is \$375. Find the number of elms and the number of maples.

SOLUTION

Let x represent the number of elm seedlings in the shipment. Since the shipment contained 27 seedlings, the number of maples is found by subtracting the number of elms from 27.

$$27 - x = \text{number of maples}$$

If each elm seedling costs \$17, then x elm seedlings will cost $17x$ dollars. Also, the cost of $(27 - x)$ maple seedlings at \$11 each is $11(27 - x)$. The total cost of the shipment was \$375. A table can be very helpful in identifying the knowns and unknowns.

	COST PER SEEDLING	NUMBER OF SEEDLINGS	TOTAL COST
Elms	\$17	x	$17x$
Maples	\$11	$(27 - x)$	$11(27 - x)$
Totals		27	375

The information in the table is used to develop the following equation.

$$\textbf{Cost of elms + Cost of maples = Total cost}$$
$$17x \quad + \quad 11(27 - x) \quad = \quad 375$$

Now solve this equation.

$$17x + 297 - 11x = 375 \qquad \text{Use distributive property.}$$
$$6x + 297 = 375 \qquad \text{Combine terms.}$$
$$6x = 78 \qquad \text{Subtract 297 from each side.}$$
$$x = 13 \qquad \text{Divide each side by 6.}$$

There were $x = 13$ elm seedlings and $(27 - 13) = 14$ maple seedlings.

QUICK CHECK 9

A beer-bottling company ordered 2100 more 12-ounce bottles than 1-quart bottles. The cost of the 12-ounce bottles was \$.08 each, and the cost of the 1-quart bottles was \$.11 each. The total cost was \$310.50 not including shipping. Find the number of each type of bottle ordered.

4.2 Exercises

MyMathLab®

*The shaded sections below contain solutions to help you get a **QUICK START** on the various types of exercises.*

Write the following as mathematical expressions. Use x as the variable. Be sure and use parentheses as needed.

1. 27 plus a number $27 + x$

2. the sum of a number and $16\frac{1}{2}$ $x + 16\frac{1}{2}$

3. a number added to 22 _____

4. 6.8 added to a number _____

5. 4 less than a number _____

6. 12 fewer than a number _____

7. subtract $3\frac{1}{2}$ from a number _____

8. subtract a number from 5.4 _____

9. triple a number _____

10. the product of a number and 9 _____

11. three-fifths of a number _____

12. four-thirds of a number _____

13. the quotient of 9 and a number _____

14. the quotient of a number and 11 _____

15. 16 divided by a number _____

16. a number divided by 4 _____

17. the product of 2.1 and the sum of 4 and a number _____

18. the quantity of a number plus 4, divided by 9 _____

19. 7 times the difference of a number and 3 _____

20. the difference of a number and 2, multiplied by 7 _____

Write mathematical expressions for each of the following.

21. PURCHASING CDs   Find the cost of 12 CDs at y dollars each. $12y$

22. TUITION FEES   Find the cost of x students paying tuition of $2800 each. $2800x$

23. LIVESTOCK FEED   The demand forecast for next month is 472 tons of livestock feed. Find the amount that should be ordered if inventory is x tons. _____

24. COMPUTER USERS   Eighty-three of the x employees have computers. How many do not have computers? _____

25. UNION MEMBERSHIP   A company has 73 employees of whom x are members of a union. How many employees are not union members? _____

26. CARD SALES   The inventory of a small card shop is valued at $73,000. The value of the greeting cards is x. Find the value of the rest of the inventory. _____

27. TEXTBOOK PURCHASES   A college bookstore paid $20,210 to purchase x textbooks for a biology class. Find the cost of one textbook. _____

28. ADMISSION FEES   A lodge paid $1853 for tickets for its x members to visit the state capitol. Find the cost of one ticket. _____

29. CHARITABLE DONATIONS   Robin has 21 books on computers. She donates x of them to the school library. How many does she have left? _____

30. VIDEO STORE   A video rental store is x years old. How old will it be in 8 years? _____

⚠️ C indicates an exercise that is related to the Case in Point feature.

Solve the following application problems. Steps 1–7 are repeated here for your convenience—use them.

Solving Applied Problems

Step 1   Read the problem carefully. A sketch may help.

Step 2   Identify the unknown and choose a variable to represent it. If possible, write any other unknowns in terms of the same variable.

Step 3   Translate the problem into an equation.

Step 4   Solve the equation.

Step 5   Answer the question(s) asked in the problem.

Step 6   Check your solution using the original words of the problem.

Step 7   Be sure your answer is reasonable.

31. Four times a number, plus 6 equals 58. Find the number.

$$4x + 6 = 58$$
$$4x = 52$$
$$x = 13$$

31. 13 _____

32. Seventeen times a number, plus 5 equals 107. Find the number.

$$17x + 5 = 107$$
$$17x = 102$$
$$x = 6$$

32. 6 _____

33. Six times the quantity of 4 minus a number is 15. Find the number.

33. _____

34. Twelve times the quantity of a number less 1 is 72. Find the number.

34. _____

35. When 6 is added to a number, the result is 7 times the number. Find the number.

35. _____

36. If 6 is subtracted from three times a number, the result is 4 more than the number. Find the number.

36. _____

37. When 5 times a number is added to twice the number, the result is 10. Find the number.

37. _____

38. If 7 times a number is subtracted from 11 times the number, the result is 9. Find the number.

38. _____

39. SOUND SYSTEM   Last month, Ben Jamison sold 17 more sound systems than did the other salesperson at the store. If the two salespeople sold a total of 101 systems, find the number sold by Jamison.

39. _____

40. SODA SALES   A grocery store sold 19 more cases of Coke than Sprite. Given that 43 cases were sold, find the number of cases of Coke sold.

40. _____

41. SHIP BUILDING   One hundred eighty-five more people work in building the ships than are in management, accounting, finance, and marketing. Given a total of 229 employees, find the number working in building ships.

41. _____

42. EXCHANGE PROGRAM   Twenty-one students went on a student exchange program to Hong Kong. There were 11 more women than men. Find the number of women.

42. _____

43. WATER SKIS   A new set of slalom water skis are priced at $314.10 which is 9/10ths of the original price. Find the original price to the nearest dollar.

43. _____

44. INTERNATIONAL SHIPMENTS   Because of unusually high handling and freight charges, Western Oil Equipment charges $\frac{5}{4}$ of the list price for an item shipped to Indonesia. Find the list price of an item that was charged at $725.

44. _____

45. COMMERCIAL BUILDING   Jane Anderson purchased a commercial building and plans to fix it up. The building can be used for both retail stores and office space. She thinks she can get a total annual rent of $135,000, with $3\frac{1}{2}$ times as much rent coming from retail stores as from office space. Find the rent she expects from office space and also the rent she expects from retail stores.

45. _____

46. MATERIAL   Karen Cherie has a piece of fabric that is 106 inches long. She wishes to cut it into two pieces so that one piece is 12 inches longer than the other. What should be the length of each piece?

46. _____

47. HARLEY DAVIDSON Excluding managers, there are 22 full-time employees working at a large Harley Davidson shop. New employees receive $9.50 per hour, while more experienced workers average $12.90 per hour. The company spends $273.60 per hour in wages, not counting benefits. Find the number of each type of worker.

47. _____

48. VEGETABLE SALES Florida Vegetables, Inc. makes $0.10 on a head of lettuce and $0.08 on a bunch of carrots. Last week, a total of 12,900 heads of lettuce and bunches of carrots were sold, with a total profit of $1174. How many heads of lettuce and how many bunches of carrots were sold?

48. _____

49. NISSAN SALES Profits on Nissan Altimas and Sentras average $1200 and $850, respectively, at one dealership. The total profit in a month in which they sold 120 of these models was $130,350. Find the number of each sold.

49. _____

50. AUTO REPAIR One week, revenue from the 95 repairs at an auto repair shop totaled $20,040. The average charges for repairs on personal and commercial vehicles were $250 and $180 respectively. Find the number of each type of vehicle repaired.

50. _____

51. Are the problems in this section difficult for you? Explain why or why not. Explain two things you would recommend to a classmate who is having difficulty.

52. Write out the steps necessary to solve an applied problem. (See Objective 3.)

QUICK CHECK ANSWERS

1. $y + 7$

2. $19 - s$

3. $7(9 + t)$

4. $94 = 12(p + 2.5)$

5. $\dfrac{17 - r}{12} = 14$

6. 7 men, 21 women

7. 51 employees

8. utility bonds, $5 million; New York City bonds, $19 million

9. 2850 12-ounce bottles; 750 1-quart bottles

4.3 Business Formulas

OBJECTIVES

1 Evaluate formulas for given values of the variables.

2 Solve formulas for a specific variable.

3 Use standard business formulas to solve word problems.

4 Evaluate formulas containing exponents.

OBJECTIVE 1 Evaluate formulas for given values of the variables. Many of the most useful rules and procedures in business are given as **formulas** which are equations showing how one number is found from other numbers. One of the single most useful formulas in business is the one for simple interest.

$$\text{Interest} = \text{Principal} \times \text{Rate} \times \text{Time}$$

When written out in words, as shown, a formula can take up too much space and be hard to remember. For this reason, it is common to *use letters as variables for the words* in a formula. Many times the first letter in each word of a formula is used, to make it easier to remember the formula. By this method, the formula for simple interest is written as follows.

$$\text{Interest} = \text{Principal} \times \text{Rate} \times \text{Time}$$
$$I \quad = \quad P \quad \times \quad R \quad \times \quad T$$

By using letters to express the relationship among interest, principal, rate, and time, we have generalized the relationship so that any value can be substituted into the formula. Once, three values are substituted into the formula, we can find the value of the remaining variable.

Evaluating a Formula

EXAMPLE 1 Use the formula $I = PRT$ to find I if $P = \$7000$, $R = .09$, and $T = 2$.

SOLUTION

Substitute $\$7000$ for P, .09 for R, and 2 for T in the formula $I = PRT$. Remember that writing P, R, and T together as PRT indicates the product of the three letters.

$$I = PRT$$
$$I = \$7000(.09)(2)$$

Multiply on the right to get the solution.

$$I = \$1260$$

QUICK CHECK 1

Use $F = ma$ to find F if $m = 1700$ and $a = 9.8$.

Evaluating a Formula

EXAMPLE 2 Use $I = PRT$ to find P if $I = \$5760$, $R = .06$, and $T = 3$.

SOLUTION

Substitute the given numbers for the letters of the formula.

$$I = PRT$$
$$\$5760 = P(.06)(3)$$
$$5760 = .18P$$
$$\frac{5760}{.18} = \frac{.18P}{.18} \qquad \text{Divide both sides by .18.}$$
$$\$32{,}000 = P$$

QUICK CHECK 2

Use the formula $I = PRT$ to find I if $P = \$40{,}000$, $T = 1$, and $R = .0125$.

Evaluating a Formula   ▼**EXAMPLE 3**   Solve for rate (R) given $M = \$12{,}270$, $P = \$12{,}000$, and $T = .5$ in the equation $M = P(1 + RT)$.

SOLUTION

$$M = P(1 + RT)$$
$$\$12{,}270 = \$12{,}000(1 + R \cdot .5)$$
$$12{,}270 = 12{,}000 + 12{,}000 \cdot R \cdot .5 \qquad \text{Use the distributive property.}$$
$$12{,}270 = 12{,}000 + 6000 \cdot R$$
$$12{,}270 - \mathbf{12{,}000} = 12{,}000 + 6000 \cdot R - \mathbf{12{,}000} \qquad \text{Subtract 12,000 from each side.}$$
$$270 = 6000 \cdot R$$
$$\frac{270}{\mathbf{6000}} = \frac{6000 \cdot R}{\mathbf{6000}} \qquad \text{Divide by 6000.}$$
$$.045 = R$$

Rate is .045, or 4.5%.

QUICK CHECK 3

Solve for rate (R) if $M = \$8300$, $P = \$8000$, and $T = .5$ in the equation $M = P(1 + RT)$.

OBJECTIVE 2 Solve formulas for a specific variable. Sometimes, you may need to rearrange a formula to solve for a particular variable. For example, rearrange the formula $I = PRT$ to solve for the variable P as follows.

$$I = PRT$$
$$\frac{I}{RT} = \frac{PRT}{RT} \qquad \text{Divide both sides by } RT.$$
$$\frac{I}{RT} = P, \quad \text{or} \quad P = \frac{I}{RT}$$

Solving a Formula for a Specific Variable   ▼**EXAMPLE 4**   Solve for T in the formula $M = P(1 + RT)$. This formula gives the maturity value (M) of an initial amount of money (P) invested at a specific rate (R) for a certain period of time (T).

SOLUTION

Start by using the distributive property on the right side.

$$M = P(1 + RT)$$
$$M = P + PRT$$

Now subtract P from both sides.

$$M - P = P + PRT - P$$
$$M - P = PRT$$

Divide each side by PR.

$$\frac{M - P}{PR} = \frac{PRT}{PR}$$
$$\frac{M - P}{PR} = T, \quad \text{or} \quad T = \frac{M - P}{PR}$$

QUICK CHECK 4

Solve $S = (kT - 12)$ for T.

Solving a Formula for a Specific Variable

EXAMPLE 5

Solve for T in the formula $D = \dfrac{B}{MT}$.

SOLUTION

This formula gives the discount rate (D) of a note in terms of the face value (B), the time of a note (T), and the maturity value (M). Solve for T.

$$D = \frac{B}{MT}$$

$$DMT = \frac{B}{MT}MT \qquad \text{Multiply both sides by } MT.$$

$$DMT = B$$

$$\frac{DMT}{DM} = \frac{B}{DM} \qquad \text{Divide both sides by } DM.$$

$$T = \frac{B}{DM}$$

> **QUICK CHECK 5**
>
> Solve $T = \dfrac{R}{JK}$ for J.

OBJECTIVE 3 Use standard business formulas to solve word problems. In the following examples, application problems that use some common business formulas are solved.

Finding Gross Sales

EXAMPLE 6

Find the gross sales amount from selling 481 fishing lures at $2.65 each.

SOLUTION

The formula for gross sales is $G = NP$, where N is the number of items sold and P is the price per item. To find the gross sales from selling 481 fishing lures at $2.65 each, use the formula.

$$G = NP$$

$$G = 481(\$2.65)$$

$$G = \mathbf{\$1274.65}$$

The gross sales will be $1274.65.

> **QUICK CHECK 6**
>
> Find the gross revenue from selling 27 cases of wine at $156 each.

Finding Selling Price

EXAMPLE 7

A retailer purchased a pleasure boat for $2170. It then adds a markup of $650 before placing it on the lot to sell. Find the selling price.

SOLUTION

The selling price is found by adding the cost of the item and the markup.

$$S = C + M$$

The variable C is the cost and M is the markup, which is the amount added to the cost to cover expenses and profit. The selling price is found as shown.

$$S = \$2170 + \$650$$

$$S = \mathbf{\$2820}$$

The selling price is $2820.

> **QUICK CHECK 7**
>
> A discount Web retailer buys software for $26.92 each and marks them up by $8.07 each. Find the selling price.

OBJECTIVE 4 Evaluate formulas containing exponents. Exponents are used to show repeated multiplication of a quantity called the *base*. For example,

Exponent: the number of times the base appears as a factor

$$x^2 = x \cdot x$$

Base: the quantity being multiplied.

Similarly,

$$z^3 = z \cdot z \cdot z \quad \text{and} \quad 5^4 = 5 \cdot 5 \cdot 5 \cdot 5 = 625$$

Forecasting Monthly Sales **EXAMPLE 8** After significant research, Ben James believes that the dollar amount of Chevrolet vehicles that can be sold in one state can be found as using the following equation.

$$S = \$40 + 16.2 \times A^2$$

▼ **CASE IN POINT** Both advertising (A) and sales (S) are in millions of dollars. Estimate sales for July if advertising is $1.4 million.

SOLUTION

Substitute $1.4 into the equation for advertising and solve for S to find the forecast.

$$S = \$40 + 16.2 \times A^2 \qquad \text{Multiply.}$$
$$S = \$40 + 16.2 \times (\$1.4)^2$$
$$S = 40 + 16.2 \times 1.96 \qquad \text{Evaluate exponent first.}$$
$$S = 40 + 31.752$$
$$S = 71.752$$

Based on the model, July sales are forecast to be $71,752,000.

QUICK CHECK 8

Stress on a suspension cable on a bridge can be estimated using $S = 7.2(\text{weight})^2 + 3480$. Find the stress if the weight is 29 tons.

▼ **4.3 Exercises**   MyMathLab®

*The shaded sections below contain solutions to help you get a **QUICK START** on the various types of exercises.*

In the following exercises a formula is given, along with the values of all but one of the variables in the formula. Find the value of the variable that is not given. Round to the nearest hundredth, if applicable.

1. $I = PRT; P = \$4600, R = .085, T = 1\frac{1}{2}$ **$586.50**

2. $F = ma; m = 820, a = 12$ **9840**

3. $P = B \times R; B = \$168,000, R = .06$ _____

4. $B = \dfrac{P}{R}; P = \$1200, R = .08$ _____

5. $s = c + m; c = \$14, m = \$2.50$ _____

6. $m = s - c; s = \$24,200, c = \$2800$ _____

7. $P = 2L + 2W; P = 40, W = 6$ _____

8. $P = 2L + 2W; P = 340, L = 70$ _____

9. $P = \dfrac{I}{RT}; T = 3, I = 540, R = .08$ _____

10. $M = P(1 + RT); R = .15, T = 2, M = 481$ _____

11. $y = mx^2 + c; m = 3, x = 7, c = 4.2$ _____

12. $C = \$5 + \$.10N; N = 38$ _____

13. $M = P(1 + i)^n; P = \$640, i = .02, n = 8$ _____

14. $M = P(1 + i)^n; M = \$2400, i = .05, n = 4$ _____

15. $E = mc^2; m = 7.5, c = 1$ _____

16. $x = \dfrac{1}{2}at^2; t = 5, x = 150$ _____

17. $A = \frac{1}{2}(b + B)h; A = 105, b = 19, B = 11$ _____

18. $A = \frac{1}{2}(b + B)h; A = 70, b = 15, B = 20$ _____

19. $P = \frac{S}{1 + RT}; S = 24{,}600, R = .06, T = \frac{5}{12}$ _____

20. $P = \frac{S}{1 + RT}; S = 23{,}815, R = .09, T = \frac{11}{12}$ _____

Solve each formula for the indicated variable.

21. $A = LW$; for L

$A = LW$

$\dfrac{A}{W} = \dfrac{LW}{W}$

$L = \dfrac{A}{W}$

22. $d = rt$; for t

$d = rt$

$\dfrac{d}{r} = \dfrac{rt}{r}$

$t = \dfrac{d}{r}$

21. $L = \dfrac{A}{W}$ _____

22. $t = \dfrac{d}{r}$ _____

23. $PV = nRT$; for V

24. $I = PRT$; for R

23. _____

24. _____

25. $M = P(1 + i)^n$; for P

26. $R(1 - DT) = D$; for R

25. _____

26. _____

27. $P = \dfrac{A}{1 + i}$; for i

28. $M = P(1 + RT)$; for R

27. _____

28. _____

29. $P = M(1 - DT)$; for D

30. $P = \dfrac{M}{1 + RT}$; for R

29. _____

30. _____

◭ indicates an exercise that is related to the Case in Point feature.

31. $A = \frac{1}{2}(b + B)h$; for h **32.** $P = 2L + 2W$; for L **31.** _____

32. _____

Solve the following application problems.

33. CARNIVAL A carnival purchases 1800 stuffed animals to give to people who win at carnival games. Given a total cost of $4320, find the cost per stuffed animal.   **33.** $2.40

          y = cost per stuffed animal

    1800 · y = $4320

$$\frac{1800y}{1800} = \frac{4320}{1800}$$

       y = $2.40

34. WEB PAGES A retailer paid $1305 to a college student who built and added 15 pages to the firm's Web site. Find the cost per Web page.   **34.** $87

       c = cost per Web page

   15 · c = $1305

$$\frac{15c}{15} = \frac{1305}{15}$$

     c = $87

35. MUSICAL INSTRUMENTS The Guitar Shoppe bought 6 sets of bongo drums and 7 quality Alvarez guitars for $2445.80. The guitars cost $269 apiece. Find the cost for a set of bongo drums.   **35.** _____

36. REFRIGERATORS An appliance store bought 8 large refrigerators and 10 washer/dryer combination sets. The store's cost for a washer/dryer was $462 and the total paid for all of the appliances was $10,860. Find the cost of a refrigerator.   **36.** _____

37. CLOTHING STORE The weekly salary for each salesperson at a clothing store is found using the formula $S = \$280 + .05x$, where $x =$ employee's total sales for the week. Find the salary of two employees with the following weekly sales: **(a)** $2940 and **(b)** $4450.   **37.** _____

38. **MUSTANG**   Adam Nguyen needs $5000 for a down payment on a new Mustang. He has $4650 which he invests in an investment called a master limited partnership that pays 6% interest per year. Estimate the number of months he must wait to have the required down payment.

38. _____

39. **COMPUTER CHIPS**   A computer chip manufacturer had net sales of $230 million with returns equal to $\frac{1}{40}$ of gross sales. Find gross sales rounded to the nearest million given that net sales equals gross sales less returns.

39. _____

40. **BRIDAL SHOP**   One month, the Bridal Shop had net sales of $33,000 and return(s) of $\frac{1}{12}$ of gross sales. If net sales equal gross sales minus returns, find gross sales.

40. _____

41. **MOVIES**   The manager of one theatre marks up the cost of chocolate covered raisins by $\frac{3}{4}$ of the cost of the raisins. Find the cost to the nearest cent if the theatre sells a box of raisins for $4.00. (*Hint*: Selling price is cost plus markup.)

41. _____

42. **COLLEGE TEXTBOOKS**   One college bookstore chain marks up the books it sells by an average of 33%. Find the cost to the bookstore of a book they sell for $195. (Hint: Selling price is cost plus markup.)

42. _____

43. **PIZZA**   Last year, the expenses at Mack's Pizzeria were $\frac{5}{6}$ of the total revenue and the remainder was profit. The profit, or the total revenue less expenses, was $107,400. Find the total revenue.

43. _____

44. **GAMING**   Best Gameworks has expenses that run $\frac{15}{16}$ of revenue. One month's profit (the difference between revenue and expenses) was $18,000. Find the revenue.

44. _____

In Exercises 45–49, use the formula I = PRT, where I = interest in dollars, P = principal or loan amount, R = interest rate written as a decimal, and T = time in years.

45. **FINDING INTEREST**   Find the interest if principal of $5200 is invested at $7\frac{1}{2}\%$ (or .075) for one year.

45. _____

46. **LOAN TO AN UNCLE**   Ben Cross loaned $8000 to his uncle for 4 years and received $1920 in interest. Find the interest rate.

46. _____

47. **AUTO PARTS STARTUP**   Terry Twitty made a $22,000 loan so that Melissa Graves could start an auto parts business. The loan was for 2 years, and interest was $5720. Find the rate of interest.

47. _____

48. **FINDING TIME**   Fred Tausz loaned $39,000 to his sister. The loan was at 7% (or 0.07), with interest of $13,650. Find the time for the loan.

48. _____

49. **STUDENT LOAN**   Joan Summers borrowed $5850 (*P*) from her brother to help pay for her last year in college. They agreed to an interest rate (*R*) of 3% and a final interest amount (*I*) of $702. Find the time.

49. _____

In Exercises 50–52, use M = P(1 + RT) where M = maturity value, P = principal or loan amount, R = annual interest rate written as a decimal, and T = time in years.

50. **MATURITY VALUE**   Mary Scott invests $1000 in a bond fund that she hopes will yield 8% per year (or .08) for 5 years. What maturity value (*M*) will she have in her account at the end of 5 years?

50. _____

51. **SAVING**   John Wood had $4560 in his retirement account after 2 years. The account paid 7% (or .07) per year. How much did John initially deposit in his account?
$[M = P(1 + RT)]$

51. _____

52. **ANTIQUES** Jan Reus borrowed $12,500 from her uncle to help start an antique shop. She repaid $14,750 exactly 2 years later. Find the interest rate. $[M = P(1 + RT)]$

52.

Solve using the equation given. Note that M = maturity value, P = principal or loan amount, i = annual interest rate, and n is the number of years.

53. **LOAN AMOUNT** Bill Abel paid a maturity value of $5989.50 on a 3-year note with annual interest of 10% (or .10). Use $M = P(1 + i)^n$ to solve for the amount borrowed.

53. _____

54. **INHERITANCE** Maybelle Jackson inherited $8500 when her grandfather died. She placed the money in a dividend paying bond fund that pays 3.5% per year and plans to leave it there for 20 years until she retires. Use $M = P(1 + i)^n$ to solve for the maturity value. (Hint: Assume the price of the bond fund remains constant.)

54.

55. Write a step-by-step explanation of the procedure you would use to solve the equation $A = P + PRT$ for R. (See Objective 2.)

56. Formulas are used in business, physics, biology, chemistry, engineering, and many other places. Why are formulas so commonly used? (See Objective 1.)

QUICK CHECK ANSWERS

1. $F = 16,660$

2. $I = \$500$

3. $R = 7.5\%$

4. $T = \dfrac{(S + 12)}{k}$

5. $J = \dfrac{R}{KT}$

6. $4212

7. $34.99

4.4 Ratio and Proportion

OBJECTIVES

1 Define a ratio.
2 Set up a proportion.
3 Solve a proportion for unknown values.
4 Use proportions to solve problems.

OBJECTIVE 1 Define a ratio. A **ratio** is a quotient of two quantities that is used to *compare* the quantities. The ratio of the number a to the number b is written in any of the following ways.

$$a \text{ to } b, \qquad a{:}b, \qquad \frac{a}{b}$$

All are pronounced "a to b" or "a is to b." This last way of writing a ratio is most common in mathematics, while $a{:}b$ is perhaps more common in business.

Writing Ratios **EXAMPLE 1** Write a ratio in the form $\frac{a}{b}$ for each word phrase. Notice in each example that the number mentioned first is always the numerator.

SOLUTION

(a) The ratio of 5 hours to 3 hours is $\frac{5}{3}$.

(b) To find the ratio of 5 hours to 3 days, *first convert 3 days to hours*. Since there are 24 hours in 1 day, **3 days** $= 3 \cdot 24 =$ **72 hours**. Then the ratio of 5 hours to 3 days is the quotient of 5 and 72.

$$\frac{5}{72}$$

(c) The ratio of $700,000 in sales to $950,000 in sales is written this way.

$$\frac{\$700{,}000}{\$950{,}000}$$

Reduce to write this ratio in lowest terms.

$$\frac{\$700{,}000}{\$950{,}000} = \frac{14}{19}$$

QUICK CHECK 1

Write 40 sheep to 15 goats as a ratio.

Writing Ratios **EXAMPLE 2** Burger King sold the following items in a one-hour period last Friday afternoon.

70 bacon cheeseburgers
15 plain hamburgers
30 salad combos
45 chicken sandwiches
40 fish sandwiches

Write ratios for the following items sold:

(a) bacon cheeseburgers to fish sandwiches

(b) salad combos to chicken sandwiches

(c) plain hamburgers to salad combos

(d) fish sandwiches to total items sold

SOLUTION

(a) $\dfrac{\text{bacon cheeseburgers}}{\text{fish sandwiches}} = \dfrac{70}{40} = \dfrac{7}{4}$

(b) $\dfrac{\text{salad combos}}{\text{chicken sandwiches}} = \dfrac{30}{45} = \dfrac{2}{3}$

(c) $\dfrac{\text{plain hamburgers}}{\text{salad combos}} = \dfrac{15}{30} = \dfrac{1}{2}$

(d) $\dfrac{\text{fish sandwiches}}{\text{total items sold}} = \dfrac{40}{200} = \dfrac{1}{5}$

QUICK CHECK 2

Use the data from Example 2 to write a ratio for the sum of bacon cheeseburgers and plain hamburgers, to salad combos.

OBJECTIVE 2 Set up a proportion. A ratio is used to compare two numbers or amounts. A **proportion** says that two ratios are equal, as shown here.

$$\frac{3}{4} = \frac{15}{20}$$

A proportion can be simplified by multiplying both sides of the equation by the product of the two denominators.

$$\frac{a}{b} = \frac{c}{d}$$

$$\frac{a}{\cancel{b}} \cdot \cancel{b}d = \frac{c}{\cancel{d}} \cdot b\cancel{d} \qquad \textbf{Multiply both sides by the product of two denominators.}$$

$$ad = bc$$

Thus, $\frac{a}{b} = \frac{c}{d}$ only if the cross products $a \cdot d$ and $b \cdot c$ are equal to one another. This **method of cross products** can be used to determine if a proportion is true.

Method of Cross Products

The proportion

$$\frac{a}{b} = \frac{c}{d}$$

is true if the cross products $a \cdot d$ and $b \cdot c$ are equal (that is, if $ad = bc$).

Determining If a Proportion Is True

EXAMPLE 3 Decide whether the following proportions are true.

(a) $\dfrac{3}{5} = \dfrac{12}{20}$ **(b)** $\dfrac{2}{3} = \dfrac{9}{16}$

SOLUTION

(a) Find each cross product.

$$\frac{3}{5} = \frac{12}{20}$$

$$3 \times 20 \overset{?}{=} 5 \times 12$$

$$60 = 60$$

Since the cross products are equal, the proportion is true.

(b) Find the cross products.

$$\frac{2}{3} = \frac{9}{16}$$

$$2 \times 16 \overset{?}{=} 3 \times 9$$

$$32 \neq 27 \qquad \textbf{Not equal.}$$

This proportion is false, so $\dfrac{2}{3} \neq \dfrac{9}{16}$.

Quick TIP

The symbol $\neq$ means "not equal to."

QUICK CHECK 3

Decide whether the following proportion is true or false: $\dfrac{2}{9} = \dfrac{8}{18}$.

OBJECTIVE 3 Solve a proportion for unknown values. Four numbers and/or variables are used in a proportion. If any three of the values are known, the fourth can be found. The two methods to solve a proportion are to:

1. multiply both sides by the product of the two denominators or
2. use the method of cross products.

Solving a Proportion **EXAMPLE 4**

Find the value of the unknowns. Use the first method for **(a)** and the second method for **(b)**.

(a) $\dfrac{3}{5} = \dfrac{x}{40}$ (b) $\dfrac{3}{10} = \dfrac{5}{k}$

SOLUTION

(a) Solve for the unknown by multiplying both sides of the equation by the product of the denominators.

$$\frac{3}{5} = \frac{x}{40}$$

$$\frac{3}{5} \cdot (5 \cdot 40) = \frac{x}{40} \cdot (5 \cdot 40) \qquad \text{Multiply both sides by product of denominators.}$$

$$120 = 5x$$

$$\frac{120}{5} = \frac{5x}{5} \qquad \text{Divide both sides by 5.}$$

$$24 = x, \quad \textbf{or} \quad x = 24$$

(b) Solve for the unknown using the method of cross products.

$$\frac{3}{10} = \frac{5}{k}$$

$$3k = 50 \qquad \text{Use method of cross products.}$$

$$\frac{3k}{3} = \frac{50}{3}$$

$$k = \frac{50}{3} = 16\frac{2}{3}$$

QUICK CHECK 4
Find y in the following proportion: $\dfrac{7}{y} = \dfrac{84}{228}$.

Solving Proportions **EXAMPLE 5**

A food wholesaler charges a restaurant chain $83 for 3 crates of fresh produce. How much should it charge for 5 crates of produce?

SOLUTION

Let x be the cost of 5 crates of produce. Set up a proportion with one ratio the number of crates and the other ratio the costs. Use this pattern.

$$\frac{\text{Crates}}{\text{Crates}} = \frac{\text{Cost}}{\text{Cost}}$$

Now substitute the given information.

$$\frac{3}{5} = \frac{83}{x}$$

→ 3 crates cost $83
→ 5 crates cost $x

Use the cross-products to solve the proportion.

$$3x = 5(83)$$

$$3x = \$415$$

$$x = \$138.33 \qquad \text{(rounded to the nearest cent)}$$

The 5 crates cost $138.33.

QUICK CHECK 5

A fish wholesaler sells 40 pounds of fresh salmon for $232. Estimate the cost of 300 pounds of salmon.

OBJECTIVE 4 Use proportions to solve problems. Proportions are used in many practical applications, as shown in the next two examples.

Solving Applications — **EXAMPLE 6**

A firm in Hong Kong and one in Thailand agree to jointly develop an engine-control microchip to be sold to North American auto manufacturers. They agree to split the development costs in a ratio of 8:3 (Hong Kong firm to Thailand firm), resulting in a cost of $9,400,000 to the Hong Kong firm. Find the cost to the Thailand firm.

SOLUTION

Let x represent the cost to the Thailand firm, then

$$\frac{8}{3} = \frac{9,400,000}{x}$$

$$8x = 3 \cdot 9,400,000 \qquad \text{Cross multiply.}$$

$$8x = 28,200,000$$

$$x = \mathbf{3,525,000} \qquad \text{Divide by 8.}$$

The Thailand firm's share of the costs is $3,525,000.

QUICK CHECK 6

Two real estate developers agree to a project estimated to cost $17.6 million. They decide to split costs in a ratio of 7:4. Find the cost to each.

Solving Applications — **EXAMPLE 7**

James McIntosh wants to cut a tree down in his front yard, but he is worried about it falling into his garage. He needs to know the height of the tree. One morning, he notices that his own 6-foot body casts an 8-foot shadow at the same time that a typical tree casts a 34-foot shadow. Find the height of the tree.

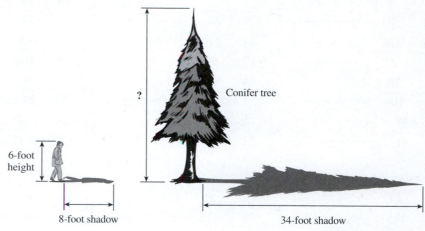

SOLUTION

Set up a proportion in which the height of the tree is given the variable name x.

$$\frac{6}{8} = \frac{x}{34}$$

$$6 \cdot 34 = 8 \cdot x \qquad \text{Cross multiply.}$$

$$\frac{204}{8} = \frac{\cancel{8} \cdot x}{\cancel{8}} \qquad \text{Divide by 8.}$$

$$x = 25.5 \text{ feet}$$

The height of the tree is 25.5 feet.

QUICK CHECK 7

Late afternoon one day, a 20-foot flagpole casts a 32-foot shadow. Find the shadow cast by a boy 4 feet tall.

▼ 4.4 Exercises

MyMathLab®

The shaded sections below contain solutions to help you get a **QUICK START** on the various types of exercises.

Write the following ratios. Write each ratio in lowest terms.

1. 18 kilometers to 64 kilometers $\dfrac{9}{32}$

2. 18 defects out of 580 items $\dfrac{9}{290}$

3. 216 students to 8 faculty _____

4. $80 in returns to $8360 in sales _____

5. 8 men to 6 women _____

6. 12 feet to 1 inch _____

7. 30 kilometers (30,000 meters) to 8 meters _____

8. 30 inches to 5 yards _____

9. 90 dollars to 40 cents _____

10. 148 minutes to 4 hours _____

11. 4 dollars to 10 quarters _____

12. 35 dimes to 6 dollars _____

13. 20 hours to 5 days _____

14. 6 days to 9 hours _____

15. $.80 to $3 _____

16. $1.20 to $.75 _____

17. $3.24 to $.72 _____

18. $3.57 to $.42 _____

Decide whether the following proportions are true or false.

19. $\dfrac{3}{5} = \dfrac{21}{35}$ T _____

20. $\dfrac{6}{13} = \dfrac{30}{65}$ T _____

21. $\dfrac{9}{7} = \dfrac{720}{480}$ _____

22. $\dfrac{54}{14} = \dfrac{270}{70}$ _____

23. $\dfrac{69}{320} = \dfrac{7}{102}$ _____

24. $\dfrac{17}{19} = \dfrac{72}{84}$ _____

25. $\dfrac{19}{32} = \dfrac{33}{77}$ _____

26. $\dfrac{19}{30} = \dfrac{57}{90}$ _____

27. $\dfrac{110}{18} = \dfrac{160}{27}$ _____

28. $\dfrac{46}{17} = \dfrac{212}{95}$ _____

29. $\dfrac{32}{75} = \dfrac{61}{108}$ _____

30. $\dfrac{28}{75} = \dfrac{224}{600}$ _____

31. $\dfrac{7.6}{10} = \dfrac{76}{100}$ _____

32. $\dfrac{95}{64} = \dfrac{320}{217}$ _____

33. $\dfrac{2\frac{1}{4}}{5} = \dfrac{9}{20}$ _____

34. $\dfrac{\frac{3}{4}}{80} = \dfrac{\frac{9}{8}}{120}$ _____

35. $\dfrac{4\frac{1}{5}}{6\frac{1}{8}} = \dfrac{27}{41}$ _____

36. $\dfrac{1\frac{1}{2}}{12} = \dfrac{5\frac{1}{4}}{42}$ _____

37. $\dfrac{8.15}{2.03} = \dfrac{61.125}{15.225}$ _____

38. $\dfrac{423.88}{17.119} = \dfrac{330.6264}{13.35282}$ _____

Solve the following proportions.

39. $\dfrac{x}{15} = \dfrac{49}{105}$ 7 _____

40. $\dfrac{y}{35} = \dfrac{27}{315}$ 3 _____

41. $\dfrac{6}{9} = \dfrac{r}{108}$ _____

42. $\dfrac{16}{41} = \dfrac{112}{I}$ _____

43. $\dfrac{63}{s} = \dfrac{3}{5}$ _____

44. $\dfrac{260}{390} = \dfrac{x}{3}$ _____

45. $\dfrac{1}{2} = \dfrac{r}{7}$ _____

46. $\dfrac{2}{3} = \dfrac{5}{s}$ _____

47. $\dfrac{\frac{3}{4}}{6} = \dfrac{3}{x}$ _____

48. $\dfrac{3}{x} = \dfrac{11}{9}$ _____

49. $\dfrac{12}{P} = \dfrac{23.571}{15.714}$ _____

50. $\dfrac{86.112}{57.408} = \dfrac{k}{15}$ _____

🔺 indicates an exercise that is related to the Case in Point feature.

51. Explain the difference between ratio and proportion. (See Objective 2.)

52. Explain cross products using the rules of algebra. (See Objective 2.)

Solve the following application problems.

53. **TICKET SALES**   One Ticketmaster outlet sold 350 rock-concert tickets in 2 days. At that rate, find the number of tickets it can expect to sell in 9 days.

$$\frac{350}{2} = \frac{x}{9}$$

$$350 \cdot 9 = 2x$$

$$2x = 3150$$

$$x = 1575 \text{ tickets}$$

53. 1575 tickets

54. **BLOOD CELLS**   A 170-pound person has about 30 trillion blood cells. Estimate the number of blood cells in a 140-pound person to the nearest tenth of a trillion.

$$\frac{170}{30} \text{ trillion} = \frac{140}{x} \text{ trillion}$$

$$170x = 30 \cdot 140$$

$$170x = 4200$$

$$x = 24.7 \text{ trillion} \quad (\text{rounded})$$

54. 24.7 trillion

55. **REAL ESTATE DEVELOPMENT**   Mike George paid $215,000 for a 5-unit apartment house. Find the cost for a 12-unit apartment house.

55. _____

56. **TIGER FOOD**   A 450-pound circus tiger eats 15 pounds of meat per day. How many pounds of meat would you expect a 360-pound tiger to eat per day?

56. _____

57. **SWIMMING**   Penny Thorpe can swim 400 meters in a nearby lake in 7.1 minutes. At this same rate, estimate the amount of time it will take her to swim one mile (1609 meters). Round to the nearest tenth of a minute.

57. _____

58. **BISCUITS**   A biscuit recipe that feeds 7 requires 2 cups of flour. How much flour is needed for enough biscuits to feed a church group of 125? Round to the nearest whole number.

58. _____

59. GLOBAL WARMING The concentration of carbon dioxide in the atmosphere has increased from 315 parts per million to 395 parts per million in the past 50 years. During the same period of time, the global average temperature increased by 1.2°F. Estimate the amount of further increase in global average temperature to the nearest tenth of a degree, if the concentration of carbon dioxide (CO_2) in the atmosphere increases from 395 parts per million up to 550 parts per million, as predicted by some.

59. _____

60. SEA LEVELS Many scientists believe that global warming contributes to the melting of ice in glaciers, on Greenland, and at both poles and thus contributes to rising sea levels. Assume sea levels rise at a constant rate of 1.1 inches per decade (10 years) and estimate the rise in sea level between 2015 and 2100.

60. _____

61. MAP READING The distance between two cities on a road map is 2 inches. Actually, the cities are 120 miles apart. The distance between two other cities is 17 inches. How far apart are these cities?

61. _____

62. WOMAN'S CLOTHING SHOP Martha Vinn opened a woman's clothing shop and had sales of $3720 during the first 3 weeks. At that rate, estimate sales for the first 4 weeks.

62. _____

63. SALES OF HEALTH FOOD Natural Harvest had sales of $274,312 for the first 20 weeks of the year. Estimate sales for the entire 52-week year.

63. _____

64. PARTNERSHIP PROFITS Chester and Gaines have a partnership agreement that calls for profits to be paid in the ratio of 2:5, respectively. Find the amount that goes to Chester if Gaines receives $45,000.

64. _____

65. OIL PROFITS The two partners in Alamo Energy agreed to split profits in a ratio of 3:8. If the first partner received $48,000 in profits one year, find the profit earned by the second partner.

65. _____

66. ROCK CONCERT   A blues group held a concert in a city of 650,000 people and 8200 people attended. At the same rate, find the number they can expect to attend in a city with 1,000,000 people.

66. _____

67. SONGBIRD MIGRATION   Small songbirds in one area migrate at about 20 miles per hour whereas eider ducks migrate at 35 miles per hour. How far would the eider ducks migrate in the same amount of time it would take songbirds to migrate 200 miles?

67. _____

68. ISLAND AREA   Indonesia has an area of 741,101 square miles and is made up of 13,677 islands. Assume the United States, with an area of 3,618,770 square miles, were similarly broken up into islands. How many islands would there be (to the nearest whole number)?

68. _____

69. ICEBERG VOLUME   Seven-eighths of an iceberg is below the water since icebergs are made up of freshwater, which is not as dense as seawater. Find the amount of an iceberg that is under water if the amount above water has a volume of 500,000 cubic meters. (*Hint:* $1 - \frac{7}{8} = \frac{1}{8}$ above water.)

69. _____

70. AUTO PRODUCTION   An auto plant produces 3 red sports models for every 7 blue family models. Find the number of red sports models produced if the plant produces 868 blue family models.

70. _____

71. JAPANESE YEN   Benjamin Lopez was in Japan for 2 months on a business trip. Find the number of U.S. dollars he will receive for 20,355 Japanese yen if $1 U.S. can be exchanged for 95 yen. Round to the nearest cent.

71. _____

72. WORKING IN CHINA   Gina Harden was offered a job as a teacher at an elite private high school in Beijing at an annual salary of 471,200 yuan. Find the salary in U.S. dollars if 6.70 yuan can be exchanged for $1 U.S. Round to the nearest cent.

72. _____

▼ Chapter 4   Quick Review

Chapter Terms *Review the following terms to test your understanding of the chapter. For each term you do not know, refer to the page number found next to that term.*

addition rule [**p. 124**]

cross product [**p. 151**]

distributive property [**p. 128**]

equation [**p. 124**]

left side [**p. 124**]

like terms [**p. 127**]

method of cross product [**p. 151**]

multiplication rule [**p. 124**]

proportion [**p. 151**]

ratio [**p. 150**]

reciprocal [**p. 126**]

right side [**p. 124**]

solution [**p. 124**]

substitute [**p. 124**]

term [**p. 124**]

unlike terms [**p. 127**]

variable [**p. 124**]

CONCEPTS

EXAMPLES

4.1 Use the addition rule to solve basic equations.

Add or subtract the same number from both sides of the equation.

Solve $x - 17.5 = 50$.

$$x - 17.5 = 50$$
$$x - 17.5 + 17.5 = 50 + 17.5 \quad \textbf{Add 17.5}$$
$$x = 67.5$$

4.1 Use the multiplication rule to solve basic equations.

Multiply or divide both sides of the equation by the same number.

Solve $6x = 72$.

$$6x = 72$$
$$\frac{6x}{6} = \frac{72}{6} \quad \textbf{Divide by 6}$$
$$x = 12$$

4.1 Solve more complicated equations.

Use the preceding addition and multiplication rules. Move all terms with only numbers to one side of the equation and all terms with variables to the other side.

Solve $10y = 8y + 42$.

$$10y = 8y + 42$$
$$10y - 8y = 8y + 42 - 8y \quad \textbf{Subtract 8y}$$
$$2y = 42$$
$$\frac{2y}{2} = \frac{42}{2} \quad \textbf{Divide by 2}$$
$$y = 21$$

4.1 Solve equations with parentheses.

First use the distributive property to remove the parentheses; then solve.

Solve $15(p - 1) = 3p + 2$.

$$15(p - 1) = 3p + 2$$
$$15p - 15 = 3p + 2 \quad \textbf{By distributive property}$$
$$15p - 15 - 3p = 3p + 2 - 3p \quad \textbf{Subtract 3p}$$
$$12p - 15 = 2$$
$$12p - 15 + 15 = 2 + 15 \quad \textbf{add 15}$$
$$12p = 17$$
$$\frac{\cancel{12}p}{\cancel{12}} = \frac{17}{12} \quad \textbf{Divide by 12}$$
$$p = 1\frac{5}{12}$$

4.2 Translate phrases into expressions.

7 plus a number

sum of a number and 12

a number minus $\frac{1}{2}$

product of 2 and a number

a number multiplied by 19

a number divided by .68

8 times the sum of a number and 1

Any letter can be used as a variable.

$$7 + x$$
$$y + 12$$
$$z - \frac{1}{2}$$
$$2A$$
$$19t$$
$$\frac{T}{.68}$$
$$8(P + 1)$$

CONCEPTS	EXAMPLES

4.2 Solve a basic application problem.

Read problem carefully. Define variables.
Write an equation and solve for the unknown.
Check to make sure the answer is reasonable.

The sum of two consecutive odd numbers is 96. Find both numbers.
Let x be the smaller number. Then $(x + 2)$ is the larger number.

$$x + (x + 2) = 96$$
$$2x + 2 = 96$$
$$2x = 94$$
$$x = 47 \quad \text{and} \quad (x + 2) = 49$$

4.3 Evaluate a formula given values.

Substitute known values into the formula and solve for the unknown.

Use $I = PRT$ to find I when $P = \$10,000$, $R = 4.5\%$, and $T = 1$.

$$I = PRT$$
$$I = \$10,000 \cdot .045 \cdot 1$$
$$I = \$450$$

4.3 Solve a formula for a variable.

Isolate the variable of interest on one side of the equation.

Solve $I = PRT$ for P.

$$I = PRT$$
$$\frac{I}{RT} = \frac{P\cancel{RT}}{\cancel{RT}}$$
$$\frac{I}{RT} = P, \quad \text{or} \quad P = \frac{I}{RT}$$

4.3 Evaluate formulas with exponents.

Substitute known values into the formula and solve for the unknown.

Use $M = P(1 + i)^n$ with $P = \$5000$, $i = 5\%$, and $n = 3$ to find M.

$$M = P(1 + i)^n$$
$$M = \$5000\,(1 + .05)^3$$
$$M = 5000\,(1.05)^3$$
$$M = 5000 \cdot 1.157625$$
$$M = \$5788.13 \quad \text{(rounded)}$$

4.4 Determine if a proportion is true.

Check to see that cross products are equal to one another.

Is $\dfrac{4}{5} = \dfrac{28}{35}$ true?

$$4 \cdot 35 \overset{?}{=} 5 \cdot 28 \quad \textbf{Use cross products}$$
$$140 = 140$$

The proportion is true.

4.4 Solve a proportion for an unknown.

Use the method of cross products and solve the resulting equation.

Find x: $\dfrac{35}{17} = \dfrac{x}{153}$.

$$35 \cdot 153 = 17x \quad \textbf{Use cross products}$$
$$5355 = 17x$$
$$\frac{5355}{17} = \frac{\cancel{17}x}{\cancel{17}}$$
$$x = 315$$

4.4 Use a proportion to solve a problem.

1. Define the unknown variable.
2. Set up the proportion.
3. Use the method of cross products.
4. Solve the equation.

A hiker walked 5.8 miles in 2 hours. At this rate, estimate the number of hours needed to hike 10 miles.

Let x = number of hours needed.

$$\frac{5.8 \text{ miles}}{2 \text{ hours}} = \frac{10 \text{ miles}}{x \text{ hours}}$$
$$5.8x = 2 \cdot 10 \quad \textbf{Use cross products}$$
$$5.8x = 20$$
$$\frac{\cancel{5.8}x}{\cancel{5.8}} = \frac{20}{5.8}$$
$$x = \textbf{3.4 hours} \quad \text{(rounded)}$$

Case Study

FORECASTING SALES AT ALCORN'S BOUTIQUE

Jane Alcorn had sold items on eBay for several years but felt it was time to open a retail store. After thinking about the options and competition, she decided to open a shop specializing in women's clothing. Sales were slow for her first few months and she began to wonder how much she should be spending on advertising. So, she decided to keep track of the monthly amount spent on advertising and the monthly sales as shown.

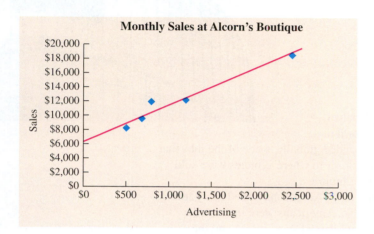

Jane's son Benton used statistics to help find the equation that was a best fit for the data. The equation is shown as the straight line in the graph. He told his mother it might not help much since it did not take into account factors such as seasonality or competition. And of course, Alcorn still had to decide where to advertise and exactly what the advertisements should look like. But she thought the equation might give her some idea of how much she should spend on advertising each month.

1. Estimate sales for advertising of $800 and $2000 if Sales = $6500 + $4.95 · Advertising.

   1. _____

2. Ah, Alcorn thought, this is easy. If you increase advertising from $800 up to $2000, then sales go up from $10,500 to $16,500. So an increase in advertising expenses of $1200 results in an increase in sales of $6000. Her gross profit margin on the fashion goods she carried in her tiny boutique was 50%. Find the increased gross profit by multiplying the 50% by the increase in sales.

   2. _____

3. Therefore, an increase in advertising of $1200 results in $3000 more gross profit. Given this information, Alcorn's first thought was to borrow $5000 from a bank and advertise a lot. Then she began to wonder. What suggestions do you have for her? Should she borrow $5000 and advertise? Why or why not (based on your intuition)?

   3. _____

INVESTIGATE

List all of the factors you can think of that can influence sales at a small, local store. You may wish to talk to the manager or owner of store and compare to your list.

▼ Case in Point Summary Exercise

GENERAL MOTORS

www.GM.com

Facts:

- 1908: Founded
- 1982: Built huge factory in Spain
- 2009: Files for bankruptcy
- 2010: Emerges from bankruptcy
- 2013: Over 200,000 employees

In some respects, General Motors (GM) *is* the story of globalization. It was one of the most successful companies in the world in the 1960s under the gifted manager Alfred Sloan. As it expanded globally, some of the jobs that had gone to Americans were moved overseas, partly to be closer to where vehicles were sold but also to cut costs. Labor costs were much lower in other countries.

Gasoline prices increased sharply during the 1970s and many Americans turned away from GM products and bought cars from Toyota, Honda, or Nissan. Americans were interested in the smaller, high-quality cars built by the Japanese. The weakened state of GM and the financial crisis of 2008–2010 forced the company to file for bankruptcy in 2009 when the U.S. government stepped in to help. But the company has since recovered.

Ben James received a bachelor's degree in statistics and a master's degree in business administration. He has worked at GM for several years. Among other things, he studies data such as that shown in the following two figures and develops equations to forecast demand.

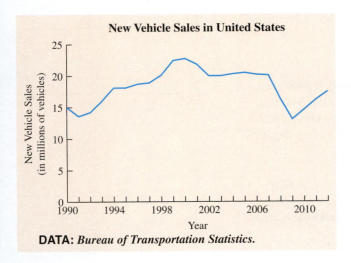

DATA: *Bureau of Transportation Statistics.*

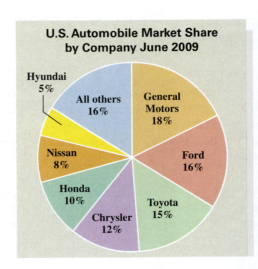

1. What can you learn from the two figures?

2. Many factors are involved in making a forecast. To illustrate, use the following equation to make a monthly forecast of car sales (in thousands) in one area given Advertising = \$6.2 (millions), Economic Growth = 2.8% (.028), and Level of Competition = .6. (See Section 4.2, Examples 1–8.)

   $\text{Sales} = 34.8 + 5.3 \cdot \text{Advertising} + 485 \cdot \text{Economic Growth} - 34.2 \cdot \text{Level of Competition}$

2. _____

3. GM has responded to increasing competition, and rapid economic growth in China by building and selling cars in China. About 1 out of every 8 vehicles sold in China is built by GM. Forecast monthly GM sales in China using the following equation (in thousands) when Advertising = $5.3 (millions), Economic Growth = 6.5%, and Level of Competition = .7. (See Section 4.3, Examples 1–8.)

3. _____

Sales = $50.9 + 9.6 \cdot$ Advertising $+ 720 \cdot$ Economic Growth $- 28.7 \cdot$ Level of Competition

4. In one European country, the sales of GM products increased from 23,850 to 36,400 in the third year that GM was in that market. Use a proportion to estimate the number of sales in the third year in a neighboring country with a very similar economy, if year two sales were 14,910. (See Section 4.4, Examples 5–7.)

4. _____

Discussion Question: *Many factors other than those listed here affect sales of new automobiles. Think about your own family or a family you know and list things that influence the purchase of an automobile, new or used.*

▼ **Chapter 4**   Test

To help you review, the numbers in brackets show the section in which the topic was discussed.

Solve each equation for the unknown.   **[4.1]**

1. $x + 45 = 96$ _____

2. $r - 36 = 14.7$ _____

3. $8t + 45 = 175.4$ _____

4. $4x - 6 = 15$ _____

5. $\dfrac{s}{6} = 43$ _____

6. $\dfrac{5z}{8} = 85$ _____

7. $\dfrac{m}{4} - 5 = 9$ _____

8. $5(x - 3) = 3(x + 4)$ _____

9. $6y = 2y + 28$ _____

10. $3r - 7 = 2(4 - 3r)$ _____

11. $.15(2x - 3) = 5.85$ _____

12. $.6(y - 3) = .1y$ _____

In Exercises 13–22, a formula is given, along with the values of all but one of the variables in the formula. Find the value of the variable that is not given.   **[4.3]**

13. $I = PRT; P = 2800, R = .09, T = 2$ _____

14. $S = C + M; C = 275, M = 49$ _____

15. $G = NP; N = 840, P = 3.79$ _____

16. $M = P(1 + RT); P = 420, R = .07, T = 2\dfrac{1}{2}$ _____

17. $R = \dfrac{D}{1 - DT}; D = .04, T = 5$ _____

18. $A = \dfrac{S}{1 + RT}; S = 12{,}600, R = .12, T = \dfrac{5}{12}$ _____

19. $T = \dfrac{D}{S}; T = 100, S = 2$ _____

20. $\dfrac{I}{PR} = T; P = 1000, R = .05, T = 1\dfrac{1}{2}$ _____

21. $d = rt; r = .07, t = 12$ _____

22. $I = PRT; P = 500, R = .08, T = 3$ _____

In Exercises 23–28, solve for the indicated variables. **[4.3]**

23. $A = LW$; for W _____

24. $d = rt$; for r _____

25. $I = PRT$; for T _____

26. $P = 1 + RT$; for R _____

27. $A = P + PRT$; for T _____

28. $R(1 - DT) = D$; for R _____

In Exercises 29–34, write the ratio in lowest terms. **[4.4]**

29. 250 pesos to 1250 pesos _____

30. 45 women to 110 men _____

31. \$1.20 to 75¢ _____

32. 20 hours to 5 days _____

33. 35 dimes to 6 dollars _____

34. 30 inches to five yards _____

In Exercises 35–40, decide whether the proportions are true or false. **[4.4]**

35. $\dfrac{2}{3} = \dfrac{42}{63}$ _____

36. $\dfrac{6}{9} = \dfrac{36}{52}$ _____

37. $\dfrac{18}{20} = \dfrac{56}{60}$ _____

38. $\dfrac{12}{18} = \dfrac{8}{12}$ _____

39. $\dfrac{420}{600} = \dfrac{14}{20}$ _____

40. $\dfrac{7.6}{10} = \dfrac{76}{100}$ _____

In Exercises 41–48, solve the proportions for the unknown. **[4.4]**

41. $\dfrac{y}{35} = \dfrac{25}{5}$ _____

42. $\dfrac{15}{s} = \dfrac{45}{117}$ _____

43. $\dfrac{a}{25} = \dfrac{4}{20}$ _____

44. $\dfrac{6}{x} = \dfrac{4}{18}$ _____

45. $\dfrac{z}{20} = \dfrac{80}{200}$ _____

46. $\dfrac{25}{100} = \dfrac{8}{m}$ _____

47. $\dfrac{1}{2} = \dfrac{r}{7}$ _____

48. $\dfrac{2}{3} = \dfrac{5}{s}$ _____

Solve the following application problems. **[4.2–4.4]**

49. The sum of an unknown and eight is twenty. Find the unknown.

49. _____

50. The sum of four plus an unknown equals fifty-one. Find the unknown.

50. _____

51. An unknown times thirty equals one thousand eight hundred. Find the unknown.

51. _____

52. Twenty-four equals three times an unknown. Find the unknown.

52. _____

53. Three times an unknown plus five is equal to fifty. Find the unknown.

53. _____

54. Four plus seven times an unknown is eighteen. Find the unknown.

54. _____

55. The sum of two consecutive whole numbers is equal to ninety-one. Find the numbers.

55. _____

56. The sum of two consecutive odd whole numbers is equal to two hundred forty. Find both numbers.

56. _____

57. Tom throws some coins onto a table. His twin brother Joe throws coins worth twice as much onto the table. The total value of the coins on the table is $2.61. How much money did Joe place on the table?

57. _____

58. A business math class has 47 students, with 9 more women than men. Find the number of men and women in the class.

58. _____

59. Cajun Boatin' Inc. bought 5 small boats and 3 skiffs for $14,878. A small boat costs $1742. Find the cost of a skiff.

59. _____

60. Mike Anderson bought a 4-unit apartment house for $172,000. Use a proportion to find the cost of a 10-unit apartment house.

60. _____

61. The tax on a $40 item is $3. Find the tax on a $160 item.

61. _____

62. Sam's phones bought 17 smart phones for $1942.25. Find the cost of one phone.

62. _____

63. The bookstore at Hudson Community College has a markup that is $\frac{1}{4}$ its cost on a book. Find the cost to the bookstore of a novel selling for \$25.

63. _____

64. An unknown principal (P) loaned out at 8% for $1\frac{3}{4}$ years yields a maturity value (M) of \$1368. Use $M = P(1 + RT)$ to find the principal.

64. _____

65. Explain why all terms with a variable should be placed on one side of the equation, and all terms without a variable should be placed on the other side, when solving an equation.   **[4.1]**

66. In your own words, explain the terms *formula*, *ratio*, and *proportion*.   **[4.3–4.4]**

▼ Chapters 1–4   Cumulative Review

CHAPTERS 1–4

To help you review, the numbers in brackets show the section in which the topic was introduced.

Round each of the following numbers as indicated.   **[1.1, 1.3]**

1. 65,462 to the nearest hundred

2. 4,732,489 to the nearest thousand

3. 78.35 to the nearest tenth

4. 328.2849 to the nearest hundredth

1. _____

2. _____

3. _____

4. _____

Solve the following problems.   **[1.1–1.5]**

5.
$$\begin{array}{r} 351 \\ 763 \\ 2478 \\ +\ \ 17 \\ \hline \end{array}$$

6.
$$\begin{array}{r} 45{,}867 \\ -\ 37{,}985 \\ \hline \end{array}$$

7.
$$\begin{array}{r} 634 \\ \times\ \ \ 38 \\ \hline \end{array}$$

8.
$$\begin{array}{r} 2450 \\ \times\ \ 320 \\ \hline \end{array}$$

9. $6290 \div 74 =$ ____

10. $22{,}899 \div 102 =$ _____

11. $.46 + 9.2 + 8 + 17.514 =$ _____

12.
$$\begin{array}{r} 45.36 \\ -\ 23.7 \\ \hline \end{array}$$

13.
$$\begin{array}{r} 29.8 \\ \times\ \ .41 \\ \hline \end{array}$$

14.
$21.8\overline{)396.76}$

Solve the following application problems.

15. Felix Schmid decides to establish a budget. He will spend $700 for rent, $325 for food, $420 for child care, $182 for transportation, $300 for other expenses, and he will put the remainder in savings. If his monthly take-home pay is $2025, find his savings.   **[1.1]**

15. _____

16. Clancy Strock wrote a feature article called "I know … I was there" for each issue of *Reminisce* magazine. He has written an article for each monthly issue of the magazine for 15 years. How many of these monthly articles has he written?   **[1.1]**

16. _____

17. Software Depot had a bank balance of $29,742.18 at the beginning of April. During the month, the firm made deposits of $14,096.18 and $6529.42. A total of $18,709.51 in checks was paid by the bank during the month. Find the firm's checking account balance at the end of April.   **[1.4]**

17. _____

18. Cara Groff pays $128.11 each month to the Bank of Brazil. How many months will it take her to pay off $4099.52?   **[1.5]**

18. _____

Solve the following problems.   **[2.1–2.4]**

19. Write $\dfrac{48}{54}$ in lowest terms. _____

20. Write $8\frac{1}{8}$ as an improper fraction. _____

21. Write $\dfrac{107}{15}$ as a mixed number. _____

22. $1\dfrac{2}{3} + 2\dfrac{3}{4} =$ _____

23. $5\dfrac{7}{8} + 7\dfrac{2}{3} =$ _____

24. $6\dfrac{1}{3} - 4\dfrac{7}{12} =$ _____

25. $8\frac{1}{2} \times \frac{9}{17} \times \frac{2}{3} = $ _____

26. $3\frac{3}{4} \div \frac{27}{16} = $ _____

Solve the following application problems.

27. The size of a prison cell at Alcatraz Prison in the San Francisco Bay is 5 feet by 9 feet. The average size of a shark cage is 5 feet by $6\frac{1}{2}$ feet. How many more square feet are there in the prison cell than in the shark cage?

27. _____

28. To prepare for the state real estate exam, Mia Dawson studied $5\frac{1}{2}$ hours on the first day, $6\frac{1}{4}$ hours on the second day, $3\frac{3}{4}$ hours on the third day, and 7 hours on the fourth day. How many hours did she study altogether?   **[2.3]**

28. _____

29. The storage area at American River Raft Rental has four sides and is enclosed with $527\frac{1}{24}$ feet of security fencing around it. If three sides of the yard measure $107\frac{2}{3}$ feet, $150\frac{3}{4}$ feet, and $138\frac{5}{8}$ feet, find the length of the fourth side.   **[2.3]**

29. _____

30. Play-It-Now Sports Center has decided to divide $\frac{2}{3}$ of the company's profit-sharing funds evenly among the eight store managers. What fraction of the total amount will each receive?   **[2.4]**

30. _____

Solve the following problems.   **[2.5]**

31. Change .65 to a fraction.

31. _____

32. Change $\frac{2}{3}$ to a decimal. Round to the nearest thousandth.

32. _____

Solve the following problems.   **[3.1–3.4]**

33. Change $\frac{7}{8}$ to a percent. _____

34. Change .25% to a decimal. _____

35. Find 35% of 6200 home loans. _____

36. Find 134% of $80. _____

37. 275 sales is what percent of 1100 sales? _____

38. 375 patients is what percent of 250 patients? _____

Solve the following application problems.

39. Currently there are 38,990 movie screens in the United States. It is expected that only 400 screens will be added in the next five years. Find the percent to be added.

39. _____

40. A Bose Home Theater System normally priced at $2499.99 is on sale for 15% off. Find the amount of discount and the sales price. Round to the nearest cent.   [3.2]

40. _____

41. Bookstore sales of the *Physicians' Desk Reference*, which contains prescription drug information, rose 13.7% this year. If sales this year were 111,150 copies, find last year's sales. Round to the nearest whole number.   [3.5]

41. _____

42. After deducting 11.8% of total sales as her commission, George-Ann Hornor, a salesperson for Marx Toy Company, deposited $35,138.88 to the company account. Find the total amount of her sales.   [3.5]

42. _____

43. The number of Facebook users increased by 225 times in one year. Find the percent increase.   [3.1]

43. _____

44. The value of a stock used to be 6 times what it is worth today. The value today is what percent of the past value? Round to the nearest tenth of a percent. Show your work, explaining how you arrived at your answer.   [3.1]

44. _____

WHERE'S THE BEEF?   *The United States exported 2.3 billion pounds of beef. Use the circle graph below to solve Exercises 45–48.*   [3.2]

Numbers in the News

"Meating" Demand
Where the 2.3 billion pounds of beef exported from the United States went.

Mexico 23%
South Korea 15%
Canada 10%
Others 7%
Japan 45%

DATA: USDA Economic Research Service, U.S. Department of Agriculture.

45. (a) What percent of the exported beef was shipped to Japan, Mexico, and South Korea combined? **(b)** Find the total number of pounds exported to these three countries.

(a) _____

(b) _____

46. (a) What percent of the exported beef was shipped to countries other than Japan, Mexico, and South Korea combined? **(b)** Find the total number of pounds exported to these three countries.

(a) _____

(b) _____

47. How much more beef was exported to Japan than to South Korea?

47. _____

48. How much more beef was exported to Mexico than to Canada?

48. _____

Solve each equation for the unknown. **[4.1]**

49. $9r - 23 = 31$ _____

50. $\dfrac{3}{4}t = 120$ _____

51. $5y - 10 = 26$ _____

52. $20 + 5x = 83 - x$ _____

Find the value of the variable that is not given. **[4.3]**

53. $I = PRT; P = \$45,000, R = .015,$ $T = .5$ _____

54. $d = rt; r = 378, t = 8.5$ _____

55. $A = P + PRT; A = 1368, P = 1200,$ $T = 2$ _____

56. $M = P(1 + i)^n; n = 6, i = 0.02,$ $M = \$42,231.09$ _____

Solve the equation for the variable indicated. **[4.3]**

57. Solve $I = PRT$ for T. _____

58. Solve $PV = nRT$ for P. _____

59. Solve $M = P(1 + i)^n$ for P. _____

60. $A = \dfrac{S}{1 + RT}$ for R. _____

Write the ratio in lowest terms. **[4.4]**

61. 500 euros to 725 dollars _____

62. 24 ounces to 15 gallons _____

63. 14 lockers to 40 minutes _____

64. 630 apples to 168 cans _____

Solve the following application problems.

65. The sum of an unknown and 47 is 93. Find the unknown. **[4.2]**

65. _____

66. The sum of two consecutive odd numbers is 228. Find the numbers. **[4.2]**

66. _____

67. A shoe retailer marks up the price of running shoes manufactured in China by 68%. Much of the markup goes to pay the costs of the retailer. Find the cost to the retailer if the selling price is $89.

67. _____

68. Forty-seven students signed up for a two-week travel/study trip to Greece. There were 9 more women than men. Find the number of men and women. **[4.2]**

68. _____

69. The cost of replacing a roof on a 1450 square foot house is $6600. Find the cost to replace the roof on a 2400 square foot house. Round to the nearest dollar. **[4.4]**

69. _____

70. A 32 unit apartment complex generates total monthly rents of $21,920. Assuming comparable rents, estimate the total monthly rent generated by a 70 unit complex. **[4.4]**

70. _____

5 Bank Services

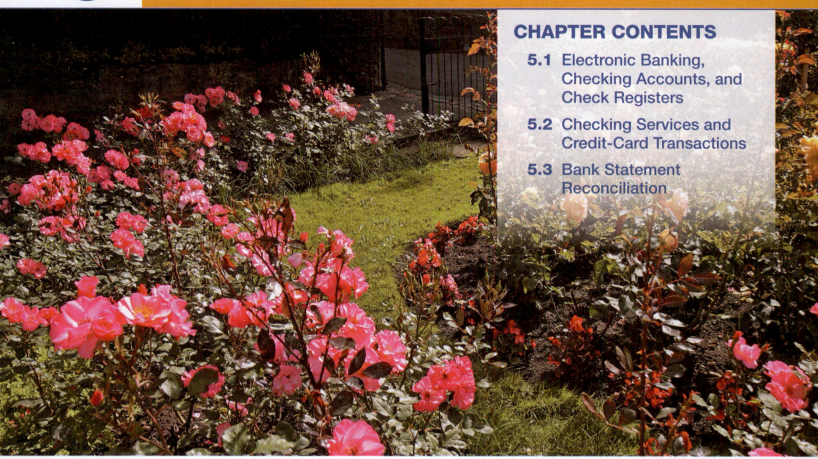

CHAPTER CONTENTS

5.1 Electronic Banking, Checking Accounts, and Check Registers

5.2 Checking Services and Credit-Card Transactions

5.3 Bank Statement Reconciliation

▼ CASE IN POINT

BARBARA WIFFY owns a small nursery named Rose Gardens. Although she sells all types of outdoor trees and shrubs, her specialty is roses. For the best quality roses, she has always bought from Jackson & Perkins Wholesale, Inc. This firm has research scientists who experiment with hybridizing roses with the goal of creating new, beautiful flowers.

As her business began to grow, Barbara Wiffy carefully looked at several different banks and talked to bank managers before choosing a bank. She knows how important the right bank and bankers are for a business owner.

Individuals and businesses use banks to hold funds and for many other purposes. Historically, banks offered few services other than checking accounts, savings accounts, and making loans. They make money by taking deposits and lending the funds out at a higher interest rate. Today, banks offer automated teller machines, electronic banking, credit and debit cards, note collection, investment services, mobile banking, guaranteed checks, and even payroll services for firms. Banks charge for many of these services. In this chapter, you will discover recent trends in banking and learn how to write checks, make deposits, and reconcile account balances.

▼ 5.1 Electronic Banking, Checking Accounts, and Check Registers

OBJECTIVES

1 Compare traditional versus electronic banking.

2 Know the types of checking accounts.

3 Identify the parts of a check.

4 Calculate the monthly service charges.

5 Identify the parts of a deposit slip.

6 Identify the parts of a check stub.

7 Complete the parts of a check register.

▼ **CASE IN POINT** As a business owner, Barbara Wiffy receives payments in all these ways: cash, checks, credit cards, debit cards, electronic payments, and even traveler's checks. In turn, she pays bills using checks, credit cards, debit cards, and electronic payments. She chose a bank that will support her growing company by efficiently handling all these types of payments.

OBJECTIVE 1 Compare traditional versus electronic banking. Banking has changed! **Traditional banking** required paper checks and people and managers used check registers to record checks and deposits. Although some people and a few small businesses still use traditional banking, most now use **electronic banking**, also referred to as **online banking**. The following table shows some of the many features in an electronic world.

Feature	Description
Automated Teller Machine (ATM)	Worldwide network used to make deposits, transfer money, pay bills, or get cash. Use may result in a charge.
Debit Card	A card that looks like a charge card, but results in an immediate withdrawal from your account. It's use requires a **personal identification number (PIN).**
Direct Deposit/Direct Payment	Allows for direct deposits to be made into an account or direct payments to be made from an account.
Electronic Commerce	Buying or selling products or services over the Internet.
Electronic Payments/ Electronic Funds Transfer (EFT)	Allows you to electronically transfer funds or pay bills. Used extensively by businesses as well as individuals.
Mobile Banking	Used to check balances, make transactions and payments, and apply for credit using a mobile device such as a smart phone or personal digital assistant.
Mobile Ticketing	Refers to the process of purchasing and obtaining tickets using a smartphone or other mobile device.
Pay by Phone	Allows funds to be transferred by phone.
Prepaid Card	A card with a prepaid balance.
Smart Card	A card with a microchip that can be used to make payments.
Point of Sale (POS)	Refers to the register in a store where a transaction occurs. Data is uploaded from registers to databases and then to banks.

Let's compare the four common payment systems for a customer making a purchase at a merchant such as Wal-Mart.

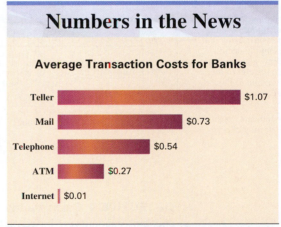

Payment Method

Check	Depending on the amount of the check, the teller may ask for identification, some of which is written on the back of the check. The check is soon deposited in Wal-Mart's local bank, which electronically requests payment from the customer's bank through a clearing house.
Credit Card	The customer swipes the card through the card reader. Depending on the amount of the charge and whether the customer has purchased there before, he or she may be asked to sign the credit slip. Often, the merchant's system will electronically check to make sure the credit card is valid.
Debit Card	The customer swipes the card through the reader and enters his or her personal identification number (PIN). Wal-Mart immediately routes the charge to a bank, which authorizes payment and debits the account balance.
Mobile Payments	Numerous firms, including Wal-Mart, are working on mobile payment systems which will allow customers to make purchases using smart phones or other electronic devices.

Traditional banking using paper checks was slow, sometimes requiring a week for a check to be processed. Today checks are processed quickly and most electronic transactions are completed almost instantly. In 2000, 50% of all consumer payments were made by paper check. Today, fewer than 20% of all such payments are made by check. Clearly, the era of paper checks is being replaced by electronic payments, debit cards, credit cards, ATMS, and mobile payments.

Banks led the change toward the use of electronic banking. Why? It reduces costs as you can see in the bar chart. The cost of a banking transaction on the internet is about 1% of the cost of the same transaction done using a teller. Electronic transfers have lowered costs by reducing the need for tellers, bookkeepers, and other staff and thereby allowed the bank to do more with less.

Numbers in the News

Average Transaction Costs for Banks

Teller	$1.07
Mail	$0.73
Telephone	$0.54
ATM	$0.27
Internet	$0.01

DATA: *msnmoney.com (or Jupiter Communications).*

However, electronic banking is not without problems. For example, it is relatively easy to authorize a payment(s) for which you do not have available funds. This may occur when a payroll check is for less than expected, yet the date for a scheduled payment arrives. This has resulted in up to ten charges for insufficient funds in one day for some individuals. Clearly, account balances should be monitored carefully and continuously.

Another problem is unauthorized use of your account, or even identity theft. **Identity theft** occurs when someone gathers enough information about you to fraudulently establish credit cards or borrow money using your name and personal information. It can be very difficult to stop the thief since it is difficult to find him or her. It is extremely important to protect

Thief from the Past

Thief of Today

your financial information as well as your log-on ID and password to all financial accounts. Experts recommend using complex passwords that cannot easily be discovered by criminals. They also recommend destroying documents that include credit-card numbers, account numbers, Social Security numbers, and all bank records.

Your **credit history** is important. Retailers, banks, mortgage companies, car finance companies and others look at your credit history before deciding whether to lend you money. Three credit bureaus keep track your **credit history**: Equifax, Experian, and TransUnion. It is a good idea to check your credit history at these three firms at least once a year to reduce the risk of people literally stealing your financial identity. You can go to the respective company websites or to www.annualcreditreport.com to check your credit history.

OBJECTIVE 2 **Know the types of checking accounts.** Checking accounts are used by individuals and businesses for daily transactions. The two basic types of checking accounts are discussed here. There are dozens of variations of these account types.

Personal checking accounts are used by individuals. The bank usually charges for the printing of checks and often charges a monthly fee for any checking account whose balance falls below a minimum amount at any time during the month. Individuals usually have the option of receiving a debit and/or credit card, as well as the ability to use ATMs and pay bills or receive deposits electronically. Some accounts pay a small amount of **interest**.

Business checking accounts often receive more services and have greater activity than do personal accounts. For example, banks often collect debts on behalf of businesses. The bank automatically credits the amount to the business account.

OBJECTIVE 3 **Identify the parts of a check.** Although many transactions are done electronically today, there are still hundreds of millions of checks written each year. So it is important to understand how to write a check.

OBJECTIVE 4 **Calculate the monthly service charges.** Service charges for business checking accounts are based on the average balance for the period covered by the statement. This average balance determines the **maintenance charge per month**, to which a **per-debit charge** (per-check charge) is added. The charges generally apply without regard to the amount of account activity. The following table shows typical bank charges for a business checking account.

Average Balance	Maintenance Charge Per Month	Per-Check Charge
Less than $500	$12.00	$.20
$500–$1999	$7.50	$.20
$2000–$4999	$5.00	$.10
$5000 or more	0	0

Other fees that some business have been charged by banks include **overdraft fees, coin counting fees, photocopying fees**, and **dormant account fees**. Use the information from the table above in the next example.

Finding the Checking-Account Service Charge

 EXAMPLE 1

Find the monthly service charge for the following business accounts.

(a) Omni Computer, 38 checks written, average balance $983

Based on the average balance of $983, the maintenance charge is $7.50 and the per-check charge is $.20.

$$\textbf{Charge} = \textbf{Maintenance charge} + \textbf{Per-check charge}$$
$$= \qquad \$7.50 \qquad + 38 \text{ checks} \times \$.20$$
$$= \qquad \$7.50 \qquad + \$7.60$$
$$= \qquad \$15.10$$

(b) Jamison Auto Repair, 62 checks written, average balance $4632.25

Based on the average balance, the maintenance charge is $5.00 and the per-check charge is $.10.

$$\text{Charge} = \text{Maintenance charge} + \text{Per-check charge}$$
$$= \qquad \$5.00 \qquad + \textbf{62 checks} \times \textbf{\$.10}$$
$$= \qquad \$5.00 \qquad + \$6.20$$
$$= \qquad \$11.20$$

⊞ The calculator solutions to this example use chain calculations, with the calculator observing the order of operations.

(a) 7.5 [+] 38 [×] .2 [=] 15.1   **(b)** 5 [+] 62 [×] .1 [=] 11.2

Note: Refer to Appendix B for calculator basics.

QUICK CHECK 1

Find the monthly service charge for the following business accounts.

(a) Towne Florist, 76 checks written, average balance $2180

(b) On-Line Books, 58 checks written, average balance $1850

OBJECTIVE 5 Identify the parts of a deposit slip. Cash and checks are placed into an account using a **deposit slip** or **deposit ticket**, as shown here. The account number is printed at the bottom in magnetic ink. The slip contains blanks for entering any currency (bills) or coins (change) as well as any checks that are to be deposited.

It is necessary to **endorse** the back of a check within 1.5 inches of the edge as shown in the figure on the next page, before depositing it in a bank. A **blank endorsement** is simply the signature of the person being paid. A lost check with a blank endorsement can be cashed by anyone finding the check. It is better to use a **restricted endorsement** which includes "For Deposit Only" followed by other information such as the name of a person or company and checking account number. A restricted check that is lost is worthless to anyone finding the check. A **special endorsement** is used to pass the check on to someone else.

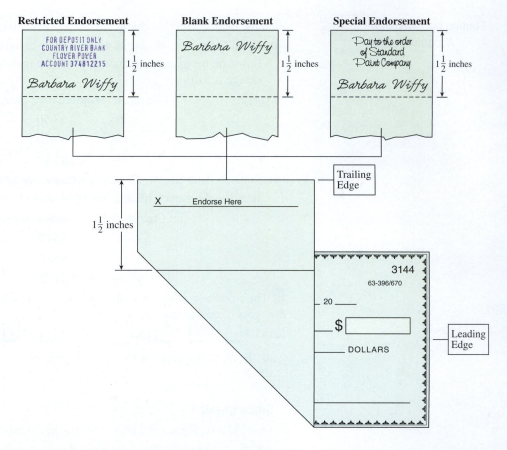

After being endorsed, a check may be deposited along with the deposit slip listing the check and showing the account number to which the check is to be deposited. Once the funds are transferred, the check is **canceled** and no longer valid. Photos are taken of both sides of the original check and kept by the bank which destroys the original check. The information on the back of a check shown below shows the processing history of the check. Banks use photos of checks to save the time and costs of mailing the checks back. This has saved **transaction costs. Processing checks** in this fashion has also reduced the **float time** which is the time between writing a check and the time funds are transferred out of the payor's account.

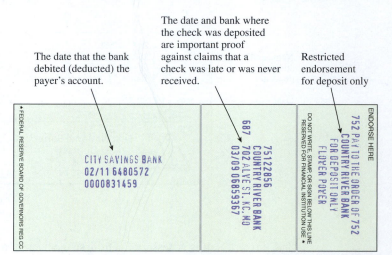

OBJECTIVE 6 Identify the parts of a check stub. Managers and individuals must keep careful records of all deposits, checks, and electronic fund transfers so that they know how much money they have and also have accurate information needed to prepare tax returns and financial statements. Although most businesses keep records on computers today, we will show the ideas using **check stubs** and **registers** since the ideas are transferable to the computer. **Total** refers to the balance from the bottom of the previous check stub. Add deposits and subtract the amount of this check and add or subtract other charges/credits to find the **balance** in the account. Although paying the bills is tedious work, accurate and quick payment of bills forms the backbone of electronic commerce.

Completing a Check Stub

EXAMPLE 2

Check number 2724 was made out on June 8 to Lillburn Utilities as payment for water and power. Assume that the check was for $182.15, that the balance brought forward is $4245.36, and that deposits of $337.71 and $193.17 have been made since the last check was written. An electronic payment for $820.36 was made to James Carpenter. Complete the check stub.

SOLUTION

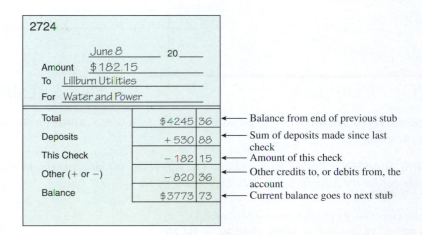

2724		
June 8 20 ____		
Amount $182.15		
To Lillburn Utilities		
For Water and Power		
Total	$4245	36
Deposits	+ 530	88
This Check	− 182	15
Other (+ or −)	− 820	36
Balance	$3773	73

- Balance from end of previous stub
- Sum of deposits made since last check
- Amount of this check
- Other credits to, or debits from, the account
- Current balance goes to next stub

QUICK CHECK 2

Use the check stub to find the balance forward. Check number 3502 is made out on November 15, 2014 to City Hall for $273.28 for garbage collection. The balance brought forward was $6750.17 and deposits of $1876.22 and $879.65 have been made since the last check was written. An ATM withdrawal of $200 was also made.

3502		
_____ 20 ____		
Amount		
To		
For		
Total		
Deposits		
This Check		
Other (+ or −)		
Balance		

OBJECTIVE 7 Complete the parts of a check register. Although a few people use check stubs to keep track of funds, most use a **check register**, also called a **transaction register,** which can either be on paper or created using computer software. The check register is used to keep track of all **transactions** including deposits, checks, ATM withdrawals, refunds, and electronic deposits or payments.

Check Register

CHECK NO.	DATE	TRANSACTION DESCRIPTION	AMOUNT OF WITHDRAWAL	✓	AMOUNT OF DEPOSIT/CREDIT	BALANCE
		BALANCE BROUGHT FORWARD ⟶				3518 72
electronic	5/8	Swan Brothers	378 93			3139 79
1436	5/8	Class Acts	25 14			3114 65
1437	5/9	Mirror Lighting	519 65			2595 00
	5/10	Deposit			3821 17	6416 17
electronic	5/10	Woodlake Auditorium	750 00			5666 17
	5/12	Deposit			500 00	6166 17
1438	5/12	Rick's Clowns	170 80			5995 37
1439	5/14	Y.M.C.A.	219 17			5776 20
	5/14	ATM	120 00			5656 20
	5/15	Deposit			326 15	5982 35
electronic	5/16	Stage Door Playhouse	825 00			5157 35
electronic	5/17	Gilbert Eckern	1785 00			3372 35
	5/19	Deposit			1580 25	4952 60

5.1　Exercises

MyMathLab®

The shaded sections below contain solutions to help you get a **QUICK START** *on the various types of exercises.*

CHECKING CHARGES　*Use the table on page 176 to find the monthly checking-account service charge for the following accounts. (See Example 1.)*

1. Rose Gardens, 92 checks, average balance $4618
$5.00 + (92 × $.10) = $5.00 + $9.20 = $14.20

　1. $14.20

2. Fresh Choice Restaurant, 114 checks, average balance $3318
$5.00 + (114 × $.10) = $5.00 + $11.40 = $16.40

　2. $16.40

3. Pest-X, 40 checks, average balance $491

　3. _____

4. Kent's Keys, Inc., 76 checks, average balance $468

　4. _____

5. Budget Dry Cleaning, 48 checks, average balance $1763

　5. _____

6. Direct Connection, 272 checks, average balance $8205

　6. _____

7. Software and More, 72 checks, average balance $516

　7. _____

8. Mart & Bottle, 74 checks, average balance $875

　8. _____

indicates an exercise that is related to the Case in Point feature.

MAINTAINING BANK RECORDS *Use the following information to complete each check stub.* (See Example 2.)

	Date	To	For	Amount of this Check	Total from previous Stub	Deposits	Other
9.	Mar. 8, 2014	Wayne Plumbing	Septic	$1835.42	$6215.13	$135; $1459.12	$100 cash withdrawal
10.	Nov. 4, 2014	Target	Misc.	$85.45	$1239.56	$122	$35 credit
11.	Oct. 7, 2014	PetSmart	Pet Food	$138.94	$2105.09	$832.47	$280.65 electronic payment

9.

```
857

Date       _____
Amount     _____
To         _____
For        _____

Total          |      |
Deposits       |      |
This Check     |      |
Other (+ or −) |      |
Balance        |      |
```

10.

```
1248

Date       _____
Amount     _____
To         _____
For        _____

Total          |      |
Deposits       |      |
This Check     |      |
Other (+ or −) |      |
Balance        |      |
```

11.

```
735

Date       _____
Amount     _____
To         _____
For        _____

Total          |      |
Deposits       |      |
This Check     |      |
Other (+ or −) |      |
Balance        |      |
```

12. List and explain at least six parts of a check. Draw a sketch showing where these parts appear on a check. (See Objective 3.)

13. Discuss the advantages and disadvantages of electronic banking. (See Objective 1.)

14. Write an explanation of two types of check endorsements. Describe where these endorsements must be placed. (See Objective 5.)

15. Explain in your own words the factors that determine the service charges on a business checking account. (See Objective 4.)

c COMPLETING CHECK STUBS *Using the information provided for 2014, complete the following check stubs for Rose Gardens.* **The balance brought forward for check stub 5311 is $7223.69.** *(See Example 2.)*

Checks Written

Number	Date	To	For	Amount
5311	Oct. 7	Julie Davis	Seeds	$1250.80
5312	Oct. 10	Post Office	Postage	$39.12
5313	Oct. 15	United Parcel	Shipping	$356.28

Deposits Made

Date	Amount
Oct. 8	$732.18
Oct. 9	$23.32
Oct. 13	$1025.45

Electronic Payments

Date	Amount
Oct. 8	$650.07
Oct. 12	$147.32

16.

5311	**Rose Gardens**	
Date	_____	
Amount	_____	
To	_____	
For	_____	
Total		
Deposits		
This Check		
Other (+ or −)		
Balance		

17.

5312	**Rose Gardens**	
Date	_____	
Amount	_____	
To	_____	
For	_____	
Total		
Deposits		
This Check		
Other (+ or −)		
Balance		

18.

5313	**Rose Gardens**	
Date	_____	
Amount	_____	
To	_____	
For	_____	
Total		
Deposits		
This Check		
Other (+ or −)		
Balance		

BANK BALANCES *In Exercises 19–22, complete the balance column in the following company check registers after each check or deposit transaction. Electronic payments are indicated by elec. (See Objective 7.)*

19. Rose Gardens

CHECK NO.	DATE	TRANSACTION DESCRIPTION	AMOUNT OF WITHDRAWAL	✓	AMOUNT OF DEPOSIT/CREDIT	BALANCE
		BALANCE BROUGHT FORWARD →				9628 35
1221	10/4	Delta Contractors	215 71			
elec.	10/5	Hand Fabricating	573 78			
1222	10/5	Photo Specialties	112 15			
	10/6	Deposit			753 28	
	10/8	Deposit			1475 69	
elec.	10/9	Young Marketing	426 55			
elec.	10/11	Wholesale Supply	637 93			
	10/11	ATM (fuel)	65 62			
elec.	10/14	Light and Power Utilities	248 17			
	10/16	Deposit			335 85	
1223	10/16	License Board	450 50			

20. Ontime Marketing

CHECK NO.	DATE	TRANSACTION DESCRIPTION	AMOUNT OF WITHDRAWAL	✓	AMOUNT OF DEPOSIT/CREDIT	BALANCE
		BALANCE BROUGHT FORWARD →				1629 86
elec.	7/3	Ahwahnee Hotel	250 45			
862	7/5	Willow Creek	149 00			
863	7/5	Void				
	7/7	Deposit			117 73	
elec.	7/9	Del Campo High School	69 80			
	7/10	Deposit			329 86	
	7/12	Deposit			418 30	
864	7/14	Big 5 Sporting Goods	109 76			
865	7/14	Dr. Yates	614 12			
866	7/16	Office Supplies	32 18			
	7/16	Deposit			520 95	

21. Stencils by Loree

CHECK NO.	DATE	TRANSACTION DESCRIPTION	AMOUNT OF WITHDRAWAL		✓	AMOUNT OF DEPOSIT/CREDIT		BALANCE	
		BALANCE BROUGHT FORWARD →						832	15
elec.	3/17	AirTouch Cellular	257	29					
elec.	3/18	Curry Village	190	50					
	3/19	Deposit				78	29		
	3/21	Deposit				157	42		
1123	3/22	San Juan District	38	76					
elec.	3/23	Macy's Gourmet	175	88					
	3/23	Deposit				379	28		
1124	3/24	Class Video	197	20					
1125	3/24	Water World	25	10					
1126	3/25	Bel Air Market	75	00					
	3/29	Deposit				722	35		

22. Beverly's Event Planning

CHECK NO.	DATE	TRANSACTION DESCRIPTION	AMOUNT OF WITHDRAWAL		✓	AMOUNT OF DEPOSIT/CREDIT		BALANCE	
		BALANCE BROUGHT FORWARD →						3852	48
elec.	12/6	Web Masters	143	16					
elec.	12/7	Water and Power	118	40					
	12/8	Deposit				286	32		
	12/10	ATM (cash)	80	00					
2312	12/11	Ann Kuick	986	22					
elec.	12/11	Account Temps	375	50					
	12/13	Deposit				1201	82		
elec.	12/14	Central Chevrolet	735	68					
2313	12/15	Miller Mining	223	94					
	12/13	Deposit				498	01		
2314	12/18	Federal Parcel	78	24					

5.2 Checking Services and Credit-Card Transactions

OBJECTIVES

1 Identify bank services available to customers.

2 Understand interest-paying checking plans.

3 Understand credit card, debit card, and mobile payment fees.

Students and Credit Card Debt (2009)	
Undergraduates with a credit card	84%
Average number of credit cards	4.6
Put tuition on credit card	30%
Average balance	$3173
Undergraduates who regularly pay off balance at end of month	17%
Undergraduates who believe they need more education on financial management	84%

Source: salliemae.com.

OBJECTIVE 1 Identify bank services available to customers. Most business checking-account fees are determined by either the average balance or the minimum balance in the account, together with specific charges for each service performed by the bank. Some of the services provided by banks, along with the *typical charges*, are listed here.

- **ATM cards** are used as debit cards when making point-of-sale purchases. There is usually no fee to use an ATM at any branch of your bank. However, the use of ATMs belonging to any other bank may result in a charge of up to $2.50 and use of an ATM in another country may cost $5 per transaction.

- An **overdraft** occurs when a check is written for which there are **nonsufficient funds (NSF)** in the checking account and the customer has no overdraft protection, also referred to as bouncing a check. The typical charge to the writer of the "bad" check is $25 to $35 per bad check. The same charge occurs when a check is returned because it was improperly completed.

- **Overdraft protection** is given when an account balance is insufficient to cover the amount of a check and an overdraft occurs. Charges for overdraft protection vary among banks.

- A **returned-deposit item** is a check that was deposited and then returned to the bank, usually because of lack of funds in the account of the person or firm writing the check. A common charge to the depositor of the check is $25.

- A **stop-payment order** is a request by a depositor that the bank not honor a check the depositor has written ($30 per request).

- A **cashier's check** is a check written by the financial institution itself and is viewed as being as good as cash ($8 per check). The payee's name is put on the cashier's check.

- A **money order** is a purchased instrument that is often used in place of cash and is sometimes required instead of a personal or business check ($4 each). The payee should be written on the money order by the purchaser immediately after purchase to avoid it being cashed by someone who finds or steals the money order.

- A **notary service** is an official certification of a signature on a document that is required on certain business documents. Occasionally this service is free to customers, but there is usually a charge ($10).

- **Online banking** or banking on the Internet allows customers to perform many banking functions from their home or place of business. This service is usually free.

OBJECTIVE 2 Understand interest-paying checking plans. Federal regulations allow banks to offer checking and savings accounts that pay interest. Interest rates are currently very low due to the lingering effects of the financial crisis that began in 2008, but those rates are likely to increase in the future. **Money market accounts** are interest bearing accounts that require a higher balance and can often be used like a checking account. Before the financial crisis, money market accounts paid higher interest rates and yet still gave the depositor the flexibility of withdrawing funds. Today, the rates paid on money market accounts are also very low. Banks also offer longer-term investments called **certificates of deposit (CDs)** which offer higher interest rates. They are discussed in Chapter 10.

OBJECTIVE 3 Understand credit card, debit card, and mobile payment fees. Businesses are charged fees whether customers pay using **credit cards, debit cards**, or using a device such as a smartphone to make a **mobile payment**. Actually, when you think about it, businesses also have costs when paid in cash – they have to protect the cash against theft which requires safes, armored car shipments, guards, and other processes to prevent theft. So, businesses have costs no matter which method is used for payments.

After a customer has made a *credit-card* charge at a merchant, information on the transaction is transferred over the internet to the bank through the bank's processor as shown in the following figure. The processor then shares the information with the merchant's bank as well as the issuer of the credit card. The issuer of the credit card accumulates charges for the month and sends a bill to the card owner on a monthly basis. The statement may include returned items with credits to the card owner.

"How It Works" Diagram

In contrast, debit cards result in an immediate charge to the card holder's bank account. The use of debit cards has become very popular as evidenced by the $2 trillion per year in debit charges and a continuing growth rate of over 15% per year.

Mobile payments can be made by tapping or waving smartphones above a device owned by the merchant. A disadvantage of mobile payments is that there is no paper record, so it can be difficult to correct an improper charge. Mobile payment systems continue to change rapidly.

Method of Payment	Charges
Credit card	2% or more of the amount of the charge
Debit card	average of 24 cents per swipe
Mobile payment	Supports credit card, debit card and prepaid card payment options. Costs vary widely.

You may have noticed that gasoline costs sometimes differ depending on which payment method is used. Now you know why – the merchant has higher costs when a customer pays with a credit card and many merchants try to pass the extra costs on to customers. However, merchants know that ease of payment results in increased sales, so they are usually willing to pay the fees. Nevertheless, you should be aware that merchants mark up the prices of products to include these costs.

Find the net deposit for credit card sales using these steps.

Finding Net Deposit for Credit-Card Sales:

1. Net credit-card sales = Total credit-card sales − Total credit-card refunds
2. Total fee = Appropriate percent × Net credit-card sales
3. Net deposit = Net credit-card sales − Total fee

Find the Fees and Net Deposit on Credit-Card Sales

 EXAMPLE 1

Here are some credit-card sales and credit-card refunds made one afternoon at Rose Gardens. Find the total credit-card sales, the total-credit card refunds, and the net credit-card sales. Then find the bank fee charged, assuming a fee of 2% of the net credit-card sales. Finally, find the amount deposited to Rose Garden's checking account.

▼ CASE IN POINT

Credit-Card Sales		Credit-Card Refunds
$82.31	$146.50	$43.83
$38.18	$78.80	$85.95
$249.33	$470.15	
$46.80	$320.90	

SOLUTION

Adding the numbers given above results in credit-card sales of $1431.97 and credit-card refunds of $129.78. Then find the net credit-card sales as follows.

$$\text{Total sales} = \$1432.97$$
$$\text{Total refunds} = -129.78$$
$$\textbf{Net sales} \quad \textbf{\$1303.19}$$

The bank fee is 2% of net credit card sales.

$$\textbf{Bank fee} = \textbf{2\% of \$1303.19}$$
$$= \textbf{\$26.06} \quad \textbf{(rounded)}$$

Finally, find the amount deposited to Rose Garden's checking account.

$$\text{Amount} = \$1303.19 - \textbf{\$26.06} = \$1277.13$$

Quick TIP

Cash rewards on prior Master-Card and Visa charges are really a rebate on previous purchases.

QUICK CHECK 1

Assume a fee of 2.25% and find the amount deposited to a business owner's account based on the following credit-card transactions.

Sales: $532.15, $650.19, $127.45, $314.98
Refunds: $120.15

▼ 5.2 Exercises

MyMathLab®

The shaded sections below contain solutions to help you get a QUICK START on the various types of exercises.

COLLEGE BOOKSTORE   *A college bookstore accepts cash, checks, debit cards, credit cards, and mobile payments. The following credit-card transactions occurred in the first hour of business one morning.*

Sales		Refunds
$66.68	$18.95	$62.16
$119.63	$496.28	$106.62
$53.86	$21.85	$38.91
$178.62	$242.78	
$219.78	$176.93	

1. What is the total amount of the credit-card sales?
   $66.68 + $119.63 + $53.86 + $178.62 + $219.78 + $18.95 + $496.28 + $21.85 + $242.78 + $176.93 = $1595.36

   1. **$1595.36**

2. Find the total of the credit-card refunds.
   $62.16 + $106.62 + $38.91 = $207.69

   2. **$207.69**

3. Find credit-card sales less refunds.

3. _____

4. If the fee paid by the business is 2.5%, find the amount of the charge at the statement date.

4. _____

5. Find the amount of the credit given to Mak's Tune and Smog after the fee is subtracted.

5. _____

 CREDIT-CARD DEPOSITS *Rose Gardens does most of its business on the Internet and accepts credit cards. In a recent period, the business had the following credit-card charges and credits. (See Examples 1 and 2.)*

Sales		Refunds
$78.56	$38.15	$29.76
$875.29	$18.46	$102.15
$330.82	$22.13	$71.95
$55.24	$707.37	
$47.83	$245.91	

6. What is the total amount of the credit-card sales?

6. _____

7. Find the total of the credit-card refunds.

7. _____

8. Find credit-card sales less refunds.

8. _____

9. If the bank charges Rose Gardens a 3% fee, find the amount of the charge at the statement date.

9. _____

10. Find the amount of the credit given to Rose Gardens after the fee is subtracted.

10. _____

CREDIT-CARD DEPOSITS *Jay Jenkins owns Campus Bicycle Shop near a college campus. The shop sells new and used bicycle parts and does a major portion of its business in adjustments and repairs. The following credit-card charges and credits took place during a recent period.*

Sales		Refunds
$7.84	$98.56	$13.86
$33.18	$318.72	$58.97
$50.76	$116.35	
$12.72	$23.78	
$9.36	$38.95	
$118.68	$235.82	

11. Find the total amount of the credit-card sales.

11. _____

12. Find the total of the credit-card refunds.

12. _____

 indicates an exercise that is related to the Case in Point feature.

13. Find credit-card sales less refunds.

13. _____

14. If the fee paid by the shop is 2%, find the amount of the charge at the statement date.

14. _____

15. Find the amount of the credit given to Campus Bicycle Shop after the fee is subtracted.

15. _____

CREDIT-CARD DEPOSITS   *Kaare Taylor Photo Studios had the following credit-card transactions during a recent period.*

Sales		Refunds
$14.86	$76.15	$43.15
$49.70	$226.17	$17.06
$183.60	$63.95	
$238.75	$111.10	
$18.36	$77.86	
$52.08	$132.62	

16. Find the total amount of the credit-card sales.

16. _____

17. Find the total of the credit-card refunds.

17. _____

18. Find credit-card sales less refunds.

18. _____

19. If the fee paid by the shop is 2.5%, find the amount of the charge at the statement date.

19. _____

20. Find the amount of credit given to Kaare Taylor Studios after the fee is subtracted.

20. _____

21. List and describe in your own words four services offered to business checking-account customers. (See Objective 1.)

22. The merchant accepting a credit card from a customer must pay a fee of 2% or more of the transaction amount. Why is the merchant willing to do this? Who really pays this fee? (See Objective 3.)

▼ 5.3 Bank Statement Reconciliation

OBJECTIVES

1 Know the importance of reconciling a checking account.

2 Reconcile a bank statement.

3 List the outstanding checks.

4 Find the *adjusted bank balance* or *current balance.*

▼ CASE IN POINT   Barbara Wiffy, owner of Rose Gardens, knows the importance of keeping accurate checking-account records. She has received customers' checks drawn on accounts with nonsufficient funds (NSF), but with great pride she says, "I have never written a bad check."

OBJECTIVE 1 Know the importance of reconciling a checking account. Each month, a bank creates a **bank statement** that shows all activity in the account for the month including checks, debits, ATM transactions, electronic funds transfers, service charges, interest, and fees such as the fees on credit card sales found in the previous section. The bank statement is available either on paper or electronically on the bank's website. Here are a few reasons business owners look carefully at their bank statements every month:

1. The fees charged by the bank vary from month to month.
2. A deposited check may be returned due to insufficient funds. The amount of the check and any fees must be deducted from the account balance. **Returned checks** are also called **bounced checks**.
3. A scheduled deposit may not have been made.
4. The account holder may have made an error in the check register or when entering data into the firm's computer system.
5. Although rare, bank employees may make an error.

Managers often separate duties to help prevent employee theft. For example, they often require one person to examine the bank statement for any mistakes but requires a different person to write a check or authorize a payment. Writing a check without sufficient funds in the account is called **bouncing a check**. The penalty for bouncing a check can be both financial and legal. Banks charge high fees for bouncing a check and a bounced check can get you in trouble with the law.

OBJECTIVE 2 Reconcile a bank statement. The process of checking the bank statement against the check register is called **reconciliation**. The following bank statement is for Rose Gardens.

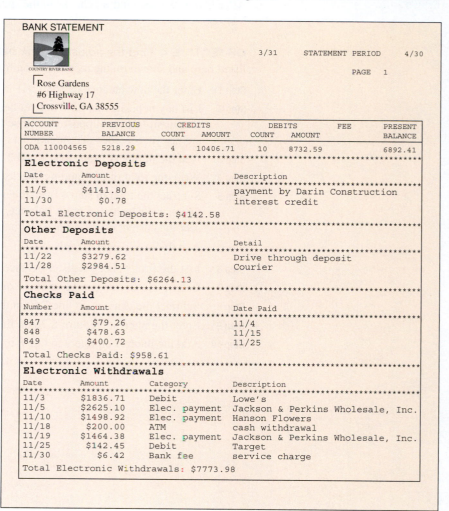

BANK STATEMENT

COUNTRY RIVER BANK

			3/31	STATEMENT PERIOD	4/30

PAGE   1

Rose Gardens
#6 Highway 17
Crossville, GA 38555

ACCOUNT NUMBER	PREVIOUS BALANCE	CREDITS COUNT	CREDITS AMOUNT	DEBITS COUNT	DEBITS AMOUNT	FEE	PRESENT BALANCE
ODA 110004565	5218.29	4	10406.71	10	8732.59		6892.41

Electronic Deposits

Date	Amount	Description
11/5	$4141.80	payment by Darin Construction
11/30	$0.78	interest credit

Total Electronic Deposits: $4142.58

Other Deposits

Date	Amount	Detail
11/22	$3279.62	Drive through deposit
11/28	$2984.51	Courier

Total Other Deposits: $6264.13

Checks Paid

Number	Amount	Date Paid
847	$79.26	11/4
848	$478.63	11/15
849	$400.72	11/25

Total Checks Paid: $958.61

Electronic Withdrawals

Date	Amount	Category	Description
11/3	$1836.71	Debit	Lowe's
11/5	$2625.10	Elec. payment	Jackson & Perkins Wholesale, Inc.
11/10	$1498.92	Elec. payment	Hanson Flowers
11/18	$200.00	ATM	cash withdrawal
11/19	$1464.38	Elec. payment	Jackson & Perkins Wholesale, Inc.
11/25	$142.45	Debit	Target
11/30	$6.42	Bank fee	service charge

Total Electronic Withdrawals: $7773.98

Notice the variety of items shown including electronic deposits when customers pay Rose Gardens electronically, other deposits, checks, and electronic withdrawals, which include electronic payments, ATM withdrawals, debits, and bank fees.

Electronic transfers are easy to track since they show up very quickly on the bank's computer system. Checks are different. For example, you may send your aunt a check for her birthday that she does not deposit for five weeks. A firm often has written checks that do not yet show up on the bank statement. These unpaid checks are called **checks outstanding**. Since electronic funds transfers usually result in a prompt change in the bank balance, we ignore them here.

Reconciling a Checking Account

 EXAMPLE 1 The bank statement for Rose Gardens shown on the previous page shows a balance of $6892.41 after a bank service charge of $6.42 and an interest credit of $.78. The check register for Rose Gardens shows a current balance of $7580.38. Reconcile the account as follows.

 CASE IN POINT

OBJECTIVE 3 List the outstanding checks. Find the checks outstanding by comparing the list of checks on the bank statement against the list of checks written by the firm. You may wish to put a check mark on the bank statement and/or check register as you compare them. In particular, note any differences in the amounts for any check. Here are the outstanding checks.

Number	Amount
846	$42.73
852	$598.71
853	$68.12
857	$79.80
858	$160.30

After listing the outstanding checks in the space provided on the form, total them. The total is $949.66.

OBJECTIVE 4 Find the *adjusted bank balance* or *current balance*. Follow the steps listed here and shown on the reconciliation form on the next page.

Step 1 Enter the new balance of $6892.41 in the space at the top of the reconciliation form.

Step 2 List any deposits that have not yet been recorded by the bank. These are called **deposits in transit (DIT)**. Suppose that Rose Gardens has deposits of $892.41 and $739.58 that are not yet recorded. These numbers are written at step 2 on the form.

Step 3 Add the numbers from steps 1 and 2. At this point, the total is $8524.40.

Step 4 Write the total of outstanding checks. The total is $949.66.

Step 5 Subtract the total in step 4 from the amount from step 3. The result here is $7574.74, which is the **adjusted bank balance**, or the **current balance.** This number should represent the current checking-account balance.

Now look at the firm's own records.

Step 6 List the firm's check register balance of $7580.38 on line 6 on the reconciliation form.

Step 7 Enter total service charge of $6.42 on line 7.

Step 8 Subtract the charges on line 7 from the checkbook balance on line 6 to get $7573.96.

Step 9 Enter the interest credit of $.78 on line 9. This is interest paid on money in the account.

Step 10 Add the interest on line 9 to line 8 to get $7574.74, the same result as in step 5.

Since the result from step 10 is the same as the result from step 5, the account is **balanced** (reconciled). The correct current balance in the account is $7574.74.

Reconciliation			Compare the list of checks paid by the bank with your records. List and total the checks not yet paid.

Checks Outstanding	
Number	Amount
846	$ 42	73
852	598	71
853	68	12
857	79	80
858	160	30
Total	$ 949	66

(1) Enter new balance from bank statement: $ 6892.41

(2) List any deposits made by you and not yet recorded by the bank:
    +   892.41
    +   739.58
    + _____
    + _____

(3) Add all numbers from lines above.
    Total: 8524.40

(4) Write total of checks outstanding: − 949.66

(5) Subtract (4) from (3).
    This is adjusted bank balance: $ 7574.74

To reconcile your records:

(6) List your checkbook balance: $ 7580.38

(7) Write the total of any fees or charges deducted by the bank and not yet subtracted by you from your checkbook: −   6.42

(8) Subtract line (7) from line (6).   7573.96

(9) Enter interest credit: (Add to your checkbook)   +   .78

(10) Add line (9) to line (8).
    Adjusted checkbook balance. $ 7574.74

New balance of your account; this number should be same as (5).

QUICK CHECK 1

Find the current balance for a checking account given the following: balance from bank statement, $7622.18; checks outstanding of $318.36, $1752.44, $738.35, $66.78; and deposits in transit of $1197.22 and $578.91.

There are several typical reasons checking accounts do not balance.

Why Checking Accounts Do Not Balance

- Forgetting to enter a check, a debit, an electronic payment, or an ATM withdrawal.
- Transposing numbers (writing $961.20 as $916.20, for example).
- Making addition or subtraction errors.
- Forgetting to subtract one of the bank service fees, such as those charged for a returned check or for ATM use at a different bank.
- Having checks that are altered or forged.

It is necessary to carefully compare the check register (or computerized account records) to the bank statement when an account does not reconcile. It can be difficult to find any error(s) in an active account, but it is important that managers keep track of funds so that they know how much they have in an account and to reduce the risk of employee theft. Usually, errors are made by the account owner although banks make mistakes occasionally.

Bank fees vary widely and individuals with higher bank balances may have no bank fees charged whatsoever. Active firms may see charges of hundreds of dollars in bank fees every month. Before choosing a bank, look carefully at the fees they charge.

Reconciling a
Checking Account

EXAMPLE 2

Using the information in the following check register and the bank statement, reconcile the checking account. Compare the items appearing on the check register to the bank statement. A check ✓ indicates that the transaction was on the prior months bank statement, so that it does not need to be added or subtracted again.

Check Register

CHECK NO.	DATE	TRANSACTION DESCRIPTION	AMOUNT OF WITHDRAWAL	✓	AMOUNT OF DEPOSIT/CREDIT	BALANCE
		BALANCE BROUGHT FORWARD →				2782 95
elec.	7/11	Miller's Outpost	138 50	✓		2644 45
elec.	7/12	Barber Advertising	73 08			2571 37
723	7/18	Wayside Lumber	318 62	✓		2252 75
	7/24	Deposit			983 37	3236 12
724	7/25	I.R.S.	836 15			2399 97
elec.	7/26	Supplies	450 00			1949 97
725	7/28	Sacramento Bee	67 80			1882 17
726	8/2	T.V.A.	59 25			1822 92
727	8/3	Carmichael Office	97 37			1725 55
	8/6	Deposit			875 45	2601 00
ATM	8/5	ATM Cash	80 00			2521 00

Bank Statement

```
************************************************************
ACCOUNT      PREVIOUS    CREDITS            DEBIT           PRESENT
NUMBER       BALANCE   COUNT    AMOUNT   COUNT    AMOUNT    BALANCE
************************************************************
7009875433  $2325.83    2     $983.59    7     $1555.15  $1754.27
************************************************************
Electronic Deposits
Date          Amount                    Description
************************************************************
7/24         $983.37              payment from JP Morgan
8/4            $.22              interest credit
Total Electronic Deposits: $983.59
************************************************************
Other Deposits
Date          Amount                      Detail
************************************************************
Total Other Deposits: $0
************************************************************
Checks Paid
Number       Amount                     Date Paid
************************************************************
724         $836.15                      7/28
726          $59.25                      8/4
Total Checks Paid: $895.40
************************************************************
Electronic Withdrawals
Date         Amount     Category        Description
************************************************************
7/22         $73.08    elec. payment   Barber Advertising
7/30        $450.00    debit           supplies
7/30         $49.07    debit           returned check
8/4          $80.00    ATM             cash withdrawal
8/5           $7.60    Bank fee        service charge

Total Electronic Withdrawals: $659.75
```

Reconciliation

Checks Outstanding	
Number	Amount
725	$ 67 80
727	97 37
Total	$ 165 17

Compare the list of checks paid by the bank with your records. List and total the checks not yet paid.

(1) Enter new balance from bank statement: $ 1754.27

(2) List any deposits made by you and not yet recorded by the bank:
+ 875.45
+
+
+

(3) Add all numbers from lines above. Total: 2629.72

(4) Write total of checks outstanding: − 165.17

(5) Subtract (4) from (3). This is adjusted bank balance: $ 2464.55

To reconcile your records:

(6) List your checkbook balance: $ 2521.00

(7) Write the total of any fees or charges deducted by the bank and not yet subtracted by you from your checkbook: − 56.67 (Returned check and service charge)

(8) Subtract line (7) from line (6). 2464.33

(9) Enter interest credit: (Add to your checkbook) + .22

(10) Add line (9) to line (8). Adjusted checkbook balance. $ 2464.55

New balance of your account; this number should be same as (5).

Since the adjusted bank balance from step 5 is the same as the adjusted checkbook balance from step 10, the account is reconciled (balanced). The correct current balance in the account is $2464.55.

QUICK CHECK 2

Use the form in Example 2 to reconcile the following account. The checkbook of Dottie Fogel Furnishings shows a balance of $7779. When the bank statement was received, it showed a balance of $6237.44, a returned check amounting to $246.70, a service charge of $15.60, and a check-printing charge of $18.50. There were unrecorded deposits of $1442.44 and $479.50, and checks outstanding of $146.36, $91.52, $43.78, and $379.52.

5.3 Exercises

MyMathLab®

*The shaded sections below contain solutions to help you get a **QUICK START** on the various types of exercises.*

CURRENT CHECKING BALANCE *Find the current balance for each of the following accounts.*
(See Example 1.)

	Balance from Bank Statement	Checks Outstanding		Deposits Not Yet Recorded		Balance
1.	$4572.15	$225.23 $97.68	$418.25 $348.17	$816.14 $571.28		$4870.24

$$\$4572.15 - \$225.23 - \$97.68 - \$418.25 - \$348.17 + \$816.14 + \$571.28 = \$4870.24$$

2.	$6274.76	$381.40 $875.14	$681.10 $83.15	$346.65 $198.96		$4799.58

$$\$6274.76 - \$381.40 - \$875.14 - \$681.10 - \$83.15 + \$346.65 + \$198.96 = \$4799.58$$

3.	$7911.42	$52.38 $95.42	$528.02 $76.50	$492.80 $38.72		_____
4.	$9343.65	$840.71 $78.68	$665.73 $87.00	$971.64 $3382.71		_____
5.	$19,523.20	$6853.60 $795.77	$340.00 $22.85	$6724.93 $78.81		_____
6.	$32,489.50	$3589.70 $263.15	$18,702.15 $7269.78	$7110.65 $2218.63		_____

7. Explain in your own words the significance of writing a bad check. What might the cost be in dollars? What are the other consequences? (See Objective 1.)

8. What are the financial costs to a business owner who receives a bad check? What would the business owner likely do regarding this customer? (See Objective 1.)

9. Briefly describe the importance of reconciling a checking account. What benefits are derived from keeping good checking records? (See Objective 2.)

10. Suppose your checking account does not balance. Name four types of errors that you will look for in trying to correct this problem. (See Objective 4.)

RECONCILING CHECKING ACCOUNTS   *For Exercises 11 and 12, use the following table to reconcile each account and find the current balance. (See Example 1.)*

		Exercise 11.		Exercise 12.
Balance from bank statement		$6875.09		$14,928.42
Checks outstanding	421	$371.52	112	$84.76
(check number is given first)	424	$429.07	115	$109.38
	427	$883.69	117	$42.03
	429	$35.62	119	$1429.12
Deposits not yet recorded		$701.56		$54.21
		$421.78		$394.76
		$689.35		$1002.04
Bank charge		$8.75		$7.00
Interest credit		$10.71		$22.86
Checkbook balance		$6965.92		$14,698.28
Current balance		_____		_____

11.

Reconciliation

Checks Outstanding	
Number	Amount
Total	

Compare the list of checks paid by the bank with your records. List and total the checks not yet paid.

(1) Enter new balance from bank statement: _____

(2) List any deposits made by you and not yet recorded by the bank:
   + _____
   + _____
   + _____
   + _____

(3) Add all numbers from lines above.
   Total: _____

(4) Write total of checks outstanding: − _____

(5) Subtract (4) from (3).
   This is adjusted bank balance: _____

To reconcile your records:

(6) List your checkbook balance: _____

(7) Write the total of any fees or charges deducted by the bank and not yet subtracted by you from your checkbook: − _____

(8) Subtract line (7) from line (6). _____

(9) Enter interest credit: (Add to your checkbook) + _____

(10) Add line (9) to line (8).
   Adjusted checkbook balance. _____

New balance of your account; this number should be same as (5).

12.

Reconciliation

Checks Outstanding	
Number	Amount
Total	

Compare the list of checks paid by the bank with your records. List and total the checks not yet paid.

(1) Enter new balance from bank statement: _____

(2) List any deposits made by you and not yet recorded by the bank:
   + _____
   + _____
   + _____
   + _____

(3) Add all numbers from lines above.
   Total: _____

(4) Write total of checks outstanding: − _____

(5) Subtract (4) from (3).
   This is adjusted bank balance: _____

To reconcile your records:

(6) List your checkbook balance: _____

(7) Write the total of any fees or charges deducted by the bank and not yet subtracted by you from your checkbook: − _____

(8) Subtract line (7) from line (6). _____

(9) Enter interest credit: (Add to your checkbook) + _____

(10) Add line (9) to line (8).
   Adjusted checkbook balance. _____

New balance of your account; this number should be same as (5).

CHECKING-ACCOUNT RECONCILIATION *Reconcile the checking accounts for the following companies. Compare the items appearing on the bank statement with the check register. A ✓ indicates that the transaction appeared on the previous month's statement. (Codes indicate the following: RC means returned check; SC means service charge; IC means interest credit; CP means check printing charge; ATM means automated teller machine.) (See Example 2.)*

13. Rose Gardens

CHECK NO.	DATE	TRANSACTION DESCRIPTION	AMOUNT OF WITHDRAWAL	✓	AMOUNT OF DEPOSIT/CREDIT	BALANCE
		BALANCE BROUGHT FORWARD →				6669 34
elec.	2/8	Floors to Go	248 96			6420 38
762	2/9	Healthways Dist.	125 63			6294 75
	2/11	Deposit			626 34	6921 09
763	2/12	Franchise Tax	770 41	✓		6150 68
764	2/14	Foothill Repair	22 86	✓		6127 82
elec.	2/15	Yellow Pages	91 24			6036 58
	2/17	Deposit			826 03	6862 61
elec.	2/17	Morning Herald	71 59			6791 02
765	2/18	San Juan Electric	63 24			6727 78
ATM	2/22	ATM Gas	15 26			6712 52
766	2/23	West Construction	405 07			6307 45
767	2/24	Heater Repairs	525 00			5782 45
	2/26	Deposit			220 16	6002 61
768	2/28	Capital Alarm	135 76			5866 85

```
Bank Statement
*****************************************************************
ACCOUNT      PREVIOUS    CREDITS          DEBIT          PRESENT
NUMBER       BALANCE  COUNT   AMOUNT  COUNT    AMOUNT     BALANCE
*****************************************************************
2352276478  $5876.07    3    $1452.49   9    $1692.05   $5636.51
*****************************************************************
Electronic Deposits
Date      Amount               Description
*****************************************************************
2/16     $626.34              payment from Jayne Inc.
2/24        $.12              interest credit
Total Electronic Deposits: $626.46
*****************************************************************
Other Deposits
Date      Amount               Detail
*****************************************************************
2/17     $826.03              Regions Bank
Total Other Deposits: $826.03
*****************************************************************
Checks Paid
Number    Amount               Date Paid
*****************************************************************
762      $125.63              2/21
766      $405.07              2/26
767      $525.00              2/28
Total Checks Paid: $1055.70
*****************************************************************
Electronic Withdrawals
Date      Amount   Category    Description
*****************************************************************
2/16     $91.24    bill pay    Central Electric
2/17    $248.96    debit       Wal-Mart Stores
2/19     $71.59    bill pay    Michaels(crafts)
2/22    $198.17    debit       check returned due to
                               nonsufficient funds
2/22     $15.26    debit       lunch
2/27     $11.13    bank fees   service charge
Total Electronic Withdrawals: $636.35
```

Reconciliation

Checks Outstanding	
Number	Amount
Total	

Compare the list of checks paid by the bank with your records. List and total the checks not yet paid.

(1) Enter new balance from bank statement: _____

(2) List any deposits made by you and not yet recorded by the bank: + _____ + _____ + _____ + _____

(3) Add all numbers from lines above. Total: _____

(4) Write total of checks outstanding: − _____

(5) Subtract (4) from (3). This is adjusted bank balance: _____

To reconcile your records:

(6) List your checkbook balance: _____

(7) Write the total of any fees or charges deducted by the bank and not yet subtracted by you from your checkbook: − _____

(8) Subtract line (7) from line (6). _____

(9) Enter interest credit: (Add to your checkbook) + _____

(10) Add line (9) to line (8). Adjusted checkbook balance. _____

New balance of your account; this number should be same as (5).

14. Play It Again Sports

CHECK NO.	DATE	TRANSACTION DESCRIPTION	AMOUNT OF WITHDRAWAL	✓	AMOUNT OF DEPOSIT/CREDIT	BALANCE
		BALANCE BROUGHT FORWARD →				7682 07
elec.	3/3	Action Packing Supplies	451 16			7230 91
663	3/3	Crown Paper	954 29	✓		6276 62
664	3/5	ATM Cash	80 00	✓		6196 62
	3/7	Deposit			913 28	7109 90
elec.	3/10	Fairless Water District	72 37			7037 53
665	3/12	Audia Temporary	340 88			6696 65
elec.	3/13	Lionel Toys	618 65			6078 00
666	3/14	Fairless Hills Power	100 50			5977 50
	3/16	Deposit			450 18	6427 68
	3/18	Deposit			163 55	6591 23
667	3/20	Hunt Roofing	238 50			6352 73
668	3/22	Standard Brands	315 62			6037 11
669	3/23	Penny-Saver Products	67 29			5969 82
	3/24	Deposit			830 75	6800 57

Bank Statement

```
************************************************************
ACCOUNT    PREVIOUS   CREDITS          DEBIT         PRESENT
NUMBER     BALANCE  COUNT  AMOUNT  COUNT   AMOUNT    BALANCE
1278992431 $6647.78   4   $1549.49   7   $1816.41  $6380.86
************************************************************
Electronic Deposits
Date      Amount                Description
************************************************************
3/7     $913.28               Credit from Nike
3/20     $22.48               interest credit from CD
Total Electronic Deposits: $935.76
************************************************************
Other Deposits
Date      Amount                Detail
************************************************************
3/16    $450.18               Invoice A65912
3/22    $163.55               John Tyler High School
Total Other Deposits: $613.73
************************************************************
Checks Paid
Number   Amount           Date Paid
************************************************************
665     $340.88              3/16
667     $238.50              3/26
Total Checks Paid: $579.38
************************************************************
Electronic Withdrawals
Date     Amount   Category   Description
************************************************************
3/11    $451.16   bill pay   Baseball Equipment, Inc.
3/20     $72.37   debit      Office Max
3/22    $618.65   bill pay   Wells Fargo-mortgage
3/16     $82.15   debit      returned check
3/26     $12.70   bank fee   service charge
Total Electronic Withdrawals: $1237.03
```

Reconciliation

Checks Outstanding	
Number	Amount
Total	

Compare the list of checks paid by the bank with your records. List and total the checks not yet paid.

(1) Enter new balance from bank statement: _____

(2) List any deposits made by you and not
yet recorded by the bank:
+ _____
+ _____
+ _____
+ _____

(3) Add all numbers from lines above.
Total:

(4) Write total of checks outstanding: − _____

(5) Subtract (4) from (3).
This is adjusted bank balance: _____

To reconcile your records:

(6) List your checkbook balance: _____

(7) Write the total of any fees or charges deducted
by the bank and not yet subtracted by you from
your checkbook: − _____

(8) Subtract line (7) from line (6). _____

(9) Enter interest credit: (Add to your checkbook) + _____

(10) Add line (9) to line (8).
Adjusted checkbook balance. _____

New balance of your
account; this number
should be same as (5).

▼ Chapter 5 Quick Review

Chapter Terms *Review the following terms to test your understanding of the chapter. For each term you do not know, refer to the page number found next to that term.*

adjusted bank balance [p. 190]
ATM cards [p. 184]
automated teller machine (ATM) [p. 174]
balance [p. 178]
balanced [p. 191]
bank statement [p. 189]
blank endorsement [p. 177]
bounced checks [p. 189]
business checking account [p. 176]
canceled (check) [p. 178]
cashier's check [p. 184]
certificates of deposit (CDs) [p. 184]
check registers [p. 180]
check stubs [p. 178]
checks outstanding [p. 190]

coin counting fees [p. 176]
credit cards [p. 184]
credit history [p. 176]
current balance [p. 190]
debit cards [p. 174]
deposit slip [p. 177]
deposit ticket [p. 177]
deposits in transit (DIT) [p. 190]
direct deposit [p. 174]
direct payment [p. 174]
dormant account fees [p. 176]
electronic banking [p. 174]
electronic payments [p. 174]
electronic commerce (EC) [p. 174]
electronic funds transfer (EFT) [p. 174]

electronic payment [p. 174]
float time [p. 178]
identity theft [p. 175]
interest [p. 176]
maintenance charge per month [p. 176]
mobile payment [p. 184]
money market account [p. 184]
money order [p. 184]
nonsufficient funds (NSF) [p. 184]
notary service [p. 184]
online banking [p. 184]
overdraft [p. 184]
overdraft fees [p. 176]
overdraft protection [p. 184]
pay by phone [p. 174]
per-debit charge [p. 176]

personal checking account [p. 176]
personal identification number (PIN) [p. 174]
photocopying fees [p. 176]
point of sale (POS) [p. 174]
prepaid card [p. 174]
processing (check) [p. 178]
reconciliation [p. 189]
restricted endorsement [p. 177]
returned check [p. 189]
returned-deposit item [p. 184]
smart card [p. 174]
special endorsement [p. 177]
stop-payment order [p. 184]
traditional banking [p. 174]
transactions [p. 180]
transaction register [p. 180]

CONCEPTS

5.1 Checking-account service charges

A checking-account maintenance fee is usually charged and there is often a per-check charge.

5.2 Bank services offered

The checking account customer must be aware of various banking services that are offered.

5.2 Deposits with credit-card transactions

All credit-card refunds must be subtracted from total credit-card sales to find the net deposit. The fee is then subtracted from this total.

EXAMPLES

Find the monthly checking-account service charge for a business with 36 checks, given a monthly maintenance charge of $7.50 and a $.20 per check charge.

$$\$7.50 + 36(\$.20) = \$7.50 + \$7.20 =$$
$$\$14.70 \text{ monthly service charge}$$

Overdraft protection Offered to protect the customer from bouncing a check (NSF)

Debit card Used at an automated teller machine to get cash or at a merchant to make a purchase

Stop-payment order Stops payment on a check written in error

Cashier's check A check written by a financial institution, such as a bank, and that is viewed to be as good as cash

Money order An instrument used in place of cash

Notary service An official certification of a signature or document

Online banking Allows customers to perform many banking functions on the Internet

The following are credit-card charges and credits.

Charges		Credits
$28.15	$78.59	$21.86
$36.92	$63.82	$19.62

(a) Find total charges.

$$\$28.15 + \$36.92 + \$78.59 + \$63.82 = \$207.48$$

| CONCEPTS | EXAMPLES |

EXAMPLES

(b) Find total credits.

$$\$21.86 + \$19.62 = \$41.48$$

(c) Find gross deposit.

$$\$207.48 - \$41.48 = \$166$$

(d) Given a 3% fee, find the amount of the charge.

$$\$166 \times .03 = \$4.98$$

(e) Find the amount of credit given to the business.

$$\$166 - \$4.98 = \$161.02$$

5.3 Reconciliation of a checking account

A checking-account customer must periodically reconcile checking-account records with those of the bank or financial institution. Use a bank statement and reconciliation form to do this.

The accuracy of all checks written, deposits made, service charges incurred, and interest paid is checked and verified. The customer's checkbook balance and bank balance must be the same for the account to reconcile, or balance.

Case Study

BANKING ACTIVITIES OF A RETAILER

Jessica Lange owns her own high-end hair salon and employs several hair stylists. Customers usually pay using either a debit card or a credit card, but they sometimes write checks or pay with cash. Her credit-card sales last week were $8752.40. During the same period, she had $573.94 in credit refunds and she pays fees of $2\frac{1}{2}\%$ on the net credit-card sales.

The balance at the beginning of the week was $4228.34. Checks outstanding were $758.14, $38.37, $1671.88, $120.13, $2264.75, $78.11, $3662.73, $816.25, and $400. Lange had credit-card and bank deposits of $458.23, $771.18, $235.71, $1278.55, $663.52, and $1475.39 that were not recorded.

1. Find the net deposit given credit-card sales and refunds.   1. _____

2. Find the fee on the net credit-card sales.   2. _____

3. What is the total of the checks outstanding?   3. _____

4. Find the total of the deposits that were not recorded.   4. _____

5. Find the current balance in the account.   5. _____

INVESTIGATE

Look at your bank statement and identify any fees you pay and interest you earn. Name three factors other than cost that are important to you when selecting a bank. Does your bank meet your needs, or can you find one better suited to your situation?

Case in Point Summary Exercise

JACKSON & PERKINS

www.jacksonandperkins.com

Facts:

- 1872: Founded
- 1901: Sold first hybridized rose
- 1939: Began selling using mail order
- 1960s: Moved growing operations to California
- 2013: Shipped more than 2 million roses and plants

The Jackson & Perkins Company was founded in 1872 to wholesale strawberry and grape plants. But it quickly found its specialty in roses. Today, the firm's research scientists grow and evaluate more than 300,000 rose seedlings each year. It takes 7 to 10 years of hybridizing work to find a handful of the best and hardiest new varieties of roses. In order to help sell flowers, marketing at Jackson & Perkins has given fun or recognizable names to specific hybridized roses, including Sweet Intoxication and Pope John Paul II.

Barbara Wiffy at Rose Gardens does not grow her own roses. Rather, she buys them from Jackson & Perkins Wholesale, Inc., marks up the prices of the roses, and then sells them to her customers. Rose Gardens is an established customer that buys a lot of roses. Wiffy often places several orders with the company during a month but usually only makes one or two electronic payments to them each month. Following are copies of Rose Gardens' check register for the month and also the bank statement. Help Wiffy reconcile the business account to see what other charges should be added and subtracted from her balance and see if there are any errors in her check register.

Check Register—Rose Gardens

Check Num.	Date	Amount of Withdrawal	Amount of Deposit	Comment	Balance
				Balance Brought Forward	$9,277.59
	6/24	$1,000.00	-	Online Transfer to Savings	$8,277.59
761	6/25	$195.00	-	Wal-Mart	$8,082.59
	6/26	$2,446.82	-	Electronic—Mortgage Payment	$5,635.77
	6/26	$4,080.97	-	Electronic—Office Max	$1,554.80
	6/27	$395.07	-	Electronic—Utilities	$1,159.73
	6/28	-	$4,500.00	Online Transfer from ***5332	$5,659.73
762	6/29	$32.34	-	CVS—Pharmacy	$5,627.39
	6/29	-	$7,550.80	Direct deposit—debit	$13,178.19
	6/30	$2,153.93	-	Electronic—Dice Plants	$11,024.26
	7/1	-	$5,781.48	Regular Deposit	$16,805.74
763	7/3	$723.35	-	Max's Remodeling	$16,082.39
	7/14	$6,230.19	-	Electronic—Jackson & Per.	$9,852.20
764	7/15	$3,290.41	-	Bacon Farms	$6,561.79
	7/15	-	$2,705.00	Regular Deposit	$9,266.79

Source: JACKSON & PERKINS.

GLEN MEADOWS BANK

Bank Statement

Period: June 17 through July 16
Year: 2014

Checking Summary		Checks	
Balance Calculation		#761	195.00
Previous Balance	9,277.59	#762	32.34
Checks	227.34		
Withdrawals	16,315.93		
Deposits	20,537.28	**Interest**	
Interest Paid	0.57	7/16	0.57
Current Balance	**13,272.17**		

Date	Description	Withdrawals	Deposits	Balance
6/24	Online Transfer—to savings	1,000.00		
6/26	Online Pmt.—Mtge. Pymt.	2,446.82		
6/26	Debit Pmt.—Office Max	4,080.97		
6/27	Online Pmt.—Utilities	395.07		
6/28	Online Transfer—from checking		4,500.00	
6/29	Direct Deposit—Numerous Debit Purchases		7,550.80	
6/30	Online Pmt.—Dice Plants	2,153.93		
7/01	Regular Deposit		5,781.48	
7/14	Online Pmt.—Jackson & Per.	6,230.19		
7/15	Regular Deposit		2,705.00	
7/16	Fee to Bank	8.95		

Reconciliation

Checks Outstanding	
Number	Amount
Total	

(1) Enter new balance from bank statement: _____

(2) List any deposits made by you and not yet recorded by the bank:
+ _____
+ _____
+ _____
+ _____

(3) Add all numbers from lines above. _____
(4) Write total of checks outstanding: − _____
(5) Subtract (4) from (3). _____

To reconcile your records:

(6) List your checkbook balance: _____

(7) Write the total of any fees. − _____

(8) Subtract line (7) from line (6). _____

(9) Enter interest credit: + _____

(10) Add line (9) to line (8). Adjusted checkbook balance. _____

New balance

So, Wiffy's check register balances this month. The only items not recorded in her check register were the bank fee of $8.95 and the interest credit of $.57. She was relieved that none of her customer checks bounced since she often has 1 or 2 bounced checks each month.

Discussion Question: *Many people no longer reconcile their checking account, effectively trusting the bank. Is it reasonable for a business with a large volume of banking activity to not reconcile its checking account? Why or why not?*

Chapter 5   Test

To help you review, the numbers in brackets show the section in which the topic was discussed.

Use the table on page 176 to find the monthly checking-account service charge for the following accounts.   **[5.1]**

1. Tino's Italian Grocery, 62 checks, average balance $1834

1. _____

2. Gifts Galore, 44 checks, average balance $2398

2. _____

3. Batista Tile Works, 27 checks, average balance $418

3. _____

Complete the following three check stubs for Mad Men Advertising in 2014. Find the balance at the bottom of each stub.   **[5.1]**

Checks Written

Number	Date	To	For	Amount
2261	Aug. 6	WBC Broadcasting	Airtime	$6892.12
2262	Aug. 8	Lakeland Weekly	Ad	$1258.36
2263	Aug. 14	W. Wilson	Freelance Art	$416.14

Deposits made: $1572 on Aug. 7, $10,000 on Aug. 10.

4.

2261	
Date	_____
Amount	_____
To	_____
For	_____
Total	$16,409 82
Deposits	
This Check	
Other (+ or −)	
Balance	

5.

2262	
Date	_____
Amount	_____
To	_____
For	_____
Total	$9517 70
Deposits	
This Check	
Other (+ or −)	
Balance	

6.

2263	
Date	_____
Amount	_____
To	_____
For	_____
Total	$9831 34
Deposits	
This Check	
Other (+ or −)	
Balance	

EMILIO RODRIGUEZ GIFTS FOR EVERYONE, INC.   *The gift shop has gifts for all occasions. Use the following information about credit-card transactions to answer the next six questions.*   **[5.2]**

Sales		Refunds
$218.68	$135.82	$45.63
$37.84	$67.45	$36.36
$33.18	$461.82	
$20.76	$116.35	
$12.72	$23.78	
$8.97	$572.18	

7. Find the total amount of credit-card sales.

7. _____

8. What is the total amount of the refunds?

8. _____

9. Find credit-card sales less refunds.

9. _____

C indicates an exercise that is related to the Case in Point feature.

10. Assuming that the bank charges the retailer a $3\frac{1}{2}$% fee, find the amount of the fee at the statement date.

10. _____

11. Find the amount of the credit given to Emilio Rodriguez Gifts For Everyone, Inc. after the fee is subtracted.

11. _____

12. Weddings by Bobbi is a regular customer of Rose Gardens. Use the information in the following table to reconcile her checking account on the form that follows. **[5.3]**

12. _____

Balance from bank statement		$4721.30
Checks outstanding	3221	$82.74
(check number is given first)	3229	$69.08
	3230	$124.73
	3232	$51.20
Deposits not yet recorded		$758.06
		$32.51
		$298.06
Bank charge		$2.00
Interest credit		$9.58
Checkbook balance		$5474.60
Current balance		_____

Reconciliation

Checks Outstanding	
Number	Amount
Total	

Compare the list of checks paid by the bank with your records. List and total the checks not yet paid.

(1) Enter new balance from bank statement: _____

(2) List any deposits made by you and not yet recorded by the bank:
  + _____
  + _____
  + _____
  + _____

(3) Add all numbers from lines above. Total: _____

(4) Write total of checks outstanding: − _____

(5) Subtract (4) from (3). This is adjusted bank balance: _____

To reconcile your records:

(6) List your checkbook balance: _____

(7) Write the total of any fees or charges deducted by the bank and not yet subtracted by you from your checkbook: − _____

(8) Subtract line (7) from line (6). _____

(9) Enter interest credit: (Add to your checkbook) + _____

(10) Add line (9) to line (8). Adjusted checkbook balance. _____

New balance of your account; this number should be same as (5).

6 Payroll

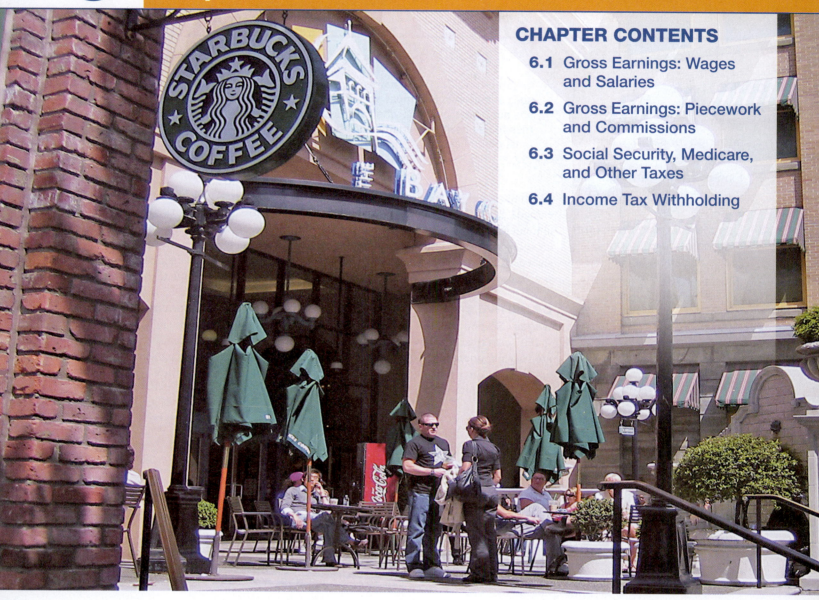

CHAPTER CONTENTS

6.1 Gross Earnings: Wages and Salaries

6.2 Gross Earnings: Piecework and Commissions

6.3 Social Security, Medicare, and Other Taxes

6.4 Income Tax Withholding

▼ CASE IN POINT

SARAH BRYNSKI worked at Starbucks when in college and was happy to be promoted to manager. She quickly discovered that completing payroll for her 15 employees was more complicated than she had anticipated. She decided to look at the history of two programs that involved deductions.

Brynski found that many elderly people suffered greatly during the Great Depression of the 1930s. The Social Security Act was passed in 1935 to help supplement the retirement income of the elderly as well as provide income for the disabled. Medicare was established in 1965 to help people 65 and over pay for hospital care, medical care, and, later,

prescriptions. Experts believe that without Social Security and Medicare, poverty would be greatly increased in the United States, especially among the elderly.

In her reading, Sarah also discovered that both Social Security and Medicare are projected to have financial problems. Without changes to the system, current projections forecast serious financial problems for Social Security by 2033 and for Medicare by 2024. Sarah realizes that these two programs are far too important to disappear, so she expects there will be some changes to both of them in the next few years.

It is important that payroll is done accurately. Making mistakes with payroll means that individuals, the state, or the federal government are not paid the correct amount(s). Calculations must be accurate and payments must be made on a timely basis.

▼ 6.1 Gross Earnings: Wages and Salaries

OBJECTIVES

1 Understand the methods of calculating gross earnings for salaries and wages.

2 Find overtime earnings for more than 40 hours of work per week.

3 Use the overtime premium method of calculating gross earnings.

4 Find overtime earnings for over 8 hours of work per day.

5 Understand double time, shift differentials, and split-shift premiums.

6 Find equivalent earnings for different pay periods.

7 Find overtime for salaried employees.

▼ **CASE IN POINT** As a manager at Starbucks, Sarah Brynski hires, schedules, and oversees employees. She must also make sure each is paid the correct amount. Occasionally, she authorizes overtime when a scheduled employee does not show up. However, she tries to use as little overtime as possible to help control costs. Businesses of every size must control costs.

The first step in preparing the payroll is to determine the **gross earnings** (the total amount earned). Several **deductions** may be subtracted from gross earnings to arrive at the **net pay**, the amount the employee actually receives. The employer must keep records to maintain an efficient business and to satisfy legal requirements. Many businesses use the services of a company such as Automatic Data Processing (ADP) to professionally prepare their payroll. Other businesses use computer software such as QuickBooks to help them complete this task.

OBJECTIVE 1 Understand the methods of calculating gross earnings for salaries and wages. Several methods are used to find an employee's pay. Salaries and wages are discussed in this section, and piecework and commission are discussed in the next section. Payroll checks are very important for livelihoods, partly since people do not have enough savings to fund their expenses for very long and so need their regular paycheck as shown below. Understanding how net pay is calculated can eliminate unwanted surprises.

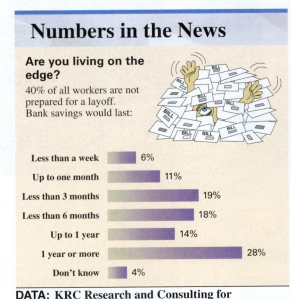

Numbers in the News

Are you living on the edge?

40% of all workers are not prepared for a layoff. Bank savings would last:

Less than a week	6%
Up to one month	11%
Less than 3 months	19%
Less than 6 months	18%
Up to 1 year	14%
1 year or more	28%
Don't know	4%

DATA: KRC Research and Consulting for Prudential Securities.

Payroll is often calculated based on hours worked. The hours worked can be stored digitally on a computer, or by using **time cards** which are shown in this section. Time cards often include: name and other personal information; the days, times, and hours worked; and the total number of hours worked. It may require the signature of the employee. Time cards are usually stamped using a special clock. The information on these cards is then transferred to a **payroll ledger** (a chart showing all payroll information) such as the one shown in Example 1.

Katie Nopper, whose payroll card is shown, is a shift manager at a local coffee shop and is paid an **hourly wage** of $14.80. Her gross earnings can be calculated with the following formula.

Gross earnings = Number of hours worked × Rate per hour

For example, if Nopper works 8 hours at $14.80 per hour, her gross earnings are

$$\text{Gross earnings} = 8 \times \$14.80 = \$118.40$$

PAYROLL CARD
NO TIME CLOCK REQUIRED

EMPL. NO. _1375_   CARD NO. _____

FULL NAME Katie Nopper   AGE (IF UNDER 18)

ADDRESS 412 Fawndale Drive   SOCIAL SECURITY NO. 123-45-6789

DATE EMPLOYED   POSITION Shift MGR   RATE $14.80

PAY PERIOD STARTING 7/23/2014   ENDING 7/27/2014

DATE	REGULAR TIME					OVER TIME		
	IN	OUT	IN	OUT	DAILY TOTALS	IN	OUT	DAILY TOTALS
7/23	8:00	11:50	12:20	4:30	8	4:30	6:30	2
7/24	7:58	12:00	12:30	4:30	8	5:00	7:30	2.5
7/25	8:00	12:00	12:30	4:32	8			
7/26	7:58	12:05	12:35	4:30	8	4:30	5:00	.5
7/27	8:01	12:00	1:00	5:00	8			

APPROVED BY _PD_   TOTAL REGULAR TIME 40   5

REGULAR DAYS WORKED 5 @ 8 HRS. @ 14.80   EARNINGS $ 592.00

ADDITIONAL COMPENSATION: VALUE OF MEALS, LODGING, GIFTS, ETC.   AMOUNT $ _____

COMMISSIONS, FEES, BONUSES, GOODS, ETC. OT 5 @ 22.²⁰   AMOUNT $ 111.00

OTHER REMUNERATIONS (KIND) $ _____

DEDUCTIONS: TOTAL EARNINGS $ 703.00

I CERTIFY THE FOREGOING TO BE A CORRECT ACCOUNT OF THE TIME WORKED AND WAGES RECEIVED:

SIGNATURE Katie Nopper   DATE PAID 8/1/2014

Completing a Payroll Ledger

EXAMPLE 1

Sarah Brynski is doing the payroll for two employees, Nelson and Orr. She must first complete a payroll ledger.

Employee	Hours Worked							Total Hours	Rate	Gross Earnings
	S	M	T	W	TH	F	S			
Nelson, L.	—	2	4	8	6	3	—		$8.40	
Orr, T.	—	3.5	3	7	6.75	7	—		$9.12	

SOLUTION

 CASE IN POINT First, find the total number of hours worked by each person.

Nelson: $2 + 4 + 8 + 6 + 3 = $ **23 hours**

Orr: $3.5 + 3 + 7 + 6.75 + 7 = $ **27.25 hours**

Then multiply the number of hours worked by the rate per hour to find the gross earnings.

	Nelson:	Orr:
	23	27.25
	× $8.40	× $9.12
	$193.20	**$248.52**

The payroll ledger can now be completed.

Employee	Hours Worked							Total Hours	Rate	Gross Earnings
	S	M	T	W	TH	F	S			
Nelson, L.	—	2	4	8	6	3	—	**23**	$8.40	**$193.20**
Orr, T.	—	3.5	3	7	6.75	7	—	**27.25**	$9.12	**$248.52**

The pay for workers varies by country and even by region within a country. The Big Mac Index shown below shows how long it takes an average worker in different countries to earn enough to buy a Big Mac at a McDonalds.

Numbers in the News

Big Mac Index

Measures how long an individual must work on average to earn enough to buy a Big Mac.

Tokyo	10 minutes
Los Angeles	11 minutes
New York	13 minutes
Budapest.......................	59 minutes
Cairo	82 minutes
Mexico City	129 minutes

DATA: *Parade Magazine*

OBJECTIVE 2 Find overtime earnings for more than 40 hours of work per week. The **Fair Labor Standards Act** covers the majority of full-time employees in the United States. It establishes a workweek of 40 hours and sets the minimum hourly wage. The law states that an **overtime** wage (a higher-than-normal wage) must be paid for all hours worked over 40 hours per workweek. Also, many companies not covered by the Fair Labor Standards Act have voluntarily followed the practice of paying a **time-and-a-half rate** ($1\frac{1}{2}$, or 1.5, times the normal rate) for any work over 40 hours per week. With the time-and-a-half rate, gross earnings are found with the following formula.

Gross earnings = Earnings at regular rate + Earnings at time-and-a-half rate

Completing a Payroll Ledger with Overtime

 EXAMPLE 2 Complete the following payroll ledger.

	Hours Worked							Total Hours		Reg.	Gross Earnings		
Employee	S	M	T	W	TH	F	S	Reg.	O.T.	Rate	Reg.	O.T.	Total
Lanier, D.	6	9	8.25	8	9	4.5	—			$8.30			
Morse, T.	—	10	6.75	9	6.25	10	4.25			$9.48			

SOLUTION

▼ CASE IN POINT   First, find the total number of hours worked.

Lanier: $6 + 9 + 8.25 + 8 + 9 + 4.5 =$ **44.75 hours**

Morse: $10 + 6.75 + 9 + 6.25 + 10 + 4.25 =$ **46.25 hours**

Both employees worked more than 40 hours. Gross earnings at the regular rate can now be found as discussed earlier. Lanier earned $40 \times \$8.30 = \$332$ at the regular rate, and Morse earned $40 \times \$9.48 = \$379.20$ at the regular rate. To find overtime earnings, first find the number of overtime hours worked by each employee.

Lanier: $44.75 -$ **40** $=$ **4.75 overtime hours**

Morse: $46.25 -$ **40** $=$ **6.25 overtime hours**

The regular rate given for each employee can be used to find the time-and-a-half rate.

Lanier: **1.5** $\times \$8.30 = \$12.45$

Morse: **1.5** $\times \$9.48 = \$14.22$

Now find the overtime earnings.

Lanier: 4.75 hours × **$12.45** per hour = **$59.14** (rounded)
Morse: 6.25 hours × **$14.22** per hour = **$88.88** (rounded)

The ledger can now be completed.

| Employee | Hours Worked | | | | | | | Total Hours | | Reg. Rate | Gross Earnings | | |
	S	M	T	W	TH	F	S	Reg.	O.T.		Reg.	O.T.	Total
Lanier, D.	6	9	8.25	8	9	4.5	—	**40**	**4.75**	$8.30	**$332.00**	**$59.14**	**$391.14**
Morse, T.	—	10	6.75	9	6.25	10	4.25	**40**	**6.25**	$9.48	**$379.20**	**$88.88**	**$468.08**

QUICK CHECK 2

Joseph Monti works 5 hours on Monday, 10 hours on Tuesday, 9.5 hours on Wednesday, 8.25 hours on Thursday, 6 hours on Friday, and 7.5 hours on Saturday. Monti is paid $9.85 per hour and time and a half for all hours over 40 per week. Find his gross earnings.

OBJECTIVE 3 Use the overtime premium method of calculating gross earnings. Gross earnings with overtime is sometimes found using the **overtime premium method**. This method produces the same result as the method used in Example 2. Add the total hours at the regular rate to the overtime hours at one-half the regular rate to arrive at gross earnings.

Overtime Premium Method

Straight-time earnings ⟵ total hours worked × regular rate
+ Overtime premium ⟵ overtime hours worked × ½ regular rate
Gross earnings

Using the Overtime Premium Method

EXAMPLE 3

This week, Holly Kelly worked 40 regular hours and 12 overtime hours. Her regular rate of pay is $17.40 per hour. Find her total gross pay, using the overtime premium method.

SOLUTION

Kelly's total hours are 40 + 12 = 52, and her overtime premium rate is .5 × $17.40 = $8.70.

52 hours × $17.40 = $904.80   regular rate earnings
12 overtime hours × $8.70 = $104.40   overtime premium
$1009.20   gross earnings

 The calculator solution uses the order of operations to find the regular earnings and the overtime earnings, and then adds these together.

52 ☒ 17.4 ⊞ 12 ☒ 17.4 ☒ .5 ⊟ 1009.2

Note: Refer to Appendix B for calculator basis.

QUICK CHECK 3

Janice Garinger worked 40 regular hours and 10 overtime hours this week. If her regular pay is $12.10 per hour, find her gross earning using the overtime premium method.

OBJECTIVE 4 Find overtime earnings for over 8 hours of work per day. Some companies pay the time-and-a-half rate for all time worked over 8 hours in any one day no matter how many hours are worked in a week. This **daily overtime** is shown in the next example.

Finding Overtime Each Day

EXAMPLE 4

One week, Jason Polanski worked the hours shown. Given that his regular pay is $10.10 per hour, find gross earnings.

	S	M	T	W	TH	F	S	Total Hours
Reg.	—	8	5	7	8	—	—	28
O.T.	—	2	—	—	4	—	—	6

SOLUTION

Polanski worked fewer than 40 hours this week. Still, his company pays time and a half for any hours over 8 in a day, so he will earn some overtime. The table shows that he worked 28 regular hours and 6 overtime hours.

$$\text{Overtime hourly pay} = \$10.10 \times 1\tfrac{1}{2} = \textbf{\$15.15 per hour}$$

Wages at regular rate: 28 hours × $10.10 = $282.80
Wages at overtime rate: 6 hours × **$15.15** = $90.90
Total gross earnings $373.70

Some careers require unusual hours and do not pay overtime for over 40 hours worked in a week or 8 hours in a day. An example is a firefighter, who may work 24 hours and then get 48 hours off.

QUICK CHECK 4

Luke Stansbury is paid $9.60 per hour and time and a half for all hours over 8 worked per day. He worked 9 hours on Monday, 6 hours on Tuesday, 12 hours on Wednesday, and 3 hours on Friday. Find his gross earnings for the week.

OBJECTIVE 5 Understand double time, shift differentials, and split-shift premiums. In addition to premiums paid for overtime, other **premium payment plans** include **double time** for holidays and, in some industries, for Saturdays and Sundays. A **shift differential** is often given to compensate employees for working less-desirable hours. For example, an additional amount per hour or per shift might be paid to swing shift (4:00 P.M. to midnight) and graveyard shift (midnight to 8:00 A.M.) employees.

Restaurant employees and nursing home employees often receive a **split-shift premium**. Hours are staggered so that the employees are on the job during only the busiest times. For example, an employee may work 4 hours, be off 4 hours, and then work another 4 hours. The employee is paid a premium because of this less-desirable schedule.

Some employers offer **compensatory time,** or **comp time,** for overtime hours worked. Instead of additional money, an employee is given time off from the regular work schedule as compensation for overtime hours already worked. Quite often, the compensatory time is calculated at $1\tfrac{1}{2}$ times the overtime hours worked. For example, 12 hours might be given as compensation for 8 hours of previously worked overtime. Occasionally, an employee is given a choice of overtime pay or comp time. Many companies reserve the use of compensatory time for their supervisory or managerial employees.

OBJECTIVE 6 Find equivalent earnings for different pay periods. The second common method of finding gross earnings uses a **salary,** a fixed amount per **pay period** (time between paychecks). Common pay periods are weekly, biweekly, semimonthly, and monthly.

Common Pay Periods

Monthly	12 paychecks each year
Semimonthly	Twice each month; 24 paychecks each year
Biweekly	Every 2 weeks; 26 paychecks each year
Weekly	52 paychecks each year

Determining Equivalent Earnings

EXAMPLE 5

A career counselor wants to compare the earnings of these employees:

Scott Perrine—weekly salary of $546   Julie Circle—semimonthly salary of $736

Tonya McCarley—biweekly salary of $1686   Bill Leonard—a monthly salary of $1818

For each, find **(a)** earnings per year, **(b)** earnings per month, and **(c)** earnings per week.

SOLUTION

Scott Perrine:
(a) $546 × **52** = $28,392 per year
(b) $28,392 ÷ **12** = $2366 per month
(c) $546 per week

Tonya McCarley:
(a) $1686 × **26** = $43,836 per year
(b) $43,836 ÷ **12** = $3653 per month
(c) $1686 ÷ **2** = $843 per week

Julie Circle:
(a) $736 × **24** = $17,664 per year
(b) $736 × **2** = $1472 per month
(c) $17,664 ÷ **52** = $339.69 per week

Bill Leonard:
(a) $1818 × **12** = $21,816 per year
(b) $1818 per month
(c) $21,816 ÷ **52** = $419.54 per week

QUICK CHECK 5

Glen Lewis receives a weekly salary of $852. Find his **(a)** earnings per year, **(b)** earnings per month, and **(c)** semimonthly earnings.

The data that follows shows that higher levels of education are usually associated with higher incomes. As you look at the data, ask yourself if you should go further in your education than you have planned.

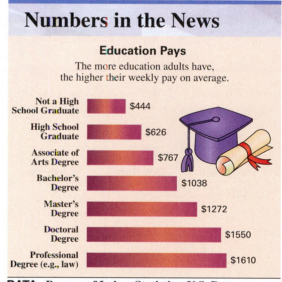

Numbers in the News

Education Pays

The more education adults have, the higher their weekly pay on average.

Not a High School Graduate	$444
High School Graduate	$626
Associate of Arts Degree	$767
Bachelor's Degree	$1038
Master's Degree	$1272
Doctoral Degree	$1550
Professional Degree (e.g., law)	$1610

DATA: Bureau of Labor Statistics, U.S. Department of Labor.

OBJECTIVE 7   Find overtime for salaried employees. A salary is ordinarily paid for the performance of a certain job, regardless of the number of hours worked. However, the Fair Labor Standards Act requires that employees in certain salaried positions receive additional compensation for overtime. Similar to a wage earner, some salaried workers are paid time and a half for all hours worked over 40 hours per week.

Finding Overtime for Salaried Employees

EXAMPLE 6

Monica Gonzales earns $936 a week as an assistant to the vice president of a community bank. A normal workweek for her is 40 hours. Find her gross earnings if she works 45 hours one week and is paid time and a half for everything over 40 hours.

SOLUTION

$$\text{Hourly equivalent to salary} = \frac{\$936}{40 \text{ hours}} = \$23.40$$

$$\text{Overtime rate} = 1\tfrac{1}{2} \times \$23.40 = \mathbf{\$35.10}$$

Find gross earnings as follows.

Regular wages	$936.00
Overtime wages **5 hours** × **$35.10** =	$175.50
	$1111.50 Gross earnings

▦ The calculator solution to this example is

936 ⊞ 936 ÷ 40 ⊠ 1.5 ⊠ 5 ⊟ 1111.5

QUICK CHECK 6

Elinor Nunes has a normal workweek of 35 hours and is paid $675.50 each week. What are her gross earnings in a week in which she works 42 hours?

▼ **6.1** Exercises   My MathLab®

The shaded sections below contain solutions to help you get a **QUICK START** *on the various types of exercises.*

Find the number of regular hours and the overtime hours (any hours over 40) for each employee. Then calculate the overtime rate (time and a half) for each employee. (See Examples 1 and 2.)

Employee	S	M	T	W	TH	F	S	Reg. Hrs.	O.T. Hours	Reg. Rate	O.T. Rate
1. Burke, E.	—	7	4	7	10	8	4	**40**	**0**	**$8.10**	**$12.15**
2. Elbern, J.	—	6.5	9	7.5	8	9.5	7			$8.24	
3. Kling, J.	3	5	8.25	9	8.5	5	—			$18.70	
4. Scholz, K.	8.5	9	7.5	8	10	8.25	—			$9.50	
5. Tomlin, M.	—	9.5	7	9	9.25	10.5	—			$11.48	

Using the information from Exercises 1–5, find the earnings at the regular rate, the earnings at the overtime rate, and the gross earnings for each employee. Round to the nearest cent. (See Example 2.)

Employee	Earnings at Reg. Rate	Earnings at O.T. Rate	Gross Earnings
6. Burke, E.	**$324**	**$0**	**$324**
7. Elbern, J.			
8. Kling, J.			
9. Scholz, K.			
10. Tomlin, M.			

Find the overtime rate, the amount of earnings at regular pay, the amount at overtime pay, and the total gross wages for each employee. Round to the nearest cent. (See Example 2.)

	Total Hours				Gross Earnings		
Employee	Reg.	O.T.	Reg. Rate	O.T. Rate	Regular	Overtime	Total
11. Deining, M.	39.5	—	$8.80	$13.20	$347.60	$0	$347.60
12. Demaree, D.	36.25	—	$10.20				
13. Snow, P.	40	4.5	$14.40				
14. Taylor, O.	40	6.75	$12.08				
15. Weyers, C.	40	4.25	$9.18				

◤**C** indicates an exercise that is related to the Case in Point feature.

Some companies use the overtime premium method to determine gross earnings. Use this method to complete the following payroll ledger. Overtime is paid at the time-and-a-half rate for all hours over 40. (See Example 3.)

		Hours Worked											Gross Earnings		
Employee	S	M	T	W	TH	F	S	Total Hours	Reg. Rate	O.T. Hours	O.T. Premium Rate	Reg.	O.T.	Total
16. Averell, B.	10	9	8	5	12	7	—	51	$11.40	11	$5.70	$581.40	$62.70	$644.10
17. Brownlee, K.	7.75	10	5	9.75	8	10	—		$9.50					
18. Carter, M.	—	12	11	8	8.25	11	—		$8.60					
19. Parks, K.	—	8.5	5.5	10	12	10.5	7		$12.50					
20. Parr, J.	—	10	9.75	9	11.5	10	—		$10.20					

Some companies pay overtime for all time worked over 8 hours in a given day. Use this method to complete the following payroll ledger. Overtime is paid at the time-and-a-half rate. (See Example 4.)

		Hours Worked						Total Hours				Gross Earnings		
Employee	S	M	T	W	TH	F	S	Reg.	O.T.	Reg. Rate	O.T. Rate	Reg.	O.T.	Total
21. Bailey, M.	—	10	9	11	6	5	—	35	6	$9.40	$14.10	$329.00	$84.60	$413.60
22. Campbell, C.	—	9	8.75	7	8.5	10	—			$9.85				
23. Ruhkala, B.	—	7.5	8	9	10.75	8	—			$10.80				
24. Salorin, B.	—	9	10	8	6	9.75	—			$17.20				
25. Warren, L.	—	9.5	8.5	7.75	8	9.5	—			$21.50				

26. In your own words, explain premium plans. Select a premium payment plan and describe it. (See Objective 5.)

27. If you were given a choice of overtime pay or compensatory time, which would you choose? Why? (See Objective 5.)

Find the equivalent earnings for each of the following salaries as indicated. (See Example 5.)

			Earnings		
	Weekly	Biweekly	Semimonthly	Monthly	Annual
28.	$496	$992	$1074.67	$2149.33	$25,792
29.	$443.08	$886.15	$960	$1920	$23,040
30.		$852			
31.				$5200	
32.					$26,100
33.	$830				
34.					$27,600

Find the weekly gross earnings for the following people who are on salary and normally work a 40-hour week. Overtime is paid at the time-and-a-half rate. (See Example 6.)

Employee	Weekly Salary	Hours Worked	Weekly Gross Earnings
35. Beckenstein, J.	$360	42	
36. de Bouchel, V.	$468	45	
37. Feist-Milker, R.	$420	43	
38. Johnson, J.	$520	56	
39. Mader, C.	$640	48	

Solve the following application problems.

40. RETAIL EMPLOYMENT Last week, Frank Nicolazzo worked 48 hours at Starbucks. Find his gross earnings for the week if he is paid $8.40 per hour and earns time and a half for all hours over 40 worked in a week.

48 − 40 = 8 overtime hours
1.5 × $8.40 = $12.60 overtime rate
40 × $8.40 = $336 regular
8 × $12.60 = $100.80 overtime
$336 + $100.80 = $436.80

40. $436.80

41. INSIDE SALES Jessica Parker is a sales associate at JC Penney and is paid $13.60 per hour for straight time and time and a half for all hours over 40 worked in a week. Find her gross earnings for a week in which she worked 52 hours.

41. _____

42. CRIMINOLOGY LAB Benito Zamora earns $12.80 per hour at his job as a lab assistant in a criminology lab. He is paid time and a half for everything worked over 8 hours in one day. Find his gross earnings for a week in which he worked the following hours: Monday, 9.5; Tuesday, 7; Wednesday, 10.75; Thursday, 4.5; and Friday, 8.75.

42. _____

43. OFFICE ASSISTANT Sheila Spinnay is an office assistant and worked 10 hours on Monday, 9.75 hours on Tuesday, 5.5 hours on Wednesday, 12 hours on Thursday, and 7.25 hours on Friday. Her regular rate of pay is $11.50 an hour, with time and a half paid for all hours over 8 worked in a given day. Find her gross earnings for the week.

43. _____

44. INSURANCE OFFICE MANAGER Alicia Klein is paid $728 a week as an insurance office manager. Her normal workweek is 40 hours. She gets paid time and a half for overtime. Find her gross earnings for a week in which she works 46 hours.

44. _____

45. **BEST BUY** A new employee in the Geek Squad at Best Buy earns $630 weekly. Find the equivalent earnings if the employee is paid (a) biweekly, (b) semimonthly, (c) monthly, and (d) annually.

(a) _____
(b) _____
(c) _____
(d) _____

46. **STORE MANAGER** Michelle Renda is assistant manager at Barnes and Noble and is paid $42,900 annually. Find the equivalent earnings if this amount is paid (a) weekly, (b) biweekly, (c) semimonthly, and (d) monthly.

(a) _____
(b) _____
(c) _____
(d) _____

47. Semimonthly pay periods result in 24 paychecks per year. Biweekly pay periods result in 26 paychecks per year. Which of these pay periods results in three checks in two months of the year? Will it always be the same two months? Explain.

48. Which would you prefer: a monthly pay period or a weekly pay period? What special budgetary issues might you consider regarding the pay period that you choose?

49. Describe the duties that a regular manager has and that regular employees do not have. Feel free to consider of a company with which you are familiar.

50. It is unusual for a new college graduate to be hired immediately as a manager responsible for more than 5-10 employees. Explain why you think this might be true.

QUICK CHECK ANSWERS

1. $236.69
2. $486.34
3. $665.50
4. $312
5. (a) $44,304 (b) $3692 (c) $1846
6. $878.15

6.2 Gross Earnings: Piecework and Commissions

OBJECTIVES

1 Find the gross earnings for piecework.

2 Determine the gross earnings for differential piecework.

3 Find the gross pay for piecework with a guaranteed hourly wage.

4 Calculate the overtime earnings for piecework.

5 Find the gross earnings using commission rate times sales.

6 Determine a commission using the variable commission rate.

7 Find the gross earnings with a salary plus commission.

OBJECTIVE 1 Find the gross earnings for piecework. The salaries and wages of the preceding section are **time rates** because they depend only on the actual time an employee is on the job. The methods described in this section are **incentive rates** because they are based on production, and pay an employee for actual performance on the job. The ten help-wanted ads from the classified section of the newspaper are for jobs offering incentive rates of pay. The ad for lathers and stucco construction workers offers piecework and hourly compensation, while the ad for truck drivers lists piece rates of 43 cents per mile (cpm). The ads for bill collectors and commercial roofing, health insurance, Better Business Bureau membership, automobile, swimming pool, and home security system sales positions pay on a commission plan.

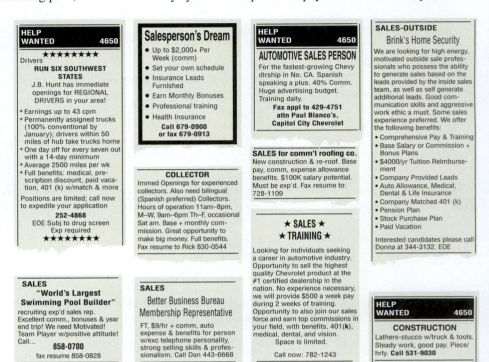

A **piecework rate** pays an employee a given amount per item produced. Gross earnings are found with the following formula.

$$\text{Gross earnings} = \text{Pay per item} \times \text{Number of items produced}$$

For example, a truck driver who drives 520 miles in one day and is paid a piecework rate of $.43 per mile has total gross earnings as follows.

$$\text{Gross earnings} = \$.43 \times 520 = \$223.60$$

Finding Gross Earnings for Piecework

EXAMPLE 1

Stacy Arrington is paid $.73 for sewing a jacket collar, $.86 for a sleeve with cuffs, and $.94 for a lapel. One week she sewed 318 jacket collars, 112 sleeves with cuffs, and 37 lapels. Find her gross earnings.

SOLUTION

Multiply the rate per item by the number of that type of item.

Item	Rate		Number		Total
Jacket collars	$.73	×	**318**	=	$232.14
Sleeves with cuffs	$.86	×	**112**	=	$96.32
Lapels	$.94	×	**37**	=	$34.78

Find the gross earnings by adding the three totals from the table.

$$\$232.14 + \$96.32 + \$34.78 = \mathbf{\$363.24}$$

QUICK CHECK 1

A production worker is paid $.58 for assembling a ceiling lamp, $1.23 for assembling a ceiling fan, and $.86 for assembling a box fan. One week a worker assembled 220 ceiling lamps, 318 ceiling fans, and 174 box fans. Find the worker's gross earnings.

OBJECTIVE 2 Determine the gross earnings for differential piecework. There are many variations to the straight piecework rate just described. For example, some rates have **quotas** that must be met, with a premium for each item produced beyond the quota. These plans offer an added incentive within an incentive. A typical **differential piece rate** plan is one where the rate paid per item depends on the number of items produced.

Using Differential Piecework

 EXAMPLE 2

Adecco is looking for individuals who enjoy working with their hands and are willing to bend, cut, and insert discrete electronic components such as integrated circuits into standard printed circuit boards and solder as required. The pay scale follows.

1–100 units	$2.10 each
101–150 units	$2.25 each
151 or more units	$2.40 each

Find the gross earnings of a worker producing **214 units**.

Quick TIP

With differential piecework, the highest amount paid applies to only the last units produced.

SOLUTION

$$\begin{array}{r} 214 \\ -\ 100 \\ \hline 114 \\ -\ 50 \\ \hline 64 \end{array}$$

← total units
← first 100 units →
← next 50 units →
← number over 150 →

100 units at $2.10 each = $210.00
50 units at $2.25 each = $112.50
64 units at $2.40 each = $153.60
214 total units = **$476.10**

The gross earnings are $476.10.

QUICK CHECK 2

Scooter Frame Company pays welders as follows: 1–150 frames, $2.85 each; 151–250, $3.20 each; and 251 or more, $3.45 each. Find the gross earnings of a worker who welds 282 frames.

OBJECTIVE 3 Find the gross pay for piecework with a guaranteed hourly wage. The piecework and differential piecework rates are frequently modified to include a guaranteed hourly pay rate. This is often necessary to satisfy federal and state laws concerning minimum wages. With this method, the employer must pay either the minimum wage or the piecework earnings, whichever is higher.

Finding Earnings with a Guaranteed Hourly Wage

 EXAMPLE 3

A tire installer at the Tire Center is paid $10.50 per hour for an 8-hour day or $1.15 per tire installed, whichever is higher. Find the weekly earnings for an employee having the following rate of production.

Quick TIP

The company guarantees that a tire installer will not earn less than $10.50 per hour or $84 ($10.50 · 8) for an 8-hour day.

Monday	85 tires
Tuesday	70 tires
Wednesday	88 tires
Thursday	68 tires
Friday	82 tires

SOLUTION

The hourly earnings for an 8-hour day are **$84 (8 × $10.50)**. The larger of hourly earnings or the piecework earnings is paid each day.

Monday   85 × $1.15 = $97.75 piece rate
Tuesday   7̶0̶ ̶×̶ ̶$̶1̶.̶1̶5̶ = $84 hourly earnings (piece rate is $80.50)
Wednesday   88 × $1.15 = $101.20 piece rate
Thursday   6̶8̶ ̶×̶ ̶$̶1̶.̶1̶5̶ = **$84 hourly earnings (piece rate is $78.20)**
Friday   82 × $1.15 = $94.30 piece rate
                                    $461.25 weekly earnings

QUICK CHECK 3

A cabinet door finisher is paid $14.70 per hour for an 8-hour day or $.95 per cabinet door finished, whichever is higher. Find the gross earnings for a worker who finished 106 doors on Monday, 127 doors on Tuesday, 152 doors on Wednesday, 120 doors on Thursday, and 138 doors on Friday.

OBJECTIVE 4 **Calculate the overtime earnings for piecework.** Piecework employees, like other workers, are paid time and a half for overtime. It is common for the overtime rate to be $1\frac{1}{2}$ times the regular rate per piece.

Calculating Earnings with Overtime Piecework

EXAMPLE 4

Jon Taylor fulfills order shipments at a large distribution center. He pulls items from stacks of inventory before handing orders to an operator who shrink wraps the order and puts an address label on it. Jon is paid $1.85 per order fulfilled during regular time and time and a half for all orders filled during overtime. Find his gross earnings for a week in which he fulfilled 293 orders during regular time and 36 orders during overtime.

SOLUTION

Gross earnings = Earnings at regular piece rate + Earnings at overtime piece rate

$$= \qquad \$1.85 \cdot 293 \qquad + \qquad \$1.85 \cdot 1\frac{1}{2} \cdot 36$$

$$= \qquad \$542.05 \qquad + \qquad \$99.90$$

$$= \mathbf{\$641.95}$$

QUICK CHECK 4

An assembler is paid $.84 for each child car seat assembled. During a recent week, she assembled 400 car seats during regular time and 138 car seats during overtime hours. If time and a half is paid for each overtime assembly, find the gross earnings for the week.

A **commission rate** pays a salesperson either a fixed percent of sales or a fixed amount per item sold. Commissions are designed to produce maximum output from the salesperson, since pay is directly dependent on sales. Different types of sales commission arrangements are discussed here.

OBJECTIVE 5 **Find the gross earnings using commission rate times sales.** With **straight commission**, the salesperson is paid a fixed percent of sales. Gross earnings are found with the following formula.

> Gross earnings = Commission rate × Amount of sales

The following data shows average incomes for some sales positions. However, the average probably does not mean a lot since some salespeople make far more than others. You can imagine that a mother of two young children who just started working as a real estate agent probably does not make anything near the income shown in the table, whereas a real estate agent who has worked in the business for years may make quite a bit more than that shown.

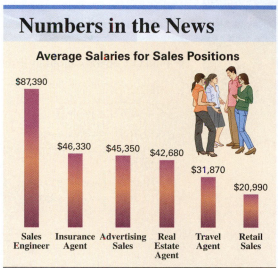

Numbers in the News

Average Salaries for Sales Positions

Sales Engineer	Insurance Agent	Advertising Sales	Real Estate Agent	Travel Agent	Retail Sales
$87,390	$46,330	$45,350	$42,680	$31,870	$20,990

DATA: Bureau of Labor Statistics, U.S. Department of Labor.

Determining Earnings Using Commission

EXAMPLE 5

A real estate broker charges a 6% commission. Find the commission on a house selling for $268,500.

SOLUTION

The commission is 6% × $268,500 = .06 × $268,500 = $16,110. The 6% is called the commission rate, or the **rate of commission**.

> ### QUICK CHECK 5
>
> An advertising sales representative is paid a 5% commission. Find the commission earned on sales of $9473.60.

Before the commission is calculated, any **returns** from customers, or any **allowances**, such as discounts, must be subtracted from sales.

Subtracting Returns When Using Commission

EXAMPLE 6

Amanda Roach, a food-supplements sales representative, had sales of $10,230 one month, with returns and allowances of $1120. If her commission rate is 12%, find her gross earnings.

SOLUTION

The returns and allowances must first be subtracted from gross sales. Then multiply the difference, net sales, by the commission rate.

$$\text{Gross earnings} = (\$10{,}230 \text{ gross sales} - \$1120 \text{ returns and allowances}) \times \mathbf{12\%}$$
$$= \$9110 \text{ net sales} \times .12$$
$$= \$1093.20 \text{ gross earnings}$$

> ### QUICK CHECK 6
>
> Nate Sellers, an Avon salesperson, had sales of $45,350 one month, with returns and allowances of $432. If his commission rate is 18%, find his gross earnings.

OBJECTIVE 6 Determine a commission using the variable commission rate. The **sliding scale**, or **variable commission**, is a method of pay designed to retain top-producing salespeople. Under such a plan, a higher rate of commission is paid as sales get larger and larger.

Finding Earnings Using a Variable Commission

EXAMPLE 7

Maureen O'Connor sells food and bakery products to businesses such as Starbucks and is paid as follows based on monthly sales.

Sales	Rate
Up to $10,000	6%
$10,001–$20,000	8%
$20,001 and up	9%

Find O'Connor's earnings if she has sales of $32,768 one month.

SOLUTION

▼ CASE IN POINT

$32,768 ← total sales
− 10,000 ← first $10,000 → $10,000 at 6% = $600.00
$22,768
− 10,000 ← next $10,000 → $10,000 at 8% = $800.00
$12,768 ← over $20,000 → $12,768 at 9% = $1149.12
$32,768 total sales   **$2549.12 total commission**

QUICK CHECK 7

Timmy Heslin sells office copiers to businesses and is paid a variable commission rate. His commission rate on sales up to $20,000 is 2%; sales of $20,001 to $30,000, 2.5%, and sales of $30,001 and up, 3%. If he has sales of $38,400, find the commission earned.

OBJECTIVE 7 Find the gross earnings with a salary plus commission. With a **salary plus commission**, the salesperson is paid a fixed sum per pay period, plus a commission on all sales. This method of payment is commonly used by large retail stores. Gross earnings with salary plus commission are found with the following formula.

> Gross earnings = Fixed amount per pay period + Amount earned on commission

Many salespeople like this method. It is especially attractive to beginning salespeople who lack selling experience. While providing an incentive, it offers the security of a guaranteed income to cover basic living costs. Occasionally, this income is an earnings advance or a **draw**, which is a loan against future commissions. This loan is paid back when future commissions are earned.

Adding Commission to a Salary

EXAMPLE 8

Jaime Bailey is paid $325 per week by Beverly's Creations, plus 3% on all sales over $500. During one week, her total sales were $2972. Find her gross earnings.

SOLUTION

Gross earnings = Weekly salary + 3% on sales above $500
= $325 + .03(**$2972** − **$500**)
= $325 + (.03 × **$2472**)
= $325 + $74.16
= $399.16

QUICK CHECK 8

Sanford Howard is paid a salary of $290 a week, plus a 4% commission on all sales over $750. Find his gross earnings for a week in which his total sales were $1870.

Commission-based earning plans may be a strong deterrent to attracting new salespeople. Many companies offer the salary plus commission and draw plans to help fill sales positions.

Subtracting a Draw to Find Earnings

EXAMPLE 9

Craig Johnson has office product sales of $36,850 for the month and is paid an 8% commission on all sales. He had draws of $850 for the month. Find his gross earnings after repaying the drawing account.

SOLUTION

$$\text{Gross earnings} = \text{Commissions} - \text{Draw}$$
$$= (.08 \times \$36,850) - \$850$$
$$= \$2948 - \$850$$
$$= \$2098$$

QUICK CHECK 9

Bob Smith has toy train sales of $18,540 for the month and is paid a 10% commission on all sales. If he had draws of $975 for the month, find his gross earnings after repaying the drawing account.

Wages vary significantly, depending on career. Look carefully at the following table which lists the median weekly wage for 50 different careers. Recall from the definition of median that half of the people make more than the median and the other half make less than the median. Those careers on the left usually require a college degree, whereas those on the right may not require a college degree but may require specialized training. Remember, it is not just about the money. It is also about finding a career that you will enjoy!

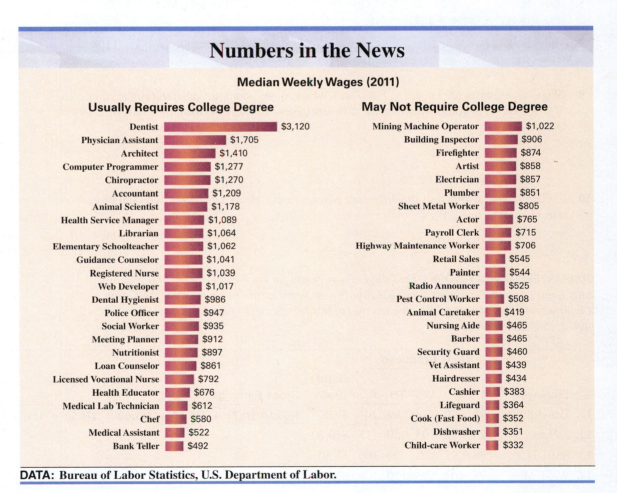

Numbers in the News

Median Weekly Wages (2011)

Usually Requires College Degree		May Not Require College Degree	
Dentist	$3,120	Mining Machine Operator	$1,022
Physician Assistant	$1,705	Building Inspector	$906
Architect	$1,410	Firefighter	$874
Computer Programmer	$1,277	Artist	$858
Chiropractor	$1,270	Electrician	$857
Accountant	$1,209	Plumber	$851
Animal Scientist	$1,178	Sheet Metal Worker	$805
Health Service Manager	$1,089	Actor	$765
Librarian	$1,064	Payroll Clerk	$715
Elementary Schoolteacher	$1,062	Highway Maintenance Worker	$706
Guidance Counselor	$1,041	Retail Sales	$545
Registered Nurse	$1,039	Painter	$544
Web Developer	$1,017	Radio Announcer	$525
Dental Hygienist	$986	Pest Control Worker	$508
Police Officer	$947	Animal Caretaker	$419
Social Worker	$935	Nursing Aide	$465
Meeting Planner	$912	Barber	$465
Nutritionist	$897	Security Guard	$460
Loan Counselor	$861	Vet Assistant	$439
Licensed Vocational Nurse	$792	Hairdresser	$434
Health Educator	$676	Cashier	$383
Medical Lab Technician	$612	Lifeguard	$364
Chef	$580	Cook (Fast Food)	$352
Medical Assistant	$522	Dishwasher	$351
Bank Teller	$492	Child-care Worker	$332

DATA: Bureau of Labor Statistics, U.S. Department of Labor.

▼ 6.2 Exercises

MyMathLab®

The shaded sections below contain solutions to help you get a **QUICK START** *on the various types of exercises.*

RECYCLING *Earth Plus pays workers $.48 per container for sorting recyclable materials. Find the daily gross earnings for each worker. (See Example 1.)*

Employee	Number of Containers	Gross Earnings	Employee	Number of Containers	Gross Earnings
1. Crossett, J.	194	**$93.12**	2. Biron, C.	292	_____
194 × $.48 = $93.12					
3. Campbell, K.	320	_____	4. Halcomb, J.	243	_____

AGRICULTURAL WORKERS *Find the daily gross earnings for each employee. (See Example 2.)*
Suppose that avocado pickers are paid as follows.

1–500 avocados	$.05 each
501–700 avocados	$.07 each
Over 700 avocados	$.09 each

Employee	Number of Avocados	Gross Earnings	Employee	Number of Avocados	Gross Earnings
5. Hoch, R.	820	**$49.80**	6. Leonard, M. K.	907	_____
(500 × $.05) + (200 × $.07) + (120 × $.09) = $49.80					
7. Matysek, J.	852	_____	8. Panunzio, K.	1108	_____

9. Wages and salaries are known as *time rates*, while commissions are called *incentive rates of pay*. Explain in your own words the difference between these payment methods. (See Objective 5.)

10. Explain in your own words the difference between a piecework rate and differential piece rate. (See Objective 2.)

GUARANTEED HOURLY WORK *Find the gross earnings for each employee by first finding the daily hourly earnings and then finding the daily piecework earnings. Each employee has an 8-hour workday and is paid $.75 for each unit of production or the hourly rate, whichever is higher. (See Example 3.)*

Employee	M	T	W	TH	F	Hourly Rate	Gross Earnings
11. Coughlin, S.	95	90	74	98	101	$8.20	**$353.60** $71.25 + $67.50 + $65.60 + $73.50 + $75.75 = $353.60
12. Jackson, S.	123	92	105	130	115	$10.20	_____
13. Shea, D.	98	92	102	96	106	$8.80	_____
14. Ward, M.	98	104	95	110	108	$9.10	_____

⚠️ C indicates an exercise that is related to the Case in Point feature.

PIECEWORK WITH OVERTIME *Find the gross earnings for each employee. Overtime is 1.5 times the normal rate per piece. (See Example 4.)*

	Units Produced			
Employee	Reg.	O.T.	Rate Per Unit	Gross Earnings
15. Shannon, B.	430	62	$.76	$397.48
16. Mc Donald, M.	530	58	$.74	_____
17. Jennings, A.	470	70	$.82	_____
18. O'Brien, K.	504	52	$.85	_____

COMMISSION WITH RETURNS *Find the gross earnings for each of the following salespeople. (See Examples 5 and 6.)*

Employee	Total Sales	Returns and Allowances	Rate of Commission	Gross Earnings
19. Mares, E.	$6210	$129	10%	$608.10
($6210 − $129) × 10% = $6081 × .1 = $608.10				
20. Peterson, J.	$5734	$415	7%	_____
21. Remington, J.	$2875	$64	15%	_____
22. Kling, J.	$3806	$108	20%	_____

VARIABLE-COMMISSION PAYMENT *Find the gross earnings for each of the following employees. (See Example 7.) Livingston's Concrete pays its salespeople the following commissions.*

6% on first $7500 in sales
8% on next $7500 in sales
10% on any sales over $15,000

Employee	Total Sales	Gross Earnings	Employee	Total Sales	Gross Earnings
23. Christensen, C.	$18,550	$1405	24. Hubbard, P.	$11,225	_____
($7500 × .06) + ($7500 × .08) + ($3550 × .10) = $1405					
25. Steed, F.	$10,480	_____	26. Goldstein, S.	$25,860	_____

SALARY PLUS COMMISSION *Fire Fighting Equipment pays salespeople as follows: $452 per week plus a commission of .9% on sales between $15,000 and $25,000, with 1.1% paid on sales in excess of $25,000. Find the gross earnings for each of the following salespeople. (No commission is paid on the first $15,000 of sales.) (See Example 8.)*

Employee	Total Sales	Gross Earnings	Employee	Total Sales	Gross Earnings
27. West, S.	$17,900	$478.10	28. Barnes, A.	$36,300	_____
$452 + $2900 × .009 = $478.10					
29. Feathers, C.	$32,874	_____	30. Maguire, J.	$28,400	_____

QUICK CHECK ANSWERS

1. $668.38   **2.** $857.90   **3.** $631.35   **4.** $509.88   **5.** $473.68   **6.** $8085.24   **7.** $902
8. $334.80   **9.** $879

▼ 6.3 Social Security, Medicare, and Other Taxes

OBJECTIVES

1 Understand FICA.
2 Find FICA tax and Medicare tax.
3 Determine the FICA tax and the Medicare tax paid by a self-employed person.
4 Find state disability insurance deductions.

▼ **CASE IN POINT**   Sarah Brynski must be able to show a new employee how her pay is calculated. It begins with total hours and hourly rate to find total income. However, there are various deductions from total income including two important federal programs: FICA (Social Security) and Medicare.

Finding gross earnings is only the first step in preparing a payroll. The employer must then subtract all required deductions from gross earnings. For most employees, these deductions include Social Security tax, Medicare tax, federal income tax withholding, and state income tax withholding. Other deductions may include state disability insurance, union dues, retirement, vacation pay, credit union savings or loan payments, purchase of bonds, uniform expenses, group insurance plans, and charitable contributions. Subtracting these deductions from gross earnings results in **net pay**, the amount the employee receives.

OBJECTIVE 1   Understand FICA.   The **Great Depression** of the 1930's was very difficult for many elderly people. President Franklin D. Roosevelt and Congress responded by passing the **Federal Insurance Contributions Act (FICA)** which created a plan called **Social Security**. The plan required all employees, employers, and self-employed individuals to make regular contributions from wages and self-employment income. In turn, it generated monthly benefits for retired workers, spouses of retired workers, and disabled workers. The table below shows that the maximum annual contribution for high earning individuals has increased from $45 (1.5% of $3000) in 1950 to $7049.40 (6.2% of $113,700) in 2013.

   Medicare was established in the 1960s to help those 65 and over, as well as younger people with disabilities, pay medical expenses. This program spreads the risk related to the costs of illness across a large group of people. It too requires contributions from employees, employers, and self-employed.

Employee Contributions

	Social Security Tax		Medicare Tax	
Year	Social Security Tax Rate	Employee Earnings Subject to the Tax	Medicare Tax Rate	Employee Earnings Subject to the Tax
1950	1.5%	$3,000	—	—
1960	3.0%	$4,800	.6%	$4,800
1970	4.2%	$7,800	1.05%	$7,800
1980	5.08%	$25,900	1.45%	$25,900
1990	6.2%	$51,300	1.45%	$51,300
2000	6.2%	$76,200	1.45%	all wages
2010	6.2%	$106,800	1.45%	all wages
2013	6.2%	$113,700	1.45%	all wages*

*The Health Care Act of 2010 results in yet higher Medicare taxes for high-income individuals and couples. We will not discuss these in the book.

   The contributions listed in the table above are paid by employees – just look at any payroll statement to see amounts withheld for FICA and Medicare. It is important to realize that the employer also pays the same rate as the employee into both systems, thereby matching employee contributions. Self-employed people pay nearly double the amount paid by workers.

   Whether a citizen or not, every employee must have a Social Security card. Applications for a Social Security card are made through Social Security offices or at most post offices. Each year the Social Security Administration sends out a statement to every worker showing past contributions and providing an estimate of future benefits. Since mistakes do occur, it is important to check the statements carefully. There is a limit of about three years, after which errors may not be corrected. You can obtain the necessary forms or get other information from the Social Security at 800-772-1213 or www.socialsecurity.gov.

The maximum earnings subject to Social Security as well as the tax rates for both Social Security and Medicare are determined by Congress. Since at least some these numbers change almost every year, we will use the following to find Social Security tax and Medicare tax throughout the book.

> **Finding Social Security and Medicare Taxes for Employees**
>
> Social Security tax = 6.2% of earnings up to $115.000*
>
> Medicare tax = 1.45% of total earnings
>
> *No Social Security tax is paid on earnings above $115,000 in one year.

You may wonder where these funds are used. Social Security provides more than one-half the income for about two-thirds of older Americans and Medicare pays medical bills for more than 50 million people. Someone in your family may either be receiving benefits now, or perhaps will receive benefits in the near future. Without Social Security and Medicare, there would be a lot more poverty among the elderly and disabled.

OBJECTIVE 2 Find FICA tax and Medicare tax. Remember to always use current rates and maximum income when finding the amount to be withheld for Social Security and Medicare.

Finding FICA Tax and Medicare Tax Help Jessica Ramirez, the manager at a local Panera Bread, find the Social Security and Medicare tax that must be withheld from the weekly earnings of two employees.

(a) Kelleher: $362.40 gross earnings   (b) Kimbrel: $468.02 gross earnings

SOLUTION

In each case, the tax is rounded to the nearest cent.

(a)   Wage × Tax rate = Tax

$362.40 × .062   = $22.47   **Social Security tax**

$362.40 × .0145 = $5.25   **Medicare tax**

(b)   Wage × Tax rate = Tax

$468.02 × .062   = $29.02   **Social Security tax**

$468.02 × .0145 = $6.79   **Medicare tax**

> **QUICK CHECK 1**
>
> Find (a) the Social Security tax and (b) the Medicare tax that must be withheld from gross earnings of $418.50.

Finding FICA Tax Shannon Woolums has earned $112,634.05 so far this year. Her gross earnings for the current pay period are $5224.03. Find her Social Security tax.

SOLUTION

The Social Security tax is paid only on the first $115,000 in earnings. First, subtract earnings to date from $115,000 to find the amount subject to Social Security tax during the current pay period.

$115,000.00   **Maximum earnings subject to Social Security tax**

− 112,634.05   **Earnings to date**

$ 2,365.95   **Amount subject to Social Security tax**

Social Security tax = $2365.95 × .062 = **$146.69**

No additional Social Security tax will be withheld for the remainder of the year.

The following table compares the contributions to social programs (similar to Social Security and Medicare in the United States) in selected countries around the world. How do U.S. workers' (employee) contributions compare with those of other countries?

Numbers in the News

Social Insurance Contributions As a Percent of Total Gross Earnings

Country	Employee	Employer
Italy	10.26%	48.00%
France	20.66%	42.57%
Sweden	33.00%	7.00%
Mexico	22.00%	3.00%
Germany	21.12%	21.12%
Japan	11.00%	12.00%
U.K.	7.08%	10.00%
Canada	5.00%	8.00%
U.S.A	7.65%	7.65%

DATA: *Benefits Report* **Europe, USA, and Canada; Watson Wyatt Worldwide, and Knight Ridder Tribune.**

OBJECTIVE 3 Determine the FICA tax and the Medicare tax paid by a self-employed person. People who are self-employed pay higher Social Security tax and higher Medicare tax than people who work for others. There is no employer to match the employee contribution, so the self-employed person pays a rate that is double that of an employee. The gross earnings of the self-employed person are first multiplied by 92.35% (.9235) to find the adjusted earnings. These adjusted earnings are then multiplied by the current rates. In our examples, the self-employed person pays 12.4% of adjusted earnings for Social Security tax and 2.9% of adjusted earnings for Medicare tax.

Finding FICA and Medicare Tax for the Self-Employed

 EXAMPLE 3

Find the Social Security tax and the Medicare tax paid by Ta Shon Williams, a self-employed Web designer who had adjusted earnings of $53,820 this year.

SOLUTION

$$\text{Social Security tax} = \$53,820 \times \textbf{12.4\%} = \$53,820 \times .124 = \$6673.68$$
$$\text{Medicare tax} = \$53,820 \times \textbf{2.9\%} = \$53,820 \times .029 = \$1560.78$$

OBJECTIVE 4 Find state disability insurance deductions. Many states have a state disability insurance (SDI) program. Qualifying employees must pay a portion of their earnings to the program. If an employee is injured and unable to work, the program pays the employee during the period of disability. The tax rate and amount subject to tax vary widely by state, but we will use an SDI deduction of 1% of gross earnings on the first $31,800 earned in a year. We assume no SDI deductions on earnings above this amount.

Finding State Disability Insurance Deductions

EXAMPLE 4

Find the state disability insurance deduction for an employee at Comet Auto Parts with gross earnings of $418 this pay period. The SDI rate is 1%, and the employee has not earned $31,800 this year.

SOLUTION

The state disability insurance deduction is $4.18 ($418 × **.01**).

QUICK CHECK 4

An employee has gross earnings of $525.80 this week. The employee has not earned $31,800 this year and the SDI rate is 1%. What is the state disability insurance deduction?

Knowing SDI Maximum Deductions

EXAMPLE 5

Jenoa Perkins has earned $29,960 so far this year. Find the SDI deduction if gross earnings this pay period are $2872. Use an SDI rate of 1% on the first $31,800.

SOLUTION

The SDI deduction will be taken on $1840 of the current gross earnings.

$31,800   maximum earnings subject to SDI
−$29,960   earnings this year
  $1,840   earnings subject to SDI

The SDI deduction is $18.40 ($1840 × .01).

QUICK CHECK 5

Linda Shirley has earned $30,780 so far this year. Her earnings this pay period are $3289. Find the SDI deduction using an SDI rate of 1% on the first $31,800.

▼ 6.3 Exercises

MyMathLab®

The shaded sections below contain solutions to help you get a **QUICK START** *on the various types of exercises.*

Find the Social Security tax and the Medicare tax for each of the following amounts of gross earnings. Assume a 6.2% FICA rate and a 1.45% Medicare tax rate. (See Example 1.)

| 1. $420 | $26.04 | $6.09 | 2. $942.50 | $58.44 | $13.67 | 3. $463.24 | | |
| 4. $606.35 | | | 5. $854.71 | | | 6. $683.65 | | |

SOCIAL SECURITY TAX *Find the Social Security tax for each employee for the current pay period. Assume a 6.2% FICA rate up to a maximum of $115,000. (See Example 2.)*

Employee	Gross Earnings This Year (So Far)	Earnings Current Pay Period	Social Security Tax
7. Dandridge, T.	$111,945.32	$6218.48	$189.39
8. Hale, R.	$112,438.75	$5200.00	$158.80
9. Hall, T.	$110,016.22	$7260.00	
10. Maurin, J.	$113,971.95	$4487.52	
11. Saraniti, S.	$114,329.75	$3053.73	
12. De Bouchel, V.	$113,974.08	$6160.86	

C indicates an exercise that is related to the Case in Point feature.

PAYROLL DEDUCTIONS *Find the regular earnings, overtime earnings, gross earnings, Social Security tax (6.2%), Medicare tax (1.45%), and state disability insurance deduction (1%) for each employee. Assume that no employee will have earned more than the FICA or SDI maximum at the end of the current pay period. Assume that time and a half is paid for any overtime in a 40-hour week. (See Examples 1–4.)*

Employee	Hours Worked	Regular Rate	Regular Earnings	Overtime Earnings	Gross Earnings	Social Security Tax	Medicare Tax	SDI Deduction
13. Garrett, R.	45.5	$9.22	$368.80	$76.07	$444.87	$27.58	$6.45	$4.45
14. Harcos, W.	47.75	$8.50	_____	_____	_____	_____	_____	_____
15. Plescia, P.	45	$14.20	_____	_____	_____	_____	_____	_____
16. Eckern, G.	45	$10.20	_____	_____	_____	_____	_____	_____
17. McIntosh, R.	47	$11.68	_____	_____	_____	_____	_____	_____
18. Wright, R.	46.75	$8.24	_____	_____	_____	_____	_____	_____

Solve the following application problems. Round to the nearest cent.

19. SOCIAL SECURITY AND MEDICARE Maria Ortega worked 43.5 hours last week at Starbucks. She is paid $8.58 per hour, plus time and a half for all hours over 40 per week. Find her **(a)** Social Security tax and **(b)** Medicare tax for the week.

Gross income is $(40 \times \$8.58) + (3.5 \times 1\frac{1}{2}) \times \$8.58 = \$388.25$
(a) Social Security tax is $.062 \times \$388.25 = \$24.07$
(b) Medicare tax is $.0145 \times \$388.25 = \$5.63$

(a) $24.07
(b) $5.63

20. SOCIAL SECURITY AND MEDICARE Chriscelle Merquillo receives 7% commission on all sales. Her sales on Monday of last week were $1412.20, with $1928.42 on Tuesday, $598.14 on Wednesday, $1051.12 on Thursday, and $958.72 on Friday. Find her **(a)** Social Security tax and **(b)** Medicare tax for the week.

(a) _____
(b) _____

21. PAYROLL DEDUCTIONS Donna Laughman is paid an 8% commission on sales. During a recent pay period, she had sales of $19,482 and returns and allowances of $193. Find the amount of **(a)** her Social Security tax, **(b)** her Medicare tax, and **(c)** her state disability insurance deduction for this pay period. (Assume the SDI rate is 1% and that earnings will not exceed $31,800.)

(a) _____
(b) _____
(c) _____

22. PAYROLL DEDUCTIONS Peter Phelps is a representative for Delta International Machinery and is paid $675 per week plus a commission of 2% on sales. His sales last week were $17,240. Find the amount of **(a)** his Social Security tax, **(b)** his Medicare tax, and **(c)** his state disability insurance deduction for the pay period. (Assume the SDI rate is 1% and that earnings will not exceed $31,800.)

(a) _____
(b) _____
(c) _____

SELF-EMPLOYMENT DEDUCTIONS *The following problems refer to self-employed individuals. These people pay a Social Security tax of 12.4% and Medicare tax of 2.9%. Find both of the taxes on the following annual adjusted earnings. (See Example 3.)*

23. Tony Romano, owner of The Cutlery, earned $58,238.74.

23. _____

24. Rachel Leach, an interior designer, earned $36,724.72.

24. _____

25. Krystal McClellan, cosmetics consultant, earned $29,104.80.

25. _____

26. Ron Morris, a Chic-Filet franchise owner, earned $78,007.14.

26. _____

27. Peggy Kelleher, shop owner, earned $26,843.60.

27. _____

28. Sadie Chambers, senior account executive, earned $92,748.32.

28. _____

29. A young person who has just received her first paycheck is puzzled by the amounts that have been deducted from gross earnings. Briefly explain both the FICA and Medicare deductions to this person. (See Objectives 1–2.)

30. Describe the difference between the FICA paid by an employee and FICA paid by a self-employed person. (See Objective 3.)

6.4 Income Tax Withholding

OBJECTIVES

1   Understand the Employee's Withholding Allowance Certificate.

2   Find the federal withholding tax using the wage bracket method.

3   Find the federal withholding tax using the percentage method.

4   Find the state withholding tax using the state income tax rate.

5   Find net pay when given gross wages, taxes, and other deductions.

6   Find the quarterly amount owed to the Internal Revenue Service.

7   Understand additional employer responsibilities and employee benefits.

▼ **CASE IN POINT**   After completing the payroll at Starbucks, all FICA taxes, Medicare taxes, and federal withholding taxes withheld from employees are sent to the Internal Revenue Service. It is essential that managers keep current with all of the changes in the tax codes that affect withholding.

The federal government relies on income taxes paid by individuals and corporations. In this section, we will talk about withholding for the **personal income tax** that must be paid by individuals. The **income tax withheld** is periodically sent by the company to the **Internal Revenue Service (IRS)**.

OBJECTIVE 1 Understand the Employee's Withholding Allowance Certificate. The income taxes withheld from a paycheck are based on the marital status and the number of **withholding allowances** claimed on the W-4 form filed with the employer. **Marital status** is based on whether an individual is married on the last day of the year. A married person with three children normally claims five allowances, one for each person in the family. However, people who want a refund when filing taxes can choose to have more withheld each pay period by decreasing the number of withholding allowances. The allowances claimed on the following W-4 form are used simply to help business estimate the amount to withhold for each employee. The exact number of allowances must be used by the employee on his tax return at the end of the year, so that the correct income tax can be calculated.

Source: Department of the Treasury Internal Revenue Service.

The amount to be withheld from each paycheck is based on **gross earnings**. Higher earners usually have larger amounts withheld. Employers may use either of two methods to determine the amount of federal withholding tax to deduct from paychecks: the **wage bracket method** and the **percentage method**. Remember, the process at this step simply results in an estimate of the amount of income tax that must be paid by the employee. The exact amount of income tax that must be paid for the year is not known until the income tax return is completed.

WAGE BRACKET METHOD

SINGLE Persons—WEEKLY Payroll Period

If the wages are —		And the number of withholding allowances claimed is —										
At least	But less than	0	1	2	3	4	5	6	7	8	9	10
		The amount of income tax to be withheld is —										
300	310	31	20	12	4	0	0	0	0	0	0	0
310	320	33	22	13	5	0	0	0	0	0	0	0
320	330	34	23	14	6	0	0	0	0	0	0	0
330	340	36	25	15	7	0	0	0	0	0	0	0
340	350	37	26	16	8	1	0	0	0	0	0	0
350	360	39	28	17	9	2	0	0	0	0	0	0
360	370	40	29	18	10	3	0	0	0	0	0	0
370	380	42	31	20	11	4	0	0	0	0	0	0
380	390	43	32	21	12	5	0	0	0	0	0	0
390	400	45	34	23	13	6	0	0	0	0	0	0
400	410	46	35	24	14	7	0	0	0	0	0	0
410	420	48	37	26	15	8	1	0	0	0	0	0
420	430	49	38	27	16	9	2	0	0	0	0	0
430	440	51	40	29	18	10	3	0	0	0	0	0
440	450	52	41	30	19	11	4	0	0	0	0	0
450	460	54	43	32	21	12	5	0	0	0	0	0
460	470	55	44	33	22	13	6	0	0	0	0	0
470	480	57	46	35	24	14	7	0	0	0	0	0
480	490	58	47	36	25	15	8	1	0	0	0	0
490	500	60	49	38	27	16	9	2	0	0	0	0
500	510	61	50	39	28	17	10	3	0	0	0	0
510	520	63	52	41	30	19	11	4	0	0	0	0
520	530	64	53	42	31	20	12	5	0	0	0	0
530	540	66	55	44	33	22	13	6	0	0	0	0
540	550	67	56	45	34	23	14	7	0	0	0	0

Source: Department of the Treasury Internal Revenue Service.

MARRIED Persons—WEEKLY Payroll Period

If the wages are —		And the number of withholding allowances claimed is —										
At least	But less than	0	1	2	3	4	5	6	7	8	9	10
		The amount of income tax to be withheld is —										
500	510	36	28	20	13	6	0	0	0	0	0	0
510	520	37	29	21	14	7	0	0	0	0	0	0
520	530	39	30	22	15	8	0	0	0	0	0	0
530	540	40	31	23	16	9	1	0	0	0	0	0
540	550	42	32	24	17	10	2	0	0	0	0	0
550	560	43	33	25	18	11	3	0	0	0	0	0
560	570	45	34	26	19	12	4	0	0	0	0	0
570	580	46	35	27	20	13	5	0	0	0	0	0
580	590	48	37	28	21	14	6	0	0	0	0	0
590	600	49	38	29	22	15	7	0	0	0	0	0
600	610	51	40	30	23	16	8	1	0	0	0	0
610	620	52	41	31	24	17	9	2	0	0	0	0
620	630	54	43	32	25	18	10	3	0	0	0	0
630	640	55	44	33	26	19	11	4	0	0	0	0
640	650	57	46	35	27	20	12	5	0	0	0	0
650	660	58	47	36	28	21	13	6	0	0	0	0
660	670	60	49	38	29	22	14	7	0	0	0	0
670	680	61	50	39	30	23	15	8	1	0	0	0
680	690	63	52	41	31	24	16	9	2	0	0	0
690	700	64	53	42	32	25	17	10	3	0	0	0
700	710	66	55	44	33	26	18	11	4	0	0	0
710	720	67	56	45	34	27	19	12	5	0	0	0
720	730	69	58	47	36	28	20	13	6	0	0	0
730	740	70	59	48	37	29	21	14	7	0	0	0
740	750	72	61	50	39	30	22	15	8	0	0	0

Source: Department of the Treasury Internal Revenue Service.

OBJECTIVE 2 **Find the federal withholding tax using the wage bracket method.** The Internal Revenue Service supplies withholding tax tables to be used with the wage bracket method. These tables are extensive, covering weekly, biweekly, semimonthly, monthly, and daily pay periods. Samples of the withholding tables are shown on this page and the next page.

WAGE BRACKET METHOD

SINGLE Persons—MONTHLY Payroll Period

If the wages are –		And the number of withholding allowances claimed is —										
At least	But less than	0	1	2	3	4	5	6	7	8	9	10
		The amount of income tax to be withheld is —										
1,600	1,640	180	132	85	49	17	0	0	0	0	0	0
1,640	1,680	186	138	91	53	21	0	0	0	0	0	0
1,680	1,720	192	144	97	57	25	0	0	0	0	0	0
1,720	1,760	198	150	103	61	29	0	0	0	0	0	0
1,760	1,800	204	156	109	65	33	2	0	0	0	0	0
1,800	1,840	210	162	115	69	37	6	0	0	0	0	0
1,840	1,880	216	168	121	73	41	10	0	0	0	0	0
1,880	1,920	222	174	127	79	45	14	0	0	0	0	0
1,920	1,960	228	180	133	85	49	18	0	0	0	0	0
1,960	2,000	234	186	139	91	53	22	0	0	0	0	0
2,000	2,040	240	192	145	97	57	26	0	0	0	0	0
2,040	2,080	246	198	151	103	61	30	0	0	0	0	0
2,080	2,120	252	204	157	109	65	34	2	0	0	0	0
2,120	2,160	258	210	163	115	69	38	6	0	0	0	0
2,160	2,200	264	216	169	121	74	42	10	0	0	0	0
2,200	2,240	270	222	175	127	80	46	14	0	0	0	0
2,240	2,280	276	228	181	133	86	50	18	0	0	0	0
2,280	2,320	282	234	187	139	92	54	22	0	0	0	0
2,320	2,360	288	240	193	145	98	58	26	0	0	0	0
2,360	2,400	294	246	199	151	104	62	30	0	0	0	0
2,400	2,440	300	252	205	157	110	66	34	2	0	0	0
2,440	2,480	306	258	211	163	116	70	38	6	0	0	0
2,480	2,520	312	264	217	169	122	74	42	10	0	0	0
2,520	2,560	318	270	223	175	128	80	46	14	0	0	0
2,560	2,600	324	276	229	181	134	86	50	18	0	0	0

Source: Department of the Treasury Internal Revenue Service.

MARRIED Persons—MONTHLY Payroll Period

If the wages are –		And the number of withholding allowances claimed is —										
At least	But less than	0	1	2	3	4	5	6	7	8	9	10
		The amount of income tax to be withheld is —										
2,200	2,240	159	123	91	60	28	0	0	0	0	0	0
2,240	2,280	165	127	95	64	32	0	0	0	0	0	0
2,280	2,320	171	131	99	68	36	4	0	0	0	0	0
2,320	2,360	177	135	103	72	40	8	0	0	0	0	0
2,360	2,300	183	139	107	76	44	12	0	0	0	0	0
2,400	2,440	189	143	111	80	48	16	0	0	0	0	0
2,440	2,480	195	148	115	84	52	20	0	0	0	0	0
2,480	2,520	201	154	119	88	56	24	0	0	0	0	0
2,520	2,560	207	160	123	92	60	28	0	0	0	0	0
2,560	2,600	213	166	127	96	64	32	1	0	0	0	0
2,600	2,640	219	172	131	100	68	36	5	0	0	0	0
2,640	2,680	225	178	135	104	72	40	9	0	0	0	0
2,680	2,720	231	184	139	108	76	44	13	0	0	0	0
2,720	2,760	237	190	143	112	80	48	17	0	0	0	0
2,760	2,800	243	196	148	116	84	52	21	0	0	0	0
2,800	2,840	249	202	154	120	88	56	25	0	0	0	0
2,840	2,880	255	208	160	124	92	60	29	0	0	0	0
2,880	2,920	261	214	166	128	96	64	33	1	0	0	0
2,920	2,960	267	220	172	132	100	68	37	5	0	0	0
2,960	3,000	273	226	178	136	104	72	41	9	0	0	0
3,000	3,040	279	232	184	140	108	76	45	13	0	0	0
3,040	3,080	285	238	190	144	112	80	49	17	0	0	0
3,080	3,120	291	244	196	149	116	84	53	21	0	0	0
3,120	3,160	297	250	202	155	120	88	57	25	0	0	0
3,160	3,200	303	256	208	161	124	92	61	29	0	0	0

Source: Department of the Treasury Internal Revenue Service.

Finding Federal Withholding Using the Wage Bracket Method

EXAMPLE 1

Benito Flores works for Best Buy. He is single and claims no withholding allowances since he prefers to get money back from the government when filing his income tax return. This choice will increase the amount withheld from his paycheck every week. Use the wage bracket method to find his withholding tax for a 30-hour workweek in which his gross earnings were $338.

Quick TIP

It is important to use the correct table when finding the amount to withhold.

SOLUTION

Use the table for single person, weekly payroll period. The earnings of $338 are found in the row for at least $330 but less than $340 and the column for 0 withholding allowances. The amount to be withheld for federal income taxes is $36. So, Flores's gross income for the week will be reduced by $36.

QUICK CHECK 1

Rachel Leach is single and claims two withholding allowances. Use the wage bracket method to find her withholding tax if her weekly gross earnings are $358.

Using the Wage Bracket Method for Federal Withholding

EXAMPLE 2

Pat Rowell is married, claims three withholding allowances, and has monthly gross earnings of $3016.47. Find her withholding tax using the wage bracket method.

SOLUTION

Use the table for married persons—monthly payroll period. Look down the two left columns, and find the range that includes Rowell's gross earnings: "at least $3000 but less than $3040." Read across the table to the column headed "3" (for the three withholding allowances). The withholding tax is $140. Had Rowell claimed five withholding allowances, her withholding tax would have been only $76.

QUICK CHECK 2

Bob Martinez has monthly earnings of $2839.78. He is married and claims four withholding allowances. Find his withholding tax using the wage bracket method.

OBJECTIVE 3 Find the federal withholding tax using the percentage method. Many companies today prefer to use the *percentage method* to determine federal withholding tax. The percentage method does not require the several pages of tables needed with the wage bracket method and is more easily adapted to computer applications in the processing of payrolls.

Percentage Method: Amount for One Withholding Allowance

Payroll Period	One Withholding Allowance
Weekly	$73.08
Biweekly	$146.15
Semimonthly	$158.33
Monthly	$316.67

Tables for Percentage Method of Withholding

TABLE 1—WEEKLY Payroll Period

(a) SINGLE person (including head of household)—

If the amount of wages (after subtracting withholding allowances) is:
Not over $41 . . . . $0

Over—	But not over—	The amount of income tax to withhold is:	of excess over—
$41	—$209	. . . $0.00 plus 10%	—$41
$209	—$721	. . . $16.80 plus 15%	—$209
$721	—$1,688	. . . $93.60 plus 25%	—$721
$1,688	—$3,477	. . . $335.35 plus 28%	—$1,688
$3,477	—$7,510	. . . $836.27 plus 33%	—$3,477
$7,510	. . . .	. . . $2,167.16 plus 35%	—$7,510

(b) MARRIED person—

If the amount of wages (after subtracting withholding allowances) is:
Not over $156 . . . . $0

Over—	But not over—	The amount of income tax to withhold is:	of excess over—
$156	—$490	. . . $0.00 plus 10%	—$156
$490	—$1,515	. . . $33.40 plus 15%	—$490
$1,515	—$2,900	. . . $187.15 plus 25%	—$1,515
$2,900	—$4,338	. . . $533.40 plus 28%	—$2,900
$4,338	—$7,624	. . . $936.04 plus 33%	—$4,338
$7,624	. . . .	. . . $2,020.42 plus 35%	—$7,624

TABLE 2—BIWEEKLY Payroll Period

(a) SINGLE person (including head of household)—

If the amount of wages (after subtracting withholding allowances) is:
Not over $83 . . . . $0

Over—	But not over—	The amount of income tax to withhold is:	of excess over—
$83	—$417	. . . $0.00 plus 10%	—$83
$417	—$1,442	. . . $33.40 plus 15%	—$417
$1,442	—$3,377	. . . $187.15 plus 25%	—$1,442
$3,377	—$6,954	. . . $670.90 plus 28%	—$3,377
$6,954	—$15,019	. . . $1,672.46 plus 33%	—$6,954
$15,019	. . . .	. . . $4,333.91 plus 35%	—$15,019

(b) MARRIED person—

If the amount of wages (after subtracting withholding allowances) is:
Not over $312 . . . . $0

Over—	But not over—	The amount of income tax to withhold is:	of excess over—
$312	—$981	. . . $0.00 plus 10%	—$312
$981	—$3,031	. . . $66.90 plus 15%	—$981
$3,031	—$5,800	. . . $374.40 plus 25%	—$3,031
$5,800	—$8,675	. . . $1,066.65 plus 28%	—$5,800
$8,675	—$15,248	. . . $1,871.65 plus 33%	—$8,675
$15,248	. . . .	. . . $4,040.74 plus 35%	—$15,248

TABLE 3—SEMIMONTHLY Payroll Period

(a) SINGLE person (including head of household)—

If the amount of wages (after subtracting withholding allowances) is:
Not over $90 . . . . $0

Over—	But not over—	The amount of income tax to withhold is:	of excess over—
$90	—$452	. . . $0.00 plus 10%	—$90
$452	—$1,563	. . . $36.20 plus 15%	—$452
$1,563	—$3,658	. . . $202.85 plus 25%	—$1,563
$3,658	—$7,533	. . . $726.60 plus 28%	—$3,658
$7,533	—$16,271	. . . $1,811.60 plus 33%	—$7,533
$16,271	. . . .	. . . $4,695.14 plus 35%	—$16,271

(b) MARRIED person—

If the amount of wages (after subtracting withholding allowances) is:
Not over $338 . . . . $0

Over—	But not over—	The amount of income tax to withhold is:	of excess over—
$338	—$1,063	. . . $0.00 plus 10%	—$338
$1,063	—$3,283	. . . $72.50 plus 15%	—$1,063
$3,283	—$6,283	. . . $405.50 plus 25%	—$3,283
$6,283	—$9,398	. . . $1,155.50 plus 28%	—$6,283
$9,398	—$16,519	. . . $2,027.70 plus 33%	—$9,398
$16,519	. . . .	. . . $4,377.63 plus 35%	—$16,519

TABLE 4—MONTHLY Payroll Period

(a) SINGLE person (including head of household)—

If the amount of wages (after subtracting withholding allowances) is:
Not over $179 . . . . $0

Over—	But not over—	The amount of income tax to withhold is:	of excess over—
$179	—$904	. . . $0.00 plus 10%	—$179
$904	—$3,125	. . . $72.50 plus 15%	—$904
$3,125	—$7,317	. . . $405.65 plus 25%	—$3,125
$7,317	—$15,067	. . . $1,453.65 plus 28%	—$7,317
$15,067	—$32,542	. . . $3,623.65 plus 33%	—$15,067
$32,542	. . . .	. . . $9,390.40 plus 35%	—$32,542

(b) MARRIED person—

If the amount of wages (after subtracting withholding allowances) is:
Not over $675 . . . . $0

Over—	But not over—	The amount of income tax to withhold is:	of excess over—
$675	—$2,125	. . . $0.00 plus 10%	—$675
$2,125	—$6,567	. . . $145.00 plus 15%	—$2,125
$6,567	—$12,567	. . . $811.30 plus 25%	—$6,567
$12,567	—$18,796	. . . $2,311.30 plus 28%	—$12,567
$18,796	—$33,038	. . . $4,055.42 plus 33%	—$18,796
$33,038	. . . .	. . . $8,755.28 plus 35%	—$33,038

> **Finding the amount of withholding using the percentage method**
>
> Step 1   Multiply the number of withholding allowances by the amount for one withholding allowance from the table.
>
> Step 2   Subtract the amount found in step 1 from gross earnings.
>
> Step 3   Find the appropriate table for percentage method of withholding and then the row.
>
> Step 4   Follow the directions in the table to find the tax to be withheld.

Finding Federal Withholding Using the Percentage Method

EXAMPLE 3

Sarah Brynski at Starbucks is married, claims two withholding allowances, and had weekly gross earnings of $690 one week. Use the percentage method to find the withholding tax.

SOLUTION

▼ CASE IN POINT

Step 1   From the table in the middle of the previous page, the amount for one withholding allowance, weekly payroll is $73.08.

Number of allowances $\times$ Amount for one allowance = 2 $\times$ $73.08 = **$146.16**

Step 2   Gross earnings $-$ Amount from step 1 = $690 $-$ **$146.16** = **$534.84**

Step 3   Use the table on the previous page for weekly payroll period, married person.

Step 4   Go to the row of **over $490 but not over $1515**.

Withholding = $33.40 plus **15% of excess over $490**

= $33.40 + **.15** · (**$543.84** − **$490**)

= $33.40 + $8.08   **rounded**

= $41.48

 The calculator solution to this example is

690 − 2 × 73.08 = 534.84 [STO]

33.40 + .15 × (RCL − $490) = 41.48

QUICK CHECK 3

Sadie Simms is married and claims three withholding allowances. Use the percentage method to find her withholding tax in a week when she has earnings of $1263.

Finding Federal Withholding Using the Percentage Method

EXAMPLE 4

Dac Kien is married, claims three withholding allowances, and receives $7850 a month working as a chemical engineer for Dupont. Use the percentage method to find his withholding tax.

SOLUTION

Step 1   The amount of one withholding allowance for monthly is $316.67.

Number of allowances $\times$ Amount for one allowance = 3 $\times$ $316.67 = **$950.01**

Step 2   Gross earnings $-$ Amount from step 1 = $7850 $-$ **$950.01** = $6899.99

Step 3   Use the table on the prior page for monthly payroll and married person.

Step 4   Go to the row of over $6567 but not over $12,567.

Withholding = $811.30 plus 25% of excess over $6567

= $811.30 + .25 · ($6899.99 − $6567)

= $894.55

QUICK CHECK 4

Howard Martin has earnings of $5735 for the month. He is married and claims four withholding allowances. Use the percentage method to find his withholding tax.

Finding Federal Withholding Using the Percentage Method

 EXAMPLE 5

Andy Herrebout is single, claims two withholding allowances, and has weekly gross earnings of $1838. Use the percentage method to find the withholding tax.

SOLUTION

One withholding allowance for weekly is $73.08.

$$\text{Number of allowances} \times \text{Amount for one allowance} = 2 \times \$73.08 = \mathbf{\$146.16}$$

$$\text{Gross earnings} - \text{Amount above} = \$1838 - \mathbf{\$146.16} = \$1691.84$$

Go to the row of over $1688, but not over $3477 on Table 1(a) for single person, weekly.

$$\text{Withholding} = \$335.35 \text{ plus } 28\% \text{ of the excess over } \$1688$$
$$= \$335.35 + .28 \cdot (\$1691.84 - \$1688)$$
$$= \$336.43$$

QUICK CHECK 5

Carol Dixon has biweekly earnings of $4350, is single, and claims two withholding allowances. Use the percentage methods to find her withholding tax.

The amount of withholding tax found using the wage bracket method will vary slightly from the amount of withholding tax found using the percentage method. Remember, both of these method just give an estimate of how much tax should be withheld. The actual income tax must be calculated at the end of the year using a federal income tax return.

OBJECTIVE 4 Find the state withholding tax using the state income tax rate. Many states and cities also have an income tax collected by withholding. Income taxes vary from state to state, with no state income tax in Alaska, Florida, Nevada, South Dakota, Texas, Washington, and Wyoming. A few states have a flat tax rate (percent of income) as a **state income tax**, while the majority of the states issue tax tables with taxes going as high as 9% and 10%. Income tax rates for a few states are shown below.

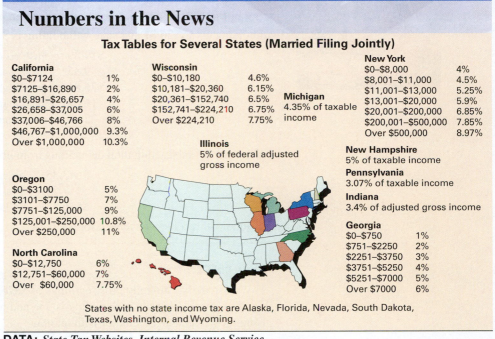

Numbers in the News

Tax Tables for Several States (Married Filing Jointly)

California		Wisconsin		New York	
$0–$7124	1%	$0–$10,180	4.6%	$0–$8,000	4%
$7125–$16,890	2%	$10,181–$20,360	6.15%	$8,001–$11,000	4.5%
$16,891–$26,657	4%	$20,361–$152,740	6.5%	$11,001–$13,000	5.25%
$26,658–$37,005	6%	$152,741–$224,210	6.75%	$13,001–$20,000	5.9%
$37,006–$46,766	8%	Over $224,210	7.75%	$20,001–$200,000	6.85%
$46,767–$1,000,000	9.3%			$200,001–$500,000	7.85%
Over $1,000,000	10.3%			Over $500,000	8.97%

Michigan 4.35% of taxable income

Illinois 5% of federal adjusted gross income

New Hampshire 5% of taxable income

Pennsylvania 3.07% of taxable income

Indiana 3.4% of adjusted gross income

Oregon	
$0–$3100	5%
$3101–$7750	7%
$7751–$125,000	9%
$125,001–$250,000	10.8%
Over $250,000	11%

North Carolina	
$0–$12,750	6%
$12,751–$60,000	7%
Over $60,000	7.75%

Georgia	
$0–$750	1%
$751–$2250	2%
$2251–$3750	3%
$3751–$5250	4%
$5251–$7000	5%
Over $7000	6%

States with no state income tax are Alaska, Florida, Nevada, South Dakota, Texas, Washington, and Wyoming.

DATA: *State Tax Websites, Internal Revenue Service.*

Finding the State Withholding Tax

EXAMPLE 6

Hilda Worthington works as a nurse in Indiana and earns $4250 for the month. Find the tax rate for Indiana from the chart and calculate the state withholding tax.

SOLUTION

Indiana has a flat tax rate of 3.4%.

$$\text{Tax} = \$4250 \times .034 = \$144.50$$

OBJECTIVE 5 Find net pay when given gross wages, taxes, and other deductions. It is common for employees to request additional deductions, such as union dues and credit union payments. The final amount of pay received by the employee equals gross earnings minus deductions. This final amount is called net pay and is given by the following formula.

Finding Net Pay

Gross earnings
$-$FICA tax (Social Security)
$-$Medicare tax
$-$Federal withholding tax
$-$State withholding tax
$-$Other deductions
Net pay

You may be thinking that is a lot of deductions, and it is. The category "other deductions" may include payments for medical care, life insurance, disability insurance, vision insurance, and retirement contributions. There may be many deductions and they differ widely from employee to employee. It is important that employers calculate these numbers carefully and correctly.

Determining Net Pay After Deductions

EXAMPLE 7

Kizzy Johnstone is married and claims three withholding allowances. Her weekly gross earnings are $643.35. Her state withholding is 2.5% of her gross income and her union dues are $25. Find her net pay using the percentage method of withholding.

SOLUTION

First find FICA (Social Security) tax, which is $39.89; then Medicare, which is $9.33. Federal withholding tax is $26.81 and state withholding is $16.08. Total deductions are

$39.89	FICA tax (6.2%)
9.33	Medicare tax (1.45%)
$26.81	federal withholding
16.08	state withholding (2.5%)
+ 25.00	union dues
$117.11	total deductions

Find net pay by subtracting total deductions from gross earnings.

$643.35	gross earnings
$-$$117.11	total deductions
$526.24	net pay

Johnstone will receive a paycheck for $526.24.

OBJECTIVE 6 Find the quarterly amount owed to the Internal Revenue Service. An employee's contribution to Social Security and Medicare must be matched by the employer.

Finding the Amount of FICA and Medicare Tax Due

EXAMPLE 8

If the employees at Fair Oaks Automotive Repair pay a total of $789.10 in Social Security tax and $182.10 in Medicare tax, how much must the employer send to the Internal Revenue Service?

SOLUTION

The employer must match this amount and send a total of $971.20 ($789.10 + $182.10 from employees) + $971.20 (from employer) = $1942.40 to the government.

> **QUICK CHECK 8**
>
> Payless Dry Cleaners withheld $461.90 in Social Security tax and $108.03 in Medicare tax from employees. How much must the employer send to the Internal Revenue Service?

In addition to withholding the employee's Social Security tax and a matching amount paid by the employer, the employer must also send the amount withheld for income tax to the Internal Revenue Service on a quarterly basis.

Finding the Employer's Amount Due the IRS

EXAMPLE 9

During a certain quarter one movie theater collected $2765.42 from its employees for FICA tax, $646.75 for Medicare tax, and $3572.86 in federal withholding tax. Compute the total amount due to the government.

SOLUTION

$2765.42	collected from *employees* for FICA tax
2765.42	equal amount paid by *employer* for FICA tax
646.75	collected from *employees* for Medicare tax
646.75	equal amount paid by *employer* for Medicare tax
3572.86	federal withholding tax
$10,397.20	total due to government

The movie theater must send $10,397.20 to the Internal Revenue Service.

> **QUICK CHECK 9**
>
> In one quarter, City Electronics collected $1953.82 in Social Security tax, $456.75 in Medicare tax, and $3780.47 in federal withholding tax from its employees. Find the total amount due to the government by the employer.

OBJECTIVE 7 Understand additional employer responsibilities and employee benefits. Each quarter, employers must file **Form 941, the Employer's Quarterly Federal Tax Return.** The form itemizes total employee wages and earnings, the income taxes withheld from employees, the FICA taxes withheld from employees, and the FICA taxes paid by the employer.

The **Federal Unemployment Tax Act (FUTA)** requires employers to pay an additional tax. This **unemployment insurance tax,** paid entirely by employers, is used to pay unemployment benefits to an individual who has become unemployed and is unable to find work. In general, all employers who paid wages of $1500 or more in a calendar quarter, or had one or more employees for some part of a day in any 20 or more different weeks, must file an employer's annual Federal Unemployment Tax (FUTA) return.

Although rates vary, the employer must pay up to 6.2% of the first $7000 in earnings for that year for each employee. Since most states have unemployment taxes, the employer is given credit for these when filing the FUTA return. As soon as the employee reaches earnings of $7000, no additional unemployment tax must be paid.

The **fringe benefits** offered today are very important to employees. These are the extras offered by the employer that go beyond the paycheck and include health care, dental care, retirement plan contributions, day care, housing, life insurance, tuition reimbursement, sick leave, vacation, profit sharing, and other benefits.

▼ 6.4 Exercises   MyMathLab®

The shaded sections below contain solutions to help you get a **QUICK START** *on the various types of exercises.*

FEDERAL WITHHOLDING TAX *Find the federal withholding tax for the following employees. Use the wage bracket method. (See Examples 1 and 2.)*

Employee	Gross Earnings	Married?	Withholding Allowances	Federal Withholding Tax
1. Safron, I.	$3128.51 monthly	yes	3	$155
2. Stanger, J.	$425.76 weekly	no	2	$27
3. Costa, P.	$507.52 weekly	yes	0	_____
4. Elle, M.	$2416.88 monthly	yes	1	_____
5. Alexander, L.	$1868.29 monthly	no	2	_____
6. Schaller, M.	$1953.35 monthly	no	1	_____
7. Moss, L.	$3012.50 monthly	yes	5	_____
8. Zagmon, B.	$391.18 weekly	no	1	_____
9. Mehta, S.	$1622.41 monthly	no	3	_____
10. Sommerfield, K.	$725.32 weekly	yes	0	_____
11. Weisner, W.	$2134.86 monthly	no	5	_____
12. NgauTibbits, C.	$748.30 weekly	yes	2	_____

STATE WITHHOLDING TAX *Use the state income tax rate given to find the state withholding tax for the following employees. Round to the nearest cent. (See Example 6.)*

Employee	Gross Weekly Earnings	State Income Tax Rate	State Withholding
13. Azzaro, J.	$245.18	2.8%	$6.87
14. Burner, P.	$368.53	3.5%	$12.90
15. Davis, L.	$466.71	6%	_____
16. Lundborg, J.	$541.45	5%	_____
17. Fox, D.	$1607.23	4.3%	_____
18. Ticarro, C.	$2802.58	4.95%	_____

🔺 indicates an exercise that is related to the Case in Point feature.

EMPLOYEE NET PAY *Use the percentage method of withholding to find federal withholding tax, a 6.2% FICA rate to find FICA tax, and 1.45% to find Medicare tax for the following employees. Then find the net pay for each employee. The number of withholding allowances and the marital status are listed after each employee's name. Assume that no employee has earned over $115,000 so far this year. (See Examples 3 and 5.)*

Employee	Gross Earnings	FICA	Medicare Tax	Federal Withholding Tax	Net Pay
19. Hamel; 4, M	$576.28 weekly	$35.73	$8.36	$12.80	$519.39
20. Guardino; 3, S	$2878.12 monthly	$178.44	$41.73	$226.12	$2431.83
21. Foster; 1, S	$3512.53 monthly				
22. Erb; 2, M	$625 weekly				
23. Terry; 3, M	$2276.83 semimonthly				
24. Galluccio; 1, S	$420.17 weekly				
25. Derma; 6, M	$2971.06 semimonthly				
26. Eddy; 2, M	$1020 weekly				
27. Wann; 3, S	$3753.18 biweekly				
28. Zamost; 2, S	$6625.24 monthly				
29. Reilly; 1, S	$1786.44 weekly				
30. Gertz; 4, M	$2618.50 biweekly				

31. Write an explanation of how to determine the federal withholding tax using the wage bracket (tax tables) method. (See Objective 2.)

32. Write an explanation of how to find the federal withholding tax using the percentage method. (See Objective 3.)

33. In your present or past job, which deductions were subtracted from gross earnings to arrive at net pay? Which was the largest deduction?

34. If you were an employer, would you prefer to use the wage bracket method or the percentage method to determine federal withholding tax? Why? (See Objectives 2 and 3.)

AMOUNT OWED THE IRS *Calculate the total amount owed to the Internal Revenue Service from each of the following firms. (See Example 9.)*

Firm	FICA Tax Collected from Employees	Medicare Tax Collected from Employees	Total Federal Withholding Tax	Amount Due IRS
35. Starbucks	$1483.59	$342.37	$5096.13	$8748.05
36. Atlasta Ranch	$265.36	$61.24	$4111.68	_____
37. Tony Balony's	$8212.18	$1895.37	$33,117.42	_____
38. Plescia Produce	$212.78	$49.10	$958.68	_____
39. Todd Consultants	$7271.39	$1678.24	$26,423.84	_____
40. Hartmann Shoes	$6538.42	$1508.87	$22,738.57	_____

Use the percentage method of withholding, a FICA rate of 6.2%, a Medicare rate of 1.45%, an SDI rate of 1%, and a state withholding tax of 3.4% in the following problems.

41. MARKETING REPRESENTATIVE David Horwitz, an industrial salesperson, has weekly earnings of $975. He is married and claims four withholding allowances. His deductions include FICA, Medicare, federal withholding, state disability insurance, state withholding, union dues of $15.50, and credit union savings of $100. Find his net pay for a week in February.
Net pay = $975 − $60.45 − $14.14 − $62.30 − $9.75 − $33.15 − $15.50 − $100 = $679.71

41. $679.71

42. STARBUCKS DISTRICT MANAGER Awanata Jackson, district manager for Starbucks, has earnings of $1147 in one week of March. She is single and claims four withholding allowances. Her deductions include FICA, Medicare, federal withholding, state disability insurance, state withholding, a United Way contribution of $15, and a savings bond of $100. Find her net pay for the week.

42. _____

43. EDUCATIONAL SALES Karen Jordon, a salesperson for Weber Scientific, is paid a salary of $410 per week plus 7% of all sales over $5000. She is single and claims two withholding allowances. Her deductions include FICA, Medicare, federal withholding, state disability insurance, state withholding, credit union savings of $50, a Salvation Army contribution of $10, and dues of $15 to the National Association of Professional Saleswomen. Find her net pay for a week in April during which she had sales of $11,284 with returns and allowances of $424.50.

43. _____

44. TRAVEL-AGENCY SALES Scott Salman, a travel agent, is paid on a variable commission, is married, and claims four withholding allowances. He receives 3% of the first $20,000 in sales, 4% of the next $10,000 in sales, and 6% of all sales over $30,000. This week he has sales of $45,550 and the following deductions: FICA, Medicare, federal withholding, state disability insurance, state withholding, a retirement contribution of $45, a savings bond of $50, and charitable contributions of $20. Find his net pay after subtracting all of his deductions.

44. _____

45. HEATING-COMPANY REPRESENTATIVE   Evelyn Beaton, a commission sales representative for Alternative Heating Company, is paid a monthly salary of $4200 plus a bonus of 1.5% on monthly sales. She is married and claims three withholding allowances. Her deductions include FICA, Medicare, federal withholding, state disability insurance, no state withholding, credit union savings of $150, charitable contributions of $25, and a savings bond of $50. Find her net pay for a month in which her sales were $42,618. The state in which Beaton works has no state income tax.

45. _____

46. RIVER RAFT MANAGER   River Raft Adventures pays its manager, Kathryn Speers, a monthly salary of $2880 plus a commission of .8% based on total monthly sales volume. In May, River Raft Adventures has total sales of $86,280. Speers is married and claims five withholding allowances. Her deductions include FICA, Medicare, federal withholding, state disability insurance, state withholding of $159.30, credit union payment of $300, March of Dimes contribution of $20, and savings bonds of $250. Find her net pay for May.

46. _____

QUICK CHECK ANSWERS

1. $17
2. $88
3. $116.46
4. $496.50
5. $861.50
6. $140.29 (rounded)
7. $6648.30
8. $1139.86
9. $8601.61

Chapter 6   Quick Review

Chapter Terms *Review the following terms to test your understanding of the chapter. For each term you do not know, refer to the page number found next to that term.*

allowances [**p. 219**]

commission rate [**p. 218**]

compensatory (comp) time [**p. 210**]

daily overtime [**p. 209**]

deductions [**p. 206**]

differential piece rate [**p. 217**]

double time [**p. 210**]

draw [**p. 220**]

Fair Labor Standards Act [**p. 208**]

Federal Insurance Contributions Act (FICA) [**p. 224**]

Federal Unemployment Tax Act (FUTA) [**p. 237**]

Form 941 [**p. 237**]

fringe benefits [**p. 237**]

Great Depression [**p. 224**]

gross earnings [**p. 206**]

hourly wage [**p. 206**]

incentive rates [**p. 216**]

income tax withheld [**p. 230**]

Internal Revenue Service (IRS) [**p. 230**]

marital status [**p. 230**]

Medicare [**p. 224**]

net pay [**p. 206**]

overtime [**p. 208**]

overtime premium method [**p. 209**]

pay period [**p. 210**]

payroll ledger [**p. 206**]

percentage method [**p. 230**]

personal income tax [**p. 230**]

piecework rate [**p. 216**]

premium payment plans [**p. 210**]

quotas [**p. 217**]

rate of commission [**p. 219**]

returns [**p. 219**]

salary [**p. 210**]

salary plus commission [**p. 220**]

SDI deduction [**p. 227**]

shift differential [**p. 210**]

sliding scale [**p. 219**]

Social Security [**p. 224**]

split-shift premium [**p. 210**]

state income tax [**p. 235**]

straight commission [**p. 218**]

time-and-a-half rate [**p. 208**]

time card [**p. 206**]

time rates [**p. 216**]

unemployment insurance tax [**p. 237**]

variable commission [**p. 219**]

wage bracket method [**p. 230**]

withholding allowances [**p. 230**]

CONCEPTS

EXAMPLES

6.1 Gross earnings

Gross earnings = Hours worked × Rate per hour

40 hours worked at $8.40 per hour

Gross earnings = **40** × $8.40 = $336

6.1 Gross earnings with overtime

First, find the regular earnings. Then, determine overtime pay at overtime rate. Finally, add regular and overtime earnings.

Gross earnings =
Earnings at regular rate + Earnings at time-and-half rate

40 regular hours at $8.40 per hour
10 overtime hours at time and a half

Gross earnings = (40 × $8.40) + (**10 × $8.40 × 1.5**)

= $336 + $126

= $462

6.1 Common pay periods

Pay Period	Paychecks Per Year
Monthly	12
Semimonthly	24
Biweekly	26
Weekly	52

Find the earnings equivalent of $2800 per month for other pay periods.

$$\text{Semimonthly} = \frac{\mathbf{\$2800}}{\mathbf{2}} = \$1400$$

$$\text{Biweekly} = \frac{\mathbf{\$2800 \times 12}}{\mathbf{26}} = \$1292.31$$

$$\text{Weekly} = \frac{\mathbf{\$2800 \times 12}}{\mathbf{52}} = \$646.15$$

6.1 Overtime for salaried employees

First, find the hourly equivalent. Next, multiply the hourly equivalent rate by the overtime hours by 1.5. Finally, add overtime earnings to the salary.

Salary is $648 per week for 40 hours. Find the earnings for 46 hours.

$648 ÷ **40** = $16.20 per hour

$16.20 × **6** × **1.5** = $145.80 overtime

$648 + $145.80 = $793.80

6.2 Gross earnings for piecework

Gross earnings = Pay per item × Number of items

Items produced, 175; pay per item, $.65; find the gross earnings.

$.65 × 175 = $113.75

CONCEPTS	EXAMPLES
6.2 Gross earnings for differential piecework The rate paid per item produced varies with level of production.	1–100 items, \$1.35 each 101–150 items, \$1.45 each 151 or more items, \$1.60 each Find the gross earnings for producing 214 items. $100 \times \$1.35 = \$135.00$ first 100 units $50 \times \$1.45 = \$72.50$ next 50 units $\underline{64 \times \$1.60 = \$102.40}$ number over 150 214 total items \$309.90 total earnings
6.2 Overtime earnings on piecework Gross earnings = Earnings at regular rate + Earnings at overtime rate	Items produced on regular time, 530; items produced on overtime, 110; piece rate \$.60; find the gross earnings. Gross earnings = $(530 \times \$.60) + 110(1.5 \times \$.60) = \$318 + \$99$ $= \$417$
6.2 Straight commission Gross earnings = Commission rate × Amount of sales	Sales of \$25,800; commission rate is 5%. $.05 \times \$25,800 = \$1290$
6.2 Variable commission Commission rate varies at different sales levels.	Up to \$10,000, 6% \$10,001–\$20,000, 8% \$20,001 and up, 9% Find the commission on sales of \$32,768. $.06 \times \$10,000 = \$600.00$ first \$10,000 $.08 \times \$10,000 = \$800.00$ next \$10,000 $.09 \times \$12,768 = \textbf{\$1149.12}$ amount over \$20,000 **\$32,768** **\$2549.12** total commission
6.2 Salary and commission Gross earnings = Fixed earnings + Commission	Salary, \$450 per week; commission rate, 3%; find the gross earnings on sales of \$6848. Gross earnings = $\$450 + (.03 \times \$6848) = \$450 + \$205.44$ $= \$655.44$
6.2 Commission with a drawing account Gross earnings = Commission − Draw	Sales for month, \$38,560; commission rate, 7%; draw, \$750 for month; find the gross earnings. Gross earnings = $(.07 \times \$38,560) - \$750 = \$2699.20 - \$750$ $= \$1949.20$
6.3 FICA; Social Security tax The gross earnings are multiplied by the tax rate. When the maximum earnings are reached, no additional FICA is withheld that year.	Gross earnings, \$458; Social Security tax rate, 6.2%; find the Social Security tax. $\$458 \times .062 = \$28.40$
6.3 Medicare tax The gross earnings are multiplied by the Medicare tax rate. Medicare tax is paid on all earnings.	Gross earnings, \$458; Medicare tax rate, 1.45%; find the Medicare tax. $\$458 \times .0145 = \$6.64$
6.3 State disability insurance deductions Multiply the gross earnings by the SDI tax rate. When the maximum earnings are reached, no additional taxes are paid in that year.	Gross earnings, \$2880; SDI tax rate, 1%; find SDI tax. $\$2880 \times .01 = \$28.80$

CONCEPTS	EXAMPLES
6.4 Federal withholding tax—wage bracket A tax must be paid on the total earnings. Look up the amount in the wage bracket table.	Single employee, 3 allowances, weekly earnings of $468. Find the amount to withhold. Wage bracket table for single, weekly, row with at least $460 but less than $470, 3 allowances. Withholding = **$22**
6.4 Federal withholding tax—percentage A tax must be paid on the total earnings. 1. Multiply number of withholding allowances by the amount for one allowance from table. 2. Find gross earnings – amount in step 1. 3. Use the appropriate table and row. 4. Follow the directions in the table.	Single employee, 2 withholding allowances, weekly earnings of $535. Find the amount to withhold. 1. 3 allowances $\times$ $73.08 = $219.24 2. $535 $-$ $219.24 = $315.76 3. Table for single, weekly, row for over $209 but not over $721 4. $16.80 + 15% of excess over $209 $16.80 + .15 $\times$ ($315.76 $-$ $209) = $32.81
6.4 State withholding tax Tax is paid on total earnings. No maximum as with FICA.	Married employee with weekly earnings of $692; find the state withholding tax given a state withholding tax rate of 4.5%. **4.5%** $\times$ **$692** = .045 $\times$ $692 = $31.14
6.4 Quarterly report, Form 941 Filed each quarter and calculated as follows: FICA paid by employees FICA paid by employer Medicare paid by employees Medicare paid by employer + Federal withholding tax paid by employees Total to be sent to the IRS	If quarterly FICA withheld from employees is $5269, Medicare tax is $1581, and federal withholding tax is $14,780, find the total owed to the IRS by the employer. (**$5269** + **$1581**) $\times$ **2** + $14,780 = $28,480

Case Study

PAYROLL: FINDING YOUR TAKE-HOME PAY

Janice Wong receives an annual salary of $42,536, which is paid weekly. Her normal work-week is 40 hours, and she is paid time and a half for all overtime. She is single and claims one withholding allowance. Her deductions include FICA, Medicare, federal withholding, state disability insurance, state withholding, credit union payments of $125, retirement deductions of $75, association dues of $12, and a Diabetes Association contribution of $25. Find each of the following for a week in which she works 52 hours.

1. Regular weekly earnings   1. _____

2. Overtime earnings   2. _____

3. Total gross earnings   3. _____

4. FICA   4. _____

5. Medicare   5. _____

6. Federal withholding using the percentage method   6. _____

7. State disability insurance deduction   7. _____

8. State withholding (Assume that the state income tax rate is 4.4%.)   8. _____

9. Net pay   9. _____

10. Find the percent of her total gross earnings that she actually receives, rounded to the near-   10. _____
    est tenth of a percent. It is amazing how much is withheld, isn't it?

INVESTIGATE

Look at the statement that you (or a parent or friend) received with your last paycheck. Be certain that your gross earnings are correct. Understand and check all of the deductions made by your employer. Subtract all deductions from your gross earnings to be certain that your net pay is accurate.

▼ Case in Point Summary Exercise

PAYROLL AT STARBUCKS

www.ssa.gov

Facts:

- 1935: Social Security Act passed
- 1937: First Social Security taxes collected
- 1965: Medicare established
- 2013: More than 50 million people receive Social Security payments
- 2013: More than 50 million people receive Medicare benefits

Sarah Brynski is busy running a Starbucks and thinking about inventory, making sure the store looks great, ensuring good service, hiring good people, motivating employees, maintaining inventories, calculating wages, deducting correct amounts for the various taxes, and getting the payroll done on time every week. She is also interested in finding ways to increase sales since part of her income is based on sales. Overtime is paid for more than 40 hours a week, the state tax rate is 3.07%, and the state disability income rate (SDI) is 1%.

1. Use the percentage method and help her calculate the weekly payroll for the employees listed.

Employee	Hourly Wage	Hours Worked	Total Pay	FICA	Medicare	Federal Tax	State Tax	SDI	Other	Net Pay
Betinez, S., 1	$8.75	28	_____	_____	_____	_____	_____	_____	$0	_____
Parton, M., 2	$12.25	45	_____	_____	_____	_____	_____	_____	$25	_____
Dickens, S., 0	$9.35	30	_____	_____	_____	_____	_____	_____	$10	_____

2. Assume Brynski receives a base salary of $450 per week plus a commission of 6% of sales over $5000. Do her weekly payroll for a week with $8432 in sales.

Employee	Base Salary	Comm.	Total Pay	FICA	Medicare	Federal Tax	State Tax	SDI	Other	Net Pay
Brynski, M., 2	_____	_____	_____	_____	_____	_____	_____	_____	$65	_____

3. Find the amount Brynski must send to the Internal Revenue Service for these employees.

4. Find the amount Brynski must send to the state including income tax and disability insurance.

Discussion Question: *Actually, payroll calculations in large firms are usually done at a corporate or regional office using specialized software. Describe the advantages of such a system for local managers as well as for the corporation.*

Source: PAYROLL AT STARBUCKS, www.SSA.GOV.

▼ Chapter 6 Test

To help you review, the numbers in brackets show the section in which the topic was discussed.

Complete the following payroll ledger. Find the total gross earnings for each employee.
Time and a half is paid on all hours over 40 in one week. [**6.1**]

Employee	Hours Worked	Reg. Hrs.	O.T. Hrs.	Reg. Rate	Gross Earnings
1. Bianchi	46.5	___	___	$10.80	_____
2. Hanna	47.5	___	___	$8.60	_____

Solve the following application problems.

3. Judy Martinez is paid $34,060 annually. Find the equivalent earnings if this amount is paid (**a**) weekly, (**b**) biweekly, (**c**) semimonthly, and (**d**) monthly. [**6.2**]

(a) _____
(b) _____
(c) _____
(d) _____

4. At Jalisco Electronics, assemblers are paid according to the following differential piece rate scale: 1–20 units in a day, $4.50 each; 21–30 units, $5.50 each; and $7 each for every unit over 30. Adrian Ortega assembled 70 units in one week. Find his gross pay. [**6.2**]

4. _____

5. Rheonna Winston receives a commission of 6% for selling a $235,500 house. One-half of the commission goes to the broker and one-half of the remainder to another salesperson. Winston gets the rest. Find the amount she receives. [**6.2**]

5. _____

An employee is paid a salary of $9800 per month. If the current FICA rate is 6.2% on the first $115,000 of earnings, and the Medicare tax rate is 1.45% of all earnings, how much should be withheld for (a) FICA tax and (b) Medicare tax during the following months? [**6.3**]

6. March: (**a**) _____ (**b**) _____   7. December: (**a**) _____ (**b**) _____

Find the federal withholding tax using the wage bracket method for each of the following employees. [**6.4**]

8. Ahearn: 2 withholding allowances, single, $415.82 weekly earnings

8. _____

9. Zanotti: 2 withholding allowances, married, $675.25 weekly earnings

9. _____

10. Allgier: 3 withholding allowances, married, $3190.20 monthly earnings

10. _____

11. Yeoman: 4 withholding allowances, single, $2046.75 monthly earnings

11. _____

12. Benner: 5 withholding allowances, married, $2864.47 monthly earnings

12. _____

Find the net pay for each of the following employees after FICA, Medicare, federal withholding tax, state disability insurance, and other deductions have been taken out.. Assume that none has earned over $115,000 so far this year. Assume a FICA rate of 6.2%, Medicare rate of 1.45%, and a state disability insurance rate of 1%. Use the percentage method of withholding. [**6.3 and 6.4**]

13. Murphy: $1852.75 monthly earnings, 1 withholding allowance, single, $37.80 in other deductions

13. _____

14. Pupek: $1028 weekly earnings, 3 withholding allowances, married, state withholding of $50.50, credit union savings of $50, contribution of $20

14. _____

15. Comar: $677.92 weekly earnings, 6 withholding allowances, married, state withholding of $22.18, union dues of $14, charitable contribution of $15

15. _____

Solve the following application problems.

16. Joseph Flores is paid $452 per week plus a commission of 2% on all sales. Flores sold $712 worth of goods on Monday, $523 on Tuesday, $1002 on Wednesday, $391 on Thursday, and $609 on Friday. Returns and allowances for the week were $114. Find the employee's **(a)** Social Security tax (6.2%), **(b)** Medicare tax (1.45%), and **(c)** state disability insurance deduction (1%) for the week. **[6.3 and 6.4]**

(a) _____
(b) _____
(c) _____

17. Neta Fitzgerald earned $112,375.60 so far this year. This week she earned $2649.78. Find her **(a)** FICA tax and **(b)** Medicare tax for this week's earnings. **[6.3]**

(a) _____
(b) _____

For Exercises 18 and 19, find (a) the Social Security tax and (b) the Medicare tax for each of the following self-employed people. Use a FICA tax rate of 12.4% and a Medicare tax rate of 2.9%. **[6.3]**

18. Kirby: $36,714.12

(a) _____
(b) _____

19. Biondi: $42,380.62

(a) _____
(b) _____

20. The employees of Quick-Lube paid a total of $418.12 in Social Security tax last month, $96.48 in Medicare tax, and $1217.34 in federal withholding tax. Find the total amount that the employer must send to the Internal Revenue Service.

20. _____

7 Mathematics of Buying

CHAPTER CONTENTS

7.1 Invoices and Trade Discounts

7.2 Series Discounts and Single Discount Equivalents

7.3 Cash Discounts: Ordinary Dating Methods

7.4 Cash Discounts: Other Dating Methods

▼ CASE IN POINT

BED BATH & BEYOND INC. owns and operates a chain of home-furnishing specialty stores selling items such as bed linens, bath accessories, cookware, kitchen utensils, and small electric appliances. Customer service in a family-style atmosphere is an essential part of the firm's marketing strategy. The firm gives more authority to store managers than most other chains. Store managers even decide which of the firm's 30,000+ products to carry in their stores.

Jack Williams works in the main offices of Bed Bath & Beyond in the purchasing department. He works with firms that supply Bed Bath & Beyond with products. His job requires that he remain in close contact with marketing to make sure he knows what is selling and what is not selling. He also needs to understand consumer trends since products are often ordered months before they are available for sale in the stores. The last thing he wants to do is order products that no one will buy.

Williams works every day with suppliers to get the biggest discount possible. He knows that controlling costs is very important in maintaining profits. Besides, part of his salary is based on a bonus. The better the firm does, the more he makes. So, he has every incentive to help keep costs low and the right products flowing smoothly to the company stores.

Managing inventories is at the heart of retailing. Look at the generalized **supply chain**, or **distribution chain**, below showing **raw materials, suppliers, manufacturer, wholesaler (distributor),** and **retailer.** The retailer may sell products in a store and/or through a website. Prices are marked up at each step in the supply chain to pay expenses such as salaries, but firms also require profit.

Supply Chain

7.1 Invoices and Trade Discounts

OBJECTIVES

1   Complete an invoice.
2   Understand common shipping terms.
3   Identify invoice abbreviations.
4   Calculate trade discounts and understand why they are given.
5   Differentiate between single and series discounts.
6   Calculate each series discount separately.
7   Use complements to calculate series discounts.
8   Use a table to find the net cost equivalent of series discounts.

▼ CASE IN POINT   Since he works with invoices every day in his job in purchasing at Bed Bath & Beyond, Jack Williams must have a good understanding of trade discounts, cash discounts, and shipping terms.

OBJECTIVE 1   Complete an invoice. An **invoice,** such as the one from J.B. Sherr Co. on the next page, is a document issued by a seller to a buyer. It is used to record the details of a transaction. It is a **sales invoice** for the seller, but a **purchase invoice** for the buyer. It shows the quantity ordered, number shipped, the **unit price,** and the **extension total** which is the number of items shipped multiplied by the unit price for the item. The **invoice total** is the sum of the extension totals. Today, most firms send and receive invoices electronically.

Trade and cash discounts, discussed later in this chapter, *are never applied to shipping and insurance charges*. For this reason, shipping and insurance charges are often not included in the invoice total, so the purchaser must add them to the invoice total to find the total amount due. In the J. B. Sherr Co. invoice, the freight (shipping) charges of $38.90 are included in the INVOICE TOTAL.

OBJECTIVE 2   Understand common shipping terms. Some common terms found on invoices are defined.

Free on board (FOB) shipping point	Buyer pays for shipping costs. Ownership of goods passes to the purchaser prior to the shipment.
FOB destination	Seller pays the shipping charge and retains ownership until goods reach the destination.
Cash on delivery (COD)	Payment for goods is made at the time of delivery.
Free alongside ship (FAS)	Goods are delivered to the dock with all freight charges to that point paid by the seller.

Since goods can be damaged, lost, or stolen during shipment, it is important for everyone to know which firms own products that are in shipment. That is the only way it will be clear which firm must pay for goods lost or damaged while in shipment.

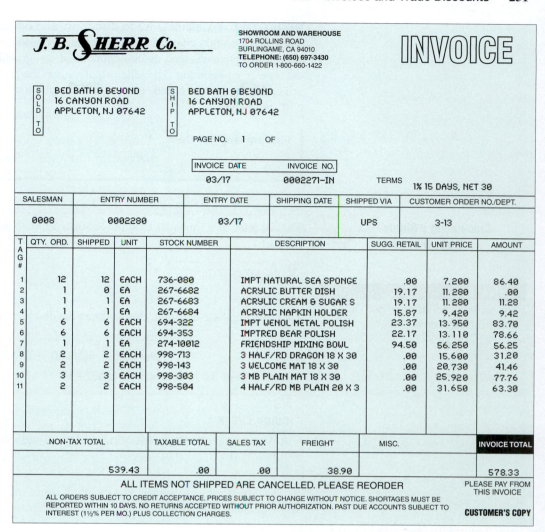

OBJECTIVE 3 Identify invoice abbreviations. Some abbreviations commonly used on invoices to identify measurements, quantities, shipping terms, and discounts are shown in the table.

Invoice Abbreviations

ea.	each	drm.	drum
doz.	dozen	cs.	case
gro.	gross (144 items)	pr.	pair
gr gro.	great gross (12 gross)	C	Roman numeral for 100
qt.	quart	M	Roman numeral for 1000
gal.	gallon (4 quarts)	cwt.	per hundredweight
bbl.	barrel	cpm.	cost per thousand
cL	centiliter	lb.	pound
L	liter	oz.	ounce
in.	inch	g	gram
ft.	foot	kg	kilogram
yd.	yard	ROG	receipt of goods
mm	millimeter	ex. or x	extra dating
cm	centimeter	FOB	free on board
m	meter	EOM	end of month
km	kilometer	COD	cash on delivery
ct.	crate	FAS	free alongside ship

OBJECTIVE 4 Calculate trade discounts and understand why they are given. **Trade discounts** are often given to businesses that buy products from other firms. Trade discounts vary due to price changes, quantity purchased, geographic location, seasonal fluctuations, and the level of competition. The seller usually gives the price of an item as its **list price** (suggested price), but then offers a trade discount that is subtracted from the list price, resulting in the **net cost** (**net price**).

> **Finding the Net Cost**
>
> Net cost = List price − Trade Discount

Calculating a Single Trade Discount   **EXAMPLE 1**   The list price of a Cuisinart food processor is $298.80, and the trade discount is 25%. Find the net cost.

CASE IN POINT

SOLUTION

First find the trade discount; then subtract the discount from the list price of $298.80.

$$\text{Trade discount} = 25\% \text{ of } \$298.80 = \mathbf{\$74.70}$$
$$\text{Net cost} = \$298.80 - \mathbf{\$74.70} = \$224.10$$

The net cost of the food processor is $224.10.

Quick TIP

The trade discount does not depend on the date.

> **QUICK CHECK 1**
>
> A wine refrigerator has a list price of $589.99 and a trade discount of 35%. Find the net cost.

The advertisements suggest that the retail stores may have received a large trade discount, allowing them to sharply reduce the price to the customers.

OBJECTIVE 5 Differentiate between single and series discounts. In Example 1, a **single discount** of 25% was offered. Sometimes two or more discounts are combined into a **series discount**, also called **chain discount**. This results in successive discounts as shown in the next example.

OBJECTIVE 6 Calculate each series discount separately. Three methods can be used to calculate a series discount and net cost. The first of these is **calculating discounts separately**.

Calculating Series Trade Discounts   **EXAMPLE 2**   Bed Bath & Beyond is offered a series discount of 20/10 on a Cooking with Calphalon stainless steel cookware set with a list price of $150. Find the net cost after the series discount.

CASE IN POINT

SOLUTION

Apply the first discount in 20/10, which is 20%.

$$\text{Discount} = \mathbf{20\% \text{ of list price of } \$150}$$
$$= \mathbf{\$30}$$
$$\text{Amount after first discount} = \$150 - \mathbf{\$30} = \$120$$

Now apply the second discount in 20/10, which is 10%. Importantly, apply the discount to the amount after the first discount, or $120.

$$\text{Discount} = 10\% \text{ of discounted price of } \$120$$
$$= \mathbf{\$12}$$
$$\text{Net cost} = \$120 - \mathbf{\$12} = \$108$$

The net cost is $108.

QUICK CHECK 2

A 12-place setting of stainless steel flatware is list priced at $249.99. If a series discount of 10/15 is offered, what is the net cost after the series discount is taken?

It is important to *never add series discounts together*. For example, a 20/10 discount is not the same as a 30% discount. Apply the discounts sequentially, or one after the other.

OBJECTIVE 7 Use complements to calculate series discounts. Complements can also be used to find series discounts. The **complement** of a discount is found by subtracting the decimal form of the discount from 1 as shown.

Discount	Decimal Equivalent	Finding the Complement		Complement
10%	.1	1 − .1	=	.90
20%	.20	1 − .2	=	.80
25%	.25	1 − .25	=	.75
30%	.30	1 − .3	=	.70
62%	.62	1 − .62	=	.38

The complement of the discount is the portion actually paid. For example, a 10% discount means that 90% must be paid, and a 25% discount means that 75% must be paid. The complements can be used to find **the net cost equivalent**, which is then used to find the net cost after the discount.

Finding the Discount Using Net Cost Equivalent

1. Find the complement of each discount in the series discount.
2. Find the net cost equivalent by multiplying the complements from step 1.
3. The net cost after the discount is the list price times the net cost equivalent found in step 2.

Using Complements to Find the Net Cost

EXAMPLE 3

Kitchen Crafters is offered a series discount of 20/10 on a George Foreman Grilling Machine with a list price of $180. Find the net cost after the series discount.

SOLUTION

Apply the preceding steps to find the net cost after the discount.

	Discount	Decimal Equivalent	Finding the Complement		Complement
Step 1	20%	.2	1 − .2	=	.8
	10%	.1	1 − .1	=	.9

Step 2   Net cost equivalent $= .8 \times .9 = .72$

Step 3   Net cost after discount $=$ List price $\times$ Net cost equivalent
$$= \quad \$180 \quad \times \quad .72$$
$$= \$129.60$$

To find the actual discount, subtract the net cost after discount from the original price.

$$\text{Discount} = \text{Original price} - \text{Net cost after discount}$$
$$= \quad \$180 \quad - \quad \$129.60$$
$$= \$50.40$$

 On many calculators, you can subtract the discount percents from the list price in a series calculation.

$$180 \boxed{-} 20 \boxed{\%} \boxed{-} 10 \boxed{\%} \boxed{=} 129.6$$

Note: Refer to Appendix B for calculator basics.

QUICK CHECK 3

A supplier offers a series discount of 25/15 on a waffle iron. If the list price of the waffle iron is $135, use the complement with respect to 1 of each of the single discounts to find **(a)** the net cost and **(b)** the amount of the discount.

Using Complements to Solve Series Discounts

 EXAMPLE 4

The list price of a Heartland 30-inch combination gas and electric stove is $3095. Find the net cost after a series discount of 20/10/10.

SOLUTION

Start by finding the complements with respect to 1 of each discount.

series discount ────────→ 20/10/10

Find complements with respect to 1. ────→ .8   .9   .9

Multiply complements. ────→ .8 × .9 × .9 = **.648**   net cost equivalent

$$\begin{array}{rl} \$3095 & \text{list price} \\ \times \quad \textbf{.648} & \textbf{net cost equivalent} \\ \hline \$2005.56 & \text{net cost} \end{array}$$

QUICK CHECK 4

A 25-cubic-foot bottom-freezer refrigerator is list priced at $2249.99. What is the net cost after a series discount of 15/20/5?

It is important *not to round* the net cost equivalent. Doing so will often result in a net cost that is not correct.

OBJECTIVE 8 Use a table to find the net cost equivalent of series discounts. Finally, a table such as the following one can be used to find the net cost equivalents for common series discounts. Look in the left column for the first one or two discounts in the series discount. Then, look across the top of the table for the last discount in the series discount. For example, a 10/10/20 series discount has a net cost equivalent of .648.

Net Cost Equivalents of Series Discounts

	5%	10%	15%	25%	30%	35%	40%
5	.9025	.855	.8075	.7125	.665	.6175	.57
10	.855	.81	.765	.675	.63	.585	.54
10/5	.81225	.7695	.72675	.64125	.5985	.55575	.513
15	.8075	.765	.7225	.6375	.595	.5525	.51
15/10	.72675	.6885	.65025	.57375	.5355	.49725	.459
20	.76	.72	.68	.6	.56	.52	.48
20/15	.646	.612	.578	.51	.476	.442	.408
25	.7125	.675	.6375	.5625	.525	.4875	.45
25/20	.57	.54	.51	.45	.42	.39	.36
25/25	.534375	.50625	.478125	.421875	.39375	.365625	.3375
30	.665	.63	.595	.525	.49	.455	.42
40	.57	.54	.51	.45	.42	.39	.36

It does not matter which discount is listed first, since the complements are simply being multiplied. So a 15/20/5 discount is the same as a 20/15/5 discount, whose net cost equivalent can be found in the table.

Using a Table of Net Cost Equivalents

EXAMPLE 5

Use the previous table to find the net cost equivalents of the following series discounts.

(a) 10/10   (b) 20/10   (c) 25/25/5   (d) 35/20/15

SOLUTION

First find the row and column needed to read the net cost equivalent from the table, then get the net cost equivalent.

(a) Row 10, Column 10%:   Net cost equivalent = .81

(b) Row 20, Column 10%:   Net cost equivalent = .72

(c) Row 25/25, Column 5%:   Net cost equivalent = .534375

(d) There is no row 35/20 corresponding to the first two numbers in 35/20/15. But 35/20/15 is the same thing as 15/20/35 or as 20/15/35. Using the last of these, go to Row 20/15 and Column 35%:   Net cost equivalent = .442

QUICK CHECK 5

Use the table of net cost equivalents to find the net cost equivalents of the following series discounts: (a) 30/5, (b) 10/40, (c) 20/15/10, (d) 10/5/5.

7.1 Exercises   MyMathLab®

*The shaded sections below contain solutions to help you get a **QUICK START** on the various types of exercises.*

USING INVOICES   *Compute the extension totals and the invoice total for the following invoices.*

HOME ACCESSORIES WHOLESALERS

Sold to: Kitchen Crafters
10100 Fair Oaks Blvd.
Fair Oaks, CA 95628

Date: June 10
Order. No.: 796152
Shipped by: UPS
Terms: Net

	Quantity	Order No./Description	Unit Price	Extension Total
1.	6 doz.	pastry brush, wide	$37.80 doz.	$226.80
2.	3 gro.	napkins, cotton	$12.60 gro.	$37.80
3.	9 doz.	cherry pitters	$14.04 doz.	
4.	8	food processors (3 qt.)	$106.12 ea.	
5.	53 pr.	stainless tongs	$68.12 pr.	
6.			Invoice Total	
			Shipping and Insurance	$85.60
7.			Total Amount Due	

J & K'S MUSTANG PARTS New and Used			

Sold to: Dave's Auto Body & Paint
4443-B Auburn Blvd.
York, PA 17402

Date: July17
Order. No.: 100603
Shipped by: Emery
Terms: Net

	Quantity	Order No./Description	Unit Price	Extension Total
8.	24	filler tube gaskets	$2.25 ea.	
9.	12 pr.	taillight lens gaskets	$4.75 pr.	
10.	6 pr.	taillight bezels to body	$10.80 pr.	
11.	2 gr.	door panel fasteners	$14.20 gr.	
12.	18	bumper bolt kits	$16.50 ea.	
13.			Invoice Total	
			Shipping and Insurance	$139.40
14.			Total Amount Due	

ABBREVIATIONS ON INVOICES   *What does each of the following abbreviations represent?*

15. ft. <u>foot</u>

16. sk. <u>sack</u>

17. pr. _____

18. gr. gro. _____

19. kg _____

20. qt. _____

21. cs. _____

22. gro. _____

23. drm. _____

24. yd. _____

25. L _____

26. cpm. _____

27. gal. _____

28. cwt. _____

29. COD _____

30. FOB _____

31. Name six items that appear on an invoice. Try to do this without looking at an invoice. (See Objective 1.)

32. Explain in your own words the difference between *FOB shipping point* and *FOB destination*. In each case, who pays for shipping and when does ownership of the merchandise transfer? (See Objective 2.)

Using complements (with respect to 1) of the single discounts, find the net cost equivalents for each of the following discounts. Do not round. (See Examples 3 and 4.)

33. 10/20 <u>.9 × .8 = .72</u>

34. 20/20 <u>.8 × .8 = .64</u>

35. 10/10/10 <u>.9 × .9 × .9 = .729</u>

36. 15/20/25 <u>.85 × .8 × .75 = .51</u>

37. 25/5 _____

38. 5/15 _____

39. 40/30/20 _____

40. 20/20/10 _____

41. 50/10/20/5 _____

42. 25/10/20/10 _____

indicates an exercise that requires a written response.

C indicates an exercise that is related to the Case in Point feature.

Find the net cost of each of the following list prices. Round to the nearest cent.
(See Examples 1–4.)

43. $418 less 20/20 $267.52 _____

44. $148 less 25/10 $99.90 _____

45. $16.40 less 5/10 _____

46. $860 less 20/40 _____

47. $1260 less 15/25/10 _____

48. $8.80 less 40/10/20 _____

49. $380 less 20/10/20 _____

50. $2008 less 10/5/20 _____

51. $22 less 10/15 _____

52. $25 less 30/20 _____

53. $980 less 10/10/10 _____

54. $8220 less 30/5/10 _____

55. $2000 less 10/40/10 _____

56. $1630 less 10/5/10 _____

57. $1250 less 20/20/20 _____

58. $1410 less 10/20/5 _____

59. Identify and explain four reasons that might cause series trade discounts to change.
(See Objective 5.)

60. Explain the difference between a single trade discount and a series or chain trade discount.

61. Explain what a complement (with respect to 1 or 100%) is. Give an example.
(See Objective 7.)

62. Using complements, explain how to find the net cost equivalent of a 25/20 series discount. Explain why a 25/10/10 series discount is not the same as a 25/20 discount.
(See Objective 7.)

Solve the following application problems in trade discount. Round to the nearest cent.

63. **VIDEO PLAYER** The list price of a Zune 120 GB MP3/Video Player is $299.99. If the series discount offered is 10/10/25, what is the net cost after trade discounts?
$.9 \times .9 \times .75 = .6075$
$\$299.99 \times .6075 = \$182.24$

63. $182.24 _____

64. **NURSING-CARE PURCHASES** Roger Wheatley, a restorative nursing assistant (RNA), finds that the list price of one dozen adjustable walkers is $1680. Find the cost per walker if a series discount of 40/25 is offered.

64. _____

65. **KITCHEN ISLAND**   Kitchen Crafters purchases a tile-topped wooden kitchen island list priced at $480. It is available at either a 10/15/10 discount or a 20/15 discount. **(a)** Which discount gives the lower price? **(b)** Find the difference in net cost.

(a) _____

(b) _____

66. **HARDWARE PURCHASE**   Oaks Hardware purchases an extension ladder list priced at $120. It is available at either a 10/10/10 discount or a 15/15 discount. **(a)** Which discount gives the lower price? **(b)** Find the difference.

(a) _____

(b) _____

67. **TRIPOD PURCHASE**   The list price of an aluminum tripod is $65. It is available at either a 15/10/10 discount or a 15/20 discount. **(a)** Which discount gives the lower price? **(b)** Find the difference.

(a) _____

(b) _____

68. **LIQUID FERTILIZER**   Continental Fertilizer Supply offers a series discount of 10/20/20 on major purchases. If a 58,000-gallon tank (bulk) of liquid fertilizer is list priced at $27,200, what is the net cost after trade discounts?

68. _____

69. **HOME BEVERAGE FOUNTAINS**   Bed Bath & Beyond receives a 10/5/20 series trade discount from a supplier. If they purchase 4 dozen Bella Home beverage fountains list priced at $468 per dozen, find the net cost.

69. _____

70. **WHOLESALE AUTO PARTS**   Kimara Swenson, an automotive mechanics instructor, is offered mechanics' net prices on all purchases at Foothill Auto Supply. If mechanics' net prices mean a 10/20 discount, how much will Swenson spend on a dozen sets of metallic brake pads that are list priced at $648 per dozen?

70. _____

71. **GRAPHIC ARTS**   Hewlett Packard introduces a new high-speed, Indigo Digital Press that can be used to print brochures, business cards, posters, and photos at a list price of $126,300. Find the net cost if a trade discount of 5/20/5 is given on the first ten sold.

71. _____

72. **DANCE SHOES**   How much will Giselle, a dance instructor, pay for three dozen pairs of dance shoes if the list price is $144 per dozen and a series discount of 10/25/30 is offered?

72. _____

73. **TRADE-DISCOUNT COMPARISON**   The Door Store offers a series trade discount of 30/20 to its builder customers. Robert Gonzalez, a new employee in the billing department, understood the 30/20 terms to mean 50% and computed this trade discount on a list price of $5440. How much difference did this error make in the amount of the invoice?

73. _____

74. FIBER OPTICS Pam Gondola has a choice of two suppliers of fiber optics for her business. Tyler Suppliers offers a 20/10/25 discount on a list price of $5.70 per unit. Irving Optics offers a 30/20 discount on a list price of $5.40 per unit. **(a)** Which supplier gives her the lower price? **(b)** Find the amount saved if she buys 12,500 units from the lower-priced supplier. (*Hint:* Do not round.)

(a) _____

(b) _____

QUICK CHECK ANSWERS

1. $383.49

2. $191.24

3. (a) $86.06 **(b)** $48.94

4. $1453.49

5. (a) .665 **(b)** .54 **(c)** .612 **(d)** .81225

7.2 Series Discounts and Single Discount Equivalents

OBJECTIVES

1 Express a series discount as an equivalent single discount.

2 Find the list price given the series discount and the net cost.

▼ CASE IN POINT At Bed Bath & Beyond, Jack Williams pays close attention to all invoices received from suppliers. He knows that the invoices sometimes have mistakes on them, and he wants to minimize mistakes, particularly overpayments to suppliers.

OBJECTIVE 1 Express a series discount as an equivalent single discount. Series or chain discounts are often expressed as a single discount rate. Find a **single discount equivalent** to a series discount by subtracting the net cost equivalent from 1. This discount is equivalent to the series discount and is always written as a percent.

> **Finding the Single Discount Equivalent**
>
> Single discount equivalent = 1 − Net cost equivalent

Finding a Single Discount Equivalent **EXAMPLE 1**
If the Optimum Energy Company offered a 20/10 discount to wholesale accounts on all heating, ventilation, and cooling systems, what was the single discount equivalent?

SOLUTION

series discount ⟶ 20/10

Find complements with respect to 1. ⟶ .8   .9

Multiply complements. ⟶ .8 × .9 = **.72**   net cost equivalent

$$
\begin{array}{rl}
1.00 & \text{base (100\%)} \\
-\ .72 & \text{net cost equivalent (remains)} \\
\hline
.28 & \text{discount is 28\%}
\end{array}
$$

The single discount equivalent of a 20/10 series discount is 28%.

QUICK CHECK 1

Baltimore Wholesale Electric offers a 30/20 discount on wholesale purchases of all small appliances. What is the single discount equivalent?

OBJECTIVE 2 Find the list price given the series discount and the net cost. Sometimes the net cost after trade discounts is given, along with the series discount, and the list price must be found.

Solving for the List Price **EXAMPLE 2**
Find the list price of a Kohler kitchen sink that has a net cost of $243.20 after trade discounts of 20/20.

SOLUTION

Use a net cost equivalent. Start by finding the percent paid, using complements.

series discount ⟶ 20/20

complements with respect to 1 ⟶ .8 × .8 = **.64**   remains (net cost equivalent)

Thus **64**% of the list price was paid. Find the list price with the standard percent formula.

$$R \quad \times \quad B \quad = \quad P$$

64% of list price = $243.20

or

$$B = \frac{P}{R} = \frac{243.2}{.64} = \$380 \text{ list price}$$

The list price of the sink is $380.

QUICK CHECK 2

After trade discounts of 10/30, the net cost of a 10-quart crock pot is $62.36. Find the list price.

Solving for the List Price   Find the list price of a Bunn 10-cup Generation home brewer having a series discount of 10/30/20 and a net cost of $60.48.

▼ CASE IN POINT
SOLUTION

Use complements to find the percent paid.

series discount ⟶ 10 / 30 / 20

complements with respect to 1 ⟶ .9 × .7 × .8 = **.504** remains (percent paid)

Therefore, **.504** of the list price is $60.48. Use the formula for base.

$$B = \frac{P}{R} = \frac{\$60.48}{.504} = \$120 \text{ list price}$$

The list price of the Bunn home brewer is $120. Check this answer as in Example 3.

QUICK CHECK 3

Find the list price of an Oster Toaster Oven having a series discount of 10/10/10 and a net cost of $43.73.

Notice that Examples 2 and 3 are decrease problems similar to those shown in **Section 3.5** in **Chapter 3**. They are still base problems but may look different because the discount is now shown as a series of two or more discounts rather than a single percent decrease as in **Chapter 3**. If you need help, refer to **Section 3.5**.

▼ **7.2 Exercises**   My**MathLab**®

The shaded sections below contain solutions to help you get a **QUICK START** *on the various types of exercises.*

Find the net cost equivalent and the single discount equivalent of each of the following series discounts. Do not round net cost equivalents or single discount equivalents. (See Example 1.)

	Series Discount	Net Cost Equivalent	Single Discount Equivalent
1.	10/20	.72	28%
	.9 × .8 = .72; 1.00 − .72 = 28%		
2.	10/10	.81	19%
	.9 × .9 = .81; 1.00 − .81 = 19%		

Series Discount	Net Cost Equivalent	Single Discount Equivalent
3. 20/15	_____	_____
4. 25/25	_____	_____
5. 10/30/20	_____	_____
6. 5/10/15	_____	_____
7. 20/10/10/20	_____	_____
8. 25/10/5/20	_____	_____

9. Using complements, show that the single discount equivalent of a 25/20/10 series discount is 46%. (See Objective 1.)

10. Suppose that you own a business and are offered a choice of a 10/20 trade discount or a 20/10 trade discount. Which do you prefer? Why? (See Objective 1.)

Find the list price, given the net cost and the series discount. (See Examples 3 and 4.)

11. Net cost $518.40; trade discount 20/10
$.8 \times .9 = .72;$ $518.40 \div .72 = 720

   11. $720 _____

12. Net cost $813.75; trade discount 30/25

   12. _____

13. Net cost $1559.52; trade discount 5/10/20

   13. _____

14. Net cost $2697.30; trade discount 10/10/10

   14. _____

15. Net cost $265.39; trade discount 10/20/5

   15. _____

16. Net cost $613.60; trade discount 25/25

   16. _____

17. Net cost $4312.40; trade discount 5/10/15

   17. _____

18. Net cost $43.17; trade discount 5/40

   18. _____

▲ᴄ indicates an exercise that is related to the Case in Point feature.

Solve the following application problems. Round to the nearest cent.

19. **BRACELET**   A bracelet had a net cost to a jeweler of $68.72 after a series trade discount of 10/10/5. Find the list price to the jeweler.
.9 × .9 × .95 = .7695; $68.72 ÷ .7695 = $89.30

19. $89.30

20. **IPAD**   Apple offers a 5/5 discount to a charitable organization on its new iPad resulting in a net cost of $450.35. Find the list price.

20. _____

21. **GPS**   After a series trade discount of 20/20, a GPS had a net cost of $132.54. Find the list price.

21. _____

22. **NINTENDO**   After a series trade discount of 10/5, a new Nintendo game had a net cost of $18.69. Find the list price.

22. _____

Solve the following two review application exercises on trade discounts.

23. **COMPARING DISCOUNTS**   A S'mores Maker Kit has a list price of $39.95 and is offered to wholesalers with a series discount of 20/10/10. The same appliance is offered to Kitchen Crafters (a retailer) with a series discount of 20/10. **(a)** Find the wholesaler's price. **(b)** Find Kitchen Crafters' price. **(c)** Find the difference between the two prices.

(a) _____
(b) _____
(c) _____

24. **STAINLESS STEEL GRILL**   A stainless steel gas grill is list priced at $495. The manufacturer offers a series discount of 25/20/10 to wholesalers and a 25/20 series discount to retailers. **(a)** What is the wholesaler's price? **(b)** What is the retailer's price? **(c)** What is the difference between the prices?

(a) _____
(b) _____
(c) _____

QUICK CHECK ANSWERS

1. 44%   **3.** $59.99
2. $98.98

7.3 Cash Discounts: Ordinary Dating Methods

OBJECTIVES

1 Calculate net cost after discounts.

2 Use the ordinary dating method.

3 Determine whether cash discounts are earned.

4 Use postdating when calculating cash discounts.

OBJECTIVE 1 Calculate net cost after discounts. **Cash discounts** are offered by sellers to encourage prompt payment by customers. In effect, the seller is saying, "Pay me quickly and receive a discount." Businesses often borrow money for their day-to-day operation. Immediate cash payments from customers *reduce* the need for the seller to borrow money, but may *increase* the need to borrow money by the customers. Still, many businesses pay quickly in order to get the maximum discount and minimize costs. Managers must constantly work to keep costs low.

> **Finding the Net Cost**
>
> Net cost = (List price − Trade discount) − Cash discount

The cash discount on the Rutherford Chocolate invoice below is shown at the bottom right corner following TERMS. Many companies state the exact amount of the cash discount on the invoice. Others require a calculation to find the discount.

OBJECTIVE 2 Use the ordinary dating method. There are many methods for finding cash discounts, but nearly all of these are based on the **ordinary dating method**. The methods discussed here and in the next section are the most common in use today. The ordinary dating method of cash discount is expressed on an invoice as

2/10, n/30   or   **2/10, net 30**

which is read as "two ten, net thirty." Interpret this as follows: A 2% discount applies if the invoice is paid within 10 days of the invoice date. If no payment is made within 10 days, then the full invoice amount must be paid within 30 days of the invoice date. If no payment is made by the end of 30 days from the invoice date, then a penalty may apply.

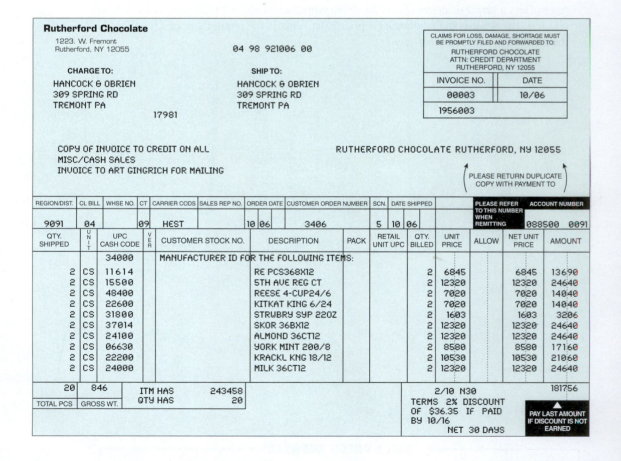

To find the due date of an invoice, use the number of days in each month, given in the following chart.

The Number of Days in Each Month

30-Day Months	31-Day Months		Exception
April	January	August	February
June	March	October	(28 days normally;
September	May	December	29 days in leap year)
November	July		

The number of days in each month of the year can also be remembered using the following rhyme and "knuckle" methods:

Rhyme Method:
30 days hath September,
April, June, and November.
All the rest have 31, except
February, which has 28 and
in a leap year 29.

Knuckle Method:

Leap years occur every four years: 2016, 2020, 2024, etc.

OBJECTIVE 3 Determine whether cash discounts are earned. Find the date that an invoice is due by counting from the next day after the date of the invoice. The date of the invoice is never counted. Another way to determine due dates is to add the given number of days to the starting date. For example, to determine 10 days from April 7, add the number of days to the date $(7 + 10 = 17)$. The due date, or 10 days from April 7, is April 17.

When the discount date or net payment date falls in the next month, the number of days remaining in the current month is found by subtracting the invoice date from the number of days in the month. Then find the number of days in the next month needed to equal the discount period or net payment period. For example, determine the date that is 15 days from October 20.

$$
\begin{array}{rl}
31 & \text{days in October} \\
-\ 20 & \text{the beginning date is October 20} \\
\hline
11 & \text{days remaining in October}
\end{array}
$$

$$
\begin{array}{rl}
15 & \text{total number of days} \\
-\ 11 & \text{days remaining in October} \\
\hline
4 & \text{November (future date)}
\end{array}
$$

Therefore, November 4 is 15 days from October 20.

Finding Cash Discount Dates

 EXAMPLE 1

A Hershey invoice is dated January 2 and offers terms of 2/10, net 30. Find **(a)** the last date on which the 2% discount may be taken and **(b)** the net payment date.

SOLUTION

(a) Beginning with the invoice date, January 2, the last date for taking the discount is January 12 (**2 + 10**).

(b) The net payment date is February 1 (**31 − 2** = 29 days remaining in January plus 1 day in February.)

QUICK CHECK 1

An invoice is dated June 8 and offers terms of 3/15, net 30. Find **(a)** the last date on which the 3% discount may be taken and **(b)** the net payment date.

Finding the Amount Due on the Invoice

 EXAMPLE 2

An invoice received by Bed Bath & Beyond for $840 is dated July 1 and offers terms of 2/10, n/30. If the invoice is paid on July 8 and the shipping and insurance charges, which were FOB shipping point, are $35.60, find the total amount due.

▼ CASE IN POINT

SOLUTION

Since the invoice was paid in 7 days ($8 - 1 = 7$), which is less than the 10-day requirement identified by 2/10, the 2% cash discount applies.

$$\text{Cash discount} = 2\% \text{ of } \$840 = \mathbf{\$16.80}$$

$$\begin{aligned}\text{Amount due} &= \text{Invoice amount} - \text{Cash discount} \\ &= \qquad \$840 \qquad - \qquad \mathbf{\$16.80} \\ &= \$823.20\end{aligned}$$

However, the shipping and insurance charges must be added to the amount due.

$$\begin{aligned}\text{Total to be paid} &= \textbf{Amount due } + \textbf{ Shipping and insurance charges} \\ &= \quad \$823.20 \quad + \qquad \$35.60 \\ &= \$858.80\end{aligned}$$

The total amount due is $858.80.

QUICK CHECK 2

An invoice received for $2830.15, is dated March 21, and offers 3/15, n/30. If the invoice is paid on April 4 and the shipping and insurance charges are $124.96, find the amount due.

In the previous example, the cash discount was not applied to the shipping and insurance charges. This is true in general. Shipping and insurance charges are not eligible for cash discounts. First, deduct applicable trade and cash discounts. Then, add the shipping and insurance charges to find the total amount due.

OBJECTIVE 4 Use postdating when calculating cash discounts. In the ordinary dating method, the cash discount date and net payment date are both counted from the date of the invoice. Occasionally, an invoice is **postdated**. This may be done to give the purchaser more time to take the cash discount on the invoice or may be to more closely fit the accounting practices of the seller. The seller places a date that is after the actual invoice date, sometimes labeling it **AS OF**. For example, the following Bakersfield Clothing invoice is dated 07/25/14 AS OF 08/01/14. Both the cash discount period and the net payment date are counted from 08/01/14 (August 1). This results in giving additional time for the purchaser to pay the invoice and receive the discount.

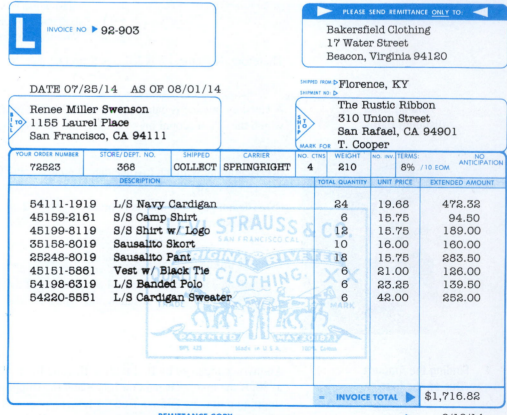

Using Postdating AS OF with Invoices

EXAMPLE 3

An invoice for a shipment of Henkels cutlery from Germany is dated October 21 AS OF November 1 with terms of 3/15, n/30. Find **(a)** the last date on which the cash discount may be taken and **(b)** the net payment date.

ONLY 199.99

HENKELS PREMIER CLASSIC 15-PIECE SET

Includes five kitchen knives, six steak knives, fork, shears, steel, and block

SOLUTION

(a) Beginning with the postdate (AS OF) of November 1, the last date for taking the discount is November 16 (**1 + 15**).

(b) The net payment date is December 1 **(29 days remaining in November and 1 day in December)**.

QUICK CHECK 3

An invoice for Waterford Crystal from Ireland is dated August 24 AS OF September 1 with terms of 1/10, n/30. Find **(a)** the last date on which the cash discount may be taken and **(b)** the net payment date.

Determining Cash Discount Due Dates for a Sliding Scale

EXAMPLE 4

An invoice from Cellular Products is dated May 18 and offers terms of 4/10, 3/25, 1/40, n/60. Find **(a)** the three final dates for each cash discount and **(b)** the net payment date.

SOLUTION

(a) The three final cash discount dates are

4% if paid by May 28	10 days from May 18
3% if paid by June 12	25 days from May 18
1% if paid by June 27	40 days from May 18

(b) The net payment date is July 17 (20 days beyond the cash discount period).

QUICK CHECK 4

An invoice is dated April 14 and offers terms of 3/10, 2/30, 1/40, n/60. Find **(a)** the three final dates for each cash discount and **(b)** the net payment date.

Never take more than one of the cash discounts. *With all methods of giving cash discounts, if the net payment period is not given, the net payment due date is assumed to be 20 days beyond the cash discount period.* After that date, the invoice is considered overdue. If either the final discount date or the net payment date is on a Sunday or holiday, the next business day is used. Many companies consider that payment is made when it is received. In non-retail transactions, payment is considered to be made when it is mailed.

▼ ## 7.3 Exercises   MyMathLab®

The shaded sections below contain solutions to help you get a **QUICK START** *on the various types of exercises.*

Find the final discount date and the net payment date for each of the following. (See Examples 1 and 3.)

	Invoice Date	AS OF	Terms	Final Discount Date	Net Payment Date
1.	May 4		2/10, n/30	May 14	June 3
2.	Apr. 12		3/10, net 30	April 22	May 12
3.	June 30	July 10	3/15, n/60	_____	_____
4.	Nov. 7	Nov. 18	3/10, n/40	_____	_____
5.	Sept. 11		4/20, n/30	_____	_____
6.	July 31		2/15, net 20	_____	_____

Solve for the amount of discount and the total amount due on each of the following invoices.
Add shipping and insurance charges if given. (See Examples 2 and 4.)

	Invoice Amount	Invoice Date	Terms	Date Invoice Paid	Shipping and Insurance	Amount of Discount	Total Amount Due
7.	$85.18	Nov. 2	2/10, net 30	Nov. 11	$8.72	$1.70	$92.20
	$85.18 − $1.70 + $8.72 = $92.20						
8.	$66.10	Mar. 8	6/10, n/30	Mar. 14	$4.39	$3.97	$66.52
	$66.10 − $3.97 + $4.39 = $66.52						
9.	$78.07	May 5	net 30	June 1	$3.18		
10.	$294	Apr. 5	net 30	May 2	$16.20		
11.	$1080	July 8	5/10, 2/20, n/30	July 26	$62.15		
12.	$1282	July 1	4/15, net 40	July 7	$21.40		

13. Describe the difference between a trade discount and a cash discount. Why are cash discounts offered? (See Objective 1.)

14. Using 2/10, n/30 as an example, explain what an ordinary dating cash discount means. (See Objective 2.)

Solve the following application problems. Round to the nearest cent.

⚠️ 15. **CATERING COMPANY**   Bed Bath & Beyond offers cash discounts of 4/10, 2/20, net 30 to all catering companies. An invoice is dated June 18 amounting to $4635.40 and is paid on July 7. Find the amount needed to pay the invoice.
June 18 to July 7 = (30 − 18) + 7 = 19 days
Discount is 2%; $4635.40 × .98 = $4542.69

15. $4542.69

16. **RUSSIAN ELECTRICAL SUPPLIES**   A shipment of electrical supplies is received from the Lyskovo Electrotechnical Works. The invoice is dated March 8, amounts to $6824.58, and has terms of 2/15, 1/20 AS OF March 20. Find the amount needed to pay the invoice on April 2.

16. _____

17. **POLICE CRUISERS**   Based on a purchase of 100 police cars, a city is offered a discount of 5/5/2 with terms of net 30. Find the net price if the list price of the 100 cars was $2,604,000 and the invoice was paid within 30 days.

17. _____

⚠️ indicates an exercise that is related to the Case in Point feature.

18. GEORGE FOREMAN GRILL A George Foreman
Rotisserie Grill is list priced at $59.99 with a trade
discount of 20/5/10 and terms of 4/10, n/30. Find
the cost to Kitchen Crafters assuming that both discounts are earned.

18. _____

19. FINDING DISCOUNT DATES An invoice is dated January 18 and offers terms of
6/10, 4/20, 1/30, n/50. Find **(a)** the three final discount dates and **(b)** the net payment
date.

(a) _____
(b) _____

20. FINDING DISCOUNT DATES An invoice with terms of 4/15, 3/20, 1/30, n/60 is dated
September 4. Find **(a)** the three final discount dates and **(b)** the net payment date.

(a) _____
(b) _____

21. AS OF DATING An invoice is dated March 28 AS OF April 5 with terms of 4/20, n/30.
Find **(a)** the final discount date and **(b)** the net payment date.

(a) _____
(b) _____

22. AS OF DATING An invoice is dated May 20 AS OF June 5 with terms of 2/10, n/30.
Find **(a)** the final discount date and **(b)** the net payment date.

(a) _____
(b) _____

23. How do you remember the number of days in each month of the year? List the months and
the number of days in each. (See Objective 2.)

24. Explain in your own words how AS OF dating (postdating) works. Why is it used? (See
Objective 4.)

QUICK CHECK ANSWERS

1. (a) June 23 **(b)** July 8
2. $2870.21

3. (a) September 11 **(b)** October 1
4. (a) April 24; May 14; May 24 **(b)** June 13

▼ 7.4 Cash Discounts: Other Dating Methods

OBJECTIVES

1 Solve cash discount problems with end-of-month dating.

2 Use receipt-of-goods dating to solve cash discount problems.

3 Use extra dating to solve cash discount problems.

4 Determine credit given for partial payment of an invoice.

▼ **CASE IN POINT** In addition to the ordinary dating method of cash discounts, several other cash discount methods are in common use. Jack Williams at Bed Bath & Beyond must be able to understand and use each of these. He works with many invoices every-day and sees a wide variety of discounts.

OBJECTIVE 1 Solve cash discount problems with end-of-month dating. This section discusses several other methods of finding cash discounts. **End-of-month** and **proximo** dating, abbreviated **EOM** and **prox.**, are treated the same. For example, both

3/10 EOM   and   **3/10 prox.**

mean that 3% may be taken as a cash discount if payment is made by the 10th of the month that follows the sale. The 10 days are counted from the *end of the month* in which the invoice is dated. For example, an invoice dated July 14 with terms of 3/10 EOM would have a discount date 10 days from the end of the month, or the 10th of August (August 10).

Since this is a method of increasing the length of time during which a discount may be taken, it has become common business practice to add an extra month when the date of an invoice is the 26th of the month or later. For example, if an invoice is dated March 25 and the discount offered is 3/10 EOM, the last date on which the discount may be taken is April 10. *However, if the invoice is dated March 26 (or any later date in March) and the cash discount offered is 3/10 EOM, then the last date on which the discount may be taken is May 10.*

The practice of adding an extra month when the invoice is dated the 26th of a month or after is used *only* with the end-of-month (proximo) dating cash discount. It does *not* apply to any of the other cash discount methods.

Using End-of-Month Dating   If an invoice from Oster is dated June 10 with terms of 3/20 EOM, find **(a)** the final date on which the cash discount may be taken and **(b)** the net payment date.

SOLUTION

(a) The discount date is July 20 (20 days after the end of June).

(b) When no net payment due date is given, common business practice is to allow 20 days after the last discount date. The net payment date is August 9, which is **20 days** after the last discount date (July 20), since no net payment date is given.

SALE 59.99
OSTER TOASTER OVEN/BROILER

Muffins not included.

QUICK CHECK 1

An invoice from Pearson Education, Inc., is dated February 15 with terms of 2/10 EOM. Find **(a)** the final date on which the discount may be taken and **(b)** the net payment date.

Using Proximo Dating   Find the amount due on an invoice of $782 for some Black and Decker Belgian waffle makers dated August 3, if terms are 1/10 prox. and the invoice is paid on September 4.

SOLUTION

The last date on which the discount may be taken is September 10 (**10 days** after the end of August). September 4 is within the discount period, so the discount is earned. The 1% cash discount is computed on $782, the amount of the invoice. Subtract the discount ($782 × **.01** = $7.82) from the invoice amount to find the amount due.

$782.00	invoice amount
− 7.82	**cash discount (1%)**
$774.18	amount due

QUICK CHECK 2

An invoice for some gourmet cookbooks is for $1475 and dated October 17. Find the amount due if the invoice terms are 3/20 proximo and the invoice is paid on November 18.

Note: With all methods of cash discounts, if the net payment period is not given, the net payment due date is assumed to be *20 days beyond the cash discount date*.

OBJECTIVE 2 Use receipt-of-goods dating to solve cash discount problems. Receipt-of-goods dating, abbreviated **ROG**, offers cash discounts determined from the date on which goods are actually received. This method is often used when shipping time is long. The invoice might arrive immediately over the Internet, but the goods may take several weeks. Under the ROG method of cash discount, the buyer is given the time to receive and inspect the merchandise and then is allowed to benefit from a cash discount. For example, the discount

3/15 ROG

allows a 3% cash discount if the invoice is paid within 15 days from receipt of goods. The date that goods are received is determined by the delivery date. If the invoice was dated March 5 and goods were received on April 7, the last date to take the 3% cash discount would be April 22 (April 7 plus 15 days). The net payment date, since it is not stated, is 20 days after the last discount date, or May 12 (April 22 plus 20 days).

Using Receipt-of-Goods Dating | **EXAMPLE 3**

Best Buy received an invoice dated December 12, with terms of 2/10 ROG. The goods were received on January 2. Find **(a)** the final date on which the cash discount may be taken and **(b)** the net payment date.

SOLUTION

(a) The discount date is January 12 (**10 days** after receipt of goods, January 2 plus **10 days**).

(b) The net payment date is February 1 (**20 days** after the last discount date).

> **QUICK CHECK 3**
>
> An invoice from Silver Specialties is dated June 4, with terms of 4/15 ROG. The merchandise was received on July 25. Find **(a)** the final date on which the cash discount may be taken and **(b)** the net payment date.

Working with ROG Dating | **EXAMPLE 4**

Find the amount due to Sir Speedy on an invoice of $285 for printing services, with terms of 3/10 ROG, if the invoice is dated June 8, the goods are received June 18, and the invoice is paid June 30.

SOLUTION

The last date to take the 3% cash discount is June 28, 10 days after June 18. Since the invoice is paid on June 30, 2 days after the last discount date, **no cash discount may be taken**. The entire amount of the invoice must be paid.

$285   invoice amount
−   **0**   **no cash discount**
─────
$285   amount due

> **QUICK CHECK 4**
>
> Find the amount due on an invoice of $896, with terms of 4/20 ROG, if the invoice is dated March 10, the goods are received April 28, and the invoice is paid on May 15.

OBJECTIVE 3 Use extra dating to solve cash discount problems. Extra dating (**extra, ex., or x**) gives the buyer additional time to take advantage of a cash discount. For example, the discount

2/10−50 extra   or   **2/10−50 ex.**   or   **2/10−50 x**

allows a 2% cash discount if the invoice is paid within 10 + 50 = 60 days from the date of the invoice. The discount is expressed as 2/10−50 ex. (rather than 2/60) to show that the 50 days are *extra*, or in addition to the normal 10 days offered.

There are several reasons for using extra dating. A supplier might extend the discount period during a slow sales season to generate more sales or to gain a competitive advantage. For example, the seller might offer Christmas merchandise with extra dating to allow the buyer to take the cash discount after the holiday selling period.

Using Extra Dating An invoice for Oster blenders is dated November 23 with terms of 2/10–50 ex. Find **(a)** the final date on which the cash discount may be taken and **(b)** the net payment date.

SOLUTION

(a) The discount date is January 22 (**7 days** remaining in November + 31 days in December = 38; thus, **22 more days** are needed in January to total 60).

(b) The net payment date is February 11 (**20 days** after the last discount date).

QUICK CHECK 5

An invoice is dated July 7 with terms of 1/10–60 ex. Find **(a)** the final date on which the cash discount may be taken and **(b)** the net payment date.

Understanding Extra Dating | **EXAMPLE 6** | An invoice from Wind Turbines & Solar, Inc., is dated August 5, amounts to $8180, offers terms of 3/10–30 x, and is paid on September 12. Find the net payment.

SOLUTION

Step 1 The last day to take the 3% cash discount is September 14 (**August 5 + 40 days = September 14**). Since the invoice is paid on September 12, the **3%** discount may be taken.

Step 2 The **3%** cash discount is computed on $8180, the amount of the invoice. The discount to be taken is $245.40.

Step 3 Subtract the cash discount from the invoice amount to determine the amount of payment.

$8180.00	invoice amount
− $245.40	**3% cash discount**
$7934.60	amount of payment

QUICK CHECK 6

An invoice for $5412 is dated May 22 and offers terms of 2/20–40 x. If the invoice is paid on July 15, what is the amount of payment due?

Quick TIP

In Example 6, the amount of payment may be found by multiplying the invoice amount by 100% − 3%, or 97%. Here, $8180 × .97 = $7934.60 is the amount of payment.

OBJECTIVE 4 Determine credit given for partial payment of an invoice. Occasionally, a customer may pay only a portion of the total amount due on an invoice. If this **partial payment** is made within a discount period, the customer is entitled to a discount on the portion of the invoice that is paid.

If the terms of an invoice are 3%, 10 days, then only 97% (100% − 3%) of the invoice amount must be paid during the first 10 days. So, for each $.97 paid, the customer is entitled to $1.00 of credit. When a partial payment is made, the credit given for the partial payment (base) is found by dividing the partial payment by the complement of the cash discount percent. Then, to find the balance due, subtract the credit given from the invoice amount. The cash discount is found by subtracting the partial payment from the credit given.

Finding Credit for
Partial Payment

EXAMPLE 7

Dave's Body and Paint receives an invoice for $1140 dated March 8 that offers terms of 2/10 prox. A partial payment of $450 is made on April 5. Find **(a)** the amount credited for the partial payment, **(b)** the balance due on the invoice, and **(c)** the cash discount earned.

SOLUTION

(a) The cash discount is earned on the $450 partial payment made on April 5 (April 10 was the last discount date). The amount paid ($450) is part of the base (amount for which credit is given).

$$100\% - 2\% = 98\%$$

The rate 98% is used to solve for base using the formula Base $= \dfrac{\text{Part}}{\text{Rate}}$.

$$B = \frac{P}{R}$$

$$B = \frac{450}{98\%} = \frac{450}{.98} = \$459.18$$

The amount credited for partial payment is $459.18.

(b) Balance due = Invoice amount − Credit given
Balance due = $1140 − **$459.18** = $680.82

(c) Cash discount = Credit given − Partial payment
Cash discount = **$459.18** − $450 = $9.18

A calculator solution to this example includes these three steps.
First, find the amount of credit given.

450 ⟦÷⟧ .98 ⟦=⟧ 459.18 (rounded) ⟦STO⟧

Then, store the amount of credit and subtract this amount from the invoice amount to find the balance due.

1140 ⟦−⟧ ⟦RCL⟧ ⟦=⟧ 680.82

Finally, subtract the partial payment from the amount of credit given to find the cash discount.

⟦RCL⟧ ⟦−⟧ 450 ⟦=⟧ 9.18

QUICK CHECK 7

Central Parts receives an invoice for $1082 dated September 14 that offers terms of 2/20 prox. A partial payment of $590 is paid on October 15. Find **(a)** the amount credited for the partial payment, **(b)** the balance due on the invoice, and **(c)** the cash discount earned.

Cash discounts are important, and a business should make the effort to pay invoices early to earn the cash discounts. In many cases, the money saved through cash discounts has a great effect on the profitability of a business. Often, companies will borrow money to enable them to take advantage of cash discounts. The mathematics of this type of loan is discussed in **Section 8.1**, Simple Interest.

▼ 7.4 Exercises

MyMathLab®

The shaded sections below contain solutions to help you get a QUICK START on the various types of exercises.

Find the discount date and net payment date for each of the following. (The net payment date is 20 days after the final discount date. See Examples 1, 3, and 5.)

	Invoice Date	Terms	Date Goods Received	Final Discount Date	Net Payment Date
1.	Feb. 8	3/10 EOM		Mar. 10	Mar. 30
2.	July 6	2/10 EOM		_____	_____

Invoice Date	Terms	Date Goods Received	Final Discount Date	Net Payment Date
3. July 14	2/15 ROG	Sept. 3	_____	_____
4. Jan. 15	3/15 ROG	Feb. 5	_____	_____
5. Nov. 22	1/10–20 x		_____	_____
6. Apr. 12	3/15–50 ex.		_____	_____

Solve for the amount of discount and the amount due on each of the following invoices. Round to the nearest cent. (See Examples 2, 4, and 6.)

Invoice Amount	Invoice Date	Terms	Date Goods Received	Date Invoice Paid	Amount of Discount	Amount Due
7. $682.28	June 4	3/20 ROG	July 25	Aug. 10	$20.47	$661.81
$20.47 discount; $682.28 − $20.47 = $661.81 due						
8. $12.38	Mar. 29	2/15 ROG	Apr. 15	Apr. 30	_____	_____
9. $356.20	May 17	3/15 prox.		June 12	_____	_____
10. $11,480	Apr. 6	2/15 prox.		Apr. 30	_____	_____
11. $2935.40	Jul. 24	4/20 EOM		Aug. 10	_____	_____
12. $1380	May 28	1/15 EOM		June 10	_____	_____
13. $23.95	Aug. 2	3/10–20 extra		Sept. 1	_____	_____
14. $3250.60	Oct. 17	3/15–20 ex.		Oct. 20	_____	_____

15. Quite often there is no mention of a net payment date on an invoice. Explain the common business practice when no net payment date is given. (See Objective 1.)

16. Describe why ROG dating is offered to customers. Use an example in your description. (See Objective 2.)

Solve the following application problems. Round to the nearest cent.

 17. **KITCHEN APPLIANCES** Nostalgia Kitchen Appliances offers terms of 2/10–30 ex. to stimulate slow sales in the winter months. Bed Bath & Beyond purchased $2382.58 worth of appliances and was offered the above terms. If the invoice was dated November 3, find (a) the final date on which the cash discount may be taken and (b) the amount paid if the discount was earned.

(a) **Dec. 13**

(b) **$2334.93**

(a)
```
  27    days remain in November
+ 13    days in December
  40    days is December 13
```

(b) $2382.58 × .02 = 47.651 = $47.65 discount
$2382.58 − $47.65 = $2334.93 paid

 indicates an exercise that is related to the Case in Point feature.

18. CANADIAN FOOD PRODUCTS   Vanitha Evans, a wholesaler of Canadian food products, offers terms of 4/15–40 ex. to encourage sales. In a recent order, a retailer purchased $9864.18 worth of Canadian foods and was offered the above terms. If the invoice was dated March 10, find **(a)** the final date on which the cash discount may be taken and **(b)** the amount paid if the discount was earned.

(a) _____

(b) _____

19. GLOBAL POSITIONING SYSTEMS   A recent invoice for 24 Garmin Nuvi 50 systems amounting to $6720.50 was dated February 20 and offered terms of 2/20 ROG. If the equipment was received on March 20 and the invoice was paid on April 8, find the amount due.

19. _____

20. WHEELS WITH BLING   Scott Ryder purchased some 21-inch and 23-inch custom wheels for his performance auto parts store and was offered a cash discount of 2/10 EOM. The invoice amounted to $7218.80 and was dated June 2. The wheels were received 7 days later, and the invoice was paid on July 7. Find the amount necessary to pay the invoice in full.

20. _____

21. ENGLISH SOCCER EQUIPMENT   An invoice dated December 8 is received with a shipment of soccer equipment from England on April 18 of the following year. The list price of the equipment is $2538, with allowed series discounts of 25/10/10. If cash terms of sale are 3/15 ROG, find the amount necessary to pay in full on April 21.

21. _____

22. CRYSTAL FROM IRELAND   Bed Bath & Beyond receives an invoice for Waterford crystal from Ireland amounting to $5382.40 and dated May 17. The terms of the invoice are 5/20–90 x and the invoice is paid on September 2. Find the amount necessary to pay the invoice in full.

22. _____

23. PARTIAL INVOICE PAYMENT   PetSmart receives an invoice amounting to $2016.90 with terms of 8/10, net 30 and dated August 20 AS OF September 1. If a partial payment of $1350 is made on September 8, find **(a)** the credit given for the partial payment and **(b)** the balance due on the invoice.

(a) _____

(b) _____

24. FROZEN YOGURT   Yogurt for You receives an invoice amounting to $263.40 with terms of 2/20 EOM and dated September 6. If a partial payment of $150 is made on October 15, find **(a)** the credit given for the partial payment and **(b)** the balance due on the invoice.

(a) _____

(b) _____

25. **DISCOUNT DATES**   An invoice received by Auto Zone is dated May 12 with terms of 2/10 prox. Find **(a)** the final date on which the discount may be taken and **(b)** the net payment date.

(a) _____

(b) _____

26. **DISCOUNT DATES**   An invoice from Dollar Distributors is dated November 11 with terms of 3/20 ROG, and the goods are received on December 3. Find **(a)** the final date on which the cash discount may be taken and **(b)** the net payment date.

(a) _____

(b) _____

27. **AMOUNT DUE**   Find the amount due on an invoice of $1525 with terms of 1/20 ROG. The invoice is dated October 20, goods are received December 1, and the invoice is paid on December 20.

27. _____

28. **PAYMENT DUE**   Find the payment that should be made on an invoice dated September 28, amounting to $4680, offering terms of 2/10–50 x and paid on November 25.

28. _____

29. **PARTIAL INVOICE PAYMENT**   An invoice received for Spode china has terms of 3/15–30 x and is dated May 20. The amount of the invoice is $4402.58, and a partial payment of $3250 is made on July 1. Find **(a)** the credit given for the partial payment and **(b)** the balance due on the invoice.

(a) _____

(b) _____

30. **AUTOMOTIVE**   Orange County Motorcycles makes a partial payment of $8726 on an invoice of $17,680.38. If the invoice is dated April 14 with terms of 4/20 prox. and the partial payment is made on May 13, find **(a)** the credit given for the partial payment and **(b)** the balance due on the invoice.

(a) _____

(b) _____

31. Write a short explanation of partial payment. Why would a company accept a partial payment? Why would a customer make a partial payment? (See Objective 4.)

32. Of all the different types of cash discounts presented in this section, which type seemed most interesting to you? Explain your reasons.

QUICK CHECK ANSWERS

1. **(a)** March 10   **(b)** March 30
2. $1430.75
3. **(a)** August 9   **(b)** August 29
4. $860.16
5. **(a)** September 15   **(b)** October 5
6. $5303.76
7. **(a)** $602.04   **(b)** $479.96
   (c) $12.04

▼ Chapter 7   Quick Review

Chapter Terms   *Review the following terms to test your understanding of the chapter. For each term you do not know, refer to the page number found next to that term.*

amount [**p. 250**]
AS OF [**p. 266**]
cash discount [**p. 264**]
chain discount [**p. 252**]
COD (cash on delivery) [**p. 250**]
complement [**p. 253**]
distribution chain [**p. 250**]
end of month (EOM) [**p. 270**]
extension total [**p. 250**]

extra dating (extra, ex., x) [**p. 271**]
FAS (free alongside ship) [**p. 250**]
FOB (free on board) [**p. 250**]
FOB destination [**p. 250**]
invoice [**p. 250**]
invoice total [**p. 250**]
list price [**p. 252**]
manufacturer [**p. 250**]
net cost [**p. 252**]

net cost equivalent [**p. 253**]
net price [**p. 252**]
ordinary dating method [**p. 264**]
partial payment [**p. 272**]
postdated "AS OF" [**p. 266**]
prox. [**p. 270**]
proximo [**p. 270**]
purchase invoice [**p. 250**]
receipt-of-goods dating [**p. 271**]
retailer [**p. 250**]

ROG [**p. 271**]
sales invoice [**p. 250**]
series discount [**p. 252**]
single discount [**p. 252**]
single discount equivalent [**p. 260**]
suppliers [**p. 250**]
supply chain [**p. 250**]
trade discounts [**p. 252**]
unit price [**p. 250**]
wholesaler [**p. 250**]

CONCEPTS

EXAMPLES

7.1 Trade discount and net cost

First find the amount of the trade discount. Then use the formula for net cost.

Net cost = List price − Trade discount

List price, $28; trade discount, 25%; find the net cost.

$$\text{Discount} = \$28 \times .25 = \$7$$
$$\text{Net cost} = \$28 - \$7 = \$21$$

7.1 Complements with respect to 1 (100%)

The complement is the number that must be added to a given discount to get 1 or 100%.

Find the complement of each with respect to 1.

Discount	Decimal Equivalent	Finding the Complement		Complement
20%	.2	1 − .2	=	.8
32%	.32	1 − .32	=	.68

7.1 Complements and series discounts

The complement of a discount is the percent paid. Multiply the complements of the series discounts to get the *net cost equivalent*.

Series discount, 10/20/10; find the net cost equivalent.

$$\begin{array}{ccc} 10/ & 20/ & 10 \\ \downarrow & \downarrow & \downarrow \end{array}$$
$$.9 \times .8 \times .9 = .648$$

7.1 Net cost equivalent (percent paid) and net cost

Multiply the net cost equivalent (percent paid) by the list price to get the net cost.

List price, $280; series discount, 10/30/20; find the net cost.

$$\begin{array}{ccc} 10/ & 30/ & 20 \\ \downarrow & \downarrow & \downarrow \end{array}$$
$$.9 \times .7 \times .8 = .504 \text{ percent paid}$$
$$\text{Net cost} = .504 \times \$280 = \$141.12$$

7.2 Single discount equivalent to a series discount

Often needed to compare one series discount to another, the single discount equivalent is found by multiplying the complements of the individual discounts to get the net cost equivalent, then subtracting from 1.

$$1 - \frac{\textbf{Net cost}}{\textbf{equivalent}} = \frac{\textbf{Single discount}}{\textbf{equivalent}}$$

What single discount is equivalent to a 10/20/20 series discount?

$$\begin{array}{ccc} 10/ & 20/ & 20 \\ \downarrow & \downarrow & \downarrow \end{array}$$
$$.9 \times .8 \times .8 = .576$$
$$1 - .576 = .424 = 42.4\%$$

CONCEPTS	EXAMPLES

7.2 Finding list price, given the series discount and the net cost

First, find the net cost equivalent, percent paid. Then use the standard percent formula to find the list price (base).

$$B = \frac{P}{R}$$

New cost, $224; series discount, 20/20; find list price.

$$20/\ 20$$
$$\downarrow\ \ \ \downarrow$$
$$.8 \times .8 = \textbf{.64}$$

$$B = \frac{P}{R} = \frac{224}{.64} = \$350 \text{ list price}$$

7.3 Number of days and dates

30-Day Months	31-Day Months
April	All the rest
June	except February with
September	28 days (29 days in leap year)
November	

Date, July 24; find 10 days from date.

July 31 − **24** = 7 days remaining in July

```
        10     total number of days
      −  7     days remaining in July
  August 3     (future date)
```

7.3 Ordinary dating and cash discounts

With ordinary dating, count days from the date of the invoice. Remember:

$$2/\ \ 10,\ \ n/\ 30$$
$$\downarrow\ \ \ \downarrow\ \ \ \ \downarrow\ \ \ \downarrow$$
$$\%\ \ \text{days},\ \ \text{net}\ \ \text{days}$$

Invoice amount $182; terms 2/10, n/30; find the cash discount and amount due.

Cash discount: $182 \times$ **.02** = $3.64

Amount due: $182 − **$3.64** = $178.36

7.4 Cash discounts with end-of-month dating (EOM or proximo dating)

The final discount date and the net date are counted from the end of the month. If the invoice is dated the 26th or after, add the entire following month when determining the dates. If not stated, the net date is 20 days beyond the discount date.

Terms, 2/10 EOM; invoice date, Oct. 18; find the final discount date and the net payment date.

Final discount date:
November 10, which is 10 days from the end of October

Net payment date:
November 30, which is 20 days beyond the discount date

7.4 Receipt-of-goods (ROG) dating and cash discounts

Time is counted from the date goods are received to determine the final cash discount date and the net payment date. If not stated, the net date is 20 days beyond the discount date.

Terms, 3/10 ROG; invoice date, March 8; goods received, May 10; find the final discount date and the net payment date.

Final discount date:
May 20 (May 10 + 10 days)

Net payment date:
June 9 (May 20 + 20 days)

7.4 Extra dating and cash discounts

Extra dating adds extra days to the usual cash discount period, so 3/10–20 x is the equivalent to 3/30. If not stated, the net date is 20 days beyond the discount date.

Terms, 3/10–20 x, invoice date, January 8; find the final discount date and the net payment date.

Final discount date:
February 7 (23 days in January + 7 days in February = 30)

Net payment date:
February 27 (February 7 + 20 days)

7.4 Partial payment credit

When only a portion of an invoice amount is paid within the cash discount period, credit will be given for the partial payment. Use the standard percent formula

$$B = \frac{P}{R}$$

where the credit given is the base, the partial payment is the part, and (100% − cash discount) is the rate.

Invoice, $4000; terms, 2/10, n/30; invoice date, Oct. 10; partial payment of $2000 on Oct. 15. Find credit given for partial payment and the balance due on the invoice.

$$B = \frac{P}{R} = \frac{\$2000}{100\% - 2\%} = \frac{\$2000}{.98}$$

Credit = $2040.82
Balance due = $4000 − $2040.82 = $1959.18

Case Study

GEORGE FOREMAN

George E. Foreman was born on January 10, 1949, in Marshal, Texas. He grew up on the tough streets of Houston's Fifth Ward area, and as a young kid he was always getting into trouble. He joined the Job Corps and his life changed. One of the counselors noticed that he was always into fights, so he decided that George should put all of his energy into something positive. This started his boxing career. George Foreman sold his brand and naming rights to Salton in 1999, but he is still involved with advertising grills. Today, "if there is one thing George Foreman knows, it's good cooking."

1. Kitchen Crafters purchased George Foreman Super Searing Grills that were list priced at $149.99. If the supplier offered a trade discount of 20/20, find the cost of one dozen grilling machines.

2. The list price of a George Foreman Evolve Grill is $119.99. The manufacturer gives a 25/10 trade discount and offers a cash discount of 3/15, net/30. Find the cost to Kitchen Crafters if both discounts are earned and taken.

3. The list price of a *George Foreman Knock-Out-the-Fat Barbecue and Grilling Cookbook* is $16.95. If the cookbook is offered at a reduced price of $13.95 when purchased on the Internet, what is the percent of markdown? Round to the nearest tenth of a percent.

INVESTIGATE

Talk with a manager of a retail business that sells products. Ask what kinds of trade and cash discounts are standard in their particular line of business. Do they take their earned discounts? Are these discounts important to them? Who is responsible for making sure that discounts are taken? Do they do any of their purchasing electronically? How does electronic purchasing work?

▼ Case in Point Summary Exercise

DISCOUNTS AT BED BATH & BEYOND

www.bedbathandbeyond.com

Facts:

- 1971: First formed
- 1985: Opened first superstore
- 1992: Listed on public stock exchange
- 2013: More than 1000 stores and $10 billion in revenue

Jack Williams works in a very active department called purchasing. He works with store managers, marketing, and supply companies. His job is to have the right product, in the right amount, at the lowest cost, where and when it's needed. With more than 1000 stores, that is a very tough job! Of course, there are others that work with him in the department.

In early September, Williams placed an order with one vendor for products having a combined list price of $27,393. The vendor offered trade discounts of 20/10/10. The invoice arrived through the computer system the next day. It was dated September 4, had terms of 3/15 EOM, and showed a shipping charge of $748.38. Find the following.

1. The total amount of the invoice excluding shipping

1. _____

2. The final discount date

2. _____

3. The net payment date

3. _____

4. The amount necessary to pay the invoice in full on October 11, including the shipping

4. _____

5. Suppose that on October 11 the invoice is not paid in full, but a partial payment of $10,000 is made instead. Find the credit given for the partial payment and the balance due on the invoice including shipping.

5. _____
_____

Discussion Question: *Have you thought about a career in purchasing? All firms that carry inventory have purchasing departments that work with people inside their own company and suppliers to keep the right products on the shelves. See what you can find out about this career on the Web. You may wish to search for the American Purchasing Society.*

Source: DISCOUNTS AT BED BATH & BEYOND, www.bedbathandbeyond.com.

▼ Chapter 7 Test

To help you review, the numbers in brackets show the section in which the topic was discussed.

Find the net cost (invoice amount) for the following. Round to the nearest cent. [7.1]

1. List price: $348.22 less 10/20/10

1. _____

2. List price: $1308 less 20/25

2. _____

Find (a) the net cost equivalent and (b) the single discount equivalent for the following series discounts. [7.2]

3. 30/10

(a) _____

(b) _____

4. 20/10/20

(a) _____

(b) _____

Find the final discount date for the following. [7.4]

Invoice Date	Terms	Date Goods Received	Final Discount Date
5. Feb. 10	4/15 EOM	Feb. 16	_____
6. May 8	2/10 ROG	May 20	_____
7. Dec. 8	4/15 prox.	Jan. 5	_____
8. Oct. 20	2/20–40 extra	Oct. 31	_____

9. The following invoice was paid on November 15. Find (a) the invoice total, (b) the amount that should be paid after the cash discount, and (c) the total amount due, including shipping and insurance. [7.1–7.4]

(a) _____

(b) _____

(c) _____

GOURMET KITCHEN WHOLESALER

Terms: 2/10, 1/15, n/60   November 6

Quantity	Description	Unit Price	Extension Total
16	tablecloths, linen	@ 35.00 ea.	
8	rings, napkin	@ 6.50 ea.	
4 cases	cups, ceramic	@ 25.30 ea.	
12	bowls, 1 qt. stainless	@ 6.30 ea.	
		(a) Invoice Total	
		Cash Discount	
		(b) Due after Cash Discount	
		Shipping and Insurance	$38.75
		(c) Total Amount Due	

Solve the following application problems involving cash and trade discounts.
Round to the nearest cent.

10. The Sports Authority made purchases at a net cost of $46,746 after a series discount of 20/20/20. Find the list price. **[7.2]**

10. _____

11. An invoice of $3168 from Scottish Importers has cash terms of 4/20 EOM and is dated June 5. Find **(a)** the final date on which the cash discount may be taken and **(b)** the amount necessary to pay the invoice in full if the cash discount is earned. **[7.4]**

(a) _____
(b) _____

12. Mel's Diner purchased paper products list priced at $696 less series discounts of 10/20/10, with terms of 3/10–50 extra. If the retailer paid the invoice within 60 days, find the amount paid. **[7.4]**

12. _____

13. The Fireside Shop offers chimney caps for $120 less 25/10. The same chimney cap is offered by Builders Supply for $111 less 25/5. Find **(a)** the firm that offers the lower price and **(b)** the difference in price. **[7.1]**

(a) _____
(b) _____

14. The amount of an invoice from Cloverdale Creamery is $1780 with terms of 2/10, 1/15, net 30 with shipping charges of $120.39. The invoice is dated March 8. **(a)** What amount should be paid on March 20? **(b)** What amount should be paid on April 3? **[7.3]**

(a) _____
(b) _____

15. Diamond Consulting receives an invoice dated November 23 for $2514 with terms of 3/15 EOM with shipping and insurance charges of $88.50. If the invoice is paid on December 14, find the amount necessary to pay the invoice in full. **[7.4]**

15. _____

16. Jim Havey receives an invoice amounting to $2916 with cash terms of 3/10 prox. and dated June 7. If a partial payment of $1666 is made on July 8, find **(a)** the credit given for the partial payment and **(b)** the balance due on the invoice. **[7.4]**

(a) _____
(b) _____

8 Mathematics of Selling

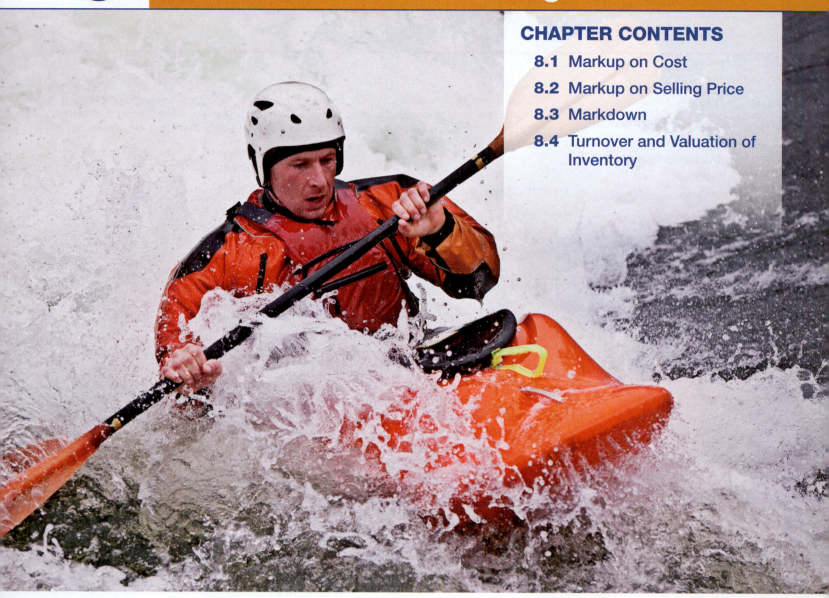

CHAPTER CONTENTS

8.1 Markup on Cost

8.2 Markup on Selling Price

8.3 Markdown

8.4 Turnover and Valuation of Inventory

▼ CASE IN POINT

JAMES SMELTER works in inventory management at REI, one of the great retail companies totally devoted to outdoor activities. The firm was started by 23 experts in mountain climbing and, today employees still design many of the products. It carries products for many types of outdoor activities, including camping, hiking, mountain climbing, skiing, paddling, snowboarding, snowshoeing, and kayaking.

REI's easy-to-navigate Internet store offers more than 40,000 products. The firm allocates 3% of operating income for donations that support the outdoors. If you are interested in working for a company that treks to Nepal, check the REI website since they organize trips to many wild places in the world. REI has been on Fortune's list of the 100 Best Companies to work for in America for 11 years in a row.

REI is now the largest consumer cooperative in the nation, with more than three million members and 80 stores. As a cooperative, REI is owned by its members. If you become a member and buy products from REI, you will receive a refund check at the end of the year based on company profits and the amount of your purchases.

The success of a business depends on many things. For example, managers must understand their customers and the competition. They must also control costs and know how to price their products and services. This chapter is about markup, which is the difference between selling price and purchase price.

▼ 8.1 Markup on Cost

OBJECTIVES

1 Recognize the terms used in selling.

2 Use the basic formula for markup.

3 Calculate markup based on cost.

4 Apply percent to markup problems.

▼ **CASE IN POINT** James Smelter must determine the appropriate selling price for a shipment of backpacks just received at REI. He must be careful since a price that is too high results in backpacks that cannot be sold and customers that shop elsewhere. Yet a price that is too low may result in a loss on the backpacks.

OBJECTIVE 1

Recognize the terms used in selling

The terms used in markup are summarized here.

Cost is the amount paid to the manufacturer or supplier after trade and cash discounts have been taken. Shipping and insurance charges are included in cost.

Selling price is the price at which merchandise is offered for sale to the public.

Markup, margin, or **gross profit** is the difference between the cost and the selling price. These three terms are often used interchangeably.

Operating expenses, or **overhead,** include the expenses of operating the business, such as wages and salaries of employees, rent for buildings and equipment, utilities, insurance, and advertising. Even an expense like postage can add up when making thousands or millions of shipments.

Net profit (**net earnings**) is the amount (if any) remaining for the business after operating expenses and the cost of goods have been paid. Income tax is computed on net profit.

OBJECTIVE 2 Use the basic formula for markup. Managers mark up the cost of an item before selling it. For example, assume a backpack costs REI $176.92 and that it is marked up by $53.07 before putting it up for sale. The basic **markup formula** that follows shows that the selling price is the sum of the cost and the markup.

$$\textbf{Selling price} = \textbf{Cost} + \textbf{Markup}$$
$$S = C + M$$
$$= \$176.92 + \$53.07$$
$$= \$229.99$$

In general, the markup should be large enough to cover all associated operating expenses, such as wages and rent, and to have some left over for profit. However, smaller markups are sometimes used during a storewide sale to encourage customers to shop at the store or when trying to quickly move outdated products out of the store. Look at the following related to the backpack.

Cost	$176.92		C	$176.92
+ Markup	$53.07	or	+ M	$53.07
Selling price	$229.99		S	$229.99

Cost is the amount paid to a supplier and includes shipping costs. Any markup remaining after paying operating expenses is profit.

Markup problems often give two of the values in the basic formula ($S = C + M$) and ask you to find the unknown value, as shown in Example 1.

Using the Basic Markup Formula

EXAMPLE 1

REI received three different types of snowshoes in one shipment. Use the basic markup formula to find the unknown for each of the following.

(a)
    C $34.48
   +M $13.40
   ——————
    S $

(b)
    C $ 83.82
   +M $
   ——————
    S $124.99

(c)
    C $
   +M $ 68.17
   ——————
    S $227.24

SOLUTION

▼ CASE IN POINT

(a)
    C $34.48
   +M $13.40
   ——————
    S **$47.88**

(b)
    C $ 83.82
   +M **$ 41.17**
   ——————
    S $124.99

(c)
    C **$159.07**
   +M $ 68.17
   ——————
    S $227.24

$R = \dfrac{P}{B}$

OBJECTIVE 3 Calculate markup based on cost. Since manufacturers often talk about inventories in terms of cost, they often use the phrase **markup on cost**, in which markup is stated as a percent of cost. This is an application of the basic percent equation introduced in Chapter 3 with the base being cost, or 100%.

Finding Markup on Cost

$$\text{Markup on cost} = \frac{\text{Amount of markup}}{\text{Cost}} \qquad \textbf{State as a percent.}$$

Assume an iPod that costs a retailer $90 sells for $126. Further, assume that the markup is on cost which is the base, or 100%. The unknown values indicated in the table are found just below the table by referencing 1, 2, and 3.

```
          100%   C   $ 90
  ② ——→     %   M   $       ←—— ①
  ③ ——→     %   S   $126
```

The three missing values in the table are found as follows.

1. Selling price = Cost + Markup   or

    Markup = Selling price − Cost
      = $126   − $90 = $36

2. **Markup as a percent of Cost = Markup ÷ Cost**
      = $36   ÷ 90 = 40%

3. **Selling price as a percent of Cost = Selling price ÷ Cost**
      = $126   ÷ $90 = 140%

The completed table looks as follows.

```
          100%   C   $ 90
           40%   M   $ 36
          ————————————————
          140%   S   $126
```

Notice that the percents in the left column add to 140%, just as the amounts in the right column add to $126. Also notice that all percents are given in terms of cost, which is the base, or 100%.

OBJECTIVE 4 Apply percent to markup problems.

Solving for Percent of Markup on Cost

EXAMPLE 2

The manager of a discount store bought hiking boots manufactured in Mexico for $60 and plans to sell them for $81 a pair. Find the percent of markup based on cost.

SOLUTION

Set up the problem using the table form given earlier. Since this problem is related to markup based on cost, cost is the base, or 100%. All other percents *must be in terms of cost.*

100%	*C*	**$60 base**
? %	*M*	$?
? %	*S*	$81

Find the unknown values as follows.

$$\text{Markup} = \text{Selling price} - \text{Cost}$$
$$= \$81 - \$60 = \$21$$

$$\text{Markup percent} = \text{Markup} \div \text{Cost}$$
$$= \$21 \div \$60 = 35\%$$

$$\text{Selling price percent} = 100\% + \text{Markup percent}$$
$$= 100\% + 35\% = 135\%$$

The following table shows that the markup based on cost is 35% and that the selling price is 135% of cost.

100%	*C*	**$60 base**
35%	*M*	$21
135%	*S*	$81

 The calculator solution to the first part of this example is as follows.

(81 − 60) ÷ 60 = .35

Note: Refer to Appendix B for calculator basics.

QUICK CHECK 2

A retail buyer purchased some pedometers at a cost of $12 and will sell them for $16. What is the percent of markup based on cost? Round to the nearest tenth of a percent.

Now we try a different type of example using markup on cost.

Finding Cost When Cost Is Base

EXAMPLE 3

Olympic Sports places a markup on a 50-lb iron barbell set of $16, which is 50% based on cost. Find the cost and the selling price.

Quick TIP

It is important to first find the base (the cost in this problem) and then find the other values in the table.

SOLUTION

Set up the table using the fact that the markup of 50% based on cost is $16. Cost is the base, or 100%. Cost is not known.

100%	*C*	**$? base**
50%	*M*	$16
? %	*S*	$?

Find the cost using the fact that markup of $16 is 50% of cost.

$$\text{Markup} = 50\% \times \text{Cost}$$
$$\$16 = .5 \times C$$

Divide both sides of the equation by .5 to find

$$C = \$16 \div .5 = \$32$$

Complete the table by adding the percent and dollar columns to find the totals.

100%	*C*	**$32 base**
+ 50%	*M*	+$16
150%	*S*	$48

The weight set costs the retailer $32 and is marked up by $16. The selling price of $48 is 150% of the cost of $32.

QUICK CHECK 3

A 6-foot billiard table has a markup of $84, which is 35% based on cost. Find the cost and the selling price.

Finding the Markup and the Selling Price

EXAMPLE 4

Find the markup and the selling price for an Adidas hooded sweatshirt if the cost is $23.60 and the markup is 45% of cost.

SOLUTION

Use the information given to set up the problem.

100%	C	$23.60	base
45%	M	$?	
? %	S	$?	

The percent column totals to 145%. Use the basic percent equation to find the following.

$$M = 45\% \text{ of Cost} = .45 \times \$23.60 = \$10.62$$

The selling price can be found either by adding the cost of $23.60 to the markup of $10.62, or as follows:

$$S = 145\% \text{ of Cost} = 1.45 \times \$23.60 = \$34.22$$

The table shows that the selling price of the hooded sweatshirt is $34.22.

100%	C	$23.60	base
45%	M	$10.62	
145%	S	$34.22	

This calculator solution uses the percent add-on feature found on many calculators.

23.6 [+] 45 [%] [=] 34.22

QUICK CHECK 4

The cost of some women's slippers is $45. If the markup is 22% of cost, find the markup and the selling price.

Finding Cost When Cost Is Base

EXAMPLE 5

REI sells a lightweight down sleeping bag rated for very cold weather for $308. If the markup on cost is 40%, find the amount that REI pays for one sleeping bag. Then find the markup.

SOLUTION

CASE IN POINT   The cost is 100% and the markup is 40%, so the selling price is 140% of cost.

100%	C	$?	base
40%	M	$?	
140%	S	$308	

It is important to notice that *the base is not known* in this example. So, use the basic percent equation to find the base or think through it as follows:

140% of Cost = Selling price

$$1.40 \times C = S$$
$$1.40 \times C = \$308 \quad \text{**Substitute \$308 for S.**}$$
$$C = \frac{\$308}{1.40} \quad \text{**Divide both sides by 1.40.**}$$
$$C = \$220$$

So, the sleeping bag cost $220. Finally, markup = selling price − cost.

$$M = S - C$$
$$= \$308 - \$220 = \$88$$

All values are given in the table.

100%	C	$220	base
40%	M	$ 88	
140%	S	$308	

Check the answer by making sure that both column totals are correct.

QUICK CHECK 5

Target sells a 2-pack of cotton socks for $4.99. If the markup is 30% on cost, how much can they afford to pay for the socks (cost)? Round to the nearest cent.

Finding the Cost and the Markup

 EXAMPLE 6

The retail price of a 50-inch portable basketball system is $549.99. The retailer has operating expenses of 29.5% and wants a 5.5% profit, both based on cost, on this item. First find the total percent of markup on cost; then find cost and markup.

SOLUTION

Add operating expense and profit percents to find the percent markup on cost required by the retailer.

$$\text{Markup on cost} = \text{operating expense} + \text{profit}$$
$$= \quad\quad 29.5\% \quad\quad + 5.5\%$$
$$= 35\%$$

Now set the problem up in the table form.

100%	C	$?	base
35%	M	$?	
→? %	S	$549.99	

The percent column total is 135%. Find the base (cost) as follows.

$$\text{Cost} = \frac{\text{Selling Price}}{\text{Rate}} = \frac{\$549.99}{1.35}$$
$$= \$407.40$$

$$\text{Markup} = \text{Selling price} - \text{Cost}$$
$$= \quad \$549.99 \quad - \$407.40$$
$$= \$142.59$$

The final table is shown.

100%	C	$407.40	base
35%	M	$142.59	
135%	S	$549.99	

The cost is $407.40 and the markup is $142.59.

> **Quick TIP**
>
> Remember, when calculating markup on cost, *cost is always the base* and 100% always goes next to cost.

QUICK CHECK 6

The selling price of a telescope is $64.99. If the markup is $40% of cost, find the cost and the markup to the nearest cent.

8.1 Exercises

MyMathLab®

*The shaded sections below contain solutions to help you get a **QUICK START** on the various types of exercises.*

Solve for the missing numbers. Markup is based on cost. Round dollar amounts to the nearest cent.
(See Examples 1–6.)

1.

100%	C	$12.40
40%	M	$ 4.96
140%	S	$ 17.36

2.

100%	C	$5.40
25%	M	$1.35
125%	S	$6.75

3.

%	C	$
%	M	$
120%	S	$32.60

4.   %   C $
  50%   M $ 50.00
    %   S $

5.   %   C $
  30%   M $ 50.40
    %   S $

6. 100%   C $78.00
    %   M $17.94
    %   S $

Find the missing numbers. Round rates to the nearest tenth of a percent and dollar amounts to the nearest cent. (See Examples 1–6.)

	Cost Price	Markup	% Markup on Cost	Selling Price
7.	$9.00	$2.70	30%	$11.70
8.	$36.00	$7.20	20%	$43.20
9.	$12.00	$7.20	_____	_____
10.	_____	_____	100%	$68.98
11.	$153.60	_____	_____	$215.04
12.	_____	$54.38	50%	_____
13.	_____	$8.45	_____	$42.25
14.	$7.75	_____	28%	_____

15. Markup may be calculated on cost or on selling price. Explain why most manufacturers use cost as base when calculating markup. (See Objective 1.)

16. Write the markup formula in vertical form. Define each term. (See Objective 2.)

Solve the following application problems, using cost as a base. Round rates to the nearest tenth of a percent and dollar amounts to the nearest cent.

17. **EXERCYCLE**   REI pays $330.30 for a ProForm Exercycle, and the markup is 45% of cost. Find the markup.

  100%   C $330.30 base
    45%   M $?
  145%   S $
  P = B × R = $330.30 × .45 = 148.635 = $148.64

17. $148.64 _____

18. **SKI JACKETS**   REI offers ski jackets, sizes S, M, and L, for $138. If the markup is 35% of cost, find the cost.

18. _____

19. **RESPONDER BACKPACK**   The cost to a retailer of a responder backpack used in emergency situations is $84.96. The retailer uses a markup of 40% based on cost. Find the selling price.

19. _____

 indicates an exercise that is related to the Case in Point feature.

20. **WEIGHT-TRAINING BOOKS** Gold's Gym sells weight-training books for $15.60 per copy. If this includes a markup of 50% on cost, find the cost.

20. _____

21. **TABLE-TENNIS TABLES** Target purchases TIGA table-tennis tables at a cost of $180 each. If the company's operating expenses are 16% of cost, and a net profit of 7% of cost is desired, find the selling price of one table-tennis table.

21. _____

22. **TEXTBOOKS** A college bookstore pays $128.50 for the business math textbook you are currently reading. The bookstore is small and has a fairly high operating expense of 25.4%. The manager of the bookstore also wants a profit of 8.1%. Find the selling price per book and total selling price for 50 books.

22. _____

23. **OUTDOOR LIGHTING** Patios Plus sold an outdoor lighting set for $119.95. The markup on the set was $23.99. Find **(a)** the cost, **(b)** the markup percent on cost, and **(c)** the selling price as a percent of cost.

(a) _____
(b) _____
(c) _____

24. **GOLF CLUBS** Olympic Sports had a markup of $46.64 on golf clubs sold for $222.64. Find **(a)** the cost, **(b)** the markup percent on cost, and **(c)** the selling price as a percent of cost.

(a) _____
(b) _____
(c) _____

25. **TRACTOR PARTS** Bismark Tractor put a markup of 26% on cost on a part for which it paid $450. Find **(a)** the selling price as a percent of cost, **(b)** the selling price, and **(c)** the markup.

(a) _____
(b) _____
(c) _____

26. **CUSTOM-MADE JEWELRY** A jewelry dealer sold custom-made necklaces at a selling price that was 250% of his cost. If the markup is $135, find **(a)** the markup percent on cost, **(b)** the cost, and **(c)** the selling price.

(a) _____
(b) _____
(c) _____

QUICK CHECK ANSWERS

1. (a) $33 **(b)** $26 **(c)** $83

2. 33.3%

3. $240 cost; $324 selling price

4. $9.90 markup; $54.90 selling price

5. $3.84

6. $46.42 cost; $18.57 markup

8.2 Markup on Selling Price

OBJECTIVES

1 Understand the phrase *markup based on selling price*.

2 Solve markup problems when selling price is the base.

3 Use the markup formula to solve variations of markup problems.

4 Determine the percent markup on cost and the equivalent percent markup on selling price.

5 Convert markup percent on cost to markup percent on selling price.

6 Convert markup percent on selling price to markup percent on cost.

7 Find the selling price for perishables.

CASE IN POINT REI faces stiff competition across a range of products from large retailers such as Academy Sports + Outdoors. It also faces serious competition from smaller specialty ski stores when selling items such as skis. In fact, competition is usually very serious for most businesses.

OBJECTIVE 1 Understand the phrase *markup based on selling price*. Markup on cost, discussed in the previous section, is often used by manufacturers. However, retailers often compare business operations to sales revenue and therefore often prefer to use **markup on selling price**. In this case, markup is stated as a percent of selling price.

Finding Markup on Selling Price

$$\text{Markup on selling price} = \frac{\text{Amount of markup}}{\text{Selling price}}$$

The same basic markup formula is used when using markup on selling price: $C + M = S$.

OBJECTIVE 2 Solve markup problems when selling price is the base. The table form used for these problems is identical to that of the previous section. However, *selling price is now the base* rather than cost. Since selling price is the base, put 100% adjacent to selling price, as shown.

? %	C	$	?
%	M	$	
100%	S	**$**	**base**

Solving for Markup on Selling Price

EXAMPLE 1

To remain competitive, REI sells Body Glove Sunglasses for only $39.99. They pay $35 for each pair and calculate markup on selling price. Find the amount of markup, the percent of markup on selling price, and the percent of cost on selling price.

SOLUTION

Set up the problem.

?%	C	$35.00	
?%	M	$?	
100%	S	$39.99	base

$$\text{Markup} = \text{Selling price} - \text{Cost}$$
$$= \$39.99 \quad - \$35 = \$4.99$$

Solve for either of the rates and subtract the result from 100% to find the other. For example, here we solve for the markup rate using the basic percent formula.

$$R = \frac{P}{B}$$

$$\text{Rate} = \frac{\text{Part}}{\text{Base}}$$
$$= \frac{\$4.99}{\$39.99}$$
$$= 12.5\% \quad \textbf{(rounded)}$$

Cost as a percent of selling price can be found either by subtracting 100% − 12.5%, or by dividing the cost of $35 by the selling price of $39.99. Notice that percents are rounded to the nearest tenth of a percent.

87.5%	C	$35.00	
12.5%	M	$ 4.99	
100.0%	S	**$39.99**	base

Here, selling price is the base and is associated with 100%. The markup in this example is very low—REI will probably take a loss on these sunglasses, but managers hope the low price will bring customers into the store.

QUICK CHECK 1

The cost of a two-piece exercise suit is $13.50 and the selling price is $19.99. Find **(a)** the amount of markup, **(b)** the percent of markup on selling price, and **(c)** the percent of cost on selling price.

Markups vary widely from industry to industry and from business to business. This variation is a result of different costs of merchandise, operating costs, levels of profit margin, and local competition. The next table shows average markups for different types of retail stores.

Average Markups for Retail Stores (Markup on Selling Price)

Type of Store	Markup	Type of Store	Markup
General merchandise stores	29.97%	Furniture and home furnishings	35.75%
Grocery stores	22.05%	Bars	52.49%
Other food stores	27.31%	Restaurants	56.35%
Motor vehicle dealers (new)	12.83%	Drug and proprietary stores	30.81%
Gasoline service stations	14.47%	Liquor stores	20.19%
Other automotive dealers	29.57%	Sporting goods and bicycle shops	29.72%
Apparel and accessories	37.64%	Gift, novelty, and souvenir shops	41.86%

(*Source:* Sole-proprietorship income tax returns, U.S. Treasury Dept., Internal Revenue Service, Statistics Division.)

OBJECTIVE 3 Use the markup formula to solve variations of markup problems. As with problems where markup is based on cost, this basic formula may be used for all markup problems in which selling price is the base. In each of these examples, the selling price has a percent value of 100%.

Finding Cost When Selling Price Is Base

 EXAMPLE 2

A Kmart® employee needs a 35% markup on selling price in order to have a markup of $5.16 on a pair of "PRO CLASSIC" Batting Gloves. How much can Kmart afford to pay for each pair of gloves?

SOLUTION

Cost as a percent of selling price is found by subtracting 35% from 100% to find 65%.

65%	C	$?
35%	M	$5.16
100%	S	$? **base**

Find the selling price as follows.

$$\text{Markup} = \textbf{35\% of selling price}$$
$$\$5.16 = .35 \times S$$

Divide both sides by .35 to find the selling price.

$$S = \$5.16 \div .35 = \$14.74 \quad \textbf{base} \quad \textbf{(rounded)}$$

Finally, find cost by subtracting.

$$C = S - M = \$14.74 - \$5.16 = \$9.58$$

The final table is shown here.

65%	C	$ 9.58
35%	M	$ 5.16
100%	S	$14.74

QUICK CHECK 2

The manager of a golf pro shop wants a 15% markup on selling price so that she can have a markup of $13.50 on a Tiger Lee fairway wood golf club. How much can she afford to pay for each club?

Finding Markup When Selling Price Is Given

 EXAMPLE 3

Marilyn Westby must calculate the markup on a Wilson youth tennis racket. The selling price of the tennis racket is $15.99, and the markup is 20% of selling price. Find the markup.

SOLUTION

Cost as a percent of selling price is found by subtracting 20% from 100% to find 80%.

80%	C	$?
20%	M	$
100%	S	**$15.99** **base**

Solve for the missing values using $P = R \times B$:

$$\text{Markup} = \$15.99 \times .2 = \$3.20$$

The markup is $3.20.

Quick TIP

If the rate for cost, 80%, had been used in the formula, the result would have been the cost.

QUICK CHECK 3

The selling price of a three-pack of tennis balls is $3.95, and the markup is 25% of selling price. Find the markup.

Finding Markup When Cost Is Given

 EXAMPLE 4

Find the markup on a dartboard made in England if the cost is $27.45 and the markup is 25% of selling price.

SOLUTION

Subtract 25% from 100% to find that cost is 75% of selling price.

75%	C	$27.45?
25%	M	$?
100%	S	$? **base**

First, solve for selling price.

$$\text{Cost} = 75\% \text{ of Selling price}$$
$$\$27.45 = .75 \times S$$
$$S = \$27.45 \div .75 \qquad \textbf{Divide both sides by .75.}$$
$$S = \$36.60$$

Finally:

$$\text{Markup} = \text{Selling price} - \text{Cost} = \$36.60 - \$27.45$$
$$= \$9.15$$

Here is the completed table.

75%	C	$27.45
25%	M	$ 9.15
100%	S	**$36.60** base

Quick TIP

Remember, when calculating markup on selling price, *selling price* is *always the base* and 100% always goes next to selling price.

QUICK CHECK 4

What is the markup on a sleeping bag if the cost is $40.80 and the markup is 32% of selling price?

OBJECTIVE 4 **Determine the percent markup on cost and the equivalent percent markup on selling price.** Sometimes a markup based on cost must be compared with a markup based on selling price. For example, a salesperson who sells to both manufacturers which use markup on cost and to retailers which use markup on selling price might have to make conversions from one markup method to the other. Make these comparisons by first computing the markup on cost and then the markup on selling price.

Determining Equivalent Markups

Benito's Fishing Lures, Inc., makes and sells a lot of fishing lures and struggles to keep costs very low. One particular lure has a cost of $2.10 and is sold to distributors and wholesalers for $3.20. Find the percent markup on cost and also the percent markup on selling price.

SOLUTION

First set up the problem using *cost as the base*, or 100%.

100%	C	**$2.10** base
? %	M	$?
? %	S	$3.20

$$\text{Markup} = S - C = \$3.20 - \$2.10 = \$1.10$$
$$\text{Markup as a percent of cost} = \$1.10 \div \$2.10 = 52.4\% \quad \textbf{(rounded)}$$
$$\text{Selling price as a percent of cost} = 100\% + 52.4\% = 152.4\%$$

Next, set up the table with *selling price as the base*, or 100%. The markup of $1.10 remains the same and can be entered in the table.

? %	C	$2.10
? %	M	$1.10
100%	S	**$3.20** base

$$\text{Cost as a percent of selling price} = \$2.10 \div \$3.20 = 65.6\% \quad \textbf{(rounded)}$$
$$\text{Markup as a percent of selling price} = 100\% - 65.6\% = 34.4\%$$

This example shows that a 52.4% markup on cost results in the same dollar markup as a 34.4% markup on selling price. In other words, a 52.4% markup on cost is equivalent to a 34.4% markup on selling price.

QUICK CHECK 5

The cost of a Razor A3 Kick Scooter is $45 and it sells for $59.99. Find **(a)** the percent of markup on cost and **(b)** the percent of markup on selling price.

Some people in the retail business use markup on cost and others use markup on selling price. Neither is better than the other—the two just represent different ways to talk about the same thing. Some companies and managers tend to use one of them, and other companies and managers tend to use the other.

OBJECTIVE 5 Convert markup percent on cost to markup percent on selling price. Another method for markup comparisons is to use **conversion formulas**.

> **Converting Markup Percent on Cost to Markup Percent on Selling Price**
>
> $$\frac{\% \text{ markup on cost}}{100\% + \% \text{ markup on cost}} = \% \text{ markup on selling price}$$

Converting Markup on Cost to Markup on Selling Price

EXAMPLE 6 Convert a markup of 25% on cost to its equivalent markup on selling price.

SOLUTION

Use the formula for converting markup percent on cost to markup percent on selling price.

$$\frac{\% \text{ markup on cost}}{100\% + \% \text{ markup on cost}} = \% \text{ markup on selling price}$$

$$\frac{25\%}{100\% + 25\%} = \frac{25\%}{125\%} = \frac{.25}{1.25} = .20 = 20\%$$

As shown, a markup of 25% on cost is equivalent to a markup of 20% on selling price.

The markup on cost (25%) is divided by 100% plus the markup on cost.

$$25 \boxed{\%} \boxed{\div} \boxed{(} 100 \boxed{\%} \boxed{+} 25 \boxed{\%} \boxed{)} \boxed{=} 0.2$$

QUICK CHECK 6

Convert a markup of 100% on cost to a markup on selling price.

OBJECTIVE 6 Convert markup percent on selling price to markup percent on cost.

> **Converting Markup Percent on Selling Price to Markup Percent on Cost**
>
> $$\frac{\% \text{ markup on selling price}}{100\% - \% \text{ markup on selling price}} = \% \text{ markup on cost}$$

Converting Markup on Selling Price to Markup on Cost

EXAMPLE 7 Convert a markup of 20% on selling price to its equivalent markup on cost.

SOLUTION

Use the formula for converting markup percent on selling price to markup percent on cost.

$$\frac{\% \text{ markup on selling price}}{100\% - \% \text{ markup on selling price}} = \% \text{ markup on cost}$$

$$\frac{20\%}{100\% - 20\%} = \frac{20\%}{80\%} = \frac{.2}{.8} = .25 = 25\%$$

A markup of 20% on selling price is equivalent to a markup of 25% on cost.

QUICK CHECK 7

Convert a markup of 40% on selling price to a markup on cost.

The following table shows common markups expressed as percent on cost and as percent on selling price. A table like this is helpful to anyone using markup equivalents on a regular basis.

Markup Equivalents

Markup on Cost	Markup on Selling Price
20%	$16\frac{2}{3}$%
25%	20%
$33\frac{1}{3}$%	25%
50%	$33\frac{1}{3}$%
$66\frac{2}{3}$%	40%
75%	$42\frac{6}{7}$%
100%	50%

OBJECTIVE 7 Find the selling price for perishables. When a business sells items that are perishable (such as baked goods, fruits, or vegetables), the fact that some items will spoil and cannot be sold must be considered when determining the selling price of each item that is sold.

The bar graph below shows the top 10 retailers in the United States. Which of these companies do you think considers perishables as part of their business operations? More than one-half of them sell groceries as part of the product line.

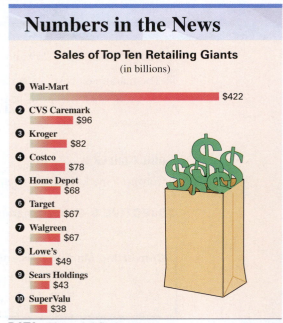

Numbers in the News

Sales of Top Ten Retailing Giants
(in billions)

1. Wal-Mart — $422
2. CVS Caremark — $96
3. Kroger — $82
4. Costco — $78
5. Home Depot — $68
6. Target — $67
7. Walgreen — $67
8. Lowe's — $49
9. Sears Holdings — $43
10. SuperValu — $38

DATA: Financial Statements.

Finding Selling Price for Perishables

EXAMPLE 8

The Bagel Boy bakes 60 dozen bagels at a cost of $2.16 per dozen. If a markup of 50% on selling price is needed and 5% of the bagels remain unsold and will be donated to a shelter, find the selling price per dozen bagels.

SOLUTION

Step 1   Find the total cost of the bagels.

$$\text{Cost} = 60 \text{ dozen} \times \$2.16 = \$129.60$$

Step 2   Find the selling price, using a markup of 50% of selling price.

50%	C	$129.60
50%	M	$
100%	S	$? **base**

$$\text{Base} = \frac{\text{Part}}{\text{Rate}} = \frac{\$129.60}{.5} = \$259.20$$

The total selling price is $259.20.

Step 3   Find the number of dozen bagels that will be sold. Since 5% will not be sold, 95%(100% − 5%) will be sold.

$$95\% \times 60 \text{ dozen} = \textbf{57} \text{ dozen bagels sold}$$

The selling price of $259.20 must be received from the sale of **57** dozen bagels.

Step 4   Find the selling price per dozen bagels by dividing the total selling price by the number of dozen bagels sold.

$$\frac{\$259.20}{57} = \$4.55 \text{ selling price per dozen} \quad (\text{rounded})$$

A selling price of $4.55 per dozen gives the desired markup of 50% on selling price while allowing for 5% of the bagels to be unsold.

QUICK CHECK 8

The Cookie Jar bakes 80 dozen cookies at a cost of $1.08 per dozen. If a markup of 60% on selling price is needed and 10% of the cookies remain unsold and will be donated, find the selling price per dozen cookies.

▼ 8.2 Exercises

MyMathLab®

The shaded sections below contain solutions to help you get a QUICK START on the various types of exercises.

Solve for the missing numbers. Markup is based on selling price. Round dollar amounts to the nearest cent. (See Examples 1–4.)

1.	75%	C	$21.00
	25%	M	$ 7.00
	100%	S	$28.00

2.	60%	C	$18.60
	40%	M	$12.40
	100%	S	$31.00

3.		C	$145.00
		M	
	100%	S	$250.00

4.	$66\frac{2}{3}$%	C	
		M	$ 89.00
		S	

5.	50%	C	$2025
		M	
		S	

6.	65%	C	
		M	$ 527.80
		S	

Find the missing quantities by first computing the markup on one base and then computing the markup on the other. Round rates to the nearest tenth of a percent and dollar amounts to the nearest cent. (See Example 5.)

	Cost	Markup	Selling Price	% Markup on Cost	% Markup on Selling Price
7.	$1920	$480.00	$2400.00	25%	20%
8.	$357.52	$78.48	$436.00	22%	18%
9.	$13.80	_____	_____	_____	38%
10.	$33.75	_____	$67.50	_____	_____
11.	_____	$300.00	_____	40%	_____
12.	$5.15	_____	$15.45	_____	_____

Find the equivalent markups on either cost or selling price using the appropriate formula. Round to the nearest tenth of a percent. (See Examples 6 and 7.)

	Markup on Cost	Markup on Selling Price		Markup on Cost	Markup on Selling Price
13.	100%	$\dfrac{100\%}{100\% + 100\%} = \frac{1}{2} = .5 = 50\%$ **50%**	14.	_____	20%
15.	18%	_____	16.	50%	_____

17. Use the table on page 292 to find the three types of retail stores with the lowest markups. Why do markups differ so much from one type of retail store to another?

C indicates an exercise that is related to the Case in Point feature.

18. To have a markup of 100% or greater, the markup must be calculated on cost. Show why this is always true. (See Objective 6.)

Solve the following application problems. Round rates to the nearest tenth of a percent and dollar amounts to the nearest cent.

19. HOME-WORKOUT EQUIPMENT Olympics Sports has a markup of $437.50 on an Epic Perspective treadmill. If this is a 35% markup on selling price, find **(a)** the selling price, **(b)** the cost, and **(c)** the cost as a percent of selling price.

(a) _____

(b) _____

(c) _____

20. SWIMMING POOL PUMP Leslie's Pool Supply pays $187.19 for a new pool pump. If the markup is 28% on the selling price, find **(a)** the cost as a percent of selling price, **(b)** the selling price, and **(c)** the markup.

(a) _____

(b) _____

(c) _____

21. BLOUSES Jana's Boutique purchased 20 blouses for $930. It sold 12 of the blouses for $85 each, 5 blouses for $68 each, and the remaining blouses for $49 each. Find **(a)** the total amount received for the blouses, **(b)** the total markup, **(c)** the markup percent on selling price, and **(d)** the equivalent markup percent on cost.

(a) _____

(b) _____

(c) _____

(d) _____

22. RIVER-RAFT SALES Olympic Sports purchased a job lot of 380 river rafts for $7600. If they sold 158 of the rafts at $45 each, 74 at $35 each, 56 at $30 each, and the remainder at $25 each, find **(a)** the total amount received for the rafts, **(b)** the total markup, **(c)** the markup percent on selling price, and **(d)** the equivalent markup percent on cost.

(a) _____

(b) _____

(c) _____

(d) _____

23. SELLING BANANAS The produce manager at Tom Thumb Market anticipates that 10% of the bananas purchased will spoil and will have to be thrown out. If she buys 500 pounds of bananas for $.56 per pound and wants a markup of 45% on the selling price, find the selling price per pound of bananas.

23. _____

24. POTTERY-SHOP SALES The Aztec Pottery Shop finds that 15% of their production cannot be sold. If they produce 100 items at a cost of $12.90 each and desire a markup of 40% on selling price, find the selling price per item.

24. _____

QUICK CHECK ANSWERS

1. (a) $6.49 **(b)** 32.5%
  (c) 67.5%

2. $76.50

3. $.99

4. $19.20

5. (a) 33.3%
  (b) 25%

6. 50%

7. 66.7%

8. $3 per dozen

▼ Supplementary Application Exercises on Markup

Solve each of the following application problems. Round rates to the nearest tenth of a percent and dollar amounts to the nearest cent.

1. **DRUMS**   Baytown Music pays $1040 for a Yamaha extreme electronic drum set. Find the markup if the markup percent on cost is 53.8%.

1. _____

2. **BED IN A BAG**   A complete comforter and sheet set has a cost of $132 to the retailer and is marked up 45% on cost. Find the markup.

2. _____

3. **SNOWBOARD**   What percent of markup on cost must be used if an Atlantis Snowboard costing $335 is sold for $399?

3. _____

4. **WINE**   Benjamin's Discount Wines sells a particular bottle of wine for $15.95. If it pays an average of $9.97 per bottle, find the percent markup on cost.

4. _____

5. **AUTOMOTIVE SUPPLIES**   An auto-parts dealer pays $41.88 per dozen cans of Chevron Techron fuel-injector cleaner and the markup is 50% on selling price. Find the selling price per can.

5. _____

6. **DIGITAL THERMOMETERS**   A local pharmacy pays $102.50 for twenty-five digital thermometers. Find the selling price to the pharmacy per thermometer if the markup is 50% of selling price.

6. _____

7. **CEILING FANS**   The Fan Gallery's cost for a ceiling fan is $92.82 and its markup is 22% on the selling price. Find the selling price.

7. _____

 8. **FLY-FISHING**   REI pays $62.40 for a fly rod and marks it up 35% on selling price. Find the selling price.

8. _____

9. **GOLF CART**   A dealer pays $112.40 for an Express 180 golf cart. The markup is 24% on selling price. Find **(a)** the cost as a percent of selling price, **(b)** the selling price, and **(c)** the markup.

(a) _____
(b) _____
(c) _____

10. **DOUBLE-PANE WINDOWS**   Eastern Building Supply pays $3808 for all the double-pane windows needed for the back wall of a 3-bedroom, 2-bath home. If the markup on the windows is 15% on selling price, what is **(a)** the cost as a percent of selling price, **(b)** the selling price, and **(c)** the markup?

(a) _____
(b) _____
(c) _____

 indicates an exercise that is related to the Case in Point feature.

11. **COMMUNICATION EQUIPMENT** A discount store purchased DVD players at a cost of $288 per dozen. If the store needs 20% of cost to cover operating expenses and 15% of cost for the net profit, what are **(a)** the selling price of a DVD player and **(b)** the percent of markup on selling price?

(a) _____

(b) _____

12. **BOWLING EQUIPMENT** The Bowlers Pro-Shop determines that operating expenses are 23% of selling price and desires a net profit of 12% of selling price. If the cost of a team shirt is $29.25, what are **(a)** the selling price and **(b)** the percent of markup on cost?

(a) _____

(b) _____

13. **MOUNTAIN BIKE** REI advertises mountain bikes for $199.90. If the store's cost is $2100 per dozen, what are **(a)** the markup per bicycle, **(b)** the percent of markup on selling price, and **(c)** the percent of markup on cost?

(a) _____

(b) _____

(c) _____

14. **FLASH DRIVE** Office Depot advertises 32 GB USB 2.0 flash drives for $49.99. Their cost is $449.91 per dozen. Find **(a)** the markup per flash drive, **(b)** the percent of markup on selling price, and **(c)** the percent of markup on cost.

(a) _____

(b) _____

(c) _____

15. **LONG-STEMMED ROSES** Farmers Flowers purchased 12 gross of long-stemmed roses at a cost of $1890. If 25% of the roses cannot be sold and a markup of 100% on cost is needed, find the regular selling price per dozen roses.

15. _____

16. **SPORTSWEAR** Olympic Sports buys 2000 baseball caps at $5.00 per hat. If a markup of 50% on selling price is needed and 5% of the caps are damaged and cannot be sold, what is the selling price of each cap?

16. _____

▼ 8.3 Markdown

OBJECTIVES

1 Define the term *markdown* when applied to selling.
2 Calculate markdown, reduced price, and percent of markdown.
3 Define the terms associated with loss.
4 Determine the break-even point and operating loss.
5 Determine the amount of a gross or absolute loss.

▼ **CASE IN POINT** James Smelter keeps a close eye on inventory at the REI store in which he works. He notes some slow-moving winter parkas of odd colors and sizes and marks them down to move them out of the store. It is important to move slow-moving inventory out of stores to make room for other items that are in demand.

OBJECTIVE 1 Define the term *markdown* when applied to selling. When merchandise does not sell at its marked price, the price is often reduced. The difference between the original selling price and the reduced selling price is called the **markdown**, with the selling price after the markdown called the **reduced price, sale price,** or **actual selling price**. The basic **formula for markdown** is as follows.

Finding Reduced Price
Reduced price = Original price − Markdown

Finding the Reduced Price   **EXAMPLE 1** Olympic Sports has marked down an Atlas Home Fitness Center. Find the reduced price if the original price was $2879 and the markdown is 30%.

SOLUTION

The markdown is 30% of $2879, or .3 × $2879 = $863.70. Find the reduced price as follows.

OBJECTIVE 2 Calculate markdown, reduced price, and percent of markdown.

$$
\begin{array}{ll}
\$2879.00 & \text{original price} \\
-\quad 863.70 & \text{markdown (.30 × \$2879)} \\
\hline
\$2015.30 & \text{reduced price (70\% of original price)}
\end{array}
$$

Quick TIP

The original selling price is always the base or 100%, and the percent of markdown is always calculated on the original selling price.

⊞ The calculator solution to this example uses the complement, with respect to 1, of the discount.

$2879 ⊠ 〔 1 ⊟ .3 〕 ⊜ 2015.3

QUICK CHECK 1

Ski boots originally priced at $289.99 were marked down 40%. Find the reduced price.

The next example shows how to find a **percent of markdown**.

Calculating the Percent of Markdown   **EXAMPLE 2** The total inventory of coffee mugs at the local bookstore has a retail value of $785. If the mugs were sold at reduced prices that totaled $530, what is the percent of markdown on the original price?

SOLUTION

First find the amount of the markdown.

$$
\begin{array}{ll}
\$785 & \text{original price} \\
-\quad 530 & \text{reduced price} \\
\hline
\$255 & \text{markdown}
\end{array}
$$

Finding the percent of the original price that is the markdown is a rate problem. (See Chapter 3.)

$$ \text{Rate} = \frac{\textbf{Part}}{\textbf{Base}} = \frac{255}{785} = .3248 = 32.5\% \text{ markdown (rounded)} $$

The mugs were sold at a markdown of 32.5%.

Finding the Original Price

EXAMPLE 3

Bouza's Baby News offers a child's car seat at a reduced price of $63 after a 25% markdown from the original price. Find the original price.

SOLUTION

After the 25% markdown, the reduced price of $63 represents 75% of the original price. The original price, or base, must be found.

$$\text{Base} = \frac{\textbf{Part}}{\textbf{Rate}} = \frac{\$63}{.75} = \$84 \text{ original price}$$

The original price of the car seat was $84.

Check the answer by subtracting 25% of $84 from $84: $84 − (.25 × $84) = $63.

Quick TIP

In Example 3, notice that 75% is used in the formula rather than 25%. The reduced price, $63, is represented by 75%.

OBJECTIVE 3 Define the terms associated with loss. Markdowns are used to stimulate sales. They may be used when an item is not selling well, or perhaps when a firm has financial problems and needs to convert inventory to cash. However, markdowns are also used as part of a marketing strategy based on the fact that most people like the idea of getting a good deal by buying something 'on sale.'

The **break-even point** is the selling price that just covers the cost of the item plus overhead. A company does not make or lose money on items sold at the break-even point. A **reduced net profit** occurs when an item is marked down, but still sold above the break-even point. An **operating loss** occurs when the selling price is below the break-even point. Finally, an absolute loss (gross loss) occurs if the selling price is less than the amount paid for the item.

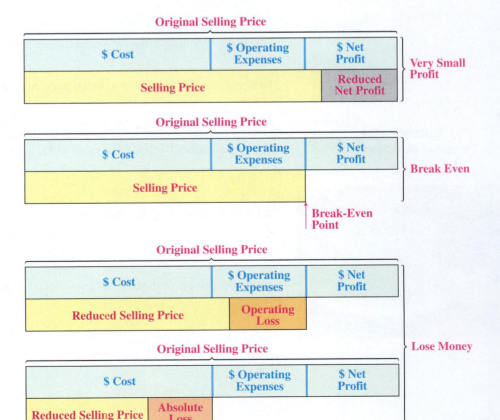

These formulas may help you.

> Break-even point = Cost + Operating expenses
> Operating loss = Break-even point − Reduced selling price
> Absolute loss = Cost − Reduced selling price

Determining a Profit or a Loss

EXAMPLE 4

Appliance Giant paid $1600 for a 60-inch LCD flat-panel HDTV. If operating expenses are 30% of cost and the television is sold for $2000, find the amount of profit or loss.

SOLUTION

Operating expenses are 30% of cost.

$$\text{Operating expenses} = .30 \times \$1600 = \$480$$

The break-even point for the LCD HDTV is

$$\text{Cost} + \text{Operating expenses} = \text{Break-even point}$$

$$\$1600 + (.3 \times \$1600) = \$1600 + \$480 = \$2080 \text{ break-even point}$$

So, the company makes a profit if the television is sold for more than the $2080 break-even point or incurs a loss if sold for less. Since the selling price is $2000, there is a loss, found as follows.

$$\$2080 - \$2000 = \$80$$

The $80 loss is an operating loss, since the selling price is less than the break-even point but greater than the cost.

The calculator solution to this example follows.

1600 [+] [(] .3 [×] 1600 [)] [−] 2000 [=] 80

QUICK CHECK 4

Big Chime Electronics paid $480 for a flat-screen television set. If operating expenses are 35% of cost and the television is sold for $600, find the amount of the operating loss.

Determining the Operating Loss and the Absolute Loss

EXAMPLE 5

A ping pong table that normally sells for $360 at Dick's Sporting Goods is marked down 30%. If the cost of the game table is $260 and the operating expenses are 20% of cost, find **(a)** the operating loss and **(b)** the absolute loss.

SOLUTION

(a) Break-even point = Cost + Operating expenses
= $260 + 20% of $260
= $312

Reduced price = $360 − (.3 × $360) = $360 − $108 = $252

Operating loss = $312 break-even point − $252 reduced price = $60

(b) The absolute or gross loss is the difference between the cost of the table and the selling price.

$$\text{Absolute Loss} = \$260 \text{ Cost} - \$252 \text{ Reduced Price} = \$8$$

QUICK CHECK 5

A propane forced-air heater normally selling for $290 is marked down 25%. If the cost of the heater is $220 and the operating expenses are 15% of cost, find **(a)** the operating loss and **(b)** the absolute loss.

The following bar graph shows the percent of adults who get an emotional high from making certain purchases. Customers love buying things—especially when they are on sale. This is valuable information to manufacturers, retailers, and all merchandisers. In fact, many large companies track your preferences and try to target you with advertising focused on your interests.

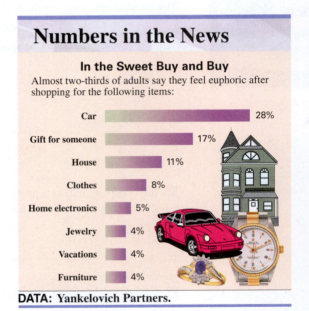

Numbers in the News

In the Sweet Buy and Buy

Almost two-thirds of adults say they feel euphoric after shopping for the following items:

Car	28%
Gift for someone	17%
House	11%
Clothes	8%
Home electronics	5%
Jewelry	4%
Vacations	4%
Furniture	4%

DATA: Yankelovich Partners.

▼ 8.3 Exercises

MyMathLab®

*The shaded sections below contain solutions to help you get a **QUICK START** on the various types of exercises.*

Find the missing quantities. Round rates to the nearest whole percent and dollar amounts to the nearest cent. (See Examples 1–3.)

	Original Price	% Markdown	$ Markdown	Reduced Price
1.	$860	25%	$215	$645
	$R = \frac{P}{B} = \frac{\$215}{\$860} = .25 = 25\%; \$860 - \$215 = \$645$			
2.	$240	40%	$96	$144
	$B = \frac{P}{R} = \frac{\$144}{.6} = \$240; \$240 - \$144 = \$96$			
3.	$61.60	_____	_____	$43.12
4.	_____	$66\frac{2}{3}\%$	_____	$3.10
5.	$6.50	_____	$1.30	_____
6.	_____	50%	$65.25	_____

Complete the following. If there is no operating loss or absolute loss, write "none."
(See Examples 4 and 5.)

	Cost	Operating Expense	Break-even Point	Reduced Price	Operating Loss	Absolute Loss
7.	$96	$24	$120	$100	$20	none
	$96 + $24 = $120; $120 − $100 = $20					
8.	$25	$8	$33	$22	$11	$3
	$25 + $8 = $33; $33 − $22 = $11; $25 − $22 = $3					
9.	$50	_____	$66	$44	_____	_____
10.	$12.50	_____	$16.50	$11	_____	_____
11.	$310	$75	_____	_____	$135	_____
12.	$156	$44	_____	_____	$60	_____

13. Give five reasons a manager may mark down the price of merchandise.

14. As a result of a markdown, there are three possible results: reduced net profit, operating loss, and absolute loss. As a business owner, which would concern you the most? Explain. (See Objectives 4 and 5.)

Solve the following application problems. Round rates to the nearest whole percent and dollar amounts to the nearest cent.

15. **GPS SYSTEMS** For accounting purposes, Best Buy prices its entire inventory of TomTom portable Global Positioning Systems at $133,509. If the original price of the inventory was $226,284, find the percent of markdown on the original price.
$226,284 − $133,509 = $92,775;
$R = \frac{P}{B} = \frac{\$92,775}{\$226,284} = .409 = 41\%$

15. __41%_____

16. **OAK DESK** An oak desk originally priced at $837.50 is reduced to $686.75. Find the percent of markdown on the original price.

16. _____

17. **ELLIPTICAL TRAINER** Olympic Sports paid $360 for a ProForm elliptical trainer. The operating expenses are $33\frac{1}{3}\%$ of cost. If they sell the elliptical trainer at a clearance price of $449.99, find the amount of profit or loss.

17. _____

18. **KAYAK** REI has an end-of-season sale, during which it sells an ocean kayak for two people for $865. If the cost was $641 and operating expenses are 28% of cost, find the amount of profit or loss.

;

18. _____

indicates an exercise that is related to the Case in Point feature.

19. TRUCK ACCESSORIES Pep Boys Automotive paid $208.50 for a pickup truck bedliner. The original selling price was $291.90, but this was marked down 35%. If operating expenses are 28% of the cost, find **(a)** the operating loss and **(b)** the absolute loss.

(a) _____

(b) _____

20. ANTIQUES American Antiques paid $153.49 for a fern stand. The original selling price was $208.78, but this was marked down 46% in order to make room for incoming merchandise. If operating expenses are 14.9% of cost, find **(a)** the operating loss and **(b)** the absolute loss.

(a) _____

(b) _____

QUICK CHECK ANSWERS

1. $173.99

2. 75%

3. $29.98

4. $48 operating loss

5. (a) $35.50 operating loss

   (b) $2.50 absolute loss

▼ 8.4 Turnover and Valuation of Inventory

OBJECTIVES

1 Determine average inventory.
2 Calculate inventory turnover.
3 Methods for tracking inventory.
4 Use the specific identification method to value inventory.
5 Determine inventory value using the weighted-average method.
6 Use the FIFO method to value inventory.
7 Use the LIFO method to value inventory.
8 Estimate inventory value using the retail method.

▼ **CASE IN POINT**   The marketing and inventory managers at REI work together to make sure they order only products that will sell. The last thing either wants is for inventory to build up needlessly in the company stores and warehouses.

OBJECTIVE 1 Determine average inventory. Several measures of the financial performance of a company are based on **average inventory**. Find average inventory by finding the average (mean) of all inventories taken during a specific interval of time, such as a month or a quarter. For example, some firms take a physical inventory only once a quarter. In that event, the average inventory for the quarter is the average of the beginning and ending inventory for the quarter.

Determining Average Inventory   **EXAMPLE 1**   Inventory at a Super Shoes store was $285,672 on April 1 and $198,560 on April 30. What was the average inventory?

SOLUTION

First add the inventory values.

$$
\begin{array}{rl}
\$285,672 & \textbf{April 1} \\
+\quad 198,560 & \textbf{April 30} \\
\hline
\$484,232 &
\end{array}
$$

Then divide by the number of times inventory was taken.

$$\frac{\$484,232}{2} = \$242,116$$

The average inventory was $242,116.

QUICK CHECK 1

Inventory on September 1 was $176,840 and on September 30 it was $153,210. Find the average inventory.

Management must carefully monitor and control the inventory of each item. Inventories can become too large due to a business recession or simply because a particular product is not popular among consumers. To reduce the inventories of slow-moving products, it may be necessary to mark prices down, increase advertising, or do both at the same time. The following ad is evidence of a sale designed to reduce inventory.

Quick TIP

When possible, save money by buying when items are on sale.

OBJECTIVE 2 Calculate inventory turnover. One measure of how well a company is doing financially is based on how fast inventory is moving, as measured by **inventory turnover**, also called **inventory turns** and **stock turnover**. Inventory turnover varies widely from one business to the next. For example, a flower shop must turn inventory over rapidly to avoid the costly waste of wilting flowers. On the other hand, a furniture store will have a lower inventory turnover since furniture often sits in a store before being sold.

Inventory turnover refers to the number of times the average inventory is turned over, or sold, during a period of time, such as a year. Businesses value inventory either at retail or at cost. For this reason, inventory turnover can be found using either of these formulas. Both are used in business.

Measuring Inventory Turnover

$$\text{Turnover at retail} = \frac{\text{Retail sales}}{\text{Average inventory at retail}}$$

$$\text{Turnover at cost} = \frac{\text{Cost of goods sold}}{\text{Average inventory at cost}}$$

The turnover ratio may be identical by using either method. The variation that often exists is caused by stolen merchandise (called **inventory shrinkage**) or merchandise that has been marked down or has become unsellable. Normally, turnover at retail is slightly lower than turnover at cost. For this reason, many businesses prefer this more conservative figure.

Finding Stock Turnover at Retail

 EXAMPLE 2

Last year, Red Clown Children's Apparel had retail sales of $559,320 and an average retail inventory of $49,601. Find the stock turnover at retail.

SOLUTION

$$\text{Turnover at retail} = \frac{\text{Retail sales}}{\text{Average inventory at retail}} = \frac{\$559{,}320}{\$49{,}601} = \textbf{11.28 at retail} \quad \textbf{(rounded)}$$

On average, the store turned over or sold the value of its entire inventory 11.3 times during the month.

QUICK CHECK 2

Painters Supply had an average retail inventory of $1,120,400 and retail sales of $1,833,080. Find the stock turnover at retail.

Finding Stock Turnover at Cost

 EXAMPLE 3

If the average inventory value at cost for Red Clown Children's Apparel in Example 2 was $27,260 and the cost of goods sold was $341,340, find the stock turnover at cost.

SOLUTION

$$\text{Turnover at cost} = \frac{\text{Cost of goods sold}}{\text{Average inventory at cost}} = \frac{\$341{,}340}{\$27{,}260} = \textbf{12.52 at cost} \quad \textbf{(rounded)}$$

Notice that the two turnover values from Examples 2 and 3 are similar, as expected.

QUICK CHECK 3

If the cost of goods sold by Painters Supply in Quick Check 2 was $1,204,300 and the average inventory at cost was $761,872, find the stock turnover at cost.

The stock turnover is useful for comparison purposes only. Many trade organizations publish such operating statistics to permit businesses to compare their operation with the industry as a whole. In addition to this, management uses these rates to compare turnover from period to period and from department to department.

OBJECTIVE 3 Methods for tracking inventory. It is important for managers to track inventory moving along the supply chain, sitting in warehouses, and on shelves in stores. Only by tracking inventory can they cut down on theft, figure out what is selling and what is not selling, prevent the waste of a buildup in unneeded inventory, and move inventory quickly to locations where it is needed. Years ago, managers used **periodic inventory** systems, which required a

RFID Chip

physical inventory at specific intervals, such as the end of each quarter. However, today, most firms have moved to **perpetual inventory** systems, also called **continuous inventory** systems. These inventory systems continually track the quantity and availability of inventory.

A number of technologies have been developed to help track inventory in perpetual inventory systems. One of the first techniques and one that is still used today is the **universal product code (UPC)**. This technique requires a tag with black stripes, called a **barcode**, to be imprinted on each item in inventory. The tag can be scanned at cash registers or other readers. A disadvantage of the UPC technique is the requirement that it be scanned with light. As a result, the UPC code has to be visible and directed toward the machine reading the code. You may have watched cashiers as they repeatedly scan an item at the cash register trying to get the machine to read the code.

Many firms use **radio frequency identification (RFID)** chips, which are read using **electronic product code (EPC)** devices. The giant retailer Walmart was one of the first to adopt this technology when it required all suppliers to put RFID chips on pallets and cases. Although some RFID chips have tiny batteries, most use energy emitted from the machine reading them to respond with an electronic signal. One advantage of RFID chips is that they do not have to be pointed at the machine reading the information on the chip. Another advantage is that they can be very small and inexpensive.

RFID chips can also be read quickly, as evidenced by new toll-booth technologies, which read the information stored on RFID chips on the windshields of automobiles driving through the booth at 50 miles per hour. In the future, the same RFID chips that allow managers to monitor inventory may be used to electronically provide cooking instructions to a smart oven or microwave.

There are four major methods used for inventory valuation: the specific identification method; the weighted-average method; the first-in, first-out method; the last-in, first-out method; and the retail method.

OBJECTIVE 4 Use the specific identification method to value inventory. The **specific identification method** is useful when items are easily identified and costs do not fluctuate. Each item is cost-coded with either numerals or letters. These costs are then added to find ending inventory.

Since the cost of many items changes with time, there may be several of the same item in stock that were purchased at different costs. For this reason, many businesses prefer taking inventory at retail. The retail value of all identical items is the same.

OBJECTIVE 5 Determine inventory value using the weighted-average method. The **weighted average (average cost)** of inventory involves finding the average cost of an item and then multiplying the number of items remaining by the average cost per item.

Using Weighted Average (Average Cost) Inventory Valuation

 EXAMPLE 4

Suppose REI made the following purchases of the Explorer internal frame backpack during the year.

Beginning inventory	20 backpacks at $70
January	50 backpacks at $80
March	100 backpacks at $90
July	60 backpacks at $85
October	40 backpacks at $75

At the end of the year, there are 75 backpacks in inventory. Use the weighted-average method to find the inventory value.

SOLUTION

Find the total cost of all the backpacks.

Beginning inventory	20 × $70 = $1400
January	50 × $80 = $4000
March	100 × $90 = $9000
July	60 × $85 = $5100
October	40 × $75 = $3000
Total	270 $22,500

Find the average cost per backpack by dividing this total cost by the number purchased.

$$\frac{\$22{,}500}{270} = \$83.33 \text{ (rounded)}$$

Since the average cost is \$83.33 and 75 backpacks remain in inventory, the weighted-average method gives the inventory value of the remaining backpacks as $\$83.33 \times 75 = \$6249.75$.

▦ The calculator solution to this example has several steps. First, find the total number of backpacks purchased and place the total in memory.

$$20 \boxed{+} 50 \boxed{+} 100 \boxed{+} 60 \boxed{+} 40 \boxed{=} 270 \boxed{\text{STO}}$$

Next, find the total cost of all the backpacks purchased and divide by the number stored in memory. This gives the average cost per backpack.

$$20 \boxed{\times} 70 \boxed{+} 50 \boxed{\times} 80 \boxed{+} 100 \boxed{\times} 90 \boxed{+} 60 \boxed{\times} 85 \boxed{+}$$
$$40 \boxed{\times} 75 \boxed{=} \boxed{\div} \boxed{\text{RCL}} \boxed{=} 83.3333$$

Finally, round the average cost to the nearest cent and multiply by the number of backpacks in inventory to get the weighted average inventory value.

$$83.33 \boxed{\times} 75 \boxed{=} 6249.75$$

QUICK CHECK 4

Dick's Sporting Goods made the following purchases of the Iron Horse BMX bicycle during the year.

Beginning inventory	20 bicycles at \$115
February	30 bicycles at \$95
April	50 bicycles at \$100
June	40 bicycles at \$110
August	80 bicycles at \$105
November	60 bicycles at \$130

At the end of the year, there are 85 bicycles in inventory. Use the weighted-average method to find the inventory value.

The cost of items purchased by the retailer is one of the greatest influences on the final retail price. The factors affecting cost include the quality of the product, the quantity purchased, and the geographic location of the purchaser. The following graphic shows the average price paid for a tennis racket in various countries around the world.

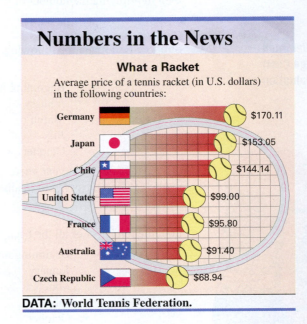

Numbers in the News

What a Racket

Average price of a tennis racket (in U.S. dollars) in the following countries:

Country	Price
Germany	\$170.11
Japan	\$153.05
Chile	\$144.14
United States	\$99.00
France	\$95.80
Australia	\$91.40
Czech Republic	\$68.94

DATA: World Tennis Federation.

OBJECTIVE 6 Use the FIFO method to value inventory. The **first-in, first-out (FIFO)** **method** of inventory valuation assumes a natural flow of goods through the inventory. The first goods to arrive are the first goods to be sold, so the last items purchased are the items remaining in inventory.

Using FIFO to Determine Inventory Valuation

EXAMPLE 5

Use the FIFO method to find the inventory value of the 75 backpacks from REI in Example 4.

SOLUTION

▼ CASE IN POINT   With the FIFO method, the 75 remaining backpacks are assumed to consist of the 40 backpacks bought in October and 35 (75 − 40 = 35) backpacks from the previous purchase in July. The value of the inventory is:

October	40 backpacks at $75 = $3000	value of last 40
July	35 backpacks at $85 = $2975	value of previous 35
	75 valued at $5975	

The value of the backpack inventory is $5975 using the FIFO method.

QUICK CHECK 5

Use the FIFO method to find the inventory value of the 85 bicycles from Dick's Sporting Goods in Quick Check 4.

OBJECTIVE 7 Use the LIFO method to value inventory. The **last-in, first-out (LIFO) method** of inventory valuation assumes a flow of goods through the inventory that is just the opposite of the FIFO flow. With LIFO, the goods remaining in inventory are those goods that were first purchased.

Using LIFO to Determine Inventory Valuation

EXAMPLE 6

Use the LIFO method to value the 75 backpacks in inventory at REI in Example 4.

SOLUTION

▼ CASE IN POINT   The calculation starts with the beginning inventory and moves through the year's purchases, resulting in 75 backpacks still in stock. The beginning inventory and January purchases come to 70 backpacks, so the cost of 5 more (75 − 70 = 5) backpacks from the March purchase is needed.

Beginning inventory	20 backpacks at $70 = $1400	value of first 20
January	50 backpacks at $80 = $4000	value of next 50
March	5 backpacks at $90 = $ 450	value of last 5
Total	75 valued at $5850	

The value of the backpack inventory is $5850 using the LIFO method.

QUICK CHECK 6

Use the LIFO method to value the 85 bicycles in inventory at Dick's Sporting Goods in Quick Check 4.

Depending on the method of valuing inventories that is used, REI may show the inventory value of the 75 backpacks as follows.

Average cost method	$6249.75
FIFO	$5975
LIFO	$5850

The preferred inventory valuation method is determined by management on the advice of an accountant.

OBJECTIVE 8 Estimate inventory value using the retail method. An estimate of the value of inventory may be found using the **retail method of estimating inventory**. With this method, the cost of goods available for sale is found as a percent of the retail value of the goods available for sale during the same period. This percent is then multiplied by the retail value of inventory at the end of the period. The result is an estimate of the inventory at cost.

Estimating Inventory Value Using the Retail Method

EXAMPLE 7

The inventory on December 31 at an Apple store in the mall was $129,200 at cost and $171,000 at retail. Purchases during the next three months were $165,400 at cost, $221,800 at retail, and net sales were $168,800. Use the retail method to estimate the value of inventory at cost on March 31.

SOLUTION

Step 1   Find the value of goods available for sale (inventory) at cost and at retail.

At cost	At retail	
$129,200	$171,000	beginning inventory
+ 165,400	+ 221,800	purchases
$294,600	$392,800	goods available for sale
	− 168,800	net sales
	$224,000	March 31 inventory at retail

Step 2   Find the retail value of current inventory.

Step 3   Now find the percent of the value of goods available for sale at cost to goods available for sale at retail (cost ratio).

$$\frac{\$294,600 \quad \text{goods available for sale at cost}}{\$392,800 \quad \text{goods available for sale at retail}} = .75 = 75\% \ (\text{cost ratio})$$

Step 4   Finally, the estimated inventory value at cost on March 31 is found by multiplying inventory at retail on March 31 by 75% (cost ratio).

Ending inventory at retail × % (cost ratio) = Inventory at cost

$224,000 × .75 = $168,000 March 31 inventory at cost

QUICK CHECK 7

At the end of June, Solar Solutions had an inventory of $87,500 at cost and $125,000 at retail. During the next three months, there were purchases of $103,200 at cost, $147,600 at retail, and net sales were $185,000. Use the retail method to estimate the value of inventory at cost at the end of September.

▼ 8.4 Exercises   MyMathLab®

*The shaded sections below contain solutions to help you get a **QUICK START** on the various types of exercises.*

Find the average inventory in each of the following. (See Example 1.)

Date	Inventory Amount at Retail	Average Inventory	Date	Inventory Amount at Retail	Average Inventory
1. July 1	$18,300		**2.** January 1	$42,312	
October 1	$26,580		July 1	$38,514	
December 31	$23,139	$22,673	December 31	$30,219	$37,015
$68,019 total of inv. ÷ 3 = $22,673			$111,045 total of inv. ÷ 3 = $37,015		
3. January 1	$65,430		**4.** January 31	$69,480	
April 1	$58,710		April 30	$55,860	
July 1	$53,410		July 31	$80,715	
October 1	$78,950		October 31	$88,050	
December 31	$46,340	_____	January 31	$63,975	_____

⚠C indicates an exercise that is related to the Case in Point feature.

Find the stock turnover at cost and at retail in each of the following. Round to the nearest hundredth. (See Examples 2 and 3.)

	Average Inventory at Cost	Average Inventory at Retail	Cost of Goods	Retail Sales	Turnover at Cost	Turnover at Retail
5.	$84,320	$127,690	$1,104,600	$1,782,300	13.10	13.96

$1,104,600 \div $84,320 = 13.10; $1,782,300 \div $127,690 = 13.96$

6.	$15,140	$24,080	$67,408	$106,193	4.45	4.41

$67,408 \div $15,140 = 4.45$ at cost; $106,193 \div $24,080 = 4.41$ at retail

7.	$68,080	$125,240	$573,330	$951,900	_____	_____
8.	$38,074	$48,550	$260,420	$330,060	_____	_____
9.	$180,600	$256,700	$846,336	$1,196,222	_____	_____
10.	$411,580	$780,600	$1,905,668	$3,559,536	_____	_____

Find the inventory values using (a) the weighted-average method, (b) the FIFO method, and (c) the LIFO method for each of the following. Round to the nearest cent if necessary. (See Examples 4–6.)

Purchases	Now in Inventory	Weighted-Average Method	FIFO Method	LIFO Method
11. Beginning inventory: 10 units at $8 June: 25 units at $9 August: 15 units at $10	20 units	$182	$195	$170

($455 purchases ÷ 50) × 20 = $9.10 × 20 = $182 average cost method

$$\begin{array}{ll} & 15 \times \$10 = \$150 \\ + & 5 \times \$9 = \$\ 45 \\ \hline & 20 \qquad \$195 \text{ FIFO} \end{array}$$

$$\begin{array}{ll} & 10 \times \$8 = \$\ 80 \\ + & 10 \times \$9 = \$\ 90 \\ \hline & 20 \qquad \$170 \text{ LIFO} \end{array}$$

12. Beginning inventory: 80 units at $14.50 July: 50 units at $15.80 October: 70 units at $13.90	90 units	_____	_____	_____
13. Beginning inventory: 50 units at $30.50 March: 70 units at $31.50 June: 30 units at $33.25 August: 40 units at $30.75	75 units	_____	_____	_____
14. Beginning inventory: 700 units at $1.25 May: 400 units at $1.75 August: 500 units at $2.25 October: 600 units at $3.00	720 units	_____	_____	_____

15. Identify three types of businesses that you think would have a high turnover. Identify three types of businesses that you think would have a low turnover.

16. Which departments in a grocery store do you think have the highest turnover? Which ones have the lowest turnover? Why do you think this is true?

Solve the following application problems. Round stock turnover to the nearest hundredth.

17. STOCK TURNOVER AT COST The Glass Works has an average inventory at cost of $62,920, and cost of goods sold for the same period is $341,648. Find the stock turnover at cost.

$$\frac{\$341,648}{\$62,920} = 5.43 \text{ turnover at cost}$$

17. <u>5.43 turnover at cost</u>

18. STOCK TURNOVER AT RETAIL Jumbo Market has an average canned-fruit inventory of $4484 at retail. Retail sales of canned fruit for the year were $98,669. Find the stock turnover at retail.

18. _____

19. SPRAY-PAINT INVENTORY The Graphic Hobby House made purchases of assorted colors of spray paint during the year as follows.

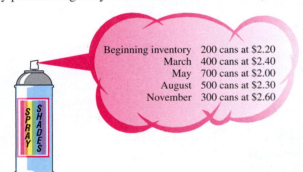

Beginning inventory	200 cans at $2.20
March	400 cans at $2.40
May	700 cans at $2.00
August	500 cans at $2.30
November	300 cans at $2.60

(a) _____
(b) _____
(c) _____

At the end of the year, they had 450 cans of spray paint in stock.

(a) Find the inventory value using the weighted-average method.
(b) Find the inventory value using the FIFO method.
(c) Find the inventory value using the LIFO method.

20. SPORT T-SHIRTS Adams Import made the following purchases of sport T-shirts made in Taiwan: beginning inventory was 650 shirts at $3.80 each; June, 500 shirts at $4.20 each; September, 450 shirts at $3.95 each; and December, 600 shirts at $4.05 each. An inventory at the end of the year shows that 775 T-shirts remain. **(a)** Find the inventory value using the weighted-average method. **(b)** Find the inventory value using the FIFO method. **(c)** Find the inventory value using the LIFO method.

(a) _____
(b) _____
(c) _____

21. ATHLETIC SOCKS REI made the following purchases of wool socks.

Beginning inventory	200 packages at $3.10
May	250 packages at $3.50
August	300 packages at $4.25
October	280 packages at $4.50

(a) _____
(b) _____
(c) _____

An inventory at the end of October shows that 320 packages remain. **(a)** Find the inventory value using the weighted-average method. **(b)** Find the inventory value using the FIFO method. **(c)** Find the inventory value using the LIFO method.

22. **ATHLETIC SHOES**   The beginning inventory and purchases of shoes made by The Sports Authority this year are as shown.

Beginning inventory	300 pairs at $21.60
March	400 pairs at $24.00
August	450 pairs at $24.30
November	350 pairs at $22.50

An inventory at the end of December shows that 530 pairs of shoes remain. **(a)** Find the inventory value using the weighted-average method. **(b)** Find the inventory value using the FIFO method. **(c)** Find the inventory value using the LIFO method.

(a) _____

(b) _____

(c) _____

23. **PIANO REPAIR** The September 30 inventory at Liverpool Piano Repair was $43,750 at cost and $62,500 at retail. Purchases during the next three months were $51,600 at cost, $73,800 at retail, and net sales were $92,500. Use the retail method to estimate the value of the inventory at cost on December 31.

23. _____

24. **EVALUATING INVENTORY** Cell Phones Plus had an inventory of $27,000 at cost and $45,000 at retail on March 31. During the next three months, they made purchases of $108,000 at cost and $180,000 at retail and had net sales of $162,000. Use the retail method to estimate the value of inventory at cost on June 30.

24. _____

25. In your opinion, what are the benefits to a merchant who is using RFID chips to electronically track inventory?

26. Which of the three inventory valuation methods discussed in this section is most interesting to you? Explain how this method determines inventory value.

QUICK CHECK ANSWERS

1. $165,025
2. 1.64 at retail
3. 1.58 at cost
4. $9334.70 weighted average

5. $10,425 FIFO
6. $8650 LIFO
7. $61,320 inventory at cost

Chapter 8 Quick Review

Chapter Terms *Review the following terms to test your understanding of the chapter. For each term you do not know, refer to the page number found next to that term.*

absolute loss [**p. 302**]

actual selling price [**p. 301**]

average inventory [**p. 307**]

barcode [**p. 309**]

break-even point [**p. 302**]

continuous inventory systems [**p. 309**]

conversion formulas [**p. 295**]

cost [**p. 295**]

electronic product code (EPC) [**p. 309**]

first-in, first-out (FIFO) method [**p. 310**]

formula for markdown [**p. 301**]

gross loss [**p. 302**]

gross profit [**p. 284**]

inventory shrinkage [**p. 308**]

inventory turns [**p. 307**]

inventory turnover [**p. 307**]

last-in, first-out (LIFO) method [**p. 311**]

margin [**p. 301**]

markdown [**p. 301**]

markup [**p. 284**]

markup on cost [**p. 285**]

markup formula [**p. 284**]

markup on cost [**p. 285**]

markup on selling price [**p. 291**]

net earnings [**p. 284**]

net profit [**p. 284**]

operating expenses [**p. 284**]

operating loss [**p. 302**]

overhead [**p. 284**]

percent of markdown [**p. 301**]

periodic inventory [**p. 308**]

perpetual inventory [**p. 309**]

physical inventory [**p. 309**]

radio frequency identification (RFID) [**p. 309**]

reduced net profit [**p. 302**]

reduced price [**p. 301**]

retail method of estimating inventory [**p. 311**]

sale price [**p. 301**]

selling price [**p. 284**]

specific identification method [**p. 309**]

stock turnover [**p. 307**]

universal product code (UPC) [**p. 309**]

weighted-average (average cost) method [**p. 309**]

CONCEPTS

EXAMPLES

8.1 Finding the markup on cost

	100%	Cost	base
	% +	**Markup**	**?**
	%	Selling price	

Cost is base. Use the basic percent formula.

$$P = B \times R$$

	100%	C	$160	base
rate	25%	M	**$?**	
	%	S	$	

$$P = B \times R$$
$$P = \$160 \times .25$$
$$P = \$40 \text{ markup}$$

8.1 Calculating the percent of markup

	100%	C	$	base
rate	**?%**	M	$	
	%	S	$	

Solve for rate.

	100%	C	$420	base
rate	**?%**	M	$	
	%	S	$546	

$$\$546 - \$420 = \$126 \text{ markup}$$

$$R = \frac{P}{B} = \frac{126}{420}$$

$$R = 30\%$$

8.1 Finding the cost and the selling price

	100%	C	$?	**base**
	%	M	$	
	%	S	$?	

Solve for base.

	100%	C	$?	base
rate	50%	M	$56	
	%	S	$?	

$$B = \frac{P}{R} = \frac{56}{.5}$$

$$B = \$112 \text{ cost}$$

$$\$112 + \$56 = \$168 \text{ selling price}$$

8.2 Finding the markup on selling price

	%	C	$	
	%	M	$?	**part**
	100%	S	$	base

Solve for part.

	%	C	$	
rate	25%	M	$?	**part**
	100%	S	$6.00	base

$$P = B \times R$$
$$P = \$6.00 \times .25$$
$$P = \$1.50$$

CONCEPTS	EXAMPLES

8.2 Finding the cost

	%	C	$?	part
	%	M	$	
	100%	S	$	base

	%	C	$?	part
rate	35%	M	$87.50	
	100%	S	$	base

$$B = \frac{P}{R} = \frac{87.5}{.35} = \$250 \text{ selling price}$$

$$\$250 - \$87.50 = \$162.50 \text{ cost}$$

8.2 Calculating the selling price and the markup

	%	C	$	
	%	M	$?	
	100%	S	$?	base

	%	C	$150	
rate	25%	M	$?	
	100%	S	$?	base

$$100\% - 25\% = 75\% \text{ cost}$$

$$B = \frac{P}{R} = \frac{150}{.75} = \$200 \text{ selling price}$$

$$\$200 - \$150 = \$50 \text{ markup}$$

8.2 Converting markup on cost to markup on selling price

Use the formula

$$\% \text{ markup on selling price} = \frac{\% \text{ markup on cost}}{100\% + \% \text{ markup on cost}}$$

Convert 25% markup on cost to markup on selling price.

$$\% \text{ markup on selling price} = \frac{25\%}{100\% + 25\%}$$

$$= \frac{.25}{1.25} = .2 = 20\%$$

8.2 Converting markup on selling price to markup on cost

Use the formula

$$\% \text{ markup on cost} = \frac{\% \text{ markup on selling price}}{100\% - \% \text{ markup on selling price}}$$

Convert 20% markup on selling price to markup on cost.

$$\% \text{ markup on cost} = \frac{20\%}{100\% - 20\%}$$

$$= \frac{.2}{.8} = .25 = 25\%$$

8.2 Finding the selling price for perishables

1. Find total cost and selling price.
2. Subtract the quantity not sold to find the number that are sold.
3. Divide the total sales by the number of sellable units to get selling price per unit.

60 doughnuts cost 25¢ each; 10 are not sold; 50% markup on selling price; find selling price per doughnut.

$$\text{Cost} = 60 \times \$.25 = \$15$$

	%	C	$15	part
rate	50%	M	$	
	100%	S	$?	base

$$B = \frac{P}{R} = \frac{15}{.5} = \$30$$

$$60 - 10 = 50 \text{ doughnuts sold}$$

$$\$30 \div 50 = \$.60 \text{ per doughnut}$$

8.3 Finding the percent of markdown

Markdown is always a percent of the original price.
Use the formula

$$R = \frac{P}{B}$$

$$\text{Markdown percent} = \frac{\text{Markdown amount}}{\text{Original price}}$$

Original price, $76; markdown, $19; find the percent of markdown.

$$R = \frac{P}{B} = \frac{19}{76} = .25$$

$$R = 25\% \text{ markdown}$$

8.3 Calculating the break-even point

The cost plus operating expenses equals the break-even point.

Cost, $54; operating expenses, $16; find the break-even point.

$$\$54 \text{ cost} + \$16 \text{ operating expenses} = \$70 \text{ break-even point}$$

CONCEPTS	EXAMPLES

8.3 Finding operating loss

The difference between the break-even point and the reduced price (when below the break-even point) is the operating loss.

Break-even point, $70; reduced price, $58; find the operating loss.

$$\begin{array}{rl} \$70 & \text{break-even point} \\ -\$58 & \textbf{reduced price} \\ \hline \$12 & \text{operating loss} \end{array}$$

8.3 Finding absolute loss (gross loss)

When the reduced price is below cost, the difference between the cost and reduced price is the absolute loss.

Cost, $54; reduced price, $48; find the absolute loss.

$54 \text{ cost} - \textbf{\$48 reduced price} = \$6 \text{ absolute loss}$

8.4 Determining average inventory

Inventory is taken two or more times. Totals are added together, then divided by the number of inventories taken to get the average.

Inventories, $22,635, $24,692, and $18,796; find the average inventory.

$$\frac{\$22,635 + \$24,692 + \$18,796}{3}$$

$$= \frac{\$66,123}{3} = \$22,041 \text{ average inventory}$$

8.4 Finding turnover at retail

Use the formula

$$\text{Turnover} = \frac{\text{Retail sales}}{\text{Average inventory at retail}}$$

Quarterly retail sales, $893,724; average inventory at retail, $87,620; find turnover at retail.

$$\frac{\$893,724}{\mathbf{\$87,620}} = 10.2 \text{ at retail}$$

8.4 Finding turnover at cost

Use the formula

$$\text{Turnover} = \frac{\text{Cost of goods sold}}{\text{Average inventory at cost}}$$

Quarterly cost of goods sold, $257,747; average inventory at cost, $32,960; find turnover at cost.

$$\frac{\$257,747}{\mathbf{\$\,32,960}} = 7.82 \text{ at cost} \quad \text{(rounded)}$$

8.4 Using specific identification to value inventory

Each item is cost coded, and the cost of each of the items is added to find total inventory.

Individual cost of each item in inventory is: item 1, $593; item 2, $614; item 3, $498; find total value of inventory.

$\mathbf{\$593 + \$614 + \$498} = \$1705 \text{ total value of inventory}$

8.4 Using weighted-average (average cost) method of inventory valuation

This method values items in an inventory at the average cost of buying them.

Beginning inventory of 20 at $75; purchases of 15 at $80; 25 at $65; 18 at $70; 22 remain in inventory. Find the inventory value.

$$\begin{array}{rl} \mathbf{20} \times \mathbf{\$75} = & \$1500 \\ \mathbf{15} \times \mathbf{\$80} = & \$1200 \\ \mathbf{25} \times \mathbf{\$65} = & \$1625 \\ \underline{\mathbf{18} \times \mathbf{\$70}} = & \underline{\$1260} \\ \text{Total } \mathbf{78} & \$5585 \end{array}$$

$$\frac{5585}{78} = \$71.60 \text{ average cost} \quad \text{(rounded)}$$

$\$71.60 \times 22 = \$1575.20 \text{ weighted-average method inventory value}$

8.4 Using first-in, first-out (FIFO) method of inventory valuation

The first items in are the first sold. Inventory is based on cost of last items purchased.

Beginning inventory of 25 items at $40; purchased on August 7, 30 items at $35; 35 remain in inventory. Find the inventory.

$$\begin{array}{rll} \mathbf{30} \times \mathbf{\$35} = & \$1050 & \text{value of last 30} \\ \underline{\mathbf{5} \times \mathbf{\$40}} = & \underline{\$\,\,200} & \text{value of previous 5} \\ \mathbf{35} & \$1250 & \text{value of inventory using FIFO} \end{array}$$

CONCEPTS	EXAMPLES

8.4 Using last-in, first-out (LIFO) method of inventory valuation

The items remaining in inventory are those items that were first purchased.

Beginning inventory of 48 items at $20 each; purchase on May 9, 40 items at $25 each; 55 remain in inventory. Find the inventory value.

$$48 \times \$20 = \$\ 960 \quad \text{value of first 48}$$
$$\underline{7 \times \$25 = \$\ 175} \quad \text{value of last 7}$$
$$\underline{55} \qquad\quad \$1135 \quad \text{value of inventory using LIFO}$$

8.4 Estimating inventory value using the retail method

$$\frac{\text{Goods available for sale at cost}}{\text{Goods available for sale at retail}} = \% \ (\text{cost ratio})$$

$$\begin{array}{c}\text{Ending inventory}\\ \text{at retail}\end{array} \times \% \ (\text{cost ratio}) = \begin{array}{c}\text{Inventory}\\ \text{at cost}\end{array}$$

Use the retail method to estimate the inventory value at cost.

	Cost	Retail
beginning inventory		
purchases	$9,000	$15,000
goods available for sale	+ 36,000	+ 60,000
	$45,000	$75,000
net sales		− 54,000
ending inventory		$21,000

$$\text{goods available for sale at cost} \quad \frac{\$45,000}{\$75,000} = .6 = 60\%$$
goods available for sale at retail

$$\$21,000 \times .6 = \$12,600 \text{ inventory value at cost}$$

▼ Case Study

MARKDOWN: REDUCING PRICES TO MOVE MERCHANDISE

Olympic Sports purchased two dozen pairs of 5th Element Adult Aggresive in-line skates at a cost of $1950. Operating expenses for the store are 25% of cost, while total markup on this type of product is 35% of selling price. Only 6 pairs of the skates sell at the original price, and the manager decides to mark down the remaining skates. The price is reduced 25% and 6 more pairs sell. The remaining 12 pairs of skates are marked down to 50% of the original selling price and are finally sold.

1. Find the original selling price of each pair of skates.

   1. _____

2. Find the total of the selling prices of all the skates.

   2. _____

3. Find the operating loss.

   3. _____

4. Find the absolute loss.

   4. _____

INVESTIGATE

Talk with the manager of a retail store. Does the store calculate markup based on cost or retail? Does the store use markdowns to promote the sale or liquidation of merchandise? How does the management decide how much to mark down merchandise? Ask the manager for an example of a product that had to be marked down so much that a gross loss resulted.

▼ Case in Point Summary Exercise

RECREATIONAL EQUIPMENT INC. (REI)

www.REI.com

Facts:

- 1938: Established by 23 mountaineers
- 2001: Exceeded 2 million members
- 2005: Annual sales passed $1 billion
- 2011: Nearly $100 million sent to members

REI is a cooperative that focuses on the great out-of-doors. Although anyone can shop at REI, the firm is owned by the members who pay a one-time fee of $20 and receive annual dividends based on company profit and the amount of each member's annual purchases.

A marketing manager was interested in a new line of off-piste skis for skiing over rugged terrain and jumping off cliffs. The manager works with James Smelter in inventory to place the following orders for two different skis.

	Model Name	Number	Total Cost
1st order	Steep Alpine	15 pairs	$4395
2nd order	Cliff Hoppers	22 pairs	$7194

1. Find the cost per pair of skis for both models.

   1. _____

2. If the markup on cost for each pair of skis is 38%, find the list price for each.

   2. _____

3. The skis were received on January 1 and a physical inventory at the end of January showed that 7 pairs of Steep Alpine and 14 pairs of Cliff Hoppers remained. Find the average inventory at cost.

   3. _____

4. Use the data for these skis to find the turnover at cost for the month of January.

   4. _____

5. The two managers are not happy with the quality of the skis and sell the remaining skis at a markdown of 40%. Find the price per pair of skis after being marked down.

   5. _____

6. Assume that operating expenses at REI are 22% of cost and determine the amount of any profit on these skis. If there was no profit, find the amount of the operating loss and/or the absolute loss.

   6. _____

Discussion Question: *Do you think firms often lose money on new products? What do you think would happen to a company that often loses money on new products? Explain.*

Source: RECREATIONAL EQUIPMENT INC. (REI), www.REI.com.

▼ Chapter 8 Test

To help you review, the numbers in brackets show the section in which the topic was discussed.

Solve for (a), (b), and (c). **[8.1 and 8.2]**

1.
100%	C	$64.00
(a)%	M	$12.80
(b)%	S	$(c)

2.
100%	C	$(b)
38%	M	$(c)
(a)%	S	$504.39

3.
(a)%	C	$134.40
(b)%	M	$(c)
100%	S	$168.00

4.
(a)%	C	$(c)
(b)%	M	$ 6.15
100%	S	$24.60

Find the equivalent markup on either cost or selling price, using the appropriate formula. Round to the nearest tenth of a percent. **[8.2]**

	Markup on Cost	Markup on Selling Price		Markup on Cost	Markup on Selling Price
5.	25%	_____	6.	100%	_____

Complete the following. If there is no operating loss or absolute loss, write "none." **[8.3]**

	Cost	Operating Expense	Break-even Point	Reduced Price	Operating Loss	Absolute Loss
7.	$160	$40	_____	$186	_____	_____
8.	$225	_____	$297	$198	_____	_____

Find the stock turnover at retail and at cost for the following. Round to the nearest hundredth. **[8.4]**

	Average Inventory at Cost	Average Inventory at Retail	Cost of Goods Sold	Retail Sales	Turnover at Cost	Turnover at Retail
9.	$14,120	$25,572	$81,312	$146,528	_____	_____

Solve the following application problems.

10. Smart Phones, Inc. buys one model of smartphone, paying $2370 per case of 20 phones. Find the asking price for each assuming a 40% markup on cost.

10. _____

11. It cost a singer-songwriter $67,300 for all of the expenses to engineer, record, mix, and promote a new music disc. The cost also included the manufacturing of 5000 discs. Assume each disc sells for $20. Find **(a)** the markup in dollars, **(b)** the markup as a percent of cost to the nearest tenth of a percent, and **(c)** the markup as a percent of selling price to the nearest tenth of a percent.

(a) _____
(b) _____
(c) _____

12. _____

☉ 12. REI buys high-tech jogging shorts manufactured in Indonesia for $195.00 per dozen pair. Find the selling price per pair if the retailer maintains a markup of 35% on selling price. **[8.2]**

13. _____

13. Restaurant Supply sells a walk-in refrigerator for $5250 while using a markup of 25% on cost. Find the cost. **[8.1]**

☉ indicates an exercise that is related to the Case in Point feature.

14. The Computer Service Center sells a DeskJet print cartridge for $37.50. If the print cartridge costs the store $22.50, find the markup as a percent of selling price. **[8.2]**

14. _____

15. REI offers a men's soft-shell waterproof jacket for $199.95. If the jackets cost $1943.52 per dozen, find **(a)** the markup, **(b)** the percent of markup on selling price, and **(c)** the percent of markup on cost. Round to the nearest tenth of a percent. **[8.1 and 8.2]**

(a) _____

(b) _____

(c) _____

16. A motorcycle originally priced at $13,875 is marked down to $9990. Find the percent of markdown on the original price. **[8.3]**

16. _____

17. Leslie's Pool Supply, a retailer, pays $285 for a diving board. The original selling price was $399, but it was marked down 40%. If operating expenses are 30% of cost, find **(a)** the operating loss and **(b)** the absolute loss. **[8.3]**

(a) _____

(b) _____

18. Carpets Plus had an inventory of $117,328 on January 1, $147,630 on July 1, and $125,876 on December 31. Find the average inventory. **[8.4]**

18. _____

Round to the nearest dollar amount.

19. Craighead Products made the following purchases of fuel tanks during the year: 25 at $270 each, 40 at $330 each, 15 at $217 each, and 30 at $284 each. An inventory shows that 45 fuel tanks remain. Find the inventory value using the weighted-average method. **[8.4]**

19. _____

20. Find the value of the inventory listed in Exercise 19 using **(a)** the FIFO method and **(b)** the LIFO method. **[8.4]**

(a) _____

(b) _____

▼ ## Chapters 5–8 Cumulative Review

CHAPTERS 5–8

The following credit-card transactions were made at the Patio Store. Answer Exercises 1–5 using this information. Round to the nearest cent. **[5.2]**

Sales			Credits
$428.80	$733.18	$22.51	$76.15
$316.25	$38.00	$162.15	$118.44
$68.95	$188.36		$13.86

1. Find the total amount of the sales slips.

1. _____

2. What is the total amount of the credit slips?

2. _____

3. Find the total amount of the deposit.

3. _____

4. Assuming that the bank charges the retailer a $1\frac{1}{4}\%$ discount charge, find the amount of the discount charge at the statement date.

4. _____

5. Find the amount of the credit given to the retailer after the fee is subtracted.

5. _____

Solve the following application problems.

6. Shaundra Brown worked 7 hours on Monday, 10 hours on Tuesday, 8 hours on Wednesday, 9 hours on Thursday, and 10 hours on Friday. Her regular hourly pay is $12.80. Find her gross earnings for the week if Brown is paid time and a half for all hours over 8 worked in a day. **[6.1]**

6. _____

7. The employees of Jena's Bakery paid a total of $968.50 in Social Security tax last month, $223.50 in Medicare tax, and $1975.38 in federal withholding tax. Find the total amount the employer must send to the Internal Revenue Service. **[6.4]**

7. _____

Find the net cost (invoice amount) for each of the following. Round to the nearest cent. **[7.1]**

8. List price $475.50, less 20/20 _____

9. List price $375, less 25/10/5 _____

Find the single discount equivalent for each of the following series discounts. **[7.2]**

10. 10/20 _____

11. 30/40/10 _____

Find the discount date and the net payment date for each of the following. The net payment date is 20 days after the final discount date. **[7.4]**

	Invoice Date	Terms	Date Goods Received	Final Discount Date	Net Payment Date
12.	May 27	2/10 ROG	June 5	_____	_____
13.	Oct. 9	3/15 EOM		_____	_____
14.	June 24	4/10–30 ex.		_____	_____

Complete the following. If there is no operating loss or absolute loss, write "none." **[8.3]**

	Cost	Operating Expense	Break-even Point	Reduced Price	Operating Loss	Absolute Loss
15.	$312	$88	_____	_____	$120	_____
16.	_____	_____	_____	$220	$112	$32

Solve the following application problems.

17. The list price of an Iron Horse BMX bike at Olympic Sports is $149.99. Find the dealer's cost if given a 20/20 trade discount and a 3/20, n/30 cash discount. Assume that the dealer earns the maximum cash discount. **[7.1 and 7.3]**

17. _____

18. Target purchases a top-selling video game for Xbox 360 paying $245 for 10 copies of the game. If the store wants a markup of 63.2% on the selling price, find the selling price per copy. **[8.2]**

18. _____

19. The Retro-Fit Window Company has an average inventory of $37,568 at cost. If the cost of goods sold for the year was $483,876, find the stock turnover at cost. Round to the nearest hundredth. **[8.4]**

19. _____

20. Inventory at a local store was taken at retail value four times and was found to be $53,820; $49,510; $60,820; and $56,380. Sales during the same period were $252,077. Find the stock turnover at retail. Round to hundredths. **[8.4]**

20. _____

21. Thunder Manufacturing made the following purchases of rivet drums during the year: 25 at $135 each, 40 at $165 each, 15 at $108.50 each, and 30 at $142 each. An inventory shows that 45 rivet drums remain. Find the inventory value, using the weighted-average method. **[8.4]**

21. _____

22. Refer to Exercise 21. Find the inventory value using **(a)** the FIFO method and **(b)** the LIFO method. **[8.4]**

(a) _____

(b) _____

9 Simple Interest

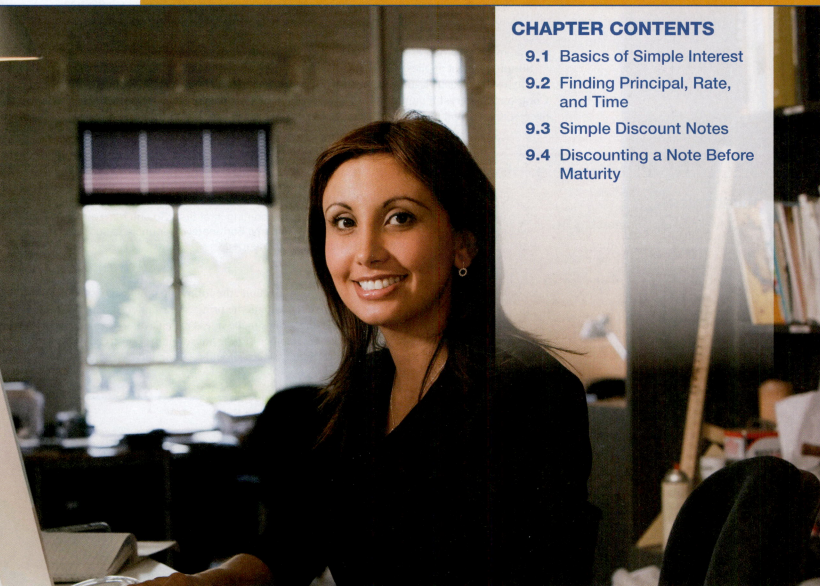

CHAPTER CONTENTS

9.1 Basics of Simple Interest

9.2 Finding Principal, Rate, and Time

9.3 Simple Discount Notes

9.4 Discounting a Note Before Maturity

▼ CASE IN POINT

APPLE INC. was founded by Steven Wozniak and Steven Jobs in 1976. Its early success was based on the Apple II and Macintosh computers. However, it revolutionized the music, phone, and book worlds with the introduction of the iPod, iPhone, and finally the iPad in 2010. In a recent quarter, Apple sold more than 20 million of these devices.

While completing her degree in Computer Information Systems at a local community college, Jessica Hernandez worked part time in one of Apple's retail stores. She continued to work at the store after graduating and receiving a promotion to assistant manager. However, she had always wanted to own her own business and finally started a business to develop web pages for businesses.

Lending occurs everywhere. Individuals borrow to buy a car, pay for college, or buy a house. Businesses borrow to make payroll, expand, build a new building, develop a new product, or pay taxes. The interest on loans can be expensive. In fact, a common cause of **bankruptcy** is too much debt and interest payments that are too high. The interest rate at which the financially strongest firms borrow is called the **prime rate**. Most other firms pay a higher interest rate. Interestingly, the Koran forbids Muslims from charging interest. Instead, Islamic banks take an ownership interest in cars, houses, or firms until they are repaid.

Simple interest applies only to the **principal**, or the original amount borrowed, and it is usually used for loans lasting less than 1 year. Simple interest is discussed in this chapter. **Compound interest** requires interest to be paid on the principal and *also* on previously earned interest. Compound interest is covered in Chapter 10.

▼ 9.1 Basics of Simple Interest

OBJECTIVES

1 Solve for simple interest.

2 Calculate maturity value.

3 Use a table to find the number of days from one date to another.

4 Use the actual number of days in a month to find the number of days from one date to another.

5 Find exact and ordinary interest.

6 Define the basic terms used with notes.

7 Find the due date of a note.

▼ CASE IN POINT   Jessica Hernandez knew that expenses on a new business would begin immediately, yet revenues would be slow coming in at first. So she realized that she would need to borrow money to start her company. Fortunately, her uncle, a successful businessperson, helped her obtain the loan she needed.

Interest rates affect the costs of many things. For example, the following graph shows the number of new houses on which construction has started and the prime rate of interest. High interest costs make it more expensive, and lower interest rates make it less expensive, to own a home. As a result, high interest rates should slow the number of new houses under construction, as happened during 1980–82. Similarly, lower interest rates should result in increased housing starts as happened in 1983 and 2002–05.

Contrary to what one would expect, new house starts fell to a historic low in 2009 even as interest rates were at historic lows. Why? The cause was the serious recession that began in 2008. The government was trying to increase demand for housing by driving interest rates to record lows. However, the high rate of unemployment and falling house prices resulted in low demand for housing. When demand is low, home builders do not start construction on many houses.

OBJECTIVE 1 Solve for simple interest. Simple interest is interest charged on the entire principal for the entire length of the loan. It is found using the formula shown in the following box. **Principal** is the loan amount, **rate** is the interest rate, and **time** is the length of the loan *in years*.

Finding Simple Interest

$$\text{Simple interest} = \text{Principal} \times \text{Rate} \times \text{Time}$$
$$I \qquad = \qquad P \quad \times \quad R \quad \times \quad T$$

When using the formula $I = PRT$:

1. Rate (R) must first be changed to a decimal or fraction.
2. Time (T) must first be converted to years.

So, for example, a rate of 7.5% should be changed to .075 and a time of 6 months should be changed to $\frac{6}{12} = .5$ year before using $I = PRT$.

Finding Simple Interest To start her business, Jessica Hernandez needs to borrow $85,000 for 9 months. Her bank would not lend her the money since she has no experience or assets. She found an individual who would lend her the money at 18.5%. However, her uncle agreed to **cosign** on a loan for her, meaning that he would have to pay the loan if Jessica failed to do so. On this basis, the bank would lend the money at 10% simple interest. Find the interest at (**a**) 18.5% and (**b**) 10%. (**c**) Then find the amount saved using the lower interest rate.

▼ CASE IN POINT

SOLUTION

(**a**) First, convert 18.5% to .185 and 9 months to $\frac{9}{12}$ year. Then substitute values into $I = PRT$ to find the interest. The principal (P) is the amount of the loan.

$$I = PRT$$
$$I = \$85,000 \times .185 \times \tfrac{9}{12} \qquad \text{Convert 18.5\% to .185}$$
$$I = \$11,793.75 \qquad \text{simple interest}$$

(**b**)
$$I = PRT$$
$$I = \$85,000 \times .10 \times \tfrac{9}{12} \qquad \text{Convert 10\% to .10 (or .1).}$$
$$I = \$6375 \qquad \text{simple interest}$$

(**c**) Difference = $11,793.75 − $6375 = $5418.75

Hernandez quickly learned an important lesson: Interest costs can be very high. She was delighted that her uncle had agreed to cosign for her. It saved her nearly $5500 in interest charges in only 9 months. Now she had to figure out how to make her business profitable!

▦ The calculator solution for part (**a**) follows:

$$85000 \;\boxed{\times}\; 18.5 \;\boxed{\%}\; \boxed{\times}\; 9 \;\boxed{\div}\; 12 \;\boxed{=}\; 11793.75$$

Note: Refer to Appendix B for calculator basics.

QUICK CHECK 1

Find the interest on a loan of $14,680 for 6 months at 9%.

OBJECTIVE 2 Calculate maturity value. The amount that must be repaid when the loan is due is the **maturity value** of the loan. Find this value by adding principal and interest.

Finding Maturity Value

$$\text{Maturity value} = \text{Principal} + \text{Interest}$$
$$M \quad\;\; = \quad P \quad + \quad I$$

Finding Maturity Value

EXAMPLE 2

Tom Swift needs to borrow $28,300 to remodel his bookstore so that he can serve coffee to customers as they browse or sit and read. He borrows the funds for 10 months at an interest rate of 9.25%. Find the interest due on the loan and the maturity value at the end of 10 months.

SOLUTION

Interest due is found using $I = PRT$, where T must be in years (10 months $= \frac{10}{12}$ year).

$$Interest = PRT$$

$$I = \$28{,}300 \times .0925 \times \frac{10}{12} = \mathbf{\$2181.46} \quad \text{(rounded)}$$

$$Maturity\ value = P + I$$

$$M = \$28{,}300 + \mathbf{\$2181.46} = \$30{,}481.46$$

QUICK CHECK 2

Find the maturity value of a loan of $48,600 at 9% for 8 months.

OBJECTIVE 3 Use a table to find the number of days from one date to another. Up to this point, the period of the loan was given in months, but it can also be given in days. Or a loan may be due at a fixed date, such as April 17, and we may have to figure out the number of days until the loan must be paid off. One way to do this is to number the days of the year as in the table on the next page.

For example, suppose it is June 11 and you want to know how many days until Christmas (December 25). In the table, June 11 is day 162 of the year and December 25 is day 359 of the year. Subtract to find the number of days until Christmas.

December 25 is day   359
June 11 is day   −162
                              197 days from June 11 to December 25

There are 197 days from June 11 to December 25.

Leap years are years with one additional day in February. If it is a leap year, June 11 is day 163 and December 25 is day 360. There are still 197 days from June 11 to December 25.

Finding the Number of Days from One Date to Another, Using a Table

EXAMPLE 3

Use the table to find the number of days from **(a)** March 24 to July 22, **(b)** April 4 to October 10, **(c)** November 8 to February 17 of the following year, and **(d)** December 2 to January 17 of the following year. Assume that it is not a leap year.

SOLUTION

(a) July 22 is day   203
March 24 is day   − 83
                              120 days from March 24 to July 22

(b) October 10 is day   283
April 4 is day   − 94
                              189 days from April 4 to October 10

(c) November 8 is day 312, so there are $365 - 312 = 53$ days from November 8 to the end of the year. Add days until the end of the year plus days into the next year to find the total.

November 8 to end of year   53
February 17 is day   + 48
                              101 days from November 8 to February 17 of next year

(d) December 2 is day 336, so there are $365 - 336 = 29$ days to the end of the year. Add days until the end of the year plus days into the next year to find the total.

December 2 to end of year   29
January 17 is day   + 17
                              46 days from December 2 to January 17 of the next year

---

QUICK CHECK 3

Find the number of days from **(a)** July 7 to November 7 and **(b)** August 25 to January 20 of the following year.

The Number of Each of the Days of the Year*

Day of Month	Jan.	Feb.	Mar.	Apr.	May	June	July	Aug.	Sept.	Oct.	Nov.	Dec.	Day of Month
1	1	32	60	91	121	152	182	213	244	274	305	335	1
2	2	33	61	92	122	153	183	214	245	275	306	336	2
3	3	34	62	93	123	154	184	215	246	276	307	337	3
4	4	35	63	94	124	155	185	216	247	277	308	338	4
5	5	36	64	95	125	156	186	217	248	278	309	339	5
6	6	37	65	96	126	157	187	218	249	279	310	340	6
7	7	38	66	97	127	158	188	219	250	280	311	341	7
8	8	39	67	98	128	159	189	220	251	281	312	342	8
9	9	40	68	99	129	160	190	221	252	282	313	343	9
10	10	41	69	100	130	161	191	222	253	283	314	344	10
11	11	42	70	101	131	162	192	223	254	284	315	345	11
12	12	43	71	102	132	163	193	224	255	285	316	346	12
13	13	44	72	103	133	164	194	225	256	286	317	347	13
14	14	45	73	104	134	165	195	226	257	287	318	348	14
15	15	46	74	105	135	166	196	227	258	288	319	349	15
16	16	47	75	106	136	167	197	228	259	289	320	350	16
17	17	48	76	107	137	168	198	229	260	290	321	351	17
18	18	49	77	108	138	169	199	230	261	291	322	352	18
19	19	50	78	109	139	170	200	231	262	292	323	353	19
20	20	51	79	110	140	171	201	232	263	293	324	354	20
21	21	52	80	111	141	172	202	233	264	294	325	355	21
22	22	53	81	112	142	173	203	234	265	295	326	356	22
23	23	54	82	113	143	174	204	235	266	296	327	357	23
24	24	55	83	114	144	175	205	236	267	297	328	358	24
25	25	56	84	115	145	176	206	237	268	298	329	359	25
26	26	57	85	116	146	177	207	238	269	299	330	360	26
27	27	58	86	117	147	178	208	239	270	300	331	361	27
28	28	59	87	118	148	179	209	240	271	301	332	362	28
29	29		88	119	149	180	210	241	272	302	333	363	29
30	30		89	120	150	181	211	242	273	303	334	364	30
31	31		90		151		212	243		304		365	31

Add 1 to each date after February 29 for a leap year.

OBJECTIVE 4 Use the actual number of days in a month to find the number of days from one date to another. The number of days between specific dates can be found using the number of days in each month of the year as shown in the table.

Number of Days in Each Month

	31 Days	30 Days	28 Days
January	August	April	February
March	October	June	(29 days in leap year)
May	December	September	
July		November	

Two other ways of remembering the number of days in each month are the rhyme method and the knuckle method, as seen below.

Rhyme Method:

30 days hath September
April, June, and November.
All the rest have 31, except
February, which has 28 and
in a leap year 29.

Knuckle Method:

Jan.　Mar.　May　July　31 days　Aug.　Oct.　Dec.

Feb.　Apr.　June　　　　　　　　　　Sept.　Nov.

30 days
(28 in Feb.)

Finding the Number of Days from One Date to Another, Using Actual Days

EXAMPLE 4

Find the number of days from **(a)** June 3 to August 14 and **(b)** November 4 to February 21.

SOLUTION

(a) June has 30 days, so there are $30 - 3 = 27$ days from June 3 to the end of June.

June 3 to the end of June	27
31 days in July	31
14 days in August	$+\ 14$
	72 days from June 3 to August 14

(b) November has 30 days, so there are $30 - 4 = 26$ days from November 4 to the end of November.

November 4 to end of November	26
31 days in December	31
31 days in January	31
21 days in February	$+\ \ 21$
	109 days from November 4 to February 21

QUICK CHECK 4

Find the number of days from March 14 to September 9.

OBJECTIVE 5　Find exact and ordinary interest. A simple interest rate is given as an annual rate, such as 7% per year. Since the rate is per year, time must also be given in years or fraction of a year when using $I = PRT$. If time is given in number of days, first change it to a fraction of a year.

Finding Time in Fraction of a Year

$$T = \frac{\text{Number of days in the loan period}}{\text{Number of days in a year}}$$

Exact interest calculations require the use of the exact number of days in the year, 365 or 366 if a leap year. **Ordinary interest**, or **banker's interest**, calculations require the use of 360 days. Banks commonly used 360 days in a year for interest calculations before calculators and computers became widely available. Today, many institutions, the government, and the Federal Reserve Bank use the exact number of days in a year in interest calculations. However, some banks and financial institutions still use 360 days. You need to be able to use both.

Finding Exact and Ordinary Interest

For exact interest: Use 365 days (or 366 days if a leap year).

$$T = \frac{\text{Number of days in a loan period}}{365}$$

For ordinary, or banker's, interest: Use 360 days for the number of days.

$$T = \frac{\text{Number of days in a loan period}}{360}$$

Example 5 shows that **ordinary interest produces more interest** for the lending institution than does exact interest.

Finding Exact and Ordinary Interest

EXAMPLE 5

Radio station KOMA borrowed $148,500 on May 12 with interest due on August 27. If the interest rate is 10%, find the interest on the loan using **(a)** exact interest and **(b)** ordinary interest.

SOLUTION

Either the table method or the method of the number of days in a month can be used to find that there are 107 days from May 12 to August 27.

(a) The exact interest is found from $I = PRT$ with $P = \$148,500$, $R = .10$, and $T = \frac{107}{365}$.

$$I = PRT$$

$$I = \$148,500 \times .1 \times \frac{107}{365} \quad \nearrow \text{Use 365 days.}$$

$$I = \$4353.29 \quad \text{(rounded)}$$

(b) Find ordinary interest with the same formula and values, except $T = \frac{107}{360}$.

$$I = PRT$$

$$I = \$148,500 \times .1 \times \frac{107}{360} \quad \nearrow \text{Use 360 days.}$$

$$I = \$4413.75 \quad \text{(rounded)}$$

In this example, the ordinary interest is $\$4413.75 - \$4353.29 = \$60.46$ more than the exact interest.

Quick TIP

Ordinary interest results in slightly more interest than exact interest. Thus ordinary interest favors those banks that use it when calculating loans.

QUICK CHECK 5

Find the exact and ordinary interest for a 200-day loan of $19,500 at 9% to the nearest cent. Then find the difference between the two interest amounts.

Use ordinary or banker's interest throughout the remainder of the book unless stated otherwise.

OBJECTIVE 6 Define the basic terms used with notes. A **promissory note** is a *legal document* in which one person or firm agrees to pay a certain amount of money, on a specific day in the future, to another person or firm. An example of a promissory note follows.

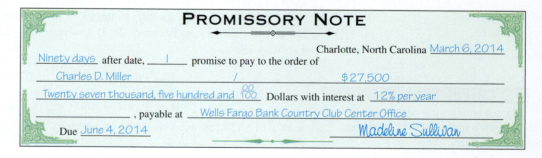

PROMISSORY NOTE

Charlotte, North Carolina March 6, 2014

Ninety days after date, I promise to pay to the order of

Charles D. Miller / $27,500

Twenty seven thousand, five hundred and 00/100 Dollars with interest at 12% per year

_____, payable at Wells Fargo Bank Country Club Center Office

Due June 4, 2014 Madeline Sullivan

This type of promissory note is called a **simple interest note**, since simple interest calculations involving $I = PRT$ are used. Here is the language of a simple interest promissory note.

Maker or **payer:** The person borrowing the money. (Madeline Sullivan in the sample note)

Payee: The person who loaned the money and who will receive the payment (Charles D. Miller in the sample note)

Term: The length of time until the note is due (90 days in the sample note)

Face value or **principal:** The amount being borrowed ($27,500 in the sample note)

Maturity value: The face value plus interest, also the amount due at maturity

Maturity date or **due date:** The date the loan must be paid off with interest (June 4 in the sample note)

Find the interest and the maturity value on the loan in the sample note above.

$$\text{Interest} = \textbf{Face value} \times \textbf{Rate} \times \textbf{Time}$$

$$\text{Interest} = \$27{,}500 \times .12 \times \frac{90}{360} = \textbf{\$825}$$

$$\textbf{Maturity value} = \textbf{Face value} + \textbf{Interest}$$

$$\text{Maturity value} = \$27{,}500 + \textbf{\$825} = \$28{,}325$$

Madeline Sullivan must pay $28,325 to Charles D. Miller on June 4, the maturity date of the note.

Banks and financial institutions lend money only to individuals and firms they believe will repay the loan with interest. Even then, banks often require **collateral** or assets such as an automobile or stock in order to make a loan. If the loan is not repaid, the bank **forecloses** on the collateral, takes ownership, and sells or liquidates it. Funds from the sale of the collateral are first used to pay off the note and the expenses of the foreclosure. Any excess is returned to the maker of the note (person who borrowed the money).

OBJECTIVE 7 Find the due date of a note. Time is in months in some promissory notes. When this occurs, the loan is due after the given number of months has passed but on the same day of the month as the original loan was made. For example, a 4-month note made on May 25 is due 4 months later on September 25. Other examples follow.

Date Made	Length of Loan	Date Due
March 12	5 months	August 12
April 24	7 months	November 24
October 7	9 months	July 7
January 31	3 months	April 30

A loan made on January 31 for 3 months would normally be due on April 31. However, there are only 30 days in April, so the loan is due on April 30. Whenever a due date does not exist, such as February 30 or November 31, use the last day of the month (February 28 or November 30 in these examples).

Finding Due Date, Interest, and Maturity Value

EXAMPLE 6

Find the due date, interest, and maturity value for a $600,000 loan made to Benson Automotive on July 31 for 7 months at 7.5% interest.

SOLUTION

Interest and principal are due 7 months from July 31 or February 31, which *does not* exist. Since February has only 28 days (unless it is a leap year), interest and principal are due on the last day of February, or February 28. If it were a leap year, the maturity value would be due on February 29.

$$I = PRT = \$600{,}000 \times .075 \times \frac{7}{12} = \textbf{\$26{,}250}$$

$$M = P + I = \$600{,}000 + \textbf{\$26{,}250} = \$626{,}250$$

A total of $626,250 must be repaid on February 28.

Quick TIP

Do not convert the period of a loan from months to days to find the due date.

QUICK CHECK 6

Find the due date for a 6-month loan made on March 31.

9.1 Exercises

MyMathLab®

*The shaded sections below contain solutions to help you get a **QUICK START** on the various types of exercises.*

Find simple interest and maturity value to the nearest cent. (See Examples 1 and 2.)

	Interest	Maturity Value
1. $3800 at 11% for 6 months	$209	$4009
$I = \$3800 \times .11 \times \frac{6}{12} = \$209$		
$M = \$3800 + \$209 = \$4009$		
2. $10,200 at 9.5% for 10 months		
3. $5500 at 8% for 1 year		
4. $18,500 at 7.5% for $1\frac{1}{4}$ years		

Find the exact number of days from the first date to the second. (See Examples 3 and 4.)

5. February 15 to April 24

From the table, February 15 is day 46; April 24 is day 114
Number of days = 114 − 46 = 68 days

5. 68

6. May 22 to August 30

6. _____

7. December 1 to March 10 of the following year

7. _____

8. October 12 to February 22 of the following year

8. _____

Find (a) the exact interest and (b) the ordinary interest for each of the following to the nearest cent. Then find (c) the amount by which the ordinary interest is larger. (See Example 5.)

9. $52,000 at $8\frac{3}{4}$% for 200 days
(a) Exact interest = $\$52,000 \times .0875 \times \frac{200}{365} = \$2493.15$
(b) Ordinary interest = $\$52,000 \times .0875 \times \frac{200}{360} = \$2527.78$
(c) Ordinary is larger by $2527.78 − $2493.15 = $34.63

(a) $2493.15
(b) $2527.78
(c) $34.63

 indicates an exercise that is related to the Case in Point feature.

10. $185,000 at 7.5% for 180 days

(a) _____

(b) _____

(c) _____

11. $29,500 at $11\frac{1}{4}$% for 120 days

(a) _____

(b) _____

(c) _____

12. $52,610 at $8\frac{1}{2}$% for 82 days

(a) _____

(b) _____

(c) _____

Identify each of the following from the promissory note shown. (See Objective 6.)

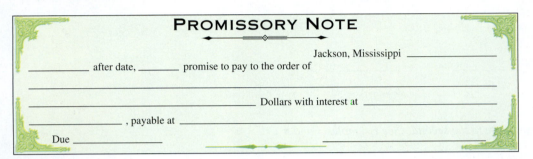

PROMISSORY NOTE

Jackson, Mississippi _____

_____ after date, _____ promise to pay to the order of

_____

_____ Dollars with interest at _____

_____ , payable at _____

Due _____

13. Maker _____   **14.** Payer _____

15. Payee _____   **16.** Face value _____

17. Term of loan _____   **18.** Date loan was made _____

19. Date loan is due _____   **20.** Maturity value _____

Find the date due, the amount of interest (rounded to the nearest cent if necessary), and the maturity value. (See Example 6.)

Date Loan Was Made	Face Value	Term of Loan	Rate	Date Loan Is Due	Maturity Value
21. Mar. 12	$4800	220 days	9%	<u>Oct. 18</u>	<u>$5064</u>

$I = \$4800 \times .09 \times \frac{220}{360} = \$264;\ M = \$4800 + \$264 = \$5064$

22. Jan. 3	$12,000	100 days	9.8%	_____	_____
23. Nov. 10	$6300	180 days	$9\frac{1}{4}$%	_____	_____
24. July 14	$20,400	90 days	$11\frac{3}{4}$%	_____	_____

Solve the following application problems. Round dollar amounts to the nearest cent.

25. INVENTORY   Benson Automotive borrows $2,000,000 at $9\frac{1}{4}$% from a bank to buy land to build a building for a new dealership. Given that the loan is for 9 months, find **(a)** the interest and **(b)** the maturity value.

SOLD

(a) $I = \$2,000,000 \times .0925 \times \frac{9}{12} = \$138,750$

(b) $M = \$2,000,000 + \$138,750 = \$2,138,750$

(a) $138,750

(b) $2,138,750

26. **LOANS BETWEEN BANKS** Wells Fargo Bank borrows $25,000,000 at 4% for 90 days from a bank in Chicago. Find **(a)** the interest and **(b)** the maturity value.

(a) _____

(b) _____

27. **ROAD PAVING** Gilbert Construction Company needs $280,000 to build a short, paved road and install all utilities in a subdivision. The company decides to borrow the funds at 10% for 180 days. In 1980, the same note would have been at a rate of 22%. Find the difference in the interest charges based on the two rates.

27. _____

28. **INTERNATIONAL BUSINESS** Lesly Pacas borrows 300,000 pesos for 90 days at 12% per year to remodel her hair salon. She lives in Guadalajara, Mexico, where the rate would have been 35% a decade ago. Find the difference in the interest charges based on the different rates.

28. _____

29. **CAPITAL IMPROVEMENT** Elizabeth Barton borrowed $13,700 to install a small rock fountain and fish pond in front of her flower shop. She signed a 90-day note on July 5 at $9\frac{1}{4}$% interest. Find **(a)** the due date and **(b)** the maturity value of the note.

(a) _____

(b) _____

30. **WEB DESIGN** On September 10, Jessica Hernandez signed a promissory note with a face value of $32,500 to help her pay the salaries of employees during the season of slow sales at her web design firm. The 90-day note is at 11% interest. Find **(a)** the due date and **(b)** maturity value of the note.

(a) _____

(b) _____

31. **HEALTH FOOD** On March 10, the owner of The Granary borrowed $80,000 on a 180-day promissory note at 10.5% interest. Find **(a)** the due date and **(b)** the maturity value of the note.

(a) _____

(b) _____

32. **CORPORATE FINANCE** On October 15, IBM borrows $45,000,000 at 8% from a bank in San Francisco and agrees to repay the loan in 120 days using ordinary interest. Find **(a)** the due date and **(b)** the maturity value.

(a) _____

(b) _____

33. **PENALTY ON UNPAID PROPERTY TAX** Joe Simpson's property tax is $3416.05 and is due on April 15. He does not pay until July 23. The county adds a penalty of 9.3% simple interest on his unpaid tax. Find the penalty using exact interest.

33. _____

34. PENALTY ON UNPAID INCOME TAX   On January 5, Helen Terry made an income tax payment that was due on September 15. The penalty was 11% simple interest on the unpaid tax of $2100. Find the penalty using exact interest.

34. _____

35. PAINT STORE   On January 31, Jackson Paints & Supplies borrowed $128,000 to build a metal building for use as a warehouse. The 8-month loan has a rate of 9.5%. Find **(a)** the due date and **(b)** the maturity value of the loan.

(a) _____
(b) _____

36. CRIMINAL JUSTICE   Harris County administrators have decided to borrow $1,850,000 to set up a branch forensic lab. The 9 month, 4.5% simple interest loan is made on the last day of May. Find **(a)** the due date and **(b)** the maturity value.

(a) _____
(b) _____

37. Explain the difference between exact interest and ordinary, or banker's, interest. (See Objective 5.)

38. List three companies that you have purchased products or services from in the past. List two reasons each of the companies may have needed to borrow money in the past.

QUICK CHECK ANSWERS

1. $660.60

2. $51,516

3. (a) 123 days   **(b)** 148 days

4. 179 days

5. $961.64 exact interest; $975 ordinary interest; difference of $13.36

6. September 30

9.2 Finding Principal, Rate, and Time

OBJECTIVES

1 Find the principal.

2 Find the rate.

3 Find the time.

Principal (P), rate (R), and time (T) were given for all problems in **Section 9.1**, and we calculated interest. In this section, interest is given, and we solve for principal, rate, or time.

OBJECTIVE 1 Find the principal. The principal (P) is found by dividing both sides of the simple interest equation $I = PRT$ by RT. See Chapter 4 for a review of algebra if needed.

$$I = PRT$$

$$\frac{I}{RT} = \frac{PRT}{RT} \quad \text{Divide both sides by } RT.$$

$$\frac{I}{RT} = P \quad \text{or} \quad P = \frac{I}{RT}$$

$$P = \frac{I}{RT}$$

The various forms of the simple interest equation can be remembered using the circle sketch shown above. In the sketch, I (interest) is in the top half of the circle, with P (principal), R (rate), and T (time) in the bottom half of the circle. Find the formula for any one variable by covering the letter in the circle and then reading the remaining letters, noticing their position. For example, cover P and you are left with $\frac{I}{RT}$.

$$\text{Principal} = \frac{\text{Interest}}{\text{Rate} \times \text{Time (in years)}} \quad \text{or} \quad P = \frac{I}{RT}$$

Note: Use banker's interest with 360 days for all problems in this section.

Finding Principal Given Interest in Days

EXAMPLE 1

Gilbert Construction Company borrows funds at 10% for 54 days to finish building a home. Find the principal that results in interest of $1560.

SOLUTION

Write the rate as .10, the time as $\frac{54}{360}$, and then use the formula for principal.

$$P = \frac{I}{RT}$$

$$P = \frac{\$1560}{.10 \times \dfrac{54}{360}}$$

$$.10 \times \frac{54}{360} = .015 \qquad \text{Simplify the denominator.}$$

$$P = \frac{\$1560}{.015} = \$104{,}000 \quad \text{Divide.}$$

The principal is $104,000.

Check the answer using $I = PRT$. The principal is $104,000, the rate is 10%, and the time is $\frac{54}{360}$ year. The interest should be, and is, $780.

$$I = \$104{,}000 \times .10 \times \frac{54}{360} = \mathbf{\$1560}$$

The calculator approach to finding the principal uses parentheses so that the numerator is divided by the entire denominator.

$$1560 \;\boxed{\div}\; \boxed{(}\; .10 \;\boxed{\times}\; 54 \;\boxed{\div}\; 360 \;\boxed{)}\; \boxed{=}\; 104{,}000$$

Quick TIP

Remember that time must be in years or fraction of a year.

Finding Principal Given Length of Loan

 EXAMPLE 2

Frank Thomas took out a loan to pay his college tuition on February 2. The loan is due to be repaid on April 15 when Thomas expects to receive an income tax refund. The interest on the loan is $151.20 at a rate of 10.5%. Find the principal.

> **QUICK CHECK 1**
>
> A 90-day loan with a rate of 12% results in interest of $285. Find the principal.

SOLUTION

First find the number of days.

26	days remaining in February
31	March
+ 15	April
72	days from February 2 to April 15

$$T = \frac{72}{360}$$

Next find the principal.

$$P = \frac{I}{RT}$$

$$P = \frac{\$151.20}{.105 \times \dfrac{72}{360}} \qquad \text{Substitute values into the formula.}$$

$$.105 \times \frac{72}{360} = .021 \qquad \text{Simplify the denominator.}$$

$$P = \frac{\$151.20}{.021} = \$7200 \qquad \text{Divide.}$$

The principal is $7200. Check the answer using the formula for simple interest.

$$I = \$7200 \times .105 \times \frac{72}{360} = \mathbf{\$151.20}$$

> **QUICK CHECK 2**
>
> A loan made on May 12 must be repaid on December 18. Find the principal given that the rate is 9% and the interest at maturity is $1551.

OBJECTIVE 2 Find the rate. Solve the formula $I = PRT$ for rate (R) by dividing both sides of the equation by PT. The rate found in this manner will be the annual interest rate.

$$I = PRT$$
$$\frac{I}{PT} = \frac{PRT}{PT} \qquad \text{Divide both sides by } PT.$$
$$\frac{I}{PT} = R \quad \text{or} \quad R = \frac{I}{PT}$$

$$R = \frac{I}{PT}$$

$$\text{Rate} = \frac{\text{Interest}}{\text{Principal} \times \text{Time (in years)}} \quad \text{or} \quad R = \frac{I}{PT}$$

Finding Rate Given Length of Loan

EXAMPLE 3

An exchange student from the United States living in Brazil deposits $5000 in U.S. currency in a Brazilian bank for 45 days. Find the rate if the interest is $75 in U.S. currency.

SOLUTION

$$\text{Rate} = \frac{I}{PT}$$

$$R = \frac{\$75}{\$5000 \times \dfrac{45}{360}}$$

$$\$5000 \times \frac{45}{360} = \$625 \qquad \text{Simplify the denominator.}$$

$$R = \frac{\$75}{\$625} = .12 \qquad \text{Divide.}$$

Convert .12 to a percent to get 12%. Check the answer using the simple interest formula.

 Solve using a calculator as follows. Notice that parentheses set off the denominator.

75 ÷ (5000 × 45 ÷ 360) = .12

QUICK CHECK 3

A 120-day loan for $15,000 has interest of $412.50. Find the rate.

Finding Rate Given Length of Loan

EXAMPLE 4

Blaine Plumbing kept extra cash of $86,500 in an account from June 1 to August 16. Find the rate if the company earned $365.22 in interest during this period of time. Round to the nearest tenth of a percent.

SOLUTION

Find the number of days using the table on page 331.

$$\begin{array}{rr} \text{August 16 is day} & 228 \\ \text{June 1 is day} & -\,152 \\ \hline & \textbf{76 days} \end{array}$$

There are 76 days from June 1 to August 16.

$$T = \frac{76}{360}$$

$$\text{Rate} = \frac{I}{PT}$$

$$R = \frac{\$365.22}{\$86,500 \times \dfrac{76}{360}} = .0200$$

The rate of interest is 2.0%.

QUICK CHECK 4

A loan of $37,000 made on February 4 results in interest of $770.83. If the loan is due on May 15, find the rate to the nearest tenth of a percent.

OBJECTIVE 3 Find the time. The time (*T*) is found by dividing both sides of the simple interest equation $I = PRT$ by PR. Note that time will be in years, or fraction of a year.

$$I = PRT$$

$$\frac{I}{PR} = \frac{PRT}{PR} \qquad \text{Divide both sides by } PR.$$

$$\frac{I}{PR} = T \quad \text{or} \quad T = \frac{I}{PR}$$

$$T = \frac{I}{PR}$$

Finding Time

$$\text{Time (in years)} = \frac{\text{Interest}}{\text{Principal} \times \text{Rate}} \quad \text{or} \quad T = \frac{I}{PR}$$

The preceding formula gives time in years, but we often need time in days or months. Find these as follows.

Finding Time

$$\text{Time in days} = \frac{I}{PR} \times 360$$

$$\text{Time in months} = \frac{I}{PR} \times 12$$

Finding Time in Days Given Principal and Rate

 EXAMPLE 5

Roberta Sanchez deposited $18,600 in an account paying 3% and she earned $217 in interest. Find the number of days that the deposit earned interest.

SOLUTION

$$T \text{ in days} = \frac{I}{PR} \times \mathbf{360}$$

$$T = \frac{\$217}{\$18,600 \times .03} \times \mathbf{360} = 140 \text{ days} \quad \text{(rounded)}$$

The money was on deposit for 140 days.

⊞ Use parentheses around the denominator of the fraction to make sure that the calculations are done in the correct order.

217 ÷ (18600 × .03) × 360 = 140

QUICK CHECK 5

A loan for $22,000 results in interest of $1283.33 at 10.5%. Find the time to the nearest day.

Simple Interest Formulas

Interest	$I = PRT$
Principal	$P = \dfrac{I}{RT}$
Rate	$R = \dfrac{I}{PT}$
Time	$T \,(\textbf{in years}) = \dfrac{I}{PR}$
	$T \,(\textbf{in months}) = \dfrac{I}{PR} \times 12$
	$T \,(\textbf{in days}) = \dfrac{I}{PR} \times 360$

All of these are modifications of the formula $I = PRT$.

9.2 Exercises

MyMathLab®

The shaded sections below contain solutions to help you get a **QUICK START** *on the various types of exercises.*

Find the principal in each of the following. Round to the nearest cent. (See Example 1.)

	Rate	Time (in days)	Interest	Principal
1.	$7\frac{3}{4}\%$	90	$271.25	**$14,000**

$$P = \frac{\$271.25}{.0775 \times \frac{90}{360}} = \$14,000$$

	Rate	Time (in days)	Interest	Principal
2.	9.5%	120	$186	**$5873.68**

$$P = \frac{\$186}{.095 \times \frac{120}{360}} = \$5873.68$$

	Rate	Time (in days)	Interest	Principal
3.	10%	80	$112	_____
4.	6%	24	$62.40	_____
5.	$8\frac{1}{2}\%$	120	$4420	_____
6.	10.5%	140	$87.20	_____

Find the rate in each of the following. Round to the nearest tenth of a percent. (See Example 3.)

	Principal	Time	Interest	Rate
7.	$7600	200 days	$498.22	**11.8%**

$$R = \frac{\$498.22}{\$7600 \times \frac{200}{360}} = 11.8\%$$

	Principal	Time	Interest	Rate
8.	$15,600	90 days	$312	_____
9.	$42,800	60 days	$677.67	_____
10.	$20,000	90 days	$625	_____
11.	$8000	4 months	$200	_____
12.	$4800	5 months	$197.60	_____

C indicates an exercise that is related to the Case in Point feature.

Find the time in each of the following. In Exercises 13–16, round to the nearest day;
in Exercises 17 and 18, round to the nearest month. (See Example 5.)

	Principal	Rate	Interest	Time
13.	$74,000	9.5%	$2343.33	120 days

$$T = \frac{\$2343.33}{\$74,000 \times .095} \times 360 = 119.9998 \text{ or } 120 \text{ days}$$

	Principal	Rate	Interest	Time
14.	$36,000	9%	$585	_____
15.	$24,000	11%	$454.70	_____
16.	$20,000	8%	$1200	_____
17.	$3500	$10\frac{1}{4}$%	$143.50	_____
18.	$8400	$7\frac{1}{4}$%	$357	_____

In each of the following application problems, find principal to the nearest cent,
rate to the nearest tenth of a percent, or time to the nearest day.

19. **SHORT-TERM SAVINGS** Hoyt Axton earned $244.80 interest in 9 months in a short-term savings account that paid 3.2% per year. Use the simple interest formula to estimate the amount initially invested.

$$P = \frac{\$244.80}{.032 \times \frac{9}{12}} = \$10,200$$

19. $10,200

20. **BANK LOAN** Citizens Bank earned $12,250 interest in 45 days from a short-term investment that paid 5.6% interest per year. Find the amount initially invested.

20. _____

21. **INVESTING IN BONDS** Joan Gretz invested $3600 in a mutual fund containing bonds. Find the rate if she earned $237.50 in interest in 250 days.

21. _____

22. **LAW ENFORCEMENT** The Smith County Police Department borrowed $120,000 for 135 days to purchase new radar-detection equipment to detect speeders. Find the rate if the interest was $4050.

22. _____

23. **PAYROLL** Jessica Hernandez borrowed $45,000 so that she could meet payroll for the quarter. She agreed to pay interest of $1881.25 in 140 days. Find the rate.

23. _____

24. **SAVING FOR RETIREMENT** Mike Jordan deposited $2000 into a Roth Individual Retirement Account (IRA) investing in a mutual fund containing corporate bonds. Find the rate if he has $2192.50 in the account 15 months later.

24. _____

25. RETIREMENT ACCOUNT   Over a period of 300 days, Shawna Johnson earned $450 interest in a retirement account paying interest at a rate of 5%. Find **(a)** the principal at the beginning of the 300 days and **(b)** the amount in the account at the end of 300 days.

(a) _____

(b) _____

26. INTEREST EARNINGS   Patterson Plumbing had an account that earned $214.67 interest in 280 days. If the interest rate was 4%, find **(a)** the principal at the beginning of the 280 days and **(b)** the amount in the account at the end of the 280 days.

(a) _____

(b) _____

27. TIME OF DEPOSIT   Benson Automotive earned $69.46 interest on a $9400 deposit in an account paying 3.5%. Find the number of days that the funds were on deposit.

27. _____

28. TIME OF DEPOSIT   Find how long Quinlan Enterprises must deposit $7500 at 6% in order to earn $243.75 interest.

28. _____

29. INTEREST RATE   Hot Air Balloon Tours, Inc. must pay the bank $23,515.27 in interest 300 days after making a loan of $328,120 to purchase hot air balloons.

29. _____

30. PENALTY ON LATE PAYMENT   James Smith lets an $1800 mortgage payment go 70 days overdue and is charged a penalty of $59.50. Find the rate of interest that was charged as a penalty. (*Note:* Penalty rates are frequently quite high.)

30. _____

31. LAPTOPS   Shanghai Computers purchased 20 laptops from a Chinese computer manufacturer. Shanghai paid the bill after 45 days, paying a finance charge of $150. If the Chinese company charges 10% interest, find **(a)** the cost of the 20 laptops excluding the interest and **(b)** the cost per laptop.

(a) _____

(b) _____

32. LAWN-MOWER   Yard Mowers, Inc., bought 15 self-propelled, riding lawn mowers from Green Lawns, Ltd. The company paid after 90 days and was charged an annual finance charge of 12% or $126. Find **(a)** the cost of the 15 lawn mowers excluding the interest and **(b)** the cost per mower.

(a) _____

(b) _____

33. PROMISSORY NOTE   Jan Rice signed a promissory note for $6400 at $11\frac{1}{2}$% interest with interest charges of $425.24. Find the term of the note to the nearest day.

33. _____

34. TIME OF DEPOSIT   The Frampton Chamber of Commerce earns $682.71 interest on a $16,385 investment at 5.5%. Find the length of time of the investment to the nearest day.

34. _____

35. HOME CONSTRUCTION   Gilbert Construction Company needs to borrow $220,000 for 1 year for materials needed to build three homes. They can borrow from either of two banks. Interest charges from Bank One would amount to $23,650, whereas interest charges from First National Bank would amount to $25,000. Find the interest rates associated with a loan from **(a)** Bank One and **(b)** First National Bank.

(a) _____

(b) _____

36. INVENTORY PURCHASE   Forest Nursery needs to borrow $9500 on February 1 to buy additional inventory and will repay the loan on July 15. Interest charges for State Bank and First National Bank are $480 and $443.60, respectively. Find the rate for **(a)** the State Bank loan and **(b)** the First National Bank loan.

(a) _____

(b) _____

37. A retired couple receives $14,000 per year from Social Security and an additional $18,000 in interest from retirement plans and lifetime savings. They need all of their income to pay expenses including medical bills. What will happen if the interest rate on their retirement plans and lifetime savings decreases significantly?

38. How would the formula for calculating time in days (given principal, interest, and rate) change if exact interest were used rather than ordinary interest?

▼ 9.3 Simple Discount Notes

OBJECTIVES

1 Define the basic terms used with simple discount notes.

2 Find the bank discount and proceeds.

3 Find the face value.

4 Find the effective interest rate.

5 Understand U.S. Treasury bills.

▼ **CASE IN POINT** Jessica Hernandez does not like to borrow money, but sometimes she must. For example, she recently had to borrow to pay her expenses when a large firm delayed its payment to her company. She had expenses that had to be paid in a timely way, but her revenue was delayed.

The following clipping shows that the federal government has the power to change interest rates. Higher interest rates make it more expensive to borrow and often slow economic growth. Lower interest rates make it cheaper to borrow and often increase economic growth. The federal government uses interest rates as a tool *to control the growth rate of the economy*. The goal is to keep the economy growing fast enough to generate jobs but not so fast as to cause inflation, which is discussed in the next chapter. So, interest rates are set in a complex way involving the government and the market.

Economists Differ

All eyes are on the Fed chairman while economists wait for the outcome of the next meeting. Economists differ in the direction they expect interest rates to go from here. Some expect the Fed to increase interest rates slightly next year, but others think rates will remain the same or decrease slightly.

In this section, we discuss **simple discount notes**, which are simply a different way to set up a promissory note based on simple interest calculations. Any note that uses simple interest calculations with a lump-sum payment can be set up *either* as a simple interest note or as a simple discount note. One type of note is *not* better than the other type of note. They merely represent two different ways to discuss the same thing. We study both because some banks use simple interest notes while others use simple discount notes.

OBJECTIVE 1 Define the basic terms used with simple discount notes. As we saw in **Section 9.2**, simple interest notes involve principal (face value or loan amount), interest rate, time, interest, and maturity value. Simple discount notes involve **proceeds (loan amount), discount rate, time, bank discount (interest),** and **face value** (or **maturity value**). Face value in a simple interest note is the amount loaned to the borrower, but it is the maturity value in a simple discount note. Simple discount notes are also called **interest-in-advance notes**, since interest is subtracted before funds are given to the borrower. A basic difference between the two types of notes is that simple interest is calculated based on principal, whereas simple discount is calculated based on maturity value, as shown in the table. College students sometimes borrow money from the government using **Stafford loans**, which are simple discount notes.

Simple Interest versus Simple Discount Notes

Type of Note	Loan Amount		Interest		Repayment Amount
Simple interest	Face value (**Principal**)	+	Interest	=	Maturity value
Simple discount	Proceeds	+	Discount (**Interest**)	=	Face value (**Maturity value**)

Note: Simple interest is calculated on the *principal*, while simple discount is calculated on the *maturity value*.

OBJECTIVE 2 Find the bank discount and proceeds. The formula for finding the bank discount is a form of the basic percent equation of Chapter 3. The formula is similar to the one used to calculate simple interest, but different letters are used since the ideas differ slightly.

Calculating Bank Discount

$$\text{Bank discount} = \text{Face value} \times \text{Discount rate} \times \text{Time}$$
$$B = M \times D \times T$$

Then, if P is the proceeds,

$$\text{Proceeds (loan amount)} = \text{Face value} - \text{Bank discount} \quad \text{or} \quad P = M - B$$

Stated in another way,

$$\textbf{Face value} = \textbf{Proceeds (loan amount)} + \textbf{Bank discount} \quad \text{or} \quad M = P + B$$

Note: Time must be given in years.

Finding Discount and Proceeds

 EXAMPLE 1 Jim Peterson signs a simple discount note with a face or maturity value of $35,000 so that he can purchase a truck with plow for his snow removal business. The banker discounts the 10-month note at 9%. Find the amount of the discount and the proceeds.

SOLUTION

Peterson *does not* receive $35,000 from the bank—that is the amount he must repay when the loan matures. Use $M = \$35{,}000$, $D = 9\%$, and $T = \frac{10}{12}$ in the formula $B = MDT$ to find the discount, which is the interest that must be paid at maturity.

$$\textit{Bank discount} = M \times D \times T$$
$$B = \$35{,}000 \times .09 \times \tfrac{10}{12} = \mathbf{\$2625}$$

The discount of **$2625** is the interest charge on the loan. The proceeds that Peterson actually receives when making the loan is found using $P = M - B$.

$$P = M - B$$
$$P = \$35{,}000 - \mathbf{\$2625} = \$32{,}375$$

Peterson signs the discount note with a face value of $35,000, but receives $32,375. Ten months later he must pay $35,000 to the bank. The difference is interest.

QUICK CHECK 1

A simple discount loan has a maturity value of $15,800, discount rate of 9%, and time of 180 days. Find the bank discount and proceeds.

Finding the Proceeds

 EXAMPLE 2 To finance a new electronic sign to put in front of a retail store, Mustang Auto signs a 6-month, simple discount note with a face value of $4500. Find the proceeds if the discount rate is 10.5%.

SOLUTION

The bank discount (B) is not known, but we do know that $B = MDT$. Therefore, we can substitute MDT in place of B.

$$P = M - B$$
$$P = M - MDT \qquad \text{Substitute } MDT \text{ in place of } B.$$
$$P = \$4500 - \left(\$4500 \times .105 \times \frac{6}{12} \right) \qquad \text{Substitute values.}$$
$$P = \$4263.75$$

Mustang Auto receives $4263.75 but must pay back $4500 in 6 months.

QUICK CHECK 2

A 220-day loan with a face value of $40,000 has a discount rate of 12%. Find the proceeds.

OBJECTIVE 3 Find the face value. If the loan amount (proceeds) of a simple discount note is known, use the following formula to find the corresponding face value.

Calculating Face Value to Achieve Desired Proceeds

$$M = \frac{P}{1 - DT}$$

where

M = Face value of the simple discount note
P = Proceeds received by the borrower
D = Discount rate used by the bank
T = Time of the loan (in years)

Note: The symbol D is the discount *rate*, not the bank discount.

Finding the Face Value   **EXAMPLE 3**   Tina Watson purchased a classic 1961 Corvette and plans to rebuild it. She needs to borrow $18,000 for 180 days. Find the face value of the 10% simple discount note that would result in proceeds of $18,000 to Watson.

SOLUTION

Use the formula.

$$M = \frac{P}{1 - DT}$$

Replace P with $18,000, D with .10, and T with $\frac{180}{360}$.

$$M = \frac{\$18,000}{1 - \left(.10 \times \dfrac{180}{360}\right)} = \$18,947.37 \quad \text{(rounded)}$$

The face value of the note is $18,947.37. However, Watson receives only $18,000 from the bank when the note is signed. She must repay $18,947.37 to the bank in 180 days.

 The problem

$$\frac{\$18,000}{1 - \left(.10 \times \dfrac{180}{360}\right)}$$

can be solved using a calculator by first finding the denominator.

1 − (.1 × 180 ÷ 360) = .95 STO
18000 ÷ RCL = 18947.37

QUICK CHECK 3

A 300-day note has proceeds of $48,000 and a discount rate of 8.8%. Find the maturity value.

Comparing Discount Notes and Simple Interest Notes   **EXAMPLE 4**   Jane Benson of Benson Automotive has been offered loans from two different banks. Each note has a face value of $75,000 and a time of 90 days. One note has a simple interest rate of 10%, and the other a simple discount rate of 10%. Benson wants to know which is the better deal.

SOLUTION

Find the interest owed on each.

Quick TIP

This example shows that a simple discount rate of 10% is not equivalent to a simple interest rate of 10%.

Simple Interest Note	Simple Discount Note
$I = PRT$	$B = MDT$
$I = \$75,000 \times .10 \times \dfrac{90}{360}$	$B = \$75,000 \times .10 \times \dfrac{90}{360}$
$I = \$1875$	$B = \$1875$

The amount of interest is the same in both notes. Now find the amount the borrower would receive.

Simple Interest Note	Simple Discount Note
Face value = $75,000	Proceeds = $M - B$ = $75,000 - $1875 = $73,125

The borrower has the use of $75,000 with the simple interest note, but only $73,125 with the simple discount note. Yet the amount of interest is identical. So, the simple interest note is the better deal for Benson in this situation. However, it is NOT true that a simple interest note is always better than a simple discount note. You must compare the terms of each to discover which is better. Find the maturity value of each note as follows.

Simple Interest Note	Simple Discount Note
$M = P + I$ = $75,000 + $1875 = $76,875	Maturity = Face value = $75,000

The differences between these two notes can be summarized as follows.

	Simple Interest Note	Simple Discount Note
Face value	$75,000	$75,000
Interest	$1875	$1875
Amount available to borrower	$75,000	$73,125
Maturity value	$76,875	$75,000

QUICK CHECK 4

Two notes both have face values of $24,000 and a time of 180 days. The first note has a simple interest rate of 9%, and the second has a simple discount rate of 9%. Find the maturity value of each.

OBJECTIVE 4 Find the effective interest rate. The federal **Truth in Lending Act** was passed in 1969 because the different ways of calculating interest were confusing. This law does not regulate interest rates, but it does require that interest rates be given in a form that can easily be compared.

The **effective rate of interest** is also called the **annual percentage rate**, the **APR**, and the **true rate**. It is the interest rate that is calculated based on the actual amount received by the borrower. The discount rate of 10% stated in Example 4 is called the **stated rate**, or **nominal rate**, since it is the rate written on the note. It is not the effective rate, since the 10% applies to the maturity value of $75,000 and *not* to the proceeds of $73,125 actually received by the borrower. The next example shows how to find the effective rate for Example 4.

Finding the Effective Interest Rate   **EXAMPLE 5**   Find the effective rate of interest (APR) for the simple discount note of Example 4.

SOLUTION

Quick TIP

The discount rate is not an interest rate to be applied to proceeds (loan amount)—rather it is applied to face value.

Find the effective rate (APR) by using the formula for simple interest: $I = PRT$. In this case, $I = 1875 (the discount), $P = $73,125$ (the proceeds), and $T = \frac{90}{360}$. Use the following formula from **Section 9.2**.

$$R = \frac{I}{PT}$$

$$R = \frac{\$1875}{\$73,125 \times \dfrac{90}{360}} = .1026 = 10.26\% \quad \text{(rounded)}$$

Thus, the 10.26% effective rate of the simple discount note is higher than the 10% effective rate of the simple interest note showing that the simple interest note is better for the borrower in this situation.

QUICK CHECK 5

Find the effective rate (APR) for a loan with a loan amount of $31,000, a time of 90 days, and interest of $891.25.

The interest rate 10.26% in Example 5 is the **effective**, or **true, rate of interest**. Federal regulations require that rates be rounded to the nearest quarter of a percent when communicated to a borrower. Note that 10.26% is closer to 10.25% than to 10.50%. Therefore, an annual percentage rate (APR) of 10.25% must be reported to someone signing a discount note with a face value of $75,000 for 90 days at a discount rate of 10%.

The table below shows two identical loans, one a simple interest loan and the other a simple discount loan. Proceeds, interest charges, terms of the loans, and maturity values are all identical.

	Simple Interest Loan	Simple Discount Loan
Proceeds	$11,100	$11,100
Interest	$900	$900
Maturity Value	$12,000	$12,000
Face Value	$11,100	$12,000
Time	10 months	10 months
Interest Rate	**9.73**%	—
Discount Rate	—	**9**%

Since the loans are identical, a 9.73% simple interest loan for 10 months is equivalent to a 9% simple discount note for 10 months. In both situations, the borrower receives $11,100 and must repay $12,000 ten months later. Therefore, the two loans have the *same effective rate*.

OBJECTIVE 5 Understand U.S. Treasury bills. The United States government borrows very large amounts of money from banks, various financial institutions, pension funds, wealthy individuals, and even foreign governments. In fact, the U.S. national debt is projected to pass $17 trillion in 2013, much of it owed to other countries such as China and Japan. Do you know how many digits are needed to write the number $17 trillion?

$$\$17 \text{ trillion} = \$1\overset{\text{trillions}}{7},\underset{\text{billions}}{000},000,000,000$$

If 17 trillion $1 bills could be stacked on top of one another, the stack would rise from the surface of the earth far past the moon. However, debt is not really in $1 bills. Think of debt as numbers written on contracts of one form or another and stored in computers. Our monetary system is not really based on paper currency. Instead, it is based on the government's backing of the dollar and (effectively) the many contractual promises to repay loans that are everywhere in our society.

The U.S. government uses **U.S. Treasury bills**, or **T-bills**, to borrow for less than one year. An individual can buy a T-bill directly from the government or indirectly through a broker such as Merrill Lynch. T-bills use discount interest.

$17 Trillion

Finding Facts About T-Bills

EXAMPLE 6

The owner of a construction company in Mexico is worried that the peso is going to devalue, or fall in value. As a result, he purchases $1,000,000 in U.S. T-bills in order to place cash in a safe place for a short period of time. The T-bills are at a 4% discount rate for 26 weeks. Find **(a)** the total purchase price, **(b)** the total maturity value, **(c)** the interest earned, and **(d)** the effective rate of interest.

SOLUTION

$M = \$1,000,000; D = .04; T = \frac{26}{52}$

(a) **Bank discount** $=$ *Face value* $\times$ *Discount rate* $\times$ *Time*
$$= \$1,000,000 \times .04 \times \tfrac{26}{52} = \$20,000$$

Purchase price $=$ *Face value* $-$ *Bank discount*
$$= \$1,000,000 - \$20,000 = \$980,000$$

(b) **Maturity value** $=$ **Face value**
$$= \$1,000,000$$

    (c) **Interest = Bank discount**

$$= \$20,000$$

    (d) **Effective rate** $= \dfrac{\text{Interest earned}}{\text{Purchase price (proceeds)} \times \text{Time}}$

$$= \frac{\$20,000}{\$980,000 \times \frac{26}{52}} = .04081 = 4.08\%$$

QUICK CHECK 6

Find **(a)** the purchase price, **(b)** the maturity value, **(c)** the interest, and **(d)** the effective rate of interest (to the nearest hundredth) for a $1,000,000, 13-week T-bill with a discount rate of 5.2%. Round to the nearest hundredth of a percent.

▼ 9.3 Exercises   MyMathLab®

The shaded sections below contain solutions to help you get a **QUICK START** *on the various types of exercises.*

Find the discount to the nearest cent, then find the proceeds. (See Example 1.)

	Face Value	Discount Rate	Time (Days)	Discount	Proceeds or Loan Amount
1.	$7800	9%	120	$234	$7566

$$B = \$7800 \times .09 \times \tfrac{120}{360} = \$234; \quad P = \$7800 - \$234 = \$7566$$

	Face Value	Discount Rate	Time (Days)	Discount	Proceeds or Loan Amount
2.	$15,000	10.25%	90	_____	_____
3.	$19,000	10%	180	_____	_____
4.	$12,500	11%	150	_____	_____
5.	$22,400	$8\frac{3}{4}\%$	75	_____	_____
6.	$18,050	8%	80	_____	_____

Find the maturity date and the proceeds for the following. Round to the nearest cent.
(See Examples 1 and 2.)

	Face Value	Discount Rate	Date Made	Time (Days)	Maturity Date	Proceeds or Loan Amount
7.	$64,000	9.5%	Mar. 22	90	Jun. 20	$62,480

$$P = \$64,000 - \left(\$64,000 \times .095 \times \tfrac{90}{360}\right) = \$62,480$$

	Face Value	Discount Rate	Date Made	Time (Days)	Maturity Date	Proceeds or Loan Amount
8.	$9500	12%	Oct. 12	100	_____	_____
9.	$10,000	$10\frac{1}{4}\%$	July 12	150	_____	_____
10.	$18,500	$9\frac{1}{4}\%$	May 1	220	_____	_____
11.	$24,000	10%	Dec. 10	60	_____	_____
12.	$8000	10.5%	Nov. 4	165	_____	_____

 indicates an exercise that is related to the Case in Point feature.

Solve each of the following application problems. Round rate to the nearest tenth of a percent, time to the nearest day, and money to the nearest cent.

13. BOAT PURCHASE   An ExxonMobil employee borrowed $6000 from First National Bank to purchase a boat. He plans to repay the loan with a Christmas bonus he is to receive in 120 days. If he borrowed the money at a discount rate of 11%, find **(a)** the discount and **(b)** the proceeds.

(a) $\underline{\$220}$
(b) $\underline{\$5780}$

(a) $B = \$6000 \times .11 \times \frac{120}{360} = \$220;$

(b) $P = \$6000 - \$220 = \$5780$

14. INCOME TAX PAYMENT   Managers at Benson Automotive sign a $48,000 simple discount note for six months for funds to pay corporate income taxes. If the discount rate is 8.5%, find **(a)** the discount and **(b)** the proceeds.

(a) _____
(b) _____

15. CHRISTMAS TREE FARM   To plant Christmas trees in another field, Tom Parsons signed a note with a face value of $25,000 at an 11% discount rate. Find the length of the loan in days if the discount is $1527.78.

15. _____

16. WEB-PAGE DESIGN   Jessica Hernandez was unable to collect funds owed her from a customer that declared bankruptcy. The shortage of cash forced Hernandez to sign a $12,200 note at a discount rate of 11% to pay her bills. She was told the interest would be $931.94. Find the length of the loan in days.

16. _____

17. CASINO   Wyatt Construction borrowed $157.25 million during the construction phase of adding a wing to a casino in Las Vegas. Management signed a 270-day note with a face value of $170 million. Find the discount rate.

17. _____

18. CELL PHONES   Ben Dayton needed funds to open a cell phone store and his uncle agreed to put up collateral for the loan. Dayton signed a 130-day simple discount note with a face value of $12,000 and proceeds of $11,523.33. Find the discount rate.

18. _____

19. NEW ROOF   Roy Gerard needs $7260 to pay for a new roof on his small home. His bank loans him money at a discount rate of 12%, and the loan is for 240 days. Find the face value of the loan so he will have $7260.

19. _____

20. TRUCKS & SPRAYERS   A regional manager at Trugreen, Inc. authorizes the borrowing of $98,300 for trucks and sprayers needed to spray yards with fertilizers and pesticides. The simple discount note has a 9.25% rate and matures in 150 days. Find the face value of the loan needed.

20. _____

21. POOR CREDIT   Cathy Cox has poor credit but she found a bank that will lend her $4200 when she uses some collateral. Still, the bank charges a 12% discount rate. Find **(a)** the proceeds if the note is for 10 months and **(b)** the effective interest rate charged by the bank.

(a) _____
(b) _____

22. **BAD CREDIT HISTORY**   Tim Garcia has a bad credit history partly due to a divorce. The bank agrees to lend him funds based on a note with a face value of $9400, but it requires him to use his truck as collateral. Even then, the bank charges him a high 16% discount rate. Find **(a)** the proceeds and **(b)** the effective rate if the note is for 7 months.

(a) _____

(b) _____

23. **INTERNATIONAL FINANCE**   A business owner in England signs a 10% discount note for 40,000 English pounds (£40,000) with a bank in London. If the proceeds are £38,833.33, find the time of the note in days.

23. _____

24. **SIMPLE DISCOUNT RATE**   A plumbing contractor receives proceeds of $4713.54 on a 12.5% simple discount note with a face value of $5000. Find the time of the note in days.

24. _____

25. **EARTHQUAKE DAMAGE**   A bridge in Japan was damaged by an earthquake. The firm repairing the bridge needs proceeds of 165 million Japanese yen (¥165,000,000) for 30 days to pay wages and buy supplies. A bank lends the funds at an 8% discount rate. Find **(a)** the face value and **(b)** the effective rate.

(a) _____

(b) _____

26. **INTERNATIONAL FINANCE**   A Malaysian electric company requires proceeds of $720,000 (local currency) and borrows from a bank in Thailand at a 12% discount rate for 45 days. Find **(a)** the face value of the note and **(b)** the effective interest rate.

(a) _____

(b) _____

27. **RACE HORSES**   Robert Johnson owns a farm and breeds race horses. To purchase three thoroughbreds, he signs a 180-day note with a maturity value of $265,000 and proceeds of $253,737.50. Find **(a)** the discount and **(b)** the true (or effective) rate.

(a) _____

(b) _____

28. **PIZZA**   To remodel a restaurant, Two Brothers Pizza signs a 250-day note with proceeds of $63,159.72 and a maturity value of $68,000. Find **(a)** the discount and **(b)** the APR.

(a) _____

(b) _____

The following exercises apply to U.S. Treasury bills, discussed at the end of this section. (Assume 52 weeks per year for each exercise, and round to the nearest hundredth of a percent.) (See Example 6.)

29. PURCHASE OF T-BILLS   A British investment firm purchases $25,000,000 in U.S. T-bills at a 6% discount rate for 13 weeks. Find **(a)** the purchase price of the T-bills, **(b)** the maturity value of the T-bills, **(c)** the interest earned, and **(d)** the effective rate.

(a) _____
(b) _____
(c) _____
(d) _____

30. T-BILLS   Nina Horn buys a $50,000 T-bill at a 5.8% discount rate for 26 weeks. Find **(a)** the purchase price of the T-bill, **(b)** the maturity value, **(c)** the interest earned, and **(d)** the effective rate of interest.

(a) _____
(b) _____
(c) _____
(d) _____

31. Explain the main differences between simple interest notes and simple discount notes. (See Objective 1.)

32. As a borrower, would you prefer a simple interest note with a rate of 11% or a simple discount note at a rate of 11%? Explain using an example. (See Example 4.)

QUICK CHECK ANSWERS

1. $711; $15,089
2. $37,066.67
3. $51,798.56
4. $25,080; $24,000
5. 11.5%

6. (a) $987,000
   (b) $1,000,000
   (c) $13,000
   (d) 5.27%

▼ 9.4 Discounting a Note Before Maturity

OBJECTIVES

1 Understand the concept of discounting a note.

2 Find the proceeds when discounting simple interest notes.

3 Find the proceeds when discounting simple discount notes.

A note is a *legal responsibility* for one individual or firm to pay a specific amount on a specific date to another individual or firm. Notes can be bought and sold just as an automobile can be bought and sold. The clipping taken from a newspaper shows firms that buy notes. This section shows how to find the value of a note that is sold before its maturity date.

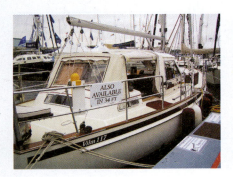

OBJECTIVE 1 Understand the concept of discounting a note. Businesses sometimes help their customers purchase products or services by accepting a promissory note rather than requiring an immediate cash payment. For example, a company that manufactures boats, a retailer that sells the boats, and a bank may do business as follows:

1. Boat manufacturer sells boats to a retailer and accepts a promissory note instead of cash.

2. Boat manufacturer needs cash and sells the note to a bank before it matures.

3. Retailer pays the maturity value of the note to the bank when due.

The bank deducts a fee from the maturity value of the note when it buys the note from the manufacturer. The fee is interest for the number of days, called the **discount period**, that the bank will hold the note until it is due. The fee charged by the bank is the **bank discount** or just **discount**. The **discount rate** is the percent used by the bank to find the discount. The process of finding the value of the note on a specific date before it matures is **discounting the note**. Both simple interest notes and simple discount notes can be discounted before they mature.

OBJECTIVE 2 Find the proceeds when discounting simple interest notes. The amount of cash actually received by the boat manufacturer on the sale of a promissory note is the **proceeds**. The bank then collects the maturity value from the maker of the note, the retailer, when it is due. These notes are usually sold with **recourse**. This means that the bank receives reimbursement from the manufacturer if the retailer does not pay the bank when the note matures. Thus the bank is protected against loss. Many banks refuse to buy these types of notes unless they have recourse.

Calculate the Proceeds When Discounting a Simple Interest Note

1. First, understand the simple interest note by finding:

   (a) the **due date** of the original note and

   (b) the **maturity value** of the original note ($M = P + I$, where $I = PRT$).

2. Then discount the simple interest note.

   (a) Find the **discount period**, which is the time (e.g., number of days) from the sale of the note to the maturity date of the note.

   (b) Find the **discount** using the formula

$$B = M \times D \times T$$

= Maturity value $\times$ Discount rate $\times$ Discount period

   (c) Find the **proceeds** after discounting the original note using $P = M - B$.

Finding Proceeds   Jameson Plumbing takes a simple interest, 180-day note from a contractor with a face value of $64,750 and a rate of 10.5%. The company sells the note to a bank 50 days later at a discount rate of 12%. Find the proceeds to the plumbing company.

SOLUTION

Step 1   ***Find the maturity value.*** The face value equals the proceeds, since this is a simple interest note.

Maturity value = Principal + Interest on the simple interest note

Maturity value = $64,750 + *PRT*   **Since** *I* = *PRT*

Maturity value = $64,750 + **$64,750 × .105** × $\frac{180}{360}$ = $68,149.38 (rounded)

Step 2   The note is discounted after 50 days, so the discount period is 180 − 50 = 130 days. This means that the buyer of the note will own it for 130 days before the note is paid off.

Use the formula *B* = *MDT*, with *M* = $68,149.38, *D* = .12, and *T* = $\frac{130}{360}$ to find the discount.

Bank discount = *MDT* = **$68,149.38** × .12 × $\frac{130}{360}$ = $2953.14

Proceeds = Maturity value of simple interest note − Bank discount

Proceeds = $68,149.38 − $2953.14 = $65,196.24

So, the following occurs:

1. A contractor signs a 180-day simple interest note with a face value of $64,750 to Jameson Plumbing.
2. After 50 days, Jameson Plumbing sells the note to a bank and receives $65,196.24 in cash.
3. The bank receives $68,149.38 on the maturity date of the loan.

QUICK CHECK 1

A simple interest note has a face value of $28,000, a rate of 9%, and a time to maturity of 240 days. It is discounted after 80 days at a rate of 11%. Find the maturity value of the simple interest note and the proceeds at the time of the discount.

Finding Proceeds   **EXAMPLE 2** Blues Recording holds a 200-day simple interest note from a rock group that agreed to pay them to record an album and produce 1000 CDs. The 12% simple interest note is dated March 24 and has a face value of $48,000. Blues Recording wishes to convert the note to cash, so they sell it to a bank on August 15. If the bank requires a discount rate of 12.5%, find the proceeds to the recording studio.

SOLUTION

Go through the two steps of discounting a note.

Step 1   *Find the maturity value.* The note is dated March 24 and is due in 200 days.

Due date: day 83 (March 24) + 200 days = day 283 (October 10)

Since this is a simple interest note, the proceeds are given but the maturity value must be found. First find the **interest** on the note if held until maturity.

$$I = \textbf{\textit{PRT}} = \$48,000 \times .12 \times \frac{200}{360} = \$3200$$

Maturity value: $48,000 + $3200 = $51,200.

Step 2   Now discount this simple interest note.

(a) *Find the discount period.* The **discount period** is the number of days from August 15, which is the date the note is discounted (sold) to the bank, to the due date of the note (October 10).

October 10 is day   283

August 15 is day   − 227

Discount period   **56 days**

Blues Recording holds the 200-day note for 200 − 56 = 144 days before they sell it. The buyer of the note holds it for 56 days before the rock group must pay off the note.

(b) *Find the bank discount.* Find the **discount** by using the formula $B = MDT$, where $M = \$51,200$, $D = 12.5\%$, and T is $\frac{56}{360}$.

$$\text{Bank discount: } \textbf{\textit{MDT}} = \$51,200 \times .125 \times \frac{56}{360} = \$995.56$$

(c) *Find the proceeds.* **Proceeds** are found by subtracting the bank discount from the maturity value.

$$P = M - B$$
$$P = \$51,200 - \$995.56 = \$50,204.44$$

Date	Transaction
March 24	Rock group signs 200-day simple interest note for $48,000.
August 15	Blues Recording sells note to bank for $50,204.44.
October 10	Bank receives $51,200 from payer (rock group).

Quick TIP

When finding the bank discount, be sure to use the maturity value of the original note.

QUICK CHECK 2

On March 27, Dayton Finance loans Jorge Rivera $9200 for 150 days at 11% simple interest. The finance company sells the note on April 24. Find the maturity value of the simple interest note and the proceeds to Dayton Finance if the note is sold at a discount rate of 12%.

It is also common for a business needing cash to sell part of its accounts receivable (money owed to the company) before it is due. The process is called **factoring**, and those who buy the accounts receivable are called **factors**. The calculations involved in factoring are the same as those for finding the discount discussed in this section.

OBJECTIVE 3 Find the proceeds when discounting simple discount notes.

Quick TIP

There are two different discounts in problems of this type. The first occurs when the original note is signed. The second discount occurs when this note is sold before maturity.

Calculate the Proceeds When Discounting a Simple Discount Note

1. First, understand the simple discount note by finding:

   (a) the **due date** of the original note,
   (b) the **discount** of the original note using $B = MDT$, and
   (c) the **proceeds** from the original note using $P = M - B$.

   The **maturity value (face value)** of the note is written on the note itself and is the value needed in step 2(b) below.

2. Then discount the simple discount note.

   (a) Find the **discount period**, which is the time (e.g., number of days) from the sale of the note to the maturity date of the note.
   (b) Find the **discount** using the formula $B = MDT$.
   (c) Find the **proceeds** after discounting the original note using $P = M - B$.

The steps for finding the proceeds at the time of sale are shown in Example 3.

Finding the Proceeds   Benson Automotive used excess cash to purchase a $100,000 Treasury bill with a term of 26 weeks at a 3.5% simple discount rate. However, the firm needs cash exactly 8 weeks later and sells the T-bill. During the 8 weeks, market interest rates changed slightly so that the bill was sold at a 3% discount rate. Find **(a)** the initial purchase price of the T-bill, **(b)** the proceeds received by the firm at the subsequent sale of the T-bill, and **(c)** the effective interest rate.

SOLUTION

(a) *Find the discount and proceeds.* The discount that Benson Automotive receives when buying the T-bill is found as follows.

$$B = MDT = \$100{,}000 \times .035 \times \frac{26}{52} = \$1750$$

The cost to the company is the maturity value minus the discount.

$$P = M - B = \$100{,}000 - \$1750 = \$98{,}250$$

Therefore, the U.S. government receives $98,250 from the sale of the T-bill.

(b) *Find the discount period, discount, and proceeds.* Now follow the steps in the table to find the proceeds Benson Automotive receives for selling the T-bill. The discount period is 18 weeks, since the T-bill is sold $26 - 8 = 18$ weeks before its due date.

The discount at the time of the sale is as follows.

$$B = MDT = \$100{,}000 \times .03 \times \frac{18}{52} = \$1038.46$$

Finally, the proceeds equal the maturity value of the T-bill ($100,000) less the discount at the time of the sale.

$$P = M - B = \$100{,}000 - \$1038.46 = \$98{,}961.54$$

(c) Benson Automotive paid $98,250 to buy the T-bill and received $98,961.54 for it 8 weeks later.

$$\text{Interest received} = \$98{,}961.54 - \$98{,}250 = \$711.54$$

$$R = \frac{\$711.54}{\$98{,}250 \times \frac{8}{52}} = 4.71\% \text{ (rounded)}$$

The company would have earned 3.5% on the T-bill had it left the Treasury bill invested until maturity. Instead, the company sold it after market interest rates rose, but before the T-bill matured. This caused the company to end up with an effective interest rate somewhat higher than the 3.5%.

QUICK CHECK 3

A 240-day discount note has a maturity value of $24,000 and a discount rate of 8%. It is sold after 100 days at a discount rate of 10.5%. Find the maturity value of the original discount note and the proceeds at the time of the sale.

▼ 9.4 Exercises   MyMathLab®

The shaded sections below contain solutions to help you get a **QUICK START** *on the various types of exercises.*

Find the discount period for each of the following. (See Examples 2 and 3, Step 2.)

	Date Loan Was Made	Length of Loan	Date of Discount	Discount Period
1.	Apr. 29	200 days	July 31	107 days
2.	July 28	120 days	Sept. 20	_____
3.	May 28	74 days	June 18	_____
4.	Sept. 17	130 days	Jan. 13	_____

Find the proceeds to the nearest cent when each of the following is discounted. (Hint: The maturity value is given.) (See Examples 1 and 2.)

	Maturity Value	Discount Rate	Discount Period	Proceeds
5.	$10,400	8.5%	90 days	$10,179

$B = \$10,400 \times .085 \times \frac{90}{360} = \$221; P = \$10,400 - \$221 = \$10,179$

	Maturity Value	Discount Rate	Discount Period	Proceeds
6.	$4800	10.3%	200 days	_____
7.	$25,000	9%	30 days	_____
8.	$3000	11%	60 days	_____

Find the maturity value of each of the following simple interest notes. Each note is then discounted at 12%. Find the discount period, the discount, and the proceeds after discounting. (See Examples 1 and 2.)

	Date Loan Was Made	Face Value	Length of Loan	Rate	Maturity Value	Date of Discount	Discount Period	Discount	Proceeds
9.	Feb. 7	$6200	90 days	$10\frac{1}{2}$%	$6362.75	Apr. 1	37 days	$78.47	$6284.28

$I = \$6200 \times .105 \times \frac{90}{360} = \$162.75; M = \$6200 + \$162.75 = \$6362.75$
Feb. 7 is day 38; Apr. 1 is day 91; $91 - 38 = 53$
Discount period $= 90 - 53 = 37$ days
$B = \$6362.75 \times .12 \times \frac{37}{360} = \$78.47$
Proceeds $= \$6362.75 - \$78.47 = \$6284.28$

	Date Loan Was Made	Face Value	Length of Loan	Rate	Maturity Value	Date of Discount	Discount Period	Discount	Proceeds
10.	June 15	$9200	140 days	12%	_____	Oct. 22	_____	_____	_____

◭ indicates an exercise that is related to the Case in Point feature.

Date Loan Was Made	Face Value	Length of Loan	Rate	Maturity Value	Date of Discount	Discount Period	Discount	Proceeds
11. July 10	$2000	72 days	11%	_____	Aug. 2	_____	_____	_____
12. May 29	$5500	80 days	10%	_____	July 8	_____	_____	_____

First, find the initial proceeds of each of the following simple discount notes. Each note is then discounted at 11%. Find the discount period, the discount, and the proceeds after discounting. (See Example 3.)

Date Loan Was Made	Maturity Value	Length of Loan	Rate	Initial Proceeds	Date of Discount	Discount Period	Discount	Proceeds at Time of Sale
13. Jan. 12	$17,800	90 days	10%	$17,355	Mar. 1	42 days	$228.43	$17,571.57

$B = MDT = \$17,800 \times .10 \times \frac{90}{360} = \$445$; $P = M - B = \$17,800 - \$445 = \$17,355$
Jan. 12 is day 12; Due date is $12 + 90 = 102$ or Apr. 12
Mar. 1 is day 60; Discount period is $102 - 60 = 42$ days
$B = MDT = \$17,800 \times .11 \times \frac{42}{360} = \$228.43$
$P = M - B = \$17,800 - \$228.43 = \$17,571.57$

Date Loan Was Made	Maturity Value	Length of Loan	Rate	Initial Proceeds	Date of Discount	Discount Period	Discount	Proceeds at Time of Sale
14. Aug. 4	$24,000	120 days	10.5%	_____	Oct. 8	_____	_____	_____
15. May 4	$32,100	150 days	9.5%	_____	July 10	_____	_____	_____
16. Apr. 30	$22,000	200 days	9%	_____	July 12	_____	_____	_____

Solve the following application problems. Round interest and discount to the nearest cent.

17. ROCK CRUSHER   First Bank loaned $360,000 for 180 days to a company purchasing a rock-crushing machine. The bank sold the 7% simple interest note 120 days later at an 8% discount rate. Find **(a)** the bank discount and **(b)** the proceeds.

(a) $4968

(b) $367,632

(a) $M = \$360,000 + (\$360,000 \times .07 \times \frac{180}{360}) = \$372,600$ (b) $P = \$372,600 - \$4968 = \$367,632$
  Discount period $= 180$ days $- 120$ days $= 60$ days
  $B = \$372,600 \times .08 \times \frac{60}{360} = \$4968$

18. **TRACTOR PURCHASE**   Cook and Daughters Farm Equipment accepts a $5800 simple interest note at 12% for 100 days, for a small used tractor. The note is dated May 12. On June 17, the firm discounts the note at the bank, at a 13% discount rate. Find **(a)** the bank discount and **(b)** the proceeds.

(a) _____

(b) _____

19. **JEWELRY**   Hanson's Jewelry signed a 180-day simple discount note with a face value of $250,000 and a rate of 9% on March 19. The lender sells the note at an 8% discount rate on June 14. Find **(a)** the proceeds of the original note, **(b)** the discount period, **(c)** the discount, and **(d)** the proceeds at the sale of the note on June 14.

(a) _____

(b) _____

(c) _____

(d) _____

20. **SEWING CENTER**   Kathy Bates, owner of Marie's Sewing Center, agreed to a 10% simple discount note with a maturity value of $18,500 on July 30. She planned to add to her inventory of sewing machines with the funds. The 120-day note is sold by the lender at a 12% discount rate on September 2. Find **(a)** the proceeds of the original note to Bates, **(b)** the discount period, **(c)** the discount, and **(d)** the proceeds at the sale of the note on September 2.

(a) _____

(b) _____

(c) _____

(d) _____

21. **FINANCING CONSTRUCTION**   To build a new warehouse, Alco Fence Co. signed a $300,000 simple interest note at 9% for 150 days with National Bank on November 20. On February 6, National Bank sold all of its notes to Bank One. Find **(a)** the maturity value of the note and **(b)** the proceeds to National Bank given a discount rate of 10.5%.

(a) _____

(b) _____

22. **BATTERY STORE**   A National Tire and Battery outlet borrowed $48,500 on a 200-day simple interest note to expand the battery store. The note was signed on December 28 and carried an interest rate of 9.8%. The note was then sold on March 17 at a discount rate of 10%. Find **(a)** the maturity value of the note and **(b)** the proceeds to the seller of the note on May 17.

(a) _____

(b) _____

23. **PURCHASE OF A T-BILL**   Elizabeth Barton bought a $25,000, 26-week T-bill at a discount rate of 6.8% on August 7. She sold it 10 weeks later at a discount rate of 7%. Find (a) Barton's purchase price, (b) the discount 10 weeks later when she sold it, (c) the proceeds to Barton, and (d) the effective interest rate rounded to the nearest hundredth of a percent for the time Barton held the note.

(a) _____

(b) _____

(c) _____

(d) _____

24. **PURCHASE OF A T-BILL**   Tina Klein bought a $10,000, 1.5%, 52-week T-bill on June 29 and sold it 26 weeks later at a discount rate of 1%. Find Klein's (a) purchase price for the T-bill, (b) the discount at time of sale, (c) the proceeds to Klein, and (d) the effective interest rate rounded to the nearest hundredth of a percent.

(a) _____

(b) _____

(c) _____

(d) _____

25. Explain the procedure used to determine the bank discount and the proceeds for a note. (See Objective 2.)

26. Explain the effect of a rise in general market interest rates on an investor who is holding notes. Give an example. (See Example 3.)

QUICK CHECK ANSWERS

1. $29,680; $28,228.98   **3.** $24,000; $23,020

2. $9621.67; $9230.39

Supplementary Application Exercises on Simple Interest and Simple Discount

The shaded sections below contain solutions to help you get a **QUICK START** *on the various types of exercises.*

There are similarities and differences between simple interest and simple discount calculations. This exercise set compares these two important concepts. First, the key similarities between the two are as follows.

1. Both types of notes involve lump sums repaid with a single payment at the end of a stated period of time.

2. The length of time is generally 1 year or less.

The following table compares simple interest and simple discount notes.

	Simple Interest Note	Simple Discount Note
Variables	I = Interest P = Principal (face value) R = Rate of interest T = Time, in years or fraction of a year M = Maturity value	B = Discount P = Proceeds D = Discount rate T = Time, in years or fraction of a year M = Maturity value (face value)
Face value	Stated on note	Same as maturity value
Interest charge	$I = PRT$	$B = MDT$
Maturity value	$M = P + I$	Same as face value
Amount received by borrower	Face value or principal	Proceeds: $P = M - B$
Identifying phrases	Interest at a certain rate Maturity value greater than face value	Discount at a certain rate Proceeds Maturity value equal to face value
Effective interest rate	Same as stated rate, R	Greater than stated rate, D

> **Quick TIP**
>
> The variable P is used for *principal or face value* in simple interest notes, but P is used for *proceeds* in simple discount notes. P represents the amount received by the borrower.

Solve the following application problems. Round rates to the nearest tenth of a percent, time to the nearest day, and money to the nearest cent.

1. The owner of Redwood Furniture, Inc., signed a 120-day note for $18,000 at 11% simple interest. Find **(a)** the interest and **(b)** the maturity value.
   (a) $I = PRT = \$18,000 \times .11 \times \frac{120}{360} = \$660$
   (b) $M = \$18,000 + \$660 = \$18,660$

   (a) $\underline{\$660}$
   (b) $\underline{\$18,660}$

2. Bill Travis signed a note for $18,500 with his uncle to start an auto repair shop on Commerce Street. The note is due in 300 days and has a discount rate of 14%. Travis hopes that a bank will refinance the note for him at a lower rate after he has been in business for 300 days. Find the proceeds.
   $B = \$18,500 \times .14 \times \frac{300}{360} = \$2158.33; P = \$18,500 - \$2158.33 = \$16,341.67$

   2. $\underline{\$16,341.67}$

 indicates an exercise that is related to the Case in Point feature.

3. Jessica Hernandez borrowed money to remodel a retail space she had leased for her computer training and Web-design business. She signed a note with a 10% simple interest rate, interest of $4800, and time of 180 days. Find the principal.

3. _____

4. Bill Abel signed a simple interest note at a rate of only 6% because he had excellent collateral—a $200,000 CD at the same bank. If the loan matures in 300 days and the interest is $9000, find the principal.

4. _____

5. Benson Automotive signed a $150,000 note at a simple discount rate of 10.5% and a discount of $8750. Find the length of the loan in days.

5. _____

6. A loan to a German bank was for $1,290,000 with a maturity value of $1,327,410 and a rate of 6%. Find the time.

6. _____

7. Jane Barber loaned her nephew $20,000 for 150 days at 9% simple interest. Find (a) the interest and (b) the maturity value.

(a) _____

(b) _____

8. John O'Neill borrowed $24,000 for 250 days at 7% simple interest. Find (a) the interest and (b) the maturity value.

(a) _____

(b) _____

9. BlueWater Pools signed a 5-month, $145,000 note at an 11.5% discount rate. Find the effective rate of interest.

9. _____

10. James Taylor signed an 80-day, $82,000 note at a 12% discount rate. Find the effective rate of interest.

10. _____

11. On October 14, Citibank loaned $10,000,000 to Fleet Mortgage Company for 180 days at a 10.5% discount rate. Find (a) the due date and (b) the proceeds.

(a) _____

(b) _____

12. On December 24, Junella Martin signed a 100-day note for $80,000 for a Jaguar. Given a discount rate of 11%, find (a) the due date and (b) the proceeds.

(a) _____

(b) _____

13. Lupe Galvez has a serious problem: two of her more energetic preschoolers keep getting out of the yard of her child-care center. She signs a note with interest charges of $670.83 to reinforce the fence around the entire yard. The simple interest note is for 140 days at 11.5%. Find the principal to the nearest dollar.

13. _____

14. Quality Furnishings accepted a 270-day, $8000 note on May 25. The interest rate on the note is 12% simple interest. The note was then discounted at 14% on August 7. Find the proceeds.

14. _____

15. On November 19, a firm accepts an $18,000, 150-day note with a simple interest rate of 9%. The firm discounts the note at 12% on February 2. Find the proceeds.

15. _____

16. Barton's Flowers accepted a $16,000, 150-day note from Wedded Bliss Catering. The note had a simple interest rate of 11% and was accepted on May 12. The note was then discounted at 13% on July 20. Find the proceeds to Barton's Flowers.

16. _____

17. Herbert Leon signed a 220-day, 10% simple interest note with a face value of $28,000. In turn, the bank he borrowed the money from sold the note 90 days later at an 11% discount rate. Find **(a)** the interest, **(b)** the maturity value, **(c)** the discount period, **(d)** the discount, and **(e)** the proceeds to the bank.

(a) _____
(b) _____
(c) _____
(d) _____
(e) _____

18. Janice Dart signed a 140-day simple discount note at a rate of 9.9% with a maturity value of $82,000. The bank she borrowed the funds from sold the note 40 days later at a 10% discount rate. Find **(a)** the discount on the original note, **(b)** the proceeds of the original note, **(c)** the discount period, **(d)** the discount at the time of sale, and **(e)** the proceeds to the bank at the time of sale.

(a) _____
(b) _____
(c) _____
(d) _____
(e) _____

19. James and Tiffany Paterson need a 220-day loan for $68,000 to open Adventure Sports Unlimited. Bank One agrees to a simple interest note with a loan amount of $68,000 at $9\frac{1}{4}$% interest. Union Bank agrees to a simple discount note with proceeds of $68,000 and a 9.5% simple discount rate. Find **(a)** the interest for the simple interest note, **(b)** the maturity value of the discount note, **(c)** the interest for the discount note, and **(d)** the savings in interest charges of the simple interest note over the discount note.

(a) _____
(b) _____
(c) _____
(d) _____

20. Gilbert Construction Company needs to borrow \$380,000 for $1\frac{1}{2}$ years to purchase some land to subdivide. One bank offers the firm a simple interest note with a principal of \$380,000 and a rate of 12%. A second bank offers the company a discount note with proceeds of \$380,000 and an 11% discount rate. **(a)** Which note produces the lower interest charges? **(b)** What is the difference in interest?

(a) _____

(b) _____

21. Show with an example that the effective interest rate is higher than the discount rate stated on a note.

22. Explain the difference in the meaning of the variable P (principal) in a simple interest note and the variable P (proceeds) in a simple discount note.

23. What is interest? Why is interest used?

24. Why might a bank use ordinary interest rather than exact interest?

▼ **Chapter 9**   Quick Review

Chapter Terms   *Review the following terms to test your understanding of the chapter. For each term you do not know, refer to the page number found next to that term.*

annual percentage rate (APR) **[p. 350]**
bank discount **[p. 347]**
banker's interest **[p. 332]**
bankruptcy **[p. 328]**
collateral **[p. 334]**
compound interest **[p. 328]**
cosign **[p. 329]**
discount **[p. 356]**
discounting the note **[p. 356]**
discount period **[p. 356]**
discount rate **[p. 356]**

due date **[p. 333]**
effective rate of interest **[p. 350]**
exact interest **[p. 332]**
face value **[p. 347]**
factoring **[p. 358]**
factors **[p. 358]**
foreclose **[p. 334]**
interest **[p. 358]**
interest-in-advance notes **[p. 347]**
loan amount **[p. 347]**

maker of a note **[p. 333]**
maturity date **[p. 333]**
maturity value **[p. 347]**
nominal rate **[p. 350]**
ordinary interest **[p. 332]**
payee of a note **[p. 333]**
payer of a note **[p. 333]**
prime rate **[p. 328]**
principal **[p. 328]**
proceeds of a note **[p. 333]**
promissory note **[p. 333]**
rate **[p. 328]**

recourse **[p. 356]**
simple discount note **[p. 347]**
simple interest **[p. 328]**
simple interest note **[p. 333]**
Stafford loan **[p. 347]**
stated rate **[p. 350]**
T-bills **[p. 351]**
term of a note **[p. 333]**
time **[p. 328]**
true rate of interest **[p. 351]**
Truth in Lending Act **[p. 350]**
U.S. Treasury bills **[p. 351]**

CONCEPTS

EXAMPLES

9.1 Finding the simple interest when time is expressed in years

1. Use the formula $I = PRT$.
2. Express R in decimal form.
3. Express time in years.
4. Substitute values for P, R, and T and multiply.

A loan of $28,000 is made for $1\frac{1}{4}$ years at 10% per year. Find the simple interest.

$$I = PRT$$
$$I = \$28,000 \times .10 \times 1.25 = \$3500$$

The simple interest is $3500.

9.1 Finding the simple interest when time is expressed in months

1. Use the formula $I = PRT$.
2. Express R in decimal form.
3. Express time in years by dividing the number of months by 12.
4. Substitute values for P, R, and T and multiply.

Find the simple interest on $24,000 for 8 months at 10%.

$$I = PRT$$
$$I = \$24,000 \times .10 \times \frac{8}{12} = \$1600$$

The simple interest is $1600.

9.1 Finding the maturity value of a loan

1. Find I using the formula $I = PRT$.
2. Find the maturity value using the formula $M = P + I$.

A loan of $8500 is made for 1 year at 9%. Find the maturity value of the loan.

$$I = PRT$$
$$I = \$8500 \times .09 \times 1 = \$765$$
$$M = P + I$$
$$M = \$8500 + \$765 = \$9265$$

The maturity value is $9265.

9.1 Finding the number of days from one date to another using a table

1. Find the day corresponding to the final date using the table.
2. Find the day corresponding to the initial date.
3. Subtract the smaller number from the larger number.

Find the number of days from February 15 to July 28.
1. July 28 is day 209.
2. Feb. 15 is day 46.
3. Number of days is

$$\begin{array}{r} 209 \\ -\ 46 \\ \hline 163 \end{array}$$

There are 163 days from February 15 to July 28.

CONCEPTS	EXAMPLES
9.1 Finding the number of days from one date to another using actual number of days in a month Add the actual number of days in each month or partial month from initial date to final date.	Find the number of days from April 20 to June 27. April 20 to April 30 **10 days** May **31 days** June **27 days** **68 days**

9.1 Finding the exact interest

Use the formula

$$I = PRT$$

with $T = \dfrac{\text{Number of days of loan}}{365}$

Find the exact interest on a $9000 loan at 8% for 140 days.

$$I = PRT$$

$$I = \$9000 \times .08 \times \frac{140}{365} = \$276.16$$

The exact interest is $276.16.

9.1 Finding the ordinary, or banker's, interest

Use the formula

$$I = PRT$$

with $T = \dfrac{\text{Number of days of loan}}{360}$

Find the ordinary interest on a loan of $14,000 at 7% for 120 days.

$$I = PRT$$

$$I = \$14,000 \times .07 \times \frac{120}{360} = \$326.67$$

The ordinary, or banker's, interest is $326.67.

9.1 Finding the due date, interest, and maturity value of a simple interest promissory note when the term of the loan is in months

1. Add the number of months in the term of the note to the initial date of note.
2. Use the formula $I = PRT$ to find interest.
3. Find the maturity value as follows.

Maturity value = Principal + Interest

Find the due date, the interest, and the maturity value of a loan made on February 15 for 7 months at 8% with a face value of $9400.

September 15 is 7 months from February 15, so the note is due on September 15.

$$I = PRT$$

$$I = \$9400 \times .08 \times \frac{7}{12} = \$438.67$$

$$M = \textbf{Principal} + \textbf{Interest}$$

$$M = \$9400 + \$438.67 = \$9838.67$$

9.1 Finding the due date of a promissory note when the term of the loan is expressed in days

Use either a table or the actual number of days in each month.

A loan is made on August 14 and is due in 80 days. Find the due date.

August 14 to August 31   17 days
September   30 days
October   31 days
  78 days

The loan is for 80 days, which is 2 days more than 78. Therefore, the loan is due on November 2.

9.2 Finding the principal given the interest, interest rate, and time

Use the formula

$$P = \frac{I}{RT}$$

$$P = \frac{I}{RT}$$

Find the principal that produces interest of $240 at 9% for 60 days.

$$P = \frac{I}{RT}$$

$$P = \frac{\$240}{.09 \times \dfrac{60}{360}} = \$16,000$$

The principal is $16,000.

CONCEPTS	EXAMPLES
9.2 Finding the rate of interest given the principal, interest, and time Use the formula $$R = \frac{I}{PT}$$ $$R = \frac{I}{PT}$$	A principal of \$8000 deposited for 45 days earns interest of \$75. Find the rate of interest. $$R = \frac{I}{PT}$$ $$R = \frac{\$75}{\$8000 \times \dfrac{45}{360}} = .075$$ Rate of interest = 7.5%.
9.2 Finding the time given the principal, rate of interest, and interest To find the time in days, use the formula $$T \text{ (in days)} = \frac{I}{PR} \times 360$$ To find the time in months, use the formula $$T \text{ (in months)} = \frac{I}{PR} \times 12$$ $$T = \frac{I}{PR}$$	Tom Jones invested \$8000 at 8% and earned interest of \$320. Find the time of the loan in days. $$T = \frac{I}{PR} \times 360$$ $$T = \frac{\$320}{\$8000 \times .08} \times 360 = 180 \text{ days}$$ The loan was for 180 days.
9.3 Finding the proceeds of a simple discount note Calculate the bank discount using the formula $B = MDT$. Then calculate the proceeds or loan amount using the formula $P = M - B$.	Karen Pattern borrows \$12,000 for 120 days at a discount rate of 9%. Find the proceeds. $$B = MDT$$ $$B = \$12,000 \times .09 \times \frac{120}{360} = \$360$$ $$P = M - B$$ $$P = \$12,000 - \$360 = \$11,640$$
9.3 Finding the face value of a simple discount note Use the formula $$M = \frac{P}{1 - DT}$$	Sam Spade needs \$15,000 for new equipment for his restaurant. Find the face value of a note that will provide the \$15,000 in proceeds if he plans to repay the note in 180 days and the bank charges an 11% discount rate. $$M = \frac{P}{1 - DT}$$ $$M = \frac{\$15,000}{1 - \left(.11 \times \dfrac{180}{360}\right)} = \$15,873.02 \text{ (rounded)}$$
9.3 Finding the effective interest rate Find the interest (B) from the formula $$B = MDT$$ Find proceeds from the formula $$P = M - B$$ Then use the formula $$R = \frac{I}{PT}$$	A 150-day, 11% simple discount note has a face value of \$12,400. Find the effective rate to the nearest tenth of a percent. $$B = \$12,400 \times .11 \times \frac{150}{360} = \$568.33$$ $$P = \$12,400 - \$568.33 = \$11,831.67$$ $$R = \frac{\$568.33}{\$11,831.67 \times \dfrac{150}{360}} = 11.5\% \text{ (rounded)}$$

CONCEPTS

EXAMPLES

9.4 Finding the proceeds to an individual or firm that discounts a simple interest note

1. If necessary, find
   (a) the **due date** of the original note and
   (b) the **maturity value** of the original note ($M = P + I$, where $I = PRT$).

Moe's Ice Cream holds a 150-day note dated March 1 with a face value of $15,000 and a simple interest rate of 9%. Moe sells the note at a discount on June 1. Assume a discount rate of 11%. Find the proceeds.

1. Due date = day 60 (March 1) + 150 days = day 210 or July 29

$$I = PRT = \$15{,}000 \times .09 \times \frac{150}{360} = \textbf{\$562.50}$$

$$M = P + I = \$15{,}000 + \textbf{\$562.50} = \textbf{\$15,562.50}$$

2. (a) Find the **discount period**, which is the time (e.g., number of days) from the sale of the note to the maturity date of the note.
   (b) Find the **discount** using the formula $B = MDT$.
   (c) Find the **proceeds** using $P = M - B$.

2. (a) The discount period is 58 days.

(b) Bank discount = MDT

$$B = \textbf{\$15,562.50} \times .11 \times \frac{58}{360} = \$275.80$$

(c) Proceeds = $M - B$

$$D = \textbf{\$15,562.50} - \$275.80 = \$15{,}286.70$$

9.4 Finding the proceeds to an individual or firm that discounts a simple discount note

1. If necessary, find
   (a) the **due date** of the original note,
   (b) the **discount** of the original note using $B = MDT$, and
   (c) the **proceeds** from the original note using $P = M - B$.

   The **maturity value (face value)** of the note is written on the note itself.

2. (a) Find the **discount period**, which is the time (e.g., number of days) from the sale of the note to the maturity date of the note.
   (b) Find the **discount** using the formula $B = MDT$.
   (c) Find the **proceeds** using $P = M - B$.

On May 10, Applecrest Orchards signed a 120-day note for $22,000 at a simple discount rate of 10%. The note was sold on June 30 at a discount rate of 10.5%. Find **(a)** the proceeds from the original note and **(b)** the proceeds at the time of sale.

(a) Due date is day 130 (May 10) + 120 days = day 250 or Sept. 7

$$B = MDT = \$22{,}000 \times .10 \times \frac{120}{360} = \textbf{\$733.33}$$

$$P = M - B = \$22{,}000 - \textbf{\$733.33} = \$21{,}266.67$$

(b) June 30 is day 181
   Discount period is 250 − 181 = 69 days

$$B = MDT = \$22{,}000 \times .105 \times \frac{69}{360} = \textbf{\$442.75}$$

(c) $P = M - B = \$22{,}000 - \textbf{\$442.75} = \$21{,}557.25$

Case Study

BANKING IN A GLOBAL WORLD:
HOW DO LARGE BANKS MAKE MONEY?

Bank of America borrowed $80,000,000 at 5% interest for 180 days from a Japanese investment house. At the same time, the bank made the following three loans, each for the exact same 180-day period:

1. A 7% *simple interest note* for $38,000,000 to a Canadian firm that extracts oil from Canadian tar sands;

2. An 8.2% *simple discount note* for $27,500,000 to a European contractor building a factory in South Africa; and

3. An 8% *simple discount note* for $14,500,000 to a Louisiana company building minesweepers in New Orleans for the British government.

   (a) Find the difference between interest received and interest paid by the bank on these funds.

   (a) _____

   (b) The bank did not loan out all $80,000,000. Find the amount it actually loaned out.

   (b) _____

   (c) Find the effective rate of interest to the nearest hundredth of a percent.

   (c) _____

   This seems like a low rate. However, this is the amount the bank earned over and above that paid out to the Japanese investment house on the same funds.

INVESTIGATE

The very idea of interest is not acceptable in Muslim countries where a bank takes partial ownership of a company when it lends to a company, at least until funds are repaid. Even in countries that do allow interest, interest rates vary considerably. Use financial newspapers, magazines, or the World Wide Web to find interest rates in three different countries and compare them to those in the United States.

▼Case in Point Summary Exercise

APPLE, INC.

www.apple.com

Facts:

- 1976: Founded
- 1984: Introduced Macintosh
- 2001: Introduced iPod
- 2003: Opened iTunes Music Store
- 2007: Introduced iPhone
- 2010: Introduced iPad

After opening her own computer and web-design business, Jessica Hernandez checked into selling Apple's popular iPhones. But she was not able to sell them since Apple allowed only a few large companies to sell them. So, Hernandez focused on computer training classes as she built her reputation designing Web pages for small firms. She knew that she needed to borrow some money as her business grew and wondered how to go about it.

1. Hernandez decided to borrow $85,000 for 10 months. She found that banks would lend to her only if she had a cosigner on the note—fortunately her uncle was a successful business owner and he agreed to cosign. Bank One offered the funds at a 10% simple discount. Find the maturity value of the loan and the discount.

   1. _____

2. Once Hernandez's uncle agreed to cosign on a loan, Union Bank offered to lend Hernandez $85,000 at 10.5% simple interest. Find the interest and maturity value.

   2. _____

3. Find the loan with the lower interest and find the difference in interest.

   3. _____

4. Find the effective interest rate for both loans to the nearest hundredth of a percent.

   4. _____

Bank	Interest	Loan Amount	Effective Rate
Bank One	$7727.27	$85,000	
Union Bank	$7437.50	$85,000	

Discussion Question: *Assume Hernandez has successfully managed her business for several years. List five reasons she may still need to borrow from time to time.*

Source: Apple, Inc., www.apple.com.

▼ Chapter 9 Test

To help you review, the numbers in brackets show the section in which the topic was discussed.

Find the simple interest for each of the following. Round to the nearest cent. **[9.1]**

1. $12,500 at $10\frac{1}{2}$% simple interest for 280 days

1. _____

2. $8250 at $9\frac{1}{4}$% simple interest for 8 months

2. _____

3. A loan of $6000 at 11% simple interest made on June 8 and due August 22

3. _____

4. A promissory note for $4500 at 10.3% simple interest made on November 13 and due March 8

4. _____

5. Joan Davies signed a 140-day simple interest note for $12,500 with a bank that uses *exact* interest. If the rate is 10.7%, find the maturity value. **[9.1]**

5. _____

6. Chez Bazan Bakery borrowed $24,300 for a new commercial oven. The simple interest loan was repaid in 6 months at $10\frac{1}{2}$%. Find the amount of the repayment. **[9.1]**

6. _____

7. Glenda Pierce plans to borrow $14,000 for a new hot tub and deck for her home. She has decided on a term of 200 days at 10.5% simple interest. However, she has a choice of two lenders. One calculates interest using a 360-day year and the other uses a 365-day year. Find the amount of interest Pierce will save by using the lender with the 365-day year. **[9.1]**

7. _____

8. Lupe Gonzalez has $6500 in her retirement account. Find the simple interest rate required for the fund to grow to $7247.50 in 15 months. **[9.2]**

8. _____

9. Hilda Heinz lends $1200 to her sister Olga at a rate of 9%. Find how long it will take for her investment to earn $100 in interest. (Round to the nearest day.) **[9.2]**

9. _____

10. A woman invested money received from an insurance settlement for 7 months at 5% simple interest. If she received $1254.17 interest on her investment during this time, find the amount that she invested. (Round to the nearest dollar.) **[9.2]**

10. _____

11. Mike Fagan needs $25,000 to expand his flower shop. Find the face value of a simple discount note that will provide the $25,000 in proceeds if he plans to repay the note in 240 days and the bank charges a 9% discount rate. **[9.3]**

11. _____

Find the discount and the proceeds for the following simple discount notes.   **[9.3]**

	Face Value	Discount Rate	Time (Days)	Discount	Proceeds
12.	$9800	11%	120	_____	_____
13.	$10,250	9.5%	60	_____	_____

14. Barbara Waters signed a simple discount note for $15,000 for 120 days at a rate of 9%. Find **(a)** the proceeds and **(b)** the effective interest rate based on the proceeds received by Waters.   **[9.3]**

(a) _____

(b) _____

15. Lizabeth Neault needed funds to open a law office. She borrowed $28,400 at 8.5% simple interest for 150 days on July 7. The bank she borrowed from sold the note at a 9% discount on August 20. Find the proceeds to the bank.   **[9.4]**

15. _____

16. A 90-day simple discount promissory note for $9200 with a simple discount rate of 11% was signed on January 25. It was discounted on March 2 at 12%. Find the proceeds at the time of the sale.   **[9.4]**

16. _____

17. A $20,000 T-bill is purchased at a 3.75% discount rate for 13 weeks. Find **(a)** the purchase price of the T-bill, **(b)** the maturity value, **(c)** the interest earned, and **(d)** the effective rate of interest to the nearest hundredth of a percent.   **[9.3]**

(a) _____

(b) _____

(c) _____

(d) _____

The following note was discounted at $12\frac{1}{2}\%$. Find the discount period, the discount, and the proceeds.   **[9.4]**

	Date Loan Was Made	Face Value	Length of Loan	Rate	Date of Discount	Discount Period	Discount	Proceeds
18.	Jan. 25	$9200	90 days	10%	Mar. 12	_____	_____	_____

19. Jan Guerra lends $9000 to her second cousin using a 180-day 10% simple interest note that was signed on October 30. Guerra subsequently has a car accident and desperately needs money, so she sells the note at a discount of 15% on January 3 to an investor. Find **(a)** the discount, **(b)** the proceeds, and **(c)** the amount of money Guerra gains or loses.   **[9.4]**

(a) _____

(b) _____

(c) _____

10 Compound Interest and Inflation

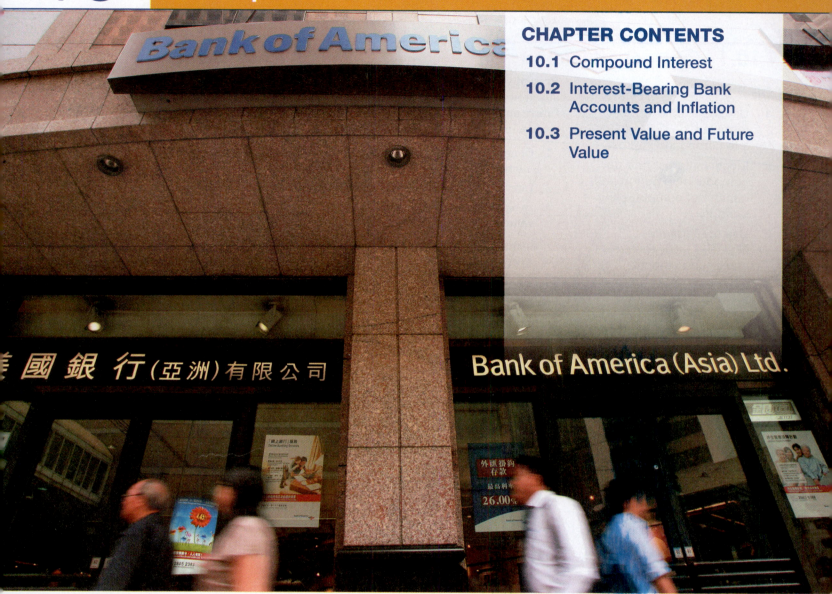

CHAPTER CONTENTS

10.1 Compound Interest

10.2 Interest-Bearing Bank Accounts and Inflation

10.3 Present Value and Future Value

▼ CASE IN POINT

In the aftermath of the financial crisis that began in 2008, Bank of America took over Countrywide Financial (home loans) and Merrill Lynch (investments) with the support and help of the U.S. government. The government was trying to soften the effects of the crisis and was actively involved in finding solvent companies to take over failing companies. Bank of America has become a giant in the global financial services world with offices all over the world.

Interest is only calculated and credited once in **simple interest** loans. On the other hand, interest is credited more often than once during the life of a **compound interest** loan. Compound interest loans are the foundations of modern finance and are very common.

▼10.1 Compound Interest

OBJECTIVES

1 Use the simple interest formula $I = PRT$ to calculate compound interest.

2 Identify interest rate per compounding period and number of compounding periods.

3 Use the formula $M = P(1 + i)^n$ to find compound amount.

4 Use the table to find compound amount.

"The most powerful force in the universe is compound interest."—Albert Einstein

Present value is the value of an investment today, right now. Money left in an investment usually grows over time. The amount in an investment at a specific future date is called the **future amount**, **compound amount**, or **future value**. The future value depends not only on the amount initially invested, it also depends on the following:

1. **Compound interest—Compound interest results in a greater future value than simple interest.**
2. **Interest rate—A higher rate results in a greater future value.**
3. **Length of investment—An investment held longer usually results in a greater future value.**

To see the effects of these, compare the future values of a $10,000 investment using the following table:

Investments A and B show the value of compound interest over simple interest.
Investments B and C show the value of a higher interest rate.
Investments C and D show the value of a longer investment period.

Investment	Term	Annual Rate	Interest	Future Value
A. Simple interest	6 years	5%	$3,000	$13,000
B. Compound interest	6 years	5%	$3,401	$13,401
C. Compound interest	6 years	8%	$5,869	$15,869
D. Compound interest	10 years	8%	$11,589	$21,589

It is no coincidence that most wealthy people are older. It takes time for compound interest to work. The graph shows the power of compound interest over time using an investment of $10,000 earning 5% and 8% per year. You can use compound interest over time to build assets.

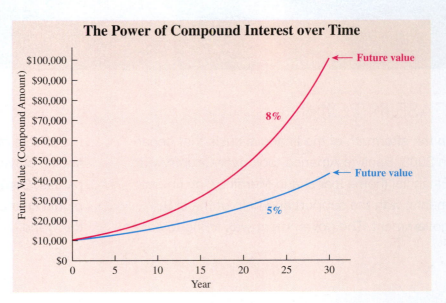

The Power of Compound Interest over Time

OBJECTIVE 1 Use the simple interest formula $I = PRT$ to calculate compound interest. **Compound interest** is interest calculated on previously credited interest in addition to the original principal. Compound interest calculations often require that interest be calculated and credited to an account more than once each year. Examples 1 and 2 show how the simple interest formula can be used to find compound interest. Later in this section, we show easier methods for finding compound interest.

Comparing Simple to Compound Interest

EXAMPLE 1

Regina Foster wants to compare simple interest to compound interest on a $2000 investment.

(a) Find the interest if funds earn 6% simple interest for 1 year.

(b) Find the interest if funds earn 6% interest compounded every 6 months for 1 year.

(c) Find the difference between the two.

(d) Find the effective rate for both.

SOLUTION

(a) Simple interest on $2000 at 6% *for 1 year* is found as follows.

$$I = PRT = \$2000 \times .06 \times 1 = \$120$$

(b) Interest compounded every 6 months means that interest must be calculated at the end of each 6-months using $I = PRT$. Add interest to principal before proceeding.

$$\text{Interest for first 6 months} = PRT = \$2000 \times .06 \times \tfrac{1}{2} = \$60$$
$$\text{Principal at end of first 6 months} = \text{Original principal} + \text{Interest}$$
$$= \$2000 + \$60 = \$2060$$

The new principal of $2060 earns interest for the second 6 months.

$$\text{Interest for second 6 months} = PRT = \$2060 \times .06 \times \tfrac{1}{2} = \$61.80$$
$$\text{Principal at end of 1 year} = \$2060 + \$61.80 = \$2121.80$$

The interest earned in the second 6 months ($61.80) is larger than that earned in the first 6 months ($60), since the first interest amount of $60 is also earning interest during the second 6 months.

$$\text{Total compound interest} = \$60 + \$61.80 = \$121.80$$

(c) Difference in interest = $121.80 − $120 = $1.80.

Compound interest results in more interest. The difference here of $1.80 seems trivial, but compound interest results in *huge differences* over time as you will see shortly!

(d) The effective interest rate is the interest for the year divided by the original investment.

Effective Interest Rate

Funds earning 6% simple interest
$$\frac{\$120}{\$2000} = 6\%$$

Funds earning 6% compounded every 6 months
$$\frac{\$121.80}{\$2000} = 6.1\% \text{ (rounded)}$$

Although they have the same nominal rate (6%), the compound interest investment has a larger effective interest rate due to compounding.

> **Quick TIP**
>
> Round interest amounts to the nearest cent each time interest is calculated.

QUICK CHECK 1

$15,000 is invested for 1 year. Find the future value based on (a) simple interest of 8% and (b) 8% interest compounded every 6 months. (c) Then find the difference between the two.

Repeat the following steps to find the future value of an investment involving compound interest.

> **Finding Future Value (Compound Amount)**
>
> 1. Use $I = PRT$ to find simple interest for the period.
>
> 2. Add principal at the end of the previous period to the interest for the current period to find the principal at the end of the current period.

Finding Compound Interest

EXAMPLE 2

The Simpsons need $5000 in 4 years for a down payment on a new car. They invest $3800 in an investment that pays 6% interest compounded annually. (a) Find the excess of compound interest over simple interest at the end of 4 years. (b) Will they have enough money to meet their goal?

SOLUTION

First calculate interest using $I = PRT$ and round to the nearest cent. Then find the new principal by adding the interest earned to the preceding principal.

(a)

Year	$P \times R \times T$ Interest	$P + I$ Compound Amount
1	$\$3800.00 \times .06 \times 1 = \$228.00$	$\$3800.00 + \$228.00 = \$4028.00$
2	$\$4028.00 \times .06 \times 1 = \$241.68$	$\$4028.00 + \$241.68 = \$4269.68$
3	$\$4269.68 \times .06 \times 1 = \$256.18$	$\$4269.68 + \$256.18 = \$4525.86$
4	$\$4525.86 \times .06 \times 1 = \$271.55$	$\$4525.86 + \$271.55 = \$4797.41$

Compound interest $= \$4797.41 - \$3800 = \$997.41$

Simple interest $= PRT = \$3800 \times .06 \times 4 = \$912$

Difference $= \$997.41 - \$912 = \$85.41$

(b) No, but almost! They will be short of their goal by $\$5000 - \$4797.41 = \$202.59$.

> **QUICK CHECK 2**
>
> Find the future amount at the end of 2 years for an $80,000 investment that earns 7% per year.

OBJECTIVE 2 Identify interest rate per compounding period and number of compounding periods. The **compounding period** is the time over which interest is calculated and added to principal. It can be annually (once a year), semiannually (two times a year), quarterly (four times a year), monthly (12 times a year), etc. The **number of compounding periods** is the number of the compounding periods per year, or in the life of the loan when talking about a loan.

Interest Compounded	Compound at the End of Every	Number of Compounding Periods in 1 Year
Semiannually	6 months	2
Quarterly	3 months	4
Monthly	1 month	12
Daily	1 day	365*

*Leap year has 366 compounding periods.

The **interest rate per compounding period** is the interest rate applied to each compounding period. It is found by dividing the annual interest rate by the number of compounding periods in a year. The total number of compounding periods is the number per year times the number of years as shown. So, a loan compounded semiannually for 4 years will be compounded every 6 months for 4 years, or 8 times.

Rate	Compounded	Number of Compounding Periods Per Year	Term	Rate Per Compounding Period	Total Number of Compounding Periods
8%	semiannually	2	4 years	$\frac{8\%}{2} = 4\%$	4 years $\times$ 2 per year $= 8$
12%	monthly	12	$2\frac{1}{2}$ years	$\frac{12\%}{12} = 1\%$	$2\frac{1}{2}$ years $\times$ 12 per year $= 30$
4%	quarterly	4	5 years	$\frac{4\%}{4} = 1\%$	5 years $\times$ 4 per year $= 20$

Finding the Interest Rate per Compounding Period and the Number of Compounding Periods

EXAMPLE 3 Find the interest rate per compounding period and the number of compounding periods for each.

(a) 5% compounded semiannually, 3 years

(b) 6% per year, compounded monthly, $2\frac{1}{2}$ years

(c) 2% per year, compounded quarterly, 5 years

SOLUTION

(a) 5% compounded semiannually is $\frac{5\%}{2} = 2.5\%$ credited at the end of each 6 months. There are 3 years $\times$ 2 periods per year $= 6$ compounding periods in 3 years.

(b) 6% per year, compounded monthly, results in $\frac{6\%}{12} = .5\%$ credited at the end of each month. There are 2.5 years $\times$ 12 periods per year $= 30$ compounding periods in 2.5 years.

(c) 2% per year, compounded quarterly, results in $\frac{2\%}{4} = .5\%$ credited at the end of each quarter. There are 5 years $\times$ 4 periods per year $= 20$ compounding periods in 5 years.

QUICK CHECK 3

A loan requires that the 8% interest be compounded quarterly for 6 years. Find the interest rate per compounding period and the number of compounding periods.

OBJECTIVE 3 Use the formula $M = P(1 + i)^n$ to find compound amount. The **formula for compound interest** uses **exponents**, which is a short way of writing repeated products. For example,

Exponent: Multiply the base by itself 3 times.

$$2 \times 2 \times 2 = 2^3$$

base

Also, $4^2 = 4 \times 4 = 16$, and $5^4 = 5 \times 5 \times 5 \times 5 = 625$.

Assume that P dollars are deposited at a rate of interest i per compounding period for n periods. Then the compound amount and the interest are found as follows. So,

$$i = \frac{\text{rate per year}}{\text{number of compounding periods in a year}} \quad \text{and } n = \text{number of compounding periods per year} \times \text{number of years}$$

Formulas for Compounding Interest
Maturity value $= M = P(1 + i)^n$ where P = initial investment
Interest $= I = M - P$ n = total number of compounding periods
                                                i = interest rate per compounding period

---

It is important to keep in mind that i is the interest rate *per compounding period*, not per year. Also, n is *the total number of compounding periods*.

Finding Compound Interest

EXAMPLE 4

An investment managed by Bank of America pays 7% interest per year compounded semiannually. Given an initial deposit of $4500, **(a)** use the formula to find the compound amount after 5 years, and **(b)** find the compound interest.

SOLUTION

(a) Interest is compounded at $\frac{7\%}{2} = 3.5\%$ every 6 months for 5 years $\times$ 2 periods per year $=$ 10 periods. Therefore, 3.5% is the interest rate per compounding period (i) and 10 is the number of compounding periods (n).

$$M = P(1 + i)^n$$
$$= \$4500 \times (1 + .035)^{10}$$
$$= \$4500 \times (1.035)^{10}$$
$$= \$6347.69 \quad (\textbf{rounded})$$

The compound amount is $6347.69.

(b)
$$I = M - P$$
$$= \$6347.69 - \$4500 = \$1847.69$$

The interest is $1847.69.

The calculator solution for part **(a)** is as follows.

 4500 ⊠ ⟮ 1 ⊞ .035 ⟯ y^x 10 ⊟ $6347.69 (rounded)

Note: Refer to Appendix B for calculator basics.

QUICK CHECK 4

Use the formula for maturity value to find the compound amount and interest on a $9000 investment at 2% compounded semiannually for 5 years.

Parents believe their children should study personal finance. The following pie chart indicates when parents believe this education should begin.

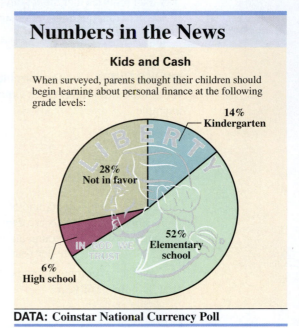

Numbers in the News

Kids and Cash

When surveyed, parents thought their children should begin learning about personal finance at the following grade levels:

14%
Kindergarten

28%
Not in favor

52%
Elementary school

6%
High school

DATA: Coinstar National Currency Poll

OBJECTIVE 4 Use the table to find compound amount. The value of $(1 + i)^n$ in the formula $M = P(1 + i)^n$ can be calculated using a calculator, or it can be found in the compound interest table below. The interest rate i at the top of the table is the interest rate *per compounding period*. The value of n down the far left (or far right) column of the table is *the total number of compounding periods*. The value in the body of the table is the compound amount, or maturity value, for each $1 in principal.

Compound Interest Table

Interest Rate Per Compounding Period

Period	1%	$1\frac{1}{2}$%	2%	$2\frac{1}{2}$%	3%	4%	5%	6%	8%	10%	Period
1	1.01000	1.01500	1.02000	1.02500	1.03000	1.04000	1.05000	1.06000	1.08000	1.10000	1
2	1.02010	1.03023	1.04040	1.05063	1.06090	1.08160	1.10250	1.12360	1.16640	1.21000	2
3	1.03030	1.04568	1.06121	1.07689	1.09273	1.12486	1.15763	1.19102	1.25971	1.33100	3
4	1.04060	1.06136	1.08243	1.10381	1.12551	1.16986	1.21551	1.26248	1.36049	1.46410	4
5	1.05101	1.07728	1.10408	1.13141	1.15927	1.21665	1.27628	1.33823	1.46933	1.61051	5
6	1.06152	1.09344	1.12616	1.15969	1.19405	1.26532	1.34010	1.41852	1.58687	1.77156	6
7	1.07214	1.10984	1.14869	1.18869	1.22987	1.31593	1.40710	1.50363	1.71382	1.94872	7
8	1.08286	1.12649	1.17166	1.21840	1.26677	1.36857	1.47746	1.59385	1.85093	2.14359	8
9	1.09369	1.14339	1.19509	1.24886	1.30477	1.42331	1.55133	1.68948	1.99900	2.35795	9
10	1.10462	1.16054	1.21899	1.28008	1.34392	1.48024	1.62889	1.79085	2.15892	2.59374	10
11	1.11567	1.17795	1.24337	1.31209	1.38423	1.53945	1.71034	1.89830	2.33164	2.85312	11
12	1.12683	1.19562	1.26824	1.34489	1.42576	1.60103	1.79586	2.01220	2.51817	3.13843	12
13	1.13809	1.21355	1.29361	1.37851	1.46853	1.66507	1.88565	2.13293	2.71962	3.45227	13
14	1.14947	1.23176	1.31948	1.41297	1.51259	1.73168	1.97993	2.26090	2.93719	3.79750	14
15	1.16097	1.25023	1.34587	1.44830	1.55797	1.80094	2.07893	2.39656	3.17217	4.17725	15
16	1.17258	1.26899	1.37279	1.48451	1.60471	1.87298	2.18287	2.54035	3.42594	4.59497	16
17	1.18430	1.28802	1.40024	1.52162	1.65285	1.94790	2.29202	2.69277	3.70002	5.05447	17
18	1.19615	1.30734	1.42825	1.55966	1.70243	2.02582	2.40662	2.85434	3.99602	5.55992	18
19	1.20811	1.32695	1.45681	1.59865	1.75351	2.10685	2.52695	3.02560	4.31570	6.11591	19
20	1.22019	1.34686	1.48595	1.63862	1.80611	2.19112	2.65330	3.20714	4.66096	6.72750	20
21	1.23239	1.36706	1.51567	1.67958	1.86029	2.27877	2.78596	3.39956	5.03383	7.40025	21
22	1.24472	1.38756	1.54598	1.72157	1.91610	2.36992	2.92526	3.60354	5.43654	8.14027	22
23	1.25716	1.40838	1.57690	1.76461	1.97359	2.46472	3.07152	3.81975	5.87146	8.95430	23
24	1.26973	1.42950	1.60844	1.80873	2.03279	2.56330	3.22510	4.04893	6.34118	9.84973	24
25	1.28243	1.45095	1.64061	1.85394	2.09378	2.66584	3.38635	4.29187	6.84848	10.83471	25
26	1.29526	1.47271	1.67342	1.90029	2.15659	2.77247	3.55567	4.54938	7.39635	11.91818	26
27	1.30821	1.49480	1.70689	1.94780	2.22129	2.88337	3.73346	4.82235	7.98806	13.10999	27
28	1.32129	1.51722	1.74102	1.99650	2.28793	2.99870	3.92013	5.11169	8.62711	14.42099	28
29	1.33450	1.53998	1.77584	2.04641	2.35657	3.11865	4.11614	5.41839	9.31727	15.86309	29
30	1.34785	1.56308	1.81136	2.09757	2.42726	3.24340	4.32194	5.74349	10.06266	17.44940	30

> **Finding Compound Amount (Future Value)**
>
> Compound amount = Principal × Number from compound interest table

Finding Compound Interest

> ◆ EXAMPLE 5

In each case, find the interest earned on a $2000 deposit.

(a) For 3 years, compounded annually at 4%

(b) For 5 years, compounded semiannually at 6%

(c) For 6 years, compounded quarterly at 8%

(d) For 2 years, compounded monthly at 12%

SOLUTION

(a) In 3 years, there are $3 \times 1 = 3$ compounding periods. The interest rate per compounding period is $4\% \div 1 = 4\%$. Look across the top of the compound interest table above for 4% and down the side for 3 periods to find **1.12486**.

$$\text{Compound amount} = M = \$2000 \times \mathbf{1.12486} = \mathbf{\$2249.72}$$
$$\text{Interest earned} = I = \mathbf{\$2249.72} - \$2000 = \$249.72$$

(b) In 5 years, there are $5 \times 2 = 10$ semiannual compounding periods. The interest rate per compounding period is $6\% \div 2 = 3\%$. In the compound interest table, look at 3% at the top and 10 periods down the side to find **1.34392**.

$$\text{Compound amount} = M = \$2000 \times \mathbf{1.34392} = \mathbf{\$2687.84}$$
$$\text{Interest earned} = I = \mathbf{\$2687.84} - \$2000 = \$687.84$$

(c) Interest compounded quarterly is compounded 4 times a year. In 6 years, there are $6 \times 4 = 24$ quarters, or 24 periods. Interest of 8% per year is $\frac{8\%}{4} = 2\%$ per quarter. In the compound interest table, locate 2% across the top and 24 periods at the left, finding the number **1.60844**.

$$\text{Compound amount} = M = \$2000 \times \mathbf{1.60844} = \mathbf{\$3216.88}$$
$$\text{Interest earned} = I = \mathbf{\$3216.88} - \$2000 = \$1216.88$$

(d) In 2 years, there are $2 \times 12 = 24$ monthly periods. Interest of 12% per year is $\frac{12\%}{12} = 1\%$ per month. Look in the compound interest table for 1% and 24 periods, finding the number **1.26973**.

$$\text{Compound amount} = M = \$2000 \times \mathbf{1.26973} = \mathbf{\$2539.46}$$
$$\text{Interest earned} = I = \mathbf{\$2539.46} - \$2000 = \$539.46$$

QUICK CHECK 5

Find the interest earned on a $5000 deposit for 4 years at 6% compounded semiannually.

USING A FINANCIAL CALCULATOR

We now show how to work Example 5(d) using a financial calculator. See Appendix C for a more detailed discussion of financial calculators and the notation used with them. But here are a few important things to keep in mind:

1. Present value (PV) is the amount of money today.

2. Future value (FV) is the amount of money at a specific date in the future.

3. The interest rate i refers to the interest rate per compounding period.

4. The symbol n refers to the number of compounding periods in the term of the investment.

   Most financial calculators use the following convention: A negative number is used for an outflow of cash from an investor, and a positive number is used for an inflow of cash to an investor. Use a financial calculator by entering the three known values; then press the key for the unknown to find its value. Since financial calculators differ greatly, you should look at the instruction booklet that comes with your calculator.

   Financial Calculator Solution Example 5(d) involves a $2000 deposit, which is the present value (PV). The unknown is the future value (FV). Since the original $2000 investment is an outflow to the investor, enter −2000 for PV. Then enter 24 (compounding periods) for n and 1% (per month) for the interest rate per compounding period. Finally, press FV to find the unknown future value.

$$-2000 \;\boxed{\text{PV}}\; 24 \;\boxed{n}\; 1 \;\boxed{i}\; \boxed{\text{FV}}\; 2539.47 \quad \text{(rounded)}$$

This answer differs by 1¢ from that found in Example 5(d) due to rounding.

The more often interest is compounded, the greater the amount of interest earned. Using a financial calculator, a compound interest table more complete than the compound interest table on page 382, or the compound interest formula will give the results of interest on $1000 shown in the following table. (Leap years were ignored in finding daily interest.)

Interest on $1000 at 8% per Year for 10 Years	
Compounded	**Interest**
Not at all (simple interest)	$ 800.00
Annually	$1158.92
Semiannually	$1191.12
Quarterly	$1208.04
Monthly	$1219.64
Daily	$1225.35

Finding Compound Interest

EXAMPLE 6

John Smith sold his truck for $15,000, which he deposited in a retirement account that pays interest compounded semiannually. How much will he have after 15 years if the funds grow at

(a) 6%?   (b) 8%?   (c) 10%?

SOLUTION

In 15 years, there are $15 \times 2 = 30$ semiannual periods. The semiannual interest rates are

(a) $\frac{6\%}{2} = 3\%$ (b) $\frac{8\%}{2} = 4\%$ (c) $\frac{10\%}{2} = 5\%$

Using factors from the table:
(a) $15,000 \times \mathbf{2.42726} = \$36,408.90$
(b) $15,000 \times \mathbf{3.24340} = \$48,651$
(c) $15,000 \times \mathbf{4.32194} = \$64,829.10$

The graph shows the growth in compound amount at these different interest rates. Importantly, annual interest earned becomes larger as the amount invested grows. In fact, many elderly people depend on interest income from the investments they have built up during their lifetimes to supplement Social Security.

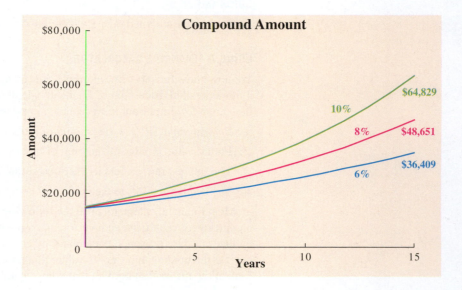

QUICK CHECK 6

A bank offers a certificate of deposit that earns 2% compounded semiannually for 3 years. Find the compound amount for an investment of $3500.

▼10.1 Exercises

MyMathLab®

*The shaded sections below contain solutions to help you get a **QUICK START** on the various types of exercises.*

Use the formula for compound amount, not the table, to find the compound amount and interest. Round to the nearest cent. (See Examples 3 and 4.)

	Compound Amount	Interest
1. $12,000 at 8% compounded annually for 4 years	$16,325.87	$4325.87

Compound interest is 8% per year for 4 years.
$$M = \$12,000 \times (1 + .08)^4 = \$12,000 \times 1.08 \times 1.08 \times 1.08 \times 1.08 = \$16,325.87$$
$$I = \$16,325.87 - \$12,000 = \$4325.87$$

2. $14,800 at 6% compounded semiannually for 4 years _____ _____

3. $28,000 at 10% compounded quarterly for 1 year _____ _____

4. $20,000 at 5% compounded quarterly for $\frac{3}{4}$ year _____ _____

Use values from the compound interest table on page 382 to find both the compound amount and the compound interest. Round the compound amount to the nearest cent. (See Examples 3–6.)

	Compound Amount	Interest
5. $32,350 at 6% compounded annually for 4 years	$40,841.23	$8491.23

Compound interest is 6% per year for 4 years.
$$M = \$32,350 \times 1.26248 = \$40,841.23; \quad I = \$40,841.23 - \$32,350 = \$8491.23$$

6. $18,000 at 1% compounded annually for 10 years _____ _____

7. $12,300 at 3% compounded semiannually for 4 years _____ _____

8. $12,500 at 8% compounded quarterly for 5 years _____ _____

9. $45,000 at 6% compounded semiannually for 5 years _____ _____

10. $82,000 at 8% compounded semiannually for 4 years _____ _____

⚠C indicates an exercise that is related to the Case in Point feature.

Find the simple interest for the period indicated. Then use table values to find the compound interest. Finally, find the difference between compound interest and simple interest. Round each to the nearest cent. (Interest is compounded annually.)

	Principal	Rate	Number of Years	Simple Interest	Compound Interest	Difference
11.	$5400	6%	4	$1296	$1417.39	$121.39
12.	$9200	5%	6	_____	_____	_____
13.	$1200	8%	15	_____	_____	_____
14.	$4625	4%	10	_____	_____	_____

Use the table to solve the following application problems. Round to the nearest cent.

15. CREDIT UNION Bill Jensen deposits $8500 with Bank of America in an investment paying 5% compounded semiannually. Find **(a)** the compound amount and **(b)** the interest in 6 years.

Compound interest is $\frac{5\%}{2}$ = 2.5% and there are 6 × 2 = 12 compounding periods.
(a) M = $8500 × 1.34489 = $11,431.57; (b) I = $11,431.57 − $8500 = $2931.57

(a) $11,431.57

(b) $2931.57

16. SAVINGS Vickie Ewing deposits her savings of $2800 in an investment paying 6% compounded quarterly and she leaves it there for 5 years. Find **(a)** the compound amount and **(b)** the interest.

(a) _____

(b) _____

17. SAVINGS Tom Blasting invested $4500 in an investment paying 8% compounded quarterly for 3 years. Find **(a)** the compound amount and **(b)** the interest.

(a) _____

(b) _____

18. INVESTMENT John Crandall deposited $6000 in an account at a bank that pays 5% compounded semiannually for 4 years. Find **(a)** the compound amount and **(b)** the interest.

(a) _____

(b) _____

19. INTERNATIONAL FINANCE Chi Tang, a businessperson from Taiwan, deposits 25,000 yuan in a Hong Kong branch of Bank of America that pays 6% compounded semiannually. Find **(a)** the balance in the account after 4 years and **(b)** the interest.

(a) _____

(b) _____

20. UNITED KINGDOM A firm in the UK places £42,000 (forty-two thousand pounds) in a bond paying 6% compounded quarterly and leaves it there as collateral for a loan. Find **(a)** the balance in the account after 1 year and **(b)** the interest.

(a) _____

(b) _____

21. INVESTMENT DECISION Bill Baxter has $25,000 to invest for a year. He can lend it to his sister, who has agreed to pay 10% simple interest for the year. Or, he can invest it with a bank at 6% compounded quarterly for a year. How much additional interest would the simple interest loan to his sister generate? Find the effective interest rate for both investments to the nearest hundredth of a percent.

21. _____

🔺 **22. MAXIMIZING INTEREST**   Bank of America has $850,000 to lend for 9 months. It can lend it to an automobile dealer at a simple interest rate of 12%, or it can lend it to a small contractor that will pay 12% compounded monthly. How much additional interest would the compound interest loan to the small business generate? Find the effective interest rate for both loans to the nearest hundredth of a percent.

22. _____

23. INTERNATIONAL FINANCE   Barton's Ltd. lends $1,400,000 for 2 years at 12% compounded monthly to an Egyptian company that manufactures tug boats. Find **(a)** the future value and **(b)** the interest.

(a) _____
(b) _____

24. CORPORATE FINANCE   Key Bank lends $4,500,000 for $1\frac{1}{2}$ years at 8% compounded quarterly to Rengen Biomedical to fund a clinical trial on a new cancer drug. Find **(a)** the future value and **(b)** the interest.

(a) _____
(b) _____

25. INVESTING   Sharon Nguyen has $25,000 to invest and believes that she will earn 6% compounded semiannually. Find the compound amount if she invests **(a)** for 2 years and **(b)** for 10 years. **(c)** Then find the additional amount earned due to the longer period.

(a) _____
(b) _____
(c) _____

26. WHICH INVESTMENT?   Jan Reus sold her home and has $18,000 to invest. She believes she can earn 8% compounded quarterly. Find the compound amount if she invests for **(a)** 3 years and **(b)** 6 years. **(c)** Then find the additional amount earned due to the longer time period.

(a) _____
(b) _____
(c) _____

27. TIME OR RATE?   Becky Hilton has a choice for her investment of $7500. She can invest it in funds she believes will earn either **(a)** 8% compounded quarterly for 2 years or **(b)** 6% compounded semiannually for 5 years. Find the future value of both. **(c)** Which is larger?

(a) _____
(b) _____
(c) _____

28. TIME OR RATE?   Manager Isat Riyadh has a choice to make regarding short-term, excess corporate cash of $330,000. He can invest it **(a)** at 6% compounded quarterly for 6 months or **(b)** at 5% compounded semiannually for 1 year. Find the future amount of both. **(c)** Which is larger?

(a) _____
(b) _____
(c) _____

29. Explain the difference between simple interest and compound interest. (See Objectives 1 and 3.)

30. Explain the difference between 8% compounded monthly for 1 year and 8% simple interest for 1 year. If you were lending money, which type of interest would you specify? Why?

31. Show the effect of both the interest rate and the period on an original investment of $2500. Decide on your own rates and time periods.

32. List five companies that you think borrow money and state why they might need the funds.

33. Explain why most wealthy people tend to be older.

QUICK CHECK ANSWERS

1. (a) $16,200   **(b)** $16,224   **(c)** $24

2. $91,592

3. 2%; 24 periods

4. $9941.60; $941.60

5. $1333.85

6. $3715.32

▼10.2 Interest-Bearing Bank Accounts and Inflation

OBJECTIVES

1 Define passbook, savings, and other interest-bearing accounts.

2 Find interest compounded daily.

3 Define time deposit accounts.

4 Define inflation and the consumer price index.

5 Examine the effect of inflation on spendable income.

6 Understand the role of the government related to inflation.

▼ CASE IN POINT Individuals, businesses, states, and even countries have money on deposit at Bank of America. These deposits can be in many forms, including checking accounts, savings accounts, money market accounts, and time deposits, such as certificates of deposits.

People sometimes think that banks have huge vaults of stored cash, but that is not the case. Banks usually have only enough cash to meet customers' needs for cash during the next few days. Most bank assets are in the loans to their many customers, rather than in cash.

OBJECTIVE 1 Define passbook, savings, and other interest-bearing accounts. **Savings accounts, passbook accounts, money market accounts,** and other interest-bearing accounts are offered by banks and credit unions and can be a safe place to deposit money. These accounts are commonly insured by the Federal Deposit Insurance Corporation (FDIC) on deposits up to $250,000. Many of these accounts require a minimum balance. Interest rates paid on these accounts have varied from less than 1% per year to more than 5% per year and are often compounded daily. The Truth in Savings Act of 1991 resulted in Regulation DD, which requires that interest on savings accounts be paid based on the *exact* number of days.

Interest-bearing checking accounts are also offered by many banks and credit unions. These accounts often have a minimum balance, such as $1500, that must be maintained, but they have the advantage that checks can be written on the account. They can be a good way to earn interest on your money as long as your balance does not fall too low, in which case the bank commonly charges a fee. It pays to earn interest when you can.

OBJECTIVE 2 Find interest compounded daily. Interest on savings accounts, passbook accounts, and other interest-bearing checking accounts is found using compound interest. It is common for banks to pay interest **compounded daily** so that interest is credited for every day that the money is on deposit.

The formula for daily compounding is *exactly* the same as the formula given in **Section 10.1**. However, because the annual interest rate must be divided by 365 (for daily compounding), the arithmetic is tedious. To avoid this, use the following special tables that give the necessary numbers for 1 to 90 days, as well as for 1 to 4 ninety-day quarters, assuming $3\frac{1}{2}\%$ interest compounded daily. Even with daily compounding, interest is often credited to an account *only at the end of each quarter* to make record keeping easier for the bank.

Note: Interest rates vary widely. No one, including the authors of this textbook, knows what interest rates will be in the future. Thus, the interest rate in this section is $3\frac{1}{2}\%$, or close to the historical average for accounts of this type.

The four quarters in a year begin on January 1, April 1, July 1, and October 1. Although some quarters have 91 or 92 days in them, we assume 90-day quarters for convenience in calculation. Assuming daily compounding and a compounding period expressed in days or quarters, compound amount and interest are found as follows.

Interest by Quarter for $3\frac{1}{2}\%$ Compounded Daily Assuming 90-Day Quarters

Number of Quarters	Value of $(1 + i)^n$
1	1.008667067
2	1.017409251
3	1.026227205
4	1.035121585

Finding Compound Amount and Interest

$$\text{Compound amount} = \text{Principal} \times \text{Number from table}$$
$$\text{Interest} = \text{Compound amount} - \text{Principal}$$

Find the value from the table below if the number of days of the deposit is 90 days or less. Use the smaller table on the previous page if time is given in number of quarters.

Values of $(1 + i)^n$ for $3\frac{1}{2}$% Compounded Daily

Number of Days n	Value of $(1 + i)^n$	n	Value of $(1 + i)^n$	n	Value of $(1 + i)^n$	n	Value of $(1 + i)^n$	n	Value of $(1 + i)^n$
1	1.000095890	19	1.001823491	37	1.003554076	55	1.005287650	73	1.007024219
2	1.000191790	20	1.001919556	38	1.003650307	56	1.005384048	74	1.007120783
3	1.000287699	21	1.002015631	39	1.003746548	57	1.005480454	75	1.007217357
4	1.000383617	22	1.002111714	40	1.003842797	58	1.005576870	76	1.007313939
5	1.000479544	23	1.002207807	41	1.003939056	59	1.005673296	77	1.007410531
6	1.000575480	24	1.002303909	42	1.004035324	60	1.005769730	78	1.007507132
7	1.000671426	25	1.002400021	43	1.004131602	61	1.005866174	79	1.007603742
8	1.000767381	26	1.002496141	44	1.004227888	62	1.005962627	80	1.007700362
9	1.000863345	27	1.002592271	45	1.004324184	63	1.006059089	81	1.007796990
10	1.000959318	28	1.002688410	46	1.004420489	64	1.006155560	82	1.007893628
11	1.001055300	29	1.002784558	47	1.004516803	65	1.006252041	83	1.007990276
12	1.001151292	30	1.002880716	48	1.004613127	66	1.006348531	84	1.008086932
13	1.001247293	31	1.002976882	49	1.004709460	67	1.006445030	85	1.008183598
14	1.001343303	32	1.003073058	50	1.004805802	68	1.006541538	86	1.008280273
15	1.001439322	33	1.003169243	51	1.004902153	69	1.006638056	87	1.008376958
16	1.001535350	34	1.003265438	52	1.004998513	70	1.006734583	88	1.008473651
17	1.001631388	35	1.003361641	53	1.005094883	71	1.006831119	89	1.008570354
18	1.001727435	36	1.003457854	54	1.005191262	72	1.006927665	90	1.008667067

Note: The value of $(1 + i)^n$ for $3\frac{1}{2}$% compounded daily for a quarter with 91 days is 1.008763788 and for a quarter with 92 days is 1.008860519.

Finding Daily Interest

Becky Gonzales received $12,500 from a divorce settlement. She plans to use the money for a down payment on a new Toyota Camry but decides to wait 60 days until the new models are out. She puts her money in a savings account earning $3\frac{1}{2}$% interest compounded daily for the 60 days. Find the amount of interest she will earn.

SOLUTION

The table value for 60 days is **1.005769730**.

$$\text{Compound amount} = \$12,500 \times \textbf{1.005769730} = \textbf{\$12,572.12}$$
$$\text{Interest} = \textbf{\$12,572.12} - \$12,500 = \$72.12$$

The additional $72.12 isn't much money to Gonzales, but she is happy to earn some interest.

QUICK CHECK 1

Find the interest if $1200 is invested in a money market account earning 3.5% compounded daily for 90 days.

The next two examples show how interest is calculated when there are several deposits and/or withdrawals within a short period of time.

Finding Interest on Multiple Deposits

EXAMPLE 2

Tom Blackmore is a private investigator who keeps his extra cash in a savings account to earn interest. On January 10, he deposited $2463 in a savings account paying $3\frac{1}{2}$% compounded daily. He deposited an additional $1320 on February 18 and $840 on March 3. Find the interest earned through April 10.

SOLUTION

Treat each deposit separately. The $2463 was in the account for 90 days (21 days in January, 28 days in February, 31 days in March, and 10 days in April). The value for 90 days from the table is **1.008667067**.

Compound amount = $2463 × **1.008667067** = **$2484.35**   first deposit plus interest

The $1320 deposited on February 18 was in the account for 51 days (10 days in February, 31 days in March, and 10 days in April).

Compound amount = $1320 × **1.004902153** = **$1326.47**   second deposit plus interest

The $840 was in the account for 38 days (28 days in March and 10 days in April).

Compound amount = $840 × **1.003650307** = **$843.07**   final deposit plus interest

The total amount in the account on April 10 is found by adding the three compound amounts.

Total in account = **$2484.35 + $1326.47 + $843.07 = $4653.89**

The preceding information is summarized in this table.

Amount	Number of Days Left in Account	Compound Amount	
$2463	90	$2484.35	
$1320	51	$1326.47	
$ 840	38	$ 843.07	
		$4653.89	**Total in account at end of quarter.**

The interest earned is the total amount in the account less the deposits.

Interest earned = **$4653.89** − ($2463 + $1320 + $840) = $30.89

QUICK CHECK 2

A money market account is opened with an $8500 deposit on April 10, and another $1500 is deposited on May 5. Find the total in the account on June 30 if funds earn $3\frac{1}{2}$% compounded daily. Also find the interest earned.

Finding Interest for the Quarter   **EXAMPLE 3**

Beth Gardner owns Blacktop Paving, Inc. She needs a place to keep extra cash, a place that will earn interest but that will allow her to get funds when needed. She opened a money market account on July 20 with a $24,800 deposit. She then withdrew $3800 on August 29 for an unexpected truck repair, and she made another withdrawal of $8200 on September 29 for payroll. Find the interest earned through October 1, given interest at $3\frac{1}{2}$% compounded daily.

SOLUTION

Quick TIP

See **Appendix C** for financial calculator solutions that do not require the use of a table.

Of the original $24,800, a total of $24,800 − $3800 − $8200 = $12,800 earned interest from July 20 to October 1 or for 274 − 201 = 73 days. Find the factor **1.007024219** from the table.

Compound amount = $12,800 × **1.007024219** = $12,889.91
Interest = $12,889.91 − $12,800 = **$89.91**

The withdrawn $3800 earned interest from July 20 to August 29 or for 241 − 201 = 40 days.

Compound amount = $3800 × **1.003842797** = $3814.60
Interest = $3814.60 − $3800 = **$14.60**

Finally, the withdrawn $8200 earned interest from July 20 to September 29 or for 272 − 201 = 71 days.

Compound amount = $8200 × **1.006831119** = $8256.02
Interest = $8256.02 − $8200 = **$56.02**

The total interest earned is ($89.91 + $14.60 + $56.02) = **$160.53.** The total in the account on October 1 is found as follows.

Deposits + Interest − Withdrawals = Balance on October 1
$24,800 + **$160.53** − ($3800 + $8200) = $12,960.53

The following information assumes that all interest is credited on the last day of the quarter.

Date	Deposit	Withdrawal	Balance
July 20	$24,800	—	$24,800
Aug. 29	—	$3800	$21,000
Sept. 29	—	$8200	$12,800
Oct. 1	$160.53 (Int.)	—	$12,960.53

QUICK CHECK 3

An account is opened with a deposit of $4000, but $3000 is withdrawn 40 days later. Find the amount in the account and the interest earned at the end of 90 days from the original deposit if interest is $3\frac{1}{2}\%$ compounded daily.

OBJECTIVE 3 Define time deposit accounts. Banks pay higher interest rates on funds left on deposit for *longer time periods* in **time deposits.** A **certificate of deposit (CD)** requires a minimum amount of money, such as $1000, to be on deposit for a minimum period of time, such as 1 year. Find the compound amount of a time deposit as follows.

Finding Compound Amount and Interest

$$\text{Compound amount} = \text{Principal} \times \text{Number from the table}$$
$$\text{Interest} = \text{Compound amount} - \text{Principal}$$

Compound Interest for Time Deposit Accounts Compounded Daily

Number of Years	1%	2%	3%	4%	5%	Number of Years
1	1.01005003	1.02020078	1.03045326	1.04080849	1.05126750	1
2	1.02020106	1.04080963	1.06183393	1.08328232	1.10516335	2
3	1.03045411	1.06183480	1.09417024	1.12748944	1.16182231	3
4	1.04081020	1.08328469	1.12749129	1.17350058	1.22138603	4
5	1.05127038	1.10516789	1.16182708	1.22138937	1.28400343	5
10	1.10516940	1.22139607	1.34984217	1.49179200	1.64866481	10

Note: This compound interest table assumes daily compounding. The compound interest table on page 382 of Section 10.1 *does not.*

Finding Interest and Compound Amount for Time Deposits

EXAMPLE 4

Tony Sanchez plans to purchase three machines for his auto-repair shop. Bank of America requires $20,000 in collateral before making the loan. Therefore, Tony deposits $20,000 with the bank in a 2-year certificate of deposit yielding 1% compounded daily. Find the compound amount and interest.

SOLUTION

Look at the table for 1% and 2 years, finding **1.02020106**.

$$\text{Compound amount} = \$20,000 \times \mathbf{1.02020106} = \mathbf{\$20,404.02} \text{ rounded}$$
$$\text{Interest} = \mathbf{\$20,404.02} - \$20,000 = \$404.02$$

QUICK CHECK 4

Find the compound amount and interest on $10,000 invested in a 4-year CD earning 2% compounded daily.

OBJECTIVE 4 Define inflation and the consumer price index. Inflation results in a continual rise in the price of goods and services. Another way to think about inflation is that a dollar is worth less each year. Either way you think about it, the end result is that inflation means you have to earn more each year to buy the same goods and services.

For example, if inflation averages 3% per year, an automobile costing $25,000 today will cost about $45,000 in 20 years. The following graph shows the increase in the average annual cost of college tuition. Is it that college costs are increasing or that the dollar is decreasing in value requiring more dollars to buy the same thing? The answer is both in this case, since annual tuition costs have increased at such a rapid rate, especially at private four-year colleges.

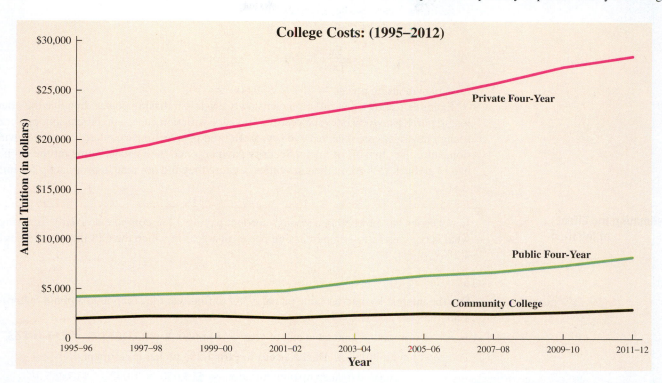

College Costs: (1995–2012)

Many people use an index called the **consumer price index (CPI)**, or **cost of living index**, to track inflation. This index is calculated by the government. It measures the average change in prices from one year to the next for a common select group of goods and services, including food, housing, fuel, utilities, apparel, transportation, insurance, health care, and even pet care. Go to the Bureau of Labor Statistics Web site (http://www.bls.gov/) to see the effect of inflation over time.

OBJECTIVE 5 Examine the effect of inflation on spendable income. Inflation reduces the buying power of a family. Example 5 shows what happens to purchasing power when a 1% pay raise is received in a year with 3% inflation. It isn't pretty!

Estimating the Effects of Inflation

EXAMPLE 5

Inflation from one year to the next was 3% as measured by the CPI.

(a) Find the effect of the increase on a family with an after-tax annual income and budget of $39,600 (after taxes).

(b) What is the overall effect if the family members receive only a 1% (after tax) increase in pay for the year?

SOLUTION

(a) This is a percent problem. The cost of the goods and services that this family buys, if they buy the common bundle of goods and services, went up by 3% as measured by the CPI.

$$.03 \times \$39{,}600 = \mathbf{\$1188}$$

Therefore, next year these same goods and services will cost the family about

$$\$39{,}600 + \mathbf{\$1188} = \mathbf{\$40{,}788}$$

(b) The family's income went up 1% after taxes, or by

$$.01 \times \$39{,}600 = \mathbf{\$396}$$

Thus,

$$\text{New income} = \$39{,}600 + \$396 = \$39{,}996$$

$$\text{Family's loss in purchasing power} = \$40{,}788 - \$39{,}996 = \mathbf{\$792}$$

Example 5 can also be solved as follows.

Inflation rate	3.0%
− Raise	1.0%
Loss	2.0%

Loss in purchasing power = 2% × $39,600 = $792

    Example 5 shows that inflation can slowly erode purchasing power. Imagine the effect of losing purchasing power every year for 10 years. Inflation can erode purchasing power even though pay raises are received every year. Retired people are particularly concerned with inflation, since they live off of Social Security payments and their estate. Some retired people have had to go back to work in their seventies because they did not plan appropriately for inflation.

Estimating the Effects of Inflation

 EXAMPLE 6

Joan Davies has $14,650 in a savings account paying $3\frac{1}{2}$% compounded daily. Ignoring taxes, what is her gain or loss in purchasing power in a year in which the CPI index increases by 4.2%?

SOLUTION

Use the interest-by-quarter table on page 389 to find that the compound amount factor for 4 quarters is **1.035121585**.

    Compound amount at end of year = $14,650 × **1.035121585** = **$15,164.53**

To keep up with inflation, Davies needs to earn 4.2% on her investment.

    Needed to keep up with inflation = $14,650 × 1.042 = **$15,265.30**

The difference of $15,265.30 − $15,164.53 = $100.77 is the loss in purchasing power. The purchasing power of Davies's savings actually went *down*, even though she earned interest for the year and her account balance grew. The problem worsens if Davies has to pay taxes on interest earned, since she will end up with even less interest.

    The opposite of inflation is **deflation**, which is a decrease in the general prices of goods and services. Deflation is relatively rare but potentially very serious. During the Great Depression of the 1930s, the prices of goods and services fell sharply in a deflationary spiral. People became worried about their savings and jobs. They also believed they could buy items more cheaply if they waited, since companies were marking down inventory to sell it. So, people postponed purchases, demand fell, and sales at firms plummeted. In turn, managers responded by laying off even more workers, causing higher unemployment and even more fear. It was a vicious cycle. In 1933, unemployment grew to (a horrible) 25% of the workforce in the U.S.

OBJECTIVE 6 Understand the role of the government related to inflation. Both inflation that is too high (prices increasing rapidly) and deflation (prices falling) can be very harmful to families and businesses. As a result, the federal government works to control inflation using tools such as interest rates, over which they have some control.

    When the economy is too "hot" and inflation is too high, the government increases interest rates, making it more expensive to borrow, thereby slowing lending and growth. When economic growth is too slow or there is a threat of deflation, the government decreases interest rates to encourage borrowing and, therefore, encourage business activity. Controlling inflation and deflation is very difficult to do, but it is a very important issue.

▼10.2 Exercises

MyMathLab®

The shaded sections below contain solutions to help you get a **QUICK START** *on the various types of exercises.*

Find the interest earned by the following. Assume $3\frac{1}{2}$% interest compounded daily.
(See Examples 1–3.)'

	Amount	Date Deposited	Date Withdrawn	Interest Earned
1.	$4800	July 6	September 30	$39.75

There are $(31 - 6) + 31 + 30 = 86$ days.
Interest is $4800 × 1.008280273 − $4800 = $39.75.

	Amount	Date Deposited	Date Withdrawn	Interest Earned
2.	$3850	January 5	February 9	$12.94

There are $(31 - 5) + 9 = 35$ days.
Interest is $3850 × 1.003361641 − $3850 = $12.94.

	Amount	Date Deposited	Date Withdrawn	Interest Earned
3.	$8200	October 4	December 7	_____
4.	$2830	May 4	June 23	_____
5.	$17,958	September 9	November 7	_____
6.	$12,000	December 3	February 20	_____

Find the compound amount for each of the following certificates of deposit. Assume daily compounding. (See Example 4.)

	Amount Deposited	Interest Rate	Time in Years	Compound Amount
7.	$3900	2%	1	$3978.78

$3900 × 1.02020078 = $3978.78

	Amount Deposited	Interest Rate	Time in Years	Compound Amount
8.	$8000	4%	1	_____
9.	$12,900	3%	10	_____
10.	$3600.40	1%	3	_____

11. Explain how you can use a time deposit to your advantage. Use an example. (See Objective 3.)

12. List five ways in which inflation affects your family. (See Objective 4.)

◬ indicates an exercise that is related to the Case in Point feature.

Solve the following application problems. If no interest rate is given, assume $3\frac{1}{2}\%$ interest compounded daily. Round to the nearest cent.

13. **SAVINGS ACCOUNT** Hilda Worth opened a savings account at Bank of America on April 1 with a $2530 deposit. She then deposited $150 on May 8 and $580 on May 24. Find **(a)** the balance on June 30 and **(b)** the interest earned through that date.

   (a) $3284.75

   (b) $24.75

   (a) The $2530 (for 90 days) becomes $2530 × 1.008667067 = $2551.93
   The $150 (for 53 days) becomes $150 × 1.005094883 = $ 150.76
   The $580 (for 37 days) becomes $580 × 1.003554076 = $ 582.06
                                                     Total is $3284.75
   (b) Interest earned is $3284.75 − ($2530 + $150 + $580) = $24.75

14. **PRINT SHOP** The manager of Quick Printing, Inc., is trying to get the most out of his assets including cash that has been sitting in a checking account that does not pay interest. He opened a savings account with a deposit of $8765 on January 4. On February 11, he deposited $936. Then, on March 21, he deposited a tax refund check for $650. Find **(a)** the balance on March 31 and **(b)** the interest earned through that date.

   (a) _____

   (b) _____

15. **SAVINGS ACCOUNT** On April 1, MVP Sports opened a savings account at Bank of America with a deposit of $17,500. A withdrawal of $5000 was made 21 days later, another withdrawal of $980 was made 12 days before July 1. Find **(a)** the balance on July 1 and **(b)** the interest earned through that date. (*Hint:* See the table footnote for 91 days.)

   (a) _____

   (b) _____

16. **SAVINGS ACCOUNT** The owner of International Magic opened a savings account at Bank of America for the extra cash in the firm. The initial deposit of $7800 was made on July 7. A withdrawal of $1500 was made 46 days later, and an additional withdrawal of $1000 was made 30 days before October 1. Find **(a)** the balance on October 1 and **(b)** the interest earned through that date.

   (a) _____

   (b) _____

17. **TIME DEPOSIT** Wes Cockrell has $4000 to deposit in a certificate of deposit, but he is debating whether to leave it there for 2 years or for 3 years. Assume 2% compounded daily in both situations, and find the compound amount in each case.

   17. _____

18. **COMPOUNDING** Georgia Pastel Fabric has $15,000 to deposit in a certificate of deposit for either 3 or 5 years. Assume 1% compounded daily in both situations, and find the compound amount in each case.

   18. _____

19. **LOAN COLLATERAL** An Italian firm deposited $800,000 in a 2-year time deposit earning 3% compounded daily with a New York bank as partial collateral for a loan. Find **(a)** the compound amount and **(b)** the interest earned.

   (a) _____

   (b) _____

20. **PUTTING UP COLLATERAL**   Joni Perez needs to borrow $20,000 to open a welding shop, but the bank will not lend her the money. Joni's uncle agrees to put up collateral for the loan with a $20,000, 4-year certificate of deposit paying 4% compounded daily. This means that the bank will take all or part of his deposit if Perez should fail to repay the loan. Find **(a)** the compound amount earned by her uncle and **(b)** the interest earned by her uncle.

(a) _____

(b) _____

21. **RETIREMENT INCOME**   The Walters accumulated $235,000 during more than 40 years of work. They originally deposited this money in a 5-year time deposit earning 3% and used the income for living expenses. On renewing the time deposit, they found that interest rates on a 5-year time deposit had fallen and that they were going to receive only 2%. Find the difference in their *annual income* due to the decline in interest rates. (*Hint:* Don't use the compound interest table.)

21. _____

22. **INHERITANCE**   Jessica Thompson inherited $80,000 and decided to put the money in one of two 4-year time deposits. The first time deposit yielded 3%, but the second yielded only 1%. Find the difference in the annual income. (*Hint:* Don't use the compound interest table.)

22. _____

23. **DETERMINING PURCHASING POWER**   A family with a spending budget of $26,500 receives an increase in wages of 3% in a year in which inflation was 4.5%. Find the net gain or loss in their purchasing power.

23. _____

24. **INFLATION AND RETIREMENT**   Ben and Martha Wheeler are retired and they have $184,500 in a savings account at Bank of America paying $3\frac{1}{2}$% compounded daily. What is their gain or loss in purchasing power from interest in a year in which inflation is 2.5%?

24. _____

25. **CORPORATE SAVINGS**   Dayton Tires has $180,000 to invest for 1 year. Find the future value if it earns **(a)** 2% per year compounded daily and **(b)** 3% per year compounded daily. **(c)** Then find the difference between the two.

(a) _____

(b) _____

(c) _____

26. **EMERGENCY CASH**   After working long days in her small business for years, Kaitlyn Plank was finally making money. Since she was still worried about emergencies, she decided to put $85,000 in an investment for 4 years. Find the future value if it earns **(a)** 2% per year compounded daily and **(b)** 4% per year compounded daily. **(c)** Then find the difference between the two.

(a) _____

(b) _____

(c) _____

27. Define inflation and discuss the government's role in controlling inflation. (See Objectives 5 and 6.)

28. Point out several differences between inflation and deflation. (See Objective 5.)

29. Define deflation and discuss how it can lead to severe problems. (See Objective 6.)

30. Describe the advantages to a family of having money in a savings account or certificate of deposit. (See Objectives 1–6.)

QUICK CHECK ANSWERS

1. $10.40

2. $10,074.35; $74.35

3. $1020.20; $20.20

4. $10,832.85; $832.85

5. $640 loss

6. $243.92

10.3 Present Value and Future Value

OBJECTIVES

1 Define the terms *future value* and *present value*.

2 Use tables to calculate present value.

3 Use future value and present value to estimate the value of a business.

OBJECTIVE 1 Define the terms *future value* and *present value*. **Future value** is the amount available at a specific date in the future. It is the amount available after an investment has earned interest. All of the values found in Sections 10.1 and 10.2 were future values.

In contrast, **present value** is the amount needed today so that the desired future value will be available when needed. For example, an individual may need to know the present value that must be invested today in order to have a down payment for a new car in 3 years. Or a firm may need to know the present value that must be invested today in order to have enough money to purchase a new computer system in 20 months. The bar chart shows present value as the value today and future value as the value at a future date.

In this section, the future value, interest rate, and term are given and the present value that must be invested today to reach the future value is calculated.

OBJECTIVE 2 Use tables to calculate present value. First, find the interest rate per compounding period (i) and the total number of compounding periods (n) of the investment. Then use these values to find the appropriate value in the Present Value of a Dollar Table. Finally, use the formula to find present value.

> **Finding Present Value**
>
> Present value (PV) = Future value $\times$ Table value

Finding Present Value EXAMPLE 1

Betty Clark needs to replace two pumps at her gas station in 3 years at an estimated cost of $12,000. What lump sum deposited today at 5% compounded annually must she invest to have the needed funds? How much interest will she earn?

SOLUTION

Step 1 The interest rate is 5% per compounding period for 3 compounding periods (years in this case). Look across the top of the table for 5% and down the left column for 3 to find **.86384**.

$$\text{Present value} = \$12,000 \times \textbf{.86384} = \textbf{\$10,366.08}$$

Step 2 Interest earned = $12,000 − **$10,366.08** = $1633.92.

Step 3 Check the answer by finding the future value of an investment of $10,366.08 in an account earning 5% compounded annually for 3 years. Use the table on page 382 to find **1.15763**.

$$\text{Future value} = \$10,366.08 \times \textbf{1.15763} = \$12,000.09$$

The reason it is not exactly $12,000 is rounding in the table value.

> **QUICK CHECK 1**
>
> Find the lump sum that must be deposited today to have a future value of $25,000 in 5 years if funds earn 6% compounded annually.

Present Value of a Dollar Table

Quick TIP

Period refers to the number of compounding periods.

Interest Rate per Compounding Period

Period	1%	$1\frac{1}{2}$%	2%	$2\frac{1}{2}$%	3%	4%	5%	6%	8%	10%	Period
1	.99010	.98522	.98039	.97561	.97087	.96154	.95238	.94340	.92593	.90909	1
2	.98030	.97066	.96117	.95181	.94260	.92456	.90703	.89000	.85734	.82645	2
3	.97059	.95632	.94232	.92860	.91514	.88900	.86384	.83962	.79383	.75131	3
4	.96098	.94218	.92385	.90595	.88849	.85480	.82270	.79209	.73503	.68301	4
5	.95147	.92826	.90573	.88385	.86261	.82193	.78353	.74726	.68058	.62092	5
6	.94205	.91454	.88797	.86230	.83748	.79031	.74622	.70496	.63017	.56447	6
7	.93272	.90103	.87056	.84127	.81309	.75992	.71068	.66506	.58349	.51316	7
8	.92348	.88771	.85349	.82075	.78941	.73069	.67684	.62741	.54027	.46651	8
9	.91434	.87459	.83676	.80073	.76642	.70259	.64461	.59190	.50025	.42410	9
10	.90529	.86167	.82035	.78120	.74409	.67556	.61391	.55839	.46319	.38554	10
11	.89632	.84893	.80426	.76214	.72242	.64958	.58468	.52679	.42888	.35049	11
12	.88745	.83639	.78849	.74356	.70138	.62460	.55684	.49697	.39711	.31863	12
13	.87866	.82403	.77303	.72542	.68095	.60057	.52032	.46884	.36770	.28966	13
14	.86996	.81185	.75788	.70773	.66112	.57748	.50507	.44230	.34036	.26333	14
15	.86135	.79985	.74301	.69047	.64186	.55526	.48102	.41727	.31524	.23939	15
16	.85282	.78803	.72845	.67362	.62317	.53391	.45811	.39365	.29189	.21763	16
17	.84438	.77639	.71416	.65720	.60502	.51337	.43630	.37136	.27027	.19784	17
18	.83602	.76491	.70016	.64117	.58739	.49363	.41552	.35034	.25025	.17986	18
19	.82774	.75361	.68643	.62553	.57029	.47464	.39573	.33051	.23171	.16351	19
20	.81954	.74247	.67297	.61027	.55368	.45639	.37689	.31180	.21455	.14864	20
21	.81143	.73150	.65978	.59539	.53755	.43883	.35894	.29416	.19866	.13513	21
22	.80340	.72069	.64684	.58086	.52189	.42196	.34185	.27751	.18394	.12285	22
23	.79544	.71004	.63416	.56670	.50669	.40573	.32557	.26180	.17032	.11168	23
24	.78757	.69954	.62172	.55288	.49193	.39012	.31007	.24698	.15770	.10153	24
25	.77977	.68921	.60953	.53939	.47761	.37512	.29530	.23300	.14602	.09230	25
26	.77205	.67902	.59758	.52623	.46369	.36069	.28124	.21981	.13520	.08391	26
27	.76440	.66899	.58586	.51340	.45019	.34682	.26785	.20737	.12519	.07628	27
28	.75684	.65910	.57437	.50088	.43708	.33348	.25509	.19563	.11591	.06934	28
29	.74934	.64936	.56311	.48866	.42435	.32065	.24295	.18456	.10733	.06304	29
30	.74192	.63976	.55207	.47674	.41199	.30832	.23138	.17411	.09938	.05731	30
31	.73458	.63031	.54125	.46511	.39999	.29646	.22036	.16425	.09202	.05210	31
32	.72730	.62099	.53063	.45377	.38834	.28506	.20987	.15496	.08520	.04736	32
33	.72010	.61182	.52023	.44270	.37703	.27409	.19987	.14619	.07889	.04306	33
34	.71297	.60277	.51003	.43191	.36604	.26355	.19035	.13791	.07305	.03914	34
35	.70591	.59387	.50003	.42137	.35538	.25342	.18129	.13011	.06763	.03558	35
36	.69892	.58509	.49022	.41109	.34503	.24367	.17266	.12274	.06262	.03235	36
37	.69200	.57644	.48061	.40107	.33498	.23430	.16444	.11579	.05799	.02941	37
38	.68515	.56792	.47119	.39128	.32523	.22529	.15661	.10924	.05369	.02673	38
39	.67837	.55953	.46195	.38174	.31575	.21662	.14915	.10306	.04971	.02430	39
40	.67165	.55126	.45289	.37243	.30656	.20829	.14205	.09722	.04603	.02209	40
41	.66500	.54312	.44401	.36335	.29763	.20028	.13528	.09172	.04262	.02009	41
42	.65842	.53509	.43530	.35448	.28896	.19257	.12884	.08653	.03946	.01826	42
43	.65190	.52718	.42677	.34584	.28054	.18517	.12270	.08163	.03654	.01660	43
44	.64545	.51939	.41840	.33740	.27237	.17805	.11686	.07701	.03383	.01509	44
45	.63905	.51171	.41020	.32917	.26444	.17120	.11130	.07265	.03133	.01372	45
46	.63273	.50415	.40215	.32115	.25674	.16461	.10600	.06854	.02901	.01247	46
47	.62646	.49670	.39427	.31331	.24926	.15828	.10095	.06466	.02686	.01134	47
48	.62026	.48936	.38654	.30567	.24200	.15219	.09614	.06100	.02487	.01031	48
49	.61412	.48213	.37896	.29822	.23495	.14634	.09156	.05755	.02303	.00937	49

Finding Present Value   **EXAMPLE 2**

The local Harley-Davidson shop has seen business grow rapidly. The owners plan to increase the size of their 6000-square-foot shop in one year at a cost of $280,000. How much should be invested in an investment earning 6% compounded semiannually to have the funds needed?

SOLUTION

The interest rate per compounding period is $\frac{6\%}{2} = 3\%$, and the number of compounding periods is 1 year $\times$ 2 periods per year $= 2$. Use the table to find **.94260**.

$$\text{Present value} = \$280,000 \times \textbf{.94260} = \$263,928$$

The difference between the $280,001.22 and the desired $280,000 is due to rounding.

QUICK CHECK 2

In 5 years, Great Lakes Dairy estimates it will need $350,000 for a down payment to purchase a nearby farm. Find the amount that should be invested today to meet the down payment if funds earn 8% compounded quarterly.

Applying Present Value   **EXAMPLE 3**

Radiux Inc. wishes to partner with a Korean company to purchase a satellite in 3 years. Radiux plans to make a cash down payment of 40% of its anticipated $8,000,000 cost and borrow the remaining funds from a bank. Find the amount Radiux should invest today in an investment earning 6% compounded annually to have the down payment needed in 3 years.

SOLUTION

First find the down payment to be paid in 3 years.

$$\text{Down payment} = .40 \times \$8,000,000 = \$3,200,000$$

This is the future value needed exactly 3 years from now. Using the present value of a dollar table on page 400 with 3 periods and 6% per period gives

$$\$3,200,000 \times \textbf{.83962} = \$2,686,784$$

Radiux must invest $2,686,784 today at 6% interest compounded annually to have the required down payment of $3,200,000 in 3 years.

Financial Calculator Solution Using data from Example 3, the future value is $3,200,000. The number of periods is 3 and the interest rate per period is 6%. Enter these values into the financial calculator with the future value being a positive number. Then press PV for the present value. It will be a negative number, indicating the outflows from Radiux.

     3200000 $\boxed{\text{FV}}$ 3 $\boxed{n}$ 6 $\boxed{i}$ $\boxed{\text{PV}}$ $-$ 2686782   (rounded to the nearest dollar)

The difference from the value found in the example is due to rounding.

QUICK CHECK 3

Mom and Pop Jenkins plan to buy a new car in 2 years and want to make a down payment of 25% of the estimated purchase price of $32,000. Find the amount they need to invest to make the down payment if funds earn 6% compounded quarterly.

OBJECTIVE 3 Use future value and present value to estimate the value of a business. Sometimes a business has such a strong growth opportunity that it is valued at more than it would be if it had normal growth. In this case, the strong growth opportunity increases the market price of the business. To estimate the value of a business with strong growth, first estimate the future value of the business 2 to 5 years in the future. Then find the present value of this amount using the appropriate discount rate.

Evaluating a Business **EXAMPLE 4** Brianna McGruder and Tanya Zoban own Extreme Sports, Inc., whose value is $120,000 today assuming normal growth. However, the partners believe the value will grow at 15% per year for the next four years. They want to take this rapid growth into consideration when valuing the business for a potential sale.

(a) Find the future value of the business in 4 years.

(b) Estimate the value of the retail store by finding the present value of the amount found in part **(a)** at 6% compounded quarterly.

SOLUTION

(a) The partners expect the business to grow at 15% per year for the next 4 years. There is no 15% column in the compound interest table of Section 10.1, so we use the formula $(1 + i)^n$, where $i = .15$ and $n = 4$.

$$\text{Future value} = \$120,000 \times (1 + i)^n$$
$$= \$120,000 \times (1 + .15)^4 = \textbf{\$209,881} \textbf{ (rounded)}$$

This is an estimate of the value of the store in 4 years.

(b) Now find the present value of $209,881 assuming 6% compounded quarterly for 4 years or at $\frac{6\%}{4} = 1.5\%$ per quarter for $4 \times 4 = 16$ compounding periods. The value from the present value of a dollar table on page 400 is **.78803**.

$$\text{Present value} = \$209,881 \times \textbf{.78803} = \$165,393 \textbf{ (rounded)}$$

Thus, the partners should ask $165,400 for their business. The rapid growth rate adds about $165,400 − $120,000 = $45,400 to the value of the business.

QUICK CHECK 4

Assuming normal growth, a clothing store is worth $100,000. But the owners believe it will grow at 9% per year for the next three years. Estimate a reasonable selling price for the business by finding the present value at 5% per year compounded semiannually.

▼10.3 Exercises

MyMathLab®

*The shaded sections below contain solutions to help you get a **QUICK START** on the various types of exercises.*

Find the present value of the following. Round to the nearest cent. Also, find the amount of interest earned.
(See Examples 1 and 2.)

	Amount Needed	Time (Years)	Interest	Compounded	Present Value	Interest Earned
1.	$12,300	3	6%	annually	$10,327.33	$1972.67
	P = $12,300 × .83962 = $10,327.33; I = $12,300 − $10,327.33 = $1972.67					
2.	$14,500	$2\frac{1}{2}$	8%	quarterly	$11,895.08	$2604.92
	P = $14,500 × .82035 = $11,895.08; I = $14,500 − $11,895.08 = $2604.92					
3.	$9350	4	5%	semiannually	_____	_____
4.	$850	10	8%	semiannually	_____	_____
5.	$18,853	11	6%	quarterly	_____	_____
6.	$20,984	9	4%	quarterly	_____	_____

Solve the following application problems.

7. **DIVORCE SETTLEMENT** Part of Abernathy's divorce settlement involves setting aside money today for college tuition for their daughter who enters college in 7 years. They estimate that the cost of four years' tuition, food, and lodging at the state university their daughter will attend will be $40,000. Find (a) the lump sum that must be invested at 4% compounded semiannually and (b) the amount of interest earned.

   (a) Lump sum = P = $40,000 × .75788 = $30,315.20
   (b) I = $40,000 − $30,315.20 = $9684.80

   (a) $30,315.20
   (b) $9684.80

8. **SELF-EMPLOYMENT** Janet Becker wishes to start her own day-care business in her home in 4 years and estimates that she will need $25,000 to do so. (a) What lump sum should be invested today at 5%, compounded semiannually, to produce the needed amount? (b) How much interest will be earned?

   (a) _____
   (b) _____

9. **FINANCING COLLEGE EXPENSES** Mrs. Lorez wants all of her grandchildren to go to college and decides to help financially. How much must she give to each child at birth if they are to have $10,000 on entering college 18 years later, assuming 6% interest compounded annually?

   9. _____

10. **BAKERY** Carlos Mora recently immigrated to the United States from Central America. His family has agreed to help him set aside the cash needed to open a small bakery in 2 years once he completes a program at a culinary institute. Find the amount they must deposit today in an investment account expected to yield 4% compounded quarterly if he needs $95,000 to open the shop in 2 years.

   10. _____

11. **EXPANDING MANUFACTURING OPERATIONS** Quantum Logic recently expanded its computer-chip assembly operations at a cost of $450,000. Management expects that the value of the investment will grow at a rate of 12% per year compounded annually for the next 5 years. (a) Find the future value of the investment. (b) Find the present value of the amount found in part (a) at a rate of 6% compounded annually. Round to the nearest dollar at each step.

    (a) _____
    (b) _____

12. **BUSINESS EXPANSION** Village Hardware expands its business at a cost of $20,000. They expect that the investment will grow at a rate of 10% per year compounded annually for the next 4 years. (a) Find the future value of the investment. (b) Find the present value of the amount found in part (a) at a rate of 6% compounded annually. Round to the nearest dollar at each step.

    (a) _____
    (b) _____

13. **VALUE OF A BUSINESS** Jessie Marquette believes her hair salon is worth $20,000 and estimates that its value will grow at 10% per year compounded annually for the next 3 years. If she sells the business, the funds will be invested at 8% compounded quarterly. (a) Find the future value if she holds onto the business. (b) What price should she insist on now if she sells the business? Round to the nearest dollar.

    (a) _____
    (b) _____

14. **VALUE OF A BUSINESS**   John Fernandez figures his bike shop is worth $88,000 if sold today and that it will grow in value at 8% per year compounded annually for the next 6 years. If he sells the business, the funds will be invested at 5% compounded semiannually. **(a)** Find the future value of the shop. **(b)** What price should he insist on at this time if he sells the business?

(a) _____

(b) _____

15. Explain the difference between future value and present value. (See Objective 1.)

16. Explain how and when to use both the compound interest table in Section 10.1 and the present value table in this section.

QUICK CHECK ANSWERS

1. $18,681.50

2. $235,539.50

3. $7101.68

4. $111,670.35

▼ # Chapter 10   Quick Review

Chapter Terms   *Review the following terms to test your understanding of the chapter. For each term you do not know, refer to the page number found next to that term.*

CD [**p. 392**]

CPI [**p. 393**]

certificate of deposit [**p. 392**]

compound amount
   [**p. 378**]

compound interest [**p. 378**]

compounded daily [**p. 389**]

compounding period [**p. 380**]

consumer price index [**p. 393**]

cost of living index [**p. 393**]

deflation [**p. 394**]

exponents [**p. 381**]

formula for compound
   interest [**p. 381**]

future amount [**p. 378**]

future value [**p. 378**]

inflation [**p. 392**]

interest-bearing checking
   accounts [**p. 389**]

interest rate per compounding
   period [**p. 380**]

money market accounts
   [**p. 389**]

passbook accounts [**p. 389**]

present value [**p. 399**]

savings accounts [**p. 389**]

simple interest [**p. 378**]

time deposit [**p. 392**]

CONCEPTS

10.1 Finding compound amount and compound interest

Find the number of compounding periods (n) and the interest rate per period (i).

Use the compound interest table to find the interest on $1.

Multiply the table value by the principal to obtain the compound amount.

Subtract principal from compound amount to obtain the interest.

10.2 Finding the interest earned when the interest is compounded daily

Find the number of days that the deposit earns interest.

Use the 90-day or 1-quarter table to calculate interest on $1.

Find compound amount using the formula

   Compound amount = Principal × Table value

Find interest earned using the formula

   Interest = Compound amount − Principal

10.2 Finding the interest on time deposits

Use the compound interest for time deposit accounts table to find the interest on $1 compounded daily.

Find the compound amount using the formula

   Compound amount = Principal × Table value

Find interest using the formula

   Interest = Compound amount − Principal

10.2 Finding the effect of inflation on a pay raise

Find the new salary by multiplying the old salary by (1 + percent increase).

Find the salary needed to offset inflation by multiplying the old salary by (1 + inflation rate).

Find the gain or loss by subtracting.

EXAMPLES

Tom Jones invested $3000 at 6% compounded quarterly for 7 years.

There are $7 \times 4 = 28$ quarters or compounding periods in 7 years.

Interest of 6% per year $= \frac{6\%}{4} = 1\frac{1}{2}\%$ per period.

Find $1\frac{1}{2}\%$ across the top of the compound interest table and 28 down the left side to find **1.51722**.

   Compound amount = $3000 × **1.51722** = $4551.66

   Interest = $4551.66 − $3000 = $1551.66

Mary Carver deposits $1000 at $3\frac{1}{2}\%$ compounded daily on May 15. She withdraws the money on July 17. Find the compounded amount and interest earned.

May 15–May 31	16 days
June	30 days
July 1–July 17	17 days
	63 days

   Table value = **1.006059089**

   Compound amount = $1000 × **1.006059089** = **$1006.06**

   Interest = **$1006.06** − $1000 = $6.06

Susan Barbee invests $50,000 in a certificate of deposit paying 3% compounded daily. Find the amount after 4 years.

   Table value for 4 years at 3% = **1.12749129**

   Compound amount = $50,000 × **1.12749129** = $56,374.56

   Interest = $56,374.56 − $50,000 = $6374.56

Leticia Jaramillo earns $45,000 per year as a computer programmer. She gets a raise of 1% in a year in which inflation is 3%. Ignoring taxes, find the effect on her purchasing power.

   New salary = $45,000 × 1.01 = **$45,450**

Salary needed to offset
inflation = $45,000 × 1.03 = **$46,350**

   Loss in purchasing power = $46,350 − $45,450 = $900

CONCEPTS	EXAMPLES
10.3 Finding the present value of a future amount Determine the number of compounding periods (*n*). Determine the interest per compounding period (*i*). Use the values of *n* and *i* to determine the table value from the present value table. Find present value from the following formula. $\quad$ Present value = Future value $\times$ Table value	Sue York must pay a lump sum of \$4500 in 6 years. What lump sum deposited today at 6% compounded quarterly will amount to \$4500 in 6 years? $\quad$ Number of compounding periods = 6 $\times$ 4 = 24 $\quad$ Interest per compounding period = $\dfrac{6\%}{4}$ = $1\frac{1}{2}\%$ **per period** $\qquad\qquad$ Table value = **.69954** $\quad$ Present value = \$4500 $\times$ **.69954** = \$3147.93

Case Study

VALUING A CHAIN OF MCDONALD'S RESTAURANTS

James and Mary Watson own a small chain of McDonald's restaurants that is valued at $2,300,000. They believe that the chain will grow in value at 12% per year compounded annually for the next 5 years. If they sell the chain, the funds will be invested at a rate of 6% compounded semiannually. They expect inflation to be 4% per year for the next 5 years. Ignore taxes, and answer the following, rounding answers to the nearest dollar at each step.

1. Find the future value of the chain after 5 years. Then find the price they should sell the chain for if they wish to have the same future value at the end of 5 years.

   1. _____

2. Find the future value of the chain if it grows at only 2% per year for 5 years. Then find the price they should ask for the chain given a 2% growth rate per year.

   2. _____

3. What future value would the chain be worth if it grew at their expected rate of inflation? Find the price they should ask for the chain if it grows at the rate of inflation.

   3. _____

4. Complete the following table.

Growth Rate	Future Value	Market Value Today
2%	_____	_____
4% (inflation)	_____	_____
12%	_____	_____

The value of the chain varies by more than one million dollars, depending on the rate of growth assumed for the business for the next 5 years.

INVESTIGATE

The interest rates that a bank pays depend on whether the money is in a checking account, money market account, savings account, or time deposit. Visit a local bank, and find the different interest rates that the bank will pay. Identify the conditions such as the minimum amount in an account, the minimum deposit, and the length of time the money must be on deposit to earn each interest rate.

▼ Case in Point Summary Exercise

BANK OF AMERICA

www.bankofamerica.com

Facts:

- 1904: Founded by son of Italian immigrants

- 1930s: Survived the Great Depression

- 2008: Acquired Countrywide Financial (home loans)

- 2009: Acquired Merrill Lynch (investments)

The financial crisis that began in 2008 was caused by a speculative bubble in home prices amidst far too much debt. As home prices fell, the excessive debt of families, banks, and other financial institutions became obvious. People spent less and tried to save or simply survive for those who had lost their jobs and homes. Corporations cut costs by laying off workers and rapidly slowing the inventory flowing in global supply chains. Home builders built far fewer homes and tried to quickly reduce debt. Banks made fewer loans and credit became very difficult to obtain. As the losses mounted, stock markets fell sharply. By the end of 2008, many governments around the world reacted to prevent another Great Depression similar to the one that occurred in the 1930s.

To keep the economic systems working, the U.S. government has spent several trillion dollars to support failing financial institutions and banks, extend unemployment benefits, increase employment, and support the sales of cars and homes. When it appeared that Countrywide Financial (home loans) and Merrill Lynch (investments) were in serious trouble, the U.S. government helped broker deals in which Bank of America took over both firms with the help of government loans and guarantees. However, Bank of America repaid the $45 billion in debt to the government at the end of 2009.

To demonstrate the effect of the recent financial crisis, we will use a small custom home builder called Horizon Homes which used Bank of America.

1. Find the gross profit for each year by multiplying gross sales by the profit margin.

Year	Gross Sales	Profit Margin	Profit or Loss
2007	$92,080,000	4.6%	_____
2008	$64,160,000	−12.3%	_____ Financial crisis begins
2009	$28,034,000	−30.5%	_____ Firm struggles to survive
2010	$24,000,000	2.0%	_____
2011	$32,060,000	1.6%	_____

2. In 1996, managers at Horizon Homes had anticipated eventual financial problems and they invested $2,500,000 earning 6% per year (ignore taxes). Find the future value of this investment in 2008 when the firm had its first big loss. Was the value of the investment enough to offset the 2008 loss?

2. _____

3. **(a)** Find the combined loss by adding the losses in 2008 and 2009. **(b)** Find the present value that needed to be set aside in 1996 assuming 6% compounded annually to offset the total losses for 2008 and 2009. *Hint:* For simplicity, assume that the total of the two years losses occurred in 2009.

(a) _____

(b) _____

4. Businesses incur risk, the possibility that bad things happen without warning. For example, a company may be adversely affected by a competitor that brings a better product to the market. Discuss what managers can do to better prepare for risk.

Discussion Question: *Do families also face risk? Explain using examples. If so, discuss what parents can do to prepare for risk.*

Chapter 10 Test

To help you review, the numbers in brackets show the section in which the topic was discussed.

In each of these problems, round to the nearest cent. Find the compound amount and the interest earned for the following.   **[10.1]**

	Amount	Rate	Compounded	Time (Years)	Compound Amount	Interest Earned
1.	$8700	4%	annually	8	_____	_____
2.	$12,000	6%	semiannually	5	_____	_____
3.	$9800	6%	semiannually	5	_____	_____
4.	$12,500	10%	quarterly	4	_____	_____

Find the interest earned by the following. Assume $3\frac{1}{2}$% interest compounded daily.   **[10.2]**

5. $6400 deposited September 24 and withdrawn December 15

5. _____

6. $63,340 deposited December 5 and withdrawn March 2

6. _____

7. $37,650 deposited December 12 and withdrawn on February 29 (leap year)

7. _____

Find the present value of the following.   **[10.3]**

	Amount Needed	Time (Years)	Rate	Compounded	Present Value
8.	$35,000	20	8%	annually	_____
9.	$15,750	7	6%	quarterly	_____
10.	$56,900	10	4%	semiannually	_____

Solve the following application problems.

11. A local branch of Gamestop, Inc., deposited $12,500 in a savings account on July 3 and then deposited an additional $3450 in the account on August 5. Find the balance on October 1 assuming an interest rate of $3\frac{1}{2}$% compounded daily.   **[10.2]**

11. _____

12. Discount Auto Insurance deposited $1800 in a savings account paying $3\frac{1}{2}$% compounded daily on January 1 and deposited an additional $2300 in the account on March 12. Find the balance on April 1.   **[10.2]**

12. _____

13. Mike George deposits $4000 in a certificate of deposit for 5 years. Find the compound amount if the interest rate is 3% compounded daily.   **[10.2]**

13. _____

14. Benton Signs places $35,000 in a 2-year certificate of deposit yielding 2% compounded daily and uses it for collateral for a loan. Find the compound amount.   **[10.2]**

14. _____

15. Liz Mulig earns $52,000 per year as a philosophy professor. She receives a raise of 2.5% in a year in which the CPI increases by 3.8%. Ignoring taxes, find the effect of the two increases on her purchasing power.   **[10.2]**

15. _____

16. James Arnosti makes $65,000 per year as an editor for a publisher. He was notified of a 1.5% raise in a year in which the CPI increased by 4%. Find the gain or loss in his purchasing power.   **[10.2]**

16. _____

17. A note for $3500 was made at 8% per year compounded annually for 3 years. Find (a) the maturity value and (b) the present value of the note assuming 5% per year compounded semiannually. **[10.3]**

(a) _____

(b) _____

18. Computers, Inc., accepted a 2-year note for $12,540 in lieu of immediate payment for computer equipment sold to a local firm. Find (a) the maturity value given a 10% rate compounded annually and (b) the present value of the note at 6% per year compounded semiannually. **[10.3]**

(a) _____

(b) _____

19. A business worth $180,000 is expected to grow at 12% per year compounded annually for the next 4 years. (a) Find the expected future value. (b) If funds from the sale of the business today would be placed in an account yielding 8% compounded semiannually, what would be the minimum acceptable price for the business at this time? **[10.3]**

(a) _____

(b) _____

20. A corporation worth $40 million is expected to grow at 8% per year compounded annually for 5 years. (a) Find the future value to the nearest million. (b) The owners then propose to sell the firm and invest the proceeds in a new venture that should grow at 12% compounded annually for 4 years. Beginning with the future value from part (a) rounded to the nearest million, find the expected future value to the nearest million at the end of 4 additional years. **[10.1]**

(a) _____

(b) _____

Chapters 9–10 Cumulative Review

CHAPTERS 9 AND 10

Round money amounts to the nearest cent, time to the nearest day, and rates to the nearest tenth of a percent.

Find the value of the unknown quantity using simple interest. Use banker's interest.   **[9.1–9.2]**

	Interest	Principal	Rate	Time		
1.	_____	$6800	8%	6 months	1.	_____
2.	_____	$6200	9.7%	250 days	2.	_____
3.	$165.28	_____	7%	100 days	3.	_____
4.	$475	_____	9.5%	180 days	4.	_____
5.	$249.38	$10,500	_____	90 days	5.	_____
6.	$733.33	$12,000	_____	200 days	6.	_____
7.	$202.22	$9100	10%	_____	7.	_____
8.	$915	$18,300	6%	_____	8.	_____

Find the discount and the proceeds.   **[9.3]**

	Face Value	Discount Rate	Time (Days)	Discount	Proceeds
9.	$9000	12%	90	_____	_____
10.	$875	$6\frac{1}{2}\%$	210	_____	_____

Find the net proceeds when each of the following is discounted.   **[9.4]**

	Maturity Value	Discount Rate	Discount Period	Net Proceeds
11.	$5000	10%	90 days	_____
12.	$12,000	9%	150 days	_____

Find the compound amounts for the following.   **[10.1]**

13. $1000 at 4% compounded annually for 5 years   13. _____

14. $3520 at 8% compounded annually for 10 years   14. _____

Find the interest earned and compound amounts for each of the following. Assume $3\frac{1}{2}\%$ interest compounded daily. **[10.2]**

	Amount	Date Deposited	Date Withdrawn	Interest Earned	Compound Amount
15.	$12,600	March 24	June 3	_____	_____
16.	$7500	Nov. 20	Feb. 14	_____	_____

Find the present value and the amount of interest earned for the following. Round to the nearest cent. **[10.3]**

	Amount Needed	Time (Years)	Interest	Compounded	Present Value	Interest
17.	$1000	7	8%	annually	_____	_____
18.	$19,000	9	5%	semiannually	_____	_____

Solve the following application problems. Use a 360-day year where applicable.

19. Cathy Cockrell signed a 180-day simple discount note with a rate of 10% and a face value of $25,000. Find **(a)** the interest and **(b)** the proceeds. **[9.3]**

(a) _____
(b) _____

20. As a project manager, Regina Foster received a bonus of $18,000 for completing a difficult project on time. She invests it at 6% compounded quarterly for 5 years. Find the future value. **[10.1]**

20. _____

21. A divorce settlement requires Samantha James to pay her ex-spouse $12,000 in 2 years. What lump sum can be invested today at 5% compounded semiannually so that enough will be available for the payment? **[10.3]**

21. _____

22. Tom Davis owes $7850 to a relative. He has agreed to repay the money in 5 months, at an interest rate of 6%. One month before the loan is due, the relative discounts the loan at the bank. The bank charges a 7.92% discount rate. How much money does the relative receive? **[9.4]**

22. _____

23. The owner of Jessica's Cookies has an extra $3200 that she puts into a savings account paying $3\frac{1}{2}\%$ per year compounded daily. Find the interest if the funds are left there for 65 days. **[10.2]**

23. _____

11 Annuities, Stocks, and Bonds

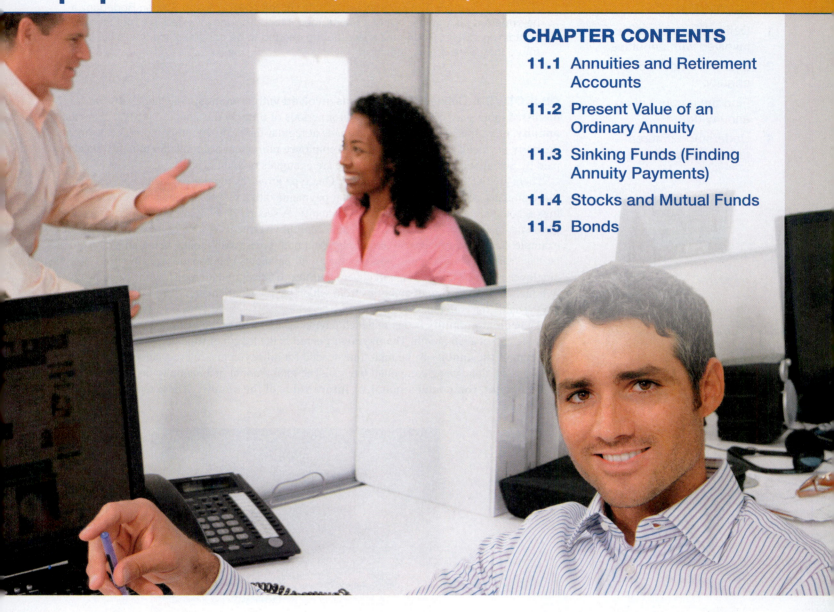

CHAPTER CONTENTS

11.1 Annuities and Retirement Accounts

11.2 Present Value of an Ordinary Annuity

11.3 Sinking Funds (Finding Annuity Payments)

11.4 Stocks and Mutual Funds

11.5 Bonds

▼ CASE IN POINT

ROMAN RODRIGUEZ received his associate of arts degree in computer information systems at American River College and then received a bachelor's degree in the same field of study at a 4-year university. He worked in various computer labs at the community college when he was a student and was very pleased when he was offered a full-time job after graduation.

The director of the Human Resources Department explained health insurance and retirement plan benefits to Rodriguez. Roman already knew that contributions he made into the retirement plan would be tax deductible, thereby reducing his current taxes. However, he was surprised to learn that the community college would match any contributions he made into the retirement plan up to 5% of his annual salary.

Roman wrote down his thoughts about the retirement plan:

1. He can put up to 5% of his income into the plan.
2. The contribution is tax deductible, thereby reducing his current income taxes.
3. The college will contribute an equal amount to his plan.
4. Funds in the plan grow income-tax free until taken out.

After looking at the numbers, Rodriguez quickly signed up to contribute 5% of his salary to his retirement plan.

413

▼11.1 Annuities and Retirement Accounts

OBJECTIVES

1   Define the basic terms involved with annuities.

2   Find the amount of an annuity.

3   Find the amount of an annuity due.

4   Understand different retirement accounts.

▼ CASE IN POINT   The benefits coordinator at the college asked Roman Rodriguez if he preferred an annuity paying a guaranteed interest or one invested in a mutual fund containing stocks. Rodriguez knew that he needed to be careful, since it was his financial future they were discussing.

OBJECTIVE 1 Define the basic terms involved with annuities.   In Chapter 10, we discussed lump sums that were invested for periods of time. In this chapter, we talk about an **annuity**, or a series of equal payments made at regular intervals. Monthly mortgage payments, quarterly payments by a company into an employee retirement account, and monthly checks paid by Social Security to a retired couple are examples of annuities.

There are two basic types of annuities. One type grows as regular payments are made and it accumulates compound interest. Regular payments into a retirement account or college savings account are examples of this type of annuity. A second type of annuity involves regular payments made out of an accumulated sum. Monthly payments from a retirement fund are an example. Retirement funds can in fact represent both types, with money being added on a regular basis while an employee is working, then with payments being made from the fund after the employee retires. This section will cover annuities that accumulate funds, while Section 11.2 will include a discussion of annuities from which payments are made. The basic terms involved are the same for both types.

An **ordinary annuity** is one in which payments are made at the end of each period, such as at the end of each month. The **payment period** is the length of time between payments and the **term of the annuity** is the total time needed for all payments. Interest calculations for annuities are done using compound interest. The total amount in an annuity on a future date is the **amount, compound amount,** or **future value of the annuity**. These terms are used interchangeably.

The amount an annuity grows to can be found using compound interest techniques from Chapter 10. For example, suppose a firm makes deposits of $3000 at the end of each year for 6 years into an investment earning 8% compounded annually. Use the compound interest tables in Section 10.1 for 5 years and 8% to find the future value of the first payment as follows:

$$\$3000 \times \mathbf{1.46933} = \$4407.99$$

The future value of the annuity is *the sum* of the compound amounts of all six payments. The annuity ends on the day of the last payment. Therefore, the last payment, which is made at the end of year 6, earns no interest.

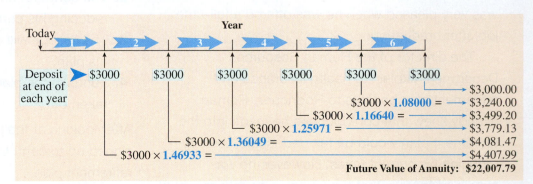

The future value of the annuity is $22,007.79. Find the total amount deposited in the annuity and interest earned as follows:

$$\text{Total deposits} = 6 \text{ years} \times \$3000 \text{ per year} = \$18,000$$

$$\text{Interest earned} = \text{Future value of annuity} - \text{Total deposits}$$

$$= \qquad \$22,007.79 \qquad - \qquad \$18,000$$

$$= \$4007.79$$

OBJECTIVE 2 **Find the amount of an annuity.** The amount of an annuity can also be found using the amount of an annuity table on page 417. The number from the table is the amount or future value of an annuity with a payment of $1. The amount of an annuity with any payment is found as follows.

> **Finding Amount of an Annuity**
>
> Amount = Payment × Number from amount of an annuity table

As a check, reconsider the annuity of $3000 at the end of each year for 6 years at 8% compounded annually. Locate 8% at the top of the table on page 417 and 6 periods in the far left (or far right) column to find **7.33593.**

$$\text{Amount} = \$3000 \times \mathbf{7.33593} = \$22,007.79$$

This amount is identical to the amount calculated earlier, but sometimes the estimates from the table differ slightly from those found using a calculator.

Finding the Value of an Annuity and Interest Earned

 EXAMPLE 1

Roman Rodriguez's employer will match his contributions into a retirement plan up to 5% of his $32,000 annual salary. In other words, the employer will put $1 into his retirement plan for every $1 Rodriguez puts into his retirement plan up to the limit. Find the future amount in 8 years if every quarter he contributes the maximum allowed assuming (a) funds earn 4% compounded quarterly and (b) funds earn 8% compounded quarterly. (c) Then find the difference between the two.

▼ CASE IN POINT

SOLUTION

$$\text{Salary per quarter} = \$32,000 \div 4 = \$8000$$

Total contributions = Rodriguez's contributions + **Employer's matching contributions**

$$= \qquad .05 \times \$8000 \qquad + \qquad \mathbf{.05 \times \$8000}$$

$$= \qquad \$400 \qquad + \qquad \mathbf{\$400}$$

$$= \$800 \text{ invested per quarter}$$

(a) Interest of $\frac{4\%}{4} = 1\%$ is earned per quarter for $8 \times 4 = 32$ quarters. Look across the top of the table for 1% and down the side for 32 periods to find **37.49407.**

$$\text{Amount} = \$800 \times \mathbf{37.49407} = \mathbf{\$29,995.26} \text{ (rounded)}$$

(b) Interest of $\frac{8\%}{4} = 2\%$ is earned per quarter for $8 \times 4 = 32$ quarters. Look across the top of the table for 2% and down the side for 32 periods to find **44.22703.**

$$\text{Amount} = \$800 \times \mathbf{44.22703} = \mathbf{\$35,381.62} \text{ (rounded)}$$

(c) Difference = $35,381.62 - $30,295.21 = **$5086.41**

> **QUICK CHECK 1**
>
> At the end of every quarter, $2000 is put into a retirement plan that earns 6% compounded quarterly. Find the future value in 5 years.

Finding the Amount of an Annuity and Interest Earned

EXAMPLE 2

At the birth of her grandson, Junella Smith commits to help pay for his college education. She decides to make deposits of $600 at the end of each 6 months into an account for 17 years. Find the **amount of the annuity** and the interest earned, assuming 6% compounded semiannually.

SOLUTION

Interest of $\frac{6\%}{2} = 3\%$ is earned each semiannual period. There are $17 \times 2 = 34$ semiannual periods in 17 years. Find 3% across the top and 34 periods down the side of the table for **57.73018**.

$$\text{Amount} = \$600 \times \mathbf{57.73018} = \$34,638.11$$

$$\text{Interest} = \$34,638.11 - (\mathbf{34} \times \mathbf{\$600}) = \mathbf{\$14,238.11} \text{ (rounded)}$$

Smith knows that a college education will cost a lot more in 17 years than it does now, but she also knows that $34,638.11 will be of great help to her grandson.

Financial Calculator Solution

In this example, payment ($600), interest rate per compounding period (3%), and number of compounding periods (34) are known. Future value is the unknown. Enter the payment as a negative number since it is an outflow of cash that Junella Smith pays each month. Finally, press the $\boxed{FV}$ key to find the future value, which is a positive value since it will be an inflow of cash to her grandson.

  $-600 \boxed{PMT} 3 \boxed{i} 34 \boxed{n} \boxed{FV} 34638.11$ (rounded)

QUICK CHECK 2

Bob Nelson deposits $250 into a retirement account at the end of every month for 30 months. The fund holds international stocks and Nelson optimistically thinks it may yield 12% compounded monthly. Find the future amount.

OBJECTIVE 3 Find the amount of an annuity due. Payments were made at the *end of each period* in the ordinary annuities discussed previously. In contrast, an annuity in which payments are made at the *beginning of each time period* is called an **annuity due.** Ordinary annuity and annuity due are just two types of annuities.

Finding the Amount of an Annuity Due

Step 1 Add 1 to the number of periods.

Step 2 Find: Amount = Payment × Number from amount of an annuity table.

Step 3 Subtract 1 payment.

Finding the Amount of an Annuity Due

EXAMPLE 3

Mr. and Mrs. Thompson set up an investment program using an *annuity due* with payments of $500 at the *beginning of each quarter*. Find **(a)** the amount of the annuity and **(b)** the interest if they make payments for 7 years into an investment expected to pay 8% compounded quarterly.

SOLUTION

(a) Step 1 Interest of $\frac{8\%}{4} = 2\%$ is earned each quarter. There are $7 \times 4 = 28$ periods in 7 years. Since it is an annuity due, add 1 period to 28, making 29 periods.

Step 2 Look across the top of the table for 2% and down the side for 29 periods to find **38.79223**.

$$\$500 \times \mathbf{38.79223} = \mathbf{\$19,396.12} \text{ (rounded)}$$

Step 3 Now subtract one payment to find the amount of the annuity due.

$$\text{Amount of annuity due} = \mathbf{\$19,396.12} - \$500 = \$18,896.12$$

(b) Subtract the 28 payments (7 years × 4 payments per year) of $500 each to find the interest.

$$\text{Interest} = \$18,896.12 - (\mathbf{28} \times \mathbf{\$500}) = \$4896.12$$

 The calculator solution to finding the interest in part **(b)** follows.

$$18896.12 \boxed{-} 28 \boxed{\times} 500 \boxed{=} 4896.12$$

Note: Refer to Appendix B for calculator basics.

Quick TIP

For an annuity due, be sure to add 1 period to the number of compounding periods and subtract 1 payment from the amount calculated.

Amount of an Annuity Table

Period											Period
					Interest Rate per Period						
n	1%	1½%	2%	2½%	3%	4%	5%	6%	8%	10%	12%	*n*
1	1.00000	1.00000	1.00000	1.00000	1.00000	1.00000	1.00000	1.00000	1.00000	1.00000	1.00000	1
2	2.01000	2.01500	2.02000	2.02500	2.03000	2.04000	2.05000	2.06000	2.08000	2.10000	2.12000	2
3	3.03010	3.04522	3.06040	3.07562	3.09090	3.12160	3.15250	3.18360	3.24640	3.31000	3.37440	3
4	4.06040	4.09090	4.12161	4.15252	4.18363	4.24646	4.31013	4.37462	4.50611	4.64100	4.77933	4
5	5.10101	5.15227	5.20404	5.25633	5.30914	5.41632	5.52563	5.63709	5.86660	6.10510	6.35285	5
6	6.15202	6.22955	6.30812	6.38774	6.46841	6.63298	6.80191	6.97532	7.33593	7.71561	8.11519	6
7	7.21354	7.32299	7.43428	7.54743	7.66246	7.89829	8.14201	8.39384	8.92280	9.48717	10.08901	7
8	8.28567	8.43284	8.58297	8.73612	8.89234	9.21423	9.54911	9.89747	10.63663	11.43589	12.29969	8
9	9.36853	9.55933	9.75463	9.95452	10.15911	10.58280	11.02656	11.49132	12.48756	13.57948	14.77566	9
10	10.46221	10.70272	10.94972	11.20338	11.46388	12.00611	12.57789	13.18079	14.48656	15.93742	17.54874	10
11	11.56683	11.86326	12.16872	12.48347	12.80780	13.48635	14.20679	14.97164	16.64549	18.53117	20.65458	11
12	12.68250	13.04121	13.41209	13.79555	14.19203	15.02581	15.91713	16.86994	18.97713	21.38428	24.13313	12
13	13.80933	14.23683	14.68033	15.14044	15.61779	16.62684	17.71298	18.88214	21.49530	24.52271	28.02911	13
14	14.94742	15.45038	15.97394	16.51895	17.08632	18.29191	19.59863	21.01507	24.21492	27.97498	32.39260	14
15	16.09690	16.68214	17.29342	17.93193	18.59891	20.02359	21.57856	23.27597	27.15211	31.77248	37.27971	15
16	17.25786	17.93237	18.63929	19.38022	20.15688	21.82453	23.65749	25.67253	30.32428	35.94973	42.75328	16
17	18.43044	19.20136	20.01207	20.86473	21.76159	23.69751	25.84037	28.21288	33.75023	40.54470	48.88367	17
18	19.61475	20.48938	21.41231	22.38635	23.41444	25.64541	28.13238	30.90565	37.45024	45.59917	55.74971	18
19	20.81090	21.79672	22.84056	23.94601	25.11687	27.67123	30.53900	33.75999	41.44626	51.15909	63.43968	19
20	22.01900	23.12367	24.29737	25.54466	26.87037	29.77808	33.06595	36.78559	45.76196	57.27500	72.05244	20
21	23.23919	24.47052	25.78332	27.18327	28.67649	31.96920	35.71925	39.99273	50.42292	64.00250	81.69874	21
22	24.47159	25.83758	27.29898	28.86286	30.53678	34.24797	38.50521	43.39229	55.45676	71.40275	92.50258	22
23	25.71630	27.22514	28.84496	30.58443	32.45288	36.61789	41.43048	46.99583	60.89330	79.54302	104.60289	23
24	26.97346	28.63352	30.42186	32.34904	34.42647	39.08260	44.50200	50.81558	66.76476	88.49733	118.15524	24
25	28.24320	30.06302	32.03030	34.15776	36.45926	41.64591	47.72710	54.86451	73.10594	98.34706	133.33387	25
26	29.52563	31.51397	33.67091	36.01171	38.55304	44.31174	51.11345	59.15638	79.95442	109.18177	150.33393	26
27	30.82089	32.98668	35.34432	37.91200	40.70963	47.08421	54.66913	63.70577	87.35077	121.09994	169.37401	27
28	32.12910	34.48148	37.05121	39.85980	42.93092	49.96758	58.40258	68.52811	95.33883	134.20994	190.69889	28
29	33.45039	35.99870	38.79223	41.85630	45.21885	52.96629	62.32271	73.63980	103.96594	148.63093	214.58275	29
30	34.78489	37.53868	40.56808	43.90270	47.57542	56.08494	66.43885	79.05819	113.28321	164.49402	241.33268	30
31	36.13274	39.10176	42.37944	46.00027	50.00268	59.32834	70.76079	84.80168	123.34587	181.94342	271.29261	31
32	37.49407	40.68829	44.22703	48.15028	52.50276	62.70147	75.29883	90.88978	134.21354	201.13777	304.84772	32
33	38.86901	42.29861	46.11157	50.35403	55.07784	66.20953	80.06377	97.34316	145.95062	222.25154	342.42945	33
34	40.25770	43.93309	48.03380	52.61289	57.73018	69.85791	85.06696	104.18375	158.62667	245.47670	384.52098	34
35	41.66028	45.59209	49.99448	54.92821	60.46208	73.65222	90.32031	111.43478	172.31680	271.02437	431.66350	35

Where will I live?

OBJECTIVE 4 Understand different retirement accounts. Many students see retirement as something very far away and mistakenly think they can wait until they are much older (say 50—ouch, that's old!) to worry about it. However, it takes a long time to save enough to retire comfortably. The clipping shows what can happen to someone who has not saved enough.

Retired Without Enough Assets...

In 2013, Tom Wheat found out that his Social Security retirement check would be $1247 per month. Given that he had his home paid for and had saved up some money, he retired. However, he has since developed diabetes and needs more money each month than he thought. Tom is almost 70 now, can no longer work, and is barely getting by on his fixed income from the government. He may need to sell his home, but where would he live?

Given that it takes years to accumulate a large amount of money, it is a good idea to start saving as soon as possible. Here are a few great features about retirement plans:

1. many firms make contributions into your plan, in addition to your salary;
2. your contributions are tax deductible;
3. funds in a retirement plan grow income tax free; and
4. funds in a retirement plan can be withdrawn early in the event of emergencies (but there may be a penalty).

Retirement plans are for everyone, *especially* recent college graduates.

Social Security is a retirement and disability program sponsored on behalf of workers sponsored by the federal government. You may have noticed FICA deductions from your paycheck – you are funding your Social Security benefits. See Chapter 6, Section 3 for more detail. However, it is difficult to live off Social Security payments alone.

Many employers have either **401(k)** or **403(b)** retirement plans into which they make regular contributions on behalf of each employee. The 401(k) plans are for those working in the private sector and the 403(b) are for various government and tax-exempt organizations. Employee contributions to either of these plans may be deductible and all funds grow income-tax free until funds are withdrawn.

Individuals who are not covered by an employer-sponsored plan may be eligible to contribute to an **individual retirement account (IRA)**. There are two types of IRAs:

Regular IRA – Deposits are usually tax deductible and grow income-tax free. Funds are subject to income taxes when withdrawn.

Roth IRA – Deposits are not tax deductible, but grow income-tax free. Funds are NOT subject to income taxes when withdrawn.

Many individuals set up IRAs at firms such as Schwab, Fidelity, or Vanguard and manage the funds themselves. The maximum allowable contribution into either type of IRA is $5500 if you are under 50, or $6500 if you are 50 or older. However, the allowable contribution may be higher in the future.

Roth IRA

WHICH IRA IS BEST FOR YOU?*		
	DEDUCTIBLE IRA	**ROTH IRA**
Tax deductible?	If you qualify	No
Taxable at withdrawal?	Yes	No
Penalty for early withdrawal?	Yes, prior to age 59½	Yes
Mandatory withdrawal age?	70½	None
Penalty-free withdrawals?	$10,000 for first-time home buyers; unlimited for education	$10,000 for first-time home buyers, after five-year wait; unlimited for education

*There are numerous rules related to each type of IRA. Research carefully before deciding which is best for you.

Regular contributions into either an IRA or a company-sponsored retirement plan are an annuity. The amount of the annuity is found using the same methods discussed earlier in this section. Payments are made at the end of each period in an ordinary annuity, and payments are made at the beginning of each year in an annuity due.

Finding the Value of an IRA

EXAMPLE
4

At 27, Joann Gretz sets up an IRA with online broker Charles Schwab, where she plans to deposit $2000 at the end of each year until age 60. Find the amount of the annuity if she invests in **(a)** a bond fund that has historically yielded 6% compounded annually versus **(b)** a stock fund that has historically yielded 10% compounded annually. Assume that future yields equal historical yields.

SOLUTION

Age 60 is $60 - 27 =$ **33 years away**, so she will make deposits at the end of each year for 33 years.

(a) Bond fund: Look down the left column of the amount of an annuity table on page 417 for 33 years and across the top for 6% to find **97.34316**.

$$\text{Amount} = \$2000 \times \textbf{97.34316} = \$194{,}686.32$$

Quick TIP

Investments can be risky. For example, stocks usually increase in value over the long term, but they may go down as well.

(b) Stock fund: Look down the left column of the table for 33 years and across the top for 10% to find **222.25154**.

$$\text{Amount} = \$2000 \times \textbf{222.25154} = \$444{,}503.08$$

The differences in the two investments are shown in the figure. Gretz wants the larger amount, but she is worried she might lose money in the stock fund. See *Exercise 20* at the end of this section to find her investment choice.

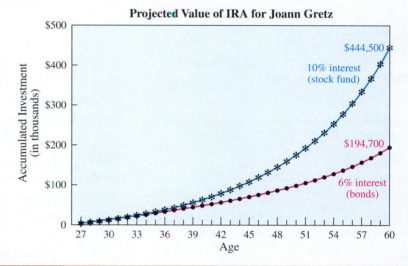

QUICK CHECK 4

Bill James plans to deposit $2500 in a regular IRA at the end of each six month period for the next 17 years until he retires. Find the future value if funds earn **(a)** 5% compounded semiannually and **(b)** 8% compounded semiannually.

Currently, more than 50 million people receive regular payments from Social Security. Workers can retire as early as age 62 and get reduced benefits, or they can wait until full retirement age and receive full benefits. The full retirement age will increase gradually until it reaches age 67 for people born after 1959. The bar graph shows the importance of Social Security to Americans.

DATA: Social Security Administration

▼ 11.1 Exercises   MyMathLab®

*The shaded sections below contain solutions to help you get a **QUICK START** on the various types of exercises.*

Find the amount of the following ordinary annuities rounded to the nearest cent. Find the total interest earned. (See Examples 1 and 2.)

Amount of Each Deposit	Deposited	Rate	Time (Years)	Amount of Annuity	Interest Earned
1. $900	annually	5%	18	$25,319.14	$9119.14
$900 × 28.13238 = $25,319.14; I = $25,319.14 − (18 × $900) = $9119.14					
2. $2900	annually	8%	5	$17,013.14	$2513.14
$2900 × 5.86660 = $17,013.14; I = $17,013.14 − (5 × $2900) = $2513.14					
3. $7500	semiannually	6%	10	_____	_____
4. $9200	semiannually	8%	5	_____	_____
5. $3500	quarterly	10%	7	_____	_____
6. $6900	quarterly	4%	4	_____	_____

Find the amount of the following annuities due rounded to the nearest cent. Find the total interest earned. (See Example 3.)

Amount of Each Deposit	Deposited	Rate	Time (Years)	Amount of Annuity	Interest Earned
7. $1200	annually	8%	5	$7603.12	$1603.12
Look up 8%, 5 + 1 = 6 periods, finding 7.33593. $1200 × 7.33593 − $1200 = $7603.12					
Interest = $7603.12 − 5 × $1200 = $1603.12					
8. $400	annually	6%	6	$2957.54	$557.54
Look up 6%, 6 + 1 = 7 periods, finding 8.39384. $400 × 8.39384 − $400 = $2957.54					
Interest = $2957.54 − 6 × $400 = $557.54					
9. $9500	semiannually	4%	9	_____	_____
10. $1800	semiannually	5%	6	_____	_____
11. $3800	quarterly	8%	3	_____	_____
12. $10,200	quarterly	10%	5	_____	_____

◩ indicates an exercise that is related to the Case in Point feature.

13. Explain the difference between an annuity and an annuity due. (See Objectives 2 and 3.)

14. Describe the differences between an IRA, a 401(k), and a 403(b). (See Objective 4.)

Solve the following application problems.

15. RETIREMENT PLANNING   Roman Rodriguez would like to know if he can retire in 35 years at age 60, when he plans to fish a lot. Assume the total deposit into his retirement account at the community college is $3800 at the end of each year and that the fund earns 6% per year. Find **(a)** the amount of the annuity and **(b)** the interest earned.

(a) $423,452.16

(b) $290,452.16

(a) Amount = $3800 × 111.43478 = $423,452.16
(b) Interest = $423,452.16 − 35 × $3800 = $290,452.16

16. SAVING FOR A HOME   Jim and Betty Collins need an additional $6500 for a down payment on a home they hope to buy in 2 years. They invest $800 at the end of each quarter in an account earning 6% compounded quarterly. Find **(a)** the amount of the annuity and **(b)** the interest earned.

(a) _____

(b) _____

17. CHILD-CARE PAYMENTS   Monique Chaney places $250 of her quarterly child support check into an annuity for the education of her child. She does this at the beginning of each quarter for 8 years into an account paying 8% per year, compounded quarterly. Find **(a)** the amount of the annuity and **(b)** the interest earned.

(a) _____

(b) _____

18. RETIREMENT   Jason Horton works for Chevron as a welder on offshore drilling rigs. His retirement plan contributions are $3800 at the beginning of each 6-month period. Assume that the account grows at 6% compounded semiannually for 15 years. Find the **(a)** future value of the annuity and **(b)** the interest earned.

(a) _____

(b) _____

19. MUTUAL FUND INVESTING   Sandra Gonzales deposits $1000 into a mutual fund containing international stocks at the end of each semiannual period for 12 years. Assume the fund earns 10% interest compounded semiannually and find the future value.

19. _____

20. T-BILL AND STOCK INVESTING   Joann Gretz (see Example 4, page 419) decides to place half of her $2000 deposit at the end of each year into the bond fund and half into the stock fund. Assume the bond fund earns 6% compounded annually and the stock fund earns 10% compounded annually. Find the amount available in 33 years.

20. _____

QUICK CHECK ANSWERS

1. $46,247.34

2. $8696.22

3. $19,864.73

4. (a) $131,532.23   **(b)** $174,644.78

▼11.2 Present Value of an Ordinary Annuity

OBJECTIVES

1   Define the present value of an ordinary annuity.

2   Use the formula to find the present value of an ordinary annuity.

3   Find the equivalent cash price of an ordinary annuity.

OBJECTIVE 1 Define the present value of an ordinary annuity. Chapter 10 was about lump sums of money. In that chapter, present value was defined as the lump sum that must be deposited in an account today so that it will grow to the required future value by a certain date. Those calculations required the interest rate per compounding period (i) and the number of compounding periods (n), as do the calculations in this chapter.

Chapter 11 is about annuities that involve periodic payments. In Section 11.1, you learned how to find the future value of an annuity. In this section, you will learn how to find the present value of an annuity. The **present value of an annuity** can be thought of in two ways. The first way is an annuity that accumulates funds. The second uses up funds that have already been accumulated to make a series of payments.

> **Present Value of an Annuity**
>
> 1.   Assume a firm needs $100,000 exactly 3 years from today. It can achieve that goal by making a single, lump-sum deposit today, or it can accumulate the $100,000 by making regular payments into an investment. The two methods are equivalent to one another. (See Example 1.)
>
> 2.   A divorced man must make a $1500 payment at the end of each quarter for child support until his son turns 16. The present value of this annuity is the amount that must be deposited today that will generate the needed payments. (See Example 2.)

OBJECTIVE 2 Use the formula to find the present value of an ordinary annuity. The present value of an annuity with periodic payments at the end of each period is found using values from the table.

> **Finding Present Value of an Annuity**
>
> $$\text{Present value of annuity} = \text{Payment} \times \frac{\text{Number from the present value}}{\text{of an annuity table}}$$

Finding the Present Value of an Annuity

 EXAMPLE 1

At the end of each quarter for 5 years, the Daily News deposits $4325 in an account paying 6% compounded quarterly. The goal is to accumulate funds for a new printing press. **(a)** Use the concepts of Section 11.1 to find the future value of the annuity. **(b)** Then find the lump sum (present value) that must be deposited today to accumulate the same future value.

SOLUTION

(a) $\frac{6\%}{4} = 1\frac{1}{2}\%$ (or 1.5%) per quarter; 5 years $\times$ 4 = 20 quarters. Use the amount of an annuity table in Section 11.1 to find **23.12367**.

$$\text{Future value} = \$4325 \times \textbf{23.12367} = \$100,009.87 \text{ (rounded)}$$

(b) It is not necessary to use this future value to find the present value of the annuity. Instead, use the present value of an annuity table with 1.5% per period and 20 periods to find **17.16864**.

$$\text{Present value} = \$4325 \times \textbf{17.16864} = \$74,254.37$$

Thus, a deposit of $4325 at the end of every quarter for 5 years has a present value today of $74,254.37. If we assume 6% compounded quarterly and ignore income taxes, each of the following has exactly the same value:

> 1. 20 end-of-quarter deposits of $4325
> 2. A future value at the end of 5 years of $100,009.87
> 3. A present value on hand today of $74,254.37

QUICK CHECK 1

Walter and Beth Bates save $1200 at the end of each quarter for 7 years. Assume 8% compounded quarterly and find both **(a)** the future value and **(b)** the present value.

The three items listed at the end of the solution to Example 1 reinforce a very important idea in finance. The value of money depends on when it is available. Generally, money available today is worth more than money available in (say) 10 years. Lenders and investors use this idea every day to create profit. Suppose a bank lends you money today. It expects the interest on the debt to be enough to pay all bank expenses, make up for bad loans, and also make a profit. So, you have to pay the bank back more than you borrowed.

Finding the Present Value **EXAMPLE 2** Tom and Brandy Barrett recently divorced. The judge gave custody of their 4-year-old son to Brandy and ruled that Tom must pay $1500 in child support to Brandy at the end of each quarter until the son turns 16. Find the lump sum that Tom must put into an account earning 6% compounded quarterly to cover the periodic payments. Find the interest earned.

SOLUTION

Quick TIP

Although the $1500 withdrawals to Brandy are at the end of each quarter, the original lump sum must be deposited at the beginning of the first year.

Payments must be made for $16 - 4 = 12$ years, or for $12 \times 4 = 48$ quarters. The interest rate per quarter is $\frac{6\%}{4} = 1.5\%$ per quarter. Look across the top of the present value of an annuity table for 1.5% and down the side for 48 payments to find **34.04255**.

$$\text{Present value of annuity} = \$1500 \times \mathbf{34.04255} = \$51,063.83$$

A deposit of $51,063.83 today will make 48 end-of-quarter payments of $1500 each. Interest earned during the 12 years is the sum of all payments less the original lump sum.

$$\text{Interest} = (48 \times \$1500) - \$51,063.83 = \mathbf{\$20,936.17}$$

QUICK CHECK 2

Find the lump sum that must be set aside today to make end-of-month payments of $1000 for 2 years, assuming 12% compounded monthly. Then find the interest earned.

Finding the Present Value **EXAMPLE 3** An American company hires a project manager to work in Saudi Arabia. The contract states that if the manager works there for 5 years, he will receive an extra benefit of $15,000 at the end of each semiannual period for the 8 years that follow. Find the lump sum that can be deposited today to satisfy the contract, assuming 6% compounded semiannually.

SOLUTION

The project manager works from years 1 to 5. He then receives two $15,000 annuity payments each year during years 6 through 13. Solve this problem in two steps.

1. *Find the present value **at the beginning of year 6** of the annuity with $15,000 payments.*
   Use $\frac{6\%}{2} = 3\%$ per compounding period and $8 \times 2 = 16$ compounding periods to find **12.56110** in the present value of an annuity table.

   $$\text{Present value of annuity} = \$15,000 \times \textbf{12.56110} = \$188,416.50$$

   This is the *present value* of the annuity needed at the beginning of year 6 to fund payments in years 6 through 13. But it is also the *future value* needed for the investment made today that will fund the eventual payments.

2. *Find the lump sum **needed today** to accumulate the $188,416.50 by the end of year 5.*
   Use the table showing present value of a dollar in Section 10.3 (page 422) with $\frac{6\%}{2} = 3\%$ per compounding period and $5 \times 2 = 10$ compounding periods to find **.74409**.

   $$\text{Present value needed today} = \$188,416.50 \times \textbf{.74409} = \$140,198.83$$

   A lump sum of $140,198.83 today will grow to $188,416.50 in 5 years. The $188,416.50 at the end of year 5 is enough to make 16 semiannual payments of $15,000 each during years 6 through 13.

Present Value of an Annuity Table

Period	1%	1½%	2%	2½%	3%	4%	5%	6%	8%	10%	Period
1	.99010	.98522	.98039	.97561	.97087	.96154	.95238	.94340	.92593	.90909	1
2	1.97040	1.95588	1.94156	1.92742	1.91347	1.88609	1.85941	1.83339	1.78326	1.73554	2
3	2.94099	2.91220	2.88388	2.85602	2.82861	2.77509	2.72325	2.67301	2.57710	2.48685	3
4	3.90197	3.85438	3.80773	3.76197	3.71710	3.62990	3.54595	3.46511	3.31213	3.16987	4
5	4.85343	4.78264	4.71346	4.64583	4.57971	4.45182	4.32948	4.21236	3.99271	3.79079	5
6	5.79548	5.69719	5.60143	5.50813	5.41719	5.24214	5.07569	4.91732	4.62288	4.35526	6
7	6.72819	6.59821	6.47199	6.34939	6.23028	6.00205	5.78637	5.58238	5.20637	4.86842	7
8	7.65168	7.48593	7.32548	7.17014	7.01969	6.73274	6.46321	6.20979	5.74664	5.33493	8
9	8.56602	8.36052	8.16224	7.97087	7.78611	7.43533	7.10782	6.80169	6.24689	5.75902	9
10	9.47130	9.22218	8.98259	8.75206	8.53020	8.11090	7.72173	7.36009	6.71008	6.14457	10
11	10.36763	10.07112	9.78685	9.51421	9.25262	8.76048	8.30641	7.88687	7.13896	6.49506	11
12	11.25508	10.90751	10.57534	10.25776	9.95400	9.38507	8.86325	8.38384	7.53608	6.81369	12
13	12.13374	11.73153	11.34837	10.98318	10.63496	9.98565	9.39357	8.85268	7.90378	7.10336	13
14	13.00370	12.54338	12.10625	11.69091	11.29607	10.56312	9.89864	9.29498	8.24424	7.36669	14
15	13.86505	13.34323	12.84926	12.38138	11.93794	11.11839	10.37966	9.71225	8.55948	7.60608	15
16	14.71787	14.13126	13.57771	13.05500	12.56110	11.65230	10.83777	10.10590	8.85137	7.82371	16
17	15.56225	14.90765	14.29187	13.71220	13.16612	12.16567	11.27407	10.47726	9.12164	8.02155	17
18	16.39827	15.67256	14.99203	14.35336	13.75351	12.65930	11.68959	10.82760	9.37189	8.20141	18
19	17.22601	16.42617	15.67846	14.97889	14.32380	13.13394	12.08532	11.15812	9.60360	8.36492	19
20	18.04555	17.16864	16.35143	15.58916	14.87747	13.59033	12.46221	11.46992	9.81815	8.51356	20
21	18.85698	17.90014	17.01121	16.18455	15.41502	14.02916	12.82115	11.76408	10.01680	8.64869	21
22	19.66038	18.62082	17.65805	16.76541	15.93692	14.45112	13.16300	12.04158	10.20074	8.77154	22
23	20.45582	19.33086	18.29220	17.33211	16.44361	14.85684	13.48857	12.30338	10.37106	8.88322	23
24	21.24339	20.03041	18.91393	17.88499	16.93554	15.24696	13.79864	12.55036	10.52876	8.98474	24
25	22.02316	20.71961	19.52346	18.42438	17.41315	15.62208	14.09394	12.78336	10.67478	9.07704	25
26	22.79520	21.39863	20.12104	18.95061	17.87684	15.98277	14.37519	13.00317	10.80998	9.16095	26
27	23.55961	22.06762	20.70690	19.46401	18.32703	16.32959	14.64303	13.21053	10.93516	9.23722	27
28	24.31644	22.72672	21.28127	19.96489	18.76411	16.66306	14.89813	13.40616	11.05108	9.30657	28

(Continued)

				Present Value of an Annuity Table (Continued)							
					Interest Rate per Period						
Period	**1%**	**1½%**	**2%**	**2½%**	**3%**	**4%**	**5%**	**6%**	**8%**	**10%**	**Period**
29	25.06579	23.37608	21.84438	20.45355	19.18845	16.98371	15.14107	13.59072	11.15841	9.36961	29
30	25.80771	24.01584	22.39646	20.93029	19.60044	17.29203	15.37245	13.76483	11.25778	9.42691	30
31	26.54229	24.64615	22.93770	21.39541	20.00043	17.58849	15.59281	13.92909	11.34980	9.47901	31
32	27.26959	25.26714	23.46833	21.84918	20.38877	17.87355	15.80268	14.08404	11.43500	9.52638	32
33	27.98969	25.87895	23.98856	22.29188	20.76579	18.14765	16.00255	14.23023	11.51389	9.56943	33
34	28.70267	26.48173	24.49859	22.72379	21.13184	18.41120	16.19290	14.36814	11.58693	9.60857	34
35	29.40858	27.07559	24.99862	23.14516	21.48722	18.66461	16.37419	14.49825	11.65457	9.64416	35
36	30.10751	27.66068	25.48884	23.55625	21.83225	18.90828	16.54685	14.62099	11.71719	9.67651	36
37	30.79951	28.23713	25.96945	23.95732	22.16724	19.14258	16.71129	14.73678	11.77518	9.70592	37
38	31.48466	28.80505	26.44064	24.34860	22.49246	19.36786	16.86789	14.84602	11.82887	9.73265	38
39	32.16303	29.36458	26.90259	24.73034	22.80822	19.58448	17.01704	14.94907	11.87858	9.75696	39
40	32.83469	29.91585	27.35548	25.10278	23.11477	19.79277	17.15909	15.04630	11.92461	9.77905	40
41	33.49969	30.45896	27.79949	25.46612	23.41240	19.99305	17.29437	15.13802	11.96723	9.79914	41
42	34.15811	30.99405	28.23479	25.82061	23.70136	20.18563	17.42321	15.22454	12.00670	9.81740	42
43	34.81001	31.52123	28.66156	26.16645	23.98190	20.37079	17.54591	15.30617	12.04324	9.83400	43
44	35.45545	32.04062	29.07996	26.50385	24.25427	20.54884	17.66277	15.38318	12.07707	9.84909	44
45	36.09451	32.55234	29.49016	26.83302	24.51871	20.72004	17.77407	15.45583	12.10840	9.86281	45
46	36.72724	33.05649	29.89231	27.15417	24.77545	20.88465	17.88007	15.52437	12.13741	9.87528	46
47	37.35370	33.55319	30.28658	27.46748	25.02471	21.04294	17.98102	15.58903	12.16427	9.88662	47
48	37.97396	34.04255	30.67312	27.77315	25.26671	21.19513	18.07716	15.65003	12.18914	9.89693	48
49	38.58808	34.52468	31.05208	28.07137	25.50166	21.34147	18.16872	15.70757	12.21216	9.90630	49
50	39.19612	34.99969	31.42361	28.36231	25.72976	21.48218	18.25593	15.76186	12.23348	9.91481	50

QUICK CHECK 3

A project manager signs a contract that will pay him a bonus of $20,000 at the end of each year for 5 years, beginning in 4 years. Assuming 4% per year, find the amount that must be set aside today to fund this benefit.

Planning for Retirement

Tish Baker plans to retire from nursing at age 65 and hopes to withdraw $25,000 per year from her retirement plan until she is 90. **(a)** If money earns 8% per year compounded annually, how much will she need at age 65? **(b)** If she deposits $2000 per year into her retirement plan beginning at age 32, and if the retirement plan earns 8% per year compounded annually, will her retirement account have enough for her to meet her goals?

SOLUTION

(a) The amount needed at age 65 is the present value of an annuity of $25,000 per year for 90 − 65 = 25 years with interest of 8% compounded annually. The present value of an annuity table is used to find the following.

$$\text{Present value} = \$25,000 \times \textbf{10.67478} = \$266,869.50$$

Baker will need $266,869.50 at age 65. This sum, at 8% compounded annually, will permit withdrawals of $25,000 per year until age 90.

(b) Baker makes payments of $2000 at the end of each year for 65 − 32 = 33 years, at 8% compounded annually. These payments form a regular annuity. The amount of an annuity table in Section 11.1 is used to find the following.

$$\text{Future value} = \$2000 \times \textbf{145.95062} = \$291,901.24$$

Quick TIP

Example 7 in Appendix C shows how a financial calculator can be used to solve a problem similar to Example 4.

The value in the retirement account at 65 (**$291,901.24**) exceeds the amount needed to fund 25 yearly withdrawals of $25,000 each (**$266,869.50**). Therefore, Tish Baker should have enough, but she will need to earn an average of 8% on her money to do so. It is very unlikely that she would earn 8% at a bank, so she will need to use stocks and bonds. But of course there is no guarantee that she will earn 8% or 9% using stocks and bonds.

Financial Calculator Solution   This problem can readily be solved using a financial calculator, although the numbers differ very slightly from those above due to rounding errors.

(a) The present value (PV) is unknown. The interest rate (i) is 8%; the payment (PMT) is $25,000; and the number of years (n) is 25. Enter the payment as a positive number since it is an inflow of cash to Tish Baker.

⊞   25000 PMT 8 i 25 n PV   −266,869.40   (rounded)

(b) The unknown is the future value (FV). The interest rate (i) is 8%; the payment (PMT) is $2000; and the number of years (n) is 33. Enter the payment as a negative number since it is a cash outflow to be paid by Tish Baker.

−2000 PMT 8 i 33 n FV $291,901.24

Since the projected future value of $291,901.24 is more than the needed amount of $266,869.40, Baker should have enough.

QUICK CHECK 4

The Smiths want to plan for retirement using an annual income of $35,000 at the end of each year for 25 years based on a rate of 5% per year. (a) Find the present value needed when they retire to generate this income. (b) If they save $20,000 at the end of each year for 15 years, will they have enough?

OBJECTIVE 3   Find the equivalent cash price of an ordinary annuity.   Payments made at different times cannot be compared directly to one another to see which is better. Rather, it is necessary to first find the present value of each payment (or series of payments) and compare these. The one that results in the larger present value is *the better of the two*. The present value that is equivalent to a payment (or series of payments) is called the **equivalent cash price**. Thus, the way to find the better deal is to compare the equivalent cash prices, which are the present values.

Comparing Methods of Investment

EXAMPLE 5

Jean Braddock offers some land to two different real estate developers. Kapton Homes offers $200,000 in cash today for the land. RealProperty offers $80,000 now as a down payment and payments of $10,000 at the end of each quarter for 4 years. Assume that money can be invested at 8% per year compounded quarterly. Which offer is better?

SOLUTION

Since payments from the two real estate developers occur over different time periods, the present value of each offer must be found to determine which is better.

The present value of Kapton Homes' offer is **$200,000**, since that payment is made now.

The present value of RealProperty's offer is the sum of the down payment plus the present value of the series of payments. Use $\frac{8\%}{4}$ = 2% per compounding period for 4 years × 4 quarters per year = 16 compounding periods. Use the present value of an annuity table to find **13.57771**.

Present value of payments = $10,000 × **13.57771** = $135,777.10
Down payment   + $80,000.00
                   Present value of RealProperty's offer   **$215,777.10**

Therefore, $215,777.10 is the equivalent cash price to $80,000 down plus 16 quarterly payments of $10,000 each.

RealProperty's offer is the better of the two by the following amount.

$215,777.10 − $200,000 = $15,777.10

QUICK CHECK 5

Ben James has two different offers for a lot: (1) $48,000 cash and (2) $12,000 down and $2659 per quarter for 12 quarters. Assuming 6% compounded quarterly, find the present value of both and determine the better of the two.

As shown in the next example, we can use the concepts in this section to estimate the present value of Social Security payments at the time of retirement. To do so, first simplify the problem by assuming that payments are made at the end of each year and that the payments remain constant. Note that increases in Social Security payments are due to inflation, so Social Security payments effectively remain constant in terms of buying power.

Finding the Present Value of Social Security Payments

EXAMPLE 6

Debra Shorter expects to receive $20,940 per year in Social Security payments. Assume that she receives these payments for 28 years and use a rate of 6% per year. Find the present value of her retirement payments.

SOLUTION

Use the present value of an annuity table with 28 years and 6% per year to find **13.40616**.

$$\text{Present value} = \$20{,}940 \times \mathbf{13.40616} = \$280{,}724.99$$

Her Social Security retirement payments have a present value of $280,724.99. In other words, the Social Security payments equate to having cash of $280,724.99 at the time of retirement.

QUICK CHECK 6

Benjamin Thomason decides to wait until age 70 to begin receiving Social Security benefits, since it will result in higher payments. Find the present value of his estimated $26,000 per year in payments assuming 5% per year and payments until his 85th birthday.

Social Security was enacted during the 1930s during the Great Depression. Benefits include monthly payments to disabled workers, the children of deceased workers, and retired workers. Today, it is common to read and hear statements that Social Security is going broke and may not be there in the future. However, most experts believe that the financial problems of Social Security can be fixed and that the system will be around for decades to come. Today, many elderly people depend on the monthly payments from Social Security to pay for food and housing.

▼11.2 Exercises

MyMathLab®

*The shaded sections below contain solutions to help you get a **QUICK START** on the various types of exercises.*

Find the present value of the following annuities. Round to the nearest cent. (See Examples 1–3.)

	Amount per Payment	Payment at End of Each	Time (Years)	Rate of Investment	Compounded	Present Value
1.	$1800	year	18	10%	annually	$14,762.54
	Present value = $1800 × 8.20141 = $14,762.54					
2.	$4100	year	7	6%	annually	$22,887.76
	Present value = $4100 × 5.58238 = $22,887.76					
3.	$2000	6 months	12	8%	semiannually	_____
4.	$1700	6 months	14	5%	semiannually	_____
5.	$894	quarter	6	4%	quarterly	_____
6.	$7500	quarter	5	10%	quarterly	_____

ⓒ indicates an exercise that is related to the Case in Point feature.

7. Explain the difference between the two ways to think of the present value of an annuity. (See Objective 1.)

8. Explain the meaning of equivalent cash price. (See Objective 3.)

Solve the following application problems. Round to the nearest cent.

9. **INJURY LAWSUIT**   The court ruled that Locan Corporation was liable in the death of an employee. The settlement called for the company to pay the employee's widow $65,000 at the end of each year for 20 years. Find the amount the company must set aside today, assuming 5% compounded annually.
   Present value of annuity = $65,000 × 12.46221 = $810,043.65

   9. $810,043.65

10. **COMPUTER REPLACEMENT**   The community college where Roman Rodriguez works sets aside an annual payment of $35,000 per year for 5 years so it will have funds to replace the personal computers, servers, and printers in the computer labs when needed. Assuming 5% compounded annually, what lump sum deposited today would result in the same future value?

    10. _____

11. **COLLEGE EXPENSES**   In addition to his scholarship, Benjamin Wink needs $8000 every 6 months for living expenses and tuition at his university. As an engineering major, it will take 5 years to complete his degree. Assume funds earn 5% per year and find (a) the lump sum that must be deposited to meet this need and (b) the interest earned.

    (a) _____
    (b) _____

12. **DISASTER RELIEF**   After a terrible cyclone in Bangladesh, an international disaster relief organization agreed to help support families in a small city who lost everything with a payment of $25,000 every quarter for 5 years. Find (a) the lump sum that must be deposited to meet this need and (b) the interest earned assuming 6% per year, compounded quarterly.

    (a) _____
    (b) _____

13. **PAYING FOR COLLEGE**   Tom Potter estimates that his daughter's college needs, beginning in 8 years, will be $3600 at the end of each quarter for 4 years. (a) Find the total amount needed in 8 years assuming 8% compounded quarterly. (b) Will he have enough money available in 8 years if he invests $700 at the end of each quarter for the next 8 years at 8% compounded quarterly?

    (a) _____
    (b) _____

14. **VAN PURCHASE**   In 4 years, Jennifer Videtto will need to purchase a delivery van for her plumbing company. She estimates it will require a down payment of $10,000 with payments of $950 per month for 36 months. (a) Find the total amount needed in 4 years assuming 12% compounded monthly. (b) Will she have enough if she invests $2200 at the end of every quarter for 4 years and earns 6% compounded quarterly?

    (a) _____
    (b) _____

15. **SELLING A RESTAURANT**   Anna Stanley has two offers for her pizza business. The first offer is a cash payment of $85,000, and the second is a down payment of $25,000 with payments of $3500 at the end of each quarter for 5 years. (a) Identify the better offer assuming 8% compounded quarterly. (b) Find the difference in the present values.

    (a) _____
    (b) _____

16. **GROCERY STORE** Adolf Hegman has two offers for his Canadian grocery company. The first offer is a cash payment of $540,000, and the second is a down payment of $240,000 with payments of $65,000 at the end of each semiannual period for 4 years. (a) Identify the better offer assuming 10% compounded semiannually. (b) Find the difference in the present values.

(a) _____

(b) _____

17. **SOCIAL SECURITY** Jessica Thames expects to receive $18,400 per year based on her deceased husband's contributions to Social Security. Assume that she receives payments for 14 years and a rate of 4% per year, and find the present value of this annuity.

17. _____

18. **SOCIAL SECURITY** Warren and Bernice White's combined Social Security payments add up to $35,400 per year. Assume payments for 20 years and a rate of 6% per year, and find the present value.

18. _____

QUICK CHECK ANSWERS

1. (a) $44,461.45 (b) $25,537.52
2. $21,243.39; $2756.61
3. $76,108.31
4. (a) $493,287.90
   (b) no, short by $61,716.70
5. $48,000; $41,003.07; $48,000 cash is the better offer.
6. $269,871.16

▼11.3 Sinking Funds (Finding Annuity Payments)

▼CASE IN POINT   Roman Rodriguez is excited! The president of the college has decided to set up a sinking fund to accumulate funds needed in 5 years for a new building that will include a gymnasium and two indoor 50-meter swimming pools, which Rodriguez plans to use. See Example 1.

OBJECTIVE 1 Understand the basics of a sinking fund. Individuals and businesses often need to raise a certain amount of money for use *at some fixed time in the future*. For example, Paul Pence needs $28,000 to purchase a truck in 3 years. Using 6% compounded quarterly and the amount of an annuity table in Section 11.1, one can guess the required payment at the end of each quarter needed to accumulate the $28,000. The interest rate is $\frac{6\%}{5} = 1.5\%$ per quarter, and the number of compounding periods is 3 years $\times$ 4 quarters per year $= 12$.

Guess of quarterly payment	From table		Future value	The guess is
$1500	$1500 $\times$ **13.04121** $=$		$19,561.82	*too low*
$2800	$2800 $\times$ **13.04121** $=$		$36,515.39	*too high*

Clearly, the method of guessing and then checking to see if it is correct works very poorly. No telling how many guesses it would take. The exact payment in this example can be found by dividing the future value of $28,000 by **13.41209**, or by using the table and methods provided in this section. In fact, this section shows how to find the periodic payment needed to achieve a specific future value at a specific date.

A fund set up to receive periodic payments is called a **sinking fund**. Sinking funds are used to provide money *to pay off a loan* in one lump sum *or to accumulate money* to build new factories, buy equipment, and so on. Large corporations and some government agencies use a form of debt called a **bond**, which is a promise to pay a fixed amount of money at some stated time in the future. Bonds are discussed in detail in Section 11.5. This section covers only the use of a sinking fund to pay off a bond when it is due.

The amount of the periodic payment needed, at the end of each period, to accumulate a fixed amount at a future date is found as follows.

> **Finding Payment Needed to Accumulate a Specific Amount**
>
> Payment $=$ Future value $\times$ Number from sinking fund table

Finding Periodic Payments

▼EXAMPLE 1

Administrators at a community college have decided to build, in 5 years, a new sports complex with two indoor 50-meter swimming pools and a large gymnasium. The cost estimate is $16,500,000. They decide to make end-of-quarter deposits into a fund expected to earn 6% compounded quarterly. Find (**a**) the amount of each quarterly payment and (**b**) the interest earned.

▼CASE IN POINT

SOLUTION

(**a**) Use $\frac{6\%}{4} = 1.5\%$ per compounding period for 5 $\times$ 4 years $= 20$ compounding periods in the sinking fund table on page 432 to find **.04325**.

$$\text{Quarterly payment} = \$16,500,000 \times \mathbf{.04325} = \mathbf{\$713,625}$$

Twenty end-of-quarter payments of $713,625 at 6% compounded quarterly will grow to $16,501,629 using the table in Section 11.1.

(**b**) Interest is the future value minus the payments.

$$\text{Interest} = \$16,501,629 - (20 \times \mathbf{\$713,625}) = \$2,229,129 \text{ (rounded)}$$

QUICK CHECK 1

A utility company needs $300 million in 6 years to build a natural gas power plant. What amount does it need to deposit at the end of each quarter into a sinking fund, if funds earn 8% compounded quarterly?

Finding the Periodic Payments

EXAMPLE 2

First Christian Church sold $100,000 worth of bonds that must be paid off in 8 years. It now must set up a sinking fund to accumulate the necessary $100,000 to pay off the debt. Find the amount of each payment into a sinking fund if the payments are made at the end of each year and the fund earns 10% compounded annually. Find the amount of interest earned.

SOLUTION

Look along the top of the sinking fund table for 10% and down the side for 8 periods to find **.08744**.

$$\text{Payment} = \$100,000 \times .08744 = \$8744$$

The church must deposit $8744 at the end of each year for 8 years into an account paying 10% compounded annually to accumulate $100,000. The interest earned is the future value less all payments.

$$\text{Interest} = \$100,000 - (8 \times \$8744) = \$30,048$$

QUICK CHECK 2

A charter airline sold $1,000,000 in bonds to buy a new aircraft. It chose to make deposits at the end of each semi-annual period to accumulate the funds needed to pay off the bonds in 4 years. Use 5% compounded semiannually and find **(a)** the payment and **(b)** the interest.

OBJECTIVE 2 Set up a sinking fund table. A **sinking fund table** is used to show the interest earned and the accumulated amount of a sinking fund at the end of each period.

Setting up a Sinking Fund Table

EXAMPLE 3

First Christian Church in Example 2 deposited $8744 at the end of each year for 8 years into a sinking fund that earned 10% compounded annually. Set up a sinking fund table for these deposits. After each calculation, round each answer to the nearest cent before proceeding.

SOLUTION

The sinking fund account contains no money until the end of the first year, when a single deposit of $8744 is made. Since the deposit is made at the end of the year, no interest is earned.

At the end of the second year, the account contains the original $8744 plus the interest earned by this money. This interest is found by the formula for simple interest.

$$I = \$8744 \times .10 \times 1 = \$874.40$$

An additional deposit is also made at the end of the second year, so that the sinking fund then contains the following total.

$$\$8744 + \$874.40 + \$8744 = \$18,362.40$$

Continue this work to get the following sinking fund table.

| | Beginning of Period | | End of Period | |
Period	Accumulated Amount	Periodic Deposit	Interest Earned	Accumulated Amount
1	$0	$8744.00	$0	$8,744.00
2	$8,744.00	$8744.00	$874.40	$18,362.40
3	$18,362.40	$8744.00	$1836.24	$28,942.64
4	$28,942.64	$8744.00	$2894.26	$40,580.90
5	$40,580.90	$8744.00	$4058.09	$53,382.99
6	$53,382.99	$8744.00	$5338.30	$67,465.29
7	$67,465.29	$8744.00	$6746.53	$82,955.82
8	$82,955.82	$8748.60	$8295.58	$100,000.00

The last payment is found as follows:

$$\text{Desired Accumulated Amount} - \text{Interest Earned during Last Period} - \text{Accumulated Amount at end of Period 7}$$

$$\$100,000 - \$8295.85 - \$82,955.82$$

Quick TIP

Normally the last payment is adjusted as needed so that the future value exactly equals the desired amount. We assume this is true from this point forward.

Sinking Fund Table

Interest Rate per Compounding Period

Period	1%	1½%	2%	2½%	3%	4%	5%	6%	8%	10%	Period
1	1.00000	1.00000	1.00000	1.00000	1.00000	1.00000	1.00000	1.00000	1.00000	1.00000	1
2	.49751	.49628	.49505	.49383	.49261	.49020	.48780	.48544	.48077	.47619	2
3	.33002	.32838	.32675	.32514	.32353	.32035	.31721	.31411	.30803	.30211	3
4	.24628	.24444	.24262	.24082	.23903	.23549	.23201	.22859	.22192	.21547	4
5	.19604	.19409	.19216	.19025	.18835	.18463	.18097	.17740	.17046	.16380	5
6	.16255	.16053	.15853	.15655	.15460	.15076	.14702	.14336	.13632	.12961	6
7	.13863	.13656	.13451	.13250	.13051	.12661	.12282	.11914	.11207	.10541	7
8	.12069	.11858	.11651	.11447	.11246	.10853	.10472	.10104	.09401	.08744	8
9	.10674	.10461	.10252	.10046	.09843	.09449	.09069	.08702	.08008	.07364	9
10	.09558	.09343	.09133	.08926	.08723	.08329	.07950	.07587	.06903	.06275	10
11	.08645	.08429	.08218	.08011	.07808	.07415	.07039	.06679	.06608	.05396	11
12	.07885	.07668	.07456	.07249	.07046	.06655	.06283	.05928	.05270	.04676	12
13	.07241	.07024	.06812	.06605	.06403	.06014	.05646	.05296	.04652	.04078	13
14	.06690	.06472	.06260	.06054	.05853	.05467	.05102	.04758	.04130	.03575	14
15	.06212	.05994	.05783	.05577	.05377	.04994	.04634	.04296	.03683	.03147	15
16	.05794	.05577	.05365	.05160	.04961	.04582	.04227	.03895	.03298	.02782	16
17	.05426	.05208	.04997	.04793	.04595	.04220	.03870	.03544	.02963	.02466	17
18	.05098	.04881	.04670	.04467	.04271	.03899	.03555	.03236	.02670	.02193	18
19	.04805	.04588	.04378	.04176	.03981	.03614	.03275	.02962	.02413	.01955	19
20	.04542	.04325	.04116	.03915	.03722	.03358	.03024	.02718	.02185	.01746	20
21	.04303	.04087	.03878	.03679	.03487	.03128	.02800	.02500	.01983	.01562	21
22	.04086	.03870	.03663	.03465	.03275	.02920	.02597	.02305	.01803	.01401	22
23	.03889	.03673	.03467	.03270	.03081	.02731	.02414	.02128	.01642	.01257	23
24	.03707	.03492	.03287	.03091	.02905	.02559	.02247	.01968	.01498	.01130	24
25	.03541	.03326	.03122	.02928	.02743	.02401	.02095	.01823	.01368	.01017	25
26	.03387	.03173	.02970	.02777	.02594	.02257	.01956	.01690	.01251	.00916	26
27	.03245	.03032	.02829	.02638	.02456	.02124	.01829	.01570	.01145	.00826	27
28	.03112	.02900	.02699	.02509	.02329	.02001	.01712	.01459	.01049	.00745	28
29	.02990	.02778	.02578	.02389	.02211	.01888	.01605	.01358	.00962	.00673	29
30	.02875	.02664	.02465	.02278	.02102	.01783	.01505	.01265	.00883	.00608	30
31	.02768	.02557	.02360	.02174	.02000	.01686	.01413	.01179	.00811	.00550	31
32	.02667	.02458	.02261	.02077	.01905	.01595	.01328	.01100	.00745	.00497	32
33	.02573	.02364	.02169	.01986	.01816	.01510	.01249	.01027	.00685	.00450	33
34	.02484	.02276	.02082	.01901	.01732	.01431	.01176	.00960	.00630	.00407	34
35	.02400	.02193	.02000	.01821	.01654	.01358	.01107	.00897	.00580	.00369	35
36	.02321	.02115	.01923	.01745	.01580	.01289	.01043	.00839	.00534	.00334	36
37	.02247	.02041	.01851	.01674	.01511	.01224	.00984	.00786	.00492	.00303	37
38	.02176	.01972	.01782	.01607	.01446	.01163	.00928	.00736	.00454	.00275	38
39	.02109	.01905	.01717	.01544	.01384	.01106	.00876	.00689	.00419	.00249	39
40	.02046	.01843	.01656	.01484	.01326	.01052	.00828	.00646	.00386	.00226	40
41	.01985	.01783	.01597	.01427	.01271	.01002	.00782	.00606	.00356	.00205	41
42	.01928	.01726	.01542	.01373	.01219	.00954	.00739	.00568	.00329	.00186	42
43	.01873	.01672	.01489	.01322	.01170	.00909	.00699	.00533	.00303	.00169	43
44	.01820	.01621	.01439	.01273	.01123	.00866	.00662	.00501	.00280	.00153	44
45	.01771	.01572	.01391	.01227	.01079	.00826	.00626	.00470	.00259	.00139	45
46	.01723	.01525	.01345	.01183	.01036	.00788	.00593	.00441	.00239	.00126	46
47	.01677	.01480	.01302	.01141	.00996	.00752	.00561	.00415	.00221	.00115	47
48	.01633	.01437	.01260	.01101	.00958	.00718	.00532	.00390	.00204	.00104	48
49	.01591	.01396	.01220	.01062	.00921	.00686	.00504	.00366	.00189	.00095	49
50	.01551	.01357	.01182	.01026	.00887	.00655	.00478	.00344	.00174	.00086	50

QUICK CHECK 3

The payments into a sinking fund are $2400 at the end of each quarter for 1 year. Assume interest of 6% compounded quarterly and construct a sinking fund table.

Frequently, an item costs more if its purchase is delayed a few years. The next example shows how to estimate the cost of a large purchase at a future date. It then shows how to find the payment needed to accumulate the necessary funds.

Finding Periodic Payments and Interest Earned

Managers at Baton Chemicals frequently travel between the corporate offices in the United States and manufacturing plants and mines in South America. The chief financial officer has decided that the firm should purchase a private jet in 4 years. The jet costs $14,800,000 today, and its cost is expected to grow at 5% per year. Find the quarterly payments needed to accumulate the necessary funds in a sinking fund in 4 years if the firm earns 6% compounded quarterly.

SOLUTION

First, find the cost (future value) of the jet in 4 years:

Use a rate of 5% per year and four compounding periods (years) in the compound interest table on page 382 to find **1.21551**.

Future cost of jet = \$14,800,000 × 1.21551 = \$17,989,548

Next, find the quarterly payment needed to accumulate $17,989,548 in 4 years:

Use a rate of $\frac{6\%}{4} = 1.5\%$ per quarter and $4 \times 4 = 16$ compounding periods in the sinking fund table to find **.05577**.

Quarterly payment = $17,989,548 × .05577 = $1,003,277.09   (rounded)

Payments of $1,003,277.09 at the end of each quarter for 4 years into a sinking fund earning 6% compounded quarterly will result in the funds needed to purchase the jet.

QUICK CHECK 4

The $19,000 cost of a compressor is increasing by 5% per year. First find the amount needed to buy the compressor in 3 years. Then find the necessary semiannual payments into a sinking fund for the purchase if funds earn 10% compounded semiannually.

Two different interest rates are involved in Example 4. The price is increasing at 5% per year compounded annually, but deposits in the sinking fund earn 6% compounded quarterly. **Interest rate spreads** such as this are common in business. For example, banks use an interest rate spread between what they pay for funds on deposit and what they charge on loans to customers.

▼11.3 Exercises   MyMathLab®

*The shaded sections below contain solutions to help you get a **QUICK START** on the various types of exercises.*

Find the amount of each payment needed to accumulate the indicated amount in a sinking fund. Round to the nearest cent. (See Examples 1–3.)

1. $12,000, money earns 5% compounded annually, 4 years
   Payment = $12,000 × .23201 = $2784.12   1. **$2784.12**

2. $125,000, money earns 6% compounded annually, 25 years
   Payment = $125,000 × .01823 = $2278.75   2. **$2278.75**

3. $8200, money earns 6% compounded semiannually, 5 years   3. _____

4. $12,000, money earns 10% compounded semiannually, 3 years   4. _____

⚠️ indicates an exercise that is related to the Case in Point feature.

5. $50,000, money earns 4% compounded quarterly, 5 years

5. _____

6. $32,000, money earns 6% compounded quarterly, 3 years

6. _____

7. $7894, money earns 12% compounded monthly, 3 years

7. _____

8. $29,804, money earns 12% compounded monthly, 2 years

8. _____

9. Explain the difference between a sinking fund (see Objective 1) and the present value of an annuity discussed in Section 11.2.

10. What is a sinking fund table? Who would use one? (See Objective 2.)

Solve each application problem. Round to the nearest cent.

11. **STUDENT UNION**   A college needs $920,000 in 3 years to remodel the student union. It decides to make payments into a sinking fund at the end of each semiannual period.
(a) Find the amount of each payment assuming 5% per year compounded semiannually.
(b) Find the total interest earned.
(a) Payment = $920,000 × .15655 = $144,026
(b) Interest = $920,000 − (6 × $144,026) = $55,844

(a) $144,026 _____
(b) $55,844 _____

12. **SCUBA DIVING**   The owner of Emerald Diving plans to buy all new scuba diving equipment to rent to divers in 5 years at a cost of $122,300. He believes that he can earn 4% compounded quarterly. Find **(a)** the amount of each of the quarterly payments needed and **(b)** the total interest earned.

(a) _____
(b) _____

13. **ACCUMULATING $1,000,000**   Kyle Anderson is 20 years old and wants to accumulate $1,000,000 by the time he is 60. He believes he can earn 8% per year by investing in stocks and bonds. Find **(a)** the amount of the annual payment needed and **(b)** the total interest earned.

(a) _____
(b) _____

14. **ALLIGATOR HUNTING**   Cajun Jack needs $45,000 in 4 years for boats used to hunt alligators. **(a)** Find the amount of each payment if payments are made at the end of each quarter with interest at 6% compounded quarterly. **(b)** Find the total amount of interest earned.

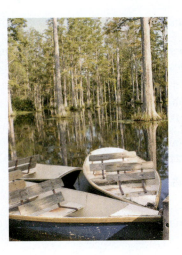

(a) _____
(b) _____

15. **X-RAY EQUIPMENT**   Newburgh Vet will need a new x-ray machine in 3 years. The owners decide to set up a sinking fund to accumulate the $82,400 needed at that time. Find the payment into the fund needed at the end of each year if money earns 2½% compounded annually. Round to the nearest dollar.

15. _____

16. **NEW AUDITORIUM**   The membership of the Green Fields Baptist Church is large and growing rapidly. The leaders of the church are planning to remodel the auditorium with special features for their televised broadcasts at a cost of $2,800,000 in 5 years. The membership has set up a sinking fund with the idea of making a payment at the end of each quarter. Find the payment needed if money earns 8% compounded quarterly.

16. _____

17. **A NEW SHOWROOM**   A Ford dealership wants to build a new showroom costing $2,300,000. It sets up a sinking fund with end-of-the-month payments in an account earning 12% compounded monthly. Find the amount that should be deposited in this fund each month if the dealership wishes to build the showroom in (a) 3 years and (b) 4 years.

(a) _____
(b) _____

18. **AIRPORT IMPROVEMENTS**   A city near Chicago sold $9,000,000 in bonds to pay for improvements to an airport. It sets up a sinking fund with end-of-the-quarter payments in an account earning 8% compounded quarterly. Find the amount that should be deposited in this fund each quarter if the city wishes to pay off the bonds in (a) 7 years and (b) 12 years.

(a) _____
(b) _____

19. **LAND SALE**   Helen Spence sells a lot in Nevada. She will be paid a lump sum of $60,000 in 4 years. Until then, the buyer pays 8% simple interest every quarter. (a) Find the amount of each quarterly interest payment. (b) The buyer sets up a sinking fund so that enough money will be present to pay off the $60,000. The buyer wants to make semiannual payments into the sinking fund. The account pays 8% compounded semiannually. Find the amount of each payment into the fund. (c) Prepare a table showing the amount in the sinking fund after each deposit.

(a) _____
(b) _____

Payment Number	Amount of Deposit	Interest Earned	Total in Account

20. **RARE STAMPS**   Jeff Reschke bought a rare stamp for his collection. He agreed to pay a lump sum of $4000 after 5 years. Until then, he pays 6% simple interest every 6 months. (a) Find the amount of each semiannual interest payment. (b) Reschke sets up a sinking fund so that money will be available to pay off the $4000. He wants to make annual payments into the fund. The account pays 8% compounded annually. Find the amount of each payment into the fund. (c) Prepare a table showing the amount in the sinking fund after each deposit.

(a) _____
(b) _____

Payment Number	Amount of Deposit	Interest Earned	Total in Account

21. **SPORTS COMPLEX**   Prepare a sinking fund table for the first four payments for the community college sports complex described in Example 1.

Payment Number	Amount of Deposit	Interest Earned	Total in Account

22. **COMMERCIAL BUILDING**   John Bangstrom plans to make a down payment of $70,000 on a commercial building for his plumbing company in 5 years. Construct a sinking fund table given semiannual payments of $6106.10 at the end of each period and an interest rate of 6% compounded semiannually.

Payment Number	Amount of Deposit	Interest Earned	Total in Account

23. **SAVING FOR COLLEGE**   Barbara Funicello hopes to go to a private college where tuition is $22,500 per year. She believes that tuition will increase at 8% for the 4 years until she plans to enter college. Find the end-of-quarter payments needed to accumulate funds to pay the first year's tuition if funds earn 6% compounded quarterly. Round to the nearest dollar.

23. _____

24. **FIRE TRUCK**   A volunteer fire department anticipates purchasing a fire truck in 3 years. Today it would cost $625,000, but the cost is increasing at 4% per year. Find the semiannual payments needed to accumulate funds to purchase the truck if funds earn 6% compounded semiannually. Round to the nearest dollar at each step.

24. _____

25. **NEW ROOF**   The manager of an apartment complex estimates she will need a new roof on one of the buildings in 5 years. Today it would cost $52,000 to reroof the building, but the cost is increasing at 8% per year. Find the semiannual payments needed to accumulate the necessary funds at 5% compounded semiannually. Round to the nearest dollar at each step.

25. _____

26. **NEW KITCHEN**   A restaurant manager believes he will need all new kitchen appliances in 2 years. The cost today is $48,800, but costs are going up at 10% per year. Find the semiannual payments needed if funds earn 5% compounded semiannually. Round to the nearest dollar.

26. _____

▼ Supplementary Application Exercises on Annuities and Sinking Funds

Solve the following application problems. Round to the nearest cent.

1. Bill Carter deposits $500 at the end of each quarter for 6 years into a mutual fund that he believes will grow at 8% compounded quarterly. Find **(a)** the future value and **(b)** the interest.

   (a) Future value = $500 × 30.42186 = $15,210.93
   (b) Interest = $15,210.93 − (24 × $500) = $3210.93

   (a) $15,210.93
   (b) $3210.93

2. For 6 years, Jessica Savage deposits $1000 at the end of each quarter into a mutual fund earning 8% per year compounded quarterly. Find **(a)** the future value and **(b)** the interest.

   (a) _____
   (b) _____

3. Mr. and Mrs. Thompson deposit $2000 at the beginning of each year for 20 years into a retirement account earning 6% compounded annually. Find **(a)** the future value and **(b)** the interest.

   (a) _____
   (b) _____

4. Jaime Navarro deposits $1000 at the end of every 6 months into a Roth IRA for 8 years at 10% compounded semiannually. Find **(a)** the future value and **(b)** the interest.

   (a) _____
   (b) _____

5. Solectron needs to purchase new equipment for its production line in 3 years. The company has been advised to deposit $135,000 at the end of each quarter into an account that managers believe will yield 10% per year compounded quarterly. Find the lump sum that could be deposited today that will grow to the same future value.

   5. _____

6. Abel Plumbing saves $12,000 at the end of every semiannual period in an account earning 6% compounded semiannually to replace several of its trucks in 5 years. Find the lump sum that could be deposited today that will grow to the same future value.

   6. _____

7. Katherine Wysong was injured when she fell on ice at work. Her employer's workers compensation insurance paid for her medical bills and must also pay her $5000 per quarter for the next 6 years. Find the lump sum that must be deposited into an investment earning 4% per year compounded quarterly needed to make the payments.

   7. _____

8. Carl and Amy Glaser recently divorced. As part of the divorce settlement, Carl must pay Amy $1000 at the end of every quarter for 8 years. Find the lump sum he must deposit into an account earning 8% per year compounded quarterly to make the payments.

   8. _____

9. Ajax Coal sets up a sinking fund to purchase a new tractor in 3 years at a price of $870,000. Find the annual payment the firm must make if funds are deposited into an account earning 8% compounded annually. Then set up a sinking fund table.

Payment Number	Amount of Deposit	Interest Earned	Total in Account

10. Swift Petrochemicals wishes to purchase a new
distillation tower costing $3,200,000 in 2 years.
Find the semiannual payment the company must
make into a sinking fund account earning 6%
compounded semiannually. Then set up a sinking
fund table.

Payment Number	Amount of Deposit	Interest Earned	Total in Account

11. Ben Jamison is 45. He wants to retire at age 65 and draw $25,000 per year from his retire-
ment plan until he turns 85. He assumes that he can earn 8% per year *before* retiring but
that he would invest more conservatively and earn 6% per year *after retiring*. **(a)** Find the
amount needed at 65 to fund his retirement. **(b)** Then find the end-of-the-year payment
into a sinking fund needed to accumulate this amount.

(a) _____

(b) _____

12. An engineer signs a contract to work in Hong Kong for 5 years. The contract specifies
that at the end of his 5 years of service, he will receive $90,000 at the end of each of the
following 3 years. Assume funds earn 6% compounded annually. **(a)** Find the amount
needed at the end of his 5 years of service to fund the payments. **(b)** Find the
end-of-year payment into a sinking fund needed to accumulate this amount.

(a) _____

(b) _____

11.4 Stocks and Mutual Funds

OBJECTIVES

1   Define the types of stock.
2   Read stock tables.
3   Find the current yield on a stock.
4   Find the stock's PE ratio.
5   Define the Dow Jones Industrial Average and the NASDAQ Composite Index.
6   Define a mutual fund.

▼ CASE IN POINT   When Roman Rodriguez began his new job, he was given the choice of investing his retirement funds in a fixed interest fund or in a fund containing stocks and/or bonds. Which should he choose? Which would you choose? Why?

Almost all large businesses and also many smaller ones are set up as **corporations**. For example, companies that we commonly refer to as Microsoft, Apple, Nike, McDonald's, and Toyota are actually corporations. **Publicly held corporations** are those owned by the public; their stocks are traded daily in markets called stock markets. **Privately held corporations** are owned by one or a few individuals, and their stock is not traded on a market. For example, your medical doctor or plumber may have organized her small business as a privately held corporation.

A corporation is a form of business that gives the owners (the stockholders) **limited liability**. You do not have to worry that lawsuits will be filed against you or your family just because you own stock in General Motors, Inc. The owners of corporations have protection through the limited-liability laws and will never lose more than they have invested in the corporation.

A corporation is set up with money, or **capital**, raised through the sale of shares of **stock**. A share of stock represents partial ownership of a corporation. If one million shares of stock are sold to establish a new firm, the owner of one share will own one-millionth of the corporation. In the past, stock ownership was indicated by **stock certificates** such as the one shown here. However, very few people hold stock certificates anymore. Rather, proof of ownership of stock is simply the regular statements and records maintained by brokerage firms.

In most states, corporations are required to have an **annual meeting**. At this meeting, open to all **stockholders** (owners of stock), the management of the firm is open to questions from stockholders. The stockholders also elect a **board of directors**—a group of people who represent the stockholders. The board of directors hires the **executive officers** of the corporation, such as the president, vice-presidents, and so on. The board of directors also often distributes a portion of any profits in the form of **dividends**, which are regular payments to stockholders.

OBJECTIVE 1 Define the types of stock. The two types of stock normally issued are **preferred stock** and **common stock**. As the name suggests, preferred stockholders *have certain rights* over common stockholders. For example, owners of preferred stock must be paid dividends *before* any dividends can be paid to owners of common stock. Also, corporate debt and preferred shareholders must be paid *before* common shareholders receive anything in the event that a corporation declares bankruptcy.

The shares of **publicly held corporations** are typically owned by many different individuals and institutions. Share prices of these firms are determined by supply and demand in public markets called **stock exchanges**. The New York Stock Exchange (NYSE) is the largest of the several exchanges in the United States. This exchange is located on Wall Street in New York City. Many foreign countries, including Japan, Taiwan, Germany, England, Canada, and Mexico, have their own stock exchanges.

OBJECTIVE 2 Read stock tables. Daily stock prices are readily found in many places on the World Wide Web, such as finance.yahoo.com or wsj.com. Information on the stock of many widely held companies such as Apple or Nike is also found in the weekly financial magazine *Barron's*. In this section, we will use data as presented in *Barron's*.

Reading the Stock Table **EXAMPLE 1**

After receiving his first paycheck from the college, Roman Rodriguez went to Best Buy to look at iPhones and MP3 players. He liked the company so well that he decided to do some research on it. Analyze the information about Best Buy stock given in the table.

▼ CASE IN POINT

| 52-Wk | | | Tick | Vol. | | | Week's | | Earnings | | | Div |
High	Low	Name	Sym	100s	Yld.	P/E	Last	Chg.	Latest Year	This Year	Next Year	Amt.
29.76	17.53	BestBuy	BBY	316525	3.7	-	18.23	−0.77	−3.36	3.62	3.76	.17

SOLUTION

(a) The highest price at which the stock sold during the year was $29.76.

(b) The lowest price the stock sold for during the year was $17.53.

(c) The ticker symbol under which the stock trades on the market is BBY.

(d) The volume of shares sold during the day was 100 × 316525 = 31,652,500 shares.

(e) The annual dividend yield is 3.7% of the current price.

(f) Best Buy had no earnings so the P/E ratio is left blank

(g) The stock closed at $18.23 at the end of last week.

(h) The price of the stock was down $0.77 compared to the close price last week.

(i) Best Buy lost $3.36 per share last year. It is expected to earn $3.62 this year and $3.76 next year.

(j) The most recent quarterly dividend was $0.17 per share.

QUICK CHECK 1

Find the information in the stock table about Beam Inc.

Individuals use **stockbrokers** to trade the stocks of publicly held companies. Regular stockbrokers charge more, but they offer financial advice. Many people trade stocks on the internet using **discount brokers** that offer less advice and a lower cost such as Schwab, E*Trade, or Fidelity.

Finding the Cost of Stocks **EXAMPLE 2**

Ignoring commissions, find Roman Rodriguez's cost for the following purchases.

(a) 500 shares of BankAm (BAC) at the close for the week

(b) 800 shares of Belo (BLC) at the low for the year

(c) Then find the combined *annual dividend* from this investment.

52-Wk							—Week's—		——Earnings——			
High	Low	Name	Tick Sym	Vol. 100s	Yld	P/E	Last	Chg.	Latest Year	This Year	Next Year	Div Amt.
69.50	53.64	Bancol ADS	CIB	13418	2.6	...	62.08	−0.57	...	4.84	5.63	.4024
15.29	8.23	Bncpsouth	BXS	20121	.3	22	14.69	−0.34	.45	.84	.94	.01
10.27	4.92	BankAm	BAC	91060	.6	8	7.07	−0.75	.01	.55	.93	.01
8.44	1.96	BankAmCIA	BACWSA	21609	...	...	3.02	−0.28	...	...	...	...
1.61	0.27	BankAmCIB	BACWSB	2662	...	...	.71	−0.06	...	...	...	...
49.99	34.50	BkHawaii	BOH	13753	3.9	13	46.33	−0.31	3.39	3.51	3.49	.45
16.50	3.99	Bkirind ADS	IRE	12097	...	...	5.12	−0.31	...	−2.17	−1.15	...
65.79	50.95	BkMntri	BMO	17094	4.9	10	57.39	+0.80	5.28	5.64	5.93	.7064
25.97	17.10	BankNY Mellon	BK	377918	2.5	11	20.77	−1.00	2.03	2.12	2.39	.13
60.68	45.79	BkNovaScotia	BNS	18487	4.2	12	51.49	...	4.62	4.72	5.10	.5345
7.00	1.82	BkAtiBop A	BBX	81112	...	...	5.95	+0.31	−2.04	...	...	...
25.95	13.38	Bankrate	RATE	27432	...	...	16.00	−0.95	−.14	.62	1.07	...
26.33	18.92	BankUnited	BKU	7466	2.8	13	23.95	+0.31	.62	1.72	1.60	.17
16.41	8.38	BarclaysADS	BCS	207469	2.5	6	9.91	−0.33	1.62	1.86	2.27	.0618
108.31	80.80	BardCR	BCR	31959	.8	27	105.71	−2.00	3.69	6.68	7.22	.20
26.00	9.35	BarnesNoble	BKS	22362	...	...	15.07	−0.16	−1.41	−.85	−.90	...
28.63	17.47	BarnesGp	B	16965	1.7	13	23.04	+0.18	1.16	1.84	2.12	.10
55.95	33.67	BarckGld	ABX	362072	2.3	8	34.57	−0.27	4.44	4.63	5.68	.20
36.45	8.52	BscEngySvs	BAS	70084	...	5	10.24	+0.89	1.14	1.54	1.29	...
62.23	47.55	Baxterint	BAX	178835	2.4	14	56.21	+1.68	3.88	4.52	4.90	.335
59.50	36.89	BaytexEnergy	BTE	14330	8.0	20	42.71	+0.81	1.88	1.54	1.82	.2137
64.00	39.33	Beam Inc	BEAM	19318	1.3	62	61.87	−0.07	5.78	2.37	2.64	.205

(*continued*)

SOLUTION

(a) 500 shares × $7.07 = $3535

(b) 800 shares × $4.36 = $3488

(c) Quarterly dividend from Bank of America = $.01 × 500 = $5
Quarterly dividend from Belo = $.08 × 800 = $64
Total quarterly dividend = $69
Total annual dividend = $69 × 4 = $276

> **QUICK CHECK 2**
> Ignore commissions and find the cost of 300 shares of Berkshire Hathaway (BRK/B) at the low for the year. Then find the *annual* dividend these shares will pay.

OBJECTIVE 3 Find the current yield on a stock. There is no certain way of choosing stocks that will increase in price. However, two **stock ratios** that people commonly look at before buying shares of a company are the **current yield** and the **price–earnings ratio**. It is used to compare the dividends paid by stocks selling at different prices. The result is commonly rounded to the nearest tenth of a percent.

Finding Current Yield

$$\text{Current yield} = \frac{\text{Annual dividend per share}}{\text{Closing price per share}}$$

| 52-Wk | | | | | | | —Week's— | | Earnings | | | |
High	Low	Name	Tick Sym	Vol. 100s	Yld	P/E	Last	Chg.	Latest Year	This Year	Next Year	Div Amt.
25.75	22.30	BeazerHomesUSAUn	BZT	7586	...	...	24.20	−1.30	...	...	...	...
3.98	1.35	BeazerHm	BZH	453528	...	...	2.68	−0.14	−2.77	−1.08	−.90	...
88.84	69.59	BectonDksn	BDX	43134	2.4	13	74.79	+0.37	5.62	5.70	6.10	.45
41.43	23.24	Belden	BDC	9431	.6	13	32.58	+0.10	2.38	2.75	3.29	.05
9.00	4.36	Belo	BLC	12515	4.9	9	6.56	+0.01	.55	.94	.74	.08
34.23	27.21	Bemis	BMS	105540	3.2	18	31.13	+0.98	1.73	2.07	2.31	.25
18.87	12.01	BenchmkElec	BHE	16607	...	19	13.77	+0.54	.87	1.17	1.39	...
39.58	27.26	Berkley	WRB	33446	1.0	13	37.45	−1.91	2.71	2.59	2.70	.09
127888	98952	BerkHathwy A	BRK/A	2410	...	...	125730	−895.00	4.14	7234.07	8070.76	...
85.35	65.35	BerkHathwy B	BRK/B	188370	...	17	83.83	−0.65	4.14	4.83	5.38	...
61.17	30.59	BerryPete A	BRY	35773	.8	...	39.98	+0.64	−4.21	3.65	4.69	.08
29.76	17.53	BestBuy	BBY	316525	3.7	...	18.23	−0.77	−3.36	3.62	3.76	.17
47.22	28.89	BigLots	BIG	32745	...	...	39.14	+0.11	2.98	3.31	3.69	...
431.74	279.86	BiglariHidgs	BH	14422	...	...	375.68	−8.32	...	26.80	26.57	...
52.13	15.42	BillBarrett	BBG	56247	...	20	21.40	+1.22	.65	.53	1.03	...
21.02	14.94	BiomdRltyTr	BMR	44813	4.6	...	18.54	−0.38	.19	.11	.25	.215
118.41	84.02	BioRadLab A	BIO	1956	...	16	98.03	−0.79	6.26	5.48	6.23	...
115.38	87.33	BioRadLab B	BIO/B	z300	...	16	99.50	+1.16	6.26	5.48	6.23	...
7.82	3.50	BltautoHidgsADS	BITA	57292	...	11	3.79	−0.32	.33	.48	.66	...
35.82	25.83	BlackHills	BKH	84281	4.6	29	32.19	+0.55	1.24	1.98	2.20	.37
209.37	137.00	BlackRock	BLK	33388	3.5	14	173.31	−2.47	12.37	13.08	14.59	1.50

Data from Barrons July 23, 2012

Finding the Current Yield

EXAMPLE 3 Use data in the stock table to estimate the current yield for Barnes and Noble (BKS) and Black Rock (BLK) rounded to the nearest tenth of a percent.

SOLUTION

$$\text{Current yield for Barnes and Noble} = \frac{\text{Annual dividend}}{\text{Closing price}} = \frac{4 \times \$.0}{\$15.07} = 0\%$$

$$\text{Current yield for Black Rock} = \frac{\text{Annual dividend}}{\text{Closing price}} = \frac{4 \times \$1.50}{\$173.31} = 3.5\%$$

QUICK CHECK 3

Find the current yield for ExxonMobil to the nearest tenth of a percent if the closing price is $85.21 and the annual dividend is $2.28.

Note that a company such as Barnes & Noble in Example 3 may not pay a dividend since it may be having financial problems and needs to keep its cash, or because it may be growing rapidly and needs the cash to finance its future growth.

OBJECTIVE 4 Find the stock's PE ratio. One number that some people use to help decide which stock to buy is the **price–earnings ratio**, also called the **PE ratio**. It is often rounded to the nearest whole number.

Finding PE Ratio

$$\text{Finding PE Ratio PE ratio} = \frac{\text{Closing price per share}}{\text{Annual net income per share}}$$

Finding the PE Ratio

EXAMPLE 4

Find the PE ratio for each of the following corporations and round to the nearest whole number.

(a) Chevron (CVX) with a closing price of $107.95 and earnings of $13.63

(b) Target (TGT) with a closing price of $60.44 and earnings of $1.44

SOLUTION

(a) PE ratio for Chevron $= \dfrac{\text{Closing price per share}}{\text{Annual net income per share}} = \dfrac{\$107.95}{\$13.63} = 8$

(b) PE ratio for Target $= \dfrac{\text{Closing price per share}}{\text{Annual net income per share}} = \dfrac{\$60.44}{\$1.44} = 42$

QUICK CHECK 4

Pfizer Inc (PFE) has a closing price of $23.60 and earnings of $0.88. Find the PE ratio to the nearest whole number.

Investors are often willing to pay more for rapidly growing companies because these companies may generate even higher profits in the near future. As a result, the PE ratios of rapidly growing companies are often higher than those of slow-growing companies.

A low PE ratio may indicate that a company is growing slowly or that it is having financial problems. It is best to compare the PE ratios of similar companies, such as oil giants ExxonMobil and Chevron. It usually is not worthwhile to compare the PE ratios of very different companies such as Wal-Mart and ExxonMobil, since they are very different types of businesses.

OBJECTIVE 5 Define the Dow Jones Industrial Average and the NASDAQ Composite Index. Both the **Dow Jones Industrial Average** and the **NASDAQ Composite Index** are used as indicators of trends in stock prices. The Dow Jones Industrial Average refers to an average of 30 specific, large industrial companies. The NASDAQ Composite Index includes price information on over 5000 companies, many of which are involved with technology. Both of these indexes are commonly quoted by television and radio, in newsprint, and on the Internet.

Dow Jones Industrial Average since 1900

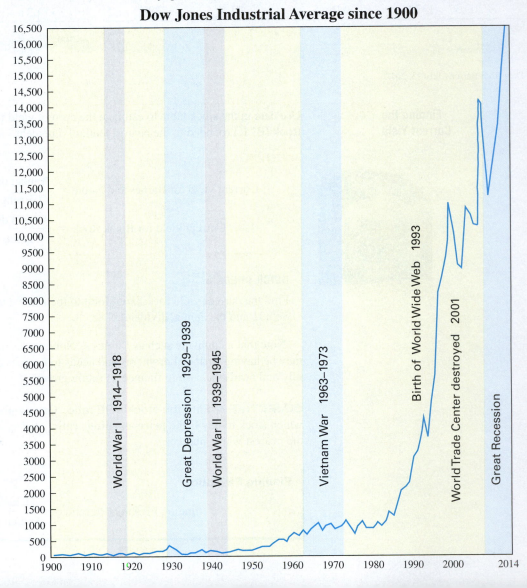

The Dow Jones Industrial Average has been widely available for over 100 years, as you can see from the graph. The Great Depression of the 1930s devastated many investors, businesses, and families. Stock prices collapsed during the early years of the depression and many companies, including banks, went bankrupt. Many people were out of work and could not find a job. The entire world was mired in the depression until World War II, when war-related activity brought us out of the depression. However, stock prices did not recover to pre-depression levels until the 1950s.

In spite of the Great Depression and the many smaller recessions in the United States, you can clearly see that the trend of stock prices has been up over the past 100 years or so. Historically, stocks have usually had a greater return on investment than savings accounts, certificates of deposit, or bonds. Most financial planners agree that stocks should be a part of any long-range investment plan.

OBJECTIVE 6 Define a mutual fund. Ownership of shares in a single company *can be risky*—the company may suffer poor financial results causing the stock price to fall. The **risk** of losing money in the stock of a single company *can be reduced* by simultaneously investing in the stocks of several different companies, especially when they are in different industries.

One way to participate in the profits of successful corporations without as much risk is to purchase shares in a mutual fund that invests in stocks. A **mutual fund** receives money from many different investors and uses the money to purchase stocks or bonds in many different companies. For example, a $1000 investment in a typical mutual fund that owns stock means that you own a very small piece of perhaps 100 different companies.

Most mutual funds are actively managed, meaning that managers are paid to buy and sell stock as they think best for investors in the fund. **Exchange-traded funds (ETFs)** are similar to mutual funds except that they tend not to be actively managed. They attempt to match the performance of an index such as the Dow Jones Average, a market sector such as energy, or a commodity such as petroleum. Essentially, ETFs are a low-cost way to purchase a portfolio with some diversification.

The next table shows that some funds *specialize* by investing in the stocks *of different types* of publicly held companies. For example, mutual funds or exchange-traded funds may specialize in large-cap (large companies), small-cap (small companies), overseas (global), or specialty (real estate, oil, banking, etc.) stocks. Many financial planners say that the first fund you should invest in is an **index fund** that tracks a broad index such as Standard & Poor's 500, which includes 500 of the largest and best-managed companies in the world. Funds that specialize in companies in one industry, such as biotechnology, or funds that specialize in international stock are usually more volatile and can be risky. However, most financial planners recommend investing some funds in international stock since the growth of emerging economies, including China and India, is so rapid.

Numbers in the News

Going Global

By mixing just two or three of these low-priced exchange-traded funds, you can create a globally diversified portfolio

Exchange-traded fund (Ticker)	Invests in
Vanguard Total Stock Market VIPERs (VTI)	U.S. stocks, all sizes
iShares S&P 500 (IVV)	Large-cap U.S. stocks
iShares S&P Midcap 400 (IJH)	Mid-cap U.S. stocks
Midcap SPDRs (MDY)	Mid-cap U.S. stocks
iShares Russell 2000 (IWM)	Small-cap U.S. stocks
iShares MSCI Japan (EWJ)	Japanese stocks
iShares MSCI Pacific Ex-Japan (EPP)	Pacific Rim, but not Japan
iShares MSCI EAFE (EFA)	Europe and Pacific Rim
iShares MSCI Emerging Markets (EEM)	Emerging markets

Comparing Investment Alternatives

EXAMPLE 5

Cynthia Peck wants to know whether she should invest her retirement monies in certificates of deposit or in a mutual fund containing stock. Assume payments of $2000 per year for 30 years and **(a)** a certificate of deposit paying 4% compounded annually or **(b)** a mutual fund containing stock that has returned 8% per year. Find the future value for both and **(c)** compare the two investments.

SOLUTION

(a) Use 4% per year and 30 years in the table in Section 11.1 to find **56.08494**.

Future value = $2000 × **56.08494** = $112,169.88

(b) Use 8% per year and 30 years in the table in Section 11.1 to find **113.28321**.

Future value = $2000 × **113.28321** = $226,566.42

(c) Difference = $226,566.42 − $112,169.88 = $114,396.54

Stocks yield more but have higher risk. Cynthia Peck will need to decide how much risk she will accept before making a decision.

Note: Neither the 4% on the certificate of deposit nor the 8% on the mutual fund is guaranteed for 30 years. Stocks may do better or worse than bank deposits in any year, but stocks tend to have higher returns over the long time periods required for retirement planning.

QUICK CHECK 5

The owner of Termites Inc. plans to deposit $15,000 at the end of each year for 10 years into an investment account. One investment would pay 5% per year, and he assumes a stock fund would continue to yield 10% per year. Find the future value of both.

▼11.4 Exercises
MyMathLab®

The shaded sections below contain solutions to help you get a QUICK START on the various types of exercises.

Find the following from the stock table on pages 442–443. (See Example 1.)

1. Low for the year for Bankrate (RATE)   1. $13.38
2. High for the year for Bard Cr (BCR)   2. $108.31
3. Most recent quarterly dividend for Big Lots (BIG)   3. _____
4. Most recent quarterly dividend for Black Hills (BKH)   4. _____
5. Volume for Berkley (WRB)   5. _____
6. Volume for Beazer Homes (BZH)   6. _____
7. PE ratio for BlackRock (BLK)   7. _____
8. PE ratio for Baytex Energy Trust (BTE)   8. _____
9. Estimated earnings per share for this year for Barck Gold (ABX)   9. _____
10. Estimated earnings per share for this year for Bank Hawaii (BOH)   10. _____
11. Dividend yield for Bank NY Mellon (BK)   11. _____
12. Dividend yield for Bancol ADS (CIB)   12. _____
13. Estimated earnings next year for Bill Barrett (BBG)   13. _____
14. Estimated earnings next year for Bemis (BMS)   14. _____
15. Change from previous week for BankNY Mellon (BK)   15. _____
16. Change from previous week for Benchmark Electric (BHE)   16. _____
17. Closing price for the week for Big Lots (BIG)   17. _____
18. Closing price for the week for Belden (BDC)   18. _____

Ignore commissions and find the cost for the following stock purchases at the closing price for the week. Then find the annual dividend that will be paid on those shares.

Stock	Number of Shares	Cost	Dividend
19. Bank of Montreal (BMO)	800	$45,912	$2260.48
800 × $57.39 = $45,912; 800 × (4 × $.7064) = $2260.48			
20. Barnes and Noble (BKS)	200	_____	_____
21. Barclays ADS (BCS)	500	_____	_____
22. Barack Gold (ABX)	300	_____	_____
23. Beam Inc (BEAM)	100	_____	_____
24. BioMed Realty Trust Inc. (BMR)	200	_____	_____

25. Define and explain **(a)** current yield and **(b)** PE ratio. (See Objectives 3 and 4.)

26. Use the chart of the Dow Jones Industrial Average and estimate the years in which stocks fell by more than 10%. (See Objective 5.)

Find the current yield for each of the following stocks. Round to the nearest tenth of a percent. (See Example 3.)

Stock	Current Price per Share	Annual Dividend	Current Yield
27. Coca-Cola (KO)	$76.58	$2.04	2.7%
$2.04 ÷ $76.58 = 2.7%			
28. Microsoft (MSFT)	$29.81	$.80	_____
29. McDonalds (MCD)	$87.91	$2.80	_____
30. Apple Inc. (AAPL)	$520.03	$12.20	_____
31. Nike (NKE)	$92.74	$1.44	_____
32. Wal-Mart (WMT)	$72.02	$1.59	_____

Find the PE ratio for each of the following. Round all answers to the nearest whole number. (See Example 4.)

Stock	Current Price per Share	Annual Net Earnings per Share	PE Ratio
33. Pepsico (PEP)	$68.73	$4.04	17
$68.73 ÷ $4.04 = 17			
34. Target (TGT)	$60.46	$4.33	_____
35. General Electric (GE)	$19.89	$1.15	_____
36. Exxon Mobil (XOM)	$84.42	$8.28	_____

37. Abercrombie & Fitch (ANF) $34.89 $1.19   _____

38. Intel (INTC) $25.00 $2.36   _____

Stock prices on consecutive days for a stock are shown next. Find the increase (decrease) in the price of each stock as a number and the percent increase (decrease) rounded to the nearest tenth of a percent.

39. $34.35, 35.20   **40.** $46.50, 45.90

_____   _____

Solve the following application problems.

41. **STOCK PURCHASE** Patsy Bonner buys 200 shares of Target at $56.30 and 100 shares of Pepsico at $68.73. Find the total cost ignoring commissions.
200 × $56.30 + 100 × $68.73 = $18,133

41. $18,133 _____

42. **WRITING A WILL** In her will, Barbara Bains stated that the trustee should purchase 300 shares of McDonalds and 200 shares of Wal-Mart and give the stock to her grandson on his 25th birthday. If the stocks are selling for $87.91 per share and $72.02 per share, respectively, find the total amount paid, ignoring broker's commissions.

42. _____

43. **CDS OR GLOBAL STOCKS** Stan Walker is comparing CDs currently yielding 2% compounded semiannually to a mutual fund with stocks that he believes will yield 8% compounded semiannually. Find the future value of an annuity with deposits of $600 every 6 months for 10 years for **(a)** the CDs and **(b)** the mutual fund. **(c)** Find the difference.

(a) _____
(b) _____
(c) _____

44. **FIXED RATE OR STOCKS** Jesica Tate plans to contribute $2500 per year to a retirement plan and is debating the use of a certificate of deposit that pays 3% per year versus an Asian stock fund that she believes will yield 10% per year. Find the future value after 12 years for **(a)** the certificate of deposit and **(b)** the stock fund. **(c)** Find the difference.

(a) _____
(b) _____
(c) _____

QUICK CHECK ANSWERS

1. (a) The highest price at which the stock sold during the year was $64.00.
   (b) The lowest price the stock sold for during the year was $39.33
   (c) The ticker symbol under which the stock trades on the market is BEAM.
   (d) The volume of shares sold during the day was 100 × 19318 = 1,931,800 shares.
   (e) The annual dividend yield is 1.3% of the current price.
   (f) The ratio of stock price to annual earnings is 62.
   (g) The stock closed at $61.87 at the end of last week.
   (h) The price of the stock was down $0.07 this week compared to last week.
   (i) Beam, Inc. earned $5.78 per share last year. It is expected to earn $2.37 this year and $2.64 next year.
   (j) The most recent quarterly dividend was $0.205 per share.

2. $19,605; $0

3. 2.7%

4. 27

5. $188,668.35; $239,061.30

11.5 Bonds

OBJECTIVES

1 Define the basics of bonds.

2 Read bond tables.

3 Find the commission charge on bonds and the cost of bonds.

4 Understand how mutual funds containing bonds are used for monthly income.

Quick TIP

Even the U.S. Government borrows using bonds. Currently, China and Japan each hold over one trillion in U.S. bonds, i.e., we owe each country over $1,000,000,000,000.

▼ CASE IN POINT   Roman Rodriguez has decided to include mutual funds holding stocks in his retirement plan, but he doesn't know about bonds. What are bonds? Should he invest in them?

OBJECTIVE 1 Define the basics of bonds. Corporations can sell shares of stock to raise funds. Shares represent ownership in the corporation. However, managers sometimes prefer to borrow money rather than issue stock. They borrow money for short-term needs from banks or insurance companies. Managers can also make long-term loans with banks, but they often prefer to borrow for the long term by issuing bonds. **Bonds** are legally binding promises (contracts) to repay borrowed money at a specific date in the future. Corporations commonly pay interest on each bond each year. Unlike shareholders, bondholders do not own part of the corporation. Countries, cities, and even churches also borrow money using bonds.

```
                    Methods Managers
                    Use to Raise Funds
        ┌───────────────────┼────────────────────────┐
   Corporate         Sell ownership              Borrow
   profits              (stock)            ┌───────────┴──────────┐
                                        Bank                  Investor
                                        loans                  loans
                                                              (bonds)
```

Here are some common terms used with bonds:

coupon rate – The interest rate stated on the bond.

face value – The amount to be repaid to the investor by the borrower when the loan matures. Corporate bonds usually have a face value of $1000. Face value is sometimes referred to as **maturity value** or **par value**.

interest – Interest is found using the face value of the bond (usually $1000), the coupon rate, and the compounding period. Most bonds require interest to be paid every six months.

issuer – The issuer is the corporation or organization that is making the loan (selling the bond).

maturity date – Date at which the bond matures and the issuer repays the face value to the current owner of the bond.

term – The length of time until the bond matures. Terms on individual bonds are determined before the bond is issued, but the terms are often in the range of 1 to 30 years.

Once issued, bonds often trade at either more than, or less than, the face value depending on prevailing interest rates.

A company is said to go **bankrupt** if it can no longer meet its financial obligations to suppliers, banks, bondholders, and others. Bankruptcy is a complex process involving management, creditors, lawyers, and courts. Generally bankruptcy lawyers are paid first. Remaining assets are then used to pay off debt, including bonds. Shareholders *do not receive anything* unless there are assets remaining after all debts have been paid. Shareholders often receive very little or nothing from a bankruptcy, and bondholders often receive only 10 to 20 cents on every dollar originally loaned.

Corporations frequently use substantial amounts of debt to build factories, expand operations, or buy other companies. The interest that must be paid on that debt is the *cost of having debt*. The larger the debt, the greater the amount of revenue the company must set aside to pay interest. As interest rates increase, companies must set aside additional money to pay interest, leaving less for other purposes including profits. On the other hand, interest costs decrease when interest rates go down.

OBJECTIVE 2 Read bond tables. The **face value**, or **par value**, of a bond is *the original amount of money* borrowed by a company. Most public corporations issue bonds with a par value of $1000. Principal and any interest due must be paid when a bond **matures**. Suppose that the owner of a bond needs money before the **maturity date** of the bond. In that event, the bond can be quickly sold through a bond dealer, such as Merrill Lynch. However, the price of the bond is determined, not by its initial price, but instead *by market conditions at the time of the sale* and the credit history of the firm. As you might expect, the bonds of a firm with poor credit history trade at much lower prices since investors worry the firm may not be able to repay its debt with interest.

Market *interest rates fluctuate widely* from year to year, yet any one bond pays exactly the same dollar amount of interest each year. If interest rates rise, investors will pay less for a bond because they want the new, higher interest yield. If interest rates fall, investors will pay more for a bond because they are satisfied with the lower yield. As a result, the price of a bond fluctuates in the opposite direction of interest rates. A bond may have a face value of $1000, but it often trades at a value different than $1000, as shown in Example 1.

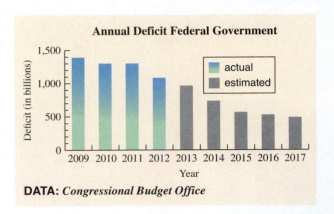

DATA: *Congressional Budget Office*

The bar chart shows that U.S. government spending has been far above revenues. The government is financing at least part of these large **deficits** by borrowing money using bonds from countries such as China and Japan. Some Experts anticipate that the excessive borrowing will result in serious inflation at some point in time which in turn will cause interest rates to increase. Other experts strongly disagree.

Working with the Bond Table

EXAMPLE 1

Brandy Barrett was in an automobile accident that put her in the hospital for 3 weeks and required months of rehabilitation. The other driver was at fault, and his insurance company paid Barrett the liability limits on his policy of $50,000. Barrett needs monthly income and is thinking about investing the funds in Goldman Sachs Group (GS) bonds that mature in 2037. Analyze the data in the table.

Company (Ticker)	Coupon	Maturity	Last Price	Last Yield	Est $Vol (000's)
Goldman Sachs Group (GS)	6.750	Oct 01, 2037	100.957	6.670	335,152

SOLUTION

(a) The ticker symbol for Goldman Sachs Group is GS.

(b) Annual interest paid per bond = 6.750% of $1000 = $67.50.

(c) The bond matures on October 1, 2037, at which time Goldman Sachs Group must pay it off.

(d) The last price at which the bond traded for the day was 100.957% of $1000.

$$\text{Last price} = 1.00957 \times \$1000 = \$1009.57$$

(e) An investor holding the bond until its maturity would earn 6.67% per year on his investment. This is often called the **yield to maturity**.

(f) The estimated volume of the bonds that sold during the week was

$$\text{Volume} = 335,152 \times \$1000 = \$335,152,000$$

QUICK CHECK 1

Analyze the data in the bond table for Bank of America (BAC) that matures in 2022.

Corporate Bonds

Company (Ticker)	Coupon	Maturity	Last Price	Last Yield	Est $ Vol (000's)
Goldman Sachs Group (GS)	5.750	Jan 24, 2022	108.728	4.605	927,056
Bank of America (BAC)	5.700	Jan 24, 2022	115.374	3.760	467,225
Morgan Stanley (MS)	6.375	Jul 24, 2042	98.697	6.474	464,519
Ebay (EBAY)	1.350	Jul 15, 2017	100.630	1.219	377,004
Goldman Sachs Group (GS)	6.750	Oct 01, 2037	100.957	6.670	335,152
Anheuser-Busch Inbev Worldwide (ABIBB)	2.500	Jul 15, 2022	101.451	2.336	276,004
United Technologies (UTX)	4.500	Jun 01, 2042	116.216	3.608	270,967
Bank of America (BAC)	5.750	Dec 01, 2017	110.625	3.552	268,930
Anheuser-Busch Inbev Worldwide (ABIBB)	3.750	Jul 15, 2042	104.370	3.513	243,555
Morgan Stanley (MS)	5.750	Jan 25, 2021	101.532	5.522	217,818
Citigroup (C)	4.450	Jan 10, 2017	107.000	2.769	216,412
Bank of America (BAC)	5.650	May 01, 2018	111.310	3.468	212,420
Stanley Black (SWK)	5.750	Jul 25, 2052	25.280	22.763	210,120
JPmorgan Chase (JPM)	4.500	Jan 24, 2022	110.505	3.208	209,823
Citigroup (C)	4.500	Jan 14, 2022	105.376	3.818	208,273
AT&T (T)	5.550	Aug 15, 2041	127.811	3.935	161,942
Comcast (CMCSA)	4.650	Jul 15, 2042	108.635	4.144	160,283
Apache (APA)	4.750	Apr 15, 2043	117.642	3.767	156,930
Wells Fargo (WFC)	3.500	Mar 08, 2022	106.021	2.782	156,770
Hewlett-Packard Co (HPQ)	4.650	Dec 09, 2021	95.123	5.317	153,311

Data from Barrons July 23, 2012

Using the Bond Table

EXAMPLE 2 Find the estimated volume sold and the last sale price of the following bonds.

(a) Citigroup (C) maturing in 2022

(b) JPmorgan Chase (JPM) maturing in 2022

(c) Anheuser-Busch Inbev Worldwide (ABIBB) maturing in 2042

SOLUTION

Company	Volume Sold	Last Sale Price per Bond
(a) Citigroup	$208,273,000	$1053.76
(b) JPmorgan Chase	$209,823,000	$1105.05
(c) Anheuser-Busch	$243,555,000	$1043.70

Notice the large volume of weekly sales. There is a lot of volume in bond markets.

QUICK CHECK 2

Find the volume sold and the last sale price for United Technologies (UTX) bonds maturing in 2042.

452 CHAPTER 11 Annuities, Stocks, and Bonds

OBJECTIVE 3 Find the commission charge on bonds and the cost of bonds. The commission for buying or selling bonds depends on the broker. These charges have fallen drastically over the past 10+ years along with the costs to buy or sell stocks due to the various discount brokerage firms on the web. The reduced costs spawned by selling on the web and competition tend to drive prices down. Today, a common charge to buy or sell a bond is $1, but commissions are even lower for large transactions.

Commission costs must be taken into account when calculating the effective interest rate of a bond. It is important to remember that the effective interest rate is not the same as the last yield. Effective interest rate is calculated by dividing the total interest the investor earns by the total cost of the bond including commissions. Last yield takes into consideration the maturity value of the bond, the time to maturity, all interest payments, and the time value of money. It does not consider commissions.

Finding the Cost to Buy Bonds

 EXAMPLE 3

Assume that the sales charge is $1 per bond, and find the following for Morgan Stanley (MS) bonds maturing in 2042.

(a) The total cost of purchasing 20 bonds

(b) The total annual interest paid on these bonds

(c) The effective interest rate to the buyer including the cost of buying the bonds

SOLUTION

(a) Total cost = (Price per bond + Sales charge per bond) × Number of bonds
$$= (\$986.97 + \$1) \times 20 = \$19{,}759.40$$

(b) Annual interest = Coupon rate × Par value of bond × Number of bonds
$$= (0.06375 \times \$1000) \times 20 = \$1275$$

(c) Effective rate $= \dfrac{\text{Total interest}}{\text{Total cost of bonds}} = \dfrac{\$1275}{\$19{,}759.40} = 6.5\%$ (rounded)

> **QUICK CHECK 3**
>
> Find the total cost, annual interest, and effective rate for 10 Goldman Sachs Group (GS) bonds maturing in 2022.

Finding the Net Amount from the Sale of Bonds

 EXAMPLE 4

Find the amount received from the sale of 50 Apache (APA) bonds maturing in 2043. Assume a commission of $1 per bond.

SOLUTION

Amount received = (Sales price of a bond − Sales charge per bond) × Number of bonds
$$= (\$1176.42 - \$1) \times 50 = \$58{,}771$$

> **QUICK CHECK 4**
>
> Find the amount received from the sale of 200 Morgan Stanley (MS) bonds maturing in 2021.

OBJECTIVE 4 Understand how mutual funds containing bonds are used for monthly income. A mutual fund can invest everything in stocks, everything in bonds, or part in stocks and part in bonds. Stock prices can be quite volatile, so financial planners recommend stock investments for people *who have a longer time horizon* over which to accumulate funds. Many planners recommend that *people invest in both stocks and bonds* during their lifetimes. Stocks may be a better investment *when investors are young*, since stocks have tended to have a higher return. Bonds may be a better investment *for investors close to retirement*, since there is less risk of losing principal in bonds and bonds pay regular interest.

Dividend paying stocks are sometimes used to generate income. However, dividend payments are not guaranteed and may be irregular. As a result, many managers of mutual funds and some individuals own bonds which have a guaranteed and regular payment stream as long as the corporation is not in bankruptcy.

Using a Bond Fund for Income **EXAMPLE 5**

Brandy Barrett from Example 1 is undergoing rehabilitation and needs safety of principal. She also needs regular interest payments to help with medical expenses. She decides to place the $50,000 received from the insurance company in a mutual fund containing bonds. **(a)** Find her annual income if the fund yields 6.5% per year. **(b)** How much would Barrett need to invest in the fund to earn $10,000 per year?

SOLUTION

(a) Use the formula for simple interest: $I = PRT$.

$$\text{Interest} = \$50,000 \times .065 = \$3250$$

(b) Again use the formula for simple interest, but now the principal (P) is unknown. Divide both sides of $I = PRT$ by RT to find the following form of the equation.

$$\text{Principal} = P = \frac{I}{RT} = \frac{\$10,000}{.065 \times 1} = \$153,846.15$$

QUICK CHECK 5

James Corporation wants $80,000 per year in interest. Find the amount the firm must invest in a bond fund yielding 6.125% to attain this annual income.

▼11.5 Exercises

MyMathLab®

The shaded sections below contain solutions to help you get a **QUICK START** *on the various types of exercises.*

Use the bond table in this section to find the following for Hewlett-Packard Co (HPQ) maturing in 2021. *(See Examples 1 and 2.)*

1. Price per bond
2. Volume of bonds sold during the week
3. Date when bonds must be paid off by Hewlett-Packard
4. Annual interest paid
5. Last yield or yield to maturity
6. Price to buy 50 of these bonds including sales charge of $1 per bond

1. $951.23
2. _____
3. _____
4. _____
5. _____
6. _____

Find the cost, including sales charges of $1 per bond, for each of the following purchases. *(See Example 3.)*

	Bond	Maturity	Number Purchased	Cost
7.	Comcast (CMCSA)	Jul 15, 2042	20	$21,747
	($1086.35 + $1) × 20 = $21,747			
8.	Stanley Black (SWK)	Jul 25, 2052	10	_____
9.	United Technologies (UTX)	Jun 01, 2042	100	_____
10.	Apache (APA)	Apr 15, 2043	25	_____
11.	Citigroup (C)	Jan 14, 2022	50	_____
12.	Anheuser-Busch (ABIBB)	Jul 15, 2022	40	_____

⚠ indicates an exercise that is related to the Case in Point feature.

454 **CHAPTER 11** Annuities, Stocks, and Bonds

13. Explain the purpose of bonds. (See Objective 1.)

14. Explain how a bondholder can estimate the effective interest rate return on the total cost of the investment, including commissions. (See Example 3.)

Solve each application problem. Assume a sales commission of $1 per bond, unless indicated otherwise, and use the table in this section. Round the rate to the nearest tenth of a percent.

15. BOND FUND Pete Chong manages bonds for a fund company. He purchases 4000 Goldman Sachs Group (GS) bonds that mature in 2037. Since this is a large purchase, the commission is only $0.20 per bond. Find **(a)** the total cost of the purchase including commissions, **(b)** the annual interest payment, and **(c)** the effective interest rate based on total cost including commissions.

(a) Total cost = ($1009.57 + $0.20) × 4000 = $4,039,080
(b) Annual interest = (.0675 × $1000) × 4000 = $270,000
(c) Effective interest rate = $270,000 ÷ $4,039,080 = 6.7%

(a) _____
(b) _____
(c) _____

16. BOND PURCHASE New York purchased 10,000 bonds issued by Apache (APA) maturing in 2043. The commission is $.20 per bond due to the large volume. Find **(a)** the total cost including commissions, **(b)** the annual interest and **(c)** the effective interest rate.

(a) _____
(b) _____
(c) _____

17. BOND PURCHASE Charles Smitten needed more income than offered by money market funds, so he purchased 25 AT&T(T) bonds maturing in 2041. Find **(a)** the total cost including commissions, **(b)** the annual interest and **(c)** the effective interest rate.

(a) _____
(b) _____
(c) _____

18. RETIREMENT FUNDS United Worker's pension administrator purchased 300 Wells Fargo (WFC) bonds maturing in 2022. Find **(a)** the total cost including commissions, **(b)** the annual interest and **(c)** the effective interest rate.

(a) _____
(b) _____
(c) _____

19. BOND FUND Bernice Clarence places $45,000 in a bond fund that is currently yielding 8% compounded annually. **(a)** Find interest for the first year. **(b)** She decides to let all interest payments remain in the account. Find the amount in the account after 10 years if the fund continues to earn 8% compounded annually.

(a) _____
(b) _____

20. **BOND FUND** The community college where Roman Rodriguez works has an endowment funded by alumni and business owners in the community. The manager of the endowment invested $500,000 in a bond fund yielding 6% compounded semiannually. Find **(a)** the interest for the first year and **(b)** the future value of the account in 8 years.

(a) _____

(b) _____

▼ Chapter 11 Quick Review

Chapter Terms *Review the following terms to test your understanding of the chapter. For each term you do not know, refer to the page number found next to that term.*

401(k) [**p. 418**]
403(b) [**p. 418**]
amount of the annuity [**p. 416**]
annual meeting [**p. 440**]
annuity [**p. 414**]
annuity due [**p. 416**]
bankrupt [**p. 449**]
board of directors [**p. 440**]
bond [**p. 430**]
capital [**p. 440**]
common stock [**p. 440**]
compound amount of the annuity [**p. 414**]
corporation [**p. 440**]
current yield [**p. 442**]
deficit [**p. 450**]
discount brokers [**p. 441**]

dividends [**p. 440**]
Dow Jones Industrial Average [**p. 444**]
equivalent cash price [**p. 426**]
ETF [**p. 445**]
exchange-traded funds (ETFs) [**p. 445**]
executive officers [**p. 440**]
face value [**p. 449**]
future value of the annuity [**p. 414**]
index fund [**p. 445**]
individual retirement account (IRA) [**p. 418**]
interest rate spreads [**p. 433**]
IRA [**p. 418**]
limited liability [**p. 440**]

mature [**p. 449**]
maturity date [**p. 450**]
mutual fund [**p. 445**]
NASDAQ Composite Index [**p. 444**]
ordinary annuity [**p. 414**]
par value [**p. 449**]
payment period [**p. 414**]
PE ratio [**p. 443**]
preferred stock [**p. 440**]
present value of an annuity [**p. 422**]
price–earnings (PE) ratio [**p. 442**]
privately held corporation [**p. 440**]

publicly held corporation [**p. 440**]
regular IRA [**p. 418**]
risk [**p. 445**]
Roth IRA [**p. 418**]
sinking fund [**p. 430**]
sinking fund table [**p. 431**]
stock [**p. 440**]
stockbrokers [**p. 441**]
stock certificates [**p. 440**]
stock exchanges [**p. 440**]
stockholders [**p. 440**]
stock ratios [**p. 442**]
term of the annuity [**p. 414**]
yield to maturity [**p. 450**]

CONCEPTS

11.1 Finding the amount of an ordinary annuity

Determine the number of periods in the annuity (n) and the interest rate per annuity period (i).
Use n and i in the annuity table to find the value of $1 at the term of annuity.
Find the value of an annuity using the formula.

Amount = Payment × Number from table

11.1 Finding the amount of an annuity due

Determine the number of periods in the annuity. Add 1 to the value and use this as the value of n.
Determine the interest rate per annuity period, and use the table to find the value of $1 at term of annuity.

The amount of the annuity is

Payment × Number from table − 1 payment

11.2 Finding the present value of an annuity

Determine the payment per period.
Determine the number of periods in the annuity (n).
Determine the interest rate per period (i).
Use the values of n and i to find the number in the present value of an annuity table.

The present value of an annuity is

Present value = Payment × Number from table

EXAMPLES

Ed Navarro deposits $800 at the end of each quarter for 7 years into an IRA. Given interest of 8% compounded quarterly, find the future value.

$$n = 7 \times 4 = 28 \text{ periods}; \ i = \tfrac{8\%}{4} = 2\% \text{ per period}$$

Number from table is **37.05121**.
Amount = $800 × **37.05121** = **$29,640.97** (rounded)

Find the amount of an annuity due if payments of $700 are made at the beginning of each quarter for 3 years in an account paying 8% compounded quarterly.

$$n = 3 \times 4 + 1 = 13; \ i = \tfrac{8\%}{4} = 2\%$$

Number from table is **14.68033**.
Amount = $700 × **14.68033** − **$700** = $9576.23

What lump sum deposited today at 8% compounded annually will yield the same total as payments of $600 at the end of each year for 10 years?

Payment = $600; n = 10
Interest = 8%
Number from table is **6.71008**.
Present value = $600 × **6.71008** = **$4026.05**

CONCEPTS	EXAMPLES

11.2 Finding the equivalent cash price

Determine the amount of the annuity payment.
Determine the number of periods in the annuity *(n)*.
Determine the interest rate per annuity period *(i)*.
Use *n* and *i* in the present value of an annuity table.
Add the present value of the annuity to the down payment to obtain today's equivalent cash price.

A buyer offers to purchase a business for $75,000 down and payments of $4000 at the end of each quarter for 5 years. Money is worth 8% compounded quarterly. How much is the buyer actually offering for the business?

Payment = $4000; $n = 5 \times 4 = 20$

Interest = $\frac{8\%}{4} = 2\%$

Number from table is **16.35143**.

Present value = $4000 \times$ **16.35143** = **$65,405.72**

Equivalent cash value = $75,000 + **$65,405.72**

= $140,405.72

11.3 Determining the payment into a sinking fund

Determine the number of payments *(n)*. Determine the interest rate per period *(i)*. Find the value of the payment needed to accumulate $1 from the sinking fund table.

Calculate the payment using

Payment = Future value $\times$ Number from table

No-Leak Plumbing plans to accumulate $500,000 in 4 years in a sinking fund for a new building. Find the amount of each semiannual payment if the fund earns 10% compounded semiannually.

$n = 5 \times 4 = 20$ periods; $i = \frac{10\%}{2} = 5\%$ per period

Number from table is **.10472**.

Payment = $500,000 $\times$ **.10472** = $52,360

11.3 Setting up a sinking fund table

Determine the required payment into the sinking fund.
Calculate the interest at the end of each period.
Add the previous total, next payment, and interest to determine the total.
Repeat these steps for each period.

A company wants to set up a sinking fund to accumulate $10,000 in 4 years. It wishes to make semiannual payments into the account, which pays 8% compounded semiannually. Set up a sinking fund table.

$$n = 4 \times 2 = 8;\ i = \frac{8\%}{2} = 4\%$$

Number from table is **.10853**.

Payment = $10,000 $\times$ **.10853** = $1085.30

Payment	Amount of Deposit	Interest Earned	Total
1	$1085.30	$0	$1085.30
2	$1085.30	$43.41	$2214.01
3	$1085.30	$88.56	$3387.87
4	$1085.30	$135.51	$4608.68
5	$1085.30	$184.35	$5878.33
6	$1085.30	$235.13	$7198.76
7	$1085.30	$287.95	$8572.01
8	$1085.11	$342.88	$10,000.00

11.4 Reading the stock table

Use the stock table in Section 11.4 to find the following information for Baytex Energy (BTE).

52 Week			Tick	Vol.			Week's		—Earnings—		
High	Low	Name	SYM	100s	Yld	P/E	Last	Chg.	Latest This Next Year Year Year		Div Amt.
59.50	36.89	Baytex Energy	BTE	14330	8.0	20	42.71	+0.81	1.88 1.54 1.82		.2137

52-week high price   52-week low price   Volume for week   Dividend yield   Price earnings ratio   Closing price   Change for the week   Last quarterly dividend

CONCEPTS	EXAMPLES
11.4 Finding the current yield on a stock To determine the current yield, use the formula $$\text{Current yield} = \frac{\text{Annual dividend}}{\text{Closing price}}$$	Find the current yield for a stock if the purchase price is \$35 and the annual dividend is \$.64. $$\text{Current yield} = \frac{\$.64}{\$35} = 1.8\% \text{ (rounded)}$$
11.4 Finding the price–earnings (PE) ratio To find the PE ratio, use the formula $$\text{PE ratio} = \frac{\text{Price per share}}{\text{Annual net income per share}}$$	Find the PE ratio for a stock priced at \$42.50 with earnings of \$2.11. $$\text{PE Ratio} = \frac{\$42.50}{\$2.11} = 20 \text{ (rounded)}$$

11.5 Reading the bond table

Use the bond table in Section 11.5 to find the following information for Morgan Stanley (MS) maturing in 2042.

Company (Ticker)	Coupon	Maturity	Last Price	Last Yield	Est Vol (000s)
Morgan Stanley (MS)	6.375	Jul 24, 2042	98.697	6.474	464,519
Pays 6.375% of $1000 per year	Matures July 24, 2042	Closed at $986.97	Yield to maturity of 6.474%	Estimated volume for the week of $464,519,000	

11.5 Determining the cost of purchasing bonds First locate the bond in the table. Find the price of the bond and multiply by \$1000. Add \$1 to this amount for commissions, then multiply by the number of bonds.	Including sales charges of \$1 per bond, find the cost of 50 Goldman Sachs Group (GS) bonds maturing in 2037. $(\$1009.57 + \$1) \times 50 = \$50,528.50$
11.5 Determining the amount received from the sale of bonds First locate the bond in the table. Find the price of the bond and multiply by \$1000. Subtract \$1 from this amount for commissions, then multiply by the number of bonds.	Find the amount received after the sales charge from the sale of 20 Citigroup (C) bonds maturing in 2017. $(\$1070.00 - \$1) \times 20 = \$21,380$
11.5 Finding the effective yield of a bond Find the cost of the bond after commission. Find the interest paid on the bond using the coupon rate. Finally, divide the interest by the cost of the bond.	Find the effective interest rate, to the nearest tenth, for a bond with a coupon rate of 3.8% and selling at 98.25. Price of bond $= .9825 \times \$1000 + \$1 =$ **\$983.50** Interest $= .038 \times \$1000 = \$38$ $$\text{Effective rate} = \frac{\$38}{\$983.50} = 3.9\% \text{ (rounded)}$$

Case **Study**

FINANCIAL PLANNING

At age 37, Paul Li decides to plan for his retirement at age 67. He currently has a net worth of about $45,000 including the equity in his home. He assumes that his employer will contribute $3500 to his retirement plan at the end of each year for the next 30 years. He plans to put one-half of his money in a mutual fund containing stocks and the other one-half in a mutual fund containing bonds.

1. Estimate Li's future accumulation if his net worth grows at 5% and the mutual funds with stocks and bonds grow at 10% and 6%, respectively.

   1. _____

2. Li is amazed that he will be able to accumulate over $600,000. However, he knows that inflation will increase his cost of living significantly in 30 years. He assumes 3% inflation and wants to find the income he needs at age 67 to have the same purchasing power as $40,000 today. (*Hint:* Look at inflation in Section 10.2 and use the compound interest table in Section 10.1.)

   2. _____

3. Li has read newspaper articles stating that Social Security benefits will be reduced in the years ahead. After some thought, he decides to be conservative and assume that Social Security will pay only the first $30,000 of the annual income he needs at age 67. Find the remaining income he will need beginning at age 67.

   3. _____

4. Li decides to plan funding for his retirement for 20 years, from ages 67 to 87. If funds earn 8% compounded annually, find the present value of the annual income that he needs at 67 based on the income from part (c).

   4. _____

5. Will his expected savings fund his retirement?

   5. _____

6. What could go wrong with his plans?

   6. _____

 INVESTIGATE

There is some discussion about the ability of Social Security to pay retirement benefits. Do you think Social Security will be around to help you during your retirement? What percent of your retirement needs do you think Social Security will pay? Try to support your views with recent articles from newspapers, magazines, or the World Wide Web.

▼ Case in Point Summary Exercise

AMERICAN RIVER COLLEGE

www.arc.losrios.edu

Facts:

- 1955: Founded
- 2012: Over 36,000 students
- 2013: Over 52% ethnically not white

American River offers students a choice of more than 70 different majors of study, including biology, engineering, hospitality management, mortuary science, collision repair, business, and even fire technology. College personnel work closely with students to help them find financial aid. Amazingly, about one-half of the students at American River College receive some kind of financial aid.

Roman Rodriguez had 3 years of experience when he went to work in Human Resources at American River College at a salary of $42,000. He began work on his 30th birthday. The college matches his contributions to his retirement plan up to 8% of his salary.

1. Rodriguez decides to contribute a total of 10% of his salary to his retirement plan. So, American River contributes 8% and he contributes a full 10% of his salary. Find the total annual contribution into the retirement plan.

   1. _____

2. For planning purposes, Rodriguez assumes he will work at American River until he is 60 and believes he can earn 8% per year in a global stock fund. Assume the contributions continue at the same level as in Exercise 1 and estimate the future value.

   2. _____

3. Assume that there are 486 faculty full-time faculty who have been at American River College for more than 8 years. If their average income is $62,940, find the annual payroll.

   3. _____

4. Based on the annual payroll in Exercise 3, estimate the annual contributions American River must make into retirement plans if all faculty contribute at least 8% of their salary into their own plans.

   4. _____

5. Assume that a wealthy donor has agreed to give American River College $250,000 per year for the next 5 years. Find the present value of these gifts, assuming 6% per year.

   5. _____

6. American River has decided to build a new classroom building and will need $8,250,000 in 7 years. They decide to make contributions into a sinking fund at the end of each 6-month period. Find the payment needed if funds earn 5% per year.

   6. _____

Chapter 11 Test

To help you review, the numbers in brackets show the section in which the topic was discussed.

Find the amounts of the following annuities. **[11.1]**

	Amount of Each Deposit	Deposited	Rate per Year	Number of Years	Type of Annuity	Amount of Annuity
1.	$1000	annually	6%	8	ordinary	_____
2.	$4500	semiannually	4%	9	ordinary	_____
3.	$30,000	quarterly	8%	6	due	_____
4.	$2600	semiannually	5%	12	due	_____

5. James Rivera earned his degree in drafting at a community college and recently began his new career. He was happy to learn that his new employer will deposit $2500 into his 401(k) retirement account at the end of each year. Find the amount he will have accumulated in 15 years if funds earn 8% per year. **[11.1]**

5. _____

6. James Rivera from Exercise 5 has also decided to invest $1000 at the end of each 6 months in an IRA that grows tax deferred. Find the amount he will have accumulated if he does this for 15 years and earns 6% compounded semiannually. **[11.1]**

6. _____

Find the present value of the following annuities. **[11.2]**

	Amount per Payment	Payment at End of Each	Number of Years	Interest Rate	Compounded	Present Value
7.	$1000	year	9	6%	annually	_____
8.	$4500	6 months	6	10%	semiannually	_____
9.	$708	month	3	12%	monthly	_____
10.	$14,000	quarter	6	8%	quarterly	_____

11. Betty Yowski borrows money for a new swimming pool and hot tub. She agrees to repay the note with a payment of $1200 per quarter for 6 years. Find the amount she must set aside today to satisfy this capital requirement in an investment earning 8% compounded quarterly. **[11.2]**

11. _____

12. Dan and Mary Foster just divorced. The divorce settlement included $650 a month payment to Dan for the 4 years until their son turns 18. Find the amount Mary must set aside today in an account earning 12% per year compounded monthly to satisfy this financial obligation. **[11.2]**

12. _____

Find the amount of each payment into a sinking fund for the following. **[11.3]**

	Amount Needed	Years Until Needed	Interest Rate	Interest Compounded	Amount of Payment
13.	$100,000	9	6%	annually	_____
14.	$250,000	10	8%	semiannually	_____
15.	$360,000	11	6%	quarterly	_____
16.	$800,000	12	10%	semiannually	_____

Solve the following application problems.

17. The owner of Hickory Bar-B-Que plans to open a new restaurant in 4 years at a cost of $200,000. Find the required semiannual payment into a sinking fund if funds are invested in an account earning 6% per year compounded semiannually.   **[11.3]**

17. _____

18. Lupe Martinez will owe her retired mother $45,000 for a piece of land. Find the required quarterly payment into a sinking fund if Lupe pays it off in 4 years and the interest rate is 10% per year compounded quarterly.   **[11.3]**

18. _____

19. George Jones purchases 200 shares of Exxon Mobil stock at $85.82 per share. Find **(a)** the total cost and **(b)** the annual dividend if the dividend per share is $2.28.   **[11.4]**

(a) _____

(b) _____

20. Belinda Deal purchases 25 IBM bonds that mature in 2021 at 95.1. They have a coupon rate of 4.2%. Find **(a)** the total cost if commissions are $1 per bond, **(b)** the annual interest, and **(c)** the effective interest rate rounded to the nearest tenth.   **[11.5]**

(a) _____

(b) _____

(c) _____

21. Explain the following.   **[11.4]**

52-Wk		Name	Tick Sym.	Vol. 100s	Yld.	P/E	Week's		Earnings			Div Amt.
High	Low						Last	Chg.	Latest Year	This Year	Next Year	
65.90	20.10	BlackDeck	BDK	74515	.8	27	63.44	+1.23	5.47	2.53	2.89	.12

22. Explain the following.   **[11.5]**

Company (Ticker)	Coupon	Maturity	Last Price	Last Yield	EST $ Vol (000s)
International Paper Co (IP)	7.950	Jun 15, 2018	117.389	5.369	209,183

12 Business and Consumer Loans

CHAPTER CONTENTS

12.1 Open-End Credit and Charge Cards

12.2 Installment Loans

12.3 Early Payoffs of Loans

12.4 Personal Property Loans

12.5 Real Estate Loans

▼ CASE IN POINT

AFTER JACKIE WATERTON received her degree in business, she went to work for Citigroup, Inc. which is one of the largest banks in the world. Since she is interested in computers and the Internet, she went to work in the department that manages electronic banking. After working there for 3 years, Waterton moved to the department that manages consumer credit. Recently, she was promoted, and she now manages a small group that works with bank customers who have major credit problems.

Debt is extremely important to every modern economy and is used daily by individuals, firms, school districts, cities, governments, and others. Individuals borrow for small and large purchases. Firms borrow to make payroll, build buildings, and pay taxes. School districts borrow to build a new school. Cities borrow to build a sports complex, and state and federal governments borrow heavily and often. When used carefully, debt is healthy and helps everyone involved. However, too much debt is a problem for students, families, firms, school districts, cities, and governments!

Debt Problems

According to the Federal Reserve Bank of New York, the average amount owed by a student borrower has nearly quadrupled in the past 10 years to an average of over $20,000. Total student debt is now close to $1 trillion ($1,000,000,000,000). Students are borrowing more to pay higher tuitions at a time when fewer scholarships are being offered. Worse yet, weak job markets make it difficult to repay the debt.

▼12.1 Open-End Credit and Charge Cards

OBJECTIVES

1 Define open-end credit.

2 Define revolving charge accounts.

3 Use the unpaid balance method.

4 Use the average daily balance method.

5 Define loan consolidation.

CASE IN POINT   Jackie Waterton has worked with many families who have serious debt problems. She often helps these families set up budgets and then tries to reduce their monthly debt payments by refinancing loans when possible.

OBJECTIVE 1 Define open-end credit. A common way of buying on credit, called **open-end credit**, has no fixed payments. The customer continues making payments until no outstanding balance is owed. With open-end credit, additional credit is often extended before the initial amount is paid off. Examples of open-end credit include most department-store charge accounts and charge cards. Individuals are given a **credit limit**, or a maximum amount that may be charged on these accounts. The lender determines the credit limit for each person based on income, assets, other debts, and credit history.

A sale paid for with a **debit card** authorizes the retailer's bank to debit the purchaser's checking account immediately upon receipt. Debit cards do not involve credit since their use results in an immediate debit, or withdrawal of funds, from an account. Debit cards are being used more and more. A Visa or MasterCard can be either a charge card or a debit card, depending on the bank and the cardholder's preference.

Quick TIP

Interest charges are often very high on revolving charge accounts, especially on cash advances. Try to minimize this type of debt and never use a credit card for a cash advance!

OBJECTIVE 2 Define revolving charge accounts. Individuals often make several charges a month to a bank card or department-store account. The charges are accumulated throughout the month on each card and billed at the end of the month. Often, the full amount owed is not paid, resulting in interest charges. Since the account may never be paid off, it is called a **revolving charge account**. Visa, MasterCard, and Discover use this method of extending credit. There are more than 3 billion credit cards in use worldwide.

According to the Federal Trade Commission, credit and charge card fraud costs cardholders and issuers hundreds of millions of dollars each year. Individuals making charges while on vacation sometimes return home to find that someone has stolen their credit card number and is using it to make purchases. Report any misuse of your credit card immediately. By law, your maximum liability is limited to $50 once you have reported the theft. Some ideas to prevent losses from theft are to:

- Keep a record of your account numbers and the phone number and address of each company in a safe place, so that you can quickly notify each of them.
- Keep an eye on your card during transactions and get it back as soon as possible.

- Save receipts to compare to billing statements.
- Open bills promptly and check the individual charges.
- Report any questionable charges promptly and in writing to the issuer of the card.

A sample copy of a credit card receipt is shown on the left. The graph on the right shows the percent of families in the United States who have a credit card and also the percent who have a balance after paying the previous month's bill. Notice that both credit-card use and loan balances have increased markedly since 1989.

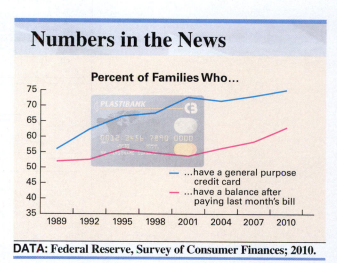

DATA: Federal Reserve, Survey of Consumer Finances; 2010.

At the end of each billing period, the customer receives a statement of payments and purchases made. An example of such an **itemized billing** is shown on page 466. Notice that it shows a variety of transactions, including new charges, refunds and payments (shown as credits), and any finance charges. The statement also shows bank fees related to exchanging currency in the event that charges were made in a foreign country.

Finance charges are interest charges beyond the cash price of an item and may include interest, credit life insurance, a time-payment differential, and carrying charges. Interest charges can be avoided if the total balance is paid by the end of the **grace period**. Grace periods range between 15 and 30 days depending on the company. Often, there is no grace period on cash advances, so that finance charges are assessed beginning immediately. Many lenders also charge **late fees** for payments that are received after the due date. **Over-the-limit fees** are charged by the lender when the borrower charges more than an approved maximum amount of debt.

OBJECTIVE 3 Use the unpaid balance method. Finance charges on open-end credit accounts may be calculated using the **unpaid balance method**. This method calculates finance charges based on the unpaid balance at *the end of the previous month*. Any purchases or returns during the current month are not used in calculating the finance charge, as you can see in the next example.

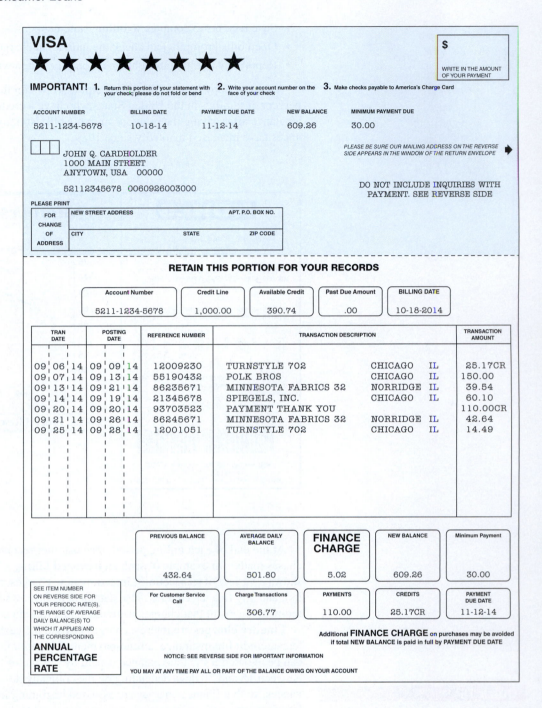

Finding Finance Charge Using the Unpaid Balance Method

EXAMPLE 1

(a) Peter Brinkman's MasterCard account had an unpaid balance of $870.40 on November 1. During November, he made a payment of $100 and used the card to purchase a puppy costing $150 for his son. Find the finance charge and the unpaid balance on December 1 if the bank charges 1.5% per month on the unpaid balance.

A finance charge of 1.5% per month on the unpaid balance would be

$$\$870.40 \times .015 = \$13.06 \text{ for the month}$$

Find the unpaid balance on December 1 as follows.

$$\$870.40 + \$13.06 + \$150 - \$100 = \$933.46$$

(b) During December, Brinkman made a payment of $50, charged $240.56 for Christmas presents, returned $35.45 worth of items, and took his family to dinner with charges of $92.45. Find his unpaid balance on January 1.

The finance charge calculated on the unpaid balance is $933.46 \times .015 = $14.00. The unpaid balance on January 1 follows.

$$\$933.46 + \textbf{\$14.00} + \textbf{\$240.56} + \textbf{\$92.45} - \textbf{\$35.45} - \textbf{\$50} = \$1195.02$$

Month	Unpaid Balance at Beginning of Month	Finance Charge	Purchases During Month	Returns	Payment	Unpaid Balance at End of Month
November	$870.40	$13.06	$150.00	—	$100	$ 933.46
December	$933.46	$14.00	$333.01	$35.45	$ 50	$1195.02

The total finance charge during the 2-month period was $13.06 + $14.00 = $27.06.

(c) Brinkman knows that his debt is increasing. He moves the balance to another charge card that charges only .8% per month. Find his savings in finance charges for January.

$$\text{Savings} = (\$1195.02 \times \textbf{.015}) - (\$1195.02 \times \textbf{.008}) = \$8.37$$

old charge card   new charge card

QUICK CHECK 1

The unpaid balance on a Visa card was $284.37. During the month, a payment of $200 was made and charges of $357.54 were added. If the finance charge is 1.2% per month on the unpaid balance, find **(a)** the finance charge for the month and **(b)** the new balance at the end of the month.

Suppose you decide to purchase a $1000 digital television set and charge it to a Visa card with finance charges of 1.5% per month on the unpaid balance. Further suppose that you make payments of $50 every month and don't charge anything else on the card. As shown in the table, it will take 24 months to pay off the television set. The $1000 television set will cost you an extra $197.83 in finance charges for a total cost of $1197.83, or nearly $1200.

Month	Unpaid Balance at Beginning of Month	Finance Charge	Payment	Unpaid Balance at End of Month
1	$1,000.00	$15.00	$50.00	$965.00
2	$965.00	$14.48	$50.00	$929.48
3	$929.48	$13.94	$50.00	$893.42
⋮	⋮	⋮	⋮	⋮
22	$143.53	$ 2.15	$50.00	$95.68
23	$ 95.68	$ 1.44	$50.00	$47.12
24	$ 47.12	$ 0.71	$47.83	$ 0.00
Totals		$197.83	$1197.83	

The cost of technology items often falls rapidly. If you had waited eight months and saved your money before buying, you might have been able to purchase the same television set for $750 cash rather than paying nearly $1200. This would have saved you 37.5%!

OBJECTIVE 4 Use the average daily balance method. Most revolving charge plans now calculate finance charges using the **average daily balance method**. First, the balance owed on the account is found at the end of each day during a month or billing period. All of these amounts are added, and the total is divided by the number of days in the month or billing period. The result is the average daily balance of the account, which is then used to calculate the finance charge.

Finding the Average Daily Balance

EXAMPLE 2

Beth Hogan's balance on a Visa card was $209.46 on March 3. Her activity for the next 30 days is shown in the table. **(a)** Find the average daily balance on April 3. Given finance charges based on $1\frac{1}{2}\%$ on the average daily balance, find **(b)** the finance charge for the month and **(c)** the balance owed on April 3.

Transaction Description		Transaction Amount
Previous balance $209.46		
March 3	Billing date	
March 12	Payment	$50.00 CR*
March 17	Walmart	$28.46
March 20	Mail order	$31.22
April 1	Auto parts	$59.10

*CR represents *credit*.

SOLUTION

(a)

Date	Unpaid Balance	Number of Days Until Balance Changes
March 3	$209.46	9
March 12	$159.46 = $209.46 − **March 12 payment of $50**	5
March 17	$187.92 = $159.46 + **March 17 charge of $28.46**	3
March 20	$219.14 = $187.92 + **March 20 charge of $31.22**	12
April 1	$278.24 = $219.14 + **April 1 charge of $59.10**	2
April 3	end of billing cycle …	31 total number of days in billing period

It is 9 days from March 3 to March 12, so the unpaid balance remains at $209.46 for 9 days.

Quick TIP

The billing period in Example 2 is 31 days. Some billing periods are 30 days (or 28 or 29 days in February). Be sure to use the correct number of days for the month of the billing period.

There are 31 days in the billing period (March has 31 days). Find the average daily balance as follows:

Step 1   Multiply each unpaid balance by the number of days for that balance.

Step 2   Total these amounts.

Step 3   Divide by the number of days in that particular billing cycle (month).

Step 1

Unpaid Balance		Days		Total Balance
$209.46	×	9	=	$1885.14
$159.46	×	5	=	797.30
$187.92	×	3	=	563.76
$219.14	×	12	=	2629.68
$278.24	×	2	=	556.48
				$6432.36 ← **Step 2**

Step 3

$$\frac{\$6432.36}{31} = \$207.50 \text{ average daily balance}$$

Hogan will pay a finance charge based on the average daily balance of $207.50.

(b) The finance charge is **.015 × $207.50** = $3.11 (rounded).

(c) The amount owed on April 3 is the beginning unpaid balance less any returns or payments, plus new charges and the finance charge.

$$\$209.46 - \$50 + (\$28.46 + \$31.22 + \$59.10) + \$3.11 = \$281.35$$

The finance charge in the previous example was small, only $3.11. Have you ever wondered how banks make money on charge cards? Let's explore this issue. Citigroup recently had a balance of just over $148 billion outstanding on credit cards. Many of these people will pay off their balances at the end of the month, resulting in no finance charges to the bank. However, assume the bank earns an average of 1.2% on credit outstanding of $105 billion and find the interest earned for a month as follows:

$$\text{Interest} = \$105{,}000{,}000{,}000 \times .012 = \$1{,}260{,}000{,}000$$

The associated one-month revenue for the bank was $1,260,000,000. Of course, the bank has a lot of expenses, but still that is a lot of revenue.

If the finance charges are expressed on a per-month basis, find the **annual percentage rate** by multiplying the monthly rate by 12, the number of months in a year. For example, $1\frac{1}{2}\%$ per month is the same as:

$$1\tfrac{1}{2}\% \times 12 = 1.5\% \times 12 = 18\% \text{ per year}$$

OBJECTIVE 5 **Define loan consolidation.** Credit can be *very easy to get* for individuals who have a good credit history and a stable job. The clipping shows that too much spending and borrowing often creates problems.

Easy Credit–Big Worry

James Machler has a degree in nursing and a great job. In the past, he has been careful with his money, even paying off an extra $80 each month on his student loans and saving a little each month. Then he decided he needed a new Lexus. Now his cash flow is tight and the clinic where he works just announced there will be some layoffs in the near future. James is suddenly very worried about his future.

Too many people get caught in a credit trap. They effectively spend more than they can afford by borrowing. They then end up with problems that can last for months or years. Below are some tips to gain control of your finances. We warn you—it takes discipline.

Gaining Control of Your Finances

1. Increase your income by investing in yourself. Choose a career you enjoy, and get training and education.

2. Make a budget and stick to it.

3. Spend less. Here are some suggestions.

   (a) Make sure you can afford your rent or mortgage payment.

   (b) Eat out less often.

   (c) Drive that old automobile one or two more years.

   (d) Purchase a less expensive automobile or reduce the number of automobiles in your family by one.

   (e) Be careful with the amount you spend on entertainment, hobbies, and travel.

   (f) Don't buy on impulse. If you want something, write it down on a piece of paper and stick it on your refrigerator for 30 days. After 30 days, ask yourself if you actually need the item.

4. Try to pay cash for things the day you buy them rather than using credit.

5. Save more by paying yourself first. Do this by saving a certain amount every month before you spend money on other things.

6. Set some money aside for emergencies.

7. Contribute to a long-range retirement plan.

Have you ever found yourself in a position where you cannot make all of your monthly payments? If so, you may be able to **consolidate your loans** into a single loan with one lower monthly payment. The new loan may have a lower interest rate and also a longer term, meaning that payments must be made for a longer period of time. This process can help you afford your monthly payments rather than defaulting on debt. **Defaulting on your debt**, or not making your payments, can mean repossession of your automobile or furniture, eviction from your apartment or house, and/or court appearances. Defaulting on your debt also ruins your credit history and can make it difficult to borrow money to buy a car or a home for years into the future.

Consolidating Loans   EXAMPLE 3

Bill and Jane Smith were married two years ago. Both were happy when they had their first child, but they needed to buy several things on credit. They now have the monthly payments shown below. The Smiths are having difficulties making the payments and they sometimes argue over money. They bank online at Citibank Direct and ask Jackie Waterton for help.

Revolving Accounts	Debt	Annual Percentage Rate	Minimum Monthly Payment
Sears	$3880.54	18%	$150
Home Depot	$1620.13	16%	$ 60
MasterCard	$3140.65	14%	$100
Visa	$4920.98	18%	$200
Total	**$13,562.30**		**Total** $510

Other Payments	Monthly Payment
Rent	$800
Jane's car payment	$315
Bill's truck payment	$268
Total	**$1383**

▼ CASE IN POINT

SOLUTION

Jackie Waterton:

1. Put the Smiths on a **strict monthly budget**.
2. Consolidated their revolving account debts into one longer-term, low-interest loan (this required a loan guarantee from Bill's father).
3. Decreased one automobile payment by refinancing the loan over a longer term.

Here are their new monthly payments.

Account	Monthly Payment	New Status
Citigroup loan for $13,562.30	$337.50	Revolving loans were consolidated
Rent	$800.00	Unchanged
Jane's car payment	$247.50	Refinanced using a longer term
Bill's truck payment	$268.00	Unchanged
	Total $1653.00	

Reduction in payments = ($510 + $1383) − $1653 = **$240 per month**

The Smiths should be all right as long as they do the following.

1. **Stay on their monthly budget.**
2. **Do not make additional credit purchases.**
3. **Continue to make all payments.**

The Smiths may end up with severe debt problems if they borrow more before the existing loan balances are significantly reduced. Borrowing more could force them to declare bankruptcy.

QUICK CHECK 3

A family refinanced the mortgage on their home, reducing the payment from $1269.45 to $1093.12. They also sold a car that had a monthly payment of $385.65 and negotiated a $50-per-month payment reduction on their second car. Find the decrease in monthly payments.

▼12.1 Exercises   MyMathLab®

The shaded sections below contain solutions to help you get a **QUICK START** on the various types of exercises.

Find the finance charge on each of the following revolving charge accounts. Assume interest is calculated on the unpaid balance of the account. Round to the nearest cent. (See Example 1.)

Unpaid Balance	Monthly Interest Rate	Finance Charge
1. $6425.40	0.8%	<u>$51.40</u>
$6425.40 × .008 = $51.40		
2. $595.35	$1\frac{1}{2}\%$	_____
3. $1201.43	$1\frac{1}{4}\%$	_____
4. $2540.33	1.2%	_____

Complete the following tables, showing the unpaid balance at the end of each month. Assume an interest rate of 1.4% on the unpaid balance. (See Example 1.)

Month	Unpaid Balance at Beginning of Month	Finance Charge	Purchases During Month	Returns	Payment	Unpaid Balance at End of Month
5. October	$437.18	_____	$128.72	$27.85	$125	_____
November	_____	_____	$291.64	—	$175	_____
December	_____	_____	$147.11	$17.15	$150	_____
January	_____	_____	$27.84	$127.76	$225	_____
6. October	$2184.60	_____	$540.68	$50.87	$200	_____
November	_____	_____	$890.27	—	$250	_____
December	_____	_____	$1240.13	$89.69	$125	_____
January	_____	_____	$384.20	—	$575	_____

7. Compare the unpaid balance method and the average daily balance method for calculating interest on open-end credit accounts. (See Objectives 3 and 4.)

8. Explain how consolidating loans may be of some advantage to the borrower. What disadvantages can you think of? (See Objective 5.)

ⓒ indicates an exercise that is related to the Case in Point feature.

Find the finance charge for the following revolving charge accounts. Assume that interest is calculated on the average daily balance of the account. (See Example 2.)

	Average Daily Balance	Monthly Interest Rate	Finance Charge
9.	$1458.25	1.4%	$20.42
	$1458.25 × .014 = $20.42		
10.	$841.60	$1\frac{1}{2}$%	$12.62
	$841.60 × .015 = $12.62		
11.	$389.95	$1\frac{1}{4}$%	_____
12.	$6320.10	0.9%	_____
13.	$1235.68	1.4%	_____
14.	$4235.47	$1\frac{3}{4}$%	_____

Solve the following application problems.

15. HOT TUB PURCHASE Betty Thomas borrowed $6500 on her Visa card to install a hot tub with landscaping around it. The interest charges are 1.6% per month on the unpaid balance. **(a)** Find the interest charges. **(b)** Find the interest charges if she moves the debt to a credit card charging 1% per month on the unpaid balance. **(c)** Find the monthly savings.

(a) _____

(b) _____

(c) _____

16. CREDIT CARD BALANCE Alphy Jurarim used a credit card from Citibank Direct to help pay for tuition expenses while in college and now owes $5232.25. The interest charges are 1.75% per month. **(a)** Find the interest charges. **(b)** Find the interest charges if he moves the debt to a credit card charging .8% per month on the unpaid balance. **(c)** Find the savings.

(a) _____

(b) _____

(c) _____

(a) Find the average daily balance for the following credit card accounts. Assume one month between billing dates using the proper number of days in the month. (b) Then find the finance charge if interest is 1.5% per month on the average daily balance. (c) Finally, find the new balance. (See Example 2.)

17. Previous balance $2340.52

November 12	Billing date	
November 20	Payment	$1000
November 21	Road bicycle & equipment	$1440.30
November 30	Flowers	$65.40

Nov. 12 to Nov. 20 = 8 days at $2340.52 gives $18,724.16
Nov. 20 to Nov. 21 = 1 day at $1340.52 gives $1340.52
Nov. 21 to Nov. 30 = 9 days at $2780.82 gives $25,027.38
Nov. 30 to Dec. 12 = 12 days at $2846.22 gives $34,154.64
8 + 1 + 9 + 12 = 30 days

$18,724.16 + $1340.52 + $25,027.38 + $34,154.64 = $79,246.70

(a) Average daily balance = $\dfrac{\$79,246.70}{30}$ = $2641.56

(b) Finance charge = $2641.56 × .015 = $39.62

(c) New balance = $2340.52 + $39.62 − $1000 + $1440.30 + $65.40 = $2885.84

(a) $2641.56

(b) $39.62

(c) $2885.84

18. Previous balance $228.95

January 27	Billing date	
February 9	Tennis-balls	$11.08
February 13	Returns	$26.54
February 20	Payment	$29
February 25	Restaurant	$71.19

(a) _____

(b) _____

(c) _____

19. Previous balance $312.78

June 11	Billing date	
June 15	Returns	$106.45
June 20	Coat	$115.73
June 24	Car rental	$74.19
July 3	Payment	$115

(a) _____

(b) _____

(c) _____

20. Previous balance $714.58

August 17	Billing date	
August 21	Mail order	$26.94
August 23	Returns	$25.41
August 27	Beverages	$31.82
August 31	Payment	$128.00
September 9	Returns	$71.14
September 11	Groceries	$110.00
September 14	Cash advance	$100.00

(a) _____

(b) _____

(c) _____

21. Previous balance $355.72

March 29	Billing date	
March 31	Returns	$209.53
April 2	Auto parts	$28.76
April 10	Pharmacy	$14.80
April 12	Returns	$63.54
April 13	Returns	$11.71
April 20	Payment	$72.00
April 21	Flowers	$29.72

(a) _____

(b) _____

(c) _____

▼12.2 Installment Loans

OBJECTIVES

1 Define installment loan.

2 Find the total installment cost and the finance charge.

3 Use the formula for approximate APR.

4 Use the table to find APR.

OBJECTIVE 1 Define installment loan. A loan is **amortized** if both principal and interest are paid off by a sequence of equal periodic payments. This type of loan is called an **installment loan**. People use installment loans for cars, boats, home improvements, and even for consolidating several loans into one affordable loan. Firms use installment loans to purchase equipment, computers, vehicles, mining equipment, etc. The graphic shows the total interest that must be paid when financing a new Ford Escape over 3, 4, and 5 years. Notice that financing the SUV over 5 years results in interest costs of $2600, thereby increasing the total cost of the $25,000 loan to $27,600 or by 10.4%.

Quick TIP

The interest rates on installments loans can be very high.

Numbers in the News

Financing Costs

The cost of financing $25,000 at 4% per year for a new Ford Escape.

Loan term (years)	Monthly payment	Interest paid
3	$738	$1568
4	$564	$2072
5	$460	$2600

Notice that the total interest paid is much higher the longer the term of the loan. It may be difficult to make the higher payments of a short-term loan, but it results in less total interest!

The federal **Truth in Lending Act** (Regulation Z) of 1969 requires lenders to disclose their **finance charge** (the charge for credit) and **annual percentage rate (APR)** on installment loans. The federal government *does not* regulate rates. Each individual state sets the maximum allowable rates and charges.

The interest rate that is **stated** (in the newspaper, a marketing brochure, or a problem in a textbook) is also called the **nominal rate**. The nominal or stated rate can differ from the annual percentage rate or APR, which is based on the actual amount received by the borrower. The APR is the *true effective annual interest rate* for a loan. Information on two loans of $1000 each is shown below. An advertisement indicates a rate of 10% for each loan, and the actual interest is $100 for each. However, the terms differ as do the APRs.

	Stated Rate	Interest	Term	APR
Loan 1	10%	$100	1 year	$R = \dfrac{I}{PT} = \dfrac{\$100}{\$1000 \times 1} = 10\%$
Loan 2	10%	$100	9 months	$R = \dfrac{I}{PT} = \dfrac{\$100}{\$1000 \times \frac{9}{12}} = 13.3\%$

The interest rates on these two loans are very different. In fact, interest rate charges vary a surprising amount from one lender to another, so it pays to shop around for the lowest APR. Furthermore, institutions usually charge a much higher interest rate for individuals with poor **credit history**. Thus, it is worth it to maintain a good credit history by paying all bills on time.

OBJECTIVE 2 Find the total installment cost and the finance charge. As shown next, the total **installment cost** includes the down payment and all subsequent payments. The **finance charge** is the difference between the total installment cost and the price if paid in cash. So, the finance charge includes interest and any fees charged by the lender.

> **Finding the Total Installment Cost, Finance Charge, and Amount Financed**
>
> Total installment cost = Down payment + Payment amount × Number of payments
>
> Finance charge = Total installment cost − Cash price
>
> Amount financed = Cash price − Down payment

Finding the Total Installment Cost

 EXAMPLE 1

Frank Kimlicko recently received his master's degree and began work at a large community college as a music professor specializing in classical guitar. He purchased an exquisite-sounding classical guitar costing $3800 with $500 down and 36 monthly payments of $109.61 each. Find **(a)** the total installment cost, **(b)** the finance charge, and **(c)** the amount financed.

SOLUTION

(a) The total installment cost is the down payment plus the total of all monthly payments.

$$\text{Total installment cost} = \$500 + (\$109.61 \times 36) = \mathbf{\$4445.96}$$

(b) The finance charge is the total installment cost less the cash price.

$$\text{Finance charge} = \mathbf{\$4445.96} - \$3800 = \$645.96$$

(c) The amount financed is $3800 − $500 = $3300.

> **Quick TIP**
>
> To find the total installment cost, add the down payment to the sum of all monthly payments.

> **QUICK CHECK 1**
>
> Robert Chu purchased a new Honda Civic costing $24,200, including taxes and licensing, with $4000 down and 48 payments of $488.25 each. Find **(a)** the total installment cost, **(b)** the finance charge, and **(c)** the amount financed.

Many students use an installment loan called a **Stafford loan** to help pay costs while in college. The government pays the interest on a *subsidized* Stafford loan while the student borrower is in school on at least a half-time basis. In contrast, the student is responsible for interest on *unsubsidized* Stafford loans. Repayment of a loan begins six months after the borrower ceases at least half-time enrollment. You can find information about Stafford loans at the financial aid office at your college or at a bank.

OBJECTIVE 3 Use the formula for approximate APR. The **approximate annual percentage rate (APR)** for a loan paid off in monthly payments can be found using the following formula.

$$\text{Approximate APR} = \frac{24 \times \text{Finance charge}}{\text{Amount financed} \times (1 + \text{Total number of payments})}$$

The formula is *only an estimate* of the APR. It is not accurate enough for the purposes of the federal Truth in Lending Act, which requires the use of tables.

Finding the Annual Percentage Rate

 EXAMPLE 2

Ed Chamski decides to buy a used car for $6400. He makes a down payment of $1200 and monthly payments of $169 for 36 months. Find the approximate annual percentage rate rounded to the nearest tenth of a percent.

SOLUTION

Use the steps outlined above.

$$\text{Total installment cost} = \$1200 + (\$169 \times 36 \text{ months}) = \mathbf{\$7284}$$
$$\text{Finance charge} = \mathbf{\$7284} - \$6400 = \$884$$
$$\text{Amount financed} = \$6400 - \$1200 = \$5200$$

Quick TIP

The precise APR can be found using a financial calculator as shown in examples in Appendix C.

Use the formula for approximate APR. Replace the finance charge with $884, the amount financed with $5200, and the number of payments with 36.

$$\text{Approximate APR} = \frac{24 \times \textbf{Finance charge}}{\textbf{Amount financed} \times (1 + \textbf{Total number of payments})}$$

$$= \frac{24 \times \$884}{\$5200 \times (1 + 36)}$$

$$= \frac{\$21,216}{\$192,400}$$

$$= .110 \; or \; 11.0\% \text{ approximate APR}$$

The approximate annual percentage rate on this loan is 11%. Example 3 shows how to find the actual APR for this loan.

QUICK CHECK 2

Bob Drake purchases a Harley-Davidson motorcycle costing $26,500. He financed the purchase at his bank with a $5000 down payment and payments of $693.74 for 36 months. Estimate the annual percentage rate to the nearest tenth of a percent.

OBJECTIVE 4 **Use the table to find APR.** Special tables must be used to find annual percentage rates *accurate enough* to satisfy federal law which requires accuracy to the nearest quarter of a percent. These tables are available from a Federal Reserve Bank or the Board of Governors of the Federal Reserve System, Washington, DC 20551. The table on page 478 shows a small portion of these tables. The APR is found from the APR table as follows.

Finding the Annual Percentage Rate (APR)

Step 1   Multiply the finance charge by $100, and divide by the amount financed.

$$\frac{\text{Finance charge} \times \$100}{\text{Amount financed}}$$

The result is the finance charge per $100 of the amount financed.

Step 2   Read down the left column of the annual percentage rate table to the proper number of payments. Go across to the number closest to the number found in Step 1. Read the number at the top of that column to find the annual percentage rate.

Finding the Annual Percentage Rate

 EXAMPLE 3

In Example 2, a used car costing $6400 was financed at $169 per month for 36 months after a down payment of $1200. The total finance charge was $884, and the amount financed was $5200. Find the annual percentage rate.

SOLUTION

Quick TIP

When using the annual percentage rate table, select the column with the table number that is closest to the finance charge per $100 of amount financed.

Step 1   Multiply the finance charge by $100, and divide by the amount financed.

$$\frac{\$884 \times \$100}{\$5200} = \$17.00 \qquad \text{Round to two decimal places for use in the table.}$$

This gives the finance charge per $100 financed.

Step 2   Read down the left column of the annual percentage rate table to the line for 36 months (the actual number of monthly payments). Follow across to the right to find the number closest to $17.00. Here, find **17.01**. Read the number at the top of this column of figures to find the annual percentage rate, 10.50%.

In this example, 10.50% is the annual percentage rate that must be disclosed to the buyer of the car. In Example 2, the formula for the approximate annual percentage rate gave an answer of 11%, which is not accurate enough to meet the requirements of the law.

QUICK CHECK 3

A refrigerator costing $1450 was financed with $100 down and 20 monthly payments of $74.95 each. Find **(a)** the finance charge, **(b)** amount financed, and **(c)** the annual percentage rate.

Finding the Annual Percentage Rate

EXAMPLE 4

Two Brothers from Italy Pizza borrowed $48,000 to remodel their store. They agreed to a note with payments of $1565.78 per month for 36 months. Find the annual percentage rate.

SOLUTION

$$\text{Total installment cost} = \$0 \text{ down payment} + \$1565.78 \times 36 = \mathbf{\$56,368.08}$$
$$\text{Finance charge} = \mathbf{\$56,368.08} - \$48,000 = \$8368.08$$
$$\text{Amount financed} = \$48,000 - \$0 \text{ down payment} = \mathbf{\$48,000}$$

Now use the formula for the APR.

$$\frac{\$8368.08 \times \$100}{\mathbf{\$48,000}} = 17.4335$$

Find the row associated with 36 payments in the annual percentage rate table. Look to the right across that row to find the number closest to 17.4335, which is 17.43. Look to the top of that column to find **10.75%**. This is the APR to the nearest quarter of a percent.

QUICK CHECK 4

An insurance agent borrowed $22,500 for new hardware and software for her growing business. She agreed to a note with payments of $858.10 per month for 30 months and put a CD up for collateral instead of making a down payment. Find the annual percentage rate.

Annual Percentage Rate Table for Monthly Payment Plans

Annual Percentage Rate (Finance Charge Per $100 of Amount Financed)

Number of Payments	10.00%	10.25%	10.50%	10.75%	11.00%	11.25%	11.50%	11.75%	12.00%	12.25%	12.50%	12.75%	13.00%	13.25%	13.50%	13.75%	Number of Payments
12	5.50	5.64	5.78	5.92	6.06	6.20	6.34	6.48	6.62	6.76	6.90	7.04	7.18	7.32	7.46	7.60	12
14	6.36	6.52	6.69	6.85	7.01	7.17	7.34	7.50	7.66	7.82	7.99	8.15	8.31	8.48	8.64	8.81	14
16	7.23	7.41	7.60	7.78	7.97	8.15	8.34	8.53	8.71	8.90	9.08	9.27	9.46	9.64	9.83	10.02	16
18	8.10	8.31	8.52	8.73	8.93	9.14	9.35	9.56	9.77	9.98	10.19	10.40	10.61	10.82	11.03	11.24	18
20	8.98	9.21	9.44	9.67	9.90	10.13	10.37	10.60	10.83	11.06	11.30	11.53	11.76	12.00	12.23	12.46	20
22	9.86	10.12	10.37	10.62	10.88	11.13	11.39	11.64	11.90	12.16	12.41	12.67	12.93	13.19	13.44	13.70	22
24	10.75	11.02	11.30	11.58	11.86	12.14	12.42	12.70	12.98	13.26	13.54	13.82	14.10	14.38	14.66	14.95	24
26	11.64	11.94	12.24	12.54	12.85	13.15	13.45	13.75	14.06	14.36	14.67	14.97	15.28	15.59	15.89	16.20	26
28	12.53	12.86	13.18	13.51	13.84	14.16	14.49	14.82	15.15	15.48	15.81	16.14	16.47	16.80	17.13	17.46	28
30	13.43	13.78	14.13	14.48	14.83	15.19	15.54	15.89	16.24	16.60	16.95	17.31	17.66	18.02	18.38	18.74	30
32	14.34	14.71	15.09	15.46	15.84	16.21	16.59	16.97	17.35	17.73	18.11	18.49	18.87	19.25	19.63	20.02	32
34	15.25	15.65	16.05	16.44	16.85	17.25	17.65	18.05	18.46	18.86	19.27	19.67	20.08	20.49	20.90	21.31	34
36	16.16	16.58	17.01	17.43	17.86	18.29	18.71	19.14	19.57	20.00	20.43	20.87	21.30	21.73	22.17	22.60	36
38	17.08	17.53	17.98	18.43	18.88	19.33	19.78	20.24	20.69	21.15	21.61	22.07	22.52	22.99	23.45	23.91	38
40	18.00	18.48	18.95	19.43	19.90	20.38	20.86	21.34	21.82	22.30	22.79	23.27	23.76	24.25	24.73	25.22	40
42	18.93	19.43	19.93	20.43	20.93	21.44	21.94	22.45	22.96	23.47	23.98	24.49	25.00	25.51	26.03	26.55	42
44	19.86	20.39	20.91	21.44	21.97	22.50	23.03	23.57	24.10	24.64	25.17	25.71	26.25	26.79	27.33	27.88	44
46	20.80	21.35	21.90	22.46	23.01	23.57	24.13	24.69	25.25	25.81	26.37	26.94	27.51	28.08	28.65	29.22	46
48	21.74	22.32	22.90	23.48	24.06	24.64	25.23	25.81	26.40	26.99	27.58	28.18	28.77	29.37	29.97	30.57	48
50	22.69	23.29	23.89	24.50	25.11	25.72	26.33	26.95	27.56	28.18	28.80	29.42	30.04	30.67	31.29	31.92	50

▼12.2 Exercises

MyMathLab®

*The shaded sections below contain solutions to help you get a **QUICK START** on the various types of exercises.*

Find the finance charge (FC) and the total installment cost (TIC) for the following.
(See Example 1.)

	Amount Financed	Down Payment	Cash Price	Number of Payments	Amount of Payment	Total Installment Cost	Finance Charge
1.	$1400	$400	$1800	24	$68.75	$2050	$250
	TIC = $400 + (24 × $68.75) = $2050; FC = $2050 − $1800 = $250						
2.	$650	$125	$775	24	$32	$893	$118
	TIC = $125 + (24 × $32) = $893; FC = $893 − $775 = $118						
3.	$150	none	$150	12	$15	_____	_____
4.	$1200	none	$1200	20	$70	_____	_____
5.	$2525	$375	$2900	18	$176	_____	_____
6.	$6388	$380	$6768	60	$136	_____	_____

Find the approximate annual percentage rate using the approximate annual percentage rate formula. Round to the nearest tenth of a percent. (See Example 2.)

	Amount Financed	Finance Charge	No. of Monthly Payments	Approximate APR
7.	$11,500	$1200	30	8.1%
	Approx. APR = $\dfrac{24 \times \$1200}{\$11{,}500 \times (1 + 30)} = 8.1\%$			
8.	$2200	$434	36	_____
9.	$7542	$1780	48	_____
10.	$4500	$650	36	_____
11.	$1852	$111.98	18	_____
12.	$8046	$973	24	_____

C indicates an exercise that is related to the Case in Point feature.

Find the annual percentage rate using the annual percentage rate table. (See Example 3.)

	Amount Financed	Finance Charge	No. of Monthly Payments	APR
13.	$1400	$185.68	24	**12.25%**

$$\frac{FC \times \$100}{AF} = \frac{\$185.68 \times \$100}{\$1400} = 13.26; \text{ from 24-payment row, APR} = 12.25\%$$

	Amount Financed	Finance Charge	No. of Monthly Payments	APR
14.	$345	$24.62	12	_____
15.	$442	$28.68	14	_____
16.	$4690	$1237.22	48	_____
17.	$1450	$132.50	18	_____
18.	$650	$73.45	24	_____

19. Explain the difference between open-end credit and installment loans. (See Section 12.1 and Objective 1 of this section.)

20. Make a list of all of the items that you have bought on an installment loan. Make another list of things you plan to buy in the next 2 years on an installment loan. (See Objective 1.)

Solve the following application problems. Use the formula on page 476 to estimate the APR, and round rates to the nearest tenth of a percent.

21. METAL LATHE Benson Fabrication purchased a new precision metal lathe for $74,800. The company made a down payment of 20% and financed the balance using 36 monthly payments of $1916.85. Find **(a)** the amount financed, **(b)** the total installment cost, and **(c)** the finance charge. **(d)** Then estimate the APR.

(a) $59,840
(b) $83,966.60
(c) $9166.60
(d) 9.9%

(a) Down payment = .2 × $74,800 = $14,960
   Amount financed = $74,800 − $14,960 = $59,840
(b) Total installment cost = $14,960 + 36 × $1916.85 = $83,966.60
(c) Finance charge = $83,966.60 − $74,800 = $9166.60
(d) Approximate APR = $\frac{24 \times \$9166.60}{\$59,840 \times (1 + 36)}$ = 9.9%

22. PLAYSET Tom and Jane Franklin bought a backyard playset with a trampoline for their grandchildren for $9400. They paid 10% down and financed the balance with 24 monthly payments of $398.24. Find **(a)** the amount financed, **(b)** the total installment cost, and **(c)** the finance charge. **(d)** Then estimate the APR.

(a) _____
(b) _____
(c) _____
(d) _____

23. ELECTRIC GUITAR Yanni Benjamin purchased a good-quality electric guitar with amplifier and financed $3600 over 12 months. The finance charge was $260. **(a)** Estimate the APR, then **(b)** find the exact APR using the table.

(a) _____
(b) _____

24. **CANNING MACHINE**   Aluminum Cans Inc. purchased a new machine to press aluminum into cans and financed $385,000 over 30 months. The finance charge was $54,411. **(a)** Estimate the APR, then **(b)** find the exact APR using the table.

(a) _____

(b) _____

Solve the following application problems and use the table to find the annual percentage rate.

25. **CHIP FABRICATION**   A Chinese computer chip manufacturer borrowed $84 million worth of Chinese yuan to purchase some sophisticated equipment. The note required 24 monthly payments of $3.88 million each. Find the annual percentage rate.

    FC $= 24 \times$ $3.88 million $-$ $84 million $=$ $9.12 million

    $$\frac{FC \times \$100}{AF} = \frac{\$9.12 \times \$100}{\$84 \text{ million}} = 10.86; \text{ from 24-payment row, APR} = 10.00\%$$

25. 10.00% _____

26. **REFRIGERATOR PURCHASE**   Sears offers a refrigerator for $1600 with no down payment, $294.06 in interest charges, and 30 equal payments. Find the annual percentage rate.

26. _____

27. **AUTO PURCHASE**   Pat Waller bought a Toyota Corolla for $20,800 including taxes and license. She made a down payment of $2000 and agreed to make 50 payments to Citibank of $472 each. Find **(a)** the amount financed, **(b)** the total installment cost, **(c)** the total interest paid, and **(d)** the APR.

(a) _____

(b) _____

(c) _____

(d) _____

28. **SKI BOAT**   James Berry purchased a ski boat costing $12,800 with $500 down and loan payments to Citibank of $399 per month for 36 months. Find **(a)** the amount financed, **(b)** the total installment cost, **(c)** the total interest paid, and **(d)** the APR.

(a) _____

(b) _____

(c) _____

(d) _____

29. **COMPUTER SYSTEM**   A contractor in Mexico City purchased a computer system for 650,000 pesos. After making a down payment of 100,000 pesos, he agreed to make payments of 26,342.18 pesos per month for 24 months. Find **(a)** the total installment cost and **(b)** the annual percentage rate.

(a) _____

(b) _____

30. **TRACTOR PURCHASE**   An electrical contractor in Hiroshima, Japan with poor credit, purchased a tractor costing 2,700,000 yen. He made a down payment of 1,000,000 yen and agreed to monthly payments of 54,855 yen for 36 months. Find **(a)** the total installment cost and **(b)** the annual percentage rate.

(a) _____

(b) _____

31. PECAN TREES Josefina Torres and her husband need $85,000 to plant pecan trees on their small farm. They pay $20,000 down and finance the balance with 40 payments of $1942.24. Find **(a)** the total installment cost and **(b)** the annual percentage rate.

(a) _____

(b) _____

32. GOAT CHEESE Toni Smith wants to produce goat cheese and needs $120,000 to purchase 400 goats. He pays $30,000 down and finances the balance with 24 monthly payments of $4253.44. Find **(a)** the total installment cost and **(b)** the annual percentage rate.

(a) _____

(b) _____

33. Should businesses be able to charge interest rates of over 20% to customers with very poor credit histories? Why or why not? If not, do you think any firm would lend to these customers?

34. Explain why it is important for the government to regulate the way in which interest rates are stated.

▼12.3 Early Payoffs of Loans

OBJECTIVES

1 Use the United States Rule for an early payment.

2 Find the amount due on the maturity date using the United States Rule.

3 Use the Rule of 78 when prepaying a loan.

OBJECTIVE 1 Use the United States Rule for an early payment. It is common for a payment to be made on a loan *before it is due*. This may occur when a person receives extra money or refinances a debt at a lower interest rate somewhere else. Prepayments of loans are discussed in this section.

The first method for calculating early loan payment is the **United States Rule**, and it is used by the U.S. government as well as most states and financial institutions. Under the United States Rule, any payment is first applied to any interest owed. The balance of the payment is then used to reduce the principal amount of the loan. We will continue to use 360-day years in the calculations of this section.

Using the United States Rule

Step 1 Find the simple interest due from the date the loan was made until the date the partial payment is made. Use the formula $I = PRT$.

Step 2 Subtract this interest from the amount of the payment.

Step 3 Any difference is used to reduce the principal.

Step 4 Treat additional partial payments in the same way, always finding interest on *only* the unpaid balance after the last partial payment.

Step 5 The remaining principal plus interest on this unpaid principal is then due on the due date of the loan.

OBJECTIVE 2 Find the amount due on the maturity date using the United States Rule. If the partial payment is not large enough to pay the interest due, the payment is simply held until enough money is available to pay the interest due. This means that a partial payment smaller than the interest due offers no advantage to the borrower—the lender just holds the partial payment until enough money is available to pay the interest owed.

Finding the Amount Due

 EXAMPLE 1

On August 14, Dr. Jane Ficker signed a 180-day note for $28,500 for a used x-ray machine for her dental office. The note has an interest rate of 10% compounded annually. On October 25, a payment of $8500 is made. **(a)** Find the balance owed on the principal after the payment. **(b)** If no additional payments are made, find the amount due at maturity of the loan.

SOLUTION

(a) Step 1 Use $I = PRT$ to find interest from August 14 to October 25 (72 days).

$$\text{Interest} = \$28{,}500 \times .10 \times \frac{72}{360} = \mathbf{\$570}$$

Step 2 Amount applied to principal = Payment − Interest
$$= \$8500 - \$570$$
$$= \mathbf{\$7930}$$

Step 3 New principal = Previous principal − Amount applied to principal
$$= \quad \$28{,}500 \quad - \quad \$7930$$
$$= \$20{,}570$$

(b) Step 4 Go on to Step 5 since there are no additional partial payments.

Step 5 The partial payment was made on day 72 of the 180-day note. Interest on the new principal of $20,570 will be for $180 - 72 = \mathbf{108}$ days.

$$\text{Interest} = \$20{,}570 \times .10 \times \frac{108}{360} = \mathbf{\$617.10}$$

$$\text{Due at maturity} = \$20{,}570 + \mathbf{\$617.10} = \$21{,}187.10$$

QUICK CHECK 1

A 200-day note, signed on April 7 for $48,300, has a rate of 9% compounded annually. A payment of $12,000 was made on June 25. Find **(a)** the balance owed on the principal after the payment on June 25 and **(b)** the amount due at maturity.

Finding the Interest Paid and Amount Due **EXAMPLE 2**

On March 1, Boston Dairy signs a promissory note for $38,500 to replace some milking equipment for their Holsteins. The note is for 180 days at a rate of 10%. The dairy makes the following partial payments: $6000 on June 9 and $3500 on July 11. Find the interest paid on the note and the amount due on the due date of the note.

SOLUTION

The first partial payment is on June 9 or, using the number of days in each month, after $(30 + 30 + 31 + 9) = 100$ days.

$$\text{Interest for 100 days} = \$38,500 \times .10 \times \frac{100}{360} = \textbf{\$1069.44} \text{ (rounded)}$$

First partial payment	$6000.00
Portion going to interest	− 1069.44
Portion going to reduce debt	**$4930.56**

Debt on June 9 *after 1st partial payment* = $38,500 − **$4930.56** = $33,569.44

The second partial payment occurs $21 + 11 = 32$ days later.

$$\text{Interest for 32 days} = \$33,569.44 \times .10 \times \frac{32}{360} = \textbf{\$298.40} \text{ (rounded)}$$

Second partial payment	$3500.00
Portion going to interest	−298.40
Portion going to reduce debt	**$3201.60**

Debt on July 11 *after 2nd partial payment* = $33,569.44 − **$3201.60** = $30,367.84

The first partial payment is made after 100 days, and the second partial payment is made after an additional 32 days. Thus, the due date of the note is $180 − 100 − 32 = 48$ days after the second partial payment.

$$\text{Interest for the last 48 days} = \$30,367.84 \times .10 \times \frac{48}{360} = \textbf{\$404.90} \text{ (rounded)}$$

$$\text{Amount due } \textit{at maturity} = \$30,367.84 + \textbf{\$404.90} = \$30,772.74$$

Date Payment Made	Amount of Payement	Applied to Interest	Applied to Principal	Remaining Balance
June 9	$6,000.00	$1069.44	$4,930.56	$33,569.44
July 11	$3,500.00	$298.40	$3,201.60	$30,367.84
At maturity	$30,772.74	$404.90	$30,367.84	$0
Total	$40,272.74	$1772.74	$38,500.00	

QUICK CHECK 2

A 120-day note has a face value of $7500 and a rate of 11.5%. A partial payment of $1700 is made after 40 days. Find **(a)** the balance owed on the principal after the partial payment and **(b)** the amount due at maturity.

OBJECTIVE 3 Use the Rule of 78 when prepaying a loan. A variation of the United States Rule, called the **Rule of 78**, is still used by many lenders for installment loans. This rule allows a lender *to earn more of the finance charge during the early months* of the loan compared with the United States Rule. Lenders typically use this rule *to protect against* early payoffs on small loans. Effectively, the lender will earn a higher rate of interest in the event of an early payoff under the Rule of 78 than under the United States Rule.

The Rule of 78 gets its name based on a loan of 12 months—the sum of the months $1 + 2 + 3 + \cdots + 12 = 78$. The finance charge for the first month is $\frac{12}{78}$ of the total charge, with $\frac{11}{78}$ in the second month, $\frac{10}{78}$ in the third month, and so on, with $\frac{1}{78}$ in the final month. The Rule of 78 can be applied to loans *with terms other than 12 months*. For example, the sum of the months in a 6-month contract is $1 + 2 + 3 + 4 + 5 + 6 = 21$. The finance charge for the first month is $\frac{6}{21}$; $\frac{5}{21}$ for the second month; and so on. Similarly, the sum of the months in a 15-month contract is $1 + 2 + \cdots + 15 = 120$. The finance charge for the first month of a 15-month contract is $\frac{15}{120}$ or $\frac{1}{8}$, and so on.

Monthly Finance Charges

Term of Loan	Month 1	Month 2	Month 3	Month 4	Month 5	Month 6	Month 7	Month 8	Month 9	Month 10	Month 11	Month 12
12 months	$\frac{12}{78}$	$\frac{11}{78}$	$\frac{10}{78}$	$\frac{9}{78}$	$\frac{8}{78}$	$\frac{7}{78}$	$\frac{6}{78}$	$\frac{5}{78}$	$\frac{4}{78}$	$\frac{3}{78}$	$\frac{2}{78}$	$\frac{1}{78}$
6 months	$\frac{6}{21}$	$\frac{5}{21}$	$\frac{4}{21}$	$\frac{3}{21}$	$\frac{2}{21}$	$\frac{1}{21}$						

The total finance charge on an installment loan is calculated when a loan is first made. Early payoff of a loan results in a lower finance charge. The portion of the finance charge that *has not yet been earned* by the lender under the Rule of 78, called **unearned interest** or **refund**, is found as follows.

Finding unearned interest

$$U = F\left(\frac{N}{P}\right)\left(\frac{1 + N}{1 + P}\right)$$

where

U = unearned interest F = finance charge

N = number of payments remaining P = original number of payments

---

Finding Unearned Interest and Balance Due

 EXAMPLE 3

Aaron Ortego borrowed $6000, which he is paying back in 24 monthly payments of $295 each. With 9 payments remaining, he decides to repay the loan in full. Find **(a)** the amount of unearned interest and **(b)** the amount necessary to repay the loan in full. Use the Rule of 78.

SOLUTION

(a) Total of all payments = 24 payments × $295 = **$7080**

Amount borrowed

Finance charge = **$7080** − $6000 = **$1080**

Find the amount of unearned interest as follows. The finance charge is $1080, the scheduled number of payments is 24, and the loan is paid off with 9 payments left. Solve as follows.

$$\text{Unearned interest} = \mathbf{\$1080} \times \frac{9}{24} \times \frac{(1 + 9)}{(1 + 24)} = \$162$$

(b) When Ortego decides to pay off the loan, he has 9 payments of $295 left.

$$\text{Sum of remaining payments} = 9 \text{ payments} \times \$295 = \mathbf{\$2655}$$

Ortego saves the unearned interest of $162 by paying off the loan early. Therefore, the amount needed to pay the loan in full is the sum of the remaining payments minus the unearned interest.

$$\text{Amount needed to repay the loan in full} = \text{Remaining payments} - \text{Unearned interest}$$
$$= \mathbf{\$2655} - \$162 = \$2493$$

QUICK CHECK 3

Simplot Maps has signed a note with a face value of $24,000 that requires 20 monthly payments of $1307.76. The manager pays the debt in full after 12 payments. Find **(a)** the finance charge, **(b)** the amount of unearned interest, and **(c)** the amount needed to repay the loan in full using the Rule of 78.

Finding Unearned Interest and Balance Due

EXAMPLE 4

The Smiths borrow $1200 for a new washer and dryer and agree to make 18 monthly payments of $74.30 each. After the 10th payment, they pay the loan in full. Find **(a)** the amount of unearned interest and **(b)** the amount needed to repay the loan in full using the Rule of 78.

SOLUTION

(a)

$$\text{Sum of payments} = 18 \text{ payments} \times \$74.30 = \textbf{\$1337.40}$$
$$\text{Finance charge} = \textbf{\$1337.40} - \$1200 = \$137.40$$

Since there are $(18 - 10) = $ **8 payments remaining** when he pays the loan off, the unearned interest is found as follows.

$$\text{Unearned interest} = \$137.40 \times \frac{8}{18} \times \frac{(1 + 8)}{(1 + 18)} = \$28.93 \text{ (rounded)}$$

(b)   The amount needed to pay the loan in full is the sum of the remaining payments less the unearned interest.

$$\text{Sum of remaining 8 payments} = 8 \text{ payments} \times \$74.30 = \textbf{\$594.40}$$
$$\text{Amount needed to repay the loan in full} = \textbf{\$594.40} - \$28.93 = \textbf{\$565.47}$$

QUICK CHECK 4

Tim O'Murphy borrows $2100 to buy a riding lawn mower and agrees to make 12 monthly payments of $186.58 each. He pays the debt in full after 6 months. Find **(a)** the finance charge, **(b)** the amount of unearned interest, and **(c)** the amount needed to repay the loan in full using the Rule of 78.

▼12.3 Exercises   MyMathLab®

The shaded sections below contain solutions to help you get a **QUICK START** *on the various types of exercises.*

Find the balance due on the maturity date of the following notes. Find the total amount of interest paid on each note. Use the United States Rule. (See Examples 1 and 2.)

	Principal	Interest	Time (Days)	Partial Payments	Balance Due	Total Interest Paid
1.	$9800	$8\frac{1}{2}\%$	150	$1800 on day 50	$8307.31	$307.31

Interest for 50 days = $9800 \times .085 \times \frac{50}{360} = $115.69
Amount of 1st payment applied to reduce debt = $1800 - $115.69 = $1684.31
Debt after 1st payment = $9800 - $1684.31 = $8115.69
Interest due at end of 150-day note = $8115.69 \times .085 \times \frac{100}{360} = $191.62
Balance due on maturity date = $8115.69 + $191.62 = $8307.31
Total interest paid = $115.69 + $191.62 = $307.31

	Principal	Interest	Time (Days)	Partial Payments	Balance Due	Total Interest Paid
2.	$7200	7.5%	120	$3000 on day 45	_____	_____
3.	$15,000	10.5%	200	$6500 on day 100	_____	_____
4.	$76,900	11%	180	$31,250 on day 75	_____	_____
5.	$18,457	12%	120	$5978 on day 34 $3124 on day 55	_____	_____
6.	$39,864	9%	105	$8458 on day 43 $11,354 on day 88	_____	_____

⚠ indicates an exercise that is related to the Case in Point feature.

Each of the following loans is paid in full before the date of maturity. Find the amount of unearned interest. Use the Rule of 78. (See Example 3.)

	Finance Charge	Total Number of Payments	Remaining Number of Payments When Paid in Full	Unearned Interest
7.	$1050	24	11	$231
8.	$422	30	16	_____
9.	$881	36	12	_____
10.	$650	24	22	_____
11.	$900	36	6	_____
12.	$1250	60	12	_____

7. $\$1050 \times \frac{11}{24} \times \frac{(1 + 11)}{(1 + 24)} = \$231$

13. Explain why banks prefer the Rule of 78 to the United States Rule in the event of prepayment. (See Objective 3.)

14. Describe a situation in which a bank might prefer a loan to be prepaid.

Solve the following application problems using the United States Rule.

15. **LANDSCAPING** Andrew Raring borrowed $8900 from Citibank to landscape his yard. The 240-day note had an interest rate of 12% compounded annually. He repaid the note in 140 days with his income-tax refund. Find **(a)** the interest due and **(b)** the total amount due.
   (a) Loan is for 140 days
      $\text{Interest} = \$8900 \times .12 \times \frac{140}{360} = \$415.33$
   (b) Amount due $= \$8900 + \$415.33 = \$9315.33$

   (a) $415.33
   (b) $9315.33

16. **COMPUTER CONSULTANT** The computer system at Genome Therapy crashed several times last year. On January 10, the company borrowed $125,000 at 11% compounded annually for 250 days to pay a consultant to work on the Novell network. However, they decide to pay the loan in full on July 1. Find **(a)** the interest due and **(b)** the total amount due.

   (a) _____
   (b) _____

17. **PARTIAL PAYMENT** Johnson Solar Technologies borrowed $92,000 on May 7, signing a note due in 90 days at 11.25% interest. On June 24, the company made a partial payment of $24,350. Find **(a)** the amount due on the maturity date of the note and **(b)** the interest paid on the note.

   (a) _____
   (b) _____

18. **REMODELING** The Second Avenue Butcher Shop financed a remodeling program by giving the builder a note for $32,500. The note was made on September 14 and is due in 120 days. Interest on the note is 9.75%. On December 9, the firm makes a partial payment of $9000. Find **(a)** the amount due on the maturity date of the note and **(b)** the interest paid on the note.

(a) _____

(b) _____

19. **INVENTORY** The Washington News orders large quantities of paper every 4 months to save on freight charges. For its last order, the firm signed a note on February 18, maturing on May 15. The face value of the note was $104,500, with interest of 11%. The firm made a partial payment of $38,000 on March 20 and a second partial payment of $27,200 on April 16. Find **(a)** the amount due on the maturity date of the note and **(b)** the amount of interest paid on the note.

(a) _____

(b) _____

20. **SURVEILLANCE CAMERAS** To help detect trespassers at night, a small security firm purchased some high-technology cameras using a note from Citibank for $32,000. The note was signed on July 26 and was due on November 20. The interest rate is 13%. The firm made a partial payment of $6000 on August 31 and a second partial payment of $11,700 on October 4. Find **(a)** the amount due on the maturity date of the note and **(b)** the interest paid on the note.

(a) _____

(b) _____

Solve the following application problems using the Rule of 78. (See Example 3.)

21. **ENGAGEMENT RING** Tom Stowe purchased a diamond engagement ring for $1150. He paid $100 down and agreed to 12 monthly payments of $95 each. After making 7 payments, he paid the loan in full. Find **(a)** the unearned interest and **(b)** the amount necessary to pay the loan in full.

    (a) Finance charge = $100 + (12 × $95) − $1150 = $90
    $U = \$90 \times \frac{5}{12} \times \frac{6}{13} = \$17.31$ (rounded)
    (b) (5 × $95) − $17.31 = $457.69

(a) $17.31

(b) $457.69

22. **GARBAGE TRUCK** Haul-it-Away, Inc., purchased a dump truck for $62,000. The owners made a down payment of $22,000 and financed the remainder with 36 payments of $1328.57 each. They paid off the note with 12 payments remaining. Find **(a)** the amount of unearned interest and **(b)** the amount necessary to pay the loan in full.

(a) _____

(b) _____

23. **PRINTING** BlackTop Printing made a $5000 down payment on a special copy machine costing $23,800. The loan agreement with Citibank called for 20 monthly payments of $1025 each. Find **(a)** the finance charge, **(b)** the unearned interest, and **(c)** the amount necessary to pay the loan in full after the 14th payment.

(a) _____

(b) _____

(c) _____

24. **MOVIE PROJECTORS** Movie 6, Inc., purchased two movie projectors at a total cost of $12,200 with a down payment of $1500. The company agreed to make 12 monthly payments of $945 each. Find **(a)** the finance charge, **(b)** the unearned interest, and **(c)** the amount necessary to pay the loan in full after the 8th payment.

(a) _____

(b) _____

(c) _____

25. **WEB DESIGN** Blackstone Web Design needed $76,800 to purchase computers, software, and network equipment. The owners paid $15,000 down and financed the balance with 30 monthly payments of $2423.89 each. Find **(a)** the total installment cost, **(b)** the finance charge, **(c)** the unearned interest, and **(d)** the amount needed to pay the loan in full after the 10th payment.

(a) _____

(b) _____

(c) _____

(d) _____

26. **ASPHALT CRUMB** Binston Asphalt borrowed $850,000 to purchase a machine that converts old tires into asphalt crumb for use as a base material under sports arenas. The company paid $200,000 of the cost up front and financed the balance with 36 monthly payments of $20,821.42 each. Find **(a)** the total installment cost, **(b)** the finance charge, **(c)** the unearned interest, and **(d)** the amount needed to pay the loan in full after the 25th payment.

(a) _____

(b) _____

(c) _____

(d) _____

QUICK CHECK ANSWERS

1. (a) $37,253.93 **(b)** $38,380.86

2. (a) $5895.83 **(b)** $6046.50

3. (a) $2155.20 **(b)** $369.46
   (c) $10,092.62

4. (a) $138.96 **(b)** $37.41
   (c) $1082.07

▼ 12.4 Personal Property Loans

OBJECTIVES

1 Define personal property and real estate.

2 Use the formula for amortization to find payment.

3 Set up an amortization schedule.

4 Find monthly payments.

▼ **CASE IN POINT**　Before she worked at Citibank, Jackie Waterton made personal property loans for a neighborhood bank. Every day she would receive many loan applications showing income, assets, and debt, as well as employment information. She would then carefully check the creditworthiness of each applicant.

OBJECTIVE 1 Define personal property and real estate. Items that can be moved from one location to another, such as an automobile, a boat, or a stereo, are called **personal property**. In contrast, land and homes cannot be moved and are called **real estate** or **real property**. Personal property loans are discussed in this section, and real estate loans are discussed in the next section.

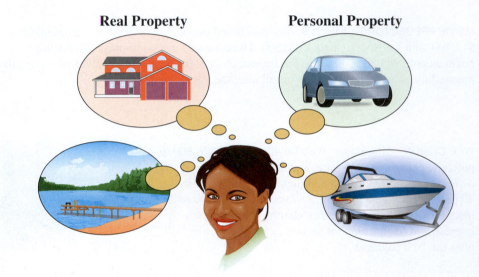

Banks, credit unions, finance companies, and many other types of companies make money through personal property loans. Typically, these loans are repaid, or **amortized**, using monthly payments. Sometimes, a buyer is not able to make the payments as promised. In that event, the lender must **repossess** the personal property and sell it to someone else. These companies charge a slightly higher interest rate to everyone to make up for loans on which they never fully recover their money. Interest rates for personal property loans vary significantly from lender to lender and from year to year, and can be high. Be sure to shop carefully before borrowing.

OBJECTIVE 2 Use the formula for amortization to find payment. The periodic payment needed at the end of each period to amortize a loan with interest i per period, over n periods, is found by using the following formula.

Finding Periodic Payment

$$\text{Payment} = \text{Loan amount} \times \text{Number from amortization table}$$

Amortizing a Loan　 **EXAMPLE 1**　Sven Yarborough earned a degree at a community college and is now a mechanic at a Ford dealership. He was so impressed with the quality of Fords that he purchased an SUV at a cost of $29,400, including tax, title, and license, after the rebate. He made a down payment of $3500 and was able to finance the balance at a rate of 6% per year for 4 years. Find **(a)** the monthly payment, **(b)** the portion of the first payment that is interest, **(c)** the balance due after one payment, **(d)** the interest owed for the second month, and **(e)** the balance after the second payment.

SOLUTION

(a) Amount financed = $29,400 − $3500 = $25,900.

Use $\frac{6\%}{12}$ = .5% per month and 4 years × 12 = 48 months in the table to find **.02349**.

Monthly payment = $25,900 × **.02349** = $608.39   (rounded)

(b) Interest for 1st month = $I = PRT$ = $25,900 × .06 × $\frac{1}{12}$ = **$129.50**

Amount of 1st payment applied to principal = $608.39 − **$129.50** = **$478.89**

(c) Balance after 1st payment = $25,900 − **$478.89** = $25,421.11.

(d) Interest for 2nd month = PRT = $25,421.11 × .06 × $\frac{1}{12}$ = **$127.11**   (rounded)

Amount of 2nd payment applied to principal = $608.39 − **$127.11** = **$481.28**

(e) Balance after 2nd payment = $25,421.11 − **$481.28** = **$24,939.83**.

QUICK CHECK 1

Marine Ltd. paid $450,000 down on a tugboat costing $1,800,000. The firm financed the balance at 6% per year for 4 years. Find **(a)** the monthly payment and **(b)** the balance after the first payment.

OBJECTIVE 3 Set up an amortization schedule.

Creating an Amortization Table

EXAMPLE 2

Clarence Thomas purchased some equipment for his car wash at a cost of $22,300. He made a down payment of $5000 and agreed to pay the balance off in quarterly payments over 2 years at 12% compounded quarterly. **(a)** Find the quarterly payment, and **(b)** show the first four payments in a table called an **amortization schedule**.

SOLUTION

(a) The amount financed is $22,300 − $5000 = $17,300. Find the factor from the table using 2 × 4 = 8 quarters and $\frac{12\%}{4}$ = 3% per quarter. Then multiply the amount financed by the factor to find the payment.

Payment = $17,300 × **.14246** = $2464.56 (rounded)

Quick TIP

Notice that interest is large at first when the debt is high but it decreases with every payment as the debt goes down.

(b)
Amortization Schedule

Payment Number	Amount of Payment	Interest for Period	Portion to Principal	Principal at End of Period
0	—	—	—	$17,300.00
1	$2464.56	$519.00	$1945.56	$15,354.44
2	$2464.56	$460.63	$2003.93	$13,350.51
3	$2464.56	$400.52	$2064.04	$11,286.47
4	$2464.56	$338.59	$2125.97	$9,160.50

QUICK CHECK 2

BlueLake Marina purchased a party barge costing $85,700 with a down payment of $20,000 and financed the balance at 8% for 4 quarters. Find the payment and construct an amortization schedule for the first 2 quarters.

Amortization Table

Interest Rate Per Period

Period	$\frac{1}{2}$%	1%	$1\frac{1}{2}$%	2%	$2\frac{1}{2}$%	3%	4%	6%	8%	10%	Period
1	1.00500	1.01000	1.01500	1.02000	1.02500	1.03000	1.04000	1.06000	1.08000	1.10000	1
2	.50375	.50751	.51128	.51505	.51883	.52261	.53020	.54544	.56077	.57619	2
3	.33667	.34002	.34338	.34675	.35014	.35353	.36035	.37411	.38803	.40211	3
4	.25313	.25628	.25944	.26262	.26582	.26903	.27549	.28859	.30192	.31547	4
5	.20301	.20604	.20909	.21216	.21525	.21835	.22463	.23740	.25046	.26380	5
6	.16960	.17255	.17553	.17853	.18155	.18460	.19076	.20336	.21632	.22961	6
7	.14573	.14863	.15156	.15451	.15750	.16051	.16661	.17914	.19207	.20541	7
8	.12783	.13069	.13358	.13651	.13947	.14246	.14853	.16104	.17401	.18744	8
9	.11391	.11674	.11961	.12252	.12546	.12843	.13449	.14702	.16008	.17364	9
10	.10277	.10558	.10843	.11133	.11426	.11723	.12329	.13587	.14903	.16275	10
11	.09366	.09645	.09929	.10218	.10511	.10808	.11415	.12679	.14008	.15396	11
12	.08607	.08885	.09168	.09456	.09749	.10046	.10655	.11928	.13270	.14676	12
13	.07964	.08241	.08524	.08812	.09105	.09403	.10014	.11296	.12652	.14078	13
14	.07414	.07690	.07972	.08260	.08554	.08853	.09467	.10758	.12130	.13575	14
15	.06936	.07212	.07494	.07783	.08077	.08377	.08994	.10296	.11683	.13147	15
16	.06519	.06794	.07077	.07365	.07660	.07961	.08582	.09895	.11298	.12782	16
17	.06151	.06426	.06708	.06997	.07293	.07595	.08220	.09544	.10963	.12466	17
18	.05823	.06098	.06381	.06670	.06967	.07271	.07899	.09236	.10670	.12193	18
19	.05530	.05805	.06088	.06378	.06676	.06981	.07614	.08962	.10413	.11955	19
20	.05267	.05542	.05825	.06116	.06415	.06722	.07358	.08718	.10185	.11746	20
21	.05028	.05303	.05587	.05878	.06179	.06487	.07128	.08500	.09983	.11562	21
22	.04811	.05086	.05370	.05663	.05965	.06275	.06920	.08305	.09803	.11401	22
23	.04613	.04889	.05173	.05467	.05770	.06081	.06731	.08128	.09642	.11257	23
24	.04432	.04707	.04992	.05287	.05591	.05905	.06559	.07968	.09498	.11130	24
25	.04265	.04541	.04826	.05122	.05428	.05743	.06401	.07823	.09368	.11017	25
26	.04111	.04387	.04673	.04970	.05277	.05594	.06257	.07690	.09251	.10916	26
27	.03969	.04245	.04532	.04829	.05138	.05456	.06124	.07570	.09145	.10826	27
28	.03836	.04112	.04400	.04699	.05009	.05329	.06001	.07459	.09049	.10745	28
29	.03713	.03990	.04278	.04578	.04889	.05211	.05888	.07358	.08962	.10673	29
30	.03598	.03875	.04164	.04465	.04778	.05102	.05783	.07265	.08883	.10608	30
31	.03490	.03768	.04057	.04360	.04674	.05000	.05686	.07179	.08811	.10550	31
32	.03389	.03667	.03958	.04261	.04577	.04905	.05595	.07100	.08745	.10497	32
33	.03295	.03573	.03864	.04169	.04486	.04816	.05510	.07027	.08685	.10450	33
34	.03206	.03484	.03776	.04082	.04401	.04732	.05431	.06960	.08630	.10407	34
35	.03122	.03400	.03693	.04000	.04321	.04654	.05358	.06897	.08580	.10369	35
36	.03042	.03321	.03615	.03923	.04245	.04580	.05289	.06839	.08534	.10334	36
37	.02967	.03247	.03541	.03851	.04174	.04511	.05224	.06786	.08492	.10303	37
38	.02896	.03176	.03472	.03782	.04107	.04446	.05163	.06736	.08454	.10275	38
39	.02829	.03109	.03405	.03717	.04044	.04384	.05106	.06689	.08419	.10249	39
40	.02765	.03046	.03343	.03656	.03984	.04326	.05052	.06646	.08386	.10226	40
41	.02704	.02985	.03283	.03597	.03927	.04271	.05002	.06606	.08356	.10205	41
42	.02646	.02928	.03226	.03542	.03873	.04219	.04954	.06568	.08329	.10186	42
43	.02590	.02873	.03172	.03489	.03822	.04170	.04909	.06533	.08303	.10169	43
44	.02538	.02820	.03121	.03439	.03773	.04123	.04866	.06501	.08280	.10153	44
45	.02487	.02771	.03072	.03391	.03727	.04079	.04826	.06470	.08259	.10139	45
46	.02439	.02723	.03025	.03345	.03683	.04036	.04788	.06441	.08239	.10126	46
47	.02393	.02677	.02980	.03302	.03641	.03996	.04752	.06415	.08221	.10115	47
48	.02349	.02633	.02938	.03260	.03601	.03958	.04718	.06390	.08204	.10104	48
49	.02306	.02591	.02896	.03220	.03562	.03921	.04686	.06366	.08189	.10095	49
50	.02265	.02551	.02857	.03182	.03526	.03887	.04655	.06344	.08174	.10086	50

OBJECTIVE 4 Find monthly payments. The loan payoff table below can be used as an alternative to the amortization table on the preceding page. The table on this page shows some higher interest rates and longer terms than the previous table. Personal property loans often have higher interest rates, since people are more likely to default on a loan for an expensive plasma television set than, say, on the loan on their home. Also, individuals with poor or no credit history and who would not qualify to buy a home must often pay a high interest rate on personal loans.

This table has a different format from the table on the preceding page. The APR is down the left column, and the number of months is across the top of this table.

> **Finding Loan Payment**
>
> Payment = Loan amount × Number from loan payoff table

Loan Payoff Table

APR	18	24	30	36	42	48	54	60	APR
				Number of Months					
8%	.05914	.04523	.03688	.03134	.02738	.02441	.02211	.02028	8%
9%	.05960	.04568	.03735	.03180	.02785	.02489	.02259	.02076	9%
10%	.06006	.04615	.03781	.03227	.02832	.02536	.02307	.02125	10%
11%	.06052	.04661	.03828	.03274	.02879	.02585	.02356	.02174	11%
12%	.06098	.04707	.03875	.03321	.02928	.02633	.02406	.02225	12%
13%	.06145	.04754	.03922	.03369	.02976	.02683	.02456	.02275	13%
14%	.06192	.04801	.03970	.03418	.03025	.02733	.02507	.02327	14%
15%	.06238	.04849	.04018	.03467	.03075	.02783	.02558	.02379	15%
16%	.06286	.04896	.04066	.03516	.03125	.02834	.02610	.02432	16%
17%	.06333	.04944	.04115	.03565	.03176	.02885	.02662	.02485	17%
18%	.06381	.04993	.04164	.03615	.03226	.02937	.02715	.02539	18%
19%	.06428	.05041	.04213	.03666	.03278	.02990	.02769	.02594	19%
20%	.06476	.05090	.04263	.03716	.03330	.03043	.02823	.02649	20%

Finding Amortization Payments

EXAMPLE 3

After a trade-in, Vickie Ewing owes $17,400 on a new Harley-Davidson motorcycle and wishes to pay the loan off in 60 months. She has found that she can finance the loan at 9% per year if she has a good credit history, but at 14% per year if she has a poor credit history.

(a) Find the monthly payment at both interest rates.

(b) Find the total finance charge at both interest rates.

(c) Find the extra cost of having poor credit.

SOLUTION

(a) Monthly payment at 9% = $17,400 × .02076 = $361.22 (rounded).

Monthly payment at 14% = $17,400 × .02327 = $404.90 (rounded).

(b) The finance charge is the sum of all of the payments minus the amount financed.

number of payments
↓

Finance charge at 9% = 60 × $361.22 − $17,400 = **$4273.20**
Finance charge at 14% = 60 × $404.90 − $17,400 = **$6894**

(c) Extra cost of poor credit = **$6894** − **$4273.20** = $2620.80.

Clearly, having a poor credit history can be very costly.

> **QUICK CHECK 3**
>
> After his down payment, Josh Crandall needs to borrow $12,800 for 48 months to buy a truck. He can finance it at 8% per year if he has excellent credit but, at 15% per year if he has poor credit. Find (a) the monthly payment at both interest rates, (b) the total finance charge for both rates, and (c) the extra cost of having poor credit.

▼ 12.4 Exercises

MyMathLab®

*The shaded sections below contain solutions to help you get a **QUICK START** on the various types of exercises.*

Find the payment necessary to amortize the following loans using the amortization table. Round to the nearest cent if needed. (See Example 1.)

	Amount of Loan	Interest Rate	Payments Made	Number of Years	Payment
1.	$6800	8%	annually	5	$1703.13
	Payment = $6800 × .25046 = $1703.13				
2.	$7500	10%	annually	6	$1722.08
	Payment = $7500 × .22961 = $1722.08				
3.	$4500	8%	semiannually	$7\frac{1}{2}$	
4.	$12,000	6%	semiannually	8	
5.	$96,000	8%	quarterly	$7\frac{3}{4}$	
6.	$210,000	12%	quarterly	8	
7.	$4876	12%	monthly	3	
8.	$6800	6%	monthly	3	

Use the loan payoff table to find the monthly payment (MP) and finance charge (FC) for each of the following loans. (See Example 3.)

	Amount Financed	Number of Months	APR	Monthly Payment	Finance Charge
9.	$5300	42	9%	$147.61	$899.62
	MP = $5300 × .02785 = $147.61; FC = (42 × $147.61) − $5300 = $899.62				
10.	$4800	24	12%	$225.94	$622.56
	MP = $4800 × .04707 = $225.94; FC = (24 × $225.94) − $4800 = $622.56				
11.	$12,000	48	13%		
12.	$8102	48	8%		
13.	$11,750	60	11%		
14.	$16,000	60	10%		

 indicates an exercise that is related to the Case in Point feature.

15. Explain the process of amortizing a loan. (See Objective 2.)

16. Explain why a loan officer at a bank might look at a credit report on someone before making a loan. What would you do if your credit report was inaccurate?

Solve the following application problems using the amortization table.

17. **FORESTRY OPERATIONS** Blackstone Logging borrowed $62,400 to purchase a used truck to haul logs. The loan has a rate of 12% per year and requires 40 monthly payments. Find **(a)** the monthly payment and **(b)** the total interest paid.

(a) $1900.70

(b) $13,628

(a) Monthly payment = $62,400 × .03046 = $1900.70

(b) Total interest = (40 × $1900.70) − $62,400 = $13,628

18. **OPENING A RESTAURANT** Chuck and Judy Nielson opened a restaurant at a cost of $340,000. They paid $40,000 of their own money and agreed to pay the remainder in quarterly payments over 7 years at 12%. Find **(a)** the quarterly payment and **(b)** the total amount of interest paid over 7 years.

(a) _____

(b) _____

19. **PRINTER** An insurance firm pays $4000 for a new high-speed color printer. It amortizes the loan for the printer in 4 annual payments at 8%. Prepare an amortization schedule for this machine.

Payment Number	Amount of Payment	Interest for Period	Portion to Principal	Principal at End of Period

20. **TRACTOR PURCHASE** Long Haul Trucking purchases a used tractor for pulling 18-wheel trailers on interstate highways at a cost of $72,000. It agrees to pay for it with a loan from Citibank that will be amortized over 9 annual payments at 8% interest. Prepare an amortization schedule for the truck.

Payment Number	Amount of Payment	Interest for Period	Portion to Principal	Principal at End of Period

Solve the following application problems. Use the loan payoff table. (See Objective 3.)

21. ELECTRONIC EQUIPMENT An engineering firm purchases specialized software for $24,500. The firm makes a down payment of $10,000 and amortizes the balance with monthly loan payments to Citibank of 11% for 4 years. Prepare an amortization schedule showing the first 5 payments.

Payment Number	Amount of Payment	Interest for Period	Portion to Principal	Principal at End of Period

22. AMORTIZING A LOAN Rebecca Reed just graduated from dental school and borrows $120,000 from Citibank to purchase equipment for her own business. She agreed to amortize the loan with monthly payments at 10% for 4 years. Prepare an amortization schedule for the first 5 payments.

Payment Number	Amount of Payment	Interest for Period	Portion to Principal	Principal at End of Period

23. SMART PHONE Ben Watson needs $50,000 to set up his own booth at a local mall. He has $15,000 and financed the balance at a high rate of 14% for 36 months since he did not have much credit history. Prepare an amortization schedule showing the first 5 payments.

Payment Number	Amount of Payment	Interest for Period	Portion to Principal	Principal at End of Period

24. SCUBA EQUIPMENT   Jessica Chien needed $280,000 for inventory for a scuba diving shop that she was opening. She had $40,000, and the bank loaned her the balance at 11% for 30 months. Prepare an amortization schedule showing the first 5 payments.

Payment Number	Amount of Payment	Interest for Period	Portion to Principal	Principal at End of Period

▼ 12.5   Real Estate Loans

OBJECTIVES

1 Determine monthly payments on a home.

2 Prepare a repayment schedule.

3 Define escrow accounts.

4 Define fixed and variable rate loans.

5 Understand your credit score.

▼ **CASE IN POINT**   Jackie Waterton's position at Citibank requires her to work with customers who have difficulty paying their bills. Since the house payment is often the largest expense for a family, she often looks to see if she can reduce the monthly payment on the mortgage.

OBJECTIVE 1   Determine monthly payments on a home. A home is *one of the most expensive purchases* that a person makes in his or her lifetime. The monthly payment for a home **mortgage** depends on the amount borrowed, the interest rate, and the term of the loan.

The bar graph shows that home **mortgage rates** have fallen from a high of over 15% in 1981–82 to record low rates of below 4% in 2012. Interest rates are a very important factor in determining the monthly payment and therefore the affordability of a particular home. If interest rates fall, people **refinance** their home loans at lower rates to reduce their monthly payments. The interest on a home loan may also be tax deductible, which can help people afford homes by reducing their income taxes.

Numbers in the News

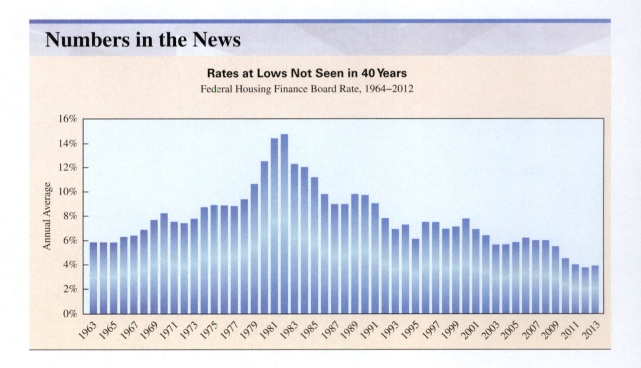

Rates at Lows Not Seen in 40 Years
Federal Housing Finance Board Rate, 1964–2012

The amount of the monthly payment is found with the methods given in Section 12.4, but different tables are used for real estate loans because of the long repayment periods. The real estate amortization table below shows the monthly payment necessary to repay a $1000 loan for differing interest rates and lengths of repayment. To use the table, first find the amount to be financed in thousands by dividing the total amount to be borrowed by $1000. Then multiply this value by the appropriate number from the table.

Real Estate Amortization Table (Principal and Interest per Thousand Dollars Borrowed)

Terms in Years	4%	$4\frac{1}{2}$%	5%	$5\frac{1}{2}$%	6%	$6\frac{1}{2}$%	7%	$7\frac{1}{2}$%	8%	Terms in Years
10	10.12	10.36	10.61	10.85	11.10	11.35	11.62	11.88	12.14	10
15	7.40	7.65	7.91	8.17	8.44	8.71	8.99	9.28	9.56	15
20	6.06	6.33	6.60	6.88	7.16	7.46	7.76	8.06	8.37	20
25	5.28	5.56	5.85	6.14	6.44	6.75	7.07	7.39	7.72	25
30	4.77	5.07	5.37	5.68	6.00	6.32	6.65	7.00	7.34	30

Understanding the Effects of Rate and Term

After making a down payment, the Stringers need to borrow $140,000 to purchase a condominium. They want to know the effect of the interest rate and term of the loan on cost. **(a)** Find the monthly payment for both 15 and 30 years at 4% and 6%. Then find **(b)** the total cost of the home with each loan and **(c)** the finance charge for each loan.

SOLUTION

(a) The amount to be financed in thousands = $140,000 ÷ $1000 = 140. Multiply this value by the appropriate factor from the real estate amortization table.

	Monthly Payment
4% interest for 15 years = 140 × **7.40** =	**$1036.00**
6% interest for 15 years = 140 × **8.44** =	**$1181.60**
4% interest for 30 years = 140 × **4.77** =	**$667.80**
6% interest for 30 years = 140 × **6.00** =	**$840.00**

Monthly payments range from $667.80 to $1181.60, depending on the interest rate and length of the loan. The lowest payment of $667.80 may look good at first, but read part **(b)** below.

(b) The total cost of the home is the sum of all payments over the respective months and years.

	Monthly Payment		Total Cost
4% interest for 15 years =	$1036.00 × 15 years × 12 months/yr	=	**$186,480**
6% interest for 15 years =	$1181.60 × 15 years × 12 months/yr	=	**$212,688**
4% interest for 30 years =	$667.80 × 30 years × 12 months/yr	=	**$240,408**
6% interest for 30 years =	$840.00 × 30 years × 12 months/yr	=	**$302,400**

(c) The finance charge, or interest cost, of each of the loans is the total cost found in part **(b)** minus the amount financed of $140,000.

Interest Cost of Purchasing the Condominium

Term of Loan	4%	6%
15 years	$46,480	$72,688
30 years	$100,408	$162,400

cheapest   most expensive

First, notice that interest adds quite a bit to the cost of the $140,000 loan. The longer term of 30 years results in a significantly lower house payment, but it also results in a much higher eventual cost. So, the longer term loan of 30 years is *not necessarily the best choice.* Clearly, higher interest rates and longer terms ADD HUGE amounts to the interest that must be paid to purchase a property.

QUICK CHECK 1

A couple plans to borrow $220,000 for 30 years to purchase a home. Find both the payment and the total 30-year cost assuming **(a)** a 4.5% rate and **(b)** a 7% rate.

Mortgage payoffs of 25 or 30 years have been common in the past. However, **accelerated mortgages**, with payoffs of 15 or 20 years, are becoming more common for the reason pointed out in Example 1—lower total costs. Mortgages with shorter terms also tend to have slightly lower interest rates.

OBJECTIVE 2 Prepare a repayment schedule. Many lenders use a computer to calculate an **amortization schedule**, also called a **repayment schedule**. This schedule separates each payment into the portion going to interest and the portion reducing the debt (principal payment).

The Zinks purchase a house by borrowing $195,000 at 7% for 30 years. Prepare a loan repayment schedule for this loan.

SOLUTION

First find the monthly payment, then use simple interest calculations for the first two months. Be sure to round to the nearest cent at each step.

$$\text{Monthly payment} = \$195 \times 6.65 = \$1296.75$$

First month:

$$\text{Interest} = PRT = \textbf{\$195,000} \times \textbf{.07} \times \tfrac{1}{12} = \$1137.50$$

monthly payment ⟶   ⟵ 1st month's interest

Amount that payment reduces principal = $1296.75 − $1137.50 = **$159.25**
Remaining debt at end of 1st month = **$195,000** − **$159.25** = $194,840.75

Every time a payment is made, interest is first subtracted from the payment. As a result, only a small portion of the first payment is applied to reduce the principal.

Second month:

$$\text{Interest} = PRT = \textbf{\$194,840.75} \times \textbf{.07} \times \tfrac{1}{12} = \textbf{\$1136.57}$$
Amount that payment reduces principal = $1296.75 − $1136.57 = **$160.18**
Remaining debt at end of 2nd month = $194,840.75 − **$160.18** = $194,680.57

These and other results are shown in the table. Notice that at first the amount applied to interest is large and the amount applied to reduce principal is small. But every month, the debt goes down, resulting in lower interest the following month, and more of each payment is applied to reduce the principal. It requires 262 months (nearly 22 years) to pay off half of the debt and only 98 months (just over 8 years) to pay off the other half of the loan.

Loan Repayment Schedule

Loan: $195,000; Term: 30 Years; Rate 7%; Payment $1296.75							
Payment Number	Interest Payment	Principal Payment	Remaining Balance	Payment Number	Interest Payment	Principal Payment	Remaining Balance
0	—	—	$195,000.00	258	$586.73	$710.02	$99,872.80
1	$1137.50	$159.25	$194,840.75	259	$582.59	$714.16	$99,158.64
2	$1136.57	$160.18	$194,680.57	260	$578.43	$718.32	$98,440.32
3	$1135.64	$161.11	$194,519.46	261	$574.24	$722.51	$97,717.81
4	$1134.70	$162.05	$194,357.41	262	$570.02	$726.73	$96,991.08
5	$1133.75	$163.00	$194,194.41	·	·	·	·
6	$1132.80	$163.95	$194,030.46	·	·	·	·
7	$1131.84	$164.91	$193,865.55	·	·	·	·
8	$1130.88	$165.87	$193,699.68	359	$19.14	$1277.61	$2,004.17
9	$1129.91	$166.84	$193,532.84	360	$11.69	$2004.17*	$0.00

*Due to rounding, the last payment needs to be a little larger to bring the debt to exactly $0.

QUICK CHECK 2

After a down payment, a couple finances a home with a loan of $128,600 at $4\frac{1}{2}$% for 20 years. First find the monthly payment, then prepare a loan repayment schedule for the first three months.

OBJECTIVE 3   Define escrow accounts. To prevent losses from unpaid taxes or uninsured damages, many lenders require **escrow accounts** (also called **impound accounts**) for people taking out a mortgage. With an escrow account, buyers pay $\frac{1}{12}$ of the total estimated property tax and insurance each month. The lender holds these funds until the taxes and insurance fall due and then *pays the bills for the borrower*. Many consumer groups oppose this practice, since the lender earns interest on the money while waiting for payments to come due. In fact, a few states require that interest be paid on escrow accounts on any homes located in those states.

Finding the Total Monthly Payment   **EXAMPLE 3**   The Campbell family borrowed $322,450 for 25 years at 5% to purchase a home with 5 acres for the two horses they own. Annual insurance and taxes on the property are $940 and $7382, respectively. Find the total monthly payment.

SOLUTION

Use the real estate amortization table to find a factor of $5.85. Add monthly insurance and taxes to the monthly payment to find the total payment.

$$\text{Monthly payment} = (322.45 \times \$5.85) + \left(\frac{\$940 + \$7382}{12}\right)$$

$$= \$1886.33 + \$693.50 = \$2579.83 \text{ per month}$$

QUICK CHECK 3

A 20-year mortgage is taken out with a debt of $147,000 and a rate of $6\frac{1}{2}$%. Taxes are estimated to be $2400 per year, and a homeowner's insurance policy costs $647 per year. Find the total monthly payment.

OBJECTIVE 4   Define fixed and variable rate loans. Home loans with fixed, stated interest rates are called **fixed-rate loans**. Many borrowers prefer fixed-rate loans, since they know that the principal and interest portion of their monthly payments will be fixed until they either sell the house or pay off the debt. In particular, it is good for a borrower (but bad for the lender) if he or she locks in a fixed-rate loan before interest rates go up. If interest rates fall after a person has borrowed money for a home, the person can usually refinance at a lower interest rate.

Another type of home loan called an **adjustable rate mortgage, or ARM**, has a **variable interest rate.** This means that the interest rate is periodically reset by the lender to either a higher or a lower rate. Usually, there is a maximum limit to the increase in the rate during any one reset. Nonetheless, higher interest rates mean higher monthly payments for home owners.

Since ARM home loans were often offered with a very low initial interest rate, millions of people chose to finance their homes using an ARM loan. Many believed that the value of the home would continue to increase along with their income, making it easy to refinance the ARM loan as needed. However, home prices reached a speculative peak in 2008 and then fell rapidly throughout most of the country through 2011. This left many homeowners **underwater**, meaning that the debt on their home was higher than the market price, the price at which the home would sell. Many underwater home buyers stopped making payments and moved out of their homes, causing banks to foreclose on homes. Banks then tried to resell the homes to other buyers.

The following bar chart shows the number of homes on which foreclosure papers were filed each month by a lender during the recent severe recession. Note that there were over 300,000 foreclosures per month in much of 2009 and most of 2010, but that number dropped to about 200,000 foreclosures per month in 2012. The very high rate at which people were losing their homes was considered a major problem by President Obama and his administration. At the time, the Federal Reserve worked to keep mortgage rates at record low levels to try to help stabilize the market.

Foreclosures of Homes in U.S. by Month

Source: Realty Trac

OBJECTIVE 5 Understand your credit score. Mortgage companies, banks, and other lending institutions determine your creditworthiness using a FICO® score. This **credit score** was established by **FICO** (Fair Isaac Corporation) in 1989, and it is based on numerical values ranging from 300 to 850. The higher the score, the higher the creditworthiness; the lower the score, the more difficult it is to get a loan at a low interest rate. Three national credit-reporting agencies have databases that contain financial information about you: Equifax, TransUnion, and Experian. Each calculates a FICO score for you. The three scores may differ slightly from one agency to the next, since they do not always have the same information about you. It is a good idea to contact at least one of the three credit reporting agencies annually to examine your credit history.

Here is how one large lender uses FICO scores:

FICO Score	Creditworthiness
above 730	excellent
700–729	good
670–699	increased scrutiny
585–669	high credit risk
below 585	very high credit risk

Your FICO score is based on a weighted average of the following factors:

1. payment history,
2. amount owed,
3. length of credit history,
4. new credit, and
5. types of credit in use.

> **Quick TIP**
>
> Higher FICO scores result in lower interest rates, whether on a personal property loan or on a home mortgage.

> **Quick TIP**
>
> Charging rates that depend on creditworthiness helps a lender ensure that its portfolio of loans remains profitable.

The largest weights in the FICO score are applied to the first two factors: payment history and amounts owed. You can control both of these factors, but you do not have control over the third factor (length of credit history), since that is partly based on age. New credit refers to the amount of new credit you have recently been given.

The higher your FICO score, the easier it is to obtain a loan and the lower the interest rate at which you borrow. The opposite is also true. Consider what will happen if you end up with too much debt and fail to make payments or start making late payments. Your credit score will fall and it will quickly become more difficult to borrow money. If you are still able to borrow, it is likely that the interest rate will be much higher, meaning that it will cost you more to borrow. It is important to protect your credit rating.

To raise your FICO score, first make sure the credit agencies do not have any false information on your records. They handle billions of pieces of information monthly, so it is easy for them to make mistakes. Your credit rating will be hurt by late payments, too many sources of credit, and high debt compared to your income. To raise your score,

- pay bills on time
- catch up on any back payments
- pay down the amount owed so that you are not using more than 30% of the credit limit on any account
- maintain credit cards for long periods of time and
- do not open new accounts too frequently

Do not expect an immediate improvement in your credit score. It may take months or perhaps even a few years to get a significant improvement, depending on your credit history.

▼ 12.5 Exercises   MyMathLab®

*The shaded sections below contain solutions to help you get a **QUICK START** on the various types of exercises.*

Use the real estate amortization table to find the monthly payment for the following loans. (See Example 1.)

	Amount of Loan	Interest Rate	Term of Loan	Monthly Payment
1.	$340,000	$4\frac{1}{2}\%$	15 years	$2601.00
	Payment = 340 × $7.65 = $2601			
2.	$263,100	4%	30 years	$1254.99
	Payment = 263.1 × $4.77 = $1254.99			
3.	$168,500	4%	25 years	_____
4.	$132,000	$6\frac{1}{2}\%$	25 years	_____
5.	$187,900	5%	20 years	_____
6.	$280,000	6%	15 years	_____

7. Explain how different interest rates can make a large difference in interest charges over a number of years. (See Example 1.)

8. Explain how interest can result in a total cost that is over twice the original loan amount when a home is financed over 30 years. (See Example 1.)

Find the total monthly payment, including taxes and insurance, for the following loans. Round to the nearest cent. (See Example 3.)

	Amount of Loan	Interest Rate	Term of Loan	Annual Taxes	Annual Insurance	Monthly Payment
9.	$98,000	7%	30 years	$1250	$560	$802.53
	98 × $6.65 = $651.70; $651.70 + + $\frac{\$1250 + \$560}{12}$ = $802.53					
10.	$195,000	5%	30 years	$4250	$727	$1461.90
	195 × $5.37 = $1047.15; $1047.15 + $\frac{\$4250 + \$727}{12}$ = $1461.90					
11.	$232,900	4%	15 years	$3250	$680	_____
12.	$195,000	5%	30 years	$3920	$850	_____

 indicates an exercise that is related to the Case in Point feature.

Amount of Loan	Interest Rate	Term of Loan	Annual Taxes	Annual Insurance	Monthly Payment
13. $149,400	$5\frac{1}{2}$%	20 years	$2840	$665	_____
14. $173,000	$6\frac{1}{2}$%	30 years	$2800	$920	_____

Solve the following application problems.

15. HOME PURCHASE   The Potters want to buy a small cottage costing $127,000 with annual insurance and taxes of $720 and $2300, respectively. They have saved $10,000 for a down payment, and they can get a 5%, 30-year mortgage from Citibank. They are qualified for a home loan as long as the total monthly payment does not exceed $1000. Are they qualified?

15. Yes, qualified

Loan amount = $127,000 − $10,000 = $117,000
Monthly payment = 117 × $5.37 = $628.29
Total payment = $628.29 + $\frac{\$720 + \$2300}{12}$ = $879.96; Yes, qualified

16. CONDOMINIUM PURCHASE   The Polinki family wants to buy a condominium that costs $225,000 with annual insurance and taxes of $850 and $3200, respectively. They plan to pay $20,000 down and amortize the balance at $4\frac{1}{2}$% per year for 25 years. They are qualified for a loan as long as the payments do not exceed $1350. Are they qualified for the loan?

16. _____

17. HOME LOAN   June and Bill Able borrow $122,500 on their home at $7\frac{1}{2}$% for 15 years. Prepare a repayment schedule for the first two payments. (See Example 2.)

Payment Number	Total Payment	Interest Payment	Principal Payment	Remaining Balance

18. ELDERLY HOUSING   Tom Ajax purchases a tiny home for his elderly mother. After a large down payment, he finances $88,600 at 5% for 10 years. Prepare a repayment schedule for the first two payments. (See Example 2.)

Payment Number	Total Payment	Interest Payment	Principal Payment	Remaining Balance

---

QUICK CHECK ANSWERS

1. (a) $1115.40; $401,544   **(b)** $1463; $526,680

2. Monthly payment = $814.04

Payment Number	Interest Payment	Principal Payment	Remaining Balance
0	—	—	$128,600.00
1	$482.25	$331.79	$128,268.21
2	$481.01	$333.03	$127,935.18
3	$479.76	$334.28	$127,600.90

3. $1350.54

▼ **Chapter 12** Quick Review

Chapter Terms *Review the following terms to test your understanding of the chapter. For each term you do not know, refer to the page number found next to that term.*

accelerated mortgages [p. 499]

adjustable rate mortgages (ARM) [p. 501]

amortization schedule [p. 499]

amortize [p. 475]

annual percentage rate [p. 475]

approximate annual percentage rate (APR) [p. 476]

average daily balance method [p. 467]

consolidate loans [p. 470]

credit history [p. 475]

credit limit [p. 464]

credit score [p. 503]

debit cards [p. 464]

defaulting on debt [p. 470]

escrow accounts [p. 501]

FICO [p. 503]

finance charges [p. 465]

fixed-rate loans [p. 501]

grace period [p. 465]

impound accounts [p. 501]

installment cost [p. 476]

installment loan [p. 475]

itemized billing [p. 465]

late fees [p. 465]

mortgage [p. 498]

mortgage rates [p. 498]

nominal rate [p. 475]

open-end credit [p. 464]

over-the-limit fees [p. 465]

personal property [p. 490]

real estate [p. 490]

real property [p. 490]

refinance [p. 498]

refund of unearned interest [p. 000]

repayment schedule [p. 499]

repossess [p. 490]

revolving charge account [p. 464]

Rule of 78 [p. 484]

Stafford loan [p. 476]

stated rate [p. 475]

Truth in Lending Act [p. 475]

underwater [p. 501]

unearned interest [p. 485]

United States Rule [p. 483]

unpaid balance method [p. 465]

variable interest rate loans [p. 501]

CONCEPTS

12.1 Finding the finance charge on a revolving charge account, using the unpaid balance method

Start with the unpaid balance of the previous month. Then find the finance charge on the unpaid balance. Next, add the finance charge and any purchases. Finally, subtract any payments made.

12.1 Finding the finance charge on a revolving charge account, using the average daily balance method

First find the unpaid balance on each day of the month. Then add up the daily unpaid balances.

Next divide the total of the daily unpaid balances by the number of days in the billing period.

Finally, calculate the finance charge by multiplying the average daily balance by the finance charge.

EXAMPLES

Debbie Mahoney's MasterCard account had an unpaid balance of $385.65 on March 1. During March, she made a $100 payment and charged $68.92. Find the finance charge and the unpaid balance on April 1 if the bank charges 1.25% per month on the unpaid balance.

$$\text{Finance charge} = \$385.65 \times .0125 = \$4.82$$

<table>
<tr><td>previous
balance</td><td>finance
charge</td><td>purchases</td><td>payment</td><td>new
balance</td></tr>
</table>

$$\$385.65 + \$4.82 + \$68.92 - \$100 = \$359.39$$

The following is a summary of a credit card account.

Previous balance		$115.45
November 1	Billing date	
November 15	Payment	$35.00
November 22	Charge	$45.00

Find the average daily balance and the finance charge if interest is 2% per month on the average daily balance.

Balance on Nov. 1 = $115.45

$$\text{Nov. } 1 - 15 = 14 \text{ days at } \$115.45$$
$$14 \times \$115.45 = \mathbf{\$1616.30}$$

Payment on Nov. 15 = $35.00
Balance on Nov. 15 = $115.45 − $35 = $80.45

$$\text{Nov. } 15 - \text{Nov. } 22 = 7 \text{ days at } \$80.45$$
$$7 \times \$80.45 = \mathbf{\$563.15}$$

Charge on Nov. 22 of $45.00
Balance on Nov. 22 = $80.45 + $45 = $125.45

$$\text{Nov. } 22 - \text{Dec. } 1 = 9 \text{ days at } \$125.45$$
$$9 \times \$125.45 = \mathbf{\$1129.05}$$

Daily balances
$$\mathbf{\$1616.30} + \mathbf{\$563.15} + \mathbf{\$1129.05} = \mathbf{\$3308.50}$$

$$\textbf{Average daily balance} = \frac{\mathbf{\$3308.50}}{30} = \$110.28$$

$$\textbf{Finance charges} = \$110.28 \times .02 = \$2.21$$

CONCEPTS	EXAMPLES
12.2 Finding the total installment cost, finance charge, and amount financed **Total installment cost** = Down payment + (Amount of each payment × Number of payments) **Finance charge (interest)** = Total installment cost − Cash price **Amount financed (principal of loan)** = Cash price − Down payment	Joan Taylor bought a leather coat for $1580. She put $350 down and then made 12 payments of $115 each. Find the total installment cost, the finance charge, and the amount financed. **Total installment cost** = $350 + (12 × $115) = $1730 **Finance charge** = $1730 − $1580 = $150 **Amount financed** = $1580 − $350 = $1230
12.2 Determining the approximate APR using a formula First determine the finance charge. Then find the amount financed. Next calculate approximate APR using the formula. **Approximate APR** $$= \frac{24 \times \text{Finance charge}}{\text{Amt. fin.} \times (1 + \text{Total number of payments})}$$	Tom Jones buys a motorcycle for $8990. He makes a down payment of $1800 and then makes monthly payments of $230 for 36 months. Find the approximate APR. **Total installment cost** = $1800 + ($230 × 36) = $10,080 **Finance charge** = $10,080 − $8990 = **$1090** **Amount financed** = $8990 − $1800 = $7190 **Approximate APR** $= \dfrac{24 \times \$1090}{\$7190 \times (1 + 36)} = 9.8\%$ (rounded)
12.2 Finding the APR using a table First determine the finance charge per $100 of amount financed, using the formula $$\frac{\text{Finance charge} \times \$100}{\text{Amount financed}}$$ Then read down the left column of the annual percentage rate table to the proper number of payments. Go across to the number closest to the number found above. Look to the top of the column to find the annual percentage rate.	Lupe Torres buys a used car for $6500. She makes a down payment of $1000 and agrees to make 24 monthly payments of $260.83. Use the table to find the APR. Finance charge = $1000 + ($260.83 × 24) − $6500 = $759.92 Amount financed = $5500 Finance charge per $100 $$\frac{\$759.92 \times \$100}{\$5500} = \textbf{13.82 (rounded)}$$ Use the 24-payment row in the table to find APR = 12.75%
12.3 Finding the amount due on the maturity date using the United States Rule First determine the simple interest due from the date the loan was made until the date of the partial payment. Then subtract this interest from the amount of the payment and reduce the principal by the difference. Next find the interest from the date of partial payment to the due date of the note, and add the unpaid balance and interest to find the amount due.	Sam Wiley signs a 90-day note on August 1 for $5000 at an interest rate of 12%. On September 15, he makes a payment of $1800. Find the balance owed on the principal. If no additional payments are made, find the amount due on the maturity date of the loan. From August 1 to September 15, there are 30 + 15 = 45 days. $$I = \$5000 \times .12 \times \frac{45}{360} = \textbf{\$75} \text{ interest due}$$ $1800 payment − 75 interest due $1725 applied to principal reduction $5000 amount owed − 1725 principal reduction **$3275 balance owed** Note is for 90 days; a partial payment was made after 45 days. Interest on $3275 will be charged for 90 − 45 = 45 days. $$I = \$3275 \times .12 \times \frac{45}{360} = \textbf{\$49.13}$$ $3275.00 principal owed + 49.13 interest **$3324.13 amount due**

CONCEPTS	EXAMPLES

12.3 Finding the unearned interest using the Rule of 78

First calculate the finance charge. Then find the unearned interest using the formula

$$U = F\left(\frac{N}{P}\right)\left(\frac{1+N}{1+P}\right)$$

where U = unearned interest
   F = finance charge
   N = number of payments remaining
   P = total number of payments

Next find the total of the remaining payments. Finally, subtract the unearned interest to find the balance remaining.

Tom Fish borrows $1500, which he is paying back in 36 monthly installments of $52.75 each. With 10 payments remaining, he decides to pay the loan in full. Find **(a)** the amount of unearned interest and **(b)** the amount necessary to pay the loan in full.

36 payments of $52.75 each for a total repayment of $36 \times \$52.75 = \$1899$.

Finance charge = $1899 − $1500 = **$399**

Unearned interest = **$399** $\times \dfrac{10}{36} \times \dfrac{(1+10)}{(1+36)} =$ **$32.95**

10 payments of $52.75 are left. These payments total

$$\$52.75 \times 10 = \$527.50$$
$$\$527.50 - \mathbf{\$32.95} = \$494.55$$

This is the amount needed to pay the loan in full.

12.4 Finding the periodic payment for amortizing a loan

First determine the number of periods for the loan and the interest rate per period.

The payment is found by multiplying the loan amount by the number from the amortization table.

Bob Smith agrees to pay $12,000 for a used car. The amount will be repaid in monthly payments over 3 years at an interest rate of 12%. Find the amount of each payment.

$$3 \times 12 = \textbf{36 periods (payments)}$$
$$\frac{12\%}{12} = \textbf{1\% per period}$$

Number from table is **.03321**.

Payment = $12,000 × **.03321** = $398.52

12.4 Setting up an amortization schedule

First find the periodic payment. Then calculate the interest owed in the first period using the formula $I = PRT$. Next subtract the value of I from the periodic payment.

This is the amount applied to the reduction of the principal. Then find the balance after the first periodic payment by subtracting the value of the debt reduction from the original amount. Now repeat the above steps until the original loan is amortized (paid off).

Terri Meyer borrows $1800. She will repay this amount in 2 years with semiannual payments at an interest rate of 8%. Set up an amortization schedule.

$$2 \times 2 = \textbf{4 periods (payments); 4\% per period}$$
$$\frac{8\%}{2} = \textbf{4\% per year}$$

Number from table is **.27549**

Payment = $1800 × **.27549** = $495.88

$$I = PRT$$

Interest owed = $1800 $\times$ .08 $\times \dfrac{1}{2} =$ $72

Debt reduction = $495.88 − $72 = $423.88

Balance of loan = $1800 − $423.88 = $1376.12

Payment Number	Amount of Payment	Interest for Period	Portion to Principal	Principal at End of Period
0	—	—	—	$1800.00
1	$495.88	$72.00	$423.88	$1376.12
2	$495.88	$55.04	$440.84	$ 935.28
3	$495.88	$37.41	$458.47	$ 476.81
4	$495.88	$19.07	$476.81	$ 0.00

CONCEPTS

EXAMPLES

12.4 Finding monthly payments, total amount paid, and finance charge

First multiply the amount to be financed by the number from the amortization table or the loan payoff table to find the periodic payment. Then find the total amount repaid by multiplying the periodic payment by the number of payments. Finally, subtract the amount financed from the total amount repaid to obtain the finance charge.

Ben Apostolides purchased a new Toyota Camry and owes $16,400 after the trade-in. He decides on a term with 50 monthly payments. Assume an interest rate of 12% compounded monthly and find the amount of each payment, total amount paid, and the finance charge.

$$\text{Monthly payment} = \$16,400 \times \mathbf{.02551} = \mathbf{\$418.36}$$

$$\text{Total amount paid} = 50 \times \$418.36 = \$20,918$$

$$\text{Finance charge} = 50 \times \mathbf{\$418.36} - \$16,400 = \$4518$$

12.5 Finding the amount of monthly home loan payments and total interest charges over the life of a home loan

Using the number of years and the interest rate, find the amortization value per thousand dollars from the real estate amortization table.

Next multiply the table value by the number of thousands in the principal to obtain the monthly payment.

Then find the total amount of the payments and subtract the original amount owed from the total payments to obtain interest paid.

Tom Begay borrowed $195,850 to buy a house. It is a 15 year loan at an interest rate of $4\frac{1}{2}\%$ and taxes and insurance will be $3800 and $750 respectively. Find the total monthly payment and the interest charges over the life of the loan.

$$\text{Payment} = \text{loan payment} + \text{payment into escrow for taxes and insurance}$$

$$\text{Payment} = 195.85 \times \$7.65 + \frac{\$3800 + \$750}{12}$$

$$= \mathbf{\$1498.25} + \$379.17$$

$$= \$1877.42$$

$$\text{Total payments} = \text{monthly loan payment} \times \text{number of years} \times \text{12 months/year}$$

$$= \$1498.25 \times 15 \text{ years} \times 12 \text{ months/year}$$

$$= \$269,685$$

$$\text{Total interest} = \text{total payments} - \text{original loan amount}$$

$$= \$269,685 - \$195,850$$

$$= \$73,835$$

Case Study

CONSOLIDATING LOANS

Roberto and Julie Hernandez are struggling to make their monthly payments. They accumulated too much debt, which was easy to do with two young kids at home. Julie works 30 hours a week and takes care of the two kids. Their credit history had been poor, but Roberto took on a second job during the evenings and they have been making payments regularly for 8 months.

1. Find the monthly payments on each of the following purchases and the total monthly payment.

Purchase	Original Loan Amount	Interest Rate	Term of Loan	Monthly Payment
Honda Accord	$18,800	12%	4 years	_____
Ford truck	$14,300	18%	4 years	_____
Home	$126,800	$6\frac{1}{2}$%	15 years	_____
2nd mortgage on home	$4,500	12%	3 years	_____
			Total	_____

2. These monthly expenses do not include car insurance ($215 per month), health insurance ($290 per month), or real estate taxes and insurance on their home ($3350 per year), among other expenses. Find their total monthly outlay for all of these expenses.

Expense	Monthly Outlay
Payments on debt from (a)	_____
Car insurance	_____
Health insurance	_____
Real estate taxes and insurance on home	_____
Total	_____

3. After discussing things with Jackie Waterton at Citibank, the Hernandez's have learned that they can (1) refinance the remaining $14,900 amount on the Honda Accord at 12% over 4 years, (2) refinance the remaining $8600 loan amount on the Ford truck at 12% over 3 years, (3) refinance the remaining $121,850 loan amount on their home at 5% over 30 years, and (4) reduce their car insurance payments by $28 per month. Complete the following table.

Item	Current Loan Amount	New Interest Rate	New Term of Loan	New Monthly Payment
Honda Accord				_____
Ford truck				_____
Home				_____
2nd mortgage on home				_____
Car insurance				_____
Health insurance				_____
Real estate taxes and insurance on home				_____
				_____

4. Find the reduction in their monthly payments.

4. _____

Part of the savings in the monthly payment came from reducing the interest rates. The remainder of the savings came from extending the loans further into the future, meaning that the Hernandez Family will, in the long run, pay more interest. But at least their current bills are reduced by $715.11 per month.

INVESTIGATE

The interest rate that you are charged for borrowing money differs depending on the bank you go to for a loan. Find current interest rates for financing a 2-year-old Toyota Camry from at least two banks in the area in which you live. Then go onto the World Wide Web and look for a lower interest rate.

▼ Case in Point Summary Exercise

UNDERWATER ON A HOME

www.citigroup.com

Facts:

- 1812: Founded in New York City
- 1914: Opened first international branch, in Argentina
- 2008: Lost $27.7 billion; Took funds from government during financial crisis
- 2010: First annual profit since 2007

Citigroup Inc. (Citi) provides various banking, lending, insurance, and investment services to individual and corporate customers worldwide. It operates more than 7200 branches and 7000 ATMs. Citi had more than $150 billion in credit-card loans outstanding in 2010 in addition to huge volumes of home loans and business loans.

The financial crisis of 2008–10 created very serious problems for Citigroup. To illustrate the nature of some of the problems, we use the example of one family: Tom and Marie Duston purchased their first home in 2008 when home loans were still very easy to get. They bought a beautiful new 4-bedroom, $2\frac{1}{2}$-bath home with a down payment of only $8500.

1. They financed the loan balance of $306,500 using an adjustable rate mortgage (ARM). The monthly payment of $1100 did not include taxes and insurance. In fact, the monthly payment was all interest, meaning that nothing was applied against the debt each month. Find the monthly payment given taxes of $6400 per year and insurance of $980 per year.

   1. _____

2. At the time of the purchase in 2008, the Dustons were told that the interest rate on their ARM loan would reset in 2011, so they knew the payments might increase. However, they were not worried since they assumed that their incomes and also the value of the house would be higher by then. But home prices fell across much of the country as did the value of their home. By 2011, an appraiser estimated that it was worth only 75% of the original loan balance of $306,500, which they still owed. They were underwater on their home! Find out what the house was worth in 2011 and the amount by which they were underwater.

   2. _____

3. The Dustons were shocked to find out that they would have to come up with $76,625 to pay off the bank loan to sell their home. They were further shocked to find out they would also need to come up with an additional $23,000 to pay various expenses, such as the real estate commission related to the sale of their home. Estimate the total amount they would have to pay to sell their home, rounded to the nearest thousand.

   3. _____

4. The Dustons did not have the funds needed, so they asked about refinancing the loan balance of $306,500. At first, the bank wanted them to pay off the loan, but it finally agreed to try to work to refinance it. The Dustons felt trapped! It was difficult to understand that they were underwater by so much given that they had made every payment on time for 3 years. With the help of a government program designed to help underwater homeowners current on their mortgage payments, the bank agreed to refinance $285,000 on the home on a 30-year fixed mortgage at 5%. The difference between the debt of $306,500 and $285,000 was essentially forgiven due to the government program. Find the new home payment not including taxes and insurance.

   4. _____

5. So the Dustons' monthly payment, not including taxes and insurance, increased from $1100 per month up to the figure found for #4 above. Find the increase in the monthly payment.

5. _____

From the Dustons' perspective: The Dustons were shocked about what had happened. They had financed their home using an ARM loan and made every payment on time for 3 years. However, the value of their home fell by 25% and they had to refinance their home in 2011 due to the nature of the ARM loan. They did not have the money needed to sell the house and pay off the debt. After a stressful period for the family, the bank finally agreed to help by refinancing $285,000 on their home. The monthly payment increased significantly. But, importantly, the home was still worth quite a bit less than they owed on it! They were still underwater and might lose more on the house later. The good news is that they were able to stay in the house.

From the bank's perspective: In 2008, the bank lent the Dustons $306,500 on an ultra-low interest ARM loan and received payments for 3 years. It was not the bank's fault that the value of the home fell by 25%. Managers essentially believed that the loss was the homeowner's responsibility. However, they found a government program that would allow the bank to forgive part of the Dustons' debt and refinance the remaining $285,000. This was still more than the house was worth. The managers were worried that the Dustons might still abandon the house. In that event, the bank would be forced to go through the lengthy and costly foreclosure process, which would probably result in further losses for the bank.

Discussion Question: *Are the Dustons right? Is the bank right? Make an argument for each side.*

▼ Chapter 12 Test

To help you review, the numbers in brackets show the section in which the topic was discussed.

Solve for following problems.

1. A cruise line needs to update some sonar equipment on one of its luxury ships that sails the Caribbean. The cost of the equipment is $214,500. The company makes a down payment of $20,000 and agrees to 24 monthly payments of $8975 per month. Find the total finance charge. **[12.1]**

1. _____

2. The balance on John Baker's MasterCard on November 1 is $680.45. In November, he charges an additional $337.32, has returns of $45.42, and makes a payment of $50. If the finance charges are calculated at 1.5% per month on the unpaid balance, find his balance on December 1. **[12.1]**

2. _____

Find the annual percentage rate, using the annual percentage rate table. **[12.2]**

Amount Financed	Finance Charge	Number of Payments	APR
3. $5280	$1010.59	36	_____
4. $1130	$149.84	24	_____

Solve the following application problems.

5. Barton Springs Landscaping buys a used truck for $18,700 and agrees to make 36 payments of $612.25 each. Find the annual percentage rate on the loan. **[12.2]**

5. _____

6. A note with a face value of $7000 is made on June 21. The note is for 90 days and carries interest of 13%. A partial payment of $2800 is made on July 17. Find the amount due on the maturity date of the note. **[12.3]**

6. _____

7. Mock Construction bought a truck and financed $7400 with 48 monthly payments of $228.14 each. Suppose the firm pays the loan off with 12 payments left. Use the Rule of 78 to find **(a)** the amount of unearned interest and **(b)** the amount necessary to pay off the loan. **[12.3]**

(a) _____

(b) _____

Find the amount of each payment necessary to amortize the following loans. **[12.4]**

8. Jenson SawLogs borrows $34,500 to buy a new electric generator. The company agrees to make quarterly payments for 2 years at 10% per year. Find the amount of the quarterly payment.

8. _____

9. Scented Candles remodeled its lobby at a cost of $36,000. It pays $6000 down and pays off the balance in payments made at the end of each quarter for 5 years. Interest is 10% compounded quarterly. Find the amount of each payment so that the loan is fully amortized.

9. _____

Find the monthly payment necessary to amortize the following home mortgages. **[12.5]**

10. $236,000, $4\frac{1}{2}$%, 15 years

10. _____

11. $134,560, 7%, 15 years

11. _____

Work the following application problems. **[12.5]**

12. Mr. and Mrs. Zagorin plan to buy a one-room cabin for $90,000, paying 20% down and financing the balance at $5\frac{1}{2}$%, for 30 years. The taxes are $960 per year, with fire insurance costing $352 per year. Find the monthly payment (including taxes and insurance).

12. _____

13. Billiards Galore purchases a commercial building for $680,000, pays 20% down, and finances the balance at 7% for 15 years. Taxes and insurance are $14,500 and $3200 per year, respectively. **(a)** Find the monthly payment. **(b)** Assume that insurance and taxes do not increase, and find the total cost of owning the building for 15 years, including the down payment.

(a) _____

(b) _____

14. Jerome Watson, owner of Watson Welding, purchases a storage building for his business and makes a $25,000 down payment. He finances the balance of $122,500 for 20 years at 8%. **(a)** Find the total monthly payment given taxes of $3200 per year and insurance of $1275 per year. **(b)** Assume that insurance and taxes do not increase, and find the total cost owning the building for 20 years (including the down payment).

(a) _____

(b) _____

Chapters 11–12 Cumulative Review

CHAPTERS 11 AND 12

Round money amounts to the nearest cent and rates to the nearest tenth of a percent.

Find the amount and interest earned of each of the following ordinary annuities. **[11.1]**

	Amount of Each Deposit	Deposited	Rate	Time (Years)	Amount of Annuity	Interest Earned
1.	$1000	annually	4%	8	_____	_____
2.	$2000	quarterly	6%	5	_____	_____

Find the amount of each annuity due and the interest earned. **[11.1]**

	Amount of Each Deposit	Deposited	Rate	Time (Years)	Amount of Annuity	Interest Earned
3.	$2500	annually	5%	6	_____	_____
4.	$1800	semiannually	8%	5	_____	_____

Find the present value of the following annuities. **[11.2]**

	Amount per Payment	Payment at End of Each	Time (Years)	Rate of Investment	Compounded	Present Value
5.	$925	6 months	11	8%	semiannually	_____
6.	$27,235	quarter	8	8%	quarterly	_____

Find the required payment into a sinking fund. **[11.3]**

	Future Value	Interest Rate	Compounded	Time (Years)	Payment
7.	$3600	8%	annually	7	_____
8.	$4500	10%	quarterly	7	_____

Solve the following application problems using 360-day years where applicable.

9. At 58, Thomas Jones knows that he needs to save more. He decides to invest $300 per quarter in a mutual fund he hopes will earn 10% compounded quarterly. Find the accumulated amount at age 65. **[11.1]**

9. _____

10. A public utility needs $60 million in 5 years for a major capital expansion. What annual payment must the firm place into a sinking fund earning 5% per year in order to accumulate the required funds? **[11.3]**

10. _____

11. Jerry Walker purchased 100 shares of stock at $23.45 per share. The company had earnings of $1.56 and a yearly dividend of $.35. Find **(a)** the cost of the purchase ignoring commissions, **(b)** the price–earnings ratio to the nearest whole number, and **(c)** the dividend yield. **[11.4]**

(a) _____

(b) _____

(c) _____

12. Martin Wicker buys 9000 GM bonds due in 2020 at 104.38 for the pension fund he manages. The coupon rate is 6.4%. Find **(a)** the cost to purchase the bonds if the commission is $1 per bond, **(b)** the annual interest from all of the bonds, and **(c)** the effective interest rate. **[11.5]**

(a) _____

(b) _____

(c) _____

13. James Thompson purchased a large riding lawnmower costing $2800 with $500 down and payments of $108.27 per month for 24 months. Find **(a)** the total installment cost, **(b)** the finance charge, and **(c)** the amount financed. **(d)** Then use the table to find the annual percentage rate to the nearest quarter of a percent. **[12.2]**

(a) _____

(b) _____

(c) _____

(d) _____

14. Abbie Spring's unpaid balance on her Visa card on July 8 was $204.37. She made a payment of $100 on July 14 and had charges of $34.95 on July 16 and $95.12 on July 30. Assume an interest rate of 1.6% per month and find the balance on August 8 using **(a)** the unpaid balance method and **(b)** the average daily balance method. **[12.1]**

(a) _____

(b) _____

15. Mayberry Pets borrows to purchase a van to transport animals and supplies. They agree to make quarterly payments on the $22,400 debt for 3 years at a rate of 8% compounded quarterly. Find **(a)** the quarterly payment and **(b)** the total amount of interest paid. **[12.4]**

(a) _____

(b) _____

16. The Hodges purchase an older 4-bedroom home for $195,000 with 5% down. They finance the balance at 5% per year for 30 years. If insurance is $720 per year and taxes are $4140 per year, find the monthly payment. **[12.5]**

16. _____

17. On January 10, Bob Jones signed a 200-day note for $24,000 to finance some work on a roof. The note was at 9% per year simple interest. Due to an unexpected income tax refund, he was able to repay $10,000 on April 15. Use the United States Rule and **(a)** find the balance owed on the principal after the partial payment. **(b)** Then find the amount due at maturity of the loan. **[12.3]**

(a) _____

(b) _____

18. Karoline Jacobs borrowed $2200 for new kitchen appliances. She agreed to pay the loan back with 8 payments of $290.69 each. After 3 payments, she decides to go ahead and pay off the loan in full. Use the Rule of 78 to find **(a)** the amount of unearned interest and **(b)** the amount needed to repay the loan in full.   **[12.3]**

(a) _____

(b) _____

19. County Squire Electrical lost a lawsuit and must pay the injured party $35,000 at the end of each semiannual period for 2 years. If the funds earn 4% per year compounded semiannually, find the amount that needs to be set aside today to fulfill this obligation.   **[11.2]**

19. _____

20. James Booker signs an employment contract that guarantees him $35,000 at the end of each year for 3 years when he retires in 4 years. If funds earn 8% per year, find the present value needed today to meet the eventual payment stream.   **[10.3 and 11.2]**

20. _____

21. Explain the terms *present value, future value*, and *annuity*.

22. Describe stocks and bonds, explaining similarities and differences.

13 Taxes and Insurance

CHAPTER CONTENTS

13.1 Property Tax

13.2 Personal Income Tax

13.3 Fire Insurance

13.4 Motor-Vehicle Insurance

13.5 Life Insurance

▼ CASE IN POINT

MARTHA SPENCER OWNS The Doll House. She specializes in antique dolls from around the world and sells a lot of antique Barbie dolls. Her business was struggling to survive in 2002 when she decided to set up a website to try to grow her business. Not only have sales increased markedly since then, but international sales have really taken off, as shown in the following bar graph. Spencer estimates that one-third of total sales in 2014 will be to overseas clients.

Spencer owns the building in which her business is located, and she has several employees. As a result, she must keep up with all the laws related to taxes and insurance. It is not fun to work through tax and insurance issues, but Spencer knows it must be done—and done well—in order for her small business to prosper.

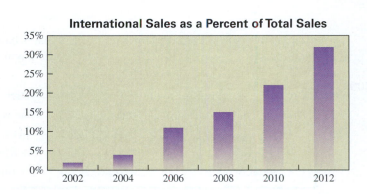

International Sales as a Percent of Total Sales

Both **taxes** and **insurance** are facts of life. In one form or another, we pay taxes to many different entities, including the federal government, states, counties, school districts, and cities. Supreme Court Justice Oliver Wendell Holmes, Jr., said, "Taxes are the price we pay to live in a civilized society." The pie chart shows the number of days per year the "average worker" works to pay various taxes. Property taxes and federal income taxes are discussed in this chapter.

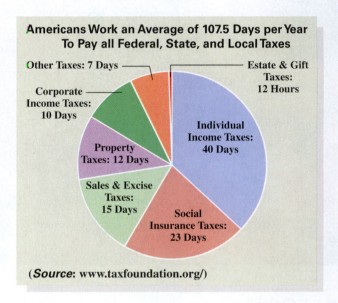

Americans Work an Average of 107.5 Days per Year To Pay all Federal, State, and Local Taxes

Other Taxes: 7 Days
Corporate Income Taxes: 10 Days
Property Taxes: 12 Days
Sales & Excise Taxes: 15 Days
Social Insurance Taxes: 23 Days
Individual Income Taxes: 40 Days
Estate & Gift Taxes: 12 Hours

(*Source*: www.taxfoundation.org/)

Individuals buy insurance to protect from catastrophic losses to their homes and automobiles and also to pay medical expenses or to pay expenses at the time of death of a family member. Companies buy insurance to protect from potential losses to buildings and property, losses due to workers injured on the job, or even lawsuits from customers. Three common types of insurance are discussed in this chapter.

▼13.1 Property Tax

OBJECTIVES

1 Define *fair market value* and *assessed value*.
2 Find the tax rate.
3 Find the property tax.
4 Express tax rate in percent, in dollars per $100, in dollars per $1000, and in mills.
5 Find taxes given the assessed value and the tax rate.

▼ CASE IN POINT   Martha Spencer was surprised by the amount of the property tax on her commercial building this year. Her taxes went up significantly and she was determined to find out why. She also wanted to know where the money was going.

Property owners must usually pay a property tax that is based on the value of their real estate. The money received from property taxes are used to pay for all of the following:

Taxes Pay for the Following:

- police protection and emergency response
- fire protection and emergency response
- 911 emergency service
- public schools
- street and sidewalk maintenance
- snow removal
- parks and recreational facilities
- activity programs for senior citizens
- libraries

Additionally, property taxes are often used to pay part of the expenses of community colleges. Without property taxes, the tuition at community colleges would be higher.

The following newspaper clipping shows the financial pressures some school districts faced during the recent financial crisis.

School District Battles Financial Problems

A local school district is struggling. The mission of the district is founded on a quality education for all, but the current financial picture is grim. Income from the state has gone down at the same time that enrollment is up slightly. The school board is asking for a small increase in the property tax rate, but board members are afraid they will not get it. Without an increase in funding, the district may have to close two schools and lay off some teachers and administrators.

OBJECTIVE 1 Define *fair market value* and *assessed value*. A local tax assessor estimates the market value of all the land and buildings in an area. The **fair market value** is the price at which a property can reasonably be expected to be sold. The fair market value could be used to find the amount of the property tax. However, many tax authorities first find what is called the **assessed value,** by multiplying the fair market value by a percent called the **assessment rate**. The assessed value is then used to calculate the property tax. In fact, the only purpose of the assessed value is for use in finding the property tax. The assessment rate varies widely from 25% in some states to 100% in others.

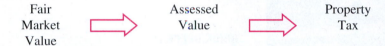

Fair Market Value → Assessed Value → Property Tax

Finding the Assessed Valuation of Property

 EXAMPLE 1

Find the assessed value for the following pieces of property owned by Martha Spencer.

(a) Home: fair market value $185,300; assessment rate 35%

(b) Business property: fair market value $328,500; assessment rate 35%

(c) Commercial lot located in a different state: fair market value $123,800; assessment rate 60%

SOLUTION

Multiply the fair market value by the assessment rate.

(a) $185,300 \times .35 = \$64,855$

(b) $328,500 \times .35 = \$114,975$

(c) $123,800 \times .60 = \$74,280$

QUICK CHECK 1

A commercial building has a fair market value of $1,480,000. If the assessment rate is 70%, find the assessed value.

Just because the assessment rate is higher in one area than another does not necessarily mean that the taxes are higher. The assessed value of the property must be multiplied by the tax rate to find the tax. (See Objective 3.)

OBJECTIVE 2 Find the tax rate. A taxing authority such as a city or community college district first estimates the revenue needed and then finds the **property-tax rate** needed to generate that amount of tax as follows.

> **Finding the Property-Tax Rate**
>
> Step 1   Identify the amount of money needed.
>
> Step 2   Find the total fair market value of all real properties in the tax district.
>
> Step 3   Find the total assessed value of all real properties in the tax district.
>
> Step 4   Property tax rate $= \dfrac{\text{Total tax amount needed}}{\text{Total assessed value}}$

Finding the Tax Rate

 EXAMPLE 2   Find the tax rate for the following school districts, rounded to the nearest hundredth of a percent.

(a) Amount needed $=$ \$14,253,000; total assessed value $=$ \$1,575,890,000

(b) Amount needed $=$ \$8,490,000; total assessed value $=$ \$983,270,000

SOLUTION

(a) Tax rate $= \dfrac{\$14,253,000}{\$1,575,890,000} = .90\%$ (rounded)

(b) Tax rate $= \dfrac{\$8,490,000}{\$983,270,000} = .86\%$ (rounded)

> **QUICK CHECK 2**
>
> A large community college district needs \$22,350,000 this year. The taxing authority has determined that the total assessed value of all the real estate in the district is \$3.48 billion. Find the property tax rate to the nearest hundredth of a percent.

OBJECTIVE 3 Find the property tax. The tax rate is applied to the assessed value to find the property tax due as follows.

> **Finding the Property Tax**
>
> $$\text{Tax} = \text{Tax rate} \times \text{Assessed value}$$

OBJECTIVE 4 Express tax rate in percent, in dollars per \$100, in dollars per \$1000, and in mills. Tax rates are stated differently by different taxing entities. However, just because they are stated differently does not mean that the tax is either higher or lower in one area than in another. Here are methods that are in common use.

Percent. Some areas express tax rates as a percent of assessed value. The yearly tax on a piece of property with an assessed value of \$174,000 at a tax rate of 2.17% follows.

$$\text{Tax} = .0217 \times \mathbf{\$174{,}000} = \$3775.80$$

Quick TIP

Remember, the assessed value is usually only a fraction of the fair market value.

Dollars per \$100.   In some areas, the tax rate is expressed as a number of dollars per \$100 of assessed value. In this event, find the tax on a piece of land by first finding the number of hundreds in the assessed value and then multiplying the number of hundreds by the tax rate. For example, assume an assessed value of \$56,300 and a tax rate of \$11.42 per \$100 of assessed value and find taxes for the year as follows.

$$\$56{,}300 \div 100 = \mathbf{563\ hundreds} \qquad \text{Divide by 100 by moving the decimal point 2 places to the left.}$$

$$\text{Tax} = \$11.42 \times 563 = \mathbf{\$6429.46} \qquad \text{Multiply by the tax rate to find tax.}$$

Dollars per $1000. In other areas, the tax rate is expressed as a number of dollars per $1000 of assessed value. If the tax rate is $98.12 per $1000, a piece of property having an assessed value of $197,000 would be taxed as follows.

$$\$197,000 = \textbf{197 thousands}$$ Move the decimal point 3 places to the left to divide by 1000.

$$\text{Tax} = \$98.12 \times \textbf{197} = \textbf{\$19,329.64}$$

Mills. Other taxing authorities express tax rates in mills or one-thousandths of a dollar. For example, a tax rate might be expressed as 46 mills. Divide the 46 mills by 1000 to find .046 per dollar of assessed value. Assuming a tax rate of 46 mills, the tax on a house assessed at $81,000 is found as follows.

46 mills = .046

$$\text{Tax} = \textbf{.046} \times \$81,000 = \textbf{\$3726}$$

The following chart shows the same tax rates written in the four different systems. Although expressed differently, the rates in each row of this chart are equivalent tax rates.

Percent	Per $100	Per $1000	In Mills
1.25%	$1.25	$12.50	12.5
3.2%	$3.20	$32	32
9.87%	$9.87	$98.70	98.7

OBJECTIVE 5 Find taxes given the assessed value and the tax rate. Property taxes are found by multiplying the tax rate by the assessed value, as shown in the following example.

Finding the Property Tax

EXAMPLE 3 Find the taxes on each of the following pieces of property. Assessed values and tax rates are given.

(a) $58,975; 8.4%   (b) $875,400; $7.82 per $100
(c) $129,600; $64.21 per $1000   (d) $221,750; 94 mills

SOLUTION
Multiply the tax rate by the assessed value.
(a) 8.4% = **.084**

$$\text{Tax} = \text{Tax rate} \times \text{Assessed value}$$
$$\text{Tax} = \textbf{.084} \times \$58,975 = \$4953.90$$

(b) $875,400 = **8754 hundreds**

$$\text{Tax} = \$7.82 \times \textbf{8754} = \$68,456.28$$

(c) $129,600 = **129.6 thousands**

$$\text{Tax} = \$64.21 \times \textbf{129.6} = \$8321.62$$

(d) 94 mills = **.094**

$$\text{Tax} = \textbf{.094} \times \$221,750 = \$20,844.50$$

QUICK CHECK 3

A home is assessed at $65,000. Find the property tax if the tax rate is (a) 3.4%, (b) $4.50 per $100, (c) $38.40 per $1000, and (d) 48.2 mills.

Not everyone pays at the same property-tax rates. For example, churches are usually exempt from property taxes. Many states give homeowners an exemption that reduces the property tax on their home. Still other states give property-tax exemptions to the elderly.

Comparing Tax Rates

EXAMPLE 4

As Ben Waller decides where to build a 60-unit apartment complex that he estimates will have a market value of $2,800,000, he considers property tax. In one county, property is assessed at 50% of market value with a tax rate of 3.2%. In a second county, property is assessed at 80% with a tax rate of 35 mills. **(a)** Find the county with the lower tax. **(b)** Find the amount saved by building in the county with the lower tax.

SOLUTION

(a) Property tax 1st county = $2,800,000 × .5 × .032 = **$44,800**
Property tax 2nd county = $2,800,000 × .8 × .035 = **$78,400**
The first county has the lower tax.

(b) Amount saved = **$78,400** − **$44,800** = $33,600 per year

---

QUICK CHECK 4

One county has a tax rate of $2.40 per $100, and a second county has a tax rate of $26.60 per $1000. Once built, a home will have an assessed value of $290,000. **(a)** Find the county with the lower tax. **(b)** Find the amount saved by building in the county with the lower tax.

▼13.1 Exercises

MyMathLab®

*The shaded sections below contain solutions to help you get a **QUICK START** on the various types of exercises.*

Find the assessed value for each of the following pieces of property. (See Example 1.)

	Fair Market Value	Rate of Assessment	Assessed Value		Fair Market Value	Rate of Assessment	Assessed Value
1.	$85,000	40%	$34,000	**2.**	$68,000	60%	$40,800
	$85,000 × .4 = $34,000				$68,000 × .6 = $40,800		
3.	$142,300	50%	_____	**4.**	$98,200	42%	_____
5.	$1,300,500	25%	_____	**6.**	$2,450,000	80%	_____

Find the tax rate for the following. Write the tax rate as a percent, rounded to the nearest tenth of a percent. (See Example 2.)

	Total Tax Amount Needed	Total Assessed Value	Tax Rate		Total Tax Amount Needed	Total Assessed Value	Tax Rate
7.	$18,300,000	$6,850,000,000	.3%	**8.**	$7,600,000	$1,752,500,000	.4%
	$18,300,000 ÷ $6,850,000,000 = .0027 = .3% (rounded)				$7,600,000 ÷ $1,752,500,000 = .0043 = .4% (rounded)		
9.	$1,580,000	$197,500,000	_____	**10.**	$2,175,000	$480,300,000	_____
11.	$1,224,000	$816,000,000	_____	**12.**	$28,630,000	$12,350,000,000	_____

Write the given tax rate using the other three methods. (See Example 3.)

	Percent	Per $100	Per $1000	In Mills
13.	4.84%	(a) $4.84	(b) $48.40	(c) 48.4
14.	(a) _____	$6.75	(b) _____	(c) _____
15.	(a) _____	(b) _____	$70.80	(c) _____
16.	(a) _____	(b) _____	(c) _____	28

---

17. What is the difference between fair market value and assessed value? How is the assessment rate used when finding the assessed value? (See Objective 1.)

18. Explain the difference between fair market value, assessed value, and property tax. (See Objectives 1, 2, and 3.)

Find the property tax for the following. (See Example 3.)

Assessed Value	Tax Rate	Tax		Assessed Value	Tax Rate	Tax
19. $86,200	$6.80 per $100	**$5861.60**		**20.** $41,300	$46.40 per $1000	_____
862 × $6.80 = $5861.60						
21. $128,200	42 mills	_____		**22.** $37,250	3.4%	_____

Solve the following application problems.

23. **REAL ESTATE TAXES**   Martha Spencer owns the real estate used by The Doll House. The property has a fair market value of $328,500, the assessment rate is 35%, and the local tax rate is 5.2%. Find the tax.

   $328,500 × .35 = $114,975; $114,975 × .052 = $5978.70

   23. $5978.70

24. **APARTMENT OWNER**   Chad LeCompte owns a four-unit apartment building with a fair market value of $248,000. Property in the area is assessed at 40% of market value, and the tax rate is 5.5%. Find the amount of the property tax.

   24. _____

25. **COMMERCIAL PROPERTY TAX**   A new FM radio station broadcasts from a building having a fair market value of $334,400. The building is in an area where property is assessed at 25% of market value, and the tax rate is $75.30 per $1000 of assessed value. Find the property tax.

   25. _____

26. **OFFICE COMPLEX**   Huron Development just purchased a modern office complex for $12,380,000. The county assesses the property at 60% of market value and has a property tax of $18.40 per $1000 of assessed value. Find the property tax.

   26. _____

27. **WALMART SUPERCENTER**   A new Walmart Supercenter is expected to have a fair market value of $32,500,000. It will be assessed at 65% and the tax rate is $2.18 per $100 of assessed value. Estimate the annual property tax.

   27. _____

28. **MOTORCYCLES**   Harley-Davidson of Lincoln has property with a fair market value of   **28.** _____
$518,600. The property is located in an area that is assessed at 35% of market value. The
tax rate is $7.35 per $100. Find the property tax.

29. **COMPARING PROPERTY TAX RATES**   In one parish (county), property is assessed at   **(a)** _____
40% of market value, with a tax rate of 32.1 mills. In a second parish, property is assessed   **(b)** _____
at 24% of market value, with a tax rate of 50.2 mills. A telephone company is trying to
decide where to place a small storage building with a fair market value of $95,000.
(a) Which parish would charge the lower property tax? **(b)** Find the annual amount saved.

30. **TAXES ON HOME**   Jacque Henri plans to build a home with a fair market value of   **(a)** _____
$240,000 in one of two neighboring counties. In Smith County, property is assessed at   **(b)** _____
30% of market value, with a tax rate of 45.6 mills. In Justin County, property is assessed
at 58% of market value with a tax rate of 38.5 mills. Find **(a)** which county has the lower
property tax and **(b)** the annual amount saved if the home is built in that county.

┌─── **QUICK CHECK ANSWERS** ───┐

1. $1,036,000   **3. (a)** $2210   **(b)** $2925   **(c)** $2496   **(d)** $3133
2. .64%   **4. (a)** first county   **(b)** $754 per year

▼ 13.2 Personal Income Tax

OBJECTIVES

1. List the four steps that determine income-tax liability.
2. Find the adjusted gross income.
3. Know the standard deduction amounts.
4. Find the taxable income and income tax.
5. List possible deductions.
6. Determine a balance due or a refund from the Internal Revenue Service.
7. Prepare a 1040A and a Schedule 1 federal tax form.

▼ **CASE IN POINT** Martha Spencer is responsible for paying all appropriate taxes related to her business as well as her personal income taxes. Since she is busy and taxes are complex, she hires an accountant to help her in her business.

The diagram below shows the president's proposed 2011 budget for the U.S. government. Notice that the largest source of income is individual **income taxes**, the topic of this section. Also notice that anticipated total spending of $3.83 trillion exceeds anticipated total revenue of $2.57 trillion, resulting in a deficit of $1.27 trillion for the year. The proposed budget includes the spending of billions to put people back to work in the aftermath of the financial crisis. The largest outlays were for defense, Social Security, and Medicare.

Many experts worry about the large deficits and increasing debt. However, the goal of the deficit spending is to get the economy growing and reduce unemployment. The idea is that a growing economy with low unemployment will result in higher tax revenues to the government in time.

One debate relates to whether those with high incomes pay enough income taxes. Although some believe that the wealthy pay no income taxes, the tax foundation states that the top 50% of all earners pay more than 97% of the individual income taxes shown in the figure below. Recent headlines suggest that the lowest 47% of all earners pay no income tax although they do pay Social Security taxes, Medicare taxes, sales taxes, and property taxes.

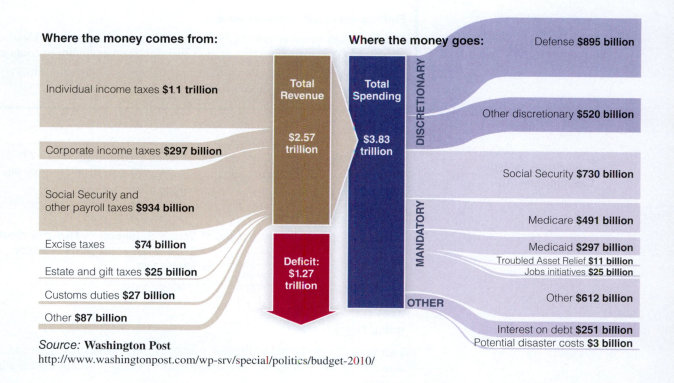

Source: **Washington Post**
http://www.washingtonpost.com/wp-srv/special/politics/budget-2010/

Most working adults in the United States are required to file an income tax return each year with the **Internal Revenue Service (IRS)**. The IRS is the branch of the U.S. government responsible for collecting income taxes. In 2014, it is estimated that over 150,000,000 personal income-tax returns will be filed in the United States and most of those will be filed electronically.

There are thousands of rules about income tax preparation and many different forms, each with its own instructions. However, many people have relatively simple income tax returns that do not require professionals to complete. No matter whether you use a professional to file your income-tax return or do it yourself, you should carefully save all records related to income and expenses. These records should be kept until the statute of limitations runs out, which is 3 years from the date the tax return was filed or 2 years from the date the tax was paid, whichever is later. The IRS can audit you during this period and it requires proof of income and deductions.

Quick TIP

Always go to the IRS for the most recent forms and laws.

Many accountants recommend that you keep records for 7 years, but you should keep records on property such as your home as long as they are needed, often longer than 3 years.

OBJECTIVE 1 List the four steps that determine income tax liability. It can be very complex to calculate the income tax for some people, but the following four steps are common to all personal tax returns.

Finding Your Income Tax Liability

Step 1   Find the adjusted gross income (AGI) for the year.
Step 2   Find the taxable income.
Step 3   Find the tax.
Step 4   Check to see if a refund is due or if money is owed to the government.

OBJECTIVE 2 Find the adjusted gross income. The first step in finding personal income tax is to find **adjusted gross income**. Adjusted gross income is the total of all income less certain adjustments. Employers are required to send out **W-2 forms** showing wages paid, federal income taxes withheld, Social Security tax withheld, and Medicare tax withheld. Other types of income such as interest, dividends, and self-employment income are shown on **1099 forms**, which are also mailed to each individual. Sample W-2 and 1099-INT forms are shown on the next page.

Finding Adjusted Gross Income

Step 1   Add amounts from all W-2 and 1099 forms along with dividends, capital gains, unemployment compensation, and tips or other employee compensation.
Step 2   From this sum, subtract adjustments such as contributions to a *regular* **individual retirement account (IRA)** or alimony payments.

EXAMPLE 1

Finding Adjusted Gross Income (AGI)

As an assistant manager at The Doll House, Jennifer Crum earned $24,738.41 last year and $1624.01 in interest from her credit union (see her W-2 and 1099 forms). She had $1500 in regular IRA contributions. Find her adjusted gross income.

SOLUTION

$$\text{Adjusted gross income} = \text{Wages} + \text{Interest} - \textbf{IRA contribution}$$
$$= \$24{,}738.41 + \$1624.01 - \$1500$$
$$= \$24{,}862.42$$

QUICK CHECK 1

Last year, Marelli Food Distribution paid marketing manager Beth Hogan $95,000. Hogan also earned $6450 in interest and contributed $2500 to an IRA. Find her adjusted gross income.

When you file your income tax return, a copy of all W-2 forms must be sent to the Internal Revenue Service along with the completed tax forms. However, the IRS does not require copies of 1099 forms to be sent unless income tax was withheld.

22222	Void ☐	**a** Employee's social security number 123-45-6789	For Official Use Only ▶ OMB No. 1545-0008	

b Employer identification number (EIN) 94-1287319	**1** Wages, tips, other compensation $24,738.41	**2** Federal income tax withheld $3275.60

c Employer's name, address, and ZIP code

The Doll House
1568 Liberty Heights Ave.
Baltimore, MD 21230

3 Social security wages $24,738.41	**4** Social security tax withheld $1533.78
5 Medicare wages and tips $24,738.41	**6** Medicare tax withheld $358.71
7 Social security tips	**8** Allocated tips

d Control number

9 Advance EIC payment	**10** Dependent care benefits

e Employee's first name and initial Jennifer	Last name Crum	Suff.

2136 old Road
Towson, MD 21285

11 Nonqualified plans	**12a** See instructions for box 12
13 Statutory employee ☐ Retirement plan ☐ Third-party sick pay ☐	**12b**
14 Other	**12c**
	12d

f Employee's address and ZIP code

15 State MD Employer's state ID number 600-5076	**16** State wages, tips, etc.	**17** State income tax	**18** Local wages, tips, etc.	**19** Local income tax	**20** Locality name

Form **W-2** **Wage and Tax Statement**

Department of the Treasury—Internal Revenue Service

9292   ☐ VOID   ☐ CORRECTED

PAYER'S name, street address, city, state, ZIP code, and telephone no. Employees Credit Union 2572 Brookhaven Drive Dundalk, MD 21222	Payer's RTN (optional)	OMB No. 1545-0112
	1 Interest income $	20__ **Interest Income**
	2 Early withdrawal penalty $	Form **1099-INT**

PAYER'S federal identification number 94-1287319	RECIPIENT'S identification number 123-45-6789	**3** Interest on U.S. Savings Bonds and Treas. obligations $1624.01	Copy A For Internal Revenue Service Center File with Form 1096.
RECIPIENT'S name Jennifer Crum		**4** Federal income tax withheld $	**5** Investment expenses $
Street address (including apt. no.) 2136 Old Road		**6** Foreign tax paid $	**7** Foreign country or U.S. possession $
City, state, and ZIP code Towson, MD 21285		**8** Tax-exempt interest $	**9** Specified private activity bond interest $
Account number (see instructions)	2nd TIN not. ☐	**10** Tax-exempt bond CUSIP no. (see instructions)	

For Privacy Act and Paperwork Reduction Act Notice. see the **2010 General Instructions for Certain Information Returns.**

Form **1099-INT**   Cat. No. 14410K   Department of the Treasury—Internal Revenue Service

OBJECTIVE 3 Know the standard deduction amounts. Most people are almost finished with their income tax return at this point. A taxpayer next subtracts the larger of either the itemized deductions or the standard deduction from adjusted gross income. Itemized deductions are described in Objective 5 in this section and are associated with several limitations based on adjusted gross income. The **standard deduction** amount is based on the taxpayer's filing status as follows.

> **Finding Standard Deduction**
>
> - $5,800 for single taxpayers
> - $11,600 for married taxpayers filing jointly
> - $5,800 for married taxpayers filing separately
> - $8,500 for head of household

A **head of household** is an unmarried person who provides a home for other people, such as a dependent child or even a dependent parent of the taxpayer.

Additional standard deductions are given for taxpayers and dependents who are blind or 65 years of age or older. The standard deduction amounts change from one year to the next. The most current amounts can be obtained from the IRS.

The next step is to find the number of **personal exemptions**. One exemption is allowed for yourself, another for your spouse if filing a joint return, and yet another exemption for each child or other dependent. A **dependent** is a child, spouse, parent, or certain other relative to whom the primary taxpayer contributes all or a major portion of necessary financial support. The number of exemptions does not depend on whether the filing status is single or married. The deduction for personal exemptions is $3700 times the number of exemptions. Here are some examples.

Filing Status and Exemptions	Total Deduction
Single individual (1 exemption)	$1 \times \$3700 = \$3700$
Married with 3 children (5 exemptions)	$5 \times \$3700 = \$18,500$
Single, head of household, 2 children (3 exemptions)	$3 \times \$3700 = \$11,100$

Taxable income is found by subtracting the standard deduction amount and personal exemptions from adjusted gross income. Taxes are then calculated based on taxable income as shown next.

OBJECTIVE 4 Find the taxable income and income tax. Taxable income is used along with data from the tax rate schedule shown next to find the income tax. As you can see from the tax rate schedules, individual income tax rates range from a low of 10% to a high of 35% depending on income and filing status. Assume a single filer has a taxable income of $37,300. Use the table for single filer below to find:

$$\text{Federal income tax} = \$4750 + \textbf{25\% of excess over \$34,500}$$
$$= \$4750 + .25 \times (\$37,300 - \$34,500)$$
$$= \$5450$$

Note that the 25% rate applies only to the excess over $34,500 and not to the entire amount of $37,300. In fact, the percent of the taxable income that goes for taxes is found as follows.

$$\frac{\text{Percent of taxable}}{\text{income paid in taxes}} = \frac{\text{Amount paid in taxes}}{\text{Taxable income}}$$

$$= \frac{\$5450}{\$37,300} = 14.6\% \quad \text{(rounded)}$$

Thus, this taxpayer must pay about 15% of taxable income in income taxes, not considering taxes related to Medicare and Social Security. The tax rates increase as income increases.

2011 Tax Rate Schedules

Schedule X—If your filing status is **Single**

If your taxable income is:		The tax is:	of the amount
Over—	But not over—		over—
$0	$8,500	·········· 10%	$0
8,500	34,500	$850.00 + 15%	8,500
34,500	83,600	4,750.00 + 25%	34,500
83,600	174,400	17,025.00 + 28%	83,600
174,400	379,150	42,449.00 + 33%	174,400
379,150	·········	110,016.50 + 35%	379,150

Schedule Y-1—If your filing status is **Married filing jointly** or **Qualifying widow(er)**

If your taxable income is:		The tax is:	of the amount
Over—	But not over—		over—
$0	$17,000	·········· 10%	$0
17,000	69,000	$1,700.00 + 15%	17,000
69,000	139,350	9,500.00 + 25%	69,000
139,350	212,300	27,087.50 + 28%	139,350
212,300	379,150	47,513.50 + 33%	212,300
379,150	··········	102,574.00 + 35%	379,150

Schedule Y-2—If your filing status is **Married filing separately**

If your taxable income is:		The tax is:	of the amount
Over—	But not over—		over—
$0	$8,500	·········· 10%	$0
8,500	34,500	$850.00 + 15%	8,500
34,500	69,675	4,750.00 + 25%	34,500
69,675	106,150	13,543.75 + 28%	69,675
106,150	189,575	23,756.75 + 33%	106,150
189,575	··········	51,287.00 + 35%	189,575

Schedule Z—If your filing status is **Head of household**

If your taxable income is:		The tax is:	of the amount
Over—	But not over—		over—
$0	$12,150	·········· 10%	$0
12,150	46,250	$1,215.00 + 15%	12,150
46,250	119,400	6,330.00 + 25%	46,250
119,400	193,350	24,617.50 + 28%	119,400
193,350	379,150	45,323.50 + 33%	193,350
379,150	··········	106,637.50 + 35%	379,150

Quick TIP

All of these figures change each year.

Find Taxable Income and the Income Tax Amount

EXAMPLE 2

Find the taxable income and income tax for each of the following.

(a) Herbert White, married filing jointly, 5 daughters, adjusted gross income $48,300

(b) Onita Fields, single, no dependents, adjusted gross income $28,400

(c) Imogene Griffin, single, head of household, 2 children, adjusted gross income $74,500

(d) Jeffy Norwood, married filing separately, 1 child, adjusted gross income $145,000

SOLUTION

(a) Herbert White + spouse + 5 daughters = 7 exemptions

$$\begin{array}{ccc} & \text{standard} & \text{deduction} & \text{taxable} \\ & \text{deduction} & \text{for exemptions} & \text{income} \end{array}$$

$$\text{Taxable income} = \$48{,}300 - \$11{,}600 - (7 \times \$3700) = \mathbf{\$10{,}800}$$

The tax rate for married filing jointly with less than \$17,000 in taxable income is 10%.

$$\text{Income tax} = .10 \times \mathbf{\$10{,}800} = \$1080$$

(b) Onita Fields = 1 exemption

$$\begin{array}{ccc} & \text{standard} & \text{deduction} & \text{taxable} \\ & \text{deduction} & \text{for exemptions} & \text{income} \end{array}$$

$$\text{Taxable income} = \$28{,}400 - \$5800 - (1 \times \$3700) = \mathbf{\$18{,}900}$$

$$\begin{aligned} \text{Income tax} &= \$850 + \mathbf{15\% \text{ of excess over } \$8500} \\ &= \$850 + .15 \times (\$18{,}900 - \$8500) \\ &= \mathbf{\$2410} \end{aligned}$$

(c) Imogene Griffin + 2 children = 3 exemptions

$$\begin{array}{ccc} & \text{standard} & \text{deduction} & \text{taxable} \\ & \text{deduction} & \text{for exemptions} & \text{income} \end{array}$$

$$\text{Taxable income} = \$74{,}500 - \$8500 - (3 \times \$3700) = \mathbf{\$54{,}900}$$

$$\begin{aligned} \text{Income tax} &= \$6330 + \mathbf{25\% \text{ of excess over } \$46{,}250} \\ &= \$6330 + .25 \times (\$54{,}900 - \$46{,}250) \\ &= \mathbf{\$8492.50} \end{aligned}$$

(d) Jeffy Norwood + 1 child = 2 exemptions

$$\begin{array}{ccc} & \text{standard} & \text{deduction} & \text{taxable} \\ & \text{deduction} & \text{for exemptions} & \text{income} \end{array}$$

$$\text{Taxable income} = \$145{,}000 - \$5800 - (2 \times \$3700) = \mathbf{\$131{,}800}$$

$$\begin{aligned} \text{Income tax} &= \$23{,}756.75 + \mathbf{33\% \text{ of excess over } \$106{,}150} \\ &= \$23{,}756.75 + .33 \times (\$131{,}800 - \$106{,}150) \\ &= \mathbf{\$32{,}221.25} \end{aligned}$$

QUICK CHECK 2

John O'Neill files jointly with his wife. They have 1 child and an adjusted gross income of \$62,300. Find their taxable income and income tax.

OBJECTIVE 5 List possible deductions. Actually, taxpayers may deduct *the larger of* **itemized deductions** *or* the standard deduction from their adjusted gross income *before* finding taxable income. This is particularly applicable to individuals who are paying interest on a home loan, but sometimes others can use this to their advantage. The most common **tax deductions** are listed next.

Medical and dental expenses: Only medical and dental expenses exceeding 7.5% of adjusted gross income may be deducted. This deduction is effectively limited to catastrophic illnesses for most taxpayers. Expenses reimbursed by an insurance company are not deductible.

Taxes: State and local income taxes, real estate taxes, and personal property taxes may be deducted (but not federal income or gasoline taxes).

Interest: Deductible interest includes interest on a home mortgage and qualified interest on other real estate. Other personal interest is not deductible.

Gifts to charity: Gifts to an eligible charity (such as a church) are deductible.

Casualty or theft losses: Losses due to a casualty (e.g., fire) or theft are deductible if not reimbursed by insurance.

Unreimbursed job expenses, tax preparation, and **miscellaneous deductions:** These expenses are deductible only if the total exceeds 2% of the taxpayer's adjusted gross income.

Using Itemized Deductions to Find Taxable Income and Income Tax

EXAMPLE 3

Kristina Kelly is single, has 1 child, and had an adjusted gross income of $58,700 last year. She paid $3240 in real estate taxes, $7280 in home mortgage interest, and donated $1200 to her church. Find her taxable income and her income tax if she files as head of household.

SOLUTION

$$\text{Itemized deductions} = \$3240 + \$7280 + \$1200 = \mathbf{\$11{,}720}$$

Her itemized deductions of $11,720 exceed the standard deduction of $5800 for a single person, so she uses the itemized deduction amount.

$$\text{Taxable income} = \$58{,}700 - \underset{\substack{\text{itemized} \\ \text{deductions}}}{\mathbf{\$11{,}720}} - \underset{\substack{\text{personal} \\ \text{exemptions}}}{(2 \times \$3700)} = \mathbf{\$38{,}580}$$

$$\begin{aligned}
\text{Income tax} &= \$1215 + \mathbf{15\% \text{ of the excess over } \$12{,}150} \\
&= \$1215 + .15 \times (\$39{,}580 - \$12{,}150) \\
&= \$5329.50
\end{aligned}$$

QUICK CHECK 3

Tom Garcia and his wife file jointly. They have no children, earned an adjusted gross income of $48,200, and paid the following: $2350 in other taxes, $6807.45 in home mortgage interest, and $500 as a charitable deduction to the Red Cross. Find their taxable income and income tax.

OBJECTIVE 6 Determine a balance due or a refund from the Internal Revenue Service. A taxpayer may have paid more to the IRS than is due. Add up the total amount of income tax paid using the W-2 forms. Usually, no taxes are withheld on 1099 forms. If the amount withheld is greater than the tax owed, the taxpayer is entitled to a refund. If the amount withheld is less than the tax owed, then the taxpayer must send the difference along with the tax return to the IRS.

Determining Tax Due or Refund

EXAMPLE 4

At age 29, Jim Clark works as a petroleum engineer for ExxonMobil, where he helps design deep, complex wells being drilled offshore Africa. His wife stays at home and takes care of their toddler. His salary last year was $123,500, and $1210 was withheld from each monthly paycheck. They file a joint return and use the standard deduction. Find the amount of income tax due to the IRS or the amount overpaid, as applicable.

SOLUTION

Adjusted gross income	$123,500	
Standard deduction	−11,600	**married filing jointly**
Personal exemptions	−11,100	**3 exemptions × $3700**
Taxable income	$100,800	

$$\begin{aligned}
\text{Income tax} &= \$9500 + \mathbf{25\% \text{ of the excess over } \$69{,}000} \\
&= \$9500 + \mathbf{.25} \times (\$100{,}800 - \$69{,}000) \\
&= \$17{,}450
\end{aligned}$$

$$\text{Amount withheld last year} = \$1210 \times 12 = \mathbf{\$14{,}520}$$
$$\text{Amount owed to IRS} = \$17{,}450 - \mathbf{\$14{,}520} = \$2930$$

The Clarks must send an additional $2930 in income taxes to the IRS with their income-tax return. Depending on the state in which they live, they may also owe some state income taxes. Although a few states do not have income taxes, most states do have them.

QUICK CHECK 4

James Benson files as head of household and has 2 children. His adjusted gross income is $59,200, and he uses the standard deduction. Last year, his employer held $280 out of every bimonthly paycheck. Find **(a)** his taxable income, **(b)** tax due, **(c)** amount withheld by his employer last year, and **(d)** either the additional amount of income taxes he owes or the amount he overpaid.

Use the simplest IRS form possible when filing your income taxes. Here are basic guidelines starting with the simplest form. Be sure to check with the IRS before choosing the tax form—the rules change often!

1040EZ (general guidelines)

1. Single or married filing jointly with no dependents
2. No adjustments to income
3. Cannot itemize
4. Limited sources of income and use of tax credits
5. Under age 65 with taxable income less than $100,000
6. Taxable interest not over $1500

1040A (general guidelines)

1. Sources of income limited to wages, interest, capital gains, and a few other categories
2. Limited adjustments to income and use of tax credits
3. Cannot itemize
4. Taxable income less than $100,000

If neither the 1040EZ nor the 1040A form applies, then you must use the 1040 form. Partnerships and corporations require a completely different set of forms.

OBJECTIVE 7 Prepare a 1040A and a Schedule 1 federal tax form. The next example shows how to complete an income tax return using **Form 1040A** and **Schedule 1 (Form 1040A)**.

Preparing a 1040A and a Schedule 1   **EXAMPLE 5**   Jennifer Crum is single and claims one exemption. Her income appears on the W-2 and 1099 forms on page 529. She contributes $1500 to a regular IRA. Crum satisfies the requirements to use Form 1040A, but she must also fill out Schedule 1 (Form 1040A), since she has more than $1500 in interest. Round figures to the nearest dollar.

Form **1040A**

Department of the Treasury—Internal Revenue Service

U.S. Individual Income Tax Return (99) 2011

IRS Use Only—Do not write or staple in this space.

OMB No. 1545-0074

Your first name and initial	Last name
Jennifer	Crum

Your social security number
1 2 3 4 5 6 7 8 9

If a joint return, spouse's first name and initial	Last name

Spouse's social security number

Home address (number and street). If you have a P.O. box, see instructions.
2136 Old Road

Apt. no.

▲ Make sure the SSN(s) above and on line 6c are correct.

City, town or post office, state, and ZIP code. If you have a foreign address, also complete spaces below (see instructions).
Towson, MD 21285

Presidential Election Campaign
Check here if you, or your spouse if filing jointly, want $3 to go to this fund. Checking a box below will not change your tax or refund.
☐ You   ☐ Spouse

Foreign country name	Foreign province/country	Foreign postal code

Filing status
Check only one box.

1 ☑ Single
2 ☐ Married filing jointly (even if only one had income)
3 ☐ Married filing separately. Enter spouse's SSN above and full name here. ▶
4 ☐ Head of household (with qualifying person). (See instructions.) If the qualifying person is a child but not your dependent, enter this child's name here. ▶
5 ☐ Qualifying widow(er) with dependent child (see instructions.)

Exemptions

If more than six dependents, see instructions.

6a ☑ **Yourself.** If someone can claim you as a dependent, **do not** check box 6a.

b ☐ **Spouse**

c **Dependents:**

(1) First name Last name	(2) Dependent's social security number	(3) Dependent's relationship to you	(4) ✔ if child under age 17 qualifying for child tax credit (see instructions)
			☐
			☐
			☐
			☐
			☐
			☐

Boxes checked on 6a and 6b **1**

No. of children on 6c who:
● lived with you
● did not live with you due to divorce or separation (see instructions)

Dependents on 6c not entered above

Add numbers on lines above ▶ **1**

d Total number of exemptions claimed.

Income

Attach Form(s) W-2 here. Also attach Form(s) 1099-R if tax was withheld.

If you did not get a W-2, see instructions.

Enclose, but do not attach, any payment. Also, please use **Form 1040-V.**

7	Wages, salaries, tips, etc. Attach Form(s) W-2.	7 $24,738
8a	**Taxable** interest. Attach Schedule B if required.	8a $1,624
b	**Tax-exempt** interest. **Do not** include on line 8a. 8b	
9a	Ordinary dividends. Attach Schedule B if required.	9a
b	Qualified dividends (see instructions). 9b	
10	Capital gain distributions (see instructions).	10
11a	IRA distributions. 11a	11b Taxable amount (see instructions). 11b
12a	Pensions and annuities. 12a	12b Taxable amount (see instructions). 12b
13	Unemployment compensation and Alaska Permanent Fund dividends.	13
14a	Social security benefits. 14a	14b Taxable amount (see instructions). 14b
15	Add lines 7 through 14b (far right column). This is your **total income.** ▶	15 $26,362

Adjusted gross income

16	Educator expenses (see instructions). 16	
17	IRA deduction (see instructions). 17 $1,500	
18	Student loan interest deduction (see instructions). 18	
19	Tuition and fees. Attach Form 8917. 19	
20	Add lines 16 through 19. These are your **total adjustments.**	20 $1,500
21	Subtract line 20 from line 15. This is your **adjusted gross income.** ▶	21 $24,862

For Disclosure, Privacy Act, and Paperwork Reduction Act Notice, see separate instructions.   Cat. No. 11327A   Form **1040A** (2011)

Form 1040A (2011)   Page **2**

Tax, credits, and payments	22	Enter the amount from line 21 (adjusted gross income).		22	$24,862

Standard Deduction for—
- People who checked any box on line 23a or 23b or who can be claimed as a dependent, see instructions.
- All others: Single or Married filing separately, $5,800

Married filing jointly or Qualifying widow(er), $11,600

Head of household, $8,500

23a Check if: ☐ **You** were born before January 2, 1947, ☐ Blind } Total boxes
☐ **Spouse** was born before January 2, 1947, ☐ Blind } checked ▶ 23a ☐

b If you are married filing separately and your spouse itemizes deductions, check here ▶ 23b ☐

24	Enter your **standard deduction** (see left margin).	24	$5,800
25	Subtract line 24 from line 22. If line 24 is more than line 22, enter -0-.	25	$19,062
26	**Exemptions.** Multiply $3,700 by the number on line 6d.	26	$3,700
27	Subtract line 26 from line 25. If line 26 is more than line 25, enter -0-. This is your **taxable income.** ▶	27	$15,362
28	**Tax,** including any alternative minimum tax (see instructions).	28	$1,879

29	Credit for child and dependent care expenses. Attach Form 2441.	29	
30	Credit for the elderly or the disabled. Attach Schedule R.	30	
31	Education credits from Form 8863, line 23.	31	
32	Retirement savings contributions credit. Attach Form 8880.	32	
33	Child tax credit (see instructions).	33	

34	Add lines 29 through 33. These are your **total credits.**	34	$0
35	Subtract line 34 from line 28. If line 34 is more than line 28, enter -0-. This is your **total tax.**	35	$1,879
36	Federal income tax withheld from Forms W-2 and 1099.	36	$3,276

If you have a qualifying child, attach Schedule EIC.

37	2011 estimated tax payments and amount applied from 2010 return.	37	
38a	**Earned income credit (EIC).**	38a	
b	Nontaxable combat pay election. 38b		
39	Additional child tax credit. Attach Form 8812.	39	
40	American opportunity credit from Form 8863, line 14.	40	
41	Add lines 36, 37, 38a, 39, and 40. These are your **total payments.** ▶	41	$3,276

Refund

42	If line 41 is more than line 35, subtract line 35 from line 41. This is the amount you **overpaid.**	42	$1,397

Direct deposit? See instructions and fill in 43b, 43c, and 43d or Form 8888.

43a Amount of line 42 you want **refunded to you.** If Form 8888 is attached, check here ▶ ☐ 43a $1,397

▶ **b** Routing number ☐☐☐☐☐☐☐☐☐   ▶ **c** Type: ☐ Checking ☐ Savings

▶ **d** Account number ☐☐☐☐☐☐☐☐☐☐☐☐☐☐☐☐☐

44	Amount of line 42 you want **applied to your 2012 estimated tax.**	44	$0

Amount you owe

45	**Amount you owe.** Subtract line 41 from line 35. For details on how to pay, see instructions. ▶	45	$0
46	Estimated tax penalty (see instructions).	46	

Third party designee

Do you want to allow another person to discuss this return with the IRS (see instructions)? ☐ **Yes.** Complete the following. ☐ **No**

Designee's name	Phone no. ▶	Personal identification number (PIN) ▶ ☐☐☐☐☐

Sign here

Joint return? See page 13. Keep a copy for your records.

Under penalties of perjury, I declare that I have examined this return and accompanying schedules and statements, and to the best of my knowledge and belief, they are true, correct, and accurately list all amounts and sources of income I received during the tax year. Declaration of preparer (other than the taxpayer) is based on all information of which the preparer has any knowledge.

Your signature	Date	Your occupation	Daytime phone number
Jennifer Crum	4/14	Assistant Manager	(410)-286-2594
Spouse's signature. If a joint return, **both** must sign.	Date	Spouse's occupation	If the IRS sent you an identity Protection PIN, enter it here (see inst.) ☐☐☐☐☐☐

Paid preparer use only

Print/type preparer's name	Preparer's signature	Date	Check ▶ ☐ if self-employed	PTIN
Firm's name ▶			Firm's EIN ▶	
Firm's address ▶			Phone no.	

Form **1040A** (2011)

Schedule 1
(Form 1040A)

Department of the Treasury—Internal Revenue Service

Interest and Ordinary Dividends for Form 1040A Filers

(99)

OMB No. 1545-0074

Name(s) shown on Form 1040A

Jennifer Crum

Your social security number

123 45 6789

Part I

Interest

(See back of schedule and the instructions for Form 1040A, line 8a.)

Note. If you received a Form 1099-INT, Form 1099-OID, or substitute statement from a brokerage firm, enter the firm's name and the total interest shown on that form.

1 List name of payer. If any interest is from a seller-financed mortgage and the buyer used the property as a personal residence, see back of schedule and list this interest first. Also, show that buyer's social security number and address.

		Amount	
Employees Credit Union	1	$1,624	

				Amount	
2	Add the amounts on line 1.		2	$1,624	
3	Excludable interest on series EE and I U.S. savings bonds issued after 1989. Attach Form 8815.		3		
4	Subtract line 3 from line 2. Enter the result here and on Form 1040A, line 8a.		4	$1,624	

Part II

Ordinary dividends

(See back of schedule and the instructions for Form 1040A, line 9a.)

Note. If you received a Form 1099-DIV or substitute statement from a brokerage firm, enter the firm's name and the ordinary dividends shown on that form.

5 List name of payer.

		Amount	
	5		

6	Add the amounts on line 5. Enter the total here and on Form 1040A, line 9a.		6	

For Paperwork Reduction Act Notice, see Form 1040A instructions.   Cat. No. 12075R   Schedule 1 (Form 1040A) 2011

▼13.2 Exercises   MyMathLab®

The shaded sections below contain solutions to help you get a **QUICK START** *on the various types of exercises.*

Find the adjusted gross income for each of the following people. (See Example 1.)

Name	Income from Jobs	Interest	Misc. Income	Dividend Income	Adjustments to Income	Adjusted Gross Income
1. R. Jacob	$22,840	$234	$1209	$48	$1200	$23,131
$22,840 + $234 + $1209 + $48 − $1200 = $23,131						
2. K. Chandler	$68,156	$285	$73	$542	$317	$68,739
$68,156 + $285 + $73 + $542 − $317 = $68,739						
3. The Hanks	$21,380	$625	$139	$184	$618	_____
4. The Jazwinskis	$33,650	$722	$375	$218	$473	_____
5. The Brashers	$38,643	$1020	$3820	$1050	$0	_____
6. The Claxtons	$93,680	$3247	$8115	$2469	$2800	_____
7. The Wheats	$21,370	$420	$0	$0	$0	_____
8. Tiny Peyton	$68,540	$1290	$480	$318	$1840	_____

Find the amount of taxable income and the tax owed for each of the following people. Use the tax rate schedule. The letter following the names indicates the marital status, and all married people are filing jointly. (See Examples 2 and 3.)

Name	Number of Exemptions	Adjusted Gross Income	Total Deductions	Taxable Income	Tax Owed
9. R. Rodriguez, S	1	$36,840	$2460	$27,340	$3676
$36,840 − $5800 − $3700 = $27,340; $850 + .15 × ($27,340 − $8500) = $3676					
10. S. Simpson, S	1	$26,190	$1248	$16,690	$2078.50
$26,190 − $5800 − $3700 = $16,690; $850 + .15 × ($16,690 − $8500) = $2078.50					
11. The Pacas, M	2	$72,450	$6040	_____	_____
12. The Laytons, M	4	$65,290	$8040	_____	_____
13. The Jordans, M	3	$99,500	$14,320	_____	_____
14. P. Jong, Head of Household	4	$162,370	$12,480	_____	_____
15. K. Tang, Married filing separately	2	$85,332	$8170	_____	_____
16. G. Begay, Head of Household	4	$58,332	$9480	_____	_____

C indicates an exercise that is related to the Case in Point feature.

Name	Number of Exemptions	Adjusted Gross Income	Total Deductions	Taxable Income	Tax Owed
17. D. Kien, Head of Household	2	$82,650	$8100	_____	_____
18. L. Dimon, M	2	$262,680	$18,350	_____	_____

Find the tax refund or tax due for the following people. The letter following the names indicates the marital status. Assume a 52-week year and that married people are filing jointly. (See Example 4.)

Name	Taxable Income	Federal Income Tax Withheld from Checks	Tax Refund or Tax Due
19. L. Karecki, S	$78,500	$1516 monthly	$2442 tax refund
$18,192 − $15,750 = $2442 refund			
20. K. Turner, S	$32,060	$347.80 monthly	_____
21. M. Hunziker, S	$23,552	$72.18 weekly	_____
22. The Fungs, M	$38,238	$119.27 weekly	_____
23. The Todds, M	$202,100	$3200 monthly	_____
24. S. Benson, HH	$160,300	$720 weekly	_____

25. List four sources of income for which an individual might receive W-2 and 1099 forms. (See Objective 2.)

26. List four possible tax deductions, and explain the effect that a tax deduction will have on taxable income and on income tax due. (See Objective 5.)

Find the tax in the following application problems.

27. **MARRIED—INCOME TAX** The Tobins had an adjusted gross income of $98,700 last year. They had deductions of $2820 for state income tax, $490 for city income tax, $4400 for property tax, $5800 in mortgage interest, and $1450 in contributions. They file a joint return and claim 5 exemptions.

27. _____

28. **SINGLE—INCOME TAX** Diane Bolton works at The Doll House and had an adjusted gross income of $34,975 last year. She had deductions of $971 for state income tax, $1864 for property tax, $3820 in mortgage interest, and $235 in contributions. Bolton claims one exemption and files as a single person.

28. _____

29. Carol Ridgeway has an adjusted gross income of $73,200 and files as head of household since she has a dependent, 9-year-old daughter. Her deductions are $7143.

29. _____

30. MARRIED—INCOME TAX   The Hernandez family had an adjusted gross income of $48,260 last year. They had deductions of $1078 for state income tax, $253 for city income tax, $3240 for property tax, $5218 in mortgage interest, and $386 in contributions. They claim three exemptions and file a joint return.

30. _____

31. HEAD OF HOUSEHOLD   Martha Spencer, owner of The Doll House, had wages of $73,800, dividends of $385, interest of $1672, and adjustments to income of $1058 last year. She had deductions of $877 for state income tax, $342 for city income tax, $4986 for property tax, $5173 in mortgage interest, and $1800 in contributions. She claims four exemptions and files as head of household.

31. _____

32. HEAD OF HOUSEHOLD   John Walker had wages of $48,200, other income of $2892, dividends of $340, interest of $651, and a regular IRA contribution of $2000 last year. He had deductions of $1163 for taxes, $5350 in mortgage interest, and $540 in contributions. Walker claims two exemptions and files as head of household.

32. _____

33. MARRIED   John and Vicki Karsten had combined wages and salaries of $64,280, other income of $5283, dividend income of $324, and interest income of $668. They have adjustments to income of $2484. Their itemized deductions are $7615 in mortgage interest, $2250 in state income tax, $3300 in real estate taxes, and $1219 in charitable contributions. The Karstens filed a joint return and claimed 3 exemptions.

33. _____

34. HEAD OF HOUSEHOLD   Jayne Binyan is single with one dependent and files as head of household. She is the chief financial officer at the university where she works, and her salary is $173,400. She has other income of $2800, interest income of $8400, and an adjustment to income of $6000 for a 401K retirement plan at work. Her itemized deductions are $14,380 in mortgage interest, $4820 in state income tax, $7800 in real estate taxes, and $6800 in charitable contributions.

34. _____

QUICK CHECK ANSWERS

1. $98,950

2. $39,600; $5090

3. $29,200; $3530

4. (a) $39,600
  (b) $5332.50
  (c) $6720
  (d) overpaid by $1387.50

▼13.3 Fire Insurance

OBJECTIVES

1 Define the terms *policy, coverage, face value*, and *premium*.

2 Find the annual premium for fire insurance.

3 Use the coinsurance formula.

4 Understand multiple-carrier insurance.

5 List additional types of insurance coverage.

▼CASE IN POINT   Martha Spencer owns the building in which The Doll House is located. A fire in that building could leave her in financial ruin. Although she hopes that there is never a fire, she carries fire insurance to protect her business in the event there is one.

Insurance protects against risk. For example, there is only a slight chance that a particular building will be damaged by fire in any year. However, the financial loss from a fire could be devastating to the owner. Therefore, people and companies pay a small fee each year to an insurance company to protect them against catastrophic losses. The insurance company collects money from many different people and companies that buy insurance and pays money to the few who suffer damages.

Insurance is important. For example, a bank requires that fire insurance be purchased on a building (or home) before it will lend the funds to the buyer. Most states require automobile drivers to buy a minimum amount of car insurance before driving. Firms large and small buy liability insurance to protect against a lawsuit or a **catastrophic event** that would be financially damaging to the company. Parents buy life insurance to support their kids in the event of a parent's untimely death. In fact, it is rare for individuals and businesses not to carry insurance for protection.

The following figure shows that most home fires begin in the kitchen. As a result, experts recommend that everyone keep a fire extinguisher in the kitchen. They also recommend that every home have fire alarms so that anyone in a burning home quickly becomes aware of the fire.

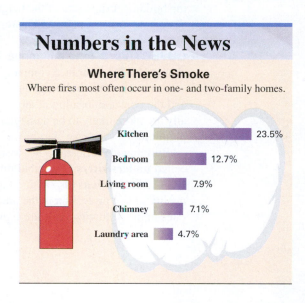

Numbers in the News

Where There's Smoke
Where fires most often occur in one- and two-family homes.

Kitchen	23.5%
Bedroom	12.7%
Living room	7.9%
Chimney	7.1%
Laundry area	4.7%

Individuals buy insurance to protect against losses due to fire, theft, illness or health problems, disability, car wrecks, lawsuits, and even death. Companies buy insurance to protect against losses due to fire, automobile accidents, employee illnesses, lawsuits, and worker accidents on the job. In this section, we talk about fire insurance.

OBJECTIVE 1 Define the terms *policy, coverage, face value,* and *premium*. The contract between the owner of a building and an insurance company is called a **policy** or an **insurance policy**. A basic fire policy provides **coverage** or protection for both the owner of the building and the company that holds the mortgage on the building. The owner of a building can also purchase coverage on the contents of the building and liability insurance in the event someone is injured while on the property. Homeowners often purchase a **homeowner's policy**, which includes all of these coverages. The graph below shows that the cost of homeowner's insurance continues to increase. However, it is important to note that much of the increase in cost is due to inflation.

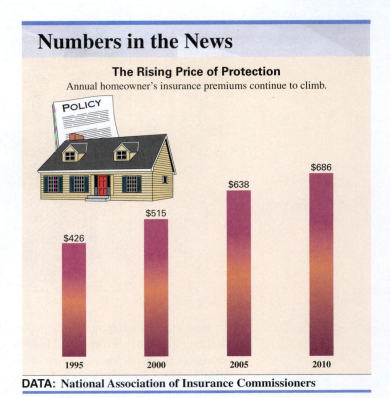

Numbers in the News

The Rising Price of Protection
Annual homeowner's insurance premiums continue to climb.

POLICY

$426 — 1995
$515 — 2000
$638 — 2005
$686 — 2010

DATA: National Association of Insurance Commissioners

The dollar value of the insurance coverage provided on a building is called the **face value** of the policy. The annual cost of the policy is called the **premium**. The premium is usually calculated based on factors such as age of the building, materials used in the construction of the building, crime rate of the neighborhood, presence of any safety features such as a sprinkler system, security system, and history of previous insurance claims on the property.

OBJECTIVE 2 Find the annual premium for fire insurance. The amount of the premium charged by the insurance company depends on several factors. Among them are the type of construction of the building, the contents and use of the building, the location of the building, and the type and location of any fire protection that is available. Wood frame buildings generally are more likely to be damaged by fire than masonry buildings and thus require a higher premium.

Building classifications are assigned to building types by insurance company employees called **underwriters**. These building categories are usually designated by letters such as A, B, and C. Underwriters also assign ratings called **territorial ratings** to each area that describe the quality of fire protection in the area. Although fire insurance rates vary from state to state, the rates in the following table are typical.

Annual Rates for Each $100 of Insurance

Territorial Rating	A		B		C	
	Building	Contents	Building	Contents	Building	Contents
1	$.25	$.32	$.36	$.49	$.45	$.60
2	$.30	$.44	$.45	$.55	$.54	$.75
3	$.37	$.46	$.54	$.60	$.63	$.80
4	$.50	$.52	$.75	$.77	$.84	$.90
5	$.62	$.58	$.92	$.99	$1.05	$1.14

Finding the Annual Fire Insurance Premium

 EXAMPLE 1

The Doll House is in a building rated class C. It is in territory 4. Find the annual premium if the replacement cost of the building is $640,000 and the contents are valued at $186,500.

SOLUTION

Building:

$$\text{Replacement cost in hundreds} = \$640,000 \div 100 = 6400$$
$$\text{Insurance premium for the building} = 6400 \times \$.84 = \$5376$$

Contents:

$$\text{Replacement cost in hundreds} = \$186,500 \div 100 = 1865$$
$$\text{Insurance premium for contents} = 1865 \times \$.90 = \$1678.50$$

Total premium: $5376 + $1678.50 = **$7054.50**

QUICK CHECK 1

A commercial building has a replacement cost of $1,480,000 and contents valued at $110,000. It has a classification of B and a territory rating of 5. Find the annual premium.

OBJECTIVE 3 Use the coinsurance formula. Most fires damage only a portion of a building and the contents. Since complete destruction of a building is rare, many owners save money by buying insurance for only a portion of the value of the building and contents. Realizing this, insurance companies place a **coinsurance clause** in almost all fire insurance policies. Effectively, the business assumes part of the risk of a loss under coinsurance.

Replacement cost refers to the cost to replace (rebuild) a building in the event it is completely destroyed. It may surprise you to learn that the replacement cost for an older building is often far greater than the fair market value, since new construction costs often exceed the value of older buildings.

Most fire insurance contracts have an 80% coinsurance clause. This clause requires the owner of the building to have an insurance policy in effect with a face value that is at least 80% of the replacement cost of the building. If the policy has a face value greater than 80%, then the insurance companies pays for all losses caused by a fire. On the other hand, if the face value is less than 80%, then the insurance company will pay only a portion of any loss. The most the insurance company will pay is the smaller amount of the loss on the face value of the policy.

Finding Amount Insurance Will Pay

$$\begin{array}{l}\text{Amount insurance company}\\ \text{will pay (assuming 80\% coinsurance)}\end{array} = \text{Amount of loss} \times \frac{\text{Amount of policy}}{80\% \text{ of replacement cost}}$$

Using the Coinsurance Formula

EXAMPLE 2

Dayton Properties owns a small apartment building with a replacement cost of $760,000. The fire insurance policy has an 80% coinsurance clause and a face value of $570,000. A fire started in the kitchen of a tenant and swept through three apartments, resulting in $144,000 in losses. Find the amount of the loss that the insurance company will pay.

SOLUTION

The policy must have a face value of at least 80% of $760,000 or $608,000 in order to receive the payment for the entire loss. Since the face value of $570,000 is less than 80% of the replacement cost, the company will pay only the following portion of the loss.

$$\text{Amount insurance company pays} = \$144,000 \times \frac{\$570,000}{\$608,000} = \$135,000$$

$$\text{Amount not paid by insurance company} = \$144,000 - \$135,000 = \$9000$$

Dayton Properties is responsible for $9000.

 The calculator solution to this example uses chain calculations and parentheses to set off the denominator. The result is then subtracted from the fire loss.

$$144{,}000 \boxed{\times} 570{,}000 \boxed{\div} \boxed{(} \boxed{(} 80 \boxed{\%} \boxed{\times} 760{,}000 \boxed{)} \boxed{=} 135{,}000$$

$$144{,}000 \boxed{-} 135{,}000 \boxed{=} 9000$$

Note: Refer to Appendix B for calculator basics.

QUICK CHECK 2

A real estate investment trust owns an office building with a replacement cost of $8,400,000 that is insured for $5,600,000. Find the amount of the loss paid for by the insurance company if a fire causes $2,300,000 in losses and the policy has an 80% coinsurance feature.

Finding the Amount of Loss Paid by the Insurance Company

EXAMPLE 3

A Swedish investment group owns a warehouse with a replacement cost of $3,450,000. The company has a fire insurance policy with a face value of $3,400,000. The policy has an 80% coinsurance feature. If the firm has a fire loss of $233,500, find the part of the loss paid by the insurance company.

SOLUTION

$$80\% \text{ of replacement cost} = .80 \times \$3{,}450{,}000 = \$2{,}760{,}000$$

The business has a fire insurance policy with a face value of more than 80% of the value of the store. Therefore, the insurance company pays the entire $233,500 loss.

QUICK CHECK 3

A plumbing company owns its own building with a replacement cost of $1,600,000. A fire results in damages of $445,000. Find the amount the insurance company will pay if the company has $1,400,000 in insurance coverage.

OBJECTIVE 4 Understand multiple-carrier insurance. A business may have fire insurance policies with several companies at the same time. Perhaps additional insurance coverage was purchased over a period of time, as new additions were made to a factory or building complex. Or perhaps the building is so large that one insurance company does not want to take the entire risk by itself, so several companies each agree to take a portion of the insurance coverage and thereby share the risk. In either event, the insurance coverage is divided among **multiple carriers**. When an insurance claim is made against multiple carriers, each insurance company pays its fractional portion of the total claim on the property.

Understanding Multiple-Carrier Insurance

Youngblood Apartments has an insured loss of $1,800,000 while having insurance coverage beyond its coinsurance requirement. The insurance is divided among Company A with $5,900,000 coverage, Company B with $4,425,000 coverage, and Company C with $1,475,000 coverage. Find the amount of the loss paid by each of the insurance companies.

SOLUTION

Start by finding the total face value of all three policies.

$$\$5,900,000 + \$4,425,000 + \$1,475,000 = \mathbf{\$11,800,000} \text{ total face value}$$

$$\text{Company A pays } \frac{\$5,900,000}{\$11,800,000} = \frac{1}{2} \text{ of the loss}$$

$$\text{Company B pays } \frac{\$4,425,000}{\$11,800,000} = \frac{3}{8} \text{ of the loss}$$

$$\text{Company C pays } \frac{\$1,475,000}{\$11,800,000} = \frac{1}{8} \text{ of the loss}$$

Since the insurance loss is $1,800,000, the amount paid by each of the multiple carriers is

$$\text{Company A: } \frac{1}{2} \times \$1,800,000 = \quad \$900,000$$

$$\text{Company B: } \frac{3}{8} \times \$1,800,000 = \quad \$675,000$$

$$\text{Company C: } \frac{1}{8} \times \$1,800,000 = \quad \underline{\$225,000}$$

$$\text{Total loss} = \$1,800,000$$

QUICK CHECK 4

A fully insured bank has $780,000 in fire damage. The coverage is divided between Company A ($1,200,000) and Company B ($800,000). Find the amount of the loss paid by each company.

If the coinsurance requirement is not met, first find the total amount of the loss paid by the insurers. Then find the amount paid by each, as shown in Example 5.

Understanding Partial Coverage and Multiple Carriers

The fire damage to a small shopping center with a replacement cost of $4,800,000 was limited to $420,000 thanks to an advanced sprinkler system. The insurance coverage is divided between Company A ($2,000,000) and Company B ($1,200,000). Find the amount of the loss paid by each, assuming management had full coverage.

SOLUTION

$$80\% \text{ of } \$4,800,000 = \mathbf{\$3,840,000}$$
$$\text{Total insurance coverage} = \$2,000,000 + \$1,200,000 = \mathbf{\$3,200,000}$$

Since the total insurance coverage is less than 80% of the replacement cost of the building, the insurance companies will pay only a portion of the total damages.

$$\text{Amount paid by insurance: } \$420,000 \times \frac{\$3,200,000}{\$3,840,000} = \mathbf{\$350,000}$$

$$\text{Paid by Company A: } \frac{\$2,000,000}{\$3,200,000} \times \mathbf{\$350,000} = \$218,750$$

$$\text{Paid by Company B: } \frac{\$1,200,000}{\$3,200,000} \times \mathbf{\$350,000} = \$131,250$$

QUICK CHECK 5

An office building with a replacement cost of $800,000 has fire damage of $100,000. The insurance coverage is divided between Company 1 ($300,000) and Company 2 ($200,000). First (a) find the amount covered by insurance, then (b) find the amount paid by each company.

The amount of money paid for insurance premiums by businesses is often small compared with other business expenses. Likewise, the average household pays only a small portion of its budget for insurance premiums. The following chart shows the percent of total household spending going to pay for insurance coverage.

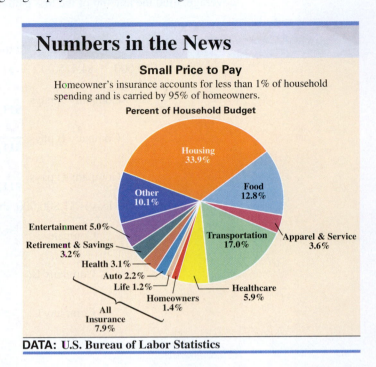

Numbers in the News

Small Price to Pay

Homeowner's insurance accounts for less than 1% of household spending and is carried by 95% of homeowners.

Percent of Household Budget

- Housing 33.9%
- Food 12.8%
- Other 10.1%
- Transportation 17.0%
- Apparel & Service 3.6%
- Entertainment 5.0%
- Retirement & Savings 3.2%
- Health 3.1%
- Auto 2.2%
- Life 1.2%
- Homeowners 1.4%
- Healthcare 5.9%
- All Insurance 7.9%

DATA: U.S. Bureau of Labor Statistics

OBJECTIVE 5 List additional types of insurance coverage. There are many other types of insurance coverages available as you can see.

Disability insurance pays monthly payments in event of disability.

Homeowner's insurance pays a homeowner in the event of fire, theft, or accidents.

Liability insurance protects business owners against lawsuit.

Long-term care insurance pays for nursing home costs.

Medical insurance pays for medical expenses.

Renter's insurance protects a renter against loss of his personal property.

Worker's compensation pays employees for injuries while on the job.

In our society, individuals, families, and business managers face risk. Experts believe that it is very important to realize where you have real risk and to cover at least some portion of that risk using insurance. Of course, it always pays to shop around to find the best deal, and finding the best insurance coverage is no different. Shop and compare to find the coverage that is best for you.

13.3 Exercises

MyMathLab®

*The shaded sections below contain solutions to help you get a **QUICK START** on the various types of exercises.*

Find the total annual premium for each of the following. Use the table on page 543.
(See Example 1.)

	Territorial Rating	Building Classification	Building Value	Contents Value	Total Annual Premium
1.	2	B	$280,000	$80,000	$1700
2.	5	A	$220,500	$105,000	$1976.10
3.	1	C	$285,000	$152,000	_____
4.	4	C	$2,325,000	$111,500	_____
5.	5	B	$782,600	$212,000	_____
6.	3	A	$596,400	$206,700	_____

Find the amount to be paid by the insurance company in the following problems. Assume that each policy includes an 80% coinsurance clause. (See Examples 2 and 3.)

	Replacement Cost of Building	Face Value of Policy	Amount of Loss	Amount Paid
7.	$1,450,000	$850,000	$96,000	$70,344.83

$1,450,000 \times .8 = \$1,160,000$ (80%); $\frac{\$850,000}{\$1,160,000} \times \$96,000 = \$70,344.83$

8.	$187,400	$140,000	$10,850	$10,132.07

$187,400 \times .8 = \$149,920$ (80%); $\frac{\$140,000}{\$149,920} \times \$10,850 = \$10,132.07$

9.	$287,000	$232,500	$19,850	_____
10.	$780,000	$585,000	$10,400	_____
11.	$218,500	$195,000	$36,500	_____
12.	$750,000	$500,000	$56,000	_____

Find the amount paid by each insurance company in the following problems involving multiple carriers. Assume that the coinsurance requirement is met. (See Example 4.)

	Insurance Loss	Companies	Coverage	Amount Paid
13.	$80,000	Company 1	$750,000	$60,000
		Company 2	$250,000	$20,000

$\frac{750,000}{1,000,000} \times \$80,000 = \$60,000$; $\frac{250,000}{1,000,000} \times \$80,000 = \$20,000$

14.	$360,000	Company A	$1,200,000	_____
		Company B	$800,000	_____

C indicates an exercise that is related to the Case in Point feature.

Insurance Loss	Companies	Coverage	Amount Paid
15. $650,000	Company 1	$1,350,000	_____
	Company 2	$1,200,000	_____
	Company 3	$450,000	_____
16. $1,600,000	Company A	$4,800,000	_____
	Company B	$800,000	_____
	Company C	$2,400,000	_____

Find the annual fire insurance premium in each of the following application problems.
Use the table on page 543.

17. COMMERCIAL BUILDING   Home Depot owns a building with a replacement cost of
$1,400,000 and with contents of $360,000. The building is class C with a territorial
rating of 5.

14,000 × 1.05 = $14,700; 3600 × $1.14 = $4104
$14,700 + $4104 = $18,804

17. $18,804

18. FIRE INSURANCE PREMIUM   James Baker owns a class-B building with a replacement
cost of $165,400. Contents are valued at $128,000. The territorial rating is 3.

18. _____

19. AIRPLANE HANGAR   Valley Crop Dusting owns an airplane hanger located in a class-B
area. It has a replacement cost of $107,500. Contents are worth $39,800. The territorial
rating is 2.

19. _____

20. INDUSTRIAL BUILDING INSURANCE   London's Dredging Equipment is in a class-C
building with a territorial rating of 4. The building has a replacement cost of $305,000
and the contents are worth $682,000.

20. _____

21. Describe three factors that determine the premium charged for fire insurance. (See Objective 2.)

22. Explain the coinsurance clause and describe how coinsurance works. (See Objective 3.)

In the following application problems, find the amount of the loss paid by (a) the insurance
company and (b) the insured. Assume an 80% coinsurance clause.

23. FIRE LOSS   The Doll House is located in a building with a
replacement cost of $328,500, but Martha Spencer insured it for
only $200,000 in order to save money on insurance premiums.
An electrical short causes a fire that results in $180,000 in damage.

(a) $328,500 × .8 = $262,800; $\frac{\$200,000}{\$262,800}$ × $180,000 = $136,986.30
(b) $180,000 − $136,986.30 = $43,013.70

(a) $136,986.30
(b) $43,013.70

24. **GIFT-SHOP FIRE LOSS** Indonesian Wonder gift shop has a replacement cost of $395,000. The shop is insured for $280,000. Fire loss is $22,500.

(a) _____

(b) _____

25. **SALVATION ARMY LOSS** The main office of the Salvation Army suffers a loss from fire of $45,000. The building has a replacement cost of $550,000 and is insured for $300,000.

(a) _____

(b) _____

26. **TRIPLEX** Fang Li purchased a small triplex that has a replacement cost of $185,000. She insures it for $111,000 and has a fire loss of $28,000 when a smoker accidently starts a fire.

(a) _____

(b) _____

In the following application problems, find the amount paid by each of the multiple carriers. Assume that the coinsurance requirement has been met.

27. **COINSURED FIRE LOSS** C. Wood Plumbing had an insured fire loss of $548,000. It has insurance coverage as follows: Company A, $600,000; Company B, $400,000; and Company C, $200,000.

A: $\frac{600,000}{1,200,000} \times \$548,000 = \$274,000$

B: $\frac{400,000}{1,200,000} \times \$548,000 = \$182,666.67$

C: $\frac{200,000}{1,200,000} \times \$548,000 = \$91,333.33$

A: $\underline{\$274,000}$

B: $\underline{\$182,666.67}$

C: $\underline{\$91,333.33}$

28. **COINSURED FIRE LOSS** Beacon Cycles had an insured fire loss of $68,500. It has insurance as follows: Company 1, $60,000; Company 2, $40,000; and Company 3, $30,000.

1: _____

2: _____

3: _____

29. **MAJOR FIRE LOSS** Gold's Gym had fire insurance coverage as follows: Company 1, $360,000; Company 2, $120,000; and Company 3, $240,000. The gym has an insured fire loss of $250,000.

1: _____

2: _____

3: _____

30. **MULTIPLE CARRIERS** Tokyo International had an insured fire loss of $2,100,000. The company has insurance as follows: Company A, $2,000,000; Company B, $1,750,000; Company C, $1,250,000.

A: _____

B: _____

C: _____

Find the amount paid by each of the multiple carriers in the following two problems. Note that the coinsurance requirement has not been met.

31. **PARTIAL COVERAGE** A building with a replacement cost of $1,200,000 has fire damages of $420,000. The insurance coverage is split between Company A ($200,000) and Company B ($300,000). Find (a) the amount of the loss covered and (b) amount paid by each company.

(a) _____

(b) _____

32. PARTIAL COVERAGE   Family Dollar owns a building with a replacement cost of
$1,800,000 that has fire and smoke damages of $310,000. The insurance coverage is split
between Company 1 ($1,000,000) and Company 2 ($400,000). Find **(a)** the amount of the
loss covered and **(b)** the amount paid by each company.

(a) _____

(b) _____

                        QUICK CHECK ANSWERS

1. $14,705   **2.** $1,916,666.67   **5. (a)** $78,125
3. $445,000   **(b)** Company A—$46,875;
4. Company A—$468,000;   Company B—$31,250
    Company B—$312,000

▼13.4 Motor-Vehicle Insurance

OBJECTIVES

1 Describe the factors that affect the cost of motor-vehicle insurance.

2 Define liability insurance.

3 Define property damage insurance.

4 Describe comprehensive and collision insurance.

5 Define no-fault and uninsured motorist insurance.

6 Apply youthful-operator factors.

7 Find the amounts paid by the insurance company and the insured.

▼ **CASE IN POINT** Martha Spencer owns a van that is used by employees of The Doll House. She insures her van, since an employee may be involved in an accident that hurts someone or damages property. Knowing that injuries can result in huge medical costs, Spencer carries more than the state-required minimum liability insurance.

OBJECTIVE 1 Describe the factors that affect the cost of motor-vehicle insurance. Automobile insurance is one of the most common types of insurance. Banks or credit unions that finance automobiles require borrowers to buy automobile insurance. Many states require automobile insurance for people living and driving in those states. As you can see from the graph, the average cost of car insurance has increased sharply.

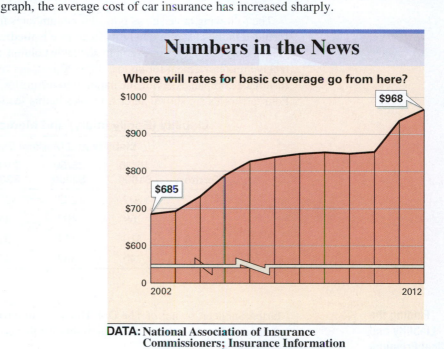

Numbers in the News

Where will rates for basic coverage go from here?

$968

$685

2002 — 2012

DATA: National Association of Insurance Commissioners; Insurance Information Institute

The **premium**, or cost, of an insurance policy is determined by **actuaries** who work for the insurance company. Actuaries look at the frequency and severity of accidents based on several factors, including

- location of the insured vehicle,
- age and sex of the driver,
- miles driven, and
- driving history of the driver.

These factors help measure the risk of insuring a particular driver, which is used to determine the premium. For example, drivers between 16 and 25 years of age are more likely to be involved in accidents and are therefore charged a higher premium. Some automobiles are more likely to be stolen than others, resulting in higher premiums for their owners. Several automobile coverages are now discussed.

OBJECTIVE 2 Define liability insurance. **Liability** or **bodily injury insurance** protects the insured in case he or she injures someone with a car. Many states have minimum amounts of liability insurance coverage set by law. The amount of liability insurance is expressed as a fraction, such as 15/30. The fraction 15/30 means that the insurance company will pay up to $15,000 for injury to one person, and a total of $30,000 for injury to two or more persons in the same accident.

However, many experts recommend liability limits of at least 100/300. This is because a single driving mistake can be very costly, as shown in the following newspaper clipping.

One Accident affects Life

Thomas Garcia has driven for 10 years and has never had an accident or a speeding ticket. However, his life changed instantly when he accidently ran through a stop sign and hit a car driven by a nurse. She is now disabled and can no longer work. Garcia's policy limits of 25/50 are not nearly enough to pay her bills, and her lawyer is taking Garcia to court. Garcia wishes that he had carried higher liability limits.

The following table shows typical premium rates for various amounts of liability coverage. Included in the cost of the liability insurance is **medical insurance** for the driver and passengers in case of injury. For example, the table column 15/30 shows that the insured can also receive reimbursement for up to $1000 of his or her own medical expenses in an accident. Insurance companies divide the nation into territories based on past claims in all areas. Four territories are shown here. All tables in this section show annual premiums.

Liability (Bodily Injury) and Medical Insurance (Per Year)

Territory	Liability and Medical Expense Limits				
	15/30 $1000	25/50 $2000	50/100 $3000	100/300 $5000	250/500 $10,000
1	$207	$222	$253	$282	$308
2	269	302	341	378	392
3	310	314	375	398	459
4	340	362	375	398	445

Finding the Liability and Medical Premium   **EXAMPLE 1**   Martha Spencer, owner of The Doll House, is in territory 2 and wants 100/300 liability coverage. Find the amount of the premium for this coverage and the amount of medical coverage included.

 CASE IN POINT

SOLUTION

Look up territory 2 and 100/300 coverage in the liability and medical insurance table to find an annual premium of $378 just for liability and medical coverage. This cost includes $5000 medical coverage.

QUICK CHECK 1

Find the annual cost, for a person living in territory 4, for 250/500 liability coverage with $10,000 in medical insurance.

OBJECTIVE 3 Define property damage insurance. Liability coverage pays if you injure someone. **Property damage coverage** pays if you damage someone else's property such as an automobile or a building. The following table shows the annual cost for various **policy limits** on property damage. You are responsible for damages above the policy limit.

Property Damage Insurance (Per Year)

Territory	Property Damage Limits			
	$10,000	$25,000	$50,000	$100,000
1	$88	$93	$97	$103
2	168	192	223	251
3	129	134	145	158
4	185	203	236	262

Finding the Premium for Property Damage

EXAMPLE 2

Find the annual premium if Martha Spencer, in territory 2, wants property damage coverage of $50,000.

▼ CASE IN POINT

SOLUTION

Property damage coverage of $50,000 in territory 2 requires a premium of $223.

> **QUICK CHECK 2**
>
> Find the premium for $100,000 in property damage coverage for a person living in territory 4.

OBJECTIVE 4 Describe comprehensive and collision insurance. Comprehensive insurance pays for damages to the insured's vehicle caused by a fire, by theft of the automobile, by vandalism (e.g., someone purposefully scratches off paint), by a tree falling onto the automobile, and by other similar events. In general, comprehensive insurance pays for damages that are not covered by collision insurance.

Collision insurance pays for repairs to the insured's vehicle when it is involved in a collision with another object.

You choose the **deductible** for both comprehensive and collision insurance when you purchase the insurance. Common deductibles for each coverage range anywhere from $200 to $2000. Higher deductibles result in a lower insurance premium. However, higher deductibles require you to pay more out of your pocket when the vehicle is damaged. So, be careful to choose a deductible that you can afford.

In the event of damages to your automobile, you pay the deductible and the insurance company pays the balance. For example, assume a tree falls on your car during a storm and that you have a $1000 deductible on your comprehension coverage. The amount that must be paid by the insured and the insurance company are shown.

Damages to your automobile	$3480
Deductible you must pay	−1000
Insurance company pays	**$2480**

Quick TIP

Lenders usually require owners to carry comprehensive and collision.

The table that follows shows typical rates for comprehensive and collision insurance, each with a $1000 deductible. The rates are determined by actuaries based on the territory in which you live, the age group of your vehicle, and the symbol based on the cost to repair your specific vehicle. Age group 1 is a vehicle that is less than 2 years of age. Age group 2 is a vehicle that is at least 2 but less than 3 years of age, and so on. Age group 6 is a vehicle 6 years of age or older.

Comprehensive and Collision Insurance (Per Year)

Territory	Age Group	Comprehensive ($1000 Deductible) Symbol			Collision ($1000 Deductible) Symbol		
		6	7	8	6	7	8
1	1	$58	$64	$90	$153	$165	$184
	2, 3	50	56	82	135	147	171
	4, 5	44	52	76	116	128	147
	6	34	44	64	92	110	128
2	1	$26	$28	$40	$89	$95	$104
	2, 3	40	52	68	80	86	98
	4, 5	20	24	34	71	77	86
	6	30	36	45	95	103	115
3	1	$70	$78	$108	$145	$157	$174
	2, 3	60	66	90	128	139	162
	4, 5	52	64	92	111	122	139
	6	48	59	63	110	132	157
4	1	$42	$46	$66	$97	$104	$124
	2, 3	36	40	58	87	94	107
	4, 5	32	38	54	77	84	94
	6	60	68	84	140	158	166

Finding the Comprehensive and Collision Premiums

 EXAMPLE 3

Martha Spencer, owner of The Doll House, is in territory 2 and has a 2-year-old minivan that has a symbol of 8. Use the comprehensive and collision insurance table to find the cost for (a) comprehensive coverage and (b) collision coverage.

▼ CASE IN POINT

SOLUTION

(a) The cost of comprehensive coverage is $68.

(b) The cost of collision coverage is $98.

> **QUICK CHECK 3**
>
> Find the premium for **(a)** comprehensive and **(b)** collision coverage for a 3-year-old vehicle in territory 4 and symbol 8.

OBJECTIVE 5 Define no-fault and uninsured motorist insurance. Some states have **no-fault** laws. Under no-fault insurance, all medical expenses and costs associated with an accident are paid to each individual by *his or her own insurance company*, no matter who is at fault. Legislators and insurance companies argue that no-fault insurance removes lawyers, courts, and juries from the process and results in quicker, less costly settlements. Others (including trial lawyers) argue that no-fault insurance leaves accident victims unable to recover all of their damages.

Most states do not have no-fault laws, thereby requiring the insurance company of the person at fault to pay for damages. A potential problem in these states is that the motorist who caused an accident either has no insurance at all or has too little insurance for the damages that occurred. **Uninsured motorist insurance** protects a vehicle owner from financial liability when hit by a driver with no insurance. **Underinsured motorist insurance** provides protection to a vehicle owner when hit by a driver who has *too little* insurance. Typical costs for uninsured motorist insurance are shown in the table at the left.

Uninsured Motorist Insurance (Per Year)

Territory	Basic Limit
1	$66
2	$44
3	$76
4	$70

Determining the Premium for Uninsured Motorist Coverage

 EXAMPLE 4

Martha Spencer, in territory 2, wants uninsured motorist coverage. Find the premium in the uninsured motorist insurance table.

▼ CASE IN POINT

SOLUTION

The premium for uninsured motorist coverage in territory 2 is $44.

> **QUICK CHECK 4**
>
> Find the annual cost of uninsured motorist coverage in territory 1.

OBJECTIVE 6 Apply youthful-operator factors. Sometimes young people think they are being charged *far too much* for automobile insurance. Insurance companies base their rates on probabilities calculated from statistical data. The graph on the next page shows that drivers under 25 are far more likely to be involved in a fatal automobile accident than drivers 25 or older. Since these younger drivers are riskier to cover, insurance companies charge higher rates for **youthful** compared to **adult** drivers. The age at which a youth becomes an adult varies from company to company. Generally, drivers under 25 are considered youthful drivers, and drivers 25 or older are considered adults.

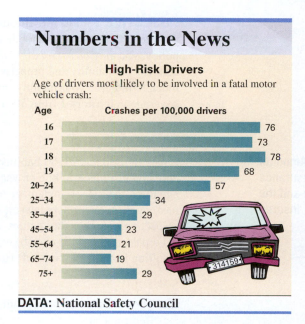

Numbers in the News

High-Risk Drivers

Age of drivers most likely to be involved in a fatal motor vehicle crash:

Age	Crashes per 100,000 drivers
16	76
17	73
18	78
19	68
20–24	57
25–34	34
35–44	29
45–54	23
55–64	21
65–74	19
75+	29

DATA: National Safety Council

The following table shows typical youthful-operator factors based on age and on whether or not the operator has taken driver's training. You can see that the factors are much higher for youthful operators who have not taken driver's training. The steps to apply these factors follow.

1. Determine the total premium for all coverages desired.
2. Multiply the total premium by the youthful-operator factor from the table.

Youthful-Operator Factor

Age	With Driver's Training	Without Driver's Training
20 or less	2.35	2.95
21–25	2.10	2.40

Using the Youthful-Operator Factor

EXAMPLE 5

Janet Ito lives in territory 4, is 22 years old, has had driver's training, and has had one speeding ticket, but was never in an accident. She drives a 5-year-old car with a symbol of 7. She wants a 25/50 liability policy, a $10,000 property damage policy, a comprehensive and collision policy, and uninsured motorist coverage. Find her annual insurance premium using the tables in this section.

SOLUTION

1. Determine the total premium for all coverages desired.

25/50 liability insurance	$362
$10,000 property damage	185
Comprehensive insurance	38
Collision	84
Uninsured motorist	+ 70
Subtotal	**$739**

2. Multiply the premium by the youthful-operator factor from the table.

$$\$739 \times 2.10 = \$1551.90$$

The calculator solution to this example uses parentheses and chain calculations.

(362 + 185 + 38 + 84 + 70) × 2.10 = 1551.9

QUICK CHECK 5

Scott Burch is 20, lives in territory 3, has not had driver's training, and drives a 3-year-old car with a symbol of 6. He wants the following coverages: 100/300 liability, $5000 medical, $50,000 property damage, uninsured motorist, and both comprehensive and collision insurance. Find the annual premium.

OBJECTIVE 7 Find the amounts paid by the insurance company and the insured. If you are at fault in an automobile accident and the damages *exceed the limits* on your insurance policy, you *may be personally liable* for the excess. You can help avoid this situation if you increase the liability and property damage limits on your policy. Sometimes, it does not cost much to increase your liability limits. For example, the additional cost of increasing liability coverage in territory 1 from 50/100 to 100/300 is only $29 per year ($282 − $253).

Finding the Amounts Paid by the Insurance Company and the Insured	**EXAMPLE 6**

James Benson has 25/50 liability limits, $25,000 property damage limits, and $500 deductible collision insurance. While on vacation, he was at fault in an accident that caused $5800 damage to his car, $3380 in damage to another car, and severe injuries to the other driver and his passenger. A subsequent lawsuit for injuries resulted in a judgment of $45,000 and $35,000, respectively, to the other parties. Find the amounts that the insurance company will pay for **(a)** repairing Benson's car, **(b)** repairing the other car, and **(c)** paying the court judgment resulting from the lawsuit. **(d)** How much will Benson have to pay the injured parties?

SOLUTION

(a) The insurance company will pay $4800 (**$5800 − $1000 deductible**) to repair Benson's car.

(b) Repairs on the other car will be paid to the property damage limits ($25,000). Here, the total repairs of $3380 are paid.

(c) Since more than one person was injured, the insurance company pays the limit of $50,000 ($25,000 to each of the two injured parties).

(d) Benson is liable for $30,000 (**$80,000 − $50,000**), the amount awarded over the insurance limits.

QUICK CHECK 6

Janet Yahn has the following coverages: 50/100 liability, $3000 medical, $25,000 property damage, and $500 deductible collision. She runs through a stop sign and hits a van with a value of $12,200. The van is destroyed and the cost to repair Yahn's car is $8600. The driver of the van had medical costs of $68,000 and Yahn had medical costs of $2800. Find each cost Yahn must pay.

▼13.4 Exercises

MyMathLab®

The shaded sections below contain solutions to help you get a **QUICK START** on the various types of exercises.

Find the annual premium for the following. (See Examples 1–5.)

Name	Territory	Age	Driver Training?	Liability	Property Damage	Comprehensive Collision Age Group	Symbol	Uninsured Motorist?	Annual Premium
1. Smyth	3	42	No	50/100	$25,000	2	7	Yes	$790
$375 + $134 + $66 + $139 + $76 = $790									
2. Thompson	4	20	Yes	25/50	$25,000	4	7	No	$1614.45
$362 + $203 + $38 + $84 = $687; $687 × 2.35 = $1614.45									
3. Shraim	3	52	No	250/500	$50,000	2	8	Yes	_____
4. Waldron	2	67	No	50/100	$100,000	1	6	Yes	_____
5. Applegate	4	35	No	100/300	$100,000	1	6	Yes	_____
6. Rodriguez	1	24	Yes	50/100	$50,000	3	8	Yes	_____

 indicates an exercise that is related to the Case in Point feature.

7. Describe four factors that determine the premium on an automobile insurance policy. (See Objective 1.)

8. Explain in your own words the difference between liability (bodily injury) and property damage. (See Objectives 2 and 3.)

Solve the following application problems.

9. ADULT AUTO INSURANCE   Bill Poole is 47 years old, lives in territory 4, and drives a 2-year-old car with a symbol of 7. He wants 250/500 liability limits, $100,000 property damage limits, comprehensive and collision insurance, and uninsured motorist coverage. Find his annual insurance premium.
$445 + $262 + $40 + $94 + $70 = $911

9. $911 _____

10. ADULT AUTO INSURANCE   Martha Spencer, owner of The Doll House, is thinking about moving from a house in territory 2 to a house in territory 3 and wants to know the effect on the insurance costs for her new car. She currently lives in territory 2 and the car has symbol 7. Her coverages are 250/500 for liability, $100,000 for property damage, comprehensive, collision, and uninsured motorist. She is 53 years old. Find the change in annual cost.

10. _____

11. YOUTHFUL-OPERATOR AUTO INSURANCE   Brandy Barrett is 23 years old, took a driver's education course, lives in territory 1, and drives a 4-year-old vehicle with a symbol of 6. She wants 50/100 liability limits, $25,000 property damage limits, comprehensive and collision insurance, and uninsured motorist coverage. Find her annual insurance premium.

11. _____

12. YOUTHFUL OPERATOR—NO DRIVER'S TRAINING   Karen Roberts' father gave her a new Honda Accord to use at college under the condition she pay her own insurance. She is 17, has not had driver's training, lives in territory 1, and her vehicle has a symbol of 6. She wants 50/100 liability limits, $25,000 property damage limits, comprehensive and collision insurance, and uninsured motorist coverage. Find her annual insurance premium.

12. _____

13. BODILY INJURY INSURANCE   Suppose your bodily injury policy has limits of 25/50 and you injure a person on a bicycle. The judge awards damages of $36,500 to the cyclist. **(a)** How much will the company pay? **(b)** How much will you pay?

(a) _____
(b) _____

14. BODILY INJURY INSURANCE   Martha Spencer, owner of The Doll House, lost control of her car while trying to find her smartphone and forced another driver off the road. The court awarded $28,000 to the driver of the other car and $8000 to a passenger of the other car. Spencer had limits of 15/30. **(a)** Find the amount the insurance company paid. **(b)** Find the amount Spencer had to pay.

(a) _____
(b) _____

15. **MEDICAL EXPENSES AND PROPERTY DAMAGE**   Wes Hanover accidentally backed into a parked car. He caused $4300 in damage to the car, and Hanover's passenger needed stitches in her forehead, which cost $850. Hanover had 15/30 liability limits, $1000 medical expense, and property damage of $10,000. Find the amount paid by the insurance company for **(a)** damages to the automobile and **(b)** medical expenses.

(a) _____

(b) _____

16. **MEDICAL EXPENSES AND PROPERTY DAMAGE**   Jessica Wallace backed into a new Mercedes and caused $12,800 in damage to the car. She also injured the vertebrae in her neck, requiring surgery costing $48,200. She had 50/100 liability limits, $10,000 in property damage, and $3000 in medical expense coverage. Find the amount paid by the insurance company for **(a)** damages to the automobile and **(b)** medical expenses.

(a) _____

(b) _____

17. **INSURANCE COMPANY PAYMENT**   A reckless driver caused Sandy Silva to collide with a car in another lane. Silva had 50/100 liability limits, $25,000 property damage limits, and collision coverage with a $100 deductible. Silva's car had damage of $1878, while the other car suffered $6936 in damages. The resulting lawsuit gave injury awards of $60,000 and $55,000, respectively, in damages for personal injury to the two people in the other car. Find the amount that the insurance company will pay for **(a)** repairing Silva's car, **(b)** repairing the other car, and **(c)** personal injury damages. **(d)** How much must Silva pay beyond her insurance coverage, including the collision deductible?

(a) _____

(b) _____

(c) _____

(d) _____

18. **INSURANCE PAYMENT**   Bob Armstrong lost control of his car and crashed into another car. He had 15/30 liability limits, $10,000 property damage limits, and collision coverage with a $100 deductible. Damage to Armstrong's car was $2980; the other car, with a value of $22,800, was totaled. The results of a lawsuit awarded $75,000 and $45,000, respectively, in damages for personal injury to the two people in the other car. Find the amount that the insurance company will pay for **(a)** repairing Armstrong's car, **(b)** repairing the other car, and **(c)** personal injury damages. **(d)** How much must Armstrong pay beyond his insurance coverage?

(a) _____

(b) _____

(c) _____

(d) _____

19. Explain why insurance companies charge a higher premium for auto insurance sold to a youthful operator. Do you think this is fair? (See Objective 6.)

20. Property damage pays for damage caused by you to the property of others. Since the average cost of a new car today is over $20,000, what amount of property damage coverage would you recommend to a friend who owns her own business?

QUICK CHECK ANSWERS

1. $445

2. $262

3. (a) $58   (b) $107

4. $66

5. $2380.65

6. $500 to repair her own car; $18,000 for medical expenses of other driver

▼13.5 Life Insurance

OBJECTIVES

1 Understand life insurance that does not accumulate cash value.

2 Understand life insurance that accumulates cash value.

3 Find the annual premium for life insurance.

4 Use premium factors with different modes of premium payment.

▼ CASE IN POINT   Martha Spencer owns the Doll House. Recently divorced, she worries about her two children should she become ill, disabled, or die. As a result, she carries medical insurance, disability insurance, and $250,000 in life insurance.

There is no doubt about it: Insurance is expensive! Yet, most of us need insurance (car, home, medical, disability, and life insurance). The graph on the left below shows that about one out of every five adults have found themselves in a situation where they wished they had more insurance. The figure on the right illustrates that many adults have some insurance through an employer.

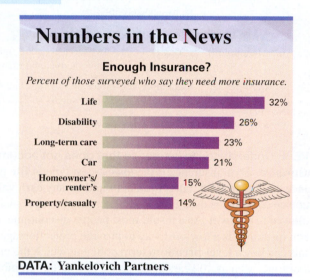

Numbers in the News

Enough Insurance?

Percent of those surveyed who say they need more insurance.

Life	32%
Disability	26%
Long-term care	23%
Car	21%
Homeowner's/renter's	15%
Property/casualty	14%

DATA: Yankelovich Partners

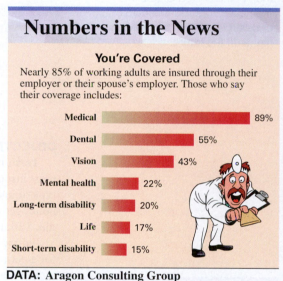

Numbers in the News

You're Covered

Nearly 85% of working adults are insured through their employer or their spouse's employer. Those who say their coverage includes:

Medical	89%
Dental	55%
Vision	43%
Mental health	22%
Long-term disability	20%
Life	17%
Short-term disability	15%

DATA: Aragon Consulting Group

People buy **life insurance** to pay for their own burial expenses, to pay off a home mortgage or a car loan, to provide for a spouse and/or children, or to pay for their children's future college expenses. Some forms of life insurance build up a cash retirement value; other forms do not. Life insurance can also be important for the owner(s) of a business. Upon the death of the business owner, life insurance proceeds can provide a company with enough money to continue until it can be sold. Alternatively, life insurance proceeds can be used by one partner of a firm to buy out the ownership interest of a deceased partner.

Quick TIP

Proceeds from a life insurance policy are generally free of income taxes.

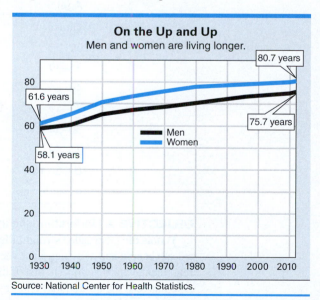

On the Up and Up

Men and women are living longer.

80.7 years

61.6 years

58.1 years

75.7 years

— Men
— Women

Source: National Center for Health Statistics.

In general, insurance rates have decreased markedly over the past 30 years for two reasons: People are living longer, as shown in the graph, and costs have fallen due to increasing competition. The increase in competition is partly a result of sales of insurance over the Internet, which lowers costs and increases the availability of information about prices. Competition often, but not always, results in reduced prices to consumers.

The following table shows the most common causes of death in the United States and includes suggestions to reduce the risk of death by each. Notice that our health risks can be reduced by doing just a few things: quit smoking, lose weight, exercise more, eat more vegetables, eat less red meat and sugar (e.g., candy and soda), and reduce salt intake. That's it! Act on these things and you will probably live longer and have a healthier, more active life.

Most Common Causes of Death

Cause	To Reduce Risk:
1. Heart disease	Quit smoking, lose weight, eat more fish and less red meat, increase physical activity
2. Cancer	Eat more vegetables, fruit, and fish
3. Stroke	Quit smoking, increase physical activity
4. Lung disease	Quit smoking, reduce salt in diet, increase physical activity
5. Accidents	Do not drink and drive
6. Alzheimer's	May be helped by exercise, eating right, staying mentally and socially active, and managing stress.
7. Diabetes	Eat more vegetables, lose weight, increase physical activity, avoid simple sugars such as candy

Source: National Institute of Health Statistics, 2010.

Quick TIP

Scientists predict that diabetes will become much more common in the United States in the near future. So this cause of death is likely to be ranked higher in the future.

OBJECTIVE 1 Understand life insurance that does not accumulate cash value.

Term insurance. Term insurance is the lowest-cost type of life insurance. It provides the most insurance per dollar spent, but it does not build up any cash values for retirement. This type of insurance coverage is usually renewable until some age, such as 70, when the insured is no longer allowed to renew it. As a result, most people discontinue term insurance before they die. Still, term insurance is a low-cost way to provide protection against an early death.

Individuals can buy a **level-premium** term policy in which the premium remains constant for a period of time, such as 10 years or 20 years. Thereafter, premiums increase rapidly.

Decreasing term insurance. This is a type of term insurance with fixed premiums commonly to age 60 or 65, but the amount of life insurance decreases periodically. An example of this is a mortgage insurance policy on a home. The amount of life insurance on the owner decreases as the amount owed to the mortgage company decreases. Many large companies provide decreasing term insurance to employees as a benefit. The table provides an example of the benefits of one particular decreasing term policy.

Quick TIP

Mortgage insurance is usually much more expensive than a regular term insurance policy. Compare prices before you buy.

Example of Death Benefits for a Decreasing Term Policy with a Premium of $11 per Month

Age	Amount of Life Insurance
Under 29	$160,000
30–34	$140,000
35–39	$120,000
40–44	$100,000
45–49	$72,000
50–54	$44,000
55–59	$28,000
60–66	$16,000
67 and over	$0

OBJECTIVE 2 Understand life insurance that accumulates cash value.

Whole life (also called **straight life, ordinary life,** or **permanent**). This type of insurance provides a death benefit and a savings plan. The insured commonly pays a constant premium until death or retirement, whichever occurs first. If the policy is in force at the time of death, a death benefit is paid. Alternatively, the insured may choose to convert the accumulated **cash value** to a retirement benefit.

Universal life. This type of insurance provides the life insurance protection of term insurance plus a tax-deferred way to accumulate assets. It sometimes allows people to establish a permanent policy at a lower premium than they would have to pay under a whole life policy, and it gives the insured more flexibility. For example, universal life can help a family obtain more insurance when young children are at home and then help accumulate savings later after the children are grown. Different investment options may be available for the portion of the premium going into retirement benefits, but the options are often limited.

Variable life. This type of insurance allows the policyholder to make choices among several investment options. It places the investment risk on the policyholder by allowing the insured to invest in any of the following: money market funds, bond funds, stock funds, or a combination of the three.

Limited-payment life insurance. Limited-payment life is similar to whole life insurance, except that premiums are paid for only a fixed number of years, such as 20. This type of insurance is thus often called 20-pay life, representing payments for 20 years. The premium for limited-payment life is higher than that for whole life policies. Limited-payment life is most appropriate for athletes, actors, and others whose income is likely to be high for several years and then decline.

Endowment policies are the most expensive type of policy since they accumulate cash more rapidly than the other types of life insurance. These policies guarantee payment of a fixed amount of money to a given individual, whether or not the insured lives. Endowment policies might be taken out by parents to guarantee a sum of money for their children's college education. Because of the high premiums, this is one of the least popular types of policies today.

OBJECTIVE 3 Find the annual premium for life insurance. Calculation of life insurance rates by actuaries is based on statistical data involving death rates, interest rates, and other factors. Women tend to live a few years longer than men, so a woman pays a lower life insurance premium than a man of the same age. Incidentally, women are more likely to be disabled than men and therefore have higher disability insurance rates than men. Use the actual age of a man to find the premium factor in the table below. However, subtract 5 from the age of a woman before finding the premium factor in the table. Remember, life insurance costs differ significantly from company to company. As always, it pays to be a knowledgeable consumer and shop for the best deal.

Annual Premium Rates* Per $1000 of Life Insurance

Age	10-Year Level Premium Term	Whole Life	Universal Life	20-Pay Life
20	1.60	4.07	3.48	12.30
21	1.65	4.26	3.85	12.95
22	1.69	4.37	4.10	13.72
23	1.73	4.45	4.56	14.28
24	1.78	4.68	4.80	15.95
25	1.82	5.06	5.11	16.60
30	1.89	5.66	6.08	18.78
35	2.01	7.68	7.45	21.60
40	2.56	12.67	10.62	24.26
45	3.45	19.86	15.24	28.16
50	5.63	26.23	21.46	32.59
55	8.12	31.75	28.38	38.63
60	14.08	38.42	36.72	45.74

*For women, subtract 5 years from the actual age. For example, rates for a 30-year-old woman are shown for age 25 in the table.

Finding Annual Premium

Annual premium = Number of thousands × Rate per $1000

Finding the Life Insurance Premium

EXAMPLE 1

Martha Spencer became the primary source of income for her family at age 35 after her divorce. At that time, she decided that she needed $250,000 in life insurance to pay off the mortgage on her home, to repay some loans at her business, and to provide for her children. Find her annual premium for **(a)** a 10-year level premium term policy, **(b)** a whole life policy, **(c)** a universal life policy, and **(d)** a 20-pay life plan.

 CASE IN POINT

SOLUTION

First, divide the desired amount of life insurance by $1000 to find the number of thousands.

$$\$250,000 \div \$1000 = 250 \text{ thousands}$$

Quick TIP
Limited-payment and endowment policies cost more, but they accumulate more money for use later in life.

Quick TIP
Individuals with health problems must pay substantially more for life insurance than healthy individuals. Other factors that increase life insurance premiums include smoking and even some hobbies such as scuba diving or bungee jumping.

Quick TIP

Use the actual age of a man when using the table of premiums. However, subtract 5 from the age of a woman before using the table.

Since Spencer is a woman, subtract 5 from her actual age before using the table ($35 - 5 = 30$). Look in the table at age 30 for the rates for each type of insurance.

		Annual Premium
(a) 10-year level premium term	$250 \times$ **1.89**	$= \$472.50$
(b) Whole life	$250 \times$ **5.66**	$= \$1415$
(c) Universal life	$250 \times$ **6.08**	$= \$1520$
(d) 20-pay life	$250 \times$ **18.78**	$= \$4695$

Spencer wanted to buy universal life because of the savings feature, which would help her save for retirement. However, she purchased the level premium term instead, since her income was limited and the level term policy was much cheaper.

QUICK CHECK 1

James Liberty is 50 and wants to buy $300,000 in life insurance. Find the annual cost for **(a)** 10-year level premium term, **(b)** whole life, **(c)** universal life, and **(d)** 20-pay life.

OBJECTIVE 4 Use premium factors with different modes of premium payment. Many companies give the insured the option of paying the premium semiannually, quarterly, or monthly. For this convenience, the policyholder *pays an additional amount* that is determined by a **premium factor**. The following table shows typical premium factors.

Premium Factors	
Mode of Payment	**Premium Factor**
Semiannually	.51
Quarterly	.26
Monthly	.0908

Using a Premium Factor The annual insurance premium on a $200,000 10-year level premium term life policy for Jane Rodriguez is $378. Use the premium factors table to find the amount of premium and the total annual cost if she pays **(a)** semiannually, **(b)** quarterly, or **(c)** monthly.

SOLUTION

	Premium		Annual Cost
(a) Semiannually:	$\$378 \times$ **.51** $= \$192.78$		$\$192.78 \times$ **2 payments/year** $= \$385.56$
(b) Quarterly:	$\$378 \times$ **.26** $= \$98.28$		$\$98.28 \times$ **4 payments/year** $= \$393.12$
(c) Monthly:	$\$378 \times$ **.0908** $= \$34.32$		$\$34.32 \times$ **12 payments/year** $= \$411.84$

QUICK CHECK 2

The annual premium on a life insurance policy is $470. Find the premium if payments are made **(a)** semiannually, **(b)** quarterly, and **(c)** monthly.

Pricing Life Insurance Shauna Jones has decided to buy $100,000 in life insurance to make sure that her kids will have funds if something happens to her. Jones is 28 and in good health. Find the monthly premium for **(a)** 10-year level premium term and **(b)** universal life.

SOLUTION

(a) 10-year level premium term:

premium factor for monthly payment

$$\text{Monthly premium} = (\$100 \times 1.73) \times .0908 = \mathbf{\$15.71} \quad \textbf{(rounded)}$$

(b) Universal life:

premium factor for monthly payment

$$\text{Monthly premium} = (\$100 \times 4.56) \times .0908 = \mathbf{\$41.40} \quad \textbf{(rounded)}$$

QUICK CHECK 3

Darryl Foster is 40 years old and wants to buy $400,000 of whole life insurance. Find the quarterly premium.

▼13.5 Exercises

MyMathLab®

*The shaded sections below contain solutions to help you get a **QUICK START** on the various types of exercises.*

Find the annual premium, the semiannual premium, the quarterly premium, and the monthly premium for each of the following. (Note: Subtract 5 years for women.) Round to the nearest cent.

	Face Value of Policy	Age of Insured	Sex of Insured	Type of Policy	Annual Premium	Semi-annual Premium	Quarterly Premium	Monthly Premium
1.	$100,000	45	F	Term	$256	$130.56	$66.56	$23.24
	$100 \times \$2.56 = \$256$; $\$256 \times .51 = \$130.56$; $\$256 \times .26 = \$66.56$; $\$256 \times .0908 = \$23.24$							
2.	$60,000	30	M	Whole life	$339.60	$173.20	$88.30	$30.84
	$60 \times \$5.66 = \$339.60$; $\$339.60 \times .51 = \$173.20$; $\$339.60 \times .26 = \$88.30$; $\$339.60 \times .0908 = \$30.84$							
3.	$35,000	40	M	20-pay life				
4.	$60,000	50	F	20-pay life				
5.	$85,000	30	M	Universal life				
6.	$150,000	60	M	Term				
7.	$75,000	21	M	Whole life				
8.	$80,000	35	F	Term				
9.	$65,000	60	M	20-pay life				
10.	$50,000	45	F	Universal life				

11. Compare level premium term insurance to universal life insurance. Which would you prefer for yourself? Why? (See Objectives 1 and 2.)

12. Describe premium factors and how they are used. How often do you prefer paying an insurance premium: annually, semiannually, quarterly, or monthly? (See Objective 4.)

🔺 indicates an exercise that is related to the Case in Point feature.

Solve the following application problems.

13. **LIFE INSURANCE**   Bill Able married on his 25th birthday. He adopted the child his wife had from a previous marriage and wanted to care for the child as his own. To protect his new family against the loss of income in the event of his death, he purchased $200,000 in 10-year level premium term. Find the annual cost.

$200,000 \div $1000 = 200$

$200 \times $1.82 = 364

13. <u>$364</u>

14. **WHOLE LIFE INSURANCE**   Jessica Smith buys a whole life policy with a face value of $100,000 at age 35. Find the annual premium.

14. _____

🔺 15. **KEY EMPLOYEE INSURANCE**   Martha Spencer owns the Doll House and has a 35-year-old key male employee whom she wants to insure for $50,000. Find the annual premium **(a)** for 10-year level term and **(b)** for whole life.

(a) _____
(b) _____

16. **20-PAY LIFE POLICY**   Luan Lee buys a $100,000, 20-pay life policy at age 45. Her son Bryan is the beneficiary and will collect the face value of the policy. **(a)** Find the annual premium. **(b)** How much will Bryan get if his mother dies after making payments for 12 years?

(a) _____
(b) _____

17. **WHOLE LIFE**   Rebecca Martinez is 35 and needs $100,000 in coverage. She opts for a whole life policy since it will also accumulate cash and force her to save. Find the annual premium and the total premiums paid if she keeps the policy to age 65.

17. _____

18. **UNIVERSAL LIFE INSURANCE**   Richard Gonsalves takes out a universal life policy with a face value of $50,000. He is 40 years old. Find the monthly premium.

18. _____

19. **PREMIUM FACTORS**   The annual premium for a whole life policy is $872. Using premium factors, find **(a)** the semiannual premium, **(b)** the quarterly premium, and **(c)** the monthly premium.

(a) _____
(b) _____
(c) _____

20. **PREMIUM FACTORS**   A universal life policy has an annual premium of $2012. Use premium factors to find **(a)** the semiannual premium, **(b)** the quarterly premium, and **(c)** the monthly premium.

(a) _____
(b) _____
(c) _____

QUICK CHECK ANSWERS

1. (a) $1689   (b) $7869   (c) $6438   3. $1317.68
   (d) $9777
2. (a) $239.70   (b) $122.20   (c) $42.68

▼ Chapter 13   Quick Review

Chapter Terms   *Review the following terms to test your understanding of the chapter. For each term you do not know, refer to the page number found next to that term.*

1099 forms [**p. 528**]
actuaries [**p. 551**]
adjusted gross income [**p. 528**]
assessed value [**p. 521**]
assessment rate [**p. 521**]
bodily injury coverage [**p. 551**]
cash value [**p. 560**]
casualty or theft losses
   [**p. 532**]
catastrophic event [**p. 541**]
coinsurance clause [**p. 543**]
collision insurance [**p. 553**]
comprehensive insurance
   [**p. 553**]
coverage [**p. 542**]
decreasing term insurance
   [**p. 560**]
deductible [**p. 553**]
dependent [**p. 530**]
disability insurance [**p. 546**]
dollars per $100 [**p. 522**]
dollars per $1000 [**p. 522**]
endowment policies [**p. 561**]

face value [**p. 542**]
fair market value [**p. 521**]
Form 1040A [**p. 534**]
gifts to charity [**p. 532**]
head of household [**p. 530**]
homeowner's policy [**p. 542**]
income tax [**p. 527**]
individual retirement account
   (IRA) [**p. 528**]
insurance [**p. 520**]
insurance policy [**p. 542**]
Internal Revenue Service
   [**p. 527**]
IRS [**p. 527**]
itemized deductions [**p. 532**]
level-premium term insurance
   [**p. 560**]
liability insurance [**p. 546**]
life insurance [**p. 559**]
limited-payment life insurance
   [**p. 561**]
long-term care insurance
   [**p. 546**]

medical and dental expenses
   [**p. 532**]
medical insurance [**p. 546**]
mills [**p. 523**]
miscellaneous deductions
   [**p. 532**]
multiple carriers [**p. 544**]
no-fault insurance [**p. 554**]
ordinary life insurance [**p. 560**]
permanent life insurance
   [**p. 560**]
personal exemptions [**p. 530**]
policy [**p. 542**]
policy limits [**p. 552**]
premium [**p. 551**]
premium factor [**p. 562**]
property damage insurance
   [**p. 552**]
property-tax rate [**p. 522**]
renter's insurance [**p. 546**]
replacement cost [**p. 543**]
Schedule 1 (Form 1040A)
   [**p. 534**]

standard deduction [**p. 530**]
straight life insurance [**p. 560**]
tax deduction [**p. 532**]
tax preparation [**p. 532**]
taxable income [**p. 530**]
taxes [**p. 532**]
term insurance [**p. 560**]
territorial ratings [**p. 542**]
underinsured motorist insurance
   [**p. 554**]
underwriters [**p. 542**]
uninsured motorist insurance
   [**p. 554**]
universal life policy [**p. 560**]
unreimbursed job expenses
   [**p. 532**]
variable life policy [**p. 561**]
W-2 forms [**p. 528**]
whole life insurance [**p. 560**]
worker's compensation [**p. 546**]
youthful operator [**p. 554**]

CONCEPTS

EXAMPLES

13.1 Fair market value and assessed value

The value of property is multiplied by a given percent to arrive at the assessed value.

Assessed value = **Assessment rate** × Market value

The assessment rate is 30%; fair market value is $115,000; find the assessed value.

$$\text{30\%} \times \$115{,}000 = \$34{,}500$$

13.1 Tax rate

The tax rate formula is

$$\text{Tax rate} = \frac{\text{Total tax amount needed}}{\textbf{Total assessed value}}$$

Tax amount needed: $3,864,400; total assessed value: $946,320,000; find the tax rate.

$$\frac{\$3{,}864{,}400}{\$946{,}320{,}000} = .00408 = .41\% \quad \text{(rounded)}$$

13.1 Tax rates in different forms

1. **Percent**: multiply by assessed value.
2. **Dollars per $100**: move decimal point 2 places to the left in assessed value and multiply.
3. **Dollars per $1000**: move decimal point 3 places to the left in assessed value and multiply.
4. **Mills**: move decimal point 3 places to the left in rate and multiply by assessed value.

Use the formula

Property tax = Assessed value × **Tax rate**

Assessed value, $90,000; tax rate, 2.5%:
$$\$90{,}000 \times \textbf{2.5\%} = \$2250$$

Tax rate, **$2.50** per $100:
$$900 \times \textbf{\$2.50} = \$2250$$

Tax rate, **$25** per $1000:
$$90 \times \textbf{\$25} = \$2250$$

Tax rate, **25 mills**:
$$\$90{,}000 \times \textbf{.025} = \$2250$$

CONCEPTS	EXAMPLES
13.2 Adjusted gross income Adjusted gross income includes wages, salaries, tips, dividends, and interest. Subtract IRA contributions and alimony.	Salary, $32,540; interest income, $875; dividends, $315; find adjusted gross income. $$\$32{,}540 + \$875 + \$315 = \$33{,}730$$
13.2 Standard deduction amounts The majority of taxpayers use the standard deduction allowed by the IRS.	$5800 for single taxpayers $11,600 for married taxpayers filing jointly or qualifying widow(er) $5800 for married taxpayers filing separately $8500 for head of household
13.2 Taxable income The larger of either the total of itemized deductions or the standard deduction is subtracted from adjusted gross income along with **$3700** for each personal exemption.	Single taxpayer, adjusted gross income, $38,500; itemized deductions, $3850; find taxable income. Note that itemized deductions are less than the standard deduction of $5800 and the personal exemption is **$3700**. $$\text{Taxable income} = \$38{,}500 - \$5800 - \$3700$$ $$= \$29{,}000$$
13.2 Tax rates There are six tax rates: 10%, 15%, 25%, 28%, 33%, and 35%.	Single: 10%; 15% over $8500; 25% over $34,500; 28% over $83,600; 33% over $174,400; 35% over $379,150 Married filing jointly: 10%; 15% over $17,000; 25% over $69,000; 28% over $139,350; 33% over $212,300; 35% over $379,150 Married filing separately: 10%; 15% over $8500; 25% over $34,500; 28% over $69,675; 33% over $106,150; 35% over $189,575 Head of household: 10%; 15% over $12,150; 25% over $46,250; 28% over $119,400; 33% over $193,350; 35% over $379,150
13.2 Balance due or a refund from the IRS If the total amount withheld by employers is greater than the tax owed, a refund results. If the tax owed is the greater amount, a balance is due.	Tax owed, $1253; tax withheld, $113 per month for 12 months. Find balance due or refund. $$\$113 \text{ withheld} \times 12 = \$1356 \text{ withheld}$$ $$\$1356 \text{ withheld} - \$1253 \text{ owed} = \$103 \text{ refund}$$
13.3 Annual premium for fire insurance The building and territorial ratings are used to find the premiums per $100 for the building and contents. The two are added.	Building value, $180,000; contents, $35,000. Premiums are: building, $.75 per $100; contents, $.77 per $100. Find the annual premium. $$\text{Building: } 1800 \text{ (hundreds)} \times \$.75 = \$1350$$ $$\text{Contents: } 350 \text{ (hundreds)} \times \$.77 = \$269.50$$ $$\text{Total premium: } \$1350 + \$269.50 = \$1619.50$$
13.3 Coinsurance formula Part of the risk of fire is taken by the insured. An 80% coinsurance clause is common. $$\begin{array}{l}\text{Loss paid by}\\\text{insurance}\\\text{company}\end{array} = \begin{array}{c}\text{Amount}\\\text{of loss}\end{array} \times \dfrac{\text{Policy amount}}{\textbf{80\% of replacement cost}}$$	Replacement cost, $250,000; policy amount, $150,000; fire loss, $40,000; 80% coinsurance clause; find the amount of loss paid by insurance company. The face value ($150,000) is less than 80% of the replacement cost ($200,000). $$\$40{,}000 \times \frac{\$150{,}000}{\$200{,}000} = \$30{,}000 \begin{pmatrix}\text{amount insurance}\\\text{company pays}\end{pmatrix}$$

CONCEPTS

EXAMPLES

13.3 Multiple carriers

Several companies insure the same property, which limits the risk of the insurance company, with each paying its fractional portion of any claim.

Insured loss, $500,000

Insurance is Company A with $1,000,000; Company B with $750,000; Company C with $250,000; find the amount of loss paid by each company.

Total insurance:

$$\$1,000,000 + \$750,000 + \$250,000 = \$2,000,000$$

Company A:

$$\frac{1,000,000}{2,000,000} \times \$500,000 = \$250,000$$

Company B:

$$\frac{750,000}{2,000,000} \times \$500,000 = \$187,500$$

Company C:

$$\frac{250,000}{2,000,000} \times \$500,000 = \$62,500$$

13.4 Annual auto insurance premium

Most drivers are required to purchase automobile insurance. The premium is determined by the types of coverage selected, the type of car, geographic territory, past driving record, and other factors.

Determine the premium: territory, 2; liability, 50/100; property damage, $50,000; comprehensive and collision, 3-year-old car with a symbol of 8; uninsured motorist coverage; driver is age 23 with driver's training.

$341	liability
$223	property damage
68	comprehensive
98	collision
44	uninsured motorist
$774 × 2.10	youthful-operator factor
= $1625.40	

13.5 Annual life insurance premium

There are several types of life policies. Use the table and multiply by the number of $1000s of coverage. Subtract 5 years from the age of women.

Premium = Number of thousands × **Rate per $1000**

Find the annual premiums on a $50,000 policy for a 30-year-old man.

(a) 10-year level premium term: 50 × **$1.89** = $94.50

(b) Whole life: 50 × **$5.66** = $283

(c) Universal life: 50 × **$6.08** = $304

(d) 20-pay life: 50 × **$18.78** = $939

13.5 Premium factors

Life insurance premiums may be paid semiannually, quarterly, or monthly. The annual premium is multiplied by the premium factor to determine the premium amount.

The annual life insurance premium is $740. Use the table to find the **(a)** semiannual, **(b)** quarterly, and **(c)** monthly premiums.

(a) Semiannual: $740 × **.51** = $377.40

(b) Quarterly: $740 × **.26** = $192.40

(c) Monthly: $740 × **.0908** = $67.19

▼ Case **Study**

FINANCIAL PLANNING FOR PROPERTY TAXES AND INSURANCE

Baker's Pottery manufactures and sells ceramic pots of all types, shapes, and styles. Planning ahead, the company set aside $53,500 to pay property taxes, fire insurance premiums, and life insurance premiums on the company president. All of these premiums happen to be due in the same month. Find each of the following.

1. The company property has a fair market value of $1,990,000 and is assessed at 75% of this value. If the tax rate is $7.90 per $1000 of assessed value, find the annual property tax.

1. _____

2. The building occupied by the company is a class-B building with a replacement cost of $1,730,000. The contents are worth $3,502,000 and the territorial rating is 4. Find the annual fire insurance premium.

2. _____

3. The president of the company is a 50-year-old woman who lost the use of her legs in an automobile accident. She needs life insurance and the company buys a $250,000, 10-year level premium life insurance policy on her. Find the semiannual premium.

3. _____

4. Find the total amount needed to pay property taxes, the fire insurance premium, and the semiannual life insurance premium.

4. _____

5. How much more than the amount needed had the company set aside to pay these expenses?

5. _____

INVESTIGATE

A recent article in *Consumer Reports* listed the top Web sites that offer to help a person shop for term life insurance. Use the Web to find information and prices for term life insurance to meet your personal life insurance needs and look at several types of life insurance products.

▼ Case in Point Summary Exercise

MATTEL INC. — TAXES AND INSURANCE

www.mattel.com

Facts:

- 1945: Founded by Elliot and Ruth Handler
- 1959: Barbie introduced
- 2004: More than one billion Barbies sold
- 2011: Sales over $5 billion

Antique dolls representing adults from the 17th and 18th centuries have been found, but they are very rare. Individual craftsmen in England made most of these earliest dolls. The craftsmen carved the dolls of wood, painted their features, and also designed the costumes for the dolls. Some of these earliest dolls are valued at more than $40,000.

The Barbie doll is the most popular fashion doll ever created. If all the Barbie dolls that have been sold since 1959 were placed head-to-toe, the dolls would circle the earth more than seven times. The most popular Barbie ever sold was the Totally Hair Barbie, which was introduced in 1992. With hair from the top of her head to her toes, more than 10 million of these dolls were sold, resulting in revenue of $100 million. With annual retail sales at an estimated $3.6 billion, Barbie is the #1 brand of doll for girls.

Martha Spencer started The Doll House and sells dolls around the world through her Web site. Her business has grown over the years, but she still carefully watches costs. She knows that she must control costs to be successful. Help her figure out some of these costs.

1. Spencer is looking at a building that she hopes to buy for what she believes is the fair market value of $310,000. However, the replacement cost is estimated to be $420,000. The assessment rate is 30% and the tax rate is $64 per $1000 of assessed value. Find the property tax for the year.

1. _____

2. Janet Chino, one of Spencer's employees, needs help estimating her income tax based on the following: wages—$28,410; interest—$212; ordinary dividends—$84; and IRA contribution—$500. Find the following: total income, adjusted gross income, taxable income, and income tax given that Chino is single and claims only 1 exemption. Use the tax rate schedules.

2. _____

3. Find the cost of fire insurance if the building in Question 1 is in territory 5 and has a building classification of C. The contents are valued at $145,000.

3. _____

4. Spencer purchases a new Toyota and buys 250/500 liability limits, $100,000 property damage, comprehensive, collision, and uninsured motorist. She is in territory 2 and the vehicle has symbol 8. Find the annual premium given that she is 35.

4. _____

5. Spencer is a 35-year old woman who is divorced and has two children. She decides to purchase $500,000 of life insurance to protect her children. Find the annual cost of 10-year level term.

5. _____

6. Find the total of all of the costs that Martha Spencer must pay. This total is only a small part of her total costs each year—clearly she has to sell a lot of dolls to pay her bills.

6. _____

Discussion Question: Is it important to pay taxes and also to buy insurance? Explain. What should happen to those who do not pay taxes? What should happen to those who do not buy required minimum amounts of insurance?

▼ Chapter 13 Test

To help you review, the numbers in brackets show the section in which the topic was discussed.

Find the following property tax rates. **[13.1]**

	Percent	Per $100	Per $1000
1.	5.76%	_____	_____
2.	_____	_____	$93.50

Find the taxable income and the tax for each of the following people. The letter following the names indicates the marital status. Assume those married file jointly. **[13.2]**

Name	Number of Exemptions	Adjusted Gross Income	Total Deductions	Taxable Income	Tax
3. J. Spalding, S	2	$68,295	$5380	_____	_____
4. The Bensons, M	4	$43,487	$8315	_____	_____

Find the tax owed in the following problems.

5. Bradkin's Toggery owns property with a fair market value of $209,200. Property in the area is assessed at 30% of fair market value with a tax rate of 3.65%. Find the annual tax. **[13.1]**

5. _____

6. The Blakely family has an adjusted gross income of $98,316. They are married and file jointly with five exemptions and deductions of $8420. **[13.2]**

6. _____

7. Kari Heen had an adjusted gross income of $44,600 last year. She had deductions of $1280 for state income tax, $3620 for property tax, $3540 in mortgage interest, and $1450 in contributions. Heen claims one exemption and files as a single person. **[13.2]**

7. _____

Find the annual fire insurance premium for the following. Use the table on page 543. **[13.3]**

8. Southside Plating owns a class-B building with a replacement cost of $780,000. Contents are valued at $128,600. The territorial rating is 5.

8. _____

9. A fourplex is valued at $220,000. The fire insurance policy (with an 80% coinsurance clause) has a face value of $150,000. If the building has a fire loss of $50,000, find the amount of the loss that the insurance company will pay.

9. _____

10. Dave's Body and Paint has an insurable loss of $72,000, while having insurance coverage beyond coinsurance requirements. The insurance is divided among Company A with $250,000 coverage, Company B with $150,000 coverage, and Company C with $100,000 coverage. Find the amount of the loss paid by each of the insurance companies.

A: _____
B: _____
C: _____

Find the annual motor-vehicle insurance premium for the following people.   **[13.4]**

Name	Territory	Age	Driver Training?	Liability	Property Damage	Comprehensive Collision Age Group	Symbol	Uninsured Motorist?	Annual Premium
11. Ramos	3	18	Yes	15/30	$10,000	5	7	Yes	_____
12. Larik	1	42	No	50/100	$100,000	1	8	Yes	_____

Find the annual premium, the semiannual premium, the quarterly premium, and the monthly premium for each of the following life insurance policies. Use the tables in Section 13.5.   **[13.5]**

	Annual	Semiannual	Quarterly	Monthly
13. Irene Chong, whole life, $28,000 face value, age 35, female	_____	_____	_____	_____
14. Gil Eckern, 20-pay life, $80,000 face value, age 40, male	_____	_____	_____	_____

Solve the following.

15. Betsy Monikens (age 28) and Jim Faber (age 30) recently married and need to buy both car and life insurance. They have one car, 4 years old, with symbol 7 and live in territory 2. Auto: 50/100 liability with $3000 in medical expense limits, $25,000 in property damage, comprehensive, $1000 deductible collision, and uninsured motorist. Life: $100,000 10-year level term on Jim and $50,000 universal life on Betsy. Find the annual cost of **(a)** the auto insurance and **(b)** the life insurance.   **[13.4 and 13.5]**

(a) _____

(b) _____

16. Jessie Hernandez's truck spun out of control on an icy road, causing an accident with another driver. Damages to his truck were $6400, damages to the other driver's vehicle were $8200, and the other driver had medical expenses of $12,900. Hernandez was not hurt and his policy showed that he had liability limits of 15/30, medical expenses of $1000, property damage of $10,000, no comprehensive or collision, and no uninsured motorist. Identify each of the costs he must pay.   **[13.4]**

16. _____

14 Depreciation

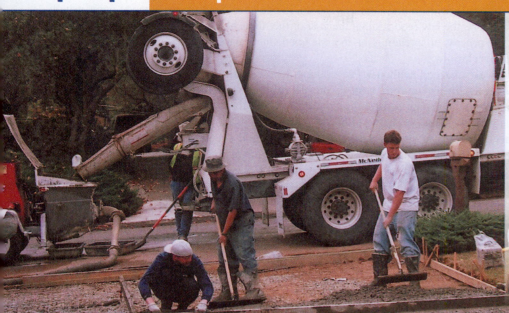

CHAPTER CONTENTS

14.1 Straight-Line Method

14.2 Declining-Balance Method

14.3 Sum-of-the-Years'-Digits Method

14.4 Units-of-Production Method

14.5 Modified Accelerated Cost Recovery System

▼ CASE IN POINT

CAPITAL CURB AND CONCRETE is owned and managed by John Goodby. The company does concrete work for building contractors and for the owners of new and existing residential and commercial properties. The company builds curbs and sidewalks, driveways and walkways, retaining walls, patios, and concrete mowing strips. To perform these services, Capital Curb and Concrete owns and maintains trucks, trailers, tractors, backhoes, trenchers, and concrete-pumping equipment.

The federal government allows businesses to deduct expenses such as salaries, payroll taxes, rent, maintenance, and utilities from revenue when determining income used to calculate income tax. However, it often does not allow firms to deduct the full cost of buildings, trucks, machines, improvements to buildings, and so on, in one year. Since these types of items usually last several years, the law requires that the cost of the items be deducted over the useful life of the item. The process of spreading the income tax deduction out over the useful life of an asset is called **depreciation**.

Over the years, several methods of computing depreciation have been used, including **straight-line, declining-balance, sum-of-the-years'-digits**, and **units-of-production**. These methods are used in keeping company accounting records and, in many states, preparing state income tax returns. Items purchased after 1981 are depreciated for federal income tax returns with the **accelerated cost recovery system** or the **modified accelerated cost recovery system**, discussed later. The use of depreciation for federal income tax purposes is detailed in Internal Revenue Service Publication 946: "How to Depreciate Property."

A company need not use the same method of depreciation for all of its various assets. For example, the straight-line method of depreciation might be used on some assets and the declining-balance method on others. Furthermore, the depreciation method used in preparing a company's financial statement may be different from the method used in preparing income tax returns.

▼14.1 Straight-Line Method

OBJECTIVES

1 Understand the terms used in depreciation.

2 Use the straight-line method of depreciation to find the amount of depreciation each year.

3 Use the straight-line method to find the book value of an asset.

4 Use the straight-line method to prepare a depreciation schedule.

▼ **CASE IN POINT** John Goodby and his accountant decide on which method of depreciation to use for the depreciable assets of Capital Curb and Concrete. A commonly used method for both accounting and tax purposes is the straight-line method of depreciation.

Cost = ?   1   2   3   4   5   . . .   Salvage value = ?
                  Useful Life (years)
         How much can be depreciated each year?

OBJECTIVE 1 Understand the terms used in depreciation. The physical assets of a company such as machinery, trucks, cars, and computers are **tangible assets**. Assets such as patents and copyrights, franchise fees, and customer lists are **intangible assets**. In general, either type of asset may be depreciated, as long as its useful life can be determined. The key terms in depreciation are summarized below.

Cost is the basis for determining depreciation. It is the total amount paid for the asset.

Useful life is the period of time during which the asset will be used. The Internal Revenue Service has guidelines for estimating the life of an asset used in a particular trade or business. However, useful life depends on the use of the asset, the repair policy, the replacement policy, obsolescence, and other factors.

Salvage value or **scrap value** (sometimes called **residual value**) is the estimated value of an asset when it is retired from service, traded in, disposed of, or exhausted. An asset may have a salvage value of zero, or **no salvage value**.

Accumulated depreciation is the amount of depreciation taken so far, a running balance of depreciation to date.

Book value is the cost of an asset minus the total depreciation to date. The book value at the end of an asset's life is equal to the salvage value. The book value can never be less than the salvage value.

OBJECTIVE 2 Use the straight-line method of depreciation to find the amount of depreciation each year. The simplest method of depreciation, **straight-line depreciation**, assumes that assets lose an equal amount of value during each year of life. For example, suppose a heavy equipment trailer is purchased by Capital Curb and Concrete at a cost of $14,100. The trailer has a useful life of 8 years and a salvage value of $2100. Find the amount to be depreciated (**depreciable amount**) using the following formula.

> **Finding Amount to be Depreciated**
>
> Amount to be depreciated = Cost − Salvage value

Here, the amount to be depreciated over the 8-year period is:

$$
\begin{array}{rl}
\$14,100 & \text{cost} \\
-\quad 2,100 & \text{salvage value} \\
\hline
\$12,000 & \text{amount to be depreciated}
\end{array}
$$

With the straight-line method, an equal amount of depreciation is taken each year over the 8-year life of the trailer. The annual depreciation for this trailer is

> **Finding Annual Depreciation**
>
> $$\text{Depreciation} = \frac{\text{Depreciable amount}}{\text{Years of life}} = \frac{\$12,000}{8} = \$1500$$

Each year during the 8-year life of the trailer, the annual depreciation will be $1500, or $\frac{1}{8}$ of the depreciable amount. The annual rate of depreciation is $12\frac{1}{2}\%$ ($\frac{1}{8} = 12\frac{1}{2}\%$).

OBJECTIVE 3 Use the straight-line method to find the book value of an asset. The book value, or remaining value, of an asset at the end of a year is the original cost minus the depreciation up to and including that year (**accumulated depreciation**). With the trailer, the book value at the end of the first year is found as follows.

$$
\begin{array}{rl}
\$14,100 & \text{cost} \\
-\quad 1,500 & \textbf{first year's depreciation} \\
\hline
\$12,600 & \text{book value at end of the first year}
\end{array}
$$

Book value is found with the following formula.

> **Finding Book Value**
>
> Book value = Cost − Accumulated depreciation

Subtract the second year's depreciation from the book value at the end of year 1 to find the book value at the end of year 2, and so on.

Finding First-Year Depreciation and Book Value

 EXAMPLE 1 KFC purchased a new low-fat chicken cooker at a cost of $26,500. The estimated life of the fryer is 5 years, with a salvage value of $3500. Find **(a)** the annual rate of depreciation, **(b)** the annual amount of depreciation, and **(c)** the book value at the end of the first year.

SOLUTION

(a) The annual rate of depreciation is 20% (5-year life = $\frac{1}{5}$ **per year = 20%**).

(b)
$$
\begin{array}{rl}
\$26,500 & \text{cost} \\
-\quad 3,500 & \text{salvage value} \\
\hline
\$23,000 & \text{depreciable amount}
\end{array}
$$

This $23,000 will be depreciated evenly over the 5-year life for an annual depreciation of $4600 ($23,000 × 20% = $4600).

(c) Since the annual depreciation is $4600, the book value at the end of the first year will be

$$
\begin{array}{rl}
\$26,500 & \text{cost} \\
-\quad 4,600 & \textbf{depreciation in the first year} \\
\hline
\$21,900 & \text{book value at the end of the first year}
\end{array}
$$

To solve Example 1 using a calculator, first use parentheses to find the depreciable amount. Next, divide to find depreciation. Finally, find the book value.

$$\boxed{(}\ 26{,}500\ \boxed{-}\ 3500\ \boxed{)}\ \boxed{\div}\ 5\ \boxed{=}\ 4600$$
$$26{,}500\ \boxed{-}\ 4600\ \boxed{=}\ 21{,}900$$

Note: Refer to Appendix B for calculator basics.

QUICK CHECK 1

Class Printers purchased a new printing press at a cost of $18,400. The estimated life of the printing press is 8 years, with a salvage value of $3600. Find **(a)** the annual rate of depreciation, **(b)** the annual amount of depreciation, and **(c)** the book value at the end of the first year.

When using straight-line depreciation, the steps to find the book value at the end of any year are as follows:

> **Finding Book Value**
>
> Step 1   Find depreciation to date by multiplying the annual depreciation times the number of years.
>
> Step 2   Subtract this value from cost to find the book value.

If an asset is expected to have **no salvage value** at the end of its expected life, the entire cost will be depreciated over its life. In Example 1, if the chicken cooker had been expected to have no salvage value at the end of 5 years, the annual amount of depreciation would have been $5300 ($26,500 × 20% = $5300).

Finding the Book Value at the End of Any Year

EXAMPLE 2

A lighted display case at Albertson's cost $3400, has an estimated life of 10 years, and has a salvage value of $800. Find the book value at the end of 6 years.

SOLUTION

The annual rate of depreciation is 10% (10-year life is $\frac{1}{10}$ or 10%).

$$\text{Depreciable amount} = \text{Cost} - \text{Salvage value}$$
$$= \$3400 - \$800 = \mathbf{\$2600}$$
$$\text{Annual depreciation} = \mathbf{\$2600} \times 10\% = \mathbf{\$260}$$
$$\text{Accumulated depreciation over 6 years} = \mathbf{\$260} \times 6 \text{ years}$$
$$= \$1560$$

Find the book value at the end of 6 years by subtracting the accumulated depreciation from the cost.

$3400	cost
− 1560	**accumulated depreciation (6 years)**
$1840	book value at the end of 6 years

After 6 years, this display case would be carried on the firm's books with a value of $1840.

> **Quick TIP**
>
> The book value helps the owner of a business estimate the value of the business, which is important when the owner is borrowing money or trying to sell the business.

QUICK CHECK 2

Two Brothers Wheel Alignment bought a new wheel alignment system for $15,900. If the salvage value of the equipment is $4500 and the estimated life is 12 years, find the book value at the end of 8 years.

OBJECTIVE 4 Use the straight-line method to prepare a depreciation schedule. A **depreciation schedule** is often used to show the annual depreciation, accumulated depreciation, and book value over the useful life of an asset. As an aid in comparing three of the methods of depreciation discussed in the text, the depreciation schedule of Example 3 and the schedules shown for the double-declining-balance (see Section 14.2) and sum-of-the-years'-digits methods (see Section 14.3) use the same pickup truck.

Preparing a Depreciation Schedule

EXAMPLE 3

Capital Curb and Concrete bought a new pickup truck for $21,500. The truck is estimated to have a useful life of 5 years, at which time it will have a salvage value (trade-in value) of $3500. Prepare a depreciation schedule using the straight-line method of depreciation.

SOLUTION

The annual rate of depreciation is 20% $\left(5\text{-year life} = \frac{1}{5}\text{ per year} = 20\%\right)$. Find the depreciable amount as follows.

$$
\begin{array}{rl}
\$21,500 & \text{cost} \\
-\quad 3,500 & \text{salvage value} \\
\hline
\$18,000 & \text{depreciable amount}
\end{array}
$$

This $18,000 will be depreciated evenly over the 5-year life for an annual depreciation of $3600 ($18,000 × 20% = $3600). This depreciation schedule includes a year zero that represents the initial purchase of the truck.

Year	Computation	Amount of Depreciation	Accumulated Depreciation	Book Value
0	—	—	—	$21,500
1	(20% × $18,000)	$3600	$3,600	$17,900
2	(20% × $18,000)	$3600	$7,200	$14,300
3	(20% × $18,000)	$3600	$10,800	$10,700
4	(20% × $18,000)	$3600	$14,400	$7,100
5	(20% × $18,000)	$3600	$18,000	$3,500

The depreciation is $3600 each year. The accumulated depreciation at the end of 5 years is equal to the depreciable amount and the book value at the end of 5 years is equal to the salvage value.

Quick TIP

If the rate is a repeating decimal, use the fraction that is equivalent to the decimal. For example, use the fraction $\frac{1}{3}$ rather than the decimal number 33.3% which is rounded.

QUICK CHECK 3

A concrete extruding machine is purchased at a cost of $4300. The machine has a useful life of 4 years and a salvage value of $700. Prepare a depreciation schedule using the straight-line method of depreciation to find the book value at the end of each year of the asset's life.

Depreciation is used with assets having a useful life of *more than one year*. The asset to be depreciated must have a predictable life. A truck can be depreciated because its useful life can be estimated, but land cannot be depreciated because its life is considered to be indefinite. For example, the graph below shows the remaining value of the pickup truck in Example 3 as it is depreciated over its useful life. The amount shown on the vertical axis in the graph represents the book value, or the value at which the truck is carried on the firm's financial statements.

Quick TIP

Sometimes the book value of an asset is close to the actual market value. At other times, the book value of an asset can end up either above or below the actual market value.

Truck Depreciation (Straight line)

Depreciable assets can be large and very expensive. For example, one utility company plans to depreciate the expected $4.9 billion cost of a new nuclear power plant over a useful life of 40 years. The income tax savings resulting from depreciation help the utility company afford the cost of building the power plant.

▼14.1 Exercises

MyMathLab®

The shaded sections below contain solutions to help you get a **QUICK START** *on the various types of exercises.*

Find the annual straight-line rate of depreciation, given the following estimated lives. (See Example 1.)

	Life	Annual Rate		Life	Annual Rate
1.	5 years	20%	**2.**	4 years	25%
	$\frac{1}{5} = 20\%$			$\frac{1}{4} = 25\%$	
3.	8 years	_____	**4.**	10 years	_____
5.	20 years	_____	**6.**	25 years	_____
7.	15 years	_____	**8.**	30 years	_____
9.	80 years	_____	**10.**	40 years	_____
11.	50 years	_____	**12.**	100 years	_____

Find the annual amount of depreciation for the following, using the straight-line method. (See Examples 1 and 2.)

13.	Cost:	$9000	**14.**	Cost:	$3400
	Estimated life:	20 years		Estimated life:	4 years
	Estimated scrap value:	None		Estimated scrap value:	$800
	Annual depreciation:	$450		Annual depreciation:	$650
	$9000 × 5% = $450			$3400 − $800 = $2600	
				$2600 × 25% = $650	

15.	Cost:	$2700	**16.**	Cost:	$8100
	Estimated life:	3 years		Estimated life:	6 years
	Estimated scrap value:	$300		Estimated scrap value:	$750
	Annual depreciation:	_____		Annual depreciation:	_____

17.	Cost:	$4200	**18.**	Cost:	$2,730,000
	Estimated life:	5 years		Estimated life:	10 years
	Estimated scrap value:	None		Estimated scrap value:	$310,000
	Annual depreciation:	_____		Annual depreciation:	_____

🔺 indicates an exercise that is related to the Case in Point feature.

Find the book value at the end of the first year for the following, using the straight-line method.
(See Examples 1 and 2.)

19. Cost: $3200
Estimated life: 8 years
Estimated scrap value: $400
Book value: **$2850**

$3200 − $400 = $2800
$2800 × 12.5% = $350
$3200 − $350 = $2850

20. Cost: $35,000
Estimated life: 10 years
Estimated scrap value: $2500
Book value: _____

21. Cost: $5400
Estimated life: 12 years
Estimated scrap value: $600
Book value: _____

22. Cost: $4500
Estimated life: 5 years
Estimated scrap value: None
Book value: _____

Find the book value at the end of 5 years for the following, using the straight-line method.
(See Examples 1 and 2.)

23. Cost: $4800
Estimated life: 10 years
Estimated scrap value: $750
Book value: **$2775**

$4800 − $750 = $4050
$4050 × 10% = $405
$405 × 5 = $2025
$4800 − $2025 = $2775

24. Cost: $16,000
Estimated life: 20 years
Estimated scrap value: $2000
Book value: _____

25. Cost: $80,000
Estimated life: 50 years
Estimated scrap value: $10,000
Book value: _____

26. Cost: $660
Estimated life: 8 years
Estimated scrap value: $100
Book value: _____

Solve the following application problems.

27. MACHINERY DEPRECIATION Capital Curb and Concrete selects the straight-line method of depreciation for a Bobcat loader costing $12,000 with a 3-year life and an expected scrap value of $3000. Prepare a depreciation schedule.

Year	Computation	Amount of Depreciation	Accumulated Depreciation	Book Value
0	—	—	—	$12,000
1	$(33\frac{1}{3}\% \times \$9000)$	$3000	$3000	$9,000
2	$(33\frac{1}{3}\% \times \$9000)$	$3000	$6000	$6,000
3	$(33\frac{1}{3}\% \times \$9000)$	$3000	$9000	$3,000

28. LABORATORY EQUIPMENT   Taconic Medical purchased new lab equipment costing $18,000, having an estimated life of 4 years and a salvage value of $1600. Prepare a depreciation schedule using the straight-line method of depreciation.

Year	Computation	Amount of Depreciation	Accumulated Depreciation	Book Value
0	—	—	—	$18,000
1				
2				
3				
4				

29. VEHICLE DEPRECIATION   Capital Curb and Concrete paid $51,200 for a $1\frac{1}{2}$-ton, dual-axle flatbed truck with an estimated life of 6 years and a salvage value of $14,000. Prepare a depreciation schedule using the straight-line method of depreciation.

Year	Computation	Amount of Depreciation	Accumulated Depreciation	Book Value
0	—	—	—	$51,200
1				
2				
3				
4				
5				
6				

30. BUSINESS FIXTURES   The Venture Center purchased a new commercial air conditioner at a cost of $7800 and estimates the useful life as 10 years, after which it will have no salvage value. Prepare a depreciation schedule, calculating depreciation by the straight-line method.

Year	Computation	Amount of Depreciation	Accumulated Depreciation	Book Value
0	—	—	—	$7800
1				
2				
3				
4				
5				
6				
7				
8				
9				
10				

31. Develop a single formula that will show how to find annual depreciation using the straight-line method of depreciation. (See Objective 1.)

32. Explain the procedure used to calculate depreciation when there is no salvage value. Why will the book value always be zero at the end of the asset's life?

33. **BARGE DEPRECIATION** A Dutch petroleum company purchased a barge for $1,300,000. The estimated life is 20 years, at which time it will have a salvage value of $200,000. Find **(a)** the annual amount of depreciation using the straight-line method and **(b)** the book value at the end of 5 years.

(a) _____

(b) _____

34. **DEPRECIATING COMPUTER EQUIPMENT** The new computer equipment at Capital Curb and Concrete has a cost of $14,500, an estimated life of 8 years, and a scrap value of $2100. Find **(a)** the annual depreciation and **(b)** the book value at the end of 4 years using the straight-line method of depreciation.

(a) _____

(b) _____

35. **DEPRECIATING MACHINERY** A bottle-capping machine costs $88,000, has an estimated life of 8 years, and has a scrap value of $16,000. Use the straight-line method of depreciation to find **(a)** the annual rate of depreciation, **(b)** the annual amount of depreciation, and **(c)** the book value at the end of the first year.

(a) _____

(b) _____

(c) _____

36. **DRILLING RIG** Transocean Drilling spent $236,000,000 to purchase a new offshore drilling rig capable of drilling to 40,000 feet. The useful life is 20 years and the salvage value is estimated to be $12,000,000. Use the straight-line method of depreciation to find **(a)** the annual rate of depreciation, **(b)** the annual amount of depreciation, and **(c)** the book value at the end of 5 years.

(a) _____

(b) _____

(c) _____

QUICK CHECK ANSWERS

1. **(a)** 12.5% rate
   (b) $1850 depreciation
   (c) $16,550 book value
2. $8300

3. year 0 = $4300
   year 1 = $3400
   year 2 = $2500
   year 3 = $1600
   year 4 = $ 700

▼ 14.2 Declining-Balance Method

OBJECTIVES

1 Describe the declining-balance method of depreciation.

2 Find the double-declining-balance rate.

3 Use the double-declining-balance method to find the amount of depreciation and the book value for each year.

4 Use the double-declining-balance method to prepare a depreciation schedule.

▼ **CASE IN POINT**   Straight-line depreciation assumes that an asset loses an equal amount of value each year of its life. This is not realistic for most of the machinery and equipment owned by Capital Curb and Concrete. For example, a new tractor loses much more value during its first year of life than during its fifth year of life.

OBJECTIVE 1 Describe the declining-balance method of depreciation. Methods of **accelerated depreciation** are used to more accurately reflect the rate at which assets actually lose value. One of the more common accelerated methods of depreciation is the **double-declining-balance method** or **200% method**. With this method, the **double-declining-balance rate** must first be found. This rate is multiplied by last year's book value to get this year's depreciation. Since the book value declines from year to year, the annual depreciation also declines, giving the origin of the name of this method.

OBJECTIVE 2 Find the double-declining-balance rate. Calculate depreciation using the double-declining-balance method by first finding the straight-line rate of depreciation. Then adjust the straight-line rate to the desired double-declining-balance rate by multiplying by 2.

Finding the 200% Declining-Balance Rate   **EXAMPLE 1**   Find the straight-line rate and the double-declining-balance (200%) rate for each of the following years of life.

SOLUTION

Years of Life	Straight-Line Rate	Double-Declining-Balance Rate
3	$33.33\% \left(\frac{1}{3}\right)$	$\times 2 = 66.67\% \left(\frac{2}{3}\right)$
4	25%	$\times 2 = 50\%$
5	20%	$\times 2 = 40\%$
8	12.5%	$\times 2 = 25\%$
10	10%	$\times 2 = 20\%$
20	5%	$\times 2 = 10\%$
25	4%	$\times 2 = 8\%$
50	2%	$\times 2 = 4\%$

QUICK CHECK 1

Find the straight-line rate and the double-declining-balance rate for **(a)** 40 years, **(b)** 6 years, **(c)** 15 years, and **(d)** 25 years.

OBJECTIVE 3 Use the double-declining-balance method to find the amount of depreciation and the book value for each year. Use the following formula and multiply the double-declining-balance rate by the declining balance. The declining balance is the total cost in the first year and the previous year's book value in following years. The answer is the amount of depreciation in that year.

> **Finding Amount of Depreciation**
>
> Depreciation = Double-declining-balance rate × Declining balance

Quick TIP

Throughout the remainder of this section and chapter, money amounts will be rounded to the nearest dollar.

Do not subtract salvage value from cost when using this method of depreciation. Rather, simply multiply the appropriate percentage by the book value remaining at the end of the prior year. It is important to remember that *book value never goes below the salvage value*. Depreciation is sometimes limited to the amount that brings the book value down to the salvage value, as we will see in Example 3.

EXAMPLE 2

Finding Depreciation and Book Value Using Double-Declining-Balance

Capital Curb and Concrete purchased a small portable storage building for $8100. It is expected to have a life of 10 years, at which time it will have no salvage value. Using the double-declining-balance method of depreciation, find the first and second years' depreciation and the book value at the end of the first and second years.

SOLUTION

The straight-line depreciation rate for property with a 10-year recovery is 10%. Therefore, the double-declining balance rate is twice that, or $10\% \times 2 = 20\%$.

$$\begin{aligned} \text{First year's depreciation} &= 20\% \text{ of declining balance} \\ &= 20\% \times 8100 \text{ cost} \\ &= \mathbf{\$1620} \end{aligned}$$

Find the book value at the end of the first year as follows.

$8100	cost
−1620	**depreciation to date**
$6480	book value at the end of the first year

$$\begin{aligned} \text{Second year's depreciation} &= 20\% \text{ of book value at end of last year} \\ &= 20\% \times \mathbf{\$6480} \\ &= \mathbf{\$1296} \end{aligned}$$

Book value at end of second year is found as follows.

$6480	Book value at the end of year 1
−1296	**Year 2 depreciation**
$5184	Book value at the end of year 2

QUICK CHECK 2

A pet store purchased a saltwater fish aquarium for $6800. It is expected to have a life of 8 years, with no salvage value. Using the double-declining-balance method of depreciation, find **(a)** the first and second years' depreciation and **(b)** the book value at the end of the first and second years.

OBJECTIVE 4 Use the double-declining-balance method to prepare a depreciation schedule. The next example shows a depreciation schedule for the pickup truck discussed in Example 3 of Section 14.1. As this example shows, the same rate is used each year with the declining-balance method, and the rate is multiplied by the declining balance, which is last year's book value. Also, the amount of depreciation in a given year may have to be adjusted so that book value is never less than salvage value.

EXAMPLE 3

Preparing a Depreciation Schedule

Capital Curb and Concrete bought a new pickup truck at a cost of $21,500. It is estimated the truck will have a useful life of 5 years, at which time it will have a salvage value (trade-in value) of $3500. Prepare a depreciation schedule using the double-declining-balance method of depreciation.

SOLUTION

The annual rate of depreciation is 40% (**20% straight-line** $\times$ **2 = 40%**). Do not subtract salvage value from cost before calculating depreciation. In year 1, the full cost is used to calculate depreciation.

Year	Computation	Amount of Depreciation	Accumulated Depreciation	Book Value
0	—	—	—	$21,500
1	(40% × $21,500)	$8600	$8,600	$12,900
2	(40% × $12,900)	$5160	$13,760	$7,740
3	(40% × $7,740)	$3096	$16,856	$4,644
4		$1144*	$18,000	$3,500
5		$0	$18,000	$3,500

Quick TIP

Never subtract the salvage value from the cost when calculating depreciation using the double-declining-balance method.

*In year 4 of the table, 40% of $4644 is $1858. If this amount were subtracted from $4644, the book value would drop below the salvage value of $3500. Since book value may *never be less than salvage value*, depreciation of $1144 ($4644 − $3500) is taken in year 4, so that book value equals salvage value. No further depreciation remains for year 5 or subsequent years. The total amount of depreciation taken over the life of the asset is the same using either the straight-line or the double-declining-balance method of depreciation.

QUICK CHECK 3

A concrete-extruding machine is purchased at a cost of $4300. The machine has a useful life of 4 years and a salvage value of $700. Prepare a depreciation schedule using the double-declining-balance method of depreciation to find the book value at the end of each year of the asset's life.

The following graph shows the remaining book value by year of the pickup truck in Example 3. It shows them using both the straight-line and double-declining-balance methods of depreciation. Notice that the book value at the end of the asset's useful life is the same (salvage value = $3500) using either method.

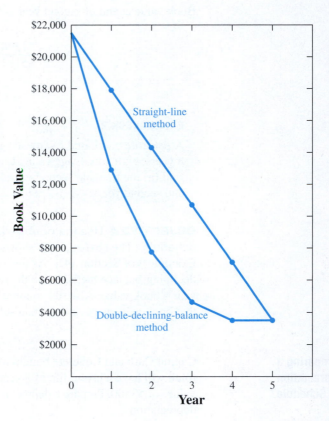

The advantage of using double-declining-balance over straight-line depreciation is that the deduction from income is greater in the early years of the useful life. In turn, this results in lower income tax in the early years. The disadvantage is that the deduction from income is much lower in the last years of the useful life. Managers are careful when choosing the depreciation methods, since they can have a material effect on income and, therefore, a significant effect on income taxes that must be paid.

▼ 14.2 Exercises

MyMathLab®

The shaded sections below contain solutions to help you get a **QUICK START** *on the various types of exercises.*

Find the annual double-declining-balance (200% method) rate of depreciation, given the following estimated lives. (See Example 1.)

	Life	Annual Rate			Life	Annual Rate
1.	5 years	40%		**2.**	20 years	10%
	$20\% \times 2 = 40\%$				$5\% \times 2 = 10\%$	
3.	8 years	_____		**4.**	25 years	_____
5.	15 years	_____		**6.**	4 years	_____
7.	10 years	_____		**8.**	30 years	_____
9.	6 years	_____		**10.**	40 years	_____
11.	50 years	_____		**12.**	100 years	_____

Find the first year's depreciation for the following, using the double-declining-balance method of depreciation. (See Example 2.)

13.	Cost:	$15,000		**14.**	Cost:	$10,800
	Estimated life:	10 years			Estimated life:	20 years
	Estimated scrap value:	$3000			Estimated scrap value:	None
	Depreciation (year 1):	$3000			Depreciation (year 1):	$1080
	$15,000 \times 20\% = $3000				$10,800 \times 10\% = $1080	

15.	Cost:	$22,500		**16.**	Cost:	$38,000
	Estimated life:	5 years			Estimated life:	40 years
	Estimated scrap value:	$500			Estimated scrap value:	$5000
	Depreciation (year 1):	_____			Depreciation (year 1):	_____

17.	Cost:	$3800		**18.**	Cost:	$11,400
	Estimated life:	4 years			Estimated life:	6 years
	Estimated scrap value:	None			Estimated scrap value:	$3500
	Depreciation (year 1):	_____			Depreciation (year 1):	_____

Find the book value at the end of the first year for the following, using the double-declining-balance method of depreciation. Round to the nearest dollar. (See Examples 1 and 2.)

19.	Cost:	$4200		**20.**	Cost:	$2500
	Estimated life:	10 years			Estimated life:	6 years
	Estimated scrap value:	$1000			Estimated scrap value:	$400
	Book value:	$3360			Book value:	_____
	$4200 \times 20\% = $840					
	$4200 - $840 = $3360 book value					

21.	Cost:	$1620		**22.**	Cost:	$11,280
	Estimated life:	8 years			Estimated life:	5 years
	Estimated scrap value:	None			Estimated scrap value:	$1600
	Book value:	_____			Book value:	_____

indicates an exercise that requires a written response.

▲ indicates an exercise that is related to the Case in Point feature.

Find the book value at the end of 3 years for the following, using the double-declining-balance method of depreciation. Round to the nearest dollar. (See Examples 1 and 2.)

23. Cost: $16,200
Estimated life: 8 years
Estimated scrap value: $1500
Book value: $6834

$16,200 × 25% = $4050 dep. year 1
$16,200 − $4050 = $12,150
$12,150 × 25% = $3038 dep. year 2
$12,150 − $3038 = $9112
$9112 × 25% = $2278 dep. year 3
$9112 − $2278 = $6834 book value year 3

24. Cost: $8500
Estimated life: 10 years
Estimated scrap value: $1100
Book value: _____

25. Cost: $6000
Estimated life: 3 years
Estimated scrap value: $750
Book value: _____

26. Cost: $75,000
Estimated life: 50 years
Estimated scrap value: None
Book value: _____

Solve the following application problems.

27. WEIGHT-TRAINING EQUIPMENT　Planet Fitness selects the double-declining-balance method of depreciation for some weight-training equipment costing $14,400. If the estimated life of the equipment is 4 years and the salvage value is zero, prepare a depreciation schedule.

Year	Computation	Amount of Depreciation	Accumulated Depreciation	Book Value
0	—	—	—	$14,400
1	(50% × $14,400)	$7200	$7,200	$7,200
2	(50% × $7,200)	$3600	$10,800	$3,600
3	(50% × $3,600)	$1800	$12,600	$1,800
4		$1800*	$14,400	$0

*To depreciate to $0 scrap value

28. STUDIO SOUND SYSTEM　A studio sound system costing $11,760 has a 3-year life and a scrap value of $1400. Prepare a depreciation schedule using the double-declining-balance method of depreciation.

Year	Computation	Amount of Depreciation	Accumulated Depreciation	Book Value
0	—	—	—	$11,760
1				
2				
3				$1,400

29. **CONVEYOR SYSTEM** Use the double-declining-balance method of depreciation to prepare a depreciation schedule for a new conveyor. Cost = $14,000; estimated life = 5 years; estimated scrap value = $2500. (Round to the nearest dollar.)

Year	Computation	Amount of Depreciation	Accumulated Depreciation	Book Value
0	—	—	—	$14,000
1				
2				
3				
4				
5				$2,500

30. **ELECTRONIC ANALYZER** Neilo Lincoln decides to use the double-declining-balance method of depreciation on an electronic analyzer that was acquired at a cost of $25,500. If the estimated life of the analyzer is 8 years and the estimated scrap value is $3500, prepare a depreciation schedule. (Round to the nearest dollar.)

Year	Computation	Amount of Depreciation	Accumulated Depreciation	Book Value
0	—	—	—	$25,500
1				
2				
3				
4				
5				
6				
7				
8				$3,500

31. Another name for the double-declining-balance method of depreciation is the 200% method. Explain why the straight-line method of depreciation is often called the 100% method. (See Objective 2.)

32. Explain why the amount of depreciation taken in the last year of an asset's life may be zero when using the double-declining-balance method of depreciation. (See Objective 4.)

33. **CARPET-CLEANING EQUIPMENT** John Walker, owner of The Carpet Solution, purchased some truck-mounted carpet-cleaning equipment at a cost of $8200. The estimated life of the equipment is 8 years, and the expected salvage value is $1250. Use the double-declining-balance method of depreciation to find the depreciation in the third year.

33. _____

34. **COMMERCIAL FISHING BOATS** A commercial fishing boat costs $717,000 and has an estimated life of 10 years and a salvage value of $225,000. Find the depreciation in the second year using the double-declining-balance method of depreciation.

34. _____

◭ 35. **EXCAVATING MACHINERY**   Reef Tours purchased a fishing boat for $39,240. It has an estimated life of 5 years with no salvage value. Use the double-declining-balance method of depreciation to find the book value at the end of the third year.

35. _____

36. **COMMUNICATION EQUIPMENT**   Laura Rogers purchased some communication equipment for her public relations firm at a cost of $19,700. She estimates the life of the equipment to be 8 years, at which time the salvage value will be $1000. Use the double-declining-balance method of depreciation to find the book value at the end of 5 years.

36. _____

◭ 37. **CONSTRUCTION POWER TOOLS**   Capital Curb and Concrete purchased a portable cement mixer at a cost of $5800. The mixer has a life of 8 years and a scrap value of $1000. Use the double-declining-balance method of depreciation to find **(a)** the annual rate of depreciation, **(b)** the amount of depreciation in the first year, **(c)** the accumulated depreciation at the end of the fifth year, and **(d)** the book value at the end of the fifth year.

(a) _____

(b) _____

(c) _____

(d) _____

38. **PRIVATE SCHOOL EQUIPMENT**   Gale Klein bought some white boards to write on for her reading clinic at a cost of $3620. The estimated life of the white boards is 5 years, with a salvage value of $400. Use the double-declining-balance method of depreciation to find **(a)** the annual rate of depreciation, **(b)** the amount of depreciation in the first year, **(c)** the accumulated depreciation at the end of the third year, and **(d)** the book value at the end of the third year.

(a) _____

(b) _____

(c) _____

(d) _____

QUICK CHECK ANSWERS

1. (a) $2\frac{1}{2}\%$, 5%

   (b) $16\frac{2}{3}\%$, $33\frac{1}{3}\%$

   (c) $6\frac{2}{3}\%$, $13\frac{1}{3}\%$

   (d) 4%, 8%

2. (a) $1700; $1275   (b) $5100; $3825

3. year 0 = $4300
    year 1 = $2150
    year 2 = $1075
    year 3 = $700
    year 4 = $700

14.3 Sum-of-the-Years'-Digits Method

OBJECTIVES

1. Understand the sum-of-the-years'-digits method of depreciation.

2. Find the depreciation fraction for the sum-of-the-years'-digits method.

3. Use the sum-of-the-years'-digits method to find the amount of depreciation for each year.

4. Prepare a depreciation schedule for the sum-of-the-years'-digits method.

OBJECTIVE 1 Understand the sum-of-the-years'-digits method of depreciation. The sum-of-the-years'-digits method of depreciation is another accelerated depreciation method. The double-declining-balance method of depreciation produces more depreciation than the straight-line method in the early years of an asset's life and less depreciation in the later years. The **sum-of-the-years'-digits method**, however, produces results in between the straight-line and the double-declining-balance methods—more than straight-line at the beginning and more than double-declining-balance at the end.

OBJECTIVE 2 Find the depreciation fraction for the sum-of-the-years'-digits method. The use of the sum-of-the-years'-digits method requires a **depreciation fraction** instead of the depreciation rate used earlier. The annual depreciation is this depreciation fraction multiplied by the depreciable amount (cost minus salvage value). The depreciation fraction decreases annually, as does the depreciation.

To find the depreciation fraction, first find the denominator, which remains constant for every year of the life of the asset. The denominator is the sum of all the years of the estimated life of the asset (sum of the years' digits). For example, if the life is 6 years, the denominator is 21, **since $1 + 2 + 3 + 4 + 5 + 6 = 21$.** The numerator of the fraction, which decreases each year, gives the number of years of life remaining at the beginning of that year.

Finding the Depreciation Fraction

EXAMPLE 1 Find the depreciation fraction for each year if the sum-of-the-years'-digits method of depreciation is used for an asset with a useful life of 6 years.

SOLUTION

First determine the denominator of the depreciation fraction. The denominator is 21 ($1 + 2 + 3 + 4 + 5 + 6 = 21$). Next determine the numerator for each year. The number of years of life remaining at the beginning of any year is the numerator.

Year	Depreciation Fraction
1	$\frac{6}{21}$
2	$\frac{5}{21}$
3	$\frac{4}{21}$
4	$\frac{3}{21}$
5	$\frac{2}{21}$
6	$\frac{1}{21}$
$\underline{21}$ ← sum of the years' digits	$\frac{21}{21}$

Quick TIP

It is common not to write these fractions in lowest terms, so that the year in question can be seen.

Under the sum-of-the-years'-digits method, an asset having a life of 6 years is assumed to lose $\frac{6}{21}$ of its value the first year, $\frac{5}{21}$ the second year, and so on. The sum of the six fractions in the table is $\frac{21}{21}$, or 1, so that the entire depreciable amount is used over the 6-year life.

QUICK CHECK 1

Find the depreciation fraction for each year if the sum-of-the-years'-digits method of depreciation is to be used for an asset with a useful life of 10 years.

A quick method of finding the sum of the years' digits is by the formula

$$\frac{n(n + 1)}{2}$$

where n is the estimated life of the asset. For example, if the life is 6 years, **6** is multiplied by **(6 + 1)**, resulting in **6 × 7**, or 42. Then 42 is divided by 2, giving 21, the same denominator used in the table. This method eliminates adding digits and is especially useful when the life of an asset is long.

OBJECTIVE 3 Use the sum-of-the-years'-digits method to find the amount of depreciation for each year. Use the following formula and multiply the depreciation fraction in any year by the depreciable amount (as in the straight-line method) to calculate the amount of depreciation in that year.

> **Finding Annual Depreciation**
>
> Depreciation = Depreciation fraction × Depreciable amount

Finding Depreciation Using the Sum-of-the Years'-Digits Method

EXAMPLE 2

Capital Curb and Concrete purchases a DitchMaster trencher at a cost of $8940. The trencher has a useful life of 8 years and an estimated salvage value of $1200. Find the first and second years' depreciation using the sum-of-the-years'-digits method.

SOLUTION

The depreciation fraction has a denominator of 36 (or **1 + 2 + 3 + 4 + 5 + 6 + 7 + 8**). The numerator in the first year is 8. The first-year fraction, $\frac{8}{36}$, is multiplied by the amount to be depreciated, $7740 ($8940 cost − $1200 salvage value).

$$\frac{8}{36} \times \$7740 = \$1720$$

The first year's depreciation is $1720.

The depreciation fraction for the second year, $\frac{7}{36}$, is multiplied by the original depreciable amount, $7740 ($8940 cost − $1200 salvage value).

$$\frac{7}{36} \times \$7740 = \$1505$$

The second year's depreciation is $1505.

> **QUICK CHECK 2**
>
> A dry cleaning plant purchases new cleaning equipment at a cost of $28,600. The equipment has a life of 6 years and a salvage value of $4600. Find the first and second years' depreciation using the sum-of-the-years'-digits method.

OBJECTIVE 4 Prepare a depreciation schedule for the sum-of-the-years'-digits method. For comparison, the next example uses the same truck as in Sections 14.1 and 14.2.

Preparing a Depreciation Schedule

EXAMPLE 3

Capital Curb and Concrete bought a new pickup truck for $21,500. The truck is estimated to have a useful life of 5 years, at which time it will have a salvage value of $3500. Prepare a depreciation schedule using the sum-of-the-years'-digits method of depreciation.

SOLUTION

The depreciation fraction has a denominator of 15 (or **1 + 2 + 3 + 4 + 5**).

Year	Computation	Amount of Depreciation	Accumulated Depreciation	Book Value
0	—	—	—	$21,500
1	$\left(\frac{5}{15} \times \$18{,}000\right)$	$6000	$6,000	$15,500
2	$\left(\frac{4}{15} \times \$18{,}000\right)$	$4800	$10,800	$10,700
3	$\left(\frac{3}{15} \times \$18{,}000\right)$	$3600	$14,400	$7,100
4	$\left(\frac{2}{15} \times \$18{,}000\right)$	$2400	$16,800	$4,700
5	$\left(\frac{1}{15} \times \$18{,}000\right)$	$1200	$18,000	$3,500

QUICK CHECK 3

A concrete-extruding machine is purchased at a cost of $4300. The machine has a useful life of 4 years and a salvage value of $700. Prepare a depreciation schedule using the sum-of-the-years'-digits method of depreciation to find the book value at the end of each year of the asset's life.

The following graph shows the book value at the end of each year for the truck in Example 3 using straight-line, double-declining-balance, and sum-of-the-years'-digits methods of depreciation. Notice that the useful life, salvage value, and book value at the end of the useful life is exactly the same for all three. In fact, the salvage value is exactly the same thing as the book value at the end of the useful life. The sum-of-the-years'-digits method generates rapid depreciation in the early years, yet also provides some depreciation in the later years.

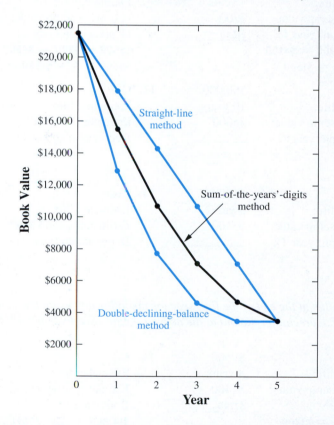

The amount of depreciation in any one year on one depreciable asset may not be large. However, depreciation on the many different depreciable assets owned by a company can amount to quite a bit. So the differences between depreciation methods can make a significant difference on income taxes.

▼14.3 Exercises   MyMathLab®

The shaded sections below contain solutions to help you get a **QUICK START** *on the various types of exercises.*

Find the sum-of-the-years'-digits depreciation fraction for the first year given the following estimated lives. (See Example 1.)

	Life	First-Year Fraction		Life	First-Year Fraction
1.	4 years	$\frac{4}{10}$	**2.**	3 years	$\frac{3}{6}$
		$4 + 3 + 2 + 1 = 10; \frac{4}{10}$			$3 + 2 + 1 = 6; \frac{3}{6}$
3.	6 years	_____	**4.**	5 years	_____
5.	7 years	_____	**6.**	8 years	_____
7.	10 years	_____	**8.**	20 years	_____

Find the first year's depreciation for the following, using the sum-of-the-years'-digits method of depreciation. Round to the nearest dollar. (See Example 2.)

9.	Cost:	$4800	**10.**	Cost:	$5600
	Estimated life:	4 years		Estimated life:	5 years
	Estimated scrap value:	$700		Estimated scrap value:	$800
	Depreciation (year 1):	$1640		Depreciation (year 1):	$1600
	$4800 - $700 = $4100			$5600 - $800 = $4800	
	$4100 \times \frac{4}{10} = $1640			$4800 \times \frac{5}{15} = $1600	

11.	Cost:	$60,000	**12.**	Cost:	$1440
	Estimated life:	10 years		Estimated life:	8 years
	Estimated scrap value:	$5000		Estimated scrap value:	None
	Depreciation (year 1):	_____		Depreciation (year 1):	_____

13.	Cost:	$18,500	**14.**	Cost:	$97,400
	Estimated life:	3 years		Estimated life:	8 years
	Estimated scrap value:	$3500		Estimated scrap value:	$11,000
	Depreciation (year 1):	_____		Depreciation (year 1):	_____

Find the book value at the end of the first year for the following, using the sum-of-the-years'-digits method of depreciation. Round to the nearest dollar. (See Example 3.)

15.	Cost:	$9500	**16.**	Cost:	$14,800
	Estimated life:	8 years		Estimated life:	10 years
	Estimated scrap value:	$1400		Estimated scrap value:	None
	Book value:	$7700		Book value:	$12,109
	$8100 \times \frac{8}{36} = $1800			$14,800 \times \frac{10}{55} = $2691	
	$9500 - $1800 = $7700			$14,800 - $2691 = $12,109	

▲ indicates an exercise that is related to the Case in Point feature.

17. Cost: $3800
Estimated life: 5 years
Estimated scrap value: $500
Book value: _____

18. Cost: $15,650
Estimated life: 6 years
Estimated scrap value: $2000
Book value: _____

Find the book value at the end of 3 years for the following, using the sum-of-the-years'-digits method of depreciation. Round to the nearest dollar. (See Example 3.)

19. Cost: $2240
Estimated life: 6 years
Estimated scrap value: $350
Book value: $890

$\frac{6}{21} + \frac{5}{21} + \frac{4}{21} = \frac{15}{21}$ dep. in 3 years
$2240 − $350 = $1890
$1890 × $\frac{15}{21}$ = $1350 dep.
$2240 − $1350 = $890

20. Cost: $27,500
Estimated life: 10 years
Estimated scrap value: None
Book value: _____

21. Cost: $4500
Estimated life: 8 years
Estimated scrap value: $900
Book value: _____

22. Cost: $6600
Estimated life: 5 years
Estimated scrap value: $1500
Book value: _____

Solve the following application problems. Round to the nearest dollar.

23. DEPRECIATING OFFICE FURNITURE   Capital Curb and Concrete uses the sum-of-the-years'-digits method of depreciation to prepare a depreciation schedule for an engineering workstation that costs $3900, has an expected life of 3 years, and has an estimated salvage value of $480.

Year	Computation	Amount of Depreciation	Accumulated Depreciation	Book Value
0	—	—	—	$3900
1	$\left(\frac{3}{6} \times \$3420\right)$	$1710	$1710	$2190
2	$\left(\frac{2}{6} \times \$3420\right)$	$1140	$2850	$1050
3	$\left(\frac{1}{6} \times \$3420\right)$	$570	$3420	$480

24. PAINT STORE   Gliddens purchased a new paint mixer at a cost of $14,400. The expected life of the mixer is 4 years, at which time the salvage value is estimated to be $2400. Complete a depreciation schedule using the sum-of-the-years'-digits method of depreciation.

Year	Computation	Amount of Depreciation	Accumulated Depreciation	Book Value
0	—	—	—	$14,400
1				
2				
3				
4				

25. COMMERCIAL FREEZER Joe's Pizzeria purchased a new freezer at a cost of $10,800. The estimated life of the freezer is 6 years, at which time the salvage value is estimated to be $2400. Complete a depreciation schedule using the sum-of-the-years'-digits method of depreciation.

Year	Computation	Amount of Depreciation	Accumulated Depreciation	Book Value
0	—	—	—	$10,800
1				
2				
3				
4				
5				
6				

26. FORKLIFT DEPRECIATION Capital Curb and Concrete purchased a new forklift. Prepare a depreciation schedule using the sum-of-the-years'-digits method of depreciation. Cost = $15,000; estimated life = 10 years; estimated scrap value = $4000.

Year	Computation	Amount of Depreciation	Accumulated Depreciation	Book Value
0	—	—	—	$15,000
1				
2				
3				
4				
5				
6				
7				
8				
9				
10				

27. Write a description of how the depreciation fraction is determined in any year of an asset's life when using the sum-of-the-years'-digits method of depreciation. (See Objective 2.)

28. If you were starting your own business, which of the three depreciation methods— straight-line, double-declining-balance, or sum-of-the-years'-digits—would you decide to use? Why?

29. WIND TURBINE Vulcan Utilities purchased several large wind turbines to generate electricity from the wind. Each turbine costs $3,200,000, has an estimated life of 10 years, and has an estimated scrap value of $650,000. Find the depreciation for the third year for each of the wind turbines.

29. _____

🔺 **30. LANDSCAPE EQUIPMENT** Capital Curb and Concrete purchased a new tractor trencher at a cost of \$32,000. The expected life of the unit is 8 years and the salvage value is expected to be \$5000. Use the sum-of-the-years'-digits method of depreciation to determine the first year's depreciation.

30. _____

31. HOSPITAL EQUIPMENT Orangevale Rental uses the sum-of-the-years'-digits method of depreciation on all hospital rental equipment. If it purchases new hospital beds at a cost of \$12,800 and estimates the life of the beds to be 10 years with no scrap value, find the book value at the end of the fourth year.

31. _____

32. COMMERCIAL CARPET First Savings Bank has installed commercial tile at a cost of \$25,200. It has a useful life of 6 years and no salvage value. Find **(a)** the first and **(b)** the second year's depreciation, using the sum-of-the-years'-digits method.

(a) _____
(b) _____

33. FAST-FOOD RESTAURANTS In-N-Out Burgers purchased a new low-fat deep-fry unit at a cost of \$12,420. The expected life of the unit is 8 years with a scrap value of \$1800. Use the sum-of-the-years'-digits method of depreciation to find **(a)** the first year's depreciation fraction, **(b)** the amount of depreciation in the first year, **(c)** the accumulated depreciation at the end of the eighth year, and **(d)** the book value at the end of the fourth year.

(a) _____
(b) _____
(c) _____
(d) _____

34. SEWER DRAIN SERVICE Armour Drain bought a new sewer line root remover for \$6725. The life of the machine is 10 years, and the scrap value is \$1500. Use the sum-of-the-years'-digits method of depreciation to find **(a)** the first year's depreciation fraction, **(b)** the amount of depreciation in the first year, **(c)** the accumulated depreciation at the end of the tenth year, and **(d)** the book value at the end of the sixth year.

(a) _____
(b) _____
(c) _____
(d) _____

QUICK CHECK ANSWERS

1. year 1 = $\frac{10}{55}$; year 2 = $\frac{9}{55}$
 year 3 = $\frac{8}{55}$; year 4 = $\frac{7}{55}$
 year 5 = $\frac{6}{55}$; year 6 = $\frac{5}{55}$
 year 7 = $\frac{4}{55}$; year 8 = $\frac{3}{55}$
 year 9 = $\frac{2}{55}$; year 10 = $\frac{1}{55}$

2. year 1 = \$6857 (rounded)
 year 2 = \$5714 (rounded)

3. year 0 = \$4300
 year 1 = \$2860
 year 2 = \$1780
 year 3 = \$1060
 year 4 = \$ 700

▼ Supplementary Application Exercises on Depreciation

Round to the nearest dollar if necessary.

1. **WAREHOUSE CONSTRUCTION** Xienshang Electronics built a new distribution center at a cost of $2,600,000. It has an estimated life of 40 years and an estimated scrap value of $400,000. Use the straight-line method of depreciation to find the book value of the distribution center at the end of 10 years.

1. _____

2. **COPY MACHINES** The UPS Store® purchased a new high-speed copy machine at a cost of $9480. Use the straight-line method of depreciation to find the amount of depreciation that should be charged off each year if the equipment has an estimated life of 4 years and a scrap value of $1500.

2. _____

3. **WOODWORKING MACHINERY** Custom Cabinets bought a lathe for turning table and chair legs at a total cost of $18,500. The estimated life of the lathe is 5 years and there is no scrap value. Find the depreciation in the first year using the double-declining-balance method of depreciation.

3. _____

4. **LANDSCAPING EQUIPMENT** Capital Curb and Concrete purchased a scraper at a cost of $22,000. If the estimated life of the scraper is 10 years, find the book value at the end of 3 years using the double-declining-balance method of depreciation.

4. _____

5. **PERSONAL ORGANIZERS** All-Pro Real Estate purchased some iPhones for its sales staff. The iPhones have a total cost of $2850, an estimated life of 6 years, and a salvage value of $600. Use the sum-of-the-years'-digits method of depreciation to find the book value of all the iPhones at the end of the third year.

5. _____

indicates an exercise that is related to the Case in Point feature.

6. BUSINESS SIGNAGE   The outdoor sign used by the Donut Palace cost $7375, has an estimated life of 10 years, and has a salvage value of $500. Use the sum-of-the-years'-digits method of depreciation to find the book value at the end of the third year.

6. _____

7. JEWELRY DISPLAY CASES   The Diamond Center installed new shatterproof display cases at a cost of $45,600. Using the straight-line method of depreciation, find the amount of depreciation that should be charged off *each year* if the estimated life of the display cases is 10 years and the scrap value is $8000.

7. _____

8. RECREATION EQUIPMENT   River Rentals purchased a sculling boat at a cost of $32,000. The estimated life of the boats is 15 years, and the scrap value is $6500. Find the book value at the end of 10 years using the straight-line method of depreciation.

8. _____

9. BUSINESS SAFE   Schools Credit Union purchased a safe at a cost of $78,000. If the estimated life of the safe is 20 years, find the book value at the end of 2 years using the double-declining-balance method of depreciation.

9. _____

10. THEATER SEATING   Music Circus just installed new seating at a total cost of $228,000. The estimated life of the seating is 10 years, there is no salvage value, and the double-declining-balance method of depreciation is used. Find the depreciation in the first year.

10. _____

11. SHUTTLE VAN   Use the sum-of-the-years'-digits method of depreciation to find the amount of depreciation to be charged off *each year* on an auto dealer's $38,600 shuttle van that has an estimated life of 4 years and a scrap value of $4400.

11. _____

_____

_____

_____

12. DIESEL TRACTOR Using the sum-of-the-years'-digits method of depreciation, find the amount of depreciation to be charged off each year on a diesel tractor purchased by Capital Curb and Concrete. The tractor has a cost of $85,000, an estimated life of 5 years, and a scrap value of $13,000.

12. _____
_____
_____
_____
_____

13. INDUSTRIAL FORKLIFT Lumber Plus buys 5 industrial lifts at a cost of $14,825 each. The life of the lifts is estimated to be 10 years and the scrap value is $3000 each. Use the sum-of-the-years'-digits method of depreciation to find the total book value of all the lifts at the end of the fourth year.

13. _____

14. CAR-WASH MACHINERY Bubble Car Wash buys new pumps for an automatic car wash at a cost of $50,950. It has a scrap value of $10,000 and an estimated life of 6 years. Use the sum-of-the-years'-digits method of depreciation to find the book value at the end of the third year.

14. _____

15. VIDEO EQUIPMENT Video Productions purchased some studio equipment manufactured in Australia. The total cost of the equipment was $21,600. It has an estimated life of 5 years and a salvage value of $2400. Use the sum-of-the-years'-digits method of depreciation to find the book value of the equipment at the end of the second year.

15. _____

16. **RESTAURANT TABLES**   Little Italy bought new dining-room tables at a cost of $14,750. The estimated life of the tables is 8 years, at which time they will be worthless. Use the double-declining-balance method of depreciation to find the book value at the end of the third year.

16. _____

17. **REFRIGERATED DISPLAY CASE**   Goldie's Delicatessen purchased a new refrigerated display case for $10,800. It has an estimated life of 10 years and a salvage value of $1500. Use the straight-line method of depreciation to find **(a)** the accumulated depreciation and **(b)** the book value at the end of the sixth year.

(a) _____

(b) _____

18. **SOFT-DRINK BOTTLING**   A small soft-drink bottler purchased two automatic filling and capping machines at a cost of $185,000 each. The machines have a scrap value of $30,000 each and an estimated life of 8 years. Use the double-declining-balance method of depreciation to find **(a)** the accumulated depreciation and **(b)** the book value of the machines at the end of the third year.

(a) _____

(b) _____

▼14.4 Units-of-Production Method

OBJECTIVES

1 Describe the units-of-production method of depreciation.

2 Use the units-of-production method to find the depreciation per unit.

3 Calculate the annual depreciation using the units-of-production method.

4 Prepare a depreciation schedule using the units-of-production method.

▼**CASE IN POINT** Capital Curb and Concrete owns a stump chipper that is used to remove tree stumps when preparing for concrete work. Since the machine is not used very often, the company's accountant suggests that the stump chipper be depreciated based on the number of hours used, rather than the number of years owned. Using this approach will be more realistic for depreciating the stump chipper and could result in faster or slower depreciation, depending on how often the chipper is used.

OBJECTIVE 1 Describe the units-of-production method of depreciation. An asset often has a useful life given in terms of **units of production**, such as hours or miles of service. For example, an airplane or truck may have a useful life given as hours of air time or miles of travel. A steel press or stamping machine may have a useful life given as the total number of units that it can produce. For these assets, the units-of-production method often is used.

The units-of-production depreciation method results in a constant amount of depreciation per unit. So, annual depreciation using units-of production depreciation will vary depending on number of units for the year. Straight-line depreciation results in a constant amount of depreciation per year, whereas double-declining-balance and sum-of-the years'-digits depreciation methods result in varying amounts of depreciation each year.

OBJECTIVE 2 Use the units-of-production method to find the depreciation per unit. Find the depreciation per unit with the following formula.

> **Finding Depreciation per Unit**
>
> $$\text{Depreciation per unit} = \frac{\text{Depreciable amount}}{\text{Units of life}}$$

For example, suppose the stump chipper owned by Capital Curb and Concrete costs $7500, has a salvage value of $1500, and is expected to operate 700 hours. Find the depreciation per hour by dividing the depreciable amount by the number of hours of life.

$$
\begin{array}{rl}
\$7500 & \text{cost} \\
- \ 1500 & \textbf{salvage value} \\
\hline
\$6000 & \text{depreciable amount}
\end{array}
$$

OBJECTIVE 3 Calculate the annual depreciation using the units-of-production method.

$$\frac{\$6000 \text{ depreciable amount}}{\textbf{700 hours of life}} = \$8.57 \text{ (rounded) depreciation per hour}$$

Use the following formula and multiply the number of hours used during the year by the depreciation per unit to find the annual depreciation.

> **Finding Annual Depreciation**
>
> $$\text{Depreciation} = \text{Number of units (hours)} \times \text{Depreciation per unit (hour)}$$

Use the formula to find depreciation during a year in which the stump chipper is used 280 hours.

$$280 \times \$8.57 = \textbf{\$2399.60 depreciation}$$

Heavy-Truck Makers Find the Good Times Are Rolling

This newspaper headline reports brisk sales of heavy-duty trucks, the ones that carry more than 33,000 pounds. These behemoth trucks, also known as Class 8s or 18-wheelers, start at a base price of $85,000 and climb as high as $140,000 and more. The useful life of these trucks often depends on the number of miles driven with accountants assigning a useful life of up to 750,000 miles. Some firms have a lot of money tied up in trucks. As a result, managers try to quickly get as much use out of the trucks as possible, sometimes driving each over 100,000 miles a year. This is done using a team of two drivers, who alternate driving. Together, the team may operate a truck for more than 15 hours a day on long-haul routes such as from California to New York.

Using Units-of-Production Depreciation

EXAMPLE 1

North American Trucking purchased a new Kenworth truck for $95,000. The truck has a salvage value of $15,000 and an estimated life of 500,000 miles. Find the depreciation for a year in which the truck is driven 128,000 miles.

SOLUTION

First find the depreciable amount.

$$\begin{array}{rl} \$95,000 & \text{cost} \\ -\ \ 15,000 & \text{scrap value} \\ \hline \$80,000 & \text{depreciable amount} \end{array}$$

Next find the depreciation per unit.

$$\frac{\$80,000 \text{ depreciable amount}}{500,000 \text{ miles of life}} = \$.16 \text{ depreciation per mile}$$

Multiply to find the depreciation for the year.

$$128,000 \text{ miles} \times \$.16 = \$20,480 \text{ depreciation for the year}$$

QUICK CHECK 1

Grayson Medical Clinic purchased an emergency generator at a cost of $19,600. The generator has a salvage value of $2500 and an estimated life of 7500 hours. Find the depreciation for a year in which the generator operated 840 hours.

Preparing a Depreciation Schedule

EXAMPLE 2

Bagel Boys purchased a packaging machine at a cost of $52,300. It has an estimated salvage value of $4000 and an expected life of 690,000 units. Prepare a depreciation schedule using the units-of-production method of depreciation. Use the following packaging schedule.

Year 1	240,000 units
Year 2	150,000 units
Year 3	90,000 units
Year 4	120,000 units
Year 5	90,000 units

SOLUTION

The depreciable amount is $48,300 ($52,300 − $4000). The depreciation per unit is

$$\frac{\$48,300}{690,000 \text{ units}} = \$.07 \text{ per unit}$$

The annual depreciation is found by multiplying the number of units packaged each year by the depreciation per unit.

			Annual Depreciation
Year 1	240,000 units × **$.07** =		$16,800
Year 2	150,000 units × **$.07** =		$10,500
Year 3	90,000 units × **$.07** =		$6,300
Year 4	120,000 units × **$.07** =		$8,400
Year 5	90,000 units × **$.07** =		$6,300
Total	**690,000 units**		**$48,300**

depreciable amount

OBJECTIVE 4 Prepare a depreciation schedule using the units-of-production method. The results above are used in the preparation of the depreciation schedule.

Year	Computation	Depreciation	Accumulated Depreciation	Book Value
0	—	—	—	$52,300
1	(240,000 × $.07)	$16,800	$16,800	$35,500
2	(150,000 × $.07)	$10,500	$27,300	$25,000
3	(90,000 × $.07)	$6,300	$33,600	$18,700
4	(120,000 × $.07)	$8,400	$42,000	$10,300
5	(90,000 × $.07)	$6,300	$48,300	$4,000

The book value at the end of year 5 is the salvage value of $4000 since all the units of production (boxes packaged in this case) have been used.

QUICK CHECK 2

Assume that the cost of the machine in Example 2 was $58,200 and the salvage value was $3000. Use the units-of-production method of depreciation and the same production schedule to prepare a depreciation schedule for the machine. Show the book value for each year.

The following newspaper clipping describes the additional interest and funding being given to the study of entrepreneurship at universities. Many community college business programs are also offering courses in entrepreneurship. This knowledge will help prepare the student who plans to start and operate his or her own business. Being a business owner and not an employee, the student will find that there will be a greater need for understanding business operations including depreciation.

Venture Capital 101: Entrepreneur Courses Increase

University classes explore start-ups, business plans

By Jim Hopkins
USA TODAY

Entrepreneurship, a subject once snubbed by universities, is taking hold on U.S. campuses.

The latest sign: The Ewing Marion Kauffman Foundation recently awarded $25 million to eight U.S. universities pledging to spread entrepreneurship education beyond business classrooms.

Recipients include the University of Rochester, which will use part of its $3.5 million to teach music students to better manage orchestras and other professional music companies.

Historically, universities prepared students to manage *Fortune* 500 companies, education experts say. Schools taught big-company finance and organizational behavior but little about start-ups, such as developing business plans and seeking venture capital.

That changed, especially in the 1990s, after research showed most jobs and innovations are created by start-ups. Also driving academic interest in entrepreneurship:

• **Demand.** More students think self-employment is a safer haven than working for big corporations. "Many saw parents downsized out of work," says John Challenger, CEO of executive outplacement consultant Challenger Gray & Christmas.

Source: USA Today.

▼14.4 Exercises   MyMathLab®

*The shaded sections below contain solutions to help you get a **QUICK START** on the various types of exercises.*

Find the depreciation per unit in the following. Round to the nearest thousandth of a dollar. (See Example 1.)

	Cost	Salvage Value	Estimated Life	Depreciation per Unit
1.	$16,800	$1800	20,000 units	$.75

$16,800 − $1800 = $15,000; $15,000 ÷ 20,000 = $.75

	Cost	Salvage Value	Estimated Life	Depreciation per Unit
2.	$22,500	$1500	60,000 units	_____
3.	$3750	$250	120,000 units	_____
4.	$7500	$500	15,000 miles	_____
5.	$37,500	$7500	125,000 miles	_____
6.	$300,000	$25,000	4000 hours	_____
7.	$175,000	$25,000	5000 hours	_____
8.	$125,000	$20,000	500,000 miles	_____

Find the amount of depreciation in each of the following. (See Example 1.)

	Depreciation per Unit	Units Produced	Amount of Depreciation
9.	$.46	55,000	$25,300

55,000 × $.46 = $25,300

	Depreciation per Unit	Units Produced	Amount of Depreciation
10.	$.18	275,000	$49,500

275,000 × $.18 = $49,500

	Depreciation per Unit	Units Produced	Amount of Depreciation
11.	$.54	32,000	_____
12.	$.73	16,500	_____
13.	$.185	15,000	_____
14.	$.032	73,000	_____
15.	$.14	22,200	_____
16.	$.075	110,000	_____

C indicates an exercise that is related to the Case in Point feature.

17. In your own words, describe the conditions in which the units-of-production method of depreciation is most applicable.

18. Use an example of your own to demonstrate how the annual depreciation amount is found using the units-of-production method of depreciation. (See Objective 3.)

Solve the following application problems. Round to the nearest dollar.

19. **DEEP FRYER**   Michael's Diner purchased a new grilling station at a cost of $6800. The expected life is 5000 hours of production, at which time it will have a salvage value of $500. Using the units-of-production method, prepare a depreciation schedule given the following production: year 1: 1350 hours; year 2: 1820 hours; year 3: 730 hours; year 4: 1100 hours.

Year	Computation	Amount of Depreciation	Accumulated Depreciation	Book Value
0	—	—	—	$6800
1	(1350 × $1.26)	$1701	$1701	$5099
2	(1820 × $1.26)	$2293	$3994	$2806
3	(730 × $1.26)	$920	$4914	$1886
4	(1100 × $1.26)	$1386	$6300	$500

20. **HEAVY-DUTY TRUCK**   Capital Curb and Concrete purchased a Kenworth truck at a cost of $87,000. It estimates that the truck will have a life of 300,000 miles and a salvage value of $15,000. Use the units-of-production method to prepare a depreciation schedule given the following production: year 1: 108,000 miles; year 2: 75,000 miles; year 3: 117,000 miles.

Year	Computation	Amount of Depreciation	Accumulated Depreciation	Book Value
0	—	—	—	$87,000

QUICK CHECK ANSWERS

1. $1915
2. year 1 = $39,000
   year 2 = $27,000
   year 3 = $19,800
   year 4 = $10,200
   year 5 = $ 3,000

14.5 Modified Accelerated Cost Recovery System

OBJECTIVES

1 Understand the modified accelerated cost recovery system (MACRS).

2 Determine the recovery period of different types of property.

3 Find the depreciation rate, given the recovery period and recovery year.

4 Use the MACRS to find the amount of depreciation.

5 Prepare a depreciation schedule using the MACRS.

CASE IN POINT Several different methods of depreciation may have been used by Capital Curb and Concrete for the company's accounting and state tax purposes. However, the modified accelerated cost recovery system (MACRS) must be used for federal income tax purposes. This means that every depreciable asset owned by the company must have a MACRS depreciation schedule and that the owner must also have an understanding of MACRS.

OBJECTIVE 1 Understand the modified accelerated cost recovery system (MACRS). A depreciation method known as the **accelerated cost recovery system (ACRS)** originated as part of the Economic Recovery Tax Act of 1981. It was later modified by the Tax Equity and Fiscal Responsibility Act of 1982 and again by the Tax Reform Act of 1984. The Tax Reform Act of 1986 brought the most recent and significant overhaul to the accelerated cost recovery system (ACRS) and applies to all property placed in service after 1986. The new method is known as the **modified accelerated cost recovery system (MACRS)**. The result is that there are now three systems for computing depreciation for *federal tax purposes*.

Federal Tax Depreciation Methods

1. The MACRS method of depreciation is used for all property placed in service after 1986.
2. The ACRS method of depreciation will continue to be used for all property placed in service from 1981 through 1986.
3. The straight-line, declining-balance, and sum-of-the-years'-digits methods continue to be used for property placed in service before 1981.

Keep two things in mind about the MACRS: First, the system is designed for tax purposes (it is sometimes called the **income-tax method**), and businesses often use some alternative method of depreciation for financial accounting purposes. Second, some states do not allow the modified accelerated cost recovery system of depreciation for finding state income tax liability. This means that businesses must use the *MACRS* on the *federal tax return* and one of the other methods on the *state tax return*.

OBJECTIVE 2 Determine the recovery period of different types of property. Under the modified accelerated cost recovery system, assets are placed in one of nine **recovery classes**, depending on whether the law assumes a 3-, 5-, 7-, 10-, 15-, 20-, 27.5-, 31.5-, or 39-year life for the asset. These lives, or **recovery periods**, are determined as follows.

Modified Accelerated Cost Recovery System (MACRS)

Useful Items
You may want to see:

Publication
- 225 Farmer's Tax Guide
- 463 Travel, Entertainment, and Gift Expenses
- 544 Sales and Other Dispositions of Assets
- 551 Basis of Assets
- 587 Business Use of Your Home

MACRS Recovery Classes

3-year property	Tractor units for use over-the-road, any racehorse that is over 2 years old, any other horse that is over 12 years old, and qualified rent-to-own property
5-year property	Automobiles, taxis, trucks, buses, computers and peripheral equipment, office machinery (typewriters, calculators), copiers, and research equipment, breeding cattle, and dairy cattle
7-year property	Office furniture and fixtures (desks, files, safes), and any property not designated by law to be in any other class
10-year property	Vessels, barges, tugs, and similar water transportation equipment
15-year property	Improvements made directly to land, such as shrubbery, fences, roads, bridges, and any single-purpose agricultural or horticultural structure, and any tree or vine bearing fruits or nuts
20-year property	Certain farm buildings such as a storage shed
27.5-year property	Residential rental real estate such as rental houses, apartments, and mobile homes
31.5-year property	Nonresidential rental real estate such as office building, stores, and warehouses if placed in service before May 13, 1993
39-year property	Nonresidential property placed in service after May 12, 1993

Finding the Recovery Period for Property

EXAMPLE 1

Capital Curb and Concrete owns the following assets. Determine the recovery period for each of them.

(a) computer equipment   (b) an industrial warehouse (built after May 12, 1993)

(c) a pickup truck   (d) office furniture   (e) a farm building (storage shed)

▼ **CASE IN POINT**

SOLUTION

Use the MACRS Recovery Classes list above.

(a) 5 years   (b) 39 years   (c) 5 years   (d) 7 years   (e) 20 years

> **QUICK CHECK 1**
>
> Determine the recovery period for each of the following assets using the MACRS recovery classes.
>
> (a) a drilling barge   (b) a taxi cab   (c) office landscaping   (d) an apartment building

OBJECTIVE 3 Find the depreciation rate, given the recovery period and recovery year. With MACRS, salvage value is ignored, so that *depreciation is based on the entire original cost of the asset.* The depreciation rates are determined by applying the double-declining-balance (200%) method to the 3-, 5-, 7-, and 10-year class properties, the 150% declining-balance method to the 15- and 20-year class properties, and the straight-line (100%) method to the 27.5-, 31.5-, and 39-year class properties. Since these calculations are repetitive and require additional knowledge, the Internal Revenue Service provides tables that show the depreciation rates. The rates are shown as percents in the table on the following page. To determine the rate of depreciation for any year of life, find the recovery year in the left-hand column and then read across to the allowable recovery period.

Notice that the number of recovery years is one greater than the class life of the property. This is because only a half-year of depreciation is allowed for the first year the property is placed in service, regardless of when the property is placed in service during the year. This is known as the **half-year convention** and is used by most taxpayers. A complete coverage of depreciation, including all depreciation tables, is included in the **Internal Revenue Service, Publication 946**, and may be obtained by contacting the IRS Forms Distribution Center or by going to www.irs.gov.

Finding the Rate of Depreciation with MACRS

EXAMPLE 2

Find the rate of depreciation given the following recovery years, and recovery periods.

	(a)	(b)	(c)	(d)
Recovery Year	3	4	2	12
Recovery Period	3 years	10 years	5 years	27.5 years

SOLUTION

(a) 14.81%   (b) 11.52%   (c) 32.00%   (d) 3.637%

	(a)	(b)	(c)	(d)
Recovery Year	4	2	20	7
Recovery Period	7	20	31.5	15

MACRS Depreciation Rates
Applicable Percent for the Class of Property

Recovery Year	3-Year	5-Year	7-Year	10-Year	15-Year	20-Year	27.5-Year	31.5-Year	39-Year
1	33.33	20.00	14.29	10.00	5.00	3.750	3.485	3.042	2.461
2	44.45	32.00	24.49	18.00	9.50	7.219	3.636	3.175	2.564
3	14.81	19.20	17.49	14.40	8.55	6.677	3.636	3.175	2.564
4	7.41	11.52	12.49	11.52	7.70	6.177	3.636	3.175	2.564
5		11.52	8.93	9.22	6.93	5.713	3.636	3.175	2.564
6		5.76	8.92	7.37	6.23	5.285	3.636	3.175	2.564
7			8.93	6.55	5.90	4.888	3.636	3.175	2.564
8			4.46	6.55	5.90	4.522	3.636	3.175	2.564
9				6.56	5.91	4.462	3.636	3.174	2.564
10				6.55	5.90	4.461	3.637	3.175	2.564
11				3.28	5.91	4.462	3.636	3.174	2.564
12					5.90	4.461	3.637	3.175	2.564
13					5.91	4.462	3.636	3.174	2.564
14					5.90	4.461	3.637	3.175	2.564
15					5.91	4.462	3.636	3.174	2.564
16					2.95	4.461	3.637	3.175	2.564
17						4.462	3.636	3.174	2.564
18						4.461	3.637	3.175	2.564
19						4.462	3.636	3.174	2.564
20						4.461	3.637	3.175	2.564
21						2.231	3.636	3.174	2.564
22							3.637	3.175	2.564
23							3.636	3.174	2.564
24							3.637	3.175	2.564
25							3.636	3.174	2.564
26							3.637	3.175	2.564
27							3.636	3.174	2.564
28							1.97	3.175	2.564
29								3.174	2.564
30								3.175	2.564
31								3.174	2.564
32								1.720	2.564
33–39									2.564
40									0.107

OBJECTIVE 4 Use the MACRS to find the amount of depreciation. MACRS is the method of depreciation that must be used on federal income taxes for property placed in service after 1986. There are three important points to remember.

1. Do not use salvage value.
2. Refer to the table to find the life of the asset for that class of property.
3. Find the depreciation amount by multiplying the appropriate percent from the table by the cost of the item.

The numbers in the MACRS table are based on the double-declining-balance method, so it yields results similar to that method.

Finding the Amount of Depreciation with MACRS Capital Curb and Concrete bought a new pickup truck for $21,500. Find the amount of depreciation for the pickup truck in the fourth year.

 CASE IN POINT

SOLUTION

A pickup truck has a recovery period of 5 years. From the table on page 607, the depreciation rate in the fourth year of recovery of 5-year property is **11.52%**. Multiply this rate by the full cost of the property to determine the amount of depreciation.

$$\textbf{11.52\%} \times \$21,\!500 = \$2476.80 = \$2477 \text{ (rounded)}$$

The amount of depreciation is $2477.

QUICK CHECK 3

Find the depreciation in year 2 for the pickup truck in Example 3.

Preparing a Depreciation Schedule with MACRS Omaha Insurance Company has purchased new office furniture at a cost of $24,160. Prepare a depreciation schedule using the modified accelerated cost recovery system.

SOLUTION

No salvage value is used with MACRS. Office desks and chairs have a 7-year recovery period. The annual depreciation rates for 7-year properties are shown in the table at the side.

Recovery Year	Recovery Percent (Rate)
1	14.29%
2	24.49%
3	17.49%
4	12.49%
5	8.93%
6	8.92%
7	8.93%
8	4.46%

OBJECTIVE 5 Prepare a depreciation schedule using the MACRS. For the furniture in Example 4, multiply the appropriate percents by $24,160 to get the results shown in the following depreciation schedule.

Year	Computation	Amount of Depreciation	Accumulated Depreciation	Book Value
0	—	—	—	$24,160
1	(14.29% × $24,160)	$3452	$3,452	$20,708
2	(24.49% × $24,160)	$5917	$9,369	$14,791
3	(17.49% × $24,160)	$4226	$13,595	$10,565
4	(12.49% × $24,160)	$3018	$16,613	$7,547
5	(8.93% × $24,160)	$2157	$18,770	$5,390
6	(8.92% × $24,160)	$2155	$20,925	$3,235
7	(8.93% × $24,160)	$2157	$23,082	$1,078
8	(4.46% × $24,160)	$1078	$24,160	$0

QUICK CHECK 4

Airport Transit purchased a new bus at a cost of $128,000. Use the MACRS method of depreciation to find the book value at the end of the fourth year.

The MACRS method of depreciation allows a rapid rate of investment recovery and at the same time results in less complicated computations. By eliminating the necessity for estimating the life of an asset and the need for using a salvage value, the tables provide a direct method of calculating depreciation.

▼ 14.5 Exercises   MyMathLab®

The shaded sections below contain solutions to help you get a **QUICK START** *on the various types of exercises.*

Use the MACRS depreciation rates table to find the recovery percent (rate), given the following recovery years and recovery periods. (See Examples 1 and 2.)

Recovery Year	Recovery Recovery Period	Percent (Rate)		Recovery Year	Recovery Recovery Period	Percent (Rate)
1. 3	5-year	19.20%	2. 5		7-year	8.93%
3. 9	10-year	_____	4. 1		3-year	_____
5. 1	5-year	_____	6. 5		20-year	_____
7. 15	27.5-year	_____	8. 11		31.5-year	_____
9. 6	5-year	_____	10. 4		27.5-year	_____
11. 14	39-year	_____	12. 4		31.5-year	_____

Find the first year's depreciation for each of the following using the MACRS method of depreciation and the MACRS depreciation rates table. Round to the nearest dollar. (See Example 3.)

13. Cost: $12,250
Recovery period: 7 years
Depreciation (year 1): $1751

14.29% rate
$12,250 × .1429 = $1751 depreciation

14. Cost: $8790
Recovery period: 5 years
Depreciation (year 1): $1758

20% rate
$8790 × .20 = $1758 depreciation

15. Cost: $430,500
Recovery period: 10 years
Depreciation (year 1):   _____

16. Cost: $72,300
Recovery period: 20 years
Depreciation (year 1):   _____

17. Cost: $48,000
Recovery period: 10 years
Depreciation (year 1):   _____

18. Cost: $12,340
Recovery period: 3 years
Depreciation (year 1):   _____

Find the book value at the end of the first year for each of the following using the MACRS method of depreciation and the MACRS depreciation rates table. Round to the nearest dollar. (See Example 4.)

19. Cost: $9380
Recovery period: 3 years
Book value: $6254

$9380 × .3333 = $3126
$9380 − $3126 = $6254 book value

20. Cost: $68,700
Recovery period: 5 years
Book value: _____

🔺 indicates an exercise that is related to the Case in Point feature.

21. Cost: $18,800
Recovery period: 10 years
Book value: _____

22. Cost: $156,000
Recovery period: 27.5 years
Book value: _____

Find the book value at the end of 3 years for each of the following using the MACRS method of depreciation and the MACRS depreciation rates table. Round to the nearest dollar. (See Example 4.)

23. Cost: $9570
Recovery period: 5 years
Book value: $2756

20% + 32% + 19.2% = 71.2% rate 3 years
$9570 × .712 = $6813.84 = $6814 dep. 3 years
$9570 − $6814 = $2756 book value year 3

24. Cost: $18,800
Recovery period: 3 years
Book value: _____

25. Cost: $136,800
Recovery period: 27.5 years
Book value: _____

26. Cost: $390,400
Recovery period: 31.5 years
Book value: _____

Solve the following application problems. Use the MACRS depreciation rates table. Round to the nearest dollar. (See Example 4.)

27. STORAGE TANK   New England Propane purchased a storage tank for $10,980. Prepare a depreciation schedule using the MACRS method of depreciation (3-year property).

Year	Computation	Amount of Depreciation	Accumulated Depreciation	Book Value
0	—	—	—	$10,980
1	(33.33% × $10,980)	$3660	$3,660	$7,320
2	(44.45% × $10,980)	$4881	$8,541	$2,439
3	(14.81% × $10,980)	$1626	$10,167	$813
4	(7.41% × $10,980)	$813*	$10,980	$0

*Due to rounding in prior years

28. COMPANY VEHICLES   Capital Curb and Concrete purchased a pickup truck at a cost of $21,500. Prepare a depreciation schedule using the MACRS method of depreciation (5-year property).

Year	Computation	Amount of Depreciation	Accumulated Depreciation	Book Value
0	—	—	—	$21,500
1				
2				
3				
4				
5				
6				

29. **OFFSHORE DRILLING** Gulf Drilling purchased a pump to circulate drilling fluids for $122,700. Prepare a depreciation schedule using the MACRS method of depreciation (10-year property).

Year	Computation	Amount of Depreciation	Accumulated Depreciation	Book Value
0	—	—	—	$122,700
1				
2				
3				
4				
5				
6				
7				
8				
9				
10				
11				

30. **RESIDENTIAL RENTAL PROPERTY** Joseph Flores purchased some residential rental real estate for $990,000. Find the book value at the end of the tenth year using the MACRS method of depreciation (27.5-year property).

30. _____

Year	Computation	Amount of Depreciation	Book Value
0	—	—	$990,000
1			
2			
3			
4			
5			
6			
7			
8			
9			
10			

31. The same business asset may be depreciated using two or more different methods. Explain why a business would do this. (See Objective 1.)

32. After learning about MACRS, what three features stand out to you as being unique to this method? (See Objective 3.)

Use the MACRS depreciation rates table in the following application problems. Round to the nearest dollar.

33. **COMMERCIAL FISHING BOAT**   Reef Fisheries purchased a new fishing boat (10-year property) for $74,125. Find the depreciation in year 8 using the MACRS method of depreciation.

33. _____

34. **SHOPPING CENTER**   A new parking lot was added to the Oak Shopping Center at a cost of $118,000. Find the depreciation in year 12 using the MACRS method of depreciation (15-year property).

34. _____

35. **LAPTOP COMPUTERS**   Capital Curb Concrete purchased two laptop computers for the office for $1700. Find the book value at the end of the third year using the MACRS method of depreciation.

35. _____

36. **DENTAL OFFICE FURNITURE**   Dr. Jill Owens Family Dentistry purchased new furniture for its patient reception area at a cost of $27,400. Find the book value at the end of the fifth year using the MACRS method of depreciation.

36. _____

37. **OFFICE BUILDING**   James Bradley purchased an office building at a cost of $860,000. Find the amount of depreciation for each of the first five years using the MACRS method of depreciation (39-year property).

Year 1: _____

Years 2–5: _____

38. **INDEPENDENT BOOKSTORE OWNERSHIP**   Maretha Roseborough, owner of the Barnstormer Bookstore, bought a building to use for her business. The cost of the building was $620,000. Find the amount of depreciation for each of the first five years using the MACRS method of depreciation (39-year property).

Year 1: _____

Years 2–5: _____

QUICK CHECK ANSWERS

1. (a) 10 years   (b) 5 years
   (c) 15 years   (d) 27.5 years
2. (a) 12.49%   (b) 7.219%
   (c) 3.175%   (d) 5.90%

3. $6880
4. $22,118

▼ Chapter 14   Quick Review

Chapter Terms   *Review the following terms to test your understanding of the chapter. For each term you do not know, refer to the page number found next to that term.*

200% method [p. 582]

accelerated cost recovery system (ACRS) [p. 605]

accelerated depreciation [p. 582]

accumulated depreciation [p. 574]

book value [p. 574]

cost [p. 574]

declining-balance [p. 574]

depreciable amount [p. 575]

depreciation [p. 574]

depreciation fraction [p. 589]

depreciation schedule [p. 576]

double-declining-balance rate [p. 582]

half-year convention [p. 606]

income tax method [p. 605]

intangible assets [p. 574]

Internal Revenue Service [p. 606]

modified accelerated cost recovery system (MACRS) [p. 605]

no salvage value [p. 574]

Publication 946 [p. 606]

recovery classes [p. 605]

recovery periods [p. 605]

residual value [p. 574]

salvage value [p. 574]

scrap value [p. 574]

straight-line method [p. 574]

sum-of-the-years'-digits [p. 574]

tangible assets [p. 574]

units-of-production [p. 574]

useful life [p. 574]

CONCEPTS

EXAMPLES

14.1 Straight-line method of depreciation

The depreciation is the same each year.

$$\text{Depreciation} = \frac{\textbf{Depreciable amount}}{\textbf{Years of life}}$$

Cost, \$4500; scrap value, \$800; life, 8 years; find the annual amount of depreciation.

$$\begin{array}{rl} \$4500 & \text{cost} \\ -\ 800 & \text{scrap} \\ \hline \$3700 & \text{depreciable amount} \end{array}$$

$$\frac{\$3700}{8} = \$462.50 \text{ depreciation each year}$$

14.1 Book value

Book value is the remaining value at the end of the year.

Book value = Cost − Accumulated depreciation

Cost, \$4000; scrap value, \$1000; life, 3 years; find the book value at the end of the first year.

$$\begin{array}{rl} \$4000 & \text{cost} \\ -\ 1000 & \text{scrap value} \\ \hline \$3000 & \text{depreciable amount} \end{array}$$

$$\frac{\$3000}{3} = \$1000 \text{ depreciation}$$

$$\begin{array}{rl} \$4000 & \text{cost} \\ -\ 1000 & \text{depreciation} \\ \hline \$3000 & \text{book value year 1} \end{array}$$

14.2 Double-declining-balance rate

First find the straight-line rate, and then adjust it. For the 200% method, **multiply by 2**.

The life of an asset is 10 years. Find the double-declining-balance (200%) rate.

$$10 \text{ years} = \textbf{10\%}\left(\frac{1}{10}\right) \textbf{straight-line}$$

$$\textbf{2} \times 10\% = 20\% \text{ per year}$$

14.2 Double-declining-balance depreciation method

First find the double-declining-balance rate, and then multiply by the cost in year 1. The rate is then multiplied by the declining book value in the following years.

Depreciation =
Double-declining-balance rate × Declining balance

Cost, \$1400; life, 5 years; find the depreciation in years 1 and 2.

$$2 \times 20\% \text{ (straight-line rate)} = 40\%$$

Year 1: **40%** × \$1400 = \$560 depreciation year 1

\$1400 − **\$560** = \$840 book value year 1

Year 2: **40%** × \$840 = \$336 depreciation year 2

CONCEPTS	EXAMPLES

14.3 Sum-of-the-years'-digits depreciation fraction

Add the years' digits to get the denominator.
The numerator is the number of years of life remaining.
The shortcut formula for finding the denominator is:

$$\frac{n(n+1)}{2}$$

Useful life is 4 years. Find the depreciation fraction for each year.

$$1 + 2 + 3 + 4 = 10 \quad \text{or} \quad \frac{4(4+1)}{2} = 10$$

Year	Depreciation Fraction
1	$\frac{4}{10}$
2	$\frac{3}{10}$
3	$\frac{2}{10}$
4	$\frac{1}{10}$

14.3 Sum-of-the-years'-digits depreciation method

First find the depreciation fraction, and then multiply by the depreciable amount.

**Depreciation =
Depreciation fraction × Depreciable amount**

Cost, $2500; salvage value, $400; life, 6 years; find depreciation in year 1.

$$\text{Depreciation fraction} = \frac{6}{21}$$

Depreciable amount = $2100 ($2500 − $400)

$$\text{Depreciation} = \frac{6}{21} \times \$2100 = \$600$$

14.4 Units-of-production depreciation amount per unit

Use the following formula.

$$\text{Depreciation per unit} = \frac{\text{Depreciable amount}}{\text{Units of life}}$$

Cost, $10,000; salvage value, $2500; useful life, 15,000 units; find depreciation per unit.

$10,000 − $2500 = $7500 depreciable amount

$$\text{Depreciation per unit} = \frac{\$7500 \text{ depreciable amount}}{15,000 \text{ units of life}} = \$.50$$

14.4 Units-of-production depreciation method

Multiply the number of units (hours) of production by the depreciation per unit (per hour).

**Depreciation =
Number of units (hours) × Depreciation per unit (hour)**

Cost, $25,000; salvage value, $2000; useful life, 100,000 units; production in year 1, 22,300 units; find the first year's depreciation.

1. $25,000 − $2000 = $23,000 depreciable amount
2. $\frac{\$23,000}{100,000} = \$.23$ depreciation per unit
3. 22,300 × $.23 = $5129 depreciation year 1

14.5 Modified accelerated cost recovery system (MACRS)

Established in 1986 for federal income tax purposes. No salvage value. Recovery periods are:

3-year	5-year	7-year
10-year	15-year	20-year
27.5-year	31.5-year	39-year

Find the proper rate from the table and then multiply by the cost to find depreciation.

Use the table, finding the recovery period column at the top of the table and the recovery year in the left-hand column. Cost, $4850; recovery period, 5 years; recovery year, 3; find the depreciation.

Rate is **19.20%** from table.

$4850 × **.192** = $931 depreciation

▼ Case Study

COMPARING DEPRECIATION METHODS

Trader Joe's purchased freezer cases at a cost of $285,000. The estimated life of the freezer cases is 5 years, at which time they will have no salvage value. The company would like to compare allowable depreciation methods and decides to prepare depreciation schedules for the fixtures using the straight-line, double-declining-balance, and sum-of-the-years'-digits methods of depreciation. Using depreciation schedules, find the answers to these questions for Trader Joe's.

1. What is the book value at the end of 3 years using the straight-line depreciation method? 1. _____

2. Using the double-declining-balance method of depreciation, what is the book value at the end of the third year? 2. _____

3. With the sum-of-the-years'-digits method of depreciation, what is the accumulated depreciation at the end of 3 years? 3. _____

4. What amount of depreciation will be taken in year 4 with each of the methods? 4. _____

_____

_____

INVESTIGATE

Identify a store or business with which you are familiar and list six of its depreciable assets. Examples could be such items as buildings, computer equipment, vehicles, and fixtures. Using the information on the MACRS method of depreciation, give the recovery period and the first-year depreciation rate for each of the six depreciable assets you listed.

Case in Point Summary Exercise

FORD MOTOR COMPANY

www.ford.com

Facts:

- 1925: Price of first Ford truck was $281
- 1950s: Cars styled for more comfort
- 2003: Celebrates 100th anniversary
- 2009–10: Weathers financial crisis without government help

In 1903, with $28,000 in cash, Henry Ford started Ford Motor Company, which is now one of the world's largest companies. Ford's greatest contribution to automobile manufacturing was the moving assembly that allowed individual workers to stay in one place and perform the same task on each vehicle as it passed by. The moving assembly line allowed Ford to cut costs and reduce prices of new automobiles so that average working families could afford them. Today, the Ford Motor Company sells a variety of vehicles under the Ford and Lincoln brands.

Capital Curb and Concrete purchased a new Ford truck for $26,500 to be used by the sales manager, who often drives to construction sites to work with customers. The firm's accountant believes that the useful life of the truck is 5 years and that the estimated salvage value is $4500.

1. Using the information above find the book value of the pickup truck after 3 years using the straight-line method of depreciation.

1. _____

2. Find the book value of the truck at the end of 3 years using the double-declining-balance method of depreciation.

2. _____

3. The company also spent $118,350 to purchase a truck that hauls concrete. Which method of depreciation must it use when calculating federal income taxes? What is the appropriate recovery class? Use this information for all of the following exercises.

3. _____

4. Find the annual depreciation, for each of the first three years, rounded to the nearest dollar.

4. _____

5. Find the book value at the end of the third year.

5. _____

6. Find the percent of the total depreciation that is taken in the first three years. Round to the nearest tenth of a percent.

6. _____

7. What is the depreciation in the year after book value reaches salvage value?

7. _____

Discussion Question: *Explain depreciation in your own words. Why is depreciation important to businesses managers?*

Chapter 14 Test

To help you review, the numbers in brackets show the section in which the topic was discussed.

Find the annual straight-line and double-declining-balance rates (percents) of depreciation and the sum-of-the-years'-digits fraction for the first year for each of the following estimated lives. **[14.1–14.3]**

Life	Straight-Line Rate	Double-Declining-Balance Rate	Sum-of-the-Years'-Digits Fraction
1. 4 years	_____	_____	_____
2. 5 years	_____	_____	_____
3. 8 years	_____	_____	_____
4. 20 years	_____	_____	_____

Solve the following application problems. Round to the nearest dollar.

5. Cloverdale Creamery purchased a soft-serve ice cream maker at a cost of $82,000. The machine has an estimated life of 10 years and a scrap value of $3000. Use the straight-line method of depreciation to find the annual depreciation. **[14.1]**

5. _____

 6. Capital Curb and Concrete purchased a new dump truck for $38,000. If the estimated life of the dump truck is 8 years, find the book value at the end of 2 years using the double-declining-balance method of depreciation. **[14.2]**

6. _____

7. Feather River Youth Camp purchased a diesel generator for $8250. Use the sum-of-the-years'-digits method of depreciation to determine the amount of depreciation to be taken during *each of the 4 years* on the diesel generator that has a 4-year life and a scrap value of $1500. **[14.3]**

Year 1: _____

Year 2: _____

Year 3: _____

Year 4: _____

8. A private road costs $56,000 and has a 15-year recovery period. Find the depreciation in the third year using the MACRS method of depreciation. **[14.5]**

8. _____

9. One water filter at Micro Brew costs $74,000, has an estimated life of 20 years, and has an estimated scrap value of $12,000. Use the straight-line method of depreciation to find the book value of the machinery at the end of 10 years. **[14.1]**

9. _____

10. Gold's Gym has added paging and intercom features to the communication systems of four stores at a cost of $2800 per store. The estimated life of the systems is 10 years, with no expected salvage value. Using the sum-of-the-years'-digits method of depreciation, find the total book value of all the systems at the end of the third year. **[14.3]**

10. _____

 indicates an exercise that is related to the Case in Point feature.

11. Table Fresh Foods purchased a machine to package its presliced garden salads. The machine costs $20,100 and has an estimated life of 30,000 hours and a salvage value of $1500. Use the units-of-production method of depreciation to find **(a)** the annual amount of depreciation and **(b)** the book value at the end of each year, given the following use information: year 1: 7800 hours; year 2: 4300 hours; year 3: 4850 hours; year 4: 7600 hours. **[14.4]**

(a) _____

(b) _____

12. The Rice Growers Cooperative paid $2,800,000 to build a new rice-drying plant. The recovery period is 39 years. Use the MACRS method of depreciation to find the book value of the rice-drying plant at the end of the fifth year.   **[14.5]**

12. _____

15 Financial Statements and Ratios

CHAPTER CONTENTS

15.1 The Income Statement

15.2 Analyzing the Income Statement

15.3 The Balance Sheet

15.4 Analyzing the Balance Sheet

▼ CASE IN POINT

APPLE, INC. gave the world the Mac computer, iPod, iPhone, iPad, iTunes, MacBook Pro, and Apple Apps (Applications). By 2012, Apple had become the most valuable company in the world. It's value later fell below ExxonMobil only to regain the lead again in late 2013. Shares of the firm trade on the NASDAQ stock exchange under the symbol AAPL. This chapter shows recent financial statements for this very successful and creative company.

Managers must keep careful records of expenses and income in order to operate the business, communicate with others about the business, provide information to lenders, and prepare tax returns. **Accountants** track the income and expenses of the firm. They are concerned with issues such as meeting payroll, paying suppliers, estimating and paying taxes, and estimating and receiving revenues. This chapter looks at some tools used in business to gauge the financial health of a firm.

▼ 15.1 The Income Statement

▼ CASE IN POINT   Apple, Inc. is a **publicly held corporation**, meaning that it is owned by shareholders that buy and sell stock in a public market. As a publicly held corporation, it must prepare and distribute financial reports. Accuracy is very important when preparing these documents since investors, banks, managers, and even competitors rely on them.

OBJECTIVE 1 Understand the terms on an income statement. Publically held companies have stringent requirements and must release financial statements such as income statements and balance sheets to the public on a quarterly basis. An **income statement** summarizes the firm's income and expenses for a specific period quarter or a year. Balance sheets are discussed later in the chapter. Here are some important definitions related to income statements.

Gross sales, or **total revenue**, is the total amount of money received from customers.
Returns are returns by customers (usually used by smaller companies and not large ones).
Net sales is the value of goods and services bought and kept by customers.

> **Finding Net Sales**
>
> $$\text{Net sales} = \text{Gross sales} - \text{Returns}$$

Cost of goods sold is the amount paid by the firm for items sold to customers.
Gross profit, or **gross profit on sales**, is the money left over after a firm pays for the cost of goods it sells.

> **Finding Gross Profit**
>
> $$\text{Gross profit} = \text{Net sales} - \text{Cost of goods sold}$$

Operating expenses, or **overhead**, is the firm's cost to run the business.
Net income before taxes is the amount earned by the firm before taxes are paid.
Net income, or **net income after taxes**, is the income remaining after income taxes are paid.

> **Finding Net Income Before and After Income Taxes**
>
> $$\text{Net income before taxes} = \text{Gross profit} - \text{Operating expenses}$$
> $$\text{Net income} = \text{Net income before taxes} - \text{Income taxes}$$

Finding Net Income   **EXAMPLE 1**   A portion of the 2011 income statement for Apple, Inc. is shown. All numbers are in millions, so total revenue of $108,249 actually refers to $108,249,000,000, or one-hundred eight billion, two hundred forty-nine million dollars. That represents the sale of a lot of electronic devices as well as music and app downloads. Check to make sure the income statement balances.

Quick TIP

Bankers and investors pore over the financial statements of publicly held corporations to determine their creditworthiness and whether they would be good investments.

SOLUTION

Apple, Inc. Consolidated Income Statement Year Ending September 23, 2011 (in millions of dollars)	
Gross Sales	$108,249
Returns	− 0
Net Sales	$108,249
Cost of Goods Sold	−$64,431
Gross Profit	$43,818
Operating Expenses	− 9,613
Net Income before Taxes	$34,205
Income Taxes	− 8,283
Net Income after Taxes	$25,922

Apple had no returns from customers and paid income taxes of $8,283,000,000, or more than $8 billion, leaving an after tax profit of $25,922,000,000. The sum of cost of goods sold, operating expenses, income taxes, and net income should equal net sales.

$$\$64{,}431 + \$9{,}613 + \$8{,}283 + 25{,}922 = \$108{,}249$$

where the terms are cost of goods sold, operating expenses, income taxes, and net income.

The income statement checks.

QUICK CHECK 1

A firm has gross sales of $5.2, cost of goods sold of $3.7, operating expenses of $.7, and income taxes of $.2, all in millions of dollars. Find the net income after taxes.

OBJECTIVE 2 Prepare an income statement. Example 1 gave the value for the cost of goods sold, but this amount would normally need to be calculated. The cost of goods sold can be found using the following formula. **Initial inventory** is the value of all goods on hand for sale at the beginning of the period. **Ending inventory** is the value of all goods on hand for sale at the end of the period.

Finding Cost of Goods Sold

        Value of initial inventory
+ Cost of goods purchased during time period
+ Freight
− Value of ending inventory
        Cost of goods sold

Preparing an Income Statement

EXAMPLE 2

In the first year of business, Decorative Stones, Inc. had $452,700 in gross sales, with returns of $38,100. Inventory at the beginning of the year was $48,800, with a cost of goods purchased of $253,700 and freight of $7430. Inventory at the end of the year was $89,090. Expenses were as follows: salaries $104,300; rent $38,800; advertising $24,300; utilities $11,600; taxes on inventory and payroll $9400; and miscellaneous expenses $13,350. The company paid no income taxes because of a slight loss in the first year. Complete an income statement using the following steps.

Preparing an Income Statement

Step 1   Enter gross sales and returns. Subtract returns from gross sales to find net sales. Net sales in this example were $414,600.

Step 2   Enter the cost of goods purchased and the freight. Add these two numbers to find total of goods available for sale.

Step 3   Add the inventory on January 1 and the total cost of goods purchased to find the total cost of goods purchased.

Step 4   Subtract the inventory on December 31 from the result of step 3. This gives the cost of goods sold.

Step 5   Subtract the cost of goods sold from net sales, which were found in step 1. The result is the gross profit.

Step 6   Enter all expenses and add them to get the total expenses.

Step 7   Subtract the total expenses from the gross profit to find the net income before taxes.

Step 8   Subtract income taxes from net income before taxes to find net income (net income after taxes).

SOLUTION

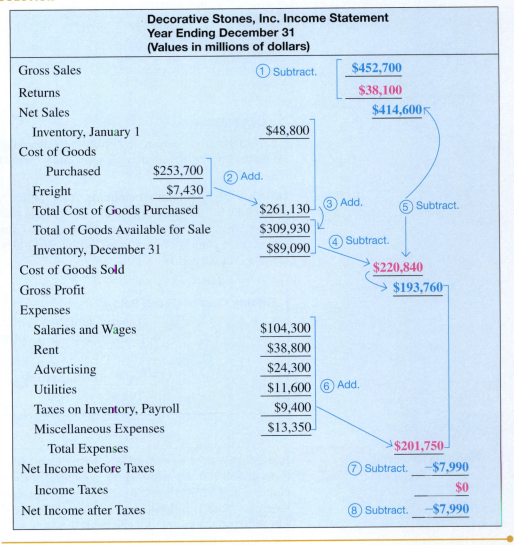

Decorative Stones, Inc. Income Statement
Year Ending December 31
(Values in millions of dollars)

Gross Sales	① Subtract.	$452,700
Returns		$38,100
Net Sales		$414,600
Inventory, January 1		$48,800
Cost of Goods		
Purchased	$253,700 ② Add.	
Freight	$7,430	
Total Cost of Goods Purchased		$261,130 ③ Add. ⑤ Subtract.
Total of Goods Available for Sale		$309,930
Inventory, December 31		$89,090 ④ Subtract.
Cost of Goods Sold		$220,840
Gross Profit		$193,760
Expenses		
Salaries and Wages		$104,300
Rent		$38,800
Advertising		$24,300
Utilities		$11,600 ⑥ Add.
Taxes on Inventory, Payroll		$9,400
Miscellaneous Expenses		$13,350
Total Expenses		$201,750
Net Income before Taxes	⑦ Subtract.	−$7,990
Income Taxes		$0
Net Income after Taxes	⑧ Subtract.	−$7,990

QUICK CHECK 2

Find the net income for a firm given the following information, in millions of dollars: Gross Sales $10.2; Returns $.1; Beginning Inventory $.3; Cost of Goods Purchased including freight $6.9; Ending Inventory $.6; Total Expenses $1.8; and Income Taxes $.5.

▼ 15.1 Exercises

MyMathLab®

*The shaded sections below contain solutions to help you get a **QUICK START** on the various types of exercises.*

Find (a) the gross profit, (b) the net income before taxes, and (c) the net income after taxes for each firm. (See Example 1.)

1. **GIFT SHOP** Janis Jacobs opened a small candle and gift shop in the mall three years ago. Last year, the cost of goods sold was $367,200, operating expenses were $228,300, income taxes were $22,700, gross sales were $685,900, and returns were $2350.
   (a) Gross profit = $685,900 − $2350 − $367,200 = $316,350
   (b) Net income before taxes = $316,350 − $228,300 = $88,050
   (c) Net income after taxes = $88,050 − $22,700 = $65,350

   (a) $316,350
   (b) $88,050
   (c) $65,350

2. **ICE CREAM SHOP** Ben's Ice Cream had quarterly net sales of $281,400, operating expenses (including wages) of $119,380, a cost of goods sold of $103,800, and paid $7240 in taxes.

   (a) _____
   (b) _____
   (c) _____

3. **APPAREL** Jill's Fashions had gross sales of $852,300 last year, with returns of $42,800. The inventory on January 1 was $174,690. A total of $345,790 worth of goods was purchased with freight of $18,107. The inventory on December 31 was $158,200. Wages and salaries were $168,240; rent was $48,200; advertising was $24,300; utilities were $11,600; taxes on inventory and payroll totaled $13,880; miscellaneous expenses totaled $21,900; and income taxes were $34,800. Complete the following income statement.

Jill's Fashions Income Statement Year Ending December 31		
Gross Sales		_____
Returns		_____
Net Sales		_____
Inventory, January 1	_____	
Cost of Goods		
Purchased	_____	
Freight	_____	
Total Cost of Goods Purchased	_____	
Total of Goods Available for Sale	_____	
Inventory, December 31	_____	
Cost of Goods Sold		_____
Gross Profit		_____
Expenses		
Salaries and Wages	_____	
Rent	_____	
Advertising	_____	
Utilities	_____	
Taxes on Inventory, Payroll	_____	
Miscellaneous Expenses	_____	
Total Expenses		_____
Net Income before Taxes		_____
Income Taxes		_____
Net Income		_____

4. Explain why a lender and an investor would want to look at an income statement before making a loan or an investment. (See Objective 1.)

5. Explain why a banker would look at your personal income statement before approving you for a loan. (See Objective 1.)

6. DENTAL-SUPPLY COMPANY New England Dental Supply is a regional wholesaler that had gross sales last year of $2,215,000. Returns totaled $26,000. Inventory on January 1 was $215,000. Goods purchased during the year totaled $1,123,000. Freight was $4000. Inventory on December 31 was $265,000. Wages and salaries were $326,000, rent was $59,000, advertising was $11,000, utilities were $12,000, taxes on inventory and payroll totaled $28,200, and miscellaneous expenses were $18,800. In addition, income taxes for the year amounted to $197,800. Complete the following income statement for this firm. (See Example 2.)

New England Dental Supply Income Statement Year Ending December 31		
Gross Sales		_____
Returns		_____
Net Sales		_____
Inventory, January 1	_____	
Cost of Goods		
Purchased	_____	
Freight	_____	
Total Cost of Goods Purchased	_____	
Total of Goods Available for Sale	_____	
Inventory, December 31	_____	
Cost of Goods Sold		_____
Gross Profit		_____
Expenses		
Salaries and Wages	_____	
Rent	_____	
Advertising	_____	
Utilities	_____	
Taxes on Inventory, Payroll	_____	
Miscellaneous Expenses	_____	
Total Expenses		_____
Net Income before Taxes		_____
Income Taxes		_____
Net Income		_____

QUICK CHECK ANSWERS

1. $.6 million, or $600,000

2. $1.2 million

15.2 Analyzing the Income Statement

OBJECTIVES

1 Compare income statements using vertical analysis.

2 Compare income statements to published charts.

3 Compare income statements using horizontal analysis.

CASE IN POINT It is important that you look carefully at the income statement of Apple, or any other company, before investing in the stock of that company. Invest only if you are convinced the company will be profitable.

OBJECTIVE 1 Compare income statements using vertical analysis. A firm can find its net income for a given period of time by going through the steps presented in the preceding section. A question that might then be asked is "What happened to each part of the sales dollar?" The first step toward answering this question is to list each of the important items on the income statement as a percent of net sales. This process is called a **vertical analysis** of the income statement.

In a vertical analysis, each item on the income statement is found as a percent of the net sales.

$$R = \frac{P}{B} \quad \text{or} \quad R = \frac{\text{Particular item}}{\text{Net sales}}$$

For example, we can use data from the 2011 income statement of Apple shown on page 621. The percent cost of goods sold is found by dividing cost of goods sold divided by net sales.

$$\text{Percent cost of goods sold} = \frac{\$64,431}{\$108,249} = 59.5\% \quad \text{(rounded)}$$

So the firm spent nearly 60% of total revenue for the cost of goods. A lot of this money went to Asia since many of the goods were produced at factories on that continent. Other companies may have either higher or lower percent cost of goods sold. For example, Microsoft Corporation writes computer software. The cost of labor to produce the software is very high (operating expense), but the cost of goods such as optical disks on which software is written is very low. So this same ratio would be tiny for Microsoft.

A **comparative income statement** is used to compare results from two or more years. It can be used to show how the company is doing over time.

Performing a Vertical Analysis First, do a vertical analysis for the 2010 and 2011 income statements for Apple and then build a comparative income statement and show the results in a table.

Apple, Inc., Consolidated Income Statement (in millions of dollars)		
Year Ending September 23	**2010**	**2011**
Gross Sales	$65,225	$108,249
Returns	− 0	− 0
Net Sales	$65,225	$108,249
Cost of Goods Sold	− 39,541	− 64,431
Gross Profit	$25,684	$43,818
Operating Expenses	− 7,144	− 9,613
Net Income before Taxes	$18,540	$34,205
Income Taxes	− 4,527	− 8,283
Net Income	$14,013	$25,922

SOLUTION

Calculate each value in the column labeled 2010 as a percent of gross sales for the year, rounded to the nearest tenth. Gross sales equals net sales for both 2010 and 2011 since there were no returns. Then do the same for 2011.

Comparative Income Statement for Apple, Inc.		
	2010	**2011**
Percent Cost of Goods Sold	$\dfrac{\$39,541}{\$65,225} = 60.6\%$	$\dfrac{\$64,431}{\$108,249} = 59.5\%$
Percent Gross Profit	$\dfrac{\$25,684}{\$65,225} = 39.4\%$	$\dfrac{\$43,818}{\$108,249} = 40.5\%$
Percent Operating Expenses	$\dfrac{\$7,144}{\$65,225} = 11.0\%$	$\dfrac{\$9,613}{\$108,249} = 8.9\%$
Percent Net Income before Taxes	$\dfrac{\$18,540}{\$65,225} = 28.4\%$	$\dfrac{\$34,205}{\$108,249} = 31.6\%$
Income Taxes	$\dfrac{\$4,525}{\$65,225} = 6.9\%$	$\dfrac{\$8,283}{\$108,249} = 7.7\%$

Quick TIP

Before deciding to invest in a company, prudent investors want to know much more about a company than what is shown in this example.

Quick TIP

Good managers constantly watch costs!

The cost of goods sold decreased from 60.6% of net sales in 2010 to 59.5% of net sales in 2011. It appears as if management controlled the costs of goods sold resulting in a slightly higher gross profit percent. Management also decreased operating expenses during the same time period from 11.0% to 8.9%, resulting in an improvement in the percent net income before taxes. Income taxes were nearly 8% of sales.

These percentages change from year to year due to many factors. So, it is important to look for trends and to try to determine the underlying causes, as we will do in Objective 3.

QUICK CHECK 1

A 2014 income statement shows the following figures in millions: Net Sales $23.5, Returns $.0, Cost of Goods Sold $12.9, and Operating Expenses $3.8. Do a vertical analysis and round each percent to the nearest tenth.

OBJECTIVE 2 Compare income statements to published charts. If you own a business or are considering investing in a business, you would be wise to compare the financial figures for that business to industry averages. Published charts of industry averages can be obtained from the federal government.

Type of Business	Cost of Goods	Gross Profit	Total Expenses*	Net Income	Wages	Rent	Advertising
Supermarkets	82.7%	17.3%	13.9%	3.4%	6.5%	.8%	1.0%
Men's and women's apparel	67.0%	33.0%	21.2%	11.8%	8.0%	2.5%	1.9%
Women's apparel	64.8%	35.2%	23.4%	11.7%	7.9%	4.9%	1.8%
Shoes	60.3%	39.7%	24.5%	15.2%	10.3%	4.7%	1.6%
Furniture	68.9%	31.2%	21.7%	9.6%	9.5%	1.8%	2.5%
Appliances	66.9%	33.1%	26.0%	7.2%	11.9%	2.4%	2.5%
Drugs	67.9%	32.1%	23.5%	8.6%	12.3%	2.4%	1.4%
Restaurants	48.4%	51.6%	43.7%	7.9%	26.4%	2.8%	1.4%
Service stations	76.8%	23.2%	16.9%	6.3%	8.5%	2.3%	.5%

*Total Expenses represents the total of all expenses involved in running the firm. These expenses include, but are not limited to, wages, rent, and advertising.

Comparing Business Ratios

 EXAMPLE 2

Gina Burton wishes to compare the business ratios of her shoe store, Burton's Shoes, to industry averages. Figures from her store and industry averages for shoe stores are shown in the table.

	Cost of Goods	Gross Profit	Total Expenses	Net Income	Wages	Rent	Advertising
Burton's Shoes	58.2%	41.8%	28.3%	13.5%	11.7%	5.6%	2.8%
Shoes (from previous chart)	60.3%	39.7%	24.5%	15.2%	10.3%	4.7%	1.6%

SOLUTION

Burton's expenses are higher than the average for other shoe stores and her net income is lower. Wages are higher—perhaps because her store is located in an area with high wages or perhaps the store is not large enough to efficiently utilize its employees. Burton also spends a higher percent than average for advertising. Perhaps she can reduce her advertising expenses without lowering sales.

QUICK CHECK 2

A furniture store has total expenses of 21.3% and cost of goods of 72%. Compare to averages.

OBJECTIVE 3 Compare income statements using horizontal analysis. Another way to analyze an income statement is to prepare a **horizontal analysis**. A horizontal analysis finds the percent of change (either increases or decreases) between the current time period and a previous time period. This comparison can expose unusual changes, such as a rapid increase in expenses or decline in net sales or profits.

Finding Percent Change

$$\% \text{ of change} = \frac{\text{Change}}{\text{Previous year's amount}}$$

Always use *last year* as the base.

Do a horizontal analysis by finding the amount of change from the previous year to the current year in dollars and as a percent. For example, the income statement of Apple on page 625 shows that net sales increased from $65,225 million in 2010 to $108,249 million in 2011.

$$\text{Increase in net sales} = \$108,249 - \$65,225 = \$43,024 \text{ million}$$

$$\text{Percent increase in net sales} = \frac{\$43,024}{\$65,225} = 66.0\% \text{ (rounded)}$$

Net sales grew by an amazing 66% in only one year! Apple, Inc. was clearly growing very rapidly for a large company.

The following graph shows the stock price for Apple (AAPL) compared to the **NASDAQ** which is mostly made up of technology companies. Note that the stock price did not do better than the NASDAQ during 2007–2009, but that it has since grown very rapidly, far outpacing the NASDAQ index.

Performing a Horizontal Analysis

EXAMPLE 3

Do a horizontal analysis for the 2010 and 2011 income statements for Apple using the data given in Example 1.

SOLUTION

Find the increase by subtracting the 2010 figure from the 2011 figure. Then divide by the 2010 figure to find the percent increase and round to the nearest tenth of a percent.

Apple, Inc. Consolidated Statement Year Ending September 23 (in millions of dollars)				
	2010	2011	Increase	Percent
Net Sales	$65,225	$108,249	$43,024	66.0%
Gross Profit	$25,684	$43,818	$18,134	70.6%
Net Income before Taxes	$18,540	$34,205	$15,665	84.5%
Income Taxes	$4,527	$8,283	$3,756	83.0%
Net Income	$14,013	$25,922	$11,909	85.0%

All of the values in the table grew by at least 66% from 2010 to 2011. Apple was clearly growing very rapidly. Note that gross profit increased by 70.6%, but income taxes increased by 83%, or at a faster rate than gross profit. An investor or lender would look carefully at all of these numbers and many other things before buying stock or lending to Apple.

Similar to most large businesses and many small ones, Apple operates in a very competitive world. It has competitors in almost all of the markets in which it operates, but it has been so well managed that it has outgrown all of its competitors. That was not always the case as evidenced by its flat stock price during 2000–2005. To continue to increase revenue and decrease costs, management is likely to continue working to:

1. increase sales outside the U.S.;
2. develop additional products to sell;
3. increase marketing efforts; and
4. decrease costs by doing even more manufacturing in low-cost countries.

QUICK CHECK 3

Partial 2014 results for a company are: Gross Sales $58.6 million and Operating Expenses $12.1 million. The same results for 2013 were: Gross Sales $61.2 million and Operating Expenses $12.9 million. Do a *horizontal comparison*.

During the past 25 years, many firms have moved manufacturing jobs to countries where wages are lower, such as Mexico, China, and India. Now there is evidence that service jobs (e.g., accountant, lawyer, and engineer) are being moved to lower-wage countries as well. Education is *the* fundamental tool you have to protect yourself and your family from a loss in job and income. It is important to continue to learn in life!

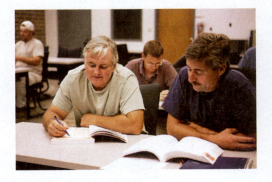

15.2 Exercises

MyMathLab®

The shaded sections below contain solutions to help you get a **QUICK START** on the various types of exercises.

Prepare a vertical analysis for each of the following firms. Round percents to the nearest tenth of a percent. (See Example 1.)

1. **SCUBA SHOPPE** Reef Scuba, Inc., had net sales of $439,000, operating expenses of $143,180, and a cost of goods sold of $198,400.

   Percent cost of goods sold $= \frac{\$198,400}{\$439,000} = 45.2\%$

   Percent operating expenses $= \frac{\$143,180}{\$439,000} = 32.6\%$

   1. __45.2%; 32.6%__

2. **COFFEE SHOP** Tatum's Coffee and Books had operating expenses of $198,400, a cost of goods sold of $287,104, and net sales of $589,250.

   2. _____

3. **GUITAR SHOP** In 2014, the Guitar Shoppe had a cost of goods sold (mostly guitars) of $243,570, operating expenses of $140,450, and net sales of $480,300.

   3. _____

4. **FLOWER SHOP** Trisha's Flowers had net sales of $294,380, operating expenses of $68,650, and a cost of goods sold of $163,890.

   4. _____

The following charts show some figures from income statements. In each case, prepare a vertical analysis by expressing each item as a percent of net sales. Then write in the appropriate average percent from the table in the book. (See Objective 2.)

5.

Gooden Drugs

	Amount	Percent	Average Percent
Net Sales	$850,000	100%	100%
Cost of Goods Sold	$570,350	____	____
Gross Profit	$279,650	____	____
Wages	$106,250	____	____
Rent	$21,250	____	____
Advertising	$12,750	____	____
Total Expenses	$209,100	____	____
Net Income before Taxes	$70,550	____	____

6.

Burger King

	Amount	Percent	Average Percent
Net Sales	$600,000	100%	100%
Cost of Goods Sold	$280,000	_____	_____
Gross Profit	$320,000	_____	_____
Wages	$160,600	_____	_____
Rent	$15,000	_____	_____
Advertising	$8,000	_____	_____
Total Expenses	$255,000	_____	_____
Net Income before Taxes	$65,000	_____	_____

7. Compare a vertical analysis to a horizontal analysis. (See Objectives 1 and 3.)

8. Why would a lender want to use both vertical and horizontal analyses before making a long-term loan to a firm?

9. Complete the comparative income statement. Round to the nearest tenth of a percent.

Hernandez Nursery Comparative Income Statement

	This Year		Last Year	
	Amount	Percent	Amount	Percent
Gross Sales	$1,856,000	_____	$1,692,000	_____
Returns	$6,000	_____	$12,000	_____
Net Sales	_____	100.0%	_____	100.0%
Cost of Goods Sold	$1,102,000	_____	$950,000	_____
Gross Profit	$748,000	_____	$730,000	_____
Wages	$252,000	_____	$248,000	_____
Rent	$82,000	_____	$78,000	_____
Advertising	$111,000	_____	$122,000	_____
Utilities	$32,000	_____	$17,000	_____
Taxes on Inv., Payroll	$17,000	_____	$18,000	_____
Miscellaneous Expenses	$62,000	_____	$58,000	_____
Total Expenses	$556,000	_____	$541,000	_____
Net Income before Taxes	_____	_____	_____	_____

10. Complete the horizontal analysis for the Hernandez Nursery comparative income statement given in Exercise 9. Round to the nearest tenth of a percent.

Hernandez Nursery Horizontal Analysis

	This Year	Last Year	Increase or (Decrease) Amount	Percent
Gross Sales	$1,856,000	$1,692,000	_____	_____
Returns	$6,000	$12,000	_____	_____
Net Sales	$1,850,000	$1,680,000	_____	_____
Cost of Goods Sold	$1,102,000	$950,000	_____	_____
Gross Profit	$748,000	$730,000	_____	_____
Wages	$252,000	$248,000	_____	_____
Rent	$82,000	$78,000	_____	_____
Advertising	$111,000	$122,000	_____	_____
Utilities	$32,000	$17,000	_____	_____
Taxes on Inv., Payroll	$17,000	$18,000	_____	_____
Miscellaneous Expenses	$62,000	$58,000	_____	_____
Net Income before Taxes	$192,000	$189,000	_____	_____

The following table gives the percents for various items from the income statements of firms in two businesses. Complete these tables by including the appropriate percents from the table on page 626. Identify any areas that might require attention by management.

	Type of Store	Cost of Goods	Gross Profit	Total Operating Expenses	Net Income	Wages	Rent	Advertising
11.	Women's apparel	66.4%	33.6%	25.3%	8.3%	8.4%	6.5%	1.9%
		____	____	____	____	____	____	____
12.	Drug store	71.2%	28.8%	26.5%	2.3%	12.9%	5.3%	2.0%
		____	____	____	____	____	____	____

13. Check on the Internet to find a graph showing the stock price of Apple, Inc. and print it out.

14. Use the Internet to find a graph of the stock-price history of a company you are familiar with.

QUICK CHECK ANSWERS

1. Returns 2.1%; Cost of Goods sold 54.9%; Operating Expenses 16.2%
2. Total Expenses are below average of 21.7%; Cost of Goods is above average of 68.9%
3. Gross Sales increased 4.4%; Operating Expenses increased 6.6%

▼ **15.3** The Balance Sheet

▼ CASE IN POINT   You also need to look at the balance sheet before deciding to buy stock in a company. The income statement shows information during an interval of time, such as a quarter or a year. In contrast, the balance sheet shows information at one point in time, such as the amount of cash Apple had on a specific day.

OBJECTIVE 1 Understand the terms on a balance sheet. An income statement show the revenues and expenses of a firm for a period of time such as a month, quarter, or year. In contrast, a **balance sheet** describes the financial condition of a firm *at one point in time*, such as the last day of a year. A balance sheet shows the **assets** of a firm, which is the total value of everything owned by a business at a particular time. Assets include property, equipment, money owed to the company, cash, and securities owned. A balance sheet also shows the amounts owed by the business to others, called **liabilities**. Think of assets as property and investments owned by a company and liabilities as debts that must be paid at some point.

Both assets and liabilities are divided into two categories, **long-term** and **current (short-term)**. Long-term generally applies to assets or liabilities with a life of more than a year. Short-term applies when the time involved is less than a year.

Assets—property and investments owned by the firm
    Current assets—cash or items that can be converted into cash within a short period of time such as a year
        Cash—amount in checking and savings accounts and money market instruments
        Accounts receivable—funds owed by customers of the firm
        Notes receivable—value of all notes owed to the firm
        Inventory—cost of merchandise that the firm has for sale
    Plant and equipment—assets that are expected to be used for more than one year (also called **fixed assets** or **plant assets**)
        Land—book value of any land owned by the firm
        Buildings—book value of any buildings owned by the firm
        Equipment—book value of equipment, store fixtures, furniture, and similar items owned by the firm

Liabilities—debts that must be paid at some point
    Current liabilities—items that must be paid by the firm within a short period of time, usually one year
        Accounts payable—amounts that must be paid to other firms
        Notes payable—value of all notes owed by the firm
    Long-term liabilities—items that will be paid after one year
        Mortgages payable—total due on all mortgages
        Long-term notes payable—total of all other debts of the firm

The difference between the total of all assets and the total of all liabilities is called the **owners' equity**, which is also referred to as **net worth** or, for a corporation, **stockholders' equity**. The relationship among owners' equity, assets, and liabilities is shown in the fundamental formula below.

$$\text{Owners' equity} = \text{Assets} - \text{Liabilities}$$
$$\text{or}$$
$$\text{Assets} = \text{Liabilities} + \text{Owners' equity}$$

OBJECTIVE 2 Prepare a balance sheet.

Preparing a
Balance Sheet

 EXAMPLE 1

On September 23, 2011, Apple's balance sheet showed the assets and liabilities shown below. Complete the balance sheet and find the stockholder's equity.

SOLUTION

Apple, Inc. Consolidated Statement Year Ending September 23, 2011 (in millions of dollars)		
ASSETS:		
Current Assets:		
Cash and short-term investments	$25,952	
Accounts receivable and other	$18,260	
Inventory	$776	
Total Current Assets	**$44,988**	sum of all current assets
Other Assets:		
Net plant and property	$7,777	
Other assets	$63,606	
Total Assets	**$116,371**	total current and other assets
LIABILITIES:		
Current Liabilities:		
Loans and accounts payable	$23,879	
Other current liabilities	$4,091	
Total Current Liabilities	**$27,970**	sum of all current liabilities
Other Liabilities:		
Long-term debt	$0	
Other long-term liabilities	$11,786	
Total Liabilities	**$39,756**	total current and other liabilities
Stockholders' Equity:	**$76,615**	Total assets − Total liabilities
Total Liabilities and Equity	$116,371	

On September 23, 2011, Apple had about $25,952,000,000 in cash and short-term investments that could quickly be converted to cash. This amount could be very different on a different day. The balance sheet gives no information about assets or liabilities for any day other than September 23, 2011. Notice that Apple had no long-term debt which is unusual since most firms have some long-term debt.

Apple had $776,000,000 in inventory as of the date of this balance sheet. This includes inventory in Apple owned stores, warehouses, and manufacturing companies and potentially even inventory in ships moving from factories in China to the U.S. Looking at the inventory sitting on shelves in retail stores, customers tend to think of inventory as always sitting around. However, managers think of inventory as products moving and moving along a global supply chain. There is no value of inventory sitting somewhere for any length of time!

Quick TIP

In the next section, we show how to analyze a balance sheet.

QUICK CHECK 1

A plumbing contractor's balance sheet shows the following assets (in thousands): Cash, $398; Accounts Receivable and other, $789; Inventory, $481, Net Plant and Property, $1047; Other Assets; $212. The liabilities were: Loans and Accounts Payable, $659; Other Current Liabilities, $241; Long-term Debt, $384, Other Long-term Liabilities, $412. Find the Stockholders' Equity.

Remember this important relationship:

Finding Stockholder's Equity

Stockholders' equity = Total assets − Total liabilities

▼15.3 Exercises

MyMathLab®

Complete the balance sheets for the following business firms. (See Example 1.)

1. **GROCERY CHAIN** Brookshire's Grocery (all figures in millions): fixtures, $28; buildings, $290; land, $466; cash, $273; notes receivable, $312; accounts receivable, $264; inventory, $180; notes payable, $312; mortgages payable, $212; accounts payable, $63; long-term notes payable, $55.

Brookshire's Grocery Balance Sheet December 31 (in millions)

ASSETS	
Current Assets	
Cash	_____
Notes Receivable	_____
Accounts Receivable	_____
Inventory	_____
Total Current Assets	_____
Plant Assets	
Land	_____
Buildings	_____
Fixtures	_____
Total Plant Assets	_____
Total Assets	_____
LIABILITIES	
Current Liabilities	
Notes Payable	_____
Accounts Payable	_____
Total Current Liabilities	_____
Long-Term Liabilities	
Mortgages Payable	_____
Long-Term Notes Payable	_____
Total Long-Term Liabilities	_____
Total Liabilities	_____
OWNERS' EQUITY	
Owners' Equity	_____
Total Liabilities and Owners' Equity	_____

2. **JETSON AIRCRAFT SALES** (All figures in thousands) Land is $8750; accounts payable total $49,230; notes receivable are $2600; accounts receivable are $37,820; cash is $14,800; buildings are $21,930; notes payable are $3780; owners' equity is $54,320; long-term notes payable are $18,740; mortgages payable total $26,330; inventory is $49,680; fixtures are $16,820 (all figures in thousands).

Jetson Aircraft Sales Balance Sheet—December 31 (in thousands)

ASSETS

Current Assets
   Cash   _____
   Notes Receivable   _____
   Accounts Receivable   _____
   Inventory   _____
      Total Current Assets   _____
Plant Assets
   Land   _____
   Buildings   _____
   Fixtures   _____
      Total Plant Assets   _____
   Total Assets   _____

LIABILITIES

Current Liabilities
   Notes Payable   _____
   Accounts Payable   _____

      Total Current Liabilities   _____
   Long-Term Liabilities
      Mortgages Payable   _____
      Long-Term Notes Payable   _____

      Total Long-Term Liabilities   _____
   Total Liabilities   _____

OWNERS' EQUITY

Owners' Equity   _____
   Total Liabilities and Owners' Equity   _____

3. Compare a balance sheet to an income statement.

4. Use the World Wide Web to find the amount of cash and equivalents at the end of the most recent fiscal year for GM and the Coca-Cola Company. Which company has more? Why do you suppose it has as much as it does?

QUICK CHECK ANSWER

1. $1,231,000

▼15.4 Analyzing the Balance Sheet

OBJECTIVES

1   Compare balance sheets using vertical analysis.

2   Compare balance sheets using horizontal analysis.

3   Find financial ratios.

OBJECTIVE 1 Compare balance sheets using vertical analysis. A balance sheet can be analyzed in much the same way as an income statement. In a **vertical analysis**, each item on the balance sheet is expressed as a percent of total assets. A **comparative balance sheet** shows the vertical analysis for two different years.

Comparing Balance Sheets **EXAMPLE 1**

First, do a vertical analysis for the 2010 and 2011 balance sheets for Apple by calculating each value as a percent of the total assets for the respective year (round percents to the nearest tenth). Then compare the percents to identify the changes.

SOLUTION

	Apple, Inc. Consolidated Statement Year Ending September 23, 2011 (in millions of dollars*)			
	2010		**2011**	
Assets:	**Amount**	**Percent**	**Amount**	**Percent**
Current Assets:				
Cash and short-term investments	$25,620	34.1%	$25,952	22.3%
Accounts receivable and other	$15,007	20.0%	$18,260	15.7%
Inventory	$1,051	1.4%	$776	0.7%
Total Current Assets	$41,678	55.4%	$44,988	38.7%
Other Assets:				
Net plant and property	$4,768	6.3%	$7,777	6.7%
Other assets	$28,737	38.2%	$63,606	54.7%
Total Assets	$75,183	100.0%	$116,371	100.0%
Liabilities:	**Amount**	**Percent**	**Amount**	**Percent**
Current Liabilities:				
Loans and accounts payable	$17,738	23.6%	$23,879	20.5%
Other current liabilities	$2,984	4.0%	$4,091	3.5%
Total Current Liabilities	$20,722	27.6%	$27,970	24.0%
Other Liabilities:				
Long-term debt	$0	0.0%	$0	0.0%
Other long-term liabilities	$6,670	8.9%	$11,786	10.1%
Total Liabilities	$27,392	36.4%	$39,756	34.2%
Stockholders' Equity:	$47,791	63.6%	$76,615	65.8%
Total Liabilities and Equity	$75,183	100.0%	$116,371	100.0%

*Rounding may cause columns to not add to percent shown.

Notice that stockholders' equity increased significantly from $47,791,000,000 to $76,615,000,000 in only one year. Wow, what an amazing growth story! Cash and short-term investments fell from 34.1% of total assets in 2010 to 22.3% of total assets in 2011, but the firm still had a lot of cash and short-term investments in 2011 at $25,952,000,000.

A careful investor would want to follow up to find out why other assets increased from 38.2% of total assets in 2010 to 54.7% of total assets in 2011. It would be prudent to also ask whether this was a one-time increase, or whether it indicates a long-term trend.

OBJECTIVE 2 Compare balance sheets using horizontal analysis. Perform a **horizontal analysis** by finding the change, both in dollars and in percent, for each item on the balance sheet from one year to the next. As before, always use the previous year as a base when finding the percents.

Using Horizontal Analysis **EXAMPLE 2** Apple's cash and short-term investments increased from $25,620 million at the end of 2010 to $25,952 million at the end of 2011. The percent increase is found as follows.

$$\text{Percent increase} = \frac{\$25,952 - \$25,620}{\$25,620} = 1.3\% \quad \text{(rounded)}$$

Complete a horizontal analysis of the current assets portion of Apple's balance sheet.

SOLUTION

	Comparative Analysis Apple, Inc. Year Ending September 23, 2011 (in millions of dollars)			
Current Assets:	**2010**	**2011**	**Amount of Increase/Decrease**	**Percent**
Cash and short-term investments	$25,620	$25,952	$332	1.3%
Accounts receivable and other	$15,007	$18,260	$3,253	21.7%
Inventory	$1,051	$776	−$275	−26.2%
Total Current Assets	**$41,678**	**$44,988**	**$3,310**	**7.9%**

Management kept cash and short-term investments at nearly the same amount. Accounts receivables and other went up significantly, probably since sales increased by so much. Interestingly, inventory fell by 26.2% even though sales were much higher. Managers probably worked hard to lean out the supply chain resulting in lower inventories and requiring fewer employees. Lower inventories mean lower costs resulting in higher profit. Current assets went up 7.9%.

OBJECTIVE 3 Find financial ratios. After preparing a balance sheet for a business firm, an accountant often calculates several different **financial ratios** for the firm. These ratios can be compared with financial ratios for other firms in the same industry or of the same size. A ratio *that is far out of line compared with other similar firms or with industry averages* might well indicate future financial difficulties.

The first two ratios we discuss are designed to measure the **liquidity** of a firm. Liquidity refers to a firm's ability to raise cash quickly without being forced to sell assets at a big loss.

Find the **current ratio** by dividing current assets by current liabilities. This ratio is read as "current assets to current liabilities," and is sometimes called **banker's ratio**.

Finding the Current Ratio

$$\text{Current ratio} = \frac{\text{Current assets}}{\text{Current liabilities}}$$

Finding the Current Ratio **EXAMPLE 3** The September 23, 2011 balance sheet for Apple shows current assets of $44,988 and current liabilities of $27,970, both in millions. Find the current ratio to the nearest hundredth.

SOLUTION

$$\text{Current ratio} = \frac{\$44{,}988}{\$27{,}970} = 1.61 \quad \text{(rounded)}$$

The current ratio is often written as 1.61 to 1, or as 1.61:1.

> **QUICK CHECK 3**
>
> A firm has current liabilities of $2.9 billion, with current assets of $1.56 billion. Find the current ratio.

Lending institutions look at the current ratio before making loans. A common rule of thumb, not necessarily applicable to all businesses, is that the current ratio should be at least 2:1. A firm with a current ratio much lower than 2 may have an increased risk of financial difficulties and may have difficulty borrowing.

Apple has a current ratio of 1.61, or slightly below the recommended value of 2. However, the value of one ratio is rarely enough to conclude whether a company is having financial difficulties. Unlike most firms, Apple has no long-term debt suggesting that a current ratio of 1.61 is not bad in this situation. Before making a decision about whether to invest in the stock of a company, one should look carefully at many different measures of financial conditions, the company, the industry, societal and other trends, management, and the economy.

One disadvantage of the current ratio is that inventory is included in current assets. In a period of financial difficulty, a firm might have trouble disposing of its inventory at a reasonable price. Some accountants think that the **acid test** of a firm's financial health is to consider only **liquid assets**: assets that either are cash or can be converted to cash quickly, such as securities and accounts and notes receivable. As a general rule, the acid-test ratio should be at least 1 to 1, so that liquid assets are at least enough to cover current liabilities.

The **acid-test ratio**, also called the **quick ratio**, is defined as follows.

> **Finding the Acid-test Ratio**
>
> $$\text{Acid-test ratio} = \frac{\text{Liquid assets}}{\text{Current liabilities}}$$

Finding the Acid-Test Ratio **EXAMPLE 4** Find the acid-test ratio for Apple using 2011 data.

SOLUTION

$$\text{Acid-test ratio} = \frac{\text{Current assets} - \text{Inventory}}{\text{Current liabilities}}$$

$$= \frac{\$44{,}988 - \$776}{\$27{,}970} = 1.58 \quad \text{(rounded)}$$

This ratio is well above the recommended value of 1, indicating financial strength.

> **QUICK CHECK 4**
>
> Find the acid-test ratio for a company with current assets of $745,600, inventory of $217,050, and current liabilities of $240,800.

A company with a large amount of capital invested should have a higher net income than a company with a small amount invested. To check on this, accountants often find the **ratio of net income after taxes to average owners' equity**. The **average owners' equity** is found by adding the owners' equity at the beginning and end of the year and dividing by 2.

> ### Finding Average Owners' Equity
> $$\text{Average owners' equity} = \frac{\text{Owners' equity at beginning} + \text{Owners' equity at end}}{2}$$

Then the ratio of net income after taxes to average owners' equity is found.

> ### Finding Ratio of Net Income After Taxes to Average Owners' Equity
> $$\frac{\text{Ratio of net income after taxes}}{\text{to average owners' equity}} = \frac{\text{Net income after taxes}}{\text{Average owners' equity}}$$

Finding the Return on Average Equity

 5

Find the 2011 ratio of net income after taxes to average owners' equity for Apple.

SOLUTION

Stockholders' equity increased from $47,791 in 2010 to $76,615 in 2011.

$$\frac{\text{Average owners' equity}}{} = \frac{\$47,791 + \$76,615}{2} = \$62,203 \quad (\text{millions})$$

Use the net income after taxes in 2011 from the income statement in Section 15.1 on page 621 to complete the following ratio.

$$\frac{\text{Ratio of net income after taxes}}{\text{to average owners' equity}} = \frac{\$25,922}{\$62,203} = 41.7\%$$

Quick TIP

Of the ratios we have looked at, the ratio of net income after taxes to average owners' equity is the only one that requires data from both the income statement and balance sheet.

> **QUICK CHECK 5**
>
> Stockholders' equity for a firm increased from $3456 at the end of 2012 to $3720 at the end of 2013, and net income after taxes during the year was $402 (all figures in thousands). Find the ratio of net income after taxes to average owners' equity.

The ratio of net income after taxes to average owners' equity should be significantly higher than the interest rate paid on savings accounts or even government bonds. Otherwise, the capital represented by these assets should be deposited in a bank account or in government bonds. After all, government bonds have *less risk* than an investment in a company. Generally, investments with a higher risk must give more reward to investors to encourage them to invest. Thus, increased risk should result in a higher return to the investor than a risk-free savings account. The ratio for Apple far exceeds the rate paid on government bonds. In fact, it is unusually high. At any rate, this illustrates that it is very difficult to truly understand how well a company is doing from a few financial ratios. It takes a lot of detective work to figure out if a company is profitable and will continue to be profitable and make an informed decision related to investment or lending.

All the ratios discussed here are more meaningful when comparing a company with another within the same industry. For example, it does not make sense to compare ExxonMobil to Apple, since the two are in very different businesses with very different capital and inventory needs. Rather, it is best to compare the financial ratios for Apple to a **direct competitor**, or one that produces similar products and/or offers similar services. However, it is difficult to find a direct competitor for Apple. This shows how difficult financial analysis can be.

The financial ratios of this section can be summarized as follows.

> ### Summary of Ratios
> $$\text{Current ratio} = \frac{\text{Current assets}}{\text{Current liabilities}} \qquad \text{Acid-test ratio} = \frac{\text{Liquid assets}}{\text{Current liabilities}}$$
>
> $$\frac{\text{Ratio of net income after taxes}}{\text{to average owners' equity}} = \frac{\text{Net income after taxes}}{\text{Average owners' equity}}$$

▼15.4 Exercises   MyMathLab®

1. **YACHT CONSTRUCTION**   Complete this balance sheet using vertical analysis. Round to the nearest tenth of a percent. (See Example 1.)

Comparative Balance Sheet for Pleasure Yacht, Inc. (in thousands of dollars)

	Amount This Year	Percent This Year	Amount Last Year	Percent Last Year
Assets:				
Current Assets				
Cash	$52,000	_____	$42,000	_____
Notes Receivable	$8,000	_____	$6,000	_____
Accounts Receivable	$148,000	_____	$120,000	_____
Inventory	$153,000	_____	$120,000	_____
Total Current Assets	_____	_____	_____	_____
Plant Assets				
Land	$10,000	_____	$8,000	_____
Buildings	$14,000	_____	$11,000	_____
Fixtures	$15,000	_____	$13,000	_____
Total Plant Assets	_____	_____	_____	_____
Total Assets	_____	100%	_____	100%
Liabilities:				
Current Liabilities				
Accounts Payable	$3,000	_____	$4,000	_____
Notes Payable	$201,000	_____	$152,000	_____
Total Current Liabilities	_____	_____	_____	_____
Long-Term Liabilities				
Mortgages Payable	$20,000	_____	$16,000	_____
Long-Term Notes Payable	$58,000	_____	$42,000	_____
Total Long-Term Liabilities	_____	_____	_____	_____
Total Liabilities	_____		_____	
Owners' Equity	$118,000	_____	$106,000	_____
Total Liabilities And Owners' Equity	_____	_____	_____	_____

2. **YACHTS** Complete the following horizontal analysis for a portion of the balance sheet for Pleasure Yacht, Inc. Note that figures are shown in thousands of dollars. Round to the nearest tenth of a percent. (See Example 1.)

Pleasure Yacht, Inc. (in thousands)

			Increase or (Decrease)	
	This Year	Last Year	Amount	Percent
Assets:				
Current Assets				
Cash	$52,000	$42,000	_____	_____
Notes Receivable	$8,000	$6,000	_____	_____
Accounts Receivable	$148,000	$120,000	_____	_____
Inventory	$153,000	$120,000	_____	_____
Total Current Assets	$361,000	$288,000	_____	_____
Plant Assets				
Land	$10,000	$8,000	_____	_____
Buildings	$14,000	$11,000	_____	_____
Fixtures	$15,000	$13,000	_____	_____
Total Plant Assets	$39,000	$32,000	_____	_____
Total Assets	$400,000	$320,000	_____	_____

In Exercises 3–6, find (a) the current ratio and (b) the acid-test ratio. Round each ratio to the nearest hundredth. (c) Do the ratios suggest that the company is financially healthy, according to the guidelines given in the text? (See Examples 3 and 4.)

3. Pleasure Yacht, Inc., has the balance sheet given above and current liabilities of $204,000.

(a) _____

(b) _____

(c) _____

4. **JUICE COMPANY** Jungle Juice has current liabilities of $356,800, cash of $32,800, notes and accounts receivable of $248,500, and an inventory valued at $82,400.

(a) _____

(b) _____

(c) _____

5. **CADILLAC DEALER** Wagner Cadillac has current assets of $2,210,350, current liabilities of $1,232,500, total cash of $480,500, notes and accounts receivable of $279,050, and an inventory of $1,450,800.

(a) _____

(b) _____

(c) _____

6. **OXYGEN SUPPLY** BlueTex Oxygen Supply has current assets of $2,234,000, current liabilities of $840,000, total cash of $339,000, notes and accounts receivable of $1,215,000, and an inventory of $680,000.

(a) _____

(b) _____

(c) _____

A portion of a comparative balance sheet is shown next. First complete the chart, and then find the current ratio and the acid-test ratio for the indicated year. Round each ratio to the nearest hundredth.

Western Auto Supply (in thousands)

	Amount This Year	Percent This Year	Amount Last Year	Percent Last Year
Current Assets				
Cash	$12,000	_____	$15,000	_____
Notes Receivable	$4,000	_____	$6,000	_____
Accounts Receivable	$22,000	_____	$18,000	_____
Inventory	$26,000	_____	$24,000	_____
Total Current Assets	$64,000	80%	$63,000	84%
Total Plant Assets	$16,000	_____	$12,000	_____
Total Assets	_____	100.0%	_____	100.0%
Total Current Liabilities	$30,000	_____	$25,000	_____

7. This year _____

8. Last year _____

Find the ratio of net income after taxes to average owners' equity for the following. (See Example 5.) Round to the nearest tenth of a percent.

9. INTERNATIONAL AIRLINE Stockholders' equity in TNA Airline, a small start-up international airline that uses small airplanes to move freight to and from Mexico, is $845,000 at the beginning of the year and $928,500 at the end of the year. Net income after taxes for the year was $54,400.

9. _____

10. TRANSMISSION REPAIR Owners' equity at Amgen Transmission was $372,600 at the beginning of the year and $402,100 at the end of the year. Net income after taxes for the year was $55,003.

10. _____

Calculate the current ratio and the acid-test ratio for the following companies. Are the companies healthy, based on the guidelines given in the text?

11. Akron Books: Current assets: $268,700
  Current liabilities: $294,200
  Liquid assets: $109,900

11. _____

12. Ashe Hair Salon: Current assets: $54,750
  Current liabilities: $17,200
  Liquid assets: $24,650

12. _____

13. Explain why the acid-test ratio is a better measure of the financial health of a firm than the current ratio. (See Objective 3.)

14. Explain why increased risk requires a higher return on investment. (See Objective 3.)

▼ Chapter 15   Quick Review

Chapter Terms   *Review the following terms to test your understanding of the chapter. For each term you do not know, refer to the page number found next to that term.*

accountant [p. 620]
acid test [p. 638]
acid-test ratio [p. 638]
assets [p. 632]
average owners' equity [p. 638]
balance sheet [p. 632]
banker's ratio [p. 637]
comparative balance sheet [p. 636]
comparative income statement [p. 625]
cost of goods sold [p. 620]
current assets [p. 632]

current liabilities [p. 632]
current ratio [p. 637]
direct competitor [p. 639]
ending inventory [p. 621]
financial ratios [p. 637]
fixed assets [p. 632]
gross profit [p. 620]
gross profit on sales [p. 620]
gross sales [p. 620]
horizontal analysis [p. 637]
income statement [p. 620]
initial inventory [p. 621]
liabilities [p. 632]

liquid assets [p. 638]
liquidity [p. 637]
long-term liabilities [p. 632]
NASDAQ [p. 627]
net income [p. 620]
net income after taxes [p. 620]
net income before taxes [p. 620]
net sales [p. 620]
net worth [p. 632]
operating expenses [p. 620]
overhead [p. 620]
owners' equity [p. 632]
plant and equipment [p. 632]

plant assets [p. 632]
publicly held corporation [p. 620]
quick ratio [p. 638]
ratio of net income after taxes to average owners' equity [p. 638]
returns [p. 620]
short-term liabilities [p. 632]
stockholders' equity [p. 632]
total revenue [p. 620]
vertical analysis [p. 625]

CONCEPTS

15.1 Finding the gross profit and net income

1. Find the net sales.
2. Determine the cost of goods sold.
3. Find gross profit from the formula.

Gross profit = Net sales − Cost of goods sold

4. Find the operating expenses.
5. Find the net income from the formula.

Net income = Gross profit − Operating expenses

15.2 Finding the percent of net sales of individual items

1. Determine net sales using the formula.

Net sales = Gross sales − Returns

2. Use the formula

$$\textbf{Percent of net sales} = \frac{\textbf{Particular item}}{\textbf{Net sales}}$$

for each item.

EXAMPLES

Candy-You-Love had a cost of goods sold of $218,509, operating expenses of $103,217, gross sales of $432,119, and no returns. Find the gross profit and net income before taxes.

Gross profit = *Gross sales − Returns − Cost of goods sold*

= $432,119 − $0 − $218,509

= **$213,610**

Net income before taxes = **Gross profit** − Operating expenses

= $213,610 − $103,217

= $110,393

Bill's Appliances lists the following information for a month.

Gross sales = $340,000   Salaries and wages = $19,000

Returns = $15,000   Rent = $8000

Cost of goods sold = $210,000   Advertising = $12,000

Express each item as a percent of net sales. Round to the nearest tenth of a percent.

Net sales = $340,000 − $15,000 = **$325,000**

Gross profit = $325,000 − $210,000 = **$115,000**

Total expenses = $19,000 + $8000 + $12,000 = **$39,000**

Net income = $115,000 − $39,000 = **$76,000**

Find all the desired percents to the nearest tenth of a percent by dividing each item by net sales.

$$\text{Percent gross sales} = \frac{\$340,000}{\$325,000} = \textbf{104.6\%}$$

$$\text{Percent returns} = \frac{\$15,000}{\$325,000} = \textbf{4.6\%}$$

$$\text{Percent cost of goods sold} = \frac{\$210,000}{\$325,000} = \textbf{64.6\%}$$

CONCEPTS

EXAMPLES

$$\text{Percent gross profit} = \frac{\$115,000}{\$325,000} = \mathbf{35.4\%}$$

$$\text{Percent expenses} = \frac{\$39,000}{\$325,000} = \mathbf{12\%}$$

$$\text{Percent salaries and wages} = \frac{\$19,000}{\$325,000} = \mathbf{5.8\%}$$

$$\text{Percent net income} = \frac{\$76,000}{\$325,000} = \mathbf{23.4\%}$$

$$\text{Percent rent} = \frac{\$8,000}{\$325,000} = \mathbf{2.5\%}$$

$$\text{Percent advertising} = \frac{\$12,000}{\$325,000} = \mathbf{3.7\%}$$

15.2 Comparing income statements with published charts

In one chart, list the percent of items from a published chart and from the particular company.

From the preceding example, prepare a vertical analysis of Bill's Appliances.

The table shows that this store has very low expenses and a slightly higher than average gross profit.

Bill's Appliances

	Cost of Goods	Gross Profit	Total Expenses	Net Income	Wages	Rent	Advertising
Bill's Appliances	**64.6%**	**35.4%**	**12%**	**23.4%**	**5.8%**	**2.5%**	**3.7%**
Appliances	66.9%	33.1%	26%	7.2%	11.9%	2.4%	2.5%

15.2 Preparing a horizontal analysis chart

1. List last year's and this year's values for each item.
2. Calculate the amount of the increase or decrease of each item.
3. Calculate the percent increase or decrease by dividing the change by last year's amount.

The results of a horizontal analysis of the portion of a business is given. Calculate the percent increase or decrease in each item.

Salmon Farm

	This Year	Last Year	Increase or (Decrease) Amount	Percent
Gross Sales	$735,000	$700,000	$35,000	**5%**
Returns	$5,000	$10,000	($5,000)	**(50%)**
Net Sales	$730,000	$690,000	$40,000	**5.8%**
Cost of Goods Sold	$530,000	$540,000	($10,000)	**(1.9%)**
Gross Profit	$200,000	$150,000	$50,000	**33.3%**

15.3 Constructing a balance sheet

List all of the current assets, other assets, current liabilities, and other liabilities on one page.

Subtract total liabilities from total assets to find stockholders' equity.

A cell phone kiosk in a local mall has cash of $28,300, accounts receivable of $49,250, and inventories of $4900. Other assets consist of equipment and a truck with a total value of $24,300. Accounts payable are $9300, and loans total $12,200. There is no long-term debt. Other liabilities amount to $12,400.

Balance Sheet

Current Assets:		Current Liabilities:	
Cash and Equivalents	$28,300	Accounts Payable	$9,300
Accounts Receivable	$49,250	Loans and Notes Payable	$12,200
Inventories	$4,900	*Total Current Liabilities*	$21,500
Total Current Assets	$82,450	Other Liabilities:	$12,400
Other Assets:		*Total Liabilities*	$33,900
Equipment and Truck	$24,300		
Total Assets	$106,750	*Stockholders' Equity*	$72,850
		Total Liabilities and Equity	$106,750

CONCEPTS	EXAMPLES

15.4 Determining the value of the current ratio

1. Determine the current assets.
2. Find the current liabilities.
3. Divide current assets by current liabilities.

Caribbean Tours has $250,000 in current assets and $110,000 in current liabilities. Find the current ratio.

$$\text{Current ratio} = \frac{\text{Current assets}}{\text{Current liabilities}}$$

$$= \frac{\$250,000}{\$110,000} = 2.27 \text{ (rounded)}$$

15.4 Finding the value of the acid-test ratio

1. Determine the liquid assets.
2. Find the current liabilities.
3. Divide liquid assets by liabilities.

If Carribean Tours has $125,000 in liquid assets, find the acid-test ratio.

$$\text{Acid-test ratio} = \frac{\text{Liquid assets}}{\text{Current liabilities}}$$

$$= \frac{\$125,000}{\$110,000} = 1.14 \text{ (rounded)}$$

15.4 Determining the ratio of net income after taxes to the average owners' equity

1. Find the net income after taxes.
2. Determine the average owners' equity for the year using the formula.

$$\text{Average owners' equity} = \frac{\text{Owners' equity at beginning} + \text{Owners' equity at end}}{2}$$

3. Divide the net income by the average owners' equity.

At the beginning of the year, Caribbean Tours had owners' equity of $140,000. At the end of the year, owners' equity was $180,000. The net income after taxes for the agency was $25,000. Find the ratio of net income after taxes to average owners' equity.

Net income after taxes = $25,000

Average owners' equity

$$= \frac{\$140,000 + \$180,000}{2} = \$160,000$$

Ratio of net income after taxes to average owners' equity

$$= \frac{\$25,000}{\$160,000} = 15.6\% \text{ (rounded)}$$

Case Study

BICYCLE SHOP

Last year, John Smarter started a business selling and repairing bicycles. He is somewhat successful, but he is tired of working 60 hours a week. With borrowed funds, Smarter believes he will be able to expand to a larger store and then hire someone to help him. The banker asked Smarter for his most recent income statement and balance sheet.

1. Prepare an income statement and find net income after taxes

Gross Sales	$238,300	Salaries and Wages	$78,690
Returns	$3,600	Rent & Utilities	$11,800
Inventory on Jan. 1	$53,400	Advertising	$3,200
Cost of Goods Purchased	$ 98,500	Miscellaneous Expenses	$4,800
Freight	$2,300	Income taxes	$3,600
Inventory on Dec. 31	$48,900		

Gross Sales	_____
Returns	_____
Net Sales	_____
Inventory, Jan. 1	_____
Cost of Goods Purchased	_____
Freight	_____
Total Cost of Goods Purchased	_____
Total of Goods Available for Sale	_____
Inventory, Dec. 31	_____
Cost of Goods Sold	_____
Gross Profit	_____
Expenses	
Salaries and Wages	_____
Rent & Utilities	_____
Advertising	_____
Miscellaneous Expenses	_____
Total Expenses	_____
Net Income before Taxes	_____
Income taxes	_____
NET INCOME AFTER TAXES	_____

2. Year-end figures for the bike shop are: $62,000 in cash, $10,700 in accounts receivable, $48,900 in inventory, land and building worth $0, improvements worth $41,500. It also has $4,300 in notes payable, and $14,800 in accounts payable. Long-term notes payable are $12,300, no mortgages. Prepare a balance sheet and find the owner's equity.

ASSETS		
Current Assets		
Cash	_____	
Accounts Receivable	_____	
Inventory	_____	
Total Current Assets		_____
Plant Assets		
Land and Buildings	_____	
Improvements	_____	
Total Plant Assets		_____
Total Assets		_____
LIABILITIES		
Current Liabilities		
Notes Payable	_____	
Accounts Payable	_____	
Total Current Liabilities		_____
Long-Term Liabilities		
Long-Term Notes Payable	_____	
Mortgages	_____	
Total Long-Term Liabilities		_____
Total Liabilities		_____
OWNERS' EQUITY		
Owners' Equity		_____
TOTAL LIABILITIES AND OWNERS' EQUITY		_____

[1]Owners' equity = Total Assets − Total Liabilities
$$= \$163{,}100 - \$31{,}400$$
$$= \$131{,}700$$

INVESTIGATE

Publicly held companies must publish their financial statements and make them available to anyone who wishes to look at them. Choose a publicly held company that you are familiar with and obtain its financial statements using the World Wide Web. Calculate the financial ratios introduced in the last section of this chapter for the company you choose (current ratio, acid-test ratio, and ratio of net income after taxes to average owners' equity).

▼ Case in Point Summary Exercise

APPLE, INC.

www.apple.com

Facts:

- 1976: Founded
- 1984: Introduced Macintosh computer
- 2001: Introduced iPod
- 2007: Introduced iPhone
- 2010: Introduced iPad
- 2011: Founder Steve Jobs passes away

Apple, Inc. was founded by Steve Jobs and Steve Wozniak on April 1, 1976 in Cupertino, California. It was originally named Apple Computer, Inc. based on its original focus on building computers. Management changed the name to Apple, Inc. in 2007 to reflect the fact that the firm was even less focused on computers and was far more focused on a variety of consumer electronics. The firm has revolutionized several industries with its creative and artful products including the iPod (music), iPhone (smart phone), iPad (books, periodicals, movies, music, games, applications, and web content), and iTunes (playing and downloading digital music and video files) among others.

Apple has about 400 retail stores in more than thirteen countries and has surpassed both Microsoft and Google in market value. It has more than 60,000 full-time employees with annual revenue of more than $100 billion per year.

1. Assume the following quarterly figures apply to a local computer and electronics store, which sells many Apple products. Prepare an income statement and find net income after taxes for the quarter.

Gross Sales	$834,200	Salaries and Wages	$193,200
Returns	$4,500	Rent & Utilities	$68,900
Inventory on Jan. 1	$84,200	Advertising	$13,900
Cost of Goods Purchased	$346,500	Insurance & Payroll Taxes	$19,400
Freight	$9,100	Miscellaneous Expenses	$18,700
Inventory on Dec. 31	$96,200	Income taxes	$37,800

Gross Sales		_____
Returns		_____
Net Sales		_____
Inventory, Jan. 1	_____	
Cost of Goods Purchased	_____	
Freight	_____	
Total Cost of Goods Purchased		_____
Total of Goods Available for Sale		_____
Inventory, Dec. 31		_____
Cost of Goods Sold		_____
Gross Profit		_____
Expenses		
Salaries and Wages	_____	
Rent & Utilities	_____	
Advertising	_____	
Insurance and Payroll Taxes	_____	
Miscellaneous Expenses	_____	
Total Expenses		_____
Net Income before Taxes		_____
Income Taxes		_____
NET INCOME AFTER TAXES		_____

2. At the end of the year, the store had the following: $84,500 in cash, $2100 in accounts receivable, land and building with a fair market value of $186,500, improvements worth $82,100. It has a note payable on store shelves with a remaining balance of $4900 and $58,400 in accounts payable for supplies. The only long-term debt is the mortgage of $134,200 on the building. Prepare a balance sheet for the firm at the end of the year and find the owner's equity.

<table>
<tr><td colspan="2" align="center">**ASSETS**</td></tr>
<tr><td>Current Assets</td><td></td></tr>
<tr><td>   Cash</td><td>_____</td></tr>
<tr><td>   Accounts Receivable</td><td>_____</td></tr>
<tr><td>   Inventory</td><td>_____</td></tr>
<tr><td>   Total Current Assets</td><td>_____</td></tr>
<tr><td>Plant Assets</td><td></td></tr>
<tr><td>   Land and Buildings</td><td>_____</td></tr>
<tr><td>   Improvements</td><td>_____</td></tr>
<tr><td>   Total Plant Assets</td><td>_____</td></tr>
<tr><td>Total Assets</td><td>_____</td></tr>
<tr><td colspan="2" align="center">**LIABILITIES**</td></tr>
<tr><td>Current Liabilities</td><td></td></tr>
<tr><td>   Notes Payable</td><td>_____</td></tr>
<tr><td>   Accounts Payable</td><td>_____</td></tr>
<tr><td>   Total Current Liabilities</td><td>_____</td></tr>
<tr><td>Long-Term Liabilities</td><td></td></tr>
<tr><td>   Long-Term Notes Payable</td><td>_____</td></tr>
<tr><td>   Mortgages</td><td>_____</td></tr>
<tr><td>   Total Long-Term Liabilities</td><td>_____</td></tr>
<tr><td>Total Liabilities</td><td>_____</td></tr>
<tr><td colspan="2" align="center">**OWNERS' EQUITY**</td></tr>
<tr><td>Owners' Equity</td><td>_____</td></tr>
<tr><td>**TOTAL LIABILITIES AND OWNERS' EQUITY**</td><td>_____</td></tr>
</table>

$$\begin{aligned}^1\text{Owners' equity} &= \text{Total assets} - \text{Total liabilities}\\ &= \$451,400 - \$197,500\\ &= \$253,900\end{aligned}$$

Discussion Question: *Explain the purpose of the income statement and balance sheet. Can an individual or family also build an income statement and balance sheet? Explain.*

▼ Chapter 15   Test

To help you review, the numbers in brackets show the section in which the topic was discussed.

1. Benni's Fish Co. had gross sales of $756,300 with returns of $285. The inventory on January 1 was $92,370, and the cost of goods purchased during the year was $465,920. Freight costs during the year were $1205. Total inventory on December 31 was $82,350. Salaries and wages totaled $84,900, advertising was $2800, rent was $42,500, utilities were $18,950, taxes on inventory and payroll were $4500, and miscellaneous expenses totaled $18,400. Income taxes were $25,450. Complete the following income statement. **[15.1]**

Benni's Fish Co.
Income Statement
Year Ending December 31

Gross Sales		_____
Returns		_____
Net Sales		_____
Inventory, January 1	_____	
Cost of Goods Purchased	_____	
Freight	_____	
Total Cost of Goods Purchased	_____	
Total of Goods Available for Sale	_____	
Inventory, December 31	_____	
Cost of Goods Sold		_____
Gross Profit		_____
Expenses		
Salaries and Wages	_____	
Rent	_____	
Advertising	_____	
Utilities	_____	
Taxes on Inventory and Payroll	_____	
Miscellaneous Expenses	_____	
Total Expenses		_____
Net Income before Taxes		_____
Income Taxes		_____
Net Income after Taxes		_____

2. Complete a horizontal analysis for the following portion of an income statement. Round to the nearest tenth of a percent. **[15.2]**

China Imports, Inc.				
Comparative Income Statement				
(in thousands)				
			Increase or (Decrease)	
	This Year	**Last Year**	**Amount**	**Percent**
Net Sales	$95,000	$60,000	_____	____
Cost of Goods Sold	$63,000	$40,000	_____	____
Gross Profit	$16,000	$12,000	_____	____

3. Complete the following chart for Alberta Heights Service Station. Express each item as a percent of net sales, and then write in the appropriate average percent from the chart on page 626. Round to the nearest tenth of a percent. **[15.2]**

Alberta Heights Service Station

	Amount (In Thousands)	Percent	Average Percent
Net Sales	$1200	100%	100%
Cost of Goods Sold	____	____	____
Gross Profit	$325	____	____
Net Income	$112	____	____
Wages	$129	____	____
Rent	$72	____	____
Total Expenses	$213	____	____

Find (a) the current ratio and (b) the acid-test ratio for each firm. (Round to the nearest hundredth.) **[15.4]**

4. J & L Construction:
Current assets: $2,482,500
Current liabilities: $1,800,200
Cash: $850,000
Notes and accounts receivable: $680,100
Inventory: $952,400

(a) _____
(b) _____

5. Ben Franklin Tobacco:
Current assets: $154,000
Current liabilities: $146,500
Cash: $22,000
Notes and accounts receivable: $32,500
Inventory: $99,500

(a) _____
(b) _____

Find the ratio of net income after taxes to average owners' equity for each of the following firms. (Round to the nearest tenth of a percent.) **[15.4]**

6. Talisman Imports:
Net income after taxes: $148,200
Owners' equity
beginning of year: $472,600
end of year: $514,980

6. _____

7. Burns Commercial Properties:
Net income after taxes: $8,465,000
Owners' equity
beginning of year: $28,346,000
end of year: $36,450,000

7. _____

16 Business Statistics

CHAPTER CONTENTS

16.1 Frequency Distributions and Graphs

16.2 Mean, Median, and Mode

Prices Available

salata 2.20 2.50
us 2.20 2.40 2.30
ange Egg Mayo 2.50 30
do & Onion 2.50
Salad 2.10
t Butter & Banana 2.40
Salami 2.20
s + One 3.50
lings 3.20
Fillings 3.60

CASE IN POINT

BEV JOHNSON has always been interested in food and restaurants. She worked in a restaurant as a teenager and then later worked in a bistro when an exchange student in France. She received her college degree in Restaurant Management and eventually opened her own business, naming it after herself: Bev's Deli. She uses statistics to help manage her business.

The word **statistics** comes from words that mean *state numbers*, or data gathered by the government, such as numbers of births and deaths. Today, the word *statistics* is used in a much broader sense to include data from business, economics, and many other fields as well as methodology for analyzing data. Statistics is a powerful and commonly used tool in business. Large companies such as The Hershey Company and Apple, Inc. use statistics to understand markets and forecast demand, as well as for many other purposes.

▼16.1 Frequency Distributions and Graphs

OBJECTIVES

1 Construct and analyze a frequency distribution.
2 Make a bar graph.
3 Make a line graph.
4 Draw a circle graph.

▼ CASE IN POINT Bev Johnson uses only fresh, high-quality ingredients at her deli, and she is quickly building a reputation for quality. However, the deli has been open only a few months, so she must continue to carefully watch sales and costs. Most restaurants fail in the first year.

OBJECTIVE 1 Construct and analyze a frequency distribution. It can be difficult to interpret or find patterns in a large group of numbers. One way of analyzing the numbers is to organize them in a table that shows the frequency of occurrence of the various numbers. This type of table is called a **frequency distribution**.

Constructing a Frequency Distribution

Bev Johnson is analyzing sales activity during her first 16 weeks in business. The weekly sales data are in thousands of dollars. Read down the columns, beginning with the left column, for successive weeks of the year.

$2.3	$5.9	$6.1	$6.4
$4.9	$4.3	$6.5	$7.2
$3.9	$4.9	$5.2	$6.1
$4.6	$5.2	$6.1	$7.2

Construct a table that shows each weekly sales amount. Then go through the data and place a **tally mark** (|) next to each corresponding value to create a frequency distribution table.

SOLUTION

Sales (Thousands)	Tally	Frequency	Sales (Thousands)	Tally	Frequency
$2.3	|	1	$5.9	|	1
$3.9	|	1	$6.1	|||	3
$4.3	|	1	$6.4	|	1
$4.6	|	1	$6.5	|	1
$4.9	||	2	$7.2	||	2
$5.2	||	2			

The frequency distribution shows that the most common weekly sales amount was $6100, although there were two weeks with each of the following in sales: $4900, $5200, and $7200.

QUICK CHECK 1

To the nearest thousand, weekly sales in the spring at a nursery were: $21, $23, $21, $25, $23, and $21. Construct a frequency distribution.

The frequency distribution given in the preceding example contains a great deal of information, perhaps more than is needed. It can be simplified by combining weekly sales into groups, forming the following grouped data. The number of groups in the left column of the grouped data table is arbitrary and usually varies between 5 and 15.

Bev's Deli Grouped Data

Sales (Thousands)	Frequency (Number of Weeks)
$2.1–$3.0	1
$3.1–$4.0	1
$4.1–$5.0	4
$5.1–$6.0	3
$6.1–$7.0	5
$7.1–$8.0	2

Analyzing a Frequency Distribution

EXAMPLE 2

When sales are $5000 or less per week, Johnson believes that she can take no salary, and the business loses money. She can take a small salary out of the company when sales are between $5000 and $10,000 per week, but she can take a good salary when sales are $10,000 or more per week.

SOLUTION

(a) During how many weeks did Johnson take no salary? 10 weeks

(b) During how many weeks did Johnson take a small salary? 6 weeks

(c) During how many weeks did Johnson take a good salary? 0 weeks

Business owners often take little or no salary for the first several months to a year after a business is started. As a result, it is very important that someone starting a business has enough financial resources to get through a year or two. Lack of sufficient planning is why so many new businesses fail.

QUICK CHECK 2

Bev's Deli needs sales of more than $5000 per week in order to break even so that all expenses (other than a salary to the owner) can be paid from sales. Use the grouped data table to find the number of weeks during which the restaurant broke even.

OBJECTIVE 2 Make a bar graph. The next step in analyzing these data is to use them to make a **graph**. A graph is a visual presentation of numerical data. One of the most common graphs is a **bar graph**, where the height of a bar represents the frequency of a particular value. A bar graph for the raw sales data follows.

Weekly Sales at Bev's Deli

Frequency (number of weeks) vs. Weekly Sales (in thousands of dollars)

Sometimes the weekly sales data varies a lot. This data can be smoothed by using the grouped data shown in the following bar graph.

The grouped data shows that sales were commonly between $4100 and $7000 per week, which is close to Johnson's breakeven level of sales of $5000 or more. However, neither of these graphs show any trend that may be occurring over time. To better understand the growth of her small business, Bev Johnson needs a graph that shows sales versus time.

OBJECTIVE 3 **Make a line graph.** Bar graphs show which numbers occurred and how many times, but do not necessarily show the order in which the numbers occurred. To discover any trends that may have developed, draw a **line graph**.

Drawing a Line Graph

EXAMPLE 3

Show the growth in sales at Bev's Deli using a line graph.

SOLUTION

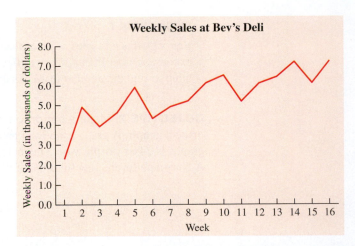

It is apparent from the line graph that sales have continued to grow in the 16 weeks that Bev Johnson has owned the deli. She is excited about the trend and determined to keep it going since her livelihood depends completely on the restaurant. Similar to many small business owners, Johnson has put everything she has into the business and plans to work hard to increase sales and make the business a success.

QUICK CHECK 3

After opening the deli, Johnson figured out that her expenses were higher than anticipated. Her break-even point is actually about $5800 in sales per week. Use the graph above to estimate the number of weeks during which Bev's deli lost money.

One advantage of line graphs is that two or more sets of data can be shown on the same graph. For example, suppose the manager of a local Radio Shack wants to compare total sales, profits, and overhead using the following historical data.

Year	Total Sales	Overhead	Profit
2010	$740,000	$205,000	$83,000
2011	$860,000	$251,000	$102,000
2012	$810,000	$247,000	$21,000
2013	$1,040,000	$302,000	$146,000

Separate lines can be made on a line graph for each category so that necessary comparisons can be made. A graph such as this is called a **comparative line graph**.

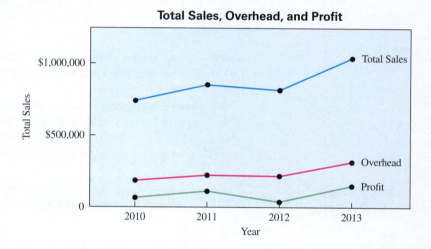

Total Sales, Overhead, and Profit

OBJECTIVE 4 **Draw a circle graph.** A sales manager for Afkin Medical Supplies records the expenses to keep a sales force on the road. First, she converts each expense to a percent of the total expenses. Then she generates the data needed to create a **pie chart**, also called **circle graph**. A pie chart has 360 **degrees** (360°). To find the number of degrees of the circle graph associated with each expense, multiply the percent by 360° as shown.

Afkin Medical Supplies – Midwest Region

Item	Expense	Percent of Total	Degrees
Travel	$246,000	30%	30% × 360° = 108°
Lodging	$180,400	22%	22% × 360° = 79° (rounded)
Food	$82,000	10%	10% × 360° = 36°
Entertainment	$82,000	10%	10% × 360° = 36°
Sales Meetings	$65,600	8%	8% × 360° = 29° (rounded)
Other	$164,000	20%	20% × 360° = 72°
Total	$820,000		Total 360°

Think of 108° as $\dfrac{108°}{360°}$ of a circle which reduces to $\dfrac{3}{10}$, and so on for the other values in the last column. The manager used the data above in Excel to create the following pie chart, which she then used in a presentation to management.

**Afrin Medical Supplies
Midwest Region**

Travel
30%

Lodging
22%

Entertainment
10%

Sales
Meetings
8%

Food
10%

Other
20%

Once you have the pie chart, you may no longer need the raw data. For example, we can use the pie chart to see that travel and lodging together accounted for 52% of the expenses by adding 30% + 22%.

Pie charts are excellent ways to view certain data and they can be used to show comparisons when one item is very small compared to another. For example, an item representing 1% of the total could be drawn as a small, but noticeable, slice of a circle graph. Pie charts are commonly used by managers, and they are often in found in newspapers and magazines.

Interpreting a Circle Graph

▶ EXAMPLE 4

Use the pie chart above and find the percent of total expenses spent on (a) food and entertainment and (b) travel and sales meetings.

SOLUTION

(a)	Food	10%
	Entertainment	10%
	Total	20%

(b)	Travel	30%
	Sales Meetings	8%
	Total	38%

QUICK CHECK 4

Use the pie chart above to find the total percent spent on sales meetings and entertainment combined.

Graphs are frequently used in business and life to communicate data. People often like graphs, since they help us visualize and therefore understand the data. For example the line graph on the left shows the average credit card debt of college students by year. The chart helps us understand that the average student credit card debt has increased rapidly over the past 10 years.

The graphic on the right shows states with the largest projected budget shortfall for fiscal year 2012. The states with the most significant problems are widely scattered and include Arizona, California, Connecticut, Illinois, Maine, Minnesota, Nevada, New Jersey, North Carolina, Vermont, and Wisconsin. Since serious shortfalls in annual budgets are problematic for states, the figure is telling us where states will be facing the largest problems in the coming years.

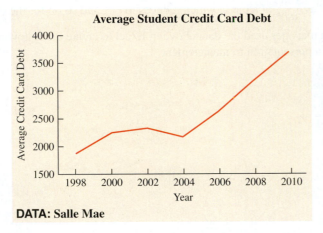

Average Student Credit Card Debt

DATA: Salle Mae

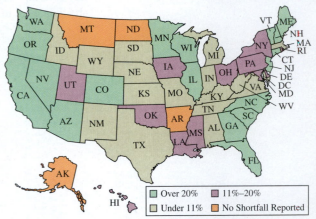

46 States Faced Budget Shortfalls in FY 2012

Shortfalls as share of General Fund Expenditures.

Over 20%   11%–20%
Under 11%   No Shortfall Reported

Beware of poorly designed graphs and charts that may mislead. For example, does the bar chart below refer to unemployment or unemployment rate? Does it refer to one region or the entire country? Was unemployment increasing over time? Was unemployment, in the last year shown, more than twice that for the first year shown?

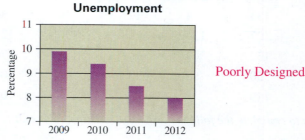

Unemployment

Poorly Designed

Source: Bureau of Labor Statistics

Actually, the graph shows the nationwide unemployment rate taken from the Bureau of Labor Statistics. Unemployment decreased from just under 10% at the end of 2009 to about 8% at the end of 2012. So, unemployment was decreasing, but not as rapidly as it may appear to you from the chart. The figure shows actual data, but its design is misleading.

▼16.1 Exercises

MyMathLab®

*The shaded sections below contain solutions to help you get a **QUICK START** on the various types of exercises.*

Answer Exercises 1–3 using the bar graph on population growth. Answer Exercises 4–6 using the line graph on people who live together.

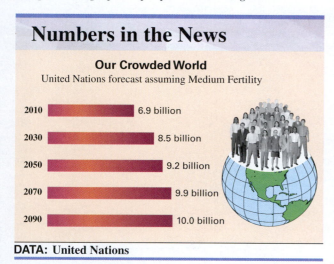

Numbers in the News

Our Crowded World
United Nations forecast assuming Medium Fertility

2010	6.9 billion
2030	8.5 billion
2050	9.2 billion
2070	9.9 billion
2090	10.0 billion

DATA: United Nations

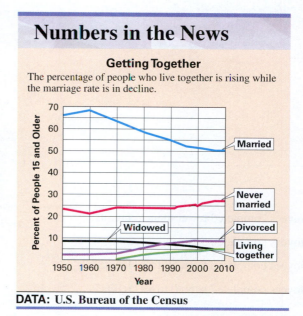

Numbers in the News

Getting Together
The percentage of people who live together is rising while the marriage rate is in decline.

DATA: U.S. Bureau of the Census

1. Estimate world population in 2020.
    (6.9 + 8.5)/2 = 7.7 billion

    1. _7.7 billion_____

2. Find the percent increase in world population from 2010 to 2090.

    2. _____

3. In 2050, assume that 56% of the world's population lives in Asia and that 5.2% of the world's population lives in the U.S. Estimate the population of Asia and of the U.S.

    3. _____

4. Approximately what percent of the U.S. population was married in 1950 and in 2010?

    4. _____

5. What has happened to the percent of people divorced during the past 60 years?

    5. _____

6. Estimate the percent of people living together in 2010.

    6. _____

The following list gives the numbers of college credits completed by 30 employees of the Franklin Bank.

College Credits
Franklin Bank Employees

74	133	4	127	20	30
103	27	139	118	138	121
149	132	64	141	130	76
42	50	95	56	65	104
4	140	12	88	119	64

Use these numbers to complete the following table. (See Examples 1 and 2.)

Number of Credits	Number of Employees
7. 0–24	4
8. 25–49	_____
9. 50–74	_____
10. 75–99	_____
11. 100–124	_____
12. 125–149	_____

13. Make a line graph using the frequencies that you found.

14. How many employees completed fewer than 25 credits?   **14.** 4 _____

15. How many employees completed 50 or more credits?   **15.** _____

16. How many employees completed from 50 to 124 credits?   **16.** _____

17. How many employees completed from 0 to 49 credits?   **17.** _____

Weekly sales in thousands of dollars are given for one Home Depot store. The numbers are in chronological order going down the columns. For example, sales for the first and fourth weeks, respectively, are $302,000 and $304,000.

302	304	318	301	330	337	335	348	339
265	275	279	283	322	349	330	325	334
315	288	299	326	325	342	328	347	

Use the numbers to complete the following table. (See Example 1.)

Sales (in thousands)	Frequency	Sales (in thousands)	Frequency
18. 260–269	1	**19.** 270–279	2
20. 280–289	_____	**21.** 290–299	_____
22. 300–309	_____	**23.** 310–319	_____
24. 320–329	_____	**25.** 330–339	_____
26. 340–349	_____		

27. Make a bar graph using your answers to Exercises 18–26.

28. Make a line graph using the original numbers.

29. How many weeks did sales equal or exceed $300,000?

30. How many weeks did sales fall below $270,000?

29. _____

30. _____

The following numbers show the scores of 80 students on a marketing test.

79	60	74	59	55	98	61	67	83	71
71	46	63	66	69	42	75	62	71	77
78	65	87	57	78	91	82	73	94	48
87	65	62	81	63	66	65	49	45	51
69	56	84	93	63	60	68	51	73	54
50	88	76	93	48	70	39	76	95	57
63	94	82	54	89	64	77	94	72	69
51	56	67	88	81	70	81	54	66	87

Use these numbers to complete the following table. (See Example 1.)

	Score	Frequency			Score	Frequency
31.	30–39	1_____		**32.**	40–49	6_____
33.	50–59	_____		**34.**	60–69	_____
35.	70–79	_____		**36.**	80–89	_____
37.	90–99	_____				

38. Make a bar graph showing your answers to Exercises 31–37.

39. How many students passed the test (passing is 70)?

40. If a grade of B is given for a score of 80 or higher, how many students received a B or better?

41. How many students failed the test (scored below 70)?

42. How many students scored from 60 to 79?

39. _____

40. _____

41. _____

42. _____

During one recent period Angela Rueben, a student, had $1400 in expenses, as shown in the following table. Find all numbers missing from the table in Exercises 43–48. (See Objective 4.)

Item	Dollar Amount	Percent of Total	Degrees of a Circle	Item	Dollar Amount	Percent of Total	Degrees of a Circle
43. Rent	$280	20%	72°	**44.** Clothing	$210	15%	54°
$\frac{72°}{360°} = .20 = 20\%$				$\frac{\$210}{\$1400} = .15 = 15\%; .15 \times 360° = 54°$			
45. Books	$140	10%	_____	**46.** Entertainment	$210	_____	54°
47. Savings	$70	_____	_____	**48.** Other	_____	_____	126°

49. Draw a circle graph using Rueben's information. (See Objective 4.)

50. What percent did Rueben spend on rent, clothing and books?

51. What percent did Rueben spend on savings and entertainment?

50. _____

51. _____

Solve the following application problems.

52. FURNITURE   Annual sales at Antique Furnishings are divided into five categories as follows.

Item	Annual Sales
Finishing materials	$25,000
Desks	$80,000
Bedroom sets	$120,000
Dining room sets	$100,000
Other	$75,000

Make a circle graph showing this distribution. (See Example 4.)

53. BOOK PUBLISHING Armstrong Publishing had 25% of its sales in mysteries, 10% in biographies, 15% in cookbooks, 15% in romance novels, 20% in science, and the rest in business books. Draw a circle graph with this information. (See Example 4.)

54. WAR DEATHS The bar chart shows an estimate of the number of Americans killed and wounded in various wars. Show this data in a circle graph. Round degrees to the nearest degree and percents to the nearest tenth of a percent. Which two wars had the highest number of killed and wounded?

Numbers in the News

Number of Americans Killed and Wounded in Wars

War	Number
American Revolutionary War (1775–93)	50,000
Civil War (1861–65)	646,000
World War I (1917–18)	321,000
World War II (1941–45)	1,076,000
Korean War (1950–53)	129,000
Vietnam War (1957–73)	212,000
Afghanistan (2001–present)	21,000
Iraq (2003–2011)	37,000

55. TOP TAX RATES   The graphic shows the highest tax rate on high-income individuals in the United States. Show the data using a bar chart. What conclusion(s) can you draw from the figure?

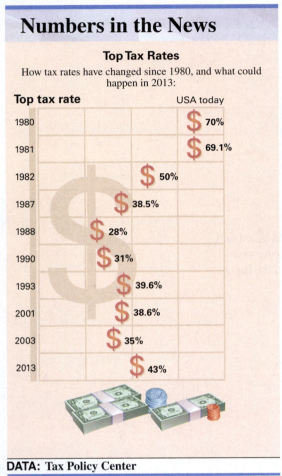

Numbers in the News

Top Tax Rates

How tax rates have changed since 1980, and what could happen in 2013:

Top tax rate	USA today
1980	70%
1981	69.1%
1982	50%
1987	38.5%
1988	28%
1990	31%
1993	39.6%
2001	38.6%
2003	35%
2013	43%

DATA: Tax Policy Center

56. List the advantages of using a graph over a table when looking for trends.

57. Cut out three graphs from newspapers or magazines and tape them to your homework assignment. Be sure to explain the data in each case.

QUICK CHECK ANSWERS

1. $21, 3; $23, 2; $25, 1

2. 10 weeks

3. 8 weeks

4. 18%

▼16.2 Mean, Median, and Mode

OBJECTIVES

1   Find the mean of a list of numbers.
2   Find the weighted mean.
3   Find the median.
4   Find the mode.

OBJECTIVE 1 Find the mean of a list of numbers. Businesses are often faced with the problem of analyzing a mass of raw data. Reports come in from many different branches of a company, or salespeople send in a large number of expense claims, for example. In analyzing all these data, one of the first things to look for is a **measure of central tendency**—a single number that shows the "middle" of the data. One such measure of central tendency is the **mean**, which is just the **average** of a collection of numbers or data.

Finding Mean

$$\text{Mean} = \frac{\text{Sum of all values}}{\text{Number of values}}$$

For example, suppose milk sales at a local 7-Eleven for each of the days last week were $86, $103, $118, $117, $126, $158, and $149. The mean sales of milk (rounded to the nearest cent) follows.

$$\text{Mean} = \frac{86 + 103 + 118 + 117 + 126 + 158 + 149}{7} = \mathbf{\$122.43}$$

One criticism of the mean is that its value *can be distorted* by one very large (or very small) value, as shown in the next example. A better measure of central tendency in cases with one abnormally large (or small) value is shown later in this section. (See Objective 3.)

Finding the Mean   Bev Johnson has promised seven of her employees at Bev's Deli that they will all work about the same number of hours. One employee commented that she worked considerably more hours than the other employees last month. The number of hours worked by each of the seven employees during the past month are given. Find the mean to the nearest hour.

$$75, 63, 76, 82, 70, 81, 149$$

SOLUTION

Add the numbers and divide by 7, since there are 7 numbers. Check that the sum of the numbers is **596**.

→distorted by the 1 large number of 149

$$\text{Mean} = \frac{\mathbf{596}}{7} = 85.14$$

The mean of 85 seems a bit large, since one employee worked a lot more hours than the other six employees. The mean without this value of 149 is the sum of the remaining 6 numbers divided by 6.

$$\text{Mean} = \frac{\mathbf{447}}{6} = 74.5$$

This value seems more in line with the average number of hours worked. Perhaps there was an unusual reason the one employee worked 149 hours (e.g., someone else was sick and could not work.)

QUICK CHECK 1

First find the mean of the following numbers: 24, 65, 25, 24, and 28. Then eliminate the largest value and find the mean of the remaining numbers.

Averages are commonly used, even in graphs. For example, the line graph at the left on the next page shows the average age at which people marry in the U.S. It shows that (on average) people are waiting to get married. The bar chart on the right shows the average number of weeks that people in the U.S. were unemployed. The average numbers of weeks of unemployment were unusually high for all ages due to high unemployment related to the continuing financial crisis. However, it was particularly high for people 35 or older, many of whom have families dependent on their income.

Numbers in the News

Older Brides and Grooms

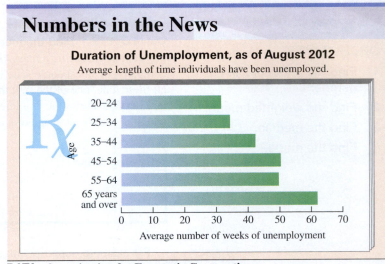

| 1960 | 1970 | 1980 | 1990 | 2000 | 2010 |

27.1
25.8
22.8
20.3

DATA: U.S. Bureau of the Census

Numbers in the News

Duration of Unemployment, as of August 2012
Average length of time individuals have been unemployed.

Age:
20–24
25–34
35–44
45–54
55–64
65 years and over

Average number of weeks of unemployment: 0 10 20 30 40 50 60 70

DATA: Organization for Economic Cooperation and Development

OBJECTIVE 2 **Find the weighted mean.** Some of the items in a list might appear more than once. In this case, it is necessary to find the **weighted mean**, or **weighted average**, where each value is the product of the number itself and the number of times it occurs.

Finding the Weighted Mean

EXAMPLE 2 Find the weighted mean of the numbers given in the following table.

Value	Frequency
3	4
5	2
7	1
8	5
9	3
10	2
12	1
13	2

SOLUTION

According to this table, the value 5 occurred 2 times, 8 occurred 5 times, 12 occurred 1 time, and so on. To find the mean, multiply each value by the frequency for that value. Then add the products. Add the values in the Frequency column to find the total number of values and then divide.

Value	Frequency	Product
3	4	12
5	2	10
7	1	7
8	5	40
9	3	27
10	2	20
12	1	12
13	2	26
Totals	**20**	**154**

$$\text{Weighted mean} = \frac{\mathbf{154}}{\mathbf{20}} = 7.7$$

QUICK CHECK 2

Find the weighted mean of the following sample of average family income in one neighborhood: 12 families, \$15,300/year; 15 families, \$19,700/year; and 22 families, \$22,450/year.

A weighted average is used to find a student's grade point average, as shown in the next example.

Finding the Grade Point Average

EXAMPLE 3

Mark Benson earned the following grades last semester. Find his grade point average to the nearest tenth. Assume A = 4, B = 3, C = 2, D = 1, and F = 0.

Course	Credits	Grade	Grade × Credits
Business Mathematics	3	A (= 4)	3 × 4 = 12
Retailing	4	C (= 2)	4 × 2 = 8
English	3	B (= 3)	3 × 3 = 9
Biology	2	A (= 4)	2 × 4 = 8
Biology Lab	2	D (= 1)	2 × 1 = 2
Totals	14		39

Quick TIP

It is common to round grade point averages to the nearest tenth.

SOLUTION

The grade point average for Benson is $\frac{39}{14}$ = 2.79 = 2.8, which is a B–. Anything between 2.5 and 3.0 is a B– at Benson's school.

This problem is solved using a scientific calculator as follows.

(4 × 3 + 2 × 4 + 3 × 3 + 4 × 2 + 1 × 2) ÷ (3 + 4 + 3 + 2 + 2) = 2.8

Note: Refer to Appendix B for calculator basics.

QUICK CHECK 3

Becky Johnson received an A in English, a C in History, and a C in Biology. All three classes are three-credit classes. An A is 4 points, a B is 3 points, and a C is 2 points. Find her grade point average to the nearest tenth.

OBJECTIVE 3 Find the median. As we saw in Example 1, the mean is a poor indicator of central tendency when there is one very large or one very small number. This effect can be avoided by using another measure of central tendency called the **median**. The median divides a group of numbers in half—half the numbers lie at or above the median, and half lie at or below the median.

The process to find the median depends on whether the list has an odd number of numbers or an even number of numbers. Find the median as follows.

Finding the Median

1. List the numbers from smallest to largest as an **ordered array**.
2. Find the median.
   (a) If there are an odd number of numbers, then the median is the number in the middle.
   (b) If there are an even number of numbers, then the median is the average of the two numbers in the middle.

Finding the Median

EXAMPLE 4

Find the median of the following weights (in pounds).

(a) 30 lb, 25 lb, 28 lb, 23 lb, 24 lb

(b) 14 lb, 18 lb, 17 lb, 10 lb, 15 lb, 19 lb, 18 lb, 20 lb

SOLUTION

(a) First list the numbers from smallest to largest.

23, 24, 25, 28, 30   ordered array

There are 5 numbers, so divide 5 by 2 to get 2.5. The next larger whole number is 3, so the median is the third number, **or 25**. The numbers 23 and 24 are less than 25, and the numbers 28 and 30 are greater than 25.

(b) First list the numbers from smallest to largest.

$$10, 14, 15, 17, 18, 18, 19, 20 \quad \text{ordered array}$$

There are 8 numbers, so divide 8 by 2 to get 4. The median is the mean of the numbers in the 4th and 5th positions.

$$\text{Median} = \frac{17 + 18}{2} = 17.5$$

QUICK CHECK 4

The heights of the students in one club at an elementary school are: 48, 41, 49, 47, and 51 inches. Find the median height.

The figure on the left shows recent data for median household income and the figure on the right shows median income by gender. Together, the charts show that there is still significant inequality in incomes in the United States. However, the two charts say *nothing about why incomes differ or what to do to bring them closer together*. Sociologists and economists study issues such as these to try to find ways to increase income equality. For example, the median is used in this data since it is a better measure than mean. The median is not distorted by a relatively few individuals with very high incomes.

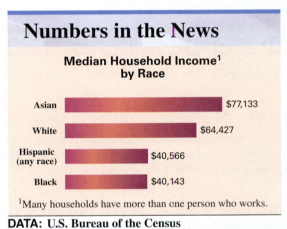

Numbers in the News

Median Household Income[1] by Race

Asian	$77,133
White	$64,427
Hispanic (any race)	$40,566
Black	$40,143

[1]Many households have more than one person who works.

DATA: U.S. Bureau of the Census

Numbers in the News

Median Household Income by Gender

Men	$33,196
Women	$20,922

DATA: U.S. Bureau of the Census

OBJECTIVE 4 Find the mode. The last important statistical measure discussed in this section is called the **mode**. The mode is the number that occurs most often. For example, if 10 students earned scores of

$$74, 81, 38, 74, 82, 80, 100, 92, 74, 85$$

on a business law examination, then the mode is 74. This is because more students obtained this score than any other score.

A data set in which every number occurs the same number of times is said to have *no mode*. A data set in which two different numbers occur the same number of times, with each occurring more often than any other number in the data set, is said to be bimodal. The prefix "bi" means two and the root "modal" refers to modes, so **bimodal** means *two modes*.

Finding the Mode   **EXAMPLE 5**

Professor Miller gave the same test to both his day and evening sections of Business Math at American River College. Find the mode of the tests given in each class. Which class has the lower mode?

(a) Day Class: 85, 92, 81, 73, 78, 80, 83, 80, 74, 69, 80, 65, 71, 65, 80, 93, 54, 78, 80, 45, 70, 76, 73, 80, 71, 68

(b) Evening Class: 68, 73, 59, 76, 79, 73, 85, 90, 73, 69, 73, 75, 93, 73, 76, 70, 73, 68, 82, 84, 77

Quick TIP

It is not necessary to place the numbers in numerical order when looking for the mode, but it helps with a large set of numbers.

SOLUTION

(a) The number **80** is the mode for the day class because it occurs more often than any other number. It occurs 6 times.

(b) The number **73** is the mode for the evening class because it occurs more often than any other number. It occurs 6 times as well.

The evening class has the lower mode.

QUICK CHECK 5

Five economists were asked to forecast the growth rate of the gross domestic product (GDP) for next year. Find the mode of their forecasts: 3.7%, 3.4%, 4.1%, 3.5%, and 3.4%.

▼ 16.2 Exercises   MyMathLab®

*The shaded sections below contain solutions to help you get a **QUICK START** on the various types of exercises.*

Find the mean for the following lists of numbers. Round to the nearest tenth. (See Example 1.)

1. Gallons of spoiled milk: 3.5, 1.1, 2.8, .8, 4.1
$\frac{3.5 + 1.1 + 2.8 + .8 + 4.1}{5} = 2.5$
  1. __2.5__

2. Weeks premature: 2, 3, 1, 4, 5, 2
$\frac{2 + 3 + 1 + 4 + 5 + 2}{6} = 2.8$
  2. __2.8__

3. Guests at board meetings: 40, 51, 59, 62, 68, 73, 49, 80
  3. _____

4. Algebra quiz scores: 32, 26, 30, 19, 51, 46, 38, 39
  4. _____

5. Number attending games: 21,900, 22,850, 24,930, 29,710, 28,340, 40,000
  5. _____

6. Annual salaries: $38,500, $39,720, $42,183, $21,982, $43,250
  6. _____

7. Average number of defects per spool: 10.6, 12.5, 11.7, 9.6, 10.3, 9.6, 10.9, 6.4, 2.3, 4.1
  7. _____

8. Weight of dogs (pounds): 30.1, 42.8, 91.6, 51.2, 88.3, 21.9, 43.7, 51.2
  8. _____

9. When is it better to use the median, rather than the mean, for a measure of central tendency? Give an example. (See Objective 3.)

10. List some situations in which the mode is the best measure of central tendency to use to describe the data. (See Objective 4.)

Find the weighted mean for the following. Round to the nearest tenth. (See Example 2.)

11.

Value	Frequency
9	3
12	4
18	2

12.3

$9 \times 3 = 27$

$12 \times 4 = 48$

$18 \times 2 = \underline{36}$

$ 9 \quad 111$

$\frac{111}{9} = 12.3$

12.

Value	Frequency
9	3
12	5
15	1
18	1

12

$9 \times 3 = 27$

$12 \times 5 = 60$

$15 \times 1 = 15$

$18 \times 1 = \underline{18}$

$10 \quad 120$

$\frac{120}{10} = 12$

13.

Value	Frequency
12	4
13	2
15	5
19	3
22	1
23	5

14.

Value	Frequency
25	1
26	2
29	5
30	4
32	3
33	5

15.

Value	Frequency
104	6
112	14
115	21
119	13
123	22
127	6
132	9

16.

Value	Frequency
243	1
247	3
251	5
255	7
263	4
271	2
279	2

Find the grade point averages for the following students. Assume that $A = 4, B = 3, C = 2, D = 1,$ and $F = 0$. Round to the nearest tenth. (See Example 3.)

17.

Credits	Grade
4	B
2	A
5	C
1	F
3	B

18.

Credits	Grade
3	A
3	B
4	B
2	C
4	D

Find the median for the following lists of numbers. (See Example 4.)

19. Number of virus attacks on a network: 140, 85, 122, 114, 98

85, 98, **114**, 122, 140

↑
Median

19. <u>114</u>

20. Cost of new laptops: $569, $478, $620, $515, $598

20. _____

21. Number of books loaned: 125, 100, 114, 150, 135, 172

21. _____

22. Calories in menu items: 346, 521, 412, 515, 501, 528, 298, 621

22. _____

23. Number of students taking business math: 37, 63, 92, 26, 44, 32, 75, 50, 41

23. _____

24. Number of orders: 1072, 1068, 1093, 1042, 1056, 1005, 1009

24. _____

Find the mode or modes for each of the following lists of numbers. (See Example 5.)

25. Porosity of soil samples: 21%, 18%, 21%, 28%, 22%, 21%, 25%

If the data are listed according to how many times each number appears,

18%, **21%**, 22%, 25%, 28%

21%

21%

↑——21% is the mode since 21% is listed more than any other number.

25. <u>21%</u>

26. Number of students graduating with honors: 85, 69, 72, 69, 103, 81, 98

26. _____

27. Age of retirees: 80, 72, 64, 64, 72, 53, 64

27. _____

28. Number of pages read: 86, 84, 83, 84, 83, 86, 86

28. _____

29. Number of fifth-grade students: 32, 38, 32, 36, 38, 34, 35, 30, 39

29. _____

30. Number of people on flights from Chicago to Denver: 178, 104, 178, 150, 165, 165, 82

30. _____

A quality-control inspector in a plant that manufactures electric motors measured the following shaft diameters (in thousandths of an inch).

35, 33, 32, 34, 35, 34, 35, 35, 34

Using these numbers, find each of the following. (Round to the nearest hundredth.)

31. The mean _____

32. The median _____

The quality-control inspector subsequently determined that he had made a mistake when he wrote 32 thousandths of an inch. Eliminate this number from the list above and find each of the following.

33. The mean _____

34. The median _____

35. If you want to avoid a single extreme value having a large effect on the average, would you use the mean or the median? Explain your answer.

36. Does an employer look at the mean, median, or mode grade on a college transcript when considering hiring a new employee? Which do you think the employer should look at? Explain.

QUICK CHECK ANSWERS

1. 33.2; 25.25

2. $19,857.14

3. 2.7

4. 48 inches

5. 3.4%

▼ Chapter 16 Quick Review

Chapter Terms *Review the following terms to test your understanding of the chapter. For each term you do not know, refer to the page number found next to that term.*

average [**p. 665**]

bar graph [**p. 655**]

bimodal [**p. 668**]

circle graph [**p. 657**]

comparative line graph [**p. 657**]

frequency distribution [**p. 654**]

graph [**p. 655**]

line graph [**p. 656**]

mean [**p. 665**]

measure of central tendency [**p. 665**]

median [**p. 667**]

mode [**p. 668**]

ordered array [**p. 667**]

pie chart [**p. 657**]

statistics [**p. 654**]

tally mark [**p. 654**]

weighted average [**p. 666**]

weighted mean [**p. 666**]

CONCEPTS

EXAMPLES

16.1 Constructing a frequency distribution from raw data

1. Construct a table listing each value and the number of times this value occurs.
2. Combine the pieces of data into groups.

Construct a frequency distribution for weekly sales, in thousands, at a small concrete plant.

$22, $20, $22, $25, $18, $19, $22, $24, $24, $29, $19

Data	Tally	Frequency
$18	|	1
$19	||	2
$20	|	1
$22	|||	3
$24	||	2
$25	|	1
$29	|	1

Class	Frequency
$18–$20	4
$21–$23	3
$24–$26	3
$27–$29	1

16.1 Constructing a bar graph from a frequency distribution

Draw a bar for each class using the frequency of the class as the height of the bar.

Construct a bar graph from the frequency distribution of the preceding example.

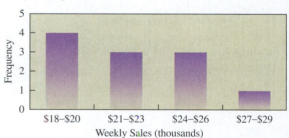

16.1 Constructing a line graph

1. Plot each year on the horizontal axis.
2. For each year, find the value of sales, and plot a point at that value.
3. Connect all points with straight lines.

Construct a line graph for the following sales data.

Year	Total Sales
2010	$850,000
2011	$920,000
2012	$695,000
2013	$975,000

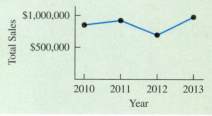

CONCEPTS

16.1 Constructing a circle graph

1. Determine the percent of the total for each item.
2. Find the number of degrees of a circle that each percent represents.
3. Draw the circle.

EXAMPLES

Construct a circle graph for the following table which lists expenses for a business trip.

Item	Amount
Car	$200
Lodging	$300
Food	$250
Entertainment	$150
Other	$100
	$1000

Item	Amount	Percent of Total
Car	$200	$\frac{\$200}{\$1000} = \frac{1}{5} = 20\%$; $360° \times 20\% = 360 \times .20 = \mathbf{72°}$
Lodging	$300	$\frac{\$300}{\$1000} = \frac{3}{10} = 30\%$; $360° \times 30\% = 360 \times .30 = \mathbf{108°}$
Food	$250	$\frac{\$250}{\$1000} = \frac{1}{4} = 25\%$; $360° \times 25\% = 360 \times .25 = \mathbf{90°}$
Entertainment	$150	$\frac{\$150}{\$1000} = \frac{3}{20} = 15\%$; $360° \times 15\% = 360 \times .15 = \mathbf{54°}$
Other	$100	$\frac{\$100}{\$1000} = \frac{1}{10} = 10\%$; $360° \times 10\% = 360 \times .10 = \mathbf{36°}$

16.1 Finding the mean of a set of numbers

1. Add all numbers to obtain the total.
2. Divide the total by the number of pieces of data.

The quiz scores for Pat Phelan in her business math course were as follows:

85   79   93   91   78   82   87   85

Find Pat's quiz average.

$$\text{Mean} = \frac{85 + 79 + 93 + 91 + 78 + 82 + 87 + 85}{8} = \mathbf{85}$$

16.2 Finding the median of a set of numbers

1. Arrange the data in numerical order from lowest to highest.
2. Select the middle value or the average of the two middle values.

Find the median for Pat Phelan's grades from the preceding example. The data arranged from the lowest to highest are

78   79   82   85   85   87   91   93

The middle two values are 85 and 85. The average of these two values is

$$\frac{85 + 85}{2} = 85$$

16.2 Finding the mode of a set of values

Determine the most frequently occurring value.

Find the mode for Pat Phelan's grades in the preceding example. The most frequently occurring score is 85 (it occurs twice), so the mode is 85.

Case **Study**

WATCHING A SMALL BUSINESS GROW

Jeremy Clark decided to call his business The Soft Touch. He opened his first kiosk selling candles and other gifts in a nearby mall on February 1. In June, he opened a second kiosk selling the same gifts. Sales at the two kiosks (stores) are shown in thousands of dollars.

	Feb.	Mar.	Apr.	May	June	July	Aug.	Sept.	Oct.
Store 1	6.5	6.8	7.0	6.9	7.5	7.8	8.0	7.6	8.2
Store 2	—	—	—	—	8.2	6.2	8.2	8.7	9.6

1. Find the median, mean, and mode sales for each store to the nearest tenth.

2. Plot sales for both stores on the same line graph, with month on the horizontal axis and sales on the vertical axis.

3. What trends are apparent from the preceding line graph?

INVESTIGATE

Find three graphs and charts using newspapers, magazines, and/or the Internet. Then explain each of them in writing. Graphs and charts can be great tools for communicating with customers, fellow workers, or even your boss. How can you make sure that a graph or chart clearly communicates the message that you wish it to convey?

Case in Point Summary Exercise

BOBBY FLAY

www.bobbyflay.com

Facts:

- 1991: Opened Mesa Grill in New York
- 1996: On Food Network for first time
- 2010: On "Boy Meets Grill" weekly on TV
- 2011: Has published 9 books

Bobby Flay opened Mesa Grill in New York City in 1991 with "a new twist on southwestern cuisine." He owns several restaurants in the New York area and also one in Las Vegas. Flay prides himself on creating a working environment in which his employees are able to express their creativity and grow professionally. His organization currently offers a $30,000 scholarship to one high school senior who plans to attend the French Culinary Institute. His most recent book, *Grilling for Life*, is about great food and healthy choices.

	October	November	December
Week 1	$7.4	$8.0	$8.9
Week 2	$8.0	$8.2	$8.9
Week 3	$7.4	$9.8	$9.2
Week 4	$8.3	$10.6	$7.1

Bobby Flay has been one of Bev Johnson's favorite TV shows for several years. She watches his shows when she has time and brings recipes from the show into her deli from time to time. Her business has continued to grow, and sales during the recent holidays are shown in thousands of dollars.

1. Find the mean and median sales for each month.

2. Make a line graph of sales versus weeks. Why do you think sales were high in the last two weeks of November and then low in the last week in December?

3. Make a pie chart using monthly sales data for October, November, and December.

Discussion Question: Is it meaningful to collect data when managing a business? It is meaningful to use the data to build graphs? Explain.

▼ Chapter 16 Test

To help you review, the numbers in brackets show the section in which the topic was discussed.

1. The following are the numbers of cases of motor oil sold per week, by a regional distributor on the East Coast, for each of the past 20 weeks.

12,450	11,300	12,800	10,850	14,100
14,900	12,300	11,600	12,400	12,900
13,300	12,500	13,390	12,800	12,500
15,100	13,700	12,200	11,800	12,600

Use these numbers to complete the following table. [**16.1**]

Cases of Motor Oil	Number of Weeks
10,000–10,999	_____
11,000–11,999	_____
12,000–12,999	_____
13,000–13,999	_____
14,000–14,999	_____
15,000–15,999	_____

2. How many weeks had sales of 13,000 cases or more? [**16.1**]

2. _____

3. Use the numbers in the table above to draw a bar graph. Be sure to put a title and labels on the graph. [**16.1**]

4. During a 1-year period, the campus newspaper at Midwest Community College had the following expenses. Find all numbers missing from the table. [**16.1**]

Item	Dollar Amount	Percent of Total	Degrees of a Circle
Newsprint	$12,000	20%	_____
Ink	$6,000	_____	36°
Wire service	$18,000	30%	_____
Salaries	$18,000	30%	_____
Other	$6,000	10%	_____

5. Draw a circle graph using the information in test question 4. [**16.1**]

6. What percents of the expenses were for newsprint, ink, and wire service? [**16.1**]

6. _____

Find the means for the following. Round to the nearest tenth if necessary.   [16.2]

7. Number attending classical music recitals: 220, 275, 198, 212, 233, 246

7. _____

8. Length of boards (centimeters): 12, 18, 14, 17, 19, 22, 23, 25

8. _____

9. Weekly commission ($): 458, 432, 496, 491, 500, 508, 512, 396, 492, 504

9. _____

10. *Volume (quarts)*	*Frequency*
6	7
10	3
11	4
14	2
19	3
24	1 _____

11. *Sales ($)*	*Frequency*
150	15
160	17
170	21
180	28
190	19
200	7 _____

Find the median for the following lists of numbers. Do not round.   [16.2]

12. Numbers of actors trying out for a part: 22, 18, 15, 25, 20, 19, 7

12. _____

13. Number of text messages received per hour: 41, 39, 45, 47, 38, 42, 51, 38

13. _____

14. Hours worked per day: 7.6, 9.3, 11.8, 10.4, 4.2, 5.3, 7.1, 9.0, 8.3

14. _____

15. Trees planted: 58, 76, 91, 83, 29, 34, 51, 92, 38, 41

15. _____

Find the mode or modes for the following lists of numbers.   [16.2]

16. Contestants' ages: 51, 47, 48, 32, 47, 71, 82, 47

16. _____

17. Customers served: 32, 51, 74, 19, 25, 43, 75, 82, 98, 100

17. _____

18. Defectives per batch: 96, 104, 103, 104, 103, 104, 91, 74, 103

18. _____

Solve the following application problems.

19. Stein's Fine Furnishings had the following sales (in thousand of dollars).

Year	Sales
2009	$754
2010	$782
2011	$853
2012	$592
2013	$680

The geographic area in which Stein's operates had a serious business recession (economic slow down) in 2012. Do you think the recession may have affected the business? Support your view by drawing a line graph.

20. Ted Smith is an analyst at Charles Schwab Corp. and receives a base salary plus a commission based on performance. His wife developed a serious illness at the beginning of 2012 and her condition slowly improved through the balance of the year. Do you think his personal problems may have influenced his work performance?

	Quarterly Commissions			
Year	Quarter 1	Quarter 2	Quarter 3	Quarter 4
2011	$14,250	$12,375	$15,750	$13,682
2012	$13,435	$14,230	$11,540	$15,782
2013	$8,207	$7,350	$10,366	$11,470

Support your view by drawing a line graph. Be sure to label the quarter in which Mrs. Smith became ill.

Appendix A

The Metric System

The metric system is a system of measurements, weights, and temperatures that is used nearly everywhere in the world other than the United States. It is a system of measurements and weights that is based on decimal numbers. Even some firms in the U.S. use the metric system, particularly those that build products that are sold in Europe or Asia. Notice that time is the same in both the English and metric systems.

Length		Weight	
1 foot	= 12 inches (in.)	1 pound (lb)	= 16 ounces (oz)
1 yard (yd)	= 3 feet (ft)	1 ton (T)	= 2000 pounds (lb)
1 mile (mi)	= 5280 feet (ft)		

Capacity		Time	
1 cup (c)	= 8 fluid ounces	1 week (wk)	= 7 days
1 pint (pt)	= 2 cups	1 day	= 24 hours (hr)
1 quart (qt)	= 2 pints (pt)	1 hour (hr)	= 60 minutes (min)
1 gallon (gal)	= 4 quarts (qt)	1 minute (min)	= 60 seconds (sec)

1 meter

1 meter is 39.37 inches.

1 yard

1 yard is 36 inches.

OBJECTIVES

1 Learn the metric system.

2 Learn how to convert from one system to the other.

Prefixes in the Metric System

deca- = 10 times

kilo- = 1000 times

deci- = $\frac{1}{10}$ times

centi- = $\frac{1}{100}$ times

milli- = $\frac{1}{1000}$ times

OBJECTIVE 1 Learn the metric system. The basic unit of length in the metric system is the **meter**. A meter is a little longer than a yard. For shorter lengths, the units **centimeter** and **millimeter** are commonly used. The prefix "centi" means hundredth, so 1 centimeter is one-hundredth of a meter. Thus

$$100 \text{ centimeters} = 1 \text{ meter} \quad \left(\text{or 1 centimeter} = \tfrac{1}{100} \text{ meter} \right)$$

The prefix "milli" means thousandth, so 1 millimeter means one-thousandth of a meter. Thus

$$1000 \text{ millimeters} = 1 \text{ meter} \quad \left(\text{or 1 millimeter} = \tfrac{1}{1000} \text{ meter} \right)$$

Meter is abbreviated m, centimeter is cm, and millimeter is mm.

Convert from centimeters to meters by moving the decimal point, as shown in the following example.

Converting Length Measurements

EXAMPLE 1

Convert the following measurements:

(a) 6.4 m to cm

(b) .98 m to mm

(c) 34 cm to m

SOLUTION

(a) A centimeter is a small unit of measure (a centimeter is about $\frac{1}{2}$ the diameter of a penny) and a meter is a large unit (a little over 3 feet), so many centimeters make a meter. Therefore, *multiply* by **100** to convert meters to centimeters.

$$6.4 \text{ m} = 6.4 \times \mathbf{100} = 640 \text{ cm}$$

(b) Multiply by **1000** to convert meters to millimeters.

$$.98 \text{ m} = .98 \times \mathbf{1000} = 980 \text{ mm}$$

(c) A meter is a large unit of measure that is a little longer than a yard. There are 100 centimeters in one meter. To convert 34 centimeters to meters, divide by 100:

$$34 \text{ cm} = \frac{34}{100} = .34 \text{ m}$$

QUICK CHECK 1

Convert 6 meters to millimeters and 3 centimeters to meters.

Long distances are measured in **kilometer** (km) units. The prefix "kilo" means one thousand. Thus,

$$1 \text{ kilometer} = 1000 \text{ meters} \quad \left(\textbf{or 1 meter} = \tfrac{1}{1000} \textbf{ kilometer} \right)$$

Since a meter is about a yard, 1000 meters is about 1000 yards, or 3000 feet. Therefore, 1 kilometer is about 3000 feet. One mile is 5280 feet, so 1 kilometer is about 3000/5280 of a mile. Divide 3000 by 5280 to find that 1 kilometer is about .6 mile.

The basic unit of volume in the metric system is the **liter** (L), which is a little more than a quart. You may have noticed that Coca Cola is sometimes sold in 2-liter plastic bottles. Again the prefixes "milli" and "centi" are used. Thus,

1 liter   1 quart

A liter equals
1.06 quarts.

$$1 \text{ liter} = 100 \text{ centiliters}$$
$$1 \text{ liter} = 1000 \text{ milliliters}$$

Milliliter (mL) and **centiliter** (cL) are such small volumes that they find their main uses in science. In particular, drug doses are often expressed in milliliters.

Weight is measured in **grams** (g). A nickel weighs about 5 grams. **Milligrams** (mg; one-thousandth of a gram) and **centigrams** (cg; one-hundredth of a gram) are so small that they are used mainly in science. A more common measure is the **kilogram** (kg), which is 1000 grams. A kilogram is equivalent to about 2.2 pounds.

1 kilogram   1 pound

A kilogram equals
2.2 pounds.

$$1000 \text{ grams} = 1 \text{ kilogram}$$

Converting Weight Measurements

EXAMPLE 2

Convert the following measurements.

(a) 650 g to kg

(b) 9.4 L to cL

(c) 4350 mg to g

SOLUTION

(a) A gram is a small unit, and a kilogram is a larger unit. Thus, *divide* by **1000** to convert grams to kilograms.

$$650 \text{ g} = \frac{650}{1000} = .65 \text{ kg}$$

(b) *Multiply* by **100** to convert liters to centiliters.

$$9.4 \text{ L} = 9.4 \times 100 = 940 \text{ cL}$$

(c) *Divide* by **1000** to convert milligrams to grams.

$$4350 \text{ mg} = \frac{4350}{1000} = 4.35 \text{ g}$$

QUICK CHECK 2

Convert 2 kilograms to grams and 700 centiliters to liters.

OBJECTIVE 2 Learn how to convert from one system to the other. Most Americans do not think in the metric system as easily as in the English system of feet, quarts, pounds, and so on. So, they find it necessary to convert from one system to the other. Approximate conversion can be made with the aid of the next table.

English-Metric Conversion Table

FROM METRIC	TO ENGLISH	MULTIPLY BY	FROM ENGLISH	TO METRIC	MULTIPLY BY
Meters	Yards	1.09	Yards	Meters	.914
Meters	Feet	3.28	Feet	Meters	.305
Meters	Inches	39.37	Inches	Meters	.0254
Kilometers	Miles	.62	Miles	Kilometers	1.609
Grams	Pounds	.00220	Pounds	Grams	454
Kilograms	Pounds	2.20	Pounds	Kilograms	.454
Liters	Quarts	1.06	Quarts	Liters	.946
Liters	Gallons	.264	Gallons	Liters	3.785

Converting Metric to English

EXAMPLE 3

Convert the following measurements.

(a) 15 meters to yards
(b) 39 yards to meters
(c) 47 meters to inches
(d) 87 kilometers to miles
(e) 598 miles to kilometers
(f) 12 quarts to liters

SOLUTION

(a) Look at the table for converting meters to yards and find the number **1.09**. Multiply 15 meters by **1.09**.

$$15 \times 1.09 = 16.35 \text{ yards}$$

(b) Read the yards-to-meters row of the table. The number **.914** appears. Multiply 39 yards by **.914**.

$$39 \times .914 = 35.646 \text{ meters}$$

(c) 47 meters = $47 \times 39.37 = 1850.39$ inches
(d) 87 kilometers = $87 \times .62 = 53.94$ miles
(e) 598 miles = $598 \times 1.609 = 962.182$ kilometers
(f) 12 quarts = $12 \times .946 = 11.352$ liters

QUICK CHECK 3

Convert a speed limit of 70 miles per hour to kilometers per hour, and convert 3 pounds to grams.

Temperature in the metric system is measured in degrees **Celsius** or **centigrade** (abbreviated C). In the Celsius scale, water freezes at 0°C and boils at 100°C. This is more sensible than degrees **Fahrenheit** (abbreviated F) in use now, in which a mixture of salt and water freezes at 0°F, and 100°F represents the temperature inside the mouth of an individual who lived in the 1700s: Gabriel Fahrenheit.

Converting from Fahrenheit to Celsius

Step 1   Subtract 32.
Step 2   Multiply by 5.
Step 3   Divide by 9.

These steps can be expressed by the following formula.

$$C = \frac{5(F - 32)}{9} = \frac{5}{9}(F - 32)$$

°F   °C

Water boils at 212°F or 100°C.

Water freezes at 32°F or 0°C.

Converting Fahrenheit to Celsius

EXAMPLE 4

Convert 68°F to Celsius.

SOLUTION

Use the steps on the previous page.

Step 1   Subtract 32: $68 - 32 = 36$

Step 2   Multiply by 5: $36 \times 5 = 180$

Step 3   Divide by 9: $\dfrac{180}{9} = 20$

Thus, 68°F = 20°C.

QUICK CHECK 4

Convert 85°F to Celsius.

Converting from Celsius to Fahrenheit

Step 1   Multiply by 9.

Step 2   Divide by 5.

Step 3   Add 32.

These steps can be expressed by the following formula.

$$F = \frac{9 \times C}{5} + 32$$

Converting Celsius to Fahrenheit

EXAMPLE 5

Convert 11°C to Fahrenheit.

SOLUTION

Use the previous steps.

Step 1   Multiply by 9: $9 \times 11 = 99$

Step 2   Divide by 5: $99 \div 5 = 19.8$

Step 3   Add 32: $19.8 + 32 = 51.8°F$

Thus, 11°C = 51.8°F.

QUICK CHECK 5

Convert 35°C to Fahrenheit.

The next example shows that $-400°C$ is equal to $-400°F$. Note that this temperature is below 0° on both scales and it is very cold. In fact, it is much colder than the inside of the freezer of your refrigerator which is probably in the neighborhood of 0°F.

Converting Celsius to Fahrenheit

EXAMPLE 6

Convert −40°C to degrees Fahrenheit.

SOLUTION

$$F = \frac{9 \times C}{5} + 32$$
$$F = \frac{9 \times (-40)}{5} + 32$$
$$F = -72 + 32$$
$$F = -40°$$

So, −40°C is equal to −40°F.

QUICK CHECK 6: CONVERT 30°C TO FAHRENHEIT

An interesting and easy way to convert from Celsius to Fahrenheit and from Fahrenheit to Celsius is shown next. It may be easier for your to remember than the equations given above, but you are effectively doing exactly the same thing. Example 7 shows how it is used.

Converting from Celsius to Fahrenheit or from Fahrenheit to Celsius:

Step 1   Add 40 to the temperature given to you.

Step 2   Multiply the sum by 9/5 if converting from Celsius to Fahrenheit or by 5/9 if converting from Fahrenheit to Celsius.

Step 3   Subtract 40 from the number found in Step 2.

Converting between Celsius and Fahrenheit

EXAMPLE 7

Use the short cut given above to convert:
(a) 15°C to Fahrenheit and
(b) 78°F to Celsius.

SOLUTION

(a) Step 1 $15 + 40 = 55$ Add 40.

Step 2 $55 \times \frac{9}{5} = 99$ Multiply by $\frac{9}{5}$.

Step 3 $99 - 40 = 59°F$ Subtract 40.

(b) Step 1 $78 + 40 = 118$ Add 40.

Step 2 $118 \times \frac{5}{9} = 65.6$ (rounded)   Multiply by $\frac{5}{9}$.

Step 3 $65.6 - 40 = 25.6°C$ Subtract 40.

QUICK CHECK 7: CONVERT (a) 10°C TO FAHRENHEIT AND (b) 65°F TO CELSIUS.

The relationship between degrees Celsius and degrees Fahrenheit is that of a straight line. You can see it on the next graph where we have plotted a few points found above and connected them with a straight line.

°Celsius VS °Fahrenheit

▼ Appendix A   Exercises   MyMathLab®

Convert the following measurements.

1. 68 cm to m _____

2. 934 mm to m _____

3. 4.7 m to mm _____

4. 7.43 m to cm _____

5. 8.9 kg to g _____

6. 4.32 kg to g _____

7. 39 cL to L _____

8. 469 cL to L _____

9. 46,000 g to kg _____

10. 35,800 g to kg _____

11. .976 kg to g _____

12. .137 kg to g _____

Convert the following measurements. Round to the nearest tenth.

13. 36 m to yards _____

14. 76.2 m to yards _____

15. 55 yards to m _____

16. 89.3 yards to m _____

17. 4.7 m to feet _____

18. 1.92 m to feet _____

19. 3.6 feet to m _____

20. 12.8 feet to m _____

21. 496 km to miles _____

22. 138 km to miles _____

23. 768 miles to km _____

24. 1042 miles to km _____

25. 683 g to pounds _____

26. 1792 g to pounds _____

27. 4.1 pounds to g _____

28. 12.9 pounds to g _____

29. 38.9 kg to pounds _____

30. 40.3 kg to pounds _____

31. One nickel weighs 5 grams. How many nickels are in 1 kilogram of nickels?   31. _____

32. Seawater contains about 3.5 grams of salt per 1000 milliliters of water. How many   32. _____
grams of salt do 5 liters of seawater contain?

33. Helium weighs about .0002 gram per milliliter. A balloon contains 3 liters of helium.   33. _____
How much does the helium weigh?

34. About 1500 grams of sugar can be dissolved in 1 liter of warm water. How much sugar   34. _____
can be dissolved in 1 milliliter of warm water?

35. Find your height in centimeters.

35. _____

36. Find your height in meters.

36. _____

Convert the following Fahrenheit temperatures to Celsius. Round to the nearest degree.

37. 104°F _____

38. 86°F _____

39. 536°F _____

40. 464°F _____

41. 98°F _____

42. 114°F _____

Convert each of the following Celsius temperatures to Fahrenheit.

43. 35°C _____

44. 100°C _____

45. 10°C _____

46. 25°C _____

47. 135°C _____

48. 215°C _____

In most cases today, medical measurements are given in the metric system. In each of the following problems, a doctor's prescription is given. Decide whether the dosage is, or is not, reasonable.

49. 1940 grams of Kaopectate after each meal

49. _____

50. 76.8 centiliters of cough syrup every 2 hours

50. _____

51. 943 milliliters of antibiotic every 6 hours

51. _____

52. 1.4 kilograms of vitamins every 3 hours

52. _____

QUICK CHECK ANSWERS

1. 6000 mm; .03 m

2. 2000 g; 7 L

3. 112.63 km per hour; 1362 g

4. 29.4°C

5. 95°C

6. 86°F

7. (a) 50°F
   (b) 18.3°C (rounded)

Appendix B

Basic Calculators

OBJECTIVES

1. Learn the basic calculator keys.
2. Understand the $\boxed{\text{C}}$, $\boxed{\text{CE}}$, and $\boxed{\text{ON/C}}$ keys.
3. Understand the floating decimal point.
4. Use the $\boxed{\%}$ and $\boxed{\text{1/x}}$ keys.
5. Use the $\boxed{x^2}$, $\boxed{y^x}$, and $\boxed{\sqrt{}}$ keys.
6. Use the $\boxed{a^{b/c}}$ key.
7. Solve problems with negative numbers.
8. Use the calculator memory function.
9. Solve chain calculations using order of operations.
10. Use the parentheses keys.
11. Use the calculator to solve problems.

Calculators are among the more popular inventions of the last four decades. Each year, better calculators are developed and their cost drops. The first all-transistor desktop calculator was introduced to the market in 1966. It weighed 55 pounds, cost $2500, and was slow. Today, these same calculations are performed quite well on a calculator costing less than $10, and today's $100 pocket calculators have more ability to solve problems than some of the early computers.

Many instructors allow their students to use calculators in business mathematics courses. Some require calculator use. Many types of calculators are available, from the inexpensive basic calculator to the more complex **scientific**, **financial**, and **graphing** calculators.

In this appendix, we discuss the basic calculator, which has a percent key, reciprocal key, exponent keys, square-root key, memory function, order of operations, and parentheses keys. In Appendix C, the financial calculator with its associated financial keys is discussed.

Quick TIP

The various calculator models differ significantly. *Use the instruction booklet that came with your calculator* for specifics about that calculator if your answers differ from those in this section.

OBJECTIVE 1 Learn the basic calculator keys. Most calculators use **algebraic logic**. Some problems can be solved by entering number and function keys in the same order as you would solve a problem by hand. Other problems require a knowledge of the order of operations when entering the problem.

Using the Basic Keys

EXAMPLE 1 Perform the following operations.

(a) 12 + 25   (b) 456 ÷ 24

SOLUTION

(a) The problem 12 + 25 is entered as

and 37 appears as the answer.

(b) Enter 456 ÷ 24 as

and 19 appears as the answer.

QUICK CHECK 1

Find 279.04 ÷ 12.8.

OBJECTIVE 2 Understand the [C], [CE] and [ON/C] keys. Most calculators have a [C] key. Pressing this key erases everything in most calculators and prepares them for a new problem. Some calculators have a [CE] key. Pressing this key erases only the number displayed, thus allowing for the correction of a mistake without having to start the problem over. Many calculators combine the [C] key and [CE] key and have an [ON/C] key. This key turns the calculator on and is also used to erase the calculator display. If the [ON/C] is pressed after the [=] key, or after one of the operation keys ([+], [−], [×], [÷]), everything in the calculator is erased. If the wrong operation key is pressed, simply press the correct key and the error is corrected. For example, in 7 [+] [−] 3 [=] 4, pressing the [−] key cancels out the previous [+] key entry.

OBJECTIVE 3 Understand the floating decimal point. Most calculators have a **floating decimal** that locates the decimal point in the final result.

Calculating with Decimal Numbers

EXAMPLE 2

Jennifer Videtto purchased 55.75 square yards of vinyl floor covering at $18.99 per square yard. Find her total cost.

SOLUTION

Proceed as follows.

$$55.75 \; [\times] \; 18.99 \; [=] \; 1058.6925$$

The decimal point is automatically placed in the answer. Since money answers are usually rounded to the nearest cent, the answer is $1058.69.

QUICK CHECK 2

Find the cost of 7 boxes of paper costing $24.87 each.

To use a machine with a floating decimal, enter the decimal point as needed. For example, enter $47 as

$$[4][7]$$

with no decimal point, but enter $.95 as follows.

$$[.][9][5]$$

One problem in utilizing a floating decimal is shown by the following example.

Placing the Decimal Point in Money Answers

EXAMPLE 3

Add $21.38 and $1.22.

SOLUTION

$$21.38 \; [+] \; 1.22 \; [=] \; 22.6$$

The final 0 is left off. Remember that the problem deals with dollars and cents, and write the answer as $22.60.

QUICK CHECK 3

Add 95.07 and 100.33.

OBJECTIVE 4 Use the [%] and [1/x] keys. The [%] key moves the decimal point two places to the left when used following multiplication or division.

Using the [%] Key

EXAMPLE 4

Find 8% of $4205.

SOLUTION

$$4205 \; [\times] \; 8 \; [\%] \; [=] \; 336.4 = \$336.40$$

QUICK CHECK 4

Find the real estate commission of 6% on a home sold for $235,000.

The $\boxed{1/x}$ key replaces a number with the reciprocal of that number.

Using the $\boxed{1/x}$ Key   **EXAMPLE 5**   Find the inverse or reciprocal of 40.

SOLUTION

$$40 \boxed{1/x} \; .025$$

QUICK CHECK 5
Find the inverse of 80.

OBJECTIVE 5 Use the $\boxed{x^2}$, $\boxed{y^x}$, and $\boxed{\sqrt{}}$ keys. The product of 3×3 can be written as follows.

The exponent (2 in this case) shows how many times the base is multiplied by itself (multiply 3 by itself or 3×3). The $\boxed{x^2}$ key can be used to quickly find the square of a number.

Using the $\boxed{x^2}$ Key   **EXAMPLE 6**   Find 5^2 and 8.5^2.

SOLUTION

$$5 \boxed{x^2} \; 25 \qquad \text{and} \qquad 8.5 \boxed{x^2} \; 72.25$$

> Pushing $\boxed{=}$ is usually not necessary when using the $\boxed{x^2}$ key.

QUICK CHECK 6
Find 25^2.

The $\boxed{y^x}$ key raises any base number y to a power x. Use as follows.
1. Enter the base number first.
2. $\boxed{y^x}$
3. Enter the exponent.
4. $\boxed{=}$

Using the $\boxed{y^x}$ Key   **EXAMPLE 7**   Find 5^3.

SOLUTION

$$5 \boxed{y^x} \; 3 \boxed{=} \; 125$$

QUICK CHECK 7
Find 4.8^3.

Since $3^2 = 9$, the number 3 is called the **square root** of 9. Square roots of numbers are written with the symbol $\sqrt{}$.

$$\sqrt{9} = 3$$

Using the ☐√ Key

EXAMPLE 8

Find each square root.

(a) $\sqrt{144}$ (b) $\sqrt{20}$

SOLUTION

(a) Enter

144 ☐√

and 12 appears in the display. The square root of 144 is 12.

(b) The square root of 20 is

20 ☐√ 4.472136

which may be rounded to the desired position.

QUICK CHECK 8

Find the square root of 729.

OBJECTIVE 6 Use the ☐a^{b/c} key. Many calculators have an ☐a^{b/c} key that can be used for problems containing fractions and mixed numbers. A mixed number is a number with both a whole number and a fraction, such as $7\frac{3}{4}$, which equals $7 + \frac{3}{4}$. The rules for adding, subtracting, multiplying, and dividing both fractions and mixed numbers are given in Chapter 2. Here, we simply show how these operations are done on a calculator.

Using the ☐a^{b/c} Key with Fractions

EXAMPLE 9

Solve the following.

(a) $\frac{6}{11} + \frac{3}{4}$ (b) $\frac{3}{8} \div \frac{5}{6}$

SOLUTION

Quick TIP

The calculator automatically shows fractions in lowest terms and as mixed numbers when possible.

(a) 6 ☐a^{b/c} 11 ☐+ 3 ☐a^{b/c} 4 ☐= $1\frac{13}{44}$

(b) 3 ☐a^{b/c} 8 ☐÷ 5 ☐a^{b/c} 6 ☐= $\frac{9}{20}$

QUICK CHECK 9

Solve $\frac{7}{8} + \frac{9}{16}$.

Using the ☐a^{b/c} Key

EXAMPLE 10

Solve the following.

(a) $4\frac{7}{8} \div 3\frac{4}{7}$ (b) $\frac{5}{3} \div 27.5$ (c) $65.3 \times 6\frac{3}{4}$

SOLUTION

(a) 4 ☐a^{b/c} 7 ☐a^{b/c} 8 ☐÷ 3 ☐a^{b/c} 4 ☐a^{b/c} 7 ☐= $1\frac{73}{200}$

(b) 5 ☐a^{b/c} 3 ☐÷ 27.5 ☐= 0.060606061

(c) 65.3 ☐× 6 ☐a^{b/c} 3 ☐a^{b/c} 4 ☐= 440.775

QUICK CHECK 10

Solve $5\frac{3}{4} \div 4\frac{1}{2}$.

OBJECTIVE 7 Solve problems with negative numbers. There are several calculations in business that result in a **negative number**, or **deficit amount**.

Working with Negative Numbers

 EXAMPLE 11

The amount budgeted for advertising last month was $4800, while $5200 was actually spent. Find the balance remaining in the advertising account.

SOLUTION

Enter the numbers in the calculator.

$$4800 \ \boxed{-} \ 5200 \ \boxed{=} \ -400$$

The minus sign in front of the 400 indicates that there is a deficit or negative amount. This value can be written as −$400 or sometimes as ($400), which indicates a negative amount. Some calculators place the minus sign after the number, as 400−.

> **QUICK CHECK 11**
>
> The following transactions were made to a checking account with a balance of $1482.05: a deposit of $185, an electronic bill payment of $122.17, and a withdrawal of $100 at an ATM machine. Find the new balance.

Negative numbers may be entered into the calculator by using the $\boxed{-}$ key before entering the number. For example, if $3000 is now added to the advertising account in Example 11, the new balance is calculated as follows.

$$\boxed{-} \ 400 \ \boxed{+} \ 3000 \ \boxed{=} \ 2600$$

The new account balance is $2600.

The $\boxed{+/-}$ key can be used to change the sign of a number that has already been entered. For example, 520 $\boxed{+/-}$ changes +520 to −520.

OBJECTIVE 8 Use the calculator memory function. Many calculators feature memory keys, which are a sort of electronic scratch paper. These **memory keys** are used to store intermediate steps in a calculation. On some calculators, a key labeled $\boxed{M}$ or $\boxed{STO}$ is used to store the numbers in the display, with $\boxed{MR}$ or $\boxed{RCL}$ used to recall the numbers from memory.

Other calculators have $\boxed{M+}$ and $\boxed{M-}$ keys. The $\boxed{M+}$ key adds the number displayed to the number already in memory. For example, if the memory contains the number 0 at the beginning of a problem, and the calculator display contains the number 29.4, then pushing $\boxed{M+}$ will cause 29.4 to be stored in the memory (the result of adding 0 and 29.4). If 57.8 is then entered into the display, pushing $\boxed{M+}$ will cause

$$29.4 + 57.8 = 87.2$$

to be stored. If 11.9 is then entered into the display, with $\boxed{M-}$ pushed, the memory will contain

$$87.2 - 11.9 = 75.3$$

The $\boxed{MR}$ key is used to recall the number in memory as needed, with $\boxed{MC}$ used to clear the memory.

Scientific calculators typically have one or more **memory registers** in which to store numbers. These memory keys are usually labeled $\boxed{STO}$ for store and $\boxed{RCL}$ for recall. For example, 32.5 can be stored in memory register 1 by

$$32.5 \ \boxed{STO} \ 1$$

or it can be stored in memory register 2 by 32.5 $\boxed{STO}$ 2, and so forth. Values are retrieved from a particular memory register by using the $\boxed{RCL}$ key followed by the number of the register. For example, $\boxed{RCL}$ 2 recalls the contents of memory register 2.

With a scientific calculator, a number stays in memory until it is replaced by another number or until the memory is cleared. The contents of the memory are saved even when the calculator is turned off.

Quick TIP

Always clear the memory before starting a problem; not doing so is a common error.

Using the Memory Registers   **EXAMPLE 12**   An elevator technician counted the number of people entering an elevator and also measured the weight of each group of people. Find the average weight per person.

Number of People	Total Weight
6	839 pounds
8	1184 pounds
4	640 pounds

SOLUTION

First find the total weight of all three groups and store in memory register 1.

$$839 \boxed{+} 1184 \boxed{+} 640 \boxed{=} 2663 \boxed{\text{STO}} 1$$

Then find the total number of people.

$$6 \boxed{+} 8 \boxed{+} 4 \boxed{=} 18$$

Finally, divide the contents of memory register 1 by the 18 people.

$$\boxed{\text{RCL}} 1 \boxed{\div} 18 \boxed{=} 147.9444444 \text{ pounds}$$

This value can be rounded as needed.

QUICK CHECK 12

The following animals were brought to the market: 7 calves with a total weight of 2989 pounds; 10 calves with a total weight of 4490 pounds; and 17 calves with a total weight of 6953 pounds. Find the average weight of a calf to the nearest tenth of a pound.

OBJECTIVE 9 Solve chain calculations using order of operations. Long calculations involving several operations (adding, subtracting, multiplying, and dividing) must be done in a specific sequence called the **order of operations** and are called **chain calculations**. The logic of the following order of operations is built into most scientific calculators and can help us work problems without having to store a lot of intermediate values.

Order of Operations

Step 1   Do all operations inside parentheses first.

Step 2   Simplify any expressions with exponents and find any square roots.

Step 3   Multiply and divide from left to right.

Step 4   Add and subtract from left to right.

Using the Order of Operations   **EXAMPLE 13**   Solve the following.

(a) $3 + 7 \times 9\dfrac{3}{4}$ (b) $42.1 \times 5 - 90 \div 4$

SOLUTION

Most calculators automatically keep track of the order of operations for us.

(a) $3 \boxed{+} 7 \boxed{\times} 9 \boxed{a^{b/c}} 3 \boxed{a^{b/c}} 4 \boxed{=} 71\dfrac{1}{4}$

(b) $42.1 \boxed{\times} 5 \boxed{-} 90 \boxed{\div} 4 \boxed{=} 188$

QUICK CHECK 13

Solve $9^2 + 2.7 \cdot 14$.

OBJECTIVE 10 Use the parentheses keys. The parentheses keys can be used to help establish the order of operations in a more complex chain calculation. For example, $\frac{4}{5+7}$ can be written as $\frac{4}{(5+7)}$, which can be solved as follows.

left-parenthesis key

right-parenthesis key

$4 \boxed{\div} \boxed{(} 5 \boxed{+} \boxed{7} \boxed{)} \boxed{=} .3333333$

Using Parentheses   **EXAMPLE 14**

Solve the following problem.

$$\frac{16 \div 2.5}{39.2 - 29.8 \times .6}$$

SOLUTION

Think of this problem as follows:

$$\frac{(16 \div 2.5)}{(39.2 - 29.8 \times .6)}$$

Using parentheses to set off the numerator and denominator will help you minimize errors.

$\boxed{(} 16 \boxed{\div} 2.5 \boxed{)} \boxed{\div} \boxed{(} 39.2 \boxed{-} 29.8 \boxed{\times} .6 \boxed{)} \boxed{=} 0.3001876$

QUICK CHECK 14

Solve $\dfrac{5^3 - 16}{253 - 4^2 \cdot 9}$

OBJECTIVE 11 Use the calculator to solve problems. Scientific calculators are great tools to help you solve problems.

Finding Sale Price   **EXAMPLE 15**

A digital camera with an original price of $560 is on sale at 10% off. Find the sale price.

SOLUTION

If the discount from the original price is 10%, then the sale price is 100% − 10% of the original price.

$560 \boxed{\times} \boxed{(} 100 \boxed{-} 10 \boxed{)} \boxed{\%} \boxed{=} 504$

On some calculators the following keystrokes will also work.

$560 \boxed{-} 10 \boxed{\%} \boxed{=} 504$

The sale price is $504.

QUICK CHECK 15

Find the price of a new home that was originally priced at $239,000 if the price was reduced by 15%.

Applying Calculator Use to Problem Solving   **EXAMPLE 16**

A home buyer borrows $125,000 at 6% on a house, for 30 years. The monthly payment on the loan is $5.996 per $1000 borrowed. Annual taxes are $3800, and fire insurance is $620 a year. Find the total monthly payment including taxes and insurance.

SOLUTION

The monthly payment is the *sum* of the monthly payment on the loan *plus* monthly taxes *plus* monthly fire insurance costs. The monthly payment on the loan is the number of thousands in the loan times the monthly payment per $1000 borrowed.

monthly taxes

$125000 \boxed{\div} 1000 \boxed{\times} 5.996 \boxed{+} 3800 \boxed{\div} 12 \boxed{+} 620 \boxed{\div} 12 \boxed{=} 1117.8333$

monthly fire insurance premium

To the nearest cent, this amount rounds to $1117.83.

QUICK CHECK 16

An investor borrows $1,200,000 on a piece of commercial property. The monthly payment on the loan is $8.43 per $1000 of debt. Annual taxes and insurance are $28,200 and $6240, respectively. Find the monthly payment.

Applying Calculator Use to Problem Solving

EXAMPLE 17

A Japanese company produces robotic dogs for the retail market. The dogs talk, cock their heads, bark, and walk. The company sells the dogs to distributors for $256.80 each.

(a) Find the revenue to the manufacturer if the company sells 26,340 robotic dogs.

(b) Find the final price to the customer if the robotic dogs are marked up an average of 87% on cost.

SOLUTION

(a) Revenue = Number sold × Price of each

26340 ⊠ 256.80 ⊟ 6764112   or $6,764,112

(b) Sales price = Cost × (1 + Markup percent)

256.80 ⊠ 1.87 ⊟ 480.216   or $480.22

QUICK CHECK 17

It cost a manufacturer an average of $38.20 per pair for each of the 180,400 pair of shoes produced in one month. The markup on the shoes is 35% based on cost. Find the total revenue to the company from the sale of the month's production.

▼ ## Appendix B   Exercises   MyMathLab®

Solve the following problems on a calculator. Round each answer to the nearest hundredth.

1.
```
   384.92
   407.61
   351.14
+   27.93
```

2.
```
   85.76
   21.94
+ 39.89
```

3.
```
  6850
   321
+ 4207
```

4.
```
   781.42
   304.59
+ 261.35
```

5.
```
  4270.41
-  365.09
```

6.
```
  3000.07
-   48.12
```

7.
```
   384.96
-  129.72
```

8. $36.84 - 12.17$

9.
```
    365
×    43
```

10.
```
   27.51
×   1.18
```

11. 3.7×8.4

12. 62.5×81

13. $\dfrac{375.4}{10.6}$

14. $\dfrac{9625}{400}$

15. $96.7 \div 3.5$

16. $103.7 \div .35$

Solve the following chain calculations. Round each answer to the nearest hundredth.

17. $\dfrac{9 \times 9}{2 \times 5}$ _____

18. $\dfrac{15 \times 8 \times 3}{11 \times 7 \times 4}$ _____

19. $\dfrac{87 \times 24 \times 47.2}{13.6 \times 12.8}$ _____

20. $\dfrac{2 \times (3 + 4)}{6 + 10}$ _____

21. $\dfrac{2 \times 3 + 4}{6 + 10}$ _____

22. $\dfrac{4200 \times .12 \times 90}{365}$ _____

23. $\dfrac{640 - .6 \times 12}{17.5 + 3.2}$ _____

24. $\dfrac{16 \times 18 \div .42}{95.4 \times 3 - .8}$ _____

25. $\dfrac{14^2 - 3.6 \times 6}{95.2 \div .5}$ _____

26. $\dfrac{9^2 + 3.8 \div 2}{14 + 7.5}$ _____

Solve the following problems. Reduce any fractions to lowest terms or round to the nearest hundredth.

27. $7\dfrac{5}{8} \div \left(1 + \dfrac{3}{8}\right)$ _____

28. $\left(5\dfrac{1}{4}\right)^2 \times 3.65$ _____

29. $\left(\dfrac{3}{4} \div \dfrac{5}{8}\right)^3 \div 3\dfrac{1}{2}$ _____

30. $\sqrt{6} \times \dfrac{3^2 + 2\frac{1}{2}}{7 \times \frac{5}{6}}$ _____

31. Describe in your own words the order of operations to be used when solving chain calculations. (See Objective 9.)

32. Explain how the parentheses keys are used when solving chain calculations. (See Objective 10.)

Solve the following application problems on a calculator. Round each answer to the nearest cent.

33. Orange County Community College Bookstore bought 397 used copies of a computer science book at a net cost of $46.40 each; 125 used copies of an accounting book at $38.40 each; and 740 used copies of a real estate text at $28.30 each. Find the total paid by the bookstore.

33. _____

34. Judy Martinez needs to file her expense account claims. She spent 5 nights at the Macon Holiday Inn at $104.19 per night and 4 nights at the Charlotte Super 8 motel at $86.80 per night. She then rented a car for 8 days at $36.40 per day. She drove the car 916 miles with a charge of $.28 per mile. Find her total expenses.

34. _____

35. In Virginia City, the sales tax is 6.5%. Find the tax on each of the following items: **(a)** a new car costing $17,908.43 and **(b)** a digital tv costing $1463.58.

(a) _____

(b) _____

36. Marja Strutz bought a two-year-old commercial fishing boat equipped for sardine fishing at a cost of $78,250. Additional safety equipment was needed at a cost of $4820, and sales tax of $7\frac{1}{4}\%$ was due on the boat and safety equipment. In addition she was charged a licensing fee of $1135 and a Coast Guard registration fee of $428. Strutz will pay $\frac{1}{3}$ of the total cost as a down payment and will borrow the balance. How much must she borrow?

36. _____

37. Becky Agnosti and her husband bought a small townhouse for $155,000. They paid $8000 down and agreed to make payments of $1002.80 per month for 30 years. By how much does the down payment and the sum of the monthly payments exceed the purchase price?

37. _____

38. Linda Smelt purchased a 20-unit apartment house for $620,000. She made a down payment of $150,000, which she had inherited from her parents, and agreed to make monthly payments of $5050 for 15 years. By how much does the sum of her down payment and all monthly payments exceed the original purchase price?

38. _____

39. Ben Hurd wishes to open a small repair shop but has only $32,400 in cash. He estimates that he will need $15,000 for equipment, $2800 for the first month's rent on a building, and about $28,000 operating expenses until the business is profitable. How much additional funding does he need?

39. _____

40. Koplan Kitchens wishes to expand their retail store. In order to do so, they must first purchase the $52,000 lot next door to them. They then anticipate $240,000 in construction costs plus an additional $57,000 for additional inventory. They have $100,000 in cash and must borrow the balance from a bank. How much must they borrow?

40. _____

41. A college bookstore buys a used textbook for $24.50 at the end of a semester and sells it at the beginning of the next semester for $60. Find the percent of markup on selling price to the nearest percent.

41. _____

42. A homebuilder spent the following when building a home: $37,800 for a cleared parcel of land with utility hookups, $59,600 for materials, and $24,300 for labor and other expenses. He then sold the home for $136,500. Find the percent markup over cost to the nearest percent.

42. _____

QUICK CHECK ANSWERS

1. 21.8
2. $174.09
3. 195.4
4. $14,100
5. .0125
6. 625
7. 110.592
8. 27
9. $1\frac{7}{16}$

10. $1\frac{5}{18}$
11. $1444.88
12. 424.5 pounds (rounded)
13. 118.8
14. 1
15. $203,150
16. $12,986
17. $9,303,228

▼ Appendix C

Financial Calculators

OBJECTIVES

1 Learn the basic conventions used with cash flows.
2 Learn the basic financial keys.
3 Understand which keys to use for a particular problem.
4 Use the calculator to solve financial problems.

Calculators are among the more popular inventions of recent times. The power and capability of calculators have increased significantly even as their cost has continued to fall. Today, programmable calculators costing less than $100 have more ability to solve problems than some of the early computers.

OBJECTIVE 1 Learn the basic conventions used with cash flows. Some financial calculators require that inflows (cash received) and outflows (cash spent) be separated. As a result, we will use the following convention in this appendix.

1. Inflows of cash (cash received) are **positive**.
2. Outflows of cash (cash paid out) are **negative**.

For example, assume that you are making regular investments into an account. Your payments are *outflows* of cash to you and should be considered *negative* numbers. The future value of your savings will eventually be returned to you as an inflow of cash, thereby as a positive number.

OBJECTIVE 2 Learn the basic financial keys. **Financial calculators** have special functions that allow the user to solve financial problems involving time, interest rates, and money. Many of the compound interest problems presented in this text can be solved using a financial calculator. Most financial calculators have financial keys similar to those shown below.

These keys represent the following functions (see Chapter 10 for a full definition of each term).

[n]—The number of compounding periods
[i]—The interest rate *per compounding period*
[PV]—Present value, the value in *today's* dollars
[PMT]—The amount of a level payment (for example, $625 per month); this is used for annuity type problems.
[FV]—Future value, the value at *some future date*

Note: Different financial calculators sometimes give slightly different answers to the same problems due to rounding.

OBJECTIVE 3 Understand which keys to use for a particular problem. Most simple financial problems require only four of the five financial keys described earlier. Both the number of compounding periods [n] and the interest rate per compounding period [i] *are needed for each financial problem*—these two keys will always be used. Which two of the remaining three financial keys ([PV], [PMT], and [FV]) are used depends on the particular problem. Using the convention described under Objective 1, one of these values will be negative and one will be positive. The process of solving a financial problem is to enter values for the three variables that are known, *then press the key for the unknown*, fourth variable.

For example, if you wish to know the future value of a series of known, equal payments, enter the specific values for n, i, and PMT. Then press FV for the result. Or, if you wish to know how long it will take for an investment to grow to some specific value at a given interest rate, enter values for PV, i, and FV. Then press n to find the required number of compounding periods.

Many financial calculators require that you enter a cash inflow as a positive number and a cash outflow as a negative number. Also, be sure to clear all values from the memory of your calculator before working a problem.

OBJECTIVE 4 Use the calculator to solve financial problems.

Finding *FV*, given *n*, *i*, and *PV* | **EXAMPLE 1**   Barbara and Ivan Cushing invest $2500 that they received from the sale of the old family car in a stock mutual fund that has recently grown at 8% compounded quarterly. Find the future value in 5 years if the fund continues to do as well.

SOLUTION

The present value of $2500 (a cash outflow is entered as a negative number) is compounded at 2% per quarter (8% ÷ 4 = 2%) for 20 quarters (5 × 4 = 20). Enter values for PV, i, and n.

$$-2500 \boxed{PV} \; 2 \boxed{i} \; 20 \boxed{n}$$

Then press FV to find the compound amount at the end of 5 years.

FV $3714.87, which is the future value

QUICK CHECK 1

A lump sum of $28,000 is deposited in a retirement account earning 10% compounded quarterly. Find the future value in 10 years.

Finding *FV*, given *n*, *i*, and *PMT* | **EXAMPLE 2**   Joan Jones plans to invest $100 at the end of each month in a mutual fund that she believes will grow at 9% per year compounded monthly. Find the future value at her retirement in 20 years.

SOLUTION

Quick TIP

The order in which data are entered into the calculator does not matter—just remember to press the financial key for the unknown value last.

Two hundred forty payments (12 × 20 = 240) of $100 each (cash outflows entered as a negative number) are made into an account earning .75% per month (9% ÷ 12 = .75%). Enter values for n, PMT, and i.

$$240 \boxed{n} \; -100 \boxed{PMT} \; .75 \boxed{i}$$

Press FV for the result.

FV $66,788.69, which is the future value

QUICK CHECK 2

Benjamin Delton deposits $2500 at the end of each year into a retirement account earning 8% per year. Find the future value in 45 years.

Any one of the four values used to solve a particular financial problem *can be unknown*. Look at the next three examples in which the number of compounding periods n, the payment amount PMT, and the interest rate per compounding period i, respectively, are unknown.

Finding *n*, given *i*, PMT, and FV
EXAMPLE 3

Mr. Trebor needs $140,000 for a new farm tractor. He can invest $8000 at the end of each month in an account paying 6% per year compounded monthly. How many monthly payments are needed?

SOLUTION

The $8000 monthly payment (cash outflow) will grow at .5% per compounding period (6% ÷ 12 = .5%) until a future value of $140,000 (cash inflow at a future date) is accumulated. Enter values for $\boxed{\text{PMT}}$, $\boxed{i}$, and $\boxed{\text{FV}}$.

$$-8000 \; \boxed{\text{PMT}} \; .5 \; \boxed{i} \; 140000 \; \boxed{\text{FV}}$$

Press $\boxed{n}$ to determine the number of payments.

$$\boxed{n} \; 17 \text{ monthly payments of \$8000 each are needed}$$

Actually, 17 payments of $8000 each into an account earning .5% per month will grow to slightly more than $140,000.

$$-8000 \; \boxed{\text{PMT}} \; .5 \; \boxed{i} \; 17 \; \boxed{n}$$

Press $\boxed{\text{FV}}$ to determine the future value.

$$\boxed{\text{FV}} \; \textbf{\$141,578.41}, \text{ which is the future value}$$

The 17th payment would need to be only

$$\$8000 - (\textbf{\$141,578.41} - \$140,000) = \$6421.59$$

to accumulate exactly $140,000.

QUICK CHECK 3

Appalachian Coal, Inc., needs $1,280,000 for a new dredge. The firm can invest $21,200 at the end of each quarter in a fund earning 2% per quarter. Find the number of quarters needed to save up the required funds.

Finding PMT, given *n*, *i*, and FV
EXAMPLE 4

Jane Abel wishes to have $1,000,000 at her retirement in 40 years. Find the payment she must make at the end of each quarter into an account earning 8% compounded quarterly to attain her goal.

SOLUTION

One hundred sixty payments (40 × 4 = 160) are made into an account earning 2% per quarter (8% ÷ 4 = 2%) until a future value of $1,000,000 (cash inflow at a future date) is accumulated. Enter values for $\boxed{n}$, $\boxed{i}$, and $\boxed{\text{FV}}$.

$$160 \; \boxed{n} \; 2 \; \boxed{i} \; 1000000 \; \boxed{\text{FV}}$$

Press $\boxed{\text{PMT}}$ for the quarterly payment.

$$\boxed{\text{PMT}} \; -\textbf{\$878.35}, \text{ which is the required quarterly payment of cash}$$

One hundred sixty payments of $878.35 at the end of each quarter into an account earning 8% compounded quarterly will grow to $1,000,000.

QUICK CHECK 4

Bill Watson has only 13 years until he retires and he wants to have $1 million at that time. He decides to make payments into a mutual fund at the end of each year, one that he hopes will earn 9% per year. Find the yearly payment needed.

Finding *i*, given *n*, PV, and FV
EXAMPLE 5

Tom Fernandez bought 200 shares of stock in an oil company at $33.50 per share. Exactly three years later, he sold the stock at $41.25 per share. Find the annual rate, rounded to the nearest tenth of a percent, that Mr. Fernandez earned on this investment.

SOLUTION

In three years, the per-share price increased from a present value of $33.50 to a future value of $41.25. The purchase of the stock is a cash outflow, and the eventual sale of the stock is a cash inflow. It is not necessary to multiply the stock price by the number of shares—the interest rate associated with the return on the investment is the same whether 1 share or 200 shares are used. Enter values for $\boxed{\textbf{n}}$, $\boxed{\textbf{PV}}$, and $\boxed{\textbf{FV}}$.

$$3\,\boxed{\textbf{n}}\ -33.50\,\boxed{\textbf{PV}}\ 41.25\,\boxed{\textbf{FV}}$$

Press $\boxed{\textbf{i}}$ for the annual interest rate.

$$\boxed{\textbf{i}}\ \textbf{7.18\%},\text{ or about 7.2\% per year}$$

Mr. Fernandez's return on his original investment grew at 7.2% per year.

> **QUICK CHECK 5**
>
> Fang Hzu bought a commercial lot for $148,400 and sold it six years later for $245,000. Find the annual interest rate to the nearest tenth of a percent.

Interest rates can have a great influence on both individuals and businesses. Individuals borrow for homes, cars, and other personal items, whereas firms borrow to buy real estate, expand operations, or cover operating expenses. A small difference in interest rates can make *a large difference* in costs over time, as shown in the next example.

Comparing Monthly House Payments

EXAMPLE 6

Hank and Francesca Wilson want to borrow $165,000 on a 30-year home mortgage. Find the monthly payment at interest rates of **(a)** 6% and **(b)** 8%. Find **(c)** the monthly savings at the lower rate and **(d)** the total savings if they make payments for the entire 30-year life of the mortgage.

SOLUTION

(a) Enter a present value of $165,000 (cash inflow) with 360 compounding periods $(30 \times 12 = 360)$ and a rate of .5% per month $(6\% \div 12 = .5\%)$ and press $\boxed{\textbf{PMT}}$ to find the monthly payment.

$$165000\,\boxed{\textbf{PV}}\ 360\,\boxed{\textbf{n}}\ .5\,\boxed{\textbf{i}}$$

$\boxed{\textbf{PMT}}$ **−$989.26** is the monthly payment.

(b) Enter the values again using a rate of .66667% $(8\% \div 12 = .66667\%$ rounded)

$$165000\,\boxed{\textbf{PV}}\ 360\,\boxed{\textbf{n}}\ .66667\,\boxed{\textbf{i}}$$

$\boxed{\textbf{PMT}}$ **$1210.72** is the monthly payment.

(c) Difference between payments $= \textbf{\$1210.72} - \textbf{\$989.26}$

$$= \$221.46 \text{ per month}$$

(d) Find the total difference in payments during the 30-year mortgage as follows.

$$\$221.46 \times 360 \text{ payments} = \$79,725.60$$

The lower rate will save a total of $79,725.60 in payments over the 30 years. Interest rates *do* make a difference!

> **QUICK CHECK 6**
>
> Bernie Slotsky borrowed $168,000 for 30 years. Find the monthly payment at interest rates of **(a)** 6.5% and **(b)** 7.5%. **(c)** Then find the difference in the monthly payments.

Planning for Retirement

EXAMPLE 7

Courtney and Nathan Wright plan to retire in 25 years and will need $3500 per month for 20 years.

(a) Find the amount needed at retirement to fund the monthly retirement payments, assuming the funds earn 9% compounded monthly while payments are being made.

(b) Find the amount of the quarterly payment they must make for the next 25 years to accumulate the necessary funds, assuming earnings of 12% compounded quarterly during the accumulation period.

SOLUTION

(a) The accumulated funds at the end of 25 years are, at their retirement, a present value that must generate a cash inflow to the Wrights of $3500 per month for 240 months ($20 \times 12 = 240$) assuming earnings of .75% per month ($9\% \div 12 = .75\%$). Enter values for $\boxed{\text{n}}$, $\boxed{\text{i}}$, and $\boxed{\text{PMT}}$.

$$240 \,\boxed{\text{n}}\, .75 \,\boxed{\text{i}}\, 3500 \,\boxed{\text{PMT}}$$

Press $\boxed{\text{PV}}$ to find the amount needed at the end of 25 years.

$$\boxed{\text{PV}} \;\; \$389,007.34 \text{ is the amount they must accumulate}$$

(b) The Wrights have 25 years of quarterly payments (100 payments that are cash outflows) in an account earning 3% per quarter ($12\% \div 4 = 3\%$) to accumulate a future value of $389,007.34. The question is what quarterly payment is required. Enter values for $\boxed{\text{n}}$, $\boxed{\text{i}}$, and $\boxed{\text{FV}}$.

$$100 \,\boxed{\text{n}}\, 3 \,\boxed{\text{i}}\, 389007.34 \,\boxed{\text{FV}}$$

Press $\boxed{\text{PMT}}$ to find the quarterly payment needed.

$$\boxed{\text{PMT}} \;\; \$640.57 \text{ is the required quarterly payment}$$

Thus, the Wrights must make 100 end-of-quarter deposits of $640.57 each into an account earning 3% per quarter in order to subsequently receive 20 years of payments of $3500 per month, assuming 9% per year during the time that payments are made.

QUICK CHECK 7

Tom and Jane Blackstone plan to retire in 20 years. At that time, they believe they will need $60,000 per year for 25 years, not including income from Social Security. **(a)** If funds earn 7% per year during retirement, find the amount needed to fund their retirement when they retire, to the nearest dollar. **(b)** Find the end-of-the-year payment they must make for the next 20 years to have the needed amount at retirement, assuming funds earn 8% per year.

▼ Appendix C Exercises   MyMathLab®

Using a financial calculator, solve the following problems for the missing quantity. Round dollar answers to the nearest cent, interest rates to the nearest hundredth of a percent, and number of compounding periods to the nearest whole number. Assume that any payments are made at the end of the period.

	n	*i*	*PV*	*PMT*	*FV*
1.	20	10%	$5800	—	_____
2.	7	8%	$8900	—	_____
3.	10	3%	_____	—	$12,000
4.	16	4%	_____	—	$8200
5.	7	8%	—	$300	_____
6.	25	2%	—	$1000	_____
7.	30	_____	—	$319.67	$12,000
8.	50	_____	—	$4718.99	$285,000
9.	360	1%	$83,500	_____	—

n	i	PV	PMT	FV
10. 180	.5%	$125,000	_____	—
11. _____	4%	$85,383	$5600	—
12. _____	2%	$3822	$100	—

Solve each of the following application problems.

13. Juanipa Manglimont inherited $23,500 from her father. She placed the money in an investment earning 6% compounded quarterly. Find the future value at the end of 5 years.

13. _____

14. At the end of each month, Tina Ramirez has $50 taken out of her paycheck and invested in an account paying .5% per month. Find the future value at the end of 14 years.

14. _____

15. After a down payment, Mr. and Mrs. Thrash borrowed $140,000 on a 30-year loan on a home at 6% per year. Find the monthly payment.

15. _____

16. Terrance Walker wishes to have $20,000 in 10 years when his son begins college. What payment must he make at the end of each quarter into an investment earning 10% compounded quarterly?

16. _____

17. The *Daily Gazette* needs $340,000 for a new printing press. The *Gazette* can invest $12,000 per month in an account paying .8% per month. Find the number of payments that must be paid before reaching the goal. Round to the nearest whole number.

17. _____

18. Cathy Cockrell anticipates that she will need $70,000 when her son Sam enters college. She can save $500 per month and earn 7% per year compounded monthly. How long will it take her to save the needed funds?

18. _____

19. Mr. and Mrs. Peters wish to build a home and must borrow $110,000 on a 30-year mortgage to do so. Find the highest acceptable annual interest rate, to the nearest tenth of a percent, if they cannot afford a monthly payment above $845.

19. _____

20. Jim Blalock needs to borrow $28,000 for a new work truck but cannot afford a payment of more than $700 per month. If a bank will finance the truck for 4 years, find the maximum interest rate Blalock can afford.

20. _____

QUICK CHECK ANSWERS

1. $75,181.79
2. $966,264.04
3. 40 quarters
4. $43,566.56
5. 8.7%

6. (a) $1061.87
   (b) $1174.68
   (c) $112.81
7. (a) $699,215
   (b) $15,279.39

Appendix D

Exponents and the Order of Operations

OBJECTIVES

1 Understand the basics of exponents.
2 Multiply and divide using exponents.
3 Apply the Order of Operations.
4 Evaluating expressions containing exponents.
5 Solving application problems.

OBJECTIVE 1 Understand the basics of exponents. Exponents show repeated multiplication of a quantity by itself. The quantity being multiplied by itself is called the **base**. The number of times it is be multiplied by itself is the **exponent**. For example, $6 \cdot 6$ can be written as follows.

Read 6^2 any of the following ways: "6 to the second power," "6 raised to the second power," or "6 squared." Note that the base is the number 6 and the exponent is the number 2, which is written in a smaller type to the upper right of the number 6. Here are several more examples.

	Read as	Base	Exponent	Equal to
5^4	"5 to the 4th power"	5	4	$5 \cdot 5 \cdot 5 \cdot 5$
x^2	"x to the 2nd power, or x squared"	x	2	$x \cdot x$
y^3	"y to the 3rd power, or y cubed"	y	3	$y \cdot y \cdot y$
e^4	"e to the 4th power"	e	4	$e \cdot e \cdot e \cdot e$

If both the base and the exponent are known, we can evaluate the term by simply multiplying.

$$6^2 = 6 \cdot 6 = 36 \quad \text{or} \quad 5^4 = 5 \cdot 5 \cdot 5 \cdot 5 = 625$$

A few important special situations involving exponents are shown in the following table.

Explanation	Examples
Any nonzero value to the power of 0 is defined to be equal to 1.	$4^0 = 1$ $x^0 = 1$ as long as x is not equal to zero
0 to the 0th power is not defined. In other words, it has no meaning and should not be used.	0^0 has no meaning y^0 is undefined when $y = 0$
Any value to the power of 1 is the value itself.	$5^1 = 5$ $z^1 = z$ $0^1 = 0$

Note that the base can be 0 as long as the exponent is not zero. For example,

$$0^3 = 0 \cdot 0 \cdot 0, \quad \text{which equals 0}$$

Writing and Evaluating Exponents

(a) Write $t \cdot t \cdot t$ and $4 \cdot 4$ using exponents.
(b) Evaluate 9^3 and $(25.1)^2$.
(c) Simplify 54^0 and x^1.

SOLUTION

(a) $t \cdot t \cdot t = t^3$ $\qquad\qquad$ $4 \cdot 4 = 4^2$
(b) $9^3 = 9 \cdot 9 \cdot 9 = 729$ $\qquad$ $(25.1)^2 = 25.1 \cdot 25.1 = 630.01$
(c) $54^0 = 1$ $\qquad\qquad\qquad$ $x^1 = x$

OBJECTIVE 2 Multiply and divide using exponents. There are several convenient rules that make it easier to work with exponents. We will show one rule at a time and give examples using both integers and variables. Then the concept behind each rule is explained using an example.

RULE 1 $X^m \cdot X^n = X^{(m+n)}$ When multiplying with the same base, add the exponents.

   Examples: $7^2 \cdot 7^3 = 7^{(2+3)} = 7^5$ Add the exponents.

   $y^4 \cdot y^2 = y^{(4+2)} = y^6$ Add the exponents.

   Concept: $7^2 \cdot 7^3 = (7 \cdot 7) \cdot (7 \cdot 7 \cdot 7) = 7^5$ The number of 7s being multiplied is found by adding the two exponents.

RULE 2 $\dfrac{X^m}{X_n} = X^{(m-n)}$ When dividing with the same base, subtract the exponents.

   Examples: $\dfrac{9^5}{9^2} = 9^{(5-2)} = 9^3$ Subtract the exponents.

   $\dfrac{Z^4}{Z^2} = Z^{(4-2)} = Z^2$ Subtract the exponents.

   Concept: $\dfrac{9^5}{9^2} = \dfrac{9 \cdot 9 \cdot 9 \cdot 9 \cdot 9}{9 \cdot 9} = 9^3$ The number of 9s remaining after canceling is found by subtracting the exponents.

RULE 3 $(X \cdot Y)^n = X^n \cdot Y^n$ Apply the exponent to both values in the parentheses.

   Examples: $(8 \cdot 9)^2 = 8^2 \cdot 9^2$ Apply the exponent to both numbers.

   $(S \cdot Z)^n = S^n \cdot Z^n$ Apply the exponent to both variables.

   Concept: $(8 \cdot 9)^2 = (8 \cdot 9) \cdot (8 \cdot 9)$ Multiply $(8 \cdot 9)$ by itself.

   $= (8 \cdot 8) \cdot (9 \cdot 9) = 8^2 \cdot 9^2$ The exponent applies to both numbers.

RULE 4 $\left(\dfrac{X}{Y}\right)^n = \dfrac{X^n}{Y^n}$ Apply the exponent to both the numerator and denominator.

   Examples: $\left(\dfrac{7}{9}\right)^2 = \dfrac{7^2}{9^2}$ Apply the exponent to both numbers.

   $\left(\dfrac{Z}{T}\right)^3 = \dfrac{Z^3}{T^3}$ Apply the exponent to both variables.

   Concept: $\left(\dfrac{7}{9}\right)^2 = \dfrac{7}{9} \cdot \dfrac{7}{9} = \dfrac{7 \cdot 7}{9 \cdot 9} = \dfrac{7^2}{9^2}$ Apply the exponent to the numerator and to the denominator.

RULE 5 $(X^m)^n = X^{m \times n}$ Multiply the two exponents.

   Examples: $(5^2)^3 = 5^{2 \cdot 3} = 5^6$ Multiply the two exponents.

   $(R^4)^2 = R^{4 \cdot 2} = R^8$ Multiply the two exponents.

   Concept: $(5^2)^3 = (5^2) \cdot (5^2) \cdot (5^2)$

   $= 5^{(2+2+2)} = 5^{3 \cdot 2} = 5^6$

Here are all the rules for working with exponents in one place.

Rules for Exponents—Quick Directions	
1. $X^m \cdot X^n = X^{(m+n)}$	Add the exponents.
2. $\dfrac{X^m}{X^n} = X^{(m-n)}$	Subtract the exponents.
3. $(X \cdot Y)^n = X^n \cdot Y^n$	Apply the exponent n to each variables in the parentheses.
4. $\left(\dfrac{X}{Y}\right)^n = \dfrac{X^n}{Y^n}$	Apply the exponent n to both the numerator and denominator of the fraction.
5. $(X^m)^n = X^{m \times n}$	Multiply the two exponents.

Note   In Rule 3, notice that $(X \cdot Y)^n$ and $X^n \cdot Y^n$ can be written without the multiplication dot ($\cdot$) as $(XY)^n$ and X^nY^n, respectively.

In Rule 1, it is important to realize that you cannot combine two values with different bases. For example, you cannot combine the following into one variable raised to a power because the bases are not the same.

$$X^2 \cdot Y^3$$

It has already been written as simply as possible unless the values for X and Y are known.

Nor can you simplify $\dfrac{y^3}{t^2}$ because these bases also differ.

Working With Exponents

▶ **EXAMPLE 2**   Simplify each of these using the preceding rules.

(a) $\dfrac{y^4}{y^2}$

(b) $(9^2)^3$

(c) $z^2 \cdot z^3$

(d) $(5 \cdot 6)^2$

(e) $\left(\dfrac{r}{S}\right)^3$

(f) T^1

(g) $x^3 \div x^3$

(h) 0^0

SOLUTION

(a) $\dfrac{y^4}{y^2} = y^{(4-2)} = y^2$

(b) $(9^2)^3 = 9^{2 \cdot 3} = 9^6$

(c) $z^2 \cdot z^3 = z^{(2+3)} = z^5$

(d) $(5 \cdot 6)^2 = 5^2 \cdot 6^2$

(e) $\left(\dfrac{r}{S}\right)^3 = \dfrac{r^3}{S^3}$

(f) $T^1 = T$

(g) $x^3 \div x^3 = x^{(3-3)} = x^0 = 1$

(h) 0^0 has no meaning; it is undefined.

QUICK CHECK 2

Simplify each using the rules given above.

(a) $\dfrac{x^5}{x^3}$

(b) $(5^3)^2$

(c) $x^4 \cdot x^2$

(d) $(x \cdot y)^2$

(e) $\left(\dfrac{x}{t}\right)^3$

(f) 7^1

(g) $y^2 \div y^2$

(h) 0^0

OBJECTIVE 3   Apply the order of operations. Every expression must be evaluated in the sequence given by the **order of operations** shown in the following table. Be careful to always do the operations in an expression in the order listed in the table.[1]

Order of Operations—Calculate from the Top Down
1. Do all operations inside parentheses.
2. Evaluate square roots and exponents.
3. Multiply and divide from left to right.
4. Add and subtract from left to right.

---

[1] More practice is given using the order of operations in the appendix on basic calculators.

To see why it is important to agree on the order of operations, look at the following. How should we evaluate it?

$$7 \cdot 8 - 3$$

Should we subtract first, or should we multiply first? A different answer is found depending on which mathematical operation is done first. There are only two math operations in the expression, namely, multiplication and subtraction. Since multiplication (item 3 in the preceding table) is listed above subtraction (item 4 in the preceding table), multiply first. Then subtract.

$$7 \cdot 8 - 3$$

$56 - 3$ First multiply 7 by 8.

53 Then subtract.

It is very important that you always use the order of operations when evaluating expressions. In complicated expressions, it is best to *do only one mathematical operation at a time* to prevent mistakes. The solution in the next example does that—only one operation is done at a time.

Evaluating Arithmetic Expressions

EXAMPLE 3

Use the order of operations to evaluate each.

(a) $7^2 - (5 \times 2)$

(b) $6 \cdot 5^3 + 3$

SOLUTION

Notice that operations are done in the sequence listed in the order of operations.

(a) $7^2 - (5 \times 2)$

$7^2 - 10$ First, evaluate the contents in the parentheses.

$49 - 10$ Next, evaluate the term with the exponent.

39 Finally, subtract.

(b) $6 \cdot 5^3 + 3$

$6 \cdot 125 + 3$ First, evaluate 5^3, which is $5 \cdot 5 \cdot 5 = 125$.

$750 + 3$ Next, multiply.

753 Finally, add.

QUICK CHECK 3

Evaluate using the order of operations.

(a) $1 + 6 \cdot 5^2$

(b) $(5 - 1)^2 \cdot 2 + 9$

OBJECTIVE 4   Evaluating expressions containing exponents. To evaluate an expression with a variable, first substitute the value of the variable into the equation. Then do the operations in the sequence listed in the order of operations to evaluate.

Evaluating an Expression with an Exponent

EXAMPLE 4

Evaluate each of the following.

(a) $X^3 - 7.8 \cdot 3$ when $X = 8$

(b) $(R - .7)^2 \cdot (9.2 - 1)$ when $R = 19$

SOLUTION

(a) $X^3 - 7.8 \cdot 3$

$8^3 - 7.8 \cdot 3$ Substitute 8 for the variable X.

$512 - 7.8 \cdot 3$ First evaluate 8^3, which is $8 \cdot 8 \cdot 8 = 512$.

$512 - 23.4$ Next, multiply.

488.6 Finally, subtract.

(b) $(R - .7)^2 \cdot (9.2 - 1)$

$(19 - .7)^2 \cdot (9.2 - 1)$ Substitute 19 for the variable R.

$(18.3)^2 \cdot (8.2)$ Do the operations inside both parentheses.

$18.3^2 \cdot 8.2$ Remove parentheses since only one number is inside each.

$334.89 \cdot 8.2$ Evaluate the exponent.

2746.098 Finally, multiply.

QUICK CHECK 4

Evaluate using the order of operations.

(a) $(y + x)^2 - 12.5$ when $y = 10$ and $x = 4$

(b) $15 + (r - 1)^2$ when $r = 4$

OBJECTIVE 5 Solving application problems. The following example shows an application that uses exponents.

Solving an Application Problem

EXAMPLE 5

The manager of Benthos Diving has perfected and patented a new valve for deep-sea scuba diving. An economist friend tells him his profit can be approximated as follows.

$$P = \$.15N^2 + \$168N - \$300,000$$

where P = annual profit and N = number of valves sold in a year. Find the expected profit if 1100 valves are sold in the first year.

SOLUTION

$$P = \$.15N^2 + \$168N - \$300,000$$
$$= .15 \cdot 1100^2 + 168 \cdot 1100 - 300,000 \quad \text{Substitute 1100 for } N.$$
$$= .15 \cdot 1,210,000 + 168 \cdot 1100 - 300,000 \quad \text{Evaluate the exponent.}$$
$$= 181,500 + 184,800 - 300,000 \quad \text{Multiply before adding.}$$
$$= 366,300 - 300,000 \quad \text{Add.}$$
$$P = \$66,300$$

The expected profit is only $66,300. The balance of the revenue is "eaten up" by costs, which include labor, materials, rent, interest on bank loans, etc.

QUICK CHECK 5

Profit at a startup pizzaria can be approximated by: $P = 0.00135n^2 + 12n - \$122,500$ where n is the number of pizzas sold in a year. Estimate profit if 8000 pizzas are sold.

▼ Appendix D Exercises   MyMathLab®

Write each using exponents.

1. $p \cdot p$

2. $3 \cdot 3$

3. $r \cdot r \cdot r$

4. $7 \cdot 7 \cdot 7$

5. $x \cdot x \cdot x \cdot x$

6. $5 \times 5 \times 5$

Evaluate each of the following.

7. 7^2

8. $(.75)^2$

9. X^0 when $X = 7$

10. 5^1

11. 19^0

12. 12^3

Simplify each of the following, leaving exponents in each answer.

13. $(t \cdot g)^4$

14. $(S^3)^2$

15. $9^2 \cdot 9^2$

16. $\dfrac{6^5}{6^3}$

17. $\left(\dfrac{3}{4}\right)^2$

18. $\dfrac{7^m}{7^n}$

19. $(x \cdot y)^2$

20. $\left(\dfrac{y}{R}\right)^3$

Evaluate the following expressions.

21. $17 - 3 \cdot 4$

22. $9 \cdot 8 - 7$

23. $5 \cdot 4^2 + 3$

24. $(9.1 - 1) \cdot 13$

25. $191 - 5^3$

26. $(14 - 7)^2 - 3 \cdot 8$

27. $\dfrac{2^5}{2^3} \cdot 5$

28. $1 - \left(\dfrac{3}{4}\right)^2$

29. $\dfrac{12^3}{12^3} \cdot 75^2$

30. $17.2^3 + (5 - 2^2)$

31. $(16 - 2 \cdot 7)^0$

32. $(4^1 + 2^3 \div 2)^1$

Substitute the value(s) for the variable(s) and then evaluate.

33. $x^2 - 4 \cdot 2; x = 13$

34. $(9 - y)^2 + 5y; y = 3$

35. $7r \div 3^2; r = 27$

36. $\left(\dfrac{s}{x}\right) - 4; s = 42, x = 6$

37. $(y^2 - 7.8) \cdot 3t; y = 10, t = 2$

38. $\left(\dfrac{12}{x}\right)^2 \cdot r^2; x = 3, r = 9$

39. $(S - 7)^n \cdot 9.2 - 1; S = 13, n = 1$

40. $\dfrac{Gr^2}{2} \cdot 7 - 2^2; G = 21, r = 6$

Solve the following application exercises.

41. The daily cost to produce a new memory chip for a smartphone is given by $C = \$.17N^2 + \$12N + \$18,900$, where $C =$ daily cost and $N =$ average number produced in a day. Find the daily cost if $N = 420$.

42. The daily profit from selling a new Barbie doll is given by $P = \$.027N^2 + \$4.50N - \$62,700$, where $P =$ daily profit and $N =$ average number sold per day. Find the daily profit if $N = 1860$.

43. The future value of an investment is given by $M = P(1 + i)^t$, where $M =$ maturity value, $P =$ amount initially invested, $i =$ interest rate per compounding period written as a decimal, and $t =$ number of compounding periods. Find the future value of a \$4800 investment expected to earn 5% per year for 4 years.

44. The future value of an investment is given by $M = P(1 + i)^t$, where $M =$ maturity value, $P =$ amount initially invested, $i =$ interest rate per compounding period written as a decimal, and $t =$ number of compounding periods. Find the future value of a \$15,000 investment expected to earn 7% per year in a mutual fund for 40 years.

QUICK CHECK ANSWERS

1. (a) $s^2; 9.7^3$ **(b)** $64; 16$ **(c)** $1; p$

2. (a) x^2 **(b)** 5^6 **(c)** x^6 **(d)** x^2y^2 **(e)** $\dfrac{x^3}{t^3}$ **(f)** 7 **(g)** 1 **(h)** undefined

3. (a) 151 **(b)** 41

4. (a) 183.5 **(b)** 24

5. \$59,900

Appendix E

Graphing Equations

OBJECTIVES

1. Understand dependent and independent variables.
2. Choose the axes and labels carefully.
3. Graph linear equations.
4. Graph nonlinear equations.

OBJECTIVE 1 Understand dependent and independent variables. A **dependent variable** is one whose value *depends on* the value of a different variable. On the other hand, an **independent variable** is one whose value *does not depend on* the value of another variable. Think about the amount of rain in the past 24 hours and amount of water flowing down a local creek. Does the amount of rain in the past 24 hours depend on the amount of water flowing down the creek? No! However, the amount of water flowing down the creek probably does depend to some degree on the amount of rain in the past 24 hours. So, the dependent variable is the amount of water flowing down the creek and the independent variable is the amount of rain in the past 24 hours. Here is an example from business.

Managers at Andiamo's Pizza have studied monthly sales and advertising data and have found that the relationship can be estimated as follows:

$$\text{Sales} = 37.5 \cdot \text{advertising} + \$12,200$$
$$S = 37.5A + 12,200$$

Since the volume of sales should depend on the amount of advertising dollars spent, the variable S (*sales* dollars) is the dependent variable and the variable A (*advertising* dollars) is the independent variable. Another way to think about it is to realize that the amount of advertising does not depend on sales. Rather, the amount of advertising is chosen by management. More advertising should call more attention to the restaurant and result in higher sales. So, sales depend on advertising.

Equations with variables have one dependent variable and at least one independent variable. Here are some common examples—the key is to decide which variable depends on the other.

Dependent Variable		Independent Variable
Real estate commission	depends on	sale price of house
Sales tax	depends on	amount of purchase
Interest earned	depends on	amount invested

Actually, there can be more than one independent variable in an equation. For example, the amount of *interest earned* in an account at a bank depends on *amount invested, interest rate,* and *length of time* funds are on deposit. In this *case, interest earned* is the dependent variable and the other three variables (*amount invested, interest rate,* and *length of time* funds are on deposit) are all independent variables.

Identifying Independent and Dependent Variables **EXAMPLE 1** Identify the independent and dependent variables for each of the following by asking yourself which variable depends on another variable or variables.

(a) Income, income tax to be paid

(b) Amount of debt on VISA card, monthly interest charge

(c) Property tax, assessed value of a house

(d) Interest rate earned, years to retirement, amount at retirement, annual investment

SOLUTION

	Dependent Variable		Independent Variable(s)
(a)	Income tax to be paid	depends on	income
(b)	Monthly interest charge	depends on	amount of debt on VISA card
(c)	Property tax	depends on	assessed value of a house
(d)	Amount at retirement	depends on	annual investment, years to retirement, and interest rate earned

QUICK CHECK 1

Identify the independent and dependent variables for each.
(a) FICA tax, wages
(b) cost of new car, sales tax

OBJECTIVE 2 **Choose the axes and labels carefully.** Data is often shown using a **line graph**, which is a graph with a line or curve drawn on it. A graph does not have the precision of an algebraic equation in that you cannot use it to find an exact number. However, line graphs are commonly used since they help convey ideas and trends so well.

Before constructing a graph, think about each axis. An **axis** is a horizontal or vertical line along the edge of a graph that usually has a **scale** with units of measurement. An axis is required in order to construct the graph, and it is an important aide to help understand the information and data in the graph. The horizontal axis is commonly used for the *independent variable,* and it is often called the **x-axis.** It should have a label below it unless the value on the axis is obvious to anyone reading the graph. Here is one choice for the x-axis for the equation introduced above: $S = 37.5A + 12{,}200$.

The purpose of a graph is to *clearly communicate* data and ideas. The x-axis above can be improved by adding a scale showing different amounts of advertising. Commonly, the amount of Advertising at the leftmost point, which is called the **origin**, is $0. However, the **origin** can be a number other than 0. Here we have added the origin at the left.

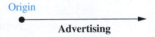

The next questions to ask are: What scale should be used for the x-axis, and how should it be labeled? A scale divides the length of the axis into sections that show amounts for the independent variable. In our example, it should be based on the amounts of advertising that managers would consider. If they would consider up to $2000 per month in advertising, then the scale should divide $2000 into 4 to 8 intervals. A reasonable label is "Advertising (in dollars)."

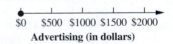

However, the following choice of a scale may also be appropriate.

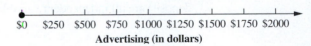

However, this last axis seems a little "too busy" with too many numbers on it, so we will use the axis just above the last one.

In a similar fashion, the **y-axis** is chosen to represent the reasonable values for the outcome of *Sales* based on the values of *Advertising* shown on the x-axis. The y-axis is commonly vertical. To determine the scale on the y-axis, first find the minimum and maximum amount of sales that are possible using the equation from above: $S = 37.5A + 12{,}200$.

Minimum sales occur if Advertising (A) is $0: $S = 37.5 \cdot \$0 + \$12{,}200 = \$12{,}200$

Maximum sales occur at the maximum $S = 37.5 \cdot \$2000 + \$12{,}200 = \$87{,}200$
    advertising of $2000:

Therefore, the scale on the y-axis should go from below $12,200 to a little over $87,200.
A reasonable scale is shown here.

Combining the x- and y-axes at the origin results in the following.

Remember, the purpose of a graph is to communicate CLEARLY. We have not yet graphed
the equation, but is there something we can do to improve the quality of the communication
in the basic graph itself? Yes, we can add a title to it. The title is very important, and it should
clearly indicate the main theme of the information or data in the graph. In our example, the title
should include some or all of the following words: Andiamo's Pizza, sales, advertising, and
monthly data. The graph should be labeled so well that you can put it aside and still understand
the graph a month or two later when you look at it again.

Sales at Andiamo's Pizza

Date Graph Developed: July 2014

Setting Up a Reasonable Graph

 EXAMPLE 2

At the request of a financial planner, the Hernandez family is setting up a personal budget. They wish to graph the amount spent per week on groceries for their family of three. Help them set up an appropriate graph.

SOLUTION

First identify the dependent and independent variables. Since the amount of food purchased depends on the week, the dependent variable is *amount of food purchased* and the independent variable is *week.* Thus, the *y*-axis label should be *Amount of Food Purchased (in dollars)* or simply *Amount Purchased (in dollars).* The *x*-axis label should be *Week* (either week number 1, 2, 3, etc., or a date associated with the first day of successive weeks such as Jan. 9, Jan. 16, Jan. 23, etc.).

To determine the scale on the *y*-axis, decide what the maximum amount of food purchased in a week might be. Assuming a maximum purchase of $300, a scale of $0, $100, $200, and $300 is reasonable. To determine the scale on the *x*-axis, decide on the number of weeks for which you wish to track the data. Assuming you want to track the data for 8 weeks, the scale would be 1, 2, 3, 4, 5, 6, 7, and 8.

Here is a reasonable graph.

Quick TIP

The first step in building a graph is to identify the independent and dependent variables.

QUICK CHECK 2

Help an economist set up a graph showing the number of homes under construction in one region versus the 30-year fixed mortgage interest rate. The number of homes under construction varies from 112,000 to 289,000 and the interest rate varies from 3% to 10%.

OBJECTIVE 3 Graph linear equations. A **linear equation** is an equation that does not have any variables raised to a power (such as x^2) or multiplied by another variable (such $x \cdot y$). Here are some examples of linear equations:

$$S = 37.5A + 12{,}200$$
$$y = 35x + 94$$
$$P = 1700 - 47.3s$$

These equations are called linear equations, since the graph of each is a straight line.

Now let's put several of these ideas together and graph the equation of sales at Andiamo's Pizza that we worked with above: $S = 37.5A + \$12{,}200$. First, note that it is a linear equation because no variable is raised to a power, nor are any variables multiplied by one another. So, the graph of the equation will be a straight line. For a straight line, we need to plot only two data points on the line graph before connecting them with a ruler. The exact same straight line results no matter which two points we use, and the same straight line would occur if we used three or more points.

Graphing a Straight Line

Step 1   Pick two different values of the independent variable.

Step 2   For each value chosen in Step 1, calculate the corresponding value of the dependent variable.

Step 3   Draw a straight line through the two points.

It is better to chose values of the independent variable that are not too close to one another. Reasonable *Advertising* expenses range from $0 to $2000, so we arbitrarily choose advertising values of $500 and $2000. Next, substitute these two values for A on the right side of the equation to find the predicted sales.

NOTE A third point can be used to check. It should be on the straight line.

Amount of *Advertising* (A)	Corresponding *Sales* (S) amount
$500	$S = 37.5 \cdot \$500 + \$12{,}200 = \$30{,}950$
$2000	$S = 37.5 \cdot \$2000 + \$12{,}200 = \$87{,}200$

The next step is to graph the following data points on the graph developed above. Often the points are written in this format: (value of independent variable, value of dependent variable), or as shown in the right column below. We sometimes refer to this notation as (x, y) where x is the value for the independent variable and y is the value for the dependent variable.

Advertising	Sales	Data Point
$500	$30,950	($500, $30,950)
$2000	$87,200	($2000, $87,200)

y-variable (dependent)

x-variable (independent)

To plot the data point ($500, $30,950), place a point directly above $500 on the *x*-axis and aligned horizontally to $30,950 on the *y*-axis. You cannot see the difference between $30,950 versus, say, $31,200 on the graph, so do the best you can. As stated earlier, graphs do not have the precision of an algebraic equation, but they often show the overall relationship more clearly than an algebraic equation. Next, plot ($2000, $87,200) by placing a dot aligned with $2000 on the *x*-axis and with $87,200 on the *y*-axis.

Sales at Andiamo's Pizza

Finally, connect the lines with a ruler.

Sales at Andiamo's Pizza

The formula $S = 37.5A + \$12{,}200$ is the algebraic form of the relationship. However, the graph is a visual representation of the same relationship. In a very real way, these are two very different ways of showing the *same information*. Graphs are extremely common in business, since they allow us to use our visual ability to quickly understand a relationship or pattern. Is it easier for you to work with a graph or an equation?

The **y-intercept** is the point at which the line intersects the *y*-axis. The *y*-axis for this graph corresponds to $0 in advertising. You can either substitute $0 into the equation in place of A and solve to find that the *y*-intercept is $12,200 or estimate the *y*-intercept by looking at the graph. Monthly sales would be $12,200 even with no advertising.

Constructing a Graph

EXAMPLE 3

The real estate commission in Albuquerque, New Mexico, is 6% of the sales price of the home. The average price of homes sold in one part of Albuquerque last month was $223,000, but prices of homes sold ranged from $100,000 to $480,000 during the month. Write an equation for commission versus sales price and graph it in a well-labeled graph.

SOLUTION

The algebraic relationship is based on the fact that *Real Estate Commission* equals 6% of *Sales Price,* so commission depends on price as follows.

$$C = .06 \times P$$

where C = Real Estate Commission

P = Selling Price of Home

Since the independent variable *Selling Price of Home* (P) ranged between $100,000 to $480,000, a reasonable scale for the *x*-axis would be $0, $100,000, $200,000, $300,000, $400,000, and $500,000. Using thousands, the scale would be $0, $100, $200, $300, $400, and $500. Although we can start the *x*-axis at $100 (in thousands) on the left since that is the lowest value of the independent variable, we choose to use $0 for the origin.

The dependent variable is *Real Estate Commission*, which can be as high as 6% of $480,000, or $28,800. So, a reasonable scale for the *y*-axis would be $0, $10,000, $20,000, and $30,000. If the label on the *y*-axis indicates that the commissions are in thousands of dollars, then the numbers shown along the axis would be $0, $10, $20, and $30.

Again, the equation is linear, so we need to plot only two data points. Remember to choose values for the independent variables that are spread out a little—we choose $100,000 and $300,000.

Independent Variable	Value of Dependent Variable	Data Point (in thousands of dollars)
$100,000	$C = .06 \times \$100{,}000 = \$6000$	($100, $6)
$300,000	$C = .06 \times \$300{,}000 = \$18{,}000$	($300, $18)

Now construct the chart with a good title, appropriate axes, and a reasonable scale.

Real Estate Commission versus Selling Price of Homes in Albuquerque, New Mexico

Quick TIP

Software such as Microsoft Excel can be used to create professional-looking graphs.

QUICK CHECK 3

Graph the following equation: Sales tax $= 0.085 \cdot S$, where S is sales not including taxes. Sales for one month range from $0 to $100,000.

OBJECTIVE 4 Graph nonlinear equations. Up to this point, we have worked only with linear equations, which graph as straight lines. However, many situations in business require **nonlinear equations**, which have graphs that are not straight lines. Compound interest calculations used daily by banks and others require the use of the following nonlinear equation. It shows how to find the maturity value of an investment of P dollars at an interest rate of i for n years.

$$M = P(1 + i)^n$$

where $M =$ total amount accumulated at the end of the investment period

$P =$ principal amount invested

$i =$ interest rate per year written as a decimal number (e.g., write 6% as 0.06)

$n =$ number of years the investment is held[3]

The dependent variable M (maturity value) depends on the three independent variables: P (original investment), i (interest rate), and n (number of years). The equation is nonlinear since it includes an exponent and also since the variable P is being multiplied by $(1 + i)$, which has a variable itself. Thus, it will not graph as a straight line. As a result, it is *necessary to plot several data points* before connecting them with a smooth line—two data points are not enough for a nonlinear graph.

Graphing an Equation that Involves Exponents

 EXAMPLE 4

Trisha Patterson inherits $8000 from her grandmother and decides to put the money into a mutual fund that she hopes will earn 5% per year. She hopes the accumulated funds will help her 2-year-old pay for college. Graph the equation $M = P(1 + i)^n$ using the data given.

SOLUTION

The original investment is $P = \$8000$ and the interest rate per year is $i = 5\%$, or .05. Putting the values for P and i into the equation simplifies it.

$$M = \$8000 \cdot (1 + .05)^n$$

Or, simpler still, as

$$M = \$8000 \cdot (1.05)^n$$

Quick TIP

Before graphing an equation with exponents or variables multiplied together, plot several points.

---

[3] Here we will work only with annual interest rate and number of years. Chapter 10 discusses several other options.

A reasonable scale for the x-axis is 0, 5, 10, 15, and 20 years. Next, find the value of M that corresponds to each of these values of the independent variable. Notice below that the largest value on the y-axis is \$21,226, so label the y-axes as Maturity Value (in thousands), and use this scale: \$0, \$5, \$10, \$15, \$20, \$25.

Dependent Variable	Maturity Value (*M*), Rounded to the Nearest Dollar
0 years	$M = \$8000 \cdot (1.05)^n = \$8000 \cdot 1.05^0 = \$8000 \cdot 1 = \$8000$
5 years	$M = \$8000 \cdot (1.05)^n = \$8000 \cdot 1.05^5 = \$8000 \cdot 1.27628 = \$10,210$
10 years	$M = \$8000 \cdot (1.05)^n = \$8000 \cdot 1.05^{10} = \$8000 \cdot 1.62889 = \$13,031$
15 years	$M = \$8000 \cdot (1.05)^n = \$8000 \cdot 1.05^{15} = \$8000 \cdot 2.07893 = \$16,631$
20 years	$M = \$8000 \cdot (1.05)^n = \$8000 \cdot 1.05^{20} = \$8000 \cdot 2.65330 = \$21,226$

Finally, plot the points (0, \$8), (5, \$10), (10, \$13), (15, \$17) and (20, \$21) and connect the points with a smooth line.

Maturity Value of \$8000 Invested at 5%

Notice that the line is not a straight line. Rather, it curves upward slightly, showing that the maturity value grows more rapidly with time. In actuality, in the later years the investment is earning interest on larger and larger amounts since interest is being paid on interest already paid to the account. Nonlinear relationships such as these are both very common and very important in business. As we will see in the chapter on annuities, the increasing amounts of interest earned over time is a key to building up investments.

QUICK CHECK 4

The chief financial officer at Siena College puts \$1,000,000 in an investment expected to earn 4.5% per year for the next 5 years. Use $M = P(1 + i)^n$ to graph the maturity value for the next five years. The variable i = interest rate as a decimal number, n = number of years of the investment, and P = original investment.

A common application of exponents uses a number represented by the symbol e, which is approximately equal to 2.7182818. This number is so commonly used in business, engineering, and scientific calculations that it can be found on most calculators. Is it on yours? Maturity value M depends on the following three things:

- The original investment of P dollars
- Invested for t years
- At an interest rate of r per year.

The formula for the maturity value assuming continuous compounding is given here.

$$M = Pe^{rt}$$

The value for e is a constant that is found on your calculator, so you will not have to key it in each time. Since e is raised to the power of r (interest rate) multiplied by t (time), the equation is nonlinear. The next example shows the huge difference both time and interest rate make in accumulating money for a future event, such as saving for an automobile or a down payment on a home.

Graphing an Equation that Uses the Number *e*

EXAMPLE 5

Sara Walker won a scratch-off lottery. After buying a Toyota Camry, she has $7000 to invest. A financial advisor shows her the difference that interest rate and length of investment can make using the following two investment options.

(a) A conservative investment expected to earn 4% per year for 10 years, or

(b) A mutual fund expected to earn 7% for 40 years.

Graph maturity value against year for both of these investment options on the same graph.

SOLUTION

It is necessary to make a separate calculation for option (a) and (b) at each of the years to be used on the *x*-axis. Option (a) is only for 10 years, so we choose to calculate the maturity values for this option for years 0, 5, and 10. However, option (b) is for 40 years, so we will calculate the maturity values for it for 0, 5, 10, 20, 30, and 40 years. Here are the calculations for maturity value for both options for 5 years, with maturity value rounded to the nearest dollar.

(a) $M = Pe^{rt} = \$7000 \cdot e^{.04 \times 5} = \$7000 \cdot e^{.2} = \$7000 \cdot 1.22140 = \$8550$

(b) $M = Pe^{rt} = \$7000 \cdot e^{.07 \times 5} = \$7000 \cdot e^{.35} = \$7000 \cdot 1.41907 = \$9933$

The remaining maturity values are calculated in the same way using the appropriate interest rate and number of years in place of the variables *r* and *t*, respectively.

The initial investment is $7000 under both option (a) and (b) above, so $7000 is the amount at time 0 for both options. Check the maturity values in the table that follows to make sure they are correct. Notice that no calculation is needed under option (a) beyond 10 years.

Maturity Values		
Year	Option (a)	Option (b)
0	$7,000	$7,000
5	$8,550	$9,933
10	$10,443	$14,096
20	*	$28,386
30	*	$57,163
40	*	$115,113

Initial investment.

Sara is amazed that a $7000 investment can grow to about $115,000 in 40 years. The amount of interest that the investment will earn in 40 years is found by subtracting the original investment from the maturity value as follows.

$$\$115,113 - \$7000 = \$108,113$$

She likes the thought of her money working for her over the years. Option (b) clearly results in far more money than option (a), but of course it takes much longer to accumulate.

The left column of the table above, labeled *Year*, shows the values for the *x*-axis. The *y*-axis of the graph should go higher than $115,113, so we choose to label it as *Maturity Value* (in thousands) with a scale of $0, $25, $50, $75, $100, $125.

Maturity Value of a $7000 Investment at 4% and 7%

The difference in the effects of the two different interest rates of 4% and 7% is shown by the difference in the two curves up to year 10. Option (b) has the higher interest rate and results in larger maturity values. So, both interest rate and time are very important to building investments. The chapter on annuities and sinking funds (Chapter 11) will show you practical ways to accumulate a large sum of money over time.

QUICK CHECK 5

Use $M = Pe^{rt}$ to graph the maturity value of a $10,000 investment ($P$), when $r = 3.5\%$ and $t = 3$ years.

▼ Appendix E Exercises   MyMathLab®

Identify the dependent and independent variable(s) based on your internal sense of which variable depends on the other(s).

		Dependent	**Independent**
1.	Interest earned, total investment	_____	_____
2.	Calories eaten, weight gain	_____	_____
3.	Profit, sales	_____	_____
4.	Number of employees, payroll	_____	_____
5.	Weight of calf, age of calf	_____	_____
6.	Total sales, number of smart phones sold	_____	_____
7.	Sales, profit, total expenses	_____	_____
8.	Size of roof, material used, cost of new roof	_____	_____

Construct a reasonable graph for each of the following.

9. FLOODING Due to severe flooding in the past, administrators in Pakistan carefully watch the flow of water in the Indus River which flows out of China and India and into Pakistan. Water flows are estimated each day based on the height of the river in meters taken at the upstream monitoring station. One of the worst floods on record occurred when the height of the water at the monitoring station peaked at 32.1 meters. It resulted in 1600 deaths and affected 14 million people.

10. MCDONALDS An entrepreneur sets up a new McDonald's franchise and plans to carefully watch weekly sales for the first 10 weeks of operation. He hopes weekly sales will approach $16,000.

11. **APPLE, INC.** An investor loves her iPad and iPhone and is debating whether to buy stock in the company that makes them, Apple Inc. She wants to look at a graph of the firm's after-tax quarterly profit for each quarter of the past year. Quarterly profits range up to nearly $8 billion.

12. **QUALITY** A quality-control inspector is concerned with the number of bottles of beer that are not being capped appropriately at a bottling machine on a production line. Although the production line runs very rapidly, he has a machine that scans every bottle for quality problems. He doesn't expect more than 30 defective bottles in an hour, and he wants a graph that will show results for a 24-hour day.

Construct the graphs indicated.

13. **MONTHLY SALES** Monthly sales for one product line are based on advertising and can be approximated by $S = 40.2A + \$17,500$. Graph this relationship if advertising does not exceed $2000 per month.

14. STOCK PRICE   Recently, the share price of LemonKing Inc. has increased with the firm's earnings per share of stock according to $S = 24.1E + \$12.3$, where S = share price and E = quarterly earnings per share of stock. Graph this relationship, assuming that earnings per share do not exceed $.90.

15. ENTREPRENEUR   Bill Thomas is thinking about working part-time tutoring gifted children. He charges $25 for each tutoring sessions with a student and will rent a small office with a total cost of $275 per month. First, write an equation for his monthly profit based on the number of students he tutors in a month. (*Hint:* monthly profit = monthly revenue − monthly expense.) Then, graph the equation assuming that he will tutor between 15 and 80 students in any given month.

16. CELL PHONE   Verizon advertises a low-cost beginner special on cell phone use to attract new users. The monthly cost is $14.95 a month plus $.07 per minute for each minute of time (excluding taxes) used for calls made in the United States. Write an equation for monthly cost versus cell phone use and graph it, assuming users do not use over 400 minutes per month.

17. LAWN MOWING Calvin Tigard is only 15, but he has decided to start a lawn-mowing business. He plans to charge an average of $40 to mow and trim each yard. He thinks that the cost of buying and maintaining the equipment needed plus operational expenses such as gasoline will be about $7 per yard mowed. Write an equation for weekly profit and graph it, assuming he does not mow more than 8 yards per week.

18. VACATION After college, Tina Duncan and her husband decide to drive the 3000 miles across the United States to visit her grandparents. They can average 60 miles per hour on the highways, but Tina is not sure how many hours per day they will drive. Write an equation to show miles driven per day based on the number of hours driven and graph it, assuming they are not willing to drive more than 10 hours in any one day.

19. COMPUTER SALES Computer Shoppe is a high-volume seller of computers on the Internet. The total cost of selling computers can be approximated by $C = \$95,000 + \$680N = \$.21N^2$, where C = total annual cost and N = number of computers sold in a month. Graph this nonlinear equation, assuming fewer than 1000 computers are sold. (*Hint:* Since it is a nonlinear equation, you must plot several different values of the independent variable before connecting points with a smooth curve.)

20. **SMARTPHONES**   Smartphones.com sells smartphones cheaply, both through their store location and on the Internet. The total weekly profit is approximated by $P = -\$85,000 + \$645N - \$.3N^2$, where P = total weekly profit and N = number of smartphones sold during the week. Use the equation to create a graph, assuming that smartphone sales range between 200 and 800 per week. (*Hint:* Since this is a nonlinear equation, you must plot several different values of the independent variable before connecting points with a smooth curve.)

QUICK CHECK ANSWERS

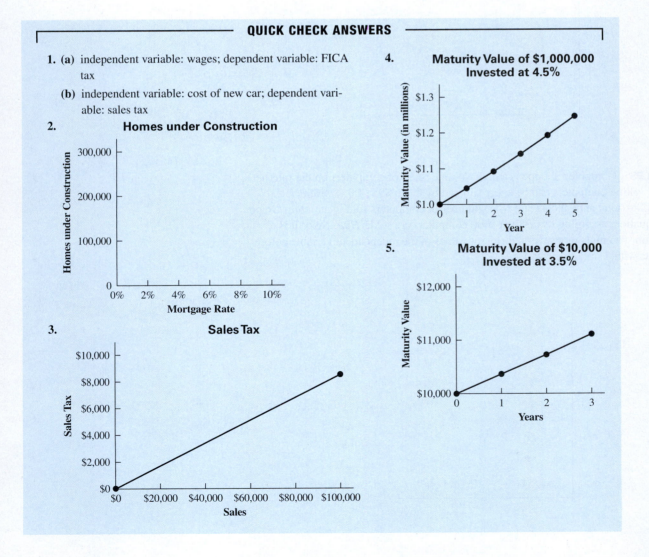

1. (a) independent variable: wages; dependent variable: FICA tax

   (b) independent variable: cost of new car; dependent variable: sales tax

2. **Homes under Construction**

3. **Sales Tax**

4. **Maturity Value of $1,000,000 Invested at 4.5%**

5. **Maturity Value of $10,000 Invested at 3.5%**

▼ Answers to Selected Exercises

CHAPTER 1

Section 1.1 Exercises (Page 9)

1. seven thousand, forty **3.** thirty-seven thousand, nine hundred one **5.** four million, six hundred fifty thousand, fifteen **7.** 2070; 2100; 2000 **9.** 46,230; 46,200; 46,000 **11.** 106,050; 106,100; 106,000 **15.** 210 **17.** 2186 **19.** 1396 **21.** 983,493 **23.** 668 **25.** 2877 **27.** 21,546 **29.** 6,088,899 **31.** Totals horizontally: $293,267; $387,795; $426,869; $373,100; $1,481,031; Totals vertically: $269,761; $267,502; $206,932; $246,587; $244,616; $245,633; $1,481,031 **33.** 9374 **35.** 117,552 **37.** 1,696,876 **39.** 8,107,899 **41.** Estimate: 12,760; Exact: 12,605 **43.** Estimate: 600; Exact: 545 **45.** Estimate: 30,000; Exact: 29,986 **47.** $37 \times 18 = 666$; 66,600 **49.** $376 \times 6 = 2256$; 22,560,000 **51.** 1241 R1 **53.** 458 R21 **57.** 2385 R5 **59.** 58 R4 **61.** two million, two hundred forty thousand **63.** three million, two hundred thousand **65.** 854,795 boxes **67.** 55,572,633 **69.** 200,000 chips **71.** 500 items per hour **73.** $4503 **75.** 128,197,000 **77.** 32,293,000 **79.** 6500 stores **81.** Dollar General; 8500 stores **83.** 2500 stores

Section 1.2 Exercises (Page 18)

1. 5208 sandwiches **3.** 100 billion fewer miles **5.** 221,555 veterans **7.** 8589 pounds **9.** $64 **11.** 6,098,400 square feet **13.** $1050 **15.** $20,961 **17.** $375 **19.** 20 seats

Section 1.3 Exercises (Page 23)

1. thirty-eight hundredths **3.** five and sixty-one hundredths **5.** seven and four hundred eight thousandths **7.** thirty-seven and five hundred ninety-three thousandths **9.** four and sixty-two ten-thousandths **13.** 438.4 **15.** 97.62 **17.** 1.0573 **19.** 3.5827 **21.** $6.00 **23.** $.58 **25.** $3.99 **27.** 3.5; 3.52; 3.522 **29.** 2.5; 2.55; 2.548 **31.** 27.3; 27.32; 27.325 **33.** 36.5; 36.47; 36.472 **35.** .1; .06; .056 **37.** $5.06 **39.** $32.49 **41.** $382.01 **43.** $42.14 **45.** $.00 **47.** $1.50 **49.** $2.00 **51.** $752.80 **53.** $26 **55.** $0 **57.** $12,836 **59.** $395 **61.** $4700 **63.** $379 **65.** $722

Section 1.4 Exercises (Page 27)

1. $40 + 20 + 9 = 69$; 68.46 **3.** $6 + 4 + 5 + 7 + 2 = 24$; 23.82 **5.** $2000 + 5 + 3 + 7 = 2015$; 2171.414 **7.** $6000 + 500 + 20 + 8 = 6528$; 6666.061 **9.** $2000 + 70 + 500 + 600 + 400 = 3570$; 3451.446 **11.** 173.273 **13.** 59.3268 **17.** $15,138.19 **19.** $5.32 per pound **21.** $20 - 7 = 13$; 13.16 **23.** $50 - 20 = 30$; 31.507 **25.** $300 - 90 = 210$; 240.034 **27.** $8 - 3 = 5$; 4.848 **29.** $5 - 2 = 3$; 3.0198 **31.** $43,815.81

Section 1.5 Exercises (Page 32)

1. $100 \times 4 = 400$; 406.56 **3.** $30 \times 7 = 210$; 231.88 **5.** $40 \times 2 = 80$; 89.352 **7.** 1.9152 **9.** 9.3527 **11.** .002448 **13.** $152.63 **15.** $418.10 **17.** 8.075 **19.** 27.442 **21.** 57.977 (rounded) **25.** $14,790 **27.** 50.9 mpg **29.** 27 months **31.** (a) .43 inch (b) 4.3 inches **33.** $129.25 **35.** (a) $70.05 (b) $25.80

Case Study (Page 39)

1. $20,496 **2.** $4372 **3.** 178 guests; $24 **4.** $46.30 **5.** 22 months

Case in Point Summary Exercise (Page 40)

1. $2190.77 **2.** 19.5 hours; $168.68 **3.** $200.56; 213 customers **4.** $673.28; $14,280.19

Chapter 1 Test (Page 41)

1. 840 **2.** 22,000 **3.** 672,000 **4.** 50,000 **5.** 900,000 **6.** $606 **7.** $8399 **8.** $21.06 **9.** $364.35 **10.** $7246 **11.** 181.535 **12.** 498.795 **13.** 133.6 **14.** 3.7947 **15.** 15.8256 **16.** 8.0882 **17.** 11.56 **18.** 350 **19.** 23.8 **20.** $125.18 **21.** $3942.90 **22.** 14.454 gallons saved **23.** $17.31 **24.** $.79 per pound (rounded) **25.** 253 seedlings **27.** $139.32

CHAPTER 2

Section 2.1 Exercises (Page 48)

1. $\frac{29}{8}$ **3.** $\frac{17}{4}$ **5.** $\frac{38}{3}$ **7.** $\frac{183}{8}$ **9.** $\frac{55}{7}$ **11.** $\frac{364}{23}$ **13.** $3\frac{1}{4}$ **15.** $2\frac{2}{3}$ **17.** $3\frac{4}{5}$ **19.** $13\frac{7}{11}$ **21.** $1\frac{62}{63}$ **23.** $7\frac{8}{25}$ **27.** $\frac{1}{2}$ **29.** $\frac{5}{8}$ **31.** $\frac{3}{5}$ **33.** $\frac{11}{12}$ **35.** 1 **37.** $\frac{7}{12}$ **41.** ✓ x ✓ x x ✓ x x **43.** ✓ ✓ ✓ ✓ ✓ x x ✓ **45.** ✓ ✓ x ✓ ✓ x ✓ ✓ **47.** ✓ x ✓ x x x x

Section 2.2 Exercises (Page 53)

1. 16 **3.** 36 **5.** 48 **7.** 42 **9.** 24 **11.** 180 **13.** 480 **15.** 2100 **19.** $\frac{3}{5}$ **21.** $\frac{8}{10}$ **23.** $\frac{1}{2}$ **25.** $\frac{17}{48}$ **27.** $1\frac{23}{36}$ **29.** $\frac{13}{14}$ **31.** $2\frac{1}{15}$ **33.** $2\frac{11}{36}$ **35.** $1\frac{13}{30}$ **37.** $\frac{9}{20}$ **39.** $\frac{7}{24}$ **43.** $\frac{23}{24}$ cubic yard **45.** $\frac{47}{60}$ inch **47.** $\frac{7}{24}$ of the contents **49.** $\frac{3}{4}$ cups **51.** $\frac{3}{16}$ inch **53.** $\frac{7}{24}$ **55.** $\frac{1}{2}$ in work and travel, and class time **57.** $\frac{1}{2}$ inch **59.** $\frac{1}{12}$ mile

Section 2.3 Exercises (Page 60)

1. $97\frac{4}{5}$ **3.** $80\frac{3}{4}$ **5.** $97\frac{7}{40}$ **7.** $53\frac{17}{24}$ **9.** $4\frac{3}{8}$ **11.** $3\frac{11}{24}$ **13.** $6\frac{1}{4}$ **15.** $3\frac{11}{12}$ **19.** $22\frac{7}{8}$ hours **21.** $116\frac{1}{2}$ inches **23.** 130 feet **25.** $1\frac{5}{8}$ cubic yards

Section 2.4 Exercises (Page 67)

1. $\frac{3}{10}$ **3.** $\frac{99}{160}$ **5.** $\frac{9}{32}$ **7.** $4\frac{3}{8}$ **9.** $9\frac{1}{3}$ **11.** $\frac{1}{3}$ **13.** $4\frac{7}{12}$ **15.** $1\frac{7}{9}$ **17.** $\frac{3}{5}$ **19.** $1\frac{1}{2}$ **21.** $\frac{2}{3}$ **23.** $2\frac{2}{3}$ **25.** $\frac{3}{20}$ **27.** $8\frac{2}{5}$ **31.** $12 **33.** $18.75 **37.** 9¢ **39.** 36 yards **41.** 12 homes **43.** $2632\frac{1}{2}$ inches **45.** 32 strawberry cheesecakes **47.** 471 gallons **49.** 88 dispensers **51.** 5 trips

Section 2.5 Exercises (Page 73)

1. $\frac{3}{4}$ **3.** $\frac{6}{25}$ **5.** $\frac{73}{100}$ **7.** $\frac{17}{20}$ **9.** $\frac{17}{50}$ **11.** $\frac{111}{250}$ **13.** $\frac{5}{8}$ **15.** $\frac{161}{200}$ **17.** $\frac{12}{125}$ **19.** $\frac{3}{80}$ **21.** $\frac{3}{16}$ **23.** $\frac{1}{625}$ **27.** .25 **29.** .375 **31.** .667 (rounded) **33.** .778 (rounded) **35.** .636 (rounded) **37.** .88 **39.** .883 (rounded)

Case Study (Page 77)

1. $288,000 **2.** $\frac{5}{12}$; $\frac{1}{4}$; $\frac{1}{12}$; $\frac{1}{16}$; $\frac{1}{16}$; $\frac{1}{8}$ **3.** Miscellaneous: $\frac{1}{8}$; Insurance: $\frac{1}{16}$; Advertising: $\frac{1}{16}$; Utilities: $\frac{1}{12}$; Rent: $\frac{1}{4}$; Salaries: $\frac{5}{12}$ **4.** 150°; 90°; 30°; 22.5°; 22.5°; 45°

Case in Point Summary Exercise (Page 78)

1. $193\frac{1}{2}$ inches **2.** $467\frac{5}{8}$ square inches **3.** $2805\frac{3}{4}$ square inches **4.** 4 side panels

Chapter 2 Test (Page 79)

1. $\frac{5}{6}$ **2.** $\frac{7}{8}$ **3.** $\frac{7}{11}$ **4.** $8\frac{1}{8}$ **5.** $4\frac{2}{3}$ **6.** $2\frac{2}{3}$ **7.** $\frac{31}{4}$ **8.** $\frac{94}{5}$ **9.** $\frac{147}{8}$ **10.** 30 **11.** 120
12. 72 **13.** $\frac{7}{8}$ **14.** $15\frac{1}{16}$ **15.** $36\frac{5}{16}$ **16.** 36 **17.** $1\frac{1}{2}$ **18.** $24\frac{1}{8}$ pounds
19. \$340 **20.** $35\frac{7}{8}$ gallons **21.** 117 pizzas; $5\frac{1}{2}$ ounces **22.** $\frac{5}{8}$ **23.** $\frac{41}{50}$
24. .25 inch **25.** .875 inch

CHAPTER 3

Section 3.1 Exercises (Page 86)

1. 25% **3.** 72% **5.** 203.4% **7.** 362.5% **9.** 87.5% **11.** .05%
13. 345% **15.** 3.08% **17.** .625 **19.** .65 **21.** .125 **23.** .125 **25.** .0025
27. .8475 **29.** 1.75 **31.** .5; 50% **33.** $\frac{7}{8}$; 87.5% **35.** $\frac{1}{125}$; .008
37. 10.5; 1050% **39.** $\frac{13}{20}$; 65% **41.** $\frac{1}{200}$; .5% **43.** $.33\overline{3}$; $33\frac{1}{3}$ %
45. $2\frac{1}{2}$; 250% **47.** $\frac{17}{400}$; .0425 **49.** 2.5; 250% **51.** $10\frac{3}{8}$; 10.375
53. $\frac{1}{400}$; .25% **55.** $\frac{3}{8}$; .375

Section 3.2 Exercises (Page 92)

1. 62 homes **3.** \$604 **5.** 4.8 feet **7.** 10,185 miles **9.** 182 cell phones
11. 148.44 yards **13.** \$5366.65 **17.** 238 people **19.** \$429.92
21. 44 females **23.** 8.95 ounces **25.** 4853 accidents **27.** (a) 28.6%
female (b) 313,099 female **29.** \$239.25 **31.** 2156 products
33. 264,552 vehicles **35.** \$51,844.20 **37.** \$6296.40 **39.** \$199.89
41. \$87.58

Section 3.3 Exercises (Page 98)

1. 2120 **3.** 325 **5.** 2000 **7.** 4800 **9.** 44,000 **11.** 20,000 **13.** \$90,320
15. 1080 **17.** 312,500 **19.** 65,400 **21.** 40,000 **25.** 110.2 million
households **27.** 7761 students **29.** \$4500 **31.** \$3333.33 **33.** 1749
owners **35.** \$185,500

Supplementary Exercises (Page 100)

1. 16 ounces **3.** \$288,150 **5.** 478,175 Mustangs **7.** 162 calories
9. \$39,000 **11.** 230 companies **13.** 55 companies

Section 3.4 Exercises (Page 104)

1. 10 **3.** 50 **5.** 28.3 **7.** 76 **9.** 4.1 **11.** 5.9 **13.** 1.3 **15.** 250 **17.** 27.8
21. 6.2% **23.** 2% **25.** 8.7% **27.** 58.0% **29.** 69.1%

Supplementary Exercises (Page 106)

1. 97 people **3.** 40% **5.** 1100 boaters **7.** \$370.14 **9.** \$568.80
11. 4% **13.** 4 million riders **15.** 62.1% **17.** China—12%;
India—55%; United States—40%; Indonesia—39%;
Brazil—25%; Pakistan—126% **19.** China—1,417,000,000;
India—1,614,000,000 **21.** 5760 items **23.** \$5886 **25.** \$6528
27. 5742 deaths **29.** (a) 36% (b) 64%

Section 3.5 Exercises (Page 113)

1. \$375 **3.** \$27.91 **5.** \$25 **7.** \$854.50 **11.** \$195,500 **13.** (a) \$950
(b) \$76 **15.** 842,857 restaurants **17.** \$66.12 **19.** 8,125,000
subscribers **21.** 21.4 million **23.** \$3864 **25.** \$145.24 million
27. 51.2 million **29.** 30,000 students **31.** 695 deaths **33.** 219

Case Study (Page 119)

Apple, Inc.—66.8%; ExxonMobil Corporation—\$84.51;
McDonalds Corp.—\$82.20; The Coca-Cola Company—\$75.76

Case in Point Summary Exercise (Page 120)

1. 3.2% **2.** \$1,181,640 **3.** \$13,488 **4.** \$82,976.25

Chapter 3 Test (Page 121)

1. 37.5% **2.** $\frac{7}{20}$ **3.** .024 **4.** $\frac{7}{50}$ **5.** 587.5% **6.** 1.75 **7.** 300 home sales
8. \$3.15 **9.** $\frac{6}{25}$ **10.** 1920 purchase orders **11.** $\frac{7}{8}$ **12.** 137.5% **13.** 43
14. 1391 **15.** \$26,563.95 **16.** 309.9 million **17.** (a) 11% (b) \$4488

per year **18.** 75% **19.** \$186.25 **20.** 1200 backpacks **21.** 6.2%
22. \$1.47 billion

CHAPTER 4

Section 4.1 Exercises (Page 130)

1. 3 **3.** 31 **5.** 3 **7.** 7 **9.** 2 **11.** 30 **13.** 7.5 **15.** 10 **17.** 4 **19.** 1.5 **21.** 7
23. 1

Section 4.2 Exercises (Page 137)

1. $27 + x$ **3.** $22 + x$ **5.** $x - 4$ **7.** $x - 3\frac{1}{2}$ **9.** $3x$ **11.** $\frac{3}{5}x$ **13.** $\frac{9}{x}$ **15.** $\frac{16}{x}$
17. $2.1(4 + x)$ **19.** $7(x - 3)$ **21.** $12y$ **23.** $472 - x$ **25.** $73 - x$
27. $\frac{20,210}{x}$ **29.** $21 - x$ **31.** 13 **33.** 1.5 **35.** 1 **37.** $1\frac{3}{7}$ **39.** 59 systems
41. 207 employees **43.** \$349 **45.** \$30,000 office; \$105,000 retail
47. 3 new; 19 experienced **49.** 81 Altimas; 39 Sentras

Section 4.3 Exercises (Page 144)

1. \$586.50 **3.** \$10,080 **5.** \$16.50 **7.** 14 **9.** 2250 **11.** 151.2
13. \$749.86 **15.** 7.5 **17.** 7 **19.** 24,000 **21.** $L = \frac{A}{W}$ **23.** $V = \frac{nRT}{P}$
25. $P = \frac{M}{(1 + i)^n}$ **27.** $i = \frac{A - P}{P}$ **29.** $D = \frac{M - P}{MT}$ **31.** $h = \frac{2A}{b + B}$
33. \$2.40 **35.** \$93.80 **37.** (a) \$427 (b) \$502.50 **39.** \$236 million
41. \$2.29 **43.** \$644,400 **45.** \$390 **47.** .13, or 13% **49.** 4 years
51. \$4000 **53.** \$4500

Section 4.4 Exercises (Page 154)

1. $\frac{9}{32}$ **3.** $\frac{27}{1}$ **5.** $\frac{4}{3}$ **7.** $\frac{3750}{1}$ **9.** $\frac{225}{1}$ **11.** $\frac{8}{5}$ **13.** $\frac{1}{6}$ **15.** $\frac{4}{15}$ **17.** $\frac{9}{2}$ **19.** T **21.** F **23.** F
25. F **27.** F **29.** F **31.** T **33.** T **35.** F **37.** T **39.** 7 **41.** 72 **43.** 105
45. $3\frac{1}{2}$ **47.** 24 **49.** 8 **53.** 1575 tickets **55.** \$516,000 **57.** 28.6 min-
utes **59.** 2.3°F **61.** 1020 miles **63.** \$713,211.20 **65.** \$128,000
67. 350 miles **69.** 3,500,000 cubic meters **71.** \$214.26 U.S.

Case Study (Page 161)

1. \$10,460; \$16,400 **2.** \$3000 **3.** Answers will vary.

Case in Point Summary Exercise (Page 162)

1. Answers will vary, but here are some obvious responses. New
vehicle sales generally grew until 2000, but they dropped off
sharply with the financial crisis that began in 2008. General
Motors has a lot of competition with sales at Ford and Toyota just
slightly lower than at GM. **2.** 60,720 vehicles **3.** 128,490 vehicles
4. 22,756 vehicles

Chapter 4 Test (Page 164)

1. 51 **2.** 50.7 **3.** 16.3 **4.** $5\frac{1}{4}$ **5.** 258 **6.** 136 **7.** 56 **8.** $13\frac{1}{2}$ **9.** 7 **10.** $1\frac{2}{3}$
11. 21 **12.** 3.6 **13.** $I = 504$ **14.** $S = 324$ **15.** $G = 3183.6$
16. $M = 493.50$ **17.** $R = .05$ **18.** $A = 12,000$ **19.** $D = 200$
20. $I = 75$ **21.** $d = .84$ **22.** $I = 120$ **23.** $\frac{A}{L}$ **24.** $\frac{d}{t}$ **25.** $\frac{I}{PR}$ **26.** $\frac{P - 1}{T}$
27. $\frac{A - P}{PR}$ **28.** $\frac{D}{1 - DT}$ **29.** $\frac{1}{5}$ **30.** $\frac{9}{22}$ **31.** $\frac{8}{5}$ **32.** $\frac{1}{6}$ **33.** $\frac{7}{12}$ **34.** $\frac{1}{6}$ **35.** true
36. false **37.** false **38.** true **39.** true **40.** true **41.** 175 **42.** 39 **43.** 5
44. 27 **45.** 8 **46.** 32 **47.** $\frac{7}{2}$ or $3\frac{1}{2}$ **48.** $\frac{15}{2}$ or $7\frac{1}{2}$ **49.** 12 **50.** 47 **51.** 60
52. 8 **53.** 15 **54.** 2 **55.** 45; 46 **56.** 119; 121 **57.** \$1.74 **58.** 19 men;
28 women **59.** \$2056 **60.** \$430,000 **61.** \$12 **62.** \$114.25 **63.** \$20
64. \$1200

Cumulative Review: Chapters 1–4 (Page 168)

1. 65,500 **3.** 78.4 **5.** 3609 **7.** 24,092 **9.** 85 **11.** 35.174 **13.** 12.218
15. \$98 **17.** \$31,658.27 **19.** $\frac{8}{9}$ **21.** $7\frac{2}{15}$ **23.** $13\frac{13}{24}$ **25.** 3 **27.** $12\frac{1}{2}$ square
feet **29.** 130 feet **31.** $\frac{13}{20}$ **33.** 87.5% **35.** 2170 home loans
37. 25% **39.** 1.03% **41.** 97,757 copies **43.** 22,500% **45.** (a) 83%
(b) 1.909 billion pounds **47.** .69 billion pounds **49.** 6 **51.** $7\frac{1}{5}$
53. $l = \$337.5$ **55.** $R = .07$ **57.** $T = \frac{I}{PR}$ **59.** $P = \frac{M}{(1 + i)^n}$ **61.** $\frac{20}{29}$
63. $\frac{7}{20}$ **65.** 46 **67.** \$52.98 **69.** \$10,924

CHAPTER 5

Section 5.1 Exercises (Page 180)

1. $14.20 **3.** $20.00 **5.** $17.10 **7.** $21.90

9.
Date	March 8, 2014
Amount	$1835.42
To	Wayne Plumbing
For	Septic
Total	$6215 13
Deposits	+1594 12
This Check	−1835 42
Other (+or −)	−100 00
Balance	$5873 83

11.
Date	October 7, 2014
Amount	$138.94
To	PetSmart
For	Pet Food
Total	$2105 09
Deposits	+832 47
This Check	−138 94
Other (+or −)	−280 65
Balance	$2517 97

17.
Date	October 10, 2014
Amount	$39.12
To	Post Office
For	Postage
Total	$5972 89
Deposits	+775 50
This Check	−39 12
Other (+or −)	−650 07
Balance	$6059 20

19. 9412.64; 8838.86; 8726.71; 9479.99; 10,955.68; 10,529.13; 9891.20; 9825.58; 9577.41; 9913.26; 9462.76 **21.** 574.86; 384.36; 462.65; 620.07; 581.31; 405.43; 784.71; 587.51; 562.41; 487.41; 1209.76

Section 5.2 Exercises (Page 186)

1. $1595.36 **3.** $1387.67 **5.** $1352.98 **7.** $203.86 **9.** $66.48 **11.** $1064.72 **13.** $991.89 **15.** $972.05 **17.** $60.21 **19.** $29.62

Section 5.3 Exercises (Page 193)

1. $4870.24 **3.** $7690.62 **5.** $18,314.72 **11.** 421 $371.52; 424 $429.07; 427 $883.69; 429 $35.62; $1719.90; $6875.09; $701.56; $421.78; $689.35; $8687.78; $1719.90; $6967.88; $6965.92; $8.75; $6957.17; $10.71; $6967.88 **13.** 765 $63.24; 768 $135.76; $199.00; $5636.51; $220.16; $5856.67; $199.00; $5657.67; $5866.85; $209.30; $5657.55; $.12; $5657.67

Case Study (Page 200)

1. $8178.46 **2.** $204.46 **3.** $9810.36 total of checks outstanding **4.** $4882.58 deposits not recorded **5.** $7274.56

Case in Point Summary Exercise (Page 201)

Checks Outstanding 763—$723.35, 764—$3290.41; Total $4013.76; $13,272.17, 0, $13,272.17, −$4013.76, $9258.41; $9266.79, −$8.95, $9257.84, $.57, $9258.41

Chapter 5 Test (Page 203)

1. $19.90 **2.** $9.40 **3.** $17.40

4.
Date	August 6, 2014
Amount	$6892.12
To	WBC Broadcasting
For	Air time
Total	$16,409 82
Deposits	
This Check	−6,892 12
Other (+ or −)	
Balance	$9517 70

5.
Date	August 8, 2014
Amount	$1258.36
To	Lakeland Weekly
For	Ad
Total	$9517 70
Deposits	+1572 00
This Check	−1258 36
Other (+ or −)	
Balance	$9831 34

6.
Date	August 14, 2014
Amount	$416.14
To	W. Wilson
For	Freelance Art
Total	$9831 34
Deposits	10,000 00
This Check	−416 14
Other (+ or −)	
Balance	$19,415 20

7. $1709.55 **8.** $81.99 **9.** $1627.56 **10.** $56.96 **11.** $1570.60 **12.** 3221 $82.74; 3229 $69.08; 3230 $124.73; 3232 $51.20; $327.75; $4721.30; $758.06; $32.51; $298.06; $5809.93; $327.75; $5482.18; $5474.60; $2.00; $5472.60; $9.58; $5482.18

CHAPTER 6

Section 6.1 Exercises (Page 212)

1. 40; 0; $12.15 **3.** 38.75; 0; $28.05 **5.** 40; 5.25; $17.22 **7.** $329.60; $92.70; $422.30 **9.** $380; $160.31; $540.31 **11.** $13.20; $347.60; $0; $347.60 **13.** $21.60; $576.00; $97.20; $673.20 **15.** $13.77; $367.20; $58.52; $425.72 **17.** 50.5; 10.5; $4.75; $479.75; $49.88; $529.63 **19.** 53.5; 13.5; $6.25; $668.75; $84.38; $753.13 **21.** 35; 6; $14.10; $329.00; $84.60; $413.60 **23.** 39.5; 3.75; $16.20; $426.60; $60.75; $487.35 **25.** 39.75; 3.5; $32.25; $854.63; $112.88; $967.51 **29.** $443.08; $886.15; $1920; $23,040 **31.** $1200; $2400; $2600; $62,400 **33.** $1660; $1798.33; $3596.67; $43,160 **35.** $387 **37.** $467.25 **39.** $832 **41.** $788.80 **43.** $556.32 **45.** (a) $1260 biweekly (b) $1365 semimonthly (c) $2730 monthly (d) $32,760 annually

Section 6.2 Exercises (Page 222)

1. $93.12 **3.** $153.60 **5.** $49.80 **7.** $52.68 **11.** $353.60 **13.** $371.90 **15.** $397.48 **17.** $471.50 **19.** $608.10 **21.** $421.65 **23.** $1405 **25.** $688.40 **27.** $478.10 **29.** $628.61

Section 6.3 Exercises (Page 227)

1. $26.04; $6.09 **3.** $28.72; $6.72 **5.** $52.99; $12.39 **7.** $189.39
9. $308.99 **11.** $41.56 **13.** $368.80; $76.07; $444.87; $27.58;
$6.45; $4.45 **15.** $568; $106.50; $674.50; $41.82; $9.78; $6.75
17. $467.20; $122.64; $589.84; $36.57; $8.55; $5.90
19. (a) $24.07 (b) $5.63 **21.** (a) $95.67 (b) $22.38 (c) $15.43
23. $7221.60; $1688.92 **25.** $3609; $844.04 **27.** $3328.61; $778.46

Section 6.4 Exercises (Page 238)

1. $155 **3.** $36 **5.** $121 **7.** $76 **9.** $49 **11.** $38 **13.** $6.87 **15.** $28.00
17. $69.11 **19.** $35.73; $8.36; $12.80; $519.39 **21.** $217.78;
$50.93; $423.37; $2820.45 **23.** $141.16; $33.01; $183.33;
$1919.33 **25.** $184.21; $43.08; $216.21; $2527.56 **27.** $232.70;
$54.42; $655.33; $2810.73 **29.** $110.76; $25.90; $342.45;
$1307.33 **35.** $8748.05 **37.** $53,332.52 **39.** $44,323.10
41. $679.71 **43.** $559.79 **45.** $3786.04

Case Study (Page 245)

1. $818 **2.** $368.10 **3.** $1186.10 **4.** $73.54 **5.** $17.20 **6.** $191.61
7. $11.86 **8.** $52.19 **9.** $602.70 **10.** 50.8%

Case in Point Summary Exercise (Page 246)

1. Betinez: $245.00; $15.19; $3.55; $13.09; $7.52; $2.45; $203.20
Parton: $581.88; $36.08; $8.44; $27.97; $17.86; $5.82; $460.71
Dickens: $280.50; $17.39; $4.07; $27.53; $8.61; $2.81; $210.09
2. $450; $205.92; $655.92; $40.67; $9.51; $36.36; $20.14;
$6.56; $477.68 **3.** FICA—$218.66; Medicare—$51.14; Federal
Taxes—$104.95; Total—$374.75 **4.** State Income Tax—$54.13;
State disability insurance—$17.64; Total—$71.77

Chapter 6 Test (Page 247)

1. 40; 6.5; $537.30 **2.** 40; 7.5; $440.75 **3.** (a) $655 weekly
(b) $1310 biweekly (c) $1419.17 semimonthly (d) $2838.33
monthly **4.** $425 **5.** $3532.50 **6.** (a) $607.60 (b) $142.10
7. (a) $446.40 (b) $142.10 **8.** $26 **9.** $39 **10.** $161 **11.** $61 **12.** $60
13. $1487.38 **14.** $737.36 **15.** $559.76 **16.** (a) $31.90 (b) $7.46
(c) $5.14 **17.** (a) $162.71 (b) $38.42 **18.** (a) $4552.55 (b) $1064.71
19. (a) $5255.20 (b) $1229.04 **20.** $2246.54

CHAPTER 7

Section 7.1 Exercises (Page 255)

1. $226.80 **3.** $126.36 **5.** $3610.36 **7.** $4935.88 **9.** $57.00
11. $28.40 **13.** $501.20 **15.** foot **17.** pair **19.** kilogram **21.** case
23. drum **25.** liter **27.** gallon **29.** cash on delivery **33.** $.9 \times .8 = .72$
35. $.9 \times .9 \times .9 = .729$ **37.** $.75 \times .95 = .7125$
39. $.6 \times .7 \times .8 = .336$ **41.** $.5 \times .9 \times .8 \times .95 = .342$
43. $267.52 **45.** $14.02 **47.** $722.93 **49.** $218.88 **51.** $16.83
53. $714.42 **55.** $972 **57.** $640 **63.** $182.24 **65.** (a) 20/15 (b) $4.08
67. (a) 15/20 (b) $.55 **69.** $1280.45 **71.** $91,188.60 **73.** $326.40
undercharged

Section 7.2 Exercises (Page 261)

1. .72; 28% **3.** .68; 32% **5.** .504; 49.6% **7.** .5184; 48.16%
11. $720 **13.** $2280 **15.** $388 **17.** $5933.81 **19.** $89.30
21. $207.09 **23.** (a) $25.89 wholesale (b) $28.76 retailer's price
(c) $2.87

Section 7.3 Exercises (Page 267)

1. May 14; June 3 **3.** July 25; Sept. 8 **5.** Oct. 1; Oct. 11
7. $1.70; $92.20 **9.** $0; $81.25 **11.** $21.60; $1120.55 **15.** $4542.69
17. $2,303,107.80 **19.** (a) Jan. 28; Feb. 7; Feb. 17 (b) Mar. 9
21. (a) Apr. 25 (b) May 5

Section 7.4 Exercises (Page 273)

1. Mar. 10; Mar. 30 **3.** Sept. 18; Oct. 8 **5.** Dec. 22; Jan. 11
7. $20.47; $661.81 **9.** $10.69; $345.51 **11.** $117.42; $2817.98
13. $.72; $23.23 **17.** (a) Dec. 13 (b) $2334.93 **19.** $6586.09
21. $1495.58 **23.** (a) $1467.39 (b) $549.51 **25.** (a) June 10
(b) June 30 **27.** $1509.75 due **29.** (a) $3350.52 (b) $1052.06

Case Study (Page 279)

1. $1151.92 **2.** $78.56 **3.** 17.7%

Case in Point Summary Exercise (Page 280)

1. $17,750.66 **2.** October 15 **3.** November 4 **4.** $17,966.52
5. $10,309.28; $8189.76

Chapter 7 Test (Page 281)

1. $225.65 **2.** $784.80 **3.** (a) .63 (b) 37% **4.** (a) .576 (b) 42.4%
5. Mar. 15 **6.** May 30 **7.** Jan. 15 **8.** Dec. 19 **9.** (a) $788.80
(b) $773.02 (c) $811.77; $560; $52; $101.20; $75.60; $788.80;
$15.78; $773.02; $811.77 **10.** $91,300.78 **11.** (a) July 20
(b) $3041.28 **12.** $437.48 **13.** (a) Builders Supply (b) $1.91
14. (a) $1882.59 (b) $1900.39 **15.** $2527.08
16. (a) $1717.53 (b) $1198.47

CHAPTER 8

Section 8.1 Exercises (Page 288)

1. 140%; $4.96; $17.36 **3.** 100%; 20%; $27.17; $5.43 **5.** 100%;
130%; $168.00; $218.40 **7.** $2.70; $11.70 **9.** 60%; $19.20
11. $61.44; 40% **13.** $33.80; 25% **17.** $148.64 markup
19. $118.94 **21.** $221.40 selling price **23.** (a) $95.96 (b) 25%
(c) 125% **25.** (a) 126% (b) $567 selling price (c) $117 markup

Section 8.2 Exercises (Page 297)

1. 75%; $21.00; $28.00 **3.** 58%; 42%; $105.00 **5.** 50%; 100%;
$2025; $4050 **7.** $1920; $2400.00 **9.** $8.46; $22.26; 61.3%
11. $750; $1050; 28.6% **13.** 50% **15.** 15.3% **19.** (a) $1250
selling price (b) $812.50 cost (c) 65% **21.** (a) $1507 (b) $577
(c) 38.3% (d) 62.0% **23.** $1.13

Supplementary Exercises (Page 299)

1. $559.52 **3.** 19.1% **5.** $6.98 **7.** $119 **9.** (a) 76% (b) $147.89
(c) $35.49 **11.** (a) $32.40 (b) 25.9% **13.** (a) $24.90 (b) 12.5%
(c) 14.2% **15.** $35.00

Section 8.3 Exercises (Page 304)

1. 25%; $645 **3.** 30%; $18.48 **5.** 20%; $5.20 **7.** $120; $20;
none **9.** $16; $22; $6 **11.** $385; $250; $60 **15.** 41% **17.** $30.01
operating loss **19.** (a) $77.15 operating loss (b) $18.77 absolute
loss

Section 8.4 Exercises (Page 312)

1. $22,673 **3.** $60,568 **5.** 13.10; 13.96 **7.** 8.42; 7.60 **9.** 4.69; 4.66
11. $182; $195; $170 **13.** $2352; $2385; $2312.50 **17.** 5.43 turnover at cost **19.** (a) $1012.50 (b) $1125 (c) $1040
21. (a) $1251.20 (b) $1430 (c) $1040 **23.** $30,660

Case Study (Page 320)

1. $125 **2.** $2062.50 **3.** $375 **4.** none

Case in Point Summary Exercise (Page 321)

1. Steep Alpine $293; Cliff Hoppers $327 **2.** Steep Alpine
$404.34; Cliff Hoppers $451.26 **3.** $9109 **4.** .54 **5.** Steep Alpine
$242.60; Cliff Hoppers $270.76 **6.** $1804.94 operating loss

Chapter 8 Test (Page 322)

1. (a) 20 (b) 120 (c) 76.80 **2.** (a) 138 (b) 365.50 (c) 138.89
3. (a) 80 (b) 20 (c) 33.60 **4.** (a) 75 (b) 25 (c) 18.45 **5.** 20%
6. 50% **7.** $200; $14; none **8.** $72; $99; $27 **9.** 5.76; 5.73
10. $165.90 **11.** (a) $6.54 (b) 48.6% (c) 32.7% **12.** $25
13. $4200 **14.** 40% **15.** (a) $37.99 (b) 19.0% (rounded)
(c) 23.5% **16.** 28% **17.** (a) $131.10 operating loss (b) $45.60
absolute loss **18.** $130,278 average inventory **19.** $12,978
weighted-average method **20.** (a) $11,775 FIFO (b) $13,350 LIFO

Cumulative Review: Chapters 5–8 (Page 324)

1. $1958.20 **3.** $1749.75 **5.** $1727.88 **7.** $4359.38 **9.** $240.47
11. 62.2% **13.** Nov. 15; Dec. 5 **15.** $400; $280; $32 **17.** $93.11
19. 12.88 turnover at cost **21.** $6489 weighted-average method

CHAPTER 9

Section 9.1 Exercises (Page 335)

1. $209; $4009 **3.** $440; $5940 **5.** 68 **7.** 99 **9.** (a) $2493.15
(b) $2527.78 (c) $34.63 **11.** (a) $1091.10 (b) $1106.25 (c) $15.15
13. Helen Spence **15.** Donna Sharp **17.** 90 days **19.** Jan. 25, 2015
21. Oct. 18; $5064 **23.** May 9; $6591.38 **25.** (a) $138,750
(b) $2,138,750 **27.** $16,800 **29.** (a) Oct. 3 (b) $14,016.81
31. (a) Sept. 6 (b) $84,200 **33.** $86.17 **35.** (a) Sept. 30
(b) $136,106.67

Section 9.2 Exercises (Page 343)

1. $14,000 **3.** $5040 **5.** $156,000 **7.** 11.8% **9.** 9.5% **11.** 7.5%
13. 120 days **15.** 62 days **17.** 5 months **19.** $10,200 **21.** 9.5%
23. 10.8% **25.** (a) $10,800 (b) $11,250 **27.** 76 days **29.** 8.6%
31. (a) $12,000 (b) $600 **33.** 208 days **35.** (a) 10.75% (b) 11.4%

Section 9.3 Exercises (Page 352)

1. $234; $7566 **3.** $950; $18,050 **5.** $408.33; $21,991.67 **7.** Jun. 20;
$62,480 **9.** Dec. 9; $9572.92 **11.** Feb. 8; $23,600 **13.** (a) $220 (b)
$5780 **15.** 200 days **17.** 10% **19.** $7891.30 **21.** (a) $3780
(b) 13.3% **23.** 105 days **25.** (a) 166,107,382.60 yen (b) 8.1%
27. (a) $11,262.50 (b) 8.9% **29.** (a) $24,625,000 (b) $25,000,000
(c) $375,000 (d) 6.09%

Section 9.4 Exercises (Page 360)

1. 107 days **3.** 53 days **5.** $10,179 **7.** $24,812.50 **9.** $6362.75; 37
days; $78.47; $6284.28 **11.** $2044; 49 days; $33.39; $2010.61
13. $17,355; 42 days; $228.43; $17,571.57 **15.** $30,829.37;
83 days; $814.09; $31,285.91 **17.** (a) $4968 (b) $367,632
19. (a) $238,750 (b) 93 days (c) $5166.67 (d) $244,833.33
21. (a) $311,250 (b) $304,713.75 **23.** (a) $24,150 (b) $538.46
 (c) $24,461.54 (d) 6.71%

Supplementary Exercises (Page 364)

1. (a) $660 (b) $18,660 **3.** $96,000 **5.** 200 days **7.** (a) $750
(b) $20,750 **9.** 12.1% **11.** Apr. 12; $9,475,000 **13.** $15,000
15. $18,208.12 **17.** (a) $1711.11 (b) $29,711.11 (c) 130 days
(d) $1180.19 (e) $28,530.92 **19.** (a) $3843.89 (b) $72,191.09
(c) $4191.09 (d) $347.20

Case Study (Page 372)

3. (a) $1,037,500 (b) $78,292,500 (c) 2.65%

Case in Point Summary Exercise (Page 373)

1. $92,727.27; $7727.27 **2.** $7437.50; $92,437.50 **3.** Simple
interest loan from Union Bank; $289.77 **4.** Bank One—10.91%;
Union Bank—10.50%

Chapter 9 Test (Page 374)

1. $1020.83 **2.** $508.75 **3.** $137.50 **4.** $148.06 **5.** $13,013.01 **6.**
$25,575.75 **7.** $11.19 **8.** 9.2% **9.** 333 days **10.** $43,000
11. $26,595.74 **12.** $359.33; $9440.67 **13.** $162.29; $10,087.71
14. (a) $14,550 (b) 9.3% **15.** $28,626.58 **16.** $9034.40
17. (a) $19,812.50 (b) $20,000 (c) $187.50 (d) 3.79% **18.** 44 days;
$144.07; $9285.93 **19.** (a) $452.81 (b) $8997.19 (c) loses $2.81

CHAPTER 10

Section 10.1 Exercises (Page 385)

1. $16,325.87; $4325.87 **3.** $30,906.76; $2906.76 **5.** $40,841.23;
$8491.23 **7.** $13,855.83; $1555.83 **9.** $60,476.40; $15,476.40
11. $1296; $1417.39; $121.39 **13.** $1440; $2606.60; $1166.60
15. (a) $11,431.57 (b) $2931.57 **17.** (a) $5707.08 (b) $1207.08
19. (a) 31,669.25 yuan (b) 6669.25 yuan **21.** $966; 10%; 6.14%
23. (a) $1,777,622 (b) $377,622 **25.** (a) $28,137.75 (b) $45,152.75
(c) $17,015 **27.** (a) $8787.45 (b) $10,079.40 (c) second is larger

Section 10.2 Exercises (Page 395)

1. $39.75 **3.** $50.48 **5.** $101.88 **7.** $3978.78 **9.** $17,412.96
13. (a) $3284.75 (b) $24.75 **15.** (a) $11,638.49 (b) $118.49
17. $4163.24; $4247.34 **19.** (a) $849,467.44 (b) $49,467.44
21. $2350 **23.** Loss of $397.50 **25.** $183,636.14; $185,481.59;
$1845.45

Section 10.3 Exercises (Page 402)

1. $10,327.33; $1972.67 **3.** $7674.01; $1675.99 **5.** $9792.06;
$9060.94 **7.** (a) $30,315.20 (b) $9684.80 **9.** $3503.40
11. (a) $793,054 (b) $592,618 **13.** (a) $26,620 (b) $20,990

Case Study (Page 407)

1. $4,053,386; $3,016,084 **2.** $2,539,384; $1,889,530
3. $2,798,295; $2,082,183 **4.** $2,539,384; $1,889,530;
$2,798,295; $2,082,183; $4,053,386; $3,016,084

Case in Point Summary Exercise (Page 408)

1. 2007—$4,235,680; 2008—$7,891,680; 2009—$8,550,370;
2010—$480,000; 2011–$512,960 **2.** $5,030,500; not enough to
offset 2008 loss **3.** (a) $16,442,050 (b) $7,708,691

Chapter 10 Test (Page 409)

1. $11,906.56; $3206.56 **2.** $16,127.04; $4127.04 **3.** $13,170.42;
$3370.42 **4.** $18,556.38; $6056.38 **5.** $50.52 **6.** $530.60
7. $286.28 **8.** $7509.25 **9.** $10,380.83 **10.** $38,291.99
11. $16,077.25 **12.** $4120.01 **13.** $4647.31 **14.** $36,428.34
15. Loss of $676 **16.** Loss of $1625 **17.** (a) $4408.99
(b) $3801.87 **18.** (a) $15,173.40 (b) $13,481.41
19. (a) $283,233.48 (b) $206,955.87 **20.** (a) $59 million
(b) $93 million

Cumulative Review: Chapters 9–10 (Page 411)

1. $272 **3.** $8500.11 **5.** 9.5% **7.** 80 days **9.** $270; $8730 **11.** $4875
13. $1216.65 **15.** $86.07; $12,686.07 **17.** $583.49; $416.51
19. $1250; $23,750 **21.** $10,871.40 **23.** $20.01

CHAPTER 11

Section 11.1 Exercises (Page 420)

1. $25,319.14; $9119.14 **3.** $201,527.78; $51,527.78 **5.** $139,509.30;
$41,509.30 **7.** $7603.12; $1603.12 **9.** $207,485.32; $36,485.32
11. $51,985.25; $6385.25 **15.** (a) $423,452.16 (b) $290,452.16
17. (a) $11,277.89 (b) $3277.89 **19.** $44,502

Section 11.2 Exercises (Page 427)

1. $14,762.54 **3.** $30,493.92 **5.** $18,991.59 **9.** $810,043.65
11. (a) $70,016.48 **(b)** $9983.52 **13. (a)** $48,879.76 **(b)** No
15. (a) First offer **(b)** $2769.99 **17.** $194,361.41

Section 11.3 Exercises (Page 433)

1. $2784.12 **3.** $715.29 **5.** $2271 **7.** $183.22 **11. (a)** $144,026
(b) $55,844 **13. (a)** $3860 **(b)** $845,600 **15.** $26,791.54
17. (a) $53,383 **(b)** $37,559 **19. (a)** $1200 **(b)** $6511.80

(c)

Payment Number	Amount of Deposit	Interest Earned	Total in Account
1	$6511.80	$0	$6511.80
2	$6511.80	$260.47	$13,284.07
3	$6511.80	$531.36	$20,327.23
4	$6511.80	$813.09	$27,652.12
5	$6511.80	$1106.08	$35,270.00
6	$6511.80	$1410.80	$43,192.60
7	$6511.80	$1727.70	$51,432.10
8	$6510.62	$2057.28	$60,000.00

21.

Payment Number	Amount of Deposit	Interest Earned	Total in Account
1	$713,625	$0	$713,625.00
2	$713,625	$10,704.38	$1,437,954.38
3	$713,625	$21,569.32	$2,173,148.70
4	$713,625	$32,597.23	$2,919,370.93

23. $1707 **25.** $6819.92

Supplementary Exercises (Page 438)

1. (a) $15,210.93 **(b)** $3210.93 **3. (a)** $77,985.46 **(b)** $37,985.46
5. $1,384,797.60 **7.** $106,216.95 **9.** $267,986.10

Payment Number	Amount of Deposit	Interest Earned	Total in Account
1	$267,986.10	$0	$267,986.10
2	$267,986.10	$21,438.89	$557,411.09
3	$267,996.02	$44,592.89	$870,000.00

11. (a) $286,748 **(b)** $6265.44

Section 11.4 Exercises (Page 446)

1. $13.38 **3.** $0 **5.** 3,344,600 **7.** 14 **9.** $4.63 **11.** 2.5% **13.** $1.03
15. −$1.00 **17.** $39.14 **19.** $45,912; $2260.48
21. $4955; $123.20 **23.** $6187; $82 **27.** 2.7% **29.** 3.2%
31. 1.6% **33.** 17 **35.** 17 **37.** 29 **39.** .85; 2.5% **41.** $18,133
43. (a) $13,211.40 **(b)** $17,866.85 **(c)** $4655.45

Section 11.5 Exercises (Page 453)

1. $951.33 **3.** Dec. 9, 2021 **5.** 5.317% **7.** $21,747 **9.** $116,316
11. $52,738 **15. (a)** $4,039,000 **(b)** $270,000 **(c)** 6.7%
17. (a) $31,977.75 **(b)** $1387.50 **(c)** 4.3% **19. (a)** $3600
(b) $97,151.40

Case Study (Page 459)

1. $620,703.67 **2.** $97,090.40 **3.** $67,090.40 **4.** $658,703.61
5. Almost, about $38,000 short. **6.** Answers will vary.

Case in Point Summary Exercise (Page 460)

1. $7560 **2.** $856,421.07 **3.** $30,588,840 **4.** $2,447,107.20
5. $1,053,090 **6.** $499,455

Chapter 11 Test (Page 461)

1. $9897.47 **2.** $96,355.40 **3.** $930,909 **4.** $86,210.18
5. $67,880.28 **6.** $47,575.42 **7.** $6801.69 **8.** $39,884.63
9. $21,316.12 **10.** $264,795.02 **11.** $22,696.72 **12.** $24,683.07
13. $8702 **14.** $8395 **15.** $5835.60 **16.** $17,976 **17.** $22,492
18. $2322 **19. (a)** $17,164 **(b)** $456 **20. (a)** $23,800 **(b)** $1050
(c) 4.4% **21.** Highest and lowest prices for the year were $65.90
and $20.10. Weekly volume was 7,451,500 shares. Dividend yield
is .8% of current price. PE ratio is 27. Stock closed at $63.44. The
stock price was up $1.23 for the week. Earnings were $5.47 last
year and are expected to be $2.53 this year and $2.89 next year.
The last quarterly dividend was $.12 per share. **22.** Annual interest
is 7.950% of $1000 = $79.50 per bond. Bond matures on June
15, 2018. Bond closed at $1173.89. Yield to maturity is 5.369%.
Estimated volume for the week is $209,183,000.

CHAPTER 12

Section 12.1 Exercises (Page 471)

1. $51.40 **3.** $15.02 **5.** October, $6.12; $419.17; November,
$419.17, $5.87, $541.68; December, $541.68, $7.58, $529.22;
January, $529.22, $7.41, $211.71 **9.** $20.42 **11.** $4.87 **13.** $17.30
15. (a) $104 **(b)** $65 **(c)** $39 **17. (a)** $2641.56 **(b)** $39.62
(c) $2885.84 **19. (a)** $312.91 **(b)** $4.69 **(c)** $285.94
21. (a) $139.71 **(b)** $2.10 **(c)** $74.32

Section 12.2 Exercises (Page 479)

1. $2050; $250 **3.** $180; $30 **5.** $3543; $643 **7.** 8.1% **9.** 11.6%
11. 7.6% **13.** 12.25% **15.** 10.25% **17.** 11.25% **21. (a)** $59,840
(b) $83,966.60 **(c)** $9166.60 **(d)** 9.9% **23. (a)** 13.3% **(b)** 13%
25. 10.00% **27. (a)** $18,800 **(b)** $25,600 **(c)** $4800 **(d)** 11.25%
29. (a) 732,212.32 pesos **(b)** 13.75% **31. (a)** 97,689.60 **(b)** 10.75%

Section 12.3 Exercises (Page 486)

1. $8307.31; $307.31 **3.** $9198.18; $698.18 **5.** $9862.15; $507.15
7. $231 **9.** $103.18 **11.** $28.38 **15. (a)** $415.33 **(b)** $9315.33
17. (a) $69,936.02 **(b)** $2286.02 **19. (a)** $41,176.11 **(b)** $1876.11
21. (a) $17.31 **(b)** $457.69 **23. (a)** $1700 **(b)** $170 **(c)** $5980
25. (a) $87,716.70 **(b)** $10,916.70 **(c)** $4930.12 **(d)** $43,547.68

Section 12.4 Exercises (Page 494)

1. $1703.13 **3.** $404.73 **5.** $4185.60 **7.** $161.93 **9.** $147.61;
$899.62 **11.** $321.96; $3454.08 **13.** $255.45; $3577
17. (a) $1900.70 **(b)** $13,628

19.

Payment Number	Amount of Payment	Interest for Period	Portion to Principal	Principal at End of Period
0	—	—	—	$4000.00
1	$1207.68	$320.00	$887.68	$3112.32
2	$1207.68	$248.99	$958.69	$2153.63
3	$1207.68	$172.29	$1035.39	$1118.24
4	$1207.70	$89.46	$1118.24	$0

21.

Payment Number	Amount of Payment	Interest for Period	Portion to Principal	Principal at End of Period
0	—	—	—	$14,500.00
1	$374.83	$132.92	$241.91	$14,258.09
2	$374.83	$130.70	$244.13	$14,013.96
3	$374.83	$128.46	$246.37	$13,767.59
4	$374.83	$126.20	$248.63	$13,518.96
5	$374.83	$123.92	$250.91	$13,268.05

23.

Payment Number	Amount of Payment	Interest for Period	Portion to Principal	Principal at End of Period
0	—	—	—	$35,000.00
1	$1196.30	$408.33	$787.97	$34,212.03
2	$1196.30	$399.14	$797.16	$33,414.87
3	$1196.30	$389.84	$806.46	$32,608.41
4	$1196.30	$380.43	$815.87	$31,792.54
5	$1196.30	$370.91	$825.39	$30,967.15

Section 12.5 Exercises (Page 504)

1. $2601.00 **3.** $889.68 **5.** $1240.14 **9.** $802.53 **11.** $2050.96
13. $1319.95 **15.** Yes, qualified **17.** Monthly payment = 122.5 ×
$9.28 = $1136.80

Payment Number	Total Payment	Interest Payment	Principal Payment	Balance of Principal
0	—	—	—	$122,500.00
1	$1136.80	$765.63	$371.17	$122,128.83
2	$1136.80	$763.31	$373.49	$121,755.34

Case Study (Page 510)

1. $495.00; $419.94; $1104.43; $149.45; $2168.82 **2.** $2168.82;
$215.00; $290.00; $279.17; $2952.99 **3.** $392.32; $285.61;
$654.33; $149.45; $187.00; $290.00; $279.17; $2237.88 **4.** $715.11

Case in Point Summary Exercise (Page 512)

1. $1715 **2.** $229,875; $76,625 **3.** $100,000 **4.** $1530.45 **5.** $430.45

Chapter 12 Test (Page 514)

1. $20,900 **2.** $932.56 **3.** 11.75% **4.** 12.25% **5.** 11% **6.** $4364.31
7. (a) $235.51 (b) $2502.17 **8.** $4811.72 **9.** $1924.50 **10.** $1805.40
11. $1209.69 **12.** $518.29 **13.** (a) $6365.56 (b) $1,281,800.80
14. (a) $1398.24 (b) $360,577.60

Cumulative Review: Chapters 11–12 (Page 516)

1. $9214.23; $1214.23 **3.** $17,855.03; $2855.03 **5.** $13,367.29
7. $403.45 **9.** (a) $11,957.94 (b) $27,257.87 **11.** (a) $2345 (b) 15
(c) 1.5% **13.** (a) $3098.48 (b) $298.48 (c) $2300 (d) 12.00%
15. (a) $2118.14 (b) $3017.68 **17.** (a) $14,570 (b) $14,952.46
19. $133,270.55

CHAPTER 13

Section 13.1 Exercises (Page 524)

1. $34,000 **3.** $71,150 **5.** $325,125 **7.** .3% **9.** 8% **11.** .2%
13. (a) $4.84 (b) $48.40 (c) 48.4 **15.** (a) 7.08% (b) $7.08
(c) 70.8 **19.** $5861.60 **21.** $5384.40 **23.** $5978.70 **25.** $6295.08
27. $460,525 **29.** (a) The second parish (b) $75.24

Section 13.2 Exercises (Page 538)

1. $23,131 **3.** $21,710 **5.** $44,533 **7.** $21,790 **9.** $27,340; $3676
11. $53,450; $7167.50 **13.** $74,080; $10,770 **15.** $69,762;
$13,568.11 **17.** $66,750; $11,455 **19.** $2442 tax refund
21. $645.56 tax refund **23.** $6257.50 due **27.** $8936 **29.** $9092.50
31. $6472.75 **33.** $5538.05

Section 13.3 Exercises (Page 547)

1. $1700 **3.** $2194.50 **5.** $9298.72 **7.** $70,344.83 **9.** $19,850
11. $36,500 **13.** $60,000; $20,000 **15.** $292,500; $260,000;
$97,500 **17.** $18,804 **19.** $702.65 **23.** (a) $136,986.30

(b) $43,013.70 **25.** (a) $30,681.82 (b) $14,318.18
27. A: $274,000 **B:** $182,666.67 **C:** $91,333.33 **29. 1:** $125,000
2: $41,666.67 **3:** $83,333.33 **31.** (a) $218,750 (b) **A:** $87,500;
B: $131,250

Section 13.4 Exercises (Page 556)

1. $790 **3.** $932 **5.** $869 **9.** $911 **11.** $1201.20 **13.** (a) $25,000;
(b) $11,500 **15.** (a) $4300; (b) $850 **17.** (a) $1778; (b) $6936;
(c) $100,000; (d) $15,100

Section 13.5 Exercises (Page 563)

1. $256; $130.56; $66.56; $23.24 **3.** $849.10; $433.04; $220.77;
$77.10 **5.** $516.80; $263.57; $134.37; $46.93 **7.** $319.50;
$162.95; $83.07; $29.01 **9.** $2973.10; $1516.28; $773.01;
$269.96 **13.** $364 **15.** (a) $100.50 (b) $384 **17.** $566 per year;
$16,980 **19.** (a) $444.72 (b) $226.72 (c) $79.18

Case Study (Page 568)

1. $11,790.75 **2.** $39,940.90 **3.** $439.88 **4.** $52,171.03 **5.** $1328.97

Case in Point Summary Exercise (Page 569)

1. $5952 **2.** $2380.40 **3.** $6063 **4.** $831 **5.** $945 **6.** $13,791

Chapter 13 Test (Page 571)

1. $5.76; $57.60 **2.** 9.35%; $9.35 **3.** $55,095; $9898.75
4. $17,087; $1713.05 **5.** $2290.74 **6.** $9382.40 **7.** $4226.50
8. $8449.14 **9.** $42,613.64 **10. A:** $36,000 **B:** $21,600 **C:** $14,400
11. $1647.35 **12.** $696 **13.** $158.48; $80.82; $41.20; $14.39
14. $1940.80; $989.81; $504.61; $176.22 **15.** (a) $678 (b) $417
16. $6400 to repair his truck

CHAPTER 14

Section 14.1 Exercises (Page 578)

1. 20% **3.** 12.5% **5.** 5% **7.** $6\frac{2}{3}$% **9.** 1.25% **11.** 2% **13.** $450
15. $800 **17.** $840 **19.** $2850 **21.** $5000 **23.** $2775 **25.** $73,000
27.

Year	Computation	Amount of Depreciation	Accumulated Depreciation	Book Value
0	—	—	—	$12,000
1	($33\frac{1}{3}$% × $9000)	$3000	$3000	$9000
2	($33\frac{1}{3}$% × $9000)	$3000	$6000	$6000
3	($33\frac{1}{3}$% × $9000)	$3000	$9000	$3000

29.

Year	Computation	Amount of Depreciation	Accumulated Depreciation	Book Value
0	—	—	—	$51,200
1	($16\frac{2}{3}$% × $37,200)	$6,200	$6,200	$45,000
2	($16\frac{2}{3}$% × $37,200)	$6,200	$12,400	$38,800
3	($16\frac{2}{3}$% × $37,200)	$6,200	$18,600	$32,600
4	($16\frac{2}{3}$% × $37,200)	$6,200	$24,800	$26,400
5	($16\frac{2}{3}$% × $37,200)	$6,200	$31,000	$20,200
6	($16\frac{2}{3}$% × $37,200)	$6,200	$37,200	$14,000

33. (a) $55,000 depreciation (b) $1,025,000 book value
35. (a) 12.5% (b) $9000 (c) $79,000

Section 14.2 Exercises (Page 585)

1. 40% **3.** 25% **5.** $13\frac{1}{3}$% **7.** 20% **9.** $33\frac{1}{3}$% **11.** 4% **13.** $3000
15. $9000 **17.** $1900 **19.** $3360 **21.** $1215 **23.** $6834 **25.** $750

27.

Year	Computation	Amount of Depreciation	Accumulated Depreciation	Book Value
0	—	—	—	$14,400
1	(50% × $14,400)	$7200	$7,200	$7,200
2	(50% × $7,200)	$3600	$10,800	$3,600
3	(50% × $3,600)	$1800	$12,600	$1,800
4		$1800*	$14,400	$0

*To depreciate to $0 scrap value.

29.

Year	Computation	Amount of Depreciation	Accumulated Depreciation	Book Value
0	—	—	—	$14,000
1	(40% × $14,000)	$5600	$5,600	$8,400
2	(40% × $8,400)	$3360	$8,960	$5,040
3	(40% × $5,040)	$2016	$10,976	$3,024
4		$524*	$11,500	$2,500
5		$0	$11,500	$2,500

*To depreciate to $2500 scrap value.

33. $1153 **35.** $8476 **37. (a)** 25% **(b)** $1450 **(c)** $4425 **(d)** $1375

Section 14.3 Exercises (Page 592)

1. $\frac{4}{10}$ **3.** $\frac{6}{21}$ **5.** $\frac{7}{28}$ **7.** $\frac{10}{55}$ **9.** $1640 **11.** $10,000 **13.** $7500 **15.** $7700
17. $2700 **19.** $890 **21.** $2400

23.

Year	Computation	Amount of Depreciation	Accumulated Depreciation	Book Value
0	—	—	—	$3900
1	$\left(\frac{3}{6} \times \$3420\right)$	$1710	$1710	$2190
2	$\left(\frac{2}{6} \times \$3420\right)$	$1140	$2850	$1050
3	$\left(\frac{1}{6} \times \$3420\right)$	$570	$3420	$480

25.

Year	Computation	Amount of Depreciation	Accumulated Depreciation	Book Value
0	—	—	—	$10,800
1	$\left(\frac{6}{21} \times \$8400\right)$	$2400	$2400	$8,400
2	$\left(\frac{5}{21} \times \$8400\right)$	$2000	$4400	$6,400
3	$\left(\frac{4}{21} \times \$8400\right)$	$1600	$6000	$4,800
4	$\left(\frac{3}{21} \times \$8400\right)$	$1200	$7200	$3,600
5	$\left(\frac{2}{21} \times \$8400\right)$	$800	$8000	$2,800
6	$\left(\frac{1}{21} \times \$8400\right)$	$400	$8400	$2,400

29. $370,909 **31.** $4887 **33. (a)** $\frac{8}{36}$ **(b)** $2360 **(c)** $10,620
(d) $4750

Supplementary Exercises (Page 596)

1. $2,050,000 **3.** $7400 **5.** $1242 **7.** $3760 **9.** $63,180
11. $13,680; $10,260; $6840; $3420 **13.** $37,575 **15.** $10,080
17. (a) $5580 **(b)** $5220

Section 14.4 Exercises (Page 603)

1. $.75 **3.** $.029 **5.** $.24 **7.** $30 **9.** $25,300 **11.** $17,280 **13.** $2775
15. $3108

19.

Year	Computation	Amount of Depreciation	Accumulated Depreciation	Book Value
0	—	—	—	$6800
1	(1350 × $1.26)	$1701	$1701	$5099
2	(1820 × $1.26)	$2293	$3994	$2806
3	(730 × $1.26)	$920	$4914	$1886
4	(1100 × $1.26)	$1386	$6300	$500

Section 14.5 Exercises (Page 609)

1. 19.2% **3.** 6.56% **5.** 20.00% **7.** 3.636% **9.** 5.76% **11.** 2.564%
13. $1751 **15.** $43,050 **17.** $4800 **19.** $6254 **21.** $16,920
23. $2756 **25.** $122,084

27.

Year	Computation	Amount of Depreciation	Accumulated Depreciation	Book Value
0	—	—	—	$10,980
1	(33.33% × $10,980)	$3660	$3,660	$7,320
2	(44.45% × $10,980)	$4881	$8,541	$2,439
3	(14.81% × $10,980)	$1626	$10,167	$813
4	(7.41% × $10,980)	$813*	$10,980	$0

*due to rounding in prior years

29.

Year	Computation	Amount of Depreciation	Accumulated Depreciation	Book Value
0	—	—	—	$122,700
1	(10% × $122,700)	$12,270	$12,270	$110,430
2	(18% × $122,700)	$22,086	$34,356	$88,344
3	(14.4% × $122,700)	$17,669	$52,025	$70,675
4	(11.52% × $122,700)	$14,135	$66,160	$56,540
5	(9.22% × $122,700)	$11,313	$77,473	$45,227
6	(7.37% × $122,700)	$9,043	$86,516	$36,184
7	(6.55% × $122,700)	$8,037	$94,553	$28,147
8	(6.55% × $122,700)	$8,037	$102,590	$20,110
9	(6.56% × $122,700)	$8,049	$110,639	$12,061
10	(6.55% × $122,700)	$8,037	$118,676	$4,024
11	(3.28% × $122,700)	$4,024*	$122,700	$0

*due to rounding in prior years

33. $4855 **35.** $490 **37. Year 1:** $21,165; **Years 2–5:** $22,050

Case Study (Page 615)

1. $114,000 **2.** $61,560 **3.** $228,000 **4.** $57,000 straight-line; $24,624
double-declining-balance; $38,000 sum-of-the-years'-digits

Case in Point Summary Exercise (Page 616)

1. $13,300 **2.** $5724 **3.** MACRS; 5-year property **4.** $23,670;
$37,872; $22,723 **5.** $34,085 **6.** 71.20% **7.** No additional depre-
ciation is allowed

Chapter 14 Test (Page 617)

1. 25%; 50%; $\frac{4}{10}$ **2.** 20%; 40%; $\frac{5}{15}$ **3.** $12\frac{1}{2}$; 25%; $\frac{8}{36}$ **4.** 5%; 10%;
$\frac{20}{210}$ **5.** $7900 **6.** $21,375 **7. Year 1:** $2700; **Year 2:** $2025; **Year 3:**
$1350; **Year 4:** $675 **8.** $4788 **9.** $43,000 **10.** $5702 **11. (a)** Year 1:
$4836; Year 2: $2666; Year 3: $3007; Year 4: $4712 **(b)** Year 1:
$15,264; Year 2: $12,598; Year 3: $9591; Year 4: $4879
12. $2,443,924

CHAPTER 15

Section 15.1 Exercises (Page 623)

1. (a) $316,350 **(b)** $88,050 **(c)** $65,350 **3.** Gross Sales, $852,300; Returns, $42,800; Net Sales, $809,500; Inventory, January 1, $174,690; Cost of Goods Purchased, $345,790; Freight, $18,107; Total Cost of Goods Purchased, $363,897; Total of Goods Available for Sale, $538,587; Inventory, December 31, $158,200; Cost of Goods Sold, $380,387; Gross Profit, $429,113; Salaries and Wages, $168,240; Rent, $48,200; Advertising, $24,300; Utilities, $11,600; Taxes on Inventory, Payroll, $13,880; Miscellaneous Expenses, $21,900; Total Expenses, $288,120; Net Income before Taxes, $140,993; Income Taxes, $34,800; Net Income, $106,193

Section 15.2 Exercises (Page 629)

1. 45.2%; 32.6% **3.** 50.7%; 29.2% **5.** Cost of Goods Sold, 67.1%, 67.9%; Gross Profit, 32.9%, 32.1%; Wages, 12.5%, 12.3%; Rent, 2.5%, 2.4%; Advertising, 1.5%, 1.4%; Total Expenses, 24.6%, 23.5%; Net Income before Taxes, 8.3%, 8.6% **9.** Gross Sales, 100.3%, 100.7%; Returns, .3%, .7%; Net Sales, $1,850,000, $1,680,000; Cost of Goods Sold, 59.6%, 56.5%; Gross Profit, 40.4%, 43.5%; Wages, 13.6%, 14.8%; Rent, 4.4%, 4.6%; Advertising, 6.0%, 7.3%; Utilities, 1.7%, 1.0%; Taxes on Inv., Payroll, .9%, 1.1%; Miscellaneous Expenses, 3.4%, 3.5%; Total Expenses, 30.1%, 32.2%; Net Income before Taxes, $192,000, 10.4%, $189,000, 11.3% **11.** 64.8%, 35.2%, 23.4%, 11.7%, 7.9%, 4.9%, 1.8%

Section 15.3 Exercises (Page 634)

1. Cash, $273; Notes Receivable, $312; Accounts Receivable, $264; Inventory, $180; Total Current Assets, $1029; Land, $466; Buildings, $290; Fixtures, $28; Total Plant Assets, $784; Total Assets, $1813; Notes Payable, $312; Accounts Payable, $63; Total Current Liabilities, $375; Mortgages Payable, $212; Long-Term Notes Payable, $55; Total Long-Term Liabilities, $267; Total Liabilities, $642; Owners' Equity, $1171; Total Liabilities and Owners' Equity, $1813

Section 15.4 Exercises (Page 640)

1. Cash, 13%, 13.1%; Notes Receivable, 2%, 1.9%; Accounts Receivable, 37%, 37.5%; Inventory, 38.3%, 37.5%; Total Current Assets, $361,000, 90.3%, $288,000, 90%; Land, 2.5%, 2.5%; Buildings, 3.5%, 3.4%; Fixtures, 3.8%, 4.1%; Total Plant Assets, $39,000, 9.8%, $32,000, 10%; Total Assets, $400,000, $320,000; Accounts Payable, .8%, 1.3%; Notes Payable, 50.3%, 47.5%; Total Current Liabilities, $204,000, 51%, $156,000, 48.8%; Mortgages Payable, 5%, 5%; Long-Term Notes Payable, 14.5%, 13.1%; Total Long-Term Liabilities, $78,000, 19.5%, $58,000, 18.1%; Total Liabilities, $282,000, 70.5%, $214,000, 66.9%; Owners' Equity, 29.5%, 33.1%; Total Liabilities and Owners' Equity, $400,000, 100%, $320,000, 100% **3. (a)** 1.77 **(b)** 1.02 **(c)** No, current ratio is low **5. (a)** 1.79 **(b)** .62 **(c)** No, acid-test ratio is low **7.** 2.13; 1.27 **9.** 6.1% **11.** .91; .37; not healthy; very low liquidity

Case Study (Page 647)

1. Gross Sales, $238,300; Returns, $3,600; Net Sales, $234,700; Inventory, Jan. 1, $53,400; Cost of Goods Purchased, $98,500; Freight, $2,300; Total Cost of Goods Purchased, $100,800; Total of Goods Available for Sale, $154,200; Inventory, Dec. 31, $48,900; Cost of Goods Sold, $105,300; Gross Profit, $129,400; Salaries and Wages, $78,690; Rent & Utilities, $11,800;

Advertising, $3,200; Miscellaneous Expenses, $4,800; Total Expenses; $98,490, Net Income Before Taxes, $30,910; Income taxes, $3,600; Net Income After Taxes, $27,310 **2.** Cash, $62,000; Accounts Receivable, $10,700; Inventory, $48,900; Total Current Assets, $121,600; Land and Buildings, $0; Improvements, $41,500; Total Plant Assets, $41,500; Total Assets, $163,100; Notes Payable, $4,300; Accounts Payable, $14,800; Total Current Liabilities, $19,100; Long-term Notes Payable, $12,300; Mortgages, $0; Total Long-Term Liabilities, $12,300; Total Liabilities, $31,400; Owners' equity, $131,700; Total Liabilities and Owners' Equity, $163,100

Case in Point Summary Exercise (Page 649)

1. Gross Sales, $834,200; Returns, $4,500; Net Sales, $829,700; Inventory, Jan. 1, $84,200; Cost of Goods Purchased, $346,500; Freight, $9,100; Total Cost of Goods Purchased, $355,600; Total of Goods Available for Sale, $439,800; Inventory, Dec. 31, $96,200; Cost of Goods Sold, $343,600; Gross Profit, $486,100; Salaries and Wages, $193,200; Rent & Utilities, $68,900; Advertising, $13,900; Insurance and Payroll taxes, $19,400; Miscellaneous Expenses, $18,700; Total Expenses, $314,100; Net Income Before Taxes $172,000; Income taxes, $37,800; Net Income After Taxes, $134,200 **2.** Cash, $84,500; Accounts Receivable, $2,100; Inventory, $96,200; Total Current Assets, $182,800; Land and Buildings, $186,500; Improvements, $82,100; Total Plant Assets, $268,600; Total Assets, $451,400; Notes Payable, $4,900; Accounts Payable, $58,400; Total Current Liabilities, $63,300; Long-term Notes Payable, $0; Mortgages, $134,200; Total Long-Term Liabilities, $134,200; Total Liabilities, $197,500; Owners' equity, $253,900; Total Liabilities and Owners' Equity $451,400

Chapter 15 Test (Page 651)

1. Gross Sales, $756,300; Returns, $285; Net Sales, $756,015; Inventory, January 1, $92,370; Cost of Goods Purchased, $465,920; Freight, $1,205; Total Cost of Goods Purchased, $467,125; Total of Goods Available for Sale, $559,495; Inventory, December 31, $82,350; Cost of Goods Sold, $477,145; Gross Profit, $278,870; Salaries and Wages, $84,900; Rent, $42,500; Advertising, $2,800; Utilities, $18,950; Taxes on Inventory and Payroll, $4,500; Miscellaneous Expenses, $18,400; Total Expenses, $172,050; Net Income Before Taxes, $106,820; Income Taxes, $25,450; Net Income After Taxes, $81,370 **2.** Net Sales, $35,000, 58.3%; Cost of Goods Sold, $23,000, 57.5%; Gross Profit, $4,000, 33.3% **3.** Cost of Goods Sold, $875, 72.9%, 76.8%; Gross Profit, 27.1%, 23.2%; Net Income, 9.3%, 6.3%; Wages, 10.8%, 8.5%; Rent, 6%, 2.3%; Total Expenses, 17.8%, 16.9% **4. (a)** 1.38 **(b)** .85 **5. (a)** 1.05 **(b)** .37 **6.** 30.0% **7.** 26.1%

CHAPTER 16

Section 16.1 Exercises (Page 659)

1. 6.9 billion **3.** 5,152,000,000 Asians; 478,400,000 Americans **5.** It has increased. **7.** 4 **9.** 6 **11.** 5

13.

Employees with College Credits

15. 23 **17.** 7 **19.** 2 **21.** 1 **23.** 2 **25.** 6

27.

Weekly Sales for the Chain

29. 20 **31.** 1 **33.** 13 **35.** 17 **37.** 8 **39.** 38 **41.** 42 **43.** 20% **45.** 36°
47. 5%, 18°

49.

Angela Rueben's Expenses

51. 20%

53.

Revenues for Armstrong Publishing

55.

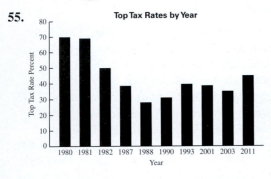

Top Tax Rates by Year

Section 16.2 Exercises (Page 669)

1. 2.5 **3.** 60.3 **5.** 27,955 **7.** 8.8 **11.** 12.3 **13.** 17.2 **15.** 118.8 **17.** 2.6
19. 114 **21.** 130 **23.** 44 **25.** 21% **27.** 64 **29.** Bimodal with modes
32 and 38 **31.** 34.11 **33.** 34.38

Case Study (Page 675)

1. Store 1 mean = $7.4; Store 2 mean = $8.2; Store 1 median = $7.5;
Store 2 median = $8.2; Store 1 has no mode; Store 2 mode = $8.2
2.

Sales at The Soft Touch

3. Sales at Store 2 are growing faster than at Store 1.

Case in Point Summary Exercise (Page 676)

1. October $7775, $7700; November $9150, $9000; December
$8525, $8900
2. In the United States, sales at many restaurants are typically
high during mid-to late November associated with shopping for
Christmas and then low during the week of Christmas.

Weekly Sales at Bev's Deli

3.

Sales at Bev's Deli

Chapter 16 Test (Page 677)

1. 1, 3, 10, 3, 2, 1 **2.** 6
3.

Weekly Motor Oil Sales

4. Newsprint, 72°; Ink, 10%; Wire Service, 108°; Salaries, 108°;
Other, 36°
5.

Expenses at Dallas Community College

6. 60% **7.** 230.7 **8.** 18.8 centimeters **9.** $478.90 **10.** 11.3 **11.** 173.7
12. 19 **13.** 41.5 **14.** 8.3 **15.** 54.5 **16.** 47 **17.** no mode **18.** bimodal,
103 and 104

19.

Stein's Fine Furnishings Annual Sales

It appears that the recession had an effect on the business.

20.

Sales Commission for Ted Smith by Quarter for 2011-2013

It appears that Mr. Smith's work was affected.

APPENDICES

Appendix A Exercises (Page A-6)

1. .68 m **3.** 4700 mm **5.** 8900 g **7.** .39 L **9.** 46 kg **11.** 976 g
13. 39.2 yards **15.** 50.3 m **17.** 15.4 feet **19.** 1.1 m
21. 307.5 miles **23.** 1235.7 km **25.** 1.5 pounds **27.** 1861.4 g
29. 85.6 pounds **31.** 200 nickels **33.** .6 g **37.** 40°C **39.** 280°C
41. 37°C **43.** 95°F **45.** 50°F **47.** 275°F
49. Not reasonable **51.** Not reasonable

Appendix B Exercises (Page B-8)

1. 1171.60 **3.** 11,378 **5.** 3905.32 **7.** 255.24 **9.** 15,695 **11.** 31.08
13. 35.42 **15.** 27.63 **17.** 8.1 **19.** 566.1397059 = 566.14 (rounded)
21. .625 = .63 (rounded) **23.** 30.57004831 = 30.57 (rounded)
25. 0.915966387 = .92 (rounded) **27.** $5\frac{6}{11}$
29. .493714286 = .49 (rounded) **33.** $44,162.80
35. (a) $1164.05 **(b)** $95.13 **37.** $214,008 **39.** $13,400 **41.** 59%

Appendix C Exercises (Page C-5)

1. $39,019.50 **3.** $8929.13 **5.** $2676.84 **7.** $1.5% **9.** $858.89
11. 24 **13.** FV = $31.651.09 **15.** PMT = $839.37
17. n = 26 **19.** i = 8.5%

Appendix D Exercises (Page D-5)

1. p^2 **3.** r^3 **5.** x^4 **7.** 49 **9.** 1 **11.** 1 **13.** t^4g^4 **15.** 9^4 **17.** $\dfrac{3^2}{4^2}$

19. x^2y^2 **21.** 5 **23.** 83 **25.** 66 **27.** 20 **29.** 5625 **31.** 1 **33.** 161 **35.** 21
37. 553.2 **39.** 54.2 **41.** $53,928 **43.** $5834.43

Appendix E Exercises (Page E-10)

1. Interest earned; Total Investment **3.** Profit; Sales **5.** Weight of Calf; Age of Calf **7.** Profit; Sales. Total Expenses

9.

Water Height at Monitoring Station on Indus River

11.

Quarterly Profit at Apple Inc.

13.

Sales based on Advertising

15.

Monthly Profit

17.

Weekly Profit Based on Number of Yards Mowed

19.

Monthly Costs at Computer Shoppe

Glossary

401 (k): A retirement plan for individuals working for private-sector companies.

403 (b): A retirement plan for employees of public schools and certain tax-exempt organizations.

A

Absolute, or gross, loss: The loss resulting when the selling price is less than the cost.

Accelerated depreciation: A technique to increase the depreciation taken during the early years of an asset's useful life.

Accelerated mortgages: Mortgages with payoffs of less than 30 years, such as 15, 20, or 25 years.

Accountant: A person who maintains financial data for a firm or individual and then prepares the income tax return.

Accounts payable: A business debt that must be paid.

Accumulated depreciation: A running balance or total of the depreciation to date on an asset.

Acid-test ratio: The sum of cash, notes receivable, and accounts receivable, divided by current liabilities.

ACRS (Accelerated cost recovery system): A depreciation method introduced as part of the Economic Recovery Tax Act of 1981.

Actual rate of interest: The true annual percentage rate that can be used to compare loans.

Actuary: A person who determines insurance premiums.

Addends: The numbers added in an addition problem.

Addition rule: The same number may be added or subtracted on both sides of an equation.

Adjustable rate mortgage: A home loan where the interest rate is adjusted up or down depending on a benchmark interest rate.

Adjusted bank balance: The actual current balance of a checking account after reconciliation.

Adjusted gross income: An individual's or family's income for a year, including all sources of income, and after subtracting certain expenses, such as moving expenses.

Algebraic logic: Rules used by most calculators for entering and evaluating arithmetic expressions.

Allowances: The number of allowances chosen by the taxpayer determines the amount withheld from gross income during the year.

American Express: A widely accepted credit card that requires an annual fee.

Amortization table: A table showing breaking a regular payment into interest and that which reduces debt. It also shows remaining debt.

Amortize: The process of paying off a loan with a sequence of periodic payments over a period of time.

Amount of an annuity: The future value of the annuity.

Amount of depreciation: The dollar amount of depreciation taken. This is usually an annual figure.

Annual meeting: Corporations have annual meetings for stockholders.

Annual percentage rate (APR): The true annual percentage rate which can be used to compare loans. The federal Truth-in-Lending Act requires lenders to state the APR.

Annual percentage rate table: A table used to find the annual percentage rate (APR) on a loan or installment purchase.

Annual rate of depreciation: The percent or fraction of the depreciable amount or declining balance to be depreciated each individual year of an asset's useful life.

Annuity: Periodic payments of a given, fixed amount of money.

Annuity due: An annuity whose payments are made at the beginning of a time period.

APR (Annual percentage rate): The true annual percentage rate that can be used to compare loans. It is required by the federal Truth-in-Lending Act.

"AS OF": A later date that appears on an invoice. The given sales terms may start at this time.

Assessed value: The value of a piece of property. Set by the county assessor, assessed value is used in figuring property taxes.

Assessment rate: The assessed valuation of a property is found by multiplying the fair market value by the assessment rate.

Asset: An item of value owned by a firm.

ATM (Automated teller machine): A machine that allows bank customers to make deposits, withdrawals, and fund transfers.

Automatic savings transfer account: A bank account that automatically transfers funds from one account to another.

Average: *See* mean.

Average cost method: An inventory valuation method whereby the cost of all purchases during a time period is divided by the number of units purchased.

Average daily balance method: A method used to calculate interest on open-end credit accounts.

Average inventory: The sum of all inventories taken divided by the number of times inventory was taken.

Average owner's equity: Sum of owner's equity at the beginning and end of the year divided by 2.

B

Bad check: A check that is not honored because there are insufficient funds in the checking account.

Balance brought forward (Current balance): The amount left in a checking account after previous checks written have been subtracted.

Balanced: In agreement. When the bank statement amount and the depositor's checkbook balance agree, they are balanced.

Balance sheet: A summary of the financial condition of a firm at one point in time.

Bank discount: A bank fee charged on a note. It is subtracted from the face value to find the proceeds loaned.

Banker's interest: A method used to calculate interest by dividing exact number of days by 360.

Banker's ratio: *See* current ratio.

Bank statement: A monthly statement prepared by a bank that lists all charges and deposits to a checking account. Historically banks mailed the statements, but many people now look at their monthly statements on the web.

Bankrupt: A company or individual whose liabilities exceed assets can declare bankruptcy, which is a legal process of working with debtors to pay off debts.

Bar code: A code placed on the side of a product that allows it to be scanned and then recognized and priced by a computer system.

Bar graph: A graph using bars to compare various numbers.

Base: The starting point or reference point or that to which something is being compared.

bbl.: Abbreviation for *barrel*.

Bimodal: A set of data with two modes.

Blank endorsement: A signature on the back of a check by the person to whom the check is made.

Board of directors: A group of people who represent the stockholders of a corporation.

Bodily injury insurance: A type of automobile insurance that protects a driver in case he or she injures someone with a car.

Bond: A contractual promise by a corporation, government entity, or church to repay borrowed money at a specified rate and time.

Book value: The cost of an asset minus depreciation to date.

Break-even point: The cost of an item plus the operating expenses associated with the item. Above this amount, a profit is made; below it, a loss is incurred.

Broker: A person who sells stocks, bonds, and other investments owned by others.

Business account: The type of checking account used by businesses.

bx.: Abbreviation for *box*.

C

C: Roman numeral for 100.

Canceled check: A check is canceled after the amount of the check has been transferred from the payer's bank account into the account of the receiver of the check.

Cancellation: A process used to simplify multiplication and division of fractions.

Capital: The amount of money originally invested in a firm. The difference between the total of all the assets and the total of all the liabilities is called the capital or net worth.

Capital gains: Profits made on investments such as stocks or real estate.

cart.: Abbreviation for *carton*.

Cash discount: A discount offered by the seller allowing the buyer to take a discount if payment is made within a specified period of time.

Cashier's check: A check written by a financial institution, such as a bank, that is guaranteed by the institution.

Cash value: Money that has built up in an ordinary life insurance policy.

Casualty or theft loss: Loss due to a casualty (e.g. fire or theft) that is deductible on a personal income tax return.

Catastrophic event: A major (harmful) event that occurs rarely. For example, a financial crisis is a catastrophic event that can devastate the finances of families.

Centi-: A prefix used in the metric system meaning hundredth. (For example, a centiliter is one one-hundredth of a liter.)

Centimeter: One one-hundredth of a meter. There are 2.54 centimeters to an inch.

Central tendency: The middle of a set of data.

Certificate of deposit (CD): A savings account in which a minimum amount of money must be deposited and left for a minimum period of time.

Chain calculations: Long calculations done on a calculator.

Chain discount: Two or more discounts that are combined into a single discount.

Check 21 Act: A federal law that took effect in October 2004 and allows banks to take electronic photos of all cancelled checks and exchange checks electronically, so the banks no longer have to mail cancelled checks.

Check register: A table usually found in a checkbook that is used by the check writer to list all checks written, deposits and withdrawals made, and ATM transactions.

Checks outstanding: Checks written that have not reached and cleared the bank as of the statement date.

Check stub: A stub attached to a check and retained as a record when a check is written.

Circle graph: A circle divided into parts that are labeled and often colored or shaded to show data.

COD: A method of shipping goods that requires cash on delivery of goods.

Coinsurance: The portion of a loss that must be paid by the insured.

Coin counting fee: A fee charged by banks to count the coins deposited by firms handling a lot of coins such as a vending company.

Collateral: Assets foreclosed on by a lender should the borrower default on payments.

Collision insurance: A form of automobile insurance that pays for car repairs in case of an accident.

Commission: A fee charged by a broker for buying and selling either stocks or bonds.

Commissions: Payments to an employee that represent a certain percent of the total sales produced by the employee's efforts.

Common denominator: Two or more fractions with the same denominator are said to have common denominators.

Common stock: Ownership of a corporation, held in portions called shares.

Comparative balance sheet: An analysis for two or more periods that compares asset categories such as cash.

Comparative income statement: A vertical analysis for two or more years that compares incomes or balance sheet items for each year analyzed.

Comparison graph (Comparative line graph): A graph showing how two or more things change with respect to one another.

Compensatory time (Comp time): Time off given to an employee to compensate for previously worked overtime.

Compound amount: The future value of an investment.

Compounding period: The interval of time at which interest is added to the account. For example, interest compounded quarterly results in interest being added to the account every quarter.

Compound interest: Interest charged or received on both principal and interest.

Comprehensive insurance: A form of automobile insurance that pays for damage to a car caused by fire, theft, vandalism, and weather.

Consolidated statement: A financial statement showing the combined results of all subsidiaries of a firm.

Consumer price index (CPI): A measure of the cost of living calculated by the government and used to estimate inflation.

Continuous inventory systems: Inventory systems that continuously monitor inventory levels.

Conventional loan: A loan made by a bank, savings and loan, or other lending agency that is not guaranteed or insured by the federal government.

Corporation: A form of business that gives the owners limited liability.

Cosign: Signing a loan with someone else. Parents sometimes cosign at the bank on a car loan applied for by their son or daughter. The cosigner must pay back the loan if the primary borrower does not.

Cost: The total cost of an item, including shipping, insurance, and other charges. Most often, the cost is the basis for calculating depreciation of an asset.

Cost (Cost price): The price paid to the manufacturer or supplier after trade and cash discounts have been taken. This price includes transportation and insurance charges.

Cost of goods sold: The amount paid by a firm for the goods it sold during the time period covered by an income statement.

Cost of living index: A measure of the cost of living calculated by the government and used to estimate inflation. It is the same as the consumer price index or CPI.

Country club billing method: A billing method that provides copies of original charge receipts to the customer.

cpm.: Abbreviation for *cost per thousand*.

Credit card (transactions): The purchase or sale of goods or services using a credit card in place of cash or a check.

Credit history: The history built up by an individual when purchasing things and making payments. A lender checks a person's credit history before making a loan.

Credit score: Three national credit-reporting agencies (Equifax, TransUnion, and Experian) keep financial records on U.S. citizens and calculate a credit score on each indicating the credit-worthiness of that individual. Also called a FICO score.

Credit union: A financial institution similar to a bank, except that it is owned by its member customers.

Credit union share draft account: A credit union account that may be used as a checking account.

Cross-products: The equal products obtained when each numerator of a proportion is multiplied by the opposite denominator.

cs.: Abbreviation for *case*.

ct.: Abbreviation for *crate*.

ctn.: Abbreviation for *carton*.

Current assets: Cash or items that can be converted into cash within a given period of time, such as a year.

Current liability: Debts that must be paid by a firm within a given period of time, such as a year.

Current ratio: The quotient of current assets and current liabilities.

Current yield: The annual dividend per share of stock divided by the current price per share.

cwt.: Abbreviation for *per hundredweight* or *per one hundred pounds*.

D

Daily interest charge: The amount of interest charged per day on a loan.

Daily overtime: The amount of overtime worked in a day.

Debit card: A card that results in a debit to a bank account when the card is used for a purchase.

Decimal: A number written with a decimal point, such as 4.3 or 7.22.

Decimal equivalent: A decimal that has the same value as a fraction.

Decimal point: The starting point in the decimal system (.).

Decimal system: The numbering system based on powers of 10 and using the 10 one-place numbers 0, 1, 2, 3, 4, 5, 6, 7, 8, and 9, which are called *digits*.

Declining-balance depreciation: An accelerated depreciation method.

(200%) Declining-balance method: An accelerated method of depreciation using twice, or 200% of, the straight-line rate.

Decrease problem (Difference problem): A percentage problem in which something is taken away from the base. It may require you to find the base.

Decreasing term insurance: A form of life insurance in which the insured pays a fixed premium until age 60 or 65, with the amount of life insurance decreasing periodically.

Deductible: An amount paid by the insured, with the balance of the loss paid by the insurance company.

Deductions: Amounts that are subtracted from the gross earnings of an employee to arrive at the amount of money the employee actually receives.

Defaulting on debt: Failure to pay back a debt.

Deficit: Refers to a shortfall in revenue. The U.S. government currently has large deficits.

Deflation: Occurs when prices of goods and services fall over time.

Denominator: The number below the line in a fraction. For example, in the fraction $\frac{7}{9}$, 9 is the denominator.

Dependents: An extra deduction is allowed on income taxes for each dependent.

Deposits in transit: Deposits that have been made but have not yet been recorded by a bank.

Deposit slip: A slip for listing all currency and checks that are part of a deposit into a bank account.

Depreciable amount: The amount of an asset's value that can be depreciated.

Depreciation: The decrease in value of an asset caused by normal use, aging, or obsolescence.

Depreciation schedule: A schedule or table showing the depreciation rate, amount of depreciation, book value, and accumulated depreciation for each year of an asset's life.

Difference (Remainder): The answer in a subtraction problem.

Differential piece rate: A rate paid per item that depends on the number of items produced.

Digits: One-place numbers in the decimal system. They are 0, 1, 2, 3, 4, 5, 6, 7, 8, and 9.

Direct competitor: A firm that produces products or offers services very similar to another company.

Direct deposit: Allows deposits (such as payroll) to be made directly into your account.

Direct payment: Allows you to authorize electronic payments from your account.

Disability coverage: Insurance coverage in the event of a disability.

Discount: (1) To reduce the price of an item. (2) The amount subtracted from the face value of a note to find the proceeds loaned.

Discount broker: A stockbroker who charges a reduced fee to customers (and, generally, reduced services).

Discount date: The last date on which a cash discount may be taken.

Discounting a note: Cashing or selling a note before the note is due from the maker.

Discount method of interest: A method of calculating interest on a loan by subtracting the interest from the amount of the loan. The borrower receives the amount borrowed less the discounted interest.

Discount period: The discount period is the period from the time of sale of a note to the note's due date.

Discount rate: The discount rate is a percent that is multiplied by the face value and time to find bank discount.

Discover: A credit card that sometimes pays the cardholder back a percentage of the amount charged.

Distributive property: The property that states the product of the sum of two numbers equals the sum of the individual products; that is $a(b + c) = ab + ac$.

Dividend: (1) The number being divided by another number in a division problem. (2) A return on an investment; money paid by a company to the holders of stock.

Divisor: The number being divided into the dividend.

Dormant account fee: A fee charged by a bank for an account that is no longer in use.

Double-declining balance: A method of accelerated depreciation that doubles depreciation in the early years compared to straight-line depreciation.

Double time: Twice the regular hourly rate. A premium often paid for working holidays and Sunday.

Dow Jones Industrial Average: A frequently quoted average price of the stocks of 30 large industrial companies.

doz.: Abbreviation for *dozen*.

Draw: A draw is an advance on future earnings.

Drawing account: An account from which a salesperson can receive payment against future commissions.

drm.: Abbreviation for *drum*.

E

ea.: Abbreviation for *each*.

Effective rate: The true rate of interest.

Effective rate of interest: The true annual percentage rate that can be used to compare loans. It is required by the federal Truth-in-Lending Act.

Electronic banking: Banking activities that take place over a network, such as the World Wide Web.

Electronic bill pay: Allows bills to be paid using the Internet.

Electronic commerce: Purchases that take place over a network, such as the World Wide Web.

Electronic funds transfer: Moving money electronically over a network, such as the World Wide Web.

Electronic payment: Bills that are paid using the Internet.

Electronic product code: A tag on a product that includes information about that product. It may succeed the bar code.

End-of-month dating (EOM): A system of cash discounts in which the time period begins at the end of the month the invoice is dated. *Proximo* and *prox.* have the same meaning.

Endowment policy: A life insurance policy guaranteeing the payment of a fixed amount of money to a given individual whether or not the insured person lives.

Equation: Two algebraic expressions that are equal to one another.

Escrow account into which monies are paid: *See* impound account.

Exact interest: A method of calculating interest based on 365 days per year.

Exchange traded funds (ETFs): These funds are similar to mutual funds except they are not as actively managed. A particular ETF tries to match the performance of an index such as the Dow Jones Averages or perhaps a market sector such as energy.

Executive officers: The top few officers in a corporation.

Expenses: The costs a firm must pay to operate and sell its goods or services.

Extension total: The number of items purchased times the price per unit.

Extra dating (ex., x): Extra time allowed in determining the net payment date of a cash discount.

F

Face value: The amount shown on the face of a note.

Face value of a bond (Par value of a bond): The amount the company has promised to repay.

Face value of a policy: The amount of insurance provided by the insurance company.

Factoring: The process of selling accounts receivable for cash.

Factors: Companies that buy accounts receivable.

Fair Labor Standards Act: A federal law that sets the minimum wage and also a 40-hour workweek.

Fair market value: The price for which a piece of property could reasonably be expected to be sold in the market.

FAS (Free alongside ship): A method of shipping goods in which the seller pays for transportation of the goods to the port from which they will be shipped. The buyer of the goods must pay for all costs in moving the goods from the shipping port to his facility.

Federal Insurance Contributions Act (FICA): An emergency measure passed by Congress in the 1930s that established the so-called social security tax. *See* FICA tax.

Federal Reserve Bank: Today, all banks are part of the Federal Reserve system. The Federal Reserve is our national bank.

Federal Truth-in-Lending Act: An act passed in 1969 that requires all interest rates to be given as comparable percents.

Federal Unemployment Tax Act (FUTA): An Act that requires employers to pay an unemployment insurance tax. The tax is paid to the federal government.

FHA loan: A real estate loan that is insured by the Federal Housing Administration, an agency of the federal government.

FICA tax (Social Security tax): The amount of money deducted from the paychecks of almost all employees, used by the federal government to pay pensions to retired people, survivors' benefits, and disability.

FICO: Three national credit-reporting agencies (Equifax, Trans Union, and Experian) keep financial records on U.S. citizens and calculate a credit score on each indicating the credit-worthiness of that individual. Also called a credit score.

FIFO: A method of inventory accounting in which the first items received are considered to be the first ones shipped.

Finance charge: The difference between the cost of something paid for in installments and the cash price.

Financial ratio: A number found using financial data that is used to compare different companies within the same industry.

Fixed assets: Assets owned by a firm that will not be converted to cash within a year.

Fixed liabilities: Items that will not be paid off within a year.

Fixed-rate loan: A loan made at a fixed, stated rate of interest.

Flat-fee checking account: A checking account in which the bank supplies check printing, a bank charge card, and other services for a fixed charge per month.

Float: The time between an actual deposit to an account and the moment those funds are available for use.

Floating decimal: A feature on most calculators that positions the decimal point where it should be in the final answer.

FOB (Free on board): A notation sometimes used on an invoice. "Free on board shipping point" means the buyer pays for shipping. "Free on board destination" means the seller pays for shipping.

Foreclose: The process by which a lender takes back the property when payments are not made.

Form 941: The Employer's Quarterly Federal Tax Return form that must be filed by the employer with the Internal Revenue Service.

Form 1040A: The form used by most federal income taxpayers.

Form 1040EZ: A simplified version of the 1040A federal income tax form.

Fraction: An indication of a part of a whole. (For example, $\frac{3}{4}$ means that the whole is divided into 4 parts, of which 3 are being considered.)

Frequency distribution table: A table showing the number of times one or more events occur.

Fringe benefits: Benefits offered by an employer, not including salary, that can include medical, dental, life insurance, and day care for employee's children.

Front-end rounding: Rounding so that all digits are changed to zero except the first digit.

Future amount: The value of an investment at a future date. It is the same as future value.

Future value: The value, at some future date, of an investment.

G

GI (VA) loan: A loan guaranteed by the Veterans Administration and available only to qualified veterans.

Grace period: The period between the due date of a payment and the time the lending institution assesses a penalty for the payment being late, usually a few days after the payment is due.

Gram: The unit of weight in the metric system. (A nickel weighs about 5 grams.)

Graph: A visual presentation of numerical data.

Great Depression: A period of time in the 1930s when global economic activity was greatly reduced and unemployment levels soared to beyond 25% in many countries.

Gr gro. (Great gross): Abbreviation for 12 gross ($144 \times 12 = 1728$).

Gro.: Abbreviation for *gross*.

gross: A dozen dozen, or 144 items.

Gross earnings: The total amount of money earned by an employee before any deductions are taken.

Gross loss: *See* absolute loss.

Gross profit: The difference between the amount received from customers for goods and what the firm paid for the goods.

Gross profit on sales: *See* gross profit.

Gross sales: The total amount of money received from customers for the goods or services sold by the firm.

H

Half-year convention: Method of depreciation used for the first year the property is placed in service.

Head of household: An unmarried person who has dependents can use the head of household category when filing income taxes.

High: The highest price reached by a stock during the day.

Homeowner's policy: An insurance policy that covers a home against fire, theft, and liability.

Horizontal analysis: An analysis that shows the amount of any change from last year to the current year, both in dollars and as a percent.

I

Identity theft: When someone gathers enough information about you to fraudulently establish credit cards or borrow money using your name and personal information.

Impound account (Escrow account): An account at a lending institution into which taxes and insurance are paid on a monthly basis by a borrower on real estate. The lender then pays the tax and insurance bills from this account when they become due.

Improper fraction: A fraction with a numerator larger than the denominator. (For example, $\frac{7}{5}$ is an improper fraction; $\frac{1}{9}$ is not.)

Incentive rate: A payment system based on the amount of work completed.

Income statement: A summary of all the income and expenses involved in running a business for a given period of time.

Income tax: The tax based on income that both individuals and corporations are required to pay to the federal government and sometimes to a state.

Income tax withholding: Federal income tax that the employer withholds from gross earnings.

Income-to-monthly-payment ratio: A ratio used to determine from an income standpoint whether a prospective borrower meets the lender's qualifications.

Increase problem (Amount problem): A percentage problem in which something has been added to the base. Usually the base must be found.

Index fund: A mutual fund that holds the stocks that are in a particular market index such as the Dow Jones Industrial Average.

Indicator words: Key words that help indicate whether to add, subtract, multiply, or divide.

Individual retirement account (IRA): An account designed to help people prepare for future retirement.

Inflation: Inflation results in a continuing rise in the cost of goods and services. *See* consumer price index (CPI).

Installment loan: A loan that is paid off with a sequence of periodic payments.

Insurance: Individuals and firms purchase insurance from insurance companies to protect them in the event of an unexpected loss.

Insured: A person or business that has purchased insurance.

Insurer: The insurance company.

Intangible assets: Assets such as patents, copyrights, or customer lists that have a value that cannot be immediately converted to cash, unlike jewelry or stocks.

Interest: A charge paid for borrowing money or a fee received for lending money.

Interest-bearing checking account: A checking account that earns interest.

Interest-in-advance notes: *See* simple discount note.

Interest rate per compounding period: Interest rates are usually given on an annual basis; however the interest rate per compounding period is needed when making many financial calculations.

Interest rate spread: The difference between the interest rate charged to borrowers and the interest rate paid to depositors.

Internal Revenue Service: The branch of the U.S. federal government responsible for collecting taxes.

Internet banking: Banking done over the Internet.

Inventory: The value of the merchandise that a firm has for sale on the date of balance sheet.

Inventory-to-net-working-capital ratio: Inventory divided by working capital, where working capital is current assets minus current liabilities.

Inventory turnover: The number of times during a certain time period that the average inventory is sold.

Inventory turns: The number of times a year that a firm turns over its average inventory.

Invoice: A printed record of a purchase and sales transaction.

Invoice amount: List price minus trade discounts.

Invoice date: The date an invoice is printed.

Itemized billing method: A billing method that provides an itemization of the customer's charge purchases but not copies of the original charge receipts.

Itemized deductions: Tax deductions, such as interest, taxes, and medical expenses, that are listed individually on a tax return in order to affect the total amount of taxes payable at the end of the year.

J

Joint return: An income tax return filed by both husband and wife.

K

Kilo-: A prefix used in the metric system to represent 1000.

Kilogram: A unit of weight in the metric system meaning 1000 grams. One kilogram is about 2.2 pounds.

Kilometer: One thousand meters. A kilometer is about .6 mile.

L

Late fees: Fees required because payments were made after a specific due date.

Least common denominator: The smallest whole number that all the denominators of two or more fractions evenly divide into. (For example, the least common denominator of $\frac{3}{4}$ and $\frac{5}{6}$ is 12.)

Left side: The left-hand side of an equation.

Level premium: A level premium insurance policy requires the same payment throughout its life.

Liability: An expense that must be paid by a firm.

LIFO: A method of inventory accounting in which the most recent items received are considered to be the first ones shipped.

Like fractions: Fractions with the same denominator.

Like terms: Two terms in an algebraic expression with the same variable can be added together (combined). For example, $2x + 5x = 7x$.

Limited liability: A form of protection that shields a company and its shareholders from having to pay large sums of money in the event that the company loses a lawsuit.

Limited-pay life insurance: Life insurance for which premiums are paid for only a fixed number of years.

Line graph: A graph that uses lines to compare numbers.

Liquid assets: Cash or items that can be converted to cash quickly.

Liquidity: The ability of a firm or individual to raise cash quickly without being forced to sell assets at a loss.

List price: The suggested retail price or final consumer price given by the manufacturer or supplier.

Liter: A measure of volume in the metric system. One liter is a little more than one quart.

Loan amount: The amount of a loan.

Loan reduction schedule: *See* repayment schedule.

Long-term care coverage: Insurance that pays for long-term care such as nursing home expenses.

Long-term liabilities: Money owed by a firm that is not expected to be paid off within a year.

Long-term notes payable: The total of all debts of a firm, other than mortgages, that will not be paid within a year.

Low: The lowest price reached by a stock during the day.

Lowest terms: The form of a fraction if no number except the number 1 divides evenly into both the numerator and denominator.

M

MACRS (Modified accelerated cost recovery system): A depreciation method introduced as part of the Tax Reform Act of 1986.

Maintenance charge per month: The charge to maintain a checking account (usually determined by the minimum balance in the account).

Maker of a note: A person borrowing money from another person.

Manufacturers: Businesses that buy raw materials and component parts and assemble them into products that can be sold.

Margin: The difference between cost and selling price.

Marital status: An individual can claim married, single, or head of household when filing income taxes.

Markdown: A reduction from the original selling price. It may be expressed as a dollar amount or as a percent of the original selling price.

Marketing channels: The path of products and services beginning with the manufacturer and ending with the consumer.

Markup (Margin, Gross profit): The difference between the cost and the selling price.

Markup on cost: Markup that is calculated as a percent of cost.

Markup on selling price: Markup that is calculated as a percent of selling price.

Markup with spoilage: The calculation of markup including deduction for spoiled or unsaleable merchandise.

MasterCard: A credit-card plan (formerly known as Master Charge).

Maturity value: The amount that a borrower must repay on the maturity date of a note.

Mean: The sum of all the numbers divided by the number of numbers.

Median: A number that represents the middle of a group of numbers.

Medical insurance: Insurance providing medical protection in the event of illness, accident, or injury.

Medicare tax: The amount of money deducted from the paychecks of almost all employees, used by the federal government to pay for Medicare.

Memory function: A feature on some calculators that stores results internally in the machine for retrieval and future use.

Merchant batch header ticket: The bank form used by businesses to deposit credit-card transactions.

Meter: A unit of length in the metric system that is slightly longer than one yard.

Metric system: A system of weights and measures based on decimals, used throughout most of the world.

Milli-: A prefix used in the metric system meaning thousandth. (For example, a milligram is one one-thousandth of a gram.)

Millimeter: One one-thousandth of a meter. There are 25.4 millimeters to an inch.

Mills: A way of expressing a real estate tax rate that is based on thousandths of a dollar.

Minuend: The number from which another number (the subtrahend) is subtracted.

Mixed number: A number written as a whole number and a fraction. (For example, $1\frac{3}{4}$ and $2\frac{5}{9}$ are mixed numbers.)

Mode: The number that occurs most often in a group of numbers.

Modified accelerated cost recovery system: *See* MACRS.

Money market account: An interest-bearing account offered by many banks, savings and loans, and brokerage firms. These accounts pay interest but allow the user to withdraw funds without penalty.

Money order: A document that looks similar to a check and is issued by a bank, other financial institution, or a retail store. It is often used in place of cash.

Mortgage: A loan on a home.

Mortgages payable: The balance due on all mortgages owed by a firm.

Multiple carrier insurance: The sharing of risk by several insurance companies.

Multiplicand: A number being multiplied.

Multiplication rule: The same nonzero number may be multiplied or divided on both sides of an equation.

Multiplier: A number doing the multiplying.

Mutual fund: A mutual fund accepts money from many different investors and uses it to purchase stocks or bonds of numerous companies.

N

NASDAQ composite index: A commonly quoted stock index composed of the stock prices of several technology companies.

Negative numbers: Numbers that are the opposite of positive numbers.

Net cost: The cost or price after allowable discounts have been taken. *See* net price.

Net cost equivalent: The decimal number derived from the complement of the single trade discount. This number multiplied by the list price gives the net cost.

Net earnings: The difference between gross margin and expenses. After the cost of goods and operating expenses are subtracted from total sales, the remainder is net profit.

Net income: The difference between gross margin and expenses.

Net pay: The amount of money actually received by an employee after deductions are taken from gross pay.

Net payment date: The date by which an invoice must be paid.

Net price: The list price less any discounts. *See* net cost.

Net proceeds: The amount received from the bank for a discounted note.

Net profit: *See* net earnings.

Net sales: The value of goods purchased by customers after the value of goods returned is subtracted.

Net worth (Capital, Stockholder's equity, Owner's equity): The difference between assets and liabilities.

No-fault insurance: A guarantee of reimbursement (provided by the insured's own insurance company) for medical expenses and costs associated with an accident no matter who is at fault.

Nominal rate: The interest rate stated in connection with a loan. It may differ from the annual percentage rate.

Nonsufficient funds (NSF): When a check is written on an account for which there is an insufficient balance, the check is returned to the depositor for nonsufficient funds.

No scrap value: The value of an item is assumed to be zero at the end of its useful life.

Notes payable: The value of all notes owed by a firm.

Notes receivable: The value of all notes owed to a firm.

NOW account (Negotiable order or withdrawal): Technically a savings account with special withdrawal privileges. It looks the same and is used the same as a checking account.

Numerator: The number above the line in a fraction. (For example, in the fraction $\frac{5}{8}$, 5 is the numerator.)

O

Odd lot: Fewer than 100 shares of stock.

Open-end credit: Credit with no fixed number of payments. The consumer continues making payments until no outstanding balance is owed. Most credit cards offer open-end credit

Operating expenses (Overhead): Expenses of operating a business. Wages, salaries, rent, utilities, and advertising are examples.

Operating loss: The loss resulting when the selling price is less than the break-even point.

Ordered array: A list of numbers arranged from smallest to largest.

Order of operations: The rules that are used when evaluating long arithmetic expressions.

Ordinary annuity: An annuity whose payments are made at the end of a given period of time.

Ordinary dating: A method for calculating the discount date and the net payment date. Days are counted from the date of the invoice.

Ordinary interest: A method of calculating interest, assuming 360 days per year. *See* banker's interest.

Ordinary life insurance (Whole life insurance, Straight life insurance): A form of life insurance whereby the insured pays a constant premium until death or retirement, whichever occurs first. Upon retirement, monthly payments are made by the company to the insured until the death of the insured.

Other expenses: Certain expenses that are deductible on a personal income tax return.

Overdraft: An event that results when there is not enough money in a bank account to cover a check that is written from that account.

Overdraft fee: A fee charged when a bank account is in overdraft.

Overhead: Expenses involved in running a firm. *See* operating expenses.

Over-the-limit fees: Fees charged when the balance on a credit-card account exceeds the account's credit limit.

Overtime: The number of hours worked by an employee in excess of 40 hours per week or 8 hours per day.

Owner's equity: *See* net worth.

P

Part: The result of multiplying the base times the rate.

Partial payment: A payment made on an invoice that is less than the full amount of the invoice.

Partial product: Part of the process of getting the answer in a multiplication problem.

Par value of a bond: *See* face value of a bond.

Passbook account: A type of savings account for day-in and day-out savings.

Pay by phone: Bill payments authorized by phone.

Payee: The person who lends money and will receive repayment on a note.

Payer of a note: A person borrowing money from another person. *See* maker of a note.

Payroll: A record of the hours each employee of a firm worked and the amount of money due each employee for a given pay period.

Payroll card: A card maintained by employers showing the name of employee, dates of pay period, days, times, and hours worked.

Payroll ledger: A chart showing all payroll information.

Percent (Rate): Some parts of a whole: hundredths, or parts of a hundred. (For example, a percent is one one-hundredth. Two percent means two parts of a hundred, or $\frac{2}{100}$.)

Percentage method: A method of calculating income tax withholding that is based on percentages.

Per debit charge: A charge per debit made on an account.

Periodic inventory: A physical inventory taken at regular intervals.

Permanent life insurance: Life insurance that can be continued until death, regardless of the age of the insured.

Perpetual inventory: A continuous inventory system normally involving a computer.

Personal account: The type of checking account used by individuals.

Personal computer banking: Banking using a personal computer and the Internet.

Personal exemption (Exemption): A deduction allowed each taxpayer for each dependent and the taxpayer himself or herself.

Personal identification number (PIN): A lettered or numbered code that allows a person with a credit or debit card to gain access to credit or cash.

Personal property: Property such as a boat, a car, or a stereo.

Photocopying fee: A fee charged by a bank to photocopy records.

Piecework: A method of pay by which an employee receives so much money per item produced or completed.

Plant assets: *See* fixed assets.

Point-of-sale terminal: A machine that allows a customer to make purchases using a credit or debit card.

Policy: A contract outlining the insurance agreement between an insured and an insurance company.

Policy limits: The maximum amount that an insurance company will pay as defined in the policy.

Postdating: Dating in the future; on an invoice, "AS OF" dating.

pr.: Abbreviation for *pair*.

Preferred stock: A type of stock that offers investors certain rights over holders of common stock.

Premium: The amount of money charged for insurance policy coverage.

Premium factor: A factor used to adjust an annual insurance premium to semiannually, quarterly, or monthly.

Premium payment plan: An additional payment for extra service such as overtime.

Prepaid card: A card on which a user has stored monetary value which allows her to make purchases.

Present value: The amount that must be deposited today to generate a specific amount at a specific date in the future.

Price-earnings (PE) ratio: The price per share divided by the annual net income per share of stock.

Prime interest rate: The interest rate banks charge their largest and most financially secure borrowers.

Prime number: A number that can be divided without remainder by exactly two distinct numbers: itself and 1.

Principal: The amount of money either borrowed or deposited.

Privately held corporation: A corporation that has relatively few owners, or perhaps a single owner. Its stock is not traded on a large exchange such as the New York Stock Exchange.

Proceeds: The amount of money a borrower receives after subtracting the discount from the face value of a note.

Product: The answer in a multiplication problem.

Promissory note: A business document in which one person agrees to repay money to another person within a specified amount of time and at a specified rate of interest.

Proper fraction: A fraction in which the numerator is smaller than the denominator. (For example, $\frac{2}{3}$ is a proper fraction; $\frac{9}{5}$ is not.)

Property damage insurance: A type of automobile insurance that pays for damages that the insured causes to the property of others.

Proportion: A mathematical statement that two ratios are equal.

Proximo (Prox.): *See* end-of-month dating.

Publicly held corporations: Corporations that are owned by the public and have stock that trades freely.

Purchase invoice: A list of items purchased, prices charged for the items, and payment terms.

Q

Qualifying for a loan: A person applying for a loan is said to qualify if his or her credit history, income, and financial statement satisfy the requirements of the lending institution.

Quick ratio: The quotient of liquid assets and current liabilities.

Quota: An expected level of production. A premium may be paid for surpassing quota.

Quotient: The answer in a division problem.

R

Radio frequency identification (RFID): A chip that responds to an electronic scan with information about the product.

Rate: Parts of a hundred. *See* percent.

Rate of interest: The percent of interest charged on a loan for a certain time period.

Ratio: A comparison of two numbers often shown as a fraction.

Real estate: Real property such as a home or a parcel of land.

Receipt-of-goods dating (ROG): A method of determining cash discounts in which time is counted from the date that goods are received.

Reciprocal: A fraction formed from a given fraction by interchanging the numerator and denominator.

Reconciliation: The process of checking a bank statement against the depositor's own personal records.

Recourse: Should the maker of a note not pay, the bank may have recourse to collect from the seller of the note.

Recovery classes: Classes used to determine depreciation under the modified accelerated cost recovery system.

Recovery period: The life of property depreciated under the accelerated cost recovery system.

Recovery year: The year of life of an asset when using the MACRS method of depreciation.

Reduced net profit: The situation that occurs when a markdown decreases the selling price to a point that is still above the break-even point.

Refinance: Borrowers can go to a lender and refinance their existing loan with a different interest rate, period, and payment.

Regulation DD: A Federal Reserve System document that specifies how interest paid to savers is to be calculated.

Regulation Z: A Federal Reserve System document that implements the Truth-in-Lending Act.

Renter's coverage: Insurance that covers only the possessions of a renter and not the house or apartment in which the possessions are kept.

Repayment schedule: A schedule showing the amount of payment going toward interest and principal and the remaining debt after each payment has been made.

Repeating decimals: Decimal numbers that do not terminate but that contain a series of digits or numbers that repeat.

Replacement cost: The cost of replacing property that is completely destroyed.

Repossess: The taking back of property by a lender when payments have not been made to the lender.

Residual value: *See* scrap value.

Restricted endorsement: A signature or imprint on the back of a check that limits the ability to cash the check.

Retailer: A business that buys from wholesalers and sells to consumers.

Retail method: A method used to estimate inventory value at cost that utilizes both cost and retail amounts.

Returned check: A check that was deposited and then returned due to lack of funds in the payer's account.

Return on average total assets: Net income divided by average total assets.

Returns: The total value of all goods returned by customers.

Revolving charge account: A charge account that never has to be paid off.

Right side: The right-hand side of an equation.

Risk: The potential of losing part or all of an investment.

Roth IRA: Contributions to a Roth Individual Retirement Account (Roth IRA) are not deductible when made. However, funds in the account grow tax free and withdrawals are not taxed once the account holder reaches a certain age.

Rounding: Writing a number with fewer digits of accuracy.

Rounding whole numbers: Reduction of the number of nonzero digits in a whole number.

Round lot: A multiple of 100 shares of stock.

Rule of 78: A method of calculating a partial refund of interest that has already been added to the amount of a loan. This calculation is done when the loan is paid off early.

S

Salary: A fixed amount of money per pay period.

Salary plus commission: Earnings based on a fixed salary plus a percent of all sales.

Sale price: The price of an item after markdown.

Sales invoice: *See* purchase invoice.

Sales tax: A tax placed on sales to the final consumer. The tax is collected by the state, county, or local government.

Salvage value: *See* scrap value.

Savings account: An interest-paying account that allows day-to-day savings and withdrawals.

Schedule 1: The part of the 1040A federal tax form that is used to list all interest and dividends.

Scrap value (Salvage value): The value of an asset at the end of its useful life. For depreciation purposes, this is often an estimate.

SDI deduction: State disability insurance pays the employee in the event of disability and is paid for by the employee.

Self-employed people: People who work for themselves instead of for the government or for a private company.

Series discount: *See* chain discount.

Shift differential: A premium paid for working a less desirable shift, such as the swing shift or the graveyard shift.

Simple discount note: A note in which the interest is deducted from the face value in advance.

Simple interest: Interest received on only the principal.

Simple interest note: A note in which interest = principal × interest rate × time in years.

Single discount equivalent: A series, or chain, discount expressed as a single discount.

Single return: An income tax return filed by a single person.

Sinking fund: A fund set up to receive periodic payments in order to pay off a debt at some time in the future.

sk.: Abbreviation for *sack*.

Sliding scale: Commissions that are paid at increasing levels as sales increase.

Smart card: A card with a microchip that receives electronic signals, makes calculations, and sends signals. It is sometimes used for identification.

Social Security tax: *See* FICA tax.

Solution: The number that makes an equation true when it is substituted in place of the variable.

Special endorsement: A signature on the back of a check that passes the ownership of the check to someone else.

Specific identification method: An inventory valuation method that identifies the cost of each item.

Split-shift premium: A premium paid for working a split shift, for example, for an employee who is on 4 hours, off 4 hours, and then on 4 hours.

Square root: The square root of 49 is 7, since $7 \times 7 = 49$.

Stafford loan: A loan taken out by college students to help pay tuition.

Standard deduction: A tax preparer may use the higher of the itemized deductions or the standard deduction established by the government.

Stated rate: The interest rate stated in connection with a loan. It may differ from the annual percentage rate.

State income tax: An income tax that is paid to a state government on income earned in that state.

Statement: Usually sent out monthly by the bank, a list of all charges and deposits made against and to a checking account.

Statement fee: A fee charged by some banks for a paper copy of a monthly statement.

Statistics: Refers both to data and to the techniques used in analyzing data.

Stock: A form of ownership in a corporation that is measured in units called *shares*.

Stockbroker: A person who buys and sells stock at the stock exchange.

Stock exchange: An institution where stock shares are bought and sold.

Stockholders: Individuals who own stock in a particular company.

Stockholder's equity: *See* net worth.

Stock ratios: Ratios calculated from the financial statements of a company—used to determine the financial health of the firm.

Stock turnover: *See* inventory turnover.

Stop payment: A request from a depositor that the bank not honor a check that the depositor has written.

Straight commission: A salary that is a fixed percent of sales.

Straight life insurance: *See* ordinary life insurance.

Straight-line depreciation: A depreciation method in which depreciation is spread evenly over the life of the asset.

Substitution: Method for checking the solution to an equation.

Subtrahend: The number being subtracted or taken away in a subtraction problem.

Sum: The total amount; the answer in addition.

Sum-of-the-years'-digits method: An accelerated depreciation method that results in larger amounts of depreciation taken in earlier years of an asset's life.

Supply chain: The chain of businesses and processes involved with moving raw materials, components, and final goods to the end user.

T

Tangible assets: Assets such as a car, machinery, or computers.

Taxable income: Adjusted income subject to taxation.

Tax deduction: Any expense that the Internal Revenue Service allows taxpayers to subtract from adjusted gross income.

Taxes: Individuals and corporations must pay taxes to government entities such as schools, cities, counties, states, and the federal government. Here are a few of the many types of taxes: sales taxes, property taxes, gasoline taxes, income taxes, and estate taxes.

Tax preparation: The preparation of an income tax return that is then sent to the Internal Revenue Service.

T-bill: A short-term note issued by the federal government that pays interest to the holder of the note. Issuing T-bills allows the federal government to raise cash without having to borrow money from a bank and pay interest.

Telephone transfer account: An interest-bearing checking account into which funds may be transferred by the customer over the telephone.

Term: A number, variable, or product or division of a number and a variable, such as $5x$ or $7 + b$.

Term insurance: A form of life insurance providing protection for a fixed length of time.

Term of an annuity: The length of time that an annuity is in effect.

Term of a note: The length of time between the date a note is written and the date the note is due.

Terms: The area of an invoice where cash discounts are indicated if any are offered. The words "terms discount" are often used in place of "cash discount."

Territorial ratings: Ratings used by insurance companies that describe the quality of fire protection in a specific area.

Texting: A method of communicating to a cell phone(s). Some banks communicate with account holders by texting.

Time-and-a-half rate: One and one-half times the normal rate of pay for any hours worked in excess of 40 hours per week or 8 hours per day.

Time card: A card filled out by an employee that shows the number of hours worked by that employee.

Time deposit account: A savings account in which the depositor agrees to leave money on deposit for a certain period of time.

Time rate: Earnings based on hours worked, not for work accomplished.

Total installment cost: Includes the down payment plus the sum of all payments.

Total revenue: The total of all revenue from all sources.

Trade discount: A discount offered to businesses. This discount is expressed either as a single discount (like 25%) or a series discount (like 20/10) and is subtracted from the list price.

Traditional banking: A method of banking involving the use of paper checks and check registers to record deposits and checks.

Transaction: An event that is recorded such as withdrawing cash, etc.

Transaction register: Shows the checks written and deposits made on a checking account.

True rate of interest: *See* effective rate of interest.

Turnover at cost: The cost of goods sold, divided by the average inventory at cost.

Turnover at retail: Sales, divided by the average inventory at retail.

U

Underinsured motorist: A motorist who does not carry enough insurance to cover the costs of an accident.

Underwater: The situation where homeowners owe more on their home than it is worth.

Underwriters: Term applied to any insurer. Usually associated with an insurance company.

Unearned interest: Interest that a company has received but has not yet earned so that it is not shown in revenues.

Uniform product code (UPC): The series of black vertical stripes seen on products in stores that cashiers scan. Also called the *bar code*.

Uninsured motorist insurance: Insurance coverage that covers the insured when involved in an accident with a driver who is not insured.

United States Rule: The rule by which a loan payment is first applied to the interest owed, with the balance used to reduce the principal amount of the loan.

Unit price: The cost of one item.

Units-of-production: A depreciation method by which the number of units produced determines the depreciation allowance.

Universal life policy: A policy whose premiums flow into a general account from which the insurance company makes investments.

Unlike fractions: Fractions with different denominators.

Unlike terms: Two terms in an algebraic expression that do not have the same variables, so they cannot be added together. For example, $2x + 5y$ are unlike terms and cannot be combined into one term.

Unpaid-balance method: A method used to calculate interest on open-end credit accounts.

Unreimbursed job expenses: Certain expenses that are deductible on a personal income tax return.

Useful life: The estimated life of an asset. The Internal Revenue Service gives guidelines of useful life for depreciation purposes.

V

Valuation of inventory: Determining the value of merchandise in stock. Four common methods are specific-identification, average cost, FIFO, and LIFO.

Variable: A letter that stands for a number.

Variable commission: A commission whose rate depends on the total amount of the sales.

Variable interest rate loan: A loan on which the interest rate can go up or down.

Variable life policy: A life insurance policy that allows the owner to invest the funds within the policy in different types of investments.

Vertical analysis: The listing of each important item on an income statement as a percent of total net sales or each item on a balance sheet as a percent of total assets.

Visa: A credit-card plan (formerly known as Bank Americard).

W

Wage: A rate of pay expressed as a certain amount of dollars per hour.

Wage bracket method: A method of calculating income tax withholding that is based on tables that list income ranges.

Weighted average method: A method for calculating the arithmetic mean for data where each value is weighted (or multiplied) according to its importance.

Whole life insurance: *See* ordinary life insurance.

Whole number: A number with no fraction or decimal part.

Wholesaler: A business that buys directly from the manufacturer or other wholesalers and sells to the retailer.

Withholding allowance: An allowance for the employee, spouse, and dependents that determines the amount of withholding tax taken from gross earnings.

Withholding tax: The funds withheld from an employee's paycheck and sent to the federal or state government on behalf of that individual.

With recourse: An understanding that the seller of a note is responsible for payment of the note if the original maker of the note does not make payment. The note is sold with recourse.

Worker's compensation: Insurance purchased by companies to cover employees against work-related injuries.

W-2 form: The wage and tax statement given to the employee each year by the employer.

W-4 form: A form usually completed at the time of employment, on which an employee states the number of withholding allowances being claimed.

Y

Yield to maturity: The interest rate yield to the maturity of a bond or other financial instrument. It includes any interest payments, time to maturity, and payoff at maturity.

Youthful operator: A driver of a motor vehicle who is under a certain age, usually 25.

Subject Index

A

Absolute loss, 303–304
Accelerated cost recovery system (ACRS), 574, 605
Accelerated depreciation, 582
Accelerated mortgages, 499
Accountants, 620
Accounts payable, 632
Accounts receivable, 632
Accumulated depreciation, 574, 575
Acid test, 638
Acid-test ratio, 638, 639
ACRS. *See* Accelerated cost recovery system
Actual selling price, 301
Actuaries, 551
Addends, 3
Addition
    of decimal numbers, 25
    of fractions, 50, 52
    of mixed numbers, 58–59
    verbal expressions involving, 132–133
    of whole numbers, 3–4
Addition rule, 124
Adjustable rate mortgages (ARMs), 501
Adjusted bank balance, 190, 191
Adjusted gross income (AGI), 528
ADP. *See* Automatic Data Processing
Adult operators, 554
AGI. *See* Adjusted gross income
Alcorn's Boutique, 161
Algebraic logic, B-1
Allowances, 219
American River College, 413, 460
Amortization, 475, 490
Amortization schedule, 491, 499–500
Amortization tables, 492, 498
Amount
    in addition, 3
    of annuities, 414
    on invoices, 250
Annual meetings, 440
Annual percentage rate (APR)
    in average daily balance method, 469
    formula for, 476–477
    legislation on, 475
    simple discount notes, 350, 351
    tables in calculating, 477–478
Annuities
    amount of, 414
    case studies, 413, 459–460
    defined, 414
    due, 416–417
    finding amount of, 415–416
    present value of ordinary, 422–427
    reasons to buy, 414
    sinking funds and, 430–433
    terminology, 414–415
Apple, Inc., 327, 373, 440, 441, 619, 649–650, 654
Application problems
    equations in solving, 134–136
    estimating answers in, 15–16
    indicator words in, 15
    solving, D-5
    solving for rate in, 103
    steps in solving, 15, 16–18, 134, 138

Approximate annual percentage rate (APR), 476
AS OF dating, 266
Assessed value, 521
Assets, 632
ATMs. *See* Automated Teller Machines
Automated Teller Machines (ATMs), 174, 184
Automatic Data Processing (ADP), 206
Automobiles. *See* Motor vehicles
Average (statistical), 665
Average cost method, 309
Average daily balance method, 467–469
Average inventory, 307
Average owners' equity, 638
Axis, defined, E-2

B

Baker's Pottery, 568
Balance brought forward, 179
Balanced bank accounts, 191
Balance sheets, 632–633, 636–639
Bank accounts, interest-bearing, 389
Bank discount, 347, 348, 356. *See also* Discounts
Banker's interest, 332
Banker's ratio, 637
Banking
    account reconciliation, 189–192
    accounts with interest, 176, 389
    case studies, 173, 200–202
    checking account types, 176
    check registers, 180
    check stubs, 178
    credit-card sales in, 184–186
    deposit slips in, 176–178
    parts of a check, 176
    service charges, 176–177, 191
    services available, 184
    traditional *vs.* electronic, 174–176
Bank of America, 372, 377, 408
Bankruptcy, 328, 449
Bank statements, 189–192
Barcodes, 309
Bar graphs, 655–656
Barron's, 441
Base. *See also* Percent(s)
    defined, 89, D-1
    exponents, 144
    finding, 96–97
    markup on selling price as, 291–292
    terminology associated with, 90
Bed Bath & Beyond, 249, 280
Bev's Deli, 653
Bimodal data sets, 668
Blank endorsements, 177
Boards of directors, 440
Bodily injury insurance, 551
Bonds
    commission charge and cost of, 452
    defined, 430, 449
    monthly income from, 452–453
    tables, 449–451
Bond tables, 449–451
Book value, 574, 575–576. *See also* Depreciation
Borrowing, subtraction, 5, 59–60

Bounced checks, 189
Break-even point, 302
Brynski, Sarah, 205
Building classifications, 543
Buildings, on balance sheet, 632
Business checking accounts, 176
Business formulas. *See* Formulas
Buying. *See also* Cash discounts
    case studies, 249, 279–280
    creating invoices, 250, 251
    invoice abbreviations, 251
    series discounts, 252–255, 260–261
    shipping terminology, 250–251
    supply chain, 250
    trade discounts, 252

C

Calculating discounts separately, 252–253
Calculators, B-1–B-8, C-1–C-5
Canceled checks, 178
Cancellation, 63
Capital (financial), 440
Capital Curb and Concrete, 573, 616
Carrying (addition), 58–59
Cars. *See* Motor vehicles
Cash, on balance sheet, 632
Cash discounts. *See also* Buying
    dating methods, 264–267, 270–273
    earned *vs.* not earned, 265–266
    finding net cost after, 264
    on postdated invoices, 266–267
Cashier's check, 184
Cash on delivery (COD), 250
Cash value, 560
Casualty or theft losses, 532
Catastrophic events, 541
CDs. *See* Certificates of deposit
Celsius (C) temperature, A-3–A-5
Centigrade (C) temperature, A-3–A-4
Centigrams (cg), A-2
Centiliters (cL), A-2
Centimeters, A-1–A-2
Century 21, 81–82, 120
Certificates of deposit (CDs), 184, 392
Chain calculations, B-6
Chain discounts, 252
Challenger, John, 602
Charity donations, 532
Checking accounts, 176, 389. *See also* Banking
Check processing, 178
Checks, 175, 176, 189
    outstanding, 190, 191
Check stubs, 178
Chevron, 444
Circle graphs, 657–659
Citigroup, Inc., 463, 512–513
COD. *See* Cash on delivery
Coin counting fees, 176
Coinsurance clauses, 543
Collateral, 334
Collision insurance, 553–554
Commas, defined, 2
Commission charge, 452
Commission rate, 218–221
Common denominators, 50, 52–53
Common fractions, 44, 64. *See also* Fractions

Common stock, 441
Comparative balance sheet, 636
Comparative income statement, 625–626
Comparative line graphs, 657
Compensatory time (comp time), 210
Complement of a discount, 253–254
Compound amount, 378, 414
Compounding periods, 380–381
Compound interest. *See also* Interest
    on bank accounts, 389–392
    case studies, 377, 407–408
    compounding periods in, 380–381
    defined, 378
    formula for, 381–382
    future value and, 399–402
    inflation and, 392–394
    present value and, 399–402
    simple interest formula in, 378–380
    simple interest *vs.*, 328, 378
    students learning about, 382
    tables in calculating, 382–384
    time and power of, 378
Comprehensive insurance, 553–554
Consolidating your loans, 470
Consumer price index (CPI), 393
Continuous inventory systems, 309
Contributions (retirement account), 528. *See also* Gifts to charity
Conversion formulas, 295
Corporations, 440
Cosigners, 329
Cost (bonds), 452
Cost (depreciation), 574
Cost (selling), 284
Cost of goods sold, 620, 621
Cost of living index, 393
Countrywide Financial, 377, 408
Coupon rate, 449
Coverage (insurance), 542
CPI. *See* Consumer price index
Credit cards, 175. *See also* Debt
    consumer finance statistics, 465
    merchant fees on, 186
    other payment methods *vs.*, 175
    students using, 184, 464, 658
Credit-card sales, 184–186
Credit history, 176, 475
Credit limits, 464
Credit scores, 503
Cross products, 151, 152
Current assets, 632
Current balance, 190
Current liabilities, 632
Current ratio, 637, 639
Current yield, 442–443

D

Daily compounding, 380, 389–392. *See also* Compound interest
Daily overtime, 209–210
Data analysis. *See* Statistics
Days
    in finance charge calculations, 468–469
    in simple interest loans, 330–332
    worked to pay taxes, 520
Death, reducing risk of, 560
Debit cards, 174, 175, 184, 464. *See also* Credit cards
Debt. *See also* Credit cards; Loans
    case studies, 463, 510–513
    cost of having, 449
    credit score impacting, 503

defaulting on, 470
    government problem with, 449, 450
    loan consolidation, 469–470
    open-end credit, 464
    revolving charge accounts, 464–465
    tips for avoiding, 469
Decimal equivalents, 72
Decimal numbers
    addition of, 25
    case studies, 2, 39, 40
    converting fractions to, 72
    converting percents to, 84
    creating fractions from, 71
    creating percents from, 82–83
    defined, 21
    in depreciation, 577
    dividing, 30–32
    estimating, 25–26
    fractional percents as, 85–86
    multiplying, 29–30
    reading, writing, and rounding, 21–22
    subtraction of, 26
Decimal parts, 21
Decimal points, 2, B-2
Decimal system, 2
Declining-balance depreciation, 574, 582–584, 591, 605
Decrease problems, 110–113, 261
Decreasing term insurance, 560
Deductible (insurance), 553
Deductions, 206. *See also* Payroll; Tax deductions
Defaulting on your debt, 470
Deficit amounts, B-4–B-5
Deflation, 394
Denominators, 44
Dental expenses, deducting, 532
Dependents, 530
Dependent variables, E-1–E-2
Deposits, 174, 390–391
Deposits in transit (DIT), 190
Deposit slips, 177–178
Deposit ticket, 177
Depreciable amount, 575
Depreciation
    case studies, 573, 615–616
    choosing method of, 584
    declining-balance, 574, 582–584
    formulas, 575, 582, 590, 600
    modified accelerated cost recovery system, 605–608
    straight-line, 574–577
    sum-of-the-years'-digits, 589–591
    taxes and, 574, 584, 591, 605, 606
    terminology, 574
    units-of-production, 600–602
Depreciation fractions, 589–590
Depreciation per unit, 600
Depreciation schedules
    double-declining balance method, 583–584
    modified accelerated cost recovery system, 608
    straight-line method, 576–577
    sum-of-the-years' digits method, 590–591
    units-of-production method, 602
Depression. *See* Great Depression
Diabetes, 560
Difference (subtraction), 5
Differential piece rate, 217
Digits, 2
Direct deposits, 174
Direct payments, 174
Disability insurance, 226–227, 546

Discount brokers, 441
Discounting the note, 356
Discount period, 356, 358, 359
Discount rate, 347, 356
Discounts. *See also* Cash discounts; Simple discount notes
    bank, 347, 348, 356
    complements of, 253–254
    on notes, 356, 358, 359
    series, 252–255, 260–261
    on shipping and insurance, 250
    trade, 252
Discover card, 464
Distance (metric system), A-2, A-3
Distribution chain, 250
Distributive property, 128
DIT. *See* Deposits in transit
Dividends, 7, 440
Divisibility rules, 47
Division
    of decimals, 30–32
    of fractions, 65, 66
    of mixed numbers, 65
    rules of divisibility, 47
    using exponents, D-2–D-3
    verbal expressions involving, 133
    of whole numbers, 3, 7–9
Divisor, 7, 65
Dollars per $100, property tax as, 522
Dollars per $1000, property tax as, 523
The Doll House, 519, 569–570
Donations, 532
Dormant account fees, 176
Double-declining-balance method, 582–584
Double-declining-balance rate, 582
Double time, 210
Dow Jones Industrial Average, 444–445
Draws, 220
Due annuities, 416–417
Due date
    calculating, 265–267, 270–271, 359
    of promissory note, 334
Dugally, Tom, 81

E

Earnings, 206–208, 209. *See also* Payroll
EC. *See* Electronic commerce
Economic Recovery Tax Act of 1981, 605
Education, pay relating to, 211. *See also* Students
Effective rate of interest, 350, 351
EFT. *See* Electronic funds transfer
Einstein, Albert, 378
Electronic banking, 174. *See also* Banking
Electronic commerce (EC), 174
Electronic funds transfer (EFT), 174
Electronic payments, 174
Electronic product code (EPC) devices, 309
Employee's Withholding Allowance Certificate (W-4 form), 230–231
Employer's Quarterly Federal Tax Return (Form 941), 237
Ending inventory, 621
End-of-month (EOM) dating, 270–271
Endorsements, on checks, 177, 178
Endowment policies, 561
English-metric conversion table, A-3
English system, A-1, A-2–A-3
Entrepreneurship, 602
Equations. *See also* Formulas
    in application problem solutions, 134–136
    case studies, 161–163

combining like terms in, 127–128
defined, 124
distributive property in, 128–129
as mathematical expressions, 132–133
multiple operations in solving, 126–127
rules for solving, 124–126
steps in solving, 129
terminology of, 124
from words, 133–134
Equipment, on balance sheet, 632
Equivalent cash price, 426–427
Escrow accounts, 501
Estimation, 15–16, 25–26
ETFs. *See* Exchange-traded funds
E*Trade, 441
Ewing Marion Kauffman Foundation, 602
Exact interest, 332
Exchange-traded funds (ETFs), 445
Executive officers, 440
Exponents, 144, 381, D-1–D-5
    division using, D-2–D-3
    evaluating expressions, D-4–D-5
    multiplication using, D-2–D-3
Expressions, 124
Extension totals, 250
Extra (ex., x) dating, 271–272
Exxon Mobil, 444

F

Face value, 333, 347, 349, 449, 542
Factoring, 358
Factors, 358
Fahrenheit, Gabriel, A-3
Fahrenheit (F) temperature, A-3–A-5
Fair Isaac Corporation (FICO), 503
Fair Labor Standards Act, 208
Fair market value, 521
FAS. *See* Free alongside ship
FDIC. *See* Federal Deposit Insurance
    Corporation
Federal Deposit Insurance Corporation (FDIC),
    389
Federal Insurance Contributions Act (FICA),
    224. *See also* Social Security
Federal Reserve Bank, 332, 477
Federal Reserve System, 477
Federal Unemployment Tax Act (FUTA), 237
Federal withholding, 231–235, 236
FICA. *See* Federal Insurance Contributions Act
FICO. *See* Fair Isaac Corporation
Fidelity, 418, 441
FIFO method. *See* First-in, first-out method
Finance charges, 465, 476
Financial calculators, B-1, C-1–C-5
Financial ratios, 637–639. *See also* Formulas
Financial statements
    balance sheet, 632–633, 636–639
    case studies, 619, 647–650
    income statements, 620–622, 625–626
Fire insurance, 541–546
First-in, first-out (FIFO) method, 310–311
Fixed assets, 632
Fixed-rate loans, 501
Flay, Bobby, 676
Floating decimal, B-2
Float time, 178
Fogle, Jared, 18
Food Network, 676
Ford Motor Company, 616
Forecasting, 123, 162–163. *See also* Formulas
Foreclosures, 334, 501–502
Foreman, George E., 279

Form 941, 237
Form 1099, 528, 529
Form 1040A, 534–537
Form 1040EZ, 534
Formula for compound interest, 381–382
Formula for markdown, 301
Formulas. *See also* Equations
    amortization, 490–491
    annual percentage rate, 476–477
    balance sheet accounts, 632, 633, 638–639
    for base, 96
    case studies, 161–163
    coinsurance, 543–544
    conversion, 295
    defined, 141
    depreciation, 575, 582, 590, 600
    evaluating, 141–142, 144
    income statement accounts, 620, 621, 625, 627
    inventory turnover, 307–308
    for percent, 89
    present value, 399, 422
    property taxes, 522
    for rate, 102
    ratios and proportion, 150–153
    simple interest, 378–380
    solving for specific variables, 142–143
    in solving word problems, 143
    stock ratios, 442–444
Form W-2, 528, 529
Form W-4, 230–231
401(k) plans, 418
403(b) plans, 418
Fractions. *See also* Mixed numbers
    adding and subtracting, 50, 52
    case studies, 43, 77, 78
    common denominator, 52–53
    converting decimals to, 71
    converting mixed numbers to, 45
    converting percents to, 84–85
    creating decimals from, 72
    creating mixed numbers from, 45–46
    creating percents from, 83–84
    defined, 44
    in depreciation, 589–590
    dividing, 65, 66
    least common denominator, 50–52
    lowest terms, 46–47
    multiplying, 63, 66
    of percents, 85–86
    rules of divisibility, 47
    types of, 44–45
Free alongside ship (FAS), 250
Free on board (FOB) destination, 250
Free on board (FOB) shipping point, 250
Frequency distributions, 654–655
Fringe benefits, 237
Front-end rounding, 4–5
FUTA. *See* Federal Unemployment Tax Act
Future amount, 378
Future value
    of the annuity, 414
    in business valuation, 401–402
    calculating, 379–380, 399–401
    defined, 378
    present value *vs.*, 399

G

Gender, household income by, 668
General Motors (GM), 123, 162–163, 440
George Foreman grills, 279
Gifts to charity, 532
GM. *See* General Motors
Google, 649

Government. *See also* Federal Reserve Bank;
    Legislation
    debt problems, 449, 450, 658
    income and expense statistics, 527
    inflation affected by, 394
    interest rates affected by, 347
    issuing T-bills, 351–352, 359–360
Grace periods, 465
Grade point averages, 667
Grams (g), A-2, A-3
Graphing calculators, B-1
Graphing equations, E-1–E-9
    linear, E-4–E-7
    nonlinear, E-7–E-9
Graphs, 655–659
Great Depression, 427, 444, 445
Gross earnings. *See also* Payroll
    calculating, 206–208, 209
    defined, 206
    education relating to, 211
    finding net earnings from, 236
    insurance as percent of, 226
Gross loss, 303
Gross profit, 284, 620
Gross profit on sales, 620
Gross sales, 620

H

Half-year convention, 606
Head of household, 530
Health Care Act of 2010, 224
Hernandez, Jessica, 327
The Hershey Company, 654
Holmes, Oliver Wendell, Jr., 520
Home Depot, 43, 78
Homeowners, insurance spending by, 546
Homeowner's insurance policies, 542, 546
Horizontal analysis, 627–628, 637
Hourly wage, 206, 217–218
Housing, interest rate affecting, 328
Hundredths, 82. *See also* Percent(s)

I

Impound accounts, 501
Improper fractions, 44. *See also* Fractions
Incentive rates, 216
Income, median, 668
Income statements, 620–622, 625–626
Income taxes. *See also* Internal Revenue
    Service (IRS); Taxes
    finding balance due or refund on, 533–534
    finding liability for, 528
    finding taxable income, 531–532
    forms, 529, 534–537
    on life insurance proceeds, 560
    recordkeeping guidelines, 528
    reporting, 528
    standard deduction, 530
    on W-2 forms, 529
Income tax liability, 528
Income tax method, 605
Income tax withholdings, 230–237. *See also*
    Taxes
Increase problems, 110–113
Independent variables, E-1–E-2
Index funds, 445
Indicator words, 15
Individual retirement accounts (IRAs),
    418–419, 528
Industry average charts, 626
Inflation, 392–394
Initial inventory, 621

Inspection, 50
Installment cost, 476
Installment loans, 475–478
Insurance. *See also* Medicare; Social Security
    case studies, 519, 568–570
    coinsurance formula, 543–544
    discounts on, 250
    finding annual premium for, 542–543
    fire, 541–546
    life, 559–562
    motor vehicle, 551–556
    multiple-carrier, 544–546
    other types of, 546
    people needing more, 559
    as percent of earnings, 226
    rising cost of, 542
    role of, 520, 541
    terminology, 542
    unemployment insurance tax, 237
Insurance policies, 542
Intangible assets, 574
Interest. *See also* Compound interest; Simple
    interest
    banker's, 332
    defined, 176, 449
    effective rate of, 350, 351
    ordinary, 332
    in simple discount notes, 347
    tax-deductible, 532
    tax reporting, 528, 529
    unearned, 485–486
    variable, 501–502
Interest-bearing bank accounts, 184,
    389–392. *See also* Banking; Compound
    interest
Interest-bearing checking accounts, 389
Interest-in-advance notes, 347
Interest paid (checking accounts), 184, 389
Interest payments, 97
Interest rate per compounding period, 380
Interest rates, 97. *See also* Rates
Interest rate spreads, 433
Internal Revenue Service (IRS). *See also*
    Income taxes; Taxes
    on depreciation, 574
    Publication 946, 606
    quarterly payment to, 236–237
    on retirement plans, 419
    role of, 528
Internet banking, 174
Inventory. *See also* Selling
    average, 307
    on balance sheet, 632
    initial and ending, 621
    tracking methods, 308–309
    turnover, 307
    valuation methods, 309–312
Inventory shrinkage, 308
Inventory turns, 307
Investments, finding amount of, 97. *See also*
    specific investments
Invoices, 250, 251. *See also* Buying
Invoice totals, 250
IRAs. *See* Individual retirement accounts
Itemized billing, 465, 466
Itemized deductions, 532–533

J

J. B. Sherr Co., 250, 251
Jackson & Perkins Wholesale, Inc., 173,
    201–202
James, Ben, 123
Jobs, Steve, 327

K

Kilograms (kg), A-2
Kilometers (km), A-2
Knuckle method, 332
Kohl's, 465

L

Land, on balance sheet, 632
Last-in, first-out (LIFO) method, 311
Late fees, 465
Layoffs, preparing for, 206
LCD. *See* Least common denominator
Least common denominator (LCD), 50–52
Left side (equations), 124
Legislation
    on banking, 389
    on loans, 350, 475
    on payroll, 205, 208, 224–227, 237
    on taxes, 605
Length (metric system), A-1–A-2, A-3
Level-premium term policy, 560
Liabilities, 440, 632
Liability insurance, 546, 551
Life expectancies, 559
Life insurance, 559–562
LIFO method. *See* Last-in, first-out method
Like fractions, 50
Like terms, 127–128
Limited liability, 440
Limited-payment life insurance, 561
Linear equations, graphing, E-4–E-7
Line graphs, 656–657, E-2
Liquid assets, 638
Liquidity, 637–638
List price, 252, 260–261
Loan amount, 347
Loan consolidation, 469–470, 510–511
Loan payoff table, 493
Loans. *See also* Debt; Real estate loans
    amount of, 347
    early payoff of, 483–486
    installment, 475–478
    personal property, 490–493
Long-term care insurance, 546
Long-term liabilities, 632
Long-term notes payable, 632
Losses, 302–304, 532
Lowest terms, 46–47

M

MACRS. *See* Modified accelerated cost recov-
    ery system
Maintenance charge per month, 176
Makers (promissory notes), 333
Manufacturing, in supply chain, 250
Margin, defined, 284
Marital status, 230
Markdown, 301–304
Markup, 284, 292
Markup formula, 284–288, 292–294
Markup on cost, 285, 294–295
Markup on selling price, 291–297
Markup percent, 286–288, 295–296
Marriage, average age for, 665–666
MasterCard, 186, 464, 466
Mathematical models, 134
Mattel Inc., 569
Maturity (bonds), 449
Maturity date, 333, 450
Maturity value
    defined, 333

in finding proceeds, 359
    formula for, 329–330, 357, 358
    in simple discount notes, 347
McDonald's, 407, 440
Mean, 665–667
Measure of central tendency, 665
Median, 667–668
Medical expenses, 532, 666
Medical insurance, 546, 552
Medicare. *See also* Insurance
    finding amount of, 225–226
    history of, 205, 224–225, 246
    on W-2 forms, 529
    withholding for, 224
Memory keys, B-5–B-6
Merrill Lynch, 351, 377, 408, 450
Mesa Grill, 676
Meters, A-1–A-2
Method of cross products, 151
Method of prime numbers, 50–51
Metric system, A-1–A-4
Microsoft, 440, 649
Milligrams (mg), A-2
Milliliters (mL), A-2
Millimeters, A-1–A-2
Mills, property tax as, 523
Minuend, 5
Miscellaneous deductions, 532
Mixed numbers. *See also* Fractions
    addition of, 58–59
    converting fractions to, 46
    converting to fractions, 45–46
    defined, 44
    dividing, 65
    multiplying, 63–65
    subtracting, 59–60
Mobile banking, 174
Mobile payments, 175, 184
Mobile ticketing, 174
Mode, 668–669
Modified accelerated cost recovery system
    (MACRS), 574, 605–608
Money market accounts, 184, 389
Money order, 184
Monthly compounding, 380. *See also*
    Compound interest
Months, length of each, 265, 330–332
Mortgage insurance, 560
Mortgage rates, 498
Mortgages, 498. *See also* Real estate loans
Mortgages payable, 632
Motor vehicles
    cost of financing, 475
    insurance, 551–556
Multiple-carrier insurance, 544–546
Multiplicand, 6
Multiplication
    of decimals, 29–30
    of fractions, 63, 66
    of mixed numbers, 63–65
    by omitting zeros, 6–7
    using exponents, D-2–D-3
    verbal expressions involving, 133
    of whole numbers, 3, 5–6
Multiplication rule, 124
Multiplier, 6
Mutual funds, 445–446, 452–453

N

NASDAQ Composite Index, 444
Negative cash flow, C-1
Negative numbers, B-4–B-5

Net cost, 252, 260–261, 264
Net cost equivalent, 253–255
Net earnings, 284
Net income, 620
    after taxes, 620, 638
    before taxes, 620
Net pay, 206, 236. *See also* Payroll
Net price, 252
Net profit, 284, 302
Net sales, 620
Net worth, 632
New York Stock Exchange (NYSE), 440
Nike, 440, 441
No-fault insurance, 554
Nominal rates, 350, 475
Nonlinear equations, graphing, E-7–E-9
Nonsufficient funds (NSF), 184. *See also*
    Returned checks
No salvage value, 574, 576
Notary service, 184
Notes. *See* Simple discount notes
Notes payable, 632
Notes receivable, 632
NSF. *See* Nonsufficient funds
Numerator, 44
NYSE. *See* New York Stock Exchange

O

Olympic Sports, 320
Omitting zeros, multiplication by, 6–7
1099 Interest Income form, 528, 529
Online banking, 174, 184
Open-end credit, 464
Operating expenses, 284, 620
Operating loss, 302–304
Operations, mathematical, 3, 126–127. *See also*
    specific types
Ordered arrays, 667
Order of operations, B-6, D-3–D-4
Ordinary annuity, 414. *See also* Annuities
Ordinary dating method, 264–265
Ordinary interest, 332
Ordinary life insurance, 560
Origin, defined, E-2
Original numbers, 9
Overdraft fees, 176
Overdraft protection, 184
Overdrafts, 184
Overhead, 284, 620
Over-the-limit fees, 465
Overtime. *See also* Payroll
    daily, 209–210
    legislation on, 208
    for piecework, 216–218
    salaried employees, 211–212
    weekly, 208–209
Overtime premium method, 209
Owners' equity, 632, 638

P

Parentheses keys, B-7
Part (percent problems), 89, 90
Partial payments, 272–273
Partial products, 6
Par value, 449
Passbook accounts, 389
Pay by phone, 174
Payees (promissory notes), 333
Payers (promissory notes), 333
Payment period, 414
Payments. *See also* Amortization schedule

in bank statement reconciliation, 200
    direct, 174
    electronic, 174
    methods, 175, 185
    mobile, 175, 184
    monthly loan, 493
Pay periods, 210–211, 233–235
Payroll. *See also* Overtime; Salary; Wages
    case studies, 205, 245–246
    commission, 218–221
    common pay periods for, 210–211
    employer filing responsibilities, 237
    federal withholding tax, 231–235
    gross earnings calculations, 206–208, 209
    net pay after deductions, 236
    piecework, 216–218
    quarterly IRS payments, 236–237
    state withholding tax, 235–236
    tax calculations, 224–227
Payroll ledger, 206
PE ratio. *See* Price-earnings ratio
Percent(s)
    basic formula, 89
    case studies, 81–82, 119, 120
    creating decimals from, 84
    creating fractions from, 84–85
    defined, 82
    finding base in, 96–97
    finding rate in, 102–103
    fractional, 85–86
    increase and decrease problems, 110–113
    of markdown, 301–302
    of markup, 286–288, 295–296
    problem components, 89
    problem format, 91–92
    property tax as, 522
    sales tax calculation, 90–91
    solving for part, 89–90
    terminology, 90
    writing decimals as, 82–83
    writing fractions as, 83–84
Percentage method, 233–235
Percent formula, 89
Per-check charge (per-debit charge), 176
Per-debit charge (per-check charge), 176
Periodic inventory systems, 308
Perishables, selling price for, 296–297
Permanent life insurance, 560
Perpetual inventory systems, 309
Personal checking accounts, 176
Personal exemptions, 530
Personal finance, students studying, 382
Personal identification number (PIN), 174, 175
Personal income tax, 230
Personal property, *vs.* other property types, 490
Personal property loans, 490–493
Photocopying fees, 176
Physical inventory, 309
Piecework rates, 216–218
Pie charts, 657
PIN. *See* Personal identification number
Plant and equipment, 632
Plant assets, 632
Point of sale (POS), 174
Policies (insurance), 542
Policy limits, 552
POS. *See* Point of sale
Positive cash flow, C-1
Postdating, 266–267
Preferred stock, 441
Premium (insurance), 542, 551, 561–562
Premium factor, 562
Premium payment plans, 210

Prepaid card, 174
Prepayment of loans, 483–486
Present value, 378
    of an annuity, 422–427
    in business valuation, 401–402
    formula, 399, 422
    future value *vs.*, 399
    tables in calculating, 399–401
Present value tables, 424–425
Price-earnings (PE) ratio, 442, 443–444
Prime numbers, 50–51
Prime rate, 328
Principal, 328, 333, 339–340
Privately held corporations, 440
Proceeds, 348, 356–358
Processing checks, 178
Processing information (checks), 178
Products (multiplication), 6
Promissory notes, 333–334
Proper fractions, 44. *See also* Fractions
Property damage coverage, 552
Property tax, 520–524, 568. *See also* Taxes
    formula, 522
Property-tax rate, 522
Proportions, 151–153. *See also* Equations;
    Formulas
Proximo (prox.) dating, 270–271
Publication 946, 606
Publicly held corporations, 440
Purchase invoice, 250

Q

Quarterly compounding, 380. *See also*
    Compound interest
Quarterly interest, 380, 391–392
QuickBooks, 206
Quick ratio, 638
Quotas, 217
Quotient, 7, 45, 133

R

Race, household income by, 668
Radio frequency identification (RFID) chips,
    309
Rate of commission, 219
Rates. *See also* Compound interest; Percent(s);
    Simple interest
    affecting future value, 378
    government power over, 347
    in percent problems, 89
    in simple interest formula, 328
    solving for, 103, 340–341
Ratings, for fire insurance, 543
Ratio of net income after taxes to average
    owners' equity, 638
Ratios, 150–153, 626–627. *See also* Equations;
    Formulas
Raw materials, in supply chain, 250
Real estate, 490, 532
Real estate amortization table, 498
Real estate loans
    accelerated, 499
    escrow accounts on, 501
    finding monthly payments on, 498–499
    fixed *vs.* variable rate, 501–502
    repayment schedules for, 499–500
Real property, 490
Reasonable graphs, setting, E-4
Receipt-of-goods (ROG) dating, 271
Reciprocals, 126
Reconciliation (bank statements), 189–192

Recourse, 356
Recovery classes, 605–606
Recovery periods, 605–606
Recreational Equipment Inc. (REI), 283, 321
Reduced net profit, 302
Reduced price, 301–302
Refinancing, 498
Refund (loan prepayment), 485
Registers, 178
Regular IRAs, 418
Regulation DD, 389
Regulation Z, 475
REI. *See* Recreational Equipment Inc.
Renter's insurance, 546
Repayment schedules, 499–500
Replacement cost, 543
Repossession, 490
Residual value, 574
Restricted endorsement, 177, 178
Retail, 250, 292. *See also* Buying; Selling
Retail method of estimating inventory, 311–312
Retirement accounts. *See* Annuities; Individual retirement accounts (IRAs)
Retirement plans, self-employed, 119
Returned checks, 189. *See also* Nonsufficient funds (NSF)
Returned-deposit item, 184
Returns (merchandise), 219, 620
Revolving charge accounts, 464–465
RFID chips. *See* Radio frequency identification chips
Rhyme method, 332
Right side (equations), 124
Risk, to shareholders, 445
Rochester, University of, 602
Rodriguez, Roman, 413
ROG dating. *See* Receipt-of-goods dating
Rose Gardens, 173, 201–202
Roth IRAs, 418
Rounding, 2–4, 21–22, 254
Rule of 78, 484–486
Rules for solving equations, 124–126
Rules of divisibility, 47

S

Salary, 210–212. *See also* Payroll
Salary plus commission, 220–221
Sale price, 301
Sales, earnings based on, 218–221
Sales invoice, 250
Sales tax, 90–91, 96–97
Salvage value, 574, 583
Savings, in layoff preparations, 206
Savings accounts, 389. *See also* Banking
Scale, defined, E-2
Schedule 1 (Interest and Ordinary Dividends for Form 1040A Filers), 537
School district funding, 521. *See also* Students
Schwab, 418, 441
Scientific calculators, B-1
Scrap value, 574
SDI deductions. *See* State disability insurance deductions
Self-employment, 119, 226
Selling. *See also* Inventory
    case studies, 283, 320–321
    markdown, 301–304
    markup, 284–288, 291–297
    price of perishables, 296–297
    terminology, 284

Selling price, 284, 291–297
Semiannual compounding, 380. *See also* Compound interest
Series discounts, 252–255, 260–261
Service charges (banking), 176–177, 191
Shift differentials, 210
Shipping, 250
Short-term liabilities, 632
Simple discount notes. *See also* Simple interest
    discounting, 356–358
    finding bank discount and proceeds, 348
    finding effective interest rate, 350–351
    finding face value, 349–350
    simple interest notes *vs.*, 347
    terms used with, 347
    U.S. Treasury bills, 351–352
Simple interest. *See also* Interest; Simple discount notes
    affecting costs, 328
    case studies, 327, 372–373
    compound interest *vs.*, 328
    exact and ordinary, 332–333
    finding number of days, 330–332
    finding principal, rate, and time, 339–342
    formula for, 141, 378–380
    maturity value, 329–330
    note due dates, 334
    note terminology, 333–334
    solving for, 328–329
    vs. compound interest, 378
Simple interest notes, 333
Single discount equivalents, 260
Single discounts, 252
Sinking funds, 430–433
Sinking funds table, 431–433
Sliding scale commissions, 219–220
Sliding scale discounts, 267
Smart card, 174
Smelter, James, 283
Smoking, statistics by age, 84
Social Security. *See also* Insurance
    financial state of, 427
    finding amount of, 225–226
    history of, 224–225, 246
    multi-country comparison, 226
    in retirement planning, 419
    on W-2 forms, 529
    withholding for, 224
Social Security Act, 205, 246
The Soft Touch, 675
Solutions (equations), 124
Special endorsement, 177, 178
Specific identification method, 309
Split-shift premium, 210
Stafford loans, 347, 476
Standard deduction, 530
Starbucks, 205, 246
State disability insurance (SDI) deductions, 226–227
Stated rates, 350, 475
State income tax, 235–236, 532
Statistics
    case studies, 653, 675–676
    defined, 654
    frequency distributions, 654–655
    graphs, 655–659
    mean, 665–667
    median, 667–668
    mode, 668–669
Stock
    capital from sale of, 440
    finding current yield on, 442–443
    finding daily prices of, 441–442

    indexes, 444–445
    in mutual funds, 445–446
    price-earnings ratio on, 443–444
    types of, 440–441
Stockbrokers, 441
Stock certificates, 440
Stock exchanges, 440
Stockholders, 440
Stockholders' equity, 632
Stock ratios, 442–443
Stocks, capital from sale of, 440
Stock tables, 441–442
Stock turnover, 307. *See also* Inventory
Stop-payment order, 184
Straight commission, 218
Straight life insurance, 560
Straight-line depreciation
    other methods *vs.*, 583–584, 591
    overview, 574–577
    tax regulations, 605
Strict monthly budget, 470
Students
    credit card use by, 184, 464, 658
    grade point average calculations, 667
    pay linked to education level, 211
    personal finance education for, 382
    school funding for, 521
Subsidized Stafford loans, 476
Substitutions (equations), 124
Subtraction
    of decimals, 26
    of fractions, 50, 52
    of mixed numbers, 59–60
    verbal expressions involving, 132–133
    of whole numbers, 3, 5
Subtrahend, 5
SUBWAY, 1, 18, 40
Sum (addition), 3
Sum-of-the-years'-digits depreciation, 574, 589–591, 605
Suppliers, 250
Supply chain, 250

T

Table of days, 331
Tally marks, 654
Tangible assets, 574
Taxable income, 530
Tax deductions, 530, 532–533
Tax Equity and Fiscal Responsibility Act of 1982, 605
Taxes. *See also* Income taxes; Internal Revenue Service (IRS)
    calculating federal, 231–235, 236
    calculating state, 235–236
    case studies, 519, 568–570
    days worked to pay, 520
    deductible, 532
    depreciation and, 574, 584, 591, 605, 606
    home loan interest reducing, 498
    payroll, 224–227
    property, 520–524
    on retirement accounts, 418
    sales, 90–91, 96–97
Tax Foundation, 527
Tax preparation, 532
Tax rate schedules, 531
Tax Reform Act of 1984, 605
Tax Reform Act of 1986, 605
T-bills, 351–352, 359–360
Temperature (metric system), A-3–A-4
Tennis rackets, cost of, 310

Term
    of the annuity, 414
    defined, 449
Term (promissory note), 333
Term insurance, 560
Terms (equations), 124
Territorial ratings, 542
Theft losses, 532
Time. *See also* Compound interest; Simple interest
    affecting future value, 378
    in metric system, A-1
    in simple discount notes, 347
    in simple interest formula, 328
    solving for, 341–342
Time-and-a-half rate, 208
Time cards, 206
Time deposits, 392
Time rates, 216
Total (in addition), 3
Total balance, 178
Total revenue, 620
Toyota, 440
Trade discounts, 252
Trader Joe's, 615
Traditional banking, 174. *See also* Banking
Trailing zeros, 25
Transaction costs, 175, 178
Transaction register, 180
True rate, 350, 351
Truth in Lending Act, 350, 475
Truth in Savings Act of 1991, 389
200% method, 582

U

Underinsured motorist insurance, 554
Underwater homeowners, 501

Underwriters, 542
Unearned interest, 485–486
Unemployment insurance tax, 237
Uninsured motorist insurance, 554
United States Rule, 483–484
Unit price, 250
Units of production, 600
Units-of-production depreciation, 574, 600–602
Universal life insurance, 560–561
Universal product code (UPC), 309
Unlike fractions, 50, 52
Unlike terms, 127
Unpaid balance method, 465–467
Unreimbursed job expenses, 532
Unsubsidized Stafford loans, 476
UPC. *See* Universal product code
U.S. Treasury bills, 351–352, 359–360
Useful life, 574, 577

V

Vanguard, 418
Variable commission, 219–220
Variable interest rates, 501–502
Variable life insurance, 561
Variable rate loans, 501–502
Variables (equations), 124
Variables, choosing dependent and independent, E-1–E-2
Vertical analysis, 625–626, 636
Visa, 186, 464, 466
Volume (metric system), A-1, A-2, A-3

W

Wage bracket method, 231–233
Wages, 221, 528, 529. *See also* Payroll
Wal-Mart, 444

Weekly overtime, 208–209
Weight (metric system), A-1, A-2, A-3
Weighted average, 666–667
Weighted-average method, 309–310
Weighted mean, 666–667
W-4 form, 230–231
Whole life insurance, 560
Whole numbers
    adding, 3–4
    application problems, 15–18
    case studies, 2, 39, 40
    defined, 2
    dividing, 3, 7–9
    dividing decimals by, 30–31
    fractions in operations with, 66
    multiplying, 3, 5–6
    rounding, 2–4
    subtracting, 3, 5
Wholesale, in supply chain, 250
Wiffy, Barbara, 173
Withholding allowance, 230–231
Woodline Moldings and Trim, 77
Word problems, 132–133, 143
Worker's compensation, 546
Wozniak, Steven, 327
W-2 Wage and Tax Statement, 528, 529

X

x-axis, E-2
X (extra) dating, 271–272

Y

y-axis, E-2
Yield to maturity, 450
y-intercept, E-6
Youthful operators, 554–555

▼ Credits

Page 300: Comstock Images/Getty Images; Page 301: Db238/ Fotolia; Page 302: Stockbyte/Getty Images; Page 303: Palto/ Shutterstock; Page 305: (t) Jupiterimages/Creatas/Getty Images; Page 305: (b) Kraig Scarbinsky/Photodisc/Getty Images; Page 308: Joshhh/Fotolia; Page 309: (t) Sufi/Shutterstock; Page 309: (c) Hbas/Shutterstock; Page 309: (b) Maygutyak/ Fotolia; Page 310: Parcan/Shutterstock; Page 312: Caro/Alamy; Page 314: Frances L Fruit/Shutterstock; Page 315: Bloomua/ Fotolia; Page 320: (l) Ultimathule/Shutterstock; Page 320: (r) 2happy/Shutterstock; Page 321: Tamix115/Fotolia; Page 325: Gradt/Fotolia

Chapter 9

Page 327: (t) Avava/Shutterstock; Page 327: (b) Oleksiy Maksymenko Photography/Alamy; Page 329: Nick White/ Cultura/Getty Images; Page 333: Courtesy of Stanley Salzman; Page 336: Portadown/Shutterstock; Page 337: (t) Gennadiy Poznyakov/Fotolia; Page 337: (b) Adisa/Fotolia; Page 338: Ifong/Shutterstock; Page 339: Lev/Fotolia; Page 342: Berc/ Fotolia; Page 345: (t) Martha Andrews/Fotolia; Page 345: (b) Nikolai Sorokin/Fotolia; Page 346: Pyzata/Fotolia; Page 349: Core Imagery/Alamy; Page 353: Courtesy of Stanley Salzman; Page 354: Shirley/Fotolia; Page 356: Courtesy of Stanley Salzman; Page 358: GoodMood Photo/Fotolia; Page 362: Aurelie and Morgan David de Lossy/Cultura/Getty Images; Page 373: Neil Fraser/Alamy.

Chapter 10

Page 377: Richard A. Brooks/AFP/Getty Images; Page 378: Harris & Ewing Collection/Library of Congress Prints and Photographs Division [LC-DIG-hec-31012]; Page 379: Evox Productions/Drive Images/Alamy; Page 384: Hemera/Getty Images; Page 389: DNY59/E+/Getty Images; Page 396: Ian Pilbeam/Alamy; Page 397: Andres Rodriguez/Fotolia; Page 399: Tony Mathews/Shutterstock; Page 401: Photos by Cally/Alamy; Page 403: Robert Hunt/E+/Getty Images; Page 407: Kevin Britland/Alamy; Page 408: Leonid Serebrennikov/Alamy.

Chapter 11

Page 413: IS362/Image Source Plus/Alamy; Page 414: Paul Moore/Fotolia; Page 416: Monkey Business/Fotolia; Page 421: Pressmaster/Fotolia; Page 425: Michael Jung/Fotolia; Page 427: Nancy Louie/E+/Getty Images; Page 428: (t) Damon Higgins/ ZUMA Press/Newscom; Page 428: (b) Deshakalyan Chowdhury/ AFP/Getty Images; Page 430: Guillermo Lobo/iStockphoto 360/Getty Images; Page 431: Nagel Photography/Shutterstock; Page 433: Comstock Images/Getty Images; Page 434: (t) Olga Khoroshunova/iStockphoto 360/Getty Images; Page 434: (b) Jason Poston/Shutterstock; Page 436: Ernest Prim/Fotolia; Page 438: (t) Kenneth Summers/Shutterstock; Page 438: (b) Nigel Hicks/Alamy; Page 439: Pack-Shot/Shutterstock; Page 443: TJP/Alamy; Page 447: Beth Anderson/Pearson Education, Inc.; Page 449: Ellen Isaacs/Alamy; Page 460: Rabbit75_fot/Fotolia.

Chapter 12

Page 463: MAXFX/Fotolia; Page 467: R. Gino Santa Maria/ Shutterstock; Page 472: EMF Images/Fotolia; Page 473:

Jupiterimages/Comstock/Thinkstock; Page 474: Africa Studio/ Fotolia; Page 478: Dick Luria/Photodisc/Getty Images; Page 480: Michael Flippo/Fotolia; Page 481: Msujan/Shutterstock; Page 482: Dimasobko/Fotolia; Page 483: Keith Brofsky/ Photodisc/Getty Images; Page 484: Branex/Fotolia; Page 486: Iriana Shiyan/Fotolia; Page 487: Manfredxy/Shutterstock; Page 488: (t) Tirc83/E+/Getty Images; Page 488: (b) Tad Denson/ Shutterstock; Page 489: Rui Vale Sousa/Shutterstock; Page 491: Sascha Burkard/Fotolia; Page 495: Skaljac/Fotolia; Page 497: Dorling Kindersley, Ltd./Alamy; Page 500: Sergej Razvodovskij/ Fotolia; Page 510: Andres Rodriguez/Fotolia.

Chapter 13

Page 519: David Coll Blanco/Alamy; Page 524: The Focus Mantra/Shutterstock; Page 522: Susan Law Cain/Shutterstock; Page 525: (t) Matthew Dixon/iStockphoto/Thinkstock; Page 525: (b) Kevin Foy/Alamy; Page 529: (t) U.S Internal Revenue Service; Page 529: (b) U.S Internal Revenue Service; Page 531: U.S Internal Revenue Service; Page 533: 2xSamara.com/ Shutterstock; Page 535: U.S Internal Revenue Service; Page 540: Wong Sze Fei/Fotolia; Page 540: (t) Video1/E+/Getty Images; Page 540: (b) Farina 3000/Fotolia; Page 545: Il-fede/Fotolia; Page 546: (l) Monkey Business Images/Shutterstock; Page 546: (r) Lisa S./Shutterstock; Page 548: Gary/Fotolia; Page 553: Eyetronic/Fotolia; Page 557: Courtesy of Stanley Salzman; Page 558: AnKudi/Fotolia; Page 562: H. Tuller/Shutterstock; Page 564: Wong Sze Fei/Fotolia; Page 568: George Doyle/ Stockbyte/Getty Images; Page 572: Daniel Hassard/E+/Getty images.

Chapter 14

Page 573: Courtesy of Stanley Salzman; Page 575: Ian Dagnall/ Alamy; Page 577: (t) Art-222/Fotolia; Page 577: (b) Petr Nad/ Shutterstock; Page 579: Courtesy of Stanley Salzman; Page 586: Goran Bogicevic/Fotolia; Page 590: Texas Stock Photo/Alamy; Page 594: Irabel8/Shutterstock; Page 597: V. Rumi/Fotolia; Page 598: Photoiron/Fotolia; Page 600: Marina Lohrbach/Fotolia; Page 601: Zuchero/Fotolia; Page 604: Wolfgang Spunbarg/ PhotoEdit, Inc.; Page 612: Courtesy of Stanley Salzman.

Chapter 15

Page 619: Oleksiy Maksymenko Photography/Alamy; Page 622: Autumn's Memories/Shutterstock; Page 623: Paul Matthew Photography/Shutterstock; Page 628: Lisa F. Young/Shutterstock; Page 629: (t) DJ Mattaar/Shutterstock; Page 629: (b) Vetkit/ Fotolia; Page 630: Kruwt/Fotolia; Page 632: Mindweb2/Fotolia; Page 640: Alexey Stiop/Shutterstock; Page 642: Gwright/Alamy; Page 647: Michael Blann/Digital Vision/Thinkstock; Page 651: Bernard van Dierendonck/LOOK Die Bildagentur der Fotografen GmbH/Alamy; Page 652: Deligodin Evgeny/Shutterstock.

Chapter 16

Page 653: Catherine Yeulet/iStock/Thinkstock; Page 661: Digital Visions Network; Page 665: Jupiterimages/Photos.com/ Thinkstock; Page 669: Courtesy of Gary Clendenen; Page 675: Pavel L Photo and Video/Shutterstock; Page 676: Matt Sayles/ Invision/AP Images; Page 679: Digital Visions Network.

Percent Formula	Part $=$ Base $\times$ Rate or $P = B \times R$ or $P = BR$
Markup Formula	Cost $+$ Markup $=$ Selling price or $C + M = S$

Converting Markup Percent on Cost to Selling Price

$$\text{Markup on selling price} = \frac{\text{Markup on cost}}{100\% \,+\, \text{Markup on cost}}$$

Converting Markup Percent on Selling Price to Cost

$$\text{Markup on cost} = \frac{\text{Markup on selling price}}{100\% \,-\, \text{Markup on selling price}}$$

Terms Associated with Loss

Original Selling Price

$ Cost	$ Operating Expenses	$ Net Profit

Selling Price   Absolute Loss   Breakeven Point

Selling Price   Operating Loss

Selling Price   Reduced Net Profit

Stock Turnover

$$\text{Turnover at retail} = \frac{\text{Retail sales}}{\text{Average inventory at retail}} \qquad \text{Turnover at cost} = \frac{\text{Cost of goods sold}}{\text{Average inventory at cost}}$$

Simple Interest   The *simple interest*, I, on a principal of P dollars at a rate of interest R per year for T years is given by $I = PRT$.

Number of Days in Each Month

31 Days		30 Days	28 Days
January	August	April	February
March	October	June	(29 days in leap year)
May	December	September	
July		November	

Types of Interest   The method for forming the *time fraction* used for T in the formula $I = PRT$ is summarized as follows:

The *numerator* is the *exact number* of days in a loan period.
The *denominator* is one of the following:
- *exact interest* assumes 365 days in a year and uses 365 as denominator.
- *ordinary*, or *banker's interest* assumes 360 days in a year and uses 360 as denominator.

Interest, Principal, Rate, and Time Formulas

Interest: $I = PRT$ Principal: $P = \dfrac{I}{RT}$ Rate: $R = \dfrac{I}{PT}$

Time: Time in days $= \dfrac{I}{PR} \times 360$ Time in years $= \dfrac{I}{PR}$

Maturity Value   The *maturity value* M of a loan having a principal P and interest I is given by $M = P + I$.

Simple Interest and Simple Discount

	Simple Interest Note	Simple Discount Note
	$I =$ Interest	$B =$ Discount
	$P =$ Principal (face value)	$P =$ Proceeds
	$R =$ Rate of interest	$D =$ Discount rate
	$T =$ Time, in years or fraction of a year	$T =$ Time, in years or fraction of a year
	$M =$ Maturity value	$M =$ Maturity value
Face value	Stated on note	Same as maturity value
Interest charge	$I = PRT$	$B = MDT$
Maturity value	$M = P + I$	Same as face value
Amount received by borrower	Face value or principal	Proceeds: $P = M - B$
Identifying phrases	Interest at a certain rate	Discounted at a certain rate
	Maturity value greater than face value	Proceeds
		Maturity value equal to face value
True annual interest rate	Same as stated rate R	Greater than stated rate D

Compound Interest   If P dollars are deposited at a rate of interest t per period for n periods, then the *compound amount* M, or the final amount of deposit, is

$$M = P(1 + i)^n$$

The interest earned I is

$$I = M - P$$

(Use the compound interest table.)